lonely planet

Kaua'i p476

Ni'ihau p474

O'ahu p62

Moloka'i p440

Lana'i p424

Maui p312

Kaho'olawe p422

Hawai'i the Big Island p172

THIS EDITION WRITTEN AND RESEARCHED BY

Sara Benson,

Amy C Balfour, Adam Karlin, Adam Skolnick,

Paul Stiles, Ryan Ver Berkmoes

PLAN YOUR TRIP

ON THE ROAD

LONELY PLANET / GETTY IMAGES ©

LEI-MAKING P619

DEBORAH RUST / GETTY IMAGES ©

GECKO

WAYNE LEVIN / GETTY IMAGES ©

KEALAKEKUA BAY STATE HISTORICAL PARK P211

Contents

ON THE ROAD

HIGHWAY TO LANA'I CITY P428

Contents

UNDERSTAND

SURVIVAL GUIDE

SPECIAL FEATURES

Welcome to Hawaii

It's easy to see why Hawaii has become synonymous with paradise. Just look at these sugary beaches, Technicolor coral reefs and volcanoes beckoning adventurous spirits.

Natural Beauty

Snapshots of these islands scattered in the cobalt blue ocean are heavenly, without the need for any tourist-brochure embellishment. As tropical getaways go, Hawaii couldn't be easier or more worth the trip, although visiting these Polynesian islands isn't always cheap. Whether you're dreaming of swimming in waterfall pools or lazing on golden-sand beaches, you'll find what you're looking for here. Sunrises and sunsets are so spectacular that they're cause for celebration all by themselves.

Go Play Outside

Just as in days of old, life in Hawaii is lived outdoors. Whether it's surfing, swimming, fishing or picnicking with the *'ohana* (extended family and friends) on weekends, encounters with nature are infused with the traditional Hawaiian value of *aloha 'aina* – love and respect for the land.

Start by going hiking across ancient lava flows, up craggy volcanic peaks and along fluted *pali* (sea cliffs). Learn to surf, the ancient Hawaiian sport of 'wave sliding,' then snorkel or dive with bountiful tropical fish, giant manta rays and sea turtles. Kayak to a deserted offshore island or hop aboard a winter whale-watching cruise. Back on land, crawl through hollowed-out lava tubes, gallop with *paniolo* (Hawaiian cowboys) along mountain ranch trails or zipline through cloud forests.

Island Style

Floating alone in the middle of the Pacific, Hawaii maintains its own sense of self apart from the US mainland. Spam, shave ice, surfing, ukulele and slack key guitar music, hula, pidgin, 'rubbah slippah' – these are just some of the touchstones of everyday life. Pretty much everything here feels easygoing, low-key and casual, bursting with genuine aloha and fun. You'll be equally welcome whether you're a globe-trotting surf bum, a beaming couple of honeymooners or a big family with rambunctious kids.

Modern Multiculturalism

Hawaii is as proud of its multicultural heritage as it is of island-born US President Barack Obama. Here descendants of ancient Polynesians, European explorers, American missionaries and Asian plantation immigrants mix and mingle. In contemporary Hawaii, multiculturalism is the rule, not the exception. Arts and cultural festivals keep diverse community traditions alive, from Hawaiian hula and outrigger canoe races to Japanese *taiko* drumming and modern-day surfing championships.

Why I Love Hawaii

By Sara Benson, Coordinating Author

On my first trip to Hawaii, I landed on Maui almost broke and with my luggage lost in transit. No problem: I camped by the beach, plucked ripe guava from trees and spent days hiking in Haleakalā National Park. Since that serendipitous first island sojourn, I've lived and traveled around the archipelago, from the Big Island's geological wonderland to the emerald river valleys of Kaua'i to the big city of Honolulu, whose backstreets now seem as familiar as my own hometown. When it comes to Hawaii, I'm always ready to go again. *Hana hou*!

For more about our authors, see page 680

Above: 'Akaka Falls (p266), Hawai'i the Big Island

Hawaii

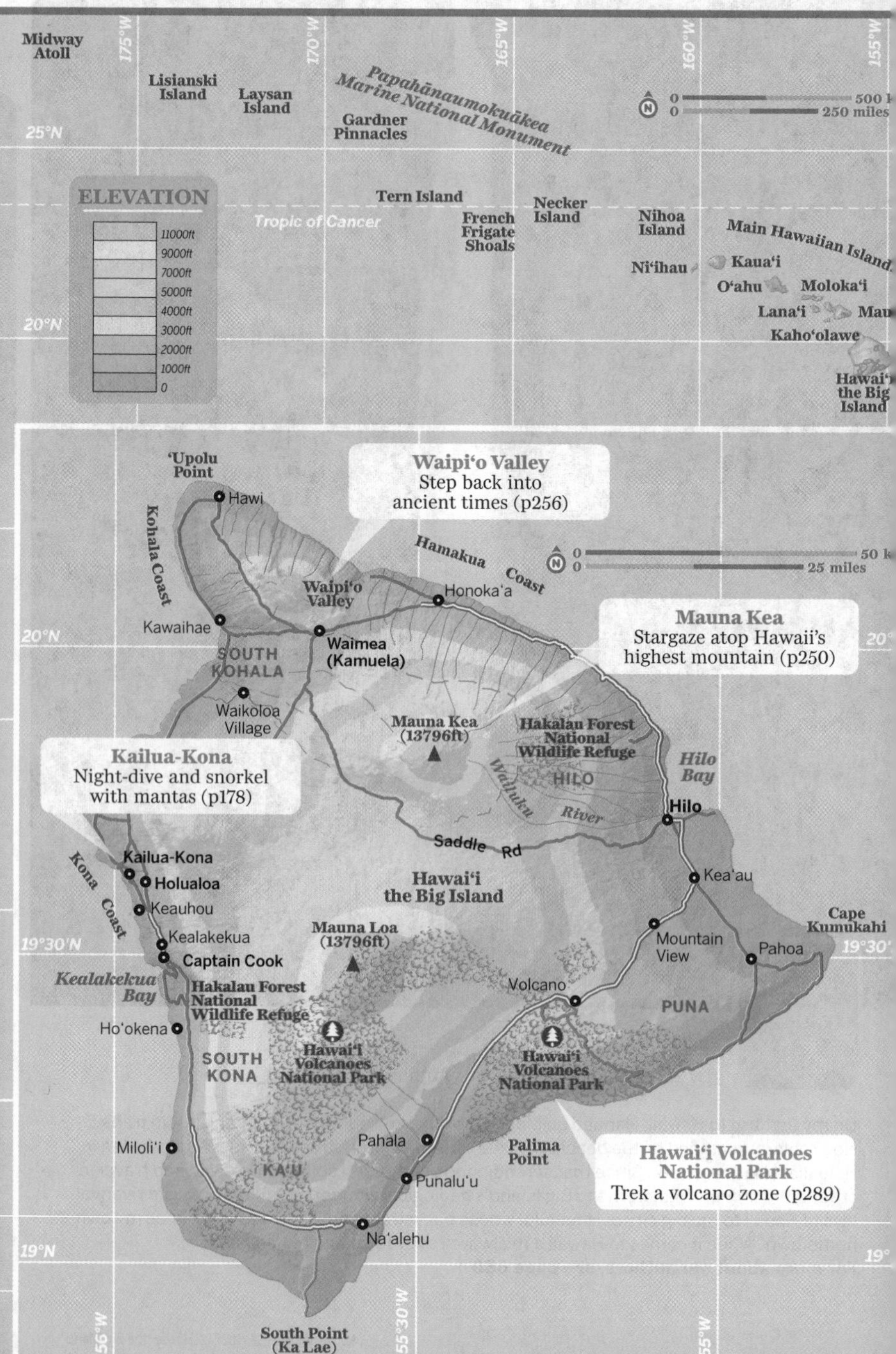

Midway Atoll
Lisianski Island
Laysan Island
Papahānaumokuākea Marine National Monument
Gardner Pinnacles
Tern Island
French Frigate Shoals
Necker Island
Nihoa Island
Ni'ihau
Main Hawaiian Islands
Kaua'i
O'ahu
Moloka'i
Lana'i
Kaho'olawe
Hawai'i the Big Island
Tropic of Cancer
ELEVATION
11000ft
9000ft
7000ft
5000ft
4000ft
3000ft
2000ft
1000ft
0
25°N
20°N
175°W
170°W
165°W
160°W
155°W
250 miles
'Upolu Point
Hawi
Kohala Coast
Hamakua Coast
Waipi'o Valley
Step back into ancient times (p256)
Honoka'a
Kawaihae
Waimea (Kamuela)
SOUTH KOHALA
Waikoloa Village
Mauna Kea
Stargaze atop Hawaii's highest mountain (p250)
Mauna Kea (13796ft)
Hakalau Forest National Wildlife Refuge
HILO
Wailuku River
Hilo Bay
Hilo
Saddle Rd
Kailua-Kona
Night-dive and snorkel with mantas (p178)
Kona Coast
Kailua-Kona
Holualoa
Keauhou
Kealakekua
Captain Cook
Kealakekua Bay
Hawai'i the Big Island
Kea'au
Mountain View
Pahoa
Cape Kumukahi
Mauna Loa (13796ft)
Volcano
PUNA
Hakalau Forest National Wildlife Refuge
Ho'okena
SOUTH KONA
Hawai'i Volcanoes National Park
Hawai'i Volcanoes National Park
Miloli'i
Pahala
Palima Point
Hawai'i Volcanoes National Park
Trek a volcano zone (p289)
KA'U
Punalu'u
Na'alehu
South Point (Ka Lae)
25 miles
20°N
19°30'N
19°N
156°W
155°30'W
155°W

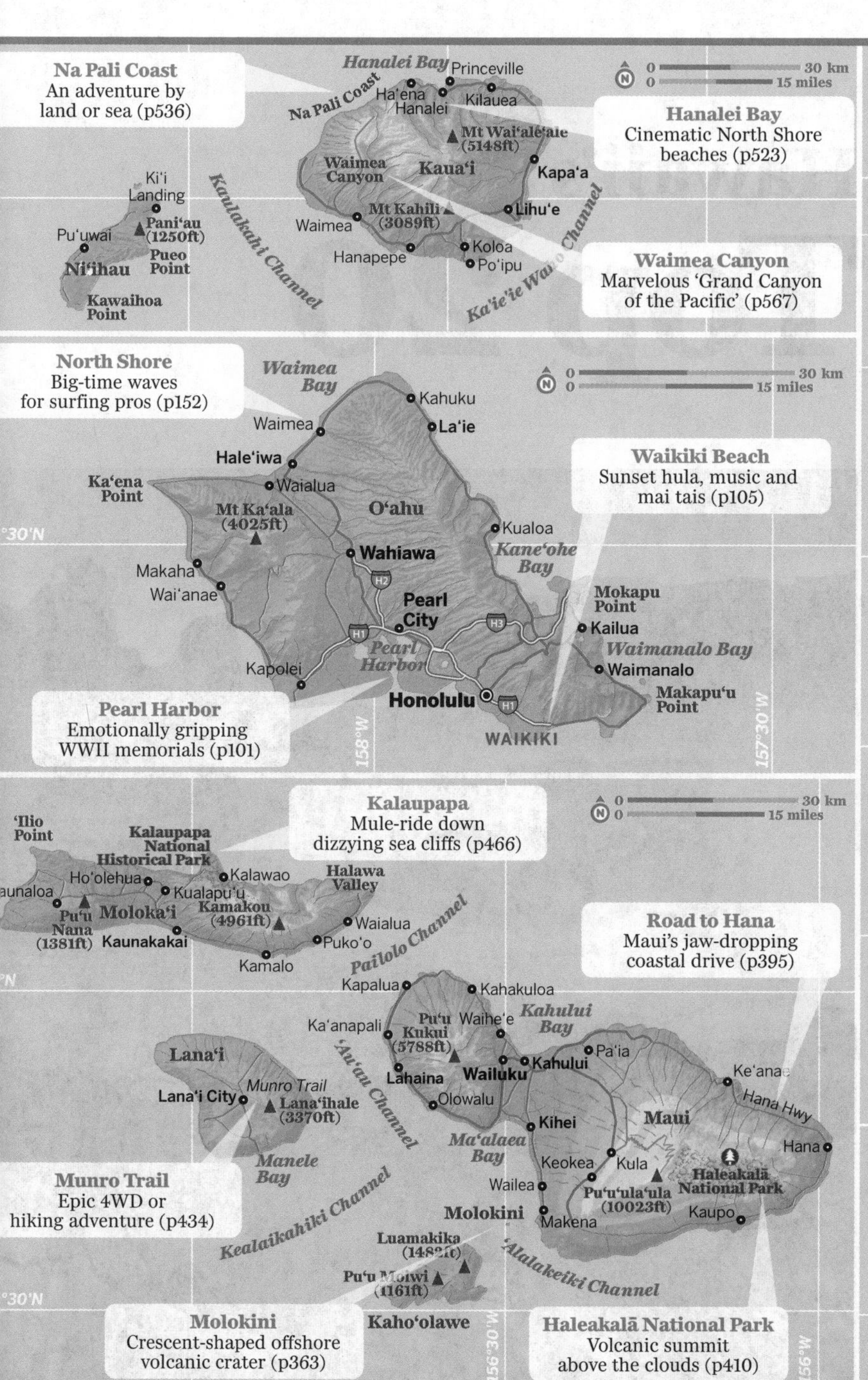

Na Pali Coast
An adventure by land or sea (p536)
Hanalei Bay
Cinematic North Shore beaches (p523)
Waimea Canyon
Marvelous 'Grand Canyon of the Pacific' (p567)
Hanalei Bay
Princeville
Ha'ena
Hanalei
Kilauea
Na Pali Coast
Mt Wai'ale'ale (5148ft)
Waimea Canyon
Kaua'i
Kapa'a
Mt Kahili (3089ft)
Lihu'e
Waimea
Hanapepe
Koloa
Po'ipu
Kaulakahi Channel
Ka'ie'ie Waho Channel
Ki'i Landing
Pani'au (1250ft)
Pu'uwai
Ni'ihau
Pueo Point
Kawaihoa Point
0 30 km
0 15 miles
North Shore
Big-time waves for surfing pros (p152)
Waikiki Beach
Sunset hula, music and mai tais (p105)
Pearl Harbor
Emotionally gripping WWII memorials (p101)
Waimea Bay
Kahuku
Waimea
La'ie
Hale'iwa
Ka'ena Point
Waialua
O'ahu
Mt Ka'ala (4025ft)
Kualoa
Kane'ohe Bay
Wahiawa
Makaha
Wai'anae
Pearl City
Mokapu Point
Kailua
Waimanalo Bay
Waimanalo
Pearl Harbor
Kapolei
Honolulu
Makapu'u Point
WAIKIKI
H1
H2
H3
30'N
158°W
157°30'W
Kalaupapa
Mule-ride down dizzying sea cliffs (p466)
Road to Hana
Maui's jaw-dropping coastal drive (p395)
Munro Trail
Epic 4WD or hiking adventure (p434)
Molokini
Crescent-shaped offshore volcanic crater (p363)
Haleakalā National Park
Volcanic summit above the clouds (p410)
'Ilio Point
Kalaupapa National Historical Park
Ho'olehua
Kalawao
Kualapu'u
Halawa Valley
Pu'u Nana (1381ft)
Moloka'i
Kamakou (4961ft)
Waialua
Kaunakakai
Puko'o
Kamalo
Pailolo Channel
Kapalua
Kahakuloa
Ka'anapali
Pu'u Kukui (5788ft)
Waihe'e
Kahului Bay
Pa'ia
Lahaina
Wailuku
Kahului
Ke'anae
Hana Hwy
Olowalu
Kihei
Maui
Hana
Lana'i
Munro Trail
Lana'i City
Lana'ihale (3370ft)
'Au'au Channel
Ma'alaea Bay
Keokea
Kula
Haleakalā National Park
Manele Bay
Wailea
Pu'u'ula'ula (10023ft)
Kealaikahiki Channel
Molokini
Makena
Kaupo
Luamakika
Pu'u Moaiwi (1161ft)
'Alalakeiki Channel
Kaho'olawe
30'N
156°30'W
156°W

Hawaii's Top 20

1

Hawai'i Volcanoes National Park

1 And you thought Earth was firm ground. Set on the sloping hillside of the world's tallest volcano, this fantastic national park (p289) will remind you that nature is very much alive. An extensive network of trails encompasses lava flows, steam vents, lava tubes and, if you wish, wild backcountry. Alternatively, you can take in many of the major sights by car in one long downhill drive. The highlight is the stunning panorama of Halema'uma'u, an enormous crater spewing tons of ash into the sky.

Na Pali Coast

2 The Na Pali Coast (p536) should top everyone's Kaua'i to-do list. Make a gentle oceanic journey by boat, with motors or sails or, for true sea adventure, pit your paddle and kayak against the elements: wind, swell and sunshine. For hikers, Ke'e Beach is the entry point for the rugged 11-mile-long Kalalau Trail. This trek will transport you to a place distant and distinct from all others, with verdant cliffs soaring above a sloping valley abundant with fruit trees, naked hippies and solace seekers.

MINT IMAGES - FRANS LANTING / GETTY IMAGES ©

2

MINT IMAGES - FRANS LANTING / GETTY IMAGES ©

RON DAHLQUIST / GETTY IMAGES ©

Road to Hana

3 Hold on tight! Of all the jaw-droppingly dramatic drives in Hawaii, this is the Big Kahuna. A roller coaster of a ride, the Hana Hwy (p395) twists down into jungly valleys and back up towering cliffs, curling around 600 twists and turns along the way. Fifty-four one-lane bridges cross nearly as many waterfalls – some eye-popping torrents, others soothing and gentle. But the ride's only half the thrill. Get out and swim in a Zen-like pool, hike a ginger-scented trail or savor some coconut ice cream.

Waikiki Beach

4 Waikiki (p105) is back, baby. Hawaii's most famous beach resort may be a haven for tacky plastic lei, coconut-shell bikini tops and motorized hip-shaking hula dolls. But real aloha and chic modernist style have revived this prototypical paradise. Beachboys surf legendary waves by day and after sunset tiki torches are lit at Kuhio Beach Park. Every night hula dancers sway to ancient and modern rhythms – backed by famous island musicians strumming slack key guitars and ukuleles – at oceanfront hotels, bars and even shopping malls.

Puna's Lava Tours

5 The Big Island is a raw place. Creation occurs daily here as a jagged, stark coast is carved out by fire, wind and water. You can witness this handiwork before your very eyes in Puna (p281). Hike over steaming black lava fields or take a boat skimming over indigo waves to places where Pele, goddess of fire and volcanoes, bleeds her molten fury into the Pacific even as building-sized waves crash against the lava flow. The primal power of this clash of elements is unforgettable.

Haleakalā National Park

6 As you hike down into the belly of Haleakalā (p410), the first thing you notice is the crumbly, lunar-like landscape. Then you experience the eerie quiet – the only sound is the crunching of volcanic cinders beneath your feet. The path continues through an unearthly world, a tableau of stark lava and ever-changing clouds. Russet cinder cones rise from the crater floor. Looking back toward the summit, eyes focused on the steep crater walls, it's impossible not to be awed by the raw beauty of Sliding Sands Trail.

Pearl Harbor

7 Hawaii's active US military bases, particularly on O'ahu, attest to its strategic importance. For the most dramatic reminder of the reasons why, visit the USS *Arizona* Memorial (p102), a somber site commemorating WWII's Pearl Harbor attack and the lives lost. Nearby, military history buffs can climb inside a sub, tour the hangars of the Pacific Aviation Museum (p103) and stand on the decks of the 'Mighty Mo' (p103), where Imperial Japan formally surrendered in 1945.

Bottom: USS *Arizona* Memorial

6

7

8

9

Hanalei Bay

8 Voted nicest beach in the USA many times over, this crescent-shaped bay (p523) will suit both passive and active beach-goers. Surfers can charge massive (and some beginner) waves while onlookers amble along the 2 miles of glorious sandy shore. Surf lessons are available near the pier, and most afternoons see locals and visitors alike firing up the BBQ, cracking open a brew and humbly watching the daylight fade. Without a doubt, beach life is *the* life here.

Molokini

9 Hawaiian legend says that Molokini (p363) was a beautiful woman turned to stone by a jealous Pele, goddess of fire and volcanoes. Today Molokini is the stuff of legends among divers and snorkelers. The crescent-shaped rock, about three miles from the South Maui coast, is the rim of a volcanic crater. The shallow waters cradled within are a hospitable spot for coral and a calling card for more than 250 fish species. For an iconic Hawaii dive, this is the place.

Surfing O'ahu's North Shore

10 When giant rollers come crashing in, head to O'ahu's North Shore (p152) for a glimpse of Hawaii's rock stars of the ocean (you can also spot them riding pro-worthy waves at Ho'okipa Beach, p381, over on Maui). No need to pull out a camera lens larger then a howitzer – you can practically look these surfers in the eye as they paddle into monster surf. Or experience the adrenaline rush for yourself by learning to ride *da kine* (the best kind of) waves. Hang loose, brah!

Waimea Canyon

11 Formed by millions of years of erosion and the collapse of the volcano that formed Kaua'i, the 'Grand Canyon of the Pacific' (p567) stretches 10 miles long, 1 mile wide and more than 3600ft deep. Waimea Canyon Lookout (p568) provides panoramic views of rugged cliffs, crested buttes and deep valley gorges. While the lookout is easily accessible by car, hiking trails allow the adventurous a chance to delve to the canyon floor and survey its interior, satisfying all curiosities – or creating even more.

Hawaii's Cuisine

12 Forget about pineapple upside-down cake and mai tais. Hawaii is a multicultural taste explosion, influenced by the Pacific Rim but rooted in the islands' natural bounty. The first Polynesians brought staples such as *kalo* (taro) and *niu* (coconut). Plantation immigrants added global flavors: Japanese rice, Chinese noodles, Portuguese sweet bread and more. Over time flavors fused to become simply 'local' (p602). Be brave and eat everything in sight – it's all *'ono grinds* (good eats).

Below: *Kalua* pork

Waipi'o Valley

13 A stunning tropical valley at the end of the road. A mysterious green bowl full of ghosts and legends. A sacred site. A retreat from the outside world. Waipi'o's (p256) special distillation of all these makes it irresistible. Many choose to snap it from the panoramic overlook, one of the Big Island's most iconic views. Others trek down to the valley floor, where they stroll a black sand beach, hike back into a natural botanical garden and peer at distant waterfalls. Access is limited beyond that, only enhancing the mystery.

12

13

KARL LEHMANN / GETTY IMAGES ©

FRANCO BANFI / GETTY IMAGES ©

Hulopo'e Beach

14 The free public park (p435) at the main beach on company-run Lana'i is maintained by the same gardeners who manicure the Four Seasons resorts – so, predictably, it's lovely. The postcard-perfect crescent of curving white-sand is enjoyed by all, from locals taking the kids for a swim, to tourists on day trips from Maui; many a visitor has ended up losing track of time here. Be sure to have a break from lounging on the sand and take advantage of the amazing snorkeling and walks to ancient Hawaiian sites.

Munro Trail

15 The Munro Trail (p434), an exhilarating 12-mile adventure, follows a surviving forest across the hills above Lana'i's one and only town. Passing through groves of rare native plants and otherworldly Norfolk Island pines, the trail was once a Hawaiian footpath through a patchwork of taro farms, which drew on the frequent rainfall. On a clear day along the route you can see all of the inhabited Hawaiian islands except for distant Kaua'i and Ni'ihau. Just listening to the myriad birdcalls will have you singing your own song.

Night Diving & Snorkeling with Mantas

16 It may seem like an alien world but the ocean's wonders become accessible to all on the Big Island. Take a night snorkeling or scuba-diving trip near Kailua-Kona (p184) and come face to face, and sometimes belly to...the equivalent body part, with enormous Pacific manta rays. These graceful giants glide like dark angels beneath you, dancing a shadowy ballet that is heart-wrenchingly beautiful and utterly fascinating. Best of all, you need no real skill in the water to enjoy this incredible wildlife adventure.

17

18

PHILIP ROSENBERG / GETTY IMAGES ©

Stargazing atop Mauna Kea

17 Star light, star bright, the first star I see tonight...whoops, scratch that. Up here (p250), where the night skies are brighter than almost anywhere on Earth, stars – even galaxies – sear the night white and choosing the first is near impossible. Not to worry: with telescopes (free!) set up for visitors to browse the sky's celestial glory, you don't have to choose just one. Get here by sunset for a heavenly double feature or be a real maverick and opt for sunrise. Are you up for it?

Kalaupapa Mule Ride

18 On the Molokai Mule Ride (p468), from a lofty perch more than 1600ft above Moloka'i's Kalaupapa Peninsula (p466), you'll ride a surefooted steed down a steep trail with dizzying switchbacks; the views of the Kalaupapa National Historical Park below are spectacular. At the bottom you'll learn the dramatic tales of Hawaii's former colony for people with Hansen's disease (leprosy). It's eerie and isolated, but you'll take heart from the stories of people who lived here, including not one but two saints.

Old Lahaina Luau

19 Cold mai tais and sweet-smelling lei welcome guests to Maui's most authentic luau (p330), a place of warm aloha where Hawaiian history, culture and culinary prowess are the focus. Highlights? The unearthing of the *imu*-cooked pig, the dancing of the *hula kahiko* and, of course, the savoring of the feast – a table-topping spread of hearty salads, fresh fish, and grilled and roasted meats. On Kaua'i, tantalize the senses with a thrilling evening of hula, fire-dancing and feasting at Luau Kalamaku (p489).

Above right: Old Lahaina Luau

Farmers Markets

20 Wanna meet the locals? Just find the nearest farmers market. Besides being places to pick up the islands' freshest papaya, pineapples, macadamia nuts, honey and more, Hawaii's farmers markets are also celebrations of community. You might meet a traditional *kahuna lapa'au* (healer) extolling the virtues of *noni* (Indian mulberry); tipple a coconut-husk cup full of a mildly sedative brew made from *'awa* (kava); or find a handwoven *lauhala* (pandanus leaf) hat. If you're craving island-style fun and cultural authenticity, start here.

SHELDON LEVIS / GETTY IMAGES ©

Need to Know

For more information, see Survival Guide (p637)

Currency

US dollar ($)

Languages

English, Hawaiian

Visas

Generally not required for stays of 90 days or less for citizens of Visa Waiver Program (VWP) countries with ESTA approval.

Money

ATMs widely available. Credit cards widely accepted; often required for reservations (eg hotels, car rentals). Traveler's checks (US dollars) sometimes accepted. Tipping customary.

Cell Phones

Coverage spotty outside developed areas; US carrier Verizon has the best network. International travelers need GSM multiband phones; buy prepaid SIM cards locally.

Time

Hawaiian–Aleutian Standard Time (GMT/UMC minus 10 hours)

When to Go

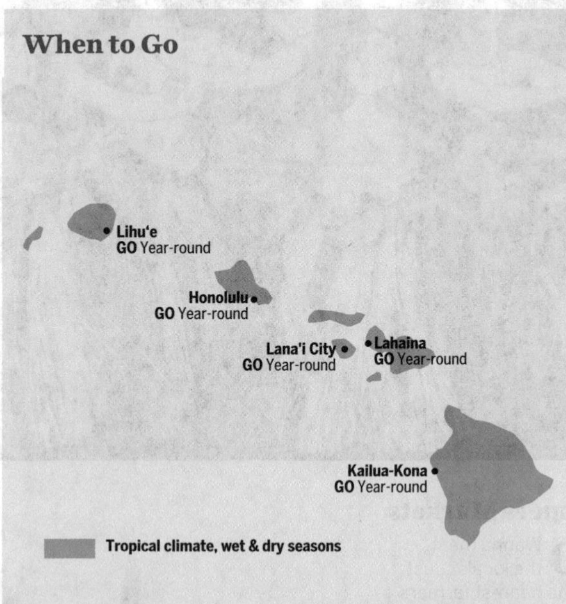

High Season
(Dec–Apr & Jun–Aug)

- Accommodation prices up 50–100%
- Christmas to New Year's, and Easter are most expensive and busy
- Winter is wetter (best for whale watching and surfing), summer is hotter (festivals galore)

Shoulder
(May & Sep)

- Crowds and prices drop slightly between schools' spring break and summer vacation
- Temperatures mild, with mostly sunny cloudless days, some scattered showers
- Statewide Aloha Festivals throughout September

Low Season
(Oct–Nov)

- Fewest crowds, airfares at their lowest from US mainland and Canada
- Accommodation rates drop – around 50% less than in high season
- Weather is dry, hot and extremely humid (not ideal for hiking)

Useful Websites

Hawaii Visitors and Convention Bureau (www.gohawaii.com) Official tourism site; comprehensive events calendar and multilingual planning guides.

Hawaii Magazine (www.hawaiimagazine.com) All-island news, entertaining features, festival coverage and travel tips.

Lonely Planet (www.lonelyplanet.com/usa/hawaii) Destination info, accommodations bookings, travelers' forums and more.

Honolulu Star-Advertiser (www.staradvertiser.com) State's biggest daily newspaper.

Important Numbers

Hawaii's area code (808) is not used when making local calls, but must be used when calling between islands. Dial 1 before any toll-free or long-distance call, including to Canada (for which international rates apply).

USA's country code	☎1
International access code	☎011
Operator	☎0
Emergency (ambulance, fire & police)	☎911
Directory assistance	☎411

Exchange Rates

Australia	A$1	$1.03
Canada	C$1	$0.97
China	Y10	$1.60
Euro zone	€1	$1.30
Japan	¥100	$1.04
New Zealand	NZ$1	$0.82
UK	UK£1	$1.50

For current exchange rates see www.xe.com

Daily Costs

Budget: Less than $100

- Dorm bed: $20–35
- Semiprivate room in hostel: $50–80
- Local plate lunch: $5–10
- Bus fare (one way): $1–2.50

Midrange: $100–250

- Double room in midrange hotel or B&B: $100–250
- Rental car (excluding insurance and gas): from $35/150 per day/week
- Dinner at a casual sit-down restaurant: $20–40

Top End: Over $250

- Beach resort hotel room or one-bedroom condo rental: over $250
- Three-course meal with a cocktail in a top restaurant: $75–120

Opening Hours

Opening hours may be longer in hub cities, major towns and tourist resorts, shorter in rural areas.

Banks 8:30am–4pm Mon-Fri, some to 6pm Fri & 9am–noon or 1pm Sat

Bars Usually noon–midnight daily, some to 2am Thu–Sat

Businesses & government offices 8:30am–4:30pm Mon-Fri; some post offices 9am–noon Sat

Restaurants breakfast 6–10am, lunch 11:30am–2pm, dinner 5–9:30pm

Shops 9am–5pm Mon-Sat, some also noon–5pm Sun; shopping malls keep extended hours

Arriving in Hawaii

Honolulu International Airport (HNL; see p66)

Car 25 to 45 minutes' drive to Waikiki via Hwy 92 (Nimitz Hwy/Ala Moana Blvd) or H-1 (Lunalilo) Fwy

Taxis Metered, usually $35 to $45 to Waikiki (more during rush hour), plus 15% tip and 35¢ per bag

Door-to-door shuttles $13–15 one way ($24–30 round-trip) to Waikiki; operate 24 hours (every 20 to 60 minutes)

Buses TheBus 19 or 20 to Waikiki ($2.50) every 20 to 60 minutes from 6am to 11pm daily (large baggage prohibited)

Getting Around

Most interisland travel is by plane. Ferries only connect Maui with Moloka'i and Lana'i. Renting a car is usually necessary if you want to explore.

Car Drive on the right. Rental cars should always be reserved in advance; rates typically are lowest for airport pick-ups/drop-offs. Consider skipping a rental car if you're staying at Waikiki Beach on O'ahu.

Bus Oahu's TheBus network is extensive but doesn't stop at some popular tourist sights, beaches and hiking trailheads. On Maui, Kaua'i, the Big Island and Moloka'i, infrequent public buses primarily serve commuters and residents.

Bicycle Not practical for island-wide travel due to narrow highways, heavy traffic, high winds and changeable weather.

For much more on **getting around**, see p649

What's New

Aulani

Complete with character breakfasts, water slides and a kids' club, Disney's $800 million oceanfront resort and spa has made a huge splash at Ko Olina on O'ahu. (p166)

Pearl Harbor

If you haven't been to Hawaii's most famous WWII-era monuments and memorials recently, come back for the brand-new interactive museum that's absolutely free to visit. (p102)

Lana'i

On this ex-pineapple-plantation island, tech billionaire Larry Ellison plans to build another resort and spur 'green growth' with solar energy, a desalination plant and small farms. (p436)

Hawai'i Volcanoes National Park

With the grand reopening of Volcano House, Kilauea's ongoing eruption and the Kahuku Unit wilderness, this star national park is bigger and better than ever. (p300)

Kealakekua Bay

Due to overcrowding, watercraft have been temporarily banned. But intrepid travelers can still hike in to enjoy a peaceful snorkel among tropical fish and coral. (p211)

Agritourism

As Hawaii's 'food sovereignty' movement gains momentum, ever more island farms are letting visitors tour their traditional taro fields and taste organic fruit plucked right from the trees.

Food Trucks

Kaukau (lunch) wagons are nothing new in Hawaii. But a modern food truck revolution has taken off, from Honolulu's city streets to surf beaches.

Stand Up Paddle Surfing

Stand up paddle surfing (aka SUP) is taking over ever more of Hawaii's beaches and bays. Good news: even beginners can get the hang of it. (p47)

Ziplines

Wanna fly through cloud forests? Ziplines are skyrocketing in popularity on the bigger islands, with each new tour operator dreaming up more thrilling adventures. (p54)

Town & Street Parties

From Honolulu's First Friday celebrations in Chinatown to Maui's town parties, many new arts, cultural, music and food events are bringing locals and tourists together outdoors.

Microbrews & Spirits

Microbreweries (p605) are popping up all around the bigger islands and you'll find a few local distillers such as Kaua'i's Koloa Rum Company (p489) offering tropical tastes too.

For more recommendations and reviews, see **lonelyplanet.com/usa/hawaii**

If You Like...

Beaches

Think of Hawaii, and you're instantly dreaming about golden sands backed by tropical palm trees, right? With six main islands and hundreds of miles of coastline, you'll be spoiled for choice.

Waikiki Learn to surf, board a sunset 'booze cruise' and catch a hula show under the stars on O'ahu (p105)

Ho'okipa Beach Near Pa'ia on Maui, this is a pilgrimage spot for both pro windsurfers and surfers – and spectators (p381)

Mauna Kea Beach Kauna'oa Bay provides the Big Island's most Hollywood-worthy crescent of white sand (p233)

Hanalei Bay Arguably Kaua'i's most postcard-perfect beach, it embraces surfers, bodyboarders and beach bums (p523)

Hulupo'e Beach Fronting azure Manele Bay on Lana'i, ferries drop off daytrippers at this sun-kissed playground (p435)

Twenty Mile Beach On Moloka'i's wild east side, don a snorkel mask to explore a rocky reef-protected lagoon (p455)

Waterfalls & Swimming Holes

Get ready to wade through the mud and step over slippery tree roots on jungly trails, all so you can swim in a crystal-clear pool under a rainforest cascade.

'Ohe'o Gulch In Haleakalā National Park, Maui's best-known series of waterfalls and natural pools tumble down into the sea (p419)

Wailua Falls You might recognize Kaua'i's famous twin cascades from the opening scenes of TV's *Fantasy Island* (p482)

Manoa Falls A short family-friendly hike in O'ahu's shady Ko'olau Range above downtown Honolulu (p85)

Rainbow Falls Just outside Hilo on the Big Island, visit these misty falls in the early morning to catch their namesake (p271)

Waipi'o & Waimanu Valleys Earn Hawai'i's most epic waterfall views after some rugged hiking in the Big Island's emerald amphitheater valleys (p256)

Moa'ula & Hipuapua Falls Hire a local hiking guide to discover these falls deep inside Moloka'i's Halawa Valley (p457)

IF YOU LIKE... HAWAIIAN MUSIC & HULA

Many oceanfront hotels and bars, especially at Waikiki Beach on O'ahu (p123), host live Hawaiian music and hula dance performances nightly. Admission is usually just the cost of a cocktail.

Hiking & Backpacking

Hawaii's islands have as many adventures to offer landlubbers as water babies. Take your pick among scores of footpaths, from easy waterfall and botanical garden strolls to overnight volcano treks.

Haleakalā National Park Cloud forest walks and volcano summit trails wind through Maui's high-altitude wilderness (p415)

Kalalau Trail Hawaii's best-known backpacking route traces the cliffs and stream-cut valleys of Kaua'i's jewel-like Na Pali Coast (p537)

Hawai'i Volcanoes National Park For thrills, nothing beats trekking through the geological wonderland ruled by Pele, goddess of fire and volcanoes (p296)

Kalaupapa Peninsula Snake down sky-high sea cliffs to Moloka'i's unique national historical park (p466)

Makiki Forest Recreation Area Climb to knife-edged summits with 360-degree panoramic views in Honolulu's windblown Ko'olau Range (p86)

Ka'ena Point State Park Stride past Hawaiian monk seals out to land's end on O'ahu (p170)

Scenic Drives

Are you ready to roll? These islands may be small, but you can still take scenic drives up volcano summits, into cloud forests, over high *pali* (cliffs) and through *paniolo* (Hawaiian cowboy) country.

Road to Hana Curving down Maui's lushest coast, this roller-coaster route passes dozens of waterfalls and crosses 54 stone bridges (p395)

O'ahu's Windward Coast Leave behind the urban jungles of Honolulu and Waikiki for the island's down-home countryside (p134)

Haleakalā Crater Rd A drive up Maui's biggest volcano measures 37 miles from sea to summit, boasting the steepest elevation gain of any road on earth (p421)

Chain of Craters Road Drop almost 4000ft through the Big Island's active volcano zone to where fiery lava once buried the road (p294)

Munro Trail Rent a jeep (or grab a mountain bike) to challenge Lana'i's red-dirt 4WD route (p434)

Small Towns

For an authentic taste of everyday life in Hawaii, spend a day in places where the pace of life is slower, the smiles are genuinely friendly and aloha overflows.

(Top) Wailua River (p496), Kaua'i

(Bottom) *Loco moco* (rice, fried egg and a hamburger doused in gravy, p602)

Hana When you're ready to unplug and get away from it all, eastern Maui's hidden hamlet beckons (p404)

Hilo Not even a tsunami could keep this old-school Big Island bayside town down for the count (p267)

Hale'iwa Surf culture meets laid-back country life in O'ahu's North Shore hub (p158)

Hanapepe Calling itself Kaua'i's 'biggest little town,' this Westside valley has been revitalized by the arts (p558)

Holualoa A heritage village that time has passed by, tucked among Kona's mountainside coffee fields on the Big Island (p197)

Hanalei Browse the quirky shops, grab a farm-fresh plate lunch and wax your surfboard on Kaua'i's North Shore (p522)

Kaunakakai A Native Hawaiian stronghold on Moloka'i, this dusty, old-fashioned village has heart (p447)

History

From Polynesian wayfarers through the arrival of 19th-century Christian missionaries, sugar barons and plantation immigrants to the modern US military, Hawaii's story is often written on the land.

USS Arizona Memorial Pay your respects to those who died in the Japanese attack on O'ahu's Pearl Harbor in 1941 (p102)

Pu'uhonua o Honaunau National Historical Park Gaze into the eyes of *ki'i* (deity images) at an ancient place of refuge on the Big Island (p214)

Lahaina Once a rowdy whaling port and Christian mission, this West Maui harbor town gives glimpses of its historic past (p318)

Mo'okini Luakini Heiau Visit a windswept Hawaiian temple and the birthplace of King Kamehameha I (p239)

Bishop Museum Uncover traditional and contemporary Hawaiian culture inside Honolulu's biggest museum (p83)

Wailua River Paddle a kayak along Kaua'i's sacred waterway, historically home to high chiefs and lava-rock heiau (p496)

Festivals

There's always a party going on somewhere in Hawaii. With outrigger canoe races, food festivals and hula competitions, you won't run out of excuses to extend your trip.

Aloha Festivals September brings colorful celebrations of Hawaiian arts and culture statewide (p28)

Merrie Monarch Festival On Easter Sunday, 'the Olympics of hula' happens in Hilo on the Big Island (p275)

Triple Crown of Surfing Gnarly winter waves and giant swells bring out the pros and thousands of spectators on O'ahu's North Shore (p158)

Kona Coffee Cultural Festival For anyone addicted to Hawai'i's richest, most potent brews, head to the Big Island in November (p187)

Pan-Pacific Festival Celebrate Hawaii's multiethnic heritage with Polynesian dancing and *taiko* drumming in Honolulu in June (p89)

Food & Drink

There are so many *'ono grinds* (good eats) in Hawaii that you might find yourself eating more than three times a day – even before *pau hana* (happy hour) rolls around!

Mixed-plate lunches Asian and European dishes mix with the indigenous flavors of the islands

Kalua pig & huli-huli chicken Get a mouthful of smokin' roasted and rotisserie meats – basically, Hawaii-style barbecue

Loco moco The breakfast of champions: rice, fried egg and a hamburger patty doused in gravy

Crack seed Got a sweet tooth? A salty, sour or spicy craving? Hawaii's Chinese-inspired dried-fruit candy snacks satisfy

Poke Hawaii's version of a marinated raw-fish salad, perfect for beach picnics

'Awa A mildly intoxicating traditional Polynesian brew made from the kava plant

Shave ice Nothing tastes better after a hot day at the beach

Month by Month

TOP EVENTS

Aloha Festivals, September

Triple Crown of Surfing, November & December

Merrie Monarch Festival, March & April

Mele Mei, May

Hawaii International Film Festival, October

January

Typically Hawaii's wettest and coolest month, January is when tourist high season gets into full swing, with snowbirds escaping winter elsewhere. The Martin Luther King Jr holiday on the third Monday is especially busy.

Chinese New Year

On the second new moon after the winter solstice, usually between mid-January and mid-February, look for lion dances, firecrackers, street fairs and parades. Honolulu's celebrations (p89) are the biggest; festivities on Hilo (Hawai'i the Big Island) and Lahaina (Maui) are notable too.

February

Peak tourist season continues, with weekends around Valentine's Day (February 14) and Presidents Day (third Monday) usually booked solid at resorts. Winter storms bring more rainfall and cooler temperatures.

Waimea Town Celebration

Over two action-packed days in mid-February, more than 10,000 folks gather in Waimea (Kaua'i) to celebrate with canoe and foot races, a rodeo, lei-making contests and live music. (p564)

Maui Whale Festival

Throughout the winter, Maui celebrates its most famous visitors – migratory humpback whales – with a family-oriented slate of events, including a winter whale count and live entertainment and kids' activities on Whale Day in mid-February. (p367)

March

It's another busy month to visit Hawaii, despite lingering rainfall. College students and families take a one- or two-week 'spring break' around Easter, falling in March or April.

Honolulu Festival

In mid-March, this three-day festival celebrates the harmony of Pacific Rim cultures. It's a unique blend of Hawaii, Asia and Polynesia, with a craft fair and live music and dance performances, culminating in a grand parade followed by a fireworks show. (p89)

Prince Kuhio Day

All islands honor the March 26 birthday of Prince Kuhio Kalaniana'ole, the man who would've become king if Queen Lili'uokalani hadn't been overthrown. Kaua'i bustles with a two-week arts and cultural festival, featuring a canoe race, lei-making and ukulele workshops and Hawaiian storytelling. (p548)

April

As peak tourist season ends, Hawaii's resorts start to slow down after Easter as college students and families finish their 'spring break.' Rainstorms lessen, too.

Merrie Monarch Festival

On the Big Island, Easter Sunday (late March/early April) kicks off Hilo's week-long celebration of Hawaiian arts and culture. Action revolves around the Olympics of hula competitions, which draws top troupes from all islands, the US mainland and abroad. (p275)

East Maui Taro Festival

On Maui, the rural town of Hana throws its biggest party for two weekend days in late April, with poi (pounded taro paste) making, a local arts-and-crafts fair, Hawaiian hula dancing and lots of island music. (p406)

Waikiki Spam Jam

How much does Hawaii love Spam? Residents consume almost seven million cans each year. Waikiki's wacky one-day street festival in late April probably accounts for 10,000 all by itself, prepared hundreds of ways – that's *'ono grinds*! (good eats). (p113)

Maui Onion Festival

For a weekend in late April/early May, Maui's famously sweet onions inspire delicious events, appealing to island chefs and visiting gourmands alike. Live music, recipe cook-off contests and an outdoor beer garden all happen in Ka'anapali. (p338)

May

Crowds thin and prices drop slightly between spring break and summer vacation. Temperatures remain mild, with mostly sunny and cloudless days. Hotels sell out for the Memorial Day holiday weekend in late May.

Mele Mei

O'ahu's month-long celebration of Hawaiian music (p89) stretches from late April to late May, with ukulele and slack key guitar workshops, concerts and hula performances, all leading up to Na Hoku Hanohano, Hawaii's version of the Grammy Awards.

Lei Day

Across Hawaii the ancient tradition of lei making gets its own holiday on May 1. O'ahu crowns a lei queen in Waikiki; Lihu'e's Kaua'i Museum holds a lei-making competition; and Hilo hosts lei-making demonstrations and Hawaiian storytelling on the Big Island.

Moloka'i Ka Hula Piko

According to Hawaiian oral history, Moloka'i is the birthplace of hula. In early May, this three-day hula festival draws huge crowds to its sacred hula performances and Hawaiian *ho'olaule'a* (celebration). (p444)

June

Before most families start taking summer vacations, visitors in early June can take advantage of warm, dry weather and discounts on hotels and flights.

Pan-Pacific Festival

In Honolulu, this three-day festival in early June combines family-friendly celebrations of Hawaiian and Japanese cultures, with hula dancing, *taiko* drumming, live music and folk-art workshops, ending with a huge parade and block party in Waikiki (p114).

King Kamehameha Day

On June 11, this state holiday is celebrated on all islands. Honolulu's statue of Kamehameha is ceremoniously draped with lei, followed by a grand parade. Later in the month, the capital city's King Kamehameha Hula Competition is one of Hawaii's biggest contests (p89).

Kapalua Wine & Food Festival

Hawaii's longest-running culinary extravaganza attracts taste-makers for three days in early June to Kapalua resort in West Maui. Show up for cooking demonstrations by TV celebrity chefs and wine tastings with master sommeliers. (p345)

Pineapple Festival

In late June or early July this festival celebrating Lana'i's special relationship with the pineapple is the island's main bash, featuring kid-friendly activities, live music and food in Lana'i City. (Never mind that Lana'i no longer grows any of its own pineapples!) (p432)

July

Temperatures rise and rain is scarce. School summer vacations and the July 4 national holiday make this one of the busiest travel months. Book early and expect high prices.

Independence Day

Across the islands, Fourth of July celebrations inspire fireworks and fairs, but maybe the most fun is had at rodeos held in the *paniolo* (Hawaiian cowboy) towns of Waimea (Kamuela) on the Big Island (p246) and Makawao on Maui (p389).

Prince Lot Hula Festival

On the third Saturday in July, one of O'ahu's premier Hawaiian cultural festivals showcases noncompetitive hula performances in a garden setting at a former royal retreat, giving it a graceful, traditional feeling. (p90)

Koloa Plantation Days Celebration

On Kauai's south shore, this 10-day festival in late July is a huge celebration of the island's sugar-plantation and *paniolo* (Hawaiian cowboy) heritage. It includes a parade, rodeo, traditional games, live entertainment, movies and historical walks. (p541)

August

Families taking summer vacations keep things busy all around the islands. Hot, sunny weather prevails, especially on the islands' leeward sides. Statehood Day is celebrated on the third Friday of the month.

Hawaiian International Billfish Tournament

Kailua-Kona, on the Big Island, is the epicenter of big-game fishing, and for more than 50 years this has been Hawaii's grand tournament. It's accompanied by almost a week of festive entertainment in late July or early to mid-August. (p187)

Hawaiian Slack Key Festival

In Waikiki, free open-air concerts by ukulele and slack key guitar legends, with food and craft vendors and guitar exhibits and demonstrations, happen in late August. Spin-off events take place during other months on the Big Island, Maui and Kaua'i. (p114)

September

After Labor Day weekend in early September, crowds start to fade away at beach resorts as students go back to school. Hot summer temperatures continue.

Aloha Festivals

Begun in 1946, the Aloha Festivals are the state's premier Hawaiian cultural celebration, an almost nonstop series of events on all the main islands during September. On O'ahu, look for a Hawaiian royal court procession and Waikiki's block party. For a full schedule, visit www.alohafestivals.com.

Queen Lili'uokalani Canoe Race

In Hawaii, traditional outrigger canoeing is alive and well, and fall is the big season for long-distance events. Everything kicks off over Labor Day weekend with these races along the Big Island's Kona Coast.

Hawai'i Food & Wine Festival

Hawaii's hottest chefs and most lauded artisan farmers gather for this homegrown culinary celebration, with stellar farm-to-table food and cocktail and wine tastings in Honolulu in early to mid-September. (p90)

Kaua'i Mokihana Festival

In mid-September, Kaua'i's week-long contemporary Hawaiian arts and cultural festival includes a three-day hula competition with a beachside royal court procession (p487), as well as the Kaua'i Composers Contest & Concert in Lihu'e (p487).

Na Wahine O Ke Kai

Held in late September (weather permitting), this is the powerful all-women sister event of the all-male Moloka'i Hoe in early October. Both legendary long-distance outrigger canoe races traverse the 41-mile Ka'iwi Channel between Moloka'i and O'ahu. (p444)

October

The slowest month for visiting Hawaii, October brings travel bargains

on hotels and flights. Weather is reliably sunny, but very humid when the tradewinds don't blow.

Kohala Country Fair

During the first week of October, the Big Island's biggest county fair shows off its country pride with equestrian demonstrations, Spam-carving and tug-of-war contests, an arts-and-crafts show, live Hawaiian music and more fun activities for kids. (p242)

Coconut Festival

You can't call yourself a Coconut Festival and not get a little nutty. In fact, Kapa'a on Kaua'i gets downright silly, with two days of pie-eating contests, coconut crafts, recipe cookoffs, live entertainment and hands-on activities for kids in early October. (p503)

Eo e Emalani I Alaka'i

On Kaua'i, Koke'e State Park reenacts Queen Emma's historic 1871 journey to Alaka'i Swamp with a powerful one-day festival in early or mid-October. It's full of authentic hula and Hawaiian music performances and traditional crafts. (p574)

Ironman Triathlon World Championship

This legendary triathlon on the Big Island's Kona coast is the ultimate endurance contest, combining a 2.4-mile ocean swim, 112-mile bike race and 26.2-mile marathon. Watch more than 1800 athletes push their own limits in mid-October. (p187)

Maui Ukulele Festival

Herald Hawaii's favorite stringed musical instrument outdoors at the Maui Arts & Cultural Center on a mid-October Sunday, with guest appearances by stars like Jake Shimabukuro and Kelly Boy De Lima. (p353)

Hawaii International Film Festival

In mid-October, this highly regarded celebration of Pacific Rim cinema screens over 200 Asian, Polynesian and Hawaii-made films at multiple venues, with the main action in Honolulu (for a full schedule of screenings, see www.hiff.org).

Halloween

On Maui, Lahaina's Halloween celebration (p325) was once so huge it was dubbed 'Mardi Gras of the Pacific.' It's been scaled back, but is still a great street party. Other places to get festive on October 31 include Waikiki Beach on O'ahu.

November

Toward the end of the month, vacationing crowds and scattered rainfall start returning to Hawaii. Thanksgiving on the fourth Thursday is a popular and pricey time to visit.

Moku O Keawe

In early November, this three-day Big Island hula festival draws top hula *halau* (schools) from Hawaii, Japan and the US mainland to competitions, workshops and a marketplace for hula fashions and traditional crafts in Waikoloa. (p226)

Kona Coffee Cultural Festival

For 10 days during the harvest season in early November, the Big Island celebrates its Kona brews with a cupping competition, a coffee-picking contest, coffee farm tours, live concerts, a lantern-lit parade and multicultural festivities. (p187)

Triple Crown of Surfing

O'ahu's North Shore – specifically Hale'iwa, Sunset Beach and Pipeline – hosts pro surfing's ultimate contest, known as the Triple Crown of Surfing. Thrill-a-minute competitions for women and men run from mid-November through mid-December, depending on when the surf's up. (p158)

December

As winter rainstorms return and temperatures cool slightly, peak tourist season begins in mid-December, with the Christmas to New Year's holiday period extremely busy – and expensive.

Honolulu Marathon

Held on the second Sunday in December, the Honolulu Marathon is Hawaii's biggest and most popular foot race. It attracts almost 20,000 runners every year (more than half hailing from Japan), making it one of the world's top 10 largest marathons. (p90)

Plan Your Trip
Itineraries

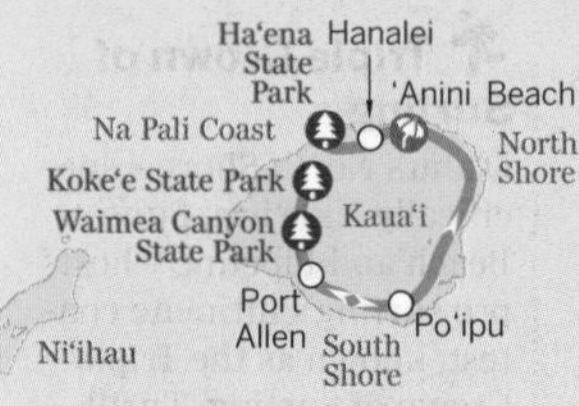

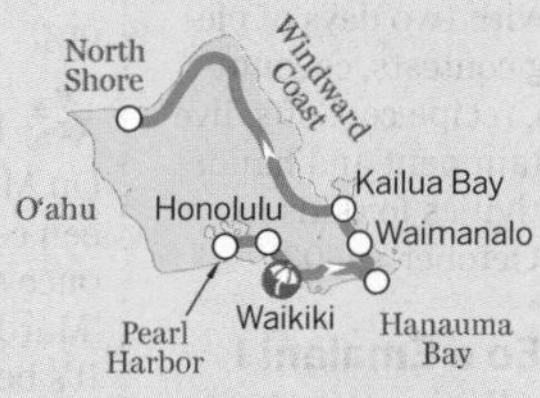

LONELY PLANET / GETTY IMAGES ©

O'ahu & Kaua'i

Think of this as your 'town and country' trip to Hawaii. Start off in the breezy streets of Honolulu, sleeping in mod style at the classic beach resort of Waikiki. Then trade the big-city buzz for the small-town scene on verdant Kaua'i.

Touch down for four days on O'ahu amid the skyscrapers of **Honolulu**. Between sessions at the beaches of **Waikiki**, eat your heart out in the capital, go clubbing and art-gallery hopping in Chinatown, visit the Bishop Museum and 'Iolani Palace, experience WWII history at **Pearl Harbor**, enjoy live Hawaiian music and hula at sunset, hike up **Diamond Head** and tour Doris Duke's incomparable **Shangri La**.

Now relax. Heading east, spend a morning snorkeling at **Hanauma Bay**. In the afternoon, swim off the white-sand beaches of **Waimanalo** or surf, kayak, windsurf and kiteboard at **Kailua Bay**. Wend your way along the **Windward Coast**, with its jungly hiking trails, ancient lava-rock fishponds and captivating offshore islands. Save at least an afternoon to savor the world-famous beaches of the **North Shore**. In winter, watch big-wave

Po'ipu (p542), Kaua'i

surfers carving; in summer, snorkel with sea turtles.

Hop a plane over to Kaua'i, full of heart-stopping scenery, for the next six days. Start off nice and easy in **Po'ipu** with a lazy snooze on the sunny beaches of the **South Shore** or head straight to **Port Allen** for a snorkeling or scuba-diving boat trip. Then lace up your hiking boots and spend a day in **Waimea Canyon State Park** and **Koke'e State Park**, where you can traverse knife-edged 2000ft-high cliffs and peek into the 'Grand Canyon of the Pacific.'

Giddy-up back around to Kaua'i's **North Shore**, which deserves a couple of days. Get in some swimming, snorkeling and windsurfing at **'Anini Beach**, and check out the beach-bum town of **Hanalei** for surfing and stand up paddle boarding on the bay or kayaking a peaceful river. Road trips hardly get more scenic than the drive to the very end of the road at **Ha'ena State Park**.

OK, ready? **Na Pali Coast State Park** is what's left: in summer, kayak 17 miles beside Kaua'i's epic sea cliffs; otherwise, backpack 11 miles to Ke'e Beach. Either way, you've saved the best for last.

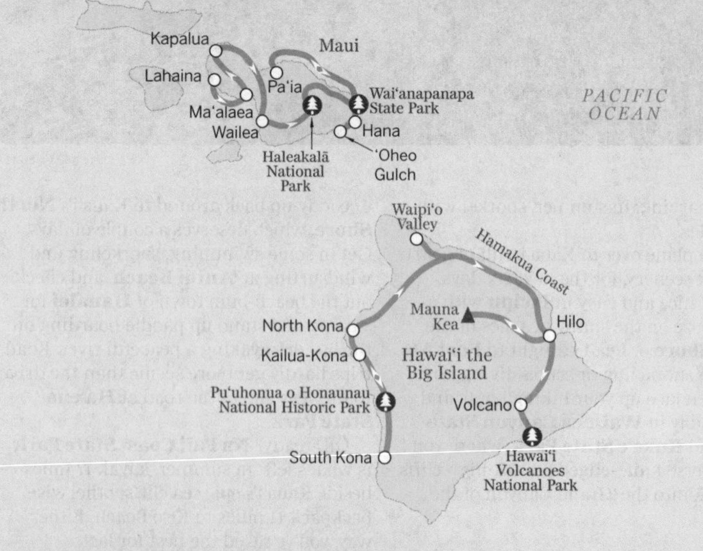
Maui
Kapalua
Lahaina
Pa'ia
Ma'alaea
Wailea
Wai'anapanapa State Park
Hana
'Oheo Gulch
Haleakalā National Park
PACIFIC OCEAN
Waipi'o Valley
Hamakua Coast
Mauna Kea
Hilo
North Kona
Kailua-Kona
Hawai'i the Big Island
Pu'uhonua o Honaunau National Historic Park
Volcano
South Kona
Hawai'i Volcanoes National Park

RON DAHLQUIST / GETTY IMAGES ©

BRIGITTE MERZ / GETTY IMAGES ©

Top: Haleakalā National Park (p410), Maui
Bottom: Lahaina (p318), Maui

2 WEEKS Maui & Hawai'i

Looking for tropical adventures you can brag about? Hit up Maui for its postcard-perfect honeymoon beaches, serpentine coastal drives and hang-loose surf scene. When you're ready for bigger thrills, jet to Hawai'i the Big Island, where erupting volcanoes, mysterious valleys and deserted beaches await.

With less than a week to spend on Maui, start in the old whaling town of **Lahaina** with its pirates' treasure chest of historical sites. In winter, spot whales breaching offshore or take a whale-watching boat tour from **Ma'alaea**. For golden-sand beaches idyllic for swimming and snorkeling, drive north up the coast to bayfront **Kapalua** and south to the resorts of **Wailea** and beyond.

Make sure you get to **Haleakalā National Park**. Spend a day hiking around an ancient volcano and catching sunrise from the summit. Then drive the cliff-hugging **Road to Hana**, stopping to kick back on the black-sand beach at **Wai'anapanapa State Park**. Go past Hana for a bamboo rainforest hike and to take a dip in the cascading waterfall pools of **'Ohe'o Gulch**. Backtrack up the coast to the surf town of **Pa'ia**, chowing *'ono grinds* (delicious food) and admiring the daredevil windsurfers at Ho'okipa Beach.

The Big Island can take a week and then some. Base yourself half the time in **Kailua-Kona**, alternating trips to the beaches – especially those in **North Kona** and on the **South Kohala** 'Gold Coast' – with feeling the ancient mana (spiritual essence) at **Pu'uhonua o Honaunau National Historical Park** and tasting the produce at the coffee farms of **South Kona**. Take a leisurely drive along the **Hamakua Coast**, making sure to gaze out on **Waipi'o Valley**, if not to hike down to the wild beach.

Walk around harborfront **Hilo**, exploring its historic architecture, the downtown farmers market and the excellent 'Imiloa Astronomy Center of Hawai'i and Pacific Tsunami Museum. Don't miss detouring up to **Mauna Kea** for an evening of stargazing. Spend at least a full day in **Hawai'i Volcanoes National Park**: hike the otherworldly Kilauea Iki Trail, drive along the Chain of Craters Road and hopefully trek or take a boat ride to see some hot lava glowing fiery red after dark. Afterward retreat to your own rainforest cottage B&B in nearby **Volcano**.

10 DAYS O'ahu & Hawai'i

Go big or go home – if that's your motto then pair Hawaii's busiest island with its biggest. Beach-resort chic, ancient heiau (temples) set beside taro fields, mountainous hiking trails and azure bays with white-sand beaches let you experience the best of almost everything Hawaii offers.

Start on the capital island of O'ahu, basing yourself in **Kailua** for five days. Among the many sights around **Honolulu**, don't miss the WWII memorials at **Pearl Harbor** or the Honolulu Academy of Arts. Snorkel one morning at **Hanauma Bay** and in the afternoon hike to Honolulu's Manoa Falls after visiting the Lyon Arboretum. Take a class in lei making, hula dancing or ukulele playing in **Waikiki**, where you can end the day with a sunset catamaran 'booze cruise' or live Hawaiian music and hula at oceanfront bars.

Drive up the **Windward Coast**, stopping at scenic beaches and to hike into the misty Ko'olau Mountains. Keep going past the coves of **Turtle Bay** to end up on the **North Shore**, famous for its big-wave surfing in winter. Stroll and grab a shave ice in **Hale'iwa**, then take a joy-ride flight at Dillingham Airfield. Dip your toes into the lagoons at **Ko Olina** before cruising up the workaday **Wai'anae Coast** for a windy walk in **Ka'ena Point State Park**.

Mosey over to the Big Island and book a B&B in **South Kona** for a few nights. For ocean adventures, go scuba diving or snorkeling at night with manta rays around **Kailua-Kona** and hike in to snorkel at **Kealakekua Bay** or nearby Two-Step. Down in Ka'u, hike to Green Sands Beach near windswept **Ka Lae**, the USA's southernmost geographical point. Next up, **Hawai'i Volcanoes National Park**, home of the world's longest-running volcanic eruption, offers alien-looking moonscapes for hiking.

Spend a night or two in **Hilo**, taking time to drive partway up **Mauna Kea** for stargazing after dark. After rolling up and down along the **Hamakua Coast**, amble the old sugar-plantation town of **Honoka'a** before stepping into ancient **Waipi'o Valley**. Giddyup through **Waimea (Kamuela)**, a *paniolo* (Hawaiian cowboy) outpost, into the quiet countryside of North Kohala: hike into sculpted **Pololu Valley**, circle around **Mo'okini Heiau** and wander quaint **Hawi**.

M SWEET / GETTY IMAGES ©

ANN CECIL / GETTY IMAGES ©

Top: Waikiki Beach (p105), Waikiki, O'ahu
Bottom: Shrimp Shack (p149), Punalu'u, O'ahu

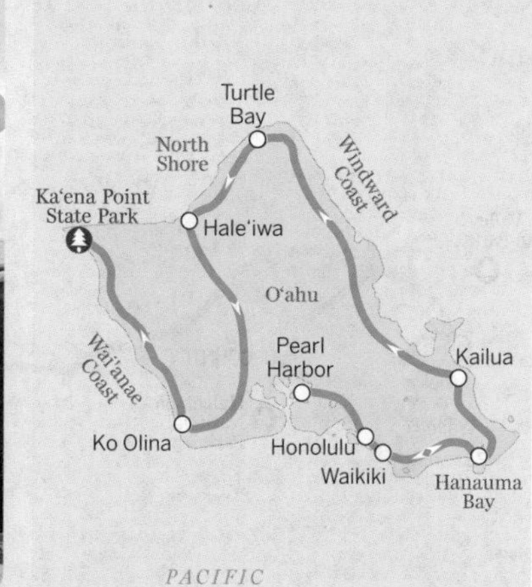
Turtle Bay
North Shore
Windward Coast
Ka'ena Point State Park
Hale'iwa
O'ahu
Wai'anae Coast
Pearl Harbor
Kailua
Ko Olina
Honolulu
Waikiki
Hanauma Bay
PACIFIC OCEAN

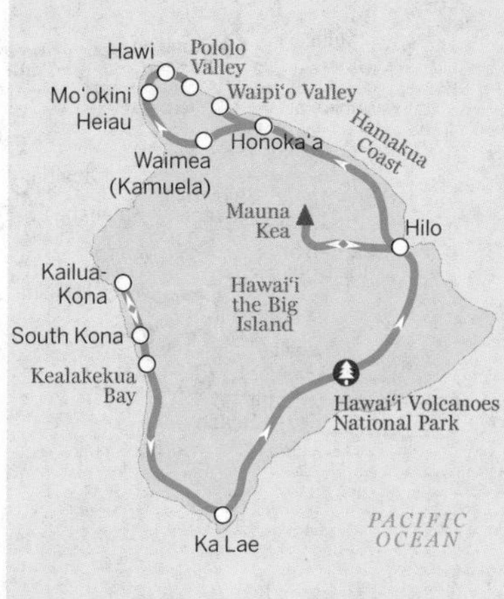
Hawi
Pololo Valley
Mo'okini Heiau
Waipi'o Valley
Honoka'a
Hamakua Coast
Waimea (Kamuela)
Mauna Kea
Hilo
Kailua-Kona
Hawai'i the Big Island
South Kona
Kealakekua Bay
Hawai'i Volcanoes National Park
Ka Lae
PACIFIC OCEAN

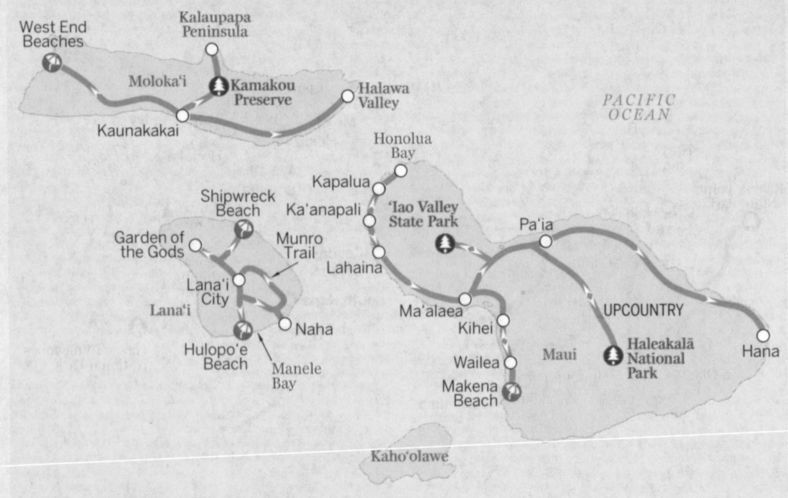
West End Beaches
Kalaupapa Peninsula
Moloka'i
Kamakou Preserve
Halawa Valley
Kaunakakai
PACIFIC OCEAN
Honolua Bay
Kapalua
Shipwreck Beach
Ka'anapali
'Iao Valley State Park
Pa'ia
Garden of the Gods
Munro Trail
Lahaina
Lana'i City
Lana'i
Naha
Hulopo'e Beach
Manele Bay
Ma'alaea
Kihei
UPCOUNTRY
Haleakalā National Park
Hana
Wailea
Maui
Makena Beach
Kaho'olawe

JOHN ELK / GETTY IMAGES ©

RON DAHLQUIST / GETTY IMAGES ©

op: Kalaupapa National Historical Park (p466), Moloka'i
Bottom: Garden of the Gods (p438), Lana'i

Maui, Lana'i & Moloka'i

You've got time, you've got money and you want outdoor experiences and peaceful relaxation in equal measure. But you're also willing to rough it when the rewards – hidden waterfalls, geological wonders – make it worthwhile. Mix up Maui, Lana'i and Moloka'i for an unforgettable island-hopping journey by airplane and possibly boat.

First, spend five or six days on **Maui**. Make it easy on yourself by getting a resort hotel room or a condo for your entire stay at **Ka'anapali** or **Kapalua** in West Maui or **Kihei** or **Wailea** in South Maui. Immerse yourself in the whaling history of **Lahaina** or take a whale-watching cruise from **Ma'alaea**. When it's beach time, some of Hawaii's wildest coastal strands are nearby, like **Honolua Bay** or Makena's **Big Beach**.

Take one full day to hike the summit moonscapes of **Haleakalā National Park** and another to lazily drive down the **Road to Hana**, stopping off for waterfall hikes and to buy fresh coconuts, before looping back to the laid-back surf town of **Pa'ia**. If you've got time to spare, visit the small farms, botanical gardens and ranches of Maui's **Upcountry**, where you can take a horseback ride or go ziplining. Before you head back to Kahului's airport, admire the legendary jungle spire at **'Iao Valley State Park**.

Next, hop over to **Lana'i** and take your pick of world-class resorts located in **Lana'i City** and at **Manele Bay**, staying three nights. Things have been a little hectic so far, so play a round of golf, snorkel at **Hulopo'e Beach** or take in the vistas from the **Munro Trail**. To really get away from it all, rent a 4WD and head for the **Garden of the Gods**, **Shipwreck Beach** or down the dusty track to **Naha**.

Last, spend four or five days on **Moloka'i**. Check into a condo or beachfront B&B after arriving in small-town **Kaunakakai**. Day one: explore **East Moloka'i**, checking out **Halawa Valley** and perhaps a waterfall or two. Day two: trek to the **Kalaupapa Peninsula** and munch macadamia nuts at Purdy's Farm. Day three: head out to the remote beaches of the island's **West End** or penetrate the dense forests of the **Kamakou Preserve**. Days four and five: relax.

The Big Four: O'ahu, Maui, Hawai'i & Kaua'i

If you want to live in the scenery – and not just admire it – take a month off on O'ahu, Maui, Hawai'i and Kaua'i. Find the truly off-the-beaten-track adventures of a lifetime and plenty of traditional and contemporary Hawaiian culture, not to mention sunset mai tais galore.

If the jam-packed beaches of **Waikiki** and modern high-rises of **Honolulu** seem too hectic, ease into your 'rubbah slippahs' on the island's longest sandy beach at **Waimanalo**. Rent a beach cottage in **Kailua** or anywhere along O'ahu's **North Shore**, where world-class surfing beaches are calm enough for swimming and snorkeling in summer. To really leave the tourist crowds behind, get to know the **Wai'anae Coast**, where big-wave surfers worship at **Makaha Beach**.

Near Maui's old whaling port of **Lahaina**, laze on West Maui's beautiful beaches. Drive north around the peninsula, stopping to snorkel in summer at **Honolua Bay**, then get on the scenic, narrow cliffside **Kahekili Highway**. Swing down to **South Maui** and book a snorkel cruise to **Molokini Crater**, or check out migratory whales in winter at **Kihei**. After you ascend to the summit of **Haleakalā National Park** and snake down the **Road to Hana**, find your way back to civilization on the rugged **Pi'ilani Highway**.

A week on the Big Island is barely enough but it'll have to do. Soak up the sunshine north of **Kailua-Kona**, where you can hike or 4WD to gorgeous strands like Makalawena Beach in **Kekaha Kai State Park** or the giant **Puako Tide Pools** for snorkeling with tropical fish. After you drive past the lava deserts of **Ka'u** and round Hawaii's southernmost tip at **Ka Lae**, stop off at **Hawai'i Volcanoes National Park** before losing track of time in the hippie paradise of **Puna**.

Kaua'i is Hollywood's ready-made movie set. These soul-inspiring canyons, cliffs, waterfalls, rivers, bays and beaches are more than just pretty backdrops, however. Kayak past sacred temples along the **Wailua River**, then glimpse rainy Mt Wai'ale'ale while hiking the rolling **Kuilau Ridge & Moalepe Trails**. If you have kids, splash around at **Lydgate Beach Park**. Charming **Kapa'a** is worth a wander before bedding down in peaceful **Kilauea**, a jumping-off point to the sleepy backwaters of Kaua'i's **North Shore**.

Top: Pi'ilani Highway (p409), Maui
Bottom: Humpback whale off Kailua-Kona (p186), Hawai'i the Big Island

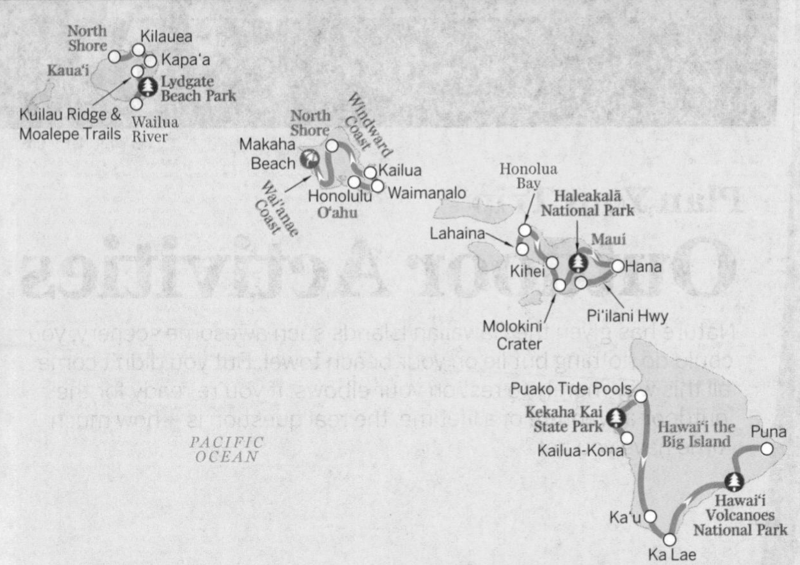
North Shore
Kilauea
Kapa'a
Kaua'i
Lydgate Beach Park
Kuilau Ridge & Moalepe Trails
Wailua River
North Shore
Windward Coast
Makaha Beach
Kailua
Waimanalo
Honolulu
O'ahu
Wai'anae Coast
Honolua Bay
Haleakalā National Park
Lahaina
Maui
Kihei
Hana
Pi'ilani Hwy
Molokini Crater
Puako Tide Pools
Kekaha Kai State Park
Kailua-Kona
Hawai'i the Big Island
Puna
Hawai'i Volcanoes National Park
Ka'u
Ka Lae
PACIFIC OCEAN

Viewpoint, Na Pali Coast, Kaua'i

Plan Your Trip

Outdoor Activities

Nature has given the Hawaiian Islands such awesome scenery, you could do nothing but lie on your beach towel. But you didn't come all this way merely to rest on your elbows. If you're ready for the outdoor adventure of a lifetime, the real question is – how much time have you got?

JAMES OSMOND / GETTY IMAGES ©

Best Time to Go for...

Kayaking May–Sep

Snorkeling & Scuba Diving Apr–Oct

Surfing Nov–Mar

Swimming Year-round

Whale Watching Jan–Mar

Windsurfing & Kitesurfing Jun–Aug

Hiking Apr–Sep

Top Adrenaline-Fueled Experiences

Surf the giant waves of Pipeline off O'ahu's North Shore (p155)

Kayak the Na Pali Coast past Hanalei on Kaua'i (p536)

Night dive or snorkel with manta rays on the Kona coast of Hawai'i the Big Island (p184)

Hike and backpack around Haleakalā's volcanic summit on Maui (p410)

Ride a mule down Moloka'i's sea cliffs to the Kalaupapa Peninsula (p466)

Rent a 4WD Jeep to drive the Munro Trail on Lana'i (p434)

At Sea

The Pacific Ocean – you probably noticed it on the way over. Here are all the ways Hawaii lets you play in it.

Beaches & Swimming

When it comes to swimming beaches, you'll be spoiled for choice in Hawaii. Coastal strands come in a rainbow of hues and an infinite variety of textures – with sand sparkling white, tan, black, charcoal, green or orange, or scattered with sea-glass, pebbles and boulders, and cratered with lava-rock tide pools.

By law, all beaches in Hawaii are open to the public below the high-tide line. Private landowners can prevent access to their shoreline from land, but not by watercraft. Resort hotel beaches provide limited beach-access parking spots for the public, occasionally charging a small fee.

Most of Hawaii's hundreds of state and county beach parks have basic restrooms and outdoor cold-water showers; about half are patrolled by lifeguards. A few parks have gates that close during specified hours or sometimes they're signposted as off-limits from sunset until sunrise.

Nudity is legally prohibited on all public beaches in Hawaii. However, at a scant handful of beaches going nude or topless sunbathing by women is grudgingly tolerated. Law enforcement at de facto nude beaches can vary, from absolutely nothing to a stern verbal warning to a written ticket with a mandatory fine and possible court appearance.

Swimming with captive and wild dolphins is a controversial activity in Hawaii; see p634 for more information.

Best Swimming Spots & Seasons

Water temperatures are idyllic, ranging from 72°F to 80°F year-round. You can usually find somewhere to swim, no matter what time of year you visit: when it's rough or rainy on one side of any island, it'll usually be calm and clear on another. Only on Moloka'i is the swimming not great; there, incessant winds often make ocean waters too rough year-round.

Each island has four distinct coastal areas – north shore, south shore, leeward (west) coast and windward (east) coast – each with its own peculiar weather and water conditions. As a rule, the best places to swim in the winter are along the south shores, and in summer, along the north shores. Keep this in mind when deciding where to book your accommodations.

Ocean Safety Tips

Never turn your back on the ocean. Waves and water conditions can change abruptly, so pay attention and never swim alone. Drowning is the leading cause of accidental death for tourists. To check on current beach hazard warnings, visit http://oceansafety.ancl.hawaii.edu/alerts.

Rogue waves All waves are not the same. They often come in sets: some bigger, some smaller.

Sometimes one really big 'rogue wave' sweeps in and literally catches sunbathers napping.

Shorebreaks Waves breaking close to shore are called shorebreaks. Smaller ones are great for bodysurfing. Large shorebreaks, though, can slam down hard enough to knock you out.

Undertows These occur when large waves wash back into incoming surf, often on sloped beaches. If one pulls you under the water, don't panic. Go with the current until you get beyond the wave.

Rip currents These fast-flowing ocean currents can drag swimmers out into deeper water. Anyone caught in a rip should either go with the flow until it loses power or swim parallel to shore to slip out of it.

Tsunami See p646.

Bodysurfing & Bodyboarding

Sure, you might not be able to bodysurf like a ballet dancer – like local kids do – but anybody can give it a go and have some fun with it. Bodysurfing doesn't require any special equipment, and once you've found the groove for catching waves, it's good times ahead. Bodyboarding is even easier, because you've got a three-foot-long piece of foam to hang on to. Some bodyboarders and bodysurfers wear webbed gloves and flipper-like fins to help propel themselves through the water.

Except in the gnarliest or calmest surf, you can bodysurf or bodyboard on almost any beach. Ideal locations are beaches with sandy shorebreaks where the inevitable wipeouts will be less painful and/or dangerous. If you're new to either bodysurfing or bodyboarding, don't underestimate small-looking waves – they can roll you just like five-footers.

DON'T GET STUNG!

Stings from jellyfish and Portuguese man-of-war (aka bluebottles) occur in Hawaii's tropical waters. Even touching a bluebottle hours after it has washed up onshore can result in burning stings. Jellyfish are often seen eight to 10 days after a full moon, when they float into Hawaii's shallow near-shore waters, especially on O'ahu at Waikiki. When this happens, some public beaches may be closed for safety. For more information, visit www.808jellyfish.com.

Diver and white-tip reef shark

Best Beaches for Bodysurfing & Bodyboarding

O'ahu	Sandy Beach (p132)
	Makapu'u Beach Park (p134)
	Kapahulu Groin (Kuhio Beach Park, p109)
Hawai'i the Big Island	White (Magic) Sands Beach (p178)
	Hapuna Beach (p233)
Maui	Big Beach (Makena State Park, p379)
	DT Fleming Beach Park (p343)
Kaua'i	Brennecke's Beach (p543)
	Hanalei Bay (p523)

Diving

Hawaii's underwater scenery is every bit the equal of what's on land: you can dive shipwrecks and lava tubes, listen to whales singing and go nose-to-nose with sharks and manta rays.

Ocean temperatures are perfect for scuba diving, averaging 72°F to 80°F at the surface year-round. Even better than

Makapu'u Beach Park (p134), O'ahu

the bathwater temperature is the visibility, which is usually perfect for seeing the plethora of fish, coral and other sea creatures. November through March aren't the best months for diving though, when winter rainstorms and winds bring rougher seas and higher waves to Hawaii.

Dive costs range widely depending on gear, dive length, location and so on, but in general, two-tank dives including all gear rental average $100 to $165. Remember to bring your dive certification card from home.

Some dive operators offer a beginners' 'discover scuba' option, which includes brief instruction, and possibly swimming-pool practice, followed by a shallow beach or boat dive. No previous experience is necessary, but you must be a strong swimmer. These introductory dives generally cost $130 to $180, depending on your location and whether or not a boat is used.

If you don't already know how to dive, Hawaii is a great place to learn. **PADI** (Professional Association of Diving Instructors; www.padi.com) open-water certification courses can be completed in as few as three days, usually from around $500 per person.

Best Scuba-Diving Spots

O'ahu	Hanauma Bay (p131)
	Three Tables & Sharks Cove (Pupukea Beach, p155)
	Sunken ship & airplane wreck dives
Hawai'i the Big Island	Off the Kona Coast (p182)
	Night dives with manta rays (p184)
Maui	Offshore Molokini Crater (p363)
	Makena Landing (p378)
Lana'i	Cathedrals (Manele Bay, p435)
Moloka'i	Pala'au barrier reef (p443)
Kaua'i	South Shore (p538)
	Makua (Tunnels) Beach (p533)
	Neighboring Ni'ihau Island (p523 and p546)
Papahānaumokuākea Marine National Monument	Midway Atoll (p577)

MARK S. COSSLETT / GETTY IMAGES ©

Kitesurfing at Kite Beach (p350), Maui

To find more Hawaii dive spots, pick up Lonely Planet's *Diving & Snorkeling Hawaii* or a waterproof, rip-proof *Franko's Dive Map* (www.frankosmaps.com), sold at convenience shops, outdoor outfitters and island bookstores.

Dive Safety Tips

- Ensure your travel medical kit contains treatment for coral cuts and tropical ear infections, as well as the standard problems.
- Have a dive medical before you leave your home country – your dive operator may not always ask about medical conditions that are incompatible with diving.
- Check that your travel and/or health insurance covers decompression illness, or get specialized dive insurance through the **Divers Alert Network** (DAN; www.diversalertnetwork.org).
- Don't go for a helicopter or plane ride or ascend to high altitudes on Hawaii's volcanoes (eg Haleakalā on Maui, Mauna Kea or Mauna Loa on the Big Island) for at least 24 hours before or after scuba diving.

Fishing

The sea has always been Hawaii's breadbasket. You'll see locals casting from shore, and no fishing license is required to join them (only freshwater or commercial fishing requires licensing). However, byzantine statewide regulations govern exactly what you can catch and when; for details ask Hawaii's **Division of Aquatic Resources** (http://hawaii.gov/dlnr/dar).

Most visiting anglers are more interested in deep-sea sportfishing for such legendary quarry as ahi (yellowfin tuna), swordfish, spearfish, mahimahi (dolphinfish) and, most famous of all, Pacific blue marlin, which can reach 1000lb ('granders'). Hawaii has some of the world's best sportfishing, chiefly off the Big Island's Kona Coast, as well as Moloka'i and Kaua'i. For a full-day trip, expect to pay from $150 to $200 per person on a shared or private charter boat.

Kayaking

Only Kaua'i offers river kayaking, but sea kayakers will find heavenly bits of coastline and offshore islets beckoning across the archipelago. Indeed, there are many beaches, bays and valleys that can be reached in no other way but from the open ocean.

Best Places to Kayak

O'ahu	Kailua Beach (p138)
Hawai'i the Big Island	Puako Bay (p232)
	Pebble Beach (p216)
Maui	Makena (p378)
	Honolua Bay (p345)
Moloka'i	Pali Coast (p458)
	South Coast (p443)
Kaua'i	Na Pali Coast (p536)
	Wailua River (p496)
	Hanalei River (p523)

Kitesurfing

Kitesurfing, also called kiteboarding, is a little like strapping on a snowboard, grabbing a parachute and sailing over the water. It's an impressive feat to watch, and if you already know how to windsurf, surf or wakeboard, there's a good chance you'll

Top: Snorkeling in a volcanic crater
Bottom: Kayaking to offshore islands (p139), Lanikai, O'ahu

ANN CECIL / GETTY IMAGES ©

master it quickly. Any place that's good for windsurfing is also good for kitesurfing. The best winds usually blow in summer.

Maui dominates the attention of kitesurfers, aspiring or otherwise. Near Kahului's airport, windsurfing shops offer rentals and instruction at Kite Beach (p349), while experts brave Ho'okipa Beach in Pa'ia (p381) during kiteboarding contests only. O'ahu's Kailua Beach (p138) is another great place to learn. On Kaua'i's south shore, Kawailoa Bay (p543) is popular, while windy Moloka'i (p442) calls to pros.

Sailing

The most common sailing excursion is a two-fer: a catamaran cruise that doubles as a snorkel, dive or whale-watching tour. Sometimes passengers who don't snorkel or dive can pay a reduced fare to ride along. But if your sole desire is to feel the sails luff with wind as you tack into the open ocean, then seek out each island's small boat harbor and start talking to captains.

Best Boat Trip Departure Points

O'ahu	Waikiki (p112)
Hawai'i the Big Island	Honokohau Harbor (p200)
Maui	Lahaina (p324)
	Ka'anapali (p336)
	Ma'alaea (p362)
Moloka'i	Kaunakakai Harbor (p443)
Kaua'i	Port Allen (p556)
	Waimea (p563)

Snorkeling

Coming to Hawaii and not snorkeling is like climbing the Eiffel Tower and closing your eyes – the most bright and beautiful underwater city in the world lies at your feet, and all you need is some molded plastic and antifog gel to see it. If you can swim, Hawaii's magnificent coral reefs are yours. In addition to more than 500 species of often neon-colored tropical fish, endangered sea turtles are sometimes spotted, and you may see manta rays, spinner dolphins, jacks, sharks and other impressive predators.

Every island has fantastic shoreline snorkeling spots, in addition to snorkel cruises that deliver you to places you can't swim to.

Best Places to Snorkel

O'ahu	Hanauma Bay (p131)
	Pupukea Beach (p155)
Hawai'i the Big Island	Night snorkeling with manta rays off the Kona coast (p184)
	Kapoho Tide Pools (p287)
	Two-Step (p215)
	Kahalu'u Bay (p194)
Maui	Molokini Crater (p363)
	Malu'aka Beach (p378)
	'Ahihi-Kina'u Natural Area Reserve (p380)
	Pu'u Keka'a (Black Rock) (p335)
Lana'i	Hulopo'e Beach (p435)
Moloka'i	Dixie Maru Beach (p473)
	Twenty Mile Beach (p455)
Kaua'i	Makua (Tunnels) Beach (p533)
	Po'ipu Beach (p544)

Snorkel Rental & Safety Tips

- Gear rental – including snorkel, mask, fins and usually a bag to carry them in – costs from around $10 a day or $25 per week, depending on the quality of the gear.
- It may be a worthwhile investment to bring or buy your own high-quality mask, if you plan on snorkeling more than once or twice.
- As a rule, snorkel early – morning conditions are often best, and if everyone else is sleeping, they won't be crowding the water and kicking up sand to mar visibility.
- Snorkelers often forget – whoops! – about putting sunblock on their back (or to wear a T-shirt) and more importantly, watching the waves.
- Follow coral-reef etiquette: don't touch any coral, which are living organisms; watch your fins to avoid stirring up sand and breaking off pieces of coral; and finally, don't feed the fish.
- Review our ocean safety tips on p41.

Helpful Resources for Snorkelers

There are myriad marine life and snorkel guides to Hawaii but photographer John Hoover publishes some great ones: snorkelers should pick up *Hawaii's Fishes* or the waterproof pocket guide *Reef Fish Hawaii*, while tide-pool enthusiasts might grab *Hawaii's Sea Creatures*. Hoover's *Ultimate Guide to Hawaiian Reef Fishes, Sea Turtles,*

Pro surfer in action at Ho'okipa Beach Park (p381), Maui

Dolphins, Whales and Seals covers everything. Island hoppers can peruse Lonely Planet's *Diving & Snorkeling Hawaii*.

Surfing & Stand Up Paddling (SUP)

Ancient Hawaiians invented surfing (calling it *he'e nalu*, 'wave sliding'). In Hawaii today surfing is both its own intense subculture as well as a part of everyday island life. Hawaii's biggest waves roll in to the islands' north shores from November through March. Summer swells, which break along the south shores, are smaller and more infrequent.

Surf lessons and board rentals are available at just about every tourist beach that has rideable waves. The latest trend is stand up paddling (SUP) – which, as the name implies, means standing on the surfboard and using a paddle to propel yourself along flat water or waves. It takes coordination to learn, but it's easier than regular surfing.

With its overwhelming variety and abundance of surf spots, O'ahu is where all the major pro surfing competitions happen; its epic North Shore is home to surfing's Triple Crown competition, which draws thousands of roadside spectators every November and December. All of the main islands have good, even great surfing breaks, but with more laid-back scenes.

PADDLING POLYNESIAN-STYLE

Hawai'i was settled by Polynesians who paddled outrigger canoes across 2000 miles of open ocean, so you could say canoeing was Hawaii's original sport. Early Europeans were awestruck at the skill Hawaiians displayed in their canoes – timing launches and landings perfectly, and paddling among the waves with the graceful agility of dolphins. Today outrigger canoe clubs race throughout the islands. The most impressive long-distance events happen in fall, starting with the Queen Lili'uokalani Canoe Race (p28) on the Big Island's Kona Coast, followed by races across the Ka'iwi Channel from Moloka'i all the way to O'ahu.

Surf Etiquette

As a visitor in Hawaii, there are some places you go, and some places you don't. Locals are usually willing to share surf spots that have become popular tourist destinations but they reserve the right to protect other 'secret' surf grounds. As a newbie in the lineup, don't expect to get every wave that comes your way. There's a definite pecking order and, frankly, tourists are at the bottom. That being said, usually if you give a wave, you'll get a wave in return. Be generous in the water, understand your place and surf with a smile. At famous breaks where surfers can be ferociously territorial, such as O'ahu's Banzai Pipeline, ask a local for an introduction.

Helpful Resources for Surfers

Surf News Network (www.surfnewsnetwork.com) Comprehensive island weather-and-wave reports online.

Surfrider Foundation (www.surfrider.org) Nonprofit organization that helps protect the ocean and Hawaii's beaches and coastline.

Humpback whale breaching off Moloka'i's shore (p443)

Whale Watching

Each winter about 10,000 North Pacific humpback whales migrate to the shallow coastal waters off the Hawaiian Islands to breed, calve and nurse. Boat tours of the **Hawaiian Islands Humpback Whale National Marine Sanctuary** (http://hawaiihumpbackwhale.noaa.gov) are a hot-ticket item, especially during the peak migration season (January through March). Maui's western coastline (p323), Lana'i's eastern shore and Moloka'i's south shore are the whales' biggest birthing and nursing grounds, but the Big Island's west coast also sees activity, including the acrobatic breaching displays for which humpbacks are famous. All of these islands offer whale-watching tours and have areas where you can spot whales from shore, including from Maui's sanctuary headquarters (p365).

BEST SURF BEACHES & BREAKS

- O'ahu (p70)
- Hawai'i the Big Island (p183)
- Maui (p319)
- Lana'i (p433)
- Moloka'i (p444)
- Kaua'i (p487)

Windsurfing

With warm waters and steady winds, Hawaii ranks as one of the world's premier spots for windsurfing. Generally, the best winds blow from June through September, but trade winds will keep windsurfers – somewhere, at least – happy all year.

As O'ahu's North Shore is to surfing, so Maui's Ho'okipa Beach (p381) is to windsurfing: a dangerous, fast arena where the top international windsurfing competitions sort out who's best. The other islands have windsurfing, but they don't reach Maui's pinnacle. Only Moloka'i, bracketed by wind-whipped ocean channels, provides an equivalent challenge for experts.

Mere mortals might prefer windsurfing Maui's Kanaha Beach (p349) or Ma'alaea Bay (p361). If you're looking to learn, O'ahu's Kailua Beach (p138) is consistently windy year-round and home to top-notch schools. Other windsurfing spots on O'ahu include Diamond Head (p128) near

Mountain bikers in Waimea Canyon (p569), Kaua'i

Waikiki and the North Shore's Backyards (p154). Kaua'i has only one prime spot for windsurfers: 'Anini Beach (p515). On the Big Island, check out 'Anaeho'omalu Beach (p224). Bring your own gear to windsurf Moloka'i's challenging Pailolo and Kaiwi Channels (p442).

On Land

As Hawaii's volcanoes have risen above the ocean's surface, they've evolved into one of the planet's richest and most varied ecosystems – no wonder some call it paradise.

Caving

Funny thing, lava. As the top of a flow cools and hardens, the molten rock beneath keeps moving. When the eruption stops and the lava drains, what's left behind is an underground maze of tunnels like some colossal ant farm. Many of these lava tubes are cultural as well as ecological wonders, since ancient Hawaiians used them as burial chambers, water caches, temporary housing and more.

Being the youngest and still volcanically active, Hawai'i the Big Island is a caving hotspot, with six of the world's 10 longest lava tubes. Ka'u's Kanohina cave system (p310), managed by the **Cave Conservancy of Hawai'i** (www.hawaiicaves.org), has 20 miles of complex tunnels, while Kea'au's Kazumura Cave (p282) is even longer.

Other islands have fewer caving opportunities, but off Maui's Road to Hana, **Ka'eleku Caverns** (☎tel, info 248 7308; www.mauicave.com; admission US$11.95; ⏲10:30am-4:30pm Mon-Sat) is a short lava-tube system that even kids can explore.

Cycling & Mountain Biking

Quality trumps quantity when it comes to cycling and mountain biking in Hawaii. Cyclists will find the most bike-friendly roads and organizational support on O'ahu and the Big Island, but all of the main islands have bicycle rentals as well as trails and 4WD roads that double as two-wheel, pedal-powered adventures.

BILL BACHMANN / GETTY IMAGES ©

Ko'olau Golf Club (p145), O'ahu

Best Places to Ride & Race

O'ahu	Ka'ena Point Trail (p171)
	'Aiea Loop Trail (p103)
	Maunawili Trail (p135)
Hawai'i the Big Island	Ironman Triathlon World Championship (p187)
	Hawai'i Volcanoes National Park (p296)
	Waimea Trail (p247)
	Puna Coast & South Point (p281)
Maui	Haleakalā's Skyline Trail & Crater Rd (p417)
	Polipoli Spring State Recreation Area
Lana'i	Munro Trail (p434)
Moloka'i	Moloka'i Forest Reserve (p443)
Kaua'i	Waimea Canyon (p569)
	Powerline Trail (p518)

Helpful Resources for Cyclists

➡ Although somewhat dated, *Mountain Biking the Hawaiian Islands* by John Alford is a good trail guide covering all the islands. The author also guides rides and multisport adventure tours on O'ahu (visit www.bikehawaii.com).

➡ Check the **Hawaii Bicycling League** (www.hbl.org) website to find local bike shops, group rides and races, as well as links to cycling maps, regulations and safety tips.

Golf

Golfing is as popular with locals as with the PGA Tour, which always finds some excuse to visit Hawaii. Beach resorts host some of the most lauded, challenging and beautiful courses. While playing on one of these elite championship courses can easily cost over $200 a round, Hawaii has dozens of well-loved, much more affordable municipal courses boasting scenery you probably can't get back home. Afternoon 'twilight' tee times are usually discounted. Club rentals are sometimes available.

For a statewide overview of privately owned courses and country clubs that are open to the public, visit **Tee Times Hawaii** (www.teetimeshawaii.com).

Hang Gliding & Paragliding

Remove the engine and flying becomes an ecofriendly adrenaline rush. On O'ahu, glider rides (and skydiving) are offered at the North Shore's Dillingham Airfield (p163). On Maui, take a tandem paraglider ride on the slopes of Haleakalā volcano starting from Kula (p393) or Hana (p405). On Kaua'i, book a ride in an ultralight (p559) from Port Allen airport.

Helicopter & Airplane Tours

Far and away the most popular places to visit by air are Kaua'i's remote Na Pali Coast (p519) and the Big Island's active volcanic zone (p271). Flying over these areas provides unforgettable vantages and experiences you simply can't get any other way. Helicopter tours are also a popular way to see Maui (p352), where some air tours include a jaunt over to Moloka'i's towering Pali Coast (p458).

That said, helicopter and airplane tours negatively impact Hawaii's environment, both in noise generated and fuel burned.

Hiking & Backpacking

Hikers will find that, mile for mile, these tiny islands almost cannot be topped for heart-stopping vistas and soulful

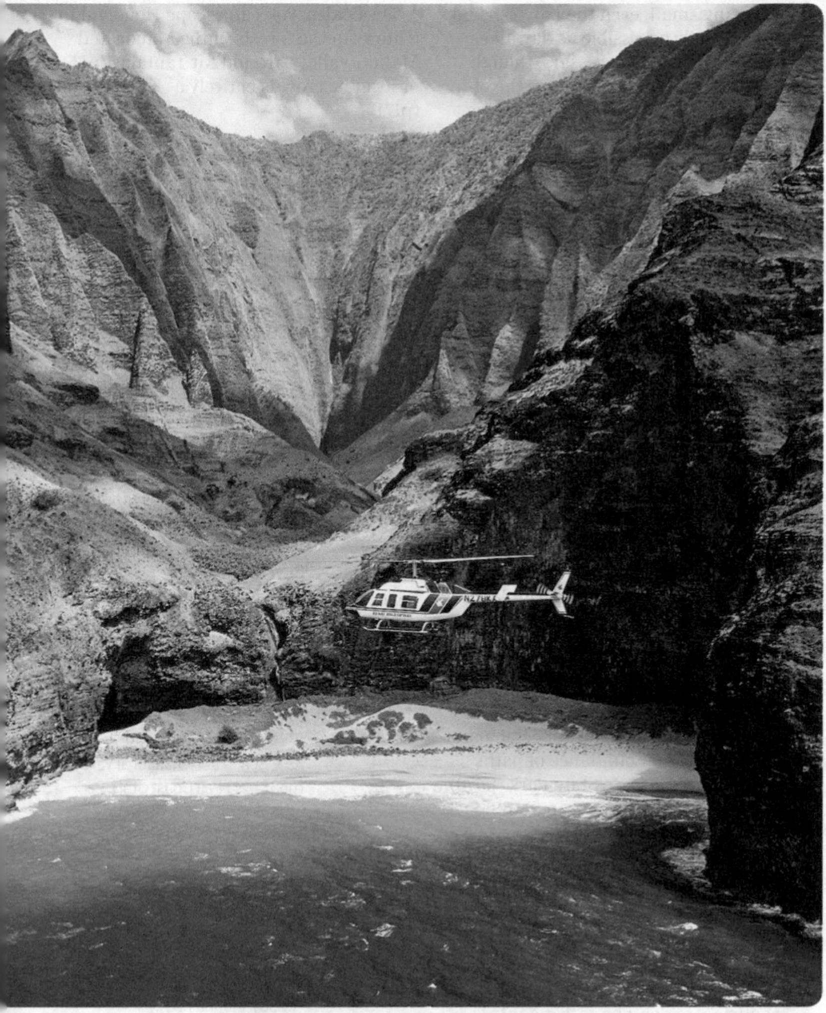

Top: Helicopter tour (p484), Na Pali Coast, Kaua'i

Bottom: Paragliding (p163) over Makapu'u Point, O'ahu

AARON BLACK / GETTY IMAGES ©

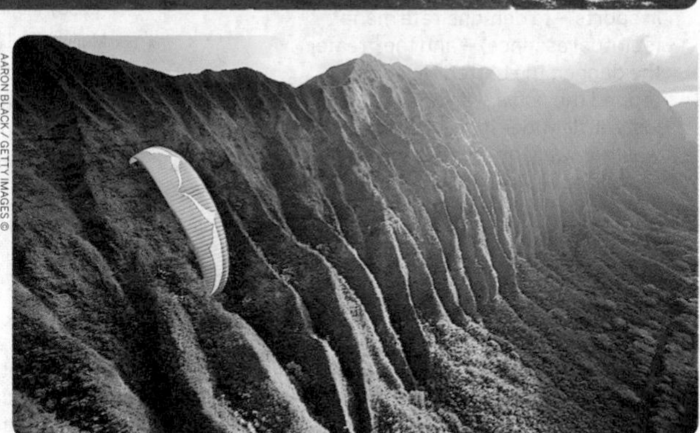

beauty. Being small, even the most rugged spots are usually accessible as day hikes. Backpacking is rarely necessary, though when it is the rewards so outstrip the effort it's almost ludicrous. Start exploring Hawaii's public trails on the state-run **Na Ala Hele** (http://hawaiitrails.ehawaii.gov) website.

Trespassing on private land or government land not intended for public use is illegal, no matter how many people you see do it. Show respect for all 'Kapu' or 'No Trespassing' signs – not just for legal reasons, but also for your own safety.

Best Islands for Hiking

For variety, **Hawai'i the Big Island** wins by a nose. Hawai'i Volcanoes National Park (p296) contains an erupting volcano, plus steaming craters, lava deserts and native rainforests. Then there are the two nearly 14,000ft mountains to scale – Mauna Loa (p255) and Mauna Kea (p252).

The volcano on **Maui** may be dormant, but Haleakalā National Park (p410) provides awe-inspiring descents across the summit's eroded moonscape. The Road to Hana (p395) offers many short excursion hikes to waterfalls and through rainforest.

The legendary Kalalau Trail (p537) on **Kaua'i**'s Na Pali Coast edges spectacularly fluted sea cliffs. An abundance of paths crisscross clifftop Koke'e State Park (p570) and cavernous Waimea Canyon (p568).

ANCIENT HAWAII'S EXTREME SPORTS

Never let it be said that ancient Hawaiians didn't know how to play. Every ruler had to prove his prowess in sports – to demonstrate mana (spiritual essence) – and the greater the danger, the better. No contest topped the *holua* – an ancient sled just a little wider than a book, on which Hawaiians raced down mountains at speeds of up to 50mph. Not every sport was potentially deadly, though many involved gambling – like foot and canoe racing, wrestling and *'ulu maika* (stone bowling). Annual makahiki celebrations featuring feasting, hula dancing, religious ceremonies and sports competitions lasted for four months.

On **O'ahu**, you can escape Honolulu in a hurry in the forests of the Manoa and Makiki Valleys around Mt Tantalus (p85) or lose the crowds entirely at Ka'ena Point (p171).

Best Day Hikes with Views

O'ahu	Ka'ena Point Trail (p171), Ka'ena Point State Park
	Kuli'ou'ou Ridge Trail (p130), Southeast Coast
Hawai'i the Big Island	Kilauea Iki Trail (p297), Hawai'i Volcanoes National Park
	Pololu Valley Trail (p243), North Kohala
Maui	Sliding Sands (p415), Halemau'u (p416) & Pipiwai (p420) Trails, Haleakalā National Park
	Waihe'e Ridge Trail (p349), Kahekili Hwy
Lana'i	Koloiki Ridge Trail (p428), Lana'i City
Moloka'i	Kalaupapa Peninsula (p466), Kalaupapa Peninsula
	Halawa Valley (p457), East Moloka'i
Kaua'i	Cliff & Canyon Trails (p572), Koke'e State Park
	Ke'e Beach to Hanakapi'ai Valley (p538), Na Pali Coast State Park

Best Backcountry Hikes & Backpacking Treks

Hawai'i the Big Island	Mauna Loa Trail (p299), Hawai'i Volcanoes National Park
	Humu'ula-Mauna Kea Summit Trail (p253), Mauna Kea
	Muliwai Trail (p258), Waipi'o & Waimanu Valleys
Maui	Kaupo Trail (p416), Haleakalā National Park
Moloka'i	Pepe'opae Trail (p462), Kamakou Preserve
Kaua'i	Kalalau Trail (p537), Na Pali Coast State Park

Hiking Safety Tips

- A hat, sunscreen and lots of water are always mandatory; coastal trails can bake you to a crisp and cause heat exhaustion or life-threatening

Horseback riding (p548) along Kaua'i's south shore, near Po'ipu

heatstroke, especially when walking across sun-reflective lava.

➡ If you're looking to spend hours (or days) on the trail, bring hiking boots and lightweight rainproof clothing – weather is changeable, and trails can be rocky, uneven and muddy.

➡ If you'll be tackling a mountain summit, carry a fleece or down jacket (even in summer).

➡ Always bring a flashlight: in the middle of the ocean it gets dark fast after sunset, and trails can take longer than expected to finish due to the uneven terrain or accidentally getting lost.

➡ All freshwater – whether flowing or from a pond – must be treated before drinking. Avoid giardiasis and leptospirosis (see p642).

➡ Depending on the hike, potential environmental hazards range from vog (p642) to flash floods and waterfalls (p646), which are not always safe for swimming.

Horseback Riding

All of the main islands have ranches for memorable horseback rides. But the Big Island and Maui have the richest living *paniolo* (Hawaiian cowboy) culture and the most extensive riding opportunities. On Moloka'i, saddle up a mule for the switchbacking trail down the sea cliffs to the Kalaupapa Peninsula (p468).

Running

Hawaii's scenery enhances almost any sport, and running is no exception.

Best Marathons & Fun Runs

➡ **Honolulu Marathon** (p90) On O'ahu in December.

➡ **Volcano Art Center Rain Forest Runs** (http://volcanoartcenter.org/rain-forest-runs) On the Big Island in August.

➡ **Maui Marathon** (p353) In September.

➡ **Kaua'i Marathon** (www.thekauaimarathon.com) In September.

Best Triathlons

➡ **Ironman Triathlon World Championship** (p187) On the Big Island's Kona coast in October; star athletes swim 2.4 miles, cycle 112 miles and run 26.2 miles. One of sport's ultimate endurance contests.

- **Ironman 70.3 Hawaii** (www.ironman703hawaii.com) Half an Ironman; run in June on the Big Island's Kohala coast.
- **Tinman Hawaii Triathlon** (www.tinmanhawaii.com) In Honolulu in July.
- **Xterra World Championship** (www.xterraplanet.com/maui) Maui's off-road event, in October.

Stargazing

Astronomers are drawn to Hawaii's night sky the way surfers are drawn to the islands' big waves. The view from Mauna Kea volcano on the Big Island is unmatched in clarity and it has more astronomical observatories than any mountain on earth. On Mauna Kea's summit road, the visitor information station hosts free public stargazing programs (p252). During the daytime, catch a family-friendly planetarium show at Hilo's educational 'Imiloa Astronomy Center (p269), also on the Big Island, or at Honolulu's Bishop Museum (p83) on O'ahu.

Astronomical observatories on Maui's towering Haleakalā volcano study the sun, not the stars, and they aren't open to the public. Nevertheless, Haleakalā National Park rangers lead free stargazing programs (p414), usually on summer weekends. Top-end resort hotels, especially on Maui and the Big Island, occasionally offer stargazing programs using high-quality telescopes for guests.

Tennis

If you bring your own racket and balls, free public tennis courts are found in just about every major island town. However, as with golf courses, upscale resorts really pull out the stops, and at many of these you'll find immaculate tennis courts of professional-level quality, sometimes with pro shops, round-robin tournaments and partner-matching. Resorts and hotels typically reserve their courts for guests only, but sometimes allow nonguests to rent tennis equipment and court time.

Ziplining at Skyline Eco-Adventures (p393), Kula, Maui

Ziplining

Another outdoor-activity fad that's growing in Hawaii is ziplining – a thrilling ride among the treetops that was first developed as a tourist adventure in the rainforest canopy of Costa Rica and is infiltrating jungles everywhere. The only skill required is the ability to hang on (including to your lunch). Kaua'i (p483), Maui (p316), O'ahu (p145) and the Big Island (p265) all offer zipline thrills.

Plan Your Trip

Travel with Children

With its phenomenal natural beauty, Hawaii always appeals to honeymooners, but it's also perfect for families. Instead of hanging out in shopping malls, kids can enjoy sand beaches galore, snorkel amid tropical fish, zipline in forest canopies and even watch lava flow. Then get out of the sun for a spell by visiting museums, aquariums and historical attractions, from WWII battleships to ancient temples.

Hawaii for Kids

There's not too much to worry about when visiting Hawaii with kids, as long as you keep them covered in sunblock. Here, coastal temperatures rarely drop below 65°F and driving distances are relatively short. Just don't try to do or see too much, especially not if it's your first trip to Hawaii. Slow down and hang loose!

Eating Out & Entertainment

Hawaii is a family-oriented and unfussy place, so most restaurants welcome children; notable exceptions are some high-end resort dining rooms. Children's menus and high chairs are usually available everywhere – but if a high chair is a necessity at every meal, bring a collapsible seat.

If restaurant dining is inconvenient, no problem. Eating outdoors at a beach

Best Islands for Kids

O'ahu

Waikiki Beach is stuffed full of family-friendly accommodations. Everything else on the island is less than a half-day's drive away, from hiking Diamond Head to snorkeling at Hanauma Bay.

Maui

Rent a family-sized condo and relax on Maui's sunny leeward shores. Kids' eyes will pop on a winter whale-watching cruise or when catching the sunrise high atop Haleakalā volcano.

Kaua'i

Calm beaches and rivers are perfect places for the pint-sized set to get wet, and older kids can learn to surf. Don't forget to peer into the 'Grand Canyon of the Pacific' and at the stunning sea cliffs of the Na Pali Coast before you leave.

Hawai'i the Big Island

Horseback riding like a *paniolo* (Hawaiian cowboy), ziplining through forests and hopping on a boat to see red-hot lava flow are just a few of Hawai'i's unforgettable experiences for kids.

park is among the simplest and best island pleasures. Pack finger foods for a picnic, pick up fruit from farmers markets, stop for smoothies at roadside stands and order plate lunches at drive-in counters.

Grocery and convenience stores stock national brands. A kid who eats nothing but Cheerios will not go hungry here. But the local diet, with its variety of cuisines and plethora of sweet treats, may tempt kids away from mainland habits.

Commercial luau might seem like cheesy Vegas dinner shows to adults, but many kids love the flashy dances and fire tricks. Children typically get discounted tickets (and sometimes free admission when accompanied by a paying adult).

If parents need a night out to themselves, the easiest and most reliable way to find a babysitter is to ask a hotel concierge, or else contact **Nannies Hawaii** (☎754-4931; http://nannieshawaii.com/).

Children's Highlights

Restaurants, hotels and attractions that especially welcome children and have good facilities for families are marked throughout this guide with the family-friendly icon (👪). Each island destination chapter also includes specific advice about the best family-friendly things to see and do, including on O'ahu (p100), Maui (p322), Kaua'i (p500), Hawai'i the Big Island (p182), Moloka'i (p449) and Lana'i (p432).

Beaches

Kuhio Beach Sand, surf and outrigger canoe rides at Waikiki. (p109)

Ko Olina Lagoons Artificial pools for splashing around on O'ahu. (p166)

'Anaeho'omalu Beach Sunsets on the Big Island's Kohala coast. (p224)

Wailea Beach South Maui's gentlest crescent-shaped strand. (p374)

Baby Beach Kaua'i's shallow South Shore waters beckon. (p544)

Water Adventures

Hanauma Bay Snorkel in a giant outdoor fishbowl on O'ahu. (p131)

Ma'alaea Winter whale-watching cruises with Maui's Pacific Whale Foundation. (p361)

Hulopo'e Beach Snorkeling and sailing in Lana'i's Manele Bay. (p435)

AM I OLD ENOUGH?

Although you can't hike the steepest trails or go scuba diving when traveling with a toddler, parents will find plenty of outdoor family fun for all ages on the bigger islands. Some activities require that children be of a certain age, height or weight to participate. Always ask about restrictions when making reservations to avoid disappointment – and tears.

To learn to surf Kids who can swim comfortably in the ocean are candidates for lessons. Teens can usually join group lessons, although younger kids may be required to take private lessons.

To take a snorkel cruise Depending on the outfit and type of boat (catamaran, raft), tours sometimes set minimum ages, usually from five to eight years. Larger boats might allow tots as young as two to ride along.

To ride in a helicopter Most tour companies set minimum ages (eg two to 12 years) and some also set minimum body weights (eg 35lb). Toddlers must be strapped into their own seat and pay the full fare.

To go ziplining Minimum age requirements range from five to 12 years, depending on the company. Participants must also meet weight minimums (usually 50lb to 80lb).

To ride a horse For trail rides the minimum age ranges from seven to 10 years, depending on the outfitter. It helps if your child already has some riding experience. Short pony rides may be offered to younger kids.

Puna Ride a boat to see fiery lava empty into the ocean, on the Big Island. (p284)

Lihu'e (p481) & **Wailua** (p492) Many family-friendly aquatic adventure tours depart from these small towns on Kaua'i.

Hiking

Manoa Falls O'ahu's family-favorite forest hike climbs above downtown Honolulu. (p85)

Diamond Head Summit an extinct volcanic tuff cone outside Waikiki, on O'ahu. (p128)

Hawai'i Volcanoes National Park Trek the Big Island's active volcanic moonscape or crawl through a lava tube. (p289)

Haleakalā National Park Step onto Maui's biggest volcano above the clouds and through a bamboo forest by waterfall pools. (p410)

Waimea Canyon (p567) & **Koke'e State Park** (p569) Dizzying clifftop lookouts, native birds and flora await on Kaua'i's Westside.

Land Adventures

Kualoa Ranch Movie and TV set tours and trail rides on O'ahu's Windward Coast. (p147)

Piiholo Ranch Maui's biggest zipline adventure on the slopes of Haleakalā volcano. (p388)

Dahana Ranch Genuine *paniolo* (Hawaiian cowboy) trail rides on the Big Island. (p246)

Moloka'i Mule Ride Navigate mile-high *pali* (sea cliffs) in the saddle down to the Kalaupapa Peninsula. (p468)

Cultural & Historical Sites

Waimea Valley Botanical gardens, archeological sites and waterfall swimming on O'ahu's North shore, with poi-pounding, lei-making and hula-dancing lessons too. (p156)

Old Lahaina Luau Hawaii's most authentic, aloha-filled luau comes with music, dancing and an *imu*-cooked whole roasted pig, on Maui. (p330)

Pearl Harbor Squeeze inside a WWII-era submarine, pace a battleship's decks or become a virtual-reality pilot, on O'ahu. (p101)

Kamokila Hawaiian Village Outrigger canoe rides, tropical fruit trees and replicas of ancient Hawaiian houses, on Kaua'i. (p493)

Na Mea Hawai'i Traditional and sacred *hula kahiko* dancing and chanting dramatically performed inside Hawai'i Volcanoes National Park, on the Big Island. (p299)

HELPFUL BOOKS & WEBSITES

➡ *Travel with Children* (Lonely Planet) is loaded with valuable tips and amusing tales, especially for first-time parents.

➡ **Lonely Planet** (www.lonelyplanet.com) Ask questions and get advice from other travelers in the Thorn Tree's online 'Kids to Go' and 'USA' forums.

➡ **Go Hawaii** (www.gohawaii.com) The state's official tourism site lists family-friendly activities, special events and more – easily search the site using terms like 'kids' or 'family'.

➡ **Parents Connect** (www.parents-connect.com/parents/family-travel/) Encyclopedia of everything first-time family travelers need to know; search the site for destination-specific tips for Hawaii vacations.

Museums

Bishop Museum Polynesian war clubs, feathered masks, an exploding faux-volcano and eye-opening planetarium sky shows in urban Honolulu. (p83)

Hawaii Children's Discovery Center Best rainy-day indoor playground for tots and schoolchildren, not far from Waikiki Beach. (p88)

'Imiloa Astronomy Center of Hawai'i Hands-on multimedia astronomy museum and 3D planetarium in Hilo, on the Big Island. (p269)

Whalers Village Museum Let kids imagine themselves aboard a 19th-century whaling ship, complete with harpoons and scrimshaw carvings, in West Maui. (p336)

Aquariums, Zoos & Farms

Maui Ocean Center USA's largest tropical aquarium has kid-sized viewing ports. (p361)

Waikiki Aquarium University-run aquarium sits beside O'ahu's most popular beach. (p110)

Ocean Rider Seahorse Farm (p220) Unique family-friendly tour spot on Hawai'i the Big Island.

Pana'ewa Rainforest Zoo and Gardens Free kiddie zoo with walking trails, outside Hilo on the Big Island. (p270)

Surfing Goat Dairy Take a tour and pet the goats, or join in evening chores and milking duties, on Maui. (p392)

Planning

To get the most out of taking a family trip to Hawaii, plan ahead. When choosing the time of year to visit, keep in mind that the windward sides of the islands get more rain and and much higher waves during winter that may nix swimming for kids.

What to Pack

Hawaii's small-town vibe means that almost no place – apart from top-chef's restaurants and five-star resorts – is formal, whether in attitude or attire. There's no need to pack your kids' designer jeans or collector-worthy kicks. Let 'em wear T-shirts, shorts and rubbah slippah (flip-flops) just about anywhere you go.

Hawaii's main islands have tourist convenience shops, such as the ubiquitous ABC Store, where you can buy or rent inexpensive water-sports equipment (eg floaties, snorkel sets, boogie boards), so there's no need to lug them from home, unless your kids have super-specialized gear. Baby supplies, such as disposable diapers and infant formula, are sold everywhere, but for the best selection and prices, shop in bigger island towns and cities.

If you do forget some critical item, **Baby's Away** (☎on Hawai'i the Big Island 800-996-9030, on Lana'i 800-942-9030, on Maui 800-942-9030, on O'ahu 800-496-6386; www.babysaway.com) rents cribs, strollers, car and booster seats, high chairs, backpacks, beach equipment and more. Major car-rental companies are required to provide infant and child-safety seats, but only if you reserve them in advance (typically $10 per day, maximum $50 per rental).

Where to Stay

When setting up a home base, choose accommodations based on your family's activity and sightseeing priorities. Resorts offer spectacular swimming pools and other distractions, along with kids' activity day camps and on-call babysitting services. But parents might prefer the convenience and cost savings of having a full kitchen and washer/dryer, which many condominiums and vacation rentals offer.

Always ask about policies and bedding before booking any accommodations. Children often stay free when sharing a hotel or resort room with their parents, but only if they use existing bedding. Cots and rollaway beds may be available (usually for an additional fee). At condos, kids above a certain age might count as extra guests and entail an additional nightly surcharge; at a few, children are not allowed. Kids and even babies are welcome at many island B&Bs and vacation rentals, but not all.

Regions at a Glance

Ready to go island hopping? Wherever you travel around the Hawaiian Islands, fantastic beaches, friendly faces and *'ono grinds* (good eats) are practically guaranteed. Be swept up by the kinetic energy of the capital island, O'ahu. Hang loose on Maui, which offers a little something for everyone, from honeymooners to beach bums. Be awed by towering sea cliffs on ancient Kaua'i, then gape at new land being birthed by volcanoes on the Big Island, Hawaii's youngest island. Escape to total resort luxury on Lana'i or get back to the land on rural Moloka'i, where Native Hawaiian traditions run strong. Whatever kind of paradise you're seeking, the Aloha State has it – all you have to do is open your mind, and your heart.

O'ahu

Beaches
Food
Culture

Town & Country

Three-quarters of Hawaii residents call 'the Gathering Place' home. It's crowded – so everyone rubs elbows on the bus and city sidewalks. Yet miles of beaches and forest trails are just a short drive from Honolulu's museums and historical monuments.

Endless Feast

If you do nothing else on O'ahu, eat. And then eat some more. Food trucks, island farmers markets and fusion menus by Hawaii's star chefs – they're all here, waiting to be tasted.

Multicultural Modernism

O'ahu lets you take the pulse of multiracial Hawaii, which confounds census categories. East and West embrace as ancient Hawaiian traditions greet the 21st century.

p62

Hawai'i the Big Island

Hiking
Culture
Wildlife

Trail Junkies Unite!

Kilauea, Earth's most active volcano, conjures up a dreamscape for hikers: emerald valleys, icy waterfalls, lava flows, rainforest and some of the loftiest summits your boots will ever struggle to top.

Cultural Border Crossing

On the Big Island culture is participatory – absorbed, rather than simply observed. You're invited to create a lei, dance a hula and watch as giant *ulua* (trevally) are caught the old Hawai'i way.

Undersea Adventures

Spinner dolphins leap, sea turtles glide and coral gardens are packed with highlighter-bright fish. In winter humpback whales steal the show.

p172

Maui

Beaches
Hiking
Food

Suntans & Surfboards

Maui's sandy shores are ready-made for beach towels, but the ocean encourages adventure – kayaking, kiteboarding, snorkeling, stand up paddling and, if you dare, surfing on some of the planet's biggest waves.

Trails Galore

The island's trails wind through a bamboo forest, climb to ridgetops, wander past waterfalls and crunch through a cindery volcanic national park. Choose from easy strolls to hardy backcountry treks.

Locavore Heaven

Grass-fed beef from Upcountry pastures, day-boat fish and bountiful organic gardens ensure Maui's chef-driven restaurants always have the raw ingredients to whip up their famed creations.

p312

Lana'i

Remoteness
History
Beaches

'South Pacific'

Ignoring the great views of other islands, Lana'i feels like an isolated bit of subtropical pleasure far from the rest of the world. And given that new owner Larry Ellison wants to make the island self-sufficient, its sense of remoteness will only increase.

Pineapples

Nearly the entire island was planted with pineapples, which were exported around the world, for much of the 20th century. The crops are gone but the vintage plantation town of Lana'i City is timeless.

Hulopo'e Beach

Lana'i's one main beach is a beaut: a long crescent of sand on a bay good for snorkeling, backed by a tidy, uncrowded park.

p424

Moloka'i

Culture
History
Activities

Most Hawaiian

More than 50% of Moloka'i's people have indigenous heritage. Locals favor preservation of land and culture over schemes promoting tourism. Yet there is aloha spirit everywhere and visitors find a genuine – rather than a paid-for – welcome.

Saint Damien

A young priest who traveled to Moloka'i's remote Kalaupapa Peninsula in 1873 to care for leprosy patients is the USA's first saint. Today the spectacular peninsula is a national park offering one of Hawaii's top adventures.

Halawa Valley

This end-of-the-road valley once was home to hundreds of sacred taro patches. Guides take you on a trail past ancient temples to waterfalls pounding into swimmable pools.

p440

Kaua'i

Lifestyle
Beaches
Landscape

Northern Bubble

The North Shore is home to many who came to check in and stayed to tune out. Surfing, hiking and a contagious (if not invasive) laid-back vibe perpetuate the northern lifestyle.

Sunny Po'ipu

The most consistently sunny area on the island, Po'ipu is like a tropical version of sleep-away camp. Smiles abound on the South Shore as most days offer activities and beach days galore, along with postcard sunsets.

Canyons & Cliffs

The rugged terrain on the Garden Island ranges from gaping chasms to dramatic coastal cliffs, balanced out by copious verdant flora. It is exemplary of Mother Earth's highest potential for land creation.

p476

On the Road

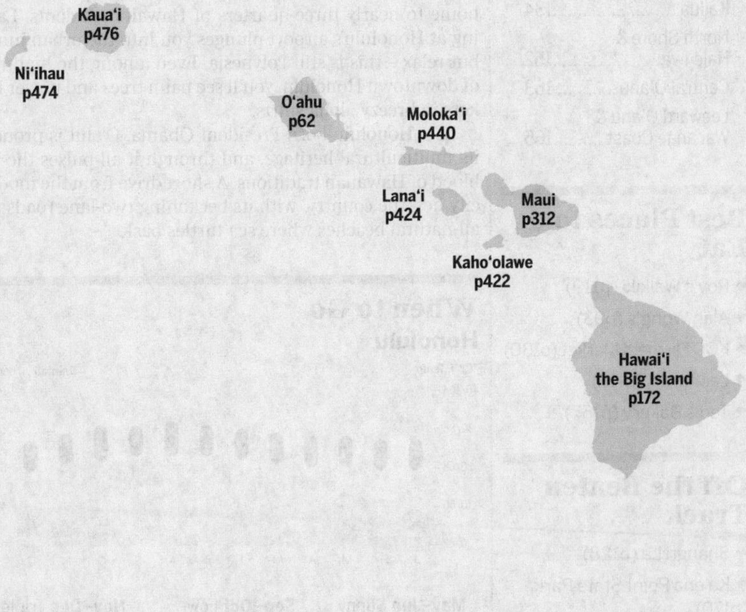

Kaua'i p476

Ni'ihau p474

O'ahu p62

Moloka'i p440

Lana'i p424

Maui p312

Kaho'olawe p422

Hawai'i the Big Island p172

O'ahu

Includes ➡

Best Places to Eat

- Roy's Waikiki (p119)
- Alan Wong's (p93)
- KCC Farmers Market (p130)
- Leonard's (p117)
- Ted's Bakery (p157)

Off the Beaten Track

- Shangri La (p128)
- Ka'ena Point State Park (p170)
- Malaekahana State Recreation Area (p151)
- Kuli'ou'ou Ridge Trail (p130)
- Kolekole Pass (p164)

Why Go?

O'ahu is not just a transit point en route to the Neighbor Islands. It's the thrill-of-a-lifetime adventure. Here you can surf the North Shore's giant waves, hike atop knife-edged *pali* (cliffs), dive into Hanauma Bay's outdoor fishbowl, go windsurfing or kayak to uninhabited islands off Kailua – and still be back in Waikiki for sunset drinks.

Nicknamed 'The Gathering Place,' the capital island is home to nearly three-quarters of Hawaii's residents. Landing at Honolulu's airport plunges you into the urban jungle, but relax – this is still Polynesia. Even among the high-rises of downtown Honolulu, you'll see palm trees and power brokers in breezy aloha shirts.

Like Honolulu-born President Obama, O'ahu is proud of its multicultural heritage, and through it all pulses the lifeblood of Hawaiian traditions. A short drive from the modern city lies 'the country,' with its beckoning two-lane roads and all-natural beaches where sea turtles bask.

When to Go

Honolulu

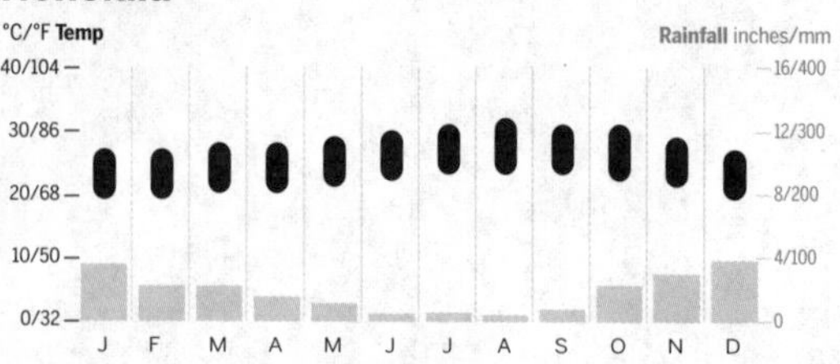

May–Jun Sunny skies; fewer crowds after Easter's spring break before summer vacation.

Sep–Oct Low-season discounts; big festivals in Honolulu and Waikiki.

Nov–Dec Triple Crown of Surfing sweeps the North Shore.

History

Around AD 1450, Ma'ilikukahi, the ancient *mo'i* (king) of O'ahu, moved his capital to Waikiki, a coastal wetland known for its fertile farmlands and abundant fishing, as well as being a place of recreation and healing. O'ahu's fall to Kamehameha the Great in 1795 signaled the beginning of a united Hawaiian kingdom. Kamehameha later moved his royal court to Honolulu ('Sheltered Bay').

In 1793 the English frigate *Butterworth* became the first foreign ship to sail into what is now Honolulu Harbor. In the 1820s, Honolulu's first bars and brothels opened to international whaling crews just as prudish Protestant missionaries began arriving from New England. Honolulu replaced Lahaina as the capital of the kingdom of Hawai'i in 1845. Today Hawaii's first church is just a stone's throw from 'Iolani Palace.

In the 1830s, sugar became king of O'ahu's industry. Plantation workers from Asia and Europe were brought to fill the island's labor shortage. The names of some of Honolulu's richest and most powerful plantation families – Alexander, Baldwin, Cooke and Dole – read like rosters from the first mission ships. The 19th century ended with the Hawaiian monarchy violently overthrown at Honolulu's 'Iolani Palace, creating a short-lived independent republic dominated by sugar barons and ultimately annexed by the USA.

After the bombing of Pearl Harbor on December 7, 1941, O'ahu was placed under martial law during WWII. As many civil rights were suspended, a detention center for Japanese Americans and resident aliens was established on Honolulu's Sand Island, and later an internment camp was built in the Honouliuli area of central O'ahu. The US federal government didn't apologize for these injustices until 1988.

After WWII, modern jet-age travel and baby-boom prosperity provided O'ahu with a thriving tourism business to replace its declining shipping industry. In the 1970s, the Hawaiian renaissance flowered, especially on the University of Hawai'i at Manoa campus and after the successful wayfaring voyage of the *Hokule'a* canoe to Tahiti, first launched from O'ahu's Windward Coast.

By the 1980s, rampant tourist development had overbuilt Waikiki and turned some of O'ahu's agricultural land into water-thirsty golf courses and sprawling resorts. The island's last sugar mills closed in the 1990s, leaving O'ahu more heavily dependent on tourism than ever. Debates about economic diversification and the continuing US military presence continue today.

National, State & County Parks

Although O'ahu is Hawaii's most populous island, nature awaits right outside Waikiki's high-rise hotels. About 25% of the island is protected as natural areas. The entire coastline is dotted with beaches, while the lush mountainous interior is carved by hiking trails, including in forest reserves rising above Honolulu's steel skyscrapers.

Most county beach parks are well-maintained with free parking, public restrooms, outdoor cold-water showers, lifeguards and picnic areas. Some of the North Shore's most famous surfing breaks are offshore from modest-looking county parks. The Wai'anae Coast doesn't register on many tourists' itineraries; its beach parks are blessedly free of crowds, save for locals.

State parks include iconic Diamond Head State Monument, where hikers can summit a landmark volcanic tuff cone, and idyllic, crescent-shaped Hanauma Bay, the island's premier snorkeling spot. At O'ahu's lesser-known state parks, you can visit ancient heiau ruins and rebuilt fishponds or take panoramic photos from beaches, lighthouses and clifftop lookouts.

Although O'ahu has no national parks, the federal government oversees WWII Valor in the Pacific National Monument (including the USS *Arizona* Memorial) at Pearl Harbor, James Campbell National Wildlife Refuge on the Windward Coast and the Hawaiian Islands Humpback Whale National Marine Sanctuary encompassing offshore waters.

Camping

You can pitch a tent at many county and some state parks spread around the island, but none are close to Waikiki. Most private campgrounds and those county beach parks that have recommendable campgrounds are found along the Windward Coast.

All county and state park campgrounds on O'ahu are closed on Wednesday and Thursday nights; some are open only on weekends. Ostensibly, these closures are for park maintenance, but also to prevent semi-permanent encampments by homeless people, especially along the Wai'anae Coast.

Choose your campground carefully, as roadside beach parks can be late-night hangouts for drunks, drug dealers and gang members. O'ahu's safest campgrounds with

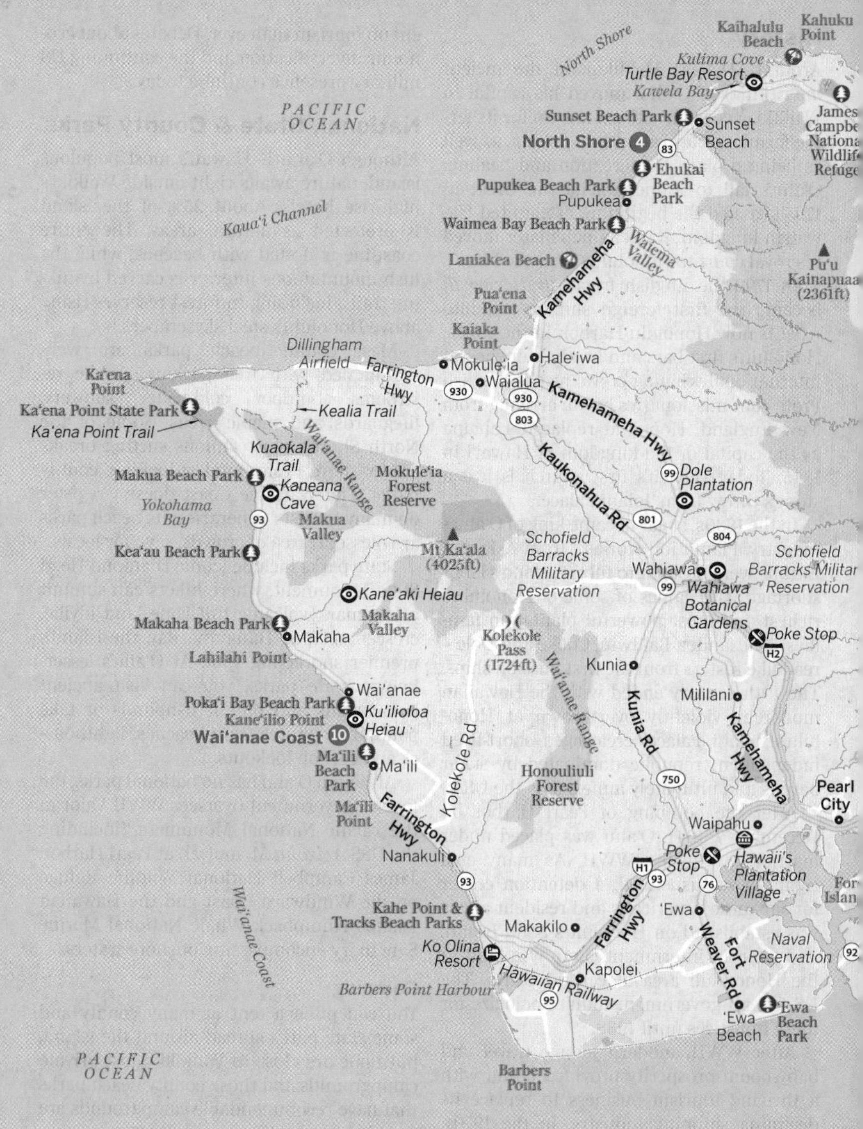

O'ahu Highlights

1 Swizzle sunset mai tais while slack key guitars play at **Waikiki** (p105)

2 Be moved by WWII history at **Pearl Harbor** (p101)

3 Snorkel and dive with tropical marine life at **Hanauma Bay** (p131)

4 Surf giant winter waves on the **North Shore** (p152)

5 Cruise past rural valleys, wild beaches and roadside shrimp trucks on the **Windward Coast** (p134)

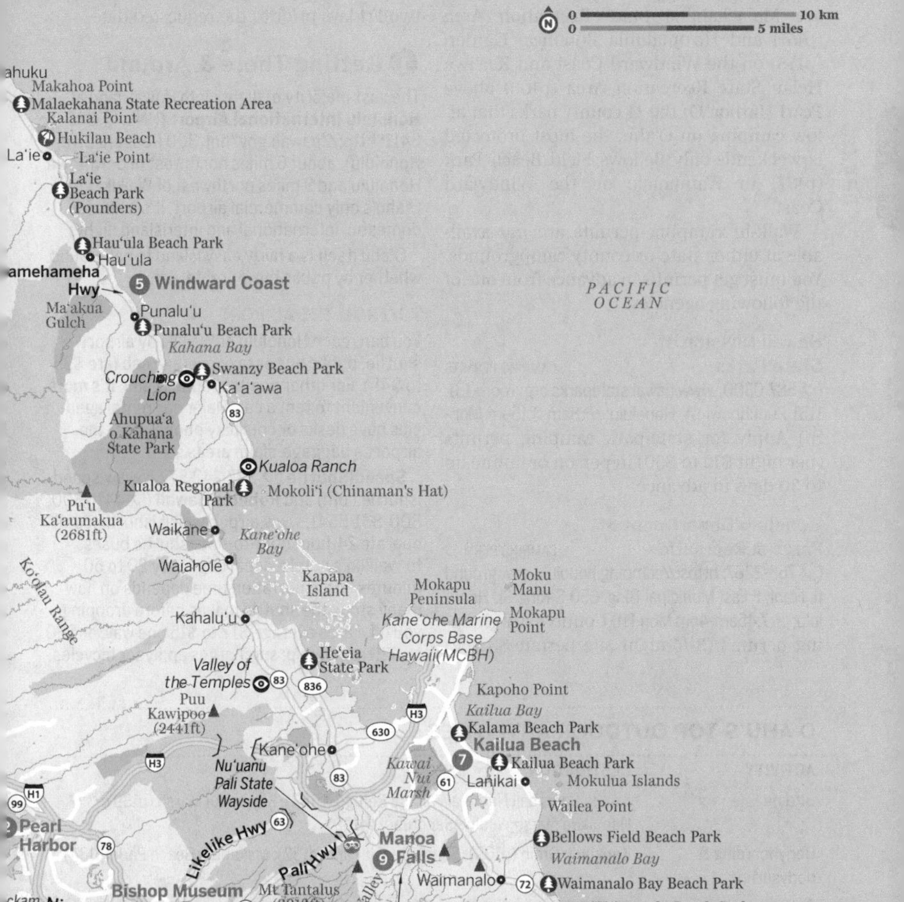

6 Go gallery hopping, shopping and clubbing in Honolulu's **Chinatown** (p76)

7 Kayak to deserted offshore islands from **Kailua Beach** (p139)

8 Inspect royal feathered capes and ancient Hawaiian temple carvings at the **Bishop Museum** (p83)

9 Hike into Honolulu's green belt to lacy **Manoa Falls** (p85)

10 Get lost on the untrammeled beaches of the **Wai'anae Coast** (p165)

24-hour security guards and locked gates are Malaekahana State Recreation Area (p151) and Hoʻomaluhia Botanical Garden (p145) on the Windward Coast and Keaʻiwa Heiau State Recreation Area (p103) above Pearl Harbor. Of the 14 county parks that allow camping on Oʻahu, the most protected is weekends-only Bellows Field Beach Park (p137) in Waimanalo on the Windward Coast.

Walk-in camping permits are *not* available at either state or county campgrounds. You must get permits in advance from one of the following agencies:

Hawaii Division of State Parks CAMPING PERMITS (☎587-0300; www.hawaiistateparks.org; room 131, 1151 Punchbowl St, Honolulu; ⊙8am-3:15pm Mon-Fri) Apply for state-park camping permits (per night $12 to $30) in person or online up to 30 days in advance.

Honolulu Department of Parks & Recreation CAMPING PERMITS (☎768-2267; https://camping.honolulu.gov; ground fl, Frank F Fasi Municipal Bldg, 650 S King St, Honolulu; ⊙7:45am-4pm Mon-Fri) County-park camping permits (3-/5-night site permit $32/52) are issued in person or online no sooner than two Fridays prior to the requested date.

Getting There & Around

The vast majority of flights into Hawaii land at **Honolulu International Airport** (HNL; ☎836-6411; http://hawaii.gov/hnl; 300 Rodgers Blvd, Honolulu), about 6 miles northwest of downtown Honolulu and 9 miles northwest of Waikiki. Oʻahu's only commercial airport, it's a hub for domestic, international and interisland flights.

Oʻahu itself is a fairly easy island to get around, whether by public bus or rental car.

TO/FROM THE AIRPORT

You can reach Honolulu or Waikiki by airport shuttle, public bus or taxi (average cab fare $35 to $45). For other points around Oʻahu, it's more convenient to rent a car. Major car-rental agencies have desks or courtesy phones near the airport's baggage-claim areas.

SpeediShuttle (☎877-242-5777; www.speedishuttle.com) and **Roberts Hawaii** (☎441-7800, 800-831-5541; www.airportwaikikishuttle.com) operate 24-hour door-to-door shuttle buses to Waikiki's hotels, departing every 20 to 60 minutes. Transportation time depends on how many stops the shuttle makes before dropping you off. Fares average $12 to $15 one way, or $20 to $30 round-trip; surcharges apply for bicycles,

OʻAHU'S TOP OUTDOOR ACTIVITIES

ACTIVITY	DESTINATION
Birding	James Campbell National Wildlife Refuge (p152); Kawai Nui Marsh (p139); Hamakua Marsh Wildlife Sanctuary (p139)
Bodyboarding & bodysurfing	Kapahulu Groin (p109); Sandy Beach Park (p132); Makapuʻu Beach Park (p134)
Golf	Ala Wai Golf Course (p113); Olomana Golf Links (p137); Koʻolau Golf Club (p145); Pali Golf Course (p145)
Hang gliding, paragliding & skydiving	Dillingham Airfield (p163)
Hiking	Manoa Falls Trail (p85); Diamond Head State Monument (p128); Kuliʻouʻou Ridge Trail (p130); Kaʻena Point Trail (p171)
Horseback riding	Kualoa Ranch (p147); Makaha Valley Riding Stables (p169)
Kayaking	Kailua Beach Park (p138)
Mountain biking	ʻAiea Loop Trail (p103); Maunawili Trail (p135); Kaʻena Point Trail (p171)
Scuba diving & snorkeling	Hanauma Bay Nature Preserve (p131); Pupukea Beach Park (p155)
Surfing	Waikiki (p105); North Shore (p152); Makaha Beach Park (p169)
Swimming	Ala Moana Beach Park (p69); Waikiki (p105); Waimanalo (p135); Kualoa (p146); Ko Olina Lagoons (p166)
Tennis	Ala Moana Beach Park (p69); Waikiki (p105)
Windsurfing & kiteboarding	Kailua Beach Park (p138); Sunset Beach Park (p154)

O'AHU IN...

One Day

Got only a day in the sun? Then it's all about you and **Waikiki**, baby. Laze on the sand, learn to surf, pose for a pic with the Duke Kahanamoku statue and catch the sunset torch lighting and hula show at Kuhio Beach Park (p109). After dark, join the buzzing crowds for dinner and drinks along oceanfront Kalakaua Ave, or find 'local grinds' and watering holes on neighborhood side streets.

Three Days

The next day get up early to snorkel at **Hanauma Bay**, then hike up **Diamond Head** or to the lighthouse atop **Makapu'u Point** in the afternoon. Reward yourself with sunset mai tais on a **catamaran cruise** or at the Halekulani's House Without a Key (p123) beach bar. Spend a full morning or afternoon exploring the capital city of **Honolulu**, with its top-notch museums and historical sites, then dive into **Chinatown**'s arts, shopping, food and nightlife scenes. Take time to detour to the mighty WWII memorials at **Pearl Harbor**.

Five Days

Switch over to island time and take everything mo' slowly. Rent a car or hop on a bus over to the surf-kissed **North Shore** and **Windward Coast**. Stop off wherever white-sand beaches catch your eye, or to explore tiny towns like **Hale'iwa** and **Kailua**. Complete your circle-island tour by cruising past the wide-open horizons of the **Wai'anae Coast** for a windy walk out to **Ka'ena Point**.

surfboards, golf clubs and extra baggage. Reservations are helpful, but not always required for airport pick-ups. For return trips, reserve at least 48 hours in advance.

You can reach downtown Honolulu, Ala Moana Center and Waikiki via TheBus 19 or 20. Buses fill up fast, so catch them at the first stop inside the airport in front of the interisland terminal; the next stop is outside the main terminal's Lobby 4. Buses run every 20 minutes from 6am to 11pm daily; the regular fare is $2.50. Luggage is restricted to what you can hold on your lap or stow under the seat (maximum size 22" x 14" x 9").

The easiest driving route to Waikiki is via the Nimitz Hwy (Hwy 92), which becomes Ala Moana Blvd. Although this route hits local traffic, it's hard to get lost. For the fast lane, take the H-1 (Lunalilo) Fwy eastbound, then follow signs 'To Waikiki.' On the return trip to the airport, beware of the poorly marked interchange where H-1 and Hwy 78 split; if you're not in the right-hand lane then, you could end up on Hwy 78 by mistake. The drive between the airport and Waikiki takes about 25 minutes without traffic; allow at least 45 minutes during weekday rush hours.

BICYCLE

It's possible to cycle around O'ahu, but consider taking TheBus to get beyond Honolulu metro-area traffic. Hawaii's **Department of Transportation** (http://hawaii.gov/dot/highways/Bike) publishes a *Bike O'ahu* route map, available free online and at downtown Honolulu's Bike Shop (p87), which also offers top-quality bicycle rentals in Kailua (p144).

BUS

O'ahu's public bus system, **TheBus** (☎848-5555; www.thebus.org; ⏲infoline 5:30am-10pm), is extensive but most hiking trails and some popular viewpoints are beyond its reach, (necessitating access to a car). Ala Moana Center is Honolulu's central bus transfer point. Each bus route can have a few different destinations; buses generally keep the same number inbound and outbound.

Although buses are fast and frequent, you can't set your watch by them. Especially in Waikiki, buses sometimes bottleneck, with one packed bus after another passing right by crowded bus stops (you can't just flag a bus down anywhere along its route).

All buses are wheelchair-accessible and have front-loading racks that accommodate two bicycles at no extra charge – just let the driver know first.

Bus Fares & Passes

The one-way adult fare is $2.50 (children aged six to 17 $1). Use coins or $1 bills; bus drivers don't give change. One free transfer (two-hour time limit) is available from the driver.

A $25 visitor pass valid for unlimited rides over four consecutive days is sold at Waikiki's ubiquitous ABC Stores and **TheBus Pass Office**

(☎848-4444; 811 Middle St; ⏰7:30am-4pm Mon-Fri).

A monthly bus pass ($60), valid for unlimited rides during a calendar month (not just any 30-day period), is sold at TheBus Pass Office, 7-Eleven convenience stores and Foodland and Times supermarkets.

Seniors (65 years and older) and anyone with a physical disability can buy a $10 discount ID card at TheBus Pass Office entitling them to pay $1 per one-way fare or $5/30 for a pass valid for unlimited rides during one calendar month/year.

CAR, MOTORCYCLE & MOPED

Avis, Budget, Dollar, Enterprise, Hertz and National have rental cars at Honolulu International Airport. Alamo and Thrifty operate about a mile outside the airport off Nimitz Hwy (airport courtesy shuttles available). It's more convenient to rent from a company with its lot inside the airport; on the drive back to the airport, all highway signs lead to on-site airport car returns.

Most major car-rental agencies have multiple branch locations in Waikiki, usually in the lobbies of resort hotels. Although the best rental rates are usually offered at Honolulu's airport, Waikiki branches can be less hassle (and less expensive, given steep overnight parking costs at Waikiki hotels) if you're only renting a car for a day.

In Waikiki, independent car-rental agencies may offer much lower rates, especially for one-day rentals and 4WD vehicles. They're also more likely to rent to drivers under 25. Some also rent mopeds and motorcycles, and a few specialize in smart cars and hybrid vehicles (see p127).

Hawaii Campers (☎222-2547; www.hawaiicampers.net) rents pop-top campervans equipped with kitchens, memory-foam mattresses and more (from $130 per day plus taxes and surcharges; five-day minimum rental). But you'll also need to pay separately for campsites and reserve camping permits in advance.

Times vary depending upon traffic, but following are typical driving times and distances from Waikiki:

DESTINATION	MILES	TIME
Diamond Head	3	10min
Hale'iwa	37	55min
Hanauma Bay	11	25min
Honolulu International Airport	9	25min
Ka'ena Point State Park	46	70min
Kailua	17	30min
Ko Olina	29	45min
La'ie	38	65min
Nu'uanu Pali Lookout	11	20min
Sunset Beach	43	65min
USS *Arizona* Memorial	15	30min

TAXI

Taxis have meters and charge $3.10 at flagfall, plus $3.20 per mile and 50¢ per suitcase or backpack. They're readily available at the airport, resort hotels and shopping centers. Otherwise, you'll probably have to call for one. TheCab (p101) offers islandwide service.

USEFUL THEBUS ROUTES

ROUTE NO	DESTINATION
A City Express!	UH Manoa, Ala Moana Center, downtown Honolulu, Chinatown, Aloha Stadium
E Country Express!	Waikiki, Ala Moana Center, Waterfront Plaza, Aloha Tower, downtown Honolulu
2 & 13	Waikiki, Kapahulu Ave, Honolulu Convention Center, downtown Honolulu, Chinatown; also Honolulu Museum of Art and Bishop Museum (No 2)
4	Waikiki, UH Manoa, downtown Honolulu, Queen Emma Summer Palace
6	UH Manoa, Ala Moana Center, downtown Honolulu
8	Waikiki, Ala Moana Center
19 & 20	Waikiki, Ala Moana Center, Ward Centers, Waterfront Plaza, Aloha Tower, downtown Honolulu, Chinatown, Honolulu International Airport; also USS *Arizona* Memorial (No 20)
22	'Beach Bus' (no service Tuesday): Waikiki, Diamond Head, Koko Marina, Sandy Beach, Hanauma Bay, Sea Life Park
23	Ala Moana, Waikiki, Diamond Head, Hawai'i Kai (inland), Sea Life Park
42	Waikiki, Ala Moana, Downtown Honolulu, Chinatown, USS *Arizona* Memorial (limited hours)
52 & 55	'Circle Isle' buses: Ala Moana Center, North Shore, Windward Coast
57	Ala Moana, Queen Emma Summer Palace, Kailua, Waimanalo, Sea Life Park

> **AVOIDING CAR BREAK-INS**
>
> When visiting O'ahu's beach parks, hiking trails or 'secret' spots off the side of the highway, take all valuables with you. Don't leave anything visible inside your car or stowed in the trunk. Car break-ins – and on O'ahu, that means not just rental cars but also locals' vehicles – are common all over the island and can happen within a matter of minutes. Some locals leave their cars unlocked to avoid the hassles of broken windows or jimmied door locks.

TOURS

Prices usually include Waikiki pick-ups and drop-offs; ask when booking.

Roberts Hawaii (☎800-831-5541, 539-9400; www.robertshawaii.com) Conventional bus and van sightseeing tours, including marathon full-day 'Circle Island' trips (adult/child from $61/38) and 'Stars & Stripes' military history itineraries (from $62/45).

E Noa Tours (☎800-824-8804, 591-2561; www.enoa.com) With knowledgeable guides certified in Hawaiiana, smaller buses circle the island (adult/child from $75/53) and explore Pearl Harbor (from $27/25).

Hawaiian Escapades (☎888-331-3668; www.hawaiianescapades.com) Waterfall walks, circle-island adventures, ghost-hunting trips and *Hawaii Five-O* and *Lost* TV location tours (half-/full-day from $65/130) in minibuses and vans.

HONOLULU

POP 337,256

You can't claim to have really gotten to know O'ahu if you never even leave Waikiki. Venture to downtown Honolulu not just for its unmatched collection of historical sites, museums and gardens – including the USA's only royal palace – but also to eat your way through the pan-Asian markets and poke around the alleyways of Chinatown, where 19th-century whalers once brawled.

Then escape the concrete jungle for a hike up into the lush valleys nestled beneath the jagged Ko'olau Mountains, especially in the forest reserves around Mt Tantalus. At sunset, walk along Honolulu's historic harborfront or splash in the ocean at Ala Moana Beach Park. After dark, hit up Chinatown's fusion kitchens, bars and nightclubs. You won't even miss Waikiki, we promise.

Beaches

Ala Moana Beach Park BEACH

(Map p80; 1201 Ala Moana Blvd; P) Opposite the Ala Moana Center shopping mall, this city fave is fronted by a broad, golden-sand beach nearly a mile long. It's hugely popular, yet big enough that it never feels too crowded. For swimmers, the deep channel that runs the length of the beach can be a hazard – it drops off suddenly to overhead depths.

The peninsula jutting from the east side of the park is **Magic Island**. During the school year, outrigger-canoe teams practice here in the late afternoon. In summer it's a hot surfing spot. Year-round, there's a postcard-worthy sunset walk around the peninsula's perimeter, within an anchor's toss of sailboats pulling in and out of neighboring Ala Wai Yacht Harbor.

The park has full facilities, including ball fields, lighted tennis courts, picnic tables, restrooms, outdoor showers and lifeguard towers. City residents come here to go running after work, play volleyball and have weekend picnics with the *'ohana* (extended family and friends). Beach wheelchairs for visitors with mobility issues are loaned out between 9am and 4:30pm daily from the food concession stands; call ☎768-3033 for information. Smoking is now banned at this park.

Sights

Downtown

★**'Iolani Palace** PALACE

(Map p72; ☎info 538-1471, tour reservations 522-0832/0823; www.iolanipalace.org; 364 S King St; grounds admission free, adult/child 5-12yr basement galleries $7/3, self-guided audio tour $15/6, guided tour $22/6; ⏰9am-5pm Mon-Sat, last tickets sold at 4pm) Perhaps no other place evokes a more poignant sense of Hawaii's history than this royal palace where plots and counterplots simmered. The building has been painstakingly restored to its former glory, although many original royal artifacts were lost or stolen before work began. Today the only way to see the palace's handsome interior is by taking a tour.

When this regal palace was commissioned by King David Kalakaua (1874–1891), the Hawaiian monarchy observed many of the diplomatic protocols of the Victorian world. The king traveled abroad meeting with leaders around the globe and received foreign emissaries at 'Iolani Palace, completed in 1882.

Although the palace was modern and opulent for its time, it did little to assert Hawaii's sovereignty over powerful US-influenced business interests, who overthrew the kingdom in 1893. Two years after the coup, the former queen, Lili'uokalani, who had succeeded her brother David to the throne, was convicted of treason and spent nine months imprisoned inside the palace in an upstairs bedroom. Soon the palace served as the capitol of the republic, then the territory and later the state of Hawaii.

Guided group tours of the palace are typically offered between 9am and 10am Tuesday and Thursday, and 9am and 11:15am Wednesday, Friday and Saturday. Alternatively, self-guided tours are usually available from 9am to 5pm Monday, 10:30am to 5pm on Tuesday and Thursday, and noon to 5pm on Wednesday, Friday and Saturday. Children under age five are not allowed on palace tours.

Sometimes you can join a guided tour on the spot, but it's advisable to call ahead for reservations and to double-check schedules, especially during busy periods. If you're short on time or the tours are sold out, head downstairs to the basement's museum exhibits, which include royal regalia, historical photographs and reconstructions of the palace kitchen and chamberlain's office.

Outside in the palace grounds, the former Royal Household Guards **barracks** is now the ticket booth. Near a huge banyan tree, thought to have been planted by Queen Kapi'olani, is a domed **pavilion** that was originally built for King Kalakaua's coronation in 1883; the Royal Hawaiian Band gives free concerts here from noon to 1pm most Fridays.

★Hawai'i State Art Museum MUSEUM
(Map p72; ☎586-0900; www.hawaii.gov/sfca; 2nd fl, No 1 Capitol District Bldg, 250 S Hotel St; ⊙10am-4pm Tue-Sat, 6-9pm 1st Fri of each month) FREE With its vibrant, thought-provoking collections, this eclectic museum showcases modern and contemporary art from Hawaii's multicultural communities. Although small,

LOCAL KNOWLEDGE

O'AHU'S BEST SURF BEACHES & BREAKS

With some of the most diverse surf breaks in all of the Hawaiian Islands, boarders of all skill levels can find what they're looking for on O'ahu.

In Waikiki, slow and mellow combers provide the perfect training ground, allowing beginners to gain some confidence. Board rental outfits abound on Waikiki Beach, where beachboys are always on hand to give lessons at spots like nice-and-mellow **Queens**, mushy left- and right-handed **Canoes**, gentle but often crowded **Populars** and ever-popular **Publics**. In Honolulu proper, **Ala Moana** offers a heavy tubing wave. Waves in these places are biggest during summer, when south swells arrive from New Zealand and Tahiti.

Reckon yourself a serious surfer? A pilgrimage to the famed North Shore is mandatory. In winter, when the waves can reach heights of more than 30ft, spots like **Waimea Bay**, **Pipeline** and **Sunset Beach** beckon to the planet's best professional surfers. Watch out for turf-protective locals, some organized into surfer gangs.

While home to some great waves, O'ahu's Wai'anae Coast has even more turf issues; the locals who live and surf here cherish this area and are trying to hold onto their Hawaiian culture and community. In the winter, large west swells can make for big surf at places like **Makaha Beach**, but tread lightly: locals know each other, so there will be no question that you're from out of town.

If you're looking for a multipurpose wave, **Diamond Head Beach** is friendly to short-boarders, longboarders, windsurfers and kiteboarders. For adrenaline-charged bodysurfing, **Sandy Beach** and **Makapu'u Beach** near the island's southeast point are ideal. If you go out there, do so with caution: the pounding waves and shallow bottom have caused serious neck and back injuries.

Surf News Network (☎596-7873; www.surfnewsnetwork.com) runs a recorded surf-conditions phone line that reports winds, wave heights and tide information.

Greater Honolulu & Pearl Harbor

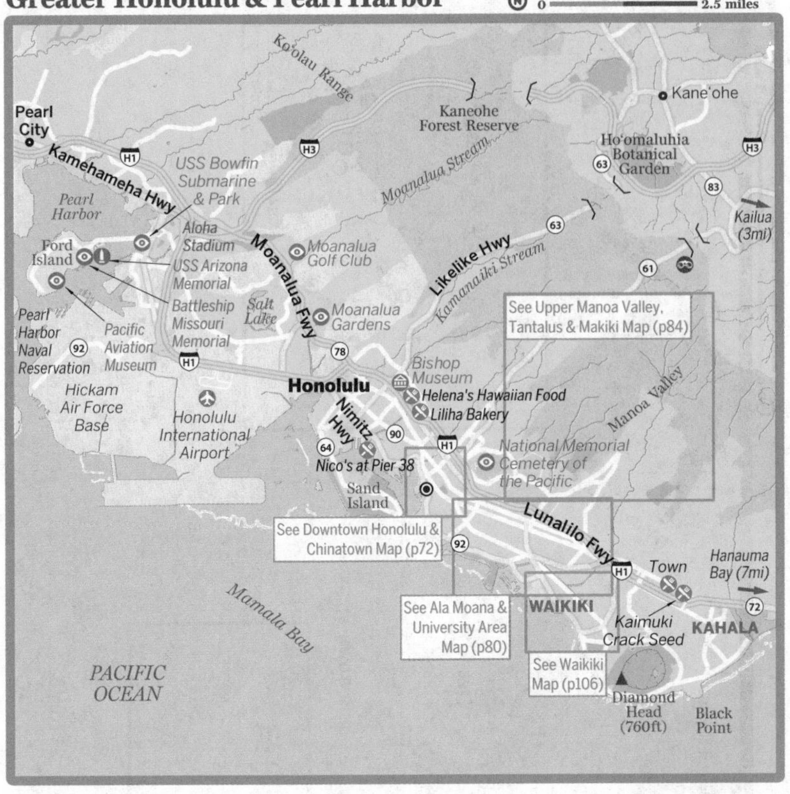

it inhabits a grand 1928 Spanish Mission Revival–style building, formerly a YMCA. Upstairs are revolving exhibits of paintings, sculptures, fiber art, photography and mixed media, while downstairs the former swimming-pool courtyard has been transformed into an airy sculpture garden.

On display inside the indoor galleries is an intriguing mix of European, Asian and Polynesian art forms and traditions, all having shaped a unique aesthetic that captures the soul of Hawaii's islands. Drop by at noon on the last Tuesday of the month for free one-hour 'Art Lunch' lectures, or from 11am to 3pm on the second Saturday for hands-on family activities.

Mission Houses Museum MUSEUM
(Map p72; ☎447-3910; www.missionhouses.org; 553 S King St; 1hr guided tour adult/child 6-18yr & college student with ID $10/6; ⏱10am-4pm Tue-Sat, guided tours usually 11am, noon, 1pm, 2pm & 3pm) Occupying the original headquarters of the Sandwich Islands mission that forever changed the course of Hawaiian history, this modest museum is authentically furnished with handmade quilts on the beds and iron cooking pots in the stone fireplaces. Taking a guided tour is the only way to peek inside any of the buildings.

Protestant missionaries packed more than their bags when they left Boston; they also brought a prefabricated wooden house, now called the **Frame House**, with them around the Horn. Designed to withstand cold New England winter winds, the small windows instead block out Honolulu's cooling tradewinds, keeping the two-story house hellaciously hot and stuffy. Erected in 1821, it's the oldest wooden structure in Hawaii.

The 1831 coral-block **Chamberlain House** was the early mission's storeroom, a necessity because Honolulu had few shops in those days. Upstairs are hoop barrels,

Downtown Honolulu & Chinatown

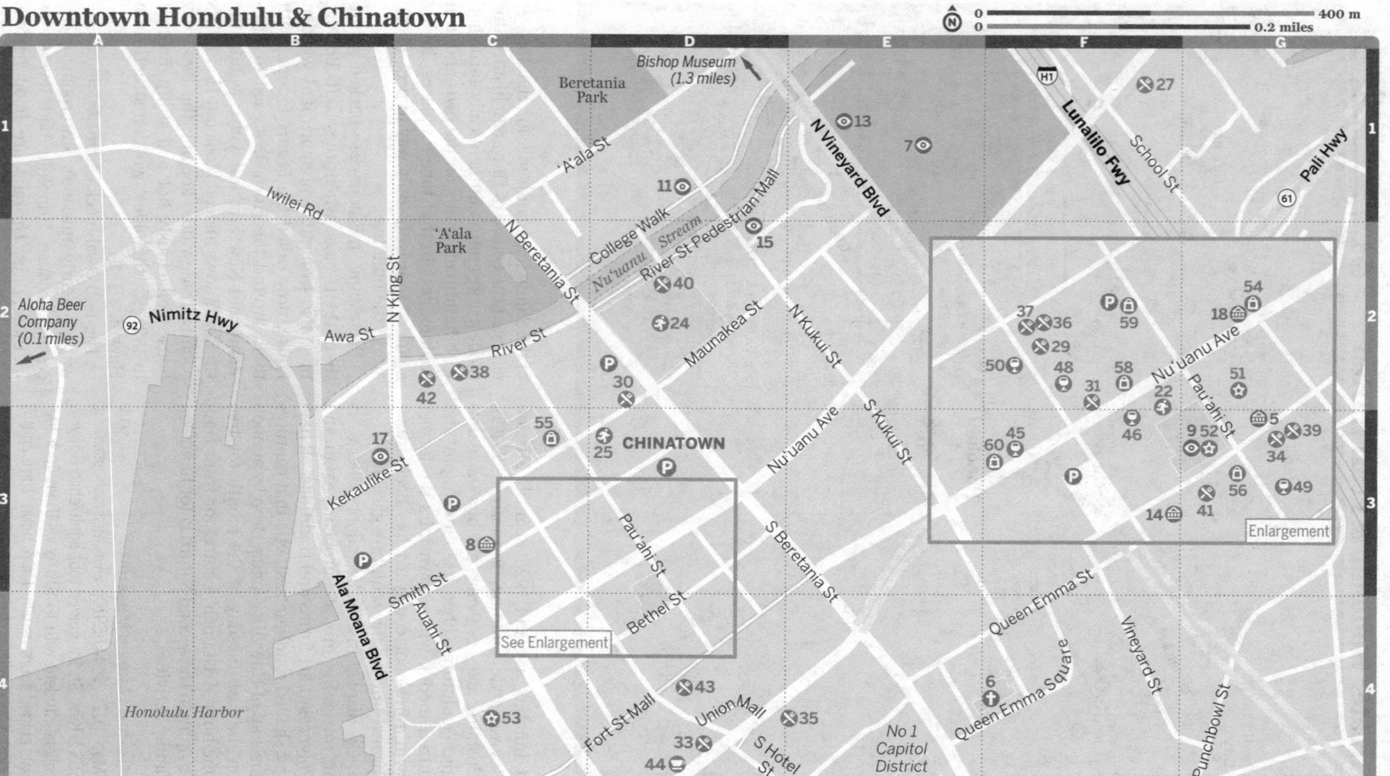

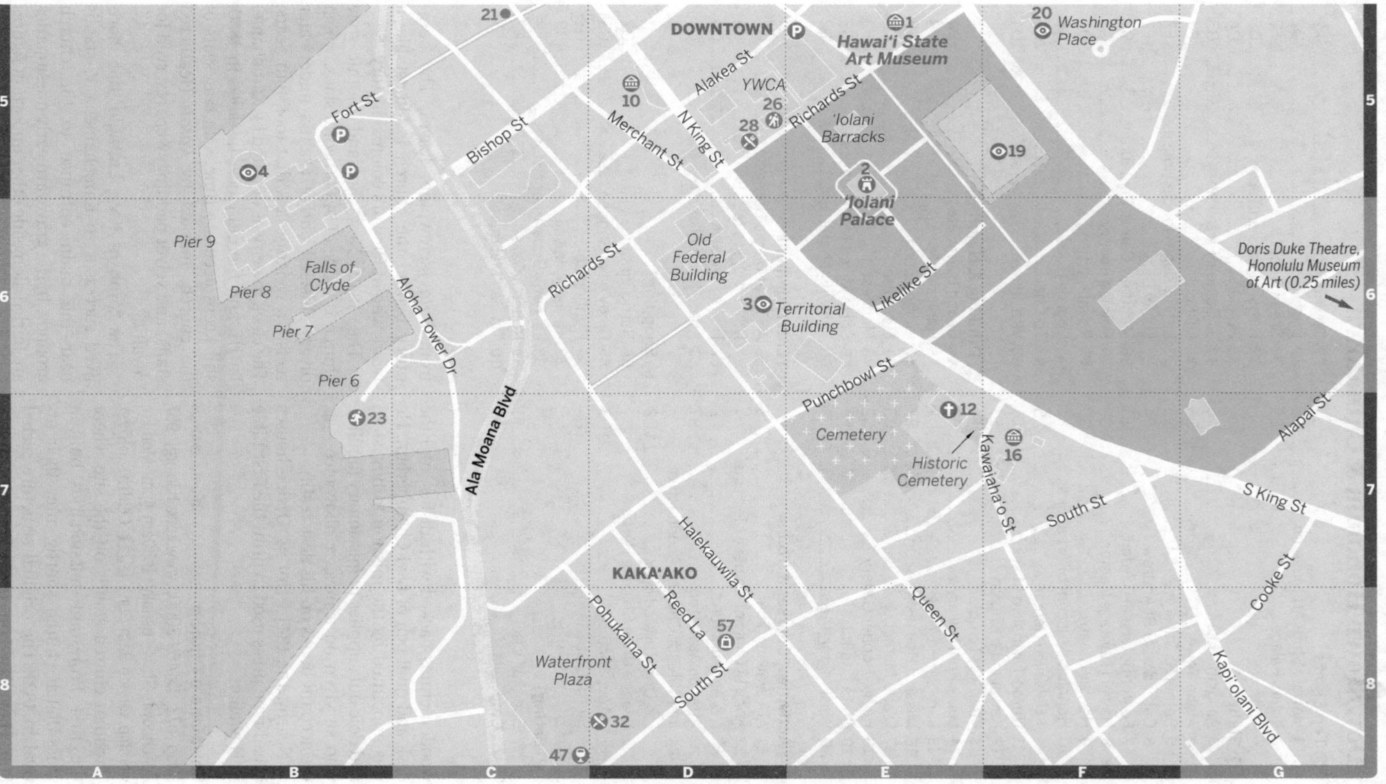
DOWNTOWN
Hawai'i State Art Museum
Washington Place
Alakea St
YWCA
Richards St
'Iolani Barracks
Fort St
Bishop St
Merchant St
N King St
'Iolani Palace
Pier 9
Falls of Clyde
Pier 8
Pier 7
Pier 6
Aloha Tower Dr
Richards St
Old Federal Building
Territorial Building
Likelike St
Doris Duke Theatre, Honolulu Museum of Art (0.25 miles)
Punchbowl St
Cemetery
Historic Cemetery
Ala Moana Blvd
Kawaiaha'o St
Alapai St
S King St
South St
Halekauwila St
KAKA'AKO
Reed La
Pohukaina St
Waterfront Plaza
South St
Queen St
Cooke St
Kapi'olani Blvd
21
20
1
10
26
28
19
2
4
3
12
16
23
57
32
47
A
B
C
D
E
F
G
5
6
7
8

Downtown Honolulu & Chinatown

Top Sights
1 Hawai'i State Art Museum....E5
2 'Iolani Palace....E5

Sights
3 Ali'iolani Hale....D6
4 Aloha Tower....B5
5 Bethel St Gallery....G3
6 Cathedral of St Andrew....F4
7 Foster Botanical Garden....E1
8 Hawai'i Heritage Center....C3
9 Hawaii Theatre....G3
10 Honolulu Museum of Art at First Hawaiian Center....D5
11 Izumo Taishakyo Mission....D1
12 Kawaiaha'o Church....E7
13 Kuan Yin Temple....E1
14 Louis Pohl Gallery....F3
15 Lum Sai Ho Tong....D2
16 Mission Houses Museum....F7
17 O'ahu Market....B3
18 Pegge Hopper Gallery....G2
19 State Capitol....F5
20 Washington Place....F5

Activities, Courses & Tours
21 AIA Walking Tour....C5
22 Anna Li Clinic of Chinese Medicine & Acupuncture....F2
23 Atlantis Adventures....B7
24 Institute for Chinese Acupuncture & Oriental Medicine....D2
25 Leanne Chee Chinese Herbs & Acupuncture....D3
26 Sierra Club....D5

Eating
27 Bangkok Chef....F1
28 Cafe Julia....D5
29 Downbeat....F2
30 Duc's Bistro....D2
31 Green Door....F2
32 Hiroshi Eurasian Tapas....D8
33 Hukilau....D4
34 JJ Dolan's Pizza Pub....G3
35 Lil' Soul....E4
36 Little Village Noodle House....F2
37 Lucky Belly....F2
38 Mabuhay Cafe & Restaurant....C2
39 Rakuen Lounge....G3
40 Royal Kitchen....D2
41 Soul de Cuba....G3
42 To Chau....C2
43 Vita Juice....D4

Drinking & Nightlife
44 Beach Bum Cafe....D4
45 Hank's Cafe....F3
46 Indigo Lounge....F3
47 M Nightclub....C8
48 Manifest....F2
49 SoHo Mixed Media Bar....G3
50 Thirtyninehotel....F2

Entertainment
51 ARTS at Marks Garage....G2
Dragon Upstairs....(see 45)
52 Hawaii Theatre....G3
53 Kumu Kahua Theatre....C4

Shopping
54 Barrio Vintage....G2
55 Cindy's Lei Shoppe....C3
56 Fighting Eel....G3
57 Kamaka Hawaii....D8
58 Lai Fong Department Store....F2
59 Roberta Oaks....F2
60 Tin Can Mailman....F3

wooden crates packed with dishes, and the desk and quill pen of Levi Chamberlain. He was appointed by the mission to buy, store and dole out supplies to missionary families, who survived on a meager allowance – as the account books on his desk testify.

Nearby, the 1841 **Printing Office** houses a lead-type press used to print the first Bible in Hawaiian.

Kawaiaha'o Church CHURCH
(Map p72; ☎469-3000; www.kawaihao.org; 957 Punchbowl St; ⊙usually 8:30am-4pm Mon-Fri, worship service 9am Sun) FREE O'ahu's oldest Christian church stands on the site where the first Protestant missionaries built a grass-thatch church shortly after their arrival in 1821. The original structure seated 300 Hawaiians on *lauhala* mats, woven from *hala* (screwpine) leaves. The **cemetery** behind the church is almost like a who's who of Hawaii's colonial history.

The 1842 New England Gothic–style church is made of 14,000 coral slabs, which divers chiseled out of O'ahu's underwater reefs – a weighty task that took four years. The clock tower was donated by Kamehameha III, and the old clock, installed in 1850, still keeps accurate time. The rear seats of the church, marked by *kahili* (feathered staffs) and velvet padding, were reserved for royalty.

The **tomb of King Lunaiilo**, the short-lived successor to Kamehameha V, stands near the main entrance to the church grounds. In the graveyard early missionaries are buried alongside other important figures of the day, including Sanford Dole, who became Hawai'i's first territorial governor after Queen Lili'uokalani was overthrown.

State Capitol NOTABLE BUILDING

(Map p72; ☎586-0178; 415 S Beretania St; ⊙7:45am-4:30pm Mon-Fri) FREE Built in the architecturally interesting 1960s, Hawaii's state capitol is not your standard gold dome. It's a poster-child of conceptual postmodernism: the two cone-shaped legislative chambers represent volcanoes; the supporting columns symbolize palm trees; and a large pool encircling the open-air rotunda represents the Pacific Ocean surrounding the Hawaiian Islands.

On the east side of the capitol stands a highly stylized **statue of Father Damien**, the 19th-century Belgian priest who lived and worked among patients with Hansen's disease (formerly called leprosy) who were forcibly exiled to the island of Moloka'i, before dying of the disease himself. In 2009, Damien was canonized as Hawaii's first Catholic saint.

Symbolically positioned between the palace and the state capitol is a bronze **statue of Queen Lili'uokalani**, Hawaii's last reigning monarch. Lili'uokalani holds the constitution that she wrote in 1893 in a failed attempt to strengthen Hawaiian rule; 'Aloha 'Oe,' a popular song she composed; and *Kumulipo*, the ancient Hawaiian chant of creation.

Ali'iolani Hale HISTORICAL BUILDING

(Map p72; www.jhchawaii.net; 417 S King St; ⊙8am-4pm Mon-Fri) FREE The first major government building constructed by the Hawaiian Kingdom in 1874, today this dignified Italianate structure houses the Hawaii Supreme Court. The ground-floor **King Kamehameha V Judicial History Center** has thought-provoking displays about martial law during WWII and the early Hawaiian monarchy. Outside, a **statue of Kamehameha the Great** points toward 'Iolani Palace.

The 'House of Heavenly Kings' was designed by Australian architect Thomas Rowe to be a royal palace, although it was never used as such. Pass through the security checkpoint at the street-level entrance to visit the Judicial History Center's exhibits, then plop yourself down in the judge's chair inside a restored 1913 courtroom.

Just northeast of the building, the bronze statue of Kamehameha I was cast in 1880 in Florence, Italy, by American sculptor Thomas Gould. The current statue is a recast, because the first statue was lost at sea near the Falkland Islands. The original statue, which was later recovered from the ocean floor, now stands in Kapa'au on Hawai'i the Big Island, where Kamehameha I was born.

Aloha Tower LANDMARK

(Map p72; www.alohatower.com; 1 Aloha Tower Dr; ⊙9:30am-5pm; P) FREE Built in 1926, this 10-story landmark at Pier 9 was once Honolulu's tallest building. In the nostalgic pre-WWII days when all tourists to Hawaii arrived by boat, this icon – inscribed with 'Aloha' on its four-sided clock tower – greeted every visitor. Take the elevator to the tower's top-floor observation deck for sweeping 360-degree views of the city and waterfront.

Cruise-ship passengers still disembark at the hulking terminal next door to the tower. Walk over and peek through the terminal's windows or step inside to see colorful murals depicting bygone Honolulu.

Self-parking at the adjacent Aloha Tower Marketplace costs $1.50 per hour for the first three hours, then $3 every 30 minutes (flat rate $5 after 4pm weekdays and all day on weekends).

Washington Place HISTORICAL BUILDING

(Map p72; ☎586-0248; http://governor.hawaii.gov/about/historic-washington-place/; 320 S Beretania St; ⊙tours by appointment only, usually at 10am Thu) FREE Surrounded by stately trees, this colonial-style mansion was erected in 1847

HONOLULU'S BEST FREE THRILLS

- ➡ Catch sunset from Magic Island at Ala Moana Beach Park (p69)
- ➡ Gaze out to sea atop the Aloha Tower (p75)
- ➡ Peruse downtown's Hawai'i State Art Museum (p70)
- ➡ Hike to Manoa Falls (p85) and the Nu'uanu Valley Lookout
- ➡ Hobnob on First Fridays (p95) in Chinatown
- ➡ Hear the Royal Hawaiian Band at 'Iolani Palace (p69)
- ➡ Learn to speak Hawaiian and make flower lei at Native Books/Nā Mea Hawaii (p88)
- ➡ Party at the Honolulu Festival (p89) or Pan-Pacific Festival (p89)

by US sea captain John Dominis. The captain's son, also named John, became the governor of O'ahu and married the Hawaiian princess who became Queen Lili'uokalani. After the queen was released from house arrest at 'Iolani Palace in 1896, she lived at Washington Place until her death in 1917.

A plaque near the sidewalk outside is inscribed with the words to 'Aloha 'Oe,' the farewell anthem that Lili'uokalani composed. For tour reservations, call at least two days in advance and bring photo ID. No large bags or backpacks are allowed inside the house, where photography is strictly limited.

Honolulu Museum of Art at First Hawaiian Center ART GALLERY
(Map p72; ☎526-0232; http://honolulumuseum.org; 999 Bishop St; ⊙8:30am-6pm Mon-Fri) FREE
Inside the high-rise First Hawaiian Bank headquarters, this tiny gallery curated by the Honolulu Museum of Art (p78) livens up the briefcase district with changing exhibits of modern and contemporary works, often mixed-media, ceramic or fabric art. The building itself features an artistic four-story glass wall incorporating 185 prisms. Free guided gallery tours are given at noon on the first Friday of the month.

Cathedral of St Andrew CHURCH
(Map p72; ☎524-2822; www.saintandrewscathedral.net; 229 Queen Emma Sq; ⊙usually 8:30am-4pm Mon-Fri, tours 11:50am Sun; P) FREE
Dedicated in 1886, this French Gothic cathedral was King Kamehameha IV's homage to the architecture and faith of the Church of England. After becoming friends with Queen Victoria, the king and his consort, Queen Emma, founded the Anglican Church of Hawaii in 1861. Historical tours usually meet by the pulpit after the 10:30am Sunday worship service; call ahead to confirm.

For a free concert, the largest pipe organ in the Pacific is sonorously played every Wednesday from 12:15pm until 12:45pm.

FLOWER POWER

Chinatown herbalists are both physicians and pharmacists, with walls full of small wooden drawers, each filled with a different herb. They'll size you up, feel your pulse and listen to you describe your ailments before deciding which drawers to open, mixing herbs and flowers and wrapping them for you to take home and boil together. Find traditional herbalists at the **Institute for Chinese Acupuncture & Oriental Medicine** (Map p72; ☎521-2288; www.orientalmedicine.edu; Suite 203-B, Chinatown Cultural Plaza, 100 N Beretania St), **Anna Li Clinic of Chinese Medicine & Acupuncture** (Map p72; ☎537-1133; 1121 Nu'uanu Ave) or **Leanne Chee Chinese Herbs & Acupuncture** (Map p72; ☎533-2498; 1159 Maunakea St).

⊙ Chinatown

The location of this mercantile district is no accident. Between Honolulu's port and what was once the countryside, shops selling goods to city folks and visiting ship crews alike sprang up. Many of these shops were opened by 19th-century Chinese laborers who had finished their sugarcane plantation contracts. The most successful entrepreneurs have long since moved out of this low-rent district into the suburbs, making room for newer waves of mostly Southeast Asian immigrants.

The scent of burning incense still wafts through Chinatown's buzzing markets, fire-breathing dragons spiral up the columns of buildings and steaming dim sum awakens even the sleepiest of appetites. Explore this revitalized neighborhood's cutting-edge art galleries and fashion boutiques, rub shoulders with locals over a bowl of noodles, consult with an herbalist and buy a flower lei or shop for 20th-century Hawaiiana antiques.

Foster Botanical Garden GARDEN
(Map p72; ☎522-7066; www.co.honolulu.hi.us/parks/hbg/fbg.htm; 50 N Vineyard Blvd; adult/child 6-12yr $5/1; ⊙9am-4pm, guided tours usually 1pm Mon-Sat, closed Dec 25 & Jan 1; P)
Tropical plants you've only ever read about can be spotted in all their glory at this botanical garden, which took root here in the 1850s. Among its rarest specimens are the Hawaiian *loulu* palm and the East African *Gigasiphon macrosiphon,* both thought to be extinct in the wild. A free self-guided tour booklet is available at the garden entrance.

Several of the garden's towering trees are the largest of their kind in the USA. Oddities include the cannonball tree, the sausage tree and the double coconut palm capable of producing a 50lb nut – watch your head! Follow your nose past fragrant vanilla vines and

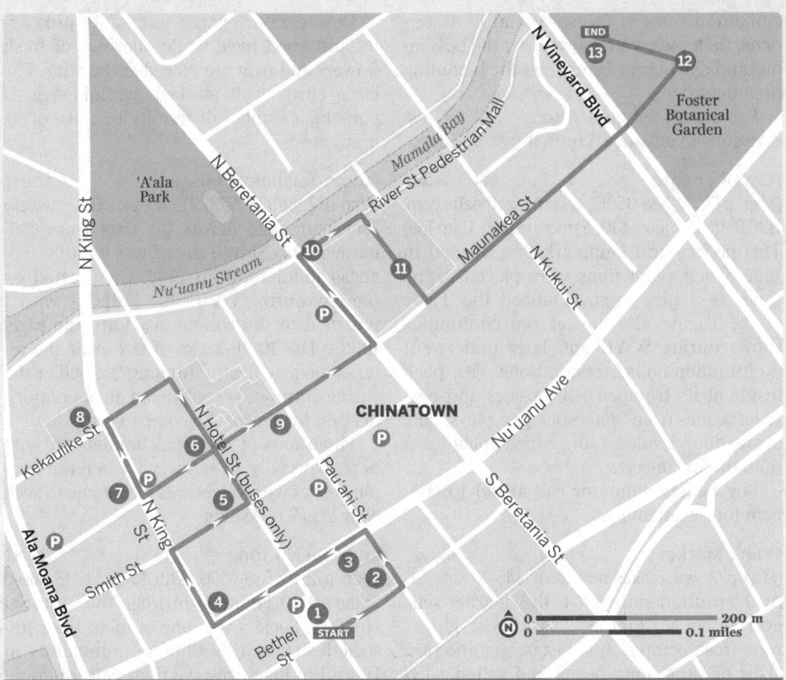

City Walk
Historical Chinatown

START CHINATOWN GATEWAY PLAZA
END FOSTER BOTANICAL GARDEN
LENGTH 1 MILE; ONE TO TWO HOURS

Honolulu's most foot-trafficked neighborhood, Chinatown, is also its most historic. Start at 1 **Chinatown Gateway Plaza** at the stone lions. Walk northeast to the neoclassical 1922 2 **Hawaii Theatre** (p78), nicknamed the 'Pride of the Pacific,' then continue around the corner.

On Nu'uanu Ave, the now-abandoned 3 **Pantheon Bar** was a favorite of sailors in days past – even King David Kalakaua imbibed here. The avenue's granite-block sidewalks are themselves relics, built with the discarded ballasts of 19th-century trading ships. At the corner of King St, peek into the 4 **First Hawaiian Bank**, with its antique wooden teller cages that cameoed in the TV show *Lost*.

Poke your head into the community-run 5 **Hawai'i Heritage Center** (p78) before turning left onto seedy Hotel St, historically Honolulu's red-light district and now a row of trendy lounges, nightclubs, eateries and coffeehouses. At the corner of Maunakea St, the ornate facade of the 6 **Wo Fat Building** resembles a Chinese temple. The building – and, incidentally, also the villain of the *Hawaii Five-O* TV series – is named after Honolulu's oldest restaurant, which opened here in 1882 (it's now closed).

On King St, continue past the red pillars coiled with dragons outside the 7 **Bank of Hawaii** to the corner of Kekaulike St and venture inside the buzzing 1904 8 **O'ahu Market** (p78). Heading north on Maunakea St, you'll pass 9 **lei shops** where skilled artisans string and braid blossom after blossom, filling the air with the scent of pikake.

Down by the riverside, the 10 **statue of Dr Sun Yat-sen**, a Chinese revolutionary, stands guard over the senior citizens playing checkers at stone tables outdoors. Cut through the courtyard of the 11 **Chinatown Cultural Plaza**. Back on Maunakea St, cross over Vineyard Blvd to the venerable 12 **Kuan Yin Temple** (p78), originally built in 1880. Finish with a peaceful stroll around the mid-19th-century 13 **Foster Botanical Garden** (p76).

cinnamon trees in the spice and herb gardens, then pick your way among the poisonous and dye plants. Don't miss the blooming orchid gardens.

For docent-led guided tours, call for reservations in advance. Limited free parking.

Hawaii Theatre HISTORICAL BUILDING

(Map p72; ☎528-0506; www.hawaiitheatre.com; 1130 Bethel St; tours $10; ⌚tours usually 11am Tue) This neoclassical landmark first opened in 1922, when silent films were played to the tunes of a pipe organ. Dubbed the 'Pride of the Pacific', the theater ran continuous shows during WWII and later underwent multimillion-dollar restorations. To peek inside at its trompe-l'oeil mosaics and bas-relief scenes from Shakespearean plays, take a one-hour guided tour, which includes a mini organ concert.

Buy tickets online or call ahead to confirm tour availability.

O'ahu Market MARKET

(Map p72; www.chinatownhi.com; 145 N King St) An institution since 1904, this market sells everything a Chinese cook needs: ginger root, fresh octopus, quail eggs, jasmine rice, slabs of tuna, long beans and salted jellyfish. It's always crowded with cart-pushing grandmothers and downtown office workers doing their grocery shopping. You owe yourself a bubble tea if you spot a pig's head among the stalls.

Hawai'i Heritage Center MUSEUM

(Map p72; ☎521-2749; 1040 Smith St; adult/child 5-18yr $1/25¢, walking tour $5; ⌚9am-2pm Mon-Sat) Local volunteers with family ties to the community run this small but welcoming gallery, which offers changing historical and cultural exhibitions about O'ahu's Chinese immigrants and other ethnic groups. Two-hour guided walking tours of Chinatown usually depart at 9:30am on Wednesday and Friday; call ahead to check schedules.

Kuan Yin Temple TEMPLE

(Map p72; 170 N Vineyard Blvd; ⌚usually 7am-5pm) FREE With its green ceramic-tile roof and bright red columns, this ornate Chinese Buddhist temple is Honolulu's oldest. The temple is dedicated to Kuan Yin, boddhisattva of mercy, whose statue is the largest in the prayer hall. Respectful visitors are welcome inside the richly carved interior, which is pervaded by the sweet smell of burning incense.

Devotees burn paper 'money' for prosperity and good luck, while offerings of fresh flowers and fruit are placed at the altar. The large citrus fruit stacked pyramid-style is pomelo, a symbol of fertility because of its many seeds.

Izumo Taishakyo Mission TEMPLE

(Map p72; ☎538-7778; 215 N Kukui St; ⌚usually 8am-5pm) FREE Across the river from Chinatown, this Shintō shrine was built by Japanese immigrants in 1906. Confiscated by the city during WWII, the property wasn't returned to the community until the early 1960s. The 100lb sacks of rice near the altar symbolize health. Ringing the bell at the shrine entrance is considered an act of purification for those who come to pray.

Thousands of good-luck amulets are sold here, especially on January 1, when the temple heaves with celebrants who come to seek New Year's blessings.

Lum Sai Ho Tong TEMPLE

(Map p72; ☎536-6590; 1315 River St; ⌚closed to the public) Founded in 1889, the Lum Sai Ho Tong Society was one of more than 100 societies started by Chinese immigrants in Hawaii to help preserve their cultural identity. The society's Taoist temple honors the goddess Tin Hau, a child who rescued her father from drowning and was later deified. The devout may claim to see her apparition when traveling by boat.

The upstairs temple is generally not open to the public, but you can admire its colorfully painted exterior from the sidewalk below.

Ala Moana & Around

Ala Moana, meaning 'Path to the Sea,' shares its name with a coastal boulevard connecting downtown Honolulu and Waikiki, passing the city's biggest beach park and Hawaii's largest shopping mall.

★Honolulu Museum of Art MUSEUM

(Map p80; ☎532-8700; www.honolulumuseum.org; 900 S Beretania St; adult/child 4-17yr $10/5, all free 1st Wed & 3rd Sun of each month; ⌚10am-4:30pm Tue-Sat, 1-5pm Sun, also 6-9pm last Fri of the month Jan-Oct; P 🚻) Near downtown's historical district, this jewel of a museum may be the biggest surprise of your trip to O'ahu. It covers the artistic traditions of almost every continent, with exceptional Asian collections. Plan on spending a few hours here, perhaps having lunch at the cafe and joining a tour of Shangri La (p128), Doris Duke's enchanting estate near Diamond Head.

Behind the museum's classical facade are airy garden and fountain courtyards. Inside the galleries are masterpieces by Monet, Matisse and O'Keeffe; galleries of Greek and Roman antiquities and Italian Renaissance paintings; major works of American modern art; ancient Japanese woodblock prints by Hiroshige and Hokusai; Ming dynasty Chinese calligraphy and painted scrolls; Indian temple carvings; war clubs and masks from Papua New Guinea – and so much more.

Formerly called the Honolulu Academy of Arts, the museum was founded in 1927 by Anna Rice Cooke, an heiress who created an art collection that would reflect the diversity of the island's local population. She wanted this to be a place where children born in Hawaii could come and examine their own cultural roots – and perhaps just as importantly, discover something about their neighbors – all through the window of works of art.

Entry tickets are also good for same-day admission to the museum's satellite galleries and sculpture garden at Spalding House (p81). Check the museum website for more special exhibitions and events, including gallery tours, family-friendly Sundays, films and concerts at the Doris Duke Theatre (p98), and social 'ARTafterDARK' parties with live entertainment, food and drinks.

Validated parking at the Honolulu Museum of Art School lot, just southeast of the museum (enter off Beretania or Young Sts), costs $3 for four hours (flat rate after 4pm $4). From Waikiki, take TheBus 2.

University Area

In the foothills of Manoa Valley, this collegiate neighborhood has a youthful collection of cool cafes and boutique shops, eclectic restaurants and boisterous bars.

University of Hawai'i at Manoa UNIVERSITY
(UH Manoa; Map p80; ☎956-8111; http://manoa.hawaii.edu; 2500 Campus Rd; P) Born too late for the tweedy academic architecture of the mainland, UH Manoa is the central campus of the statewide university system. Filled with shade trees and well-bronzed students from around Polynesia, UH Manoa has strong academic programs in astronomy, marine sciences and Hawaiian, Asian and Pacific studies. It's free to tour the campus and browse its arts and cultural exhibits.

Free one-hour w
emphasizing hi
ally leave fro
info 956-7137; www
Campus Rd; 8:30
on Monday, Wedne
ervations are necess
minutes beforehand a
tion and ID office upstai
walking tour of outdoo
other works by notable Ha
for a free *Campus Art* brochu

A short walk downhill fro
Center, the **John Young Museu**
(Map p80; ☎956-3634; www.outreach.ha
jymuseum; Krauss Hall, 2500 Dole St; 11a
Mon-Fri, 1-4pm Sun) FREE houses a 20th
tury Hawaii painter's eclectic collection
artifacts from around the Pacific, Africa an
Asia, including ceramics, pottery and sculpture. Although it only fills a couple of rooms, it's worth a quick look.

On the east side of campus, the **East-West Center** (Map p80; ☎944-7111; www.eastwestcenter.org; 1601 East-West Rd) aims to promote mutual understanding among the peoples of Asia, the Pacific and the USA. Changing exhibitions of art and culture are displayed in the center's **EWC Gallery** (Map p80; 1st fl, Burns Hall; usually 8am-5pm Mon-Fri, noon-4pm Sun) FREE. A short walk further north you'll find a replica royal **Thai pavilion** and **Japanese garden**. Check the center's online calendar for multicultural programs, including lectures, films, concerts and dance performances.

Designated visitor parking on the Upper Campus costs $2 per half hour (flat rate after 4pm $6).

Upper Manoa Valley, Tantalus & Makiki

North of the university campus, roads wind uphill into Honolulu's green belt, passing historic homes before entering forest reserves around Mt Tantalus. Further west above downtown's high-rises, Makiki Heights is the neighborhood where President Obama spent much of his boyhood.

Lyon Arboretum GARDENS
(☎info 988-0456, tour reservations 988-0461; www.hawaii.edu/lyonarboretum; 3860 Manoa Rd; suggested donation per person $5, guided tour $5; 8am-4pm Mon-Fri, 9am-3pm Sat, tours usually 10am Mon-Fri; P) Beautifully unkempt

oana & University Area

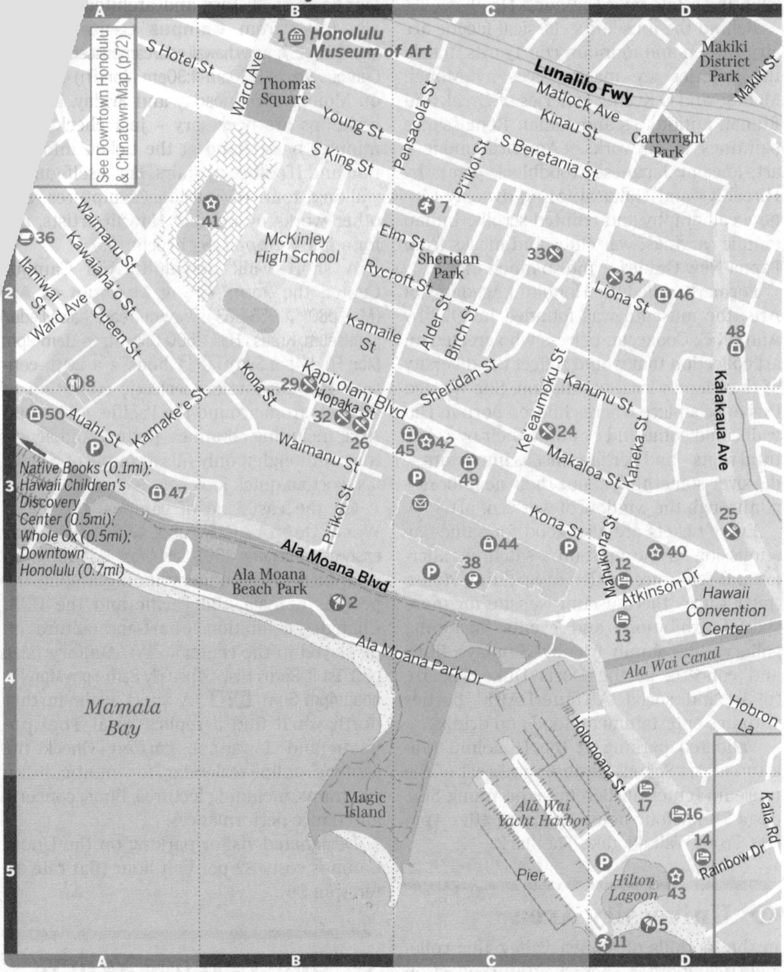

See Downtown Honolulu & Chinatown Map (p72)

walking trails wind through this highly regarded 200-acre arboretum, founded by sugar-plantation owners in 1918 and managed today by the University of Hawaiʻi. This is not your typical overly manicured tropical flower garden, but a mature and largely wooded arboretum, where related rainforest species cluster in a seminatural state.

Among the plants in the Hawaiian ethnobotanical garden are *ʻulu* (breadfruit), *kalo* (taro) and *ko* (sugarcane) brought by early Polynesian settlers; *kukui*, once harvested to produce lantern oil; and *ti*, which was used for medicinal purposes during ancient times and for making moonshine after Westerners arrived. To reserve your spot on a guided tour, call at least 24 hours in advance.

If you hike uphill for about a mile along a signposted dirt jeep road, a narrow, tree-root-entangled footpath continues to seasonal **ʻAihualama Falls**, a lacy cliffside cascade (no swimming).

From Ala Moana Center or University Ave, catch TheBus 5 to Manoa Valley and get off at the last stop, then walk 0.6 miles uphill past Paradise Park to the end of Manoa Rd. Limited free parking.

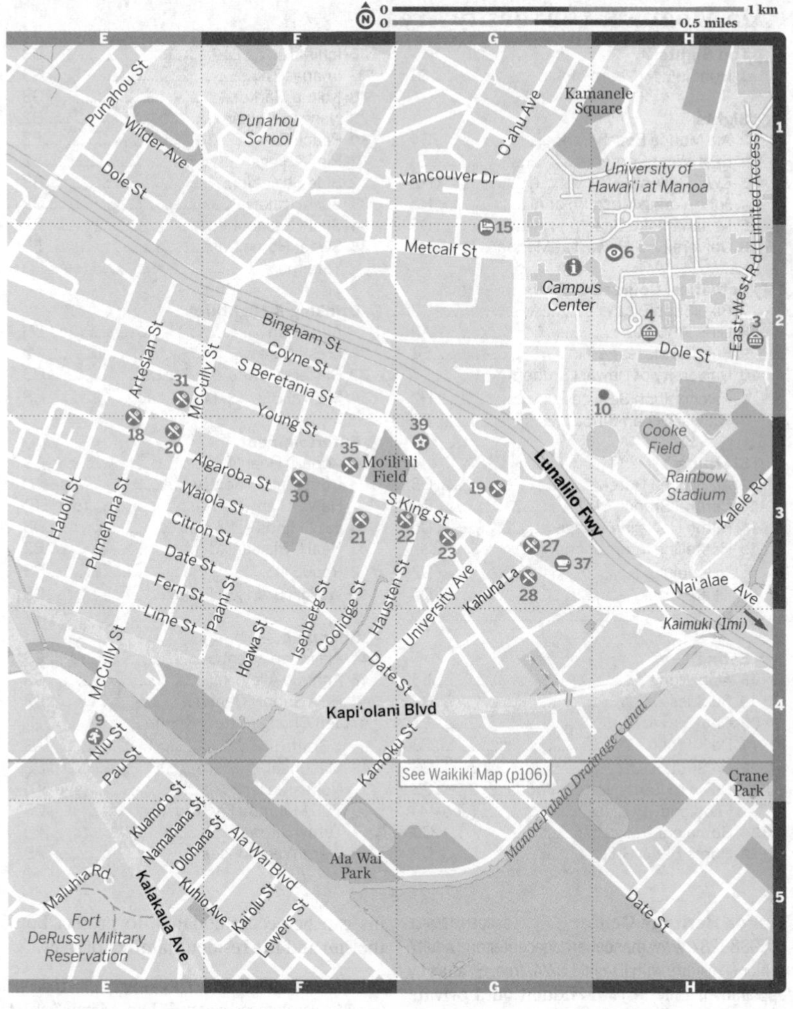

Honolulu Museum of Art at Spalding House MUSEUM

(☎526-1322; www.honolulumuseum.org; 2411 Makiki Heights Dr; adult/child 4-17yr $10/5, all free 1st Wed of each month; ⏰10am-4pm Tue-Sat, noon-4pm Sun, tours usually 1:30pm Tue-Sun; Ⓟ) At an estate house with meditative sculpture and flowering gardens, this small museum features changing exhibits of paintings, sculpture and other artwork dating from the 1940s onward by Hawaii-born, mainland and international artists. The lawn pavilion shelters the museum's most prized piece, an environmental installation by David Hockney based on his sets for Ravel's opera *L'Enfant et les sortilèges*.

Admission tickets are valid for same-day entry at downtown's much bigger Honolulu Museum of Art (p78). Downstairs, the modest Spalding House Cafe serves drinks, desserts and light lunches; reserve ahead for a romantic picnic basket for two to enjoy on the museum's grassy lawn.

From Waikiki, take TheBus 2 or 13 toward downtown Honolulu and get off at Alapa'i St. From the corner of Alapa'i and King Sts, catch TheBus 15 bound for Pacific Heights, which stops at the museum.

Ala Moana & University Area

Top Sights
1 Honolulu Museum of Art....B1

Sights
2 Ala Moana Beach Park....B4
East-West Center....(see 3)
3 EWC Gallery....H2
4 John Young Museum of Art....H2
5 Kahanamoku Beach....D5
6 University of Hawai'i at Manoa....H2

Activities, Courses & Tours
7 Bike Shop....C2
8 Girls Who Surf....A2
9 Sukotai Massage 1....E4
10 University of Hawai'i Student Recreation Services....H2
11 Waikiki Ocean Club....D5

Sleeping
12 Ala Moana Hotel....D3
13 Central Branch YMCA....D4
14 Hilton Hawaiian Village....D5
15 Hostelling International (HI) Honolulu....G2
16 Ilikai....D5
17 Modern....D5

Eating
18 Alan Wong's....E3
19 Bubbies....G3
20 Chef Mavro....E3
21 Da Kitchen....F3
22 Da Spot....G3
23 Down to Earth Natural Foods....G3
Foodland....(see 44)
24 Gomaichi....C3
25 Home Bar & Grill....D3
26 Ichiriki....B3
27 Imanas Tei....G3
28 Kokua Market....G3
29 Nanzan Girogiro....B2
30 Peace Cafe....F3
31 Pint & Jigger....E2
32 Side Street Inn....B3
33 Sushi Izakaya Gaku....C2
34 Sushi Sasabune....D2
35 Sweet Home Café....F3
Yataimura....(see 44)

Drinking & Nightlife
Addiction....(see 17)
36 Fresh Cafe....A2
37 Glazers Coffee....G3
38 Mai Tai Bar....C3

Entertainment
39 Anna O'Brien's....G3
Doris Duke Theatre....(see 1)
HawaiiSlam....(see 36)
40 Jazz Minds Art & Café....D3
41 Neal S Blaisdell Center....B2
42 Republik....C3
43 Waikiki Starlight Luau....D5

Shopping
44 Ala Moana Center....C3
45 Antique Alley....C3
46 Hula Supply Center....D2
47 Jeff Chang Pottery & Fine Crafts....A3
48 Manuheali'i....D2
Nohea Gallery....(see 50)
49 T&L Muumuu Factory....C3
Tutuvi Sitoa....(see 27)
50 Ward Warehouse....A3

Manoa Heritage Center GARDEN, TEMPLE
(☎988-1287; www.manoaheritagecenter.org; adult/senior & military with ID/child $7/4/free; ⊙tours by appointment only; 🅿) Hidden on a private family's estate in the lush upper Manoa valley, the centerpiece of this unique Hawaiian heritage site is a stone-walled agricultural heiau surrounded by Hawaiian ethnobotanical gardens that include rare native and Polynesian-introduced plants. Walking tours are led by knowledgeable volunteers and staff eager to share island lore and Hawaiian traditions.

During an educational tour, kids can take a turn at the *konane* board (a Hawaiian version of checkers), then get their hands dirty learning how taro was traditionally farmed. Try to call at least a week in advance for tour reservations and to get directions. No walk-ins can be accommodated, to protect both the site and the resident family's privacy.

Pu'u 'Ualaka'a State Wayside LOOKOUT
(www.hawaiistateparks.org; ⊙7am-7:45pm Apr-1st Mon in Sep, to 6:45pm 1st Tue in Sep-Mar; 🅿) At this hillside park, sweeping views extend from Diamond Head on the far left, across Waikiki and downtown Honolulu, to the Wai'anae Range on the right. The sprawling UH Manoa campus is easily recognized by its sports stadium. You can even gaze into the green mound of Punchbowl crater. The airport is visible on the coast and Pearl Harbor beyond that.

It's less than 2.5 miles up Round Top Dr from Makiki St to the park entrance, from where it's another half-mile drive to the lookout (bear left at the fork).

Greater Honolulu

★Bishop Museum MUSEUM

(Map p71; ☎infoline 847-3511, planetarium 848-4136; www.bishopmuseum.org; 1525 Bernice St; adult/child 4-12yr/senior $20/15/17; ⏲9am-5pm Wed-Mon; P 👪) Like Hawaii's version of the Smithsonian Institute in Washington, DC, this museum showcases a remarkable array of cultural and natural history exhibits. It ranks among the world's very best Polynesian anthropological museums. Founded in 1889, it originally housed only Hawaiian and royal artifacts. Today the museum also has high-tech interactive science exhibits for kids and O'ahu's only planetarium.

The recently renovated main gallery, the **Hawaiian Hall**, resides inside a dignified three-story Victorian building. Displays covering the ancient history of Hawaii include a *pili*-grass thatched house, carved *ki'i* (deity images), *kahili* (feathered staffs used at royal funerals and coronations), shark-toothed war clubs and traditional *kapa* cloth made by pounding the bark of the paper mulberry tree. Don't miss the feathered cloak once worn by Kamehameha the Great, created entirely from the yellow feathers of the now-extinct *mamo* – some 80,000 birds were caught and plucked to create this single adornment. Upper-floor exhibits delve further into *ali'i* (royal) history, traditional daily life and the close relationship between Hawaiians and the natural world.

Fascinating exhibits inside the adjacent two-story **Pacific Hall**, reopening after renovations in late 2013, cover the cultures of Polynesia, Micronesia and Melanesia. You could spend hours gazing at astounding and rare ritual artifacts, from elaborate dance masks and ceremonial costumes to carved canoes and tools of warfare. Next door, the museum's modern wing, the **Castle Memorial Building**, hosts traveling exhibitions.

Across the Great Lawn, the state-of-the-art, family oriented **Science Adventure Center** uses eye-popping multimedia exhibits and demonstrations to explain Hawaii's natural environment, letting kids walk through an erupting model volcano and virtually take a mini-sub dive. Screened several times daily, **planetarium** movies highlight traditional Polynesian methods of wayfaring (navigation), along with astronomy and the telescope observatories atop Mauna Kea. Daytime showings are free with your museum admission ticket.

A **gift shop** off the main lobby sells books on the Pacific not easily found elsewhere, as well as some high-quality Hawaiian crafts and souvenirs. The on-site Café Pulama serves local and Hawaiian plates, lighter lunches, drinks and desserts. Check the museum website for special exhibitions and events, including summer concerts under the stars, family-friendly activities and after-dark planetarium shows.

From Waikiki or downtown Honolulu, take TheBus 2 to School St/Middle St to the intersection of School St and Kapalama Ave; walk one block *makai* (seaward) on Kapalama Ave, then turn right on Bernice St. By car, take eastbound H-1 Fwy exit 20, turn right on Houghtailing St, then left on Bernice St. Free on-site parking.

National Memorial Cemetery of the Pacific CEMETERY

(☎532-3720; www.cem.va.gov/cems/nchp/nmcp.asp; 2177 Puowaina Dr; ⏲8am-5:30pm Sep 30-Mar 1, 8am-6:30pm Mar 2-Sep 29, 7am-7pm on last Mon in May; P) FREE About 2 miles northeast of downtown Honolulu surrounded by freeways and residential neighborhoods is a bowl-shaped crater, nicknamed Punchbowl, formed by a long-extinct volcano. Ancient Hawaiians sacrificed to appease the gods now share the crater floor with the buried remains of nearly 50,000 US soldiers, many of whom were killed in the Pacific during WWII.

Early Hawaiians called the crater Puowaina ('hill of human sacrifices'). It's believed that the slain bodies of *kapu* (taboo) breakers

OFF THE BEATEN TRACK

TANTALUS–ROUND TOP SCENIC DRIVE

Offering skyline views to drivers and cyclists alike, the Tantalus–Round Top Scenic Drive climbs almost to the top of Mt Tantalus (2013ft), aka Pu'u 'Ohi'a. Bamboo, ginger, elephant-eared taro and eucalyptus trees make up the roadside profusion of tropical plants, as vines climb to the tops of telephone poles and twist their way across the wires. Starting above downtown Honolulu and the H-1 Fwy, this 10-mile circuit is a two-way loop called Tantalus Dr on its western side, Round Top Dr to the east. Many hiking trails branch off the loop, which passes by Pu'u 'Ualaka'a State Wayside.

Upper Manoa Valley, Tantalus & Makiki

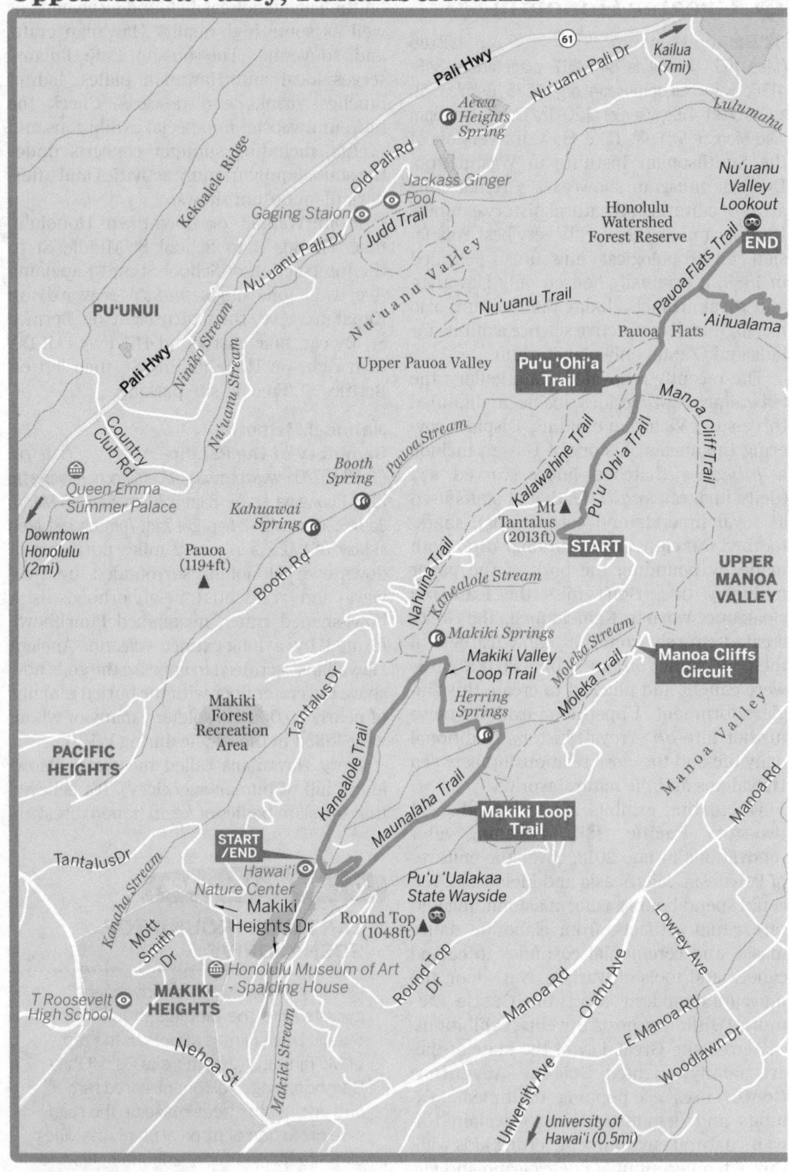

were ceremonially cremated upon the altar of a heiau here. The crater may also have been used for secretive royal burials.

In the modern US military cemetery, the remains of Ernie Pyle, the distinguished war correspondent who covered both world wars and was hit by machine-gun fire on Ie-shima during the final days of WWII, lie in section D, grave 109. Five stones to the left, at grave D-1, is the marker for Ellison Onizuka, the Big Island astronaut who perished in the 1986 *Challenger* space-shuttle disaster.

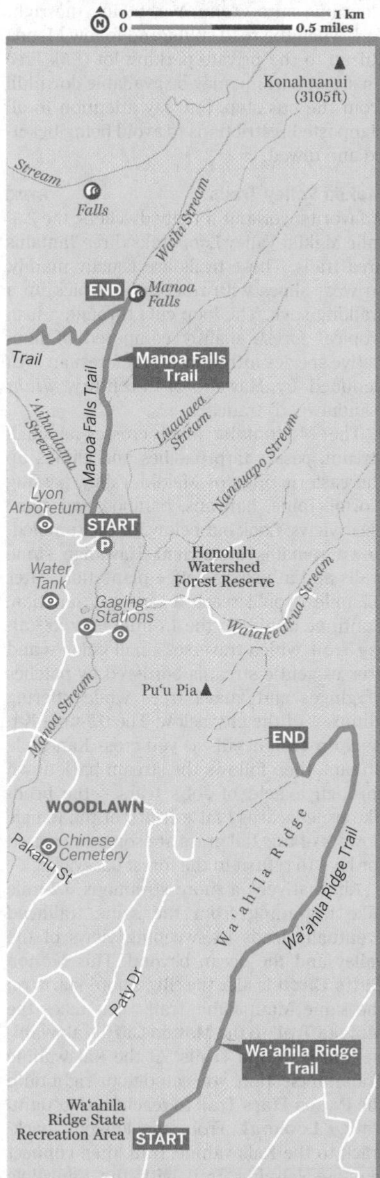

For plum views of the city and Diamond Head, head up to the lookout by bearing left after passing through the main cemetery gates. Special events held at the cemetery include Memorial Day ceremonies and an Easter sunrise Christian church service.

From Waikiki, take TheBus 13 or 42 toward downtown Honolulu and get off at Alapa'i St, then transfer to TheBus 15 bound for Pacific Heights, which stops a 15-minute uphill walk from the cemetery entrance. If you're driving, there's a marked exit on your right as you start up the Pali Hwy – watch closely, because it comes up quickly. You then follow the signs through twisting, narrow residential streets.

Queen Emma Summer Palace HISTORICAL BUILDING

(Map p84; ☎595-3167; www.daughtersofhawaii.org; 2913 Pali Hwy; adult/child $6/1; ⏲9am-4pm, last guided tour 3pm; P) In the heat and humidity of summer, Queen Emma, Kamehameha IV's royal consort, used to slip away to this genteel hillside retreat, now a historical museum. The Greek Revival-style building recalls an old Southern plantation house, with its columned porch and high ceilings. The interior now looks much as it did in Queen Emma's day, decorated with period furniture and royal memorabilia.

Forgotten after Queen Emma's death in 1885, this stately home was slated to be razed and the estate turned into a public park. The Daughters of Hawai'i, whose members are all descendants of early missionary families, rescued it. Docents will show you around the house, pointing out a koa-wood cabinet displaying a set of china from England's Queen Victoria and the elaborate feather cloaks and capes once worn by Hawaiian royalty.

Take TheBus 4 from Waikiki, the UH Manoa area or downtown Honolulu, or board bus 55, 56 or 57 at Ala Moana Center or downtown. Be sure the bus driver knows where you're going, so you don't miss the stop. If you're driving, look for the entrance near mile marker 2 on the northbound Pali Hwy (Hwy 61).

Activities

Hiking

Some of O'ahu's most popular hiking trails lead into the solitudinous forests of the rainy, windy Ko'olau Range above downtown.

★Manoa Falls Trail HIKING

(👪) One of Honolulu's most rewarding short hikes, the 1.6-mile round-trip Manoa Falls Trail runs above a rocky streambed through lush vegetation. Wild orchids and red ginger grow near the falls, which drop about 100ft into a small, shallow pool. Falling rocks and

HIKE LIKE A LOCAL

To find more hiking trails island-wide, visit the website of the government-sponsored **Na Ala Hele Hawaii Trail & Access System** (http://hawaiitrails.ehawaii.gov). For group hikes, check the calendar published by **Honolulu Weekly** (www.honoluluweekly.com) or with the following organizations:

➡ **Hawaiian Trail & Mountain Club** (http://htmclub.org; donation per hike $3) Volunteer-run hiking club that arranges intermediate to challenging group hikes on weekends all over the island. Trail descriptions and safety tips available online.

➡ **Sierra Club** (Map p72; www.hi.sierraclub.org/oahu; 1040 Richards St; donation per hike adult/child under 14yr $5/1;) The Hawaii chapter of this nonprofit national organization leads weekend hikes and other outings around O'ahu, including volunteer opportunities to rebuild trails and combat invasive plants.

leptospirosis make swimming unsafe, and it's illegal to venture beyond the established viewing area.

Tall tree trunks lining the often muddy, slippery path include *Eucalyptus robusta*, with soft, spongy, reddish bark; flowering orange African tulip trees; and other arboreals that creak like wooden doors in old houses.

Just before reaching Manoa Falls, the inconspicuous **'Aihualama Trail** branches off west of a chain-link fence, offering broad views of Manoa Valley starting just a short way up the path. The trail soon enters a bamboo forest with some massive old banyan trees, then contours around a ridge and switchbacks up. For a satisfying 5.5-mile round-trip hike, turn right onto the **Pauoa Flats Trail**, which leads up to the **Nu'uanu Valley Lookout**, where it's possible to peer through a gap in the steep *pali* (cliffs) over to the Windward Coast.

From the Ala Moana Center, take hourly TheBus 5 Manoa Valley to the end of the line, from where it's a 0.5-mile uphill walk past Treetops Restaurant through Paradise Park to the trailhead. By car, follow University Ave north of the UH Manoa campus. Continue onto O'ahu Ave, taking the right fork when the road splits, and follow Manoa Rd up to the private parking lot ($5). Free on-street parking may be available downhill from the bus stop, but pay attention to all signposted restrictions to avoid being ticketed and towed.

Makiki Valley Trails HIKING

A favorite workout for city dwellers, the 2.5-mile Makiki Valley Loop links three Tantalus area trails. These trails are usually muddy, so wear shoes with traction and pick up a walking stick. The loop cuts through a lush tropical forest, mainly composed of non-native species introduced to reforest an area denuded by Hawaii's 19th-century *'iliahi* (sandalwood) trade.

The **Maunalaha Trail** crosses a small stream, passes taro patches and climbs up the eastern ridge of Makiki Valley, passing Norfolk pine, banyans, bamboo and some clear views. Look out below for the tumbled-down remains of ancient Hawaiian stone walls and a historic coffee plantation. After 0.7 miles, you'll reach a four-way junction. Continue uphill on the 1.1-mile **Makiki Valley Trail**, which traverses small gulches and crosses gentle streams bordered by patches of ginger and guava trees while offering glimpses of the city below. The 0.7-mile **Kanealole Trail** begins as you cross Kanealole Stream, then follows the stream back down through a field of Job's tears – the bead-like psuedocarps ('false fruit') of the female flowers of this tall grass are sometimes used for lei – to return to the forest baseyard.

Alternatively, a more strenuous 6.2-mile hike beginning from the same trailhead eventually leads to sweeping views of the valley and the ocean beyond. This **Manoa Cliffs Circuit**, aka the 'Big Loop,' starts on the same Maunalaha Trail, then takes the **Moleka Trail** to the **Manoa Cliff**, **Kalawahine** and **Nahuina Trails**. At the Kalawahine Trail intersection, you can detour right onto the **Pauoa Flats Trail** to reach the **Nu'uanu Valley Lookout**. From the lookout, backtrack to the Kalawahine Trail, then connect via the Nahuina Trail with the Kanealole Trail, which rolls downhill back to the forest baseyard.

The starting point for both hiking loops is **Makiki Forest Recreation Area** (2135 Makiki Heights Dr) FREE, less than 0.5 miles up Makiki Heights Dr from Makiki St. Where the road makes a sharp left turn, drive straight ahead through an open green gate into the forest baseyard. Park along the shoulder just inside the gate or in a small unpaved parking lot, then follow the signs and walk along the hillside nature path toward the main trailheads near the Hawai'i Nature Center (p88), which organizes family-friendly hikes and outdoor education programs.

From downtown, take TheBus 15, which runs into Pacific Heights. Get off near the intersection of Mott-Smith Dr and Makiki Heights Dr near the Spalding House art museum, then walk about 0.5 miles southeast along Makiki Heights Dr to the forest baseyard. From Waikiki, take TheBus 4 Nu'uanu to the corner of Wilder Ave and Makiki St, then walk 0.3 miles northeast up Makiki St, veering left onto Makiki Heights Dr and walking another 0.4 miles uphill to the baseyard.

Wa'ahila Ridge Trail HIKING

Popular with families, this boulder-strewn trail offers a cool retreat amid Norfolk pines and endemic plants, with ridgetop views of the city and Waikiki. Rolling up and down a series of saddles and knobs before reaching a grassy clearing, the 4.8-mile trail covers a variety of terrain in a short time, making an enjoyable afternoon's walk for novice hikers.

Look for the Na Ala Hele trailhead sign just past the picnic tables deep inside **Wa'ahila Ridge State Recreation Area** (www.hawaiistateparks.org; end of Ruth Pl; ⏲7am-7:45pm Apr 1-1st Mon in Sep, to 6:45pm 1st Tue in Sep-Mar 31) FREE, at the back of the St Louis Heights subdivision east of Manoa Valley.

By car, follow Wai'alae Ave east of the university area into the Kaimuki neighborhood, turning left at the stoplight onto St Louis Dr. As you drive uphill, veer left onto Bertram St, turn left onto Peter St, then left again onto Ruth Pl, which runs west into the park. From Waikiki, TheBus 14 St Louis Heights stops every hour or two at the intersection of Peter and Ruth Sts, about 0.5 miles from the trailhead.

Cycling

Road cyclists looking for an athletic workout often head up the Tantalus–Round Top Scenic Drive (see the boxed text, p83).

Bike Shop CYCLING

(Map p80; ☎596-0588; www.bikeshophawaii.com; 1149 S King St; per day rental bicycle $20-85, car rack $5; ⏲9am-8pm Mon-Fri, 9am-5pm Sat, 10am-5pm Sun) Honolulu's Bike Shop rents top-quality road and mountain bikes and can provide maps of suggested cycling routes around the city and the island. An annual membership ($20) in its cycling team lets you join weekend, quarterly and women-only group rides and take advantage of support services at races.

Surfing

You'll find beginner and intermediate-level surf breaks at Ala Moana Beach Park (p69).

Girls Who Surf SURFING, SUP

(Map p80; ☎772-4583; www.girlswhosurf.com; 1020 Auahi St; 2hr lesson from $99, rental per hour/day bodyboards $5/15, surfboards from $10/30, SUP sets $18/47; ⏲8am-6pm) Learn how to surf

MR OBAMA'S NEIGHBORHOOD

US President Barack Obama, who grew up in Makiki Heights, said that 'Hawaii's spirit of tolerance… became an integral part of my world view, and a basis for the values I hold most dear' (*Punahou Bulletin*: 1999). He has also said that Hawaii is a place for him to rest and recharge, and every year he returns to O'ahu for a family vacation.

In 1999, Obama said, 'When I'm heading out to a hard day of meetings and negotiations, I let my mind wander back to Sandy Beach, or Manoa Falls… It helps me, somehow, knowing that such wonderful places exist and [that]…I'll always be able to return to them' (*Punahou Bulletin*).

If you want to walk in Obama's footsteps, here are some of his favorite places:

- Manoa Falls Trail (p85)
- Rainbow Drive-In (p118)
- Kapi'olani Beach (p109)
- Hanauma Bay Nature Preserve (p131)
- Sandy Beach Park (p132)
- Olomana Golf Links (p137)

HONOLULU FOR CHILDREN

For endless sand and a children's playground, take your *keiki* (child) or teen to Ala Moana Beach Park (p69), where local families hang out. For more of Honolulu's great outdoors, head up to Manoa Valley's Lyon Arboretum (p79), then hike to Manoa Falls (p85). Indoors, the Bishop Museum (p83) is entertaining for kids of all ages, or drop by the interactive family art center in the basement of the Honolulu Museum of Art (p78).

➡ **Hawaii Children's Discovery Center** (☎524-5437; www.discoverycenterhawaii.org; 111 'Ohe St; adult/senior/child 1-17yr $10/6/10; ⏰9am-1pm Tue-Fri, 10am-3pm Sat & Sun; P 👪) On a rainy day when you can't go to the beach, consider dropping by this hands-on museum for families. Opposite Kaka'ako Waterfront Park, the building was once the city's garbage incinerator, as evidenced by the surviving smokestack. Interactive science and cultural exhibits are geared toward elementary school-aged children, preschoolers and toddlers.

The Fantastic You! exhibit explores the human body, allowing kids to walk through a mock human stomach. In the Your Town section, kids can drive a play fire engine or conduct a TV interview. Hawaiian Rainbows and Your Rainbow World introduce Hawaii's multicultural heritage, while Rainforest Adventures highlights Hawaii's natural environment and conservation.

From Waikiki, take TheBus 19, 20 or 42, then walk around 0.3 miles makai (seaward) from the nearest bus stop on Ala Moana Blvd at Kolua St. Limited free parking.

➡ **Hawai'i Nature Center** (☎955-0100; www.hawaiinaturecenter.org; 2131 Makiki Heights Dr; program fees from $10; 👪) Inside the woodsy Makiki Forest Recreation Area, this small nonprofit community center conducts family oriented environmental education programs, day camps and guided weekend hikes for ages six and up. Reservations are usually required; check the online calendar or call ahead for details.

or stand up paddle surf (SUP) with safety-conscious group lessons taught by women at beaches near Waikiki and Ko Olina, with free Waikiki hotel pick-ups. For board rentals, delivery to Waikiki or Ala Moana Beach typically costs $10 extra.

Whale Watching

Prime-time for whale watching is winter, when migratory North Pacific humpbacks visit Hawaii.

Atlantis Adventures WHALE WATCHING
(Map p72; ☎800-548-6262; www.atlantisadventures.com; Pier 6, 1 Aloha Tower Dr; tour adult/child 7-12yr from $79/39; 👪) Usually departing at noon daily between late December and early April, Atlantis runs whale-watching cruises aboard the *Navatek I*, a high-tech catamaran designed to minimize rolling. Lasting two to 2½ hours, tours include a light breakfast or a lunch buffet. Reservations are essential; for discounts, book online or look for coupons in the free tourist magazines available around town.

Golf

Moanalua Golf Club GOLF
(☎839-2311; www.mgchawaii.com; 1250 Ala Aolani St; green fees $45; ⏰by reservation only Mon-Fri) Built in 1898 by a missionary family, Hawaii's oldest golf club offers a fairly quick round with straight fairways and nine holes that can be played twice from different tees. The eighth hole has killer views of the city skyline and Diamond Head.

Courses

★ **Native Books/ Nā Mea Hawaii** ARTS, CULTURE
(☎596-8885; www.nativebookshawaii.com; Ward Warehouse, 1050 Ala Moana Blvd) This community-oriented independent bookstore and gift shop hosts free classes, workshops and demonstrations in hula dancing, Hawaiian language, traditional feather-lei making and *lauhala* weaving, ukulele playing and more. Go online or call for current schedules and to check if pre-registration is required.

University of Hawai'i Student Recreation Services FITNESS, ARTS
(Map p80; ☎956-6468; www.manoa.hawaii.edu/studentrec/; 1337 Lower Campus Rd; most classes $10-65) UH Manoa offers a variety of short-term indoor recreation courses open to the public. Some classes, including hula, Tahi-

tian dance, tai chi, yoga and ukulele, meet once or twice weekly during a month-long session. Outdoor recreation trips and classes, including a variety of watersports, are usually only open to UH community members and guests.

Tours

For inexpensive guided walking tours of Chinatown, contact the Hawai'i Heritage Center (p78).

★AIA Walking Tour WALKING TOUR
(Map p72; ☎628-7243; www.aiahonolulu.org; 828 Fort St Mall; per person $10; ⏲usually 9am-11:30am Sat) Guided by professional architects, these architectural walking tours with a historical slant will literally change your perspective on downtown Honolulu's capitol district. Reservations required. Self-guided architectural walking tour booklets ($5) are available at the office between 8am and 4:30pm weekdays.

Hawaii Food Tours VAN TOUR
(☎926-3663; www.hawaiifoodtours.com; per person from $99) Designed by a former chef and restaurant critic, this four-hour lunchtime 'hole-in-the-wall' tour samples Chinatown noodle factories, island plate-lunch kitchens, famous bakeries, candy shops and more. Reservations required.

O'ahu Ghost Tours WALKING TOUR
(☎877-597-7325; www.oahughosttours.com; adult/child from $39/29) Hear spooky 'chicken skin' stories and go hunting for paranormal orbs on hokey, but amusing guided walking tours of Honolulu's haunted places. No skeptics allowed; reservations required.

Festivals & Events

Some of Honolulu's biggest parties also spill over into Waikiki (p113).

Chinese New Year CULTURE, ARTS
(www.chinatownhi.com) From late January to mid-February, Chinatown's lunar new year festivities include a night market and a parade with lion dancers and firecrackers.

★Honolulu Festival ARTS, CULTURE
(www.honolulufestival.com) In mid-March, this three-day celebration of Asian-Pacific cultural exchange features live music, dance and drama performances and an arts-and-crafts fair.

★Mele Mei MUSIC, ARTS
(www.melemei.com) Mostly in May, a month-long celebration of Hawaiian music with workshops, live concerts and hula performances leads up to Hawaii's prestigious Na Hoku Hanohano Awards.

Lantern Floating Hawaii CULTURE
(www.lanternfloatinghawaii.com) On Memorial Day (the last Monday in May), the souls of the dead are honored with a Japanese floating-lantern ceremony after sunset at Ala Moana Beach Park's Magic Island.

Pan-Pacific Festival ARTS, CULTURE
(www.pan-pacific-festival.com) Three days of Japanese, Hawaiian and South Pacific entertainment in early June, with music, dancing and *taiko* drumming.

King Kamehameha Hula Competition HULA
(http://hulacomp.webstarts.com) One of Hawaii's biggest hula contests, with hundreds

BE YOUR OWN TOUR GUIDE

Unlike on the Neighbor Islands, you won't necessarily need to rent a car or take a tour to explore O'ahu. You can travel at your own pace, and save money – not to mention the environment – by circling the island on O'ahu's public transit system, TheBus (p67).

Starting from the Ala Moana Center near Waikiki, TheBus 52 Wahiawa 'Circle Isle' bus goes clockwise up Hwy 99 to Hale'iwa. Be sure to ask the driver for a free transfer upon boarding. In Hale'iwa, continue on TheBus 55 Kane'ohe 'Circle Isle' bus to Turtle Bay, on the island's northern tip, then down the Windward Coast and back over the Pali Hwy to Ala Moana Center. Both routes operate every 15 to 30 minutes from around 6am until 9:30pm daily; if you ride nonstop, the entire circle-island trip takes about four hours.

For a shorter excursion from Waikiki, you can make a scenic loop around southeast O'ahu by taking TheBus 22 'Beach Bus' (no service on Tuesday) to Sea Life Park, then transfer to TheBus 57 toward Kailua and back over the Pali Hwy to Ala Moana Center, from where several buses run back to Waikiki. With fast connections, this loop takes about 2½ hours.

of dancers competing at the Neal S Blaisdell Center in late June.

Prince Lot Hula Festival HULA
(www.mgf-hawaii.org) The state's oldest and largest noncompetitive hula event at the Moanalua Gardens on the third Saturday in July.

★**Hawai'i Food & Wine Festival** FOOD
(www.hawaiifoodandwinefestival.com) Star chefs, sustainable farms and food lovers come together for a long weekend of wining and dining in early September.

Talk Story Festival STORYTELLING
(http://www1.honolulu.gov/parks/programs/;) Storytellers and sign-language interpreters gather for two nights at Ala Moana Beach Park in mid-October; Friday is usually spooky stories.

★**Hawaii International Film Festival** CINEMA
(www.hiff.org) A celluloid celebration of Pacific Rim, Asian and homegrown films, including world premieres, in late October.

King Kalakaua's Birthday MUSIC, CULTURE
(www.iolanipalace.org) Victorian-era decorations and a concert of traditional monarchy-era music by the Royal Hawaiian Band at 'Iolani Palace on November 16.

Honolulu Marathon SPORTS
(www.honolulumarathon.org) One of the world's 10 biggest marathons runs on the second Sunday of December.

Sleeping

Honolulu doesn't have much in the way of accommodations. Most tourists stay by the beach in Waikiki.

Hostelling International (HI) Honolulu HOSTEL $
(Map p80; ☎946-0591; www.hostelsaloha.com; 2323-A Seaview Ave; dm $20-23, r $50-56; ⊙reception 8am-noon & 4pm-midnight;) Along a quiet residential side street near the UH Manoa campus, a short bus ride from Waikiki, this tidy, low-slung house has sex-segregated dorms and basic private rooms that are sunny and fan-cooled. There's a kitchen, laundry room, lockers and two free parking spaces. Some students crash here while looking for apartments, so it's often full (maximum seven-night stay).

Central Branch YMCA HOSTEL $
(Map p80; ☎941-3344; www.ymcahonolulu.org; 401 Atkinson Dr; s/d $55/75, with shared bathroom $45/65;) Opposite the Ala Moana Center, the ol' Y lets unfussy budget travelers book basic, well-worn rooms with shared bathrooms or slightly larger en suite rooms on single-sex or co-ed floors. Perks include an Olympic-sized swimming pool and a gym. Traffic noise, a general lack of cleanliness and an institutional atmosphere are downers.

Ala Moana Hotel HOTEL $$
(Map p80; ☎866-956-4262, 955-4811; www.alamoanahotelhonolulu.com; 410 Atkinson Dr; r/ste from $155/285;) Neighboring the Ala Moana Center shopping mall, this high-rise condotel near the convention center has executive-strength rooms with bland trimmings. Prices rise on higher floors with city or ocean views – request the Waikiki Tower for a lanai (balcony). Expect to share the check-in line with conventioneers and airline crews. Free in-room wired internet; lobby wi-fi costs extra. Parking $20.

Airport Honolulu Hotel HOTEL $$
(☎866-956-4262, 836-0661; www.outrigger.com; 3401 N Nimitz Hwy; r from $110;) For a quick layover, your best choice among Honolulu's handful of airport-area hotels is this nondescript chain snoozing beside a noisy freeway. A small outdoor swimming pool helps while away flight delays. Rates include free lobby wi-fi, in-room internet access (wireless or wired) and complimentary 24-hour airport shuttles. Parking $25.

Eating

If O'ahu weren't so far away from the US mainland, you'd hear a lot more buzz about this multiethnic chowhound capital. Watch for **Eat the Street** (www.streetgrindz.com), a monthly outdoor rally for food trucks and street-food vendors. During **Restaurant Week Hawaii** (www.restaurantweekhawaii.com) in mid-November, many local restaurants offer dining-out discounts and prix-fixe menus.

Downtown

Some places here are only open for weekday lunch, serving downtown's office crowd.

Vita Juice HEALTHY $
(Map p72; www.freewebs.com/vitajuice; 1111-C Fort St Mall; items $3-7; 7am-5pm Mon-Fri;) Mobbed by students, this orange-walled juice and smoothie bar takes the concept of 'brain food' seriously, with exotic ingredients from Amazonian acai and Tibetan goji berries to green tea and ginseng.

★**Hiroshi Eurasian Tapas** FUSION $$
(Map p72; 533-4476; www.hiroshihawaii.com; Waterfront Plaza, 500 Ala Moana Blvd; shared plates $9-17, mains $26-29; 5:30-9:30pm; P) Chef Hiroshi Fukui puts a Japanese twist on Pacific Rim fusion styles, from Big Island baby abalone with ginger and roasted brown-butter sauce to Portuguese sausage potstickers swirled with truffled *ponzu* (Japanese citrus) sauce. Order tropical martinis and fresh-fruit sodas at the bar, or duck next door to vivacious Vino, an Italian tapas and wine bar. Reservations essential.

Lil' Soul SOUTHERN $$
(Map p72; 735-7685; http://pacificsoulhawaii.com; 1111 Bishop St; mains $8-15; 11am-3pm Mon-Fri) Authentic, rib-sticking Southern soul food with a Motown soundtrack in Honolulu? Chef Sean Priester is all smiles as he dishes up island-grown cabbage coleslaw, buttermilk fried chicken, shrimp with cheesy grits and sassy black-eyed-pea chili. Chicken-and-waffles plates sell out quick.

Cafe Julia CAFE $$
(Map p72; 533-3334; http://cafejuliahawaii.com; 1040 Richards St; mains $8-24; 9am-1pm Sun, 11am-2pm Mon-Fri, 4-9pm Wed-Fri) Inside the landmark 1920s Laniakea YWCA building, designed by California architect Julia Morgan, this sunny courtyard cafe lists a fresh, light menu of salads, sandwiches and seafood dishes at lunch and Saturday brunch, emphasizing island-grown, often organic ingredients. Reservations recommended.

Hukilau LOCAL $$
(Map p72; 523-3460; www.dahukilau.com/honolulu; Executive Centre, 1088 Bishop St; mains $11-20; 11am-2pm & 3-9pm Mon-Fri) A friendly tiki-themed sports bar hides underground inside downtown's highest high-rise hotel. Huge sandwiches, salads and burgers aren't as tempting as only-in-Hawaii specialties like miso-braised pork, slow-roasted *kalua* pork with kim-chi saimin (local-style noodle soup) and classic *pupu* (snacks) like ahi *poke* (marinated raw fish).

Chinatown

This historic downtown neighborhood is packed with open-air markets, hole-in-the-wall noodle kitchens, dim sum palaces, pan-Asian kitchens and fusion resto-lounges.

Bangkok Chef THAI $
(Map p72; http://bangkokchefexpress.com; 1627 Nu'uanu Ave; mains $8-10; 10:30am-9pm Mon-Sat, noon-8pm Sun) Eating here feels strangely like eating out of someone's garage, but who cares when the Thai curries, noodle dishes and savory salads taste exactly like they're from a Bangkok street cart? Dessert is mango ice cream over sticky rice topped with salty peanuts, or tapioca pudding cups in a rainbow of flavors – try Okinawan sweet potato or taro.

To Chau VIETNAMESE $
(Map p72; 1007 River St; mains $7-10; 8:30am-2:30pm) Always busy, To Chau holds fast to its reputation for Honolulu's best *phõ* (Vietnamese noodle soup). Beef, broth and vegetables – the dish is a complete meal in itself, but the menu also includes other Vietnamese standards. Just over a dozen tables inside equals long queues underneath the restaurant's battered-looking sign outside.

Downbeat DINER $
(Map p72; www.downbeatdiner.com; 42 N Hotel St; mains $5-15; 11am-midnight Mon, to 3am Tue-Thu, to 4am Fri & Sat, to 10pm Sun;) This shiny late-night diner with lipstick-red booths posts a serious comfort-food menu of salads, sandwiches, burgers and heaping breakfasts of *loco moco* (dish of rice, fried egg and hamburger patty topped with gravy or other condiments) and island sweet-bread French toast. Otto's cheesecake is unbelievably addictive.

Royal Kitchen CHINESE $
(Map p72; http://royalkitchenhawaii.com; Chinatown Cultural Plaza, 100 N Beretania St; snacks $1-2.50, plate lunches $5-8; 5:30am-4:30pm Mon-Fri, 6:30am-4:30pm Sat, 6:30am-2:30pm Sun) Facing the riverside pedestrian mall, this harried takeout shop is worth finding for its *manapua* (steamed or baked buns) with sweet and savory fillings like *char siu* (Chinese BBQ pork), chicken curry, sweet potato, *kalua* pig or black sugar.

★**Lucky Belly** ASIAN, FUSION $$
(Map p72; 531-1888; www.luckybelly.com; 50 N Hotel St; mains $8-14; 11am-2pm & 5pm-midnight Mon-Sat) Where Japanese pop art hangs over

sleek bistro tables packed elbows-to-shoulders, this arts district noodle bar crafts hot and spicy Asian fusion bites, knock-out artisanal cocktails and amazingly fresh, almost architectural salads that the whole table can share. A 'Belly Bowl' of ramen soup topped with buttery pork belly, smoked bacon and pork sausage is carnivore heaven.

Little Village Noodle House CHINESE **$$**
(Map p72; ☎545-3008; www.littlevillagehawaii.com; 1113 Smith St; mains $8-22; ⏲10:30am-10:30pm Sun-Thu, to midnight Fri & Sat; ❄) If you live for anything fishy in black-bean sauce, this is Honolulu's gold standard. Starring on an eclectic regional Chinese menu, dishes are served garlicky, fiery or with just the right dose of saltiness. Bonuses: air-con and free parking out back. Reservations recommended.

Soul de Cuba CUBAN **$$**
(Map p72; ☎545-2822; www.souldecuba.com; 1121 Bethel St; mains $10-24; ⏲11am-10pm Mon-Thu, to 11pm Fri & Sat, to 8:30pm Sun) Sate your craving for Afro-Cuban food and out-of-this-world *mojitos* inside this fashionable restaurant near Chinatown's art galleries. Stick with family recipe classics like *ropa vieja* (shredded beef in tomato sauce), *bocadillos* (sandwiches, served till 5pm) and black-bean soup. Reservations helpful.

Rakuen Lounge SUSHI **$$**
(Map p72; ☎524-0920; http://rakuenlounge.com; 1153 Bethel St; shared plates $4-16; ⏲3pm-2am Tue-Sat) Shiny happy groups of friends share endless plates of sushi rolls, fresh seafood salads and bowls of spicy garlic edamame. A top-shelf list of sake and cocktails infused with Asian flavors like Thai basil or lychee make this chill lounge a sleeper hit, especially for late-night noshes when clubbing in Chinatown.

Duc's Bistro FUSION **$$**
(Map p72; ☎531-6325; www.ducsbistro.com; 1188 Maunakea St; mains $16-26; ⏲11am-2pm Mon-Fri, 5-10pm daily) Honolulu's bigwigs hobnob at this swank French-Vietnamese bistro with a tiny bar. Buttery escargot, fire-roasted eggplant with lime dressing, tangy green-papaya salad and pan-fried fish with mango relish round out the haute-fusion menu. A small jazz combo serenades most evenings. Reservations advised.

Green Door SOUTHEAST ASIAN **$$**
(Map p72; ☎533-0606; 1110 Nu'uanu Ave; mains $7-13; ⏲11:30am-2:30pm Mon-Fri, 6-8:30pm Wed-Sat) Behind the lime-green-painted door, service is infamously slow and brusque. But the food is worth sticking around for, especially Nyonya (Straits Chinese-Malaysian) classics such as coconut-chicken curry. With just four tables squeezed inside, waits can be very long.

Mabuhay Cafe & Restaurant FILIPINO **$$**
(Map p72; 1049 River St; mains $6-13; ⏲10am-9pm) Red-and-white checked tablecloths and a jukebox should clue you in that this is a mom-and-pop joint. They've been cooking up pots full of succulent, garlic-laden pork *adobo* (spicy marinaded meat) and *kare-kare* (oxtail stew) on this same sketchy street corner since the 1960s.

JJ Dolan's Pizza Pub PIZZA **$$**
(Map p72; www.jjdolans.com; 1147 Bethel St; pizzas from $16; ⏲11am-2am Mon-Sat) Two guys running a sociable Irish pub in Chinatown, baking NYC-style pizza and pouring cold beer. What's not to like?

Ala Moana & Around

A bevy of locally famous restaurants are hidden around Ala Moana Center mall.

Home Bar & Grill LOCAL **$**
(Map p80; 1683 Kalakaua Ave; shared plates $6-15; ⏲2pm-2am) Run by fun-loving young chefs who graduated from Alan Wong's kitchens, this sports bar with a karaoke machine and dartboards lets buddies meet up for *pau hana* (happy hour) and scarf comfort-food faves like tater-tot nachos, kim-chi fried rice and garlicky chicken with chips. Parking lot $5.

Yataimura JAPANESE **$**
(Map p80; www.shirokiya.com; 2nd fl, Shirokiya, Ala Moana Center, 1450 Ala Moana Blvd; most items $2-12; ⏲10am-10pm) Forget about the fast food downstairs in Ala Moana Center's food court. Head to the upper level of Japanese department store Shirokiya to unlock a beer garden and boisterous food-stall marketplace that's a gold mine of takeout meals, from *bentō* boxes to hot *takoyaki* (fried minced-octopus balls).

Foodland SUPERMARKET **$**
(Map p80; Ala Moana Center, 1450 Ala Moana Blvd; ⏲5am-10pm Mon-Sat, 6am-8pm Sun) Full-service supermarket at Hawaii's biggest mall has a good range and is a good option for self-catering.

Whole Ox DELI $$
(☎699-6328; http://wholeoxdeli.com; 327 Keawe St; mains $10-35; ⊙9:30am-3pm Mon-Sat, 5:30-9:30pm Tue-Sat) An unlikely place for a butcher shop and deli, this Kaka'ako industrial warehouse cafe with floor-to-ceiling windows and modern minimalist decor is all about the meat, whether you're gorging on foie-gras poutine, a 21-day dry-aged burger or house-made meatloaf and pickles.

Ichiriki JAPANESE $$
(Map p80; ☎589-2299; http://ichirikinabe.com; 510 Pi'ikoi St; mains lunch $12-25, dinner $22-38; ⊙11am-2pm daily, 5-11pm Sun-Thu, to midnight Fri & Sat) An authentic Japanese *nabemono, shabu-shabu* and *sukiyaki* restaurant stirs island-grown vegetables and savory meats into hot pots sized for sumo wrestlers. Bring a big group to maximize the pig-out factor without breaking your piggy bank. Reservations recommended.

Gomaichi JAPANESE $$
(Map p80; www.rikautsumi.com/demo/gomaichi; 631 Ke'eaumoku St; mains $8-11; ⊙11am-2pm & 5:30-8:45pm Mon-Sat) This squeaky-clean ramen shop's name roughly translates as 'No 1 Sesame.' Die-hard fans agree the *tantan* noodle soup in spicy sesame broth reigns supreme, especially if you get an extra order of falling-apart *char siu* pork.

Side Street Inn LOCAL $$
(Map p80; ☎591-0253; www.sidestreetinn.com; 1225 Hopaka St; plate lunch $7-10, shared dishes $10-20; ⊙2pm-2am, takeout only 10am-2pm Mon-Fri) The outside looks like hell, and the sports-bar atmosphere hardly rates on a Zagat's survey, but this late-night gathering spot is where you'll find some of Honolulu's top chefs hanging out in the Naugahyde booths after work. Divinely tender *kalbi* short ribs and pan-fried pork chops are what locals crave most. Reservations advised. Also at 614 Kapahulu Ave near Waikiki.

Sushi Sasabune JAPANESE $$
(Map p80; ☎947-3800; 1417 S King St; most shared dishes $12-36; ⊙noon-2pm Tue-Fri, 5:30pm-10pm Tue-Sat) Honolulu's top-shelf choice for sushi purists, hands down. If you're going to go all out for the *omakase* tasting menu, be prepared to shell out over $120 per person for more than a dozen courses of fresh Pacific seafood, personally chosen by the sushi chefs who deftly work their knives behind the counter. Reservations essential.

★**Alan Wong's** HAWAII REGIONAL CUISINE $$$
(Map p80; ☎949-2526; www.alanwongs.com; 3rd fl, 1857 S King St; mains $35-60; ⊙dinner from 5pm) An innovative co-founder of Hawaii Regional Cuisine, Alan Wong creatively reinterprets immigrants' culinary traditions inside a nondescript office building (which, sadly, lacks views). Fresh seafood and island-grown produce get spotlighted, including at bimonthly 'farmers series' dinners. Order the chef's stand-out signature dishes, such as ginger-crusted *onaga* (red snapper) and twice-cooked *kalbi* short ribs. Reservations essential. Valet parking available downstairs.

Alan Wong's more casual Pineapple Room restaurant inside Macy's department store at the Ala Moana Center dishes out express lunches daily and weekend breakfasts for much less moolah.

★**Nanzan Girogiro** JAPANESE $$$
(Map p80; ☎521-0141; www.guiloguilo.com; 560 Pensacola St; chef's tasting menu $50-60; ⊙dinner from 6pm Thu-Mon) A culinary alchemist, Japanese chef Matsumoto-san imports his hometown of Kyoto's traditional *kaiseki ryōri* (multicourse meals of seasonal, small dishes) and infuses it with Hawaii-grown fruits and vegetables, wild seafood and, frankly, magic. Inside an art gallery, bar seats ring an open kitchen, where pottery bowls open to reveal tastes like tea-soaked rice topped with delicately poached fish. Reservations required.

Sushi Izakaya Gaku JAPANESE $$$
(Map p80; ☎589-1329; 1329 S King St; most shared plates $4-40; ⊙5-11pm Mon-Sat) Known mostly by word-of-mouth, this *izakaya* (Japanese bar serving food) beats the competition with adherence to tradition and supremely fresh sushi and sashimi. A spread of savory and sweet, hot and cold dishes includes hard-to-find specialties like *chazuke* (tea-soaked rice porridge) and *natto* (fermented soybeans). Reservations essential, or cross your fingers for an open table after 7pm.

Chef Mavro FUSION $$$
(Map p80; ☎944-4714; www.chefmavro.com; 1969 S King St; multicourse tasting menus from $85; ⊙6-9pm Tue-Sun) At Honolulu's most avant-garde restaurant, maverick chef George Mavrothalassitis creates conceptual dishes like *kabocha* (Japanese pumpkin) coconut custard and Big Island abalone confit, each paired with Old and New World wines. Sometimes

the cutting-edge experimental cooking, like the half-empty atmosphere, falls flat. Reservations required.

University Area

Internationally flavored eateries cluster south of the UH Manoa campus, a short bus ride from Waikiki.

Da Spot INTERNATIONAL $
(Map p80; 2469 S King St; smoothies $3-5, plate lunches $6-10; ⏲10:30am-9:30pm Mon-Sat) A converted auto mechanic's garage is home base for this chef duo's world fusion and island-flavored plate lunches, plus three dozen flavor combinations of smoothies. Egyptian chicken, southeast Asian curries, gyro sandwiches and homemade baklava will leave you stuffed.

Peace Cafe HEALTHY $
(Map p80; www.peacecafehawaii.com; 2239 S King St; mains $8-10; ⏲11am-9pm Mon-Sat, to 3pm Sun; ✎) Vegan home-cooking specials are scribbled on the chalkboard at this simple storefront cafe. Pick a Popeye miso-tahini spinach sandwich or a light lunch box with Moroccan chickpea stew. Green-tea lattes, *mochi* (Japanese sticky-rice cakes) and soy ice cream are dairy-free delights.

Down to Earth Natural Foods SUPERMARKET $
(Map p80; www.downtoearth.org; 2525 S King St; ⏲7:30am-10pm; ✎) Natural-foods supermarket with a bountiful salad bar, custom-made sandwiches and fresh juices and smoothies.

Kokua Market SUPERMARKET $
(Map p80; www.kokua.coop; 2643 S King St; ⏲8am-9pm; ✎) Hawaii's only natural-foods co-op offers an organic salad bar and a vegan-friendly deli for takeout meals.

Bubbies ICE CREAM $
(Map p80; www.bubbiesicecream.com; Varsity Center, 1010 University Ave; items $2-6; ⏲noon-midnight Mon-Thu, to 1am Fri & Sat, to 11:30pm Sun;) Homemade tropical ice cream, including bite-sized frozen *mochi* treats.

Sweet Home Café TAIWANESE $
(Map p80; ☎947-3707; 2334 S King St; shared dishes $2-8; ⏲4-11pm) You won't believe the lines outside this strip-mall kitchen. At long, wooden tables inside, there're steaming hot pots squat, filled with stewed lemongrass beef, sour cabbage, mixed tofu or Asian pumpkin squash, plus your pick of spicy dipping sauces and extra lamb, chicken or tender beef tongue on the side. Make reservations, arrive early or expect to wait an hour or more.

Pint & Jigger GASTROPUB $$
(Map p80; ☎744-9593; http://pintandjigger.com; 1936 S King St; shared plates $4-13; ⏲4:30pm-midnight Mon & Wed, 4:30pm-2am Tue & Thu-Sat, 8am-midnight Sun) Red-brick walls and high-top tables make this gastropub, not too far west of the UH Manoa campus, trendy enough for aspiring 20- and 30-something foodies, who mix-and-match craft beers and cocktails with noshes like guava wood-smoked sausage sliders and Scotch eggs.

Da Kitchen HAWAII REGIONAL CUISINE $$
(Map p80; www.da-kitchen.com; 925 Isenberg St; meals $9-18; ⏲11am-9pm Mon-Sat) This crowded neighborhood storefront is where you'll find Hawaiian and local food just so dang *'ono* (delicious) that it has even been served at the White House for O'ahu-born President Obama. Deep-fried Spam *musubi* (rice balls) and tempura-battered fish and chips are massive hits.

★**Imanas Tei** JAPANESE $$$
(Map p80; ☎941-2626; 2626 S King St; most shared dishes $5-30; ⏲5-11:30pm Mon-Sat) A chorus shouts *'Irrashaimase!'* as you walk through the door of this *izakaya* with polished dark wooden tables. Booze it up with sake as you graze a seemingly endless menu of sushi and epicurean and country Japanese cooking, including crowd-pleasing *nabemono* meat and vegetable stews. Reserve a few days in advance or stand in line for open seating after 7pm.

Greater Honolulu

Tasty off-the-beaten-track spots are scattered around the metro area, especially in the low-key Kaimuki neighborhood along Wai'alae Ave, east of UH Manoa.

Liliha Bakery BAKERY $
(www.lilihabakeryhawaii.com; 515 N Kuakini, cnr Liliha St; items from $2, mains $6-10; ⏲24hr, except closed 8pm Sun-6am Tue) This retro bakery has been causing neighborhood traffic jams for its coco puffs (cream-filled pastries) since the 1950s. Still hungry? Grab a counter seat in Liliha's all-night coffee shop for a hearty plate of *loco moco* or mahimahi with eggs.

Kaimuki Crack Seed SWEETS $
(1156 Koko Head Ave; snacks from $2; usually 9am-6:30pm Mon-Sat;) Mom-and-pop candy store scoops homemade crack seed from overflowing glass jars and dispenses frozen slushies spiked with *li hing mui* (salty dried plums).

Helena's Hawaiian Food HAWAII REGIONAL CUISINE $$
(http://helenashawaiianfood.com; 1240 N School St; meals $9-20; 10:30am-7:30pm Tue-Fri) Walking through the door is like stepping into another era at this humble Honolulu institution. The menu is mostly à la carte dishes, some smoky and salty, others sweet or spicy. Start with *poi* (fermented taro), then add *pipi kaula* (beef jerky), *kalua* pig, fried butterfish or squid cooked in coconut milk, and voila! You've got a mini luau to go.

Town FUSION $$
(735-5900; www.townkaimuki.com; 3435 Wai'alae Ave; mains breakfast & lunch $5-16, dinner $16-26; 7am-2:30pm daily, 5:30-9:30pm Mon-Thu, to 10pm Fri & Sat) The motto at this buzzing Kaimuki bistro with urban coffeeshop decor is 'local first, organic whenever possible, with aloha always.' Yoga divas and muscled surfers dig into the chef's daily changing farm-to-table menu, including grass-fed beef burgers and salads that taste as if they were just plucked from a backyard garden.

Nico's at Pier 38 SEAFOOD, LOCAL $$
(www.nicospier38.com; 1133 N Nimitz Hwy; breakfast & lunch plates $6-13, dinner mains $13-16; 6:30am-9pm Mon-Sat, 10am-4pm Sun) French chef Nico cranks up Hawaii's belly-filling comfort food with fresh catches from Honolulu's nearby fish auction. Local faves include *furikake*-crusted ahi with garlic-cilantro dip, grilled pork chops drizzled with soy-butter sauce and beer-steamed clams. Casual outdoor tables are within spitting distance of the sea.

FIRST FRIDAYS IN CHINATOWN

Chinatown's somewhat seedy Nu'uanu Ave and Hotel St are surprisingly cool places for a dose of urban art and culture, shopping, live music and nightlife during **First Friday Honolulu** (www.firstfridayhawaii.com), held from 5pm to 9pm on the first Friday of each month. What was once a low-key art walk has become almost too big for its britches. A giant block party now rocks out to live music and DJs, with food trucks and over-21 wristbands for getting into Chinatown's bumpin' bars and clubs. Be prepared to queue behind velvet ropes.

Drinking & Nightlife

For up-to-date listings of live-music gigs, DJ club nights, movies, theater and cultural events, check the TGIF section in the **Honolulu Star-Advertiser** (www.honolulupulse.com), which comes out on Friday, and the free tabloid **Honolulu Weekly** (www.honoluluweekly.com), published every Wednesday.

Wherever you go at night, any self-respecting bar or lounge has a *pupu* menu to complement the liquid sustenance. A key term to know is *pau hana* (literally 'stop work'), pidgin for 'happy hour.' Chinatown's buzzing nightlife scene revolves around Nu'uanu Ave and Hotel St, once Honolulu's notorious red-light district.

★Thirtyninehotel LOUNGE, CLUB
(Map p72; 599-2552; www.thirtyninehotel.com; 39 N Hotel St; 4pm-2am Tue-Sat) More arty than clubby, this upstairs multimedia space is a gallery by day, low-key lounge after dark. DJs don aloha wear for weekend spins, while rock bands test the acoustics some nights. Nearby **Bar 35** serves over 100 bottled beers and dishes up fusion pizzas; you'll find more DJs and live bands there and at **Next Door**. All three places are on the same side of the same sketchy block of Hotel St.

M Nightclub CLUB, LOUNGE
(Map p72; http://mnlhnl.com; Waterfront Plaza, 500 Ala Moana Blvd; admission after 10pm Fri & Sat $10; 4:30pm-midnight Tue-Thu, 4:30pm-4am Fri, 8pm-4am Sat) Flickering votive candles, flair bartenders who juggle bottles of Grey Goose and Patron and table service at sexy white couches backlit with purple hues – this restaurant-nightclub hybrid is as close as Honolulu gets to Vegas. An insider crowd of dressed-to-kill locals bumps shoulders on the dance floor ruled by electronica DJs. Grab happy-hour martinis at neighboring **Bambu**.

Mai Tai Bar BAR
(Map p80; www.maitaibar.com; Ho'okipa Tce, 3rd fl, Ala Moana Center, 1450 Ala Moana Blvd; 11am-1am;) A happening bar in a shopping

mall? We don't make the trends, we just report 'em. During afternoon and late-night happy hours, this spring-break-style sports bar is packed with a see-and-flirt crowd listening to live island grooves and watching pro sports games on giant-screen TVs. For a boogie, join the cougarish dance divas at the mall's **Pearl Ultralounge**.

La Mariana Sailing Club BAR
(www.lamarianasailingclub.com; 50 Sand Island Access Rd; ⏲11am-9pm) Irreverent and kitschy, this 1950s tiki bar by the marina is filled with yachties and long-suffering locals. Classic mai tais are as decent as the other signature tropical potions, complete with tiki-head swizzle sticks. Grab a waterfront table and dream of sailing to Tahiti. Skip the bland *pupu*, though.

Manifest BAR, CAFE
(Map p72; http://manifesthawaii.com; 32 N Hotel St; ⏲7am-2am Mon-Fri, 8am-2am Sat; 📶) Smack in the middle of Chinatown's art scene, this lofty apartment-like space with provocative photos and paintings by local artists is a serene coffee shop by day and a cocktail bar by night, with hipster events like movie and trivia nights and DJ sets (often no cover charge).

★ **Beach Bum Cafe** CAFE
(Map p72; www.beachbumcafe.com; 1088 Bishop St; ⏲6:30am-6:30pm Mon-Thu, 6:30am-4pm Fri, 7am-1pm Sat; 📶) 🍃 In downtown's high-rise financial district, this connoisseur's coffee bar serves 100% organic, grown-in-Hawaii beans, roasted in small batches and hand-brewed one perfect cup at a time. Chat with the owner as you sip the rich flavors of Big Island, Maui, Kaua'i and Moloka'i coffee farms.

Hank's Cafe BAR
(Map p72; www.thedragonupstairs.com; 1038 Nu'uanu Ave; ⏲3pm-2am Mon-Sat, to midnight Sun) You can't get more legit than this neighborhood dive on the edge of Chinatown. Owner Hank Taufaasau is a jack-of-all-trades when it comes to the barfly business: the walls are decorated with Polynesian-themed art, live music rolls in many nights and regulars call it home.

SoHo Mixed Media Bar CLUB, BAR
(Map p72; http://sohomixedmediabar.com; 80 S Pau'ahi St; ⏲9pm-2am Tue-Sat) DJs spin deep house, hip hop, funk, mash-ups and retro sounds for two giant dance floors packed by a college-aged crowd. On First Fridays, this may be ground zero for Chinatown's biggest party scene. The joint jams with loud, live local bands some weeknights.

Fresh Cafe CAFE
(Map p80; ☎688-8055; http://freshcafehi.com; 831 Queen St; ⏲7am-1am Mon-Thu, 7am-1:30am Fri & Sat, noon-7pm Sun; 📶) Alternative coffeehouse brings bohemians and hipsters to the up-and-coming Kaka'ako industrial district. Sip a Vietnamese coffee, pikake iced tea or Thai latte and nosh on healthy soups and sandwiches. Some nights their 'Loft in Space' warehouse stages live music, films, poetry slams and artistic-minded social events.

Lion Coffee CAFE
(☎847-3600; www.lioncoffee.com; 1555 Kalani St; ⏲6am-5pm Mon-Fri, 9am-3pm Sat; 📶) In an out-of-the-way warehouse, Hawaii coffee giant sells bags of beans roasted straight-up (like 100% Kona 24-Karat and Diamond Head espresso blend) or tropically flavored (chocolate macadamia-nut, toasted coconut etc). Ask the coffee-bar staff for a free taste. Call ahead to reserve a free factory tour.

Aloha Beer Company MICROBREWERY
(http://alohabeer.com; 580 N Nimitz Hwy; ⏲3pm-10pm Sun-Thu, to 11pm Fri & Sat) Next to Sam Choy's Breakfast, Lunch & Crab restaurant, sip Hawaii-made Aloha Lager and Kiawe Honey Porter by shiny brewing vats and sports TVs. A six-beer sampler costs just $10, but the food is blah. Call ahead for brewery tours.

Indigo Lounge LOUNGE
(Map p72; www.indigo-hawaii.com; 1121 Nu'uanu Ave; ⏲5pm-midnight Tue, to 1:30am Wed-Sat) Indigo restaurant shakes up tropical-fruit-flavored martinis during happy hours in its svelte lounge showing off opium-den chic. Live jazz sometimes plays during the week, with old-school and electronica DJs slotted in on the weekends.

Glazers Coffee CAFE
(Map p80; www.glazerscoffee.com; 2700 S King St; ⏲7am-11pm Mon-Thu, 7am-9pm Fri, 8am-11pm Sat & Sun; 📶) They're serious about brewing stiff espresso drinks and batch-roasted coffee at this university students' hangout, with comfy sofas, jazzy artwork and plentiful electrical outlets for your gizmos.

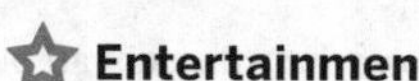

Entertainment

Live Music

If traditional and contemporary Hawaiian music tickles your ears, go straight to Waikiki (p123).

Republik LIVE MUSIC
(Map p80; ☎941-7469; http://jointherepublik.com; 1349 Kapi'olani Blvd; ⊙lounge 6pm-2am Mon-Sat, concert schedules vary) Honolulu's most intimate concert hall for touring and local acts – indie rockers, punk and metal bands, and more – has a graffiti-bomb vibe and backlit black walls that trippily light up. Buy tickets for shows in advance, to make sure you get in and also to save a few bucks.

Dragon Upstairs LIVE MUSIC
(Map p72; ☎526-1411; www.thedragonupstairs.com; 2nd fl, 1038 Nu'uanu Ave; admission $5-10; ⊙usually 7pm-2am) With funky artwork and lots of mirrors, this hideaway above Hank's Cafe hosts a rotating line-up of older jazz cats, from experimental bands and bop trios to piano-and-vocal soloists. Check the online calendar, which pegs blues travelers, DJs and eclectic world beats too.

Anna O'Brien's LIVE MUSIC
(Map p80; ☎946-5190; http://annaobriens.com; 2440 S Beretania St; ⊙usually to 2am daily) A college dive bar, part roadhouse and part Irish pub, this reincarnation of Anna Bananas goes beyond its retro-1960s 'Summer of Love' roots to book reggae, alt-rock and punk bands, singer-songwriters and blues jams.

DON'T MISS

HONOLULU'S TOP 10 HAWAIIANA SHOPS

- Bishop Museum (p83)
- Native Books/Nā Mea Hawaii (p88)
- Honolulu Museum of Art (p78)
- Cindy's Lei Shoppe (p99)
- Bailey's Antiques & Aloha Shirts (p125)
- Na Lima Mili Hulu No'eau (p125)
- Manuheali'i (p98)
- Tin Can Mailman (p99)
- Kamaka Hawaii (p99)
- Hula Supply Center (p99)

Jazz Minds Art & Café LIVE MUSIC
(Map p80; ☎945-0800; www.honolulujazzclub.com; 1661 Kapi'olani Blvd; cover charge $10, plus 2-drink minimum; ⊙9pm-2am Mon-Sat) Don't let the nearby strip clubs necessarily turn you off. This tattered Tokyo-esque dive pulls in Honolulu's most offbeat jazz talent – swing, fusion, funk, neo-soul and blues sounds. Validated parking $5.

Performing Arts

★**Hawaii Theatre** PERFORMING ARTS
(Map p72; ☎528-0506; www.hawaiitheatre.com; 1130 Bethel St) Gorgeously restored, this historic Chinatown landmark is a major venue for dance, music and theater. Performances include live Hawaiian bands and international touring acts to modern dance, contemporary plays and film festivals. The theater also hosts the annual Ka Himeni 'Ana contest in which famous Hawaiian falsetto-style singers compete.

Neal S Blaisdell Center PERFORMING ARTS
(Map p80; ☎768-5252; www.blaisdellcenter.com; 777 Ward Ave) Honolulu's cultural lynchpin, this performing-arts center hosts symphonic and chamber-music concerts, opera performances and ballet recitals, prestigious hula competitions, Broadway shows, arts-and-crafts fairs and more. Occasionally big-name pop and rock touring acts play here instead of at Aloha Stadium. Parking is available from $6.

ARTS at Marks Garage PERFORMING ARTS
(Map p72; ☎521-2903; www.artsatmarks.com; 1159 Nu'uanu Ave; ⊙gallery 11am-6pm Tue-Sat, show schedules vary) At the cutting edge of the Chinatown arts scene, this community gallery and performance space puts on a cornucopia of live shows, from improv comedy, burlesque and fringe theater nights to conversations with artists, live Hawaiian music or electronica DJs.

Kumu Kahua Theatre PERFORMING ARTS
(Map p72; ☎536-4441; www.kumukahua.org; 46 Merchant St) In the restored Kamehameha V Post Office building, this little 100-seat nonprofit community theater premieres works by contemporary playwrights about mulicultural island life, often peppered richly with Hawaiian pidgin.

HawaiiSlam PERFORMING ARTS
(Map p80; www.hawaiislam.com; Fresh Cafe, 831 Queen St; admission before/after 8:30pm $3/5; ⊙8:30pm 1st Thu of each month) One of the

USA's biggest poetry slams, here international wordsmiths, artists, musicians, MCs and DJs share the stage. Sign-up for aspiring spoken-word stars starts at 7:30pm.

Cinemas

★Doris Duke Theatre CINEMA
(Map p80; ☎532-8768; www.honolulumuseum.org; Honolulu Museum of Art, 900 S Beretania St; admission $10) Inside an art museum, this intimate movie house showcases independent and avant-garde cinema, foreign films, retro revivals and mind-bending experimental shorts. Look for screenings of ground-breaking Hawaii and Pacific Rim documentaries. Buy tickets online in advance.

Movie Museum CINEMA
(☎735-8771; www.kaimukihawaii.com; 3566 Harding Ave; admission $5; ⏲showtimes usually noon-9pm Thu-Mon) This Kaimuki neighborhood spot is a sociable place to watch classic oldies, foreign flicks and indie films in a tiny theater equipped with digital sound and just 20 comfy Barcalounger recliners. Bring your own snacks and drinks. Reservations recommended.

Shopping

Although not a shopping powerhouse like Waikiki, Honolulu's unique shops offer plenty of local flavor, from traditional flower lei and ukulele makers to antiques stores and island-brand clothing boutiques.

Ala Moana Center MALL
(Map p80; www.alamoanacenter.com; 1450 Ala Moana Blvd; ⏲9am-9pm Mon-Sat, 10am-7pm Sun; 👪) This open-air shopping mall and its nearly 300 stores could compete on an international runway. Thrown into the mix are a handful of made-in-Hawaii specialty shops such as Crazy Shirts for tees, Reyn Spooner and Tori Richards for aloha shirts, Maui WaterWear and Loco Boutique for swimsuits and board shorts, Town & Country Surf and Local Motion for surfwear and Na Hoku jewelry.

★Ward Warehouse MALL
(Map p80; www.wardcenters.com; 1050 Ala Moana Blvd; ⏲10am-9pm Mon-Sat, to 6pm Sun) Across the street from Ala Moana Beach, this mini-mall has many one-of-a-kind island shops, including Native Books/Nā Mea Hawaii, which sells gourmet foodstuffs, wooden koa bowls, handmade jewelry, authentic Hawaiian quilts and oodles of books, CDs and DVDs. Drop by Rix Island Wear for aloha shirts and Noa Noa or Tiare Teiti for batik-printed, Polyneisan-inspired fashions.

Nohea Gallery ARTS & CRAFTS
(Map p80; www.noheagallery.com; Ward Warehouse, 1050 Ala Moana Blvd; ⏲10am-9pm Mon-Sat, to 6pm Sun) A meditative space amid the shopping-mall madness, this respected high-end art gallery displays beautifully handcrafted jewelry, glassware, pottery, sculptures, woodworks, tropical prints and paintings, with 90% of the works made in Hawaii. On some sunny weekends, artisans from around the islands demonstrate their craft on the sidewalk outside.

Manuheali'i CLOTHING
(Map p80; www.manuhealii.com; 930 Punahou St; ⏲9:30am-6pm Mon-Fri, 9am-4pm Sat, 10am-3pm Sun) Look to this island-born shop for original and modern designs. Flowing rayon

CHINATOWN ART GALLERIES

Pick up a free map from any of Chinatown's two dozen art galleries, most within a two-block radius of the Hawaii Theatre (p78). Eclectic works by up-and-coming island artists in all types of media can be found at ARTS at Marks Garage (p97). It stays open later during First Friday Honolulu (p95) events, as do the following well-established galleries:

➡ **Bethel St Gallery** (Map p72; www.bethelstreetgallery.com; 1140 Bethel St; ⏲11am-4pm Tue-Fri, 11am-3pm Sun) Artist-owned cooperative exhibits a mixed plate of island artworks, from blown-glass sculptures to abstract paintings.

➡ **Pegge Hopper Gallery** (Map p72; www.peggehopper.com; 1164 Nu'uanu Ave; ⏲11am-4pm Tue-Fri, to 3pm Sat) Represents the namesake artist's distinctive prints and paintings depicting voluptuous island women.

➡ **Louis Pohl Gallery** (Map p72; www.louispohlgallery.com; 1142 Bethel St; ⏲11am-2pm Tue, to 5pm Wed-Sat) Paintings by contemporary island artists and a former 'living treasure' of Hawaii.

dresses take inspiration from the traditional muumuu, but are transformed into fresh contemporary looks. Hawaiian musicians often sport Manuheali'i's bold-print silk aloha shirts. Also in Kailua (p143).

Cindy's Lei Shoppe ARTS & CRAFTS
(Map p72; ☎536-6538; www.cindysleishoppe.com; 1034 Maunakea St; ⏲usually 6am-7pm Mon-Sat, to 6pm Sun) This inviting little street-corner shop sells lei made of *maile* (a native twining plant), lantern *ilima* (a native groundcover) and Micronesian ginger, as well as more common orchids and plumeria. A half dozen other lei shops on nearby streets will also pack lei for you to carry back home on the plane.

Fighting Eel CLOTHING
(Map p72; www.fightingeel.com; 1133 Bethel St; ⏲10am-6pm Mon-Sat) Within a lei's throw of Chinatown's other fashion-forward and lifestyle boutiques like Owens & Co and La Muse, this homegrown Honolulu brand is known for its flowy dresses, skirts and tunics that you can toss over your head before hitting the beach or glam up for a big night out. Also in Kailua (p143).

Kamaka Hawaii MUSIC
(Map p72; ☎531-3165; www.kamakahawaii.com; 550 South St; ⏲8am-4pm Mon-Fri) Skip right by those tacky shops selling cheap plastic and wooden ukuleles. Kamaka specializes in handcrafted ukuleles made on O'ahu since 1916, with prices starting at around $500. Its signature is an oval-shaped 'pineapple' ukulele that has a more mellow sound. Call ahead to ask about free 30-minute factory tours, usually given at 10:30am Tuesdays to Fridays.

Tin Can Mailman ANTIQUES, BOOKS
(Map p72; http://tincanmailman.net; 1026 Nu'uanu Ave; ⏲11am-5pm Mon-Thu, to 4pm Fri & Sat) If you're a fan of vintage tiki wares and 20th-century books about the Hawaiian Islands, you'll fall in love with this little Chinatown antiques shop. Thoughtfully collected treasures include 20th-century jewelry and ukuleles, silk aloha shirts, tropical-wood furnishings, vinyl records, rare prints and tourist brochures from the post-WWII tourism boom.

Island Slipper SHOES
(www.islandslipper.com; Ward Warehouse, 1050 Ala Moana Blvd; ⏲10am-9pm Mon-Sat, to 8pm Sun) Scores of stores sell flip-flops (aka 'rubbah slippah') across Honolulu and Waikiki, but nobody carries such ultracomfy suede, leather and neoprene styles – all made right here in Hawaii since 1946 – let alone so many sizes, from petite to giant.

Tutuvi Sitoa CLOTHING
(Map p80; www.tutuvi.com; 2636 S King St; ⏲10am-5pm Mon-Sat) Near the UH Manoa campus, designer Colleen Kimura's Polynesian-themed storefront floats unique T-shirts, dresses, *pa'u* (modern hula-style) skirts, *lavalava* (pareo) beach wraps, aloha shirts and natural-fiber sandals, all handmade and screen-printed with designs drawn from nature, like banana leaves, hibiscus and forest ferns.

Roberta Oaks CLOTHING
(Map p72; www.robertaoaks.com; 19 N Pau'ahi St; ⏲10am-6pm Mon-Fri, to 4pm Sat) At the bleeding edge of Chinatown's modern fashion evolution, here men's tailored shirts – aloha-print or *palaka* (plantation-style checkered) – are even more appealing than the women's strappy sundresses and super-short board shorts.

Hula Supply Center SOUVENIRS
(Map p80; www.hulasupplycenter.com; 1481 S King St; ⏲10:30am-5:30pm Mon-Sat) For more than 60 years, Hawaiian musicians and hula dancers have come here to get their *kukui* (candlenut) lei, calabash drum gourds, Tahitian-style raffia skirts and coconut bras, nose flutes and the like. Even if you don't dance, swing by for a *kapa*-print aloha shirt, a teach-yourself-hula DVD or a CD of Hawaiian music and traditional chants.

Jeff Chang Pottery & Fine Crafts ARTS & CRAFTS
(Map p80; ☎591-1440; www.wardcenters.com; Ward Centre, 1200 Ala Moana Blvd; ⏲9am-9pm Mon-Sat, to 6pm Sun) Not everything at this mall gallery is island-made, but it's all handcrafted. Striking *raku* (Japanese rustic-style pottery) molded by Chang himself sits beside hand-turned bowls of tropical hardwoods, art jewelry and blown glass by some of Hawaii's best artisans. On some Sundays, Chang offers interactive classes in wheel-throwing and *raku*-firing techniques ($25, including a take-home piece).

T&L Muumuu Factory CLOTHING
(Map p80; www.muumuufactory.com; 1423 Kapi'olani Blvd; ⏲9am-6pm Mon-Sat, 10am-4pm Sun) Near Ala Moana Center, this kitschy

outlet is beloved by *tutu* (grandmothers), to whom polyester represents progress. Bold-print muumuus run in sizes from supermodel skinny to queen, and *pa'u* skirts are just funky enough to wedge into an urban outfit.

Barrio Vintage CLOTHING
(Map p72; www.barriovintage.com; 1160 Nu'uanu Ave; ⏲11am-6pm Tue-Thu, to 7pm Fri, to 5pm Sat) One-of-a-kind fashions from decades past jostle against one another on the racks of this Chinatown secondhand shop, showing off mod dresses and skirts for women, hip jackets and pants for men, designer handbags and glamazon shoes.

Lai Fong Department Store ANTIQUES
(Map p72; ☎781-8140; 1118 Nu'uanu Ave; ⏲usually 11am-7pm Mon, noon-8pm Fri, 11am-4pm Sat) A long-time Chinatown tenant, this family owned shop has a hodgepodge of antiques and knickknacks in all price ranges, from Chinese silk and brocade clothing to jade jewelry and vintage postcards of Hawaii from the early 20th century. Call to check hours or for off-hours appointments.

Antique Alley ANTIQUES
(Map p80; ☎941-8551; www.portaloha.com/antiquealley; 1347 Kapi'olani Blvd; ⏲12pm-5pm) Delightfully crammed full of rare collectibles and Hawaiiana, this shop that cameoed on *Antiques Roadshow* sells everything from poi pounders to vintage hula dolls and Matson cruise-liner artifacts. Call ahead to make sure it's open.

ℹ Orientation

Honolulu's compact downtown set the stage for the 19th-century fall of the Hawaiian monarchy, all just a lei's throw from the harborfront where whaling ships once docked. Nearby, the narrow streets of Chinatown are packed with open-air markets, antiques shops, art galleries and bars. Southeast of downtown heading toward Waikiki, Ala Moana is Honolulu's beach. The University of Hawai'i at Manoa campus is further inland, as are the upper Manoa Valley and Makiki Heights neighborhoods, which are gateways to Honolulu's green belt of forest-reserve lands.

ℹ Information

DANGERS & ANNOYANCES

Chinatown's skid rows include blocks of Hotel St. Drug dealing and crime are prevalent in this neighborhood, particularly along Nu'uanu Stream; the River St pedestrian mall should be avoided after dark.

EMERGENCY

Honolulu Police Department (☎529-3111; www.honolulupd.org; 801 S Beretania St) For nonemergencies (eg to report a theft).

Police, Fire & Ambulance (☎911) For emergencies.

INTERNET ACCESS

Cheap fly-by-night cybercafes near the UH Manoa campus stay open late.

FedEx Office (www.fedex.com/us/office; per hr $12; 📶) Ala Moana (1500 Kapi'olani Blvd; ⏲7:30am-9pm Mon-Fri, 10am-6pm Sat, noon-6pm Sun); Downtown (590 Queen St; ⏲7am-11pm Mon-Fri, 9am-9pm Sat & Sun); University Area (2575 S King St; ⏲24hr; 📶) Self-serve, pay-as-you-go computer terminals and wi-fi, plus digital-photo printing stations.

Hawaii State Library (☎586-3500; www.librarieshawaii.org; 478 S King St; ⏲10am-5pm Mon & Wed, 9am-5pm Tue, Fri & Sat, 9am-8pm Thu; 📶) The main branch of the

O'AHU FOR CHILDREN

- Outrigger canoe rides, swimming and a free sunset torch lighting and hula show at Waikiki's Kuhio Beach Park (p109)
- Touch tanks at the educational, eco-conscious Waikiki Aquarium (p110)
- Planetarium shows and exploding faux volcanoes at Honolulu's Bishop Museum (p83)
- Hiking to Manoa Falls (p85) or summiting Diamond Head (p128)
- Snorkeling at Hanauma Bay Nature Preserve (p131)
- Wading into Ko Olina Lagoons (p166) near Disney's Aulani (p166) resort
- Steam-train rides and a giant maze at the Dole Plantation (p164)
- Movie and TV filming tours at Kualoa Ranch (p147)
- Walking the decks of Pearl Harbor's Battleship Missouri Memorial (p103)
- Rainy-day indoor fun for tots at Hawaii Children's Discovery Center (p88)

state system; there are also 23 neighborhood library branches around O'ahu. All accept internet terminal reservations (temporary nonresident card $10); some offer free wi-fi.

MEDIA

Honolulu Star-Advertiser (www.staradvertiser.com) In Honolulu's daily newspaper, look for 'TGIF,' Friday's events and entertainment pull-out section. Its website Honolulu Pulse (www.honolulupulse.com) reviews food, music, theater, bars and nightclubs.

Honolulu Magazine (www.honolulumagazine.com) Glossy monthly magazine covers the arts, culture, fashion, shopping, lifestyle and cuisine.

Honolulu Weekly (www.honoluluweekly.com) Free weekly tabloid with a calendar of museum and gallery exhibits, live music and DJ club events, cultural classes, volunteering and outdoor activities.

KHET (cable channel 10) Hawaii public TV (PBS).

KHPR (88.1FM) Hawaii Public Radio; classical music.

KIKU (cable channel 9) Multicultural community TV programming.

KINE (105.1FM) Contemporary Hawaiian music.

KIPO (89.3FM) Hawaii Public Radio; news, jazz and world music.

KQMQ (91.3FM) Island-style music and Hawaiian reggae.

KTUH (90.3FM) UH Manoa student-run radio.

MEDICAL SERVICES

Hyperbaric Medicine Center (☎851-7032, 851-7030; www.hyperbaricmedicinecenter.com; 275 Pu'uhale Rd) For scuba divers with the bends.

Longs Drugs (☎949-4781; www.cvs.com/longs; 2470 S King St; ⏲24hr) Convenient 24-hour pharmacy near UH Manoa.

Queen's Medical Center (☎538-9011; www.queensmedicalcenter.net; 1301 Punchbowl St; ⏲24hr) O'ahu's biggest, best-equipped hospital has a 24-hour emergency room.

Straub Clinic & Hospital (☎522-4000; www.straubhealth.org; 888 S King St; ⏲24hr) Operates a 24-hour emergency room downtown and also nonemergency clinics.

POST

Ala Moana Post Office (☎800-275-8777; www.usps.com; ground fl, Ala Moana Center, 1450 Ala Moana Blvd; ⏲9am-5pm Mon-Fri, to 4:30pm Sat)

ℹ Getting Around

For ground transportation to/from the airport, see p66. For bicycle rentals, call the Bike Shop (p87).

BUS

The Ala Moana Center mall is O'ahu's central transfer point for TheBus (p67). Several direct bus routes run between Waikiki and Honolulu's other neighborhoods.

CAR

Downtown Honolulu and Chinatown are full of one-way streets, traffic is thick and parking can be tight, so consider taking TheBus instead of driving.

Honolulu traffic jams up during rush hours, from 7am to 9am and 3pm to 6pm on weekdays. Expect heavy traffic in both directions on the H-1 Fwy during this time, as well as on the Pali and Likelike Hwys headed into Honolulu in the morning and away from the city in the late afternoon.

Parking

Hourly parking is available at several municipal parking lots and garages around downtown. On-street metered parking is hard to find on weekdays, easier on weekends; bring quarters.

Major shopping centers usually have free parking for customers. The Aloha Tower Marketplace offers paid parking: on weekdays after 4pm and all day on weekends and holidays, a $5 flat-rate applies; otherwise, it's $1.50 per hour for the first three hours, then $3 for each additional 30 minutes.

TAXI

You'll probably have to call for a taxi:

TheCab (☎422-2222; www.thecabhawaii.com)

Charley's Taxi (☎877-531-1333, 233-3333; www.charleystaxi.com)

City Taxi (☎524-2121; www.citytaxihonolulu.com)

PEARL HARBOR

The WWII-era rallying cry 'Remember Pearl Harbor!' that once mobilized an entire nation resonates dramatically on O'ahu. It was here that the surprise Japanese attack on December 7, 1941 hurtled the US into war in the Pacific. Every year around 1.6 million tourists visit Pearl Harbor's unique collection of war memorials and museums, all clustered around a bay west of Honolulu where oysters were once farmed.

Today Pearl Harbor is home to an active and mind-bogglingly enormous US naval base. Anyone looking for a little soul-soothing peace and quiet, especially after a solemn visit to the USS *Arizona* Memorial, can head up into the misty Ko'olau Mountains above the harbor, where an ancient Hawaiian temple and forested hiking trails await.

PEARL HARBOR: A SURPRISE ATTACK

December 7, 1941 – 'a date which will live in infamy,' President Franklin D Roosevelt later said – began at 7:55am with a wave of over 350 Japanese planes swooping over the Ko'olau Range headed toward the unsuspecting US Pacific Fleet in Pearl Harbor.

The battleship USS *Arizona* took a direct hit and sank in less than nine minutes, trapping its crew beneath the surface. The average age of the 1177 enlisted men who died on the ship was just 19 years. It wasn't until 15 minutes after the bombing started that American anti-aircraft guns began to shoot back at the Japanese warplanes. Twenty other US military ships were sunk or seriously damaged and 347 airplanes were destroyed during the two-hour attack.

In hindsight, there were two significant warnings prior to the attack that were disastrously dismissed or misinterpreted. More than an hour before Japanese planes arrived, USS *Ward* spotted a submarine conning tower approaching the entrance of Pearl Harbor. The *Ward* immediately attacked with depth charges and sank what turned out to be one of five midget Japanese submarines attempting to penetrate the harbor. Then at 7:02am a radar station on the north shore of O'ahu reported planes approaching. Even though they were coming from the west rather than the east, the planes were assumed to be from the US mainland – a fatal mistake.

Sights & Activities

The offshore shrine at the sunken USS *Arizona*, part of the multi-state **WWII Valor in the Pacific National Monument** (www.nps.gov/valr/), is Hawaii's most-visited tourist attraction. Nearby are two other floating historical sites: the USS *Bowfin* submarine (aka the 'Pearl Harbor Avenger') and the battleship USS *Missouri*, where General Douglas MacArthur formally accepted the Japanese surrender at the end of WWII. Together, for the USA, these military sites represent the beginning, middle and end of the war.

To visit all three sites, as well as the Pacific Aviation Museum, dedicate a full day, preferably starting on a weekday morning when it's less crowded. All of Pearl Harbor's attractions are wheelchair-accessible and closed on Thanksgiving, Christmas and New Year's Day.

Book guided tours in advance online (www.pearlharborhistoricsites.org and www.recreation.gov), or buy same-day tickets and discount sightseeing packages in person at the visitor center's **Aloha Court**. A one-day pass to Pearl Harbor's main attractions costs $55/30 per adult/child, or get a two-day pass ($65/35) valid over a seven-day period.

★ **USS Arizona Memorial** MUSEUM, MEMORIAL
(☎422-3300; www.nps.gov/valr; 1 Arizona Memorial Pl; tours free, tour reservation fee $1.50; ⏰7am-5pm, boat tours 8am-3pm) **FREE** One of the USA's most significant WWII sites, this somber monument commemorates the Pearl Harbor attack and its fallen service members with an offshore shrine reachable by boat. At the recently rebuilt visitor center back on land, a modern multimedia museum displays rare WWII memorabilia and a model of the battleship, as well as historical photos and oral history.

Offshore, the USS *Arizona* Memorial was built over the midsection of the sunken USS *Arizona*, with deliberate geometry to represent initial defeat, ultimate victory and eternal serenity. In the furthest of three chambers inside the shrine, the names of crewmen killed in the attack are engraved onto a marble wall. In the central section are cutaways that allow visitors to see the skeletal remains of the ship, which even now oozes about a quart of oil each day into the ocean. In its rush to recover from the attack and prepare for war, the US Navy exercised its option to leave the servicemen inside the sunken ship; they remain entombed in its hull, buried at sea. Visitors are asked to maintain respectful silence at all times.

On land, among the most interesting exhibits at the visitor center's **museum galleries** are islanders' testimonies about the unease before the attack (maybe it wasn't as much of a surprise to residents as it was to the military) and the frank look at the discriminatory treatment of Japanese Americans during the war. A self-guided **waterfront walk** passes interpretive signs illustrating how the attack unfolded in the now-peaceful harbor. The center's **bookstore** sells just about every book and movie ever produced on the Pearl Harbor attack and WWII's Pacific theater, as well as illustrated maps of the battle.

Boat tours to the shrine depart every 15 minutes from 8am until 3pm (weather permitting). For the 75-minute tour program, which includes a 23-minute documentary film on the attack, make reservations online (fee per ticket $1.50) at www.recreation.gov at least a few days before your visit. Free first-come, first-serve tickets are also available in person at the visitor center's Aloha Court, but during peak season when more than 4000 people take the tour daily, the entire day's allotment of tickets may be gone by 10am and waits of a few hours are not uncommon, so arrive early.

★Battleship Missouri Memorial MUSEUM, MEMORIAL

(☎877-644-4896, 455-1600; www.ussmissouri.com; 63 Cowpens St, Ford Island; admission incl tour adult/child 4-12yr from $22/11; ⏲8am-4pm Sep-May, to 5pm Jun-Aug) The last battleship built at the end of WWII, the USS *Missouri* provides a unique historical 'bookend' to the US campaign in the Pacific during WWII. Nicknamed the 'Mighty Mo' (it's bigger than the RMS *Titanic*), this decommissioned battleship saw action during the decisive WWII battles of Iwo Jima and Okinawa.

The USS *Missouri* is now docked on Ford Island, just a few hundred yards from the sunken remains of the USS *Arizona*. During a self-guided audio tour, you can poke about the officers' quarters, browse exhibits on the ship's history and stride across the deck where General MacArthur accepted the Japanese surrender on September 2, 1945. Guided battle-station tours, which are sometimes led by knowledgeable US military veterans, are worth the extra time and expense.

To visit the memorial, board the mandatory Ford Island visitor shuttle bus (bring photo ID) outside the visitor center's Aloha Court.

USS Bowfin Submarine Museum & Park MUSEUM, PARK

(☎423-1341; www.bowfin.org; 11 Arizona Memorial Dr; park admission free, museum adult/child 4-12yr $5/3, incl self-guided submarine audio tour $10/4; ⏲7am-5pm, last entry 4:30pm) If you have to wait an hour or two for your USS *Arizona* Memorial tour to begin, this adjacent park harbors the moored WWII-era submarine USS *Bowfin* and a somewhat dated niche museum that traces the development of submarines from their origins to the nuclear age, including wartime patrol footage. Undoubtedly, the highlight is clambering aboard a historic submarine.

Launched on December 7, 1942, one year after the Pearl Harbor attack, the USS *Bowfin* sank 44 enemy ships in the Pacific by the end of WWII. A self-guided audio tour explores the life of the crew – watch your head below deck! Children under age four are not allowed aboard the submarine for safety reasons.

As you stroll around the surrounding waterfront park, peer through the periscopes and inspect a Japanese *kaiten* (suicide torpedo), the marine equivalent of a kamikaze pilot's plane, developed as a last-ditch effort by the Japanese military near the end of WWII.

Pacific Aviation Museum MUSEUM

(☎441-1000; www.pacificaviationmuseum.org; 319 Lexington Blvd, Ford Island; adult/child 4-12yr $20/10, incl guided tour $30/20, flight simulator add $10; ⏲9am-5pm, last entry 4pm) Still a work in progress, this military aircraft museum covers WWII through the US conflicts in Korea and Vietnam. The first aircraft hangar has been outfitted with exhibits on the Pearl Harbor attack, the Doolittle Raid on mainland Japan in 1942 and the pivotal Battle of Midway, when the tides of WWII in the Pacific turned in favor of the Allies.

Authentically restored planes on display here include a Japanese Zero and a Dauntless navy dive bomber. Walk next door to explore the MiG Alley Korean War exhibit or take a guided tour to look behind the scenes at restoration work in Hangar 79's replica WWII-era maintenance shop.

To visit the museum, board the mandatory Ford Island visitor shuttle bus (bring photo ID) outside the visitor center's Aloha Court.

Kea'iwa Heiau State Recreation Area PARK

(www.hawaiistateparks.org; off 'Aiea Heights Dr, 'Aiea; ⏲7am-7:45pm April-1st Mon in Sep, to 6:45pm 1st Tue in Sep-Mar) FREE In the hills above Pearl Harbor, this park protects the ruins of **Kea'iwa Heiau**, a Hawaiian stone temple used by *kahuna lapa'au* (herbalist healers). For hikers and mountain bikers, the park's steep and sometimes muddy, but nevertheless scenic 4.8-mile **'Aiea Loop Trail** starts from the top of the paved driving loop road and ends back at the campground.

In ancient times, kahuna grew scores of medicinal plants on the heiau grounds. Among those still found here are *noni* (Indian mulberry), whose pungent yellow fruit was used to treat heart disease; *kukui* (candlenuts), a laxative; and *ti* leaves, which were wrapped around a sick person to break a fever. The heiau itself was believed to possess life-giving energy that could be channeled by kahuna.

If you follow the hiking loop trail, you'll eventually be rewarded with sweeping vistas of Pearl Harbor, Diamond Head and the Ko'olau Range. About two-thirds of the way along the trail, the wreckage of a C-47 cargo plane that crashed in 1943 can be spotted through the foliage on the east ridge.

The park's few campsites are well-maintained, but there's not a lot of privacy and it rains frequently at this elevation. Facilities include covered picnic pavilions with BBQ grills, restrooms, outdoor showers, drinking water and a payphone. There's a resident caretaker by the front gate, which is locked at night. Camping is not permitted on Wednesday and Thursday nights; advance permits are required (see p63).

From Honolulu or Waikiki, drive west on the H-1 Fwy, then merge onto Hwy 201 W and take the Stadium/'Aiea turnoff and merge onto Moanalua Rd. Turn right onto 'Aiea Heights Dr, which winds up through a residential area for over 3 miles to the park. From downtown Honolulu, TheBus 11 'Aiea Heights stops about 1.8 miles downhill from the park entrance every hour or so.

Tours

Widely advertised in Waikiki, Pearl Harbor tours range from big buses to excursions in WWII-era amphibious armored vehicles ('ducks'). These tours don't add much, if anything, to the experience of visiting the memorials and museums. Besides, commercial tour boats aren't allowed to disembark at the USS *Arizona* Memorial.

Eating

The visitor center's Aloha Court has cheap fast-food concession stands. On Ford Island, the Battleship *Missouri* Memorial and Pacific Aviation Museum both have cafes. Down-home local eateries are flung west along the Kamehameha Hwy (Hwy 99) near Pearlridge Center mall in 'Aiea, or detour to Waipahu's Poke Stop (p166).

Forty Niner Restaurant DINER $

(98-110 Honomanu St, 'Aiea; mains $4-9; 7am-8pm Mon-Thu, to 9pm Fri & Sat) This little 1940s noodle shop and soda fountain may look abandoned, but its old-fashioned saimin (local-style noodle soup) is made with a secret-recipe broth that keeps locals coming back. Garlic chicken lunch plates and, for breakfast, mac-nut waffles and coconut pancakes aren't half bad either.

★**The Alley** LOCAL $$

(488-6854; www.aieabowl.com/restaurant.htm; 99-115 'Aiea Heights Dr, 'Aiea; mains $7-17; 7am-9:30pm Sun-Wed, to midnight Thu-Sat;) Attached to a bowling alley, this Hawaiian soul-food restaurant with retro Naugahyde booths dishes up pan-seared *furikake 'ahi* sandwich with crispy fries and Asian-spiced braised pork shoulder with brown rice – save room for lemon crunch cake, too. Owned by two *braddahs* (brothers), one of whom is a classically trained chef, this casual kitchen is almost always jumpin'.

Chun Wah Kam Noodle Factory ASIAN, LOCAL $$

(www.chunwahkam.com; Waimalu Shopping Center, 98-040 Kamehameha Hwy, 'Aiea; items $1-8, meals $7-12; 7:30am-7pm Mon-Sat, 8:30am-4pm Sun) Fanatics line up for *manapua* stuffed with anything from *char siu* pork or guava BBQ pork to purple sweet potatoes. Ginormous mix-and-match plate lunches are forgettable, however. This mini-mall is chockablock with many more Asian and local joints like **Shiro's Saimin Haven**, **Egoziku Ramen** and **Baldwin's Sweet Shop** for shave ice.

Information

Strict security measures are in place at Pearl Harbor's memorials, museums and visitor centers. You are not allowed to bring in any items that allow concealment (eg purses, camera bags, fanny packs, backpacks, diaper bags). Wallets and personal-sized cameras and camcorders are allowed. Don't lock valuables in your car; instead use the **storage facility** (per item $3; 6:30am-5:30pm) off to the right outside the visitor center's main entrance.

Getting There & Away

The entrance to Pearl Harbor's historic sites is off the Kamehameha Hwy (Hwy 99), southwest of Aloha Stadium. From Honolulu or Waikiki, take H-1 west to exit 15A (Arizona Memorial/Stadium), then follow the signs to the USS *Arizona* Memorial, not those pointing toward Pearl Harbor's military base. Visitor parking is free.

From Waikiki, bus 42 ('Ewa Beach) is the most direct, running twice hourly beginning around 6am, taking just over an hour each way; slower TheBus 20 also stops here.

WAIKIKI

POP 27,150

Waikiki – just the name alone will have you thinking of boundless horizons, Pacific sunsets and hula dancers gently swaying to the beat of island rhythms. Once the playground of Hawaiian royalty, this remains O'ahu's quintessential beach.

After emerging from the long shadow of WWII, Waikiki recaptured the popular imagination as an idyllic tropical island vacation complete with flower lei, aloha shirts and romance. Celebrities like Elvis sang about it and strummed a ukulele, while bronzed beachboys walked on water thanks to their long wooden surfboards.

Today Waikiki has reinvented itself. Although tacky tiki drinks and resort luau featuring all-you-can-eat buffets and Samoan fire-knife dancing are still a fixture on the scene, Hawaii's most-visited beach is moving beyond plasticky mass tourism, with stylish resort hotels, fashion-forward boutiques and sophisticated restaurants and cocktail lounges.

A lazy morning of lying on the white sand here is only the start of the fun. Take a surfing lesson, sip a mai tai as the sun drops into the sea, listen to lilting slack key guitars, and just enjoy life. It's for good reasons that everyone's here.

History

Fed by mountain streams from Manoa Valley, Waikiki ('Spouting Water') was once a fertile wetland of *kalo lo'i* (taro fields) and fishponds. In 1795 when Kamehameha the Great conquered O'ahu, he brought his royal court here. For almost the next century, Waikiki became a privileged royal retreat.

In the 1880s, Honolulu's wealthier citizens started building gingerbread-trimmed cottages along the narrow beachfront. Tourists arrived in 1901, when the Moana opened its doors as Waikiki's first luxury hotel, built on a former royal compound. The next year a tram line connected Waikiki with downtown Honolulu, and city folk crowded aboard for weekend beach outings.

Tiring quickly of the pesky mosquitoes that thrived in Waikiki's wetlands, beachgoers petitioned to have the 'swamps' brought under control. In 1922 the Ala Wai Canal was dug to divert streams and dry out the wetlands. Old Hawaii lost out: local farmers had the water drained out from under them and Waikiki's water buffaloes were quickly replaced by tourists.

In the 'Roaring Twenties,' the Royal Hawaiian hotel opened to serve passengers arriving on luxury ocean liners from San Francisco. During WWII, this 'Pink Palace' was turned into an R&R playground for US Navy sailors on shore leave. As late as 1950, surfers could still drive their cars right up onto Waikiki Beach and park on the sand. But by then passenger jets had started making regularly scheduled flights to Hawaii, and mainland tourism boomed.

Beaches

The 2-mile stretch of white sand commonly called Waikiki Beach runs from the Hilton Hawaiian Village down to Kapi'olani Park. Along the way, the beach changes names and personalities. In the early morning, quiet seaside paths belong to walkers and joggers. By midmorning it looks like a resort beach – watersports concessionaires and lots of tourist bodies sprawled on beach mats catching rays. At noon, it gets packed and it can be challenging to walk along the sand without stepping on anyone.

Waikiki is good for swimming, bodyboarding, surfing, sailing and other watersports most of the year, and there are lifeguards and outdoor showers scattered along the beachfront. Between May and September, summer swells make the water rougher for swimming, but great for surfing. For snorkeling, head to Sans Souci Beach or Queen's Surf Beach.

As the beachfront has become more developed, private landowners have constructed seawalls and offshore barriers (called groins) to protect their properties. In doing so, they've blocked the natural forces of sand accretion, which has made erosion a serious problem. Some of Waikiki's legendary white sands have been recently reclaimed through an offshore pumping project.

On O'ahu, smoking has now been banned at some public beaches and parks, including Waikiki's Kahanamoku, Kuhio and Kap'iolani Beaches.

The following beaches are listed geographically from northwest to southeast.

Waikiki

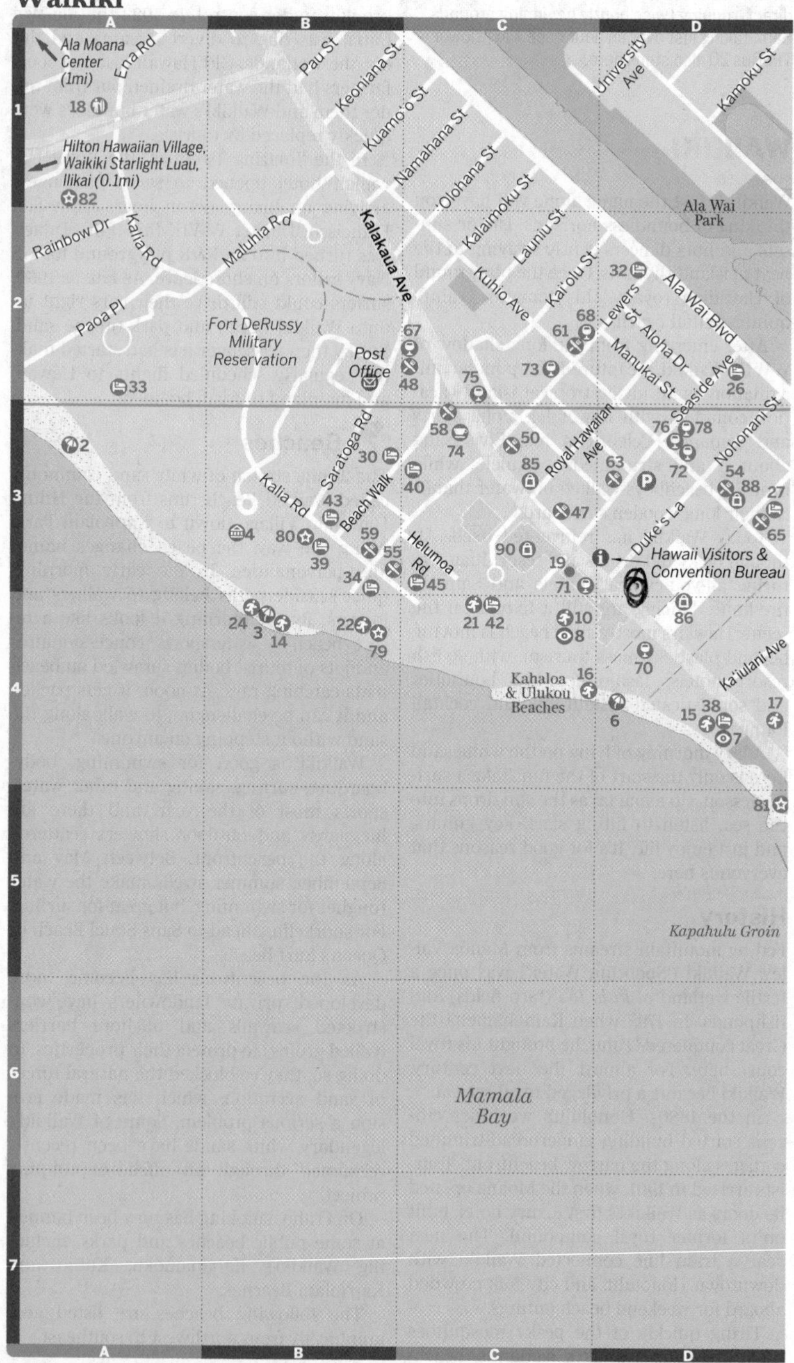
Ala Moana Center (1mi)
Ena Rd
Pau St
Keoniana St
Kuamo'o St
Namahana St
'Olohana St
Kalaimoku St
Launiu St
Kai'olu St
University Ave
Kamoku St
Hilton Hawaiian Village, Waikiki Starlight Luau, Ilikai (0.1mi)
Rainbow Dr
Kalia Rd
Maluhia Rd
Kalakaua Ave
Kuhio Ave
Ala Wai Park
Ala Wai Blvd
Lewers St
Aloha Dr
Manukai St
Seaside Ave
Nohonani St
Paoa Pl
Fort DeRussy Military Reservation
Post Office
Saratoga Rd
Beach Walk
Helumoa Rd
Royal Hawaiian Ave
Duke's La
Hawaii Visitors & Convention Bureau
Kahaloa & Ulukou Beaches
Ka'iulani Ave
Kapahulu Groin
Mamala Bay

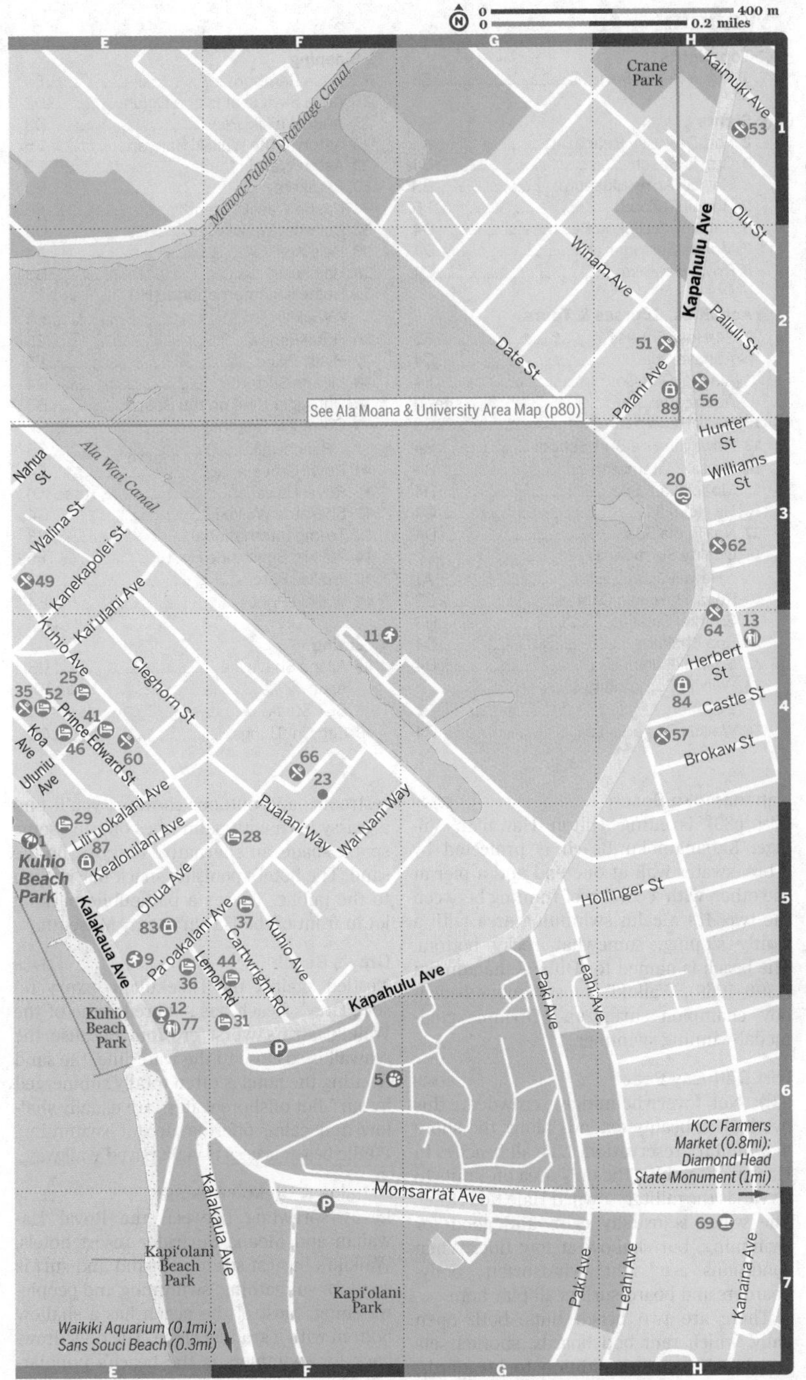
0 400 m
0 0.2 miles
Crane Park
Kaimuki Ave
Manoa-Palolo Drainage Canal
Kapahulu Ave
Olu St
Winam Ave
Paliuli St
Date St
Palani Ave
See Ala Moana & University Area Map (p80)
Hunter St
Williams St
Ala Wai Canal
Nahua St
Walina St
Kanekapolei St
Kai'ulani Ave
Kuhio Ave
Cleghorn St
Herbert St
Castle St
Brokaw St
Prince Edward St
Koa Ave
Uluniu Ave
Lili'uokalani Ave
Kealohilani Ave
Pualani Way
Wai Nani Way
Kuhio Beach Park
Ohua Ave
Kalakaua Ave
Pa'oakalani Ave
Cartwright Rd
Lemon Rd
Hollinger St
Paki Ave
Leahi Ave
KCC Farmers Market (0.8mi); Diamond Head State Monument (1mi)
Monsarrat Ave
Kapi'olani Beach Park
Kapi'olani Park
Kanaina Ave
Waikiki Aquarium (0.1mi); Sans Souci Beach (0.3mi)

Waikiki

Top Sights

1 Kuhio Beach Park E5

Sights

2 Fort DeRussy Beach A3
3 Gray's Beach B4
4 Hawai'i Army Museum B3
5 Honolulu Zoo F6
6 Kahaloa & Ulukou Beaches D4
7 Moana Surfrider D4
8 Royal Hawaiian C4

Activities, Courses & Tours

9 24-Hour Fitness E5
10 Abhasa Spa C4
11 Ala Wai Golf Course F4
AquaZone .... (see 9)
12 Hans Hedemann Surf E6
13 Hawaiian Fire Surf School H4
14 Maita'i Catamaran B4
15 Moana Lani Spa D4
16 Na Hoku II C4
17 Na Ho'ola Spa D4
18 Quality Surfboards Hawaii A1
19 Royal Hawaiian Center C3
20 Snorkel Bob's H3
21 Spa Khakara C4
22 SpaHalekulani B4
23 Waikiki Community Center F4
24 Waikiki Rigger B4

Sleeping

25 Aqua Bamboo E4
26 Aqua Skyline at Island Colony D2
27 Aqua Waikiki Pearl D3
28 Aston at the Waikiki Banyan F5
29 Aston Waikiki Circle E5
30 Breakers B3
31 Castle Waikiki Grand F6
32 Coconut Waikiki D2
33 Hale Koa A2
34 Halekulani B3
35 Hostelling International (HI) Waikiki E4
36 Hotel Renew E5
37 Hyatt Place F5
38 Moana Surfrider D4
39 Outrigger Reef on the Beach B3
40 Outrigger Regency on Beachwalk C3
41 Royal Grove E4
Royal Hawaiian .... (see 10)
42 Sheraton Waikiki C4
43 Trump International B3
44 Waikiki Beachside Hostel F5
45 Waikiki Parc C3
46 Waikiki Prince E4

Eating

47 Ailana Shave Ice C3
Azure .... (see 10)
BLT Steak .... (see 43)
48 Eggs 'n' Things C2

Kahanamoku Beach BEACH
(Map p80) Fronting Hilton Hawaiian Village, Kahanamoku Beach is protected by a breakwater wall at one end and a pier at the other, with a coral reef running between the two. It's a calm swimming area with a gently sloping, somewhat rocky bottom. The beach is named for Duke Kahanamoku (1890–1968), Waikiki's most famous beachboy, champion surfer and Olympic gold-medal-winning swimmer.

Fort DeRussy Beach BEACH
(👪) Not overwhelmingly crowded, this overlooked beauty extends along the shore of a military reservation. Like all beaches in Hawaii, it's public; the only area off-limits to civvies is the military-owned Hale Koa Hotel. The water is usually calm and good for swimming, but shallow at low tide. When conditions are right, windsurfers, bodyboarders and board surfers all play here.

There are two beach huts, both open daily, which rent bodyboards, snorkel sets and beach gear. In addition to lifeguards, restrooms and outdoor showers, you'll find a grassy lawn with palm trees offering some sparse shade, an alternative to frying on the sand. The hotel's poolside snack bar is open to the public. There's a pay public parking lot in front of the Hawai'i Army Museum.

Gray's Beach BEACH
Nestled against the Halekulani luxury resort, Gray's Beach has suffered some of the Waikiki strip's worst erosion. Because the seawall is so close to the waterline, the sand fronting the hotel is often totally submerged by surf, but offshore waters are usually shallow and calm, offering decent swimming. Public beach access is via a paved walkway.

Kahaloa & Ulukou Beaches BEACH
Lazily sprawling between the Royal Hawaiian and Moana Surfrider resort hotels, Waikiki's busiest stretch of sand and surf is great for sunbathing, swimming and people-watching. Most of the beach has a shallow bottom with a gradual slope. The only drawback for swimmers is the beach's popular-

49 Food Pantry ... E3
50 Gyū-kaku ... C3
51 Haili's Hawaiian Foods ... H2
52 Iyasume ... E4
53 Leonard's ... H1
54 Marukame Udon ... D3
Me BBQ ... (see 41)
55 Nōbu ... B3
56 Ono Seafood ... H2
57 Rainbow Drive-In ... H4
58 Ramen Nakamura ... C3
59 Roy's Waikiki ... B3
60 Ruffage Natural Foods ... E4
Sansei Seafood Restaurant & Sushi Bar ... (see 9)
61 Siam Square ... C2
62 Tokkuri Tei ... H3
63 Tropical Dreams ... D3
64 Uncle Bo's ... H4
65 Veggie Star Natural Foods ... D3
66 Waikiki Farmers Market ... F4

Drinking & Nightlife

67 Arnold's Beach Bar & Grill ... C2
68 Bacchus ... C2
69 Diamond Head Cove Health Bar ... H7
70 Duke's Waikiki ... D4
71 Five-O Bar & Lounge ... C3
72 Fusion Waikiki ... D3
73 Genius Lounge ... C2
74 Gorilla in the Cafe ... C3
Hula's Bar & Lei Stand ... (see 31)
75 In Between ... C2
Island Vintage Coffee ... (see 19)
76 LoJax ... D3
77 LuLu's ... E6
RumFire ... (see 42)
78 Tapa's Lanai Bar ... D3
Wang Chung's ... (see 52)

Entertainment

'Aha 'Aina ... (see 10)
Beach Bar ... (see 15)
79 House Without a Key ... B4
80 Kani Ka Pila Grille ... B3
81 Kuhio Beach Hula Show ... D5
Mai Tai Bar ... (see 10)
Moana Terrace ... (see 9)
Royal Grove ... (see 71)
82 Tapa Bar ... A1

Shopping

83 Angels by the Sea ... E5
84 Bailey's Antiques & Aloha Shirts ... H4
Bob's Ukulele ... (see 9)
85 DFS Galleria ... C3
86 International Market Place ... D4
87 Loco Boutique ... E5
88 Muse ... D3
89 Na Lima Mili Hulu No'eau ... H2
Newt at the Royal ... (see 10)
Reyn Spooner ... (see 42)
90 Royal Hawaiian Center ... C3

ity with beginner surfers and the occasional catamaran landing hazard.

Queens and **Canoes**, Waikiki's best-known surf breaks, are just offshore, and sometimes there are scores of surfers lined up on the horizon waiting to catch a wave. Paddle further offshore to **Populars** (aka 'Pops'), favored by longboarders.

There are restrooms, outdoor showers, a snack bar, surfboard lockers and beach-gear rental stands further south at **Waikiki Beach Center**, near the police substation.

★Kuhio Beach Park BEACH

(👪) A Hollywood-worthy superstar, this beach is perfect for everything from swimming to outrigger canoe rides. On its eastern end is **Kapahulu Groin**, a walled storm drain topped by a walkway jutting into the ocean. A low stone breakwater, called **The Wall**, runs out parallel to the beach. Built to control sand erosion, it has formed two nearly enclosed swimming pools.

The pool closest to Kapahulu Groin is tops for swimming, with the water near the breakwater reaching overhead depths. However, because circulation is limited, the water gets murky, with a noticeable film of suntan oil. The 'Watch Out Deep Holes' sign refers to holes in the pool's sandy bottom created by swirling currents; waders should be cautious in the deeper part of the pool.

Kapahulu Groin is one of Waikiki's hottest bodyboarding spots. If the surf's right, you can find a few dozen bodyboarders, mostly teenagers, riding the waves. These experienced local kids thrillingly ride straight for the groin's cement wall and then veer away at the last moment. They also walk out onto the Wall, but that can be dangerous due to a slippery surface and the breaking surf.

Kapi'olani Beach Park BEACH

Where did all the tourists go? South of Kapahulu Groin, this peaceful stretch is backed by banyan trees and grassy lawns. Here you'll find far less hubbub than in front of Waikiki's beachfront hotels. It's a popular weekend picnicking spot for local families, who unload the kids to splash in the water.

DON'T MISS

O'AHU'S BEST BEACHES

➡ Kuhio Beach Park (p109) – Waikiki's always-busy oceanfront carnival

➡ Hanauma Bay (p131) – snorkeling even kiddies can enjoy

➡ Sandy Beach (p132) – bodyboarding only for the fearless

➡ Waimanalo (p135) – O'ahu's longest, calmest golden strand

➡ Kailua (p138) – swimming, kayaking, stand up paddle surfing, windsurfing and kiteboarding

➡ Kualoa (p146) – the Windward Coast's prettiest ocean views

➡ Malaekahana State Recreation Area (p151) – wild, untamed windward O'ahu beach

➡ Pipeline (p155) – the North Shore's epic surfing break

➡ Pupukea (p155) – superb summertime snorkeling and diving

➡ Makaha (p169) – the Wai'anae Coast's big-wave beach

Park facilities include restrooms, outdoor showers and BBQ grills.

Queen's Surf Beach is the nickname for the widest section of Kapi'olani Beach. The strand in front of the pavilion is popular with Waikiki's gay community, and its sandy bottom offers decent swimming. The beach between Queen's Surf and the Wall is shallow and has broken coral. The offshore surfing break, called **Publics**, gets some good waves in winter.

At the Diamond Head end of the beach park, the 1920s **Natatorium** (http://natatorium.org; 2815 Kalakaua Ave) is on the National Register of Historic Places. This 100m-long saltwater swimming pool was constructed as a memorial for soldiers who died in WWI. Two Olympic gold medalists – Johnny Weissmuller and Duke Kahanamoku – swam in the tide-fed pool. It remains closed to the public, awaiting renovations or demolition.

Sans Souci Beach Park BEACH

At the Diamond Head edge of Waikiki, Sans Souci (aka Kaimana Beach) is a prime sandy stretch of oceanfront for sunbathing, swimming and snorkeling even further away from Waikiki's frenzied tourist scene. Next door to the New Otani Kaimana Beach Hotel, locals often come here for their daily swims. Limited beach facilities include a lifeguard tower and outdoor showers.

A shallow coral reef close to shore makes for calm, protected waters and provides reasonably good snorkeling. More coral can be found by following the Kapua Channel as it cuts through the reef, although if you swim out, beware of strong currents that can pick up. Always check conditions with a lifeguard before venturing out. Visitors with mobility issues can reserve beach wheelchairs, available free of charge, by calling ☎923-1555 in advance.

Sights

Let's be honest: you're probably just here for the beach. Waikiki's handful of diversions for landlubbers include two historical hotels, spas, a popular golf course and an aquarium. All along the shoreline, surfboard-shaped signs – part of the **Waikiki Historic Trail** (www.waikikihistorictrail.com) – point out local history and lore.

★**Waikiki Aquarium** AQUARIUM

(☎923-9741; www.waquarium.org; 2777 Kalakaua Ave; adult/child 5-12yr/youth 13-17yr $9/2/4; ⏰9am-5pm, last entry 4:30pm; 👪) Next to a living reef on Waikiki's shoreline, this university-run aquarium features a jaw-dropping ocean predator gallery and dozens of tanks re-creating different Pacific reef habitats. It's a great place to identify the colorful coral and fish you've already glimpsed while snorkeling. An outdoor tank is home to rare Hawaiian monk seals that can't return to the wild.

Among the kid-friendly exhibits, look for rare fish species from the Northwestern Hawaiian Islands, as well as hypnotic moon jellies and flashlight fish that host bioluminescent bacteria. Especially hypnotizing are the Paluan chambered nautiluses with their unique spiral shells – this is the world's first aquarium to breed these endangered creatures in captivity.

Check the website or call to make reservations for special family events and fun kids' educational programs such as meeting the monk seals or exploring the ocean reef at night.

Moana Surfrider HISTORICAL BUILDING

(☎922-3111; www.moana-surfrider.com; 2365 Kalakaua Ave; ⏰tours usually 11am Mon, Wed & Fri)

FREE Christened the Moana Hotel when it opened in 1901, this hotel resembles a beaux-arts style plantation inn. Guided tours start upstairs from the lobby with a video screening at the mezzanine **museum**, which displays period photographs and hotel memorabilia, including scripts from the famed *Hawaii Calls* radio show that was broadcast from the banyan courtyard between 1935 and 1975.

Back in the early 20th century, when Waikiki was an exclusive neighborhood for Hawaiian royalty and Honolulu business tycoons, early guests of the Moana Hotel included aristocrats, princes and Hollywood movie stars. Still today the historic hotel embraces a seaside courtyard with a giant banyan tree where island musicians and hula dancers often perform in the evenings.

Royal Hawaiian HISTORICAL BUILDING

(☎923-7311; www.royal-hawaiian.com; 2259 Kalakaua Ave; ⏲tours usually 2pm Tue & Thu) FREE With its Spanish Moorish-style turrets and archways, this beautifully restored 1927 art deco hotel is a Waikiki landmark. Dubbed the 'Pink Palace,' its guest list once read like a who's who of A-list celebrities, from royalty to Rockefellers, plus pop-culture stars like Charlie Chaplin and Babe Ruth. Today, historic tours explore the architecture and lore of this grand dame.

The hotel is a throwback to the era when Rudolph Valentino was *the* romantic idol and tourist travel to Hawaii was by Matson Navigation luxury liner. Join a free guided tour or stop by the concierge desk to pick up a self-guided tour brochure and then stroll through the gardens where Queen Ka'ahumanu's summer palace once stood.

Hawai'i Army Museum MUSEUM

(www.hiarmymuseumsoc.org; 2161 Kalia Rd; donations welcome, audio tour $5; ⏲9am-5pm Tue-Sat, last entry 4:45pm; P) FREE At Fort DeRussy, this special-interest museum showcases an almost mind-numbing array of military paraphernalia as it relates to Hawaii's history, starting with shark-tooth clubs used by Kamehameha the Great. Concentrating on the US military presence in Hawaii, extensive exhibits include displays on the 442nd, the Japanese American regiment that became the most decorated US Army unit in WWII, and a rooftop Cobra helicopter.

Validated museum parking at Fort DeRussy costs $2 for the first hour, plus $1.25 each additional hour.

Honolulu Zoo ZOO

(☎971-7171; www.honoluluzoo.org; cnr Kapahulu & Kalakaua Aves; adult/child 4-12yr $14/6; ⏲9am-4:30pm; P 👪) Arguably in need of renovations and more spacious enclosures, this small-scale zoo on the north side of Kapi'olani Park features some 300 species spread across over 40 acres of tropical greenery. In the aviary near the entrance you'll spot some rare native birds, including the *'io* (Hawaiian hawk), *nene* (Hawaiian goose) and Laysan duck.

Check the online calendar for family-friendly twilight tours, dinner safaris and overnight campouts (make reservations). The zoo parking lot costs $1 per hour, but there's often free parking on Monsarrat Ave.

Activities

In the mornings, runners pound the pavement next to **Ala Wai Canal**; in the late afternoon, outrigger canoe teams ply the canal's waters en route to Ala Wai Yacht Harbor. **Kapi'olani Park** (http://kapiolanipark.net; off Kalakaua & Paki Aves) FREE has tennis courts and sports fields for soccer and softball, even cricket. For an indoor workout, **24-Hour Fitness** (☎923-9090; www.24hourfitness.com; 2490 Kalakaua Ave; daily/weekly pass $25/75; ⏲24hr) has a small, fully equipped gym and group exercise classes.

WAIKIKI'S SORCERERS & SURFERS

On the Diamond Head side of Waikiki's police substation, four quite ordinary-looking boulders are actually the legendary **Wizard Stones of Kapaemahu**, said to contain the secrets and healing powers of four 16th-century Tahitian sorcerers who visited Hawaii.

Just further east is a bronze **statue of Duke Kahanamoku** standing with one of his longboards and fresh flower lei draped around his neck. Considered the father of modern surfing, Duke made his home in Waikiki and traveled around the world giving surfing demonstrations, from Sydney to New York. Some surfers have taken issue with the placement of the statue – Duke is standing with his back to the sea, a position they say he never would've taken in real life.

Waikiki Ocean Club WATER SPORTS

(Map p80; ☎855-380-6800, 380-6800; www.waikikioceanclub.com; adult/child under 4yr/youth 4-15yr $89/25/69; ⊙9am-5pm;) Zip over from the Hilton's pier to this aquatic theme park moored offshore, where you can bounce on a trampoline, swivel down water slides or test the triple-level diving deck, then go ocean snorkeling or swimming. Add-on activities such as sea kayaking, quad boating and helmet diving all cost extra. Make reservations a few days in advance, especially for weekend visits.

Surfing

Waikiki's gentler winter breaks are best for beginners. Surfing lessons (from $75 for a two-hour group class) and surfboard, boogie board and stand up paddleboard (SUP) rentals (per day $10 to $100) can be arranged at Kuhio Beach Park's concession stands. Based in nearby Ala Moana, Girls Who Surf (p87) offers surfing lessons with free transportation to/from Waikiki.

★ **Hawaiian Fire Surf School** SURFING

(☎737-3743; www.hawaiianfire.com; 3318 Campbell Ave; 2hr group/private lesson from $109/159;) With small-group classes taught by real-life firefighters, this safety-conscious surf school offers free pick-ups from Waikiki and transportation to/from a quiet beach on Leeward O'ahu's coast.

Hans Hedemann Surf SURFING

(☎924-7778; www.hhsurf.com; Park Shore Waikiki, 2586 Kapahulu Ave; 2hr group/semiprivate/private lesson $75/125/150; ⊙8am-5pm) Learn to surf, bodyboard or stand up paddle surf at this pro surfer's well-established school, conveniently opposite the beach. Rental boards available.

Quality Surfboards Hawaii SURFING

(☎947-7307; www.qualitysurfboardshawaii.com; 1860 Ala Moana Blvd; ⊙8am-8pm) The name's no lie: hit this local surfer's shop for board, SUP, snorkel and beach gear rentals. Call 48 hours ahead for free surfboard delivery and pick-up (two-day minimum rental).

Diving & Snorkeling

To really see the gorgeous stuff – coral gardens, manta rays and exotic tropical fish – head out on a boat trip (per snorkeler/diver from $40/120). Many dive shops also rent snorkel gear and scuba-diving equipment and arrange boat trips daily.

O'ahu Diving DIVING

(☎721-4210; www.oahudiving.com) Specializes in first-time experiences (from $120) for beginning divers without certification, deep-water boat dives all around O'ahu and PADI open-water certification and refresher classes.

AquaZone DIVING, SNORKELING

(☎866-923-3483, 923-3483; www.aquazonescuba.com; Marriott Waikiki Beach Resort, 2552 Kalakaua Ave) This dive shop and tour outfitter lets snorkelers ride along on dive-boat trips. Catamaran snorkeling adventures with sea turtles depart twice daily. Gear rentals and free pool lessons available.

Snorkel Bob's SNORKELING

(☎800-262-7725, 737-2421, 735-7944; www.snorkelbob.com; 702 Kapahulu Ave; ⊙8am-5pm) Snorkel mask, fins and wetsuit rental rates vary depending on the gear quality and accessories packages. Ask about corrective-lens masks if you wear glasses or contacts.

LET'S SAIL AWAY

Several catamaran cruises leave right from Waikiki Beach – just walk down onto the sand, step into the surf and hop aboard. A 90-minute, all-you-can-drink 'booze cruise' costs $25 to $40 per adult. Reservations are recommended, especially for sunset sails.

➜ **Maita'i Catamaran** (☎800-462-7975, 922-5665; www.leahi.com;) Ahoy! A white catamaran with green sails offers the biggest variety of boat trips, including reef snorkeling, moonlight cruises and a sunset mai tai sail (kids allowed).

➜ **Na Hoku II** (☎554-5990; www.nahokuii.com) With unmistakable yellow-and-red-striped sails, this hard-drinkin', spring-break-style catamaran shoves off five times daily from in front of the Barefoot Bar at Duke's Waikiki.

➜ **Waikiki Rigger** (☎922-2210; http://waikikibeachsailing.com;) Family-friendly snorkeling trips, high-speed daytime sailings and yes, a sunset booze cruise on a sleek silver catamaran with white sails.

WAIKIKI'S BEST SPAS

What's a beach vacation without a little pampering? Especially with Hawaii's traditions of *lomilomi* ('loving touch') and *pohaku* (hot stone) massage, coupled with gentle aloha spirit. Call ahead for appointments at the following.

➡ **SpaHalekulani** (931-5322; www.halekulani.com; Halekulani, 2199 Kalia Rd) Serene couples' tandem suites, Polynesian massage and foot-pounding rituals with a gorgeous ocean-view setting.

➡ **Abhasa Spa** (922-8200; www.abhasa.com; Royal Hawaiian Hotel, 2259 Kalakaua Ave) Hawaiian massage and body-cocoon treatments in cabanas set amid tropical gardens.

➡ **Na Ho'ola Spa** (923-1234; http://waikiki.hyatt.com; Hyatt Regency, 2424 Kalakaua Ave) *Limu* (seaweed), mud and *noni* (Indian mulberry) wraps, plus macadamia-nut exfoliation and coconut moisturizers.

➡ **Moana Lani Spa** (237-2535; www.moanalanispa.com; Moana Surfrider, 2365 Kalakaua Ave) Kona coffee and vanilla facials, pineapple and tea wraps and ginger-coconut sea-salt scrubs.

➡ **Spa Khakara** (685-7600; www.khakara.com; Sheraton Waikiki, 2255 Kalakaua Ave) Tiny space specializing in organic, holistic and all-natural spa treatments, including coconut and *kukui* (candelnut) oils.

➡ **Sukotai Massage 1** (Map p80; 946-7117; http://thaimassagehonolulu.com; Hawaiian Monarch, 444 Niu St) Wonderfully traditional Thai and Hawaiian massage at half the price of beachfront resort spas.

Golf

Ala Wai Golf Course GOLF
(info 733-7387, reservations 296-2000; www1.honolulu.gov/des/golf/alawai.htm; 404 Kapahulu Ave; green fees $26-52) With views of Diamond Head, this flat 18-hole, par-70 layout scores a Guinness World Record for being the world's busiest golf course. Visitors may reserve tee times three days in advance. Otherwise, get there early in the day and put your name on the waiting list – your entire party will need to wait at the course. Driving range and rental clubs and carts available.

Courses

Waikiki Community Center HAWAIIANA, ARTS & CRAFTS
(923-1802; www.waikikicommunitycenter.org; 310 Pa'oakalani Ave; most classes $5-15) Try your hand at the ukulele, hula dancing, yoga or a variety of island arts and crafts. Instructors at this homespun community center are brimming with aloha. Call or go online for schedules; pre-registration may be required.

Royal Hawaiian Center HAWAIIANA, ARTS & CRAFTS
(922-2299; www.royalhawaiiancenter.com; 2201 Kalakaua Ave) FREE Gargantuan shopping mall offers complimentary weekday Hawaiian cultural and arts-and-crafts classes, including quilting, lei making, hula dancing, ukulele playing and *lomilomi* massage. Call or check the website for schedules.

Festivals & Events

Waikiki loves to party. Every Friday night, starting around 7:45pm, the Hilton Hawaiian Village shoots off a big ol' fireworks show, visible from the beach and sounding like thunder inside hotel rooms.

Duke Kahanamoku Challenge CULTURE, SPORTS
(www.waikikicommunitycenter.com;) Outrigger canoe and stand up paddleboarding races, local food, traditional Hawaiian games, arts-and-crafts vendors and live entertainment in late February.

Honolulu Festival ARTS, CULTURE
(www.honolulufestival.com) Be energized by Hawaiian, Asian and pan-Pacific cultural performances, followed by a festive parade along Kalakaua Ave and a fireworks show in mid-March.

Waikiki Spam Jam FOOD
(www.spamjamhawaii.com;) In late April, this street festival goes nuts for Hawaii's favorite canned-meat product, with food vendors, live music and entertainment galore.

Pan-Pacific Festival ARTS, CULTURE
(www.pan-pacific-festival.com) Hula dancing, Japanese *taiko* drumming, an arts-and-crafts fair, and a huge parade and *ho'olaule'a* (block party) happen in early June.

Na Hula Festival ARTS, CULTURE
(www1.honolulu.gov/parks/programs) In early August, hula *halau* (schools) and the Royal Hawaiian Band gather for two days of music and dance celebrations at the Waikiki Shell.

Hawaiian Slack Key Guitar Festival MUSIC, ARTS
(www.slackkeyfestival.com) Traditional Hawaiian guitar and ukulele music, food vendors and an arts-and-crafts fair take place at Kapi'olani Park in mid-August.

Aloha Festivals ARTS, CULTURE
(www.alohafestivals.com) During a statewide cultural festival held every September, Waikiki is known for its royal court ceremonies, parade and *ho'olaule'a*.

Sleeping

On Waikiki's beachfront strip, mostly along Kalakaua Ave, you'll find a few historic hotels and luxury resorts, as well as chains catering to the package-tour crowd. If stepping out of your room and digging your toes in the sand isn't a must, smaller hotels inside 1960s and '70s high-rises and apartment buildings off Kuhio Ave and near Ala Wai Canal may have rooms at half the price.

Be aware that the term 'ocean view' and its cousins 'ocean front' and 'partial ocean view' are all liberally used and may require a periscope to spot the waves. 'City', 'garden' or 'mountain' views may be euphemisms for overlooking the parking lot. When making reservations, peruse detailed property maps online or call a reservations agent to ask which tower or building has optimal views.

Overnight parking averages $15 to $30, whether for valet or self-parking. Increasingly, hotels are also charging mandatory 'resort fees,' which tack another $10 to $25 per day onto your final bill. Resort fees may cover internet connections, local and toll-free phone calls and fitness room access, or no extra perks at all, but regardless, you'll have to pay.

Designed for both business and leisure travelers, island-owned **Aqua Hospitality** (www.aquahospitality.com) boutique hotels sometimes offer free high-speed internet and complimentary continental breakfast.

O'AHU'S BEST FAMILY-FRIENDLY HOTELS

- Aulani, a Disney resort and spa (p166)
- Hilton Hawaiian Village (p115)
- Sheraton Waikiki (p117)
- Outrigger Reef on the Beach (p117)
- Hyatt Place (p115)

★Hostelling International (HI) Waikiki HOSTEL $
(☎926-8313; www.hostelsaloha.com; 2417 Prince Edward St; dm $25-28, d $58-64; ⊙reception 7am-3am; P@🛜) Inside a converted low-rise, aqua-painted apartment building, this tidy hostel has fan-cooled private rooms and single-sex dormitories, a common kitchen, coin-op laundry, lockers and boogie boards to borrow. No smoking, alcohol, curfew or daytime lockout. Reservations strongly recommended; a plane ticket proving arrival or departure within three weeks and an out-of-state or Neighbor Island ID are required at check-in. Limited self-parking ($5).

Waikiki Prince HOTEL $
(☎922-1544; www.waikikiprince.com; 2431 Prince Edward St; r $70-85; P❄🛜) What ocean views? Never mind the cramped check-in office either. A standout budget option, this 1970s apartment complex on an anonymous side street holds two dozen compact, cheery rooms with kitchenettes. Free lobby wi-fi during office hours only. Weekly discounts available. Limited self-parking ($15) by reservation.

Waikiki Beachside Hostel HOSTEL $
(☎866-478-3888, 923-9566; www.waikikibeachside-hostel.com; 2556 Lemon Rd; dm $20-37, semiprivate r $70-79; P@🛜) Like most private hostels on back-alley Lemon Rd, this aging apartment complex attracts an international party crowd with plenty of budget-friendly amenities, from a 24-hour internet cafe to surfboard and moped rentals. Although security and cleanliness can be lax, each dormitory (co-ed or women-only) has a full kitchen and telephone. Limited self-parking ($7).

Royal Grove HOTEL $
(☎923-7691; www.royalgrovehotel.com; 151 Uluniu Ave; r $55-125; ❄@🏊) Zero frills but plenty of aloha characterize this candy-colored pink low-rise courtyard motel, a favorite of

'snowbird' retirees who return each winter. At this home-away-from-home with a pet bird and a piano in the lobby, all rooms have kitchenettes. Economy rooms in the older Mauka Wing are non-stop noisy and lack air-con. Ask about weekly rates.

★ Hotel Renew BOUTIQUE HOTEL **$$**
(☎888-485-7639, 687-7700; www.hotelrenew.com; 129 Pa'oakalani Ave; r from $180; P ❄ @ ☰) Just a block from the beach, this eco-savvy boutique hotel has attentive concierge staff who provide chilled drinks upon arrival, morning coffee with pastries and beach gear to freely borrow. Design-savvy accommodations show off platform beds, projection-screen TVs, Japanese-style robes and soothing dark-wood furnishings. It's romantic enough for honeymooners, and also gay-friendly. No swimming pool.

Lotus BOUTIQUE HOTEL **$$**
(☎800-367-5004, 923-2249; www.aqualotus.com; 2885 Kalakaua Ave; r from $180; P ❄ @ ☰) At the distant Diamond Head edge of Waikiki, adjacent to Sans Souci Beach, Aqua's Balinese-inspired boutique hotel has hip, cutting-edge design. If you don't mind being far away from the crowds, it's a calming sanctuary offering free yoga classes, beach gear to borrow and morning coffee and evening wine in the lobby lounge, with its flickering candles. No pool, sorry.

Outrigger Regency on Beachwalk CONDO HOTEL **$$**
(☎866-956-4262, 922-3871; www.outrigger.com; 255 Beach Walk; 1br/2br from $199/269; P ❄ @) Spacious condo suites inside this modern high-rise are designed with earth- and jewel-toned furnishings and bold artwork. All have full kitchens, but no bathtubs; some have lanai with peek-a-boo ocean views. Step outside the downstairs lobby and you're right on buzzing Beach Walk. Free in-room wired internet. Limited pay self-parking. Off-site swimming pool.

Waikiki Parc BOUTIQUE HOTEL **$$**
(☎800-422-0450, 921-7272; www.waikikiparc.com; 2233 Helumoa Rd; r $200-415; P ❄ @ ☰ ≈) Epitomizing new-wave Waikiki, this affordably hip hangout mixes nostalgic touches like plantation-shuttered windows with minimalist contemporary furnishings. Although the pint-sized guest rooms are cool and modern, they're not nearly as chic as Nobu sushi bar and lounge downstairs. For serenity, head to the rarely crowded rooftop ocean-view pool and cabanas. Front-desk staff are top class.

Hilton Hawaiian Village RESORT **$$**
(Map p80; ☎800-445-8667, 949-4321; www.hilton-hawaiianvillage.com; 2005 Kalia Rd; r from $215; P ❄ @ ☰ ≈) On the Fort DeRussy side of Waikiki, Waikiki's largest oceanfront hotel is practically a self-sufficient tourist fortress of towers, restaurants, bars and shops. It's geared almost entirely to families and package tourists, with recently renovated contemporary rooms and a swimming pool lagoon. Expect check-in lines to move as slowly as airport-security checkpoints.

Aqua Bamboo BOUTIQUE HOTEL **$$**
(☎866-326-8423, 954-7412; www.aquabamboo.com; 2425 Kuhio Ave; r from $149, studio/1br ste from $169/199; P ❄ @ ☰ ≈) Looking for a meditative retreat from Waikiki's concrete jungle? Recently refreshed, this ecoconscious boutique hotel even has a small saltwater pool, should you tire of the ocean. Book a stylishly minimalist room, a studio with a kitchenette or a suite with a full kitchen. Free in-room wired internet and lobby and poolside wi-fi.

Hyatt Place HOTEL **$$**
(☎800-233-1234, 922-3861; www.hyattplacewaikikibeach.com; 175 Pa'oakalani Ave; r incl breakfast from $169; P ❄ @ ☰ ≈) Forget about humdrum high-rise hotels that have seen far better days. This ultra-contemporary, value-conscious chain goes above and beyond with full breakfasts, an outdoor pool deck, a cardio workout room, a high-tech business center and grab-and-go cafes. Rooms are smallish, but families with kids can request sleeper sofas or rollaway beds.

Coconut Waikiki BOUTIQUE HOTEL **$$**
(☎866-974-2626, 923-8828; www.jdvhotels.com; 450 Lewers St; r from $150; P ❄ @ ☰ ≈) This Joie de Vivre boutique hotel captures retro-modern style with atomic starburst mirrors in the hallways and cool mint-green rooms, each with its very own private lanai. Although some rooms are pygmy-hippo-sized, all have pillowtop beds, work desks, coffeemakers, microwaves and mini fridges. A small exercise room is well-equipped, but the pool is barely big enough to dip your toes in.

Aston at the Waikiki Banyan CONDO HOTEL **$$**
(☎877-997-6667, 922-0555; www.astonwaikikibanyan.com; 201 Ohua Ave; 1br from $145; P ❄ @

) Appealing most to families, this all-suites high-rise hotel is a short walk from the aquarium, the zoo and, of course, the beach. Roomy, but sometimes beat-up suites come with a full kitchen and a living-room sofabed. Let your kids loose on the pool deck, playground, tennis and basketball courts, and putting green. In-room wi-fi costs extra.

Aqua Skyline at Island Colony CONDO HOTEL **$$**
(923-2345; www.skylineislandcolony.com; 445 Seaside Ave; studio/1br apt from $159/229;) Overlooking the Ala Wai Canal, this 44-floor apartment building tucks away a few floors way up high that have been reimagined in a chic way by the Aqua Hospitality boutique-hotel chain. Spacious studio and one-bedroom suites with IKEA-esque decor have kitchenettes and private lanai, but no in-room internet. Free lobby wi-fi.

Aston Waikiki Circle HOTEL **$$**
(877-997-6667, 923-1571; www.astonwaikikicircle.com; 2464 Kalakaua Ave; r from $155;) This circular building must have been *très* chic back in the playful era of postmodernism. Today it's all about value, not fashion. About half of the renovated contemporary rooms, all with lanai, enjoy a full ocean view, but they aren't big enough to practice hula in, and there's no pool. In-room wi-fi costs extra.

Breakers HOTEL **$$**
(800-426-0494, 923-3181; www.breakers-hawaii.com; 250 Beach Walk; r $130-220;) Squeezed by luxury high-rise hotels, this Polynesian-style hotel is a throwback to another era. You'll either love or hate the old, creaky facilities and simply basic kitchenette rooms. Studios on the 2nd floor have lanai and Japanese *shōji* (sliding paper-screen) doors. Free poolside and lobby wi-fi are erratic. Limited free self-parking.

Aqua Waikiki Pearl HOTEL **$$**
(922-1616, 866-406-2782; www.aquaresorts.com; 415 Nahua St; r from $120, 1br ste from $209;) Centrally located near Waikiki's nightlife, this high-rise hotel with a downstairs sports bar is an honest bargain. Spacious, elementary rooms each have a microwave, mini-fridge and coffeemaker, or book a one-bedroom suite with a full kitchen. Free in-room wired internet and lobby and poolside wi-fi. Limited pay self-parking.

Ilikai CONDO HOTEL **$$**
(Map p80; 866-536-7973, 954-7417; www.ilikaihotel.com; 1777 Ala Moana Blvd; ste from $199;) At the far edge of Waikiki near Ala Wai Yacht Harbor, this humble timeshare condo high-rise is as close to the Ala Moana Center mall as to the beach. Recently redone with island-style decor, spacious studio suites here have full kitchens and private lanai. Free in-room wired internet and lobby wi-fi.

Castle Waikiki Grand CONDO HOTEL **$$**
(800-367-5004, 923-1814; www.waikikigrand.com; 134 Kapahulu Ave; r/ste from $165/205;) Gay-friendly condotel rents compact rooms and studios (some with kitchenettes) that vary from horrifying to heavenly. View online photos with some skepticism. Much lower rates are available for internet bookings. Ask about weekly discounts. Limited pay self-parking.

Hale Koa HOTEL **$$**
(800-367-6027, 955-0555; www.halekoa.com; 2055 Kalia Rd; r $90-290;) This high-rise hotel fronting Fort DeRussy Beach is reserved for active and retired US military personnel only. Ask for more recently renovated Ilima Tower rooms. In-room wired internet, lobby and poolside wi-fi, and parking cost extra.

★Halekulani RESORT **$$$**
(800-367-2343, 923-2311; www.halekulani.com; 2199 Kalia Rd; r from $490;) With modern sophistication, this resort hotel lives up to its name, which means 'House Befitting Heaven.' It's an all-encompassing experience of gracious living, not merely a place to crash. Peaceful rooms are equipped with all mod-con gadgets like high-tech entertainment centers, along with deep soaking tubs and expansive lanai. Luxury suites include one personally designed by Vera Wang.

★Royal Hawaiian HISTORIC HOTEL **$$$**
(866-716-8110, 923-7311; www.royal-hawaiian.com; 2259 Kalakaua Ave; r from $400;) The aristocratic Royal Hawaiian was Waikiki's first luxury hotel. Now the Spanish Moorish–style 'Pink Palace' looks better than ever, thanks to multimillion-dollar renovations. Rooms in the historic section maintain classic appeal, though many guests prefer the modern high-rise tower's ocean views. Spa suites come adorned in carved

teak, bamboo and mosaic glass, with cabana daybeds on the lanai.

Modern BOUTIQUE HOTEL **$$$**
(Map p80; 888-970-4161, 943-4161; www.themodernhonolulu.com; 1775 Ala Moana Blvd; r from $290; P) Whimsical postmodernity is hotel designer Ian Schrager's signature, from a revolving bookcase that hides the lobby bar to contemporary video art in the hallways. Terraced ocean-view rooms and suites are crisp, chic and elemental, showing off teak doors, Frette linens and marble baths. A lanai deck pool overlooks Ala Wai Yacht Harbor. It's a 10-minute walk from the beach.

Sheraton Waikiki RESORT **$$$**
(866-716-8109, 922-4422; www.sheratonwaikiki.com; 2255 Kalakaua Ave; r from $325; P) Sleek high-rise chain megahotel is ginormous enough to accommodate package-tour groups and business conferences alike. No-surprises contemporary rooms are crisply clean. Facing the beach, a 'superpool' amphibious playground keeps the kiddies entertained with a 70ft-long waterslide, while adults retreat to the ocean-view infinity pool. There's also a fitness center and drop-off child-care programs. In-room wired internet and lobby wi-fi cost extra.

Moana Surfrider HISTORIC HOTEL **$$$**
(866-716-8112, 922-3111; www.moana-surfrider.com; 2365 Kalakaua Ave; r from $350; P) Waikiki's most historic beach hotel retains much of its colonial character, with high plantation-style ceilings, Hawaiian artwork on the walls and koa-wood rocking chairs beckoning on the front veranda. Compact rooms have been upgraded with 21st-century amenities. Expect to be dodging wedding parties in the bustling hotel lobby. In-room wired internet and lobby and poolside wi-fi cost extra. Pay self-parking off site.

Outrigger Reef on the Beach RESORT **$$$**
(866-956-4262, 923-3111; www.outriggerreef.com; 2169 Kalia Rd; r from $265; P) Forget the hoity-toity attitudes of the Outrigger's higher-priced beachfront neighbors. Here the Hawaiiana flows from the handmade outrigger canoe in the Polynesian-style lobby through hula dancing, and ukulele and lei-making classes. Rooms are modern and functional enough for the mostly suburban crowd. Free in-room wired internet and lobby and poolside wi-fi.

Trump International CONDO HOTEL **$$$**
(877-683-7401, 683-7777; www.trumpwaikikihotel.com; 223 Saratoga Rd; studio/1br ste from $399/649; P) With an enviable position on Waikiki Beach Walk, this luxury tower lets you live the high life. Urbane apartment suites have panoramic windows, kitchens, marble baths and plenty of space to relax. The 6th-floor infinity pool and sundeck should ease the pain of not being right on the beach, just a five-minute walk away. Perks for kids include board games and beach bags to borrow.

Eating

Warning: many of Waikiki's restaurants are overpriced and not worth eating at, no matter how enticing the ocean views. On beachfront Kalakaua Ave, chains like the Hard Rock Cafe and the Cheesecake Factory cater to hungry tourists, while a few stand-out restaurants are run by Hawaii's top chefs. Inland Kuhio Ave abounds with cheaper grazing and takeout joints. On the outskirts of Waikiki, neighborhood eateries, drive-ins and bakeries line up along Kapahulu Ave.

★**Leonard's** BAKERY **$**
(www.leonardshawaii.com; 933 Kapahulu Ave; pastries from $1; 5:30am-10pm Sun-Thu, to 11pm Fri & Sat) It's impossible to drive by Leonard's eye-catching vintage 1950s neon sign without stopping in. This Portuguese bakery is famous all over O'ahu for its *malasadas* (sweet, fried dough rolled in sugar), served oven-fresh and warm. Try the *haupia*

O'AHU'S BEST SWEET TREATS

- Leonard's (p117) – hot-out-of-the-oven, sugary *malasadas*
- Liliha Bakery (p94) – coco-puff pastries that cause traffic jams
- Bubbies (p94) – rainbow-colored *mochi* ice cream
- Kaimuki Crack Seed (p95) – salty, sweet and sour dried fruit
- Lanikai Juice (p142) – O'ahu's premier fresh-fruit smoothies
- Matsumoto's (p160) – North Shore's classic shave-ice stand
- Dole Plantation (p164) – cones of frozen-pineapple soft-serve whip

(coconut-cream) or *liliko'i* (passion fruit) filling, and you'll be hooked for life. Pick up a souvenir 'got malasadas?' T-shirt, too. Free parking.

Me BBQ LOCAL $
(151 Uluniu Ave; meals $5-12; 7am-8:45pm Mon-Sat;) This streetside takeout counter has zero atmosphere, but you can chow down at sidewalk picnic tables or tote your plate lunch to the beach. Succulent *kalbi* short ribs and spicy kimchi are house specialties, but the wall-sized picture menu also features local-flavor combos with chicken *katsu* (breaded cutlet), fried squid and more.

Ailana Shave Ice SHAVE ICE $
(http://ailanashaveice.com; Waikiki Shopping Plaza, 2250 Kalakaua Ave; snacks $3-6; 10am-9pm;) With homemade syrups like *haupia* and peanut-butter caramel, Ailana is the new king of Honolulu's shave-ice scene. Build up your sugar-snow mountain with a scoop of Dave's ice cream and azuki beans. Service is smiley, but slow. Also at 1430 Koa St opposite the Ala Moana Center mall.

Rainbow Drive-In LOCAL $
(www.rainbowdrivein.com; 3308 Kanaina Ave; meals $4-9; 7am-9pm;) Started by a Hawaii-born US Army cook after WWII, this classic drive-in is wrapped in rainbow-colored neon. At the takeout counter, construction workers, surfers and gangly teens order all the local favorites: *loco moco,* teriyaki burgers, plate lunches, sweet-bread French toast and more. Free parking.

Ono Seafood SEAFOOD $
(747 Kapahulu Ave; mains $7-12; usually 9am-6pm Mon & Wed-Sat, 10am-3pm Sun) At this addictive, made-to-order *poke* shop, show up early before they run out. Half-and-half rice bowls let you sample two varieties of *poke*, including ever-popular spicy ahi and *tako* (octopus) with *shōyu* (soy sauce). Look for the blue awning outside. Limited free parking is available.

Diamond Head Market & Grill LOCAL $
(www.diamondheadmarket.com; 3158 Monsarrat Ave; meals $8-17; market 6:30am-9pm, grill 7am-10:30am & 11am-9pm;) Step inside this neighborhood market with a bakery and gourmet deli for beach picnics, or walk up to the takeout counter outside by the picnic tables for *char siu* pork and wasabi ahi plate lunches, portobello-mushroom burgers and tropical-fruit pancakes. Free parking.

Iyasume JAPANESE $
(www.tonsuke.com/eomusubiya.html; 2410 Koa Ave; dishes $2-7; 6:30am-4pm) This hole-in-the-wall kitchen keeps busy making *musubi* (rice balls) stuffed with seaweed, salmon roe, sour plums and even Spam. Other rare specialties are Japanese-style curry and salmon-roe rice bowls. In a hurry? Grab a *bentō* boxed lunch with *mochiko* (batter-fried) chicken to go.

Veggie Star Natural Foods HEALTHY $
(417 Nahua St; 10am-8pm Mon-Sat;) Stocking organic, all-natural and healthy groceries, this tiny market also blends tropical fruit smoothies and puts together gluten-free sandwiches, veggie burritos, vegan chili and salads to go.

Ruffage Natural Foods HEALTHY $
(2443 Kuhio Ave; dishes $4-8; 9am-6pm;) Pint-sized health-food store whips up real-fruit smoothies to revitalize your whole bod and a short menu of passable veggie burgers, tofu scrambles and avocado-sprouts sandwiches and wraps.

Tropical Dreams ICE CREAM $
(http://tropicaldreamsicecream.com; 334 Seaside Ave; items from $2; 11:30am-9:30pm;) Homemade ice cream from Hilo on the Big Island treats you right with Kona coffee, mac-nut, mango cream and other Hawaii-inspired flavors.

Food Pantry SUPERMARKET $
(2370 Kuhio Ave; 6am-1am) More expensive than bigger chain supermarkets (all outside Waikiki), but cheaper than convenience stores.

Waikiki Farmers Market MARKET $
(www.waikikicommunitycenter.org; Waikiki Community Center, enter off Ohua Ave; 7-11:30am Tue & Fri;) Fresh produce stands and island food vendors set up in this community center parking lot twice weekly.

★ **Marukame Udon** JAPANESE $
(www.facebook.com/marukameudon; 2310 Kuhio Ave; dishes $2-8; 7am-9am & 11am-10pm;) Off-duty military personnel, Asian tourists, retirees babysitting a brood of grandkids, budget backpackers and hotel employees all love this cafeteria-style Japanese noodle shop. Watch thick *udon* noodles get rolled, cut and boiled right in front of you, then stack mini plates of oversized tempura and *musubi* on a self-service tray, washing

it all down with iced barley tea. Lines are loooooong.

Haili's Hawaiian Foods HAWAIIAN **$$**
(http://hailishawaiianfood.com; 760 Palani Ave; meals $11-16; ⏲10am-7pm Tue-Thu, 10am-8pm Fri & Sat, 11am-3pm Sun) Haili's has been cooking up homegrown Hawaiian fare since the 1950s. Locals shoehorn themselves into cheery booths for heaping dishes of *kalua* pig, *lomilomi* salmon and *laulau* (meat wrapped in *ti* leaves and steamed) served with poi (mashed taro) or rice, grilled ahi plate lunches, bowls of tripe or pastele stew, *pipi kaula* (Hawaiian beef jerky) and fat tortilla wraps.

Tokkuri Tei JAPANESE, LOCAL **$$**
(☎732-6480; 449 Kapahulu Ave; most shared plates $6-25; ⏲11am-2pm Mon-Fri, 5:30pm-midnight Mon-Sat, 5-10pm Sun) Wear your rubbah slippah to this upbeat neighborhood *izakaya* and sushi bar crafting contemporary reinterpretations of Japanese standards – try the Big Island abalone or *hamachi kama* (yellowtail cheek). Shelves behind the bar store regulars' private bottles of sake and *shōchū* (potato liquor). Make reservations, or be prepared to wait. Valet parking available.

Uncle Bo's ASIAN, FUSION **$$**
(☎735-8311; www.unclebosrestaurant.com; 559 Kapahulu Ave; shared plates $8-15, mains $19-27; ⏲5pm-2am) Boisterous groups of friends devour this classy gastropub's endless list of *pupu* with island flair, from the Thai street-style grilled chicken to *kalua* pig nachos with wonton chips. For dinner, feast on market-fresh seafood like baked *opah* (moonfish) with parmesan-*panko* (Japanese bread-crumb) crust. Reservations recommended.

Gyū-kaku JAPANESE **$$**
(☎926-2989; www.gyu-kaku.com; 307 Lewers St; shared plates $3-24; ⏲11:30am-midnight) Starving surfers will love this grill-it-yourself Japanese BBQ joint. Settle in for Kobe ribeye steak, *kalbi* short ribs, garlic shrimp and enoki mushrooms, served with plentiful sweet and spicy marinades and dips. Show up for happy-hour specials (before 6:30pm or after 9:30pm) or lunchtime set-menu deals. Also at 1221 Kapi'olani Blvd.

Siam Square THAI **$$**
(2nd fl, 408 Lewers St; mains $11-16; ⏲11am-10pm;) It's Waikiki's most authentic Thai restaurant, although that's not saying too much. You want it spicy? Work to convince your server that you can handle Thai-hot *larb* pork salad or fried fish with chili sauce. Service is standoffish, but the kitchen works so fast and furiously, you may not mind.

Ramen Nakamura JAPANESE **$$**
(2141 Kalakaua Ave; mains $9-14; ⏲11am-11:30pm) You'll have to strategically elbow aside Japanese tourists toting Gucci and Chanel bags just to sit down here. Then you're free to dig into hearty bowls of oxtail or *tonkotsu* (pork-bone broth) ramen soup with crunchy fried garlic slices on top. It's usually worth the wait. Cash only.

Eggs 'n' Things BREAKFAST **$$**
(www.eggsnthings.com; 343 Saratoga Rd; mains $9-18; ⏲6am-2pm & 5-10pm;) Never empty, this cutesy but overhyped diner dishes up seriously overpriced banana macadamia-nut pancakes topped with your choice of honey, guava or coconut syrup, and fluffy omelets with Portuguese sausage for jetlagged tourists. Kids' menu available.

Sansei Seafood Restaurant & Sushi Bar JAPANESE, FUSION **$$**
(☎931-6286; www.sanseihawaii.com; 3rd fl, Marriott Waikiki Beach Resort, 2552 Kalakaua Ave; most shared plates $3-20, mains $16-35; ⏲5:30-10pm Sun-Thu, to 1am Fri & Sat) From the mind of ground-breaking chef DK Kodama, this Pacific Rim menu rolls out everything from 'new look' fusion sushi and traditional Japanese sashimi to Dungeness crab ramen with black-truffle broth. Tables on the torch-lit veranda get prime sunset views. Queue for the early bird special: 50% off all food ordered before 6pm on Sundays and Mondays; night owls get the same deal after 10pm on Fridays and Saturdays. Reservations advised.

★ **Roy's Waikiki** HAWAII REGIONAL CUISINE **$$$**
(☎923-7697; www.royshawaii.com; 226 Lewers St; mains $30-42, 3-course prix-fixe menu without/with wine pairings $47/67; ⏲11am-9:30pm Sun-Thu, to 10pm Fri & Sat) A torch-lit incarnation of Roy Yamaguchi's island-born chain is perfect for a flirty date or just celebrating the good life with friends. The ground-breaking chef doesn't actually cook in the kitchens here, but his signature *misoyaki* (grilled with miso paste) butterfish, blackened ahi, macadamia-nut-encrusted mahimahi and deconstructed sushi rolls always appear on the menu. Molten-chocolate soufflé for dessert is a must. Reservations essential.

O'ahu

Gaze at royal Hawaiian feathered capes and ancient temple carvings in Honolulu, then swizzle sunset mai tais while slack key guitars strum at Waikiki Beach. Set your watch to island time to snorkel in Hanauma Bay, cruise the waterfall-laden Windward Coast and hit the North Shore's world-renowned surf beaches.

1

2

THEBIGPINEAPPLE / GETTY IMAGES ©

4

JOHN ELK / GETTY IMAGES ©

1. Makapu'u Point (p133)
This lookout located at O'ahu's easternmost tip provides picture-perfect coastal views.

2. Ho'omaluhia Gardens (p144)
O'ahu's biggest botanical garden is nestled below the Ko'olau Range.

3. Waikiki Nightlife (p122)
Head to Waikiki's Kalakaua Ave for all the tropical drinks you could possibly desire.

4. 'Iolani Palace (p69)
Completed in 1882, this Honolulu palace played host to key moments in Hawaii's history.

3

LINDA CHING / GETTY IMAGES ©

Azure SEAFOOD **$$$**
(☎921-4600; www.azurewaikiki.com; Royal Hawaiian, 2259 Kalakaua Ave; mains $38-52, 5-course tasting menu $75; ⏲5:30am-9pm) At this award-winning oceanfront kitchen, seafood fresh from Honolulu's fish auction, such as Kona lobster, *onaga* (red snapper) and *ono* (white-fleshed wahoo), is exquisitely prepared with finishing touches like red Hawaiian sea salt and organic farm produce on the side. Wrought-iron Moroccan lamps glowing above white leather banquettes add an exotic element to the already swoon-worthy atmosphere. Reservations recommended.

BLT Steak STEAKHOUSE, SEAFOOD **$$$**
(☎683-7440; www.e2hospitality.com/blt-steak-waikiki/; Trump International, 223 Saratoga Rd; mains $26-52; ⏲5-10pm Sun-Thu, to 11pm Fri & Sat) A trendy NYC import, chef Laurent Tourondel's steakhouse has top-choice cuts broiled at 1700°F and finished off with herb butter and no fewer than nine sauces. The daily blackboard of specials shows off fresh catches like Hawaiian lobster and a raw bar of oysters. With walnut floors, chocolate-colored leather chairs and an outdoor patio, the atmosphere is date-worthy. Reservations recommended.

Nobu JAPANESE, FUSION **$$$**
(☎237-6999; www.noburestaurants.com/waikiki; Waikiki Parc, 2233 Helumoa Rd; shared dishes $5-48, mains $30-40; ⏲restaurant 5:30-10pm Sun-Thu, to 10:30pm Fri & Sat, lounge 5pm-midnight daily) Globe-trotting Iron Chef Nobu Matsuhisa's elegant seafood tapas tastes right at home by the beach. Broiled black cod with miso sauce, new-style sashimi with spicy sauces drizzled on top, and Japanese-Peruvian *tiradito* (seviche) rank among Nobu's signature tastes. A low-lit cocktail lounge serves appetizing small (truthfully, microscopic) bites and 'sake-tinis.' Reservations advised.

Drinking & Nightlife

Waikiki is tourist central with all the telltale signs, such as fruity umbrella drinks and coconut bikini bras. But underneath all of the commoditized cheesiness, authentic Hawaiian music and hula dancing have made a joyful comeback, especially at beachfront bars. If you're after spring-break party spots and dive bars, hit Kuhio Ave after dark. For a current calendar of live music, DJ dance clubs and other daytime and nightlife events, check with **Honolulu Weekly** (www.honoluluweekly.com).

Addiction CLUB
(Map p80; ☎943-5800; www.addictionnightclub.com; Modern, 1775 Ala Moana Blvd; ⏲10:30pm-3am Thu-Sun) Superstar mainland and international DJs spin at this boutique hotel's chic nightspot with an upscale dress code (no shorts, flip-flops or hats). The dance floor gets so packed, you may end up accidentally knocking boots with a stranger. For a chill scene and artisanal cocktails, the downstairs lobby's svelte **The Study** bar is craftily hidden behind a revolving bookcase.

RumFire BAR
(www.rumfirewaikiki.com; Sheraton Waikiki, 2255 Kalakaua Ave; ⏲11am-midnight, live music usually 5-8pm Tue-Sun) Cabinets full of vintage rum, flirty beachfront fire pits and contemporary Hawaiian musicians bring crowds of friends and first dates to this sexy lounge. By day, the same resort's **Edge of Waikiki** poolside bar has equally gorgeous ocean views, knock-out cocktails and live Hawaiian music with solo hula dancers after sunset.

Arnold's Beach Bar & Grill BAR
(www.arnoldsbeachbarwaikiki.com; 339 Saratoga Rd; ⏲10am-2am) Down an alleyway next to the Eggs 'n' Things diner, this grass-shack dive bar with a smoky patio is where beach bums knock back cheap microbrews in the middle of a sunny afternoon. Down a stiff 'TikiTea' while staring at the posters of half-nekkid hula pin-up girls.

Duke's Waikiki BAR
(www.dukeswaikiki.com; Outrigger Waikiki on the Beach, 2335 Kalakaua Ave; ⏲7am-midnight, live music usually 4-6pm Fri-Sun, 9:30pm-12am Fri & Sat) This is a raucous, surf-themed party scene mostly for baby boomers, with lots of drunken souvenir photo-taking and vacationland camaraderie. Sunday afternoon concerts by big-name Hawaiian musicians like Henry Kapono can't help but spill out onto the sand.

★**Gorilla in the Cafe** CAFE
(www.facebook.com/gorillahawaii; 2155 Kalakaua Ave; ⏲6:30am-10:30pm) Owned by Korean TV star Bae Yong Joon, this artisan coffee bar brews Waikiki's biggest selection of 100% Hawaii-grown beans from independent farms all around the islands. Handmade pourovers are worth the extra wait, or just grab a fast, hot espresso or creamy frozen coffee concoction blended with banana.

Island Vintage Coffee CAFE

(www.islandvintagecoffee.com; 2nd fl, Royal Hawaiian Center, 2301 Kalakaua Ave; ⏲6am-11pm) If you prefer your latte sweetened with Hawaiian honey, or an iced mocha tricked out with macadamia nuts and coconut drizzle, get in line behind all of the other tourists at this cutesy upstairs coffee shop, with open-air lanai table seating. Also at the Ala Moana Center mall.

LuLu's BAR

(www.luluswaikiki.com; 2nd fl, Park Shore Waikiki, 2586 Kalakaua Ave; ⏲7am-2am) Brush off your sandy feet at Kuhio Beach, then head over to this surf-themed bar and grill with lanai views of the ocean and Diamond Head. After happy hour, acoustic acts and local bands take over some nights. DJs crank up the beats after 10pm on weekends.

Five-O Bar & Lounge SPORTS BAR

(www.five-o-bar.com; 2nd fl, Bldg B, Royal Hawaiian Center, 2233 Kalakaua Ave; ⏲11am-2am) You won't spot any *Hawaii Five-0* stars hiding out at this shopping-mall bar, but you can still twirl the swizzle stick in your mai tai or belly up to the polished native-wood bar for *kalua* pork sliders and BBQ nachos during extended happy hours (11am to 6pm daily).

Diamond Head Cove Health Bar CAFE

(www.diamondheadcove.com; 3045 Monsarrat Ave; ⏲10am-8pm Mon & Sat, 9am-11pm Tue-Thu, 9am-8pm Fri, 10am-11pm Sun) Why rot your guts with the devil's brew when you can chill out with a coconut-husk bowl of *'awa* (kava, Polynesia's mildly intoxicating, mouth-numbing elixir made from the *Piper methysticum* plant)? Local musicians jam here some nights.

Genius Lounge LOUNGE

(www.geniusloungehawaii.com; 3rd fl, 346 Lewers St; ⏲6pm-2am) This glowing candle-lit hideaway is strictly for ultracool hipsters and lovebirds. East-West tapas bites let you nibble on squid tempura or deep-fried garlic as you sit back and sip imported Japanese sake, letting cutting-edge electronica and indie tunes spin.

☆ Entertainment

Hawaiian Music & Hula

All of the following showtimes are subject to change; call ahead to check. There's no cover charge (admission fee) for performance at resort hotel bars and restaurants, although you're expected to at least buy one drink once you sit down.

★ House Without a Key LIVE MUSIC, HULA

(☎923-2311; www.halekulani.com; Halekulani, 2199 Kalia Rd; ⏲7am-9pm, live music usually 5:30-8:30pm) Named after a 1925 Charlie Chan novel set in Honolulu, this genteel open-air oceanfront bar sprawled beneath a century-old kiawe tree simply has no doors to lock. A sophisticated crowd gathers for sunset cocktails, Pacific panoramas, live Hawaiian music and solo hula dancing by former Miss Hawaii beauty queens.

★ Kuhio Beach Hula Show LIVE MUSIC, HULA

(☎843-8002; www.honolulu.gov/moca; Kuhio Beach Park, off Kalakaua Ave; ⏲usually 6pm-7pm or 6:30pm-7:30pm Tue, Thu, Sat & Sun, weather permitting; 👪) FREE It all begins by the Duke Kahanamoku statue with the sounding of a conch shell and torch lighting after sunset. Then lay out your beach mat on the grassy hula mound for an authentic Hawaiian music and dance show. It's full of aloha, and afterward the amateur performers often hang around the stage to chat and pose for photos with tourists.

Mai Tai Bar LIVE MUSIC, HULA

(☎923-7311; www.royal-hawaiian.com; Royal Hawaiian, 2259 Kalakaua Ave; ⏲10am-midnight, live music usually 6-10pm Tue-Sun) At this low-key oceanfront bar (no preppy resort wear required), let yourself be mesmerized by Hawaiian musical duos and lithe hula dancers. Even if you don't dig who's playing that night, the signature Royal Mai Tai still packs a punch and romantic views of the breaking surf extend all the way down to Diamond Head.

Beach Bar LIVE MUSIC, HULA

(☎921-4600; www.moana-surfrider.com; Moana Surfrider, 2365 Kalakaua Ave; ⏲10:30am-midnight, live music usually 12:30-1:30pm & 6-9pm) Inside one of Waikiki's historical hotels, soak up the sounds of classical and contemporary Hawaiian musicians playing underneath the banyan tree where the mid-20th-century *Hawaii Calls* radio program was broadcast worldwide. Solo hula dancers usually perform from 6pm nightly.

Kani Ka Pila Grille LIVE MUSIC

(☎924-4990; www.outriggerreef.com; Outrigger Reef on the Beach, 2169 Kalia Rd; ⏲11am-10pm, live music usually 6-9pm) After happy hour ends, some of the island's best traditional and contemporary Hawaiian musicians play their hearts out and crack jokes here. On many Wednesday nights, slack key guitar master

GAY & LESBIAN WAIKIKI

Waikiki's LGBT community is tightly knit, but full of aloha for visitors. The free monthly magazine **Odyssey** (www.odysseyhawaii.com) covers the scene. It's available at the friendly, open-air **Hula's Bar & Lei Stand** (www.hulas.com; 2nd fl, Castle Waikiki Grand, 134 Kapahulu Ave; 10am-2am;), which has ocean views of Diamond Head. Stop by for drinks and to meet a variety of new faces, play pool and boogie. More svelte **Bacchus** (www.bacchus-waikiki.com; 2nd fl, 408 Lewers St; noon-2am) is an intimate wine bar and cocktail lounge with happy-hour specials, shirtless bartenders and Sunday afternoon beer busts. For nonstop singalongs, seek out **Wang Chung's** (http://wangchungs.com; 2410 Koa Ave; 5pm-2am), a living-room-sized karaoke bar.

Tiki-themed **Tapa's Restaurant & Lanai Bar** (www.tapaswaikiki.com; 407 Seaside Ave; 2pm-2am Mon-Fri, from 9am Sat & Sun) is a bigger chill-out spot with bear-y talkative bartenders, pool tables, a jukebox and karaoke nights. Around the corner, **Lo Jax Waikiki** (http://lojaxwaikiki.com; 2nd fl, 2256 Kuhio Ave; noon-2am;) is a gay sports bar with drag shows and weekend DJs. Next door **Fusion Waikiki** (www.fusionwaikiki.com; 2nd fl, 2260 Kuhio Ave; 10pm-4am) is a divey nightclub with weekend drag shows. Hidden up an alley a few blocks away, **In Between** (2155 Lau'ula St; noon-2am), a laid-back neighborhood bar, attracts an older crowd for 'the happiest of happy hours.'

By day, have fun in the sun at Queen's Surf Beach (p109) and (illegally clothing-optional) Diamond Head Beach (p128). At night, check into the gay-friendly Castle Waikiki Grand (p116) or Hotel Renew (p115).

Cyril Pahinui brings down the house. Grab a seat in the hotel lobby's lounge and eavesdrop for free.

Royal Grove LIVE MUSIC, HULA

(922-2299; www.royalhawaiiancenter.com; ground fl, Royal Hawaiian Center, 2201 Kalakaua Ave; schedules vary) FREE Inside a sprawling shopping mall, catch Hawaiian music and hula performances here almost every evening, as well as twice-weekly lunchtime shows by Polynesian Cultural Center performers and twice-monthly concerts by the Royal Hawaiian Band.

Tapa Bar LIVE MUSIC

(949-4321; www.hiltonhawaiianvillage.com; ground fl, Tapa Tower, Hilton Hawaiian Village, 2005 Kalia Rd; 10am-11pm, live music usually 7:30-10:30pm Mon-Thu, 8-11pm Fri & Sat, 5-10:30pm Sun) It's worth navigating through the gargantuan Hilton resort to this Polynesian-themed open-air bar on Friday and Saturday nights just to see Jerry Santos and Olomana, one of the top Hawaiian musical groups performing on O'ahu today.

Moana Terrace LIVE MUSIC

(922-6611; 2nd fl, Marriott Waikiki Beach Resort, 2552 Kalakaua Ave; 11am-11pm, live music usually 6:30-9:30pm;) Come for mellow sunset happy-hour drinks at this open-air poolside bar, just a lei's throw from Kuhio Beach. Slack key guitarists, ukulele players and falsetto singers make merry, with famous faces often on stage Thursday and Sunday nights.

Luau

'Aha 'Aina LUAU

(921-4600; www.royal-hawaiian.com/dining/ahaaina; Royal Hawaiian, 2259 Kalakaua Ave; adult/child 5-12yr from $175/97; 5:30-9:30pm Mon) Graciously set on the manicured oceanfront lawns of the historic Royal Hawaiian hotel, this sit-down dinner show is like a three-act musical play narrating the history of Hawaiian *mele* (songs) and hula dancing, starting from ancient times. Tickets are high-priced and top-notch food comes in small portions, but there's an open bar.

Waikiki Starlight Luau LUAU

(Map p80; 947-2607, 949-5828; www.hiltonhawaiianvillage.com/luau; Hilton Hawaiian Village, 2005 Kalia Rd; adult/child 4-11yr from $102/51; 5:15am-8pm Sun-Thu, weather permitting;) Rooftop luau offers an all-you-can-eat buffet-style dinner with just two complimentary mai tais. An enthusiastic, if not exactly authentic Polynesian show features fire dancing that's a crowd-pleaser, especially for families. Free validated parking.

Shopping

Catwalk designer boutiques surround the glitzy **DFS Galleria** (www.dfsgalleria.com/en/hawaii/; 330 Royal Hawaiian Ave; 9am-11pm).

Only-in-Hawaii brands such as Noa Noa and Honolua Surf Co line lower Lewers St, while upstart boutiques hide on streets off Kalakaua Ave and Kuhio Blvd. Ubiquitous **ABC Stores** (www.abcstores.com) are the place to pick up beach mats, sunblock, snacks and sundries, 'I got lei'd in Hawaii' T-shirts and motorized grass-skirted hula girls for the dashboard of your car.

★Bailey's Antiques & Aloha Shirts CLOTHING, ANTIQUES
(http://alohashirts.com; 517 Kapahulu Ave; ⏲10am-6pm) There's no place like Bailey's, which has without a doubt O'ahu's best collection of aloha shirts. Racks are crammed with thousands of collector-worthy vintage and reproduction shirts in every conceivable color and style, from 1920s kimono-silk classics to 1970s day-glo polyester specials. Among the new generation of shirts, Bailey's only carries Hawaii-made labels like Mamo and RJC.

Na Lima Mili Hulu No'eau LEI
(✆732-0865; 762 Kapahulu Ave; ⏲usually 9am-4pm Mon-Sat) The late Aunty Mary Louise Kaleonahenahe Kekuewa's daughter and granddaughter keep alive the ancient craft of feather lei-making at this small storefront, whose name means 'the skilled hands that touch the feathers.' It can take days to produce a single feather lei, prized by collectors. Call ahead to check opening hours or make an appointment for a personalized lesson.

Reyn Spooner CLOTHING
(www.reynspooner.com; Sheraton Waikiki, 2259 Kalakaua Ave; ⏲8am-10:30pm) Since 1956, Reyn Spooner's subtle reverse-print preppy aloha shirts have been the standard for Honolulu's power brokers and socialites. The Waikiki flagship store is a bright, mod and clean-lined store, carrying men's shirts and board shorts. Also at the Ala Moana Center and Kahala Mall. Ask about downtown **Reyn's Rack** to score discounts on factory seconds.

Royal Hawaiian Center MALL
(www.royalhawaiiancenter.com; 2201 Kalakaua Ave; ⏲10am-10pm) Not to be confused with the Royal Hawaiian resort next door, Waikiki's

ISLAND SOUNDS

You might be surprised to learn that some of Hawaii's leading local musicians play regular gigs at Waikiki's resort hotels and bars. Here are some stars to watch out for:

- **Jake Shimabukuro** The 'Jimi Hendrix of the uke' has been lured away from the islands by record companies, but sometimes plays live shows in his hometown, Honolulu.
- **Henry Kapono** Kapahulu-born singer-songwriter is O'ahu's renaissance man, putting out innovative Hawaiian rock albums since the 1970s.
- **Brothers Cazimero** O'ahu-born, Hawaiian heritage–conscious duo (12-string guitar and bass) played in Peter Moon's legendary Sunday Manoa band in the early '70s.
- **Jerry Santos and Olomana** Strumming traditional and contemporary Hawaiian tunes, these ukulele and guitar players from Windward O'ahu have been performing for decades.
- **Martin Pahinui** The son of late slack key master Gabby Pahinui is a gifted vocalist and often performs with guitarist George Kuo and former Royal Hawaiian Band leader Aaron Mahi.
- **Kapena** Founding member and band leader Kelly Boy De Lima is a ukulele star whose children have joined in to carry on the *ohana*'s musical legacy.
- **Keawe 'Ohana** Some say the granddaughter of the late great *ha'i* singer Genoa Keawe sounds just like Aunty Genoa in her younger days.
- **Sam Kapu III** Part of another musical dynasty, Sam Kapu performs traditional ukulele music and contemporary three-part harmonies with his trio.
- **Makana** O'ahu-born singer-songwriter who studied guitar with Sonny Chillingworth is a leading proponent of slack key world-fusion rock.
- **Natural Vibrations** 'Natty Vibes' is a fave among O'ahu's Jawaiian (island reggae) groups.

biggest shopping center sprawls across four levels and multiple buildings. Inside you'll find mostly name-brand international chains, but also a handful of Hawaii-born labels like Crazy Shirts and Dakine, Hawaiiana art galleries, island jewelry stores and lei stands.

Loco Boutique CLOTHING
(www.locoboutique.com; 2490 Kalakaua Ave; ⌚9am-11pm) Your old bikini from da mainland just doesn't measure? Fix the sitch quick by combing the racks of this Hawaii-born swimwear shop. Hundreds of mix-and-match bikinis, tankinis, board shorts, rash guards and rompers come in a rainbow of colors and retro, sexy and splashy styles. Also at the Ala Moana Center and Ward Warehouse malls.

Angels by the Sea CLOTHING
(http://angelsbytheseahawaii.com; Marriott Waikiki Beach Resort, 2552 Kalakaua Ave; ⌚8am-10pm) Hard to find inside a mega chain hotel, this airy boutique owned by a Vietnamese fashion designer (who was once crowned Ms Waikiki) is a gem for handmade beaded jewelry and hobo bags, effortlessly beautiful resort-style dresses, tunic tops and aloha shirts in tropical prints of silk and linen.

Muse WOMEN'S CLOTHING
(www.musebyrimo.com; 2310 Kuhio Ave; ⌚10am-11pm) Blousy, breezy feminine fashions are what's sewn by this LA designer, whose cotton-candy tissue tanks, lighter-than-air sundresses, flowing maxi-dresses, floppy hats and beaded sandals are a serious addiction for Tokyo jetsetters. Also in Kailua (p143).

International Market Place SOUVENIRS
(www.internationalmarketplacewaikiki.com; 2330 Kalakaua Ave; ⌚10am-9pm) At this kitschy outdoor market revolving around a gigantic banyan tree, more than 100 touristy stalls sell everything from plastic seashell necklaces to hibiscus-print sarongs, with live music or Polynesian dancing almost nightly. Step inside island-born **T&C Surf** for quality surfboards and apparel.

Bob's Ukulele MUSIC
(www.bobsukulele.com; Marriott Waikiki Beach Resort, 2552 Kalakaua Ave; ⌚9am-noon & 5-9pm) Avoid those cheap, flimsy imported ukuleles sold at so many Waikiki shopping malls. Instead let the knowledgeable staff here teach you about island-made ukes handcrafted from native woods, including by Honolulu's Kamaka Hawaii (p99) factory.

Newt at the Royal CLOTHING
(www.newtattheroyal.com; Royal Hawaiian, 2259 Kalakaua Ave; ⌚9am-9pm) With yesteryear Hollywood panache, Newt specializes in Montecristi Panama hats – classic men's fedoras, plantation-style hats and women's high-quality *fino* toppers. Everything's neat as a pin and top-drawer quality.

Orientation

Technically, Waikiki is a district of the city of Honolulu. It's bounded on two sides by Ala Wai Canal, on another by the ocean and on the fourth by Kapi'olani Park. Three parallel roads cross Waikiki: one-way Kalakaua Ave alongside the beach; Kuhio Ave, the main drag inland for pedestrians and buses; and Ala Wai Blvd, which borders Ala Wai Canal.

Information

DANGERS & ANNOYANCES

Never leave your valuables unattended on the beach. At night, it can be risky to stroll along the beach or Ala Wai Canal, whether alone or in groups. After dark on Kuhio Ave, prostitutes aggressively solicit male tourists, while drunk male tourists sometimes harass women passersby.

Day or night, you won't be able to walk down Kalakaua Ave without encountering timeshare salespeople, often sitting behind the desk of a so-called 'activity center' advertising free luau, sunset cruises or $10-per-day car rentals. Caveat emptor.

EMERGENCY

Waikiki Police Substation (☎723-8562; www.honolulupd.org; 2405 Kalakaua Ave; ⌚24hr) If you need help, or just friendly directions, at Kuhio Beach Park.

INTERNET ACCESS & TELEPHONE

Most hotels offer wired high-speed connections in guest rooms, but only limited wi-fi in the lobby and pool areas (daily surcharges of $10 or more may apply). Free wi-fi is available at a few coffee shops, restaurants and bars.

Da Kine Cellular & Da Internet Cafe (http://dakinecellular.com; 2463 Kuhio Ave; wi-fi/internet terminal per hr $5/8; ⌚9am-10pm; wi-fi) Pay-as-you-go internet terminals and wi-fi, and cell (mobile) phone and SIM card sales, next door to a coin-op laundromat.

Hula's Bar & Lei Stand (www.hulas.com; 2nd fl, Waikiki Grand, 134 Kapahulu Ave; ⌚10am-2am; wi-fi) Free wi-fi and two internet terminals inside a gay-oriented bar.

ING Direct Café (http://cafes.ingdirect.com/honolulu/; 1958 Kalakaua Ave; ⏲8am-7pm Mon-Fri, to 4pm Sat;)

Cheap coffee, air-con and free wi-fi and internet computer terminals.

Waikiki Beachside Hostel Internet Café (www.waikikibeachsidehostel.com; 2556 Lemon Rd; internet terminal per hr $7; ⏲24hr;) Pay-as-you-go internet terminals available to nonguests as well.

MEDICAL SERVICES

Find all-night pharmacies and 24-hour hospital emergency rooms in Honolulu (p101).

Doctors on Call (www.straubhealth.org) North Waikiki (☎973-5250; www.straubhealth.org; 2nd fl, Rainbow Bazaar, Hilton Hawaiian Village, 2005 Kalia Rd; ⏲8am-4:30pm Mon-Fri); South Waikiki (☎971-6000; www.straubhealth.org; ground fl, Sheraton Princess Kaiulani, 120 Ka'iulani Ave; ⏲24hr) Nonemergency walk-in clinics accept some travel health-insurance policies.

MONEY

There are 24-hour ATMs all over Waikiki, including at these full-service banks:

Bank of Hawaii (www.boh.com; 2155 Kalakaua Ave; ⏲8:30am-4pm Mon-Thu, 8:30am-6pm Fri, 9am-1pm Sat) International banking and currency exchange on the 3rd floor.

First Hawaiian Bank (www.fhb.com; 2181 Kalakaua Ave; ⏲8:30am-4pm Mon-Thu, to 6pm Fri) Lobby displays Hawaii history murals by French artist Jean Charlot.

POST

Post Office (☎800-275-8777; www.usps.com; 330 Saratoga Rd; ⏲9am-4:30pm Mon-Fri, to 1pm Sat)

TOURIST INFORMATION

Freebie tourist magazines containing discount coupons such as *This Week O'ahu* and *101 Things to Do* can be found in street-corner boxes, in hotel lobbies and at Honolulu's airport.

Hawaii Visitors & Convention Bureau (HVCB; ☎800-464-2924, 923-1811; www.gohawaii.com; suite 801, Waikiki Business Plaza, 2270 Kalakaua Ave; ⏲8am-4:30pm Mon-Fri) Business office hands out the same free visitor maps and brochures you can get more easily at the airport.

ℹ Getting There & Around

For ground transportation to/from Honolulu International Airport, see p66.

BICYCLE

Several shops in Waikiki rent beach cruisers or commuter bikes from about $20 per day, with discounts for multiday or weekly rentals. For top-quality road and mountain-bike rentals, call Honolulu's Bike Shop (p87).

BUS

Several TheBus (p67) routes run frequently through Waikiki, with most stops along Kuhio Ave. Just outside Waikiki, the Ala Moana Center mall is O'ahu's central bus transfer point.

CAR

Several international car-rental agencies have branch offices in Waikiki, but rates are usually higher than at the airport. For eco-friendly car rentals, consider the following:

808 Smart Car Rentals (☎735-5000; http://smartcartours.com; 444 Niu St) At the Hawaiian Monarch Hotel, small, fuel-efficient and convertible smart cars are easy to park and can be driven islandwide.

Green Car Hawaii (☎877-664-2748; www.greencarhawaii.com) Book ahead online for hourly and daily car-sharing rentals of hybrid sedans and SUVs. Check in at self-serve smartphone locations or partner hotels' valet parking desks.

Parking

Most hotels charge $20 to $35 per night for valet or self-parking. The **Waikiki Trade Center Parking Garage** (2255 Kuhio Ave, enter off Seaside Ave) and next-door **Waikiki Parking Garage** (333 Seaside Ave) offer competitively priced hourly and flat-fee early bird, day, evening and overnight rates. At the far edge of Waikiki, there's a free parking lot along Monsarrat Ave beside Kapi'olani Park with no time limit, while Waikiki's cheapest metered lot (25¢ per hour, four-hour limit) is off Kapahulu Ave by the zoo; neither of these public lots is particularly safe for rental cars.

MOPED & MOTORCYCLE

Mopeds may seem like a great way of getting around Waikiki, but they can be more expensive to rent than a car. Drivers should have previous experience navigating urban traffic. Independent agencies renting mopeds and motorcycles are scattered all around Waikiki.

TAXI

Taxi stands are found at resort hotels and shopping malls. For islandwide taxi service, call TheCab (p101).

TROLLEY

The motorized **Waikiki Trolley** (☎593-2822; www.waikikitrolley.com; adult/child 4-11yr 4-day pass $52/20, 7-day pass $58/22) runs three color-coded lines that connect Waikiki with the Ala Moana Center and downtown Honolulu. These services don't offer much in the way of value compared with TheBus, however. Purchase passes at the **DFS Galleria Waikiki Trolley Stop & Ticket Booth** (www.waikikitrolley.

com; 330 Royal Hawaiian Ave) or the **Royal Hawaiian Center Trolley Stop & Ticket Booth** (www.waikikitrolley.com; 2201 Kalakaua Ave), or buy online for less.

DIAMOND HEAD & SOUTHEAST COAST

Cue the *Hawaii Five-0* music and pretend to be a movie star as you cruise past the glamorous suburbs of Kahala and Hawai'i Kai. The Kalaniana'ole Hwy (Hwy 72) becomes a slow-and-go coastal drive that swells and dips like the sea itself as it rounds ancient volcanic Koko Head. The snorkeling hot spot of Hanauma Bay, hiking trails to the top of Diamond Head and windy Makapu'u Point, and O'ahu's most famous bodysurfing beaches are all just a short bus ride or drive from Waikiki. Save time for hidden delights like Shangri La, billionaire Doris Duke's former mansion, now a trove of Islamic art.

Diamond Head & Kahala

A massive backdrop to Waikiki and the wealthy Kahala neighborhood, Diamond Head is O'ahu's best-known landmark, sitting alongside off-the-beaten-path surfy beaches.

Beaches

From Waikiki, TheBus 22 (no service Tuesday) runs by these beaches once or twice hourly.

Kuilei Cliffs Beach Park BEACH
(3450 Diamond Head Rd) In the shadow of Diamond Head, this rocky beach draws experienced windsurfers when the tradewinds are blowing. Surfers take over the waves when the swells are up. The little public beach park has outdoor showers, but no other facilities. Park in the paved lots off Diamond Head Rd, just east of the lighthouse, then follow the paved footpath down to the beach.

Diamond Head Beach Park BEACH
(3300 Diamond Head Rd) Bordering the lighthouse, this rocky beach draws surfers, snorkelers and tide-poolers, plus a few picnickers. The narrow strand north of the lighthouse is popular with gay men, who pull off Diamond Head Rd onto dead-end Beach Rd, then walk along the shore to find a little seclusion and (illegally) sunbathe au naturel.

Wai'alae Beach Park BEACH
In between Kahala's multimillion-dollar mansions, a half-dozen shoreline access points provide public rights-of-way to the beach, but the swimming ain't grand – it's mostly shallow, with sparse pockets of sand. One picturesque exception is the beach near Kahala's resort. Here you'll find a sandy strand where Wai'alae Stream flows into the sea toward a shallow offshore reef.

Sights & Activities

★ **Diamond Head State Monument** HIKING
(www.hawaiistateparks.org; off Diamond Head Rd btwn Makapu'u & 18th Aves; admission per pedestrian/car $1/5; 6am-6pm, last trail entry 4:30pm;) The historic trail to the summit of Diamond Head, a volcanic tuff cone, was built in 1908 to service military observation stations along the crater rim. Although it's a fairly steep 0.8-mile hike to the top, the trail is fully paved and plenty of people of all ages make it. The return trip takes about an hour.

The trail, which passes through several tunnels and up dizzying staircases, is mostly open and hot, so bring plenty of water and wear a hat and sunscreen. The windy summit affords fantastic 360-degree views of the southeast coast to Koko Head and west to the Wai'anae Range. A lighthouse, coral reefs and surfers waiting to catch a wave are visible below.

From Waikiki, take TheBus 23 or 24, which run once or twice hourly; from the closest bus stop, it's a 20-minute walk to the trailhead. By car, take Monsarrat Ave to Diamond Head Rd and turn right immediately after passing Kapi'olani Community College.

★ **Shangri La** HISTORIC BUILDING
(532-3853; www.shangrilahawaii.org; 2½hr tour incl transportation $25; tours usually 9am, 10:30am & 1:30pm Wed-Sat, closed early Sep-early Oct) Once called 'the richest little girl in the world,' heiress Doris Duke (1912–93) had a lifelong passion for Islamic art and architecture that was first inspired by a visit to the Taj Mahal during her honeymoon voyage to India in 1935. You can only visit her former estate on a guided tour departing from downtown's Honolulu Museum of Art (p78).

During her honeymoon, Doris stopped on O'ahu, fell in love with the island and decided to build a private seasonal residence on Black Point. She made Shangri La into an intimate sanctuary rather than an ostentatious mansion. Over the next six decades,

Southeast Coast

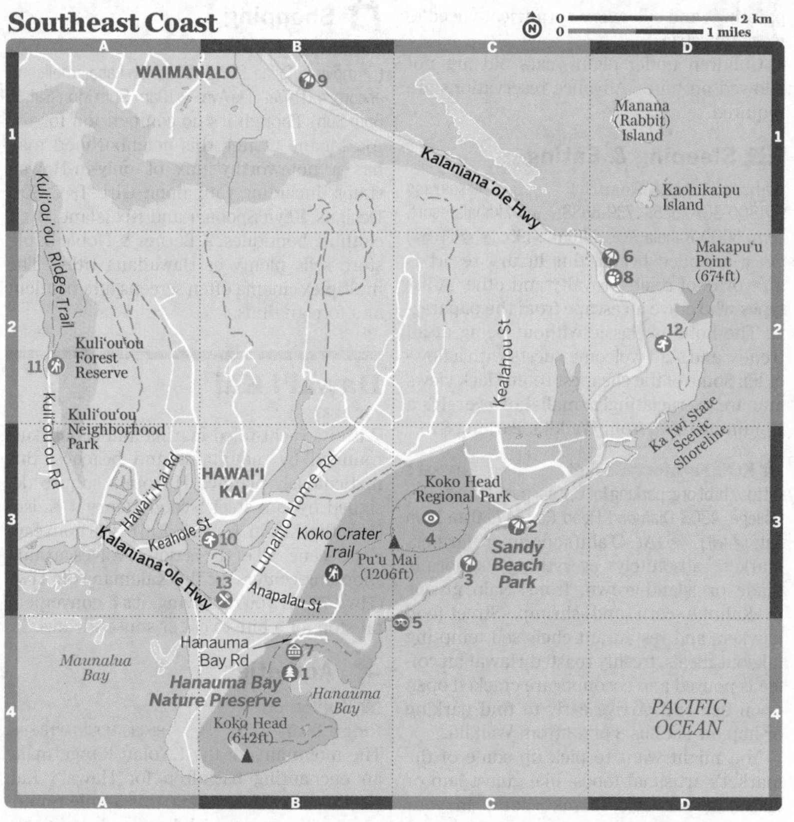

Southeast Coast

Top Sights
1 Hanauma Bay Nature Preserve........... B4
2 Sandy Beach Park C3

Sights
Halona Blowhole ....(see 3)
3 Halona Cove C3
4 Koko Crater Botanical Garden............ C3
5 Lana'i Lookout........................... C4
6 Makapu'u Beach Park D2
7 Marine Educational Center................ B4
8 Sea Life Park............................ D2
9 Waimanalo Beach Park.................... B1

Activities, Courses & Tours
10 H_2O Sports Hawaii B3
Island Divers............................ (see 10)
11 Kuli'ou'ou Ridge Trail.....................A2
12 Makapu'u Point Lighthouse Trail D2

Eating
Bubbie's..................................(see 13)
Kale's Natural Foods..................... (see 10)
13 Kona Brewing Company......................B3
Moena Cafe ....(see 13)

Drinking & Nightlife
Island Brew Coffeehouse .... (see 10)

she traveled the globe from Indonesia to Istanbul, collecting priceless Islamic art and shipping it back to Hawaii.

One of the true beauties of Shangri La is its harmony with the natural environment. Finely crafted interiors open to embrace gardens and fountain courtyards. Artworks blend with architecture to represent a theme or region, like in the restored interior of an 18th-century Syrian merchant's house. Duke's extensive art collections also include gemstone-studded enamels, glazed ceramic paintings and silk *suzanis* (intricate needlework tapestries).

Children under eight years old are not allowed on tours. Advance reservations are required.

Sleeping & Eating

Kahala Hotel & Resort RESORT $$$

(800-367-2525, 739-8888; www.kahalaresort.com; 5000 Kahala Ave; r from $495;) On a secluded beach, this luxury resort is a favorite of celebs, royalty and other A-list types who crave an escape from the paparazzi. The hotel is classic without being at all trendy, and staff welcome guests with a flower lei. Some of the cheapest rooms lack views and are excruciatingly small, however. It's a 15-minute drive from Waikiki. Parking $25.

★KCC Farmers Market MARKET $

(http://hfbf.org; parking lot C, Kapi'olani Community College, 4303 Diamond Head Rd; 7:30am-11am Sat;) At O'ahu's premier farmers market, absolutely everything is locally made or island-grown, from 'Nalo greens to Kahuku corn and shrimp. Street-food hawkers and restaurant chefs sell tempting takeout meals, freshly roasted Hawaiian coffee is poured and coconuts are cracked open upon demand. Arrive early to find parking or hop on TheBus 3 or 23 from Waikiki.

You might want to pick up some of the market's artisanal foods, like guava jam or Hawaiian sea salt, to take home in your suitcase.

Whole Foods SUPERMARKET $

(http://wholefoodsmarket.com; Kahala Mall, 4211 Wai'alae Ave; 7am-10pm;) This natural-foods grocery store stocks organic and Hawaiian produce and is handy for takeout meals from the vegetarian-friendly deli and hot-and-cold salad bar.

Hoku's PACIFIC RIM $$$

(739-8760; www.kahalaresort.com; Kahala Hotel & Resort, 5000 Kahala Ave; Sun brunch adult/child 6-12yr $65/33, dinner mains $30-65; 10am-2pm Sun, 5:30-10pm Wed-Sun) Executive chef Wayne Hirabayashi's elegant East–West creations, such as braised short ribs with avocado tempura and wok-fried whole fish, pair exquisitely with a world-ranging wine list. The oceanfront Sunday brunch buffet stars all-you-can-eat king crab legs and a chocolate dessert fountain. Make reservations and inquire about the dress code.

Kahala Mall MALL

(movie infoline 593-3000; www.kahalamallcenter.com; 4211 Wai'alae Ave; 10am-9pm Mon-Sat, to 6pm Sun) Though it's no competition for the Ala Moana Center, this neighborhood mall has a noteworthy mix of only-in-Hawaii shops, including Cinnamon Girl, T&C Surf Designs, Reyn Spooner and Rix Island Wear clothing boutiques. A Barnes & Noble bookstore sells plenty of Hawaiiana titles. The multiplex cinema often screens independent and foreign films.

Hawai'i Kai

POP 29,875

With its yacht-filled marina and canals surrounded by mountains and beaches, this meticulously planned Honolulu suburb designed by late steel tycoon Henry J Kaiser (he's the Kai in Hawai'i Kai) is a nouveau-riche scene. All of the action revolves around shopping centers off the Kalaniana'ole Hwy (Hwy 72). If you're driving, it's a convenient pit stop for a bite to eat or sunset drinks.

Activities

★Kuli'ou'ou Ridge Trail HIKING, MOUNTAIN BIKING

The mountains of the Ko'olau Range make an enchanting backdrop for Hawai'i Kai. Northwest of the marina, this 5-mile round-trip trail is open to hikers and mountain bikers. After winding upward on forested switchbacks, you'll make a stiff but satisfying ascent along a ridgeline to a windy summit for heart-stopping 360-degree views.

From the summit, you can spy Koko Head, Makapu'u Point, the Windward Coast, Diamond Head and Honolulu. The trail, which may be partly overgrown with vegetation, starts from the brown-and-yellow Na Ala Hele trailhead sign at the end of Kala'au Pl, which branches right off Kuli'ou'ou Rd, about a mile *mauka* (inland) from the Kalaniana'ole Hwy (Hwy 72).

H_2O Sports Hawaii WATER SPORTS

(396-0100; www.2osportshawaii.com; Hawai'i Kai Shopping Center, 377 Keahole St) The marina is flush with tour operators and water-sports outfitters that can hook you up with jet packs, water skis, banana boats, bumper tubes, parasailing trips, wakeboarding, scuba dives, speed sailing – whatever gets your adrenaline pumping. Just be prepared to pay plenty; check online for advance booking discounts.

Island Divers DIVING, SNORKELING
(www.oahuscubadiving.com; Hawai'i Kai Shopping Center, 377 Keahole St) Friendly, five-star PADI operation offers boat dives ($85 to $175 per person) for all skill levels, including expert-level wreck dives. If you're a novice, staff can show you the ropes and take you to calm, relatively shallow waters. Snorkelers can ride along on dive boats for $40 each, including snorkel-gear rental.

Eating & Drinking

Kale's Natural Foods SUPERMARKET $
(www.kalesnaturalfoods.com; Hawai'i Kai Shopping Center, 377 Keahole St; mains $6-11; ⏲8am-8pm Mon-Fri, to 5pm Sat & Sun;) Near a Safeway supermarket, this healthy-minded grocery store has a takeout deli-cafe with a smoothie bar.

Bubbie's ICE CREAM $
(www.bubbiesicecream.com; Koko Marina Center, 7192 Kalaniana'ole Hwy; items $2-6; ⏲10am-11pm Sun-Thu, to midnight Fri & Sat;) Tropically flavored and *mochi* ice cream across from a Foodland supermarket.

Kona Brewing Company PUB $$
(☎396-5662; www.konabrewingco.com; Koko Marina Center, 7192 Kalaniana'ole Hwy; mains $12-28; ⏲11am-10pm;) With tiki torches overhanging the marina, this Big Island import is known for its microbrewed beers, especially Longboard Lager and Castaway IPA. Live Hawaiian music some nights that occasionally brings out big-name musicians like Led Ka'apana. Island-style *pupu*, wood-fired pizzas, seafood, burgers and salads are filling but forgettable.

Moena Cafe CAFE $$
(☎888-7716; www.moenacafe.com; Koko Marina Center, 7192 Kalaniana'ole Hwy; mains $8-13; ⏲6:30am-3pm) Farm-fresh salads, grilled panini and all-day breakfasts of crepes, crab eggs Benedict and short-rib *loco moco* bring hungry crowds of locals back to this simple storefront kitchen. Service is not exceptionally fast, but it's almost always worth the wait for a table just to taste this chef's island-style recipes.

Island Brew Coffeehouse CAFE
(www.islandbrewhawaii.com; Hawai'i Kai Shopping Center, 377 Keahole St; ⏲6am-6pm Mon-Fri, 7am-6pm Sat & Sun) With umbrella-shaded tables gazing out at the marina, this unhurried hangout individually brews cups of Hawaii-grown coffee – try richly roasted 100% Kona, Ka'u or Maui Mokka. Thai ice tea, espresso drinks, baked goodies and acai fruit bowls will also refuel you.

Hanauma Bay Nature Preserve

A swirling palette of sapphire and turquoise hues mix together in modern-art abstractions inside the bowl-shaped bay, ringed by the remnants of an eroded volcano. Just below the sparkling surface are coral reefs, some of which may be 7000 years old. You'll see schools of glittering silver fish, bright blue flashes of parrotfish and perhaps sea turtles so used to snorkelers that they'll go eyeball to face mask with you. Despite its protected status as a marine-life conservation district since 1967, this beloved **nature preserve** (☎396-4229; www.honolulu.gov/parks/facility/hanaumabay; Hanauma Bay Rd, off Hwy 72 (Kalaniana'ole Highway); adult/child under 13yr $7.50/free; ⏲6am-6pm Wed-Mon Nov-Mar, to 7pm Wed-Mon Apr-Oct;) is still a threatened ecosystem, constantly in danger of being loved to death – an average of 3000 people hit the beach each day.

Sights & Activities

Past the ticket windows at the park entrance is the award-winning **Marine Educational Center** (http://hbep.seagrant.soest.hawaii.edu/; 100 Hanauma Bay Rd;) run by the University of Hawai'i. The interactive, family-friendly displays teach visitors about the unique geology and ecology of the bay. Everyone should watch the 12-minute video, intended to stagger the crowds and inform you about environmental precautions before snorkeling. Down below at beach level you'll find snorkel-gear rental concessions, lockers, lifeguards and restrooms.

The bay is well protected from the vast ocean by various reefs and the inlet's natural curve, making conditions favorable for **snorkeling** year-round. The fringing reef closest to shore has a large, sandy opening known as the **Keyhole Lagoon**, which is the best place for novice snorkelers. The deepest water is 10ft, though it's very shallow over the coral. The Keyhole is well protected and usually very calm. Because most visitors are beginners, this is also the most crowded part of the bay later in the day and visibility can be poor as a result. Be careful not to step on the coral or to accidentally knock it with your fins. Feeding the fish is strictly prohibited.

For confident snorkelers and strong swimmers, it's better on the outside of the reef, where there are large coral heads, bigger fish and fewer people. To get there follow the directions on the sign board or ask the lifeguard at the southern end of the beach. There are two channels on either side of the bay that experience very strong currents. Don't attempt to swim outside the reef when the water is rough or choppy. Not only could the currents sweep you away, but the sand will be stirred up and visibility poor.

For **scuba diving**, you'll have the whole bay to play in, with crystal-clear water, coral gardens and sea turtles. Beware of currents when the surf's up, especially those surges near the shark-infested **Witches' Brew**, on the bay's right-hand side, and the humorously nicknamed **Moloka'i Express**, a treacherous current on the left-hand side of the bay's mouth.

Information

Hanauma Bay Nature Preserve is operated by the county of Honolulu. To beat the crowds, especially during peak summer season, arrive as soon as the park opens. Mondays and Wednesdays tend to be busier, because the park is closed Tuesdays.

All built park facilities are wheelchair-accessible. Beach wheelchairs for visitors with mobility issues are available free of charge from the information kiosk between 8am and 4pm on a first-come, first-served basis.

Getting There & Away

Hanauma Bay is 10 miles east of Waikiki along the Kalaniana'ole Hwy (Hwy 72). The parking lot sometimes fills by mid-morning, after which all drivers will be turned away, so the earlier you get there the better. Parking costs $1.

From Waikiki, TheBus 22 (nicknamed the 'Beach Bus') runs twice hourly to Hanauma Bay, except on Tuesdays, when the park is closed; the one-way trip takes about 45 minutes. Buses leave Waikiki between 8am and 4pm (until 4:45pm on Saturday, Sunday and holidays); the corner of Kuhio Ave and Namahana St is the first stop, and buses can fill up shortly thereafter. Buses back to Waikiki leave Hanauma Bay between 11am and 5:25pm (until 5:55pm on weekends and holidays).

Koko Head Regional Park

With mountains on one side and a sea edged by bays and beaches on the other, the drive along this coast rates among O'ahu's best. The highway rises and falls as it winds its way round the eastern tip of the Ko'olau Range, looking down on stratified rocks, lava sea cliffs and other fascinating geological formations. At last, you've left the city behind.

Beaches

Halona Cove — BEACH

This gem-like beach is where the steamy love scene with Burt Lancaster and Deborah Kerr in *From Here to Eternity* (1953) was filmed. There's no lifeguard on duty, and when the surf's up, this beach really earns its nickname 'Pounders' – so never turn your back on the sea. With strong offshore currents, it's best to stay out of the water.

To reach the cove, carefully scramble down the faint path from the south side of the Halona Blowhole parking lot.

★Sandy Beach Park — BEACH

(8800 Kalaniana'ole Hwy) Here the ocean heaves and thrashes like a furious beast. This is one of O'ahu's most dangerous beaches, with a punishing shorebreak, powerful backwash and strong rip currents. Expert bodysurfers spend hours trying to mount the skull-crushing waves, as crowds gather to watch the daredevils being tossed around. When the swells are big, bodyboarders hit the beach's multiple breaks.

Sandy Beach is wide, very long and, yes, sandy, but this is no place to frolic. Dozens of people are injured every year, some with just broken arms and dislocated shoulders, but others with serious spinal injuries. Red flags flown on the beach indicate hazardous water conditions. Even if you don't see flags, always check with the lifeguards before entering the water.

Not all the action is in the water. The grassy strip on the inland side of the parking lot is used by people looking skyward for their thrills – it's both a hang glider landing site and a popular place for flying kites. On weekends, you can usually find a food truck selling plate lunches and drinks in the parking lot. The park has picnic tables, restrooms, outdoor showers and sparse shade trees. Smoking is now banned at this park.

From Waikiki, TheBus 22 stops here twice hourly (no service Tuesday); the trip takes about an hour.

Sights & Activities

Lana'i Lookout LOOKOUT

FREE Less than a mile east of Hanauma Bay, a **roadside lookout** offers a panorama on clear days of several Hawaiian islands: Lana'i to the right, Maui in the middle and Moloka'i to the left. About 0.5 miles further east, at the highest point on a sea cliff known as Bamboo Ridge, look for a little **fishing shrine**.

The temple-like mound of rocks surrounds a statue of Jizō, a Japanese Buddhist deity and guardian of fishers. The statue is often decked in flower lei and surrounded by sake cups. There's a little roadside pull-off in front of the shrine.

Halona Blowhole LOOKOUT

FREE Just follow all of the tour buses to find this famous blowhole. Here ocean waves surge through a submerged tunnel in the rock and spout up through a hole in the ledge. Ignore the temptation to disregard the warning signs and walk down toward the blowhole, as several people have been fatally swept off the ledge by rogue waves.

The action depends on water conditions – sometimes the blowhole is barely discernible, while at other times it's a showstopper. Before it goes off, you'll hear a gushing sound of air being forced out by the rushing tidal waters.

Koko Crater Botanical Garden GARDENS

(www1.honolulu.gov/parks/hbg/kcbg.htm; end of Kokonani St; ⏲ sunrise-sunset, closed Dec 25 & Jan 1) FREE According to Hawaiian legend, Koko Crater is the imprint left by the magical flying vagina (yes, really) of Kapo, sent from the Big Island to lure the pig-god Kamapua'a away from her sister Pele, goddess of fire and volcanoes. Today inside this volcanic tuff cone is a quiet botanical garden planted with aloes, cacti and other exotic and native dryland species.

You'll probably have the interconnecting loop trails to yourself. To get here, turn inland off the Kalaniana'ole Hwy (Hwy 72) onto Kealahou St, opposite Sandy Beach. After around 0.5 miles, turn left onto Kokonani St, then continue on a rough, unpaved road past the equestrian center. From Waikiki, TheBus 23 stops once or twice hourly near the corner of Kealahou St and Kalohelani St, just over 0.3 miles from the garden entrance.

Makapu'u Point

Makapu'u Point and its coastal lighthouse mark O'ahu's easternmost tip. On the north side of the point, a scenic roadside lookout gazes down at aqua waters bordered by white sand and black lava beds. Offshore is **Manana Island**, an aging volcanic crater once populated by feral rabbits that now harbors burrowing wedge-tailed shearwaters. Curiously, it somewhat resembles the head of a rabbit, ears folded back. In front is smaller, flat **Kaohikaipu Island**, another seabird sanctuary.

TheBus 22 (no service Tuesday) and 23 from Waikiki via Hawai'i Kai and TheBus 57 from Kailua and Waimanalo all stop at Makapu'u Beach and Sea Life Park, but not at the lighthouse trailhead.

THE BATTLE OF NU'UANU

O'ahu was the linchpin conquered by Kamehameha the Great in his campaign to unite the Hawaiian Islands under his rule. In 1795, on the rural beaches of Waikiki, Kamehameha landed his fleet of canoes to battle Kalanikupule, the *mo'i* (king) of O'ahu.

Heavy fighting started around Puowaina ('Hill of Sacrifice,' now nicknamed Punchbowl), and continued up Nu'uanu Valley. But O'ahu's spear-and-stone warriors were no match for Kamehameha's troops, which included a few Western sharpshooters.

O'ahu's defenders made their last stand at the narrow ledge near the current-day Nu'uanu Pali Lookout. Hundreds were driven over the top to their deaths. A century later, during the construction of the Old Pali Hwy, more than 500 skulls were found at the base of the cliffs.

Some O'ahu warriors, including their king, escaped into the forest. When Kalanikupule surfaced a few months later, he was sacrificed by Kamehameha to the war god Ku. Kamehameha's taking of O'ahu was the last battle ever fought between Hawaiian warriors.

Beaches

Makapu'u Beach Park BEACH

(41-095 Kalaniana'ole Hwy) Opposite Sea Life Park, this is one of O'ahu's top winter bodyboarding and bodysurfing spots, with waves reaching 12ft and higher. Like Sandy Beach, it's strictly the domain of experts who can handle rough water and dangerous currents. In summer, when the waves disappear, calm waters may allow swimming. The beach park has restrooms, outdoor showers, drinking water and lifeguards.

Sights & Activities

★Makapu'u Point Lighthouse Trail HIKING

(www.hawaiistateparks.org; off Makapu'u Lighthouse Rd; 7am-7:45pm Apr-1st Mon in Sep, 7am-6:45pm 1st Tue in Sep-Mar) South of the lookout, the mile-long service road up to a red-roofed lighthouse (no public entry) is closed to private vehicles, but you can park in the paved lot and hike in. Although not difficult, it's a steady uphill walk and conditions can be hot and very windy. Spectacular coastal views await – in winter, you might spot migratory whales offshore.

Avoid the temptation to climb down the rocks to the lighthouse, as that's illegally trespassing on federal property. The ligthhouse trail is now part of the **Ka Iwi State Scenic Shoreline**. Starting near the trailhead parking lot, newer dirt paths roll downhill to the ocean, where you'll find pocket beaches for swimming, sunbathing and snorkeling.

Sea Life Park THEME PARK

(259-2500; www.sealifeparkhawaii.com; 41-202 Kalaniana'ole Hwy; adult/child 3-11yr $30/20, parking $5; 10:30am-5pm;) More like a circus than an aquarium, Hawaii's only marine park offers a mixed bag of run-down attractions that, frankly, aren't worth your time. The park's 300,000-gallon aquarium is filled mostly with marine animals not found in Hawaiian waters. Theme-park entertainment includes choreographed animal shows and pool encounters with imported Atlantic bottlenose dolphins, a controversial activity (see p634).

There's also a penguin habitat, a turtle lagoon and a seabird 'sanctuary' with native *'iwa* (great frigate bird). The park works to rehabilitate some injured seabirds and also maintains a breeding colony of green sea turtles, releasing young hatchlings back into the wild.

WINDWARD COAST & KAILUA

On O'ahu's most verdant coast, *pali* (cliffs) are shrouded in mist as often as they are bathed in glorious sunshine. Tropical showers guarantee that everything glistens with a hundred shades of green, all dazzlingly set against the Windward Coast's turquoise bays and white-sand beaches. Repeat visitors to O'ahu often make this side of the island their adventure base camp, whether they've come to kayak, windsurf, snorkel, dive or just laze on the sand.

Enticing beaches are found here, especially around Waimanalo and Kailua, but many shoreline spots further north along the coast are too silted to be much more than a snapshot. Once you've left behind the suburbs of Kailua and Kane'ohe, the rest of the Windward Coast is surprisingly rural, dotted with family farms and taro patches. The Kamehameha Hwy narrows to a modest two-lane road running the length of the entire coast, doubling as Main St for small towns along the way.

Pali Highway

Slicing through the emerald Ko'olau Range, the Pali Hwy (Hwy 61) soars and winds between Honolulu and Kailua. If it has been raining heavily, seemingly every fold and crevice in the jagged *pali* will have a fairyland waterfall streaming down into the valley. An ancient Hawaiian footpath once wound its way perilously over these cliffs; in 1845, the path was widened into a horse trail and later into a cobblestone carriage road. The modern highway wasn't completed until 1962.

Sights & Activities

★Nu'uanu Pali State Wayside LOOKOUT

(www.hawaiistateparks.org; Pali Hwy [Hwy 61]; parking per vehicle $3; sunrise-sunset) Don't miss this ridge-top park's sweeping vistas of windward O'ahu from a height of 1200ft. From the signposted lookout you can see Kane'ohe straight ahead, Kailua to the right, and Mokoli'i Island and the coastal fishpond at Kualoa to the far left. The funneling winds are so strong you can lean against them, and it's often cool enough to warrant a jacket.

A pedestrian-only section of the Old Pali Hwy winds down from the right of the lookout, ending abruptly at a barrier near the current highway about a mile away. Few people realize the road is here, let alone venture down it. It's worth walking just five minutes down the paved path for a photo op with magnificent views looking back up at the snaggle-toothed Ko'olau Range and out across the broad valley.

As you get back on the highway, it's easy to miss the signs near the parking lot exit, and instinct could send you in the wrong direction. Go left toward Kailua or right toward Honolulu. Several TheBus routes travel the Pali Hwy, but none stop at the lookout.

Maunawili Falls Trail HIKING
(http://hawaiitrails.ehawaii.gov) Reaching a small waterfall alongside a muddy, mosquito-infested stream, the 2.5-mile round-trip Maunawili Falls Trail is a family-friendly hike that ascends and descends flights of wooden stairs and crosses Maunawili Stream several times. This trail connects with the 10-mile **Maunawili Trail**, which gently contours around ridges and valleys in the Ko'olau Range between the Pali Hwy and Waimanalo town.

To reach the main Maunawili Falls trailhead, drive over the Pali Hwy from Honolulu, then take the *second* right-hand exit onto A'uloa Rd. At the first fork veer left onto Maunawili Rd, which ends in a residential subdivision. Look for a gated trailhead-access road on the left; nonresidents may not drive or park along this road. Instead, park along nearby residential streets that aren't gated. Respect local residents by not loitering or being noisy while walking along the road.

Waimanalo

POP 5450

The proudly Hawaiian community of Waimanalo sprawls alongside O'ahu's longest beach, where the white sands stretch for miles, within view of offshore islands and a coral reef that keeps breaking waves at a comfortable distance. Small hillside farms in 'Nalo, as it's often called, grow many of the fresh leafy greens served in Honolulu's top restaurants.

Beaches

As elsewhere at O'ahu's beaches, don't leave any valuables in your car to avoid break-ins and theft.

★ **Waimanalo Bay Beach Park** BEACH
(41-043 Aloiloi St, off Kalaniana'ole Hwy [Hwy 72]) Just over a mile north of the town center,

Maunawili Trail System

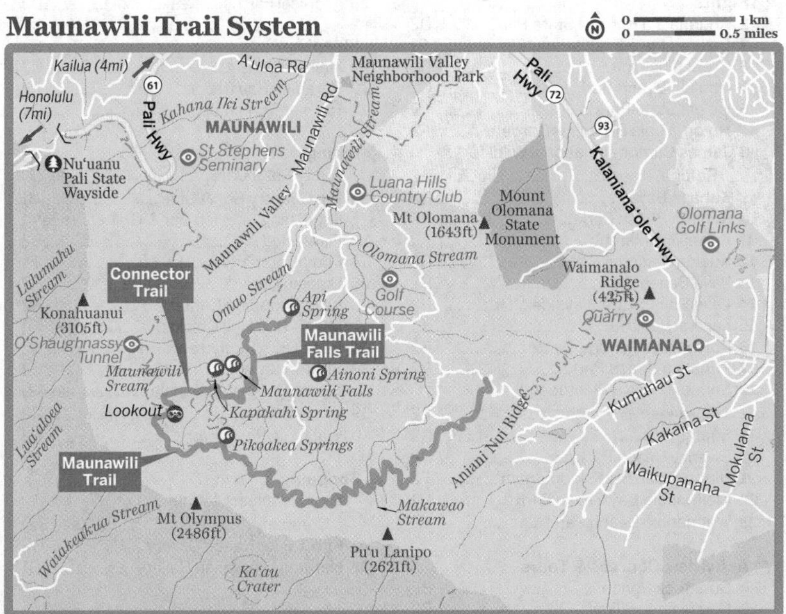

Windward Coast

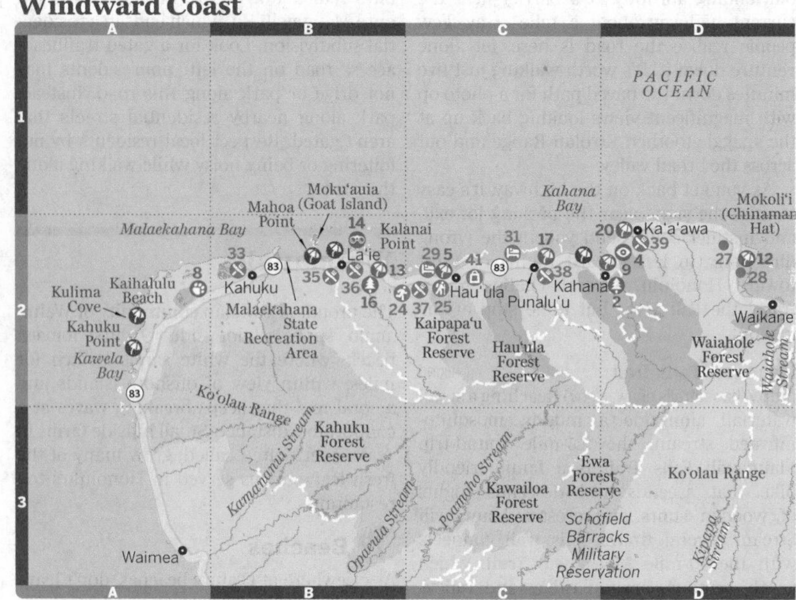

Windward Coast

Top Sights
1 Valley of the Temples & Byōdō-In E2

Sights
2 Ahupua'a o Kahana State Park D2
3 Bellows Field Beach Park G1
4 Crouching Lion D2
5 Hau'ula Beach Park C2
6 He'eia State Park E2
7 Ho'omaluhia Botanical Garden F2
8 James Campbell National Wildlife Refuge A2
9 Kahana Bay D2
10 Kalama Beach Park F1
11 Kawai Nui Marsh F2
12 Kualoa Regional Park D2
13 La'ie Beach Park B2
14 La'ie Point State Wayside B2
15 Lanikai Beach F1
16 Polynesian Cultural Center B2
17 Punalu'u Beach Park C2
18 Senator Fong's Plantation & Gardens E2
19 Shangri La G3
20 Swanzy Beach Park D2
21 Ulupo Heiau State Monument F2
22 Waimanalo Bay Beach Park G1
23 Waimanalo Beach Park G1

Activities, Courses & Tours
24 Gunstock Ranch B2
25 Hau'ula Loop Trail C2
26 Ka'iwa Ridge (Lanikai Pillboxes) Trail F1
27 Kualoa Ranch D2
28 Tropical Farms D2

Sleeping
29 Hale Ko'olau C2
30 Paradise Bay Resort E2
31 Pat's at Punalu'u C2

Eating
Aunty Pat's Café .... (see 27)
32 Big Country Bar & Grill G1
Crouching Lion Inn Bar & Grill .... (see 4)
33 Fiji Market B2
34 Food Company F1
35 Hukilau Cafe B2
36 La'ie Shopping Center B2
Mike's Huli Huli Chicken .... (see 30)
37 Papa Ole's Kitchen C2
38 Shrimp Shack C2
Sweet Home Waimanalo .... (see 42)
39 Uncle Bobo's D2
40 Waiahole Poi Factory E2

Shopping
East Honolulu Clothing Company .... (see 32)
41 Kim Taylor Reece Gallery C2
42 Naturally Hawaiian Gallery G1

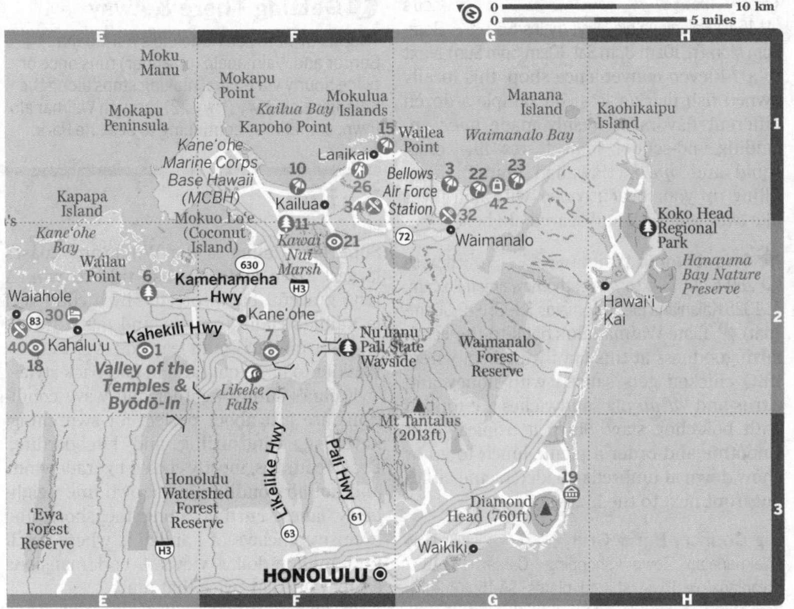

the bay's biggest waves break onshore, drawing dedicated board surfers and bodysurfers. Backed by a wide swath of ironwoods, you'll find a thick mane of blond sand for long walks and ocean ogling. Facilities include picnic tables, BBQ grills, restrooms, outdoor showers, lifeguards and 10 just-OK, tree-shaded campsites.

Bellows Field Beach Park BEACH
(Tinker Rd, off Kalaniana'ole Hwy [Hwy 72]; usually open to public noon Fri-8am Mon, gates closed 8pm-6am) Fronting Bellows Air Force Station, this is a long beach with fine sand bordered by ironwood trees. Small shorebreak waves are good for beginner bodysurfers and board surfers. The beach is open to civilians only on national holidays and weekends. There are lifeguards, outdoor showers, restrooms, drinking water and 50 campsites nestled among the trees by the beach.

TheBus 57 stops in front of the park entrance road, just north of Waimanalo Bay Beach Park; from the bus stop, it's a 1.5-mile walk in to the beach.

Waimanalo Beach Park BEACH
(Kalaniana'ole Hwy [Hwy 72]) By the side of the highway, this strip of soft white sand has little puppy waves that are excellent for swimming. The park has a shady patch of ironwood trees and views of Manana (Rabbit) Island and Makapu'u Point to the south. Camping is allowed in an open area near the road, but it's uninviting.

Southeast of the town center, the community park also offers a grassy picnic area, children's playground, ball courts, drinking water, restrooms, outdoor showers and lifeguards.

Activities

Olomana Golf Links GOLF
(259-7926; www.olomanagolflinks.com; 41-1801 Kalaniana'ole Hwy; green fees incl cart rental $65-95) LPGA star Michelle Wie got her start and President Obama regularly swings his clubs here during his vacations on O'ahu. With a dramatic backdrop of the Ko'olau Range, two challenging nine-hole courses are played together as a regulation 18-hole, par-72 course. Facilities include a driving range, a pro shop with club rentals and a restaurant.

Sleeping & Eating

All of Waimanalo's public beach parks allow camping with an advance county camping permit (see p63).

Tersty Treats SEAFOOD $

(41-1540 Kalaniana'ole Hwy; mains $6-12; ⌚11am-8pm Mon-Fri, 10am-8pm Sat, 10am-5pm Sun) Next to a 7-Eleven convenience shop, this locally owned fish market lets you sample a dozen different flavors of freshly made *poke*, including old-school luau tastes like crab, squid and *opihi* (Hawaiian limpet). Keep filling up your beach cooler with deli faves like *char siu* pork and seared ahi belly.

★ **Sweet Home Waimanalo** LOCAL $$

(☎259-5737; http://sweethomewaimanalo.com; 41-1025 Kalaniana'ole Hwy; mains $8-13; ⌚9:30am-7pm) Taste Waimanalo's back-to-the-earth farm goodness at this family kitchen, where BBQ chicken gets sauced with honey and citrus and *kalua* pig sandwiches are topped with bok-choy slaw. Slurp a tropical fruit smoothie and order a picnic lunch to go or chow down at umbrella-shaded picnic tables out front next to the highway.

Big Country Bar & Grill PUB $$

(Waimanalao Town Shopping Center, 41-1537 Kalaniana'ole Hwy; shared plates $5-15; ⌚2pm-2am Mon-Sat, to midnight Sun) At this neighborhood watering hole with sports TVs and a karaoke machine, Hawaiian musicians and live bands take to the stage after 8pm on Thursday to Sunday nights. Local grinds like Asian stir-fries and fresh fish are plated big, and drinks are super cheap. Famous **Dave's Ice Cream** shop is a few doors down.

Shopping

Naturally Hawaiian Gallery ARTS & CRAFTS

(www.patrickchingart.com; 41-1025 Kalaniana'ole Hwy; ⌚9:30am-5:30pm) Inside a converted gas station, browse handmade works by O'ahu artists, including wooden koa bowls, carved bone fishhook pendants and other jewelry. Owner Patrick Ching sells his own naturalist paintings, prints and illustrated books here.

East Honolulu Clothing Company CLOTHING, SOUVENIRS

(www.doublepawswear.com; Waimanalo Town Shopping Center, 41-537 Kalaniana'ole Hwy; ⌚9am-5pm) Striking, graphic tropical-print fabrics used to make casual apparel here are designed and silk-screened in-house. This fashion studio provides local hula *halau* (schools) with costumes, and they'll even customize a flowy dress or aloha shirt just for you.

Getting There & Away

TheBus 57 between Honolulu's Ala Moana Center and Waimanalo (one hour) runs once or twice hourly via Kailua, making stops along the Kalaniana'ole Hwy (Hwy 72) through Waimanalo town, sometimes continuing to Sea Life Park.

Kailua

POP 38,635

Suburban Kailua is the Windward Coast's largest town, a fairly easy title to win. A long graceful bay protected by a coral reef is Kailua's claim to fame, and many travelers returning to O'ahu leapfrog over touristy Waikiki to hang out here in laid-back style.

Kailua's sunny weather and wave conditions are just about perfect for swimming, kayaking, windsurfing and kiteboarding. Beach cottages, mostly cooled by tradewinds and not air-conditioning, crowd into neighborly lanes. Further along the shore, the exclusive enclave of Lanikai is where you'll find million-dollar views – and mansions easily valued at twice that much.

In ancient times Kailua (meaning 'two seas') was a place of legends and home to Hawaiian chiefs, including Kamehameha the Great (briefly) after he conquered O'ahu. Once rich in stream-fed agricultural land, fishing grounds and protected canoe landings, Kailua was home to at least three temples, one of which you can still visit.

Beaches

★ **Kailua Beach Park** BEACH

(off Kawailoa Rd;) A wide arc of white sand drapes around the jewel-colored waters of Kailua Bay, with formidable volcanic headlands pinning either side and islets rising offshore. The beach has a gently sloping sandy bottom with usually calm waters, good for swimming year-round, especially in the morning. In the afternoons, winds pick up and transform the bay into a windsurfing and kiteboarding rink.

Sea turtles poke their heads above the gentle waves, while back on land residents swap gossip during daily dog walks. The beach park has the usual public facilities, including lifeguard towers, drinking water, restrooms and outdoor showers. On weekdays, beach wheelchairs for visitors with mobility issues are freely available to borrow, but only with advance reservations (call ☎233-7300).

Lanikai Beach BEACH

(off Mokolua Dr) Southeast of Kailua Beach Park, Lanikai is fronted by what was once one of Hawaii's prettiest stretches of powdery white sand. Today the beach is shrinking, as nearly half of the sand has washed away as a result of retaining walls built to protect the neighborhood's multimillion-dollar mansions. Still, it's a rare beauty, at its best during full-moon phases.

Beyond Kailua Beach Park, the coastal road turns into one-way A'alapapa Dr, which loops back around as Mokulua Dr, passing almost a dozen narrow public-access walkways to the beach. On weekends, parking on the road's shoulders fills up fast.

Kalama Beach Park BEACH

(248 N Kalaheo Ave) On the northern side of Kailua Bay, this beach has a rougher shorebreak, making it popular with experienced bodyboarders. When waters are calm, you'll find families with kids sunning themselves and splashing around here, while locals run along the soft sands. The park has restrooms and outdoor showers, but no lifeguards or drinking water. Access the beach by walking across the grassy lawn.

Sights

Ulupo Heiau State Monument TEMPLE

(www.hawaiistateparks.org; ⊙sunrise-sunset) FREE Construction of this imposing platform temple was traditionally attributed to *menehune*, the 'little people' who legends say created much of Hawaii's stonework, finishing each project in one night. Fittingly, Ulupo means 'night inspiration.' In front of the temple, thought to have been a *luakini* (temple dedicated to war god Ku) used for human sacrifice, is an artist's rendition of how it probably looked in the 1700s.

The temple is a mile southwest of downtown Kailua, hidden behind the YMCA at 1200 Kailua Rd. Coming over the Pali Hwy from Honolulu, take Uluoa St, the first left after passing the Hwy 72 junction, then turn right on Manu Aloha St and right again on Manu O'o St.

Kawai Nui Marsh PARK

(www.kawainuimarsh.com; off Kaha St; ⊙7am-7pm) FREE One of Hawaii's largest freshwater marshes, Kawai Nui provides flood protection for Kailua town and habitat for endangered Hawaiian waterbirds. The inland water catchment has one of the largest remaining fishponds used by ancient Hawaiians. Legend says the edible mud of the fishpond was once home to a *mo'o* (lizard spirit). A wheelchair-accessible recreational path leads around the marsh.

Park at the end of Kaha St, off Oneawa St, just over a mile northwest of Kailua Rd.

WORTH A TRIP

PADDLING TO KAILUA'S OFFSHORE ISLANDS

Three of Kailua's pretty little offshore islands are seabird sanctuaries, accessible only by kayak. Landings are allowed on **Popoi'a (Flat) Island**, off the south end of Kailua Beach Park. The magical twin Mokulua Islands, **Moku Nui** and **Moku Iki**, sit directly off Lanikai. It's possible to kayak to them from Kailua Beach Park. Landings are prohibited on smaller Moku Iki, but you can step ashore at Moku Nui, which has a beautiful beach and, if you hike around to the island's back side, a protected ocean cove with even better swimming and snorkeling.

Hamakua Marsh Wildlife Sanctuary WILDLIFE RESERVE

(http://hawaii.gov/dlnr/; off Hamakua Dr; ⊙sunrise-sunset) FREE Downstream from Kawai Nui Marsh, this tiny nature preserve provides more habitat for rare waterbirds, including the *koloa maoli* (Hawaiian duck), *ae'o* (Hawaiian black-necked stilt), *'alae ke'oke'o* (Hawaiian coot) and *'alae 'ula* (Hawaiian moorhen). Bird-watching is best after heavy rains. To keep these endangered birds wild, please do not feed them. Park off Hamakua Dr, behind Down to Earth natural-foods store.

Activities

There are a handful of watersports outfitters that have in-town shops, where you can arrange private or group lessons (from $130) and guided tours (from $100), and rent gear, including kayaks (single/tandem from $45/55), SUP sets (from $59), windsurfing rigs (from $70), surfboards (from $20), snorkel sets (from $12) and boogie boards (from $8).

★ **Kailua Sailboards & Kayaks, Inc** WATER SPORTS

(☎888-457-5737, 262-2555; www.kailuasailboards.com; Kailua Beach Center, 130 Kailua Rd; ⊙8:30am-

Kailua

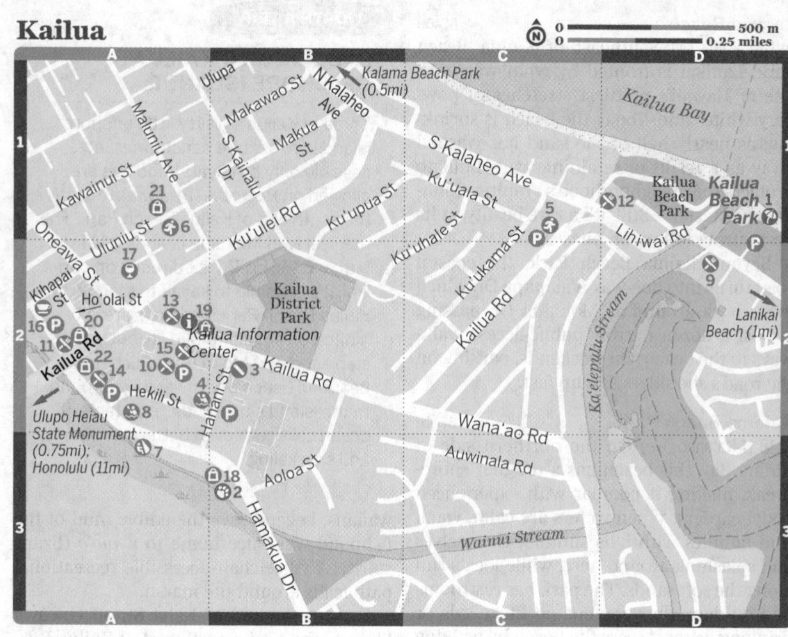

5pm Mon-Sat) Energetic all-round water-sports outfitter offers kayaking, surfing, windsurfing, SUP and boogie board rentals, plus lessons and guided tours, just a short walk from Kailua Beach Park.

Twogood Kayaks Hawaii KAYAKING
(☎262-5656; www.twogoodkayaks.com; 134-B Hamakua Dr; ⊙9am-6pm Mon-Fri, 8am-6pm Sat & Sun) Free delivery of rental kayaks to Kaelepulu Stream beside Kailua Beach Park. The shop also rents snorkel gear and boogie boards. Kayak adventure packages include round-trip Waikiki shuttle service.

Naish Hawaii WINDSURFING, KITEBOARDING
(☎262-6068; www.naish.com; 155-C Hamakua Dr; ⊙9am-5:30pm) Owned by windsurfing champion Robby Naish, this is *the* place for windsurfing and kiteboarding lessons and also rental gear, including 'woodie' surfboards and SUP sets.

Kailua Ocean Adventures CANOEING
(☎554-5911; www.kailuaoceanadventures.com; 348 Hahani St; ⊙8am-5pm Mon-Fri, to noon Sat;) Hawaiian outrigger canoe paddling trips on Kailua Bay and to offshore islands are fun for both adults and children. Surfboard, SUP, snorkel gear and bicycle rentals available.

Aaron's Dive Shop DIVING
(☎888-847-2822, 262-2333; www.hawaii-scuba.com; 307 Hahani St; ⊙7am-7pm Mon-Fri, to 6pm Sat, to 5pm Sun) Sea caves, lava tubes, coral gardens and WWII shipwrecks can all be explored with this five-star PADI operation, which boats all over O'ahu and also teaches scuba classes and certification courses.

Ka'iwa Ridge (Lanikai Pillboxes) Trail HIKING
(http://hawaiitrails.ehawaii.gov; off Kaelepulu Dr) Identified by the WWII 'pillboxes' (concrete bunkers) that it passes, this barren two-mile round-trip trail is steep and always slippery – either with wet mud or dry, loose dirt. Make it to the top for head-spinning views of the Mokulua Islands off Kailua Bay and the lofty Ko'olau Range. The trailhead is hidden in the residential neighborhood of Lanikai.

Coming from Kailua Beach, turn right off A'alapapa Dr onto Ka'elepulu Dr and park uphill just beyond the country club. On the *makai* (ocean) side of the street, look for a brown-and-yellow Na Ala Hele sign marking a dirt path beside a chain-link fence.

Lomilomi Hana Lima MASSAGE, SPA
(☎253-0303; www.lomilomihanalima.com; 2nd fl, Kailua Square, 315 Uluniu St; 1hr massage from $90; ⊙9am-5pm Mon-Fri) Spoil yourself with a

Kailua

Top Sights
1 Kailua Beach Park........D1

Sights
2 Hamakua Marsh Wildlife Sanctuary...B3

Activities, Courses & Tours
3 Aaron's Dive Shop........B2
4 Kailua Ocean Adventures........A2
5 Kailua Sailboards & Kayaks, Inc........C1
6 Lomilomi Hana Lima........A1
7 Naish Hawaii........A3
8 Twogood Kayaks Hawaii........A2

Eating
9 Buzz's........D2
Cinnamon's Restaurant........(see 6)
10 Kailua Farmers Market........A2
11 Kalapawai Cafe........A2
12 Kalapawai Market........D1
13 Lanikai Juice........A2
14 Prima........A2
15 Whole Foods........A2

Drinking & Nightlife
16 ChadLou's Coffee Lounge........A2
17 Kailua Town Pub & Grill........A2

Shopping
Fighting Eel........(see 15)
18 Island Glassworks........B3
19 Kailua Shopping Center........A2
Lily Lotus........(see 15)
Manoa Chocolate........(see 6)
20 Manuheali'i........A2
21 Muse Room........A1
22 Mu'umu'u Heaven........A2

traditional Hawaiian *lomilomi* or *pohaku* massage, a soothing body wrap with honey and healing *noni* or an organic facial at this small meditative spa. Reservations advised.

Aloha Yoga Kula YOGA
(☎772-3520; www.alohayogakula.com; classes $10-20; ⊙class schedules vary) Drop-in group classes in a variety of yoga styles (basic, vinyasa, anusara, gentle, even vayu aerial) happen at different locations several times daily except Sunday.

Sleeping

Kailua has no hotels, but suburban home-style B&Bs and vacation rentals abound, some just a short walk from the beach. Most are nonsmoking, don't accept credit cards, require an advance deposit and multiple-night stays, charge a one-time cleaning fee and are legally prohibited from offering hot breakfasts. The majority are unlicensed, whether they're managed by local vacation-rental agencies or listed on websites such as **Vacation Rentals by Owner** (VRBO; www.vrbo.com), **HomeAway** (www.homeaway.com) and **Air B&B** (www.airbnb.com). Book online or call ahead (not just from the airport!) a few weeks or even months in advance. The following places have purposefully not been mapped, to discourage last-minute guests without reservations from just showing up at the door.

Manu Mele Bed & Breakfast B&B **$$**
(☎262-0016; www.manumele.net; d $100-120; ❄ 📶 🏊) Just 100 steps from the beach, these peaceful, contemporary island-style guest rooms feel light and bright. Creature comforts include private parking and entrances, plush seven-layer beds with Hawaiian quilts and, unusually, a swimming pool. Rates include complimentary breakfast baked goods and fruit on your first morning.

Kailua Guesthouse B&B **$$**
(☎888-249-5848, 261-2637; www.kailuaguesthouse.com; d $129-159; 📶) Not too far from downtown, this contemporary home rents out two blissfully quiet studio suites that open onto lanai overhanging with plumeria blossoms. Modern amenities include flat-screen TVs with DVD players, digital in-room safes and kitchenettes. Weekly rates available.

Paradise Palms Bed & Breakfast B&B **$$**
(☎254-4234; www.paradisepalmshawaii.com; d $110-120; ❄ 📶) It'll feel like you're visiting long-lost relatives at this tidy suburban home with designer-looking decor. Beds claim most of the limited space inside, but guest rooms with private entrances also have kitchenettes stocked with breakfast fixings like baked goods, fruit, coffee and tea.

Sheffield House B&B **$$**
(☎262-0721; www.hawaiisheffieldhouse.com; d $129-169; 📶) A 10-minute walk from Kailua Beach, this house sports beachy cottage decor. Surrounded by tropical gardens, both the smaller guest room and the larger studio suite have a kitchenette where complimentary pastries, fruit and juice for your first breakfast await. Kids allowed.

Eating & Drinking

Kailua has dozens of places to eat, from fast-food joints to upscale restaurants, but many are mediocre and overpriced. Following are some above-par recommendations.

O'AHU'S BEST B&B & VACATION-RENTAL AGENCIES

➡ **Affordable Paradise** (☎261-1693; www.affordable-paradise.com) Biggest selection of B&B rooms, apartments, bungalows and rental houses in Kailua, Lanikai and near Diamond Head.

➡ **Pat's Kailua Beach Properties** (☎261-1653; www.patskailua.com) Family-run agency books dozens of budget-conscious options around Kailua and Lanikai, from studio cottages to multi-bedroom family homes.

➡ **Lanikai Beach Rentals** (☎261-7895; www.lanikaibeachrentals.com) Beautiful, contemporary island-style studios, beach cottages, apartments and private homes in Lanikai and Kailua.

➡ **Hawaii's Best Bed & Breakfast** (☎800-262-9912, 262-5030; www.bestbnb.com) Handpicked studio apartments, beach houses, villas, cottages and condos around the Windward Coast, North Shore and Leeward O'ahu.

★ **Lanikai Juice** HEALTHY $
(www.lanikaijuice.com; Kailua Shopping Center, 600 Kailua Rd; snacks & drinks $4-8; ⏲6am-8pm Mon-Fri, 7am-7pm Sat & Sun) With fresh fruit grown by local farmers getting blended and poured into biodegradable cups, this juice bar makes addictive smoothies with names like Ginger 'Ono and Lanikai Splash. In the morning, neighborhood yoga fanatics devour overflowing bowls of granola topped with acai berries, apple bananas and grated coconut at sunny sidewalk tables.

Whole Foods SUPERMARKET $
(http://wholefoodsmarket.com/stores/kailua; Kailua Town Center, 629 Kailua Rd; ⏲7am-10pm;) Emphasizing organic, natural and locally sourced food, this supermarket offers deliciously healthy options. Grab a hot meal from the full-service deli – sandwiches, BBQ meats or tacos, anyone? – or graze the pizza, *poke*, sushi and salad bars. Island-made gelato is sold at the coffee kiosk up front. Come for happy-hour drinks and *pupu* at the supermarket's Windward Bar.

Kalapawai Market DELI, SUPERMARKET $
(www.kalapawaimarket.com; 306 S Kalaheo Ave; items $2-12; ⏲6am-9pm) En route to the beach, everyone stops at this 1930s landmark to stock their picnic basket with made-to-order sandwiches and market-fresh salads. Early morning regulars help themselves to fresh coffee. Back in the town center, its sister **Kalapawai Cafe** (☎262-2354; www.kalapawaimarket.com/section/cafe; 750 Kailua Rd; dinner mains $14-24; ⏲6am-9pm Mon-Thu, to 9:30pm Fri & Sat, from 7am Sun) serves haute bistro dinners in a candlelit dining room and also has a gourmet takeout deli.

Kailua Farmers Market MARKET $
(http://hfbf.org; Kailua Town Center, 609 Kailua Rd; ⏲5-7:30pm Thu;) Artisan breads, organic fruit and veggies and filling plate meals, from island-style BBQ to Filipino stew, are sold by stall vendors in the parking garage behind Longs Drugs.

Food Company LOCAL $$
(☎262-6640; http://foodcompanykailua.com; Enchanted Lake Shopping Center, 1020 Keolu Dr; mains restaurant $5-10, cafe $9-26; ⏲restaurant 8am-8pm Tue-Fri, market & cafe 10:30am-8:30pm Tue-Thu, to 9pm Fri & Sat) One side of this delish catering company (the 'original' restaurant) slings mountain-high plate lunches that could easily feed two people and equally gobstopping breakfasts (until 11am) of macnut banana French toast, *loco moco* and more. The upscale 'new' market-cafe side offers chef's seafood and pasta daily specials, as well as takeout sandwiches, wraps and salads made with local greens.

Cinnamon's Restaurant BREAKFAST $$
(☎261-8724; www.cinnamonsrestaurant.com; Kailua Square, 315 Uluniu St; mains $7-13; ⏲7am-2pm;) Local families pack this crowded cafe, decorated like your eccentric aunt's house, for airy chiffon pancakes drowning in guava syrup, sweet-bread French toast, eggs Benedict mahimahi, curried chicken-and-papaya salad and omelettes with *kalua* pork and *laulau* ingredients.

Prima ITALIAN $$
(☎888-8933; www.primahawaii.com; 108 Hekili St; mains $15-20; ⏲5-10pm) Next to Foodland supermarket, all-black-clad servers circulate in a sleek dining room outfitted with Eames chairs and a polished mahogany

bar. Crispy wood-oven-fired pizzas, creamy pastas, seafood appetizers and small plates of farm-fresh vegetable sides mostly hit the mark.

Buzz's STEAKHOUSE $$$
(☎261-4661; http://buzzsoriginalsteakhouse.com; 413 Kawailoa Rd; mains lunch $9-17, dinner $16-38; ⏲11am-3pm & 4:30-9:30pm) By the canal across from Kailua Beach, this old-school hangout has a tiki-lit lanai, kitschy decor plus an old-school menu of charbroiled fish and burgers at lunch or kiawe-grilled surf-and-turf at dinner. Waits are long, service only so-so.

ChadLou's Coffee Lounge CAFE
(www.chadlous.com; 45 Kihapai St; snacks & drinks $2-8; ⏲7am-8pm Mon-Fri, to 7pm Sat & Sun; 📶) This laid-back coffee shop with comfy sofas and chairs is where friends chat over espresso drinks, blended frozen coffees and ice-cream floats or cookie sandwiches. Peruse locally made jewelry, art and souvenirs while you wait.

Kailua Town Pub & Grill PUB
(http://kailuatownpub.com; 26 Ho'olai St; ⏲11am-1:30am Mon-Fri, 6am-1:30am Sat, 8am-1:30am Sun) This faux-Irish bar has 30 beers on tap, tasty from-scratch Bloody Marys, gourmet burgers, fish and chips and big-screen sports TVs.

Shopping

Downtown Kailua abounds with whimsical, cutting-edge fashion boutiques, beachy souvenir shops and island art galleries.

Kailua Shopping Center GIFTS, BOOKS
(600 Kailua Rd; ⏲most shops open daily, hours vary) Start your souvenir shopping downtown at this strip mall opposite Macy's department store. Pick up Hawaiiana books and beach reads at **Bookends**, tropically scented lotions and soaps at **Lanikai Bath & Body** or beachy home accents, tote bags and kids' toys at **Sand People**.

Mu'umu'u Heaven CLOTHING, HOMEWARES
(www.muumuuheaven.com; 767 Kailua Rd; ⏲10am-6pm Mon-Sat, 11am-4pm Sun) Fun and funky, this chic contemporary boutique crafts flowing tropical-print dresses, skirts and feminine tops, all handmade from vintage muumuus. A second set of rooms displays equally colorful housewares and original island art.

Manoa Chocolate FOOD
(http://manoachocolate.com; 2nd fl, Kailua Square, 315 Uluniu St; ⏲10am-6pm Tue-Sun) Expensive, but utterly delicious handmade chocolate gets processed from cacao bean to foil-wrapped bar inside this workshop. Sample the goat's milk, Hawaiian sea salt, pineapple or chili pepper flavors before you buy.

Island Glassworks ARTS & CRAFTS
(☎263-4527; http://islandglassworks.com; 171-A Hamakua Dr; ⏲usually 9am-4pm Mon-Wed & Fri, by appointment Sat) Part glassblowing factory, part art gallery, here you can peruse one-of-a-kind pieces like calabash-shaped vases and bowls with elemental color palettes. Call ahead to check hours or sign up for classes.

Lily Lotus CLOTHING
(www.lilylotus.com; Kailua Town Center, 609 Kailua Rd; ⏲10am-6pm Mon-Sat, 11am-4pm Sun) Honolulu-born Momi Chee has made an international name for herself designing yoga wear for women and men. Her Kailua flagship shop also vends eco-friendly gifts and jewelry.

Manuheali'i CLOTHING
(www.manuhealii.com; 5 Ho'olai St; ⏲9:30am-6pm Mon-Fri, 9am-4pm Sat, 10am-3pm Sun) Branch of the famous Honolulu designer's showroom, with modern aloha-print styles for men, women and kids.

Fighting Eel CLOTHING
(www.fightingeel.com; Kailua Town Center, 629 Kailua Rd) Another fashion-savvy import from over the *pali*, this time from Honolulu's Chinatown arts district.

Muse Room WOMEN'S CLOTHING
(www.musebyrimo.com; 332 Uluniu St; ⏲10am-5pm) Beachy, dreamy and grown-up girly styles inspired by Waikiki and LA.

Information

Kailua Information Center (☎888-261-7997, 261-2727; www.kailuachamber.com; Kailua Shopping Center, 600 Kailua Rd; ⏲10am-4pm Mon-Fri, 10am-2pm Sat, also sometimes 10am-1pm Sun) Free local maps and brochures.

Kailua Public Library (☎266-9911; www.librarieshawaii.org; 239 Ku'ulei Rd; ⏲10am-5pm Mon, Wed, Fri & Sat, 1-8pm Tue & Thu) Free reservable internet terminals with a temporary nonresident library card ($10).

Morning Brew (http://morningbrewhawaii.com; Kailua Shopping Center, 600 Kailua Rd; per hr $6; ⏲6am-9pm Sun-Thu, to 10pm Fri & Sat; 📶) Pay internet terminals and free wi-fi with purchase at this crowded coffee shop.

U-Wash-N-Dry Laundromat (11 Ho'olai St; ⏲24hr) Convenient self-service coin-op laundromat.

Getting There & Around

Outside of weekday morning and afternoon rush hours, it's normally a 25-minute drive between Honolulu and Kailua along the Pali Hwy (Hwy 61).

From Honolulu's Ala Moana Center, TheBus routes 56 and 57 run over the *pali* to downtown Kailua (40 to 50 minutes, one to three hourly). TheBus 57 continues from Kailua to Waimanalo (20 minutes) and sometimes Sea Life Park (30 minutes). For Kailua Beach or Lanikai, transfer in downtown Kailua at the corner of Kailua Rd and Oneawa St to TheBus 70 (every 60 to 90 minutes).

Kailua Sailboards & Kayaks, Inc (p139) rents single-speed beach cruisers (per half-day/full day/week $20/25/85) not far from Kailua Beach Park. Bicycle rentals are also available from the following:

Hawaii B-Cycle (http://hawaii.bcycle.com; 24hr/30-day pass $5/30; ⏲5am-10pm) Davis Building (767 Kailua Rd); Hahani Plaza (515 Kailua Rd) Hawaii's first bike-sharing system lets you pay for a pass online or at on-street kiosks. Borrow a shiny cruiser bicycle for a quick trip around town, then return it to any B-station.

Bike Shop (☎261-1553; www.bikeshophawaii.com; 270 Ku'ulei Rd; rentals per day/week from $20/100; ⏲10am-7pm Mon-Fri, 9am-5pm Sat, 10am-5pm Sun) Top-quality beach cruiser, mountain bike and performance road-bike rentals, plus repairs, parts, cycling gear and maps.

Kane'ohe

POP 34,600

Although Kane'ohe is blessed with Hawaii's biggest reef-sheltered bay, its largely silty waters are not good for swimming. Neighboring the Marine Corps Base Hawaii (MCBH), this workaday town doesn't receive nearly as many tourists as the surf-and-sun village of Kailua, but it has a few attractions worth stopping for.

Two highways run north–south through Kane'ohe. The coastal Kamehameha Hwy (Hwy 830) is slower but more scenic. The inland Kahekili Hwy (Hwy 83) goes past the Valley of the Temples. Both highways merge into the Kamehameha Hwy (Hwy 83).

Sights & Activities

★Valley of the Temples & Byōdō-In — TEMPLE

(http://www.byodo-in.com; 47-200 Kahekili Hwy; temple adult/child under 13yr/senior $3/1/2; ⏲9am-5pm) The Valley of the Temples is an interdenominational cemetery that is famously home to Byōdō-In, a replica of a 900-year-old temple in Uji, Japan. The temple's perfect symmetry is a classic example of Japanese Heian architecture, with rich vermilion walls set against the verdant fluted cliffs of the Ko'olau Range.

In the main hall, a 9ft-tall gold-leaf-covered Buddha is positioned to catch the first rays of morning sunlight. Outside, wild peacocks roam beside a koi pond and a garden designed to symbolize the Pure Land of Amitabha Buddhism. The three-ton brass bell is said to bring peace and good fortune to anyone who rings it – and so, of course, everyone does.

From Honolulu's Ala Moana Center, TheBus 65 stops hourly near the cemetery entrance on the Kahekili Hwy, from where it's a winding 0.5-mile walk uphill to the temple from the security gate.

Ho'omaluhia Botanical Garden — GARDENS

(☎233-7323; www1.honolulu.gov/parks/hbg/hmbg.htm; 45-680 Luluku Rd; ⏲9am-4pm, closed Dec 25 & Jan 1) FREE Nestling beneath the dramatic *pali* at the foot of the Ko'olau Range, O'ahu's biggest botanical garden is planted with 400 acres of trees and shrubs hailing from the world's tropical regions. This peaceful nature preserve is networked by semi-marked, grassy and often muddy trails near an artificial reservoir (no swimming).

A small visitor center features displays on the park's history, flora and fauna, and Hawaiian ethnobotany. Call ahead to register for two-hour guided nature hikes, usually departing at 10am Saturday and 1pm Sunday.

The park is at the end of Luluku Rd, over a mile *mauka* (inland) from the Kamehameha Hwy. TheBus 55 stops behind the Windward City Shopping Center, opposite the start of Luluku Rd; the visitor center is a 1.6-mile uphill walk from there.

He'eia State Park — PARK

(☎235-6509; www.hawaiistateparks.org; 46-465 Kamehameha Hwy; ⏲7am-7:45pm Apr-1st Mon in Sep, 7am-6:45pm 1st Tue in Sep-Mar) FREE Despite looking slightly abandoned, this park offers picturesque views of **He'eia Fishpond**, an impressive survivor from the days when stone-walled ponds used for cultivating fish for royalty were common on Hawaiian shores. Near the park entrance, there's a traditional Hawaiian outrigger canoe shed and workshop. Just offshore to the southeast, the island of **Mokuo Lo'e** was once a royal playground.

Its nickname 'Coconut Island' comes from the trees planted there by Princess Bernice Pauahi Bishop in the mid-19th century. During WWII, the US military used it for R&R. Today the Hawai'i Institute of Marine Biology occupies much of the island, which you might recognize from the opening scenes of the *Gilligan's Island* TV series.

Call ahead to reserve kayak rentals (available until 1pm daily) or a three-hour morning kayak tour including snorkeling and a light lunch (adult/child 4-12yr $100/80).

Likeke Falls Trail HIKING

(👪) Ready for a hidden waterfall? This 2-mile round-trip trail winds through a forest of native and exotic trees up into the misty Ko'olau Range. Taking about an hour, the family-friendly hike starts from the upper end of the Ko'olau Golf Club parking lot. Enter off Kionaole Rd, just west of the Kamehameha Hwy (Hwy 83) near the H-3 Fwy junction.

Walk through the chain-link gate uphill along a paved maintenance road. Veer left before the water tank onto a well-used trail that ascends a set of wooden steps over moss-covered rocks and gnarled tree roots. This shady forest path eventually emerges onto a cobblestone road that keeps climbing. Watch for the (often muddy) side trail leading off to your right toward a hidden 20ft-high waterfall (no swimming), where the only sounds are tumbling water and tropical birdsong.

Due to the danger of flash floods, do not start this hike if rain is forecast or dark clouds are visible in the sky. Obey any 'Kapu' or 'No Trespassing' signs, as public access could be revoked at any time.

Ko'olau Golf Club GOLF

(☎247-7088; www.koolaugolfclub.com; 45-550 Kionaole Rd; green fees $110-145) O'ahu's toughest championship course is scenically nestled beneath the soaring Ko'olau Range. For practice, there's a driving range, as well as putting and chipping greens. Club and handcart rentals are available. Reserve tee times in advance.

Pali Golf Course GOLF

(☎info 266-7612, reservations 296-2000; www1.honolulu.gov/des/golf/pali.htm; 45-050 Kamehameha Hwy; green fees $20-52) This municipal 18-hole hillside course has stunning mountain views, stretching across to Kane'ohe Bay. Club and handcart rentals are available. Reserve tee times in advance.

Bay View Mini-Putt & Zipline ZIPLINING

(☎247-6464; http://bayviewminiputt.com; 45-285 Kane'ohe Bay Dr; ⏲10am-6pm Sun-Fri, to 8pm Sat; 👪) At a mini golf course, O'ahu's only zipline is a very short ride for beginners. All riders must be at least six years old, weigh between 60lb and 250lb and wear closed-toed shoes with a heel strap (no high heels).

Sleeping

The beach town of Kailua nearby has many more places to bed down and fuel up.

Ho'omaluhia Botanical Garden CAMPGROUND $

(☎233-7323; https://camping.honolulu.gov; 45-680 Luluku Rd; 3-night campsite permit $32; ⏲9am Fri-4pm Mon) This county-run garden offers grassy campsites from 9am Friday until 4pm Monday. With overnight guard and gates that open after-hours only for pre-registered campers, it's among O'ahu's safest places to camp. Limited amenities include restrooms, outdoor showers and picnic tables. Advance county-camping permits are required (see p63); validate them inside the visitor center (open until 4pm daily). No alcohol allowed.

Paradise Bay Resort HOTEL $$

(☎239-6658, 800-735-5071; http://paradisebayresorthawaii.com; 47-039 Lihikai Dr; studio/1br/2br incl continental breakfast from $229/250/250; ❄📶) On a point overlooking the bay, the Windward Coast's only hotel (it's more like a motel) is a step above vacation rentals. Casual, earth-toned contemporary rooms with kitchenettes are spacious, if noise-prone. Twice-weekly happy hours with food, drinks and live entertainment and a Saturday-morning bay cruise are complimentary. Usually there's a two-night minimum stay (daily resort fee $25).

Getting There & Away

TheBus 55 leaves Honolulu's Ala Moana Center every 30 to 60 minutes, taking about an hour to reach Kane'ohe. TheBus 56 runs once or twice hourly between Kailua and Kane'ohe. From Kane'ohe, TheBus 55 trundles north once or twice hourly along the Kamehameha Hwy to Turtle Bay and Hale'iwa, taking about an hour to reach La'ie.

Kahalu'u & Waiahole

Driving north along the Kamehameha Hwy (Hwy 83), you'll cross the bridge beside Kahalu'u's unusual-sounding Hygienic Store (formerly owned by the Hygienic Dairy company). There you'll make a physical and cultural departure from the gravitational pull of Honolulu. You've officially crossed into 'the country,' where the highway becomes a two-laner and the ocean shares the shoulder as you cruise past sun-dappled valleys, small towns and farms past Waiahole.

Sights

Senator Fong's Plantation & Gardens GARDENS
(☎239-6775; www.fonggarden.com; 47-285 Pulama Rd, Kahalu'u; adult/child 5-12yr $14.50/9; ⏲tours usually 10:30am & 1pm Sun-Fri) A labor of love by Hiram Fong (1907–2004), the first Asian American elected to the US Senate, these flowering gardens preserve Hawaii's plant life for future generations. The Fong family offers 1½-hour, 1-mile guided tours that wind past tropical flowers, sandalwood and palm trees, and other endemic plants. Call ahead to reserve a tour.

The gardens are 0.7 miles *mauka* (inland) from the Kamehameha Hwy – turn onto Pulama Rd about 0.5 miles north of **Sunshine Arts Gallery**, where you can browse artworks by island-born painters, photographers, printmakers, sculptors and woodcarvers.

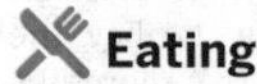

Eating

★**Waiahole Poi Factory** LOCAL $
(http://waiaholepoifactory.com; 48-140 Kamehameha Hwy, Waiahole; meals $7-11; ⏲11am-6pm) About a mile north of the Hygienic Store, this family owned roadside landmark sells *'ono* traditional Hawaiian plate lunches, baked *laulau* and squid, freshly pounded poi and seafood *poke* by the pound, and homemade *haupia* for dessert. Get here early at lunchtime, as food sells out fast.

Mike's Huli Huli Chicken FOOD TRUCK $
(https://sites.google.com/site/mikeshulihulichicken/; 47-525 Kamehameha Hwy, Kahalu'u; meals $7-11; ⏲11am-dusk) Just north of the Hygienic Store, a few food trucks regularly park. As seen on TV's Food Network, 'Monkey Mike' not only rotisserie roasts birds, but also bakes *kalua* pork and minces *lomilomi* salmon. Wait until you reach Kahuku to try the Windward Coast's famous garlic shrimp, though.

A LEGENDARY LIZARD

That eye-catching peaked volcanic islet you see offshore from Kualoa Regional Park is **Mokoli'i** ('little lizard'). According to legend, it's the tail of a *mo'o* (lizard spirit) slain by the goddess Hi'iaka and thrown into the ocean. Following the immigration of Chinese laborers to Hawaii, this cone-shaped island also came to be called Chinaman's Hat, a nickname that persists today, regardless of political correctness.

Kualoa

Although there's not a lot to see nowadays, in ancient times Kualoa was one of the most sacred places on O'ahu. When a chief stood on Kualoa Point, passing canoes lowered their sails in respect. The children of *ali'i* (royalty) were brought here to be educated, and this may have been a place of refuge where *kapu* (taboo) breakers and fallen warriors could seek sanctuary.

In 1850 Kamehameha III sold over 600 acres of land to Gerrit Judd, a missionary doctor who planted the land with sugarcane and hired Chinese immigrants to work the fields. Drought spelled the end of O'ahu's first sugar plantation in 1870. Today you can see the ruins of the mill's stone stack, and a bit of the crumbling walls, on the *mauka* side of the highway, just north of Kualoa Ranch's main entrance.

Beaches

★**Kualoa Regional Park** BEACH
(49-479 Kamehameha Hwy) Offering a postcard-worthy vista of offshore islands and ancient Hawaiian fishponds, this wide-open park is backed by magnificent mountain scenery. Palm trees shade a narrow white-sand beach that usually offers safe swimming, but watch out for jellyfish and winter waves. There are picnic areas, restrooms, drinking water, outdoor showers and sometimes lifeguards.

During low tide, fishers wade out toward **Mokoli'i**. If you go, avoid walking on the fragile island itself or disturbing its nesting seabirds. Birders will want to stroll south along the beach to **'Apua Pond**, a 3-acre brackish salt marsh on Kualoa Point that's a nesting area for the endangered *ae'o* (Hawaiian black-necked stilt). Further down the beach, the rock walls of **Moli'i Fishpond** are covered with mangrove.

Roadside camping is allowed at this county park (advance permit required; see p63), but it's often a hangout for drinking and carousing at night.

Tours

Kualoa Ranch GUIDED TOUR
(☎800-231-7321, 237-7321; www.kualoa.com; 49-560 Kamehameha Hwy; tours adult/child 3-12yr from $26/15; ⏱tours 9am-3pm;) Almost irresistibly scenic, this tour-bus destination is actually a 4000-acre working cattle ranch. If you want to see where Hurley built his *Lost* golf course, where Godzilla left his footprints or where *Jurassic Park* kids hid from dinosaurs, take a 4WD tour of filming locations. The ranch's horseback trail rides (minimum age 10 years) lack giddy-up, though.

Reserve tours online at least a few days in advance for the best rates and to avoid disappointment; walk-ups are welcome on a space-available basis.

Tropical Farms GUIDED TOUR
(☎237-1960; www.macnutfarm.com; 49-227 Kamehameha Hwy; tours $20; ⏱9:30am-5pm, tours 11am Mon-Sat) Sure, it's a kitschy tourist trap, but everything for sale here is island-grown. The open-air shop overflows with various flavors of macadamia nuts, fruit jams and sauces. Learn what guava trees and pineapple plants look like on the bus-and-boat tour that visits flowering gardens, orchards, coconut groves and a few TV and movie locations.

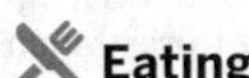

Eating

Aunty Pat's Café CAFE $$
(www.kualoa.com; 49-560 Kamehameha Hwy; meals $7-15, lunch buffet adult/child 4-11yr $16/11; ⏱7:30am-3pm;) At Kualoa Ranch's visitor center, this cafeteria lays out a filling midday buffet. Banana pancakes for breakfast and grass-fed beef burgers for lunch are cooked à la carte.

Ka'a'awa

Here the road really hugs the coast and the *pali* move right on in, with barely enough space to squeeze a few houses between the base of the cliffs and the road. Across the road from the beach park is a convenience store, gas station and hole-in-the-wall post office – pretty much the center of town, such as it is.

WHOSE LAND IS IT ANYWAY?

Not everything on the Windward Coast is as peaceful as the *lo'i kalo* (taro fields) seen alongside the Kamehameha Hwy. Large tracts of these rural valleys were taken over by the US military during WWII for training and target practice, which continued into the 1970s. After decades of pressure from locals, clean-up of ordinance and chemicals by the military is slowly getting underway. Not surprisingly, you'll encounter many Hawaiian sovereignty activists here. Spray-painted political banners and signs, Hawaii's state flag flown upside down (a sign of distress) and bumper stickers with anti-development slogans like 'Keep the Country Country' are seen everywhere.

Beaches

Swanzy Beach Park BEACH
(51-369 Kamehameha Hwy) Fronted by a shore wall, this narrow neighborhood beach is used mainly by fishers. You'll see kids splashing around and local families picnicking and camping here on weekends. Roadside camping is permitted from noon on Friday through 8am on Monday, but the nine sites can be noisy and aren't recommended; an advance county permit is required (see p63).

Sights

Crouching Lion MOUNTAIN
The Crouching Lion is a landmark rock formation just north of mile marker 27 on the Kamehameha Hwy. According to legend, the rock is a demigod from Tahiti who was cemented to the mountain during a jealous struggle between the volcano goddess Pele and her sister Hiiaka. When he tried to free himself by crouching, he was instead turned to stone.

To spot the lion, stand at the Crouching Lion Inn restaurant sign with your back to the ocean and look straight up to the left of the coconut tree at the cliff above.

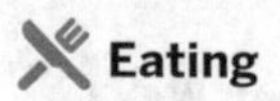

Uncle Bobo's LOCAL $

(www.unclebobos.com; 51-480 Kamehameha Hwy; mains $5-13; 11am-5pm Tue-Fri, to 6pm Sat & Sun) You don't usually find buns baked from scratch at a Hawaiian BBQ joint, where a local family dishes up smoked brisket and ribs, grills mahimahi tacos and other island faves done right. The cheery yellow dining room is small, but the beach park across the street has ocean-view picnic tables.

Crouching Lion Inn Bar & Grill RESTAURANT $$

(237-8981; 51-666 Kamehameha Hwy; mains $12-27; 11am-9pm, bar to midnight) Sharing real estate with its namesake landmark, this tour-bus restaurant has country roosters parading around the parking lot. Day-trippers stop in for light lunches of bland salads and sandwiches. In the evening, tiki torches are lit for cocktails and just-OK *pupu* on a sunset-view lanai.

Kahana

In ancient Hawai'i, all of the islands were divided into *ahupua'a* – pie-shaped land divisions that ran from the mountains to the sea – providing everything Hawaiians needed for subsistence. Modern subdivisions and town boundaries have erased this traditional organization almost everywhere except here, O'ahu's last publicly owned *ahupua'a*.

Before Westerners arrived, the Kahana Valley was planted with wetland taro, which thrived in the rainy valley. Archaeologists have identified the remnants of over 120 agricultural terraces and irrigation canals, as well as the remains of a heiau, fishing shrines and numerous *hale* (house) sites.

In the early 20th century the lower valley was planted with sugarcane, which was hauled north to Kahuku via a small railroad. During WWII the upper valley was taken over by the US military and used to train soldiers in jungle warfare. Today some locals come here to hunt feral pigs on weekends.

Beaches

Kahana Bay BEACH

(www.hawaiistateparks.org; Kamehameha Hwy [Hwy 83]) Although many of Kahana's archaeological sites are inaccessibly deep in the valley, impressive **Huilua Fishpond** is visible from the highway and can be visited simply by walking down to the beach. Managed by the state park, the beach itself offers mostly safe swimming with a gently sloping sandy bottom. Watch out for the riptide near the bay's southern reef break.

There are restrooms, outdoor showers, picnic tables and usually drinking water. Ten roadside campsites (advance state-park camping permit required; see p63) don't offer much privacy, and they're mostly a locals' hangout.

Sights & Activities

Ahupua'a o Kahana State Park PARK, HIKING

(www.hawaiistateparks.org; Kamehameha Hwy [Hwy 83]; sunrise-sunset) FREE In spite of over 40 years of political controversy and failed plans for a living-history village, this park is currently still open to visitors. Starting near the community center, the gentle, 1.2-mile round-trip **Kapa'ele'ele Trail** runs along a former railbed and visits a fishing shrine and a bay-view lookout, then follows the highway back to the park entrance.

Park before the residential neighborhood, then walk 0.6 miles further up the valley road to the start of the less well-maintained **Nakoa Trail**, a 3.5-mile rainforest loop that confusingly crisscrosses Kahana Stream and bushwhacks through thick vegetation. It borders a designated hunting area, so wear bright colors and don't hike alone.

Both of these trails can be very slippery and muddy when wet. Don't attempt the Nakoa Trail if any rain is forecast or dark clouds are visible in the sky, due to the danger of flash floods.

The signposted park entrance is a mile north of Crouching Lion Inn. Turn *mauka* (inland) past the picnic tables and drive up the valley road to an unstaffed orientation center on your left, where hiking pamphlets with trail maps are available outside by the educational boards.

Punalu'u

POP 1165

This sleepy seaside community is a string of houses along the Kamehameha Hwy (Hwy 83) that most visitors drive by en route to the North Shore's big surf scene.

Punalu'u Beach Park BEACH

(Kamehameha Hwy [Hwy 83]) At this long, narrow swimming beach, an offshore reef protects the shallow waters in all but stormy weather. Be cautious of strong currents near the mouth of the stream and in the channel leading out from it, especially during high surf. The roadside park has restrooms, outdoor showers and picnic tables.

Sleeping & Eating

Pat's at Punalu'u CONDO **$$**

(☎255-9840; 53-567 Kamehameha Hwy; ⊙studio/1br from $100/125;) Largely residential and looking a bit neglected from the outside, this oceanfront condominium houses privately owned units that are spacious, if well-worn. It's best for repeat island visitors, or those who truly want to get away from it all. There's no front desk; rentals are handled by local real-estate agents and vacation-rental websites like **VRBO** (www.vrbo.com) and **HomeAway** (www.homeaway.com).

Shrimp Shack SEAFOOD **$$**

(http://shrimpshackoahu.com; 53-352 Kamehameha Hwy; meals $10-18; ⊙10am-5pm) Bite into deep-fried coconut or garlic-butter shrimp imported from Kaua'i or a seafood plate lunch of snow-crab legs, all made to order in a sunny, yellow-painted food truck. For dessert, down a Kona iceberg (hot coffee poured over vanilla ice cream) or step inside neighboring **Ching's Punalu'u Store** for addictive homemade butter *mochi*.

Shopping

Kim Taylor Reece Gallery ART

(www.kimtaylorreece.com; 53-866 Kamehameha Hwy; ⊙noon-5pm Mon-Wed, by appointment Thu-Sun) Reece's sepia-toned photographs of traditional Hawaiian *hula kahiko* dancers in motion are widely recognized, but it's his images of Kalaupapa, a place of exile on Moloka'i, that haunt. The artist's gallery inhabits an airy, light-filled two-story house on the *mauka* side of the highway north of town.

Hau'ula

POP 4150

Aside from a couple of gas pumps, a general store and a 7-Eleven convenience shop, just about the only point of interest in this small coastal town is the beach. Behind the commercial strip is a misty backdrop of hills and majestic Norfolk pines, where secluded trails head into forest-reserve land.

Beaches

Hau'ula Beach Park BEACH

(Kamehameha Hwy [Hwy 83]) This ironwood-shaded in-town beach has a shallow, rocky bottom that isn't appealing for swimming but does attract snorkelers. Waves occasionally get big enough for local kids to ride, while families picnic on the grass. Roadside camping with an advance county permit (see p63) is allowed here and at Kokololio Beach Park further north, though you probably won't get a good night's sleep, due to roadside noise and other annoyances.

Activities

Hau'ula Loop Trail HIKING, MOUNTAIN BIKING

This tranquil trail, which clambers through Waipilopilo Gulch and onto a ridge over Kaipapa'u Valley, rewards hikers with views of the lush interior of the Ko'olau Range. Native flora blooms all along the way, including sweet-smelling guava and octopus trees with tentacle-like branches of reddish-pink flowers. This moderate 2.5-mile lollipop loop hike takes about 1½ hours. Wear bright safety colors to alert hunters.

The signposted trailhead appears at a sharp bend in Hau'ula Homestead Rd above the Kamehameha Hwy, north of Hau'ula Beach Park. Trailhead parking is unsafe due to vehicle break-ins, so leave your car by the beach and instead walk up 0.25 miles from the highway to the trailhead.

Sleeping & Eating

Hale Ko'olau VACATION RENTAL **$$**

(☎888-236-0799, 536-4263; www.halekoolau.com; 54-225 Kamehameha Hwy; 1br/2br/3br apt from $115/205/340;) It's so close to the ocean here that during high tide, surf splashes a few of the windows. Beachfront lawns, hot tubs and washer/driers are shared at this comfy, if slightly timeworn community of residential homes and bungalows, some of which have ocean views. Three-night minimum stay required.

Papa Ole's Kitchen LOCAL **$**

(www.papaoles.com; Hau'ula Shopping Center, 54-316 Kamehameha Hwy; mains $5-12; ⊙7am-9pm Thu-Mon, to 3pm Tue) Billing itself as 'da original,' Papa Ole's *'ono kine grinds* (delicious eats) are da bomb. Make your island-style plate lunch a tad healthier by choosing fresh greens instead of macaroni salad. In a strip mall north of town, sit inside the small cafe or at picnic tables facing the parking lot.

La'ie

POP 6140

Feeling almost like a big city compared with its rural neighbors, life in La'ie revolves around Brigham Young University-Hawaii (BYUH), where scholarship programs recruit students from islands throughout the Pacific. Some students work as guides at the Polynesian Cultural Center (PCC), a tourist mega complex that draws nearly a million visitors each year.

La'ie is thought to have been the site of an ancient Hawaiian *pu'uhonua* – a place where *kapu* (taboo) breakers could escape being put to death. It later became a refuge for Hawaii's Mormon missionaries, after their attempt to establish a 'City of Joseph' on the island of Lana'i failed amid an 1860s land scandal. Today, La'ie is the center of the Mormon community in Hawaii. Built in 1919, its dazzling white hillside temple (open only to church members) is the Windward Coast's most incongruous sight.

Beaches

La'ie Beach Park BEACH

(Kamehameha Hwy [Hwy 83]) A half-mile south of the PCC's main entrance, this is an excellent bodysurfing beach, but the shorebreak can be brutal, thus its nickname Pounders Beach. Summer swimming is generally good, but watch out for strong winter currents. The area around the old landing is usually the calmest.

Hukilau Beach BEACH

(Kamehameha Hwy [Hwy 83]) Just over a half-mile north of La'ie Shopping Center, this tucked-away pocket of white sand is a leisurely place for swimming in summer when waters are calm. In winter, beware of strong currents and stay out of the water any time the surf's up. The beach is named for a traditional Hawaiian method of communal fishing with dragnets.

Sights & Activities

Polynesian Cultural Center THEME PARK

(PCC; 800-367-7060; www.polynesia.com; 55-370 Kamehameha Hwy; adult/child 5-11yr from $50/36; noon-5pm Mon-Sat, closed 4th Thu of Nov & Dec 25;) Showcasing the cultures of Polynesia, this theme park operated by the Mormon church is one of O'ahu's biggest attractions, second only to the USS *Arizona* Memorial at Pearl Harbor. Continually overrun by tour-bus crowds, the nonprofit theme park revolves around eight Polynesian-themed 'villages.' Although steep, the basic admission price includes an afternoon canoe parade.

Representing Hawaii, Rapa Nui (Easter Island), Samoa, Aotearoa (New Zealand), Fiji, Tahiti, Tonga and other South Pacific islands, the ersatz villages contain traditional-looking huts and ceremonial houses, many elaborately built with twisted ropes and hand-carved posts. University students dressed in native garb gamely demonstrate poi pounding, coconut-frond weaving, handicrafts and games.

You'll pay extra for a personal guide or to attend an evening luau with a dinner buffet or a Polynesian song-and-dance revue, an animated production that's partly authentic, partly Bollywood-style extravaganza. On-site parking costs $8.

La'ie Point State Wayside LOOKOUT

(www.hawaiistateparks.org; end of Naupaka St; sunrise-sunset) FREE Crashing surf, a lava arch and a slice of Hawaiian folk history await at La'ie Point. The tiny offshore islands are said to be the surviving pieces of a *mo'o* (lizard spirit) slain by a legendary warrior. To get here from the highway, head seaward on Anemoku St, opposite La'ie Shopping Center, then turn right onto dead-end Naupaka St.

Gunstock Ranch HORSEBACK RIDING

(341-3995; http://gunstockranch.com; 56-250 Kamahameha Hwy; trail rides $89-159;) Take a *paniolo* (Hawaiian cowboy) ride on a working ranch settled beneath the lofty Ko'olau Range. Reserve ahead for scenic mosey-alongs, advanced giddy-ups, daytime picnic and moonlight trail rides, as well as pony rides for kids aged two to seven years ($39). Online booking discounts available.

Eating

Hukilau Cafe LOCAL $

(55-662 Wahinepe'e St; mains $4-9; 6am-2pm Tue-Fri, 7am-11:30am Sat) Hidden in a neighborhood on the north side of town, this hole-in-the-wall is the kind of place locals would rather keep to themselves. Big plates of local grinds, including sweet-bread French toast, *loco moco* and teriyaki beef burgers, are mostly right on. Join the oddly mixed crowd of tattooed surfers in tank tops and buttoned-down churchgoers.

La'ie Shopping Center FAST FOOD, SUPERMARKET $
(55-510 Kamehameha Hwy; most shops closed Sun) Fast-food restaurants, shops and services cluster in this mini-mall, about a half-mile north of the PCC. Foodland supermarket has a takeout deli and bakery, but doesn't sell alcohol and it's closed Sunday (this is Mormon country).

Malaekahana State Recreation Area

You'll feel all sorts of intrepid pride when you discover the wild and rugged beaches of **Malaekahana State Recreation Area** (www.hawaiistateparks.org; Kamehameha Hwy [Hwy 83]; 7am-7:45pm Apr-1st Mon in Sep, 7am-6:45pm 1st Tue in Sep-Mar) FREE. A long, narrow strip of sand stretches between Makahoa Point to the north and Kalanai Point to the south, with a thick inland barrier of ironwoods. Swimming is generally good year-round, although strong currents occur in winter.

Kalanai Point, the main section of the park, is less than a mile north of La'ie and has picnic tables, BBQ grills, camping, restrooms, drinking water and outdoor showers. Popular with families, the beach is also good for many watersports, including bodysurfing, board surfing and windsurfing.

When the tide is low and the water is calm, it's possible to wade over to **Moku'auia (Goat Island)**, a state bird sanctuary about 400yd offshore. It has a small sandy cove with good swimming and snorkeling. Be careful of the shallow coral (sharp) and sea urchins (sharper), and don't approach or disturb the nesting and burrowing seabirds. When the water is deeper, only strong swimmers knowledgeable about rip currents can make it across – ask lifeguards about current conditions.

Sleeping

Malaekahana has two of the Windward Coast's safest, most sheltered public campgrounds. Camping at Kalanai Point requires getting a state-park camping permit in advance (see p63). As with all public campgrounds on O'ahu, camping is not permitted on Wednesday and Thursday nights.

★**Friends of Malaekahana Campground** CAMPGROUND $
(293-1736; www.malaekahana.net; 56-335 Kamehameha Hwy; tent site per person $12, rental units $40-150; gates open 7am-7pm only; @) Let the surf be your lullaby and the roosters your wake-up call at Makahoa Point, about 0.7 miles north of the park's main entrance. Here the nonprofit Friends of Malaekahana maintains tent sites by the beach, very rustic 'little grass shacks,' canvas yurts and duplex cabins, providing 24-hour security, outdoor hot showers and internet access at the campground office.

Make reservations at least two weeks in advance; there's usually a two-night minimum stay.

Kahuku

POP 2615

Kahuku is an old sugar-plantation town, its roads lined with rows of wooden ex-workers' houses. Most of the old sugar mill that operated here until 1971 has been knocked down, but remnants of the smokestack and iron gears can be seen behind the post office.

DOWN ON THE FARM

Even though Kahuku's sugar mill has long since closed, locals are once again looking to the land for their livelihoods. Roadside stands sell roasted Kahuku corn, a famously sweet variety that gets name-brand billing on Honolulu menus, along with a bounty of tropical fruits and veggies. Refresh yourself with a fresh-fruit smoothie after taking a tractor-pulled tour of taro fields and orchards at **Kahuku Farms** (628-0639; http://kahukufarms.com; 56-800 Kamehameha Hwy; tours adult/child 5-12yr $15/12; 11am-4pm Fri-Mon, tours usually 2pm, call for reservations;).

Shrimp ponds on the north side of town also supply O'ahu's top restaurants, while colorful lunch trucks that cook up the crustaceans – in sweet-and-spicy sauce, for example, or fried with butter and garlic – are thick along the highway. But not all of these trucks serve shrimp and prawns actually raised in Kahuku; some trucks import the critters from other Hawaiian Islands, or even overseas.

The rest of the former mill grounds have been turned into a small shopping center with a bank, gas station and cafes.

Sights & Activities

James Campbell National Wildlife Refuge WILDLIFE RESERVE
(637-6330; www.fws.gov/jamescampbell; off Kamehameha Hwy [Hwy 83]; tours by reservation only) FREE A few miles northwest of Kahuku town heading toward Turtle Bay, this rare freshwater wetland provides habitat for four of Hawaii's six endangered waterbirds – the *'alae ke'oke'o* (Hawaiian coot), *ae'o* (Hawaiian black-necked stilt), *koloa maoli* (Hawaiian duck) and *'alae 'ula* (Hawaiian moorhen). During stilt nesting season, normally mid-February through mid-October, the refuge is off-limits to visitors.

The rest of the year you may only visit by taking a volunteer-guided tour. Finding the refuge is tricky, so ask for directions when you call ahead for tour reservations.

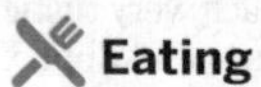

Eating

Always popular with circle-island tour groups and road trippers, Kahuku's **shrimp trucks** are usually open from 10am to 6pm daily (later in summer), depending on supply and demand. A plate of a dozen shrimp or prawns with two scoops of rice costs at least $12. Especially around lunchtime and on weekends, expect long waits at the most famous shrimp trucks.

Tita's Grill LOCAL $
(www.titasgrill.com; 56-485 Kamehameha Hwy; meals $5-15; 7am-7pm Mon-Fri, to 4pm Sat) Real local flavor defines this drive-in, where *loco moco* plates smothered in gravy, *kalbi* short ribs, *laulau* and garlicky shrimp are all cooked hot. Grab sweet bread to go.

Kahuku Grill BURGERS, SEAFOOD $
(55-565 Kamehameha Hwy; mains $8-12; 11am-9pm Mon-Sat;) On the old mill grounds in the middle of town, this tidy farmhouse-like cafe takes its sweet time cooking juicy handmade beef burgers and thickly battered coconut-fried shrimp.

Fiji Market MARKET $
(55-565 Kamehameha Hwy; mains $6-12; 9am-9pm Mon-Sat) Hidden back inside the old mill shopping complex, this Polynesian mini-mart serves up South Pacific curry plate lunches with fresh, hot roti and also imported New Zealand meat pies.

Giovanni's SEAFOOD $$
(http://giovannisshrimptruck.com; 56-505 Kamehameha Hwy; plates $13; 10:30am-6:30pm) Giovanni's white graffiti-covered shrimp truck is the original, and still a classic. Handily, neighboring trucks serve smoothies, fro-yo, shave ice and more.

Fumi's SEAFOOD $$
(www.fumiskahukushrimp.com; 56-777 Kamehameha Hwy; plates $10-13; 10am-7pm) Dig into a coconut shrimp plate lunch by the original sunset-painted food truck or next to the live-shrimp tank inside Fumi's newer building up the road.

Romy's SEAFOOD $$
(www.romyskahukuprawns.org; 56-781 Kamehameha Hwy; plates $12-17; 10am-6pm) Tented picnic tables overlook an aquaculture farm and you'll get to peel the heads-on prawns yourself. *Pani popo* (Samoan coconut buns) for dessert!

NORTH SHORE & HALE'IWA

You don't have to be a surfer, or even know much about surfing, to have heard of the North Shore. Iconic breaks such as Pipeline, Sunset and Waimea are world-famous. In winter the big swells come in and the wave heights reach gigantic proportions. The ocean rears its head in profound beauty or utter terror – depending on your point of view. In summer the gigantic waves peter out and international surf tribes migrate to the next big break – in their wake all that is left is calm water, perfect for snorkeling, diving and swimming, at those same stunning beaches.

Before the surfing revolution of the 1950s, the North Shore was little more than a collection of fishing villages, sugarcane plantations and dilapidated houses. The rebirth of board riding brought surfers, big-name pro surf competitions and eventually those eager to cash in on the trend. The North Shore is far from a sellout though – there's a strong current within the community to 'Keep the North Shore Country,' where development is treated skeptically and sustainability is the coolest concept in town.

Turtle Bay

Idyllic coves and lava beds define O'ahu's northern tip, where the Windward Coast and the North Shore meet. Turtle Bay Resort dominates this landscape with a view-perfect hotel, golf course, condo village and public-access beaches. Only time will tell if the resort's ambitious expansion plans will come to pass after a court-ordered environmental impact statement, or if tough economic times will be enough to sway locals' opposition with the promise of new jobs.

Beaches

Public beach parking at the resort costs $5 per day.

Kuilima Cove BEACH

(🚸) Just east of the hotel on Kuilima Point is a beautiful little strand known as **Bayview Beach**. On the bay's right-hand side is an outer reef that not only knocks down the waves but facilitates great snorkeling in summer – and, in winter, some moderate surf. Rent bodyboards, snorkel sets and beach gear at the resort's on-site **Sand Bar** (www.turtlebayresort.com; Turtle Bay Resort, 57-091 Kamehameha Hwy; ⏲9am-5pm).

Kaihalulu Beach BEACH

A mile's walk along the beach east of Kuilima Cove is this beautiful, curved, white-sand beach backed by ironwoods. The rocky bottom makes for poor swimming, but the shoreline attracts morning beachcombers. Continue another mile east, detouring up onto the bluff by the golf course, to reach scenic **Kahuku Point**, where fishers cast throw-nets and pole-fish from the rocks.

★**Kawela Bay** BEACH

West of Kuilima Cove, a 1.5-mile shoreline trail runs over to Kawela Bay. In winter you might spy whales cavorting offshore. After walking round **Protection Point**, named for its WWII bunker, voila! You've found Kawela Bay, with its thicket of banyan trees as seen on TV's *Lost*. For the best swimming and snorkeling, keep walking to the middle of the bay.

Activities

Hele Huli Adventure Center OUTDOORS

(☎293-6024; www.helehuli.com; Turtle Bay Resort, 57-091 Kamehameha Hwy; 🚸) Swimming and snorkeling just not exciting enough for you? Turtle Bay hotel's activity desk arranges horseback rides on forest and beach trails, surfing and stand up paddleboarding (SUP) lessons, sea-kayaking and fishing trips, kid-friendly geocaching games and more.

Turtle Bay Golf GOLF

(☎293-8574; www.turtlebayresort.com; Turtle Bay Resort, 57-091 Kamehameha Hwy; green fees $75-185; ⏲by reservation only) Turtle Bay has two top-rated 18-hole championship golf courses, one designed by George Fazio and the other by Arnold Palmer. Both abound with water views and host PGA/LPGA tour events. The pro shop offers instruction and rental clubs and carts.

Sleeping

At Turtle Bay Resort, condos are individually owned, which means you may get a slice of vacation-rental paradise or a taste of time-share hell. Choose your unit carefully after inspecting online photos and reviews. Make reservations using local real-estate agencies, using booking agencies such as the following, or websites like **VRBO** (www.vrbo.com) and **HomeAway** (www.homeaway.com). Quoted rates generally don't include taxes or a one-time cleaning fee ($80 to $200); usually there's a minimum stay of two to five nights.

Estates at Turtle Bay VACATION RENTAL $$

(☎293-0600; www.turtlebay-rentals.com; studio/1br/2br/3br from $90/125/160/200; 🏊) Amenities vary, but all condos have access to swimming pools and tennis courts.

Turtle Bay Condos VACATION RENTAL $$

(☎888-266-3690, 293-2800; http://turtlebaycondos.com; studio/1br/2br/3br from $120/150/225/385; 🏊) Weekly and monthly discounts available for a variety of condo rentals.

Team Real Estate ACCOMMODATION SERVICES $$

(☎800-982-8602, 637-3507; www.teamrealestate.com; 1br/2br from $100/150) Rental agency based in Hale'iwa that also manages a few condos at Turtle Bay.

Turtle Bay Resort RESORT $$$

(☎800-203-3650, 293-6000; www.turtlebayresort.com; 57-091 Kamehameha Hwy; r from $259, cottage/villa from $659/1090; ❄@📶🏊) Out of sync with the North Shore's beatnik-surfer vibe, Turtle Bay offers all the modern conveniences of beach resort life. Admittedly dated, every hotel room at least has an ocean view, while deluxe rooms have private lanai. More romantic options include nearby

North Shore (O'ahu)

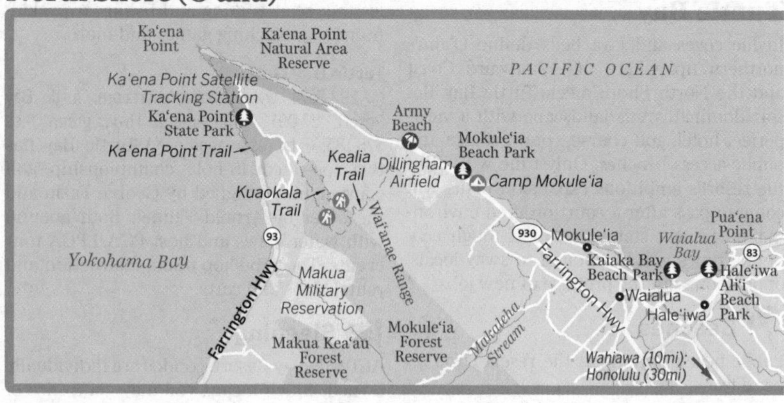

cottages, where fresh fruit is delivered daily, and ocean villas where the water splashes not far from your door.

Eating & Drinking

21 Degrees North PACIFIC RIM $$$

(☎293-6000; www.turtlebayresort.com; Turtle Bay Resort, 57-091 Kamehameha Hwy; mains $27-46, 5-course tasting menu from $75; ⏲6pm-10pm Tue-Sat) Panoramic windows with ocean views are the hallmark of this white-tablecloth dining room. Expect perfectly prepared seafood like braised Kona lobster or pepper-crusted ahi plated with Kahuku corn fritters and an organic farm salad. There's a discerning global wine list too. Tapas and cocktails are served in the lounge until 11pm daily except Monday.

Ola LOCAL, SEAFOOD $$$

(☎293-0801; www.olaislife.com; Turtle Bay Resort, 57-091 Kamehameha Hwy; mains lunch $10-24, dinner $19-58; ⏲11am-10pm) With table legs and tiki torches sticking out of the sand, this cabana stakes out an unparalleled position on the beach. When it's sunny, Ola is an irresistible spot for lunch, although the food is far from outstanding. Service is so laid-back, you might find yourself staying straight through happy hour for *pupu* like *kalua* pork nachos and ahi *poke*.

Surfer Bar BAR

(☎293-6000; www.turtlebayresort.com; Turtle Bay Resort, 57-091 Kamehameha Hwy) Big-name North Shore musicians occasionally play live sets at the resort's Surfer Bar, where the stage is set for anything from open-mic nights to surf-film screenings. Happy-hour coconut margaritas and 'lychee-tinis' are a bargain. For sunset views and live Hawaiian music some nights, head over to the resort's poolside **Hang Ten Bar & Grill** instead.

Sunset Beach to Waimea Bay

Revered for monster winter waves and having some of the best surf breaks on the planet, this stretch of coastline running from Sunset Beach all the way to Waimea Bay is a sort of loose gathering point for the world's best surfers, ardent fans and enthusiastic wannabes. Beyond the beaches, which shouldn't be ignored, lie pockets of lush green beauty. In ancient Hawai'i, the Waimea Valley was heavily settled, with the lowlands terraced in taro and ridges topped by heiau. Now blocked at the ocean by a sandbar, the river was once a passage for canoes traveling to villages upstream.

Beaches

The following beaches are listed geographically from northeast to southwest.

Sunset Beach Park BEACH

(59-104 Kamehameha Hwy) Like many North Shore beaches, this one has a seasonally split personality. In winter the big swells come in and the sand is pounded into submission by spectacularly large waves. In summer the waves calm down, making it attractive to swimmers and snorkelers, and the beach actually grows bigger. The park has restrooms, outdoor showers and a lifeguard tower.

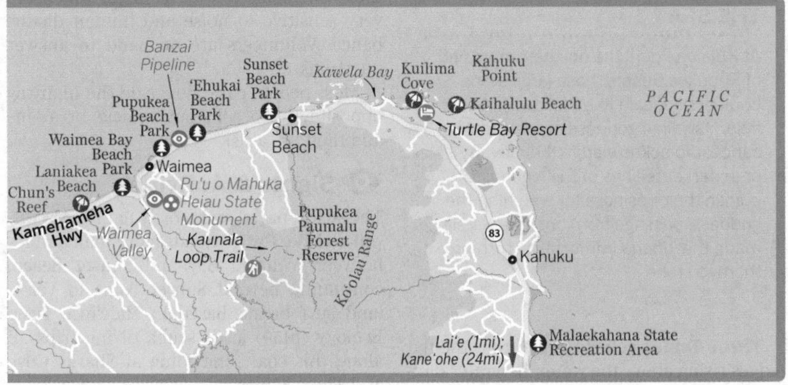

In winter, it's a hot spot for pro wave riders and the posse of followers these rock stars of the sea attract. The tremendous surf activity causes the slope of the beach to become increasingly steep as the season goes on. Though the water looks more inviting in summer, be aware there are still some nasty currents about.

Backyards is a smokin' hot reef break off Sunset Point on the northeastern side of the beach. With strong currents and a shallow reef, it draws expert windsurfers and tow surfers.

To get to the beach park, turn *makai* (seaward) off Kamehameha Hwy onto O'opuola St, near Ted's Bakery. If the beach lot is full, there's overflow parking across the street.

★'Ehukai Beach Park — BEACH

(59-337 Ke Nui Rd) 'Ehukai Beach, aka **Banzai Pipeline**, Pipeline or Pipe – call it what you want, but if it's big surf you seek, this is *the* place. It's known the world over for having the biggest, heaviest and closest-to-perfection barrels in all of wave riding. At the beach, there's a lifeguard tower, outdoor showers, restrooms, drinking water and picnic tables.

When strong westerly swells kick up in winter, these waves jack up to monster size, often topping out above 15ft before breaking on the ultrashallow reef below. For expert board riders who know what they're doing (no, a day of lessons at Waikiki Beach doesn't count), this could be surfing's holy grail. The waves break only a few yards offshore, so spectators are front-row and center. In the summer months everything calms down and there's even some decent snorkeling off this beach.

The beach parking lot is off the Kamehameha Hwy (Hwy 83), opposite Sunset Beach Neighborhood Park.

★Pupukea Beach Park — BEACH

(59-727 Kamehameha Hwy) Pupukea, meaning 'white shell,' is an unusually scenic beach, with deep blue waters protected as a marine-life conservation district and a mix of lava and white sand along a varied coastline. The long beach encompasses Three Tables to the south, Sharks Cove to the north and Old Quarry in the center, where you'll find outdoor showers and restrooms.

At **Sharks Cove**, the white-tipped reef sharks here aren't usually aggressive unless you disturb or otherwise provoke them. Just keep your distance and don't approach them. In summer, when the seas are calm, the cove has superb snorkeling (wear reef walkers to protect your tender *malihini* feet), as well as O'ahu's most popular cavern dive. Beginning divers take lessons here, while underwater caves will thrill advanced divers. Some caves are very deep and labyrinthine, and there have been a number of drownings, so only venture into them with a local expert.

At **Old Quarry**, the beach's natural rock features are jagged, sculpted and look as if they were cut by human hands, but rest assured that these features are natural. Coastal tide pools are intriguing micro-habitats for marine creatures, best explored at low tide. Be careful, especially if you have kiddies in tow, because these rocks are razor sharp.

STONE-FACED WATCHERS OF THE SEA

At Kulalua Point, the northernmost end of Pupukea Beach, those large stone boulders are said to be followers of Pele, Hawaiian goddess of fire and volcanoes. To acknowledge their loyalty – or in darker tellings of the legend, to punish their nosiness for watching the goddess' passage from onshore – Pele made the *'ohana* immortal by turning them to stone.

Three Tables gets its name from the flat ledges rising above the water. In winter dangerous rip currents flow between the beach and the tables. In summer, only when the water is calm, it's good for snorkeling and diving. You might see some action by snorkeling around the tables, but the best variety of coral and fish, as well as some small caves, lava tubes and arches, are in deeper water further out. Watch for sharp rocks and coral – and, as always, don't touch the fragile reef.

Waimea Bay Beach Park BEACH
(61-031 Kamehameha Hwy) It may be a beauty but it's certainly a moody one. Waimea Bay changes dramatically with the seasons: it can be tranquil and flat as a lake in summer, then savage in winter, with incredible waves and the island's meanest rip currents. It's usually only calm enough for swimming and snorkeling between June and September. Lifeguards are on duty daily.

Winter is prime time for surfers. On the calmer days bodyboarders are out in force, but even then sets come in hard and people get pounded. Winter watersports at this beach are not for novices. Year-round, jumping off the big rock formation that sticks out into the bay is prohibited.

Parking at this popular beach is often tight, but don't park along the highway, even if you see others doing so, because police can tow away dozens of cars at once. Beach facilities include restrooms, outdoor showers and picnic tables.

Laniakea Beach BEACH
(http://malamanahonu.org; Kamehameha Hwy [Hwy 83]) Between the highway's 3- and 4-mile markers, this narrow spit of sand is crowded with basking *honu* (green sea turtles), who migrate here from French Frigate Shoals in the remote Northwestern Hawaiian Islands. Stay back at least 20ft from these endangered sea creatures, which are very sensitive to noise and human disturbance. Volunteers are on hand to answer questions.

Most people park alongside the highway opposite the beach, but vehicle break-ins and theft are a risk.

Sights & Activities

The shady, paved and mostly flat **Ke Ala Pupukea Bike Path** extends more than 3 miles between Waimea Bay and Sunset Beach, continuing beyond Sunset Point to Velzyland surf break. Based in Hale'iwa, Deep Ecology (p159) leads scuba diving trips all along this coast, including at Sharks Cove and Three Tables.

Waimea Valley GARDENS, PARK
(☎638-7766; www.waimeavalley.net; 59-864 Kamehameha Hwy; adult/child 4-12yr $15/7.50, waterfall shuttle one-way/round-trip $4/6, guided walking tours from $5; ⏲9am-5pm; 👪) Craving more jungle than beach? This 1800-acre Hawaiian cultural and nature park, just inland from Waimea Bay, is a sanctuary of tropical tranquillity. Wander among the botanical gardens, planted with over 5000 native and exotic plant species. Amble alongside Kamananui Stream for a mile (shuttle available) to take a dip at the base of 45ft-high Waimea Falls.

Also interesting are the replicas of buildings ancient Hawaiians dwelled in and a restored heiau dedicated to Lono, god of fertility and agriculture. Daily cultural activities like lei-making, hula lessons and traditional Hawaiian games of skill and chance are designed for tour-bus crowds. Guided botanical walking tours are often given on the first and third Saturdays of the month (call ahead to check schedules).

Pu'u o Mahuka Heiau State Monument TEMPLE
(www.hawaiistateparks.org; off Pupukea Rd; ⏲sunrise-sunset) FREE A cinematic coastal panorama and a stroll around the grounds of O'ahu's largest temple reward those who venture up to this national historic landmark, perched on a bluff above Waimea Bay. It's a dramatically windswept and lonely site. Though the ruined walls leave a lot to be imagined, it's worth the drive for the commanding views, especially at sunset.

Pu'u o Mahuka means 'hill of escape' – but this was a *luakini* heiau, where human sacrifices took place. Likely dating from the 17th century, the temple's stacked-stone construction is attributed to the legendary *menehune* (the 'little people' who, according to legend, built many of Hawaii's fishponds, heiau and other stonework), who are said to have completed their work in just one night.

Do not walk around inside or atop the fragile lava-rock walls, to avoid damaging them. To get here, turn *mauka* (inland) onto Pupukea Rd by the Foodland supermarket; the monument turnoff is about 0.5 miles uphill, from where it's another roughshod 0.7 miles to the heiau.

Sleeping

Like elsewhere on the North Shore, available accommodations are mostly vacation rentals. Book online with websites like **VRBO** (www.vrbo.com), **HomeAway** (www.homeaway.com) and **Air B&B** (www.airbnb.com) or through local real-estate agencies, for example, in Hale'iwa.

Backpackers Vacation Inn & Plantation Village HOSTEL **$**
(☎638-7838; http://backpackers-hawaii.com; 59-788 Kamehameha Hwy; dm $27-30, d $62-85, studio/2br/3br cabin from $120/170/215; @📶) The only budget option around is this scruffy backpacker crash pad. In keeping with the surf-shack vibe, digs are modest to the point of being ramshackle. If you don't mind peeling paint and thrown-together decor, you'll feel right at home. Hostel dorms share baths and kitchens, while the village is a groovy collection of beach cabins, some private. The hostel is located between Waimea Bay and Pupukea Beach Park.

★**Ke Iki Beach Bungalows** VACATION RENTAL **$$**
(☎866-638-8229, 638-8229; http://keikibeach.com; 59-579 Ke Iki Rd; 1br/2br apt from $205/230; ❄📶) Just north of Pupukea Beach Park, these hideaway retreats show admittedly dated tropical flair, with rattan chairs and hammocks strung between coconut trees that fit the beachfront setting like a glove. Each of the apartment-style units has a full kitchen, cable TV, phone and wi-fi, and all guests have access to a BBQ grill and picnic tables.

The location is idyllic – oceanfront units are right on the sand, while others are just a minute's walk from the water. Cleaning surcharges ($50 to $100) apply. Ask about weekly discounts.

Eating

★**Ted's Bakery** LOCAL **$**
(www.tedsbakery.com; 59-024 Kamehameha Hwy; meals $7-16; ⏰7am-8pm; 👪) You can't get more North Shore than this quintessential takeout joint. Famous island-wide, Ted's is the place for a quick snack or a huge plate lunch (think chicken *katsu*, teriyaki beef, *kalua* pork, grilled mahimahi) that'll satisfy even hungry surfers. The chocolate-*haupia* cream pie is legendary, and there are a dozen more desserts to choose from, including guava cheesecake. The bakery is opposite Sunset Beach Park.

THAT'S WHERE EDDIE WOULD GO

Eddie Aikau was a champion surfer and Waimea lifeguard. You only have to see Waimea on a stormy winter day to know the courage it takes to wade into the water here to save a swimmer in trouble. But it was another act of heroism that spawned the slogan 'Eddie Would Go' that you'll see on bumper stickers all around the islands.

In 1978 Eddie joined an expedition to re-create ancient Polynesians' journey to Hawaii by sailing the *Hokule'a*, a replica double-hulled voyaging canoe, from O'ahu to Tahiti and back. Several hours after the craft set sail it got into trouble and capsized in rough water near Moloka'i. Eddie decided to go for help – he grabbed his surfboard and set off to paddle over a dozen miles to shore to raise the alarm. He was never seen again. His companions survived, but the legendary waterman was gone.

Today an annual big-wave surfing event, called the Quiksilver in Memory of Eddie Aikau, takes place during winter at Waimea Bay. It's invitation-only and only runs when waves are giant enough (ie 20ft minimum), meaning the bay picks the day. It doesn't happen every year and you can't predict the waves – but that's somehow fitting. People like Eddie are one in a million, and waves that honor his memory are worth the wait.

TRIPLE CROWN OF SURFING

During the North Shore's **Triple Crown of Surfing** (www.vanstriplecrownofsurfing.com) championships, touring pros compete for pride – and over $800,000 in prizes. For men, the kick-off is the Reef Hawaiian Pro at Hale'iwa Ali'i Beach Park in mid-November. The competition's second challenge, the Vans World Cup of Surfing (late November to early December), rides at Sunset Beach. The final leg, the Billabong Pipe Masters, happens in early to mid-December at Pipeline. Parallel events for world-class women surfers take place alongside the men's battles on O'ahu, but finish on Maui.

Foodland SUPERMARKET **$**
(www.foodland.com; 59-720 Kamehameha Hwy; ⏲6am-11pm) Across from Pupukea Beach Park, pick up everything you need for a beach picnic from the deli or get groceries for DIY meals.

Pupukea Grill LOCAL **$$**
(www.pupukeagrill.com; 59-680 Kamehameha Hwy; meals $9-15; ⏲11am-5pm Thu-Mon) Next to an auto service station across from Sharks Cove, this white food truck cranks out roasted veggie and grilled fish tacos, *poke* bowls, flatbread kebab wraps, garden-fresh salads, quinoa plates and fruit smoothies, all of which are better than the North Shore's typical roadside fare.

Sharks Cove Grill LOCAL **$$**
(www.sharkscovegrill.com; 59-712 Kamehameha Hwy; dishes $4-8, meals $11-16; ⏲8:30am-8:30pm) Opposite Pupukea Beach Park, order your taro burger or ahi kebab skewers from the food truck's window, then pull up a rickety seat at an umbrella-shaded table and watch the waves roll onto the beach. The food's only so-so, but the experience is totally North Shore.

Hale'iwa

POP 3970

The best way to know if the surf's up is by how busy Hale'iwa is. If the town is all hustle and bustle, then chances are the surf is flat. If you arrive into town and find it eerily quiet, check the beach – odds are the waves are pumping. It's that sort of town: it's all about the surf and everyone knows it.

Despite being a touristy hub, there's a laid-back ambience to Hale'iwa that's in perfect harmony with the rest of the North Shore. As the biggest town around, this is the place to stop for a shave ice, pick up a new bikini or board shorts, rent a longboard for the day and then hang around after sunset, wishing you could stay just a little bit longer.

Beaches

Hale'iwa has a picturesque boat harbor bounded by beach parks. The winter wave action attracts annual international surf competitions and lots of local attention.

Hale'iwa Ali'i Beach Park BEACH
(66-167 Hale'iwa Rd) Home to some of the North Shore's best surf, winter waves here can be huge, with double or triple overhead tubes not uncommon. When it's flat, local kids rip it up with their bodyboards, while newbie tourists test their skills with stand up paddleboarding (SUP). The shallow areas on the beach's southern side are generally calmest for swimming.

The park has restrooms, outdoor showers, picnic tables and lifeguards. Trivia alert: scenes from *Baywatch* were shot here.

Hale'iwa Beach Park BEACH
(62-449 Kamehameha Hwy) On the northern side of the harbor, this beach is protected by a shallow shoal and breakwater so it's usually gentle enough for swimming. There's little wave action, except for occasional winter swells that ripple into the bay. Not as pretty as Hale'iwa's other strands, this community park has a children's playground, volleyball courts, restrooms and outdoor showers.

Kaiaka Bay Beach Park BEACH
(66-449 Hale'iwa Rd) Beach bums wanting to get away from crowds head less than a mile southwest of town. There are a few shade trees, so it's a good option when temperatures climb, and turtles sometimes show up here. But if you're looking to get wet, swimming is better at other local beaches. The park has restrooms, outdoor showers, picnic tables and campsites.

Sights

North Shore Surf & Cultural Museum MUSEUM
(www.northshoresurfmuseum.com) It's impossible to separate surfing from the culture of the

North Shore. The best place to see how deep that connection runs is at this little museum, packed with vintage boards, fading photographs and some epic surf stories. At the time of writing, the museum was closed pending relocation; check the website for updates.

Historic Hale'iwa Town HISTORICAL SITE
(☎637-4558; www.gonorthshore.org; 90min walking tour $10; ⏰tours usually 3pm Wed & 9:30am Sat) In 1832 John and Ursula Emerson, the North Shore's first Christian missionaries, arrived in Hale'iwa – meaning house *(hale)* of the great frigate bird *('iwa)*. Learn more about the town's ancient Hawaiian history and missionary and sugar-plantation eras on a guided walking tour (call for reservations).

Activities

For beginner surfers, the North Shore has a few tame breaks like **Pua'ena Point**, just north of Hale'iwa Beach Park, and **Chun's Reef**, further north of town. Even if you've ridden a few waves in Waikiki, it's smart to take a lesson for an introduction to local underwater hazards. At Hale'iwa Beach Park, surf school vans rent gear and offer same-day instruction, including for stand up paddleboarding. Expect to pay at least $75 for a two-hour group surfing lesson, or $25 to $45 to rent a board for the day (with paddle $60).

Deep Ecology DIVING
(☎800-578-3992, 637-7946; www.oahuscubadive.com; 66-456 Kamehameha Hwy; dives from $95; ⏰8am-5pm) If you'd rather get under the waves than on top of them, the eco-conscious divers at Deep Ecology can sort you out. Summer shore dives explore Sharks Cove and Three Tables at nearby Pupukea Beach Park, while offshore lava tubes, coral reefs, arches and cathedrals await boat divers. Rental scuba and snorkel gear available. Ask about winter whale-watching tours.

Surf 'n' Sea WATER SPORTS
(☎637-9887; www.surfnsea.com; 62-595 Kamehameha Hwy; ⏰9am-7pm) In a ramshackle wooden building, the granddaddy of Hale'iwa surf shops rents surfboards, wetsuits, car racks, boogie boards, snorkel sets, kayaks, life jackets, bicycles, beach umbrellas and chairs by the hour, day or week. Watersports tours and lessons require advance reservations.

North Shore Surf Girls SURFING
(☎637-2977; www.northshoresurfgirls.com; ⏰by reservation only) Especially great for women and kids, these surfing, bodyboarding and SUP lessons and camps are taught by multilingual instructors, some of whom cameoed in the surf movie *Blue Crush*.

Rainbow Watersports SUP
(☎800-470-4964, 372-9304; www.rainbowwatersports.com; ⏰by reservation only) Specializing in stand up paddleboarding, Rainbow offers lessons along flat-water rivers and at calm beaches, plus paddling excursions along the North Shore with swimming and snorkeling breaks.

Sunset Surratt Surf Academy SURFING, SUP
(☎783-8657; www.surfnorthshore.com) Born and raised on the North Shore, 'Uncle Bryan' has been coaching pro surfers for decades. He and his staff teach all skill levels of surfers and stand up paddlers. Board rentals available.

North Shore Catamaran CRUISE
(☎351-9371; www.sailingcat.com; Hale'iwa Boat Harbor, cnr Hale'iwa Rd & Kamehameha Hwy; adult/child under 12yr from $60/55) Book ahead for a sunset cruise, summer snorkeling trip or winter whale-watching tour aboard a catamaran sailboat.

Tours

O'ahu Agri-Tours BUS TOUR
(☎228-7585; http://oahuagritours.com; adult/child $110/102; ⏰usually 8am-2:30pm Wed-Sun) Get back to the *'aina* (land) at the North Shore's small farms, maybe having lunch in a taro patch and tasting locally grown coffee and chocolate. Reservations required; transportation to/from Waikiki included.

Sleeping

Vacation rentals are the most common accommodations in Hale'iwa, which has no hotels. Browse vacation-rental websites such as **VRBO** (www.vrbo.com), **HomeAway** (www.homeaway.com) and **Air B&B** (www.airbnb.com), or check the bulletin boards at Celestial Natural Foods and Malama Market.

Kaiaka Bay Beach Park CAMPGROUND $
(https://camping.honolulu.gov; 66-449 Hale'iwa Rd; 5-night campsite permit $52; ⏰8am Fri-8am Wed) At Hale'iwa's only campground, beachfront sites lack much privacy. The county allows

camping except on Wednesday and Thursday nights; permits are required in advance (see p63).

Team Real Estate VACATION RENTAL **$$**
(800-982-8602, 637-3507; www.teamrealestate.com; North Shore Marketplace, 66-250 Kamehameha Hwy; studio/1br/2br/3br/4br from $60/95/150/165/250) This local real-estate agency handles a couple dozen vacation rentals on the North Shore, from duplex studio apartments to beachfront luxury homes. Book early, especially for the busy winter season. Ask about weekly, monthly and off-peak discounts.

Eating & Drinking

Most restaurants and bars are spread out along the Kamehameha Hwy (Hwy 83), Hale'iwa's main drag.

Beet Box Cafe HEALTHY **$**
(www.thebeetboxcafe.com; Celestial Natural Foods, 66-443 Kamehameha Hwy; mains $7-10; 9am-5pm Mon-Sat, to 4pm Sun;) At the back of a hole-in-the-wall market stocking good-karma organic produce and groceries, this tiny veg-friendly kitchen makes up toasted sandwiches on multigrain bread, fresh salads and all-day breakfasts of burritos, egg scrambles and acai bowls. The Beet Box's lunch wagon parks opposite Pipeline surf break outside town.

DON'T MISS

HALE'IWA'S SHAVE ICE

O'ahu's classic circle-island drive just isn't complete without stopping for shave ice at **Matsumoto's** (www.matsumotoshaveice.com; 66-087 Kamehameha Hwy; snacks $3-5; 9am-6pm;), a tin-roofed 1950s general store. Some families drive from Honolulu to the North Shore with one goal only in mind: to stand in line here and walk out with a delicious shave ice cone, drenched with island flavors, such as *liliko'i* (passion fruit), banana, mango and pineapple.

Tourists flock to Matsumoto's, but some locals prefer **Aoki's** (www.aokisshaveice.com; 66-117 Kamehameha Hwy; snacks $3-5; 11am-6:30pm;), which usually has much shorter lines. But its souvenir T-shirts aren't nearly as cool as Matsumoto's...

Kua 'Aina BURGERS **$**
(www.kua-aina.com; 66-160 Kamehameha Hwy; dishes $3-10; 11am-8pm;) A North Shore classic, Kua 'Aina has a monster-sized list of burgers and sandwiches: take your pick of grilled ahi or mahimahi, teriyaki chicken, peppery eggplant or pineapple-topped North Shore grass-fed beef patties with shoestring fries on the side.

Grass Skirt Grill LOCAL **$**
(www.grassskirtgrill.com; 66-214 Kamehameha Hwy; mains $6-13; 11am-6pm) At this local kitchen, retro surf decor on the walls fits right in with the island-style mixed plates, grilled seafood and juicy fish sandwiches, and heart-attack-worthy teriyaki cheese fries. It's good enough for a takeout meal when you're bound for the beach. Cash only.

Hale'iwa Farmers Market MARKET **$**
(www.haleiwafarmersmarket.com; Waimea Valley, 59-864 Kamehameha Hwy; 3-7pm Thu;) With live musicians and 40 vendors selling organic, seasonal edibles and artisan crafts, this farmers market stays lively. It keeps changing locations, so check the website before you go.

Waialua Bakery & Juice Bar BAKERY, DELI **$**
(66-200 Kamehameha Hwy; dishes $1-8; 10am-5pm Mon-Sat;) Next to a parking lot, drop into this hippie shack for home-baked bread and cookies, deli sandwiches, salads, smoothies and ice-cream sandwiches.

Malama Market SUPERMARKET **$**
(66-190 Kamehameha Hwy; 7am-9pm) Grab a quick bite from the deli or stock up on picnic fixin's at this modern supermarket.

Opal Thai THAI **$$**
(381-8091; Hale'iwa Town Center, 66-460 Kamehameha Hwy; mains $8-13; 11am-3pm & 5-10pm Tue-Sat;) What does a local food truck want to be when it grows up? A casual cafe with reasonable prices and a fiery, authentic menu of Thai classics such as green-papaya salad, noodles stir-fried with garlic and crab, duck curry and tom yum soup. Owner Opel will ask what kinds of flavors you like, but may insist on ordering for you – trust him only if you're not on a limited budget.

Café Hale'iwa BREAKFAST **$$**
(637-5516; 66-460 Kamehameha Hwy; mains breakfast & lunch $5-12, dinner $18-30; 7am-1:45pm daily, 6-9:30pm Tue-Sat;) This surf-style diner has been hanging around town

since the 1980s. Before a day out paddling the waves, fuel up on the sunny patio with an 'off the wall' omelette or 'breakfast in a barrel' (an egg-and-potato burrito splashed with green salsa). Candlelight transforms the joint for hit-or-miss dinners like grilled pork with North Shore farm-raised veggies.

B's Bar & Grinds LOCAL **$$**
(☎744-4125; www.bsbarandgrinds.com; Hale'iwa Town Center, 66-197 Kamehameha Hwy; shared plates $6-12, mains $12-24; ⊙11am-4pm & 6pm-midnight, bar to 2am) Groove with live acoustic acts while digging into bowls of super-fresh *poke*, baskets of truffle fries, meaty BBQ *kalua* pork sandwiches and Kahuku shrimp with corn cakes. Stick with the bar food and skip the overreaching dinner mains like pasta or curried lamb.

Luibueno's MEXICAN, SEAFOOD **$$**
(☎637-7717; http://luibueno.com; Hale'iwa Town Center, 66-165 Kamehameha Hwy; mains $6-29; ⊙11am-10:30pm, drinks only after 9:30pm; 👪) If you've never tried a beer-battered mahimahi taco or a big ol' grilled ahi burrito, take your chances at this sunset-colored faux-adobe hacienda. Along with modern Mexican fare, Luibueno's also serves decent upmarket seafood and steaks. An après-surf crowd hogs the bar while knocking back margaritas during happy hour.

Hale'iwa Food Trucks FAST FOOD **$$**
(Kamehameha Hwy [Hwy 83]; meals $8-15; ⊙open daily, hours vary) On the south side of town, between the bridge and the roundabout, locals debate which food truck in this dusty lot grills the best shrimp, but most agree **VJ's North Shore Dogs** makes dang good burgers. Back in the town center, **Roy's Kiawe Broiled Chicken** is another smokin' hot food truck (open weekends only).

Hale'iwa Joe's SEAFOOD **$$$**
(☎637-8005; www.haleiwajoes.com; 66-011 Kamehameha Hwy; mains lunch $11-19, dinner $19-40; ⊙11:30am-9:30pm) Scenically overlooking the marina, Hale'iwa Joe's is, frankly, overrated. Some of the fresh catch comes from fishing boats glimpsed outside the windows, but the execution falls short. Come for sunset cocktails and *pupu* only during happy hour (4:30pm to 6:30pm Monday to Friday).

Lanikai Juice JUICE BAR
(www.lanikaijuice.com; 66-215 Kamehameha Hwy; snacks & drinks $4-8; ⊙6am-8pm Mon-Fri, 7am-7pm Sat & Sun) Kailua's favorite stop for smoothies, fresh juice and acai bowls has branched out to Hale'iwa, with the same commitment to locally grown, often organic ingredients.

Coffee Gallery CAFE
(☎637-5355; www.roastmaster.com; North Shore Marketplace, 66-250 Kamehameha Hwy; snacks & drinks $2-6; ⊙6:30am-8pm; 📶) This mellow cafe brews freshly roasted coffee, sometimes made from Hawaii-grown beans, and espresso drinks.

Shopping

Trend-setting surf shops, eclectic boutiques and art galleries are chock-a-block along the Kamehameha Hwy, especially in the Hale'iwa Town Center and North Shore Marketplace shopping plazas.

North Shore Swimwear CLOTHING
(www.northshoreswimwear.com; North Shore Marketplace, 66-250 Kamehameha Hwy; ⊙10am-6pm) Women's wet-and-wild styles from sporty to retro cover-up to barely there, all free to mix and match. Custom orders are handmade in Hawaii.

Guava WOMEN'S CLOTHING
(www.guavahawaii.com; Hale'iwa Town Center, 66-165 Kamehameha Hwy; ⊙10am-6pm) Upscale chic boutique for beachy women's apparel like gauzy sundresses and beach cover-ups, hip denim and strappy sandals.

Kai Ku Hale HOMEWARES, GIFTS
(http://kaikuhale.com; Hale'iwa Town Center, 66-145 Kamehameha Hwy; ⊙10am-7pm) Bring island style back home with made-in-Hawaii bath products, recycled art, wood carvings, homewares and handmade jewelry.

Growing Keiki CLOTHING, CHILDREN
(http://thegrowingkeiki.com; 66-051 Kamehameha Hwy; ⊙10am-6pm; 👪) Outfit your junior surfer or budding beach bum with mini aloha shirts, sundresses, hoodies and even onesies, plus books and toys.

Hale'iwa Art Gallery ARTS & CRAFTS
(www.haleiwaartgallery.com; North Shore Marketplace, 66-250 Kamehameha Hwy; ⊙10am-6pm) This unpretentious art gallery displays works by 20-plus local and regional painters, photographers, sculptors and mixed-media artists.

Getting There & Away

From Honolulu's Ala Moana Center, TheBus 52 runs to Hale'iwa via Wahiawa once or twice hourly; the one-way ride from Honolulu takes 1¾ hours. Every hour, TheBus 55 trundles from Hale'iwa up to Turtle Bay, then down the Windward Coast, taking over two hours to reach the Ala Moana Center.

Waialua

POP 3860

If you somehow find the relatively slow pace of life on the North Shore just too hectic, try Waialua. This mill town ground to a halt in 1996, when sugar production ended. Since then locals have transformed the old mill into a crafty shopping complex and started small-scale farms raising coffee, chocolate, vanilla and much more.

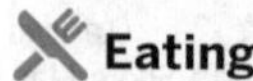

Eating

Thai and Mexican food trucks often park near the sugar mill, where the unhurried **Waialua Farmers Market** (67-106 Kealohanui St; 8:30am-noon Sat) sets up on Saturday mornings.

Pa'ala'a Kai Bakery BAKERY $
(www.pkbsweets.com; 66-945 Kaukonahua Rd; snacks & pastries $2-4; 5:30am-7pm) Take a detour down a country road to find this family-run bakery, a pilgrimage for anyone craving a 'snow puffy' (chocolate cream puff dusted with powdered sugar), which are half-price after 6pm. There's plenty here to satisfy any sweet-toothed traveler.

Shopping

Old Sugar Mill ARTS & CRAFTS, SOUVENIRS
(67-106 Kealohanui St; 9am-5pm Mon-Sat, 10am-5pm Sun) Waialua's former sugar mill has been reborn as an ever-changing hub for local artisan shops. The current line-up includes the rambling **Island X Hawaii** warehouse, which is full of vintage aloha shirts, wood handicrafts and Waialua coffee beans and chocolate, while the **North Shore Soap Factory** makes all-natural bars with tropical ingredients like *kukui* (candlenuts), pikake flowers and sumptuous coconut cream. Both shops have small displays about the building's history.

NOT LOST AFTER ALL

Does Army Beach look familiar? It appeared in the pilot of the hit TV drama *Lost*. When *Lost* first started filming here, tourists driving along the highway would see the smoking wreckage of a crashed plane sitting on the beach. Needless to say, a burned-out jetliner is an alarming site, and many called 911 to mistakenly report an emergency.

Mokule'ia to Ka'ena Point

Hello? Is there anybody out there? The vast, empty stretches of the Farrington Hwy (Hwy 930) show the last few signs of human habitation before the island terminates in the deep and fearsome ocean. The road along O'ahu's Wai'anae Coast is also called Farrington Hwy (Hwy 93), but these roads don't connect – each side reaches a dead end about 2½ miles short of Ka'ena Point.

Beaches

Mokule'ia Beach Park BEACH
(68-919 Farrington Hwy) The beach itself is a nice sandy stretch, but a rocky seabed makes for poor swimming. When waters are calm and flat in summer, snorkelers swim out along the shallow reef. During winter, the currents pick up and entering the water isn't advisable. Keen windsurfers take advantage of the consistent winds. A large grassy area has picnic tables, restrooms and outdoor showers, but no lifeguards.

Army Beach BEACH
(Farrington Hwy [Hwy 930]) Opposite the west end of Dillingham Airfield, this is the widest stretch of sand on the Mokule'ia shore. Once reserved for military personnel, the beach is now open to the public, although it's no longer maintained and there are no facilities. The beach is also unprotected and has very strong rip currents, especially during high winter surf.

Ka'ena Point State Park BEACH
(www.hawaiistateparks.org; Farrington Hwy [Hwy 930]; sunrise-sunset) From Mokule'ia's Army Beach you can drive another 1.6 miles down the road, passing still more white-sand beaches with aqua blue waters. The bit of sand off the pull-out just beyond the first state park sign has a small rock-free swimming area accessible in calm surf. Graffiti, empty liquor bottles and car break-ins are commonplace here, so exercise caution.

Activities

Honolulu Soaring SCENIC FLIGHTS
(☎637-0207; www.honolulusoaring.com; Dillingham Airfield, Farrington Hwy [Hwy 930]; rides $80-305; ⏲10am-5:30pm) The trade winds that visit O'ahu create perfect conditions for sailplanes to glide over the North Shore. Take a short scenic ride or an aerobatic one-hour flight with a hands-on mini lesson. Call ahead, as flights are weather-dependent.

Pacific Skydiving Center SKYDIVING
(☎637-7472; www.pacificskydivinghawaii.com; Dillingham Airfield, 68-760 Farrington Hwy [Hwy 930]; tandem jumps $140-340; ⏲8am-3pm) Wanna get tossed out of a perfectly good airplane? Novices can take a tandem jump attached to an instructor for the stomach-turning 14,000ft freefall, followed by a 15-minute glide back to earth. No scuba diving allowed for 24 hours beforehand. Book online for discounts.

Paradise Air HANG GLIDING
(☎497-6033; www.paradiseairhawaii.com; Dillingham Airfield, Farrington Hwy [Hwy 930]; flights $165-265; ⏲by reservation only) Soar like a bird in an ultralight powered hang glider, accompanied by a pilot instructor who may even let you take over the controls for a few minutes.

Stearman Biplane Rides SCENIC FLIGHTS
(☎637-4461; www.stearmanbiplanerides.com; Hangar B6, Dillingham Airfield, Farrington Hwy [Hwy 930]; flights $175-300; ⏲by reservation only) Loop-de-loop on an aerobatic flight, fly over the scenic North Shore or retrace the route the Japanese flew to Pearl Harbor, all in a restored 1941 Boeing biplane.

Hawaii Polo HORSEBACK RIDING
(☎220-5153; http://hawaii-polo.org; 68-539 Farrington Hwy [Hwy 930]; 90min rides $85-95; ⏲by reservation only, usually Tue, Thu & Sat) When the polo ponies aren't playing, you can ride horseback around the polo club's 100-acre stomping grounds or on the beach at sunset. Children aged eight and up welcome.

Kealia & Kuaokala Trails HIKING, BIKING
(http://hawaiitrails.ehawaii.gov; ⏲sunrise-sunset) The 5-mile round-trip **Kealia Trail** switchbacks its way up the cliffs above Dillingham Airfield, offering ocean views through a forest of ironwoods and *kukui* trees. It connects with the equally long **Kuaokala Trail**, which reaches a celebrated viewpoint over Makua Valley and the Wai'anae Range, without the hassle of securing an advance hiking permit and driving up the Wai'anae Coast (see p171).

The Kealia Trail starts at the back of Dillingham Airfield. Enter via the West Gate and just before the airfield ends, take the road marked Gate D and follow it inland about 0.4 miles. Park in the lot near the air control tower, then walk *mauka* down the gravel access road and look for a brown-and-yellow Na Ala Hele trailhead sign. Watch out for dangerous rockfall along this trail and wear bright safety colors to alert hunters of your presence.

Ka'ena Point Trail HIKING, MOUNTAIN BIKING
(www.hawaiistateparks.org; ⏲sunrise-sunset) Where the Farrington Hwy peters out, a dirt footpath heads out toward Ka'ena Point. The terrain is scrubland up to the base of the Wai'anae Range, while the shoreline is wild and windswept. You can hike or mountain bike about 2.5 miles to the point, then double-back to where you started. Parking at this trailhead is notoriously risky, however.

It's usually safer to leave your car on the state park's southern side and hike in from the Wai'anae Coast trailhead instead (see p171). To get there, backtrack east and drive south through central O'ahu then north up the Wai'anae Coast, a 50-mile trip that takes well over an hour.

Sleeping

Camp Mokule'ia CAMPGROUND $
(☎637-6241; www.campmokuleia.com; 68-729 Farrington Hwy; campsites per person $18; ⏲office 8:30am-5pm Mon-Fri, 10am-5pm Sat) Looking for solitude? Near Dillingham Airfield, this church-owned retreat is open to the public (with advance reservations) if another group hasn't prebooked. In a partially shaded ironwood grove facing the ocean, campground facilities are ultra basic, with outdoor showers and composting toilets. Skip the well-worn lodge rooms, cabins and beach house. No alcohol, drugs or smoking.

CENTRAL O'AHU

Central O'ahu is the island's forgotten backwater. Squeezed by enormous military bases, don't be surprised if you get passed on the highway by camo-painted Humvees or Black Hawk choppers buzzing overhead. A few highways head north to Wahiawa, the

OFF THE BEATEN TRACK

KOLEKOLE PASS

At 1724ft, Kolekole Pass occupies the biggest gap in the Wai'anae Range. Film buffs may recognize the landscape, as this is where WWII Japanese fighter planes appeared to fly through on their way to bomb Pearl Harbor in the classic war movie *Tora! Tora! Tora!* (1970). In reality, the planes flew along the inside of the mountain range, not through it.

Kolekole Pass, on military property above Schofield Barracks, can be visited as long as the base isn't on military alert. Bring photo ID and your rental-car contract. Access is granted by security guards at Lyman Gate off Kunia Rd (Hwy 750). Follow Lyman Rd for over 5 miles, partially alongside an infantry battle course, to reach the pass trailhead. Park on the left side of the road before reaching the security gate, which prohibits anyone without military ID from driving over to the Wai'anae Coast.

From the unmarked dirt parking pull-off, look for a short, steep hiking path with wooden steps that climb toward a viewpoint. On the way up you'll pass a large, ribbed stone allegedly used in ancient times for ritual sacrifices of fallen warriors. In Hawaiian mythology, the stone is also believed to be the embodiment of a woman named Kolekole, who took this form to become the perpetual guardian of the pass. Local lore says that if you touch the stone, bad luck may follow.

region's central town: the H-2 Fwy is the fastest option, while Kunia Rd (Hwy 750), the furthest west, is the most scenic. Moving onward from Wahiawa, rural Kaukonahua Rd (Hwy 803) and the busy Kamehameha Hwy (Hwy 99) lead through pineapple country to the North Shore.

Wahiawa

POP 17,820

Wahiawa itself isn't the sort of place that most travelers seek out, unless you're looking for a military buzz cut, a tattoo or a pawn shop. Yet the land around town was considered sacred by ancient Hawaiians, who built temples, gave birth to royal chiefs and clashed in fierce battles here.

Sights & Activities

Dole Plantation THEME PARK

(☎621-8408; www.dole-plantation.com; 64-1550 Kamehameha Hwy; visitor center admission free, maze adult/child 4-12yr $6/4, train ride $8.50/6.50, walking tour $5/4.25; ⏲9:30am-5pm; 👪) Less than 3 miles north of town, this busy tourist complex has an outdoor pineapple maze and miniature train ride that are fun for kids. Inside the gift shop is a sickly sweet overdose of everything *anana* (pineapple) – the final touch being pineapples for sale for higher prices than in local grocery stores.

After you've devoured a cone of frozen pineapple whip from the cafeteria-style **Plantation Grille**, you can get hopelessly lost in the 'world's largest' **maze**, as verified by *Guinness World Records*, with over 1.5 miles of pathways twisting through more than 14,000 plants.

A vintage-style **steam train** chugs around the plantation, taking visitors for a 20-minute narrated ride. Or you can rent an audio wand and take a self-guided **walking tour** of the plantation's gardens for an up-close look at pineapple, banana, papaya, mango, lychee, taro, coffee and cacao plants.

Wahiawa Botanical Gardens GARDENS

(☎522-7064; www1.honolulu.gov/parks/hbg/wbg.htm; 1396 California Ave; ⏲9am-4pm, closed Dec 25 & Jan 1) FREE While much of Wahiawa is drab bordering on ugly, this botanical garden about a mile east of the Kamehameha Hwy, is a 27-acre oasis. Started in the 1920s as an experiment by sugarcane farmers, it's a mix of the manicured and the wild, with pruned ornamental plants, a gully of towering tropical hardwoods, green ferns and bamboo groves. Some walking paths are wheelchair-accessible.

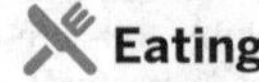

Eating

Maui Mike's FAST FOOD $

(http://mauimikes.com; 96 S Kamehameha Hwy; meals $6-9; ⏲10:30am-8:30pm; 👪) At this fast-food joint, it's chicken, chicken or chicken – fire-roasted, free-range, all-natural and super fresh. Grab some 'lava hot' dipping sauce and Cajun-spiced fries to go.

Sunny Side LOCAL, DINER $

(1017 Kilani Ave; mains $4-9; ⏲7am-2pm) The latest renovations at this side-street diner may have been done a half century ago: think plastic furniture and peeling paint. But all is forgotten when the homestyle cooking arrives (save room for wickedly delicious pie).

Da Pokeman SEAFOOD, LOCAL $

(36 N Kamehameha Hwy; meals $7-10; ⏱10:30am-6pm Mon-Sat) Take your pick of fresh *poke* (kimchi or spicy tuna, anyone?) at this storefront fish market. Keep it Hawaiian with a pork *laulau*, *lomilomi* salmon or *kalua* pig plate lunch.

Poke Stop SEAFOOD, LOCAL $$

(http://poke-stop.com; 95-1840 Meheula Pkwy, Mi'ilani; meals $8-14; ⏱8am-8:30pm Mon-Sat, to 7pm Sun) About 4 miles southeast of Wahiawa, this chef-owned grill's fresh *poke* rice bowls and plate lunches of blackened island fish, tender *kalbi* short ribs and garlic shrimp feed construction workers and hungry schoolkids. It's in a strip mall behind McDonald's, just off the H-2 Fwy (exit 5 Mi'ilani Mauka). Also in Waipahu (p166).

Getting There & Around

From Honolulu's Ala Moana Center, TheBus 52 passes through Wahiawa once or twice hourly; the one-way ride takes 1¼ hours. Buses continue north to the Dole Plantation (15 minutes) and Hale'iwa (25 minutes).

LEEWARD O'AHU & WAI'ANAE COAST

O'ahu's lost coast is full of contradictions. There is a collective feeling of the forgotten here, with the wealthier citizens of Honolulu sweeping what they don't want in their backyard under the leeward rug. You'll find the garbage dump, power plant and US military personnel and the economically disadvantaged living here. Sounds depressing? Surprisingly, it's not really.

In some ways the Wai'anae Coast is the heart and soul of O'ahu. You'll find more Native Hawaiians here than anyplace else on the island, and cultural pride is alive. The land may look parched, with mountains that almost push you into the sea, but the beaches are wide, and relatively untouched by development.

Beyond Ko Olina's luxury resorts, the stop-and-go Farrington Hwy (Hwy 93) runs the length of the Wai'anae Coast, rolling past working-class neighborhoods and strip malls on one side and gorgeous white-sand beaches on the other. Human habitation eventually gives way to velvet-tufted mountains and rocky coastal ledges near Ka'ena Point.

Waipahu

Waipahu was one of O'ahu's last plantation towns. The smokestack of its rusty sugar mill, which operated for almost a century until shutting down in 1995, is still visible on a knoll.

Sights & Activities

Hawaii's Plantation Village MUSEUM

(☎677-0110; www.hawaiiplantationvillage.org; Waipahu Cultural Garden Park, 94-695 Waipahu St; 90min tours adult/child 4-11yr $13/5; ⏱tours 10am, 11am, noon & 1pm Mon-Sat) The lives of immigrants who came to work on Hawaii's sugarcane plantations are examined at this outdoor historical museum and cultural park. Designed primarily for school field trips, the dusty, sprawling grounds encompass two dozen buildings typical of an early-20th-century plantation village. Although the village shows its age, you can still learn a lot by taking a guided tour.

Led by volunteers, walking tours visit a historic Chinese cookhouse and Japanese Shintō shrine, as well as the replica homes of the many ethnic groups – Hawaiian, Japanese, Chinese, Korean, Portuguese, Puerto

TASTY TIDBITS

- In 1901 James Dole planted O'ahu's first pineapple patch in Wahiawa.
- Today, each acre of a pineapple field can support around 30,000 plants.
- The commercial variety of pineapple grown in Hawaii is smooth cayenne.
- It takes nearly two years for a pineapple plant to reach maturity.
- Each plant usually produces just two pineapples, one in its second year and one in its third year.
- Pineapples are harvested year-round, but the long, sunny days of summer produce the sweetest fruit.
- Pineapples won't continue to ripen after they've been picked.

Rican and Filipino – who labored on Hawaii's plantations.

By car from Honolulu, take the H1 Fwy west to exit 7, turn left onto Paiwa St, then right onto Waipahu St for three blocks; the complex will be on your left. From Waikiki, TheBus 42 stops twice hourly at the Waipahu Transit Center, about a 0.6-mile walk away.

Poke Stop SEAFOOD, LOCAL $$

(http://poke-stop.com; Waipahu Town Center, 94-050 Farrington Hwy; mains $8-14; ⏲9am-7pm Mon-Sat, to 4pm Sun) It's a longish detour west of Pearl Harbor, but some folks would drive all the way across the island just for the chef's deconstructed sushi bowls, plate lunches with spicy eggplant fries, and over 20 kinds of *poke* – ahi mixed with sweet Maui onions or more unusual *'o'io* (bonefish) will leave you salivating for more. Also in Mi'ilani (p165).

Ko Olina

Don't have a beach? No problem. All it takes is a couple thousand tons of imported sand. When Kapolei's luxury resort was still on the drawing board, it lacked one key feature – a beach. In exchange for public beach access, investors were allowed to carve out four kidney-shaped lagoons from the coastline and line them with soft white sand. Recently, Disney's Aulani resort has made quite a splash here.

For snorkel trips and whale-watching and dolphin-spotting tours, book directly with Hawaii Nautical in Wai'anae, which offers free shuttle service to/from Ko Olina resorts.

Ko Olina Lagoons BEACH

(off Ali'inui Dr, Kapolei; 👪) FREE Ko Olina's artificial beaches have calm waters that are perfect for kids, although the current picks up near the opening to the ocean. A wide, paved recreational path connects all four lagoons, inviting a lazy sunset stroll. Extremely limited, but free public beach-access parking can be found by each lagoon, off Ali'inui Dr inside the resort area.

To peer at rainbow-colored tropical fish, rent snorkel sets and beach gear at the biggest lagoon furthest north. Fewer crowds visit the southernmost lagoons, with free parking often found just before the road's-end marina.

Ko Olina Golf Club GOLF

(☎676-5300; www.koolinagolf.com; 92-1220 Ali'inui Dr, Kapolei; green fees $129-189; ⏲by reservation only) At this PGA-rated championship 18-hole, par-72 golf course, mere mortals can enjoy this landscaped oasis of green. Check online for discounted rates and special packages, including Waikiki shuttle service. Rental clubs and carts and a driving range are available. Book ahead for tee times and a table at **Roy's restaurant**, serving Hawaii regional cuisine.

Ko Olina Marina FISHING, CRUISE

(☎853-4300; www.koolinamarina.com; 92-100 Waipahe Pl, Kapolei; cruises adult/child 2-13yr from $119/99) Let the friendly marina staff put you on a sunset catamaran cruise or a sportfishing charter boat.

Sleeping & Eating

★Aulani RESORT $$$

(☎674-6200, reservations 714-520-7001; http://resorts.disney.go.com/aulani-hawaii-resort/; 92-1185 Ali'inui Dr, Kapolei; r from $450; ❄@🛜🏊) It would be impossible for even the most energetic families to run out of things to do at this top-notch Disney resort and spa. Tone up at beach-body boot camp or hula the day away, then bring the kids to character meet-and-greets, storytelling hours and pool parties – and oh, yeah, the beach. The Hawaiian-inspired spa is lavish.

JW Marriott Ihilani Resort RESORT $$$

(☎800-626-4446, 679-0079; www.ihilani.com; 92-1001 Olani St, Kapolei; r from $299; ❄@🛜🏊) Right on the beach, but extremely isolated from the rest of the island, this aging hotel is at least architecturally soothing. Despite its remoteness and sky-high room rates, it's popular with wedding parties and anyone intent on avoiding the Waikiki scene who still craves a little luxury.

Ko Olina Hawaiian Bar-B-Que LOCAL $

(92-1047 Olani St, Kapolei; mains $7-13; ⏲10:30am-9pm) Escape Ko Olina's high-dollar resort dining rooms for giant plate lunches of *mochiko* chicken, BBQ short ribs, teriyaki beef, pork *katsu* and other fast food, with brown rice and green salad options. It's hidden in a strip mall, opposite **Island Country Market**, a convenience shop selling snacks, drinks and everything else needed for a day at the beach.

Kapolei Marketplace INTERNATIONAL, FAST FOOD $
(http://themarketplaceatkapolei.com; 590 Farrington Hwy, Kapolei; meals $6-12; hours vary) About a 15-minute drive east of Ko Olina, this down-to-earth strip mall is where locals eat. It's stuffed with pan-Asian noodle joints, Hawaiian BBQ places, a pancake house and a Safeway supermarket.

Entertainment

Buy tickets in advance for Ko Olina's touristy luau.

Paradise Cove LUAU
(800-775-2683, 842-5911; www.paradisecove-hawaii.com; 92-1089 Ali'inui Dr, Kapolei; adult/child 4-12yr/youth 13-20yr $88/68/78; 5-9pm;) Near the entrance to Ko Olina, this nightly luau on the beach features pan-Polynesian dancing and demonstrations of Hawaiian crafts and games for kids before the show.

Fia Fia Show LUAU
(679-4700; http://chiefsielu.com/fia-fia-show/; Marriott's Ko Olina Beach Club, 92-161 Waipahe Pl, Kapolei; adult/child $65/50; 5pm Tue;) Entertaining Polynesian performances lean heavily toward the Samoan, because that's where hilarious Chief Sielu Avea, who emcees this weekly dinner show, hails from.

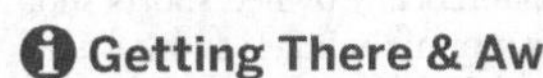

Getting There & Away

From Honolulu's airport, it's about a 30-minute drive to Ko Olina via the H-1 Fwy, taking longer in rush-hour traffic. From Waikiki, allow at least 45 minutes.

Kahe Point

A hulking power plant complete with towering smokestacks isn't the best neighbor to a beach. At **Kahe Point Beach Park** (92-301 Farrington Hwy), there isn't actually a beach, just a rocky point that's popular with fishers and snorkelers who are good swimmers and can handle strong currents. There are great coastal views, as well as picnic tables, restrooms and outdoor showers.

Further north of Kahe Point lies **Tracks Beach Park** (off Farrington Hwy [Hwy 93]), named after the train that once transported beachgoers here from Honolulu prior to WWII. Sometimes also called Hawaiian Electric Beach, the sandy shores are good for swimming in summer and great for surfing in winter.

Nanakuli

The biggest town on the Wai'anae Coast, Nanakuli has a Hawaiian Homesteads settlement with one of the largest Hawaiian populations on O'ahu. But all you'll likely see from the highway is a strip of fast-food joints.

Nanakuli Beach Park (89-269 Farrington Hwy) fronts a broad, sandy beach that lines the highway, offering swimming, snorkeling and diving during summer. In winter high surf can create rip currents and dangerous shore-breaks. This in-town community park also has a playground, sports fields, picnic tables and full beach facilities. Camping is available with an advance county permit, but it's not recommended. To get to the beach, turn *makai* (seaward) off the Farrington Hwy onto Nanakuli Ave at the traffic lights.

Ma'ili

There's not much for travelers to see here besides **Ma'ili Beach Park** (87-021 Farrington Hwy), a long, grassy roadside park with a supersized stretch of snow-white beach. Like other places on the Wai'anae Coast, ocean conditions are often treacherous in winter (which pleases surfers), but calm enough for swimming in summer. There's a lifeguard station, beach facilities and a few coconut palms providing scant shade. Camping is allowed with an advance county permit, but it isn't recommended.

Wai'anae

POP 13,180

A little rough around the edges, Wai'anae is this coast's hub for everyday services, with grocery stores, gas stations, a commercial boat harbor and a well-used beach park.

Beaches & Sights

Poka'i Bay Beach Park BEACH
(85-037 Wai'anae Valley Rd;) Protected by Kane'ilio Point and a long breakwater, this beach is a beauty. Waves seldom break inside the bay, and the sandy sea floor slopes gently, making the beach a popular spot for year-round swimming. Snorkeling is

HOMELESS IN PARADISE

Honolulu County doesn't have an accurate figure of how many people are living on its beaches, but recent estimates put the number of homeless people on O'ahu at around 4350. One out of every five of those homeless people shelters along the Wai'anae Coast.

When Hawaii's economy was strong and housing prices were soaring, many rental properties were sold, thus diminishing the available accommodations and driving up rents. Many low-income families – some with service-industry or construction jobs, others receiving some form of government assistance – simply couldn't afford the increase.

Another aggravating factor is Hawaii's stagnant stock of public housing, with waiting lists of more than 9000 people statewide. Even after evictions of squatters from beaches on the Wai'anae Coast, the island's homeless crisis continues. Without enough jobs, affordable housing or homeless shelters, where are all of these struggling families supposed to go? Many end up eking out a living in O'ahu's most impoverished district, Wai'anae, where rents are lowest.

fair near the breakwater, where fish gather around the rocks. There are restrooms, outdoor showers, drinking water, picnic tables and lifeguards.

Ku'ilioloa Heiau TEMPLE

Kane'ilio Point, along the south side of Poka'i Bay, is the site of an ancient stone temple, partly destroyed by the army during WWII and later reconstructed. When the waves aren't crashing strongly, look for little tidepools harboring marine life by the base of the heiau. To get here, turn *makai* (seaward) onto Lualualei Homestead Rd off the Farrington Hwy (Hwy 93).

Activities

★ **Hawaii Nautical** WHALE WATCHING, CRUISE

(☎234-7245; www.hawaiinautical.com; Wai'anae Boat Harbor, 85-371 Farrington Hwy; tours adult/child 4-11yr from $79/59;) Set sail on a deluxe catamaran to snorkel along the island's leeward shores, and spot dolphins and migratory humpback whales with a tour operator that truly cares about marine wildlife. Upgrade with snuba or stand up paddleboarding gear, or opt for a dive trip. Complimentary shuttle service to/from Ko Olina's resorts.

Wild Side Specialty Tours WHALE WATCHING, CRUISE

(☎306-7273; http://sailhawaii.com; Wai'anae Boat Harbor, 85-371 Farrington Hwy; tours $115-195;) Friendly tour operator sails catamarans and yachts along the Wai'anae Coast, letting the whole family snorkel with tropical fish and sea turtles and spot dolphins year-round and whales in winter. Try to reserve at least two weeks ahead; last-minute availability is limited.

Ocean Concepts DIVING

(☎800-808-3483; www.oceanconcepts.com; Wai'anae Boat Harbor, 85-371 Farrington Hwy; boat trips from $110) Full-service, five-star PADI outfitter runs scuba trips along the Wai'anae Coast including to offshore Makaha Caverns, the 29 Down sunken airplane and a WWII minesweeper ship transformed into an artificial reef. Ask about Saturday night dives. Equipment rental available.

Hale Nalu Surf & Bike WATER SPORTS, CYCLING

(☎696-5897; www.halenalu.com; 85-876 Farrington Hwy; ⏲10am-5pm) Locally owned sports shop sells and rents mountain bikes, snorkel gear, surfboards, bodyboards, stand up paddleboarding (SUP) sets and car roof racks.

Eating

At strip malls alongside the Farrington Hwy (Hwy 93), it's fast food or local grinds, all the time.

Ka'aha'aina Cafe LOCAL $

(82-260 Farrington Hwy; mains $5-10; ⏲7am-2pm Mon-Fri;) The hilltop location on the grounds of a community health clinic has its pluses and minuses – a businesslike setting but with ocean views. Tropical fruit smoothies and island-style plate lunches, piled high with *huli-huli* (rotisserie-grilled) chicken or seared ahi with garlicky aioli, are priced right.

Ono Polynesian Market MARKET $

(85-998 Farrington Hwy; meals $6-10; ⏲7am-9pm) Ready for a taste of the South Seas? A ramshackle little market across the street from the beach dishes out takeout treats like Samoan *palusami* (corned beef wrapped in taro leaves and slow-cooked in coconut milk) and Polynesian curries.

Kahumana Cafe HEALTHY $$
(☎696-8844; http://kahumanafarms.org; 86-660 Lualualei Homestead Rd; mains $10-13; ⊙11:30am-2:30pm & 6-7:30pm Tue-Sat; ☎) Way off the beaten track, this organic farm's hardwood-floored cafe has peaceful views of green fields. Fork into bountiful salads and sandwiches, macadamia-nut pesto pasta with wild-caught fish or homemade *liliko'i* cheesecake. The farm is about 2 miles *mauka* (inland) from the Farrington Hwy (Hwy 93) via Ma'ili'ili Rd; call ahead to check if they're open.

Coquitos Latin Cuisine LATIN AMERICAN $$
(☎888-4082; 85-773 Farrington Hwy; mains $8-18; ⊙11am-9pm Tue-Sat, to 4pm Sun) Inside a breezy green plantation-style house that looks like it belongs in the Caribbean or Key West, this Puerto Rican kitchen has hooked locals with its *mofongo* (mashed plantains with garlic and bacon), grilled Cuban sandwiches, shredded beef empanadas and tall *tres leches* (sponge cake) for dessert.

Makaha

POP 8280

Relatively free of tourists even today, this is where big-wave surfing got its start in the 1950s. Makaha means 'ferocious,' and long ago the valley was notorious for bandits who waited along the cliffs to ambush passing travelers, but the word could just as easily describe the stark, rugged landscape.

Beaches

Makaha Beach Park BEACH
(84-369 Farrington Hwy) Makaha Beach hosted Hawaii's first international surfing competition in 1954, and the long point break here inspired the first generation of big-wave surfers. Winter months bring huge swells that preclude swimming much of the time, but the invitingly soft stretch of golden sand is a permanent feature year-round. The beach has restrooms, outdoor showers and lifeguards.

Except for weekends and on big-surf days, you're likely to have the place virtually to yourself. In summer when waters are calm, go snorkeling with sea turtles or take a dive-boat trip to offshore Makaha Caverns with Ocean Concepts (p168).

Sights & Activities

Kane'aki Heiau TEMPLE
(☎695-8174; end of Maunaolu St; ⊙call for hours) FREE Hidden within a gated residential community in Makaha Valley, this quietly impressive heiau is one of O'ahu's best-restored sacred sites. Originally an agricultural temple dedicated to Lono, the Hawaiian god of agriculture and fertility, the site was later used as a *luakini,* a temple dedicated to the war god Ku and a place for human sacrifices.

Kamehameha the Great worshipped here and the temple remained in use until his death in 1819. Restorations by the Bishop Museum added two prayer towers, a *kapu* (taboo) house, drum house, altar and *ki'i* (deity statues), while the heiau was reconstructed using traditional ohia tree logs and *pili* grass.

To get here, turn *mauka* (inland) off Farrington Hwy (Hwy 93) onto Makaha Valley Rd. Just over a mile later, follow Huipu Dr as it briefly curves left, then right. Turn right again onto Maunaolu St, which enters Mauna Olu Estates. Sign in at the security gatehouse (bring your driver's license and car-rental contract).

At the time of writing, public access was closed indefinitely due to vandalism. Call ahead to ask if the site has since reopened.

Makaha Valley Riding Stables HORSEBACK RIDING
(☎779-8904; http://makahastables.com; 84-1042 Maunaolu St; rides from $45) Saddle up at this historic ranch for a sunset trail ride with a BBQ dinner and s'mores by the firepit, or an afternoon horseback ramble through the valley as you learn about Hawaiian culture, including traditional games and crafts. Advance reservations required.

Sleeping

Makaha has the majority of the vacation rentals available on the Wai'anae Coast. Browse listings on websites like **VRBO** (www.vrbo.com), **HomeAway** (www.homeaway.com), **Air B&B** (www.airbnb.com), **Affordable Oceanfront Condos** (www.hawaiibeachcondos.com) and **Discount Hawaii Condos** (www.discounthawaiicondos.com) or try local real-estate agencies in nearby Wai'anae, including the following:

SOULS' LEAP

Ancient Hawaiians believed that when people went into a deep sleep or lost consciousness, their souls would wander. Souls that wandered too far were drawn west to Ka'ena Point. If they were lucky, they were met here by their *'aumakua* (guardian spirit), who led their souls back to their bodies. If unattended, their souls would be forced to leap from Ka'ena Point into the endless night, never to return.

Inga's Realty, Inc VACATION RENTAL **$$**
(☎696-1616; www.ingasrealty.com; 85-910 Farrington Hwy, Wai'anae)

Hawaii Hatfield Realty VACATION RENTAL **$$**
(☎696-4499; www.hawaiiwest.com; suite 201, 85-833 Farrington Hwy, Wai'anae)

Makua Valley

As you drive north of Makaha, you won't find any more gas stations, restaurants or even towns. Wide and grassy, backed by a fan of sharply fluted mountains, the scenic Makua Valley belongs to a military reservation. A seaside road opposite its southern end leads to a little graveyard shaded by yellow-flowered trees, the only visible remnant of the community here that was forced to evacuate during WWII when the US military took over the valley for war games. Live-fire exercises have ceased, but the valley, rich in ancient Hawaiian archaeological sites, is still fenced off with barbed wire and danger signs warning of unexploded ordinance.

Beaches & Sights

Makua Beach BEACH
In ancient Hawai'i, this beach was a canoe landing site for interisland travelers. During the late 1960s, it became a backdrop for the movie *Hawaii,* starring Julie Andrews and Max von Sydow. These days there's little here beyond a nice stretch of sand opposite Makua Military Reservation. There are no lifeguards or other facilities.

Locals crawl out from their nine-to-five lives on weekends to soak up the sun at this beach. Powerful shorebreaks are popular with expert bodyboarders, and when high surf rolls in during winter, the sand practically disappears entirely. In summer, give the wild spinner dolphins plenty of room to rest – do not approach or try to swim with them.

Homeless locals sometimes camp here. Though serious crimes are rarely reported, be mindful of car break-ins and petty theft.

Kaneana Cave HISTORIC SITE
The waves that created this giant stone amphitheater receded long ago. Now the highway sits between the ocean and this cave, about 2 miles north of Kea'au Beach. *Kahuna* (priests) once performed rituals inside the cave's inner chamber, which was the legendary abode of a vicious shark-man, a shapeshifter who lured human victims into the cave before devouring them.

Some Hawaiians consider it a sacred place and won't enter the cave for fear that it's haunted by the spirits of deceased chiefs. Judging by the collection of broken beer bottles and graffiti beyond the barricades at the cave entrance, not everyone shares their sentiments.

Ka'ena Point State Park

You don't have to believe in Hawaiian legends to feel something mystical occur at this dramatic convergence of land and sea. At the far northwestern tip of the island, powerful ocean currents altered by O'ahu's landmass have been battling against each other for millennia. Waves crash onto long lava-bed fingers, sending frothy explosions skyward. All along this untamed coast, nature is at its most furiously beautiful.

Running along both sides of O'ahu's westernmost point, **Ka'ena Point State Park** (www.hawaiistateparks.org; end of Farrington Hwy [Hwy 930]; ⌚sunrise-sunset) FREE is a totally undeveloped coastal strip. Until 1947 the O'ahu Railway ran up here from Honolulu and continued around the point, carrying passengers to Hale'iwa on the North Shore. Today the US Air Force operates a satellite tracking station high on the ridges above Ka'ena Point. Originally built in the 1950s for satellite reconnaissance, those giant white golf balls perched on the hillsides now support weather, early warning, navigation and communications systems.

Don't leave anything valuable in your car. Telltale mounds of shattered windshield glass litter the road's-end parking areas. Locals advise parking close to the lifeguard tower. To decrease the odds of having your car damaged by a break-in, consider leaving the doors unlocked and the windows rolled down.

 Beaches

Yokohama Bay BEACH

(www.hawaiistateparks.org; Farrington Hwy [Hwy 930]; sunrise-sunset) Some say this is O'ahu's best sunset spot, with a blissful mile-long sandy beach that faces west. Winter brings huge pounding waves, making this a popular seasonal surfing and bodysurfing spot, but it's best left to the experts because of submerged rocks, strong rips and a dangerous shorebreak. Swimming is limited to summertime, and then only when waters are calm.

If the water's flat, it's possible to snorkel too; the easiest access is on the south side of the bay, named for the Japanese fishers who used to come here back in the railroad days. You'll find restrooms, showers and a lifeguard station at the park's southern end.

 Activities

Ka'ena Point Trail HIKING, MOUNTAIN BIKING

(www.hawaiistateparks.org; end of Farrington Hwy [Hwy 930]) An extremely windy, mostly level coastal trail runs along the old railbed for 2.5 miles from Yokohama Bay to Ka'ena Point, then continues another 2.5 miles around the point to the North Shore (see p163). Most hikers take the trail from the end of the paved road at Yokohama Bay as far as the point, then return the same way.

This hike offers fine views the entire way, with the ocean on one side and craggy cliffs on the other. Along the trail are tidepools, sea arches and blowholes that occasionally come to life on high-surf days. In addition to native and migratory seabirds, you might spot Hawaiian monk seals hauled out on the rocks or the sand – but do not approach or otherwise disturb these endangered creatures.

The trail is extremely exposed and lacks any shade, so take sunscreen and plenty of water and hike during the cooler parts of the day. Be cautious near the shoreline, as there are strong currents, and rogue waves can reach extreme heights.

Kuaokala Trail HIKING, MOUNTAIN BIKING

(https://hawaiitrails.ehawaii.gov; off Farrington Hwy [Hwy 930]) Hawaii's **Division of Forestry & Wildlife** (DOFAW; 587-0166; https://hawaiitrails.ehawaii.gov; Room 325, 1151 Punchbowl St, Honolulu) issues advance permits for the hiking and mountain-biking trail system surrounding Ka'ena Point's satellite tracking station. From a dirt parking lot, the dusty 2.5-mile one-way Kuaokala Trail climbs a high ridge into Mokule'ia Forest Reserve. On a clear day you can see Mt Ka'ala (4025ft), O'ahu's highest peak.

This land is also open to hunting, so hikers and bikers should wear bright, safety-colored clothing. Check in with your hiking permit at the station guardhouse opposite Yokohama Bay. Without a permit, the Kuaokala Trail can still be accessed via the **Kealia Trail**, starting from the North Shore's Dillingham Airfield (see p163).

Hawai'i the Big Island

Includes ➡

Best Beaches

- Hapuna Beach (p233)
- Mau'umae Beach (p233)
- Waipi'o Valley (p256)
- Manini'owali Beach (p221)
- Makalawena Beach (p221)

Best Snorkeling

- Two-Step (p215)
- Mau'umae Beach (p233)
- Kapoho Tide Pools (p287)
- Hapuna Beach (p233)

Why Go?

Hawai'i the Big Island is twice as big as the other islands combined and, thanks to a rambunctiously active volcano that periodically bleeds lava into the ocean, it's growing.

But the Big Island isn't just where raw creation occurs. It's where the fruits of that process are presented in dizzying diversity. Eight of the world's 13 climate zones exist here, encompassing Martian lava deserts, emerald jungle, paradisical valleys that front black-, white- and even *green*-sand beaches, snowcapped mountains, coral forests and an enchantingly unique population of locals, hippies, transplants, eccentrics, neighbors, bartenders, teachers and more.

You can easily be lazy here, but the Big Island really shines for adventurers. Some of the best beaches, reefs and valleys require a short hike, swim or drive over rutted roads. The beauty is astounding, and for a little effort, you get enormous rewards on your travel investment.

When to Go

Kailua-Kona

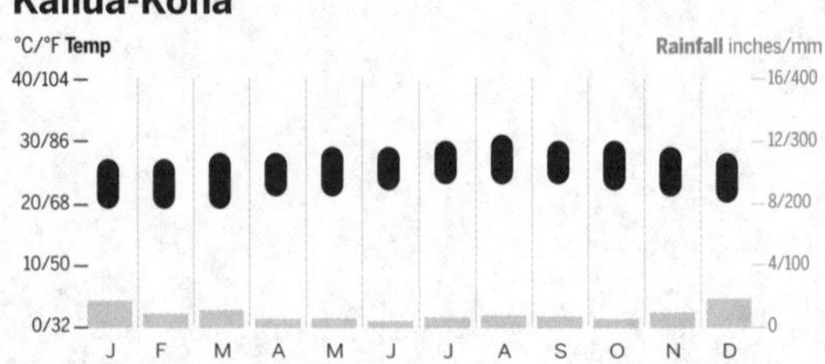

Jan Surf's up and summits are snowcapped during the Big Island 'winter.'

Late Mar–early Apr Catch the world's greatest hula at Hilo's Merrie Monarch Festival.

Oct Tenacious triathletes compete in the legendary swim-bike-run race born in Kailua-Kona.

History

The modern history of the Big Island is a tale of two cities – Kailua-Kona and Hilo – which represent the island's split personality: West Hawai'i and East Hawai'i. Kamehameha the Great, born in West Hawai'i, lived out the end of his life in Kailua, and throughout the 19th century, Hawaiian royalty enjoyed the town as a leisure retreat, using Hulihe'e Palace as a crash pad.

Yet, during the same period, Hilo emerged as the more important commercial harbor. The Hamakua Coast railroad connected Hilo to the island's sugar plantations, and its thriving wharves became a hub for agricultural goods and immigrant workers. By the 20th century the city was the Big Island's economic and political center, and Hilo remains the official seat of island government.

On April 1, 1946 the Hamakua Coast was hit by an enormous tsunami that crumpled the railroad and devastated coastal communities (such as Laupahoehoe). Hilo got the worst of it: its waterfront was completely destroyed, and 96 people were killed. The city was rebuilt, but 14 years later, in 1960, it happened again: another deadly tsunami splintered the waterfront. This time Hilo did not rebuild, but left a quiet expanse of parks separating the downtown area from the bay.

After that the sugar industry steadily declined (sputtering out in the 1990s), and the Big Island's newest income source – tourism – focused quite naturally on the sun-drenched, sandy western shores where Hawaiian monarchs once gamboled. Since the 1970s, resorts and real-estate barons have jockeyed for position and profit along the leeward coast, turning West Hawai'i into the de facto seat of power.

Today, despite escalating home prices, the Big Island is considered the most affordable island to live on (and travel around), attracting young people from across the state; and it is diversifying its economy with small farm-based agriculture and renewable energy.

National, State & County Parks

The Big Island's main attraction, Hawai'i Volcanoes National Park (p289), is one of the USA's most interesting and varied national parks. More than a million visitors come annually to drive and hike this lava and rainforest wonderland.

The Big Island is also notable for its wealth of ancient Hawaiian sights, which are preserved in several national and state historical parks. The most famous is Pu'uhonua o Honaunau (p214), an ancient place of refuge in South Kona. But Native Hawaiian history and moody landscapes can also be found at remote Mo'okini Luakini Heiau (p239) in North Kohala; snorkeling mecca Kealakekua Bay (p211), where Captain Cook met his demise; the restored fishponds of Kaloko-Honokohau (p217) near Kailua-Kona; and the imposing, majestic Pu'ukohola Heiau (p235) just south of Kawaihae.

Many of the Big Island's finest beaches lie within parkland, such as the world-renowned Hapuna Beach (p233). The beaches within Kekaha Kai State Park (p220) are also idyllic, though only Manini'owali is accessible by paved road.

Other parks worth seeking out on the Windward Coast are Kalopa State Recreation Area (p264), preserving a native forest; Laupahoehoe (p264), site of a tsunami disaster; and Akaka Falls (p266), the prettiest 'drive-up' waterfalls in Hawai'i. Though not a designated park, Waipi'o Valley shouldn't be missed.

Camping

Hawai'i has enough good campgrounds that you can enjoyably circumnavigate the island in a tent, plus there are several highly memorable backcountry camping opportunities. Some parks also offer simple cabins and DIYers can rent camper vans.

Hawai'i Volcanoes National Park has two drive-up campgrounds (one fee-paying with cabins, the other free) and several great backcountry sites. Only backcountry sites require permits (available at Visitor Emergency Operations Center).

State parks require camping permits for tent sites ($12/18 residents/non-residents)

BORED WAITING TO BOARD?

They were clever, whoever located the **Astronaut Ellison S Onizuka Space Center** (Map p218; ☎329-3441; adult/child under 12yr $3/1; ⏲8:30am-4:30pm) at the Kona International Airport. This little museum paying tribute to the Big Island native who perished in the 1986 *Challenger* space-shuttle disaster collects celestial ephemera like moon rocks and space suits; it makes an interesting way to spend some time before takeoff.

Hawai'i the Big Island Highlights

1. Gaze at stars on top of the world's tallest mountain at the summit of **Mauna Kea** (p250).
2. Explore the black-sand nooks and crannies, and chill with sea turtles, at isolated **Kiholo Bay** (p223).
3. See how dramatic Eden can be while taking in the rugged, emerald vistas of the **Waipi'o Valley** (p256).
4. Get happily lost amid magical coral gardens and multicolored reefs while snorkeling at **Two-Step** (p215).
5. Witness **Halema'uma'u Crater** (p293), the smoldering home of Pele, goddess of fire, at Hawai'i Volcanoes National Park.
6. Get in touch with the local side of Hawai'i while perusing the many museums of **Hilo** (p267).
7. Find hidden **Makalawena Beach** (p221), take pictures of its perfection, then make your friends jealous.
8. Bodysurf till the waves pound you into submission, then bodysurf some more, at **White (Magic) Sands Beach** (p178).
9. Dance a surreal underwater dance with manta rays on a nighttime snorkeling trip off **Kailua-Kona** (p184).
10. Watch the raw power of creation as Hawai'i forms itself anew on a lava flow tour (p284) in **Puna**.

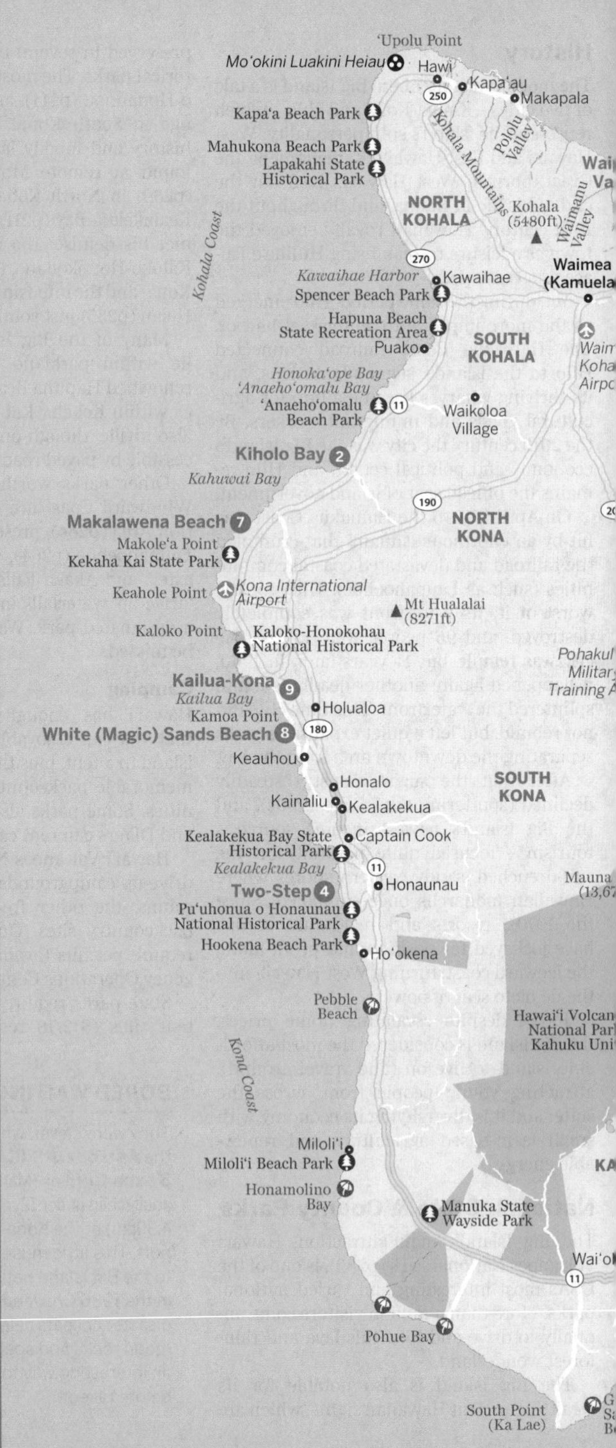

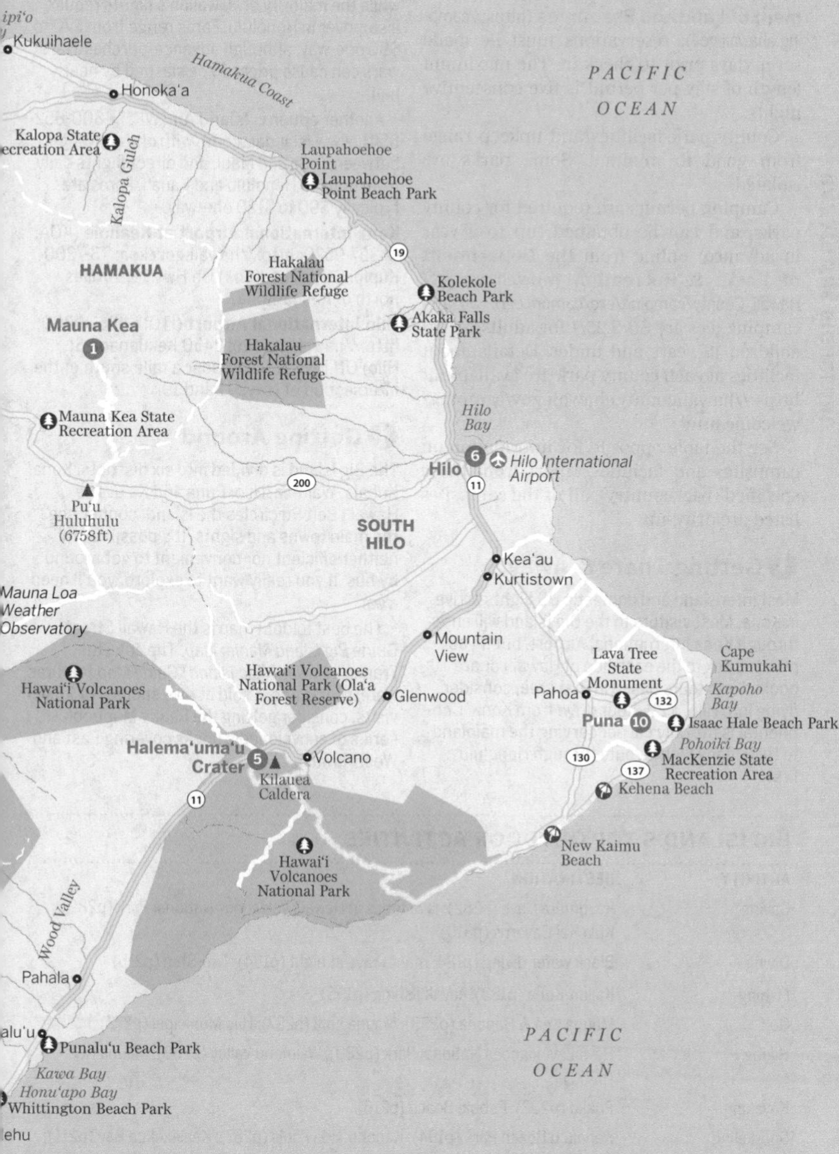

0 20 km
0 10 miles
PACIFIC OCEAN
Kukuihaele
Hamakua Coast
Honoka'a
Kalopa State Recreation Area
Kalopa Gulch
Laupahoehoe Point
Laupahoehoe Point Beach Park
19
HAMAKUA
Hakalau Forest National Wildlife Refuge
Kolekole Beach Park
Akaka Falls State Park
Mauna Kea
1
Hakalau Forest National Wildlife Refuge
Mauna Kea State Recreation Area
Hilo Bay
Hilo
6
Hilo International Airport
200
11
Pu'u Huluhulu (6758ft)
SOUTH HILO
Kea'au
Kurtistown
Mauna Loa Weather Observatory
Mountain View
Lava Tree State Monument
Cape Kumukahi
Hawai'i Volcanoes National Park
Hawai'i Volcanoes National Park (Ola'a Forest Reserve)
Glenwood
Pahoa
132
Kapoho Bay
Puna
10
Isaac Hale Beach Park
Halema'uma'u Crater
5
Kilauea Caldera
Volcano
Pohoiki Bay
130
MacKenzie State Recreation Area
137
Kehena Beach
11
New Kaimu Beach
Hawai'i Volcanoes National Park
Wood Valley
Pahala
PACIFIC OCEAN
Punalu'u Beach Park
Kawa Bay
Honu'apo Bay
Whittington Beach Park

and cabins. The easiest way to make a reservation and obtain a permit for state park cabins and campgrounds (plus those in Waimanu Valley) is via the online reservation system for the **State of Hawaii Department of Land and Resources** (https://camping.ehawaii.gov); reservations must be made seven days prior to check in. The maximum length of stay per permit is five consecutive nights.

County park facilities and upkeep range from good to minimal. Some parks are isolated.

Camping permits are required for county parks, and can be obtained (up to a year in advance) online from the **Department of Parks & Recreation** (www.ehawaii.gov/Hawaii_County/camping/exe/campre.cgi). Daily camping fees are $6/2.25/1 for adults/teens/children 12 years and under. Details about facilities at each county park are available at https://hawaiicounty.ehawaii.gov/camping/welcome.html.

See the table opposite for information on campsites and facilities. Apart from those specified (backcountry), all of the campsites listed are drive-up.

Getting There & Away

Most interisland and domestic US flights arrive in Kona. Most visitors to the Big Island will enter through Kona International Airport, but if you plan to stick to the east side of Hawai'i or are booked into tours based in that area, consider flying into Hilo, a 2½-hour drive from Kona. Continental is the only carrier serving the mainland to Hilo; many flights route through Honolulu first.

There are two major interisland carriers: **Hawaiian Airlines** (HA; ☎800-367-5320; www.hawaiianair.com) and **go!** (YV; ☎888-435-9462; www.iflygo.com). Both have multiple interisland flights daily, though go! has more direct flights, while the majority of Hawaiian's flights require a stopover in Honolulu. Fares range from $70 to $90 one-way, although advance-purchase fare wars can cause prices to be slashed by nearly half.

Another option is **Island Air** (WP; ☎800-652-6541; www.islandair.com), with one daily flight between Kona and Maui, and direct flights daily from Kona to Honolulu and Kaua'i. Fares are typically $90 to $120 one-way.

Kona International Airport at Keahole (KOA; ☎327-9520; http://hawaii.gov/koa; 73-7200 Kupipi St, Kailua-Kona) On Hwy 19, 7 miles north of Kailua-Kona.

Hilo International Airport (ITO; ☎961-9300; http://hawaii.gov/ito; 2450 Kekuanaoa St, Hilo) Off Hwy 11, just under a mile south of the intersection of Hwys 11 and 19.

Getting Around

The Big Island is divided into six districts: Kona, Kohala, Waimea, Hilo, Puna and Ka'u. The Hawai'i Belt Rd circles the island, connecting the main towns and sights. It's possible but neither efficient nor convenient to get around by bus. If you really want to explore, you'll need a car.

The best foldout map is the Hawaii Street Guide *Big Island Manini Map*. The colorful Franko's *Hawai'i (Big Island) Guide Map* features watersports and is sold at dive shops. For longer visits, consider getting the Ready Mapbook series of encyclopedic books covering East and West Hawai'i.

BIG ISLAND'S TOP OUTDOOR ACTIVITIES

ACTIVITY	DESTINATION
Caving	Kazumura Cave (p282); lava tubes in Hawai'i Volcanoes National Park (p289); Kula Kai Caverns (p310)
Diving	Black water diving (p184; manta rays at night (p184); Two-Step (p215)
Fishing	Kailua-Kona (p183); kayak fishing (p195)
Golf	Mauna Kea & Hapuna (p233); Mauna Lani (p227); Hilo Municipal (p272)
Hiking	Hawai'i Volcanoes National Park (p289); Waimanu Valley (p258); Mauna Kea (p250)
Kayaking	Puako (p232); Pebble Beach (p216)
Snorkeling	Kahalu'u Beach Park (p194); Kapoho Tide Pools (p287); Kealakekua Bay (p211); Two-Step (p215)
Stand Up Paddle Boarding	Kailua-Kona (p185); Kahalu'u Beach (p194)
Ziplining	Hamakua Coast (p265)

BIG ISLAND PARK CAMPSITES

PARK	FEATURES
Hawai'i Volcanoes National Park	
'Apua Point	Backcountry; no water; shelter
Halape Shelter	Backcountry; closes during drought; turtle nesting site
Ka'aha Shelter	Backcountry; shelter
Keauhou Shelter	Backcountry; shelter
Kulanaokuaiki Campground	Pit toilets; no water; views
Namakanipaio Campground & Cabins	Shelter; water; toilets; no showers
Napau Crater	Backcountry; no water
State Parks	
Hapuna Beach State Recreation Area	Cabins only
Kalopa State Recreation Area	Full facilities; cabins
MacKenzie State Recreation Area	Full facilities
Manuka Natural Area Reserve	Full facilties
County Parks	
Ho'okena Beach Park	Full facilities
Isaac Hale Beach Park	Full facilities; surfing
Kapa'a Beach Park	Full facilities
Kolekole Beach Park	Full facilities; surfing
Laupahoehoe Point Beach Park	Full facilities
Mahukona Beach Park	Showers; potable toilets
Miloli'i Beach Park	Showers
Punalu'u Beach Park	Full facilities; turtle nesting site
Spencer Beach Park	Full facilities
Whittington Beach Park	No potable water

TO/FROM THE AIRPORTS

Most visitors rent cars at the airport; car-hire booths for the major agencies line the road outside the arrivals area at both airports.

Shuttle-bus services typically cost as much as taxis. **Speedi Shuttle** (☎877-242-5777, 329-5433; www.speedishuttle.com) will get you to destinations up and down the Kona Coast, plus Waimea, Honoka'a and Hawai'i Volcanoes National Park (although that will cost $165-plus). Book in advance.

Taxis are curbside. The approximate fare from Hilo International Airport to downtown is $20. From Kona airport to Kailua-Kona is $30, and to Waikoloa is $55.

BICYCLE

As your primary transportation, cycling around the Big Island is easiest with the support of a tour. Though doable on one's own, it's a challenge, particularly if the weather doesn't co-operate. However, Kona – the hub for the famous Ironman Triathlon – has top-notch bike shops that sell and repair high-caliber equipment.

BUS

The island-wide **Hele-On Bus** (☎961-8744; www.heleonbus.org) will get you (most) places on the Big Island, but Sunday and holiday service is limited. Fares are $1 per ride, and a monthly pass is $300 for unlimited rides. Always check the website for current routes and schedules. Most buses originate from Mo'oheau terminal in Hilo. You cannot board with a surfboard or body-board, while luggage, backpacks and bicycles are charged $1 apiece.

CAR & MOTORCYCLE

There are companies with car-hire booths at Kona and Hilo airports. Reserve well in advance for decent rates.

Harper Car & Truck Rentals (☎800-852-9993, 969-1478; www.harpershawaii.com; 456 Kalaniana'ole Ave, Hilo) No restrictions on driving its 4WDs up Mauna Kea, but driving into Waipi'o Valley and to Green Sands Beach is prohibited. Damage to a vehicle entails a high deductible; rates are generally steeper than at major agencies.

Driving Distances & Times

To circumnavigate the island on the 230-mile Hawai'i Belt Rd (Hwys 19 and 11), you'll need about six hours.

From Hilo

DESTINATION	MILES	TIME
Hawai'i Volcanoes National Park	28	½ hr
Hawi	86	2¼ hr
Honoka'a	40	1 hr
Kailua-Kona	92	2½ hr
Na'alehu	64	1¾ hr
Pahoa	16	½ hr
Waikoloa	80	2¼ hr
Waimea	54	1½ hr
Waipi'o Lookout	50	1¼ hr

From Kailua-Kona

DESTINATION	MILES	TIME
Hawai'i Volcanoes National Park	98	2½ hr
Hawi	51	1¼ hr
Hilo	92	2½ hr
Honoka'a	61	1½ hr
Na'alehu	60	1½ hr
Pahoa	108	3 hr
Waikoloa	18	¾ hr
Waimea	43	1 hr
Waipi'o Lookout	70	1¾ hr

KAILUA-KONA

POP 11,975

Kailua-Kona, also known as 'Kaliua,' 'Kona Town' and sometimes, just 'Town,' is a love-it-or-leave-it kind of place. Along the main drag of shoreline Ali'i Dr, Kailua works hard to evoke the nonchalance of a sun-drenched tropical getaway, but in an injection-molded, bargain-priced way.

Pros: it's an easy place to book tours, what nightlife exists on the Big Island is here and the waterfront can be attractive in the right light (ie sunset). Cons: many restaurants are overrated, traffic can be a pain in the ass, and at times, this place evokes the tackiest of seaside clichés.

The following are either pros or cons depending on your attitude: Kailua has the most hotels and condos, the most tourists, the most souvenirs per square foot and is the most likely place on the island to find businesses open on Sunday.

Anyways, we like Kailua. It's a convenient base from which to enjoy the Kona Coast's beaches, snorkeling, watersports, and ancient Hawaiian sites, and seriously, that waterfront is wonderful when you're taking it in with a sweaty beer and some fresh fish.

Beaches

★White (Magic) Sands Beach Park BEACH
(Map p218; P) This small but gorgeous beach (also called La'aloa Beach) has crystal-clear turquoise waters, tall palms, little shade and possibly the best bodysurfing on the Big Island. The waves are consistent and just powerful enough to shoot you across the water without breaking your body; the sandy bay bottom helps in this regard. During high-winter surf the beach can lose its sand literally overnight, earning it the nickname 'Magic Sands.'

When the rocks and coral located past the dissapearing sands are exposed, the beach becomes too treacherous for most swimmers. Gradually the sand returns, transforming the shore back into its former beachy self.

White Sands is almost always packed, but there's little-to-no proprietary attitude from locals. Facilities include rest rooms, showers, picnic tables and a volleyball court; a lifeguard is on duty. The park is about 4 miles south of the center. Sunsets here are mind-blowing.

Old Kona Airport State Recreation Area BEACH
(Map p218; P) Visitors often overlook this quiet 217-acre park, located a mile from downtown. Admittedly, the swimming here isn't great, but this is a grand spot for a picnic. Just inside the southern entrance gate, one tidal pool is large and sandy enough to be the perfect *keiki* (child) pool. The beach area is studded with lava rock and other tide pools; the latter are occasionally occupied by napping sea turtles.

A few breaks in the lava allow entry into the water, but fishing is the main activity. Scuba divers and confident snorkelers can make for Garden Eel Cove, a short walk from the north end of the beach. The reef fish are large and plentiful, and a steep coral wall in deeper waters harbors moray eels and small caves. When the surf's up, local surfers flock to an offshore break here.

Facilities include rest rooms, showers and covered picnic tables on a lawn dotted with beach heliotrope and short coconut palms. Runners enjoy a mile-long jogging track and an adjacent complex has a playground for kids.

Oh, and you know what makes going to the beach better? Getting there by barreling down an unused airport runway. There's still a tarmac at Old Airport Park, which once was the area's airport until it was deemed too small. To get here, follow Kuakini Hwy to its end.

Sights

★Hulihe'e Palace HISTORIC BUILDING

(Map p180; ☎329-1877; www.huliheepalace.net; 75-5718 Ali'i Dr; adult/child under 18/senior $6/1/4; ⏲10am-3pm Tue-Sat) Hulihe'e Palace is a fascinating study in the rapid shift the Hawaiian royal family made from Polynesian God-kings to Westernized monarchs. Here's the skinny: Hawai'i's second governor, 'John Adams' Kuakini, built a simple two-story, lava-rock house as his private residence in 1838. After Kuakini's death, it became the favorite vacation getaway for Hawaiian royalty.

In the mid-1880s Hulihe'e Palace was thoroughly renovated by the globe-trotting King David Kalakaua, who felt it needed more polish. He stuccoed the lava rock outside, plastered it inside, and added decorative ceilings, gold-leaf picture moldings and crystal chandeliers.

Hard times befell the monarchy in the early-20th century, and the house was sold and the furnishings and artifacts auctioned off by Prince Kuhio. Luckily his wife and other royalty numbered each piece and recorded the names of bidders. In 1925 the Territory of Hawaii purchased the house to be a museum run by the Daughters of Hawai'i, a women's group dedicated to the preservation of Hawaiian culture and language. This group tracked down the furnishings and royal memorabilia, such as a table inlaid with 25 kinds of native woods, several of Kamehameha the Great's war spears and the (surprisingly small) bed of 6ft, 440lb Princess Ke'elikolani.

You'll learn these and other stories on 40-minute guided tours. The free concert series, held here at 4pm on the 3rd Sunday of each month, is a treat, with Hawaiian music and hula performed on the grass facing sparkling Kailua Bay.

Ahu'ena Heiau TEMPLE

(Map p180; www.ahuena.com; 75-5660 Palani Road) FREE After uniting the Hawaiian islands, Kamehameha the Great established his kingdom's royal court in Lahaina on Maui,

HAWAI'I THE BIG ISLAND IN...

Two Days

If you arrive in **Kona**, spend your days leeward, starting with a swim at Hapuna Beach, a kayak and snorkel at Two-Step and a visit to ancient Hawai'i at Pu'uhonua o Honaunau. Save day two for exploring the galleries in **Holualoa**, followed by a coffee-farm tour.

If you arrive in **Hilo**, browse the farmers markets and explore historic downtown before visiting 'Imiloa Astronomy Center. If the lava is flowing into the ocean, head to **Puna** at night to check it out. Then spend a day hiking Hawai'i Volcanoes National Park.

Four Days

If you've got double the time, double your fun by linking the leeward and windward itineraries with a twilight visit to **Mauna Kea** for sunset and stargazing, or a hike in Waipi'o Valley. En route you'll pass through Waimea, restaurant capital of the island: give casual Pau or powerhouse Merriman's a try.

A Week

To really make the most of the Big Island, you should give yourself a week. On top of our four-day itinerary, spend an extra day exploring Kona Coast beaches including **Kekaha Kai State Park** and Kiholo Bay before snorkeling or diving with manta rays at night. Bookend these experiences with a visit north to quaint **Hawi** and hiking the Pololu Valley. Close out your adventures with a trip to **South Point** and Green Sands Beach.

Kailua-Kona

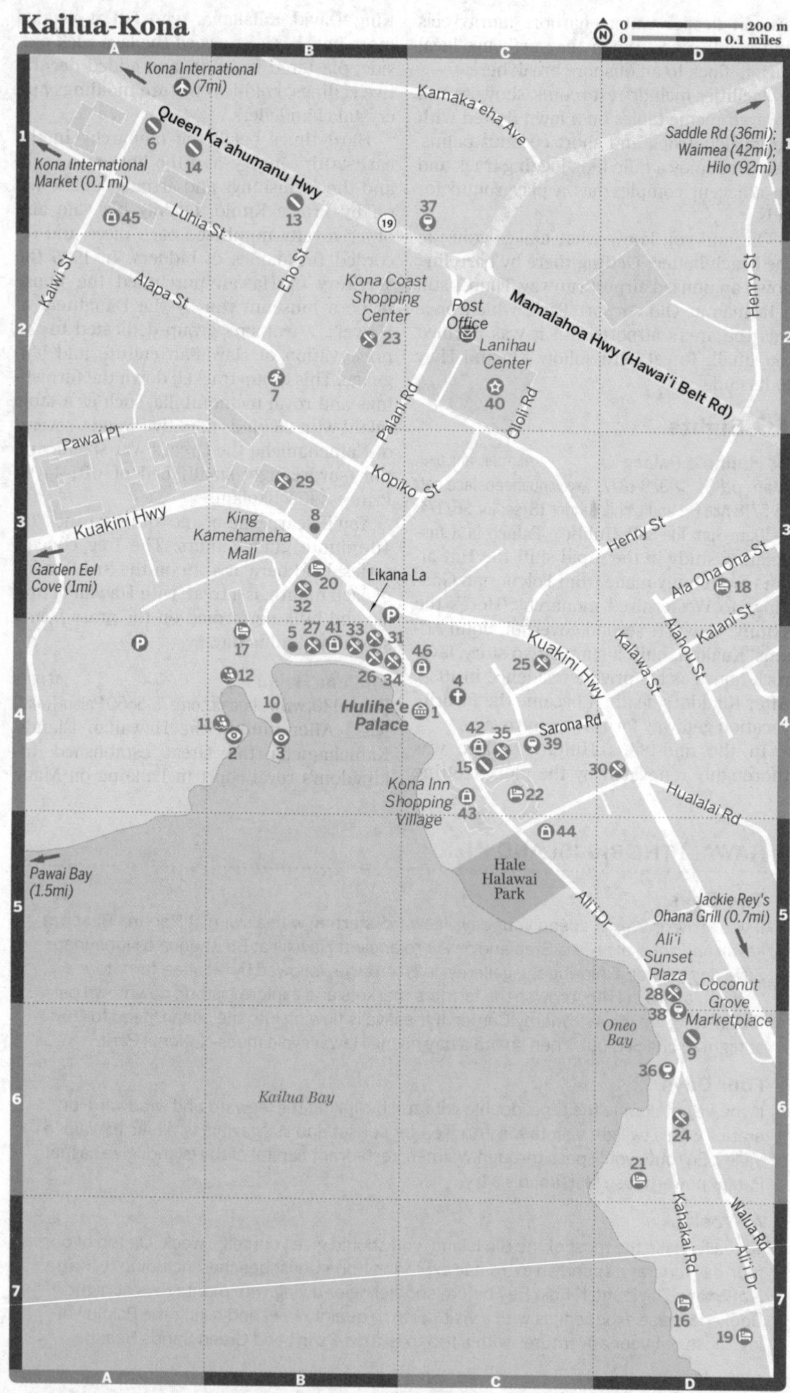

200 m
0.1 miles
Kona International (7mi)
Queen Ka'ahumanu Hwy
Kamaka'eha Ave
Saddle Rd (36mi); Waimea (42mi); Hilo (92mi)
Kona International Market (0.1mi)
Luhia St
Kaiwi St
Alapa St
Eho St
Kona Coast Shopping Center
Post Office
Lanihau Center
Mamalahoa Hwy (Hawai'i Belt Rd)
Henry St
Palani Rd
Ololi Rd
Pawai Pl
Kopiko St
Kuakini Hwy
King Kamehameha Mall
Garden Eel Cove (1mi)
Likana La
Ala Ona Ona St
Alahou St
Kalani St
Kalawa St
Hulihe'e Palace
Sarona Rd
Kona Inn Shopping Village
Hualalai Rd
Hale Halawai Park
Pawai Bay (1.5mi)
Ali'i Dr
Jackie Rey's Ohana Grill (0.7mi)
Ali'i Sunset Plaza
Coconut Grove Marketplace
Oneo Bay
Kailua Bay
Kahakai Rd
Walua Rd

Kailua-Kona

Top Sights
1 Hulihe'e Palace C4

Sights
2 Ahu'ena Heiau B4
3 Kailua Pier B4
Kona Brewing Company .... (see 29)
4 Moku'aikaua Church C4

Activities, Courses & Tours
5 Atlantis Submarines B4
6 Big Island Divers A1
7 Bikram Yoga Kona B2
8 Body Glove Historical Sunset Dinner Cruise B3
9 Jack's Diving Locker D6
10 Kailua Bay Charter Company B4
11 Kai'Opua Canoe Club B4
12 Kona Boys Beach Shack B4
13 Kona Diving Company B1
14 Kona Honu Divers A1
Lotus Center Spa .... (see 21)
15 Sandwich Isle Divers C4
Snorkel Bob's .... (see 24)
Yoga Hale .... (see 30)

Sleeping
16 Hale Kona Kai D7
17 King Kamehameha's Kona Beach Hotel B4
18 Koa Wood Hale Inn/Patey's Place D3
19 Kona Reef D7
20 Kona Seaside Hotel B3
21 Royal Kona Resort D6
22 Uncle Billy's Kona Bay Hotel C4

Eating
23 Ba-Le Kona B2
24 Basik Acai D6
25 Big Island Grill C4
26 Falafel in Paradise B4
27 Fish Hopper B4
28 Island Lava Java D5
Kanaka Kava .... (see 9)
29 Kona Brewing Company B3
KTA Super Store .... (see 23)
30 Lemongrass Bistro D4
31 Metal Mike's Twisted Pretzels B4
32 Quinn's Almost by the Sea B3
33 Rapanui Island Café B4
34 Scandinavian Shaved Ice B4
Sushi Shiono .... (see 28)
35 You Make the Roll C4

Drinking & Nightlife
Don's Mai Tai Bar .... (see 21)
36 Huggo's on the Rocks D6
Humpy's Big Island Alehouse .... (see 9)
37 Kona Town Tavern C1
38 Rosa's Cantina D6
39 Sam's Hideaway C4

Entertainment
Island Breeze Lu'au .... (see 17)
Journeys of the South Pacific .... (see 21)
40 KBXtreme C2

Shopping
41 Big Island Jewelers B4
42 Conscious Riddims Records C4
43 J. Lambus Photography C4
44 Kailua Village Farmers Market C5
45 Kona Bay Books A1
46 Na Makana C4

but he continued to use Ahu'ena Heiau as his personal retreat and temple. This is where he died in May 1819, and where his body was prepared for burial, though in keeping with tradition his bones were secreted elsewhere, hidden so securely no one has ever found them.

Reconstructed with palm-leaf shacks and carved wooden *ki'i* (statues), the small heiau (closed to the public) sits next to Kailua Pier, and the adjacent Courtyard King Kamehameha Beach Hotel uses it as a backdrop for its luau. The heiau's tiny cove doubles as a placid saltwater pool where locals fish, children swim and seniors lounge on its comma of sand at **Kamakahonu Beach**.

Kamakahonu was the name of the grand royal residence of Kamehameha; Ahu'ena Heiau is the only remaining part of that compound. A few artifacts from Kamakahonu are displayed in the lobby of the Courtyard King Kamehameha Beach Hotel, including Kamehameha's royal feather cloak *('ahu'ula)* and helmet *(mahiole)*, as well as 40 paintings by local legend Herb Kane depicting traditional Hawaiian folkways and mythology.

Moku'aikaua Church CHURCH

(Map p180; www.mokuaikaua.org; 75-5713 Ali'i Dr; 7:30am-5:30pm) Completed in 1836, Moku'aikaua Church is a handsome building with walls of lava rock held together by sand and coral-lime mortar. The posts and beams, hewn with stone adzes and smoothed with chunks of coral, are made from ohia, and the pews and pulpit are made of koa, the most prized native hardwood. The steeple tops

THE BIG ISLAND FOR CHILDREN

- Dance underwater with manta rays on a nighttime snorkeling tour out of Kailua Kona (p184)
- Trek to the ends of the Earth (or at least this island) at Green Sands Beach (Papakolea) (p308)
- Look at, but don't touch, the sea turtles sunbathing near Kiholo Bay (p223)
- Hop and swim among lava pools filled with tropical fish at Kapoho Tide Pools (p287) and Puako (p232)
- Fly over rainforest and waterfalls on a Kohala zipline adventure (p242)
- Watch molten lava pouring into the sea on a spectacular lava boat tour (p284)
- Picnic and swim at Lili'uokalani Park (p270)
- Ride the range on a horseback tour (p246)

out at 112ft, making this the tallest structure in Kailua.

Often referred to as 'the big stone church on Ali'i,' Moku'aikaua is the gestation point of Hawaiian Christianity. On April 4, 1820, the first Christian missionaries to the Hawaiian Islands sailed into Kailua Bay. When they landed they were unaware that Hawai'i's kapu system had been abolished on that very spot just a few months before.

The church is popular for weddings, and inside is a dusty model of the missionaries' ship, *Thaddeus,* and a history of their arrival.

Contemporary **services** are held at 9am on Sundays, with traditional services following at 11am. The latter features the Ohana Choir and is followed by a short lecture on the history of the church.

Kailua Pier LANDMARK

(Map p180) The town's pier, built in 1915, was once a major cattle-shipping point. Cattle driven down from hillside ranches were stampeded into the water and forced to swim out to waiting steamers, where they were hoisted aboard by sling and shipped to Honolulu slaughterhouses.

Today Kailua Pier is where locals get wet on their lunch hour, where the Ironman Triathlon starts and finishes, and the official weigh-ins happen at the annual Hawaiian International Billfish Tournament.

Kona Brewing Company MICROBREWERY

(Map p180; ☎334-2739; www.konabrewingco.com; 75-5629 Kuakini Hwy, North Kona Shopping Center; ⊙tours 10:30am & 3pm Mon-Fri)  Founded in 1994, the Big Island's first microbrewery now ships its handcrafted brews throughout the islands and beyond. Tours of this family-run Kona icon are free and include sampling.

Activities

Most of Kailua's activities focus on the sea. Coconut Grove on Ali'i Dr has a sandy volleyball court (BYO volleyball or join a pickup game).

Diving

The area's snorkeling and diving tours are gathered here, so you can see the range of options on offer.

Near the shore, divers can see steep drop-offs with lava tubes, caves and diverse marine life. In deeper waters there are 40 popular boat-dive areas, including an airplane wreck off Keahole Point. Visibility is typically 100ft, with the best conditions prevailing April through August.

Two-tank dives cost around $150. One-tank night dives and manta-ray dives are similarly priced. The larger five-star PADI operations offer certification courses for between $475 and $650 (the price goes up for smaller groups). If you're already certified but haven't been out in the water for awhile, refresher courses cost around $30.

Some snorkel outfits accommodate divers; conversely, some dive companies accommodate snorkelers.

★Jack's Diving Locker DIVING

(Map p180; ☎800-345-4807, 329-7585; www.jacksdivinglocker.com; 75-5813 Ali'i Dr, Coconut Grove Marketplace) One of the best outfits for introductory dives and courses, with extensive programs for kids. Housed at a 5000-sq-ft facility, with a store, classrooms, a tank room and a 12ft-deep dive pool, it offers boat and shore dives, as well as nighttime manta-ray dives; snorkelers are welcome on many trips. Jack's has a reputation for environmental preservation and ecofriendly moorings.

Big Island Divers DIVING
(Map p180; ☎329-6068; www.bigislanddivers.com; 74-5467 Kaiwi St) This outfit has personable staff and an expansive shop offering tours and certification courses; all boat dives are open to snorkelers.

Sandwich Isle Divers DIVING
(Map p180; ☎888-743-3483, 329-9188; www.sandwichisledivers.com; 5729 Ali'i Dr, Kona Marketplace) This smaller outfit run by a husband-and-wife team with decades of experience offers trips that feel personalized due to a six-person maximum.

Kona Diving Company DIVING
(Map p180; ☎866-463-4836, 331-1858; www.konadivingcompany.com; 74-5615 Luhia St) A well-run family-owned dive outfit that specializes in a more personalized diving experience.

Kona Honu Divers DIVING
(Map p180; ☎888-333-4668, 324-4668; www.konahonudivers.com; 74-5583 Luhia St) Well-regarded dive company that offers a big range of excursions, including nighttime manta-ray dives and Nitrox trips.

Fishing

Kona is the world's number-one spot for catching Pacific blue marlin (June to August is peak season) and is also home to ahi (yellowfin tuna), *aku* (bonito or skipjack tuna), swordfish, spearfish and mahimahi (white-fleshed fish also called 'dolphin'). Most of the world records for catches of these fish belong to Kona fishermen.

Many charter boats are listed in the *Fishing* freebie available around town and online at *Hawaii Fishing News* (www.hawaiifishingnews.com). The standard cost to join an existing party starts at $99 per person for a four-hour (half-day) trip. Otherwise, a charter for up to six people costs between $450 and $600 for a half-day, and $750 and $3500 for a full day, depending on the boat and the number of people on the trip. Prices include equipment and license.

BIG ISLAND SURF BEACHES & BREAKS

Because Hawai'i is the youngest island and its coastline is still quite rugged, it's often assumed there isn't much in the way of surfable waves. As a result places like O'ahu and Kaua'i have stolen the surf spotlight, but archaeologists and researchers believe that Kealakekua Bay (p211) is probably where ancient Polynesians started riding waves. Today a fun little left-hander called Ke'ei breaks near the bay, but it's unclear as of press time if the moratorium on kayaking in Kealakekua will extend to surfing (see p211).

Unlike its neighboring islands, whose north and south shores are the primary center of swell activity, the east and west shores are the Big Island's focal points. Because swells are shadowed by the other islands, as a general rule the surf doesn't get as big here. The Kona Coast offers the best opportunities, with north and south swell exposures, as well as offshore trade winds. Kawaihae Harbor (p235) is surrounded by several fun, introductory reefs near the breakwall,while further south, near Kekaha Kai State Park (p220), is a considerably more advanced break that challenges even the most seasoned surfers. If you have a 4WD vehicle or don't mind an hour-long hike, be sure to check out heavy reef breaks like Mahai'ula (p220) and Makalawena (p221). They break best on northwest swells, making the later winter months the prime season. A hike or 4WD is also necessary to reach popular Pine Trees (p220) at Keahole Point, near Kailua-Kona airport.

On East Hawai'i, just outside of Hilo, are several good intermediate waves. Richardson Ocean Park (p268) is a good option within Hilo, and just west of town is Honoli'i (p269), a fast left and right peak breaking into a river mouth. Further up the Hamakua Coast is Waipi'o Bay (p257); while access to the beach requires a long walk or a 4WD vehicle, the waves are worth the effort. Puna's Pohoiki Bay (p287), meanwhile, boasts three breaks and offers the island's best surfing, according to many. This is decidedly not a beginner's break – the waves crash right up on some rough rocks.

In Ka'u, locals brace a rough paddle out to catch long rides on the nearly perfect left-break at Kawa Bay. Newbies take lessons and test the waves at Kahalu'u Beach Park (p194).

Top bodyboarding and bodysurfing spots include Hapuna Beach (p233), White (Magic) Sands Beach (p178), near Kailua-Kona, and the beaches at Kekaha Kai State Park (p220).

BLACK WATER MAGIC

For many, a night snorkel or dive with Pacific manta rays is the capstone experience to their time in Hawaii. The ocean at night is spooky enough, but to see these graceful, gentle creatures (with 8ft to 14ft wing spans) glide out of the darkness and spin cartwheels as they feed is unforgettable. There are two main dive locations: the original site in front of the Sheraton Keauhou Bay Resort and a more northerly site near Garden Eel Cove. If you snorkel, you'll likely be put in the water with a floating metal ladder-rig that you'll hang onto as mantas whir beneath you. A powerful light is attached to the ladder rigs, which attracts a buffet of plankton and, subsequently, mantas.

While clutching the rig you may feel a little like someone is holding your hand, but it is illegal in the state of Hawaii to touch manta rays, and the floating ladders are a good preventative tool that wards against accidental contact. Some kayak outfits lead tours out for night manta dives that do not include the floating ladder rigs. While it is possible to enter the water yourself from an access point near the Sheraton, we do not recommend trying to do so. The currents in this area are unpredictable, the nearby rocks are sharp and the waves can become powerful in the blink of an eye; throw in the cover of night and you're asking for trouble.

Most manta night dives are two-tank dives exploring one mediocre site during sunset before heading to the manta grounds. Operators tend to offer manta dive and snorkel excursions; the former run around $150 (not including gear), the latter around $100 (mask and fins included). Check the Manta Pacific Research Foundation website (www.mantapacific.org) for manta-sighting data and guidelines for responsible manta watching.

If you really want a nighttime underwater adventure, try a **black water dive**. Sound ominous and creepy? It kind of is, but also surreal and beautiful. You'll be boated to a site offshore where you dive into the cold black waters of the open ocean. At night, the strange, bio-luminescent animals of the deep rise to the surface, creating a glow-in-the-dark rave of alien underwater life feeding all around you. Occasionally much larger, strange beasts, like 900lb bug-eyed marlin, will dart past your astonished eyes. Trust us when we say black water dives are one of the most fascinating experiences available in Hawaii. They don't take just anyone on these excursions; Jack's Diving Locker (p182), which runs an excellent Pelagic Magic black water excursion, requires night divers to have a previous night dive under their belt, as well as 10 logged dives, including one within the last year.

Next to the weigh station at Honokohau Marina, the **Charter Desk** (Map p218; ☎888-566-2487, 326-1800; www.charterdesk.com; 74-381 Kealakehe Pkwy; ⏰6am-6pm) is the main booking service.

Hawaii Big Game Fishing Club FISHING
(☎326-7902; www.hbgfc.org) Check the Hawaii Big Game Fishing Club for tournament schedules.

Outrigger Canoeing

Kona Boys Beach Shack CANOEING
(Map p180; ☎329-2345; www.konaboys.com; Kamakahonu Beach; adult/child $50/25; ⏰8am-5pm) With celebrated Hawaiian paddler Uncle Jesse as your guide, experience what original Polynesian settlers must have felt with the water rushing under their hull as they approached the volcanic shores of the Big Island. Prices for outrigger canoe trips are per person for a minimum of two people. Also rents kayaks, stand up paddleboards and surfboards, as well as offering lessons.

Kai'Opua Canoe Club CANOEING
(Map p180; ☎334-9481, 938-8577; www.kaiopua.org) This local club is dedicated to traditional outrigger canoeing. Visitors are welcome to join their recreational paddling excursions held on weekdays and Saturday mornings; there is no office for this club so check the website for times and contact details. Trips leave from Kamakahonu Beach next to Ahu'ena Heiau.

Snorkeling

Some of the island's best snorkeling is an easy drive from Kailua: to the south check out Kahalu'u Beach Park, Two-Step and Kealakekua Bay; to the north try Makalawena and Mau'umae Beach. Shops all along

Ali'i Dr rent gear for between $7 and $10 per day or $15 and $45 per week; a good choice is **Snorkel Bob's** (Map p180; ☎800-262-7725, 329-0770; www.snorkelbob.com; 75-5831 Kahakai Rd; ⏲8am-5pm), with Rx masks, baby reef shoes and more.

Boat cruises (aka 'dolphin cruises'), including snorkeling, are plentiful around Kailua. A four-hour cruise offers snorkeling in otherwise inaccessible places, the chance to spot whales and dolphins, and knowledgeable guides. When choosing, always opt for morning departures, when conditions are best.

Ultimately the captain decides the best destination for the day's conditions. The coast south of Kailua has beautiful lava cliffs and caves, while the northern coast is a flat lava shelf with great snorkeling aplenty.

Cruise prices usually include snorkeling gear, beverages and snacks. Most offer internet discounts.

★ Sea Paradise SNORKELING, CRUISE
(Map p202; ☎800-322-5662, 322-2500; www.seaparadise.com; 78-6831 Ali'i Dr; snorkel cruise adult/child $125/72, manta snorkel $89/59, 2-tank dive $145, manta dive $110) Sea Paradise offers morning snorkel cruises to Kealakekua Bay, dive trips and a sunset dinner sail on a classy 50ft catamaran with a fun and professional crew. The manta night cruises guarantee sightings (or you repeat for free).

Sea Quest SNORKELING, WHALE WATCHING
(Map p202; ☎329-7238; www.seaquesthawaii.com; Keauhou Bay; 2-snorkel cruise adult/child $96/78, whale-watching cruise $72/62) Sea Quest offers one and two-stop snorkel adventures, plus whale-watching cruises.

Fair Wind SNORKELING, DIVING
(Map p202; ☎800-677-9461, 322-2788; www.fairwind.com; Keauhou Bay; morning snorkel adult/child $129/75, afternoon snorkel $75/45) The *Fair Wind II* is a 100-passenger catamaran with two kickin' 15ft slides and a BBQ. Cruises on the luxury hydrofoil catamaran *Hula Kai* (per person including a meal $155) are longer and motor to fairly crowd-free spots. The *Hula Kai* also does a night manta trip (snorkel $99; dive $130 to $150). Divers are accommodated and they guarantee sightings or you repeat the cruise free.

Captain Zodiac SNORKELING, CRUISE
(Map p218; ☎329-3199; www.captainzodiac.com; Honokohau Harbor; half-day cruise adult/child 4-12yr $112/93) In business since 1974, Captain Zodiac makes daily trips in 24ft rigid-hull inflatable Zodiacs with up to 16 passengers and a jaunty pirate theme.

Ocean Safaris SNORKELING, KAYAK
(Map p202; ☎326-4699; www.oceansafariskayaks.com; 78-7128 Kaleiopapa Rd; manta night-snorkeling $55 per person) Based in Keauhou, just south of Kailua-Kona, Ocean Safaris conducts kayak tours of local sea caves and can take you out on a nighttime manta ray trip.

Kamanu Charters SNORKELING, CRUISE
(Map p218; ☎800-348-3091, 329-2021; www.kamanu.com; Honokohau Harbor; adult/child $90/50) Snorkel without crowds at Pawai Bay, just north of the protected waters of the Old Kona Airport State Park. Offers a night manta snorkel ($95), and the boat can be privately chartered.

Stand Up Paddle Boarding (SUP)

It's hard to explain the appeal of Stand Up Paddle Boarding. Initially the sport only seems to make surfing slower and paddling more difficult, but in fact it's a sweet blend of intense exercise, aquatic adventure and marine biology lesson. SUP delivers a core workout accompanied by dolphins, turtles and tropical fish. And the best part is anyone can do this easy and fun activity. Lessons and rentals are available at the Kona Boys Beach Shack (p184): 90-minute private lessons cost $150, one-hour rental $25), right on Kamakahonu Beach.

Surfing

What little surf there is on the Leeward Coast is not in Kailua-Kona but a short drive north at Banyans and Pine Trees, or south at Kahalu'u Beach (equipment and lessons available).

Kona Surf Adventures SURFING
(Map p218; ☎334-0033; www.konasurfadventures.com; 75-6129 Ali'i Dr; private/group lessons $150/99) Kona Surf Adventures is run by 'Kona Mike,' who comes with endorsements from novice students and veteran wave riders alike, and also offers educational tours that provide insights into Hawaiian culture.

Hawaii Lifeguard Surf Instructors SURFING
(HLSI; Map p218; ☎324-0442; www.surflessonshawaii.com; 75-5909 Ali'i Dr; group lessons $68) The instructors at HLSI have a minimum of 15 years surfing experience and are all certified lifeguards. Offers semi-private lessons for two people at $185, and private lessons for kids (age three to 10) for $98.

WORTH A TRIP

THREE RING RANCH

Dr Ann Goody is as close to a real life Dr Doolittle as you'll ever be lucky to meet. She doesn't just talk to the animals, she also fixes their broken bones and psyches. When she can, she then sets them free, but if they can't cut it in the wild they become residents of the **Three Ring Ranch Exotic Animal Sanctuary** (☎331-8778; www.threeringranch.org; suggested donation $35; ⏲tours 11am) on five lovely acres in upland Kona. Visiting the ranch is one of the most fascinating animal encounters you can experience well…anywhere.

Licensed by the US Department of Agriculture and accredited by the American Association of Sanctuaries, Three Ring currently hosts South African crowned cranes, lesser flamingos, David and Goliath (a pair of gigantic African spur-thigh tortoises) and much more, including native endangered species such as the Hawaiian owl. Amid all this wonderful wildlife, zebra Zoe is something special: rescued from the failed Moloka'i Ranch Safari Park, Zoe has amelanosis, meaning her stripes are the color of Hapuna Beach sand and her eyes the color of the sea.

Dr Goody – who incredibly has been struck by lightning, tossed by a shark and is a breast cancer survivor – is as good with people as she is with animals. This has led to enormously successful educational initiatives, including an after-school program, a resident-intern program and a residency placement program for pre-veterinarian students. Since the sanctuary's primary commitment is to the animals and their welfare, it leads two-hour tours by prior arrangement only; booking via email preferred. See the website for details.

Whale Watching

The season for humpback whales starts around January and runs to March or April.

Dan McSweeney's Whale Watch WHALE WATCHING
(Map p218; ☎888-942-5376, 322-0028; www.ilovewhales.com; 3hr-cruise adult/child $110/99) While many maritime tour operators add whale-watching trips in season, we recommend marine mammal biologist Dan McSweeney. An active researcher, he leads educational excursions where observing whales is always the main focus. Several other types of whales, and five species of dolphin, can also be seen in Kona waters year-round. Hydrophones allow passengers to hear whale songs. Book via the website or phone.

Yoga

Yoga Hale YOGA
(Map p180; ☎326-9642; http://yogahale.com; 75-5742 Kuakini Hwy) Offers a large variety of courses, from hot yoga to Bikram to vinyasa. Also does dance classes like hip-hop, ecstatic and (why not?) hula hoop.

Bikram Yoga Kona YOGA
(Map p180; ☎443-9990; www.bikramkona.com; 74-5626 Alapa St; drop-in class $16) An excellent local Bikram studio.

Tours

★Body Glove Historical Sunset Dinner Cruise CRUISE
(Map p180; ☎326-7122, 800-551-8911; www.bodyglovehawaii.com; 75-5629 Kuakini Highway; adult/child 6-17/under 5 $115/83/free; ⏲historical cruise 4pm Tue, Thu, Fri & Sat) This popular historical cruise along the Kona Coast lasts three hours and includes dinner, kickin' live music and engaging historical narration. The sunset 'booze' cruise is two hours and features an open bar. The boat is wheelchair accessible.

Kona Historical Society WALKING TOUR
(Map p202; ☎323-3222, 938-8825; www.konahistorical.org; 90-min tour $15) This worthwhile and informational walking tour covers historical sites in downtown Kailua-Kona, and includes a booklet. Ten-person minimum; tours by appointment.

Atlantis Submarines BOAT TOUR
(Map p180; ☎800-381-0237; www.atlantisadventures.com; adult/child $99/45; ⏲rides 10am) You read that right: this is a real-deal submarine tour. The underwater portion lasts 35 minutes, involves a 100ft descent into a coral crevice in front of the Royal Kona Resort and explores a couple of nearby shipwrecks. The battery-powered sub has 26 portholes and carries 48 passengers.

Kailua Bay Charter Company BOAT TOUR
(Map p180; ☎324-1749; www.konaglassbottomboat.com; Kailua-Kona Pier; 50-min tour adult/child $40/20; ⏰10:30am, 11:30am & 12:30pm) See Kailua's coastline and underwater reef from a 36ft glass-bottom boat with a pleasant crew and onboard naturalist. Easy boarding for mobility impaired passengers.

Festivals & Events

Kailua-Kona Street Fair FESTIVAL
If you're in town on the last Sunday of the month, make sure to check out the Kailua-Kona Street Fair, when local vendors, artists, craftsmen and musicians set up in booths and on stages along the north end of Ali'i Dr. The whole affair usually starts around 1pm and lasts until sunset.

Kona Brewers Festival BEER, FOOD
(☎987-9196; www.konabrewersfestival.com; admission $50) Held in mid-March, this 'just folks' festival features samples from dozens of craft breweries and gourmet eats from scores of local restaurants.

Hawaiian International Billfish Tournament FISHING
(www.hibtfishing.com) 'The grandfather of all big-game fishing tournaments' is also Kona's most prestigious. Held in late July to August, it's accompanied by a week of festive entertainment.

Ironman Triathlon World Championship SPORTS
(http://ironman.com) This legendary event, held on the Kona Coast in early October, combines a 2.4-mile ocean swim, 112-mile bike race and 26.2-mile marathon – the ultimate race, which must be completed in 17 hours or fewer.

Kona Coffee Cultural Festival COFFEE
(www.konacoffeefest.com) For 10 days during harvest season in November the community celebrates Kona coffee-pioneers and their gourmet brew. Events include a cupping competition (like a wine tasting), art exhibits, farm tours, parades, concerts and a coffee-picking race.

Sleeping

The quality of many hotels and condos along Ali'i Dr in the walkable center of Kailua-Kona trend toward fair to middling. More attractive offerings are just outside town. Reservations for all listed properties are recommended in high season.

Kona Tiki Hotel HOTEL $
(Map p218; ☎329-1425; www.konatikihotel.com; 75-5968 Ali'i Dr; r $80-145; P 🛜 ≋) The nothing-special rooms (with refrigerator, but no TV or phone) in this older three-story building would be forgettable if the intimate hush of crashing waves didn't tuck you in every night. Snug on a restless cove, the Kona Tiki is well kept, friendly and surprisingly romantic. The more expensive rooms have kitchenettes.

Casa de Emdeko CONDO $
(Map p218; ☎329-2160; www.casadeemdeko.org; 75-6082 Ali'i Dr; 1- & 2-bedroom from $95; ❄ ≋) With Spanish-tile roofs, white stucco, immaculate gardens and two pools, this vacation rental complex is stylish and restful. Units are overall up-to-date, well cared for and nicely priced.

Koa Wood Hale Inn/Patey's Place HOSTEL $
(Map p180; ☎329-9663; 75-184 Ala Ona Ona St; dm/s/d from $30/55/65; @ 🛜) This oddly named hostel is Kona's crashpad for backpackers. There's basic, clean dorms and private rooms (all with shared baths, kitchens and living rooms) on a residential street that's walking distance to Ali'i Dr. There's the usual crowd of youngsters, misfits and the heavily road-worn.

Uncle Billy's Kona Bay Hotel HOTEL $
(Map p180; ☎800-367-5102, 329-1393; www.unclebilly.com; 75-5744 Ali'i Dr; r $85-150; P ❄ 🛜 ≋) We're including Uncle Billy's because it's smack downtown and, as a result, lots of people end up here. The problem is there's lots of street noise and that retro-chic exterior devolves into old and boring grandma sheets inside.

Plumeria House APARTMENT $
(Map p218; ☎326-9255; www.plumeriahouse.com; Kilohana St; 1 bedroom $80-120; @ 🛜) Located in an upland residential neighborhood, this immaculate 800 sq ft one-bedroom unit features many convenient touches: full kitchen, filtered water, patio tables and use of washer–dryer. Wheelchair accessible; $50 cleaning fee.

★**Kona Sugar Shack** INN $$
(Map p218; ☎877-324-6444, 895-2203; www.konasugarshack.com; 77-6483 Ali'i Drive; r $150-540; P ❄ 🛜 ≋) 🍃 The Sugar Shack hits the sweet spot when it comes to vacation rentals. The friendly, artistic hosts have created an attractively funky yet homey three-room

VACATION RENTALS

Condos tend to be cheaper than hotels for longer stays, and they offer more independence for DIY types (and families). Condo vacation rentals are handled directly by owners or by property management agencies. Vacation rentals are another family-friendly option; check listings on the following websites:

- **Airbnb** (www.airbnb.com)
- **Vacation Rentals by Owner** (www.vrbo.com)
- **ATR Properties** (888-311-6020, 329-6020; www.konacondo.com)
- **Kona Hawaii Vacation Rentals** (800-244-4752, 329-3333; www.konahawaii.com)
- **Kona Rentals** (800-799-5662; www.konarentals.com)
- **Luxury Retreats Hawaii** (877-993-0100; www.fabulous-homes.com)
- **Alternative Hawaii** (283-4405; www.alternative-hawaii.com)
- **Knutson & Associates** (800-800-6202, 329-6311; www.konahawaiirentals.com)
- **SunQuest Vacations & Property Management Hawaii** (800-367-5168, 329-6438; www.sunquest-hawaii.com)

inn, mostly solar powered, with shared outdoor kitchen, a miniscule pool and lots of amenities. Best of all is the eclectic decor and general vibe; this spot feels like it's happily torn between being an art museum, attic of amazing stuff and funky gallery.

Also, the owners are great with kids. Did we mention this place is just across the street from White Sands Beach? Three-night minimum stay required; the entire house, sleeping 15, is available for rent as well.

★ Hale Kona Kai CONDO **$$**
(Map p180; 800-421-3696, 329-6402; www.hale-konakai-hkk.com; 75-5870 Kahakai Rd; 1 bedroom $170-195; P ❄ ☎ ≋) Quietly positioned on a hidden lane just walkable to downtown, this three-story block of frequently upgraded units is an excellent choice. At the time of writing there were over 20 condo units to pick from, all decorated and maintained in unique fashion, from kitschy Hawaiian Tiki-tastic to slick and modern; check the website for individual descriptions of each property. That said, all face the ocean and have lanai.

The Lilikoi Vine GUESTHOUSE **$$**
(Map p218; 808-987-9091, 808-325-9856; http://konaguesthouse.com; 73-1529 Hao Way; 1-/2-bedroom apt $110/140; P ☎) This warmly appointed property sits on an deeply green, lush upcountry lot complete with Balinese garden. There are two options for guests: the Paniolo Room, a studio flat accented by vintage touches like hardwood floors and an antique stove, and I'iwi's Nest, a two-bedroom apartment decked out in tropical-trendy artwork and accoutrement. Three-night minimum.

King Kamehameha's Kona Beach Hotel HOTEL **$$**
(Map p180; reservations 800-367-2111, 329-2911; www.konabeachhotel.com; 75-5660 Palani Rd; r $170-250; P ❄ @ ☎ ≋) One of the better options in downtown Kailua-Kona, the historic 'King Kam,' operated by Courtrad by Mariott, anchors Ali'i Dr. Chic room decor, a Herb Kawainui Kane exhibit in the lobby (open to nonguests) and free in-room wi-fi are all draws here. Walk to some of our favorite restaurants or hop over to the Kona Boys Beach Shack (p184) to try stand up paddling or sea kayaking.

Kona Bali Kai RESORT **$$**
(Map p218; 808-329-9381; www.konabalikai.com; 76-6246 Ali'i Dr; 1-/2-bedroom villa from $140/180; P ❄ ☎ ≋) This seaside resort is a collection of ambitiously titled 'villas' – we would probably call them 'nicely appointed guesthouses and condo units' – that are airy and open to natural light, have kitchenettes, and are filled with lots of neutral colors and vaguely nautical paraphernalia.

Kona Seaside Hotel HOTEL **$$**
(Map p180; 800-560-5558, 329-2455; http://seasidehotelshawaii.com; 75-5646 Palani Rd; r $110-170; P ❄ ☎ ≋) Passable downtown option. The Garden Wing is quietest; rooms with a view aren't worth the extra cash.

Royal Kona Resort RESORT $$
(Map p180; ☎329-3111, reservations 800-222-5642; www.royalkona.com; 75-5852 Ali'i Dr; r from $150, ste from $225; P ❄ @ ≋) You can't miss the Royal Kona, thrusting like a ship's prow, whose '70s Polynesian kitsch is so potent you half expect the Brady Bunch to come tumbling out of the elevator. The good-sized, freshly renovated rooms are attractive, with nice touches such as wood-shutter closet doors; corner-room lanai have tremendous views, but others lack privacy. Check out the extensive services at the **Lotus Center Spa** (Map p180; www.konaspa.com) here.

Royal Sea-Cliff Resort CONDO $$
(Map p218; ☎800-688-7444, 329-8021; www.outrigger.com; 75-6040 Ali'i Dr; studios from $150, 1-/2-bedroom from $185/325; P ❄ @ ≋) Outrigger runs the condo side of this seven-floor time-share complex like an upscale hotel, giving you the best of both worlds. Immaculate units are generous-sized and uniformly appointed with pretty furniture and lots of amenities – kitchens, washers and dryers, sauna and two oceanfront pools.

Kona Reef CONDO $$
(Map p180; ☎800-513-6708, 329-2959; www.konareefresorts.com; 75-5888 Ali'i Dr; 1 bedroom from $198; P ❄ @ ≋) Spacious, well-kept condos in a nondescript complex; you'll find drastically lower rates with internet discounts for booking online.

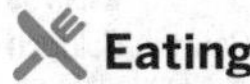

Eating

There's *'ono grinds* (good food) in Kailua-Kona, but there's also a lot of dross on Ali'i Dr. This is also by far the most expensive area for food on the island.

KTA Super Store (Map p180; www.ktasuperstores.com; 74-5594 Palani Rd, Kona Coast Shopping Center; ⏲5am-11pm) and **Island Naturals** (Map p202; www.islandnaturals.com; 74-5487 Kaiwi St; ⏲7:30am-8pm Mon-Sat, 9am-7pm Sun; 🖉) should have everything you need in the way of groceries. Each has a deli, and at KTA you'll find sushi, some of the island's best *poke* (cubed raw marinated fish), kimchi and other local specialties.

★ **Ba-Le Kona** VIETNAMESE $
(Map p180; 74-5588 Palani Rd, Kona Coast Shopping Center; sandwiches $4-7, soups & plates $9-13; ⏲10am-9pm Mon-Sat, 11am-7pm Sun; 🖉) Don't let the fluorescent-lit dining room and polystyrene plates fool you: Ba-Le serves up the sort of Vietnamese that makes you want to pack it all up and move to Hanoi. Flavors are simple, refreshing and bright, from the green-papaya salad to traditional *pho* (Vietnamese noodle soup), and rice plates of spicy lemongrass chicken, tofu, beef or roast pork.

The *banh mi* (Vietnamese baguette sandwiches) are a perfect choice for a Big Island picnic.

Da Poke Shack SEAFOOD $
(Map p218; 76-6246 Ali'i Dr; mains from $5; ⏲10am-6pm) Nope, you don't get to eat Gumby's red horse friend Pokey here (sicko). *Poke* is a local specialty that blends ceviche and sushi; raw, marinated cubes of fish mixed with soy sauce, sesame oil, some chiles, seaweed and…well, really, the sky's the limit. The point is, *poke* is wonderful, and Da Poke Shack is the spot to get it, because they offer a huge variety of *poke* creations.

It's like a salad bar, except the salad is raw fish – yum! There's barely enough room for 10 customers at the ordering counter; you eat outside on breeze-licked picnic tables, which is fine with us.

Falafel in Paradise MIDDLE EASTERN $
(Map p180; 75-5699 Ali'i Dr; mains $8-14; ⏲11am-9pm Sun-Fri, til 3:30pm Sat; 🖉) Nothing says Hawaii like Israeli–Middle Eastern cuisine, right? Hey, we love Pacific fusion as much as the next guidebook, but Falafel in Paradise brings a welcome bit of vegetarian/international flair to the dining options on Ali'i. The signature falafel is quite good, as are any variant of flatbread dipped in a delicious sauce (hummus, we're looking your way).

Quinn's Almost by the Sea SEAFOOD $
(Map p180; 75-5655 Palani Rd; mains $9-16; ⏲11am-11pm; 👪) Quinn's, while lacking a waterfront location (did you see the name of the place?), serves up the best fish and chips in Kailua-Kona. The interior is a bit divey and dark, but the outside courtyard, where most folks dine, is pleasant enough.

Kanaka Kava HAWAII REGIONAL CUISINE $
(Map p180; www.kanakakava.com; Coconut Grove Marketplace, 75-5803 Ali'i Dr; à la carte $7-8, mains $14-16; ⏲10am-10pm Sun-Wed, to 11pm Thu-Sat) We're not going to say people either love or hate kava (the juice of the *'awa* plant). In our experience, folks either hate it, or *tolerate* it, because kava, frankly, tastes like dirt. But it also tends to induce a minor, non-alcoholic buzz if you drink enough (about three cups). Anyways, some folks *do* love it: namely the

proprietors of Kanaka Kava, one of Kailua-Kona's most unique eating experiences.

Delicious organic salads are topped with fish, shellfish, chicken, tofu or *poke*. The *kalua* (traditional method of cooking) pork is phenomenal.

Metal Mike's Twisted Pretzels FAST FOOD $
(Map p180; Likana Lane; pretzels under $5; ⏲11:30am-10pm Mon-Thu, 11:30am-midnight Fri & Sat, noon-10pm Sun;) Metal Mike, who seriously looks like he spent time as a roadie for Def Leppard (that's a compliment, Mike – you rock) runs a delicious pretzel stand on a narrow alley that runs by a parking lot situated just above Ali'i Dr; look for the entrance by Scandinavian Shaved Ice. There's over a dozen kinds of pretzels and dipping sauces on offer; we say go for the savory options.

You Make the Roll SUSHI $
(Map p180; 75-5725 Ali'i Dr, Kona Marketplace; sushi rolls $5-7; ⏲11am-7pm Mon-Fri, to 4pm Sat) This high-concept hole-in-the-wall presents over 20 sushi ingredients you can combine however you like. Fat loose rolls, low prices, lots of fun and a hidden location.

Scandinavian Shaved Ice SHAVE ICE $
(Map p180; www.scandinavianshaveice.com; 75-5699 Ali'i Dr; shave ice $3.50-7.25; ⏲11am-7pm) Shave ice is served here in huge, psychedelic-colored mounds that are as big as your head and as tasty as all get-out. There's an orgy of syrup choices and plenty of board games for whiling away the hours.

Sushi Shiono SUSHI $
(Map p180; www.sushishiono.com; 75-5799 Ali'i Dr, Ali'i Sunset Plaza; sushi & rolls $4-14; ⏲lunch Mon-Fri, dinner daily) Awesomely fresh fish and a nice sake list served by a Japanese expat employing an all-Japanese all-star cast of sushi chefs.

Basik Acai HEALTH FOOD $
(Map p180; www.basikacai.com; 75-5831 Kahakai Rd; bowls $6-11; ⏲8am-4pm Mon-Sat;) Healthy, wholesome bowls bursting with goodness (granola, tropical fruit, nuts) are blended with acai for added punch. Nice ocean views from up here.

★ **Big Island Grill** HAWAII REGIONAL CUISINE $$
(Map p180; 75-5702 Kuakini Hwy; plate lunches $10, mains $10-19; ⏲7:30am-9pm Mon-Sat;) If you eat in one spot in Kailua-Kona, eat here. The grill serves Hawaii's comfort foods – aka plate lunches and *loco moco* (rice, fried egg and hamburger patty topped with thick gravy) – as fresh and flavorful as home cooking. Choose from fried chicken katsu (deep-fried fillets), fried mahimahi, shrimp tempura, beef teriyaki, *kalua* pork and more.

All meals come with two scoops of rice, potato-mac salad and rich gravy. It's always packed, but swift service is warm with aloha.

Island Lava Java CAFE $$
(Map p180; www.islandlavajava.com; Ali'i Sunset Plaza, 75-5799 Ali'i Dr; meals $9-18; ⏲6:30am-9:30pm;) This cafe is a favorite gathering spot for sunny breakfasts (and Sunday brunch) with almost-oceanside dining on the outdoor patio. The food aims for upscale diner; if it sometimes hits closer to greasy spoon, no one minds – especially since the coffee is 100% Kona, and the beef and chicken are Big Island–raised. Portions are huge, baked goods sinful and the fish Benedict delicious.

Lemongrass Bistro ASIAN $$
(Map p180; ☎331-2708; http://lemongrass-bistro.webs.com; 75-5742 Kuakini Hwy; mains from $13-35; ⏲11:00am-3pm & 5-10:30pm Mon-Fri, noon-3pm & 5-9pm Sat & Sun;) The food at Lemongrass is clean and elegant, but also hearty enough to stick to your ribs, just like the best comfort food. Try the meaty oxtail or crispy duck shellacked in a garlic soy glaze and you'll agree this is the tastiest local bridge between Eastern and Western gastronomy.

Rapanui Island Café ASIAN $$
(Map p180; 75-5695 Ali'i Dr, Banyan Court mall; lunch $6-10, dinner mains $10-16; ⏲lunch & dinner Mon-Fri, dinner Sat) This cafe's New Zealand owners know curry, which they prepare with a delicious tongue-tingly warmth. Choose from various satays, spiced pork, seafood and salads. Order the house coconut rice; and wash it down with lemongrass ginger tea or a New Zealand wine. Side note: they always play kick-butt rock music here at night.

Jackie Rey's Ohana Grill ISLAND CONTEMPORARY $$
(Map p218; ☎327-0209; www.jackiereys.com; 75-5995 Kuakini Hwy, Pottery Terrace; mains lunch $11-15, dinner $14-28; ⏲lunch 11am-9pm Mon-Fri, 5-9pm Sat & Sun;) Jackie's is one of the original Big Island restaurants that turned evolved casual Hawaii *grinds* (cuisine) into a high-end dining experience ensconsed in Polynesian kitsch. The food (think glazed short ribs, wasabi-seared ahi and killer fresh fish tacos) is pricey but served with aloha, making this place a local night-out favorite.

Kids are king here, getting their own menu, crayons for creating on the 'tablecloths' and tours of the walk-in freezer.

Kona Brewing Company AMERICAN $$
(Map p180; ☎334-2739; www.konabrewingco.com; 75-5629 Kuakini Hwy; sandwiches & salads $11-16, pizzas $15-26; ⏰11am-9pm Sun-Thu, to 10pm Fri & Sat) Good beer, green stewardship and lots of aloha: the Big Island's first microbrewery serves up one of Kona's liveliest scenes. Kona Brewing Company's latest concoctions include Oceanic Organic Saison (a singular certified-organic brew) and Suncharged Pale Ale, made using solar power. Either at the bright bar (closes an hour after the kitchen) or on the torch-lit patio, diners enjoy meal-sized salads, juicy burgers and thin-crust pizzas from a stone oven. Make reservations.

Fish Hopper AMERICAN $$
(Map p180; 75-5683 Ali'i Dr; mains $12-30; ⏰7:30am-9:30pm;) If you're jonesing for waterfront dining on the west end of Ali'i Dr, Fish Hopper's a good bet, and stands pretty well above a handful of almost identical nearby restaurants. The Hopper boasts a breeze-cooled porch and a tasty, diverse menu, offering mahimahi crusted in macadamia nuts, lobster pasta and a nice burger.

La Bourgogne FRENCH $$$
(Map p218; ☎329-6711; 77-6400 Nalani St, Kuakini Plaza, Hwy 11; mains $28-38; ⏰6-10pm Tue-Sat) At this classic French restaurant the cuisine and the presentation exude skill and refinement. Expect baked brie in puff pastry, roast duck, rabbit in white wine, foie gras and Kona's best wine list. The dining room is Parisian-intimate, and the service is good, if not always up to the food. Reservations a must.

Drinking & Nightlife

The residents of Kailua-Kona have always been adamant about not wanting their town to be another Waikiki, but this is still where you'll find the most bars on the Big Island.

Kona Town Tavern BAR
(Map p180; 75-5626 Kuakini Hwy, Unit F; ⏰6am-2am) In a city full of transplants and tourists, the Kona Town Tavern (KTT) is where the locals are: smoking, drinking 'til they're merry, rubbing elbows, giving each other crap, shootin' the breeze and generally enjoying the scene in one of the best little tropical dives anywhere. Located in a strip mall on a hill overlooking Kuakini Hwy.

Humpy's Big Island Alehouse PUB
(Map p180; www.humpyshawaii.com; 75-5815 Ali'i Dr, Coconut Grove Marketplace; ⏰9am-1am) Smack on the strip overlooking Ali'i, Humpy's would survive in touristy Kailua-Kona even if it didn't have more than three dozen beers on tap. But fresh, foamy brews bring in the locals, giving the upstairs balcony – with its sea breeze and views – special cachet.

Come by for happy hour, 3pm to 6pm on weekdays and open-mic nights on Thursdays, when a lot of the island's best (or at least most enthusiastic musicians) drop in: Humpy's opens at 7am on Sundays if an NFL game is going and has multiple screens, so you can catch most games

Huggo's on the Rocks BAR
(Map p180; www.huggos.com/all/rocksdefault.htm; 75-5828 Kahakai Rd; ⏰11:30am-midnight) Huggo's is as adjacent to the water as you're allowed to get in Kailua-Kona (ordinances now prevent other bars from getting this close to the waves). You'll be drinking under thatch roofs with live music, magic sunsets and every now and then, a spray of surf dusting your hair. In the mornings, this place reverts to **Java on the Rocks** (6am to 11am), with terrific coffee drinks and inventive breakfasts.

Sam's Hideaway BAR
(Map p180; 75-5725 Ali'i Dr; ⏰9am-2am) Sam's is a dark, cozy (OK, some might say 'dank') little nook of a bar. You'll rarely find a tourist here, but there's always locals, especially when the Hideaway hosts its frequent karaoke nights. Trust us: you haven't done Kailua-Kona until you've seen a 7ft Samoan

PARKING LOT PROBLEMS

The parking lot behind Humpy's Big Island Alehouse is convenient if you've got a designated driver and want to park near Ali'i Dr's most popular boozing strip. With that said, be careful walking back to your car later in the evening, given the level of alcohol/testosterone around and the sometime problem of locals picking fights with tourists. If you're in a group you should be fine; just keep your wits about you.

guy tear up as he belts 'The Snows of Mauna Kea.' Located a little off Ali'i Dr, behind the shops that front the main road.

Rosa's Cantina BAR
(Map p180; 75-5805 Ali'i Dr; noon-2am) Looking to dance? Rosa's is a fun bay-front bar that hosts good reggae and DJ nights several evenings a week.

Don's Mai Tai Bar BAR
(Map p180; www.royalkona.com; 75-5852 Ali'i Dr; 10am-10pm) For pure kitsch, nothing beats the shameless lounge-lizard fantasy of Don's, in the Royal Kona. Behold killer ocean views, with one of 10 different mai tais. Real fans roll in for the annual **Mai Tai Festival** held here each August.

Entertainment

Kailua-Kona's two cruise-ship friendly luau include a ceremony, a buffet dinner with Hawaiian specialties, an open bar and a Polynesian dinner show featuring a cast of flamboyant dancers and fire twirlers.

If the rain or vog (haze) is bringing you down head to **Hollywood Makalaua Stadium Cinemas** (Map p218; 327-0444; 74-5469 Kamaka'eha Ave, Makalapua Shopping Center) for the latest Hollywood flicks; or to **KBXtreme** (Map p180; 326-2695; www.kbxtreme.com; 75-5591 Palani Rd; per hr $29, shoe rental $3; 9am-midnight, bar to 2am) for some bowling fun – weekdays from 1pm to 4pm are deeply discounted and weekend nights feature 'cosmic bowling' followed by a DJ and dancing.

Journeys of the South Pacific LUAU
(Map p180; 329-3111; www.royalkona.com/luaus; Royal Kona Resort; adult/child 6-11yr $70/24; 6pm Mon, Wed & Fri) One child under six years admitted free with each paying adult.

Island Breeze Lu'au LUAU
(Map p180; 329-4969; www.islandbreezeluau.com; King Kamehameha Kona Beach Hotel; adult/child 5-12yr $74/37; 5pm Tue, Thu & Sun)

Shopping

Kailua-Kona is swamped with run-of-the-mill, dubious-quality Hawaiiana, but there's good stuff, too. You never know when you'll find that perfectly sublime kitschy, tacky something.

★ **Big Island Jewelers** JEWELRY
(Map p180; 329-8571; www.bigislandjewelers.com; 75-5695 Ali'i Dr) Family owned and operated for nearly four decades, with master jeweler Flint Carpenter at the wheel, this jewelry store offers authentic Big Island keepsakes (or rings if you need to pop the question!).

J. Lambus Photography ART
(Map p180; 989-9560; www.jlambus.com; 75-5744 Ali'i Dr, Kona Inn Shopping village) Josh Lambus is one of the finest underwater photographers in Hawaii. His work has been exhibited by the Smithsonian, and he has taken some of the first recorded snaps of several deep-sea species. Pop into his gallery, take home a picture and ask Josh about adventure activities in the area; he's extremely well-connected in the field.

Na Makana SOUVENIRS
(Map p180; 938-8577; 75-5722 Likana Lane; 9am-5pm) This odds-and-ends shop is a rarity in Kailua – offering authentic Hawaii-made gifts, books and collectibles, with unusual finds such as Japanese glass fishing floats. Opening hours vary according to the owner's schedule.

Kailua Village Farmers Market SOUVENIRS
(Map p180; www.konafarmersmarket.com; Ali'i Dr; 7am-4pm Wed-Sun) First, wander through this market where craft stalls outnumber produce stands two to one. Then purchase your coconut purses, cheap kids wear and koa wood Harleys. Do like the locals and get your fresh lei ($5) here.

Kona International Market SOUVENIRS
(Map p218; www.konainternationalmarket.com; 74-5533 Luhia St; 9am-5pm) Five large warehouse buildings make up this expansive, attractive complex, where individual stalls sell everything imaginable: beach gear, fresh fish, boutique clothing, music, gifts and crafts galore. Has a food court and ample parking.

Kona Bay Books BOOKS
(Map p180; www.konabaybooks.com; 74-5487 Kaiwi St; 10am-6pm) A good used-book store, with a nice selection of Hawaiian titles, plus used CDs.

Conscious Riddims Records MUSIC
(Map p180; 326-7685; www.consciousriddims.org; 75-5719 Ali'i Dr, Kona Marketplace; 10am-6pm Sun-Fri) This far-out joint offers a wide selection of reggae and Jawaiian (Hawaii-style reggae) music, plus clothing and *pakalolo* (marijuana) activism.

Orientation

The highways and major roads in the Kona district run parallel to the coastline, so you're unlikely to get lost. Kailua-Kona is south of the airport on Hwy 19 (Queen Ka'ahumanu Hwy), which becomes Hwy 11 (Mamalahoa Hwy) at Palani Rd. What makes navigation a bit tricky is when Queen Ka'ahumana (Hwy 19) confusingly becomes Kuakini Hwy (Hwy 11) at the intersection with Palani Rd, then connects with the historic Kuakini Hwy toward the ocean. In other words, there are two Kuakini Hwys for a stretch!

From the highway, Kaiwi St, Palani Rd and Henry St are the primary routes into town. Ali'i Dr is Kailua's main drag; the first mile, from Palani Rd to Kahakai Rd, is a pedestrian-friendly ramble lined with shops, restaurants and hotels. Ali'i Dr then continues another 4 miles along the coast to Keauhou, and is cheek-by-jowl condo complexes, vacation rentals, B&Bs, hotels and private homes.

To beat commuter traffic in and out of town, check out the Haleki'i Bypass Rd connecting Kealakekua with Keauhou.

Information

MEDIA

The Big Island's main daily newspaper is the **Hawaii Tribune-Herald** (www.hawaiitribune-herald.com). The **West Hawaii Today** (www.westhawaiitoday.com) is Kona Coast's daily newspaper.

Popular radio stations include:

KAGB 99.1 FM The Kona-side home of effervescent KAPA – Hawaii and island music.

KKUA 90.7 FM Hawaii Public Radio; classical music, talk and news.

KLUA 93.9 FM Native FM Plays island and reggae tunes.

KMWB 93.1 Classic rock.

MEDICAL SERVICES

Kona Community Hospital (☎322-9311; www.kch.hhsc.org; 79-1019 Haukapila St) Located about 10 miles south of Kailua-Kona.

CVS (75-5595 Palani Rd, Lanihau Center; ⌚8am-9pm Mon-Sat, to 6pm Sun) Centrally located drugstore and pharmacy.

MONEY

Both **Bank of Hawaii** (75-5595 Palani Rd, Lanihau Center) and **First Hawaiian Bank** (74-5593 Palani Rd, Lanihau Center) have 24-hour ATMs.

POST

Post Office (74-5577 Palani Rd, Lanihau Center; ⌚8:30am-4:30pm Mon-Fri, 9:30am-1:30pm Sat)

USEFUL WEBSITES

Big Island Visitors Bureau (www.bigisland.org) Basic info geared to the mainstream; handy calendar of events.

Kona Web (www.konaweb.com) This wonderfully helpful site has been collecting reviews from locals and visitors about the entire Big Island since 1995.

Getting There & Away

AIR

The island's primary airport is Kona International Airport at Keahole (p176), located 7 miles north of Kailua-Kona. When booking, keep in mind that late afternoon weekday traffic is brutal on southbound Hwy 19.

BUS

The **Hele-On Bus** (www.heleonbus.org; all fares $1) runs from Kailua-Kona to the town of Captain Cook (1½ hours) multiple times daily except Sunday. Twice daily except Sunday, it runs to Pahala (two hours), Hilo (3½ hours) and Waimea (1½ hours). The South Kohala resorts, meanwhile, are serviced three times a day except Sunday (1½ hours).

Another option between Kailua-Kona and Keauhou is the **Keauhou Trolley Express**, a $2 shuttle that runs daily between Kailua Pier and Keauhou Shopping Center with plenty of stops in between. For a full schedule, check www.konaweb.com/forums/shuttle.

CAR

The trip from Hilo to Kailua-Kona is 92 miles and takes 2½ hours via Waimea, a bit longer via Volcano.

To avoid snarly traffic during rush hour, try the Mamalahoa-Haleki'i Bypass Road.

Getting Around

TO/FROM THE AIRPORTS

If you're not picking up a rental car, taxis can be found curbside; the fare averages $35 to Kailua-Kona and $55 to Waikoloa. **Speedi Shuttle** (☎877-242-5777, 329-5433; www.speedishuttle.com) charges about the same, and only a couple of dollars for each additional person. Book in advance.

If you've got a rental car, a right turn out of the airport takes you south 7 miles to Kailua-Kona; left takes you up the coast to North Kona.

BICYCLE

Bicycle is an ideal way to get around Kailua.

Hawaiian Pedals (☎329-2294; www.hawaiianpedals.com; 75-5744 Ali'i Dr, Kona Inn Shopping Village; per day $20; ⌚9:30am-8pm) Rents well-used hybrid bikes for cruising.

Bike Works (☎326-2453; www.bikeworkskona.com; 74-5583 Luhia St, Hale Hana Center; per day $40-60; ⏲9am-6pm Mon-Sat, 10am-4pm Sun) Rents high-quality mountain and touring bikes for the serious cyclist; offers multiday discounts. Rentals include helmet, lock, pump and patch kit.

BUS

The Hele-On Bus (p193) and the **Keauhou Trolley Expresss** both make stops within Kailua-Kona.

CAR

Ali'i Dr, in downtown Kailua-Kona, gets very congested in the late afternoon and evening. Free public parking is available in a lot between Likana Lane and Kuakini Hwy. Shopping centers along Ali'i Dr usually provide free parking for patrons behind their center.

MOPED & MOTORCYCLE

Scooter Brothers (☎327-1080; www.scooterbrothers.com; 75-5829 Kahakai Rd; per 4hr/day/week $40/50/266; ⏲10am-6pm Mon-Sat, from 9am Wed, by reservation Sun) Get around town like a local, on a moped. The official riding area is from Waikoloa up north to Captain Cook down south.

Big Island Harley Davidson (☎635-0542; www.hawaiiharleyrental.com; 75-5633 Palani Rd; per day/week $179/763) Choose from a fleet of 19 new, well-maintained motorcycles.

TAXI

Call ahead for pickups from the following companies:

Laura's Taxi (☎326-5466; www.luanalimo.com; ⏲5am-10pm)

D&E Taxi (☎329-4279; ⏲6am-9pm)

AROUND KAILUA-KONA

Immediately south of Kailua-Kona is upscale Keauhou, a conglomeration of timeshares, condos and mainland amenities. In the mountains to the southeast is the dropped-in-amber town of Holualoa, now an intriguing artists community. Just north of Kailua-Kona is Honokohau Harbor, jump-off point for the lion's share of the area's maritime tours.

Keauhou Resort Area

Keauhou is a taste of the US mainland in the tropics, replete with chain shops and shopping centers. It's also like the mainland (well, the suburban mainland) in the sense that there is no town center, unless you count the mall. Rather, there's a collection of destinations: Keauhou Harbor for boat tours; Kahalu'u Beach for snorkeling and surfing; resorts and condos for sleeping; a farmers market and good restaurants; and a significant ancient Hawaiian settlement.

Beaches

Kahalu'u Beach Park BEACH

One of the island's most thrilling, easy-to-access (and admittedly, busiest) snorkeling spots, Kahalu'u Bay is a giant natural aquarium. Get out on the water and in seconds you're plunged into a classic medley of rainbow parrotfish, silver needlefish, brilliant yellow tangs and Moorish idols. Green sea

WORTH A TRIP

THE END OF THE WORLD

Rarely do geographic titles so convincingly live up to their names, but then comes Keauhou's **End of the World** (Kuamo'o Bay; Map p202; Ali'i Dr). A Mordoresque lava plain of jagged *'a'a* rock crinkles to the deep blue coast, and then drops steeply into the ocean. Sometimes the waves crash like thunderheads on the rocks, sometimes the ocean is calm as a pond and, often, local teenagers jump off the cliffs into the water. It's a lot of fun but is best not attempted unless you're a strong swimmer and are with a group of friends. To get here, drive all the way to the end of Ali'i Dr and look for a trail-head to the water. It's a short, rocky hike to the cliffs.

The End of the World marked the end of an era. When Kamehameha the Great's son Liholiho (Kamehameha II) was crowned king, the new monarch took major steps to abolish the rigid kapu, or taboo system that regulated daily life. So Liholiho took the then-drastic step of eating at a table with women. His cousin, Chief Kekauokalani, was incensed (or perhaps he coveted the crown, or maybe a bit of both) and challenged Liholiho to battle at the End of the World. In the resulting Battle of Kuamo'o some 300 were killed, including Kekauokalani and his wife. The dead were interned in cairns on the lava field, Liholiho's rule was firmly established, and the kapu system was broken.

turtles often swim in to feed and rest on the beach.

An ancient breakwater, which according to legend was built by the *menehune* (Hawaii's mythical race of little people), is on the reef and protects the bay.

This is a favorite surf spot that, when conditions are mellow, is ideal for beginners and for learning to SUP; when surf is high, strong rip currents make it challenging. Across the road from Kahalu'u Bay, **Kona Surf Company** (Map p202; ☎217-5329; www.surflessonskona.com; 78-6685 Ali'i Dr; board rental per day/week $25/99, surf lessons $129-175; ⊙8:30am-5pm) offers board rentals and lessons daily (reservations required), including SUP surfing ($85).

One thing not to come here for is peace and quiet. The tiny salt-and-pepper beach is hemmed in on all sides: by the busy highway, by the adjacent resort, by the covered pavilion with picnicking families and by throngs of snorkelers constantly paddling in and out of the water. Come early; the parking lot can fill up by 10am. Facilities include showers, rest rooms, picnic tables, grills, and snorkel and locker rentals. A lifeguard is on duty.

Sights & Activities

★Keauhou Farmers Market MARKET
(Map p202; www.keauhoufarmersmarket.com; 78-6831 Ali'i Dr, Keauhou Shopping Center; ⊙8am-noon Sat;) One of the Big Island's best farmers markets is at the Keauhou Shopping Center. Though small, it focuses almost solely on high-quality organic produce and products from local small farms. The warm community feeling is enhanced by live Hawaiian music and presentations by local chefs. Grab a coffee and come early!

St Peter's Church CHURCH
(Map p202) The 'Little Blue Church' is one of Hawai'i's most photographed, and a favorite for weddings. The striking sea-green and white building sits almost in Kahalu'u Bay. Built in the 1880s, St Peter's was moved from White (Magic) Sands Beach to this site in 1912. It now sits on an ancient Hawaiian religious site, Ku'emanu Heiau.

Hawaiian royalty, who surfed Kahalu'u Bay, prayed for good surf at this temple before hitting the waves.

Heiau & Historical Sites HISTORICAL SITE
(Map p202) Kahalu'u Bay is adjacent to the former Outrigger Keauhou Beach Resort, which sits where a major ancient Hawaiian settlement once existed. At the time of writing, the Outrigger had just been shut and was slated for demolition. While it seems all but certain that the sacred and historical sites will be preserved, it is unknown how they will be managed. During our visit, an easy path led from the beach into and around the protected sites

At the north end are the ruins of **Kapuanoni**, a fishing heiau, and a replica of the summer beach house of King Kalakaua next to a spring-fed pond, once either a fishpond or a royal bath. To the south are two major heiau. The first, **Hapaiali'i Heiau**, was built 600 years ago and in 2007 was completely restored by dry-stack masonry experts into a 15,000-sq-ft platform; the speculation is that the heiau was used as a sun calendar to mark the solstice and equinox. Next to Hapaiali'i is the even larger **Ke'eku Heiau**, also recently restored. Legends say that Ke'eku was a *luakini* (temple of human sacrifice); most famously, a Maui chief who tried to invade the Big Island was sacrificed here, and his grieving dogs guard the site still. Nearby petroglyphs, visible only at low tide, tell this story.

Keauhou Kahalu'u Heritage Center CULTURAL CENTER
(Keauhou Shopping Center; ⊙10am-5pm) FREE Keauhou Kahalu'u Heritage Center, an unstaffed, well-lit space in the Keauhou Shopping Center, will teach you more about the

KAYAK FISHING

Imagine landing a 25lb ahi or 35lb *ono* from a kayak – but not without a fight! A couple of professional, licensed outfitters can hook you up to do exactly that (OK, yours might be a wee bit smaller...). No experience is necessary, and due to the nature of the sport, tours are usually just you and your guide.

For fully guided tours and all gear:

➡ **Lucky Gecko Kayak Fishing** (☎557-9827; www.luckygeckokayakfishing.com; 5hr tour $150) Leaves from Keauhou Bay.

➡ **Kayak Fishing Hawai'i** (☎936-4400; www.kayakfishinghawaii.com; 6hr tour $300) Based in Kawaihae but travels islandwide.

restoration of Keauhou's heiau; it's near KTA Super Store. Displays and videos also describe *holua,* the ancient Hawaiian sport of sledding over lava rock.

Keauhou Bay HARBOUR
(Map p202) This bay, with a small boat harbor and launch ramp, is one of the most protected on the west coast. The vast majority of folks come here because they've booked, or want to book, a tour. There's a small grassy area with picnic tables, showers and rest rooms, a sand volleyball court, and the headquarters of the local outrigger canoe club onsite.

To get to the bay, turn makai (seaward) off Ali'i Dr onto Kamehameha III Rd.

Original Hawaiian Chocolate Factory GUIDED TOUR
(Map p218; ☎888-447-2626, 322-2626; www.ohcf.us; 78-6772 Makenawai St; adult/child under 12yr $10/free; ⊙tour 9am Wed, 9:30am Fri) A must for chocolate fans, these exclusive one-hour tours detail how the *only* Hawaiian chocolate is grown, harvested, processed and packaged. Samples and sales available at tour's end. By appointment only.

Courses

Keauhou Shopping Center MUSIC, DANCE
(www.keauhoushoppingcenter.com; 78-6831 Ali'i Drive) FREE **Ukulele jams** (BYO uke) are held from 6pm to 8pm Wednesday, as well as **Polynesian dance shows** at 6pm Friday. Check the website for other classes and activities.

Sleeping

Outrigger Kanaloa at Kona CONDO $$$
(Map p202; ☎322-9625, reservations 866-956-4262; www.outriggerkanaloaatkonacondo.com; 78-261 Manukai St; 1 bedroom $285-365, 2 bedroom $325-499; P ❄ @ ≈ ≋) These tropical townhouse-style condominiums are simply splendid. Large, immaculate and fully stocked, units are gathered in small, well-designed clusters that afford privacy. One-bedroom units easily fit a family of four, and you'll want to rip the kitchen out to take home. A daily maid service is included; two-night minimum stay required.

Sheraton Keauhou Bay Resort RESORT $$$
(Map p202; ☎866-716-8109, 930-4900; www.sheratonkeauhou.com; 78-128 'Ehukai St; r $220-525; ❄ @ ≈ ≋) The only bona fide resort in the Kailua-Kona area, the Sheraton boasts a sleekly modern design, over 500 rooms, upscale spa, fine dining and massive pool (with spiral slide) threading through the canyon-like atrium, but no beach. The theatrical atmosphere is topped off by the manta rays, which gather offshore nightly.

Sheraton will hit you with a $16 per night mandatory resort fee (for parking, wi-fi and other amenities). Check online for deep discounts.

Eating

For economical groceries try **KTA Super Store** (Keauhou Shopping Center; ⊙7am-10pm). Meanwhile, **Habaneros** (Map p202; ☎324-4688; Keauhou Shopping Center; à la carte $3-7, plates $7-8; ⊙9am-9pm Mon-Sat) does passable Mexican takeout.

Peaberry & Galette CAFE $
(Map p202; www.peaberryandgalette.com; Keauhou Shopping Center; crepes $8-14; ⊙7am-7pm Mon-Thu, to 8pm Fri & Sat, 8am-6pm Sun) For a dose of European hipness, order a sweet or savory crepe here. The quality of the salads and quiches is above average and the espresso machine hisses constantly, of course. Tea drinkers can get a quality fix here, too.

Kenichi Pacific JAPANESE $$$
(Map p202; ☎322-6400; www.kenichihawaii.com; Keauhou Shopping Center; sushi $5.50-10, mains $26-38; ⊙11:30am-1:30pm Tue-Fri, dinner from 5pm daily) Kenichi prepares well-executed and beautifully presented Pacific fusion cuisine. Highlights include scallops in red curry over soba noodles, grilled *ono* with a *ponzu* (Japanese citrus sauce) glaze and sweet potatoes, and sautéed shiitake mushrooms over spaghettini. The sushi and sashimi here are extraordinarily fresh.

While the mall setting doesn't affect the sleek, stylish dining room, it kills the outdoor terrace. Don't miss happy hour (4:30pm to 6:30pm), with half-price sushi rolls and drink specials.

Sam Choy's Kai Lanai HAWAII REGIONAL CUISINE $$$
(Map p202; ☎333-3434; www.samchoy.com; 78-6831 Ali'i Dr, Keauhou Shopping Center ; mains $18-36; ⊙Mon-Thu 11am-9pm, til 9:30pm Fri, Sat 8am-9:30pm, til 9pm Sun; ✎ 👪) Sam Choy is one of the pioneers of modern Hawaiian fusion cuisine, and his restaurant in the Keauhou Shopping Center remains an excellent spot to sample the genre. The dinner menu is stuffed with delicious island haute gastronomy

like orange duck glazed with honey and macadamia nuts, and lamb chops broiled with cilantro, ginger and local bird-peppers.

A 3pm to 5pm happy hour is great for a creative *pupu* menu (edamame hummus, anyone?).

Drinking & Entertainment

Haleo Luau LUAU

(Map p202; ☎866-482-9775; www.haleoluau.com; 78-128 Ehukai St, Sheraton Keauhou Bay Resort; adult/child 5-12 yr $80/50; ⏲4:30pm Mon) The Sheraton luau is a fiery hero narrative weaving together several Polynesian tales and themes.

Regal Cinemas Keauhou CINEMA

(☎324-0172; Keauhou Shopping Center) Hollywood flicks fill seven screens. Matinee and Tuesday discounts.

Shopping

Kona Stories BOOKS

(☎324-0350; www.konastories.com; Keauhou Shopping Center; ⏲10am-6pm Mon-Fri, to 5pm Sat, 11am-5pm Sun) Good independent bookstore with fun events for kids and adults.

Information

The following are all in the **Keauhou Shopping Center** (www.keauhoushoppingcenter.com):

Bank of Hawaii (⏲9am-6pm Mon-Fri, to 2pm Sat & Sun) Has a 24-hour ATM.

Keauhou Urgent Care Center (☎322-2544; www.konaurgentcare.com; ⏲9am-7pm) Treatment for minor emergencies and illness. Walk-ins OK.

Longs Drugs (⏲8am-9pm Mon-Sat, to 6pm Sun)

Post Office (⏲9am-4pm Mon-Fri, 10am-3pm Sat)

Getting There & Around

The **Keauhou Honu Express** (☎329-1688; www.konaweb.com/forums/shuttle; one-way ticket $2; ⏲9am-8pm) runs buses between Keauhou Shopping Center and Kailua Pier in Kailua-Kona, stopping at the Keauhou resorts, White (Magic) Sands Beach and elsewhere. It makes half a dozen trips into downtown Kailua-Kona. Schedules are available at Keauhou Shopping Center or any Keauhou hotel.

Holualoa

POP 8538

The further up the mountain you get from Kailua-Kona, the artsier, more residential, more rural (not to mention cooler and damper) it gets until all of these qualities mush into one misty bohemian village: Holualoa. Perched at 1400ft on the lush slopes of Mt Hualalai, this town has come a long way from its days as a tiny, one-donkey coffee crossroads. Today Holualoa's ramshackle buildings hold a stunning collection of sophisticated artist-owned galleries.

Most businesses close on Sunday and Monday.

Sights & Activities

Donkey Mill Art Center ART GALLERY

(Map p218; ☎322-3362; www.donkeymillartcenter.org; 78-6670 Hwy 180; ⏲10am-4pm Tue-Sat; 👪) FREE The Holualoa Foundation for Arts & Culture created this community art center in 2002. There are free exhibits, plus lectures and workshops – taught by recognized national and international artists – open to visitors. If you're wondering where the name comes from, the center's building, built in 1953, was once a coffee mill with a donkey

A WALK IN THE CLOUDS

Above 3000ft on the slopes of Mt Hualalai, the Kaloko Mauka subdivision is the home of the spectacular 70-acre **Kona Cloud Forest Sanctuary** (Map p218; www.konacloudforest.com). And not just any forest – a cloud forest, a moist woodland where mist and fog are constants. The sanctuary is a lush haven for native plants and birds, and thanks to a consistent carpet of ropy gray-green fog, it always feels as mysterious as it is beautiful. The sanctuary also contains demonstration gardens of non-native species, including more than 100 varieties of bamboo, which local experts study for their viability for use. Sustainable agriculture–types and horticulturists won't want to miss a visit to this well-kept Kona secret most locals don't even know about!

Hawaiian Walkways (☎800-457-7759; www.hawaiianwalkways.com; adult/child $119/99; ⏲8:30am-1pm) leads a daily morning tour to the sanctuary, including a stop at adjacent Mountain Thunder Coffee.

painted on its roof. Located 3 miles south of the village center.

Malama I'ka Ola Holistic Health Center HEALTH & FITNESS
(☎324-6644; 76-5914 Hwy 180) Holualoa's New Age ley lines converge here, where interested parties can take care of mind, body and spirit via yoga and Pilates classes, plus massage, acupuncture and other alternative skin and healthcare treatments.

Festivals & Events

During November's **Kona Coffee Cultural Festival**, Holualoa hosts a popular day-long block party called the **Coffee & Art Stroll**. The **Summer Farmfest & 'Ukulele Jam** each June is a bounty of local produce and music, and December's **Music & Light Festival** is a wonderful Christmas celebration. For more information see www.holualoahawaii.com.

Sleeping

Kona Hotel HOTEL $
(Map p218; ☎324-1155; Hwy 180; s/d $30/40) Although attractive from the outside, this pink historic boarding house (c 1926) is one of those 'only if necessary' properties. It's cheap and you get what you pay for: dirty communal bathrooms (for all rooms) and some territorial long-term residents sharing them with you.

Hale Maluhia Country Inn B&B $$
(☎329-1123; www.hawaii-bnb.com; r $87-123, cottage $157-177; P) Take an exuberant grab-bag run by a friendly couple and stuff it with elements of Japanese, Hawaiian and bohemian style and sensibility. Put it all on a jungle mountain abutting some pretty coffee plantations and boom, there's Hale Maluhia, a lovely little inn that's worth getting lost in. We're not big fans of the smallest, cheapest rooms, so go up a little in price or opt for one of the excellent private cottages.

The cottages feel like Shinto-Tropical retreat rooms designed by a Zen monk who was into the Swiss Family Robinson story.

Lilikoi Inn B&B $$
(☎333-5539; www.lilikoiinn.com; 75-5339 Mamalahoa Hwy; r incl breakfast $125-165; P) The four rooms here all have an airy, modern art-gallery-in-the-tropics kind of vibe, blending

UPCOUNTRY COFFEE TASTING

Gourmet coffee has long gone mainstream, and many farms have established visitor centers, where they give free tours and samples. See www.konacoffeefest.com/driving-tour for a list.

Mountain Thunder Coffee Plantation (Map p218; ☎888-414-5662; www.mountainthunder.com; 73-1944 Hao St; ⊙tours hourly 10am-4pm) Established in 1998, this award-winning organic farm is located in lush Kaloko Mauka, about 15 minutes from Kailua-Kona. Free 20-minute tours are detailed (and wheelchair accessible), but for a real indepth look at Kona coffee, try the VIP Tours (per person $65 to $135; reserve ahead, lunch extra) or become Roast Master for a Day (per person $199) and roast 5lb of your own beans.

Holualoa Kona Coffee Company (☎800-334-0348, 877-322-9937; www.konalea.com; 77-6261 Mamalahoa Hwy; ⊙8am-4pm Mon-Fri) The Kona Le'a Plantation in Holualoa does not use pesticides or herbicides on its beautiful organic farm; tours are excellent.

Hula Daddy Kona Coffee (☎327-9744; www.huladaddy.com; 74-4944 Hwy 180; ⊙10am-4pm Mon–Sat) The attractive tasting room of this multiple-award winner is the place for cupping seminars. See the website for directions to its upland Honokohau location.

Kona Blue Sky Coffee (☎877-322-1700; www.konablueskycoffee.com; 76-973A Hualalai Rd; ⊙9am-3:30pm Mon-Sat) In Holualoa village, this estate's tour includes the traditional open-air drying racks and a video; it has a nice gift shop. Give Maka, the handsome resident pooch, a good scratch behind the ears from us.

Rancho Aloha (☎322-9562; www.ranchoaloha.com; 75-5760 Mamalahoa Hwy) This wonderfully named spot (the owner used to be a Peace Corps volunteer in Colombia) encompasse an organic farm that harvests excellent coffee straight out of the volcanic soil.

cool monochromes with tasteful Hawaiian decor. Each comes with private entrance, and access to hot tub, plus guest laundry, kitchen and lanai. Breakfasts are restaurant-worthy.

★**Holualoa Inn** B&B **$$$**
(Map p218; ☎800-392-1812, 324-1121; www.holualoainn.com; 76-5932 Hwy 180; r $315-390, ste $350-425; P 📶 🏊) The Holualoa Inn has got oodles of class, romance and aloha. From the gleaming eucalyptus floors to the unwoven *lauhala* (hala leaf) walls and river-rock showers, serene beauty and comfort shines in every detail. Several gorgeous public rooms graced with tasteful Asian art and exquisite carved furniture segue seamlessly into the outdoor gardens and pool, while the rooftop gazebo surveys the world.

The six rooms don't disappoint, making this a peaceful, intimate retreat that you'll long remember. No TVs, phones or children under 13. There's a kitchenette for guest use. Rates listed include breakfast.

Eating

Holuakoa Gardens & Café LOCAL **$$**
(☎322-2233; Hwy 180; brunch $11-15, dinner $22-32; ⌚restaurant 10am-2:30pm & 5:30-8:30pm Mon-Fri, from 9am Sat, 9am-2:30pm Sun, cafe 6:30am-3pm Mon-Fri, from 8am Sat & Sun; 🖉) 🍃 The storefront cafe here serves espressos and sandwiches, while the organic, slow-food restaurant in the garden dishes up sophisticated yet casual bistro-style cuisine that makes the most of local produce. The creative, seasonal menu may include homemade gnocchi with morels, leeks and edamame, or grilled ahi with roasted fig and ginger fried rice. Book ahead for dinner.

This is one of Hawaii's more dedicated establishments for supporting local farmers and fishermen. You can get your own local organic produce and products at the **Saturday Farmers Market** (9am-noon) here.

Shopping

★**Studio 7 Gallery** GALLERY
(☎324-1335; 76-5920 Mamalahoa Hwy; ⌚11am-5pm Tue-Sat) Artist Hiroki Morinoue led Holualoa's artistic renaissance in the 1980s. Japanese woodblocks and sophisticated art in all media are displayed in his serene gallery.

Ipu Hale Gallery GALLERY
(Map p218; ☎322-9069; www.ipuguy.com; Hwy 180; ⌚10am-4pm Tue-Sat) This gallery sells *ipu* (gourds) decoratively carved with Hawaiian imagery using an ancient method unique to the Hawaiian island of Ni'ihau. Lost after the introduction of Western crockery, the art form was revived by a Big Island scholar just 15 years ago, and is now practiced by Michael Harburg, artist and co-owner of the gallery.

Holualoa Ukelele Gallery MUSIC
(Map p218; ☎324-4100; www.konaweb.com/ukegallery; 76-5942 Mamalahoa Hwy; ⌚11am-4:30pm Tue-Sat) In the super-cool historic Holualoa post-office building, Sam Rosen sells his handcrafted ukulele, and those of other luthiers. Sam is happy to talk story all day and show you his workshop. Drop by Wednesday nights (6pm to 8:30pm) for a ukelele jam or, if you have two weeks, take a class and build your own.

Kimura Lauhala Shop ARTS & CRAFTS
(Map p218; ☎324-0053; www.holualoahawaii.com/member_sites/kimura.html; cnr Hualalai Rd & Hwy 180; ⌚9am-5pm Mon-Fri, to 4pm Sat) 🍃 Three generations of Kimuras weave *lauhala* products here, as they have since the 1930s. Originally they purchased *lauhala* products from Hawaiian weavers to sell. When demand increased they took on the production themselves, assisted by local farming wives, who do piecework at home outside of coffee season. Don't fall prey to cheap imports – the *lauhala* hats, placemats, baskets and floor mats sold here are the real deal.

Dovetail GALLERY
(☎322-4046; www.dovetailgallery.net; 76-5942 Mamalahoa Hwy; ⌚10am-4pm Tue-Sat) Funky and cool Asian and Hawaiian-style art in this shared studio space.

Holualoa Gallery GALLERY
(☎322-8484; www.lovein.com; 76-5921 Mamalahoa Hwy; ⌚10am-5pm Tue-Sat) Matt and Mary Lovein specialize in whimsical, oversized paintings and *raku* (Japanese rustic-style) pottery.

ℹ Getting There & Away

From Kailua-Kona, turn *mauka* (inland) on Hualalai Rd off Hwy 11, and wind 3 miles up to Hwy 180; turn left for most sights. If coming from North Kona, either Hina Lani St and Palani St are straighter shots to Hwy 180 than Hualalai Rd, though they are a little indirect. From South Kona, head up Hwy 180 immediately north of Honalo.

Honokohau Harbor & Around

Almost all of Kona's catch comes in at this harbor 2 miles north of Kailua-Kona, including the 'granders' – fish weighing over 1000lb. To witness the sometimes dramatic **weigh-ins**, head to the far side of the harbor, near the gas station, at 11am or 3:30pm; the weigh-in station is behind Bite Me Bar & Grill.

The majority of snorkeling/diving tours, whale-watching tours and fishing charters booked out of Kailua-Kona leave from here. To reach the harbor, turn *makai* (seaward) on Kealakehe Rd, just a little north of mile marker 98.

Any Hele-On buses heading from Kailua-Kona to the Kohala resorts can potentially drop you off here.

Beaches

Honokohau Beach

BEACH

Just minutes from the bustle of Kailua-Kona is this beautiful hook-shaped beach with a mix of black lava, white coral and wave-tossed shells. Bring your reef shoes – you'll need them for the rocky bottom. The water is usually too cloudy for snorkeling, but you'll often see green turtles just standing on the shore.

Look for more *honu* (green sea turtles) feeding around the **'Ai'opio fishtrap**, bordered by an ancient heiau at the south end of the beach. Snorkeling and swimming is permitted here and it's perfect for *na keiki* (kids). Just don't climb on the rocks or disturb the turtles.

There's also a **Queen's Bath** (a brackish natural pool) just north of the beach. To get there, walk north from the end of the beach about 200m and look *mauka* (towards the mountain). You'll see a trail that runs to the mountain by a dozen large rock clumps. The pool is about 30m north of the largest mound.

To get to Honokohau Beach, turn right into the first harbor parking lot (look for the small public coastal access sign). Near the end of the road is the signposted trailhead; a five-minute walk on a well-beaten path leads to the beach. You can also reach Honokohau Beach along the easy Ala Hele Ike Trail starting from Kaloko-Honokohau National Historical Park.

Activities

Snorkeling & Diving

The area south of Honokohau Harbor all the way to Kailua Bay is a marine-life conservation district (accessible by boat); diving here is better than snorkeling, though nearby 'Ai'opio fishtrap is a good snorkel alternative.

Turtle Pinnacle DIVING

(Map p218) Straight out from Honokohau Harbor, this is a premier dive site for spotting turtles, which congregate here to let small fish feed off the algae and parasites on their shells.

Kaiwi Point DIVING

Off this point south of Honokohau Harbor, sea turtles, large fish and huge eagle rays swim around some respectable drop-offs.

Suck 'Em Up DIVING

The swell pulls divers through a couple of lava tubes like an amusement-park ride, near Kaiwi Point.

Kayaking

Not just for paddling anymore, kayaks now come ready to sail, surf, snorkel and even fish.

Plenty Pupule KAYAKING

(Map p218; ☎880-1400; www.plentypupule.com; 73-4976 Kamanu St, Kaloko Industrial Park, Suite 102; s/d per day kayak rental $25/32.50, kayak snorkeling ½-day tour $80; ⏲10am-6pm Tue-Sat) One of the island's top outfitters for adventure kayaking, these folks can recommend the best put-in and snorkeling spots beyond Kealakekua Bay, customize tours and teach you to kayak surf ($125). They can also take you **kayak sailing** ($195 for a half-day trip) – this can be particularly memorable during whale-watching season.

Surfing

There are a few decent breaks within striking distance of the harbor.

Ocean Eco Tours SURFING

(Map p218; ☎324-7873; www.oceanecotours.com; Honokohau Harbor; group/private surf lessons $95/150) For lessons and equipment; this is the only operator permitted to surf within the boundaries of Kaloko-Honokohau National Historical Park.

Hiking

To explore the lush upper slopes of Mt Hualalai (largely private land), your only choices are Hawaii Forest & Trail or **Hawaiian Walkways** (see boxed text, p197). See their websites for full descriptions of tours.

★ **Hawaii Forest & Trail** HIKING, TOUR
(Map p218; ☎800-464-1993, 331-8505; www.hawaii-forest.com; 74-5035B Queen Ka'ahumanu Hwy; Mauna Kea summit tour $192, birdwatching tour $178) This outfit is a top choice for those wishing to delve into the island's greenest depths. From its super popular **Mauna Kea stargazing** tour to its exclusive hikes into the **Hakalau Forest National Wildlife Refuge**, you won't regret an adventure with these experts and green stewards. The retail store sells high-quality outdoor gear, clothing, topo maps and camping equipment.

Sleeping

One of the best-kept secrets along this stretch of coast directly north of Kailua-Kona are the B&Bs tucked into the cool cloud forest on the slopes of Mt Hualalai.

Honu Kai B&B B&B $$
(Map p218; ☎292-1775, 329-8676; www.honukaibnb.com; 74-1529 Hao Kuni St; d incl breakfast $185-220; @ wi-fi) This attractive, get-away-from-it-all B&B sparkles with four plush, upscale rooms done up with rich fabrics, carved bed frames, and Asian and Hawaiian decor. Tip: book the Lani or Mahina suites and access the roof deck. A separate cottage has full kitchen, and the well-tended gardens afford privacy and seclusion, whether lounging on the huge porch or in the Jacuzzi.

Your hostess, to her chagrin, is a former Dallas Cowboys cheerleader.

Nancy's Hideaway B&B $$
(Map p218; ☎866-325-3132, 325-3132; www.nancyshideaway.com; 73-1530 Uanani Pl; studio/cottage incl breakfast $130/150; wi-fi) If you're looking for peace, quiet and privacy, the independent cottage or studio in this well-located residential neighborhood is ideal. The decor is functional and both units have kitchenettes, lanai with views and king-sized beds. Either option is perfect for a couple.

Mango Sunset B&B B&B $$
(Map p218; ☎325-0909; www.mangosunset.com; 73-4261 Mamalahoa Hwy; r $100-120; @ wi-fi) Hawaiiana-bedecked teak furnishings and bamboo accents spruce up the pretty accomodation on this organic coffee farm. The best rooms offer sweeping ocean views from a shared lanai; if you prefer your own private porch, opt for the mountain view.

Eating & Drinking

Harbor House Restaurant SEAFOOD $$
(Map p218; ☎326-4166; http://harborhouserestaurantkona.com; 74-425 Kealakehe Pkwy, Honokohau Harbor complex; mains $8-16; ⏲11am-7pm Mon-Sat, to 6pm Sun) After fishing, the place to spin your tale is a wharfside table here, chowing on a burger or excellent fish and chips. Happy hour runs from 4pm to 6pm Monday to Saturday and to 5:15pm Sunday and features 18oz 'schooners' for $2.50.

Kailua Candy Company CANDY $$
(Map p218; ☎800-622-2462, 329-2522; www.kailua-candy.com; 73-5612 Kauhola St, Kaloko Industrial Park, cnr Kamanu & Kauhola Sts; ⏲closed Sun) A detour to this chocolate shop is mandatory for every sweet tooth. Try the handmade chocolate-covered macadamia-nut *honu* (turtles), Kona coffee swirls, *liliko'i* (passion fruit) truffles or dark-chocolate-covered crystallized ginger. The cheesecake is the tastiest ever to pass our lips. They give good samples. Turn *mauka* (inland) on Hina Lani St off Hwy 19 and right on Kamanu St.

Bite Me Bar & Grill SEAFOOD $$
(Map p218; ☎960-2464; www.bitemefishmarket.com; 74-425 Kealakehe Pkwy, Honokohau Harbor complex; seafood bar & mains $9-23; ⏲6am-9pm; wi-fi, child-friendly) Steps from the harbor boat ramp, this casual place makes a logical stop for some mahimahi tacos or Longboard Lager after a day fishing or a night dive with manta rays. With a kid's menu and shady picnic tables on a patio overlooking boat traffic, it also makes a good family spot. The **fish market** here stocks more than a dozen types of local fresh fish daily.

Kona Coffee & Tea Company CAFE $
(Map p218; www.konacoffeeandtea.com; 73-5053 Queen Kaahumanu Hwy, Suite 5A; cup of coffee $3; ⏲7am-5:30pm Mon-Fri, 8am-5pm Sat, from 11am Sun; wi-fi) Life is too short for bad coffee: head here for award-winning 100% Kona. Free tastings include Peaberry, which mitigates the parking lot location.

SOUTH KONA COAST

South Kona, more than any other district of Hawaii, embodies the many strands that make up the geo-cultural tapestry of the Big Island. There is both the dry lava desert of the Kohala Coast and the womb-wet, misty

South Kona Coast

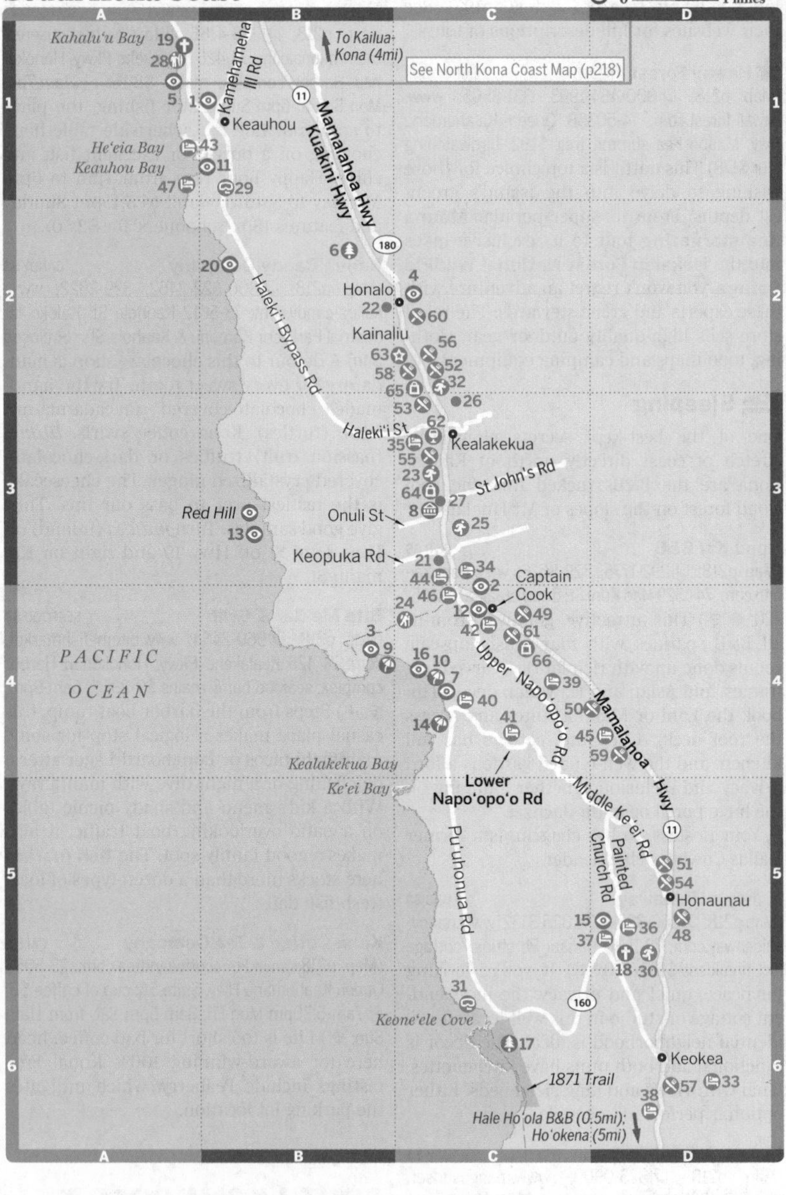

jungles of Puna and Hilo; fishing villages inhabited by country-fried Hawaiian locals next to hippie art galleries established by counterculture exiles from the mainland, next to condos plunked down by millionaire land developers.

This is the acclaimed Kona Coffee Belt, consisting of 22 miles patchworked with more than 600 small coffee farms. That there is no cost-efficient way to industrialize the hand-picking and processing of the beans contributes to the time-warp quality

South Kona Coast

Top Sights
1 Keauhou Farmers Market....B1

Sights
2 Amy BH Greenwell Ethnobotanical Garden....C4
3 Captain Cook Monument....B4
4 Daifukuji Soto Mission....C2
Greenwell Farms....(see 8)
5 Heiau & Historical Sites....A1
6 Higashihara Park....B2
7 Hiki'au Heiau....C4
8 HN Greenwell Store Museum....C3
9 Ka'awaloa Cove....B4
10 Kealakekua Bay State Historical Park....C4
11 Keauhou Bay....B1
12 Kona Coffee Living History Farm....C4
Kona Potter's Guild....(see 30)
13 Long Lava Tube....B3
14 Manini Beach....C4
15 Paleaku Gardens Peace Sanctuary....D5
16 Pali Kapu o Keoua....C4
17 Pu'uhonua o Honaunau National Historical Park....C6
18 St Benedict's Painted Church....D5
19 St Peter's Church....A1
20 The End of the World....B2

Activities, Courses & Tours
21 Adventures in Paradise....C3
22 Aloha Kayak Company....B2
23 Big Island Yoga Center....C3
24 Captain Cook Monument Trail....C4
Fair Wind....(see 11)
25 Kings' Trail Rides....C3
26 Kona Boys....C3
27 Kona Historical Society....C3
28 Kona Surf Company....A1
29 Ocean Safaris....B1
Sea Paradise....(see 11)
Sea Quest....(see 11)
30 SKEA....D5
31 Two-Step....C6
32 Yoganics Hawaii Limited....C2

Sleeping
33 Aloha Guest House....D6
34 Areca Palms Estate B&B....C3
35 Banana Patch....C3
36 Camp Aloha....D5
37 Dragonfly Ranch....D5
38 Hale Ho'ola B&B....D6
39 Ka'awaloa Plantation & Guesthouse....C4
40 Kealakekua Bay Bed & Breakfast....C4
41 Luana Inn....C4
42 Manago Hotel....C4
43 Outrigger Kanaloa at Kona....A1
44 Pineapple Park....C3
45 Pomaika'i 'Lucky' Farm B&B....D4
46 Rainbow Plantation Bed & Breakfast Inn....C4
47 Sheraton Keauhou Bay Resort....A1

Eating
Annie's Island Fresh Burgers....(see 53)
48 Bong Brothers & Sistahs....D5
49 ChoiceMart....C4
50 Coffee Shack....D4
51 Coffees 'n' Epicurea....D5
52 Donkey Balls....C2
Habaneros....(see 1)
53 Island Naturals....C3
Kenichi Pacific....(see 1)
54 Keoki's Roadside Cafe....D5
Manago Hotel....(see 42)
Mi's Italian Bistro....(see 34)
55 Orchid Isle Café....C3
Patz Pies....(see 61)
Peaberry & Galette....(see 1)
56 Rebel Kitchen....C2
Sam Choy's Kai Lanai....(see 1)
57 South Kona Fruit Stand....D6
South Kona Green Market....(see 49)
58 Standard Bakery....C2
59 Super J's....D4
60 Teshima Restaurant....C2
61 Up Country Bakery & Cafe....C4

Drinking & Nightlife
62 Korner Pocket Bar & Grill....C3

Entertainment
63 Aloha Theatre....C2
Haleo Luau....(see 47)

Shopping
64 Discovery Antiques....C3
65 Just Ukes....C2
Kimura Store....(see 65)
66 The Reading Garden....C4

of local life. But the reasons are also cultural: at the turn of the 20th century, thousands of Japanese immigrants arrived to labor as independent coffee farmers, and their influence – along with that of Chinese, Filipino and Portuguese workers – remains richly felt in Buddhist temples, fabric stores and restaurant menus.

Note that the main island belt road also goes by the names Hwy 11 and Mamalahoa

Hwy. Southbound Hele-On buses departing from Kailua-Kona for Kau can drop travelers at sights along the way.

Honalo

POP 2423

At a bend in the road past the intersection of Hwys 11 (Mamalahoa) and 180, little Honalo is your first sign that more than miles separate you from touristy Kailua.

Sights

Daifukuji Soto Mission TEMPLE

(Map p202; 322-3524; www.daifukuji.org; 79-7241 Mamalahoa Hwy; 8am-4pm Mon-Sat) The first building you see in Honalo resembles a cross between a low-slung red barn, a white-roofed villa and a Japanese shrine. Well, one out of three ain't bad: this is the Buddhist Daifukuji ('Temple of Great Happiness') Soto Mission. Slip off your shoes and admire the two ornate, lovingly tended altars.

Everyone is welcome to join **Zen meditation** sessions, tai-chi lessons and **taiko** (Japanese drum) practices, which are held across the week; call or check the website for details.

Higashihara Park PARK

(Map p202; 7am-8pm;) If you have young kids, return north a mile or so from Honalo and enjoy shady Higashihara Park. Its unique Hawaii-themed wooden play structure is both attractive and endlessly climbable. It is on the *makai* (seaward) side, between mile marker 114 and 115.

Eating

Teshima Restaurant JAPANESE, LOCAL $$

(Map p202; 79-7251 Mamalahoa Hwy; mains $13-23; 6:30am-1:45pm & 5-9pm;) For a real window into local life, grab a table at Teshima, which has dished up delicious Japanese comfort food since the 1940s. Served in an old school, dineresque atmosphere, the unpretentious country cooking is usually spot on – order *donburi* (bowl of rice and main dish), ahi sashimi, butterfish and teriyaki, or better yet, sample a bit of everything with a *teishoku* (set meal).

Four generations of Teshimas keep guests happy, be it via great food or plenty of ribbing banter.

> **BYPASS THE TRAFFIC**
>
> The long-awaited bypass road between Keauhou and Kealakekua is now open. This cut-through allows savvy drivers to avoid the worst of commuter traffic in and out of Kailua-Kona. The road connects Haleki'i Rd in Kealakekua (between mile markers 111 and 112) to Kamehameha III Rd in Keauhou and Ali'i Dr and Hwy 11 (Mamalahoa) beyond. It's open in both directions from 6:30am to 6:30pm, seven days a week.

Kainaliu

This quaint crossroads is packed with cozy shops and good places to eat, making Kainaliu a prime lunch and linger spot – handy if you get caught in the 'Kainaliu Krawl' traffic nightmare.

Check out fine Hawaiian fabrics at the long-standing **Kimura Store** (Map p202; 79-7408 Mamalahoa Hwy; 9am-6pm Mon-Sat, noon-4:30pm Sun) and then pop in to **Just Ukes** (Map p202; 323-0808; 79-7412 Mamalahoa Hwy; noon-5pm Mon & Wed-Fri, to 6:30pm Tue, to 4pm Sat) for some instruments, plus photos by the talented Kim Taylor Reece. Across the street from Just Ukes, **Yoganics Hawaii Limited** (Map p202; www.yoganicshawaii.com; 79-7401 Mamalahoa Hwy; 10am-5pm Mon-Sat) features all natural-clothing; an attached studio has yoga and belly dancing classes (drop-in $15; five-class pass $50).

The rather handsome marquee of the **Aloha Theatre** (Map p202; 322-9924; www.apachawaii.org; 79-7384 Mamalahoa Hwy; tickets $10-25) marks the location of one of the liveliest little community theaters troupes in the islands: the Aloha Performing Arts Company. Quality plays, indie films and live music are on the program here. Budget tip: buy tickets in advance to save money. Pro tip: on the opening night of locally produced shows, the cast cooks the audience dinner.

Eating

Annie's Island Fresh Burgers BURGERS $

(Map p202; www.anniesislandfreshburgers; 79-7460 Hwy 11, Mango Court; burgers $9-14; 11am-8pm;) Sometimes you just need a burger. And not just any burger. You need the sort of burger that makes you sigh and smile and go 'Damn' and feel slightly uncomfortably full afterwards. Enter Annie's, which uses local veggies and grass-fed Big Island beef to make some of the Big Island's best burgers.

KONA COAST FOR KIDS

- Turtle-spotting at Makalawena Beach (p221)
- Swimming and beachcombing at Kiholo Bay (p223)
- Snorkeling in Ka'awaloa Cove (p212)
- Meeting other kids at Manini'owali Beach (p221)

Vegetarian? No worries – dig into a portobello mushroom stuffed with parmesan cheese and bulgur while enjoying the views from the back lanai.

Rebel Kitchen AMERICAN $
(Map p202; 322-0616; www.rebelkitchen.com; 79-7399 Mamalahoa Hwy; sandwiches $7-9, mains $13-18; 11am-3pm & 5-8pm Mon-Fri;) Rebel Kitchen is well titled. There's a sense of playful anarchy when you walk in here, from the young counter staff to the punk and reggae coming out of the kitchen. You know what else comes out of the kitchen? Amazing sandwiches. We'll fight you for the blackened *ono* with cajun mayo, although you could pacify us with the jerk chicken sandwich served on a rosemary roll.

At night, the dinner menu is hearty and eschews calorie-counting for comfort food of the steak and barbeque pork-chops variety. A few vegetarian options like an eggplant sandwich or chickpea salad help balance all that meat.

Donkey Balls SWEETS
(Map p202; 322-1475; www.alohahawaiianstore.com; 79-7411 Mamalahoa Hwy; 8am-6pm) When it comes to sweets, we love Donkey Balls, and we promise it's not just for the saucy name. It's the excellent quality and diverse varities of these beefy chocolates. Sure, the pure version is amazing enough, but check the Jitter Balls, coated in 100% Kona coffee, or the Hot Board Balls, rolled in Cayenne pepper, or the Blue Balls, which come in a layer of blue-colored white chocolate… OK, maybe we're a little enamored of the saucy names.

The factory store in Kainaliu also contains a pretty excellent cafe if you need some espresso to go with your hoard of punny chocolates.

Standard Bakery BAKERY $
(Map p202; 79-7934 Mamalahoa Hwy; mains under $6.75; 5am-1pm Mon-Fri) So you want to eat local? It doesn't get more local than the Standard, a bare-bones bakery that caters to South Konans with a jonesing for delicious moon pies, extravagant cakes, donuts, spam and eggs ($2.10 – possibly the best breakfast deal on the island) and pretty *bentō* boxes (Japanese-style box lunch).

Kealakekua

POP 2019

Kealakekua means 'Path of the Gods,' a name that references a chain of 40 heiau that once ran from Kealakekua Bay to Kailua-Kona. That was back in the day. In the present, Kealakekua is a functional, friendly hamlet, with banks, a post office, a hospital and plenty of aloha.

Sights

Kona Coffee Living History Farm FARM
(Map p202; 323-3222; www.konahistorical.org; 82-6199 Mamalahoa Hwy; adult/child 5-12yr $20/5; 10am-2pm Mon-Thu, tours every hour) Many coffee-farm tours are perfunctory 15-minute affairs. This tour, run by the Kona Historical Society, an affiliate of the Smithsonian Institute, stands in stark, deep and comprehensive contrast. More than an exploration of how coffee is harvested (although you will learn the above), this is an evocative look at rural Japanese-immigrant life. The tour takes place on the Society's 5.5-acre, working coffee farm.

This was once the family farm of the Uchida clan, who lived here till 1994, but the farm has been returned to the era of the 1920s–40s. Several docents grew up on similar farms, so they speak from experience as they present the orchards, processing mill, drying roofs and main house. On the tours (which take an hour or so) you'll learn how to pick cherries, heat a bathhouse and prepare a traditional *bentō*. It's worth the high ticket price.

Greenwell Farms FARM
(Map p202; 323-2295, 888-592-5662; www.greenwellfarms.com; 81-6581 Mamalahoa Hwy; 8am-5pm) FREE This 150-acre family farm, established in 1850, is run by fourth-generation Greenwells and is one of Kona's oldest and best-known coffee plantations. It currently roasts coffee cherries from more than 200 local growers. Take a free **tour** and sample coffee and fruit at a shady picnic table.

RED-HOT GREEN ISSUES

Understanding issues that impassion locals – invasive species, resort developments, renewable energy, sovereignty – provides insight into what makes this island tick. You'll see placards, squatters, DIY projects and graffiti addressing all these in your travels.

10% Kona coffee blends These cheaper blends using foreign beans threaten local farmers who are currently fighting for recognition of Kona coffee as a Product of Designated Origin. This would protect the name and origin of Kona coffee à la Napa Valley Wines and Parmigiano-Reggiano cheese.

Coffee berry borer This destructive beetle, which had infected over 20 Kona farms by early 2011, resulted in a quarantine of Hawai'i's $30 million crop. Eradication solutions are being sought, but the bug is causing high anxiety among Kona coffee farmers.

Kealakekua Bay At the time of writing, a moratorium was in place on watercraft entering Kealakekua Bay. Pods of spinner dolphins enjoy sleeping in these waters, but locals and biologists alike have claimed the presence of hordes of snorkelers disturb their sleep.

Thirty Meter Telescope, Mauna Kea Hawai'i's most sacred spot will be home to the Thirty Meter Telescope (TMT). Slated for completion by 2018, the community is divided over this project, which will be bigger than all current observatories combined. See http://kahea.org/issues/sacred-summits for info on opposition to the TMT, and www.tmt.org for the argument in favor of the facility.

Dolphin encounters Whether in captivity or the wild, human-dolphin encounters carry potential risks for the animals. Wild dolphins may become too tired to feed, while captive 'show' dolphins can suffer from stress, infections and damaged dorsal fins.

Solar power In 2010 the Hawaiian Electric Company (HECO) sought to ban new solar-power systems, saying the excess energy they feed to the electric grid could be destabilizing. While ultimately rejected by state regulators, HECO continues to push back against smaller, distributed solar generation. The debate rages.

You can also purchase **Kona Red** (www.konared.com) here, an intriguing new superfood made from cherry pulp. The farm is between mile markers 110 and 111.

HN Greenwell Store Museum MUSEUM

(Map p202; www.konahistorical.org; Mamalahoa Hwy; adult/child $7/3; ⏲10am-2pm Mon-Thu) Next door to Greenwell Farms, the Kona Historical Society has turned the 1890 stone-and-mortar Greenwell General Store into a clever museum. Shelves and walls are meticulously stocked with brand-new or recreated dry goods and farm equipment authentic to the period. Inside, docents hand you a shopping list and a character profile (based on actual customers from Henry Greenwell's journals) from Kona's multiethnic, farming and ranching community of the 1890s.

Then…well, you shop, in a store that convincingly feels like an Old West general store, except the frontier is the Big Island. Out back, the Portuguese bread oven turns out fresh-baked bread from 11am on Thursdays. The museum is located between the mile markers 110 and 111.

Amy BH Greenwell Ethnobotanical Garden GARDEN

(Map p202; ☎323-3318; www.bishopmuseum.org/greenwell; 82-6160 Mamalahoa Hwy; adult/senior/under-12 yr $7/6/free; ⏲9am-4pm Tue-Sat, guided tours 1pm) Without pottery or metals, ancient Hawaiians fashioned most of what they needed from plants. This ethnobotanical garden preserves Hawaii's original native and Polynesian-introduced plants in a typical *ahupua'a,* the ancient land division system that ensured all Hawaiians had access to everything they needed. Plaques are informative, but guided tours are helpful to appreciate the humble grounds. Bring insect repellant. The garden is just south of mile marker 110.

Activities

Mamalahoa Hot Tubs & Massage SPA

(☎323-2288; www.mamalahoa-hottubs.com; 81-1016 St John's Church Rd; hot tub per hour for

2-people $40; ⌚by appointment noon-9pm Wed-Sat) Soak away your blisters or blues in one of two jarrah-wood tubs set in a lush garden at this mountain-side mini-oasis. The tubs, sheltered by thatched roofs, are open to the air, but privately sealed off from prying eyes. Hawaiian hot stone, *lomilomi* (traditional Hawaiian massage), Swedish, deep tissue and couples' massage are offered.

A half-hour tub and one-hour massage package will run you $150 ($285 for couples). Bottled water, towels and bathing facilities provided.

Big Island Yoga Center YOGA
(Map p202; ☎329-9642; www.bigislandyoga.com; 81-6623 Mamalahoa Hwy; class adult $14) For Iyengar yoga, Big Island Yoga Center is the place. The bright studio occupies the 2nd floor of a beautiful old house, and is stocked with mats and props. There's a donation class at 8:30am on Wednesdays and Saturdays, and 10:30am also on Saturdays.

Sleeping

Pineapple Park HOSTEL $
(Map p202; ☎877-800-3800, 323-2224; www.pineapple-park.com; 81-6363 Mamalahoa Hwy; dm $25, r shared/private bathroom $65/85; ⌚office 7am-8pm; @📶) South Kona's only hostel is a basic backpacker dive run by a friendly if iron-willed Korean proprietress. It definitely has that social hostel-like vibe, which makes up for the cramped dorms (No 10 is best) and fresher, more comfortable (but overpriced) private rooms. Bathrooms are shared.

Rainbow Plantation Bed & Breakfast Inn B&B $
(Map p202; ☎323-2393; www.rainbowplantation.com; 6327 Mamalahoa Hwy; r $89-109) An eclectic little B&B is concealed on this 3-acre macadamia-and-coffee farm, inhabited by tropical birds, koi fish and burping frogs. The ground-floor rooms are heavy on plant decor and are comfy, but we love the airy upper unit 'Crow's Nest'. Located *makai* (seaside) between mile markers 110 and 111; look for the (appropriately) rainbow-colored sign.

Check out the little shrine replete with art-deco stained glass Madonna and Child, once the property of silent film star Ramón Novarro.

Areca Palms Estate B&B B&B $$
(Map p202; ☎323-2276; www.konabedandbreakfast.com; 81-1031 Keopuka Mauka Rd; r incl breakfast $100-145; @📶) Country comfort and aloha combine seamlessly in this spotless, wooden home. The airy rooms are meticulously

SOUTH KONA RENTAL & TOURS

Outfitters along Hwy 11/Mamalahoa Hwy rent kayaks and snorkeling kits, as do a few free agents around the parking lot. All outfitters should include paddles, life jackets, backrests and scratch-free pads for strapping the kayak to your car; make sure to get a dry bag for your things.

Kona Boys (Map p202; ☎328-1234; www.konaboys.com; 79-7539 Mamalahoa Hwy, Kealakekua; single-/double-kayak full day $47/67, tours $125-250; ⌚7am-5pm) This laidback yet professional watersports outfit is the area's largest. Its kayak tours include private and group paddles to secluded Pawai Bay, sunset paddles and overnight camping.

Aloha Kayak Company (Map p202; ☎877-322-1444, 322-2868; www.alohakayak.com; 79-7248 Mamalahoa Hwy, Honalo; single-/double-/triple-kayak full-day $35/60/85, half-day $25/45/60, tours $90-130; ⌚7:30am-5pm) This popular, Hawaiian-owned outfit knows local waters, has half-day rentals (noon to 5pm) and rents glass-bottomed kayaks. Kayak tours go to Keauhou Bay and other destinations, seeking out sea caves and cliff jumping.

Adventures in Paradise (Map p202; ☎800-979-3370, 323-3005; www.bigislandkayak.com; 81-6367 Hwy 11, Kealakekua; single-/double-/triple-kayak full day $35/60/75, tours $80; ⌚8am-4pm) Friendly and professional, this outfitter makes sure beginners know what they're doing.

Hawaii Pack and Paddle (☎328-8911; www.hawaiipackandpaddle.com; 79-7493 Mamalahoa Hwy; tour adult/child 3-12yr $125/95) Offers hiking, wildlife watching, kayaking and snorkeling tours. If you're after a custom or longer kayaking-hiking adventure, this is the outfitter for you.

outfitted (lots of pillows and closet space, plus lush robes) and your hosts share their local knowledge freely. Kick back in the family room or watch the sun set in the Jacuzzi. You'll eat like royalty here, with fresh, unique breakfasts daily.

Banana Patch COTTAGE **$$**
(Map p202; ☎800-452-9017, 322-8888; www.bananabanana.com; Mamao St; studio $115, 1-/2-bedroom cottages $125/150; @) Let it all hang out in one of these comfortable, clothing-optional cottages secluded amid tropical foliage. Clean and tasteful, these units are terrific for DIYers, with full kitchen, lanai, gardens and Jacuzzi.

Eating & Drinking

Orchid Isle Café CAFE **$**
(Map p202; ☎323-2700; 81-6637 Mamalahoa Hwy; snacks $5-9; ⏰6am-5pm Mon-Fri, 7am-2pm Sat & Sun; 📶) Hang out on the lanai, surf the internet, and refuel with coffee and quiche at this relaxed coffeehouse.

Mi's Italian Bistro ITALIAN **$$**
(Map p202; ☎323-3880; www.misitalianbistro.com; 81-6372 Mamalahoa Hwy; mains $15-30; ⏰4:30-8:30pm Tue-Sun; 🖉) This intimate eatery run by a husband-and-wife team does a great job of filling South Kona's need for upscale Italian. Settle into a romantic nook and devour homemade pasta, organic veggies, wickedly good seafood corn chowder and thin-crust pizza amid a laidback, classy vibe.

Ke'ei Cafe HAWAII REGIONAL CUISINE **$$**
(☎322-9992; 79-7511 Mamalahoa Hwy; mains $15-29; ⏰11am-2pm Mon-Fri, 5-9pm Mon-Sat; P 🖉) If you're craving some fine dining while in South Kona, it's hard to do better than Ke'ei Cafe, which has carved a name out for itself as an excellent outpost of haute Hawaiian cuisine. Cracking peanut miso salad sets the stage for powerful mains like roasted chicken served with red curry sauce – or if you're in the mood, a more Western peppercorn gravy.

Finish your meal with *liliko'i* cheesecake, but beware: at time of writing, Ke'ei Cafe was cash only.

Korner Pocket Bar & Grill BAR
(Map p202; 81-970 Haleki'i St; ⏰11am-1am) This is about it when it comes to bar options in South Kona. It's a pretty local joint, and hosts live music on weekends.

Shopping

Discovery Antiques ANTIQUES
(Map p202; Mamalahoa Hwy; ⏰10am-5pm Mon-Sat, 11am-4pm Sun) Tin toys and aloha shirts, bric-a-brac and boxing gloves – you never know what you'll find at this secondhand antiques and curiosities shop.

Information

A **post office** (cnr Hwy 11 & Haleki'i St), several banks with ATMs, and the primary hospital serving the leeward side, Kona Community Hospital (p193), are all in close proximity.

Captain Cook

POP 3429

As Hwy 11/Mamalahoa Hwy winds southward, the greenery thickens and the ocean views become more compelling and it can be hard to tell where towns start and stop. Captain Cook is signaled by the historic Manago Hotel, which began in 1917 as a restaurant catering to salesmen on the then-lengthy journey between Hilo and Kona. The stout building remains a regional touchstone for travelers and residents alike.

Captain Cook is also where you access Kealakekua Bay, plus a great selection of B&Bs and down-home cooking. Sinewy Napo'opo'o Rd, which eventually becomes Middle Keei Rd, webs between the mountain and the ocean and is a pretty place to drive without an agenda. The many 'No Spray' signs are put up by organic farms (or even just homeowners) that are warding against state pesticide spraying.

Sleeping

Manago Hotel HOTEL **$**
(Map p202; ☎323-2642; www.managohotel.com; 82-6151 Mamalahoa Hwy; s $56-61, d $59-64, Japanese-style s/d $75/78) The Manago is a classic Hawai'i motel experience. A more modern block of motel-style rooms sits behind the historic building; the 2nd and 3rd floors are the hotel's quietest and enjoy ocean views, while 1st-floor digs are for smokers. The cheapest option is by far the shared-bath boarding-house rooms, which look the same today as they did over 80 years ago – that is, plain, no frills and well kept. No children under 18 are allowed back here, but a single/double runs for the ridiculously cheap rate of $33/36.

★Ka'awaloa Plantation & Guesthouse B&B $$

(Map p202; ☎323-2686; www.kaawaloaplantation.com; 82-5990 Upper Napo'opo'o Rd; r incl breakfast $130-150, cottage/ste $160/200; @ 📶) This rambling plantation home, set in more than 5 acres of lush jungle gardens abloom with tropical fruit, is one of South Kona's most romantic stays. Perhaps it's the dramatic four-poster beds, or the living-room fireplace, or the tasteful art and fine linens, or the divine outdoor shower, or the hot tub and Hawaiian steam box.

It certainly has to do with the hosts' aloha and attention to detail. Watching the sunset from the wraparound lanai, with the coast unfolding below, doesn't hurt. The suite has the only full bath (it's a doozy); a separate cottage has a kitchenette but no views.

Pomaika'i 'Lucky' Farm B&B B&B $$

(Map p202; ☎328-2112; www.luckyfarm.com; 83-5465 Mamalahoa Hwy; d incl breakfast $90-140; 📶) Rustic, bohemian charm oozes out of this macadamia-and-fruit farm run by a friendly couple who blend Southern hospitality with the best of aloha spirit. Two simple rooms share the main house, while attached are two airy 'Greenhouse' rooms with queen beds and screened windows. Separate and hidden by banana plants, the Barn is simply wonderful, a tastefully unadorned shack with screened, half-open walls and an outdoor shower – a budget traveler's jungle fantasy.

THE CAPTAIN COOK STORY

On January 17, 1779, Captain Cook sailed into Kealakekua Bay, touching off one of the most controversial months in Hawaii's history.

Cook's visit coincided with the annual makahiki festival, a four-month period when all warfare and heavy work was suspended to pay homage to Lono – the god of agriculture and peace. Makahiki was marked by an islandwide procession to collect the chief's annual tribute, which set off celebrations, sexual freedom and games.

Cook's welcome in Kealakekua Bay was spectacular: over 1000 canoes surrounded his ships and 9000 people hailed him from shore. Once landed, Cook was treated with supreme deference – feted as any ruling chief would be, with huge celebrations and overwhelming offerings. The Hawaiians also bartered for goods – particularly for metals, which they'd never seen before. Though Cook tried to keep his sailors from fraternizing with Hawaiian women, he failed utterly and ultimately gave up: Hawaiian women flocked to the boats, having sex freely and frequently in exchange for nails.

On February 4, restocked and ready to go, Cook departed Kealakekua Bay. But only a short way north he encountered a huge storm, and the *Resolution* broke a foremast. Unable to continue, Cook returned to the safety of Kealakekua Bay on February 11.

This time, no canoes rowed out in greeting. Chief Kalaniopu'u instead seemed to indicate Cook had worn out his welcome. For one, captain and crew had already depleted the Hawaiians supplies of food, plus the makahiki season had ended; the party was over.

As Hawaiian generosity decreased, petty thefts increased; insults and suspicion replaced politeness on both sides. After a rowboat was stolen, Cook ordered a blockade of Kealakekua Bay and took chief Kalaniopu'u hostage until the boat was returned.

Cook convinced Kalaniopu'u to come to the *Resolution* to resolve their disputes. But as they walked to shore, Kalaniopu'u learned that sailors had killed a lower chief attempting to exit the bay in his canoe. At this, Kalaniopu'u apparently sat and refused to continue, and a large angry crowd gathered.

Thinking to frighten the Hawaiians, Cook fired his pistol, killing one of the chief's bodyguards. Incensed, the Hawaiians attacked. In the deadly melee, Captain Cook was stabbed with a dagger and clubbed to death.

Cook's death stunned both sides and ended the battle. In the days afterward, the Hawaiians took Cook's body and dismembered it in the custom reserved for high chiefs. The Englishmen demanded Cook's body back, and in a spasm of gruesome violence torched homes and slaughtered Hawaiians – women and children included. Eventually the Hawaiians returned some bits and pieces – a partial skull, hands and feet – which the Englishmen buried at sea, as per naval tradition. However, the Hawaiians kept the bones that held the most mana (spiritual essence), such as his femurs.

Families are particularly welcome, and breakfast is a social occasion. Two-night minimum stay.

Eating

★Manago Hotel HAWAII REGIONAL CUISINE $
(Map p202; ☎323-2642; 82-6151 Mamalahoa Hwy; breakfast $4-6, dinner mains $8-14; ⏰7-9am, 11am-2pm & 5-7:30pm Tue-Sun; 👪) There are somethings you just don't miss on the Big Island. The crater of Kilauea. Snorkeling at Two-Step. Sipping 100% Kona coffee. And the dining room of the Manago. Traveling here involves crossing space *and* time; the Manago, with its woodsy paneling and linoleum floors, feels like an early 20th-century diner. But it's a diner for the population of South Kona, and that population is a blend of Japanese, Chinese, Portuguese, Filipino, a few mainlanders and Native Hawaiian.

Thus, the Manago's famous pork chops are hearty enough for a Westerner, yet come with bowls of rice and chopsticks plus diced Japanese vegetables. The liver and onions is a house specialty, while the fried whole *'opelu* (mackerel scad) is a delight. For breakfast there's a complete egg, meat, toast, juice and coffee combo for $5.50 – one of South Kona's best deals.

★Super J's LOCAL $
(Map p202; ☎328-9566; 83-5409 Mamalahoa Hwy; mains under $10; ⏰10am-6:30pm Mon-Sat) The full title of this place is 'Ka'aloa's Super J's Authentic Hawaiian,' but everyone calls it Super J's. They also call it freaking delicious. Super J's is a veritable temple to Native Hawaiian cuisine. The *laulau* (pork cooked in taro leafs) is cooked for over six hours until it's so tender it melts under your fork, the *lomolomi* (salmon and tomato salad) is damn tasty – hell, we even like the poi (steamed, mashed taro).

Best of all is the setting: you're basically eating in a very friendly Hawaiian family's living room. Don't miss this one.

Up Country Bakery & Cafe CAFE $
(Map p202; ☎323-2253; 82-6127 Mamaloha Hwy; mains under $10; ⏰8am-7pm Mon-Wed, til 9pm Thu-Sat, 9am-2pm Sun; 📶🌱👪) It's hard not to love this spot. The Up Country is decked out in bright local artwork and patronized by the greater bohemian community of South Kona, as well as anyone who happens to like great baked goods (the bagels and banana bread are incredible) and good vegetarian and vegan food. Gluten-free dishes are available as well. On weekend evenings, the Up Country dishes out some tasty southwestern fare – green chili burritos and the like.

Patz Pies PIZZERIA $
(Map p202; ☎323-8100; 82-6127 Mamalahoa Hwy; slices/pies $3.50/19; ⏰10am-8pm) Thin-crust, zesty sauce and a nice price: claims to good Noo Yawk–style pizza are not exaggerated here. Not surprisingly, Pat's a native NYer.

Keoki's Roadside Cafe SEAFOOD $
(Map p202; 83-5293 Mamalahoa Hwy; mains $6-12; ⏰9am-6:30pm Mon-Sat, till 6pm Sun) This friendly little roadside stand dishes out the best fish and chips in South Kona. The restaurant is attached to an eclectic general store, and both businesses are filled with original artwork by local artists.

Coffees 'n' Epicurea CAFE $
(Map p202; ☎328-0322; 83-5315 Mamalahoa Hwy; ⏰6:30am-6pm) A coffee-tasting room/tea bar is an unlikely place for this sublime patisserie with flaky pastries, delicate éclairs and gorgeous pies (the baker defected from the Kohala Coast resorts).

South Kona Green Market MARKET $
(Map p202; www.skgm.org; 82-6188 Mamalahoa Hwy; ⏰9am-2pm Sun) Behind the ChoiceMart, this farmers market epitomizes South Kona's diversity, with organic produce, musical performances and funky crafts.

ChoiceMart SUPERMARKET $
(Map p202; 82-6066 Mamalahoa Hwy; ⏰5am-10pm) South Kona's largest grocery store. These guys actually prepare some of the finest *poke* in the area.

Coffee Shack CAFE $$
(Map p202; ☎328-9555; www.coffeeshack.com; 83-5799 Mamalahoa Hwy; meals $9-16; ⏰7:30am-3pm) Perched precariously next to the highway, the Shack is famous for the insane views of Kealakekua Bay from its open-air deck. We can say, with no hyperbole, you may never have a cup of coffee with a better vista (and if you do, you're one lucky traveller). The food's pretty kick-butt too, especially the *loco moco*, which is one of the best variations on the dish we've had on the Big Island.

Shopping

★The Reading Garden BOOKS
(Map p202; ☎323-9540; 82-6125 Mamalahoa Hwy; ⏰ 9am-6pm Mon-Sat, from 11am Sun) The

Reading Garden is everything a secondhand bookstore should be: teetering stacks of used volumes spread about in an ordered chaos, wrapping over walls and up staircases and even extending outdoors.

Within you may be lucky enough to find incredibly friendly proprietor Marc Medler, a book enthusiast who feels like a Hawaiian version of the twinkly-eyed professor who first led the kids through the wardrobe into Narnia. His hobby is restoring rare, vintage books, and if you ask nicely, he may show you some of the amazing volumes he has on hand.

Kealakekua Bay State Historical Park

Kealakekua Bay is one of Hawai'i's seminal sites, a location that manages to blend incredible natural beauty with supreme historical importance. Besides being one of the major religious sites of Native Hawaiians, the bay marks the spot where Captain Cook, and by extension the outside world, first set foot in the archipelago, irrevocably altering the fate of the islands and their residents.

A wide, calm bay shouldered by a low lava point to the north, tall reddish *pali* (cliffs) in the center and miles of green mountain slopes to the south, the bay is both a **state park** (Map p202) and a marine-life conservation district, and is famous for its rich variety of sea life, including spinner dolphins. This entire area is considered sacred, and deserves your respect.

Napo'opo'o Rd, off Hwy 11, winds 4.5 miles down to the bay, leaving behind the lush foliage of the rainier uplands for the perpetually sunny coast; never assume that rain on the highway means rain in the bay. The road ends at the parking lot for Napo'opo'o Beach and Wharf.

Beaches

Manini Beach BEACH

(Map p202) On its southern shoreline, Kealakekua Bay is rocky and exposed to regular northwest swells, making for poor swimming and snorkeling conditions. On the other hand, Manini Beach makes a highly scenic, shady picnic spot. That said, there's scattered coral and *'a'a* (rough, jagged type of lava), so this isn't a great spot for a swim. If you're confident in the water, use a small break in the lava (to the right) to access the bay.

Surfers head to the point just south of Manini Beach. The park has portable toilets and picnic tables. From Napo'opo'o Rd, turn left on Pu'uhonua Rd, then right on Kahauloa Rd; after 0.25 mile, turn right on Manini Beach Rd and park at the blue house.

Ke'ei Bay BEACH

Continuing south on Puu'honua Rd, you'll come across Ke'ei Bay, an attractive cove that's nonetheless rough for swimming. At the bay, there's a beach, a small canoe launch and a few shacks, but no facilities – be respectful of residents here; you're essentially in their front yard.

To get there, take the ragged dirt road past the turnoff for Manini Beach (if you reach Ke'ei Transfer Station, you've gone too far). If you don't have a high-clearance vehicle, park along the dirt road and walk in.

South of here is the site of the Battle of Moku'ōhai, where, in 1782, Kamehameha the Great defeated his rival Kiwala'o and asserted his rule over West Hawai'i.

Pu'uhonua Rd continues for several miles south through scrub brush to Pu'uhonua o Honaunau National Historical Park.

KEALAKEKUA BAY'S MORATORIUM

As of 2013, Hawai'i's Department of Land and Natural Resources has instituted a moratorium on kayaks, surfboards, boogie boards and most other watercraft in Kealakekua Bay (some craft are allowed to transit the bay, but they cannot stop there). Prior to the moratorium, dozens if not hundreds of vessels were plying the bay every day, disturbing sleeping spinner dolphins and generally crowding this body of water. The moratorium was also instituted in response to the drowning death of a New York teenager in 2012.

While we cannot say for sure, we expect the moratorium to be lifted by the time you read this book. The state seems likely to allow tourism watercraft back in the bay, but companies will have to be licensed. In the meantime, you may still swim and snorkel in Kealakekua Bay (and you should!), but getting there requires hiking the Captain Cook Monument Trail (p212).

Sights

Hiki'au Heiau TEMPLE

(Map p202) Veer right at the base of Napo'opo'o Rd to reach public rest rooms and Hiki'au Heiau, a large platform temple. In front of the heiau, a stone beach makes a moody perch from which to observe the stunning scenery, but the surf is too rough to swim. Climbing on the ruins is kapu (forbidden).

Captain Cook Monument HISTORIC SITE

(Map p202) A 27ft white obelisk marking the spot where Captain Cook was killed in 1779, is perched just above Ka'awaloa Cove. In 1877, as an act of diplomacy, the Kingdom of Hawai'i gifted the 16 sq ft of land that the monument stands on to Britain. Behind the monument are the ruins of the ancient village of Ka'awaloa.

Pali Kapu o Keoua HISTORIC SITE

(Map p202) The 'sacred cliffs of Keoua' were named for a chief and rival of Kamehameha I. Numerous caves in the cliffs were the burial places of Hawaiian royalty, and it's speculated that some of Captain Cook's bones were placed here as well. High, inaccessible caves probably still contain bones.

Activities

Snorkeling

At Kealakekua Bay's north end, protected **Ka'awaloa Cove** (Map p202) is among Hawaii's premier snorkeling spots. The fish and coral are absolutely wonderful, and those with iron stomachs can swim out 100ft to hang over the blue abyss.

The water is protected from ocean swells and is exceptionally clear. Snorkeling is limited to a narrow section along the shore, where sea stars and eels weave through coral gardens, and schools of colorful fish sweep by. Confident swimmers can seek out an underwater lava arch toward the point. If you're lucky, sea turtles and spinner dolphins might join you – but remember to keep your distance from these animals, and avoid stepping on coral. In light of recent research that's revealed smaller dolphin pods and widening patches of dead coral here, we recommend considering alternative snorkel sites, such as Two-Step or Kahalu'u Bay.

Unless boat tours have been resumed, the only way to Ka'awaloa Cove is hiking the Captain Cook Monument Trail. Morning – with calm winds and reliable sunny skies – is best.

Kayaking

If the moratorium is lifted (as seems likely), look into kayaking on Kealakekua Bay (see p207). The calm waters make for a great paddle, even for novices.

Diving

There are many good dive sites clustered around Kealakekua Bay, including **Ka'awaloa Cove**, with its exceptional diversity of coral and fish in depths from about 5ft to 120ft. Other sites near here include **Hammerhead** (deep dive with pelagic action), **Coral Dome** (a big, teeming cave with a giant skylight) and **Driftwood** (featuring lava tubes and white-tip reef sharks).

In the aptly named **Long Lava Tube** (Map p202), an intermediate site just north of Kealakekua Bay, lava 'skylights' shoot light through the ceiling of the 70ft tube. You may see crustaceans, morays – even Spanish dancers. Outside are countless lava formations sheltering conger eels, triton's trumpet shells and schooling squirrelfish.

Other Activities

Captain Cook Monument Trail HIKING

(Map p202) As of this writing, the only way to snorkel Ka'awaloa Cove without renting a kayak or taking a boat tour was via hiking the Captain Cook Monument Trail. And that's frankly OK with us – Kealakekua Bay is so beautiful, but simultaneously fragile, we feel like visiting it needs to be earned.

Admittedly, the trail can be hot and buggy, but there's nice lookouts on the way down and it leads right to the snorkeling cove. The way down is an easy hour, but after a morning of snorkeling the uphill return seems twice as steep (in reality it's a 1300ft elevation gain in 1.8 miles); allow two hours to return.

To get to the trailhead, turn *makai* (seaward) off Hwy 11/Mamalahoa Hwy onto Napo'opo'o Rd; within the first tenth of a mile, park along the narrow road in one of the pullouts, wherever it's safe to do so. To find the trail entrance, count four telephone poles from the start of the road, and it's *makai* across from three tall palm trees. The trail is clear and easy to follow going down; when in doubt at a confusing spur, stay to the left. The trail ends at the place where kayakers with permits pull up on the rocks. There are no facilities at the bottom, so bring lots of water.

Returning uphill, stay right at the fork (back onto the lava ledge); left is a 4WD road that continues north along the coast for miles.

Kings' Trail Rides HORSE RIDING, TOUR
(Map p202; ☎345-0661, 323-2388; www.konacowboy.com; 81-6420 Mamalahoa Hwy; rides $135; ⏲9am-4pm Mon-Fri) Kings' leads two-hour horseback trips to the coastline just north of Kealakekua Bay. Trips include lunch and snorkeling if waters are calm.

Sleeping

Luana Inn B&B $$
(Map p202; ☎328-2612; www.luanainn.com; 82-5856 Lower Napo'opo'o Rd; r incl breakfast $180-210; ❄@🛜🏊) Some people (and properties) are perfectly suited to hosting in comfort and style. Welcome to spotless, aloha-filled Luana Inn. Each spacious, uncluttered and tastefully understated room has a private entrance and equipped kitchenette – two open right onto the pool and Jacuzzi with jaw-dropping bay views; two others are cozy private digs perfect for a couple or family.

Pick your hosts' brains over a lavish breakfast for the best of the Big Island – they've been around.

Kealakekua Bay Bed & Breakfast B&B $$
(Map p202; ☎328-8150; www.keala.com; 82-6002 Lower Napo'opo'o Rd; r $165-220, cottage $300; 🛜) You know, the breakfasts served in the Mediterranean-style mansion are reason enough to stay here. Seriously: local goat cheese, macadamia nut pancakes, fresh fruit plucked from the lush local garden – you can't go wrong. That goes for the property itself, three bright, sunlit-kissed rooms filled with cool white sheets and tropical accents, and the six-person Ohana-Kai Guesthouse, a hill-perched cottage with simply stunning views of Kealakekua Bay (which by the way, is located just a few minutes down the road).

Honaunau

POP 2567

Little more than some scattered, friendly businesses hidden amid thick coffee-and-macadamia-nut groves, Honaunau is fun to explore without a guidebook. The nearby 'Place of Refuge' remains the star attraction, but meander down Painted Church Rd, stopping at fruit stands and coffee shacks with sea views for another type of retreat.

Sights & Activities

St Benedict's Painted Church CHURCH
(Map p202; www.thepaintedchurch.org; 84-5140 Painted Church Rd) From the outside, the Painted Church doesn't look all that painted. Well, there's a coat of white, but that's hardly unusual. But step *inside* and it looks like the Gospels crashed into an art supply store. In a good way! Rarely have we seen Christian allegory come so vividly to life; the artwork isn't what we'd call elegant, but it does possess an undeniable raw energy

Catholic priest John Berchmans Velghe came to Hawai'i from Belgium in 1899. Upon taking responsibility for St Benedict's church, he moved it 2 miles up from its original location on the coast near the *pu'uhonua* (place of refuge). It's not clear whether he did this as protection from tsunami or as an attempt to rise above – both literally and symbolically – what Christians considered pagan native culture.

Father John then painted the walls with a series of biblical scenes to aid in teaching the Bible. Sayings in Hawaiian (including the admonishment 'Begone Satan!' among others) are painted on columns topped with palm fronds.

Paleaku Gardens Peace Sanctuary GARDENS
(Map p202; ☎328-8084; www.paleaku.com; 83-5401 Painted Church Rd; admission $5; ⏲9am-4pm Tue-Sat) Near the church on Painted Church Rd, these tranquil 7-acre gardens contain shrines to the world's major religions and a frankly staggeringly impressive 'Galaxy Garden,' in which famous space painter Jon Lomberg has created a scale model of the Milky Way – in plants. You'll also find yoga and tai chi classes and plenty of general good vibes

SKEA COURSE, ART
(Society for Kona's Education & Art; Map p202; ☎328-9392; www.skea.org; 84-5191 Mamalahoa Hwy) SKEA is a hotbed of activity, with Pilates, Polynesian dance and Japanese ink-painting classes, plus pidgin poetry-readings and concerts on the lawn. Check the calendar, and look for it between mile markers 105 and 106. Around the back of SKEA is the **Kona Potter's Guild** (Map p202), where you can watch potters at work and buy their unique creations.

Sleeping

Camp Aloha GUESTHOUSE $
(Map p202; ☎328-2304; konajoan@yahoo.com; 84-5210 Painted Church Rd; r $99; 🛜🏊) This excellent guesthouse is fantastic value for money. Furnishings are modern and handsome, and

relaxing by the large pool is a perfect way to wile away South Kona afternoons. The owners are friendly and hip to what's happening in the area, and serve a mean breakfast.

Dragonfly Ranch B&B $$
(Map p202; 84-5146 Keala O Keawe Rd; r incl breakfast $100-175, ste $225-250; P) Lord, bless the eccentric and the original, for without them there would be no Dragonfly Ranch. This riot of colors, prayer flags, murals and cool bric-a-brac is concealed in the scrubby forests that lead from the main road to the Place of Refuge. There's five rooms to pick from. OK, we're not fans of the seemingly Lisa Frank-inspired Dolphin Room, but the Writer's Studio is an endearing mash of whites and pale greens.

The Lomilomi suite, with its Asian and Polynesian art and hardwood accents, looks like the quarters for bohemian Hawaiian royalty, and then there's the Honeymoon Suite. Rock lava pool, shoji screens, pavillion roof, goose-down pillows, 1200-thread count sheets and mirrored canopy – hot!

Aloha Guest House B&B $$
(Map p202; 800-897-3188, 328-8955; www.alohaguesthouse.com; 84-4780 Mamalahoa Hwy; r incl breakfast $140-280; @) If you're coming all the way to Hawaii, you should have the finest digs, and damn the cost. Heady views from the lanai, guest living room and king-sized bed will make you swoon, guaranteed. The views are complemented by luxurious amenities, including organic bath products, deliciously customized bathrooms and a hot tub. The Honu room is wheelchair accessible.

WHILE YOU SNORKEL, THEY SCHEME

For many, the Big Island's remote beaches and hikes are the main event – but they also make your rental car a prime target for thieves. Follow locals' advice: leave nothing of value in your car (this includes the trunk). Places to be particularly cautious include Kehena Beach and Ahalanui Beach Park (Puna), the remote Kona Coast beaches and Ho'okena and Miloli'i.

Another tip is to leave your doors unlocked so would-be ne'er-do-wells know there's nothing of value in the car. This way, you can avoid a smashed window, which – if the confetti of broken glass in parking areas is any indication – occurs fairly frequently. This strategy can backfire, however: at Miloli'i, leaving the doors unlocked, we set off for Honomalino Beach. While we played, a cheeky local opened the door wide for stray cats to come in and pee.

Hale Ho'ola B&B B&B $$
(Map p202; 877-628-9117, 328-9117; www.halehoola.com; 85-4577 Mamalahoa Hwy; r incl breakfast $110-150; @) This friendly B&B makes for a homey, relaxed stay, with three small but comfortable rooms downstairs from the main house. Rooms have nice beds and lanai, but are packed in pretty tightly – not recommended for honeymooners or antisocial types. Best views are from the main house lanai over a big breakfast.

Eating

South Kona Fruit Stand HEALTH FOOD $
(Map p202; 328-8547; www.southkonafruitstand.com; 84-4770 Mamalahoa Hwy; smoothies $5.25–6.25, sandwiches $7–9; 9am–6pm Mon–Sat & 10am–4pm Sun) This chichi organic-produce stand sells only the cream of the crop. The cafe whips up heavenly fruit smoothies and good sandwiches, and there are nice views from the outdoor patio.

Bong Brothers & Sistahs HEALTH FOOD, DELI $
(Map p202; www.bongbrothers.com; Hwy 11; deli items $3-5; 9am-6pm Mon-Fri, noon-6pm Sun;) Food is politics at this small organic health-food store and vegetarian takeout deli. The fresh-made curries, soups and salads are mouthwateringly delicious, even when served with ornery aloha by unrepentant agricultural activists. There are cool gift items, too. It's located within an historic 1929 building.

Pu'uhonua o Honaunau National Historical Park

Standing at the end of a long semi-desert of thorny scrub and lava plains, the **national park** (Map p202; 328-2326, 328-2288; www.nps.gov/puho; 1-week pass adult/car $3/5; 7am-sunset, visitor center 8:30am-4:30pm) fronting Honaunau Bay provides one of the state's most evocative experiences of ancient Hawai'i, and easy access to some of the best snorkeling anywhere. In short, Pu'uhonua o Honaunau combines a seminal historical experience with some of the best wildlife-spotting on the island, and to access all this, you just need to be able to fit a snorkel in your mouth. The park's tongue-twister name simply means 'place of refuge at Honaunau'.

To get here, turn *makai* (seaward) on to City of Refuge Rd (about 17 miles south of Kailua-Kona). Follow the signs along the curvy road for about two miles to Pu'uhonua o Honaunau.

History

In ancient Hawai'i the kapu (taboo) system regulated every waking moment. A commoner could not look at *ali'i* (royalty) or walk in their footsteps. Women couldn't cook for men, nor eat with them. Fishing, hunting and gathering timber was restricted to certain seasons. And on and on.

Violators of kapu were hunted down and killed. After all, breaking kapu infuriated the gods, according to the Hawaiian belief system. And gods wrought volcanic eruptions, tidal waves, famine and earthquakes.

There was one loophole, however. Commoners who broke a kapu could stave off death if they reached the sacred ground of a *pu'uhonua* (place of refuge). A *pu'uhonua* also gave sanctuary to defeated warriors and wartime 'noncombatants' (men who were too old, too young or unable to fight).

To reach this *pu'uhonua* was no small feat, though. Since royals and their warriors lived on the grounds surrounding the refuge, kapu breakers had to swim through violent, open ocean, braving currents and sharks, to safety. Once inside the sanctuary, priests performed ceremonies of absolution to placate the gods. Kapu breakers could then return home to start afresh. The *pu'uhonua* at Honaunau was used for several centuries before being abandoned around 1819.

Sights & Activities

A half-mile walking tour encompasses the park's major sites – the visitor center provides a brochure map with cultural information. At midday, the park gets hot and is only partially shaded. While most of the sandy trail is accessible by wheelchair, sites near the water require traversing rough lava rock.

You enter the national park in the village-like royal grounds, where Kona *ali'i* and their warriors lived; this area's quiet spiritual atmosphere is greatly enhanced by the gently breaking waves and wind-rustled palms. **Hale o Keawe Heiau**, the temple on the point of the cove, was built around 1650 and contains the bones of 23 chiefs. It was believed that the mana (spiritual essence) of the chiefs remained in their bones and bestowed sanctity on those who entered the grounds. A fishpond, lava tree molds, a hand-carved koa canoe and a few thatched huts and shelters are scattered through here. The royal canoe landing, a tongue of sand called **Keone'ele Cove**, is a favorite resting spot for sea turtles.

Carved wooden *ki'i* (deity images) standing up to 15ft high front an authentic-looking heiau reconstruction. Leading up to the heiau is the **Great Wall** separating the royal grounds from the *pu'uhonua*. Built around 1550, this stone wall is more than 1000ft long and 10ft high. Inside the wall are two older heiau platforms and legendary standing stones.

Just south of the park's central village area, an oceanfront palm-tree grove holds one of South Kona's choicest **picnic areas**. Parking, picnic tables and BBQs face a wide slab of *pahoehoe* (smooth-flowing lava), which is littered with wave-tumbled lava-rock boulders and pockmarked with busy **tide pools** where you may encounter sea turtles. Swimming is possible but can be dicey; judge the surf and entry for yourself. Note that it's kapu to snorkel here.

After wandering the self-guided trail, you might try some wildlife watching: humpback whales can be seen offshore in winter, plus turtles and dolphins and even hoary bats can be seen here (after sunset is best).

★Two-Step SNORKELING, SWIMMING

(Map p202) Immediately north of Pu'uhonua o Honaunau National Historical Park, concealed within a (usually) placid bay, is a series of ridiculously vibrant and beautiful coral gardens where the reef and marine life seem locked in a permanent race to outstrip each other with the gaudiest color palette.

From above the water, your only indication of the action is the presence of boats leading snorkeling, diving, kayaking and SUP tours, plus the crowds gathering at the titular two steps. Leave your car in the park's lot, and hang a left outside the entrance. Alternatively, there is parking ($3) across from the snorkel entry.

There's no beach here – snorkelers step off a lava ledge beside the boat ramp into about 10ft of water, which quickly drops to about 25ft. Some naturally formed steps (hence the spot's name) make entry and exit fairly easy. It's much easier to use the steps than the boat ramp (we hear locals don't approve of the latter anyways).

Once you're in the water you'll feel like a supporting cast player in Disney's *The Little Mermaid*. Visibility is usually excellent, especially with the noon-sun overhead; good-sized reef fish and a fine variety of coral are close to shore. When the tide is rising, the water is deeper and brings in more fish. The predatory 'crown of thorns' starfish can be seen here feasting on live coral polyps. Cool, freshwater springs seep out of the ground, creating blurry patches in the water. Divers can investigate a ledge a little way out that drops off about 100ft.

1871 Trail HIKING

This pretty 2-mile round-trip hike leads to the abandoned village of Ki'ilae. The visitor center lends a trail guide describing the archaeological sites along the way. Among other things, you pass a collapsed lava tube and a tremendous, if overgrown, *holua* that *ali'i* raced sleds down. Keep your ears peeled for benign feral goats in these parts.

The steep **Alahaka Ramp** once allowed riders on horseback to travel between villages; halfway up the ramp, the **Waiu o Hina lava tube** (closed for safety reasons) opens to the sea. From the top of the ramp, the incredible vista of ocean coves and ragged cliffs is a trail highlight; for confident snorkelers, some of these coves can provide water access in calm seas. Continuing on, you reach a gate that once marked the park's boundary; this is the current Ki'ilae Village site – the ruins are pretty ruined, with almost nothing to see.

Fit hikers can walk all the way to Ho'okena Beach on this 3.5-mile trail, though it becomes increasingly rough after the Alahaka Ramp.

Festivals & Events

On the weekend closest to July 1, the park puts on a **cultural festival** (www.nps.gov/puho; ⌚9am-3pm) with traditional crafts and food, *hukilau* (net fishing), canoe rides and a 'royal court'. Park fees are waived for the festival.

Ho'okena & Around

Ho'okena is a tiny, impoverished fishing village with no businesses to speak of, but it fronts a beautiful bay with a popular charcoal-sand beach park. This is primarily a locals' spot, where large families picnic and teens hang out, blaring music from car speakers. Unlike Miloli'i, the vibe is mellow and open to outsiders and, particularly during the day, travelers should have no qualms about hanging out.

This was once a bustling village. King Kalakaua dispatched his friend Robert Louis Stevenson here in 1889 to show him a typical Hawaiian settlement; Stevenson then wrote about Ho'okena in *Travels in Hawaii*. In the 1890s Chinese immigrants moved into Ho'okena, a tavern and a hotel opened, and the town got rougher and rowdier. In those days Big Island cattle were shipped from the Ho'okena landing, but when the circle-island road was built, the steamers stopped coming and people moved away. By the 1920s the town was all but deserted.

Beaches

★Ho'okena Beach Park BEACH

The modest-sized, charcoal-colored beach here is backed by a steep green hillside. When calm, the bay's waters are good for swimming, kayaking and snorkeling (though it drops off pretty quickly). There are strong currents further out. When the winter surf is up, local kids hit the waves with bodyboards. Look for dolphins and humpback whales here from December to April.

The beach park was once grotty and unfriendly, but today it's one of the prettiest, well-maintained public spaces on the island. There's a picnic pavilion, bathrooms, showers, a concession stand and drinking water, all thanks to vigorous community organizing. You can **camp** right on the sand, at the base of the cliffs. Sites are awesome and security issues have been addressed by implementing a guard patrol, and through the activism of the **Friends of Ho'okena Beach Park** (http://hookena.org); you can obtain the required permits and rent camping gear on their website. Permits ($5) can also be obtained from the Department of Parks & Recreation. A neighborhood **potluck** is hosted Wednesday afternoons here; all are welcome.

The signed turnoff is located between mile markers 101 and 102. A narrow road winds 2 miles down to the beach. Veer left at the bottom.

Pebble Beach BEACH

Not quite pebbles, the smoky stones of this beach at the bottom of the Kona Paradise subdivision range from gumdrop- to palm-sized. This is a popular kayak put-in and offers a good dose of peace and quiet. Lounge for a bit, paddle a while or watch the sun go down.

The beach is 1 mile down very steep and winding Kaohe Rd, accessed between mile markers 96 and 97. Though Pebble Beach is reached through an ungated subdivision, there are signs saying 'private road' and 'keep out' – seek permission from locals. Also, be watchful for sneaker waves (a woman died here in 2009).

Miloli'i

Miloli'i residents highly prize the traditional lifestyle of their modest fishing village, and they are very protective of it. Compared with Ho'okena, Miloli'i feels quite prosperous: new homes blanket the hillsides (along with the remains of a 1926 lava flow), shiny pick-up trucks sit in driveways, fishermen zip around in motorized boats – all alongside makeshift shacks and older mariners patiently fixing their nets by the water. Miloli'i means 'fine twist,' and historically the village was known for its skilled sennit twisters, who used bark from the *olona* (a native shrub) to make fine cord and highly valued fishnets.

But Miloli'i is also known for its resistance to, and lack of, tourism. Villagers prefer their isolation and are not enthusiastic about visitors. At the end of the steep, winding 5-mile road to the village is a small county **beach park** with bathrooms, a covered pavilion and unremarkable camping (with a county permit). It's a pretty spot with lots of tide pools, but it's also insular and intimate, and especially on weekends, you'll feel like a stranger crashing a family reunion. Do *not* do things like pee on the side of the road; we talked with a French tourist who was almost beat up by locals for doing so. Just act with respect and avoid violating people's privacy and you'll be treated with the same esteem.

NORTH KONA COAST

If you thought the Big Island was all jungle mountains and white sand beaches, the severe North Kona Coast will come as a shock. This is more a landscape that crosses the Martian desert with Tolkien's Mordor, a place of beige deserts and black-and-rust lava fields. Yet always, at the edge of your eyesight, is the bright blue Pacific, while bits of green are sprinkled like jade flecks amid the dry. Penetrate those lava fields and you can snorkel with turtles, walk on black sand and experience an iconic Kona sunset. Turn inland and you'll see Mauna Kea, Mauna Loa (both snowcapped in winter) and, between the two, Mt Hualalai.

North Kona technically runs 33 miles along Queen Ka'ahumanu Hwy (Hwy 19), from Kailua-Kona up the Kona Coast to Kawaihae. Honokohau Harbor is an easy 2-mile drive from downtown Kailua.

Kaloko-Honokohau National Historical Park

Just north of Honokohau Harbor, this 1160-acre **national park** (Map p218; ☎326-9057; www.nps.gov/kaho; ⏰visitor center 8:30am-4pm, park 24hr) may be the island's most underappreciated ancient Hawaiian site. The main draws are two ancient fishponds and a beach frequented by *honu* (green sea turtles), but it also preserves ancient heiau and house sites (restored in 2010), burial caves, petroglyphs, *holua* and a restored 1-mile segment of the ancient King's Trail footpath. It's speculated that the bones of Kamehameha the Great were secretly buried near Kaloko.

The park takes its name from the two *ahupua'a* (ancient land divisions) it occupies. These comprise a seemingly desolate expanse of black lava, perhaps explaining the lack of visitation. If the relatively short, hot trails through this otherworldly wasteland don't appeal, you can drive and see the highlights with hardly any hiking at all. The main entrance to the park's visitor center is located off Hwy 19 between mile markers 96 and 97.

Beaches & Sights

Kaloko Fishpond HISTORIC SITE

(Map p218) At the park's northern end, Kaloko is the more interesting fishpond because its massive rock retaining wall is being completely rebuilt, so it can once again be fished in the traditional way. It also provides gorgeous views. From the park's visitor center, drive north on Hwy 19 until you reach a separate gated entrance at Kaloko Rd.

'Aimakapa Fishpond HISTORIC SITE

(Map p218) At the southern end, 'Aimakapa is the largest fishpond on the Kona Coast.

North Kona Coast

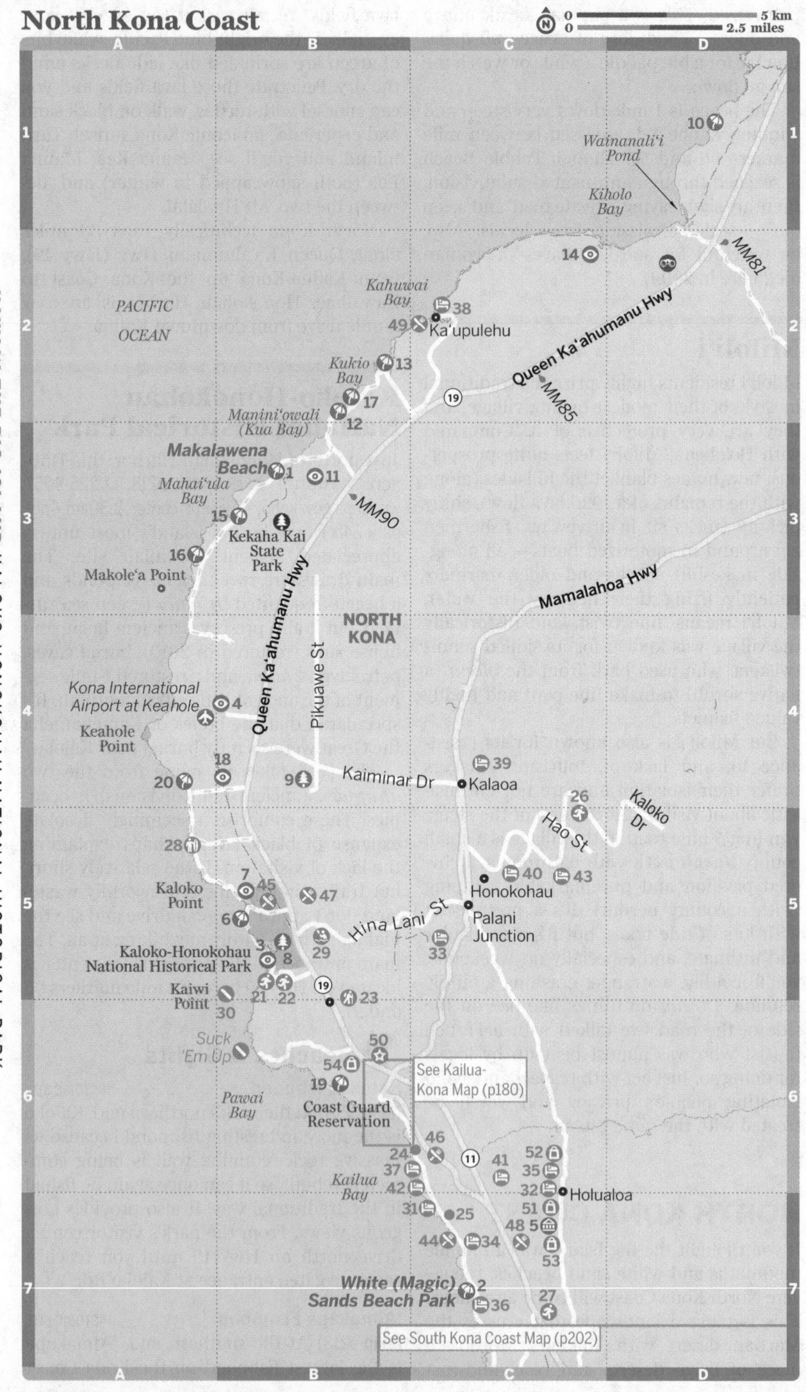

North Kona Coast

Top Sights

1 Makalawena Beach ... B3
2 White (Magic) Sands Beach Park ... C7

Sights

3 'Aimakapa Fishpond ... B5
4 Astronaut Ellison S Onizuka Space Center ... B4
5 Donkey Mill Art Center ... C7
Hawaii Gateway Energy Center ... (see 18)
6 Honokohau Beach ... B5
7 Kaloko Fishpond ... B5
8 Kaloko-Honokohau National Historical Park ... B5
Ka'upuleho Cultural Center ... (see 13)
9 Keahole Ag Park ... B4
10 Keawaiki Beach ... D1
11 Kehaka Kai State Park ... B3
12 Kikaua Beach ... B2
Kona Cloud Forest Sanctuary ... (see 26)
13 Kukio Beach ... B2
14 Luahinewai ... C2
15 Mahai'ula Beach ... B3
16 Makole'a Beach ... A3
17 Manini'owali Beach (Kua Bay) ... B2
18 Natural Energy Laboratory of Hawaii Authority ... B4
Ocean Rider Seahorse Farm ... (see 18)
19 Old Kona Airport State Recreation Area ... B6
20 Wawaloli (OTEC) Beach ... A4

Activities, Courses & Tours

Captain Zodiac ... (see 6)
21 Charter Desk ... B5
22 Dan McSweeney's Whale Watch ... B5
23 Hawaii Forest & Trail ... B5
24 Hawaii Lifeguard Surf Instructors ... C6
Kamanu Charters ... (see 6)
25 Kona Surf Adventures ... C7
26 Mountain Thunder Coffee Plantation ... C5
Ocean Eco Tours ... (see 6)
27 Original Hawaiian Chocolate Factory ... C7
28 Pine Trees ... A5
29 Plenty Pupule ... B5
30 Turtle Pinnacle ... B5

Sleeping

31 Casa de Emdeko ... C7
Four Seasons Resort Hualalai ... (see 13)
32 Holualoa Inn ... C6
33 Honu Kai B&B ... C5
34 Kona Bali Kai ... C7
35 Kona Hotel ... C6
36 Kona Sugar Shack ... C7
37 Kona Tiki Hotel ... C6
38 Kona Village Resort ... C2
39 Mango Sunset B&B ... C4
40 Nancy's Hideaway ... C5
41 Plumeria House ... C6
42 Royal Sea-Cliff Resort ... C6
43 The Lilikoi Vine ... C5

Eating

Beach Tree Bar & Grill ... (see 13)
Bite Me Bar & Grill ... (see 6)
44 Da Poke Shack ... C7
45 Harbor House Restaurant ... B5
Hualalai Grille ... (see 13)
46 Jackie Rey's Ohana Grill ... C6
47 Kailua Candy Company ... B5
Kona Coffee & Tea Company ... (see 23)
48 La Bourgogne ... C7
49 'Ulu Ocean Grill ... C2

Entertainment

50 Hollywood Makalaua Stadium Cinemas ... B6

Shopping

51 Holualoa Ukelele Gallery ... C7
52 Ipu Hale Gallery ... C6
53 Kimura Lauhala Shop ... C7
54 Kona International Market ... B6

Separated from the ocean by a high berm, it resembles a rectangular lake and is home to *ae'o* (Hawaiian black-necked stilt) and *'alae kea* (Hawaiian coot), which are both endangered native waterbirds.

Honokohau Beach BEACH

(Map p218) Adjacent to 'Aimakapa Fishpond, the salt-and-pepper Honokohau Beach is the perfect spot for sunning, strolling and even swimming when waters are calm – it makes an enjoyable sunset destination from the park.

Keahole Point

At Keahole Point the seafloor drops steeply just offshore, providing a continuous supply of both cold water from 2000ft depths and warm surface water. These are ideal conditions for ocean thermal-energy conversion (OTEC). These parts also provide top conditions for flower farming: turn right onto Kai'iminani Dr between mile markers 93 and 94 and you enter **Keahole Ag Park** (Map p218) – a top local spot for fresh lei. Enter the first driveway on your right or left and you'll find coolers full of these flowered delights sold on the honor system.

Sights & Activities

Wawaloli (OTEC) Beach BEACH

(Map p218; 6am-8pm) The Natural Energy Laboratory of Hawaii Authority (Nelha) access road leads to Wawaloli Beach, which is perfectly positioned for sunset and contains oodles of tide pools along its rocky lava coastline. Swimming conditions are poor, but the quiet beach has bathrooms and outdoor showers. Enjoy a late-afternoon picnic as waves crash, the sun falls and the kids play in a protected *keiki* pool (best at high tide). Never mind the airplanes.

Natural Energy Laboratory of Hawaii Authority BUILDING

(Map p218; Nelha; www.nelha.org; Abalone Farm Tour & Tasting adult/student & senior $18/15) That funny-looking building with the gigantic solar panels on Hwy 19 is Nelha's visitor center and crown jewel: the **Hawaii Gateway Energy Center** (Map p218). This 'zero-net energy facility' was voted one of the 10 greenest buildings in the country by the American Institute of Architects in 2007. Learn about OTEC and other research and technologies at Nelha's **public lectures** (329-8073; adult/student & senior $8/5; 10am-noon Mon-Thu); reservations required.

The **Abalone Farm Tour & Tasting** follows the lecture on Monday, Wednesday and Thursday; the **Solar Thermal Plant Tour** follows the lecture on Tuesday.

Today Nelha also sponsors a variety of commercial ventures, including aquaculture production of *ogo* (seaweed), algae and black pearls. One of Nelha's tenants is a Japanese company that desalinates pristine Hawaiian seawater and sells it as a tonic in Japan. Their huge ponds are hard to miss. Also here is **Ocean Rider Seahorse Farm** (Map p218; 329-6840; www.oceanrider.com; 73-4388 Ilikai Place; tours adult/child $36/26; tours Mon-Fri noon & 2pm), the only one of its kind in the country. Kids love it. Buy tickets in advance.

The signed turnoff to Nelha is between mile markers 94 and 95.

Pine Trees SURFING

(Map p218; 6am-8pm) Pine Trees, one of West Hawai'i's best surfing breaks, is just south of Nelha. Why Pine Trees? Early surfers spied mangrove trees near the break, which they thought were pines. No mangroves (or pines) are visible today, but the name stuck.

The break stretches along a pretty beach that is rocky enough to make swimming difficult. There is surf at a number of points depending on the tide and swell. The final bay gets the most consistent yet more forgiving waves. An incoming midtide is favorable, but as the swell picks up in winter these breaks often close out. This place attracts a crowd, so if you plan to paddle out, respect the priority of locals.

When the access road to Nelha veers to the right, look left for a rutted dirt road leading about 2 miles further south to Pine Trees. You need a high-clearance 4WD to make it, or you can walk, but it's hot. Gates close between 8pm and 6am.

Kekaha Kai State Park

The gorgeous beaches of **Kekaha Kai** (www.hawaiistateparks.org; 9am-7pm) are all the more memorable for being tucked on the far side of a vast desert of unforgiving black lava. This nearly undeveloped 1600-acre park has four beaches, only one of which has paved access. The others are best approached with a 4WD or on foot; but if you hike, come prepared with good shoes, food and lots of water. It can be brutally hot, and once you reach the sand you'll want to stay till the last drop of sunlight.

The park is 11 miles north of Kailua-Kona.

Beaches

Mahai'ula Beach BEACH

(Map p218) The park's largest, this rough, salt-and-pepper-sand beach is not great for swimming, but has good surfing during winter swells and kayaking is possible year-round. The beach has shaded picnic tables and pit toilets. Walk a few minutes north along the coast to a second, less rocky, curved tan beach with soft sand (called Magoon's) that is perfect for sunning and swimming.

Mahai'ula Beach is at the end of the park's main entrance – a ragged 1.5-mile road between mile markers 90 and 91. You can trek out here or drive, but if you go by vehicle, a 4WD is recommended. The road has been improved and 2WD cars were making the trek during our visit but you'll want to drive very carefully. The end of this road is the junction for Makalawena and Makole'a Beaches.

★ **Makalawena Beach** BEACH
(Map p218) 'Maks,' as it is often called, is almost the picture-perfect definition of an isolated, off the beaten path and (occasionally) deserted beach. If what you're after is an almost deserted, postcard-perfect scoop of pristine white-sand beach, edged by ivy-covered dunes and cupping brilliant blue-green water (are you sold?), head here.

Just realize it takes a little effort. Before the parking lot for Mahai'ula, the road junction offers two choices: go south for Makole'a Beach, or go north for Makalawena Beach. You'll be heading north. The service road to Makalawena Beach is cabled off, so you have to park and walk. Either follow the service road or follow the coastline from Mahai'ula Beach (a much nicer route, but suspect to the tides) and aim for the abandoned red houses. A rougher but more reliable route is a mile-long trail that parallels the coast. Beware: there's stretches of nothing but nasty *'a'a*. You don't want to walk this path in sandals.

After the broiling hike, it's shocking to emerge at a series of idyllic, scalloped bays with almost-glowing velvety white sand. If it's midweek, you might be the only one here. The north cove is sandier and gentler, while the southern beach is unofficially a nude sunbathing spot; don't be shocked if you see folks in their birthday suits. Swimming is splendid, but the surf can get rough and there are rocks in the water. Bodyboarding and snorkeling are also attractive, and sea turtles sightings are common. Some like to rinse off in a brackish pond behind the southernmost cove. There is no official camping, but locals often do; they don't always appreciate out-of-town tenters.

Makole'a Beach BEACH
(Map p218) At the road junction, you can drive south to Makole'a Beach, but this section of road is definitely 4WD only; in fact, it's wise to park the 4WD after 900m, where coral marks the path to the ocean. You won't get lost walking: either follow the road or follow the coastline from Mahai'ula Beach and make for the lone tree.

Makole'a lacks shade and is too rocky for good swimming, this black-sand beach is most popular with local fisherman, but its beauty rewards those who make the effort.

Manini'owali Beach (Kua Bay) BEACH
(Map p218; 9am-7pm) Welcome to another vision of paradise: a crescent-shaped white-sand beach with perfect, sparkling turquoise waters that provides for first-rate swimming and bodyboarding (especially in winter), and even pretty decent snorkeling when waters are calm. But unlike Makalawena, a paved road leads right up to it. Thus Manini'owali draws major crowds, especially on weekends.

Arrive late and cars will be parked a half mile up the road. That's reason aplenty for locals to continue grumbling about the easy access the paved road provides. The parking area has bathrooms and showers.

To get here, take the paved road between mile markers 88 and 89 (north of the main Kekaha Kai entrance). Hikers will enjoy the scenic coastal trail from here to Kukio Beach.

Ka'upulehu

Once a thriving fishing village among many dotting this length of coast, Ka'upulehu was wiped out by the 1946 tsunami and abandoned until the Kona Village Resort opened here in 1965 (ironically and sadly, the resort closed indefinitely following damage sustained as a result of the 2011 tsunami in Japan). The luxurious Four Seasons Hualalai – the island's poshest – followed in 1996. By law, these and other resorts must provide public coastal access, meaning you can enjoy some fine beaches without the resort price tag. What you can't do is hit the links at the PGA-tour **Four Seasons Hualalai Course** (325-8000; www.fourseasons.com/hualalai/golf.html; 72-100 Kaupulehu Dr), designed by golfing legend Jack Nicklaus; it's for members and guests only.

Beaches

Kikaua Beach BEACH
(Map p218) On the south end of Kukio Bay, this beach is accessed through a private country club. This lovely, quiet, tree-shaded beach contains a protected cove where kids can swim and snorkel in bathtub-calm water; around the kiawe-covered point, sea turtles line up to nap. Both this and Kukio Beach have bathrooms, showers and drinking water.

Come early, as beach parking is limited to 28 stalls and can fill up. Access is via Kuki'o Nui Rd near mile marker 87; request a pass at the gate.

Kukio Beach BEACH
(Map p218) From Kikaua Beach, you can see (and walk to) the bay's northern Kukio Beach, which is within the grounds of the Four Seasons. This picture-perfect crescent of sand is great for swimming or lounging away an afternoon. You can follow a paved footpath north past some intriguing lava-rock coastline to another beach.

To drive here, turn onto the (unsigned) Ka'upulehu Rd between mile markers 87 and 86; go to the Four Seasons gate and request a beach pass. Public parking accommodates 50 cars and almost never fills up.

Sights

Ka'upuleho Cultural Center MUSEUM
(Map p218; ☎325-8520; Four Seasons Resort; ⏰8:30am-4pm Mon-Fri) FREE We give a lot of credit to the the Four Seasons for establishing this often-overlooked Native Hawaiian cultural center. Excellent, informative displays are organized around the center's collection of 11 original paintings by Hawaiian artist Herb Kawainui Kane, each depicting an important facet of traditional Hawaiian culture. In addition, each work is accompanied by a hands-on exhibit: shake an *'uli'uli* (feathered hula rattle), test the heft of a *kapa* (mulberry tree bark) beater and examine adze heads.

It's run by Hawaiian cultural practitioners who actively link the present with the past. The center holds classes (usually open to resort guests only), but they'll happily refer you to *kumu* (teachers) directly. At the Four Seasons gate, tell them you're visiting the center.

Sleeping

The Kona Village Resort was closed due to damage sustained by the March 2011 tsunami that devastated Japan. Plans for its reopening proceed slowly. Check the website for updates.

Four Seasons Resort Hualalai RESORT $$$
(Map p218; ☎800-819-5053, 325-8000; www.fourseasons.com/hualalai; 72-100 Ka'upulehu Dr; r $700-1700, ste from $1500;) It's no accident that the Hualalai is the island's only five-diamond resort. Those accolades are earned through lavish attention to detail (fresh orchids in every room, lava rock gardens, 42in TVs, kids' robes and crayons, and multimedia library) and top-flight service. The golf course, spa and lap pool are world class, plus there's a big, well-stocked snorkel tank, including manta rays. Garden units have wonderful outdoor showers.

Eating

Beach Tree Bar & Grill INTERNATIONAL $$
(Map p218; ☎325-8000; Four Seasons Resort Hualalai; lunch mains $12-18, dinner mains $15-36; ⏰11:30am-8:30pm) Do you know what's better than enjoying tangy ceviche or one of the island's best burgers on the breezy, beachside porch of the Beach Tree on a perfect Hawaiian day? Not much. Lord, does this kitchen know what it's doing. Thin-crust brick-oven pizzas come with toothsome toppings (try the Hamakua fungi or mac nut and gorgonzola creations) and sit alongside a variety of surf-and-turf delights, including a fierce paella

The setting is equal parts romantic and casual; sunset on the sofas accompanied by traditional Hawaiian music, cocktails and *pupu* is highly recommended.

'Ulu Ocean Grill HAWAII REGIONAL CUISINE $$$
(Map p218; ☎325-8000; mains $24-38; ⏰6:30am-11am & 5:30am-9pm daily) 'Ulu means 'breadfruit,' and the 'Ulu Grill is all about that local plant (the breadfruit chips are pretty great). Actually, the 'Ulu is about local plants in general, as well as locally sourced meat and fish; 70% of its menu comes from the Big Island. The atmosphere is fine dining, but fun fine dining, with glass-ball partitions and lots of local artwork.

And the food? It's presented as a mix of *makai* (sea) and *mauka* (mountain); the former may get you curried Kona mussels and lobster wonton soup, while the latter offers heirloom tomato salads and *liliko'i* barbecued wild boar. The cherry on this sundae (or toro on the rice) is an excellent 10-seat onsite sushi lounge.

It's located ocean-side between King's Pond & Sea Shell crescents

Hualalai Grille HAWAII REGIONAL CUISINE $$$
(Map p218; ☎325-8000; Golf Clubhouse, Four Seasons Resort Hualalai; mains $30-56; ⏰5:30am-9pm) Nicknamed the 19th Hole, the Hualalai Grille is the upscale, 'resort casual' dining option at the Four Seasons. Your menu basically runs from surf (sauteed yellowtail, pan roasted snapper) to turf (ribeyes, ribs and hanger steaks). The Grille offers some very fine fine-dining, but we tend to prefer the beachy ambience of the Beach Tree.

Kiholo Bay

With its pristine turquoise waters and shoreline fringed with coconut trees, **Kiholo Bay** (⌚7am-7pm) is yet another off-the-beaten-track Big Island beauty. It's more of a series of beaches than one contiguous stretch of sand.

The main beach (near the parking lot) is pebbly and swimming is fine when seas are calm. Follow a trail south (left if facing the water) over the lava to find secluded pockets of fine black sand and, further south, a coconut grove surrounding **Luahinewai** (Map p218), a pretty spring-fed pool.

Walking north (right if facing the water), low tide reveals tide pools that are popular feeding and napping grounds for sea turtles and offer plenty of snorkeling possibilities. Inland near the end of the gravel path is a **lava tube/Queen's Bath** filled with clear freshwater; adventurous swimmers can check it out. Rumor has it other tubes in the area are some of the longest in the island. Lots of folks stop here to wash off salt water, but please note there is an actual ecosystem within the pond, and coming in while wearing suncreen can harm said environment. Just past the Queen's bath is a sandy patch with a **keiki pool** perfect for the little ones.

Keep going north. You'll pass a gargantuan private estate with a yellow mansion and tennis courts, then a huge **Balinese house**. This estate was built in Indonesia, then taken apart and reassembed here. Keep a respectful distance from this private residence, then continue on to the north end of Kiholo.

You'll see more black sand fronted by smooth *pahoehoe* lava. Follow along a circular bay, crossing a bridge over a fishpond, and you'll come to **Wainanali'i Pond**, also known as the Blue Lagoon. Green sea turtles *love* this spot; on our last visit we saw no less than 10 sunbathing on the sand. You may see them swimming around if you want to snorkel, although the presence of freshwater stream outflow clouds underwater visibility.

To get to Kiholo, turn seaward on the unmarked, graded gravel road between mile markers 82 and 83. Follow the road for a mile, taking the left-hand fork and park at the roundhouse. An alternate way in, which we prefer for the scenery, is hiking from a trailhead located by a small, rocky parking lot just north of mile marker 81. Hike along the trail at the bottom of the lot for 20 to 30 minutes (bring water), and say hi to the goats. You'll pop out just north of the Balinese house. Kiholo is a popular camping spot for locals; just be aware that there's no potable water.

Keawaiki Beach (Map p218) is just north of Kiholo Bay. This secluded black-sand strand fronts the former estate of Francis I'i Brown, an influential 20th-century Hawaiian businessman. It's fine for swimming when calm, but wear reef shoes, as sea urchins like the rocks. To get here, park between mile markers 78 and 79 on Hwy 11; there's a small lot in front of a boulder-blocked gravel road. Walk the road to the estate's fence, then follow the trail to the right around the fence to the beach.

Finally Kiholo Bay does have the largest concentration of tiger sharks in the Big Island. Once in a blue moon someone is attacked, but we wouldn't worry, as the sharks tend to swim further offshore.

SOUTH KOHALA

What began in North Kona continues in South Kohala: the sometimes plumb-straight highway cuts through sweeping coastal plains; stark lava fields alternate with barren pastures, all baking under a relentless sun. Punctuating the drive, a series of sumptuous resorts have carved green oases at the water's edge on some of the island's best beaches – making their own beaches, if necessary.

In contrast to the very modern world of the resorts, South Kohala also contains numerous ancient Hawaiian sights. Apparently, the Kohala Coast (including North Kohala) was more populated then than now, and the region is packed with village sites, heiau, fishponds, petroglyphs and historic trails.

Waikoloa Resort Area

POP 4800

Among South Kohala's resort areas, the **Waikoloa Beach Resort** (www.waikoloabeachresort.com) is the most affordable and bustling. Its mega hotels and golf courses aren't as prestigious as those further up the coast, but it does offer two shopping malls and the lion's share of events.

Note that the Waikoloa Beach Resort is not Waikoloa Village, a residential community further inland. To get to the resort area,

South Kohala

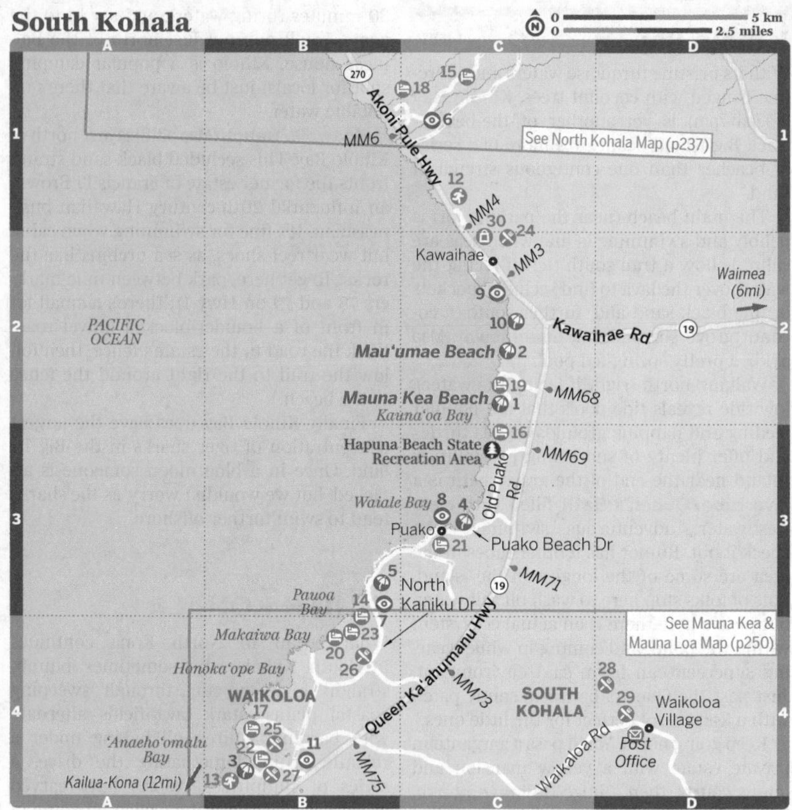

turn *makai* (seaward) just south of mile marker 76. To get to the village – for general services, such as a post office – turn *mauka* (mountainward) onto Waikoloa Rd north of mile marker 75.

Beaches

'Anaeho'omalu Beach Park BEACH

(Waikoloa Beach Dr; parking 6am-8pm) 'A Bay' boasts easy access, salt-and-pepper sand and calm waters; it's the only place suited to windsurfing on Hawai'i. Classically beautiful, it's backed by hundreds of palm trees and makes for fantastic sunset viewing. It's less crowded than Hapuna Beach further north, but it's not isolated by any stretch.

The Waikoloa Beach Marriott fronts the beach's north end, but **ancient fishponds** add a buffer zone between the two. In that area, there's decent snorkeling directly in front of the sluice gate, where you'll find coral formations, a fair variety of fish and possibly sea turtles. Drinking water, showers and restrooms are available.

'Anaeho'omalu was once the site of royal fishponds, and archaeologists have found evidence of human habitation here dating back more than 1000 years. A short footpath with interpretive plaques starts near the showers and passes fishponds, caves, ancient house platforms and a shrine.

To get here, turn left off Waikoloa Beach Dr opposite the Kings' Shops.

Sights & Activities

Waikoloa Petroglyph Preserve HISTORICAL SITE

(Waikoloa Beach Dr; admission free; dawn-dusk, tours 9:30am daily) FREE This collection of petroglyphs carved in lava rock is so easy-access that it merits a stop, although the Puako Petroglyph Preserve further north is larger and more spectacular and isn't adjacent to a shopping plaza pumping Taylor

South Kohala

Top Sights
1 Mauna Kea Beach ... C2
2 Mau'umae Beach ... C2

Sights
3 'Anaeho'omalu Beach Park ... B4
4 Beach 69 ... C3
Dolphin Quest ... (see 17)
5 Holoholokai Beach Park ... B3
Kalahuipua'a Fishponds ... (see 20)
Kalahuipua'a Historic Trail ... (see 20)
6 Pua Mau Place Botanic & Sculpture Garden ... C1
7 Puako Petroglyph Preserve ... B3
8 Puako Tide Pools ... C3
9 Pu'ukohola Heiau National Historic Site ... C2
10 Spencer Beach Park ... C2
11 Waikoloa Petroglyph Preserve ... B4

Activities, Courses & Tours
Francis I'i Brown North & South Golf Courses ... (see 20)
12 Hamakua Macadamia Nut Company ... C1
Hilton Waikoloa Village Pools ... (see 17)
Kohala Divers ... (see 30)
Mauna Lani Sea Adventures ... (see 20)
Mauna Lani Spa ... (see 20)
13 Ocean Sports ... B4
Spa Without Walls ... (see 14)
Waikoloa Beach & Kings' Courses ... (see 22)

Sleeping
14 Fairmont Orchid ... B4
15 Hale Ho'onanea ... C1
16 Hapuna Beach Prince Hotel ... C3
17 Hilton Waikoloa Village ... B4
18 Makai Hale ... C1
19 Mauna Kea Beach Hotel ... C2
20 Mauna Lani Bay Hotel & Bungalows ... B4
21 Puako B&B ... C3
22 Waikoloa Beach Marriott ... B4
23 Waikoloa Beach Resort ... B4

Eating
24 Blue Dragon Musiquarium ... C2
Brown's Beach House ... (see 14)
Café Pesto ... (see 30)
CanoeHouse ... (see 20)
Foodland Farms ... (see 26)
25 Kings' Shops ... B4
Kohala Burger & Taco ... (see 30)
Merriman's Market Café ... (see 25)
26 Monstera ... B4
27 Queens' Marketplace ... B4
Sansei Seafood Restaurant & Sushi Bar ... (see 27)
Waikoloa Kings' Shops Farmers Market ... (see 25)
28 Waikoloa Village Farmers Market ... D4
29 Waikoloa Village Market ... D4

Drinking & Nightlife
Luana Lounge ... (see 14)

Entertainment
Gathering of the Kings ... (see 14)
Legends of the Pacific ... (see 17)
Mauna Kea Hawaiian Luau ... (see 19)
Waikoloa Beach Marriott Sunset Luau ... (see 22)

Shopping
30 Kawaihae Shopping Center ... C2

Swift. Many of the petroglyphs date back to the 16th century; some are graphic (humans, birds, canoes) and others cryptic (dots, lines). Western influences appear in the form of horses and English initials.

Park at the Kings' Shops mall and walk for five minutes on the signposted path. Never touch or walk on the petroglyphs. Kings' Shops offers a free one-hour **petroglyph tour**; meet at the shopping center stage.

Ocean Sports WATERSPORTS
(☎888-724-5924, 886-6666; www.hawaiioceansports.com; 69-275 Waikoloa Beach Dr) Ocean Sports, established in 1981, monopolizes the ocean-activity market in South Kohala. Fortunately the company is well run, if slightly steep in its pricing. Cruises include whale watching ($119) and snorkeling tours ($147) aboard a 49-passenger catamaran. Kids between six and 12 years of age pay half price. Cruises depart from either 'Anaeho'omalu Bay or Kawaihae Harbor.

Waikoloa Beach & Kings' Courses GOLF
(☎886-7888; www.waikoloabeachgolf.com; 69-275 Waikoloa Beach Dr, Waikoloa Beach Marriott; guest/non-guest $135/165) The Waikoloa Beach Marriott boasts two of Hawaii's top golf courses: the coastal Beach course is known for its par-five 12th hole; the Kings' course is a little more challenging and offers Scottish-style links. Tee off later and pay less (11:30am/1pm/2pm $115/105/85). Carts are mandatory.

ANCIENT HAWAIIAN ART

Ancient Hawaiians carved *ki'i pohaku* (stone images), called petroglyphs, into *pahoehoe* (smooth lava). These mysterious carvings are most common on the Big Island, perhaps because – as the youngest island – it has the most extensive fields of *pahoehoe*. The simple images include human figures, animals and important objects such as canoes and sails. No one can prove why the Hawaiians made *ki'i pohaku* or placed them where they did. Many petroglyph fields are found along major trails or on the boundaries of *ahupua'a* (land divisions).

In addition to the Waikoloa petroglyphs, a large field remains further north along the South Kohala coast in Puako; they're also found at Hawai'i Volcanoes National Park.

Touching the petroglyphs will damage them, so never step on or make rubbings of them. Photography is fine and best done in the early morning or late afternoon, when the sun is low.

Star Gaze Hawaii STARGAZING
(☎323-3481; www.stargazehawaii.com; adult & child over 12yr/child 5-11yr $30/15; ⌚Fairmont Orchid 7:30-8:30pm Fri, Hapuna Beach Prince Hotel 8-9pm Sun & Wed, Hilton Waikoloa Village 8-9pm Tue & Thu) Take advantage of Kohala's consistently clear night skies and join professional astronomers in identifying stars using a high-powered telescope.

Dolphin Quest SWIMMING
(☎800-248-3316, 886-2875; www.dolphinquest.com; 425 Waikoloa Beach Dr, Hilton Waikoloa Village; per person from $210, family encounter $1400; ⌚9am-4pm; P) Minds differ on whether 'dolphin encounters' are good or bad. Judging by the popularity of this program, however, many willingly pay big bucks to meet this adored sea creature face to face; $210 buys you but 30 minutes of dolphin time.

Hilton Waikoloa Village Pools SWIMMING
(☎800-221-2424, 886-1234; www.hiltonwaikoloavillage.com; 425 Waikoloa Beach Dr; nonguest pool pass up to 4 people $90; 👪) Chances are, the pools at this over-the-top resort will thrill your kids. Besides the two ridiculously enormous serpentine pools (with multiple waterslides, waterfalls, hot tubs and sandy toddler areas), there's also an artificial beach on a protected lagoon (frequented by sea turtles and tropical fish) and a minigolf course. Parking per day self/valet is $15/21.

Festivals & Events

A Taste of the Hawaiian Range FOOD
(www.tasteofthehawaiianrange.com; Hilton Waikoloa Village; admission advance/door $40/60) Celebrated Big Island chefs work magic with local range-fed meats and local produce in late September or early October.

Moku O Keawe HULA
(www.mokif.com; Waikoloa Resort Area; admission per night $7-20) This early-November hula competition includes *kahiko* (ancient), *'auana* (modern) and *kupuna* (elder) categories. Set on an outdoor lawn, the vibe is international, with troupes from Japan and the US mainland.

Sleeping

Waikoloa Beach Marriott HOTEL **$$$**
(☎888-924-5656, 886-6789; www.waikoloabeachmarriott.com; 69-275 Waikoloa Beach Dr; r $200-450; P ❄ @ ᯤ ≋) The Hilton might be Waikoloa's glamour gal, but the Marriott is the solid girl next door. This airy, 555-room hotel is rather standard in design, but it fronts 'Anaeho'omalu Bay and thus boasts an awesome beach setting, plus three oceanfront pools. Rooms feature quality beds (down comforters and 300-count linens), tastefully muted decor and the expected amenities, from cable TV to refrigerator.

Internet access is wi-fi in public areas and wired in rooms. Expect a $20 'resort fee' for parking, phone, internet and other essentials. Book ahead for deep discounts.

Hilton Waikoloa Village HOTEL **$$$**
(☎800-221-2424, 886-1234; www.hiltonwaikoloavillage.com; 425 Waikoloa Beach Dr; r $225-540, ste from $720; P ❄ @ ᯤ ≋) You'll either love or hate the showy, theme-park features of this 62-acre megahotel. There's no natural beach, so its glamour is manmade. Rooms are comfy enough, but they're standard business class, not luxury (nothing's oceanfront either) – and no additional facilities (internet access, gym, kitchen appliances) are included in the nightly rate.

A monorail and covered boats let you navigate the sprawling grounds without scuffing your flip-flops, while kids splash aboard kayaks in waveless artificial waterways. There's visual interest everywhere, from a giant Buddha sculpture near the lobby to interesting collections of Polynesian and Asian art pieces or replicas along sidewalks.

It's an additional $15/21 per day for self/valet parking.

Eating

Increase your dining options beyond resort fare at two Waikoloa shopping malls: **Kings' Shops** (www.kingsshops.com; 250 Waikoloa Beach Dr), with two destination restaurants, and **Queens' MarketPlace** (www.waikoloabeachresort.com; 201 Waikoloa Beach Dr), with one big-name sushi bar, plus budget-saving food-court fare (including Subway, Dairy Queen and Arby's).

Merriman's Market Café MEDITERRANEAN **$$**
(☎886-1700; www.merrimanshawaii.com; Kings' Shops; mains $20-30; ⊙11:30am-9:30pm) Foodies from sophisticated cities might find the Mediterranean-inspired fare here unremarkable, but the kitchen does feature organic island-grown produce and fresh local fish. Lunch is better value, with salads, sandwiches, pizzas and pastas from $12 to $18.

Sansei Seafood Restaurant & Sushi Bar JAPANESE, FUSION **$$$**
(☎886-6286; www.sanseihawaii.com; Queens' MarketPlace; mains $25-50, sushi $4-22; ⊙5:30-10pm) Local celebrity chef DK Kodama will surprise you with innovative, fusion cuisine, from Dungeness-crab ramen in truffle broth to *panko*-crusted (Japanese breadcrumbs) ahi (yellowfin tuna) sushi. His succulent dry-aged beef ups the ante for a great steak. There's an extensive wine list, compliments of master sommelier Chuck Furuya, and fantastic early-bird discounts.

Waikoloa Village Market SUPERMARKET
(☎883-1088; 68-3916 Paniolo Ave, Waikoloa Highlands Center; ⊙6am-9pm) Located *mauka* (inland) of the highway in Waikoloa Village, this branch of the excellent KTA chain is a full-service grocery store with deli, bakery and ATM.

Waikoloa Village Farmers Market MARKET
(Paniolo Ave, Waikoloa Community Church; ⊙7-10am Sat) Located on inland side of the highway, in the residential Waikoloa Village community. Farmers from around the way sell produce at this local event.

Waikoloa Kings' Shops Farmers Market MARKET
(Kings' Shops; ⊙8:30am-3pm Wed) Features 100% locally grown and produced edibles (no crafts). Come for fresh seasonal produce, honey, baked goods, coffee, tea and orchids.

☆ Entertainment

For nightlife, check the **Waikoloa Nights** (www.waikoloanights.com) website for special events from rock concerts to hula shows. Concerts also regularly go down in the Kings' Shops and Queens' Marketplace. There are two ongoing luau shows in Waikoloa.

Legends of the Pacific LUAU
(☎886-1234; www.hiltonwaikoloavillage.com/dining/luau.cfm; Hilton Waikoloa Village; adult/child 5-12yr/senior & teen 13-18yr $109/54/99; ⊙5:30pm Tue, Fri & Sun) The Legends of the Pacific luau show features various South Pacific dances and includes a dinner buffet and one cocktail.

Waikoloa Beach Marriott Sunset Luau LUAU
(☎886-6789; www.waikoloabeachmarriott.com; Waikoloa Beach Marriott; adult/child 5-12yr $100/40; ⊙5pm Wed & Sat) This poolside luau is the typical commercial show with Hawaiian-style dinner buffet, open bar and Polynesian dances. The setting by 'Anaeho'omalu Bay is a plus.

Mauna Lani Resort Area

The Mauna Lani Resort Area superficially resembles its neighbors, with high-end hotels, condos and golf courses. But it deserves special attention for its significant historical sites and for the Mauna Lani Bay Hotel & Bungalows' refreshingly open attitude toward nonguests who come to explore its trails and fishponds.

Beaches

The best beaches for swimming or snorkeling are small and located around the two large hotels.

The beach fronting the Mauna Lani Bay Hotel & Bungalows is protected and relatively calm, but the water is shallow. Just 10 minutes south of the hotel by foot, in **Makaiwa Bay**, there's a small, calm lagoon fronting the Mauna Lani Beach Club condo.

To get here, park at the hotel and walk south along the path past the fishponds.

One mile south of the hotel (at the boundary of the overall resort area), there's a small salt-and-pepper beach at **Honoka'ope Bay**. When seas are calm, swimming and snorkeling are fine but not fantastic. Walk here by an old coastal trail or drive toward the golf courses and turn left at Honoka'ope Pl.

Located at the Fairmont Orchid, **Pauoa Bay** is an excellent, little-known snorkeling spot, but is accessible to guests of the hotel only.

Holoholokai Beach Park BEACH

Forget about sand and gentle waves here. Instead enjoy picnicking and strolling at this pleasantly uncrowded beach, blanketed by chunks of white coral and black lava. On the calmest days, the waters are fine for snorkeling. Facilities include restrooms, showers, drinking water, picnic tables and grills.

To get here, take Mauna Lani Dr and veer right at the circle; turn right on the marked road immediately before the Fairmont Orchid. The Puako petroglyphs are accessed from the park.

Sights

Puako Petroglyph Preserve HISTORIC SITE

With more than 3000 petroglyphs, this preserve is among the largest collections of ancient lava carvings in Hawaii. The simple pictures might not make sense to you, but viewed altogether they are fascinating and worth a visit.

The 1200m walk from Holoholokai Beach Park to the preserve adds to the experience: take the easy, well-marked Malama trail at the *mauka* (inland) side of the park.

Kalahuipua'a Historic Trail HISTORIC SITE

(68-1400 Mauna Lani Dr, Mauna Lani Bay Hotel & Bungalows; P) FREE This easy trail starts on the hotel's inland side, at a marked parking lot opposite the resort's little grocery store.

The first part of the historic trail meanders through a former Hawaiian settlement that dates from the 16th century, passing **lava tubes** once used as cave shelters and a few other archaeological and geological sites marked by interpretive plaques. Keep a watchful eye out for quail, northern and red-crested cardinals, saffron finches and Japanese white-eyes.

The trail then skirts ancient **fishponds** lined with coconut palms and continues out to the beach, where you'll find a thatched shelter with an outrigger canoe and a **historic cottage** with a few Hawaiian artifacts on display. If you continue southwest past the cottage, you can loop around the fishpond and back to your starting point (for a round-trip of about 1.5 miles).

Kalahuipua'a Fishponds HISTORIC SITE

These ancient fishponds are among the island's few remaining working fishponds and, as in ancient times, they're stocked with *'awa* (Hawaiian milk fish). Water circulates from the ocean through traditional *makaha* (sluice gates), which allow small fish to enter, but keep mature, fattened catch from escaping.

To access the fishponds directly (without taking the trail), exit the hotel lobby and go south toward the beach. They lie partly under a shady grove of coconut palms and milo (native hardwood) trees.

Activities

Mauna Lani Sea Adventures WATERSPORTS

(☎885-7883; www.hawaiiseaadventures.com; 68-1400 Mauna Lani Dr, Mauna Lani Bay Hotel & Bungalows; snorkeling tour adult & child/child 3-12 Wed & Sun $99/45, whale-watching cruise $85/45) This outfit offers three-hour morning snorkeling cruises five mornings per week; the fee applies to all, but kids pay half price on Sundays and Wednesdays. From mid-December to mid-April, 1½-hour whale-watching cruises run five afternoons per week.

Mauna Lani Sea Adventures is also the main dive operator (two-tank dive $160) here. Although Kailua-Kona is the Big Island's hub for scuba diving, the waters off Mauna Lani are perhaps even better (and also much less crowded). Divemasters are competent, friendly and flexible. Well-regarded certification courses also offered.

Francis I'i Brown North & South Golf Courses GOLF

(☎885-6655; 68-1400 Mauna Lani Dr, Mauna Lani Bay Hotel & Bungalows; guest/nonguest $160/265) The two Mauna Lani courses are among the island's top world-class golf courses. The South Course is more scenic and popular, with its signature 15th hole featuring a tee shot over crashing surf. The North Course is more challenging and interesting, however, with a par-three 17th hole within an amphitheater of black lava rock. Discounts for online bookings and twilight tee times.

Mauna Lani Spa SPA
(☎881-7922; www.maunalani.com; 68-1400 Mauna Lani Dr, Mauna Lani Bay Hotel & Bungalows; massages & facials from $159; ⏲treatments 10am-4pm) A vast indoor/outdoor space landscaped with exotic tropical flora and lava-rock sauna. Treatments are pricey, perhaps overpriced; choose something Hawaiian (eg *lomilomi* or hot stones) for the memory.

Spa Without Walls SPA
(☎887-7540; www.fairmont.com/orchid; 1 North Kaniku Dr, Fairmont Orchid; massages & facials from $169; ⏲7am-6pm) Treatments can be done in alfresco *hale* (house), hidden amid orchids, coconut palms, waterfalls, streams and lily ponds. Treatments feature botanicals from Kona coffee to *matcha* green tea. Like Mauna Lani Spa, this facility is upscale if not quite luxurious.

Festivals & Events

Kona Chocolate Festival FOOD
(☎987-8722; www.konachocolatefestival.com; Fairmont Orchid; ⏲late Mar/early Apr) The Kona Chocolate Festival is a three-day celebration of (surprise!) all things chocolate. It includes a 'chocolate symposium' of workshops and culminates in a gala evening celebration, with live music and a chocolate cook-off among island chefs. Check the website for updates on location.

Sleeping

Mauna Lani Bay Hotel & Bungalows HOTEL $$$
(☎800-367-2323, 885-6622; www.maunalani.com; 68-1400 Mauna Lani Dr; r $400-950; P ❄ 📶 🏊) Among the top South Kohala resorts, the Mauna Lani offers a wonderfully Hawaiian atmosphere. The parklike grounds feature landscaped tropical gardens, hundreds of towering coconut palms and precious historic sites, and the staff is exceptionally courteous and committed to Hawaiian culture. Rooms are modern in amenities and decor; 90% are oceanfront or ocean-view.

Rates include basic services (eg parking, phone, high-speed internet access), so there are no extra charges. This ecoconscious resort uses solar power for its daytime water-pumping needs, drought-resistant grass for the golf greens and recycled water for irrigation. It even raises endangered green sea turtles on-site.

Fairmont Orchid HOTEL $$$
(☎866-54004474, 885-2000; www.fairmont.com/orchid-hawaii; 1 North Kaniku Dr; r $360-700; P ❄ @ 📶 🏊) Elegant and almost formal (for Hawai'i), the Orchid never lets you forget that you're at an exclusive, luxury hotel. The architecture feels more continental than overtly Hawaiian, but the meticulously maintained grounds are buoyantly tropical. Rooms are quite posh, and the spa and restaurants are first-rate, adding to the pampering quality. Amenities, such as inroom internet access ($14.50 per day), are rather pricey. Self/valet parking is an additional $17/22 per day.

Eating

Monstera JAPANESE $$
(☎887-2711; www.monsterasushi.com; 68-1330 Mauna Lani Dr; plates $12-30, sushi rolls $9-25; ⏲5:30-10pm) This excellent *izakaya* (Japanese pub) venue offers a range of Japanese goodness, from classic *nigiri* (oblong-shaped sushi) and seared tuna *tataki* (quickly marinated and seared) to sizzling plates of kimchi-stir-fried pork loin and teriyaki chicken. The fresh ingredients and friendly service often attract repeat customers.

Brown's Beach House HAWAII REGIONAL CUISINE $$$
(☎887-7368; 1 North Kaniku Dr, Fairmont Orchid; mains $40-57; ⏲5:30-8:30pm Thu-Mon, til 9pm Tues & Wed) The prices might deter you but, otherwise, this oceanfront gem is virtually faultless. The service is gracious and the menu is practically a circle-island tour of the best of Hawai'i's local ingredients. Standouts include the Kohala ceviche and 'Sustainable Seafood Trio,' three types of fish from the Kona Coast.

CanoeHouse HAWAII REGIONAL CUISINE $$$
(☎881-7911; 68-1400 Mauna Lani Dr, Mauna Lani Bay Hotel & Bungalows; mains $35-44; ⏲6-9pm) The Mauna Lani's fanciest restaurant is lovely all round, with an oceanfront setting and a menu that highlights seafood and local ingredients. Salt-and-pepper snapper makes a delicious main following some local island goat-cheese, while the sweet-potato cheesecake had us gasping for more.

Foodland Farms SUPERMARKET
(☎887-6101; 68-1330 Mauna Lani Dr, Shops at Mauna Lani; ⏲6am-11pm) Full-service gourmet supermarket with an impressive deli selection that will please foodies.

Hawai'i the Big Island

The Big Island, larger than all of the other Hawaiian islands combined, contains a staggering diversity of landscapes. Moonscape lava deserts spread across the western side of the island, while thick groves of hardwood jungle cling to black sea cliffs in the east, all separated by snow-capped Mauna Kea.

1

WAYNE LEVIN / GETTY IMAGES ©

SCOTT DARSNEY / GETTY IMAGES ©

1. **Holei Sea Arch (p296)**
This rock arch has been carved out of the *pali* (cliffs) by the elements.

2. **Kealakekua Bay (p211)**
Incredible snorkeling awaits at Ka'awaloa Cove in Kealakekua Bay State Historical Park.

3. **Lava Flows (p295)**
See fire meet water as lava flows reach the ocean from Kilauea's Pu'u O'o vent.

4. **Halema'uma'u Crater (p293)**
Take a hike with a difference in Hawai'i Volcanoes National Park and see Kilauea in action.

TOSHI SASAKI / GETTY IMAGES ©

Drinking & Nightlife

For evening drinks (and a more affordable dinner), try an oceanfront bar at any resort restaurant. The **Luana Lounge** (885-2000; 1 North Kaniku Dr, Fairmont Orchid; 4-11pm) at the Fairmont is a great spot for catching a sunset and admiring local artwork.

Entertainment

Gathering of the Kings LUAU
(326-4969; http://ibphawaii.com/luaus; Fairmont Orchid; adult/child 6-12yr $99/65; Sat check-in at 4.30pm) This luau spins a thread of storytelling to highlight slightly modernized versions of Polynesian and Hawaiian dance and music; it's notable for its above average Polynesian dinner buffet and an open bar.

Puako

POP 772

Standing in contrast to the mega-resorts to the south, Puako is essentially a mile-long row of homes. The single road through 'town' is marked with numerous 'shoreline access' points. To get here, turn *makai* (seaward) down Puako Beach Dr between mile markers 70 and 71.

Heading towards Puako 'town' you'll pass the **Hokuloa United Church** on your right. This may be the cutest little white seaside church on the Big Island. Originally built in 1860, the structure fell apart and was then restored in 1990.

Beaches

The clear waters and shallow reef of Puako Bay are great for kayaking, snorkeling and diving. Rent kayaks from Plenty Pupule Adventure Sports (p200) down the coast in Honokohau Harbor. As you drive down Puako's main drag, keep an eye out for signed shoreline access points. Pull over, and boom, there's a new beach for you to explore.

Beach 69 BEACH
(Waialea Bay; 7am-8pm;) This lovely crescent of white sand is a local favorite but remains somewhat off the tourist radar. Both family- and gay-friendly, this beach is less crowded than Hapuna Beach, and its calm, protected waters are ideal for morning snorkeling. Around the boundary, shady trees provide welcome relief. Rest rooms and showers are available; no lifeguards.

From Puako Beach Dr, take the first right turn onto Old Puako Rd. Find telephone pole No 71 to the left and park. Follow the 'road' to its end, and then tramp along the footpath that runs parallel to a wooden fence. In case you're wondering, telephone pole No 71 was once numbered No 69, which gave the beach its nickname. You can also drive here from the Hapuna Beach parking lot

Sights & Activities

Puako Tide Pools LANDMARK
Puako is known for giant tide pools, set in the swirls and dips of the *pahoehoe* coastline. Some pools are deep enough to shelter live coral and other marine life. There's no sandy beach, but a narrow strip of pulverized coral and lava covers the shore.

To get to the pools, park along the road near one of six signposted 'beach access' paths. The easiest access is the southernmost path: go to the south end of the village and stop just before the 'Road Closed 500 Feet' sign. Take the short dirt road toward a small cove that's used for snorkeling and shore diving; note that the surf is generally too rough in winter. A couple of minutes' walk north brings you to a few petroglyphs, a board for *konane* (a game similar to checkers) chinked into the lava, and tide pools deep enough to cool off in.

Kohala Divers DIVING
(882-7774; www.kohaladivers.com; 61-3665 Akoni Pule Hwy; 1-/2-/3-tank dive $100/139/239; 8am-6pm) This dive outfit, based out of Kawaihae to the north, leads excellent diving trips across Kohala, includng the Puako area. One of the best trips is to a local sea turtle 'cleaning' station, where *honu* allow fish to pick parasites off their bodies.

Sleeping

It seems every other home in Puako is available as a vacation rental; see www.hawaiianbeachrentals.com and www.2papayas.com for listings.

★**Puako B&B** B&B $$
(800-910-1331, 882-1331; www.bigisland-bedbreakfast.com; 25 Puako Beach Dr; r $100-155, ste $175;) For both proximity to South Kohala beaches and a personal touch, make this inviting B&B your home base. Rooms are tastefully appointed with Hawaiian motifs, and guests are welcome to use the kitchen. The best options are the largest three, each with private sliding doors to the garden.

Proprietor Paul 'Punahele' Andrade, who grew up in this very house, is a *kumu hula* (certified hula teacher) who will gladly introduce you to Hawaiian and local culture. Rates include breakfast.

Hapuna Beach State Recreation Area

Hapuna Beach is world-famous for its magnificent, screen-saver worthy half-mile sweep of white powder sand and crystal-clear waters. Water conditions vary depending on the season; in summer waves are calm and allow good swimming, snorkeling and diving – though bear in mind, the fish population has woefully declined since the 1980s. When the surf's up in winter, the bodyboarding is awesome and the surf is reliable – the best swells tend to come from the northwest. In general, Hapuna waters are too choppy for tots or nonswimmers. Remember that waves over 3ft should be left for the experts; drownings are not uncommon here.

Due to its drive-up access and popularity, the restrooms and picnic area at this **state recreation area** (gate 7am-8pm; P) can be crowded and, at worst, grungy. Still, facilities do include pay phones, drinking water, showers, restrooms and a picnic area. Lifeguards are on duty.

To get here, take Hapuna Beach Rd just south of mile marker 69. Arrive early to snag a parking space and stake out a good spot. In 2011 the state was considering charging an entry fee for nonresidents, but a decision was still pending during research for this book. Bring industrial-strength sunscreen because there's little shade.

Outdoorsy types could bunk in one of the six state-owned **A-frame cabins** (per night residents/nonresidents $30/50) near the beach. The awesome location is perfect for sunset and moonrise watching. While run-down and makeshift for the price, the cabins are decently livable and each sleeps four people on wooden platforms (bring your own beddings). There are restrooms, showers and a cooking pavilion with a stove and fridge.

Mauna Kea Resort Area

The Mauna Kea may not have the historical heritage of resorts to the south, but it does have proximity to two of the Big Island's great beaches. Development here began when the late Laurance Rockefeller obtained a 99-year lease on the land around Kauna'oa Bay. 'Every great beach deserves a great hotel,' Rockefeller apparently said. Not everyone would agree, but he got his way here.

For dining options beyond hotel fare, head to Waimea, Kawaihae or the Waikoloa Resort Area for more variety.

Beaches

★Mauna Kea Beach BEACH

Laurance Rockefeller picked a winner in this picture-perfect beach, unofficially named after the hotel flanking it. Crescent-shaped **Kauna'oa Bay** is blanketed in powdery white sand, while the clear waters are calm and shallow (generally less than 10ft). Snorkeling is only average near the shore; go to the north end along the rocky ledge.

Best of all, the beach is never crowded. It is open to the public, but the hotel sets aside only 40 parking spaces daily for nonguests. Arrive by 9am and obtain a parking pass at the entry booth.

★Mau'umae Beach BEACH

White sand, teal water, shady trees and protected waters – and it's even more private and local than Kauna'oa Bay. What's not to love about Mau'umae? Locals are proprietary about this gem (for good reason). There's great snorkeling on either end of the bay. Only 10 parking spots are given out here, so arrive by 9am on weekdays, and possibly earlier on weekends.

To get here, go toward the Mauna Kea Beach Hotel, turn right on Kamahoi and cross two wooden bridges. Look for telephone pole No 22 on the left and park (you'll probably see a bunch of cars parked). Walk down the trail to the Ala Kahakai sign and turn left toward the beach. You can also get here from nearby Spencer Beach by walking 10 minutes on the Ala Kahakai Trail.

Activities

Ala Kahakai Trail HIKING

Here's another way to access Kauna'oa Bay: on foot. A 6-mile stretch of the 175-mile Ala Kahakai historical trail passes many of South Kohala's signature beaches. You'll also cover pristine shoreline and natural anchialine ponds impossible to see from the highway.

You can start at any point along the way; from the north, start at the southern end of Spencer Beach Park, where you'll pass thick kiawe groves until you reach Mau'umae

SACRED SITES

Ancient Hawaiians built a variety of heiau for different gods and different purposes: healing the sick, sharing the harvest, changing the weather, offering human sacrifice and succeeding in warfare. Some heiau were modest thatched structures, but others were enormous stone edifices.

Today the eroded ruins of heiau, found across the Hawaiian Islands, often only hint at their original grandeur. After Liholiho (Kamehameha II) abolished the kapu (taboo) system in 1819, many were destroyed or abandoned. But on the Big Island, two of the largest and best-preserved heiau remain: the war temple Pu'ukohola Heiau (p235) and sacrificial temple Mo'okini Luakini Heiau (p239).

The war temples were typically massive platforms built with boulders, plus covered shelters for kahuna (priests), ceremonial drums and idols of the temple's patron god. The larger the heiau, the more threatening it appeared to enemies. Indeed, the sheer magnitude of Pu'ukohola Heiau, built during Kamehameha the Great's rise to power, foreshadowed his ultimate conquest of the Hawaiian Islands.

Luakini heiau (temples of human sacrifice) were always dedicated to Ku, the war god. Only Ku deserved the greatest gift, a human life, and only the highest chiefs could order it. But human sacrifice was not taken lightly; typically people gave offerings of food to Ku. The actual act of killing was not a necessary ritual; an enemy slain in battle was acceptable. But the victim had to be a healthy man – never a woman, a child or an aged or deformed man.

Beach and eventually the Mauna Kea Resort Area, including the renowned golf course. After you navigate the Hapuna Beach Prince Hotel and then the beach, the trail continues down to Beach 69. The whole hike, especially the last leg, is scorching. Of course, you can turn back at any point. Wear strong sun protection, bring water and expect to sweat.

Mauna Kea & Hapuna Golf Courses GOLF
(☎880-3000, 882-5400; www.princeresortshawaii.com; Mauna Kea Beach Hotel, Hapuna Beach Prince Hotel; Mauna Kea course guest/nonguest $225/250, Hapuna course guest/nonguest $225/250) Golfers dream about playing the combined 36 holes of these two premier courses. The Mauna Kea course is a 72-par championship course that consistently ranks among the top courses in the USA. Designed by Robert Trent Jones Sr, it was remodeled in 2008 by his son, Rees Jones. The Hapuna course has a 700ft elevation gain and was designed by Arnold Palmer and Ed Seay.

Sleeping

Room rates vary significantly by season.

Hapuna Beach Prince Hotel HOTEL **$$**
(☎880-1111, 888-977-4623; www.princeresortshawaii.com; 62-100 Kauna'oa Dr; r $200-500; ❄📶🏊) The Mauna Kea Beach Hotel's 'sister' resort, open since 1994, boasts an ideal location on Hapuna Beach and affordable rates. The rooms are clean, spacious and come with large bathrooms, although decor is a little dated and sometimes worn. This hotel caters to Japanese tourists and even has a bilingual concierge desk. It shares amenities with the Mauna Kea, and buses transport guests between the two.

Mauna Kea Beach Hotel HOTEL **$$$**
(☎866-977-4589, 882-7222; www.maunakeabeachhotel.com; 62-100 Mauna Kea Beach Dr; r $325-760; P❄📶🏊) The grand dame of the Gold Coast is understated and quietly confident of its reputation. At first glance it might not wow you, but there is history here; guests are often returnees (some for decades) and staff includes many longtimers. Mountain and Golf view rooms are tastefully understated, while the beach front and beach club rooms blend austere yet elegant touches in the form of hardwoods and swatches of color (not to mention shady lanai). The hotel's crowning jewel, however, is simply its location on Kauna'oa Bay, arguably the best beach on the island

Entertainment

Mauna Kea Hawaiian Luau LUAU
(☎882-5707; www.princeresortshawaii.com; 62-100 Mauna Kea Beach Drive; adult/child 5-12yr $96/48; ⏲6pm Tue & Fri) This outdoor luau show features standard entertainment (thrilling fire dance, group hula) and a

gorgeous beach setting. Buffet is generous and above average; drinks are stiff but exorbitant at $15 each.

Kawaihae & Around

Kawaihae marks the transition point from the dry, rocky resorty part of Kohala to its more residential and rainy side (although Kawaihae itself is still in the dry zone). It's a drab port, where fuel tanks and cargo containers give off an industrial vibe, but there's great food, a family beach and historic heiau toward the south.

Beaches

Spencer Beach Park BEACH

Shallow, sandy and gentle, this beach doesn't have the dramatic sweep of Mauna Kea or Hapuna, but it is ideal for kids and popular with local families. Come to swim rather than to snorkel; the waters are slightly silty due to Kawaihae Harbor to the north.

Located off the Akoni Pule Hwy (Hwy 270) just north of mile marker 2, the park has a lifeguard, picnic tables, barbecue grills, restrooms, showers, drinking water and campsites. A footpath leads south to Mau'umae Beach.

The campsites are exposed and crowded together, but it's still the best camping beach north of Kona; a permit is required.

Sights & Activities

The waters of the Kohala Coast are pristine and teeming with marine life – and they're much less crowded. The reef here drops off more gradually than along the Kona Coast, so you'll probably see reef sharks, spinner dolphins, turtles and manta rays, but not large schools of tuna and other deepwater fish. Kohala is the oldest area of the Big Island: see lush coral growth and lots of lava tubes, arches and pinnacles. Contact Kohala Divers (p232) in Kawaihae's main shopping center for more information.

Pu'ukohola Heiau National Historic Site HISTORIC SITE

(☎882-7218; www.nps.gov/puhe; 62-3601 Kawaihae Rd; ⏰7:45am-4:45pm) FREE By 1790 Kamehameha the Great had conquered Maui, Lana'i and Moloka'i. But power over his home island of Hawai'i proved to be a challenge. When told by a prophet that he'd rule all the Islands if he built a heiau dedicated to his war god Kuka'ilimoku atop Pu'ukohola (Whale Hill) in Kawaihae, Kamehameha built Pu'ukohola Heiau.

It is believed that Kamehameha and his men formed a human chain 20 miles long, transporting rocks hand to hand from Pololu Valley in North Kohala. After finishing the heiau by summer 1791, Kamehameha held a dedication ceremony and invited his rival and cousin, Keoua, the chief of Ka'u. When Keoua came ashore, he was killed and taken to the *luakini* heiau (temple of human sacrifice) as the first offering to the gods. With Keoua's death, Kamehameha took sole control of the Big Island, eventually ruling all the Hawaiian Islands by 1810.

Back then Pu'ukohola Heiau was adorned with wooden *ki'i* and thatched structures, including an oracle tower, altar, drum house and shelter for the high priest. After Kamehameha's death in 1819, his son Liholiho and powerful widow Ka'ahumanu destroyed the deity images and the heiau was abandoned.

Today, only the basic rock foundation remains, but it's still a massive 224ft by 100ft, with 16ft to 20ft walls. Windswept and stark, it seems a fitting legacy of Kamehameha, whose name translates as 'the Lonely One.' To get here, turn *makai* (seaward) off the Akoni Pule Hwy halfway between mile markers 2 and 3.

Hamakua Macadamia Nut Company TOUR

(☎888-643-6688, 882-1690; www.hawnnut.com; 61-3251 Maluokalani St; ⏰8am-5pm) FREE Compared with the Hershey-owned Mauna Loa mac-nut headquarters near Hilo, this locally owned company is tiny. But the spanking-clean factory and gift shop are staffed by multigeneration locals who give tours, answer questions and otherwise emanate much aloha spirit. An ecoconscious company, it uses ground mac-nut shells (not fossil fuels) to steam-dry its nuts. Generous free samples.

Festivals

Ho'oku'ikahi Hawaiian Cultural Festival CULTURAL

(www.nps.gov/puhe; 62-3601 Kawaihae Rd, Pu'ukohola Heiau National Historic Site) Held in mid-August at Pu'ukohola Heiau, the tongue-twisting Ho'oku'ikahi Hawaiian Cultural Festival is a celebration of the folkways, traditions, arts and culture of Native Hawaiians. The public is invited to participate in well over a dozen classes that provide instruction in various Hawaiian crafts, such as woodworking and frond plaiting, or simply observe the hundreds of locals come decked in traditional dress for this impressive gala.

Sleeping & Eating

In this rural residential area, the only lodging options are B&Bs and vacation rentals.

Hale Ho'onanea B&B **$$**
(☎877-882-1653, 882-1653; www.houseofrelaxation.com; Ala Kahua Dr; ste $100-130; 📶) About 5 miles north of Kawaihae, these three B&B units set on peaceful grassy knolls 900ft above sea level are excellent value. The Bamboo Suite is priciest, but the high ceiling, hardwood floor and stunning 180-degree horizon view are worth it. The other rooms get smaller and more makeshift as the price drops, but all are clean and homey, with kitchenette, lanai, satellite TV and wi-fi.

★ **Blue Dragon Musiquarium** HAWAII REGIONAL CUISINE **$$**
(☎882-7771; www.bluedragonhawaii.com; 61-3616 Kawaihae Rd; mains $18-36; ⏲5-10pm Wed-Thu & Sun, to 11pm Fri & Sat) This roofless restaurant under towering palms has a menu of locally sourced food that's well prepared into an eclectic mix of stir-fries and curries, rib-eye steaks and teriyaki. Service is casual (and a bit distracted).

It books live jazz music almost nightly – as well as local slack key favorites such as John Keawe – creating a mood so upbeat and friendly that (aided by potent specialty cocktails) even the shyest couples can't resist the scallop of a dance floor. Music ends at 10pm, but the bar goes as long as you do, or until the staff get tired...

Kohala Burger & Taco AMERICAN **$**
(☎880-1923; www.kohalaburgerandtaco.com; 61-3665 Akoni Pule Hwy; mains under $10; ⏲11am-7pm Mon-Fri, til 4pm Sat & Sun) Do you know what's better than a big, juicy burger after hours of swimming, snorkeling, hiking or surfing? Absolutely nothing, with the possible exception of a good taco or burrito. And this place has all of the above! Kohala Burger & Taco, you just keep winning, what with your grass-fed burgers layered with slices of local avacado, and enormous wet burritos, and just gobs of awesome.

Café Pesto FUSION **$$**
(☎882-1071; www.cafepesto.com; Akoni Pule Hwy, Kawaihae Shopping Center; lunch $11-14, pizza $9-20, dinner mains $17-33; ⏲11am-9pm Sun-Thu, to 10pm Fri & Sat) This fun, stylish restaurant is a well-loved favorite, serving eclectic, innovative cuisine you might call Mediterranean with an Asian twang, or Italian with an island twist. Choose from curries and Greek salads, seafood risotto and smoked salmon alfredo, piping hot calzones and thin-crust gourmet pizza.

NORTH KOHALA

Rural North Kohala has a distinct flavor all its own – a charming, successful mix of rural farmers and local artists, Native Hawaiians and mainland transplants, plantation-era storefronts and green valleys. While still relatively untouristed, word of its charms has leaked out, and the area is slowly moving onto the beaten track. In recent years several wealthy individuals have purchased major tracts of land here, helping to limit future development.

The North Kohala peninsula is the oldest part of the Big Island, and it shows: driving up the coast from Kona, one sees a mountain range deeply cut with ravines, as opposed to the smooth slopes found elsewhere. The area is also steeped in human history, being the birthplace of King Kamehameha I. In modern times North Kohala was sugar country until the Kohala Sugar Company closed in 1975. Today the small historic towns of Hawi and Kapa'au contain enough art galleries, boutiques and distinctive eateries to succeed as tourist attractions, particularly when you add them together. The refreshing **Kohala Welcome Center** (☎889-5523; www.northkohala.org; ⏲9am-4pm Mon-Fri), located at the western entrance to Hawi, offers an excellent map to the entire area, some local history, and friendly advice from a tribe of doting mavens. Rounding the peninsula's thumb on Hwy 270, you leave the Kohala Mountains rain shadow. The land shifts steadily from a bone-dry volcanic plain to lushly tropical gulches, culminating in the Pololu Valley, the jewel of North Kohala.

Kohala Mountain Road (Highway 250)

Arguably the Big Island's best scenic drive, Kohala Mountain Rd (Hwy 250) affords stupendous views of the Kohala–Kona coastline and three majestic volcanic mountains: Mauna Kea, Mauna Loa and Hualalai. Start from Waimea, climb past an overlook, and then follow the spine of the peninsula through green pastures until you finally descend to the sea at Hawi. The name changes to Hawi Rd close to town.

Activities

Windswept pastureland. Grazing cattle. Cloud-dappled skies. North Kohala makes some folks yearn to be a *paniolo* (cowboy), at least for a day. If that's you, there are two interesting options on Kohala Mountain Rd (and one in Waimea). Be aware that in Hawaii, all liability for horseback riding rests with the rider.

★ Paniolo Adventures — HORSEBACK RIDING

(☎ 889-5354; www.panioloadventures.com; Kohala Mountain Rd; rides $69-175) 'Get off the beaten path with the original all-terrain vehicle.' And you do. Paniolo Adventures offers five different horseback rides ranging from one to four hours, enough for anyone to find their comfort level, whether it's walking or cantering. Of particular note is the Sunset Ride, allowing you to finally – ahem – ride off into the sunset.

The terrain is the beautiful 1000-acre Ponoholo Ranch, a working cattle ranch. Horses are selected for the rider's experience. All necessary equipment is provided. This is the best choice on the island for an experienced rider.

Na'alapa Stables — HORSEBACK RIDING

(☎ 889-0022; www.naalapastables.com; Kahua Ranch Rd; rides $65-85) Na'alapa Stables organizes rides across the pastures of the 8500-acre Kahua Ranch, affording fine views of the coast from its 3200ft elevation. A 2½-hour ride (9–11:30am) is available, but the 1½-hour ride (1:30–3:00pm) will satisfy most parties. There is some cantering but it's mostly a nose-to-tail ride, set at the level of the most inexperienced rider.

Turn off Route 250 between mile marker 11 and 12; it's the first building on the right.

North Kohala

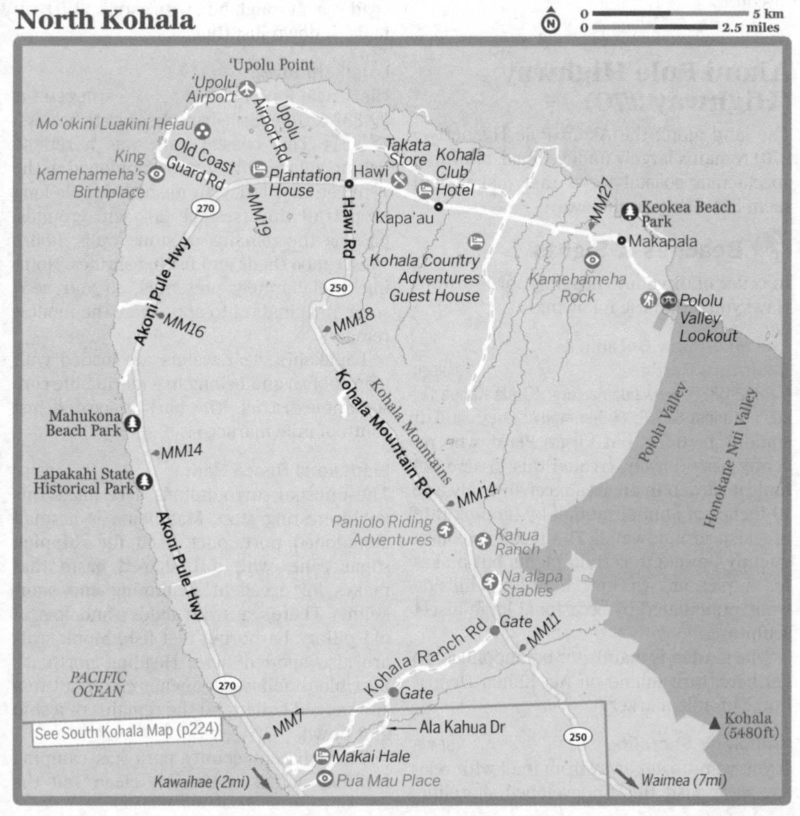

Eating

Kahua Ranch BARBECUE **$$$**

(882-7954; www.exploretheranch.com; Kahua Ranch Rd; $119 with transportation, $95 without, children 6-11 half price, under 5 free; 6-9pm Wed summer, 5:30-8:30pm Wed winter;) Hey there, city slicker – lookin' for a little down-home country BBQ? Well they've got a doozy here at the Kahua Ranch. One of the ranch owners, who missed his calling in stand-up comedy, gets things rolling with an introduction to ranching life. Busloads of lei-wearing tourists then line up for a hearty buffet dinner of chicken, steak and beer in a nearby Quonset hut.

The feast is followed by country music, line dancing, s'mores over the campfire and, best of all, Piggly Wiggly, the performing pig. Well yeeee-ha! The cheerful, longstanding event takes place on a gorgeous piece of sloping pasture with wide-open views, making sunset and stargazing by telescope a natural highlight. There's a 15% online discount.

Akoni Pule Highway (Highway 270)

The land along the Akoni Pule Hwy (Hwy 270) remains largely undeveloped, affording spectacular coastal views that make Maui seem but a short swim away.

Beaches & Sights

In order of direction, heading north toward Hawi you'll find the following:

Pua Mau Place Botanic & Sculpture Garden GARDEN

(882-0888; www.puamau.org; 10 Ala Kahua Dr; adult/student $15/5; 9am-4pm) They said it couldn't be done, but Virgin Place, who recently passed away, created this 13-acre botanical garden in an area receiving only 3 to 10 inches of annual rainfall by tapping into brackish groundwater. The result is consequently limited to certain plants but makes for a pleasant (if hot) hour-long hillside walk, punctuated by occasional large insect sculptures.

The garden is mainly for botanophiles. To get here, turn inland on Ala Kahua Dr just north of mile marker 6.

Kaiholena Shoreline BEACH

If you want to get away from it all with relative ease, visit this undeveloped shoreline. It's rocky but offers great swimming and snorkeling, including large schools of yellow tang, and you'll probably have it to yourself. There's also the ruins of an ancient settlement. Heading north on Hwy 270, turn left on the dirt road just prior to mile marker 12 and directly opposite Kaiholena Pl. The road is a bit rough but, with care, a 2WD can make it down just fine.

DON'T MISS

MAHUKONA-TO-KAPA'A WALKING TRAIL

Mahukona and Kapa'a Beach Parks are linked by a beautiful, little-known, 2-mile oceanside walking trail. From Kapa'a Beach Park, start by the old railway bed on the left, visible on the way in. From Mahukona Beach Park, go past the two-story brown metal building and park at the turn-out on the right. Scoot left around the metal pipe gate to find the trail sign. Bring water and a hat and stay on the trail.

Lapakahi State Historical Park HISTORICAL SITE

(882-6207; 8am-4pm, closed state holidays) FREE This coastal park was a remote fishing village until it was abandoned in the 19th century. Today an unshaded, mile-long **loop trail** traverses the 262-acre grounds, passing the remains of stone walls, house sites, canoe sheds and fishing shrines. Nothing is elaborately presented, so you need some imagination to appreciate the modest remains.

Lapakahi's clear waters are loaded with tropical fish and belong to a marine-life conservation district. The park is located just south of mile marker 14.

Mahukona Beach Park BEACH

The unusual surroundings here make this an interesting stop. Mahukona is a small abandoned port, once used for shipping sugar cane, with a U-shaped basin that makes for excellent swimming and snorkeling. There's a swim ladder and lots of old pilings harboring reef fish. Monk seals are also spotted here. Heading north it's possible to follow an anchor chain out to a submerged boiler and the remains of a ship 25ft down.

The adjacent county park has camping facilities and is reasonably clean, but the profusion of signs, porto-potties and trash bins makes nearby Kaiholena or Kapaa Beach Park better alternatives.

Kapa'a Beach Park BEACH

This excellent seaside park offers a covered picnic area with welcome shade, few people and public toilets. It is simple and clean, with nice coastal and Maui views, but no swimming. Camping by permit. Turn at mile marker 16.

Mo'okini Luakini Heiau TEMPLE

(373-8000; 9am-8pm, closed Wed) FREE It's off the beaten path, but this heiau near 'Upolu Point, Hawai'i's northernmost tip, is among the oldest (c AD 480) and most historically significant Hawaiian sites. Measuring about 250ft by 125ft, with walls 6ft high, the massive stone ruins sit solitary and brooding on a wind-rustled grassy plain. The only way to get here is via the horribly rutted dirt road that heads south along the shoreline from 'Upolu airport, requiring a 4WD.

Sleeping

Makai Hale B&B $$

(880-1012; www.makaihale.com; 59-411 Pupu Pl; d $175 winter, $155 summer, 2-night minimum;) Inside the gated Kohala Ranch subdivision, this well-kept B&B lies on windswept, barren volcanic slopes looking out to sea. If you like that terrain, it is the only choice for miles, and a good one. The freestanding guest wing is separated from the owner's residence by a large pool deck with Jacuzzi.

A vaulted ceiling, nice patio, kitchenette and refrigerated breakfast make this a comfortable if somewhat remote base. For larger parties, an adjoining room with private bath can be rented for an additional $85. The B&B can be accessed either from Hwy 270 or Hwy 250.

Hawi

POP 940

Hawi (hah-*vee*) can fit all of its businesses within two blocks, but it looms large in picturesque charm, notable restaurants and great shopping finds. It was once a major plantation town for the Kohala Sugar Company, and many local residents are descendants of sugar workers. Mainland transplants are bringing big money to little Hawi and leading its transformation from rustic boondocks to tourist destination. But the town offers only basic services, such as a post office, grocery store and gas station. Thank goodness, say the residents.

Sleeping

★ **Cabin in the Treeline** VACATION RENTAL $$

(884-5105; www.vacationhi.com; 56-867 Kamalei St; cabin for 2 people $169, per person thereafter $10, cleaning fee $85;) Tucked away in a treeline with gorgeous views along the length of the Hawaiian archipelago, this reproduction *paniolo* ranchhouse is so picture-perfect it stops you in your tracks at first sight. The owner has showered attention on every aspect of the structure, from the lava rock fireplace to the period plumbing, such that you would swear you have entered the 19th century.

The house is large, with an en suite master bedroom, cavernous living room and loft, sleeping six in total. Peaceful, spotless, and more than reasonably priced, this is a property that has captured the hearts of many visitors. Call for directions.

★ **Puakea Ranch** VACATION RENTALS $$$

(315-0805; www.puakearanch.com; 56-2864 Akoni Pule Hwy; cottages $249-549 plus cleaning fee;) This very laid-back, rural working ranch, set amidst rolling pastureland, offers four meticulously restored and very private ranch cottages steeped in local history. Each is on its own acre of land, with nice views to sea, and a detached bathhouse with separate hot tub converted from the original Japanese washhouses.

Ranging from two to six bedrooms, all units are self-contained, with kitchen and laundry facilities and attractive pools. Dedicated owners have crafted just the right balance of luxury and authenticity. Perfect for couples and families alike (child care available). Located on a gated dirt road 3 miles from Hawi center; call for directions.

Hawaii Island Retreat BOUTIQUE HOTEL $$$

(889-6336; www.hawaiiislandretreat.com; At Ahu Pohaku Ho'omaluhia; r $425-500;) This is not a high-end resort or boutique spa in the typical sense, but a place of spiritual retreat appealing to a particular type of person. Located on 50 acres bordered by beautiful oceanfront cliffs, it successfully separates you from the world, immersing you to the extent that you desire in a high-end, off-the-grid organic farm where peace reigns supreme.

Powered by the wind and sun, and with vast resources of fruit, vegetables and livestock, the hotel is entirely self-sufficient. There's no sacrifice of comfort, but the experience is not opulent or indulgent either. Though a bit on the concrete side of things, the purpose-built cliffside villa, which surrounds a central courtyard, offers nine spacious rooms, each worthy of a well-heeled inn. There are also seven less expensive yurts for $195, but these get extremely hot during the day. A separate spa center, with a wide-ranging therapeutic menu and lovely horizon pool with fine forest views, complements the park-like grounds.

Eating & Drinking

For groceries see **Takata Store** (889-5413; Akoni Pule Hwy; 8am-7pm Mon-Sat, to 1pm Sun).

Lighthouse Delicatessen DELI $
(889-5757; 55-3419 Akoni Pule Hwy; sandwiches $10-15; 10am-10pm Sun-Thu, to midnight Fri-Sat) This ambitious eatery began as a deli known for its tasty sandwiches and generous portions. It now offers breakfast on weekends, Sunday brunch (7am–2pm) and has recently added a bar offering craft beers and occasional live entertainment, making it Hawi's top (and only) nightspot. The shaded tables outside are the perfect place for that Reuben sandwich.

Kohala Coffee Mill CAFE $
(889-5577; 55-3412 Akoni Pule Hwy; snacks $3-5; 6am-6pm Mon-Fri, kava bar 4:30am-9pm) A comfy place to hang out and treat yourself to muffins, fresh-brewed Kona coffee and heavenly Tropical Dreams ice cream. Also check out the shave ice and fudge at adjoining **Upstairs at the Mill** (889-5015; 11am-5pm;), where you can also find internet access ($5 per 30 minutes) and art displays. In the evenings, the space becomes a **kava bar**, serving flavored versions of *'awa* plant juice.

★**Sushi Rock** SUSHI $$
(889-5900; www.sushirockrestaurant.net; 55-3435 Akoni Pule Hwy; nigiri per piece $6, sushi rolls $6-20, mains $15-28; noon-3pm & 5:30am-8pm Sun-Tue & Thu, to 9pm Fri & Sat) This ever-popular, veggie-friendly sushi bar is renowned for having reinvented the genre through its exotic flavor combos, a philosophy now extending to sandwiches, fish cakes and other entrees. Take the Pololu salad: organic greens, Gorgonzola cheese, Fuji apples and candied macadamia nuts tossed in papaya pomegranate dressing.

The owner claims the key to his success is pouring love into the food. Whether or not such transfers are possible, guests are certainly treated with great care by the hospitable staff. Arrive early.

★**Bamboo** HAWAII REGIONAL $$
(889-5555; Akoni Pule Hwy, Kohala Trade Center; lunch $11-16, dinner $25-35; 11:30am-2:30pm & 6-8pm Tue-Sat, 11:30am-2:30pm Sun;) Credited with jump-starting Hawi's revival as a tourism destination, always-packed Bamboo offers interesting takes on old stand-bys, such as mahimahi on focaccia with shredded papaya. Some elements, like the eclectic decor, are inspired by the owner's international travels.

Located in a historic building, it shares space with a gallery and gift shop (worth a look), making you feel like you're eating in a general store – which you are. Pitch-perfect for Hawi.

Shopping

★**Hawi Gallery** MUSIC
(206-235-1648; www.hawigallery.com; 55-3406 Akoni Pule Highway; 10am-5pm Mon-Sat, 11am-3pm Sun) You wouldn't necessarily think that a ukelele store would be a constant source of fascination, but this is why you come to Hawi. Owner Richard Bodien will happily take you on a trip through time and space courtesy of his vast collection, including the Cuban model made from a cigar box.

And don't miss the curvaceous Polk-a-lay-lee, a rare 1960s promotional item from a Chicago furniture store. Since you can't do this anywhere else on Earth, take advantage of it while you can. Don't forget your free guitar pick on exit, and one of the signature bumper stickers: 'Hawi Nice Day'.

Living Arts Gallery GALLERY
(www.livingartsgallery.net; 55-3435 Akoni Pule Hwy; 10:30am-5pm, to 8pm Fri) To appreciate the extraordinary amount of artistic talent nurtured by the Big Island, come here to this artists co-op. Members staff the gallery, giving you firsthand contact with some of the 65 local artists represented here. Their infectious motto: 'Take heart, make art.'

Pacifica Shell & Jewelry JEWELRY
(889-1033; 55-3410A Akoni Pule Hwy; 11am-4:30pm) Very high-quality, ocean-inspired jewelry, sculptures and models, along with

DON'T MISS

BOND HISTORIC DISTRICT

Surrounded by a large macadamia nut orchard, the 54-acre **Bond Historic District** ('Iole; 889-5151; www.iolehawaii.com; 53-496 'Iole Rd; 8am-4pm Mon-Sat) is a work in progress that is definitely worth visiting already. The district contains three historic properties all built by missionary Elias Bond (1813–62), a seminal figure in numerous aspects of Kohala life, from education to roads to the sugar industry. While fully furnished, the Bond Homestead (1889) has been uninhabited for 60 years and is currently undergoing renovations after extensive earthquake damage. The Kohala Girls School is in excellent condition and an atmospheric throwback to the merger of New England missionary sensibilities with Hawaii. So too is the Kalahikiola Congregational Church, a vital part of the Kohala community since 1855 (services 9:30am Sunday). The entire district is part of 'Iole, a 2400 acre tract extending from the Pacific Ocean into the Kohala Mountains now owned and managed by the New Moon Foundation (www.newmoonfoundation.org).

Tours ($10 per person) depart at 1:30pm Monday to Saturday, with more planned beginning summer 2013. There's also an interesting series of six short walking trails ranging from 0.5 mile to 2 miles. An information office near the car park (up 'Iole Rd, between mile markers 23 and 24) provides trail guides. 'Iole contains some beautiful tropical forest with magnificent banyan trees, so pack a picnic (no food or drinks available on site) and make an afternoon of it. If you are interested in ziplining, Big Island Eco Adventures (p242) departs from the information office as well.

an impressive seashell collection. You will be surprised to discover they produce much of the jewelry on site. Great for browsing.

Elements HANDICRAFTS
(www.elementsjewelryandcrafts.com; 55-3413 Akoni Pule Hwy; 10am-6pm) This jewelry and gift shop offers an eclectic array of unique crafts, most notably some beautiful hand-woven African wire baskets, available in limited numbers.

L Zeidman Gallery GALLERY
(Hwy 270; 10am-5pm) The exquisitely crafted, museum-quality wooden bowls and sculptures in this exclusive gallery range in price from $150 to $2500.

Kapa'au

POP 1160

Kapa'au is a former sugar town refashioned into an attractive tourist destination. Though it's not as atmospheric as Hawi, it offers just as much and is so close that you might as well consider the two towns joined at the hip.

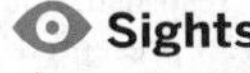

★Keokea Beach Park BEACH
(off Akoni Pule Hwy; gate 7am-11pm) While it has no beach to speak of, this park about 3.5 miles from Kapa'au has the best picnic spot around, an elevated pavilion with smashing views of a small rocky bay and the motley collection of experienced local surfers who bravely venture out into its dangerous shore breaks and strong currents.

There are lots of other picnic tables, too, if someone else has claimed the throne. The marked turnoff is about 1.5 miles before the Pololu Valley Lookout.

Kamehameha the Great Statue MONUMENT
The statue on the front lawn of the North Kohala Civic Center has a famous twin in Honolulu, standing across from 'Iolani Palace. The Kapa'au one was the original, constructed in 1880 in Florence, Italy, by American sculptor Thomas Gould. When the ship delivering it sank off the Falkland Islands, a second statue was cast from the original mold. The duplicate statue arrived in 1883 and took its place in downtown Honolulu. Later the sunken statue was recovered from the ocean floor and sent here, to Kamehameha's childhood home.

Activities

Kohala Zipline ZIPLINING
(331-3620; www.kohalazipline.com; 54-3676 Akoni Pule Highway; adult/child $159/$129) You don't have any dramatic long zips over tropical rivers here, but the fun of a forest canopy tour with nine easy zips, five elevated suspension bridges between platforms, and two

rappels. The course is new, with three-hour tours departing every half hour from 8am to 2:30pm. Check online for discounts.

ATV Outfitters ADVENTURE TOUR
(☎888-288-7288, 889-6000; www.atvoutfittershawaii.com; 53-324 Lighthouse Rd, btwn MM 24 and 25) Offers three all-terrain-vehicle (ATV) trips: a 1½-hour trip along the Kohala ditch system to a secluded beach (driver/passenger $129/80); a two-hour, 15-mile waterfall tour with a swim (driver/passenger $179/130); and a three-hour, 22-mile journey that combines both (driver/passenger $249/130). For the more adventurous at heart, ATV trips are a blast. Check online for discounts.

Kohala Ditch Adventures KAYAKING
(☎888-288-7288, 889-6000; www.kohaladitchadventures.com; 53-324 Lighthouse Rd, btwn MM 24 & 25; tour per adult/child under 12yr $139/75; ⏲Mon-Sat 7-11am & 12:15pm-4pm) After an off-road excursion by Pinzgauer, a six-wheel Austrian military vehicle, you embark on a 2.5-mile kayaking trip through historic plantation irrigation ditches, or flumes, including 10 tunnels. Lots of family fun. Nine 2½-hour tours per day. Check online for discounts.

Big Island Eco Adventures ZIPLINING
(☎889-5111; www.bigislandecoadventures.com; 53-496 'Iole Rd; tour $169) The forest wilderness near Pololu Valley is the perfect setting for a zipline canopy tour. This one combines eight zips, a suspension bridge beside a 60-foot waterfall, and snacks in the idyllic Mango Hut, plus you get to ride up to the site in a 6WD military vehicle.

The three-hour tour departs hourly between 8am and 2pm. Maximum 10 guests, 90–250lb weight range. On the right, a half-mile up 'Iole Rd; shares office with Bond Historic District. A ten-percent discount is available online.

Kamehameha Park & Golf Learning Center PARK, GOLF
(☎golf center 345-4393, gym 889-5532, pool 889-6933; ⏲pool 10-11:45am, 1-4pm) Given the size of Kapa'au, this county park offers amazing facilities. There's a huge pool, tennis courts, a gym with basketball courts and weight room, and a playground. In back you'll find a six-hole golf learning center where you can rent equipment and play all day for $30. Lessons available.

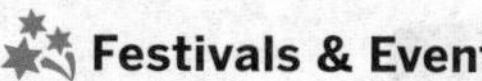

Festivals & Events

★**Kohala Country Fair** COUNTY FAIR
(www.kohalacountryfair.com; Akoni Pule Hwy opposite 'Iole Rd; ⏲9am-4pm, 1st week in Oct) FREE The Big Island's biggest county fair is a smorgasbord of local artists and food in a sea of tents. Entertainment includes a spam carving contest, frog catching, equestrian demonstrations, a tug of war, a dance competition and you never know what else.

North Kohala Kamehameha Day Celebration HISTORICAL FESTIVAL
(www.kamehamehadaycelebration.org) Join thousands who flock to Hawi and Kapa'au on June 11 to honor Kamehameha the Great in his birthplace. The spectacular parade of floral-bedecked horseback riders and floats culminates in an all-day gathering with music, crafts, hula and food.

Sleeping

Kohala Club Hotel INN $
(☎889-6793; www.kohalaclubhotel.com; 54-3793 Akoni Pule Hwy; r/cottage $56/90) Just 0.5 miles from Kapa'au, this laid-back hotel, one of the oldest on the island, offers clean en suite accommodations for an unbelievable price. The main house contains four small, no-frills rooms with either a queen bed or two twins, three of which share a common porch. The two-bedroom cottage is perfect for families. Expansion to eight rooms is underway.

Kohala Country Adventures Guest House INN $$
(☎866-892-2484, 889-5663; www.kcadventures.com; off Akoni Pule Hwy; r $85-175; 📶) If you like the country, try this relaxed house on eight acres with fruit trees, livestock and coastal views. The Sundeck Suite is great for families, with kitchenette, three beds and an open loft layout. Host Bobi Moreno puts everyone at ease. Breakfast not included.

Eating

★**Gill's Lanai** CAFE $
(☎315-1542; 54-3866 Akoni Pule Hwy; mains $6-9; ⏲11am-5pm) With its umbrella-shaded patio seating and teeny kitchen, this avocado-colored roadside food stand really belongs at the beach. The emphasis is on fresh fish, hot dogs and veggie options, creatively presented.

King's View Cafe PIZZA, SANDWICHES $
(☎889-5138; 55-3897 Akoni Pule Hwy; mains $9-11; ⏲9am-8:30pm) Across from Kamehameha

statue, this cafe offers nice big sandwiches (try the pastrami) and handmade pizzas, along with super smoothies and beer.

Minnie's DINER $
(☎889-5288; 54-3854 Akoni Pule Hwy; meals $8-13; ⊙11am-8pm Mon-Thu, 11am-3pm & 6-8:30pm Fri, 11am-3pm Sat) Fill up on burgers, sandwiches and plate lunches including mahimahi, Korean chicken and the house specialty, roast pork. Indoor/outdoor seating.

Shopping

★Dunn Gallery ARTS & CRAFTS
(☎884-5808; dunngallerywoodart.com; 54-3862 Akoni Pule Hwy; ⊙10am-5pm Tue-Sat) Of the many wood art shops on the island, this one stands alone. The distinctive works here, gathered from 30 Big Island artists, represent a museum-quality collection. Contemporary, traditional, and functional pieces range from $20 to five figures.

Ackerman Galleries GIFTS
(☎889-5138; www.ackermangalleries.com; 55-3897 Akani Pule Hwy; ⊙10am-6pm) The Ackerman family has managed to combine art and commerce for 30 years. They have two galleries within sight of each other, the Gift Gallery being the main one, with an excellent array of wooden bowls, glasswork, jewelry and other items, some of it produced by family members.

Across the street, Gary Ackerman's personal gallery offers impressionistic paintings of Hawaii and France. It is open from October to March and by request.

Rankin Gallery & Studio GALLERY
(☎889-6849; www.patricklouisrankin.net; 53-4380 Akoni Pule Hwy; ⊙11am-5pm Tue-Sat & 12-4pm Sun-Mon) Located on a deep bend in the road midway to Pololu from Kapa'au, this gallery is noted for its landscapes of Hawaii and the American West, as well as the conviviality of Patrick Rankin, a local character happy to show you around his studio.

Don't miss the adjacent Kohala Tong Wo Society building, a nicely restored temple that once served as an opium den.

Pololu Valley

Unlike its sister valley, Waipi'o, Pololu Valley has not been inhabited since the 1940s. So, instead of territorial residents, you are met by a forest reserve.

Activities

★Pololu Valley Lookout & Trail HIKING
This steep, rocky trail from the lookout to the valley floor is doable for most, thanks to switchbacks and its 0.75-mile distance. Not counting scenic stops, walking time averages 20 minutes going down and perhaps 30 coming back up. Be careful trekking after rainfall, as the mud-slicked rocks will be precarious. Walking sticks are often left at the trailhead. There are no facilities.

At the mouth of the valley lies a gorgeous black-sand beach. The surf is rough, particularly in winter, with rip currents year-round. Swimming is generally out of the question, even if you see local surfers and bodyboarders testing the waves. Monk seals come ashore here, too.

Behind the beach, a hillocky ironwood forest vibrates like some Tolkien-inspired shire wood. Deeper valley explorations are blocked by a pond, beyond which cattle roam freely (an indication you shouldn't drink the water).

Tours

Hawaii Forest & Trail WALKING TOUR
(☎800-464-1993, 331-8505; www.hawaii-forest.com; adult/child under 13yr $159/129) The Kohala Waterfalls Tour is a 1.5-mile loop that follows the Kohala Ditch Trail to waterfalls (swimming included); transportation from the Waikoloa Resort Area is included.

WAIMEA (KAMUELA)

POP 7030

The wide open plains and hilly pastures surrounding Waimea are Hawai'i the Big Island's most unexpected face. This is cattle and cowboy country, and nearly all of it, including Waimea itself, is owned, run or leased by Parker Ranch, the fifth-largest cow-calf ranch in the USA.

But don't leap to any conclusions: this is no company town. For its size, Waimea contains extraordinary depth, and one of the joys of visiting is to plumb it. From the highway all you see are bland strip malls, but closer inspection finds an extraordinary art scene, a long list of dining options, outstanding shopping, including *three* farmers markets, and a rich cowboy heritage. Then there are all the fascinating transplants – organic farmers, astronomers, artists, teachers – a most enlightened, well-traveled

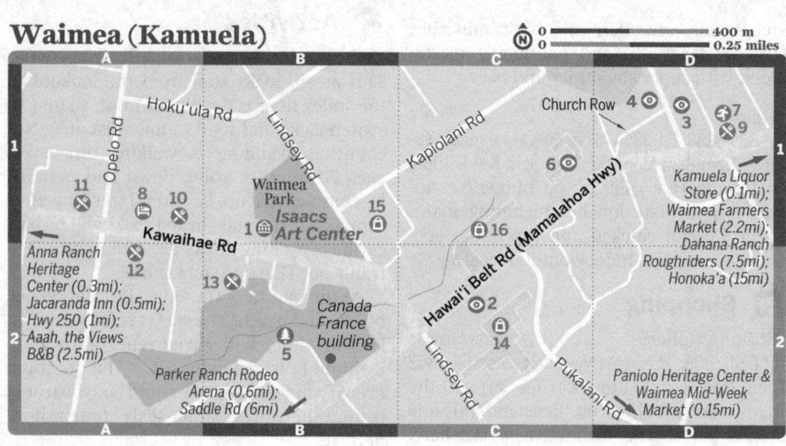

Waimea (Kamuela)

Top Sights
1 Isaacs Art Center B1

Sights
2 Hawaiian Cowboy Memorial C2
3 Imiola Congregational Church D1
4 Ke Ola Mau Loa Church D1
5 Waimea Nature Park B2
6 WM Keck Observatory Office C1

Activities, Courses & Tours
7 Mountain Road Cycles D1

Sleeping
8 Kamuela Inn A1

Eating
9 Big Island Brewhaus & Taqueria D1
10 Hawaiian Style Cafe A1
Healthways II .... (see 14)
KTA Super Store .... (see 16)
Merriman's .... (see 11)
11 Pau A1
12 Redwater Cafe A2
Starbucks .... (see 14)
Village Burger .... (see 14)
13 Waimea Coffee & Co B2

Shopping
Gallery of Great Things .... (see 13)
14 Parker Ranch Center C2
15 Parker School Farmers Market B1
Parker Sq .... (see 13)
16 Waimea Center C1
Wishard Gallery .... (see 14)

bunch whose headquarters (starting around 7am every morning) is **Starbucks** (☎887-6409; www.starbucks.com; 67-1185 Mamalahoa Highway D108, Parker Ranch Center; ⌚4:30am-9pm). Old West courtesy and small town pace prevail here, making it easy to strike up a conversation.

The town has some wonderfully wacky weather. It is split into the 'dry side' and the 'wet side,' the boundary being roughly the center of town. So while Kawaihae Rd is a desert, drive past the malls along Mamalahoa Hwy and you find yourself in green fields. Days are warm, while nights are cool up here at 2670ft, necessitating jeans and sweaters. And it can go from sun to rain in the swish of a horse's tail, so make sure that convertible top is up overnight.

For visitors, Waimea makes a good base to explore Kohala, Mauna Kea and the Hamakua Coast, since all are easily accessible; many people like retreating to the cool evenings here after a hot day on the beach. Just be aware that Waimea and Kamuela are the same place on the map. Kamuela is mainly a zip code used to differentiate this Waimea from those on O'ahu and Kaua'i. But having two different names does put one last spin on this little gem of a town.

Sights

Until the late 2000s, Waimea's main attractions were Parker Ranch's museum and

19th-century historic homes. They're now closed permanently – a sign of management difficulties at the ranch, which is even phasing out horseback rides – but there are many other worthy stops.

★Isaacs Art Center GALLERY
(☎885-5884; www.isaacsartcenter.hpa.edu; 61-1268 Kawaihae Rd; ⏰10am-5pm Tue-Sat) FREE This series of bright, spacious and charming galleries, set in a 1915 schoolhouse relocated to the site, displays an excellent collection of local and international artwork in a suitably (for the Big Island) unique setting, both down home and upscale at once. Think of it as a museum where most items are for sale.

For the most part the collection is not drawn from living artists, but the best of those past. The entryway is permanently overseen by Herb Kawainui Kane's enormous *The Arrival of Captain Cook at Kealakekua Bay in January 1779*. Other highlights include several large watercolors of tropical scenes by Ben Norris (around $10,000), which reflect a masterful style. All proceeds go to the Hawai'i Preparatory Academy scholarship fund.

Anna Ranch Heritage Center HISTORICAL SITE
(☎885-4426; www.annaranch.org; 65-1480 Kawaihae Rd; ⏰10am-3pm Tue-Fri) The life and times of Hawaii's 'first lady of ranching,' Anna Leialoha Lindsey Perry-Fiske, are celebrated at this 14-room historic ranch house. Tours (10am & 1pm; $10) must be booked in advance. There's also a self-guided outdoor tour ($5 recommended) that leads you through the history of local ranching and agriculture. A mile west of Waimea's town center.

WM Keck Observatory Office VISITOR CENTER
(☎885-7887; www.keckobservatory.org; 65-1120 Mamalahoa Hwy; ⏰10am-2pm Tue-Fri) The lobby of this working office is open to the public, offering models of the twin 10m Keck telescopes, fascinating photos, and informative volunteers. The hexagonal lawn symbolizes the mirror of each telescope. It's definitely worth visiting unless you are visiting the telescopes themselves. Check the website for occasional lectures.

Paniolo Heritage Center MUSEUM
(☎854-1541; www.paniolopreservation.org; Pukalani Rd; ⏰9am-4pm Wed) FREE In 2011 the Paniolo Preservation Society took over management of Pukalani Stables, once the center for Parker Ranch horse breeding operations, and have been creating a museum ever since. It is still in its early stages, but they have finished one large photo exhibit and a saddle-making operation.

The great reward is the personal touch: anyone here is happy to bend your ear about the history of the *paniolos*. Hours may be extending soon.

Hawaiian Cowboy Memorial MEMORIAL
(Parker Ranch Center) This large bronze sculpture by Fred Fellows, a spirited symbol of *paniolo* culture, depicts Ikua Purdy, the Parker Ranch cowboy who won the World Steer Roping Championships in 1908. On Mamalahoa Hwy facing Starbucks in Parker Ranch Center.

Church Row CHURCHES
Home to Buddhists, Mormons, Baptists and other Christians, Church Row is a living synopsis of the religious life of the Big Island, past and present. There are several noteworthy, if humble, structures along this curved street, including the much-photographed, all-Hawaiian **Ke Ola Mau Loa Church** built in 1931 (service 11am Sunday). Look for the green steeple.

Just next door is the **Imiola Congregational Church** (www.imiolachurch.com; ⏰services 9:30am) FREE, built entirely of koa in 1857, which has a beautifully varnished interior.

Activities

Mountain Road Cycles CYCLING
(☎885-7943; www.mountainroadcycles.com; 64-1066 Mamalahoa Hwy; bikes per day $30-45; ⏰9:30am-5:30pm Mon-Fri, 10am-3pm Sat) The Big Island has lots of scenic roads and few cars on them. In addition to renting bicycles, this full-service bike shop arranges moun-

PARKER RANCH

Until recently, **Parker Ranch** (www.parkerranch.com) was the nation's largest privately owned ranch, peaking at 250,000 acres. To make ends meet, however, the ranch has had to sell off parcels, including 24,000 acres to the US military in 2006. Today it's the fifth-largest cow-calf ranch in the USA, with at least 12,000 mother cows on 130,000 acres. That's 5% of the entire Big Island, producing 12 million pounds of beef annually.

tain biking and road tours starting at $50. They prefer small groups and serious riders. Located behind Big Island Brewhaus (p247).

Dahana Ranch Roughriders HORSEBACK RIDING
(☎888-399-0057, 885-0057; www.dahanaranch.com; 90min ride adult/child $80/70; ⏰rides 9am, 11am, 1pm & 3pm) Offers American quarter horses, bred and trained by third- and fourth-generation *paniolo*. These are open-range (not mountain-view) rides, available to kids as young as three years, but if you want to canter more advanced rides are also available. The ranch is 7.5 miles east of Waimea, off Old Mamalahoa Hwy. Reservations required.

Festivals & Events

Waimea Ocean Film Festival FILM
(☎854-6095; www.waimeaoceanfilm.org) Films, speakers, receptions and art exhibits engage participants in a celebration of the beauty, power and mystery of the ocean and island culture. Held every January. Local venues vary.

Waimea Cherry Blossom Heritage Festival JAPANESE FESTIVAL
(☎961-8706; waimeacherryblossom@gmail.com; Parker Ranch Center & Church Row Park) FREE Dark pink blossoms are greeted with *taiko* drumming, *mochi* (sticky rice cake) pounding and other Japanese cultural events on the first Saturday in February.

Fourth of July Rodeo RODEO
(☎885-2303; 67-1435 Mamalahoa Hwy, Parker Ranch Rodeo Arena; admission $6) Celebrating over 45 years of ranching, this event has cattle roping, bull riding and other hoopla.

Round-Up Rodeo RODEO
(☎885-5669; www.parkerranch.com; 67-1435 Mamalahoa Hwy, Parker Ranch Rodeo Arena; admission $5) This whip-cracking event is held on the first Monday in September after the Labor Day weekend.

LOCAL KNOWLEDGE

PANIOLO?

So where does *'paniolo'* come from? The first cowboys who came to the Big Island hailed from the Spanish part of North America, circa 1830. In the local diction, these *'espanoles'* soon became *'paniolos.'*

Waimea Paniolo Parade and Ho'olaule'a PARADE
(☎885-3110; www.waimeatown.org) This mid-September parade of authentic *paniolo*, island princesses and beautiful steeds begins at historic Church Row Park and makes its way through Waimea Town, followed by a fair in Waimea Park that features Hawaiian foods, games, arts and crafts, products and live entertainment.

Christmas Twilight Parade CHRISTMAS PARADE
In early December, the town gets into the Kalikimaka (Christmas) spirit with a block party.

Sleeping

Kamuela Inn HOTEL $
(☎800-555-8968, 885-4243; www.thekamuelainn.com; 1600 Kawaihae Rd; r $69-94, ste $109-119, incl breakfast; 📶) Dedicated new owners are reshaping this local institution, now half a century old, which retains its vintage motor inn feel. There is a great variety of rooms, including suites with kitchenettes or full kitchens – a budget-saver. Decor can be a bit eclectic (particularly in the executive suite) but rooms are clean, comfortable and good value. Continental breakfast provided.

At $119, Penthouse 1 is a bargain, with vaulted ceiling and a small lanai.

★**Tina's Country Cottage** COTTAGE $$
(☎+1 702-525-0289; www.homeaway.com/vacation-rental/p373121; 65-1396D Kawaihae Rd; 2-bed cottage $135) This classic one-floor plantation cottage is perfect: centrally located yet tucked away in a quiet cul-de sac, in impeccable condition and offering all amenities, including washer/dryer, flat-screen TVs, and wi-fi. Attention to detail is everywhere and the price is a bargain. The only problem: you'll have a hard time leaving the charming porch. Ask for directions.

Aaah, the Views B&B B&B $$
(☎885-3455; www.aaahtheviews.com; 66-1773 Alaneo St; r $185-195; 📶) Run by pros who understand the business of hospitality, this aptly named B&B occupies an attractive location on a babbling stream, with mountain views across a broad prairie, 3 miles west of the town center. The three rooms are well lit and take advantage of the scenery. A full breakfast is served streamside.

The Queen Room ($185) has an ingenious loft ladder, and can further be broken into

DON'T MISS

GREEN SPACE AT LAST

For all its wide-open spaces, Waimea has a surprising lack of public parks and trails. Now two related initiatives are addressing that.

The largest project of Waimea Outdoor Circle, **Waimea Nature Park** (Ulu La'au; ☎443-4482; www.waimeaoutdoorcircle.org; ⏲7am-5:30pm), not to be confused with adjacent Waimea Park, is a 10-acre green space in the center of town with picnic tables and free wi-fi (user id: 0000lulaau), that is also a native plant restoration project. An excellent booklet on the latter is available on site ($3, free if you return them). The park is surprisingly easy to miss: follow the road by the side of the large Canada France building.

Waimea Trail (www.waimeatrails.com; Waimea Park; ⏲daylight hours), an ambitious project of Waimea Trails and Greenways, also begins in the park. At time of research it follows the adjacent Waikoloa Stream (hence its local name, the 'Stream Trail') to an old military road, forming an interesting round trip hike or mountain bike of approximately 2 miles. Future plans include paving 4.8 miles of trail.

two rooms ($125, $135) that share a bath. Amenities include cable TV, DVD, phone, fridge, microwave and coffee maker.

Waimea Garden Cottages COTTAGES $$
(☎885-8550; www.waimeagardens.com; studio $150, cottages $165-180, incl breakfast; wi-fi) Located 2 miles west of town near the intersection of Kawaihae Rd and Hwy 250, these three well-done, fully stocked, and cozy country cottages offer privacy in an attractive natural setting.

The Kohala Cottage has a full kitchen, enormous tiled bath and adjacent walled garden. The Waimea Cottage offers a fireplace, kitchenette and private patio. There's also a spacious studio with great woodwork and clerestory windows near a seasonal stream. Three-day minimum stay. No laundry facilities.

Jacaranda Inn INN $$
(☎885-8813; www.jacarandainn.com; 65-1444 Kawaihae Rd; r/ste/cottage from $129/159/178; wi-fi) Built in 1897, the Jacaranda is a grand old lady struggling to maintain her dignity amidst the vicissitudes of the years. Each of the eight rooms here are indulgent, antique-filled visions, a mix of four-poster beds, opulent tiled baths, carved furniture, Jacuzzi tubs and oriental rugs over hardwood floors.

The garden is not what it once was, and occupancy ebbs and flows. Call ahead; the property has long been for sale, but promises to continue as an inn.

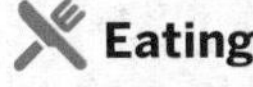

Eating

Good news: Waimea is awash in tasty, reasonably priced food. In addition to the options below, an international row of restaurants at the Waimea Shopping Center offers Italian, Japanese, Korean, Thai and Chinese cuisine, though these are largely uninspiring. Self-caterers can get all they need from **KTA Super Store** (☎885-8866; 65-1158 Mamalahoa Hwy, Waimea Center; ⏲6am-11pm), a grocer with an in-store pharmacy, and health-food store **Healthways II** (☎885-6775; 67-1185 Mamalahoa Hwy, Parker Ranch Center; ⏲9am-7pm Mon-Sat, to 5pm Sun).

★Big Island Brewhaus & Taqueria MEXICAN $
(☎887-1717; www.bigislandbrewhaus.com; 64-1066 Mamalahoa Hwy; mains $7.50-16; ⏲11am-8:30pm Mon-Sat, noon-8:30pm Sun) What could be a better choice to exemplify Waimea's defining blend of unpretentious sophistication than this intelligent new brewhouse? Owner Thomas Kerns, former brewmaster at Maui Brewing Company, already has more taste and quality in his collection of 17 house beers than do most major breweries.

Embracing the new craft beer ethos, Thomas brews outside the traditional box, exploring a wide range of styles and flavors, like the Paniolo Pale Ale, with its dash of tropical fruit, and the Golden Sabbath Belgian Ale, which has a tremendous aroma. The Brewpub is further attached to a taqueria, so you have some hot reasons for downing a five-cup sampler, although the beer outshines the food. A 2L jar of beer to go is $14.

Hawaiian Style Cafe LOCAL $
(☎885-4295; 64-1290 Kawaihae Rd, Hayashi Bldg; dishes $7.50-10; ⏲7am-1:30pm Mon-Sat, to

noon Sun) The screen door, its springs shot, slams constantly as locals gather around the horseshoe-shaped counter at this favorite island-style greasy spoon, particularly for breakfast. It delivers huge portions of *loco moco*, pancakes, *kalua* hash, poi, fried rice, burgers and more.

Village Burger BURGERS **$**
(☎885-7319; www.villageburgerwaimea.com; 67-1185 Mamalahoa Hwy, Parker Ranch Center; burgers $7.50-12; ⏰10:30am-8pm Mon-Sat, to 6pm Sun) Given the magnitude of Parker Ranch, you'd think there would be a great burger joint in town, and finally there is. Get your Big Island Beef Burger here and you'll notice the taste difference right away. Great shakes, too.

Waimea Coffee & Co CAFE **$**
(☎885-8915; www.waimeacoffeecompany.com; Kawaihe Rd, Parker Sq; sandwiches $7-8.50; ⏰6:30am-5:30pm Mon-Sat, 8am-2pm Sun; 📶) This upscale coffee shop has a devoted following for its espresso drinks and sandwiches.

Redwater Cafe HAWAII REGIONAL **$$**
(☎885-9299; www.redwater-cafe.com; 65-1299 Kawaihae Rd; mains $22-36; ⏰noon-2:30pm Mon-Fri, 5-9pm daily) This new addition has quickly risen to the top of many lists, propelled in part by the reputation of owner/chef David Abrahams, a 25-year veteran of resort kitchens on the West Coast. The decor is saloon simple, quality a bit uneven, and the menu somewhat limited, though it incorporates a fusion of global tastes: think Hawaii Regional with a twist.

A sushi bar (5pm to 9pm) and outdoor garden area provide some variety. Extensive kids menu.

Pau INTERNATIONAL **$$**
(☎885-6325; www.paupizza.com; 65-1227 Opelo Rd, Opelo Plaza; pizza $17-28; ⏰11am-8pm Mon-Fri) Order at the counter, then sit back and enjoy the salads, sandwiches, pastas and over a dozen thin-crust pizzas at this laid-back, engaging, and ever-popular eatery. The seasonal menu is ever-changing and focused on specials.

★ **Merriman's** HAWAII REGIONAL CUISINE **$$$**
(☎885-6822; www.merrimanshawaii.com; 65-1227 Opelo Rd, Opelo Plaza; lunch $10-18, dinner $30-55; ⏰11:30am-1:30pm Mon-Fri, 5:30am-8pm daily) Easily Waimea's best restaurant, and the only one that tempts you out of your flip-flops, this cornerstone of Hawaii Regional Cuisine continues to deliver impeccable meals and great service.

The professional staff guides you through a fine dining experience, supported by a creative menu fusing Hawaiian and Asian influences. The 'duo' menu option, which combines two entrees in one, is a nice way to extend your sample size. Lunch is a welcome bargain.

 Shopping

Three shopping malls line Hwy 19 through town: **Parker Ranch Center** (67-1185 Mamala hoa Hwy), where the stop signs say 'Whoa,' **Waimea Center** (65-1158 Mamalahoa Hwy) and

KECK BREAKTHROUGHS

Keck Observatory no longer contains the world's largest optical telescopes – at present that prize is held by the new 10.4m Grand Telescope of the Canaries, on the Spanish island of La Palma – but it is still arguably the most productive observatory in the world. In the past few years it has been the primary instrument for some of the greatest breakthroughs in astronomy, including:

➡ The 2011 Nobel Prize–winning discovery that the expansion of the universe is accelerating.

➡ The 2012 Crafoord Prize for the discovery of a supermassive black hole at the center of our Milky Way galaxy.

➡ The first image of a planet outside our own solar system, and the subsequent discovery of more than half of all known such 'exoplanets'.

➡ The 2012 discovery of a small planet in the so-called Goldilocks Zone (where temperatures are just right for liquid water, essential for life) of a solar system orbiting the closest Sun-like star to Earth, Tau Ceti. Do you hear that thumping sound, Dr Arroway?

Parker Sq (65-1279 Kawaihae Rd). The first two have groceries and basics, in addition to gift shops; Parker Sq aims for the more discriminating, upscale gift buyer.

★ **Gallery of Great Things** GALLERY
(☎885-7706; www.galleryofgreatthingshawaii.com; 65-1279 Kawaihae Rd, Parker Sq; ⏰9am-5.30pm Mon-Sat, 10am-4pm Sun) Is it a museum, a gallery, a trinket shop, or an antique store? This perfectly named shop is all of these, and more than enough to keep you poking about for hours amidst one great find after another.

Multicolored feather masks? Secondhand kimonos? Infrared photographs? Butterfly art? The owner has filled a cottage with items cherry-picked from around the vast Pacific region, each with a special something, a puzzling uniqueness or extraordinary flair that makes it great. If you have any weakness for curios or exotica, or simply good art, they will have to drag you away kicking and screaming.

★ **Parker School Farmers Market** MARKET
(65-1224 Lindsey Rd; ⏰8am-1pm Sat) Why Waimea has two farmers markets on the same day is a mystery, but this one edges out its rival, the Waimea Farmers Market. In the center of town, behind Parker School, it is more convenient, and attracts more varied participants, including a mobile bread oven. Look for the white tents.

Vendors emphasize organic produce and specialty items: fresh eggs, herbs and plants, local meat and honey, beautiful flowers and plenty of cooked food.

Waimea Farmers Market MARKET
(⏰7am-noon Sat) Like its Saturday morning rival, the more central Parker School Farmers Market, this is a fun and vibrant community event offering fresh produce and local gossip in equal amounts. There's a small selection of high-quality craft stalls. Located in front of the Hawaiian Home Lands office, near mile marker 55 on Hwy 19.

Waimea Mid-Week Market MARKET
(⏰9am-4pm Wed) If you can't wait until the weekend farmers markets, this smallish version offers local organic produce, island honey, handmade soaps, free-range beef, handmade jewelry, hot plate lunches and live *paniolo* music. Located in the stables at Parker Ranch, next to the growing Paniolo Heritage Center (free on market days).

DON'T MISS

MAUNA KEA POLO CLUB

After a long hiatus the Big Island once again has polo, and the field alone is worth the trip. The games are sponsored by **Mauna Kea Polo Club** (☎960-8223 Jed; www.maunakeapoloclub.com; adult/child under 12 $5/free; ⏰1pm Sun Oct–mid-Dec), and held 6.4 miles up Saddle Rd from Waimea on exclusive Waikii Ranch. More Big Island than Long Island, they are very low key, with BBQ eats and T-shirts for sale, and tailgating encouraged. It's the perfect excuse for a beautiful drive and picnic, and you might even learn something about polo. Right at Saddle Rd mile marker 59; the gate house attendant will let you in.

Wishard Gallery ART GALLERY
(☎887-2278; www.wishardgallery.com; 67-1185 Mamalahoa Hwy D104, Parker Ranch Center; ⏰9:30am-5:30pm Mon-Sat, 11am-5pm Sun) Apart from Harry Wishard's own imaginative landscapes, which pop up in houses and restaurants around the island, this gallery represents 20 other artists. Of note are Ethan Tweedie's stunning panoramas of Mauna Kea transferred to aluminum.

Kamuela Liquor Store WINE
(☎885-4674; 64-1010 Mamalahoa Hwy; ⏰8:30am-7pm Mon-Sat, 9am-5pm Sun) A wolf in sheep's clothing, this smallish shop, tucked away in a vintage building, has some of the island's best selection of wine.

ℹ Orientation

The intersection of Kawaihae Rd (Hwy 19) and Mamalahoa Hwy (Hwy 190) is Waimea's town center. Given that sea and mountains lie all around, it can be a surprisingly confusing point to navigate from, so remember this: Kawaihae Rd leads to Kawaihai (think beach) and Kohala; Mam Hwy goes past the malls toward Honoka'a and Hilo, and in the other direction to Saddle Rd.

ℹ Information

North Hawaii Community Hospital (☎885-4444; 67-1125 Mamalahoa Hwy) Emergency services available 24 hours.

Post Office (☎800-275-8777; 67-1197 Mamalahoa Hwy; ⏰8am-4:30pm Mon-Fri, 9am-noon Sat) Address all Waimea mail to 'Kamuela'.

MAUNA KEA & SADDLE ROAD

Mauna Kea

With a summit 13,796ft above sea level, Mauna Kea is the tallest volcano in the world's oceans. Measured from its roots on the ocean floor, it is even more impressive, edging out Mauna Loa to be the world's tallest mountain at 33,500ft. These statistics may create a somewhat misleading picture, however. As a massive shield volcano, with a shallow convex shape, Mauna Kea lacks the curvaceous grandeur of a classic volcanic cone, like Mt Fuji. Viewed from a few miles away, it looks more like an enormous wall in the sky.

Elevation is just one measure of Mauna Kea's stature, however. Here, nature, spirituality and science converge, and sometimes conflict. The harsh environment on the mountain is home to several endemic species, some endangered. The entire mountain, and the summit in particular, is one of the holiest places in traditional Hawaiian spirituality. And it is a shrine to the modern astronomy community as well, which has constructed the greatest collection of major astronomical telescopes in the world here. This mighty mountain has certainly attracted its share of followers, all of whom converge on the summit.

To fully appreciate Mauna Kea you should: visit the 'Imiloa Astronomy Center of Hawai'i (p269) which provides a wonderful introduction to the mountain and its history; take one or more hikes on its extensive trail system; visit the summit at sunset, an unforgettable experience; and then descend to the Visitor Information Station and participate in its evening stargazing program, equally profound in its own way. All of that can be accomplished in one fantastic day, either on your own or with a tour: a trip to the Big Island is not complete otherwise.

Mauna Kea & Mauna Loa

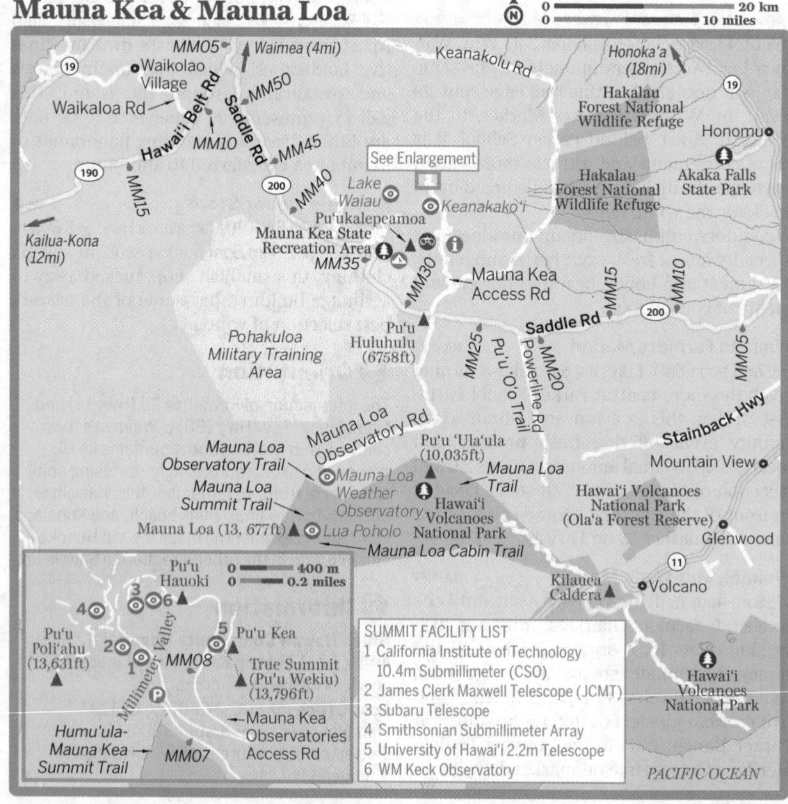

History & Environment

According to the Hawaiian creation myth, the Hawaiian Islands were created at Mauna Kea, the home of the gods. That's not too far from the geological explanation, either. Between 40,000 and 13,000 years ago, Mauna Kea's deep roots tapped into a hot spot, an area in the Earth's mantle that acts like a molten well, causing frequent eruptions. Thanks to the drift of oceanic plates, it has since slid off the hot spot, rendering the mighty mountain dormant, with the last eruption occurring some 4500 years ago.

Certain plants and animals adapted to this unique environment. Ascending the mountain, biological zones shift from rainforest to koa-and-ohia forest to open woodland to shrubs and finally (above 11,500ft) to alpine desert. Every elevation has species endemic to Hawai'i, and some found only here. Plants endemic to the summit include the bizarre Mauna Kea silversword, which takes 50 years to flower, and does so only once.

Summit creatures are restricted mostly to insects. Strangest by far is the endemic *wekiu,* a bug that increases the salt content in its bodily fluids to lower their freezing point. Further down the mountain, several of Hawai'i's endemic birds call Mauna Kea home, such as the nene and the *palila* (finch-billed honeycreeper), as well as the endangered Hawaiian bat, the *'ope'ape'a.*

Westerners arriving here in the late 1700s introduced feral cattle, goats and sheep. By the early 20th century these animals had decimated the mountain's natural environment. Animal eradication efforts, begun in the 1920s and continuing today, have helped nature partly restore itself.

In 1960 astronomer Gerard Kuiper placed a telescope on Pu'u Poli'ahu and announced that 'the mountaintop is probably the best site in the world from which to study the moon, the planets and stars.' Kuiper turned out to be right.

In 1968, the same year the first Mauna Kea observatory was built, the University of Hawai'i (UH) was granted a 65-year lease to the summit area, now called the Mauna Kea Science Reserve. The university leases property to others, and 13 telescopes are currently in operation, more than on any other single mountain, including three of the world's largest. Their combined light-gathering power is 60 times greater than the Hubble Space Telescope.

STARGAZING PLANNER

Here are some tips from the experts about the best times – celestially speaking – to visit Mauna Kea.

➡ Lunar eclipses and meteor showers are special events in this rarefied air; the Leonides in November are particularly impressive. Check **StarDate** (http://stardate.org/nightsky/meteors) for the year's meteor showers, eclipses, moon phases and more.

➡ The Milky Way streaks the night sky bright and white between January and March.

➡ Don't forget the monthly full moon. It's simply spectacular as it rises over you, seemingly close enough to touch.

Given the environmental and cultural concerns, building on Mauna Kea has led to some heated conflicts in the past. Today concerted efforts are being made to balance the needs of all stakeholders in the construction of an immense Thirty Meter Telescope (www.tmt.org). While the TMT will be the world's most accurate, multiplying by nine the collecting area of current optical telescopes, its structural footprint will be larger than any other observatory currently on Mauna Kea's summit. On the other hand, in traditional Hawaiian mythology the navel, or *piko,* is the central connection between the individual and the universe. Whatever its footprint may be, the TMT will be the greatest tether to the heavens on Earth – our planetary *piko.*

Sights

Mauna Kea Visitor Information Station
(MKVIS; ☎961-2180; www.ifa.hawaii.edu/info/vis; ⏲9am-10pm) The Mauna Kea Visitor Information Station is of modest size, but packs quite a punch. It is full of videos on astronomy, virtual observatory tours, and exhibits on the mountain's history, ecology and geology. Movies are constantly showing, and there's an interesting gift shop full of things for budding astronomers of all ages.

Also, you can puchase coffee, hot chocolate and instant noodles, or munch on freeze-dried astronaut food, and there are books and gifts for sale. Several hikes are possible from here, and at night the free stargazing program (p252) is held here.

Summit Area LANDMARK

Sunsets are phenomenal from the summit. All of Hawai'i lies below as the sun sinks into an ocean of clouds – while the telescopes silently unshutter and turn their unblinking eyes to the heavens. Look east to see 'the shadow' – the gigantic silhouette of Mauna Kea looming over Hilo.

Moonrises can be equally as impressive: the high altitude can make the moon appear squashed and misshapen, or sometimes resemble a brushfire. In any case, bring long pants, a thick coat (or lots of layers), a warm hat and gloves. It gets cold up there.

If you have a 4WD, you may drive to the summit in the daytime, but you must descend 30 minutes after sunset. It takes about half an hour to drive the 8-mile summit road; the first 4.5 miles are gravel. Just before the pavement begins, the area on the east side of the road is dubbed 'moon valley', because it's where the Apollo astronauts rehearsed with their lunar rover before their journey to the real moonscape.

Keanakako'i HISTORICAL SITE

During Mauna Kea's ice age, molten lava erupted under its glacier, creating an extremely hard basalt, which ancient Hawaiians later chipped into sharp adzes at the ancient adze quarry Keanakako'i. For 800 years, these tools were fashioned on the mountain and traded throughout the islands. Entering the fragile quarry is discouraged but not prohibited.

Just past mile marker 6 on Mauna Kea Access Rd is a parking area. Below this is the trailhead to Lake Waiau and Keanakako'i. Getting to both takes about an hour, depending on your rate of acclimatization.

★Lake Waiau LAKE

At 13,020ft this unique alpine lake is the third-highest in the USA. Thought by ancient Hawaiians to be bottomless, it's actually only 10ft deep and, despite desert conditions, never dry.

Clay formed from ash holds the water, which is fed by melted snow, permafrost and less than 15in of rainfall annually. To Hawaiians, these sacred waters are the island's *piko*. It's traditional to place a baby's umbilical cord in the water to assure good health.

WM Keck Observatory Visitor Gallery OBSERVATORY

(www.keckobservatory.org; 10am-4pm Mon-Fri) FREE Includes a display, a 15-minute video, public bathrooms and a plexiglass-enclosed viewing area inside the Keck I dome.

True Summit LANDMARK

(Pu'u Wekiu) The short 200yd trail to Mauna Kea's true summit begins opposite the UH telescope. It's harder than it looks, and it's not necessary to go to see the sunset nor claim you've summited Mauna Kea. The summit is marked by a US Geological Survey (USGS) summit benchmark and a Native Hawaiian *ahu* (altar).

Given the biting winds, high altitude and extreme cold, most people don't linger.

Activities

★Visitor Information Station Stargazing Program STARGAZING

(Mauna Kea Visitor Information Station; 6-10pm) FREE The Visitor Information Station offers a terrific nightly stargazing program. Numerous telescopes are set up outside the station, each one trained on a different celestial object. On an average night you might move from the Ring Nebula to the Andromeda Galaxy to a galactic cluster to Jupiter's moons. It is a unique and profoundly memorable experience.

The program begins with one of various films that may last up to an hour; some are better than others. How much you'll see still depends on cloud cover and moon phase, but you can call ahead if you want to double check. The busiest nights are Friday and Saturday, but there are no reservations. Special scope attachments accommodate visitors in wheelchairs.

During big meteor showers, the station staffs its telescopes for all-night star parties; call for details. And every Saturday night at 6pm it hosts a rotating series of lectures and events: 'The Universe Tonight' is an astronomy lecture held on the first Saturday; on the second Saturday students from the UH Hilo Astrophysics Club assist with stargazing; 'Malalo I Ka Lani Po' is a culture lecture on the third Saturday; and the fourth Saturday is a multigenre international music night.

Shorter Hikes HIKING

Several short walks begin at the Visitor Information Station. Off the parking lot is an area protecting the endemic silversword plant, while across the road a 10-minute uphill hike on a well-trodden trail brings you to the crest of **Pu'ukalepeamoa**, a cinder cone that offers the best sunset views near the station. Several moderate hikes also begin from the summit road.

Humu'ula-Mauna Kea Summit Trail HIKING
The 6-mile Humu'ula-Mauna Kea Summit Trail climbs nonstop about 4600ft to the top of Mauna Kea. This is a very strenuous, all-day, high-altitude hike up such steep, barren slopes that you sometimes feel you might step off the mountain into the sky. Utterly exposed to winds and the changeable weather, it makes for an eerie, primordial experience.

To do this trail, start very early – by 6am if possible. It typically takes five hours to reach the summit, and half as long coming down, and you want time to explore in between. Consult with rangers for advice, and get a map and register at the Visitor Information Station's outdoor trail kiosk before hiking. Be prepared for serious weather, as snow and 100mph winds have been known.

Park at the Visitor Information Station and walk 1000ft up the road. Where the pavement ends, go left on the dirt road, following several Humu'ula Trail signs to the trail proper. Reflective T-posts and cairns mark the route. After about an hour the summit road comes back into view on your right, and the vegetation starts to disappear. As you weave around cinder cones and traipse over crumbled *'a'a* and slippery scree, you pass various spur trails, which all lead back to the access road.

Most of the way you will be passing through the Mauna Kea Ice Age Natural Area Reserve. After about three hours a sharp, short ascent leads to Keanakako'i. The hardest, steepest part of the trail is now behind you. After another mile you reach a four-way junction, where a 10-minute detour to the left brings you to Lake Waiau. Return to the four-way junction and head north (uphill) for the final push to meet the Mauna Kea Summit Rd at a parking area. Suddenly the observatories are visible on the summit, and straight ahead is 'Millimeter Valley', nicknamed for its submillimeter and millimeter observatories. The trail officially ends at the access road's mile marker 7, but the true summit still snickers at you another 1.5 miles away.

For native Hawaiians, the summit is a region, a realm, not a point on a map. But if you really need to place a boot toe on Pu'u Wekiu, Mauna Kea's true summit, soldier on till you reach the UH 2.2m Telescope, where the short spur trail to the summit begins.

When descending, return along the shoulder of the access road rather than retracing the trail. Though the road is 2 miles longer, it's easier on the knees and easier to follow as sunlight fades. Also, it's common for hikers to get offered a lift downhill; sticking to the road increases your chances.

Alternatively, save time and energy by hitching a lift to the top from the Visitor Information Station and just walking down (about three hours).

Tours

★ Visitor Information Station Summit Tours GUIDED TOUR
(935-6268; 1pm Sat & Sun) FREE The Visitor Information Station offers free summit tours, but you must provide your own 4WD transportation (or hitch a lift from someone who does). No reservations are needed; simply arrive by 1pm to join the tour. Tours don't go in bad weather, so be sure to call ahead.

The first hour is spent watching videos about Mauna Kea as you acclimatize, then you caravan to the summit, where you hear a talk on the history and workings of the summit telescopes. The tours then visit at least one telescope, usually the WM Keck's 10m telescope. Tours depart from the summit at about 4:30pm, but most people stay for sunset and come down on their own. Pregnant women, children under 16, and those with circulatory and respiratory conditions are not allowed, nor are those who have been scuba diving in the past 24 hours.

Subaru Telescope GUIDED TOUR
(www.naoj.org/Information/Tour/Summit; 10:30am, 11:30am & 1:30pm) FREE The only public telescope tour on the summit takes in the world's largest single-piece mirror telescope up to 15 weekdays per month (40min, in English and Japanese). Advance online reservations and personal transportation required.

★ Hawaii Forest & Trail GUIDED TOUR
(800-464-1993, 331-8505; www.hawaii-forest.com; tours from $195) This excellent tour company, with diverse operations on the Big Island, has a meal stop in a tent on the ruins of a former ranch. Its guides are extremely knowledgeable, take you to the summit, and conduct a fine tour of the heavens by laser pointer. Departs from Kona, Waikoloa, and the junction of Hwy 190 and Hwy 200. Participants must be 16 years old.

Mauna Kea Summit Adventures GUIDED TOUR
(☎888-322-2366, 322-2366; www.maunakea.com; tours $192) Mauna Kea was the first company to do summit tours, starting over 20 years ago. It remains a high-quality outfit. Meals are outside at the Visitor Information Station. Picks up in Kona, Waikoloa, and the junction of Hwy 190 and Hwy 200. Participants must be 13 years old. Book online two weeks in advance for a 15% discount.

Orientation

The Mauna Kea Access Rd is near mile marker 28 on Saddle Rd. From the Saddle Rd junction, it's paved for 6 miles to the Visitor Information Station. It takes about 50 minutes from Hilo or Waimea and 1½ hours from Kailua-Kona. Past the visitor station, it's another 8 miles (half unpaved) and nearly 5000ft to the summit.

To visit the summit without a 4WD, you will need to join a Mauna Kea tour, hike or hitch a ride at the visitor station from one of the many people heading to the top with a 4WD (particularly at the start of the daily summit tour).

Note there are no restaurants, gas stations or emergency services on Saddle Rd or the mountain. Weather conditions can change rapidly, and daytime temperatures range from 50°F to below freezing. The summit can be windy, and observatory viewing rooms are colder than outside. Bring warm clothing, a heavy jacket, sunglasses and sunscreen. Especially in winter, it's a good idea to check on **weather and road conditions** (☎935-6268; http://mkwc.ifa.hawaii.edu/current/road-conditions). Even when the fog's as thick as pea soup on Saddle Rd, it's crystal clear at the mountaintop around 325 days a year.

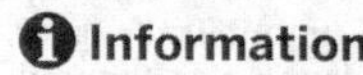

Information

The Visitor Information Station is at 9200ft, and even here some visitors might experience shortness of breath and mild altitude sickness. At the 13,796ft summit, atmospheric pressure is 60% what it is at sea level, and altitude sickness is common. Symptoms include nausea, headaches, drowsiness, impaired reason, loss of balance, shortness of breath and dehydration. The only way to recover is to descend. Kids under 16 years, pregnant women, and those with high blood pressure or circulatory conditions should not go to the summit. Nor should you scuba dive within 24 hours of visiting Mauna Kea.

The best way to avoid altitude sickness is to ascend slowly. All hikers and travelers to the summit should stop first at the visitor station for at least 30 minutes to acclimatize before continuing.

Getting There & Around

Saddle Road (Hwy 200) runs between Kona and Hilo, passing between the island's great peaks. From Kona it starts just south of mile marker 6 on Hwy 190. From Hilo, drive *mauka* (inland) on Kaumana Dr, which becomes Saddle Rd (Hwy 200). From Volcano, take Hwy 11 to Puainako which turns into Kaumana Dr. All drivers should start with a full tank of gas, as there are no gas stations on Saddle Rd.

Past the visitor station the road is suitable only for 4WD vehicles – there have been many accidents to underline this point. Over half the road is gravel, sometimes at a 15% grade, and the upper road can be covered with ice. When

SHOULD YOU BUY A SUMMIT TOUR?

To buy a summit tour or not, that is the question.

Tours have many positives: transportation from other parts of the island to the visitor station, 4WD to the summit, warm clothing, a box dinner, excellent guides with deep knowledge of astronomy, and the ease of it all. The negatives to consider include the considerable cost ($400 per couple), a fixed and limited schedule, and the herd factor.

Itinerary-wise, a typical sunset tour starts early afternoon, stops for dinner, arrives at the summit just before sunset, stays about 40 minutes (which doesn't allow for hiking), descends to the visitor station for private stargazing with a single telescope, and gets you home after 9pm. There is no tour of summit telescopes.

Now assess the DIY alternative. If you have a 4WD rental, you can do some hiking on your own, then take the summit tour from the Visitor Information Station. This includes a movie, a talk at the summit, and a visit to one of the observatories (if you only have a 2WD rental, you will need to hitch a round-trip ride from the station to the summit.) Finally, you can come back down to the visitor station for a smorgasbord of stargazing amidst multiple telescopes. You'll have to pack your dinner and bring warm clothing, but the total cost is zero, apart from the car, which you might have rented anyway. If not, a rental 4WD is a lot less than $400 a day.

descending, drive in low gear (or you can ruin your brakes), and pay attention to any signs of altitude sickness. Driving when the sun is low – in the hour after sunrise or before sunset – can create hazardous blinding conditions.

Saddle Road

Several exceptional hikes are possible from Saddle Rd. The most legendary and rewarding is the Mauna Loa Observatory Trail – the only way to get to the top in a single day.

★Mauna Loa Observatory Trail HIKING

This trail is the most recommended way to summit Mauna Loa; those who prefer a challenge above all else might consider taking the daunting, multiday Mauna Loa Trail (p299). However, make no mistake: the Observatory Trail is a difficult all-day adventure, but few 13,000ft mountains exist that are so accessible to the average hiker. This is a rare and unforgettable experience.

Day hikers do not need a permit, but if you would like to overnight at Mauna Loa Cabin, register the day before at the Kilauea Visitor Center in Hawai'i Volcanoes National Park.

To reach the trailhead, take the unsigned Mauna Loa Observatory Rd near mile marker 28 on Saddle Rd; it's nearly opposite the Mauna Kea Access Rd and adjacent to Pu'u Huluhulu. The single-lane, 17.5-mile asphalt road is in good condition but full of blind curves; the squiggled white line is to aid drivers in the fog. The road ends at a parking area just below the weather observatory at 11,150ft. There are no visitor facilities or bathrooms. From the observatory, the Mauna Loa Observatory Trail climbs up to the mountaintop.

Begin hiking by 8am; you want to be off the mountain or descending if afternoon clouds roll in. The trail is marked by cairns, which disappear in the fog. If this happens, stop hiking; find shelter in one of several small tubes and hollows along the route until you can see again, even if this means waiting till morning.

It is nearly 4 miles to the trail junction with the Mauna Loa Trail. Allow three hours for this gradual ascent of nearly 2000ft. If it weren't for the altitude, this would be a breeze. Instead, proceed slowly but steadily, keeping breaks short. If you feel the onset of altitude sickness, descend. About two hours along, you re-enter the national park, and the old lava flows appear in a rainbow of sapphire, turquoise, silver, ochre, orange, gold and magenta.

Once at the trail junction, the majesty of the summit's Moku'aweoweo Caldera overwhelms you. Day hikers have two choices: proceed another 2.6 miles and three hours along the Summit Trail to the tippy-top at 13,677ft (visible in the distance), or explore the caldera itself by following the 2.1-mile Mauna Loa Cabin Trail. If you can stand not summiting, the second option is extremely interesting, leading to even grander caldera views and a vertiginous peek into the awesome depths of Lua Poholo – a craterlike hole in the landscape.

Descending takes half as long as ascending; depending on how far you go, prepare for a seven- to 10-hour round-trip hike. Bring copious amounts of water, food, a flashlight and rain gear, and wear boots, a winter coat and a cap – it's cold and windy year-round.

Pu'u Huluhulu Trail HIKING

The easy trail up the cinder cone **Pu'u Huluhulu** or Shaggy Hill (6758ft), an ancient *kipuka* (volcanic oasis) created more than 10,000 years ago, makes a piquant appetizer before going up Mauna Kea. The 20-minute hike climbs through secondary growth to the top of the hill, from where there are panoramic views of Mauna Kea, Mauna Loa and Hualalai.

The trailhead is very near the turnoff to Mauna Kea, just past Saddle Rd's mile marker 28 heading west.

Pu'u 'O'o Trail HIKING

For a more substantial but equally peaceful ramble, try the Pu'u 'O'o Trail (also called the Power Line Rd Trail), an 8-mile loop traversing meadows, old lava flows and several pretty koa-and-ohia *kipuka* forests filled with the birdsong of Hawaiian honeycreepers. (Note: this is different from the Hawai'i Volcanoes National Park's Pu'u 'O'o Trail.)

The signed trailhead (with a small parking area) is almost exactly halfway between mile markers 22 and 23 on Saddle Rd. The trail is marked by *ahu* (stone cairns); it's easy to follow in good weather, less so in rain or fog. If in doubt, simply retrace your steps the way you came. Eventually, the trail connects with Power Line Rd (marked with a sign), a 4WD road that can be used as the return route. Note, though, that the road returns you about a mile away from the trailhead parking area.

HAMAKUA COAST

Stretching from Waipi'o Valley to Hilo, the Hamakua Coast is the rugged side of tropical paradise. Here on the windward side of the island the sea pounds cliffs, rocky shores and the occasional black sand beach, and lush tropical jungles stretch into the hills, full of waterfalls. Meanwhile, history lies close at hand. Farmers still work ancient taro patches, and well-preserved sugar plantation towns recall the region's economic heyday, when steam trains chugged along a coastline stitched together by sweeping bridges. This a great stretch of coast to drive, with numerous scenic parks along the way.

Waipi'o Valley

Beautiful and maddening, there's no doubt that Waipi'o Valley occupies a special place on an already special island, and for reasons as tangled as the boughs of a monkeypod tree. Reaching the end of Hwy 240, you look out across a spectacular natural amphitheater, as if an enormous scoop has subtracted a chunk of coastline, one of seven such valleys carved into the windward side of the Kohala Mountains. The valley goes back 6 miles, its flat floor an emerald patchwork of jungle, huts and taro patches crowned by the awesome sight of **Hi'ilawe**, a distant ribbon of white falling 1450ft, making it the longest waterfall in the state. A river winds through it all (Waipi'o means 'curving water'), to a black sand beach squeezed between dramatic running cliffs that disappear around the corner of the island.

So what's the rub? Waipi'o Valley is the one place on the Big Island where the aloha spirit has faded. The valley walls contain some very territorial residents, with a long history of disagreement with the outside world. And like all deep conflicts, this one has two sides. Some 50 in number, the residents point out that their home is sacred in

Hamakua Coast

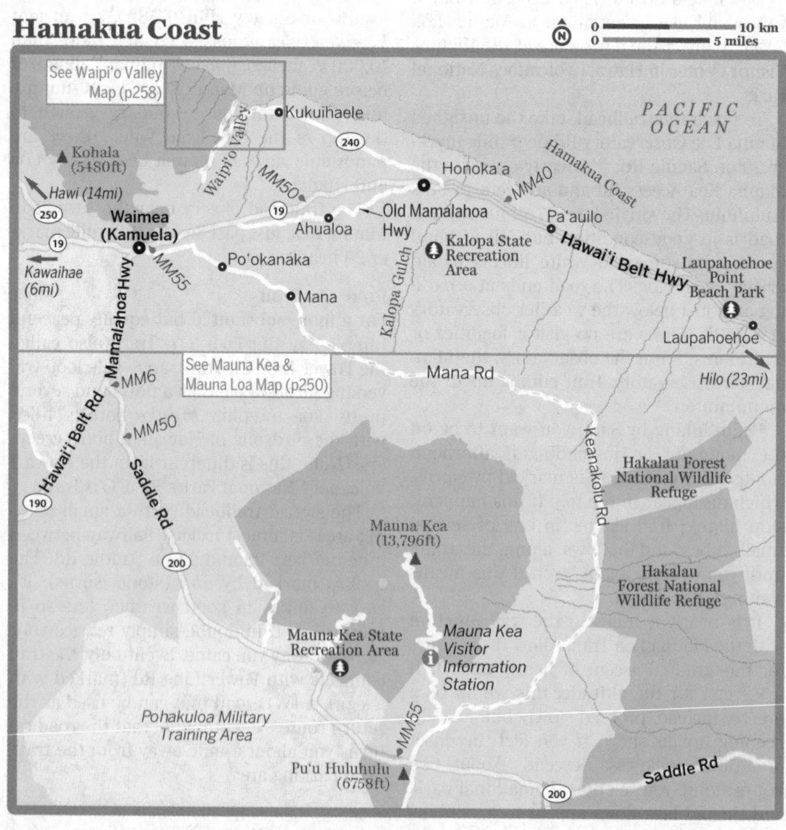

traditional Hawaiian culture, contains an intangible spiritual energy, holds a special place in Hawaii history, is limited in space, and has a natural beauty that must be protected from too many visitors. Others above the rim and beyond claim that the valley's residents simply wish to separate themselves from the outside world, for a variety of reasons ranging from misanthropy to marijuana. This is, after all, the end of the road, on an island in the middle of the Pacific Ocean. In any case, if you are of a mind that the mainland has gone mad, Waipi'o may be the last holdout, and that alone makes it irresistible.

For visitors, all of this has a practical impact: if you wish to descend into the valley, you can explore Waipi'o Beach and take the King's Trail to Nanewe Falls, but that is basically it, unless you pay for a tour (and even those are limited in range). Hiking along Waipi'o Stream to Hi'ilawe is no longer recommended as you must either traverse private land or walk in the stream itself, which is difficult and somewhat hazardous. Having said that, for the average person the beach and the King's Trail are more than enough to satisfy your curiosity, and if you want more, you can head over the ridge toward Waimanu on the Muliwai Trail and explore to your heart's content. So at the moment there is a workable treaty in place if everyone adheres to it. For those content with a photograph from afar, the scenic lookout on the rim of the valley is your destination, a place to reflect on how paradise can get so complicated.

History

Known as the Valley of the Kings, Waipi'o was the ancient breadbasket of the Big Island, and Hawai'i's political and religious center, home to the highest *ali'i*, or ruling chiefs. According to oral histories, several thousand people lived here before contact with the West, and the remains of heiau and other structures can be seen today. In 1823 William Ellis, the first missionary to descend into Waipi'o, guessed the population to be around 1300. In the 1880s Chinese immigrants began to settle in the valley's green folds, adding rice to the native taro cultivation.

In 1946 Hawai'i's most devastating tsunami struck the valley, traveling over a mile inland. Interestingly, no one perished from it; in one case an entire family hut was lifted up and put down elsewhere. But the sea salted the earth, and once the waters receded, most people resettled 'topside,' particularly in **Kukuihaele**, the small town that flanks the rim of the valley. The valley floor has been sparsely populated ever since, attracting a wide variety of nature lovers, recluses, pot farmers, hippies and locals seeking to reclaim their history. Kukuihaele is now home to vacation rentals and tour providers.

MULIWAI TRAIL SAFETY

- Streams beyond the valley are subject to flash floods. If it rains hard, choose your fords carefully.
- Don't drink untreated water. Feral animals roam the area and leptospirosis is present.
- Check shoes and sleeping bags for centipedes, which can deliver a painful bite.
- Bring a signal flare for emergencies, as sightseeing helicopters are common.

Sights & Activities

★Waipi'o Valley Lookout LOOKOUT

Located at the end of Hwy 240, this lookout provides a jawdropping view across the valley. One of Hawaii's iconic images.

★Waipi'o Valley Hike HIKING

To explore the valley on your own, first you need to get down into it, by taking the incredibly steep road from the overlook to the valley floor. Then follow the road to Waipi'o Beach and explore from one end to the other. From the far cliffs, the adventurous can follow the King's Trail to swim at Nanewe Falls.

The road down from the lookout is to be taken seriously, no matter how you tackle it. If by car, you must have a 4WD, and use your gears for braking. Do not attempt it otherwise, as the road has a 25% grade and ends in a rutted mess that becomes a quagmire when wet. The trip is about 15 minutes. If you hike down (45 minutes), make sure you have tightly fitted shoes, as the pitch of the pavement will tend to jam your toes. If you can't hitch a ride back up, the return trip can be exhausting for those not used to strenuous effort. There's no shade, so bring water.

Waipi'o Valley

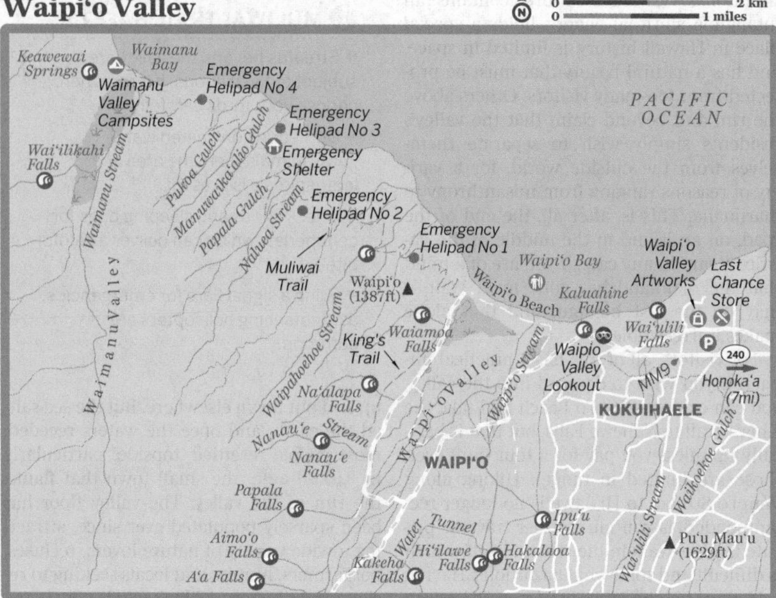

Once on the valley floor, follow the road to **Waipi'o Beach**, passing the twisted remains of some vehicles that took the quick way down. There are bathrooms near the beginning of the black sand beach, which has rip currents and a treacherous undertow, so don't even think of swimming here, even if you see local surfers in search of its daunting break. Look for spinner dolphins and whales offshore, and views of Hi'ilawe in the distance. Midway down you'll have to cross **Waipi'o Stream**, which flows into the sea; best to do so by wading in the ocean, where there are no rocks. If there has been rain, you can see **Kaluahine Falls** cascading down the cliffs from whence you came. High surf makes getting to the falls more challenging than it looks. Ahead you'll see the Muliwai Trail zig-zagging up the cliffs on the other side of the valley, on its way to distant Waimanu.

Once you near the base of the far cliffs, you will see a trail that heads inland, next to a gate. The trail shortly forks, with the Muliwai Trail heading upwards, and the **King's Trail** further inland, along a fence. If you don't mind a good workout, it's an excellent idea to climb the Muliwai to the ridgeline for an outstanding view, then return to the fork before heading along the King's Trail.

As it parallels the valley walls the King's Trail passes through a natural botanical garden. You'll encounter coffee plants, *liliko'i* (passion fruit), massive monkeypods, papaya, elephant ear, avocado and lots more, making you realize what a cornucopia the valley really is. You'll also come across small groups of friendly wild horses, the descendents of domesticated animals left behind following the tsunami.

After 45 minutes or so you'll reach a wire fence, which you can pass through, as the trail is public. Shortly thereafter the trail reaches **Nanau'e Falls**, a stepped series of three pools, and a popular swimming hole for residents, not all of whom see the necessity for clothes. This is the end of the public trail, so take a dip and head back. Don't forget your bathing suit.

Muliwai Trail HIKING

This 8-mile backcountry trail is for strong hikers who can traverse steep, slippery and potentially treacherous ground. Don't underestimate the difficulty or the beauty of this hike, which takes 6½ to eight hours and requires crossing 13 gulches – brutal to ascend and descend, but lovely nonetheless, with little waterfalls and icy cold pools for swimming.

Plan on at least two nights (ideally, three or more) of camping in Waimanu Valley. Hiking there from Waipi'o Valley takes about six hours, while the return is easier and faster. You can park your car at the signposted 24-hour parking area. Dry weather is imperative for a safe, enjoyable experience.

The Muliwai Trail begins at the base of the cliffs on the far side of the valley; you can see it zig-zagging up the cliff face as you approach. A shaded path at the end of the beach takes you to a dual trailhead: head right and up for Muliwai (straight ahead leads to the King's Trail). The ancient Hawaiian footpath now rises over 1200ft in a mile of hard laboring back and forth up the cliff face; it's nicknamed 'Z-Trail' for the killer switchbacks. Hunters still use this trail to track feral pigs. The hike is exposed and hot, so cover this stretch early.

Eventually the trail moves into ironwood and Norfolk pine forest, and tops a little knoll before gently descending and becoming muddy and mosquito-ridden. The view of the ocean gives way to the sounds of a rushing stream. The trail crosses a gulch and ascends past a sign for Emergency Helipad No 1. For the next few hours the trail finds a steady rhythm of gulch crossings and forest ascents. A waterfall at the third gulch is a source of fresh water; treat it before drinking. For a landmark, look for Emergency Helipad No 2 at about the halfway point from Waipi'o Beach. Beyond that, there's an open-sided emergency shelter with pit toilets and Emergency Helipad No 3.

Rest here before making the final difficult descent. Leaving the shelter, hop across three more gulches and pass Emergency Helipad No 4, from where it's less than a mile to Waimanu Valley. This final section of switchbacks starts out innocently enough, with some artificial and natural stone steps, but over a descent of 1200ft the trail is poorly maintained and extremely hazardous later. A glimpse of **Wai'ilikahi Falls** (accessible by a 45-minute stroll) on the far side of the valley might inspire hikers to press onward, but beware: the trail is narrow and washed out in parts, with sheer drop-offs into the ocean and no handholds apart from mossy rocks and spiny plants. If the descent is questionable, head back to the trail shelter for the night.

Waimanu Valley is a mini Waipi'o, minus the tourists. It once had a sizable settlement and contains many ruins, including house and heiau terraces, stone enclosures and old *lo'i*. In the early 19th century an estimated 200 people lived here, but the valley was abandoned by its remaining three families after the 1946 tsunami. Today you'll bask alone amid a stunning deep valley framed by cliffs, waterfalls and a boulder-strewn beach.

From the bottom of the switchbacks, Waimanu Beach is 10 minutes past the camping regulations signboard. To ford the stream to reach the campsites on its western side, avoid a rope strung across the water, which is deep there. Instead, cross closer to the ocean entry where it is shallower. Camping requires a state permit for a maximum of six nights. There are nine campsites of your choice: recommended are No 2 (full valley views, proximity to stream, grassy spot); No 6 (view of Wai'ilikahi Falls, access to the only sandy beach); and No 9 (very private at the far end of the valley, lava-rock chairs and a table). Facilities include fire pits and composting outhouses. There's a spring about 10 minutes behind campsite No 9 with a PVC pipe carrying water from a waterfall; all water must be treated.

On the return trip, be careful to take the correct trail. Walking inland from Waimanu Beach, don't veer left on a false trail-of-use that attempts to climb a rocky streambed. Instead keep heading straight inland past the camping regulations sign to the trail to the switchbacks. It takes about two hours to get to the trail shelter, and another two to reach the waterfall gulch: refill your water here (again, treat before drinking). Exiting the ironwood forest soon after, the trail descends back to the floor of Waipi'o Valley.

Tours

★ Ride the Rim DRIVING TOUR
(775-1450; www.ridetherim.com; adult/child $159/85; tours 9am & 1pm) If you want to ride an all-terrain vehicle (ATV), what better place to do it than the rim of Waipi'o Valley? Much of the trail takes you through a private forest, with a refreshing stop at a swimming hole. The highlight is a panoramic overlook stretching from Hi'ilawe across the valley to the sea.

Drivers must be 16, but children may ride with a guide. Tours depart from Waipi'o Valley Artworks.

Walking Waipi'o HIKING
(345-9505; www.walkingwaipio.com; adult/child 7-12 $120/75; tours 8am Mon-Fri) An

uncommon five-hour hiking trip on the valley floor, including some swimming, led by a valley resident.

Na'alapa Stables HORSEBACK RIDING
(☎775-0419; www.naalapastables.com; rides $85; ⏲ tours 9am & 1pm) Visit the valley floor on a 2½-hour horseback ride; children eight years and over are welcome. This longstanding business has deep roots in the valley. Tours leave from Waipi'o Valley Artworks.

Waipi'o Valley Shuttle DRIVING TOUR
(☎775-7121; www.waipiovalleyshuttle.com; adult/child $55/25; ⏲ tours 9am, 11am, 1pm & 3pm Mon-Sat) This longstanding provider offers a 1½-hour valley tour by 4WD van, an efficient choice if you don't want to walk to the bottom. Tours depart from Waipi'o Valley Artworks.

Waipi'o Valley Wagon Tours TOUR
(☎775-9518; www.waipiovalleywagontours.com; adult/child $62/31; ⏲tours 10:30am, 12:30pm & 1:30pm Mon-Sat) This 1½-hour jaunt, in a mule-drawn wagon, carts visitors around the valley floor. Tours leave from Neptune's Garden.

Waipi'o Ridge Stables HORSEBACK RIDING
(☎877-757-1414, 775-1007; www.waipioridgestables.com; rides $85-165; ⏲tours 9am) Tour around the valley rim to the top of Hi'ilawe Falls (2½ hours) or combine with a forest trail ride (five hours), ending with a picnic and swim at a hidden waterfall. Departs Waipi'o Valley Artworks.

Hawaiian Walkways HIKING
(☎457-7759; www.hawaiianwalkways.com; guided hikes adult/child $119/99) Go to waterfalls and swimming holes via a private trail along the rim. Departs Parker Ranch Center, Waimea, at 9:30am.

Sleeping

With the exception of a single yurt, there are no accommodations on the valley floor (the longstanding tree house has closed). However, there are several options in Kukuihaele, the residential community on the rim, including some cliffside properties with spectacular views.

Waipi'o Valley Yurt YURT $
(☎345-9505; www.walkingwaipio.com; Waipi'o Valley; yurt per night/week $75/450) This off-the-grid, 14-foot yurt by Waipi'o Stream is your only opportunity to stay in Waipi'o Valley. Suitably unique, it offers a kitchen with propane fridge and gas stove, and, amazingly, a hot shower. The bed sleeps two but its kitchen/living area can accommodate others. A rare opportunity to indulge your inner (or outer) hippie.

Waipio Hostel/Alegre Plantation Cottage VACATION RENTAL, HOSTEL $
(☎989-1533, 775-1533; 48-5380 Kukuihaele Rd; r $35, 2-bed upper floor $79; 📶) This simply furnished former plantation house, in largely original condition, contains a two-bedroom top floor with full kitchen and large living spaces (rented as the Alegre Plantation Cottage) and three private rooms on the lower level (the hostel) with shared bath and a choice of beds. It's in a residential neighborhood, but has sea views out back and a rock-bottom price.

★Waipio Rim B&B B&B $$
(☎775-1727; www.waipiorim.com; d $200) Private and secluded, this handsome B&B sits up in the trees on the cliff opposite the lookout, as if suspended in midair. The view of the valley from the private lanai is fabulous, and lots of windows bring it inside. You'll be lulled to sleep by the sound of the surf below. Microwave, fridge, fifth night free.

Hale Kukui Orchard Retreat VACATION RENTAL $$
(☎800-444-7130, 775-1701; www.halekukui.com; 48-5460 Kukuihaele Rd; studio/cottage/2-bed unit $187/195/221; 📶) You can't go wrong with the three rentals here: each includes a full kitchen, spacious living area, private deck, outdoor hot tub and, best of all, fantastic views of the Waipi'o Valley cliffs (which is what you're paying for).

The Orchard Cottage makes an ideal honeymoon spot. The two-bedroom unit is great value: four guests can stay without extra fees. The spacious studio also sleeps four and is great for a family on a budget. The grounds include papaya, banana, star fruit and citrus, all for the taking. Classy owners ensure a great stay. Seventh night free.

Waipi'o Valley Nanea STUDIO $$
(☎775-9194; http://waipiovalleynanea.com; 48-5530 Waipi'o Rd; studio $125, cleaning fee $35; 📶) Located three houses back from the lookout, this private and cozy studio doesn't have cliff views (except from the adjacent yard) but does offer a nice four-poster bed and plenty of tranquillity. Laundry access too.

A DRIVER'S PARADISE

While many people think of the Big Island as tropical paradise, it is also a driver's paradise. From the ocean to the top of Mauna Kea, and from the dry side to the wet side, this is one enormous area with nicely paved roads, very few people on them, and staggering views all around. It is absolutely screaming for a convertible. So without further ado, here are some of the island's greatest drives.

➡ **Saddle Road (Hwy 200)** – ever drive between the two largest peaks in the world's oceans? (p255)

➡ **Kohala Mountain Rd (Hwy 250)** – an exhilirating trip down the spine of the Kohala Peninsula. (p236)

➡ **Old Mamalahoa Hwy**.– a winding journey through the backcountry of Ahualoa.

➡ **Hamakua Coast (Hwy 19)** – twist and turn across deep tropical valleys plunging toward the ocean. (p256)

➡ **Hilina Pali Rd** – coast beneath a big sky through the volcanic wastes of Hawai'i Volcanoes National Park. (p294)

➡ **Ka'alaiki Rd** – only Ka'u locals know about this freshly paved jaunt amidst green hills and distant sea. (p305)

Cliff House Hawaii VACATION RENTAL **$$**
(☎800-492-4746, 775-0005; www.cliffhousehawaii.com; Waipi'o Rd; 2-bedroom house $199, min two nights, each additional person $35; @) Set on sprawling acres of pastureland with a stunning view of the Waipi'o cliffs, this house assures privacy and space. It's well equipped, with two bedrooms, full kitchen, comfortably sized living and dining rooms, wraparound lanai, BBQ grill, telescope, satellite TV and washer/dryer. The same parcel contains the less dramatic but still beautifully situated **Hawaii Oceanview House** (☎775-9098; www.hawaiioceanviewhouse.com; 2-bed house $165, each additional person $35).

★**Hale 'Io** VACATION RENTAL **$$$**
(☎775-0118, 775-1450; www.vrbo.com/381655; 48-5484 Kukuihaele Rd; 5-bed house per week $5000, per night thereafter $750;) What else can we say? This is the greatest vacation rental on the Big Island. The completely private 5-bedroom house sits atop a 600ft bluff with a panoramic view of the Waipi'o cliffs, Maui and a vast expanse of ocean. Festooned with three large cupolas, the house itself is like a sexy temple, bursting with color and evocative artworks inside and out.

Loads of covered outdoor space harbor alluring couches. The knockout master bedroom with attached office, dressing room, bathroom and outdoor lava rock shower is the palace within the palace. The expansive kitchen is a chef's delight, and could have fed Captain Cook's crew. The pool replicates a tropical jungle swimming hole, replete with waterfall, lava tube slide (which will keep the kids entertained all day) and beach entry. The cherry on top: the secret staircase that ascends to a rooftop room with four-poster bed. Add hawks, whales, sunsets and endless tranquillity, and you have a big problem: you won't want to leave. Ever.

Shopping

★**Waipi'o Valley Artworks** ART GALLERY
(☎800-492-4746, 775-7157, 775-0958; www.waipiovalleyartworks.com; 8am-5pm) This airy little shop wears many hats. Stop for ice cream, muffins, sandwiches and coffee. Browse through the koa wood furniture, bowls and other crafts for gifts at all price points. Arrange overnight parking for camping in Waimanu (per day $15); call first in July and August or if you want to park before 8am.

Honoka'a & Around

Who would guess that Honoka'a was once the third-largest town across Hawaii, after Honolulu and Hilo? Yet it was once the hub for both the powerful cattle and sugar industries. When those industries crashed, the town was forced to reinvent itself, and has happily succeeded.

Having diversified their crops, today's farms in upcountry Pa'auilo and Ahualoa produce the tomatoes, mushrooms and other goodies whipped up by gourmet chefs seeking the finest, freshest local ingredients.

In particular, organic farming – from goat cheese to green tea and honey – is booming.

Meanwhile, the downtown has turned to tourism. Honaka'a has become a great place for browsing chockablock antique stores and lunching on a grass-fed beef burger before heading to Waipi'o Valley – although watching the world go by might tempt you to stay awhile. If so, there are some fine places to lay your head.

Sights

NHERC Heritage Center MUSEUM
(☎775-8890; http://hilo.hawaii.edu/academics/nherc/heritagecenter.php; 45-539 Plumeria St; ⏲9am-4pm Mon-Fri, to 1pm Sat) FREE Honaka'a will make a lot more sense if you stop by this new museum. Sponsored by the Northern Hawai'i Education and Research Center, it's mainly a large photo collection documenting the plantation era and its demise, but each picture speaks a thousand words. Volunteers provide further background. At the main intersection downtown, follow Plumeria St uphill, right on Lehua St.

Tours

The Honaka'a area is the locus of interesting agri-tours. The following farms are located in **Pa'auilo** and **Ahualoa**, on the *mauka* (inland) side of the highway.

★**Volcano Island Honey Company** FARM
(☎888-663-6639, 775-1000; www.volcanoisland-honey.com; Ahualoa; 90min farm tour, min 4 people, per adult/child under 16 $35/15; ⏲9-11:30am & 1:30-4pm Mon-Thu) In the mid-1970s, former Washington DC lawyer and self-described 'good hippie' Richard Spiegel began working with bees to capture the sweet nectar of kiawe flowers. Today his thriving business boasts a startling honey – imagine a pearlescent butter. You'll see the farm, don a bee suit and sample the delicous wares on this far-more-than-average agri-tour.

The honey business becomes a springboard to the philosophy of organic farming, the state of the world, and life in general. Most amazingly, Richard manages to pull it off. For those with more than a passing interest, two B&B rooms should be open by time of publication; check the website for details. For everyone else: an 8oz jar of Rare Hawaiian Organic White Honey with Hawaiian Lilikoi is $18 and worth every cent. Reservations required. Don't miss Motta Ceramics next door.

★**Hawaiian Vanilla Company** FARM
(☎776-1771; www.hawaiianvanilla.com; Pa'auilo; 1hr farm tour per adult/child under 13 $25/10, luncheon $29; ⏲farm tours 11:30am & 1pm Mon-Sat, luncheon 12:15pm Mon-Fri) The first commercial vanilla operation in the USA, this family-run farm is a model for how agri-tourism can be done. For those wanting to taste as well as tour, the Vanilla Experience Luncheon features a gourmet, vanilla-infused meal, an informative presentation and a walking tour of the plant.

There's also an Upcountry Tea (11am Saturday, adult/child under 13 $39/15). A gift shop (10am to 5pm Monday to Saturday) offers vanilla-scented everything. Reservations required for all events.

Motta Ceramics CERAMICS
(☎775-0856; http://gordonmotta.com; 46-4030 Pu'aono Road) FREE After four decades as a potter, Gordon Motta knows a few things about throwing clay on the wheel. He also offers a free tour of his ceramics studio, located next to Volcano Island Honey. The unvarnished workshop is chock full of high quality porcelain stoneware at all stages of production, including finished gift items.

Time and weather permitting, visitors can also enjoy a brief guided tour of the 5-acre grounds. Call for reservations.

Mauna Kea Tea FARM
(☎775-1171; www.maunakeatea.com; 46-3870 Old Mamalahoa Hwy, Ahualoa; 60-90min tours for 2/3/4 people, per person $30/25/20, under 18 free) If you're into tea, organic farming and philosophical inquiry, tour this small-scale, family-run plantation. Their green and oolong teas are intended to represent the inherent 'flavor' of the land, not artificial fertilizers. Check out the website for insights into tea cultivation and to make required reservations. Internship and volunteer opportunities available.

Festivals & Events

Honoka'a Western Week FESTIVAL
(Mamane St) FREE In late May, sleepy Mamane St startles awake with a BBQ, parade, country dance, rodeo, saloon girl contest and – a global first – a golf tournament using macadamia nuts for balls.

Sleeping

Almost all accommodations are outside Honaka'a, including the Ahualoa and

Pa'auilo countryside to the east, and the rim of beautiful Waipi'o Valley to the west.

Mountain Meadow Ranch VACATION RENTAL $$
(☎775-9376; www.mountainmeadowranch.com; 46-3895 Kapuna Rd, Ahualoa; cottage $150, ste incl breakfast $115;) This equestrian ranch on 7 acres offers a well-kept two-bedroom cottage that sleeps four and includes a full kitchen, wood stove, nice lanai, and washer/dryer – an excellent family option. A separate two-room suite is available in the main house but has no kitchen and feels suburban.

★**Keolamauloa** FARMSTAY $$
(☎776-1294; www.keolamauloa.com; 43-1962 Pa'auilo Mauka Rd, Pa'auilo; house per 2/3/4 people $100/125/150, plus cleaning fee;) This well-tended, 80-year-old family homestead in Pa'auilo offers a sophisticated farmstay. The comfy two-bedroom accommodations, which sleep six (with living room futon), include full kitchen, laundry facilities, vacation gear and access to the grounds: reclaimed koa forest, fruit trees, large vegetable gardens, pond and livestock, plus distant ocean views.

Guests are encouraged, if they wish, to participate in the life of the farm, a thought-provoking exercise in sustainable living. Discounts for extended stays; surcharge for less than four nights.

★**Waipi'o Wayside B&B** B&B $$
(☎800-833-8849, 775-0275; www.waipiowayside.com; Hwy 240; r incl breakfast $110-180;) Loaded with character, this attractively furnished 1932 plantation house is a classic B&B, complete with a welcoming host who knows the island intimately. The five rooms differ markedly, but each enjoys designer touches, such as iron bed frames, a wooden Chinese barber chair, shower skylight and hardwood floors.

Common areas include a living room with books and a large-screen TV (with DVDs), plus a spacious, secluded lanai. Full, homemade organic breakfast is included. Between mile markers 3 and 4 on Hwy 240, about 2 miles north of Honoka'a.

Waianuhea B&B B&B $$$
(☎888-775-2577, 775-1118; www.waianuhea.com; 45-3503 Kahana Dr, Ahualoa; r $210-310, ste $400;) This is a very fine inn. The owners have maximized the value of their property by combining eco-thinking with fine art and design (Tiffany lamps, Philippe Starck chairs), including the appropriate use of color, suitable Asian accents, bright skylights and gleaming hardwood floors.

Nevertheless, the building never surmounts a suburban feel. Gourmet dinners (per person $58 to $68) are served with 48 hours' notice. Rates include breakfast.

Eating

Simply Natural CAFE $
(☎775-0119; 45-3625 Mamane St, Honoka'a; dishes $4-12; 9am-3pm Mon-Sat, 11am-3pm Sun;) The local choice for trendy, fun and creative breakfasts, like the taro pancakes. At lunchtime try the spicy tuna melt.

★**Café il Mondo** ITALIAN $$
(☎775-7711; www.cafeilmondo.com; 45-3626A Mamane St, Honoka'a; pizzas $12-24; 11am-8pm Mon-Sat) The best restaurant in Honaka'a, this intimate local gathering place specializes in pizzas, pastas and, best of all, enormous calzones packed to the bursting point. If you want to meet the interesting locals, sit at the long central table: it won't take long. Bring your own wine and don't hesitate to share it.

Tex Drive-In DRIVE-IN $
(☎775-0598; www.texdriveinhawaii.com; mile marker 43, Hwy 19; snacks from $1, mains $5-10; 6:30am-8pm) A *malasada* is just a donut, but Tex is famous for serving them hot and fresh. They come plain (96¢) or filled ($1.31). Tex also serves an above average plate lunch, with crisp green salads; burgers on sweet-bread buns are good, too.

Jolene's Kau Kau Korner LOCAL $
(☎775-9498; 45-3625 Mamane St, Honoka'a; sandwiches & burgers $5-8, mains $10-15; 10:30am-3:30pm daily, to 8pm Mon & Wed) Awash in local color, this simple 20-year veteran, which serves a bit of everything in generous portions, is like dining at grandma's house – and she makes a great burger.

Honoka'a Farmers Market MARKET
(Mamane St, Honoka'a; 7:30am-noon Sat) Fresh produce directly from the farmers. Located in front of Honoka'a Trading Company.

Entertainment

Honoka'a People's Theatre THEATER
(☎775-0000; Mamane St, Honoka'a; movie tickets adult/child/senior $6/3/4) In a historic building dating from 1930, this theater shows movies and hosts special events.

Shopping

★Honoka'a Marketplace HANDICRAFTS
(☎775-8255; 45-3586 Mamane St) This large, well-kept and cheerful shop contains a variety of products – sarongs, quilts, collectibles, pillows, clothing – united by their colorful, laid-back tropical vibe. Hawaiian handicrafts fuse with Indonesian and other Asian imports. The shop carries its own label, Mary Guava designs. A personal touch makes all the difference.

Big Island Grown ARTS & CRAFTS, BEAUTY
(☎775-9777; bigislandgrown@hotmail.com; 45-3626 Mamane; ⊙9am-5pm Mon-Sat) This new business offers products cherry-picked from the Big Island's farmers markets. Where else will you find bamboo shirts, essential oils distilled from Hawaiian flowers, or the branding champion, Filthy Farmgirl soap?

Honoka'a Trading Company ANTIQUES
(Mamane St, Honoka'a; ⊙10:30am-5pm) If a couple of Honoka'a aunties emptied their attics, basements and garages, it would look like this hangar-sized store. Weave between vintage aloha wear, antiques, used books (great Hawaiiana selection), rattan and koa furniture and hand-selected Hawaiian artifacts. Then talk story with the owner, an equally eclectic character.

Kalopa State Recreation Area

This 100-acre family-friendly state park, with camping (first left as you enter), cabins (second left) and various gentle trails in a quiet native forest at a cool 2000ft, is a favorite local hideaway. Camping is in an attractive grassy area surrounded by tall trees. Group cabins (eight people maximum) have bunk beds, linens and blankets, plus hot showers and a fully equipped kitchen. Permits ($60/90 for residents/nonresidents) are required. There are basically two trail systems; see the large park map standing near the cabins.

The first trail system begins where the road by the cabins dead-ends. The easy 0.7mi **Nature Trail** passes through old ohia forest, where some of the trees measure more than 3ft in diameter. Detailed trail maps are available at the beginning. Be sure to follow the trail marks as the path has grown in substantially. The **Dryland Forest Trail** begins at the small trailhead but only goes in 100 yards. A small **Polynesian Garden** contains 12 of the original 20 canoe plants (the plants first brought to Hawaii by the Polynesian voyagers for food, medicine and clothing). Don't take the **Arboretum Trail**; it's so grown in that the risk of getting lost is high.

The second trail system, and the most interesting, begins along Robusta Lane, on the left between the caretaker's house and the campground. **Robusta Trail** goes about 600yd to the edge of Kalopa Gulch, through a thick eucalyptus forest. The trail continues along the gulch rim for another mile, while several side trails branch off and loop back into the recreation area via the **Perimeter Trail**. Signage on this trail network can be confusing, and there is no map offered, so a sketch from the park map near the cabins prior to setting out would be helpful.

To get here, turn *mauka* (inland) off the Hawai'i Belt Rd at the Kalopa Dr sign, near mile marker 42. Follow park signs for 3 miles.

Laupahoehoe

Another town that had its heyday when sugar was king, Laupahoehoe is now a small community with a pleasant beach park and a handful of attractions. The great drive in from the highway descends into a verdant tropical valley.

On April 1, 1946, tragedy hit the small plantation town when a tsunami 30ft high wiped out the schoolhouse on the point, killing 20 children and four adults. After the tsunami the whole town moved uphill.

In February, the **Laupahoehoe Music Festival** (Laupahoehoe Point Beach Park; admission $10; ⊙9am-5pm, Feb) comes to the beach park to raise scholarship money for local students, with good eating, quality hula and tunes by the best local performers.

Beaches & Sights

★Laupahoehoe Point Beach Park BEACH
Only real crazy *buggahs* would swim at windy, rugged Laupahoehoe, where the fierce surf sometimes crashes up over the rocks and into the parking lot. But it is fabulously pretty, with a scenic breakwater and fingers of volcanic rock thrusting out of the waves. While relatively untouristed, there are full facilities for **camping**, restrooms and picnic tables.

Stop here to view the memorial for the 24 schoolchildren and teachers who died in the 1946 tsunami. The school stood around the breathtakingly huge banyan tree toward your right as you approach the park.

★ Laupahoehoe Train Museum MUSEUM
(☎962-6300; www.thetrainmuseum.com; 36-2377 Mamalahoa Hwy; adult/student/senior $6/3/5; ⏲9am-4:30pm Tue-Fri, 10am-2pm Sat & Sun; Ⓟ) A Big Island classic, this unassuming little museum fascinates with artifacts and photographs of the plantation railroad era, contained within an old station agent's house. Be sure to see the video of the long-gone coastal train, which reveals the amazing bridges that once curved across Hamakua valleys until, sadly, a tsunami swept them all away. Located between mile markers 25 and 26.

Sleeping & Eating

Old Jodo Temple B&B $$
(☎962-6967; www.vrbo.com/236574; r per night/week $125/750;) This historic Buddhist Temple (c 1899) offers a chance to relax in a beautiful private location deep in the tropical valley near Laupahoehoe Point, and with ocean views. More or less restored to its original condition, it's nothing fancy but the authenticity adds to its charm; you'll feel thrown back half a century at least.

Downstairs the house includes two large bedrooms (sleeps six), spacious living and dining, airy porches and full kitchen. There's also a private yoga studio upstairs with bed & bath for $150/950 per night/week. Groups can rent the whole place at a discount. Washer/dryer available.

★ Back to the 50s Highway Fountain Diner DINER $
(☎962-0808; 35-2704 Mamalahoa Hwy; burgers $4-7, plates $8-10; ⏲8am-7pm Wed & Thu, to 8pm Fri & Sat, to 3pm Sun) Nostalgia reigns in this wonderful homage to Elvis, Marilyn and the boppin' '50s. Built in a historic plantation house, the old-fashioned counter and booths set the mood for burgers (made with local beef) and shakes. The menu includes island favorites – fried *ono* (wahoo) fillets with mashed potatoes, chili bowls, and pancake and egg breakfasts. Live music Friday and Saturday.

Hakalau & Around

It's a stretch to call this a town, but there's an active residential community, which is now a mix of old-timers and newcomers. Around New Year's Eve, hundreds flock here for the annual *mochi* pounding festival at Akiko's Buddhist B&B.

Sights

Kolekole Beach Park PARK
Beneath a highway bridge, this park sits alongside Kolekole Stream in a verdant tropical valley. The river-mouth break is a local surfing and bodyboarding hot spot, but ocean swimming is dangerous. There are small waterfalls and full facilities.

HAMAKUA ZIPLINES

Ziplines are spreading like bamboo on the Hamakua Coast. So which one should you choose?

Zip Isle Zipline Adventures (☎888-947-4753, 963-5427; www.zipisle.com; $99-147; ⏲zips at 9:30am, 12:30pm & 2:30pm) A good choice for kids and anxious first-timers. There are seven gentle zips, including a dual line, and a 150ft-long suspension bridge. Located at World Botanical Gardens, to which you get free entry afterwards.

Skyline EcoAdventures Akaka Falls (☎888-878-8400; www.zipline.com; 28-1710 Honomu Rd; $179; ⏲zips at 10am, 11am, 2pm & 3pm) Skyline has the single best zip and it's a jaw dropper. The seven zips on this course get progressively longer and higher up until you find yourself sailing directly over a 250ft waterfall on an extraordinary 3,350ft ride – the best single zip on the Big Island.

Umauma Falls & Zipline Experience (☎930-9477; http://umaumaexperience.com; 31-313 Old Mamalahoa Highway; $197; ⏲zips at 10am, 11am, 1pm & 2pm) The most consistently thrilling. None of its nine zips has the grandeur of Skyline's magnificent climax, but they don't take any baby steps, cross over *lots* of waterfalls, and one makes it over 2000ft.

For other ziplines see North Kohala.

Camping is allowed with a county permit, but the narrow area can get crowded and boisterous with picnicking local families, and might not be the best choice at night. To get here, turn inland off the Hawai'i Belt Rd at the southern end of the Kolekole Bridge, about 1300yd south of mile marker 15, right before the bridge.

World Botanical Gardens GARDENS
(☎963-5427; www.wbgi.com; MM16, Hwy 19; adult/teen 13-17yr/child 5-12yr $13/6/3; ⏲9am-5:30pm) Under development since 1995, this garden remains a work in progress. It is an admirable effort but plays second fiddle to the Hawaii Tropical Botanical Garden closer to Hilo. To get here from Hwy 19, turn *mauka* (inland) near mile marker 16, at the posted sign.

Sleeping

Akiko's Buddhist Bed & Breakfast B&B $
(☎963-6422; www.akikosbnb.com; s/d $65/75, cottage $65-85; 📶) A Big Island original, this B&B is part zendo, part community center, part farm, part art studio, and all Akiko, making for a delightful stay for the holistic visitor. Rooms are simple – futons on the floor in the main house or twin beds in an adjacent house. All rooms have shared bathroom; rates include breakfast.

Two screened bungalows are small but wonderfully set in lush forest. For longer stays, ask about the Artist's Retreat. Akiko herself is a live wire who farms the 2-acre grounds, leads morning meditation, coordinates a popular end-of-year *mochi* pounding festival, and allows wi-fi 'as long as no one sees you do it.' Located in Wailea, just over 2 miles north of Honomu. Turn left at mile marker 15, then left again.

Honomu

Honomu is a quaint old sugar town that might be forgotten if it weren't for its proximity to Akaka Falls. Life here remains rural and slow paced. Main St is lined with retro wooden buildings now sprouting shops and eateries.

Sights

★**'Akaka Falls State Park** PARK
(www.hawaiistateparks.org; 'Akaka Falls Rd (Hwy 220); entry per car/pedestrian $5/1) This outstanding and convenient little park offers an enchanting and newly-renovated concrete path that loops along the lush cliffs above a river, first passing scenic Kahuna Falls (100ft), then reaching the truly grand 'Akaka Falls, which plunge 442ft into a deep green basin. These are the best of the 'tourist falls' on this coast so don't miss them.

You'll also enjoy a natural botanical garden that goes wildly into bloom during certain times of year (June to July is heliconia season). To get here turn onto Hwy 220 between mile markers 13 and 14, and head 4 miles inland. You can avoid the parking fee if you park outside the lot, but you must still pay the walk-in fee. Cash or credit cards accepted.

Sleeping & Eating

The Palms Cliff House Inn B&B $$$
(☎963-6076; www.palmscliffhouse.com; r incl breakfast $299-449; ❄📶) This elegant B&B fits the bill for those seeking a romantic splurge near resort-free Hilo. The eight ocean-view rooms are spacious (550 sq ft to 650 sq ft), with high-end furnishings and private lanai. Four have gas fireplaces and outdoor hot tubs. Guests rave about the full hot breakfasts. One qualm: rates are steep, but you might luck out during special discounts.

★**Hilo Sharks Coffee** CAFE $
(☎963-6706; www.konasharkscoffee.com; sandwiches $6-7; ⏲8am-6pm Mon-Sat, to 4pm Sun) The cafe with everything: great locally grown coffee, homemade chocolate, outdoor patios front and back, wi-fi, occasional live music, breakfast stand-bys, creative sandwiches, refreshing smoothies and attractive prices. *The* place to hang out in Honomu.

Woodshop Gallery & Café CAFE $
(☎963-6363; www.woodshopgallery.com; Hwy 220; lunch dishes $6-9; ⏲11am-5:30pm) Try a burger and lemonade here – although the menu is all good and served with aloha. Following lunch, go on a shopping spree among the extraordinary collection of handcrafted bowls, photos and blown glass.

Onomea Bay & Around

Papaikou, Onomea and Pepe'ekeo are three more plantation villages admired for their gorgeous landscape and views.

Sights & Activities

Pepe'ekeo 4-Mile Scenic Drive DRIVE
The fantastic rainforest jungle along this stretch of the Old Mamalahoa Hwy proves

that all of those annoying showers are really worthwhile. Cruising along the narrow road you cross a series of one-lane bridges spanning little streams and waterfalls.

You can begin the drive from either end, but approaching from the south (Hilo side) involves an easy right turn between mile markers 7 and 8 on the main highway – and allows you to end with a meal at What's Shakin'.

★Hawaii Tropical Botanical Garden GARDEN

(☎964-5233; www.hawaiigarden.com; adult/child $15/5; ⏲9am-4pm) This is an absolutely fabulous botanical garden, with a beautiful oceanfront setting and superb management. A nicely paved trail leads you through 2000 species of tropical plants set amid streams and waterfalls. There's a beautiful macaw aviary, too. The walk ends at Onomea Bay and takes around 1½ hours.

If you only visit one botanical garden on the island this should be it.

★Onomea Tea Company FARM

(☎964-3283; www.onomeatea.com; 27-604 Alakahi Pl; tour $25) This 9-acre tea plantation offers a very personal tour in an extraordinary setting; you'll never feel like a tourist. After seeing the garden and production facilities, which occupy an oceanfront promontory, you'll settle into the owner's elegant home for a tasting and sandwiches. Altogether flawless and reasonably priced. Reservations required.

Onomea Bay Hike HIKING

For a quick, scenic hike to the bay, take the **Na Ala Hele** trailhead on the seaward side of the road, just north of the tropical botanical garden.

After a 10-minute hike down a slippery jungle path, you'll come to a finger of lava jutting into the sea. A spur to the right leads to a couple of small waterfalls and a cove. Continuing straight brings you to the diminutive bluffs overlooking the batik blues of Onomea Bay. Hawaiian monk seals sighted here.

Eating & Drinking

★What's Shakin' HEALTH FOOD, TAKEOUT $

(☎964-3080; smoothies $6; ⏲10am-5pm) If you are doing the Pepe'ekeo 4-Mile Scenic Drive, either begin or end it here, near its northern terminus. While this charming yellow cottage looks innocuous enough, it sits on 23 acres of organic farmland, and pumps out fantastic homemade food, along with killer smoothies. The fish wraps are to die for, the help priceless.

Hilo

POP 41,000

Hilo is the beating heart of the Big Island. Hidden beneath its daily drizzle lies the most fertile soil, a world dedicated to all that is unique, natural, holistic, organic, local, personal and artistic. The result is the social version of a botanical garden, where the endless color, variety and downright quirkiness of all forms never ceases to amaze. No single word captures this special phenomenon, which applies to people, products and establishments alike: 'Hiloism' will do.

Perhaps this ongoing celebration of life's boundless creativity has something to do with the local demographics. Like other former sugar towns in Hawaii, Hilo is a diverse mix of Native Hawaiians, Japanese, Chinese, Koreans, Filipinos, Portuguese, Puerto Ricans and Caucasians, many of them descended from plantation workers. Or perhaps it also has to do with living on the edge. Knocked down by two tsunamis, threatened with extinction by Mauna Loa lava flows (most recently in 1984), and subject to the highest annual rainfall in the USA, Hilo knows more than most that life is a gift from the gods and you can see it in the vivacious attitude of the locals.

In any case, Hilo is sunny Kona's alter ego, which is why you ought to visit. The town had a life before tourism, and continues to do so, as the Big Island's commercial center. Having said that, it is off the charts in quirky museums, and has the island's best farmers market, a weekly shrine to Hiloism. The downtown begs to be walked, and there are some knockout B&Bs to stay in. Set on a calm bay along a lush coastline, Hilo also makes an ideal base for exploring Hawai'i Volcanoes National Park, Mauna Kea, Puna and the Hamakua Coast. Drizzle aside, the state's second-largest city makes a compelling argument for at least a day trip, if not home base. That is, if you have any Hiloism at all.

For a concentrated dose, see the Bayfront Hiloism Walking Tour (p277).

Beaches

Except for Honoli'i Beach Park, Hilo's beaches are all located in the Keaukaha neighborhood.

All-terrain wheelchairs are available for 'surf day' events at certain beaches on scheduled dates. For more information call ☎961-8681.

★Richardson Ocean Park BEACH

Near the end of Kalaniana'ole Ave, this pocket of black sand is Hilo's best all-round beach. There are restrooms, showers, picnic tables and a lifeguard.

During calm surf, swimming is fine, while snorkeling is good on the warmer eastern side. (Waters are cooler on the northern side due to subsurface freshwater springs.) Lava rocks create interesting nooks and crannies, and sea turtles often hang out here. High surf attracts bodyboarders.

Onekahakaha Beach Park BEACH

(Map p268) Popular with local families, this beach has a broad, shallow, sandy-bottomed pool, protected by a boulder breakwater. There are lifeguards on weekends and holidays, restrooms, showers, grassy lawns and covered pavilions.

The water is only 1ft to 2ft deep in spots at low tide, so toddlers can splash safely. An unprotected cove north of the protected pool is deeper but can be hazardous due to sea urchins and rough surf; it's best to stay inside the breakwater.

James Kealoha Beach Park BEACH

(Carl Smith Beach Park) Further along the road, this county park is best for older kids and snorkelers. Locals call it Four Miles (the distance between the park and the downtown post office). There are weekend lifeguards, restrooms, showers, covered pavilions and lots of turtles.

Hilo

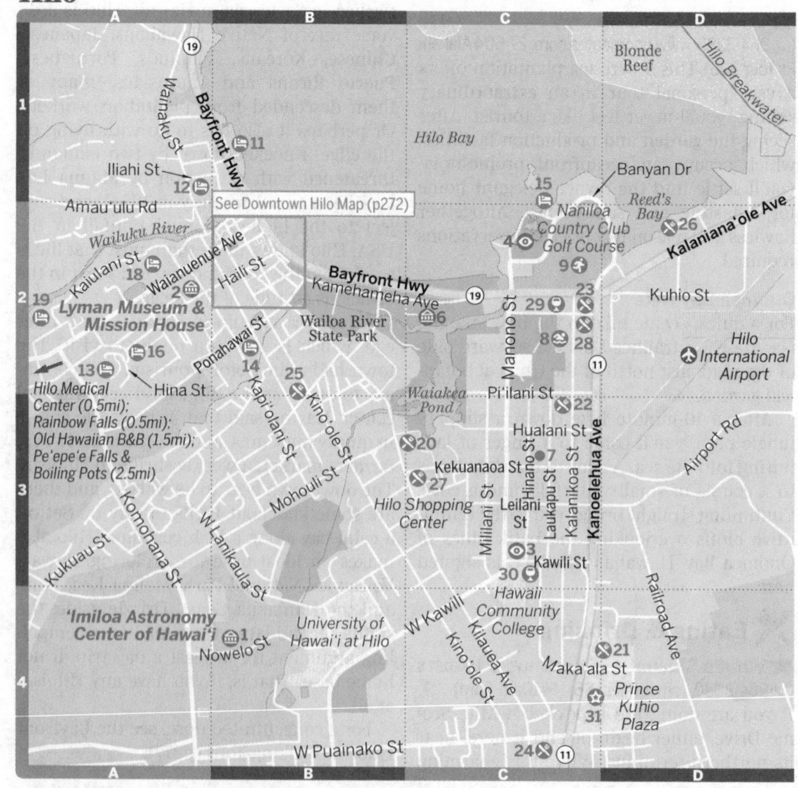

For swimming and snorkeling head to the eastern side, which contains a deep, protected basin with generally calm, clear water and pockets of white sand. The park's western side is open ocean and much rougher, without an easy entry. Locals surf here in winter or net fish.

Wai'olena and Wai'uli Beach Parks — BEACH

(Leleiwi Beach) Rocky and ruggedly pretty, these side-by-side beaches contain Hilo's best shore-dive site. You might see turtles, interesting coral growth and a variety of butterfly fish. The water is freezing until you go past the reef, and the entrance is tricky; ask for advice at Nautilus Dive Center.

Though commonly known by their former name, Leleiwi Beach, for cultural reasons the county renamed the beaches Wai'uli (dark water) and Wai'olena (light water) in January 2008.

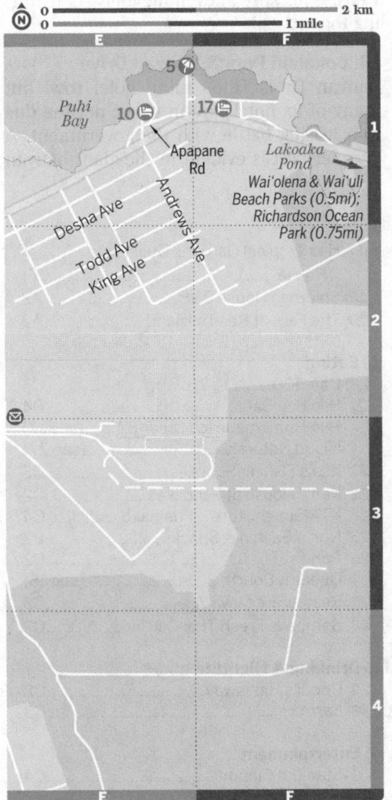

Honoli'i Beach Park — BEACH

Less than 2 miles north of downtown Hilo, this protected cove is Hilo's best surfing and bodyboarding spot. Don't come here to swim, as the adjacent river tends to muddy the waters, although it's guarded daily. There's a pleasant grassy picnic area, restrooms, showers and a lifeguard.

From Hilo take the Bayfront Hwy north; after mile marker 4, turn right onto Nahala St and then left onto Kahoa St. Park on the roadside and walk down to the park. On weekends cars are parked bumper to bumper.

Sights

★'Imiloa Astronomy Center of Hawai'i — MUSEUM

(Map p268; ☎969-9700; www.imiloahawaii.org; 600 'Imiloa Pl; adult/child 4-12yr $17.50/9.50; ⏲9am-5pm Tue-Sun) Where else but Hilo will you find a museum that merges traditional myth and modern science? And yet this extraordinary $28 million complex, which includes the world's first 3-D planetarium, manages to pull it off, providing a holistic, multifaceted view of the heavens. One planetarium show is included with admission.

'Imiloa, which means 'exploring new knowledge,' fuses modern astronomy on Mauna Kea with the Polynesian ocean voyagers, who used star maps rooted in myth, bringing the Big Bang and the Hawaiian creation story together. This is an excellent family attraction and the natural preliminary to ascending Mauna Kea itself.

★Lyman Museum & Mission House — MUSEUM

(Map p268; ☎935-5021; www.lymanmuseum.org; 276 Haili St; adult/child $10/3; ⏲10am-4:30pm Mon-Sat) This superb little museum expresses the tremendous variety of Hawaii's natural and cultural history. The adjacent Mission House, built by the Reverend David Lyman and his wife, Sarah, in 1839, adds a human element to the historical facts. Half-hour tours of the House depart 11am & 2pm.

The museum's rotating exihibits upstairs draw upon the wealth of local immigrant backgrounds, eg Chinese art, a traditional Korean house. A Hawaiian history exhibit explores sports, religion and the kapu system. Don't miss the fascinating, spherical stone used in Hawaiian games. Downstairs, geologic exhibits include fascinating examples of lava rock, an awesome mineral collection, and an equally good shell collection.

★Pana'ewa Rainforest Zoo & Gardens ZOO
(☎959-9233; www.hilozoo.com; ⏱9am-4pm, petting zoo 1:30-2:30pm Sat) FREE This very well-done global zoo is, remarkably, free. Four miles south of town, its 12 tropical acres are a pleasure to meander through, and a perfect outing for families.

The star is Namaste, a white Bengal tiger, but you'll also encounter free-roaming peacocks, monkeys, reptiles, a pygmy hippo and some of Hawaii's endangered birds. To get here, turn *mauka* (inland) off the Volcano Hwy onto W Mamaki St, just past mile marker 4.

★Pacific Tsunami Museum MUSEUM
(Map p272; ☎935-0926; www.tsunami.org; 130 Kamehameha Ave; adult/child 6-17yr $8/4; ⏱9am-4:15pm Mon-Sat) You cannot understand Hilo without knowing its history as a two-time tsunami survivor, in 1946 and 1960. This modest yet comprehensive museum is chock-full of riveting information, including a new section on the Japanese tsunami of 2011, which damaged Kona. Allow enough time to experience the multimedia exhibits, including chilling computer simulations and heart-wrenching first-person accounts.

★Mokupapapa Discovery Center MUSEUM
(Map p272; ☎933-8184; www.papahanaumokuakea.gov/education/center.html; 76 Kamehameha Ave; ⏱9am-4pm Tue-Sat) FREE Though very few people realize it, the Hawaiian archipelago extends far beyond the eight main islands to the Northwestern Hawaiian Islands, a long chain of islets and atolls containing the healthiest coral reefs in the USA. Learn more about it at this fascinating and well-done museum. Unfortunately the lasting image may be of the enormous amounts of plastic now washing ashore there.

East Hawai'i Cultural Center ART GALLERY
(Map p272; ☎961-5711; www.ehcc.org; 141 Kalakaua St; suggested donation $2; ⏱10am-4pm Mon-Sat) The best venue for local art is this downtown center, which has some truly fabulous works on display. The exhibit changes monthly, while workshops and classes on varied creative forms (eg painting, drawing, ukulele and hula) are ongoing. Check the website for special evening concerts featuring top artists.

Lili'uokalani Park & Banyan Drive PARK
Banyan Dr is Hilo's mini 'hotel row,' but many of its hotels are in tragic decline due to a leasing battle with the government. A grander past is evident in the giant banyan

Hilo

Top Sights
1 'Imiloa Astronomy Center of Hawai'i B4
2 Lyman Museum & Mission House A2

Sights
3 Hawai'i Nui Brewing C3
4 Lili'uokalani Park C2
5 Onekahakaha Beach Park E1
6 Wailoa Center & Wailoa River State Park C2

Activities, Courses & Tours
7 Big Island Candies C3
8 Ho'olulu Complex C2
9 Naniloa Country Club Golf Course C2

Sleeping
10 Arnott's Lodge E1
11 Bay House B&B B1
12 Dolphin Bay Hotel A1
13 Hilltop Legacy A2
14 Hilo Bay Hale B2
15 Hilo Hawaiian Hotel C1
16 Hilo Honu Inn A2
17 Hilo Tropical Gardens Guest House F1
18 Shipman House B&B A2
19 The Falls at Reed's Island A2

Eating
20 Cafe 100 .... C3
21 Hilo Bay Cafe D4
Hilo Homemade Ice Cream .... (see 17)
Island Naturals .... (see 27)
22 Itsu's Fishing Supplies C3
23 Ken's House of Pancakes C2
24 KTA Super Store – Puainako C4
25 Nori's Saimin & Snacks B2
26 Pond's D2
Queen's Court .... (see 15)
27 Restaurant Miwa C3
28 Sombat's Fresh Thai Cuisine C2

Drinking & Nightlife
29 Coqui's Hideaway C2
30 Karma C3

Entertainment
31 Stadium Cinemas C4

THE BIG ISLAND BY AIR

Seeing the Big Island by air adds an entirely new dimension to your visit, particularly when the doors are off. Drama depends on volcanic activity and water flow over falls. The following providers will take you skyward from Hilo Airport.

★ **Paradise Helicopters** (☎969-7392; www.paradisecopters.com). Offers a Kilauea volcano tour via two different birds. In the 4-passenger Hughes MD500 everyone gets a window, and its small size really enhances the feeling of flying. Best of all is the doors-off option, which may ruin your hairdo but enhances the trip (ever smell a volcano from the air?). The 6-pax Bell 407 is the same tour in a larger chopper with doors on. $228 per person, $205 online. Departs main terminal every hour from 7:30am to 4:30pm.

Blue Hawaiian (☎961-5600; www.bluehawaiian.com). Flies the Ecostar ($274) and A-star ($225) on a 45-minute volcano & waterfall tour departing hourly from 9am to 4pm except noon. Main terminal.

Safari Helicopters (☎969-1259; www.safarihelicopters.com). Offers a 45-minute Kilauea volcano tour ($207) and a 55-minute volcano & waterfalls tour ($229). First parking lot on left.

Iolani Air (☎800-538-7590, 329-0018; www.iolaniair.com; ⏲8am-4pm Mon-Fri). The fixed-wing option. A one-hour narrated volcano/waterfall flight is $175. Everyone gets a window. End of cargo terminal.

trees lining the road, planted in the 1930s, and in beautiful Lili'uokalani Park.

Named for Hawaii's last queen, the 30-acre Japanese garden has manicured lawns, shallow ponds, bamboo groves, arched bridges, pagodas and a teahouse. You can also stroll across the footbridge from here to Mokuola (Coconut Island), where you can swim and picnic surounded by a spectacular view of the bay, the town and majestic Mauna Kea in the distance.

Pe'epe'e Falls & Boiling Pots WATERFALL

This interesting series of falls cascading into swirling, bubbling pools (or 'boiling pots') is 2 miles past Rainbow Falls, and the better of the two sights. Restrooms available.

You might be tempted to hike closer and take a plunge, but heed the warning signs; currents are much stronger than they appear and there's a drowning in this river about once a year.

Rainbow Falls WATERFALL

A regular stop for tour buses, the lookout for this 'instant gratification' cascade is just steps from the parking lot. Depending on rainfall, the lovely 80ft waterfall can be a torrent or a trickle. Go in the morning and you'll see rainbows if the sun and mist cooperate.

Waianuenue (which means 'rainbow seen in water') is the Hawaiian name for these falls. To get here, drive up Waianuenue Ave (veer right when it splits into Kaumana Dr) about 1.5 miles from downtown Hilo; follow the signage.

Wailoa Center & Wailoa River State Park ART GALLERY

(Map p268; ☎933-0416; ⏲8:30am-4:30pm Mon, Tue, Thu & Fri, noon-4:30pm Wed) FREE This eclectic, state-run gallery hosts a variety of monthly exhibits. You might find quilts, bonsai, Chinese watercolors or historical photos, all done by locals. Surrounding the center is a quiet state park on the Wailoa River.

The main park landmark is a 14ft, Italian-made bronze statue of Kamehameha the Great, erected in 1997 and restored with gold leaf in 2004. There is also a tsunami memorial and a Vietnam War memorial.

Hawai'i Nui Brewing BREWERY

(Map p268; ☎934-8211; http://hawaiinuibrewing.com; 275 E Kawili; ⏲10am-6pm Mon-Fri) FREE This microbrewery has a small tasting room where you sample some excellent craft beer. Mauna Kea pale ale is the most popular, but don't overlook Southern Cross, a powerful Belgian ale that gives those Trappist monks a run for their money.

Activities

While Hilo's coast is lined with reefs rather than sand, the gentle waters are ideal for stand up paddleboarding (SUP). Rent a board and paddle, and launch from Mokuola

Downtown Hilo

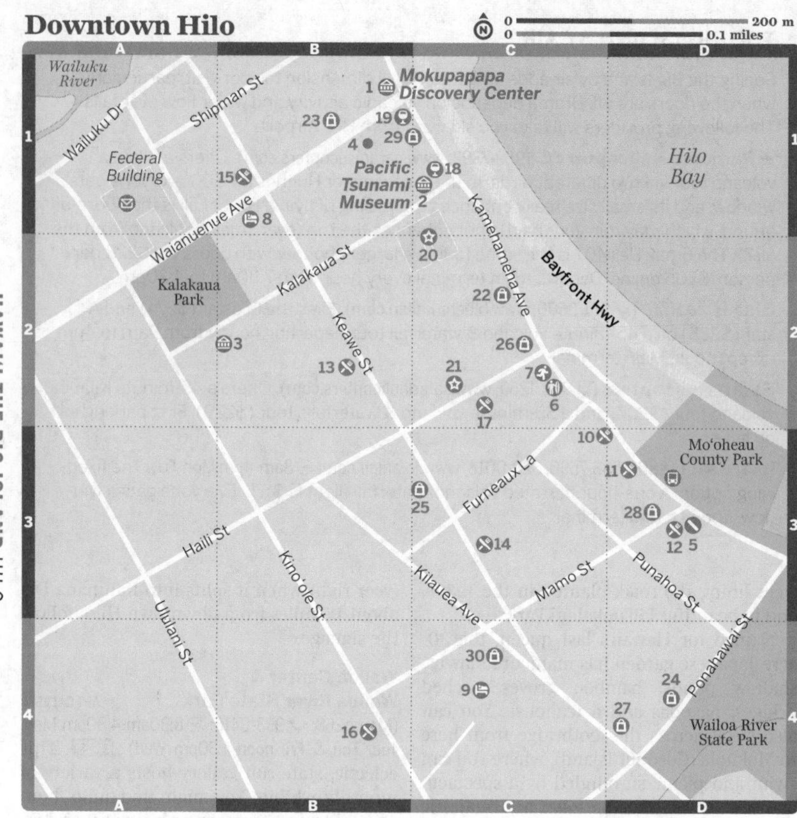

(Coconut Island), Reed's Bay or Wailoa River State Park. For surfing, head to Honoli'i Beach Park.

While diving is best on the Kona side, there are decent shore-dive spots in or near Hilo; inquire at the dive shops.

Sun & Sea Hawaii WATERSPORTS
(Map p272; ☎934-0902; sunandseahawaii@gmail.com; 244 Kamehameha Ave; SUP half/full day $45/65, 1-/2-tank shore dive $99/$129) This friendly one-stop shop for ocean sports rents SUP packages and sells a variety of snorkeling, diving and swimming gear.

Nautilus Dive Center DIVING
(Map p272; ☎935-6939; www.nautilusdivehilo.com; 382 Kamehameha Ave; 2-tank dive $85; ⏰9am-5pm Tue-Sat) Hilo's go-to dive shop since 1975 offers guided dives, PADI certification courses and general advice on shore diving. If you're a certified diver, rent here and head to the best East Hawai'i dive site at Pohoiki Bay in Puna.

Orchidland Surfboards SURFING
(Map p272; ☎935-1533; www.orchidlandsurf.com; 262 Kamehameha Ave; ⏰9am-5pm Mon-Sat, 10am-3pm Sun) For board rentals and surf gear. Owner Stan Lawrence is an expert surfer; he opened the Big Island's first surf shop in 1972.

Hilo Municipal Golf Course GOLF
(☎959-7711; 340 Haihai St; greens fee Mon-Fri $34, Sat & Sun $45) Hilo's main course (the Muni) is nicely maintained and a terrific deal. Morning tee times are favored by the local contingent.

Naniloa Country Club Golf Course GOLF
(Map p268; ☎935-3000; 120 Banyan Dr; greens fee $15) Most locals golf at the Muni, so this nine-hole course is uncrowded and boasts a pretty setting across from Lili'uokalani Park.

Downtown Hilo

Top Sights
1 Mokupapapa Discovery Center B1
2 Pacific Tsunami Museum C1

Sights
3 East Hawai'i Cultural Center B2

Activities, Courses & Tours
4 Kapoho Kine Adventures B1
5 Nautilus Dive Center D3
6 Orchidland Surfboards C2
7 Sun & Sea Hawaii C2

Sleeping
8 Hilo Bay Hostel B1
9 Lotus Garden of Hilo C4

Eating
10 Abundant Life Natural Foods C3
11 Café Pesto D3
12 Farmers Kitchen Cafe D3
13 Hilo Town Tavern B2
14 KTA Super Store – Downtown C3
15 Le Magic Pan B1
16 Short N Sweet B4
17 Surf Break Cafe C2

Drinking & Nightlife
18 Bayfront Coffee, Kava & Tea Co. C1
19 Cronies B1

Entertainment
20 Kress Cinemas C2
21 Palace Theatre C2

Shopping
22 Alan's Art & Collectibles C2
23 Big Island Book Buyers B1
24 Bryan Booth Antiques D4
25 Bytes and Bites with Pieces C3
26 Extreme Exposure Fine Art Gallery C2
27 Grapes: A Wine Store D4
28 Hilo Farmers Market D3
29 Sig Zane Designs C1
30 Still Life Books C4

Ho'olulu Complex SWIMMING
(Map p268; ☎961-8698; 260 Kalanikoa St) FREE For lap swimming, this impressive Olympic-sized, open-air pool is generally uncrowded during the day. Call for hours.

Tours

★ **Kapoho Kine Adventures** TOUR
(Map p272; ☎964-1000; www.kapohokine.com; 25 Waianuenue Ave) This well-managed and veteran tour provider has a downtown office selling an interesting variety of tours, including ziplining, Hawai'i Volcanoes National Park, helicopter tours, and (gulp) the Big Island in one day. A useful place for talking over your options. Prices vary widely.

Mauna Loa Macadamia-Nut Visitor Center FACTORY TOUR
(☎888-628-6256, 966-8618; www.maunaloa.com; Macadamia Rd; ⏲8:30am-5pm) FREE Hershey-owned Mauna Loa provides a self-guided tour of its working factory, where you can watch the humble mac nut as it moves along the assembly line from cracking to roasting to chocolate dipping and packaging.

The gift shop, of course, has every variation ready for purchase, with tasters. The factory is well signed about 5 miles south of Hilo. The 3-mile access road dips through acres of macadamia trees.

Big Island Candies CANDY TOUR
(Map p268; ☎800-935-5510, 935-8890; www.bigislandcandies.com; 585 Hinano St; ⏲8:30am-5pm) FREE This immaculate candy factory delights everyone, judging from the hordes of tourists embarking upon its free self-guided tour. Taste the chocolate and macadamia confections and you'll be hooked, too.

Festivals & Events

★ **Big Island Hawaiian Music Festival** MUSIC FESTIVAL
(☎961-5711; www.ehcc.org; 556 Waianuenue Ave, Hilo High School; adult/child $10/free) A mid-July, two-day concert featuring virtuoso musicians in ukulele, steel guitar, slack key guitar and falsetto singing.

May Day Lei Day Festival LEI FESTIVAL
(☎934-7010; www.hilopalace.com; 38 Haili St, Palace Theater) Beautiful lei displays, demonstrations, live music and hula on the first Sunday in May.

King Kamehameha Day Celebration HISTORIC DAY
(☎935-9338; Mokuola) On June 11, observe the historic reenactment of King Kamehameha's history, plus music and crafts.

Fourth of July INDEPENDENCE DAY CELEBRATION
Entertainment and food all day at Lili'uokalani Park; fireworks display from Mokuola (Coconut Island).

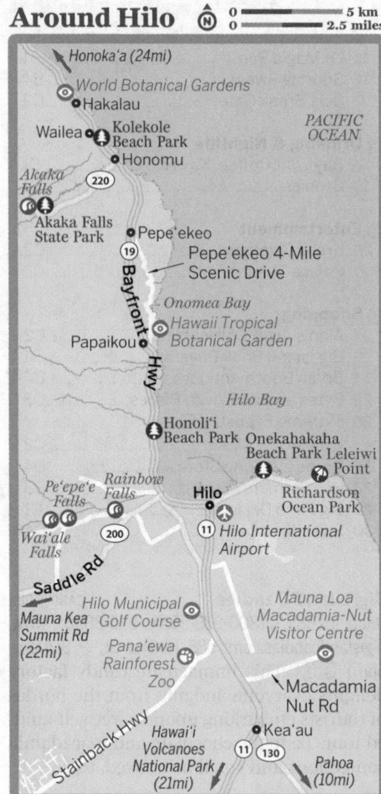

Hawai'i County Fair FAIR
(799 Pi'ilani St, Afook-Chinen Civic Auditorium; adult/student $3/2) Pure nostalgia comes to town in September, with carnival rides, games and cotton candy.

Sleeping

True to form, Hilo has no major hotel chains, but loads of fantastic one-off B&Bs, hostels and vacation rentals.

★ **Hilo Bay Hostel** HOSTEL $
(Map p272; ☎933-2771; www.hawaiihostel.net; 101 Waianuenue Ave; dm $27, r with/without bath $77/67; wi-fi) This well-managed hostel is a winner. Perfectly situated downtown, it occupies an airy historic building with hardwood floors, remarkably clean restrooms and a kitchen in which you could cook Thanksgiving dinner. The crowd is older and diverse, creating a low-key, relaxed vibe. Staff are friendly but rule sticklers (after the 11am checkout time you must leave the premises). Wine is served to guests. The private rooms facing the street, with private baths, are light and airy Hilo classics. The nice corner women's dorm has sea views and a breeze.

★ **Lotus Garden of Hilo** COTTAGES $
(Map p272; ☎936-5212; www.vrbo.com/390986; 140a Kilauea Ave; r $69-79, cottage for 2 people $120, $15 per additional person; wi-fi) These two brightly painted beachy cottages are perfect for downtown Hilo. Hidden in a lush, quarter-acre walled compound behind Still Life Books (p280), they are private, charming, reasonably priced and super convenient. One is rented as rooms, the other sleeps up to seven. Shared hot tub.

Hilltop Legacy VACATION RENTAL $
(Map p268; ☎896-2074; www.hilltoplegacy.com; 57 Hina St; r $65-119; wi-fi) This is a great budget choice. The property lies on top of a hill behind the town, with nice gardens and great views of the bay. The welcoming young proprietor has inherited a large family home (c 1930) and is renting four rooms, each with private bath and continental breakfast. The results aren't perfect, but good value.

Arnott's Lodge HOSTEL, CAMPGROUND $
(Map p268; ☎339-0921, 969-7097; www.arnottslodge.com; 98 Apapane Rd; dm $28, r with/without bath $75/65; wi-fi) Hilo's longest-running hostel remains solid value, with a variety of lodging options close to beaches. The $75 rooms are especially nice, with private garden views, ensuite baths and shared kitchen; choose the queens over the twin. Tent sites ($11 per person) include outdoor showers and kitchen access. Bike rental $7 to $12 a day.

Old Hawaiian B&B B&B $
(☎961-2816; www.thebigislandvacation.com; 1492 Wailuku Dr; r incl breakfast $85-125; wi-fi) A good choice for discriminating budget travelers, these three pleasant rooms include private entrances and tidy furnishings. The Hawaiian Room (sleeps 4) and the Bamboo Room (sleeps 3) are the best value. All open to a backyard lanai, with dining table, microwave and refrigerator. About a mile above Rainbow Falls; right Waiau, left Wailuku.

Hilo Tropical Gardens Guest House HOSTEL $
(Map p268; ☎217-9650; www.hilogardens.com; 1477 Kalaniana'ole Ave; dm $25, d $55-65; wi-fi)

Dorm and private rooms are tiny, but the lush garden setting is delightful. Shared bathrooms only. Pitch a tent (single/double $15/20) and suddenly you're camping in a jungle. Located behind Hilo Homemade Ice Cream (p278) store.

★The Inn at Kulaniapia Falls INN $$

(☎866-935-6789, 935-6789; www.waterfall.net; 1 Kulaniapia Dr; r incl breakfast $159-179, pagoda $279;) To reach this unforgettable inn you must drive 4 miles past acres of macadamia orchards to 850ft above sea level. Your reward? It's perched on a spectacular 120ft waterfall, with verdant gorge and swimming hole attached. Eight rooms (in two buildings) are exquisitely appointed with Asian antiques.

The pagoda guesthouse is a worthy splurge and includes a kitchen, laundry facilities and 1.5 bathrooms. All power is hydroelectric and off the grid. The unlit 4-mile road can be tricky at night. See website for driving directions.

★Shipman House B&B B&B $$

(Map p268; ☎934-8002; www.hilo-hawaii.com; 131 Ka'iulani St; r incl breakfast $219-249;) For the grandeur of Old Hawaii, you can't beat the Shipman House. This turreted Victorian mansion is where Queen Lili'uokalani played the grand piano, and Jack London slept in the guest cottage. The main house is perched over a lush ravine, and full of beautiful museum-quality antiques, including a fantastic collection of woodblock prints and some fascinating Hawaiiana.

The five nicely furnished rooms are thoroughly equipped with kimonos, private baths, beach gear, flashlights, even tripods. Welcoming hosts go the extra mile for guests. Convenient location near downtown Hilo.

★Orchid Tree B&B B&B $$

(☎961-9678; www.orchidtree.net; 6 Makakai Pl; r incl breakfast $150;) If you want a B&B experience but value space and privacy, try this standout near Honoli'i Beach. The Koi Room is spacious (500 sq ft) and chic, with a gleaming hardwood floor and koi pond outside. The Hula Room is even bigger, containing two beds, plus a lounging area with two plump, inviting sofas.

Outside you'll find a pool and 'surfer shack' patio facing the eastern horizon. At end of cemetery near mile marker 4 on Mamalahoa Hwy, turn onto Nahala St, then left onto Makakai.

★Hilo Honu Inn B&B $$

(Map p268; ☎935-4325; www.hilohonu.com; 465 Haili St; r incl breakfast $140-250;) In a lovely retro home, three custom-designed guest rooms accommodate different budgets. A worthy splurge, the two-bedroom Samurai Suite is utterly memorable, with genuine Japanese detailing, plus tatami mats, *furo* (soaking tub), tea room and sweeping (if distant) views of Hilo Bay.

The two-room Bali Hai Suite is tropical themed, with a delicious 'rainfall shower,' while the shower in the comfy Honu's Nest has a great mosaic reef scene. An added bonus: the owner dances a mean hula.

Hilo Bay Hale B&B $$

(Map p268; ☎800-745-5049, 640-1113; www.hilobayhale.com; 301 Ponahawai St; r $139-159;) You can't go wrong in this gorgeously restored 1912 plantation home, designed as a B&B. Two upper-floor rooms feature private lanai overlooking charming koi ponds, while

HULA'S MAIN EVENT

★Merrie Monarch Festival (☎935-9168; www.merriemonarchfestival.org; Afook-Chinen Civic Auditorium; 2-night admission general/reserved $10/15) comes to town around Easter (late March or early April) and this three-day hula competition is a phenomenal sellout attraction that turns laid-back Hilo into *the* place to be; forget about booking a last-minute hotel room in Hilo. Top hula troupes from all the islands vie in *kahiko* (ancient) and *'auana* (modern) categories. *Kahiko* performances are strong and serious, accompanied only by chanting. *'Auana* is closer to the mainstream style, with sinuous arm movements, smiling dancers and melodious accompaniment that includes string instruments. The primal chanting, meticulous choreography and traditional costumes are profoundly moving.

To guarantee a seat, order tickets by mail on December 26 (no earlier postmarks allowed); see the website for seating and payment info. The roughly 2700 tickets sell out within a month. Book your hotel room and car a year in advance.

the spacious ground-floor room boasts a palatial garden shower and its own patch of lawn. Guests have access to the charmingly retro kitchen and open-air dining lanai.

The central location lets you ditch the car for pleasant walks to the heart of downtown Hilo. For weeklong stays this place is a steal at $99 to $119 per night.

Bay House B&B B&B **$$**
(Map p268; ☎888-235-8195, 961-6311; www.bayhousehawaii.com; 42 Pukihae St; r incl breakfast $170;) Just across the Singing Bridge, find three immaculate guest rooms within eyeshot (and earshot) of the bay. Tasteful tropical theme, with classy hardwood and granite floors, each room includes a top-quality king bed, TV and private lanai (for that sunrise cup of coffee). The foyer contains a shared kitchenette and sitting area. Charming hosts are longtime residents who respect guests' privacy.

Hilo Hawaiian Hotel HOTEL **$$**
(Map p268; ☎800-367-5004, 935-9361; www.castleresorts.com; 71 Banyan Dr; r $155-240, ste from $315;) Hilo's biggest hotel's major attribute is its prime location across from Lili'uokalani Park. It's also an apt choice for those who prefer a largish hotel feel, especially with its spiffy lobby. Rooms are standard, not plush, but oceanfront units afford fantastic bay views. Book online for rooms at $105 to $135 and one-bedroom suites at $255 to $285. Lobby wi-fi.

Dolphin Bay Hotel HOTEL **$$**
(Map p268; ☎935-1466, 877-935-1466; www.dolphinbayhotel.com; 333 Iliahi St; studio/1br/2br from $109/159/179;) This family-run hotel hasn't changed much since it opened in 1968, so it's perfect for Hilo. The 18 spick-and-span apartments, all with full kitchens, TV and lanai, are a five-minute jog from downtown. Trundle beds are great for families. For longer stays, ask about the one-bedroom apartments in the **Annex** (per day/week/month $119/674/1400) across the street.

★**The Falls at Reed's Island** VACATION RENTAL **$$$**
(Map p268; ☎635-3649; www.reedsisland.com; 286 Kaiulani St; 2 people per night $275, $35 per additional person, $150 cleaning fee, minimum 3 nights) Wow! It's a hard to imagine a more dramatic location than this. The pair of architects who built this eyrie took 200 truckloads of rock off the top of a pinnacle on the Wailua River, and placed their dream house upon it.

The result is a very long and simple yet design-conscious three-bedroom cabin that holds you up in the lush canopy of a rainforest amidst the sound of roaring water. A spectacular monument to architectural vision – and right near downtown Hilo! Book well ahead.

Eating

★**Farmers Kitchen Cafe** TAKEOUT **$**
(Map p272; 57 Mamo St; mains $4-6; ⏲7am-3pm Tue-Sat;) This take-out restaurant opposite the Farmers Market is a hidden gem. It offers the tastiest homemade plate lunches around, with creative touches, like big slices of avocado on your burger, at bargain prices. If all those free samples at the market haven't filled you up, come here for lunch. Free wi-fi.

Surf Break Cafe CAFE **$**
(Map p272; ☎934-8844; 17 Haili St; breakfast sandwich $7; ⏲Mon-Sat 7am-3pm) Creative paninis and breakfast sandwiches, washed down with delicious smoothies and coffee drinks, define this surf-themed eatery. A great spot for an outdoor breakfast.

Le Magic Pan CREPERIE **$**
(Map p272; ☎935-7777; 64 Keawe Ave; crepes $12-14; ⏲7:30am-2pm Mon-Sat, 9am-2pm & 5-9pm Sun) Known for its sophisticated dinner crepes, this classy yet informal bistro also offers live jazz, daily specials, a limited wine list and, uniquely, a magic show on certain evenings. Ask the chef to share a trick.

★**Café Pesto** ITALIAN **$$**
(Map p272; ☎969-6640; www.cafepesto.com; 308 Kamehameha Ave, S Hata Bldg; pizzas $9-21, dinner $19-27; ⏲11am-9pm Sun-Thu, to 10pm Fri & Sat) This ever-popular bistro reels them in with its winning blend of Parisian flair, bayfront location, upbeat mood, and predominantly Italian menu, sparked with various international influences. Set in a historic building with high ceilings, its whirring ceiling fans mix a constant supply of conversation and music (live Wednesday to Sunday).

★**Hilo Bay Cafe** CAFE **$$**
(Map p268; ☎935-4939; www.hilobaycafe.com; Waiakea Center, 315 Maka'ala St; mains $15-26; ⏲11am-9pm Mon-Thu, to 9:30pm Fri & Sat, 5-9pm Sun) While its mall-box setting doesn't do it any favors, Hilo Bay Cafe tops many lists of the

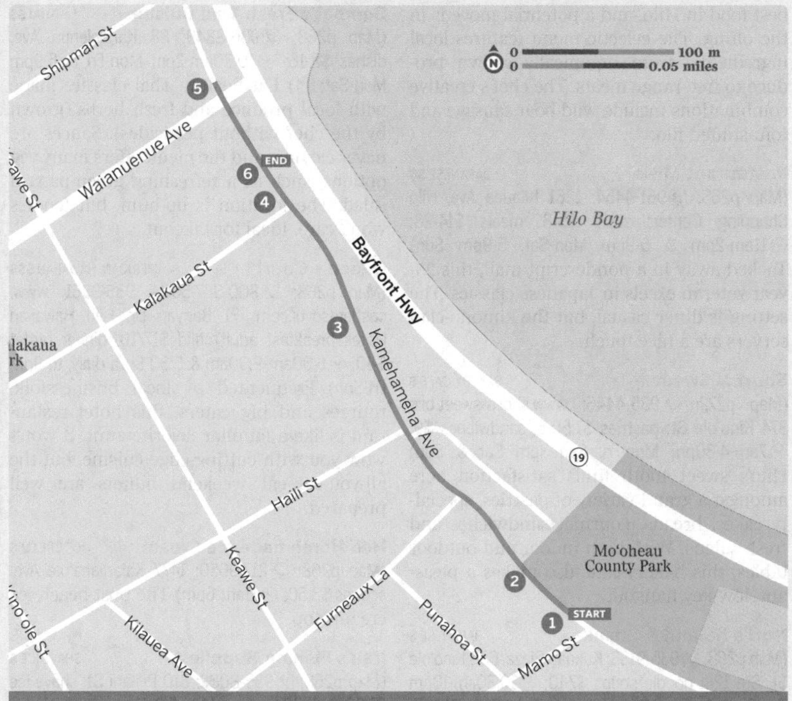

Town Walk
Bayfront Hiloism Walking Tour

START HILO FARMERS MARKET
END BAYFRONT COFFEE, KAVA & TEA CO
LENGTH 400 YARDS; HALF TO FULL DAY

Unite things that don't normally go together, and you get the creativity, the surprise, the mystery, the quirkiness, and ultimately the pleasure that defines Hilo. It's hard to put your finger on it sometimes, but by the time you finish walking the bayfront, you'll know Hiloism when you see it. Just be sure to talk to the locals: they'll happily weigh in.

The tour begins at ground zero 1 **Hilo Farmers Market** (p279), where the most surprising combinations end up in the same container on Wednesday and Sunday. Goat-milk soap, anyone? After surveying the local produce, duck into 2 **Cafe Pesto** (p276) for a fine brunch. But the questions keep coming. Is it a French bistro? An Italian pizzeria? A Spanish tapas bar? Or more Hawaii Regional Cuisine? You are now excused for wanting to flee into a dark room. So it's on to 3 **Kress Cinemas** (p279). Here you find a business that defies all the laws of economics. Where else can you see a movie these days for $2? Welcome, certainly, but what Twilight Zone have you entered? Head spinning, you now receive the double whammy: 4 **Pacific Tsunami Museum** (p270). This is a place dedicated to revisiting Hilo's own destruction – twice. No wonder they show the movies in the bank vault. You're then left wide open to a deeper shock: 5 **Mokupapapa Discovery Center** (p270). And you thought there were only eight Hawaiian Islands? Guess again – they go on for another 1500 miles. This entire place isn't what you thought! By now you have lost your moorings so completely that you need pharmaceutical support. Head back down the street to 6 **Bayfront Coffee, Kava & Tea Co** (p279), where you'll find Hilo's own licit substance, kava, ladled out at the bar. Now grasp half a coconut shell – clearly, it's time to give in – and raise a toast to Hiloism. After all, where else on the planet can you experience all that in 400 yards? Just don't be surprised when your mouth turns numb. You're not supposed to talk about it!

best food in Hilo, and a potential move is in the offing. The eclectic menu features local ingredients, from organically grown produce to free-range meats. The chef's creative combinations include wild boar sausage and tofu-stuffed filo.

Restaurant Miwa JAPANESE **$$**
(Map p268; ☎961-4454; 1261 Kilauea Ave, Hilo Shopping Center; sushi $5-8, meals $14-28; ⌚11am-2pm & 5-9pm Mon-Sat, 5-9pm Sun) Tucked away in a nondescript mall, this 25-year veteran excels in Japanese classics. The setting is diner casual, but the kimono-clad servers are a nice touch.

Short N Sweet BAKERY, CAFE **$**
(Map p272; ☎935-4446; www.shortnsweet.biz; 374 Kino'ole St; pastries $1.50-5, sandwiches $9; ⌚7am-4:30pm Mon-Fri, 8am-3pm Sat & Sun) Hilo's sweet tooth finds satisfaction here amongst a grand variety of pastries, specialty cakes, breads, gourmet sandwiches and fresh salads. With both indoor and outdoor tables, this bakery-cafe also makes a pleasant, low-key hangout.

Nori's Saimin & Snacks JAPANESE **$**
(Map p268; ☎935-9133; Kukuau Plaza, 688 Kino'ole St, Ste 124; noodle soups $7-10; ⌚10:30am-10pm Tue-Sun) Ignore the strip-mall setting. Focus on the Japanese noodle soups: tasty, filling and perfect for rainy days. Rippled saimin have an irresistibly chewy bite. Spotty service.

Hilo Town Tavern PUB **$**
(Map p272; 168 Keawe; mains $9-11; ⌚2pm-2am daily, restaurant 2-9pm) This friendly neighborhood tavern with a creative interior and outdoor terrace offers live music Tue & Thu-Sat, along with the usual pub food – burgers, pizza, sandwiches.

Pond's INTERNATIONAL **$$**
(Map p268; ☎934-7663; www.pondshilohi.com; 134 Kalanianaole Ave; mains $20-25; ⌚11am-9:30pm Sun-Thu, to midnight Fri-Sat) Noted for its great location right on the water, Pond's offers an eclectic menu of American, French and Hawaiian favorites in a comfy, summer-cottage atmosphere. Live music Thursday to Monday.

Ken's House of Pancakes DINER **$**
(Map p268; 1730 Kamehameha Ave; meals $6-12; ⌚24hr) The interior resembles any diner anywhere, but there's something comforting about a 24-hour diner with a mile-long menu. Choose from mac-nut pancakes, Spam omelettes, *kalua* (cooked in an underground pit) pig plates and steaming bowls of saimin.

Sombat's Fresh Thai Cuisine THAI **$$**
(Map p268; ☎936-8849; 88 Kanoelehua Ave; dishes $8-16; ⌚10:30am-2pm Mon-Fri & 5-9pm Mon-Sat; 🖉) Eat healthy Thai classics made with local produce and fresh herbs (grown by the chef without pesticides). Sauces are never cloying, and the menu offers many veg options, such as a refreshing green-papaya salad. The location is ho-hum, but foodies won't care. Ideal for takeout.

Queen's Court AMERICAN, HAWAIIAN **$$$**
(Map p268; ☎800-367-5004, 935-9361; www.castleresorts.com; 71 Banyan Dr, Hilo Hawaiian Hotel; breakfast adult/child $17/10, dinner buffet $40; ⌚6:30am-9:30am & 5:30-8pm daily, to 9pm Fri-Sun) Frequented by local businessfolk, retirees and big eaters, this hotel restaurant is like a familiar favorite aunt. It won't wow you with cutting-edge cuisine, but the all-you-can-eat weekend buffets are well prepared.

Hilo Homemade Ice Cream ICE CREAM **$**
(Map p268; ☎217-9650; 1477 Kalaniana'ole Ave; scoops $3.50; ⌚11am-6pm) The post-beach ice cream stop.

Itsu's Fishing Supplies SHAVE ICE **$**
(Map p268; ☎935-8082; 810 Pi'ilani St; shave ice $1.50; ⌚8:30am-5pm Mon-Fri) For generations, this family-run shop has delighted locals of all ages with soft-as-snow shave ice. The 'rainbow' (tri-flavor) is a classic.

Groceries

Besides the Farmers Market, we recommend these grocery stores:

★**KTA Super Store – Puainako** GROCERY
(Map p268; ☎959-9111, pharmacy 959-8700; 50 E Puainako St, Puainako Town Center; ⌚grocery 5:30am-midnight, pharmacy 8am-7pm Mon-Fri, from 9am Sat) Excellent locally owned chain in Puainako Town Center and downtown, KTA carries a wide selection of groceries plus an impressive deli with fresh poke, bento-box meals and other ready-to-eat items, which sell out by mid-morning. With pharmacy attached.

Abundant Life Natural Foods GROCERY
(Map p272; ☎935-7411; 292 Kamehameha Ave; ⌚8:30am-7pm Mon-Tues, Thurs-Fri, from 7am Wed & Sat, 10am-5pm Sun) Longtime downtown indie with takeout cafe (10am to 3pm Monday to Saturday) serves smoothies and wholesome sandwiches, from tamari-baked tofu to curried albacore tuna.

Drinking & Nightlife

★Coqui's Hideaway NIGHTCLUB

(Map p268; ☎935-4477; 1550 Kamehameha Ave; ⏰7am-2am Wed-Mon) This sprawling complex earns its moniker as 'the littlest big club in town,' offering pub fare, live music, a sports bar, a game room, karaoke and quite the dash of local color. All ages mix at all hours, making this tropical melting pot the best all-around nightspot in Hilo. Big bouncers round up the usual suspects.

Karma NIGHTCLUB

(Map p268; 124 Makaala St; ⏰2pm-2am Mon-Fri, 930pm-3:30am Sat) The local college crowd hangs out at this sports bar and dance club starting around midnight.

Cronies SPORTS BAR

(Map p272; ☎935-5158; www.cronieshawaii.com; 11 Waianuenue Ave; ⏰11am-9pm Mon-Thu & Sat, to 10pm Fri, to 8pm Sun) A sport-themed restaurant and bar, now going 15 years. The usual memorabilia and meat-driven menu, but all well done.

Bayfront Coffee, Kava & Tea Co BAR

(Map p272; ☎935-1155; www.bayfrontkava.com; 116 Kamehameha Ave; cup $5; ⏰noon-11pm Mon-Sat) If you're curious about kava (*'awa* in Hawaiian), try a cup at this minimalist bar. Friendly bar staff serve freshly brewed, locally grown kava root in coconut shells. Get ready for tingling taste buds and a calm buzz. Music nightly.

Entertainment

★Palace Theatre THEATER

(Map p272; ☎934-7010, box office 934-7777; www.hilopalace.com; 38 Haili St; movie tickets $8) This resurrected, historic theater is Hilo's cultural crown jewel. Its eclectic programming includes arthouse and silent films (accompanied by the house organ), music and dance concerts, Broadway musicals and cultural festivals. On Wednesday morning (from 11am to noon) it hosts *Hawai'iana Live* (adult/child $5/free), a touching, small-town intro to Hawaiian culture through storytelling, film, music, *oli* (chant) and hula.

Kress Cinemas CINEMA

(Map p272; ☎935-6777; 174 Kamehameha Ave; tickets $2) When was the last time you saw a $2 theater? Enter on Kalakaua St.

Stadium Cinemas CINEMA

(Map p268; ☎959-4595; 111 E Puainako St, Prince Kuhio Plaza; tickets adult/child 3-11yr/matinee $9.50/6.25/7.50) Typical shopping mall cinema with the usual Hollywood offerings.

Shopping

While locals flock to the chain-heavy malls south of the airport, downtown is far better for unique shops.

★Hilo Farmers Market FARMERS MARKET

(Map p272; www.hilofarmersmarket.com; cnr Mamo St & Kamehameha Ave; ⏰6am-4pm Wed & Sat) With 200 produce and craft vendors and sizeable crowds, this farmers market concentrates the creative spirit of the Big Island in one delicious, not-to-be-missed experience.

A single pass through the food tents unearths lehua honey, *liliko'i* jam, homemade chocolate, prune cakes, purple sweet potatoes, cranberry butter, pineapple curry, papaya BBQ sauce, and honeydew melon popsicles. The craft tents add to the atmosphere (don't miss the ivory nut jewelry).

★Bryan Booth Antiques ANTIQUES

(Map p272; ☎933-2500; www.bryanboothantiques.com; 94 Ponahawai St; ⏰10am-5pm Mon-Sat) The first stop for antiques in Hilo, this well-groomed shop has a bit of everything, but all of it high quality and well preserved. Your chance to find that unique piece of Hawaiiana.

Grapes: A Wine Store WINE

(Map p272; ☎933-1471; 207 Kilauea Ave; ⏰noon-6pm Tue-Sat) Wine lovers finally have a home in Hilo with this new store, which is run by some real aficionados, and packed to the rafters with global stock. Don't miss the Friday evening tasting.

Extreme Exposure Fine Art Gallery GALLERY

(Map p272; www.extremeexposure.com; 224 Kamehameha Ave; ⏰10am-8pm Mon-Sat, 11am-5pm Sun) This gallery offers some of Hawaii's finest nature photography, notably Kilauea's spectacular lava displays, and caters to all budgets, from framed prints to greeting cards. Of special note are the photos embedded in aluminum, providing a sparkling reality.

Bytes and Bites with Pieces VINTAGE

(Map p272; ☎935-3520; 264 Keawe St; ⏰10am-4pm Mon-Sat; 📶📝) Hilo's love of unique combinations is epitomized by this shop, which merges vintage furniture and collectibles with vegetarian food and the internet. The owner also does computer repairs. Hours may vary during paddling season.

Sig Zane Designs CLOTHING
(Map p272; www.sigzane.com; 122 Kamehameha Ave; ⌚9:30am-5pm Mon-Fri, 9am-4pm Sat) Legendary in the hula community, Sig Zane creates iconic custom fabrics, marked by rich colors and graphic prints of Hawaiian flora. You can spot a 'Sig' a mile away. Pricey, but this is real art.

Alan's Art & Collectibles ANTIQUES
(Map p272; ☎969-1554; 202 Kamehameha Ave; ⌚10am-4pm Mon & Wed-Fri, 1-4pm Tue, 10am-3pm Sat) Glimpse old Hawai'i in this chock-full secondhand shop: vintage glassware, household doodads, aloha shirts, vinyl LPs and scattered collectible treasures.

Big Island Book Buyers BOOKS
(Map p272; 14 Waianuenue Ave; ⌚10am-6pm Mon-Sat, 11am-5pm Sun) New books, particularly bestsellers, history and Hawaiiana. A cozy place to read, with coffee bar and couches.

Still Life Books BOOKS
(Map p272; ☎756-2919; http://stillifebooks.blogspot.com; 134 Kilauea Ave; ⌚11am-3pm Tue-Sat) Used books, with a focus on quality literature. A great place to browse and talk ideas.

Information

DANGERS & ANNOYANCES

Hilo has a relatively large homeless population. Definitely avoid Kalakaua Park and downtown alleys at night. Hilo also has a local culture fascinated with the sport of mixed martial arts (www.ufc.com), and is home to one of its champions, BJ Penn. Unfortunately some of this has spilled into local bars, so patrons are advised not to be loud or confrontational.

INTERNET ACCESS

You can access the internet as well as grab a snack at Bytes and Bites with Pieces (p279).

Hilo Public Library (☎933-8888; www.librarieshawaii.org; 300 Waianuenue Ave; ⌚11am-7pm Tue & Wed, 9am-5pm Thu & Sat, 10am-5pm Fri) If you buy a three-month nonresident library card ($10), you can use free internet terminals and check out books.

MEDICAL SERVICES

Supermarket chain KTA Super Store, with locations **downtown** (Map p272; ☎935-3751; 323 Keawe St, Downtown; ⌚7am-9pm Mon-Sat, to 6pm Sun) and in Puainako Town Center (p278), has an in-store pharmacy.

Hilo Medical Center (☎974-4700, ER 974-6800; 1190 Waianuenue Ave; ⌚24hr emergency) Near Rainbow Falls.

Longs Drugs (☎935-3357, pharmacy 935-9075; 555 Kilauea Ave; ⌚pharmacy 7am-7pm Mon-Fri, to 6pm Sat, 8am-5pm Sun) General store and pharmacy. Also at Prince Kuhio Plaza (☎959-5881, pharmacy 959-4508; 111 E Puainako St, Prince Kuhio Plaza; ⌚pharmacy 8am-8pm Mon-Fri, to 7pm Sat, to 5pm Sun).

MONEY

Bank of Hawaii (☎961-0681; 417 E Kawili St) Also with a branch at Pauahi St (☎935-9701; 120 Pauahi St).

First Hawaiian Bank (☎969-2222; 120 Waianuenue Ave)

POLICE

Police (☎935-3311; 349 Kapi'olani St) For nonemergencies.

POST

Both post offices hold general-delivery mail, but require you to complete an application in person.

Downtown Post Office (☎933-3014; 154 Waianuenue Ave; ⌚9am-4pm Mon-Fri, 12:30pm-2pm Sat) Located in the Federal Building.

Main Post Office (☎933-3019; 1299 Kekuanaoa St; ⌚8am-4:30pm Mon-Fri, 9am-12:30pm Sat) Located near Hilo airport.

Getting There & Away

AIR

Hilo International Airport (ITO; ☎934-5838; www.state.hi.us/dot/airports/hawaii/ito) All flights to Hilo are inter-island except for two Continental Airlines routes, which fly directly from Los Angeles and from San Francisco. For a disabled access guide see http://hawaii.gov/health/dcab/travel.

BUS

Hele-On Bus (www.heleonbus.org) The main Hilo station is the **Mo'oheau terminal** (329 Kamehameha Ave), where all intra-island buses originate. Check the website for current routes and schedules. All buses are wheelchair accessible.

CAR

The drive from Hilo to Kailua-Kona (via Waimea) is 92 miles and takes 2½ hours. If you're driving from Hilo to Mauna Kea, the fastest route is Puainako St, which leads into Saddle Rd. You'll shorten your travel time and reduce traffic on the winding, residential Kaumana Dr.

Getting Around

BIKE

Cycling is more recreation than transportation in Hilo. **Mid-Pacific Wheels** (☎ 935-6211; www.midpacificwheelsllc.com; 1133-C Manono St; ⊙ 9am-6pm Mon-Sat, 11am-5pm Sun) rents mountain bikes for $15 to $20 per day.

BUS

The Hele-On Bus (p280) provides comprehensive coverage of Hilo. Check the website for routes and schedules.

CAR

Numerous car-rental booths can be found outside the baggage claim area of the airport. Free parking is generally available in Hilo. Downtown street parking is free for two hours; finding [illegible] during Saturday and [illegible] ental, and [illegible] Mustang or [illegible] **loha Aina Car** [illegible] hotmail.com; [illegible] k $150-250) [illegible] Enterprising [illegible] ndhand cars are [illegible] d locals alike. [illegible] a week, airport [illegible] s must have [illegible] vn a $300 deposit. Some 4WD vehicles and a priceless Miata convertible available.

Happy Campers Hawaii (☎ 896-8777; www.happycampershawaii.com; rental per 24hr $130) offers VW Westfalia pop-top campers/Vanagons that sleep up to four. At $130 per day, and in great condition, they're a steal, with built-in kitchenettes, sink with running water, cookware, bedding and more. A great way to get around the Big Island. Pick up and drop off in Hilo.

TAXI

From the airport, taxis are located right outside the baggage-claim area. The approximate cab fare from the airport to downtown Hilo is $15. For taxi service around Hilo call **Marshall's Taxi** (☎ 936-2654) or **Percy's Taxi** (☎ 969-7060).

PUNA

The Polynesian word 'mana' is tough to translate. 'Life force,' 'energy,' and other terms are usually bandied about. But if you really want to learn mana's meaning, come to Puna, because everyone on this island agrees it is overflowing with the stuff. Here, at Hawai'i's eastern tip, rain blends with black volcanic soil to engender a fertility that is frankly astounding. Green bursts through the soil and weaves itself into thick forests of wood rooted in lava soil. The ocean beats like a hammer on the Big Island's easternmost cliffs, and in turn the water edges back as lava flows into the ocean.

Who lives here? Smack in the path of the lava flow are the homes of hippies, funky artists, alternative healers, Hawaiian sovereignty activists, *pakalolo* growers, organic farmers and off-the-grid survivalists. A nickname for all these folks, which they have adopted themselves, is Punatics. There's an extreme blend here of laid-back pliability and intense emotions.

One settles here only by accepting wildness and impermanence as the price. Puna retains dense, unspoiled portions of sometimes hallucinatory jungle as well as long-gone neighborhoods now blanketed by a thick mass of black lava. Sultry and hang-loose Puna encourages travelers to ditch the guidebook and go with the flow.

Once the Big Island frontier, these days Puna is the fastest-growing district in the state. It has some of Hawaii's most affordable land, in subdivisions that were marked out more than 50 years ago and sparsely settled – until now. The northern half of Puna is becoming one unending suburban subdivision, with the population poised to almost double within a decade. Most agree Puna faces an infrastructure crisis, not to mention an identity crisis. The fast food/chain store shopping-mall erected at the terminus of Pahoa's historic downtown in 2010 – protested by some – is indicative of the schism.

PERMACULTURE IN PUNA

Permaculture, a sustainable agriculture method wherein practitioners attempt to emulate natural ecosystems, is widespread in Puna. Many local permaculture farms are willing to offer at least free lodging for permaculture volunteers and students. **Hawaiian Sanctuary** and Hedonisia (p286) are both excellent accomodations options that double as permaculture farms and education centers. Inquire at Island Naturals (p285) or the Pahoa Museum (p283) for information on new permaculture enclaves in the district.

Kea'au & Around

POP 2253

Heading down the 'hill' from Volcano towards Hilo, you'll whisk past sugar plantations converted into subdivisions. There are some worthy lodgings tucked away in these parts, making it an attractive base between Hilo, Volcano and Puna. The main town is Kea'au, a cluster of gas stations and stores just off Hwy 11 – provision here before heading to Volcano; the two general stores there charge an arm and a leg.

At the **Hilo Coffee Mill** (☎866-982-5551, 968-1333; www.hilocoffeemill.com; 17-995 Hwy 11; ⏰7am-4pm Mon-Sat) you can taste East Hawai'i coffee and take a short, free tour at this mill-cafe with a breezy lanai for enjoying tasty sandwiches and a cup of joe.

Tours

Kazumura Cave Tours GUIDED TOUR
(☎967-7208; http://kazumuracave.com; off Volcano Hwy, past MM 22; tours from $20; ⏰by appointment) Since discovering his property lies atop the Kazumura Cave – the world's longest lava tube – Harry Schick has become an expert on lava caves and gives small tours (four to six people maximum) at low cost. On the shortest, easiest tour, participants must climb ladders and walk over rocky terrain. Age 10 and above.

Kilauea Caverns of Fire GUIDED TOUR
(☎217-2363; www.kilaueacavernsoffire.com; 1-/3-hr tours $29/79; ⏰by appointment) A more impersonal tour through Kazumura Cave; choose from an easy one-hour walk or a three-hour scramble. Call for reservations and directions.

Sleeping

Butterfly Inn B&B $
(☎800-546-2442, 966-7936; www.thebutterflyinn.com; Kurtistown; s/d with shared bathroom $55/65) Since 1987 owners Kay and Patty have welcomed women to stay at their

Puna

0 — 10 km
0 — 5 miles

See Around Hilo Map (p274)
Hilo (2.5mi)
SOUTH HILO
Stainback Hwy
MM5
Kea'au
MM11
Paradise Dr
Orr's Beach
Dan DeLuz's Woods
8th Rd
Hilo Coffee Mill
Art & Orchids B&B
Mountain View
130
MM7
Kahakai Blvd
Wa'a Wa'a
Cape Kumukahi
Kumukahi Lighthouse
11
MM15
South Kulani Rd
Kilauea Caverns of Fire
Maku'u Craft & Farmers Market
Kapoho Village Inn
Champagne Pond & Likeke Cove
Hawai'i Belt Rd
MM10
Pahoa
Lava Tree State Monument
Kapoho
132
137
Kapoho Tide Pools
Glenwood
PUNA
MM13
Hot Dog Guy
MM22
Hale Makamae B&B
Pohoiki Rd
Ahalanui Beach Park (Hot Pond)
Coconut Cotage B&B
Isaac Kepo'okalani Hale Beach Park
Kazamura Cave Tours
MM15
Kamaili Rd
A'akepa
Opihikao
MacKenzie State Recreation Area
Volcano Village (7mi); National Park Entrance (8.5mi)
Space Farmers Market
Kalani Oceanside Retreat
East Rift Zone
Pu'u 'O'o Vent
Ramashala
Kehena Beach
MM20
Star of the Sea Church
Hawai'i Volcanoes National Park
Kaimu
New Kaimu Beach
Naulu Trail
Kalapana Trail
Lava Flow Viewing Area
Kalapana (Former Village)
PACIFIC OCEAN
See Hawai'i Volcanoes National Park Map (p290)

comfortable home in Kurtistown. Two tidy rooms with private entrance share an ample kitchen, living room, dining deck, bathroom and outdoor hot tub. Single female travelers will appreciate the safe, supportive, women-only environment. Three-night minimum, or rates go up. Directions provided upon booking.

Art & Orchids B&B B&B $$
(☎877-393-1894; www.artandorchids.com; 16-1504 39th Ave; r incl breakfast $110-140;) This dreamy, relaxed haven set in an ohia forest is Puna at its best. Three airy (albeit frumpy) rooms include funky mosaic-tile baths and tons of amenities. The spacious common room has a full kitchen and cozy couches, plus there's a unique lava-rock-and-mosaic-tile swimming pool with a hot tub out back. Papermaking and mosaic classes are available, and you can make your own art in the garden gazebo.

Pahoa

POP 945

Like a weird mix of Wild West frontier town and hippie commune, Pahoa is the beating original, eclectic heart of Puna. This ramshackle, ragamuffin town, with its raised wooden sidewalks, peeling paint and unkempt bohemian edge, can easily capture your heart. It's full of oddballs and eccentrics and genuine aloha.

Sights

★Maku'u Craft & Farmers Market MARKET
(Hwy 130; ⏲8am-2pm Sun) Join the entire Puna *'ohana* (family) at the Maku'u Craft & Farmers Market, which is more like a massive village party than a market with psychics, wood carvings, massage, old junk, surfboard repair, orchids, organic honey, sarongs and jewelry, photos of the Kalapana eruption and (imagine that) fruits and vegetables. **Morning cultural workshops** (9am) give way to live music through the afternoon. Don't miss it.

Hot food includes Hawaiian, Samoan, Mexican and Thai cuisine, and more. It's located on Hwy 130 between mile markers 7 and 8.

Pahoa Museum MUSEUM
(☎430-1573; 15-2931 Pahoa Village Rd; suggested donation $3; ⏲11am-7pm) This little museum showcases Puna history and culture in all its splendid diversity, with a fair dose of New Age theory thrown in for good measure. It exhibits local artists, historical artifacts, old maps and about anything else under the sun, and spearheads many local community projects. Donations are badly needed. Please note the official opening hours can be pretty flexible.

Activities

★Jeff Hunt Surfboards SURFING
(☎965-2322; http://jeffhuntsurfboards.com; 15-2883 Pahoa Village Rd; rental per day $25; ⏲10am-5pm Mon-Sat, 11am-3pm Sun) Jeff Hunt is one of the island's best board shapers, and at his little hut you can buy one, talk surfing and rent soft-top boards.

Paradissimo Tropical Spa SPA
(☎965-8883; www.spaparadissimo.com; 15-2958 Pahoa Village Rd; facials from $25) In our estimation, there's no better way to spend a rainy afternoon than getting a good pampering here. Owner Olivia is a tender soul with talented hands and the organic spa products she uses feel like a magical alchemy for the skin. Sauna and massage also available.

Tours

Bird-watching or discovering pockets of unbridled nature along the Puna coast are highlights of guided tours in this area, but if the lava is flowing, you *must* go on a lava-spotting tour. You can depart either by boat or on foot from Kalapana (p289). Remember the four classic elements: wind, water, earth and fire? It's rare to see all four occur naturally at once, but that's exactly what happens on lava tours. Maybe those old alchemists had it right, because when the four substances combine, creation – of the Big Island itself – occurs.

LGBT PUNA

Along with hosting the island's biggest concentration of New Agers and organic farmers, Puna is also the Big Island's gay capital. While there aren't queer bars, you will find cruising and rainbow flags, plus gay-friendly places to stay, workshops and gatherings. This laidback approach to sexual orientation is also extended to lesbians and bisexuals. All hotels we list in Puna are LGBT friendly.

★ **Lava Ocean Adventures** BOAT TOUR
(☎966-4200; www.lavaocean.com; tours adult/child 6-12yr $175/125) The crew on the *Lava Kai* get you close enough to the lava that you feel the heat and smell the sulphur. It's an unforgettable experience. These expertly narrated tours motor from Isaac Hale Beach Park to the sea entry near Kalapana, where you'll see lava gushing into the ocean, boiling it on contact.

For 30 minutes watch as live lava chunks explode underwater, getting churned into a water-molten rock 'smoothie' while a new black-sand beach is built – simply awesome. Go for the sunrise tour and you'll be escorted by flying fish, leaping dolphins and maybe a rainbow. Warning: you may get seasick.

Native Guide Hawaii GUIDED TOUR
(☎982-7575; www.nativeguidehawaii.com; tour incl lunch $300, or $150 per person for 2+ groups; by appointment) Tours with Native Hawaiian and cultural practitioner Warren Costa are different. He's trained, personal, professional and he knows his land well. All-day volcano, coastal or birding tours reveal Puna mysteries that you won't unravel on your own.

Sleeping

Hawaiian Sanctuary COTTAGE $
(☎309-8010; http://sustainable-hawaii.org; MM 12, Hwy 130; r $65-85) The Sanctuary, located about 1.5 miles from Pahoa proper, is Puna at her funky best. This permaculture farm welcomes volunteers and sustainable agriculture students from around the world. If you'd just like to visit, soak up the vibe and dine on the Sanctuary's vegan food, you can stay in a series of comfortable chalets (one shaped like an odd space pod) and partake of daily activies, including yoga, meditation and hula dancing.

Island Paradise Inn HOTEL $
(☎990-0234; www.islandparadiseinn.com; 15-2937 Pahoa Village Rd; d from $40;) Smack downtown, this inn is actually a row of former plantation-worker houses that's been converted into 20 small, clean and very affordable rooms, all with private bathroom and kitchenette. Decor varies; pleasing touches (fluffy towels, stained glass) are combined with secondhand bureaus. Three-night minimum stay.

Coconut Cottage B&B B&B $$
(☎866-204-7444, 965-0973; www.coconutcottagehawaii.com; 13-1139 Leilani Ave; r incl breakfast $110-140; @) South of Pahoa in a trim residential neighborhood, this romantic, four-room B&B is full of sweet Balinese accents and little luxuries. The garden hot tub in a tiki hut and the breezy porch are attractive places to relax, a sensation that's cultivated by the warm, gracious hosts. Rooms are comfortably cozy; the largest is the detached bungalow with kitchenette. Breakfast is a feast.

Hale Makamae B&B B&B $$
(☎965-7015; www.bnb-aloha.com; 13-3315 Makamae St; studio incl breakfast $105, 1-/2-bedroom ste incl breakfast $140/160; @) In a clean-cut neighborhood, this B&B is immaculate, family-friendly and a bargain to boot. Suites are especially comfy, with well-equipped kitchenettes and enough space to kick back. All accommodations have a separate entrance onto lush gardens. Hot breakfast

PUNA BACKROADS

The old lighthouse that Pele spared isn't much – just a tall piece of white-painted metal scaffolding. But it's still rewarding to head straight across Four Corners from Hwy 132 and brave the rutted, 1.5-mile dirt road to the end of **Cape Kumukahi**. This is the easternmost point in the state, and the air that blows across it is the freshest in the world (so scientists say). Even better, the lava-covered cliffs make a gorgeous perch to contemplate this meeting of sky, sea and lava. From the parking area, walk the 4WD roads that crisscross the point – all the way to Champagne Pond and other snorkeling spots, if you're up to it.

Turn left, or north, at Four Corners, and time will seem to slow to a stop as you enter a teeming, ancient, vine-draped forest pulsing with mana. The road leads to **Wa'a Wa'a** and is passable for standard cars, but much of it is cratered, narrow and twisted. Mind the numerous 'Kapu' signs and go slow. After about 5 miles you reach boulder-strewn **Orr's Beach** shaded by ironwood trees; park here and scramble along the shore to find a spot for a quiet picnic lunch.

is served in a breakfast room bursting with orchids. Hosts are fluent in German.

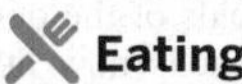

Eating

★Pahoa Fresh Fish SEAFOOD $
(☎965-8248; 15-2670 Pahoa Village Rd; mains $5-7; ⏰8am-7pm) Utterly unassuming Pahoa Fresh Fish, which has the atmosphere of the moon and is slotted in an ugly strip mall, serves, hands down, the best fish and chips on the Big Island. We don't know what the friendly lady behind the counter is doing and we don't care; we will come back for her perfectly battered and fried ono and mahimahi anytime, all the time.

Ning's Thai Cuisine THAI $
(15-2955 Pahoa Village Rd; mains $10-14; ⏰noon-9pm Mon-Sat, from 5pm Sun; ✎) Accomplished Thai is served up at this little spot; save room for the *liliko'i* or ginger ice-cream.

Mike's New York Pizzeria PIZZERIA $
(☎965-5331; 15-2945 Pahoa Village Rd; pizza slice/whole from $4/15; ⏰11am-2pm & 5-9pm Tue-Sun) We're all for Pahoa's macrobiotic goodness, but sometimes, you just need a yummy, greasy thin-crust New York-style pizza. And along comes Mike! Never have two more drastically different islands (Manhattan and Hawaii) crossed in one place, but the result is delicious.

Island Naturals HEALTH FOOD $
(Map p268; 15-1403 Pahoa Village Rd; sandwiches $6-10; ⏰7:30am-7:30pm Mon-Sat, 8am-7pm Sun; ✎) For organic produce and picnic lunches; this place has a fresh, interesting range of sandwiches, packaged salads, baked goods and hot food.

Paolo's Bistro ITALIAN $$
(Pahoa Village Rd; mains $13-26; ⏰5:30am-9pm Tue-Sun) An intimate place serving a well-executed menu of authentic northern Italian cooking. Bring your own *vino*.

★Kaleo's Bar & Grill HAWAII REGIONAL CUISINE $$
(☎965-5600; 15-2969 Pahoa Village Rd; lunch mains $9-16, dinner mains $14-30; ⏰11am-9pm; 📶) Laid-back Puna may not be the spot you expect to find fabulous fine dining, but don't forget, this district is creative as hell too. Enter Kaleo's, a wonderful restaurant that blends original menu items with an artsy, island-casual vibe. Tempura ahi roll, orzo pasta salad, coconut chicken curry and island-raised ribeye are some of the fresh, creative fare that's a staple here. Live music many nights.

THOSE DAMN COQUI

Hawai'i's most wanted alien is the Puerto Rican coqui frog, only an inch long. Why? They are loud. They make jet engines sound subdued. At sunset, coquis begin their nightly chirping (a two-tone 'ko-kee' call), which can register between 90 and 100 decibels from 2ft away. Even at a distance their chorus maintains 70 decibels, equivalent to a vacuum cleaner.

Coquis accidentally reached the Hawaiian Islands around 1988, and they've proliferated wildly on the Big Island. Around Lava Tree State Monument, densities are the highest in the state and twice that of Puerto Rico. Besides causing a nightly racket, coquis are disrupting the ecosystem by eating bugs that feed native birds. If you're in Puna and you're a light sleeper, bring ear plugs.

Drinking & Entertainment

Akebono Theater LIVE MUSIC
(☎965-9990; Pahoa Village Rd; tickets $10-20) This historical theater hosts all kinds of music, from Big Island Elvis to visiting jam bands. It's located behind Luquins.

Black Rock Cafe BAR
(15-2872 Pahoa Village Rd; ⏰7am-9pm) Half the Black Rock is an average restaurant serving passable burgers and breakfast. The other half is a bar popular with Punatics who are little more Harley Davidson than hippie. Not that it gets rough here (and hippies do show up too); the Black Rock is just a little saltier, smokier and sweatier.

Luquin's Mexican Restaurant BAR
(☎965-9990; 15-2942 Pahoa Village Rd; mains $10-19; ⏰7am-9pm) The Mexican option, with standard plate combos. Its hopping bar does a brisk business in margaritas ($14 per pint; try the *lilko'i* number). If the drinks don't get you too hungover, the breakfast here is pretty excellent too.

Sirius Coffee Connection CAFE
(15-2874 Pahoa Village Rd; ⏰7am-6pm, til 3pm Sun) This cute cafe serves good local coffee and is a bit of an unofficial community center for Puna.

Shopping

Just off the main highway, north of the historic downtown, is Pahoa Marketplace – a shopping mall with a good grocery store and hardware store. Across the highway is a contentious new shopping center with a giant Long's Drugs.

Along the main street in town is a convenience store (if you need chepaer groceries than Island Naturals), as well as **Big Island BookBuyers** (15-2901 Pahoa Village Rd; 10am-6pm Mon-Sat, 11am-5pm Sun), a well-run used bookshop.

Information

Along the main road you'll find banks, gas stations and a **post office** (15-2859 Pahoa Village Rd). There are no internet cafes in Pahoa but most businesses along the main strip of Pahoa Village Rd have wi-fi signals.

Getting There & Away

Hele-On Bus (www.heleonbus.org; fare $1) goes from Hilo to Kea'au and Pahoa 11 times a day Monday to Friday, and four times on Saturday.

Lava Tree State Monument

Entering this **park** (daylight hours) FREE beneath a tight-knit canopy of (invasive) albizia trees is an otherworldly experience. A short, easy loop **trail** passes through a tropical vision of Middle Earth, full of ferns, orchids and bamboo, and takes you past unusual 'lava trees,' which were created in 1790 when a rainforest was engulfed in *pahoehoe* from Kilauea's East Rift Zone. The lava enveloped the moisture-laden ohia trees and then receded, leaving lava molds of the destroyed trees. These mossy shells now lie scattered like dinosaur bones, adding to the park's ghostly aura. In the late afternoon the love songs of coqui frogs reverberate among the trees. To get here follow Hwy 132 about 2.5 miles east of Hwy 130.

If you plan to visit overnight, **Hedonisia** (430-9903, 430-2545; http://hedonisiahawaii.com; 13-657 Hinalo St; dm from $27, huts $55-70;) ranks up there among the world's friendly, funky hostels. What was once a junkyard has been converted into an organic farm/ramshackle accomodation compound, with Technicolor murals, simple, cozy chalets, 'dorms' where you can sleep in a comfy common area in a tent, wild pigs and a school bus. You can stay in said bus, which has been decked out in cosmic artwork, and anyone who wants to volunteer in the hostel gets discounted stays. Located about 1.7 miles from Lava Tree State Monument, and 10 minutes' drive from downtown Pahoa.

STAYING HEALTHY IN PUNA

Frolicking in tide pools and hot ponds can be tons of fun, but visitors should be aware of health risks due to the enclosed nature of these natural wonders – bacteria (including staphylococcal) have been present here in the past. To minimize risk, locals counsel visitors to go early in the morning when fewer people have been in the pools; aim to time your explorations for high tide; and try to avoid Mondays and other post-peak usage times (ie after holidays). It's essential to not enter pools with open cuts and to shower immediately after.

Kapoho

Hwy 132 goes east until it meets Red Rd at **Four Corners** (where four roads meet) near Kapoho. Once a small farming village, Kapoho became Pele's victim in January 1960 when a volcanic fissure let loose a half-mile-long curtain of fiery lava in a nearby sugarcane field. The main flow of *pahoehoe* ran toward the ocean, but a pokier offshoot of *'a'a* crept toward the town, burying orchid farms in its path. Two weeks later the lava buried Kapoho, including nearly 100 homes and businesses.

When the lava approached the sea at **Cape Kumukahi**, it parted around the lighthouse which, alone, survived. Old-timers say that the lighthouse keeper offered a meal to Pele, who appeared disguised as an old woman on the eve of the disaster, and so she spared the structure.

Red Road (Highway 137)

Winding Hwy 137 is nicknamed Red Rd because its northern portion is paved with red cinder. It's a swooping, atmospheric drive that periodically dips beneath tunnel-like canopies of milo and hala (pandanus) trees. There are many discreet paths to the shore along this road – take one for a private piece of coast.

Two side roads also make intriguing detours or shortcuts back to Pahoa: **Pohoiki Rd** connects Hwy 137 with Hwy 132, and is another shaded, mystical mana path winding through thick forest dotted with papaya orchards and wild *noni* (Indian mulberry). Further south, **Kama'ili Rd**, connecting with Hwy 130, is another pleasant country ramble.

When hunger strikes, pull up to the **Hot Dog Guy** (intersection of Hwy 132 & Pohoiki Rd; hotdogs $5-7; daily until sunset;) for some bison, reindeer or all-beef hotdogs grilled to order and nestled in a whole wheat bun.

Kapoho Beach Lots

Top-notch **snorkeling** awaits beyond the locked gates of this seaside community – perfect for a family reunion or getaway.

The *many* vacation rentals here are ideal for family getaways, with many houses boasting flexible, multiroom sleeping arrangements. One terrific option is **Pualani** (805-225-1552; www.bigislandhawaiivacation-homes.com; Kapoho Beach Lots; 2-bedroom house $145; @) a modern, open-plan home with hot tub, wraparound lanai, bikes and beach toys. Another gem is **Hale O Naia** (965-5340; www.hale-o-naia.com; Kapoho Beach Lots; r incl breakfast $90-110, ste $175), which qualifies as a Fantasy Beach House. All units feature gleaming hardwoods, ocean-view lanai, wraparound windows and use of a sauna and whirlpool tub. The sprawling Master Suite is a worthy splurge. Check airbnb.com and vrbo.com for more information.

This stretch of coast is technically open only to those living or renting within its gates. **Champagne Pond** is a famous snorkeling spot out here, but you must access it either by knowing someone in Kapoho, or via the lava road (4WD only) that leads from Kumukahi Lighthouse (because all coast in Hawai'i is technically public land, you're not trespassing in this scenario).

Kapoho Tide Pools

The best snorkeling on the Big Island's windward side is this sprawling network of **tide pools** (suggested donation $3; 7am-7pm) – officially named the Wai Opae Tide Pools Marine Life Conservation District. Here Kapoho's lava-rock coast is a mosaic of protected, shallow, interconnected pools containing a rich variety of sea life. It's easy to pool-hop for hours, tracking saddle wrasses, Moorish idols, butterfly fish, sea cucumbers and much more. For interesting coral gardens, head straight out from the blue house; sea turtles like the warm pocket a bit further south and octopuses are known to visit here.

From Hwy 137, a mile south of the lighthouse, turn onto Kapoho Kai Dr, which winds a little and dead-ends at Wai Opae; turn left and park in the lot. A $3 donation is requested by the local community, which is fair enough. There are no facilities.

This area is also peppered with vacation rentals.

Ahalanui Beach Park

It's called 'the hot pond' because of its main attraction – a large, spring-fed **thermal pool** (7am-7pm) that's set in lava rock and deep enough for swimming. It's a pretty sweet bathtub: water temperatures average 90°F (cooler with incoming tide), cement borders make for easy access, tropical fish abound and, though the ocean pounds the adjacent seawall, the pool is always calm. However, despite being regularly flushed by the sea, the pond contains a risk of bacterial infection.

The park gates are never locked – early and late soaking is the best crowd-beating strategy. The park has picnic tables, portable toilets and a lifeguard daily. Don't leave valuables in your car.

Isaac Kepo'okalani Hale Beach Park

This rocky beach park is extremely popular with locals. It encompasses restless Pohoiki Bay, where the waves are usually too rough for swimming but some of the gnarliest breaks for bodyboarding and surfing. The boat ramp area is still a popular fishing spot, and beyond that, a well-worn path leads (past a private house) to a small natural **hot pond**.

Across the road from the beach, the **camping** area consists of a pristine lawn, trim as a putting green, with 22 sites, picnic tables, BBQs, and bathrooms with flush toilets and drinking water. A security guard checks permits (folks used to squat here). Lava boat tours leave from the camping area.

MacKenzie State Recreation Area

This grove of ironwood trees edging sheer 40ft cliffs above a restless ocean is a moody, windswept spot. During the day this quiet, secluded park makes an unforgettable picnic spot. Exploring the **lava tube** just back from the precipitous ledge a moment's walk from the pavilion makes a memorable post-lunch adventure. Head into the forest facing the ledge to find the entrance (requires a short, steep descent and a little boulder scrambling); after about 20 minutes walking on uneven lava rock you'll be dumped a little ways down and across the road from the park entrance. **Camping** at MacKenzie is allowed, but not recommended due to the area's unsettling isolation, making it a site for violent crimes in the past – a long time ago, but the place retains an eerie vibe still.

About half a mile south of here is **A'akepa**, a hidden expanse of lava flats and tide pools run through with rivers of incoming surf and chartreuse ground cover. Here palm-trunk bridges cross little lagoons, lichen and pine needles drip from lava boulders like glaze on a cinnamon bun. Look for the coastal path from Hwy 137 marked by a rusted-out car.

Kehena Beach & Around

If any place captures the friendly uninhibited intensity of Puna, it's this beautiful black-sand beach at the base of rocky cliffs, shaded by coconut and ironwood trees. All types and persuasions mix easily – hippies, Hawaiians, gays, families, teens, seniors, tourists. Many come to doff their clothes but, truly, no one cares if you don't. As the drum circle plays, old guys dance with their eyes closed while parents chase their kids in the surf while others meditate, drink, swim and hang out. For a quieter experience, come early to greet the rising sun and watch the resident dolphin pod leap into the air.

The surf is *powerful*, even when 'calm,' so swim with caution. Deaths occur here every year, and you shouldn't venture beyond the rocky point at the southern end. Kehena is immediately south of mile marker 19. From the small parking lot a short, steep path leads down to the beach. Don't leave valuables in your car.

Sights

Space Farmers Market MARKET
(www.hawaiispace.com; 12-247 West Pohakupele Loop, Seaview Performing Arts Center for Education; ⌚8-11:30am Sat) Closer to mile marker 18, the Seaview subdivision is home to this farmers market. More inventive than most, here you'll find everything from tarot readers to tie-dyes and lots of organic produce and prepared foods. To get here, turn into the subdivision, turn right on Mapuana St and left on Kehauopuna St.

Sleeping

Kalani Oceanside Retreat RESORT $
(☎800-800-6886, 965-7828; www.kalani.com; tents s/d $40/55, d $115-175, treehouse $265; ⌚day passes 7:30am-8pm, Ecstatic Sun-Dance 10:30am-12:30pm Sun; @📶🏊) For the full-on retreat experience, head north up Hwy 137 (between mile markers 17 and 18) to Kalani, which occupies a 120-acre compound that hums with activity and energy. It's a fun, communal place to stay, but if you're not down with yoga, meditation, dance and alternative healing, you'll feel left out.

Massages ($90 to $180) are highly recommended. Nonguests can buy **day passes** ($20) for use of the facilities and grounds. An outdoor dining lanai (also open to nonguests) serves healthy buffet-style meals, while the rooms are all simple and breezy, with bright tropical spreads and plywood floors covered in *lauhala* mats.. Weekly **Ecstatic Sun-Dance** ($15) gatherings on Sunday are insanely popular; day care available ($5) and donations ($5) expected.

Right across the road from Kalani is the **Point** – a wild spot of coast for some contemplative solitude on a rough-hewn bench under a lone palm.

Ramashala GUESTHOUSE $
(☎965-0068; www.ramashala.com; 12-7208 Hwy 137; r $50-250; 📶) Almost directly across from Kehena Beach is this laid-back retreat. Among the red-shingled Balinese buildings, the six rooms vary wildly: from teeny rooms with a twin bed and shared bath to spacious roosts with full kitchens. Hardwood floors, furnishings and gorgeous grounds exude a spare, meditative elegance. There's a communal hot tub, and two studio spaces host weekly yoga classes.

Got a group? The entire property can be rented for $750 to $1000 per night.

LAVA VIEWING NO-NO

Hwy 130 ends at a somewhat ominous set of guard barriers. Many trekkers venture out from here to try and see the lava flow, but we are warning you: *do not attempt this without a guide*. Yes, yes: everyone will tell you it's doable and chill out and Mama Pele wants you to and all that crap. Look: people die and are seriously injured trying to hike to the lava. There are areas where the ground can give way and others with trapped bubbles of poison gas. Instead, take a tour guide from Kalapana.

Absolute Paradise B&B B&B $$
(☎888-285-1540, 965-1828; http://absoluteparadise.tv; Kipuka St; r $99-135, ste $164; wi-fi) This charming, gay-oriented, clothing-optional B&B is located near Kehena Beach and is a ton of fun. Rooms are clean, charming and filled with original design motifs, and the owners are as friendly as family. There's an emphasis on the optional in 'clothing optional', so don't fret if you want to come clad.

Kalapana (Former Village)

As with Kapoho in 1960, so it was for Kalapana 30 years later: in 1990 a redirection of the ongoing eruption buried most of this village, destroying 100 homes and obliterating what was once Hawai'i's most famous black-sand beach, Kaimu Beach.

Today Hwy 137 ends abruptly at the eastern edge of what used to be Kalapana. A few houses here were spared and sit surrounded by devastation. The dead-end now contains a modest complex catering to tourists and an outpost of the Hawaiian sovereignty movement. Grab a good burger or plate lunch at **Kalapana Village Cafe** (12-5037 Pahoa Kalapana Rd [Hwy 137]; mains $8-11; ⏰8am-9pm), or sidle up to **Uncle's Awa Bar** (⏰3-10pm), where you can try kava and rub elbows with locals. Live music goes off here a lot.

One conversation starter is the adjacent billboard display promoting the establishment of the 'lawful Hawaiian government.' The display provides a full account of Hawaiian history, past and present, from a native perspective. Visitors can contract guides here for **lava walks** (flow permitting) for $100, or arrange via Lava Ocean Adventures (p284).

Visitors should note that the entire lava flow, both here and at the lava-viewing area covers private land, and trespassing is illegal. While there are no fences or 'no trespassing' signs, know that if you walk across the flow – guided or unguided – you do so at your own risk.

Finally, a short, public-access walk across the lava leads to **New Kaimu Beach** (aka **Coconut Beach**), where hundreds of baby coconut palms surround a black comma of sand. The water is too rough to swim, but it's a reflective spot.

Highway 130

Red Rd intersects Hwy 130 (Old Kalapana Rd), which leads north to Pahoa. At mile marker 20 the 1929 **Star of the Sea Church** (⏰9am-4pm) is noted for the naive-style paintings that cover the walls and the trompe l'oeil mural behind the altar, whose illusion of depth is remarkably effective. Inside, displays recount the history of the church and of the area's missionaries, including Father (now Saint) Damien, of Moloka'i fame. The church is wheelchair accessible.

HAWAI'I VOLCANOES NATIONAL PARK & AROUND

Hawai'i Volcanoes National Park

Of all of Hawaii's marvels, none equals the elemental grandeur and raw power of the two active volcanoes contained within **Hawai'i Volcanoes National Park** (HAVO; ☎985-6000; www.nps.gov/havo; 7-day entry pass per car $10, per person on foot, bicycle or motorcycle $5). The entire island chain is the result of the volcanic processes on display here, which is nothing less than the ongoing birth of Hawaii.

The elder sibling is Mauna Loa, whose recumbent bulk slopes as gently as Buddha's belly, as if the earth's largest volcano (which constitutes over half of the Big Island's land mass) were nothing more than an overgrown hill. But, at 13,677ft, its navel is a frigid alpine desert that's snow-covered in winter.

Hawai'i Volcanoes National Park

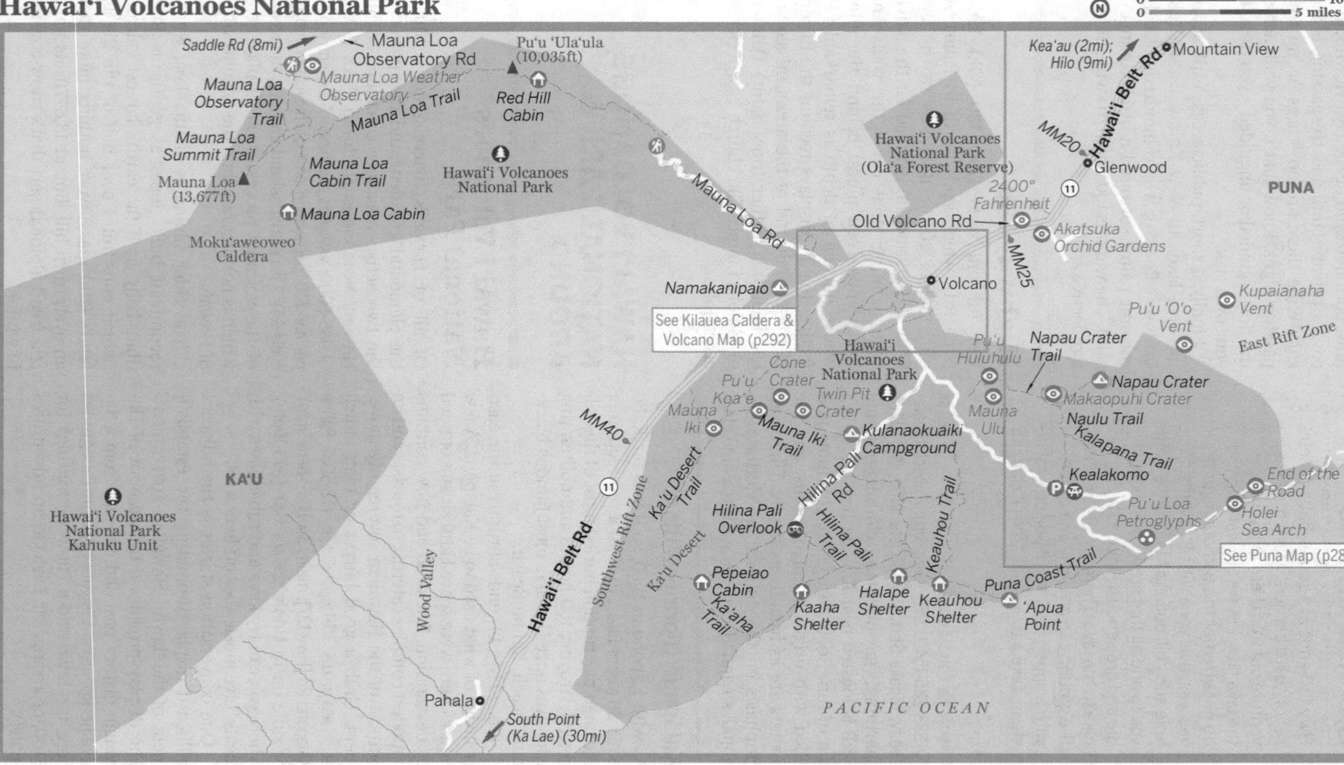

The younger sibling is Kilauea – the Earth's youngest and most active volcano. Since 1983 Kilauea's East Rift Zone has been erupting almost nonstop from the Pu'u 'O'o vent (southeast of the caldera), adding nearly 500 acres of new land to the island and providing residents and visitors with a front-row seat at one of the best shows on Earth. In 2008 new action erupted within Halema'uma'u Crater, located within the larger Kilauea Caldera (like a bubble within a cauldron). The **lava lake** here still glows molten red every night, drawing people from far and wide. In traditional Hawaiian spirituality, this is the home of the goddess Pele.

In geologic terms, Hawai'i's shield volcanoes lack the explosive gases of other volcanoes. Bomb-like explosions and geysers of lava aren't the norm: most of the time lava simply oozes and creeps along till it reaches the sea, which creates arcs of steamy fireworks. Naturally whenever Pele does send up dramatic curtains of fire people stream in from everywhere to watch.

Pele exacts a price for this entertainment. Since 1983, this side of the island has been remade. Lava blocked the coastal road to Puna in 1988, and covered the village of Kalapana in 1990. Flows then crept further west, engulfing Kamoamoa Beach in 1994, and later claiming an additional mile of road and most of Wahaula Heiau. In 2008, in addition to the Halema'uma'u eruption, a Thanksgiving Breakout vent sent lava back through Kalapana, and there is truly no telling how (or even if) lava will be flowing by the time you read this.

However, no matter what the lava is doing, there is still plenty to see. When the enormous Kuhuku Unit in Ka'u is factored in, HAVO is nearly the size of O'ahu, and contains a highly varied landscape – black-lava deserts, rainforests, grassy coastal plains, snowy summits and more. The park is Hawai'i the Big Island's best place for hiking and camping, with about 150 miles of trails, but you don't *have* to break a sweat: good roads circle the caldera and take in the main highlights of what is certainly the USA's most dynamic national park.

Sights

This vast and varied park can fill as many days as you give it, particularly if you enjoy hiking. If not, you can also drive it all in one long downhill journey, from Jaggar Museum to the suitably named End of the Road, with only one detour (Hilina Pali Rd). That's a full 50-mile day, including numerous stops. Less time? Stick to Crater Rim Dr, where many of the key sites are located. In any case, start at the Kilauea Visitor Center, just past the entrance.

Crater Rim Drive

Crater Rim Rd is an incredible 11-mile loop that starts at the Kilauea Visitor Center and skirts the rim of Kilauea Caldera. Unfortunately about a third of the road has been closed since 2008, and likely won't reopen until Pele stops venting her frustrations. But the remainder still links many of the park's main attractions, including a museum, a lava tube, steam vents, rifts, hiking trails and views of the smoking crater that'll knock your socks off. So practice your U-turns and don't miss it. It's also an excellent road for **cycling**.

Kilauea Visitor Center & Museum MUSEUM
(☎985-6017; Crater Rim Dr; ⏲7:45am-5pm) This should be your first stop. Rangers can advise you on volcanic activity, air quality, trail conditions and the best things to see based on your time. A small theater shows free short films on Kilauea and the current eruption, with spectacular footage, every hour from 9am to 4pm.

Introductory talks by rangers on subjects like park geology also occur at 9:30am and 3:30pm (combining a movie with one is a great way to begin). A board lists the day's guided hikes (normally around 15) and ranger programs (posted by 9am). Free trail pamphlets and junior-ranger program activity sheets are also available (backcountry permits are now issued by the new Visitor Emergency Operations Center, located nearby). The excellent bookstore has a plethora of volumes and videos on volcanoes, flora, hiking and Hawaiian culture and history. Wheelchairs (free) are available for exploring the park upon request; accessible areas include Waldron Ledge, Devastation Trail, Sulphur Banks Trail, Pauahi Crater and the

WHY NOT MAUNA KEA?

So why isn't Mauna Kea part of Hawaii Volcanoes National Park? Because it's not an *active* volcano. It last erupted some 4600 years ago.

Volcano Art Center. There's also an ATM, a pay phone and restrooms.

★ **Volcano Art Center** GALLERY

(☎866-967-7565; www.volcanoartcenter.org; ⊙9am-5pm) There are local art galleries, and then there is this place. Next door to the visitor center, it sells the highest quality island pottery, paintings, woodwork, sculpture, jewelry and more; a fabulous collection, ranging from $25 prints to $9000 koa rocking chairs.

It also hosts craft and cultural workshops, music concerts, plays and dance recitals; see the online events calendar.

Sulphur Banks TRAIL

Near the Volcano Art Center, wooden boardwalks weave through steaming Sulphur Banks, where numerous holes and rocky vents have been stained yellow, orange and neon green by the hundreds of tons of sulfuric gases released here daily. The smoldering, foul-smelling area looks like the aftermath of a forest fire.

A short, easy walk along the beautifully renovated and wheelchair-accessible boardwalk starts at the art center, takes in the Sulphur Banks and crosses the road to Steaming Bluff. For a longer walk, you can connect to a variety of trails, including Crater Rim Trail.

Steam Vents & Steaming Bluff VIEWPOINT

These nonsulfurous steam vents make a good drive-up photo op; they are the result of rainwater that percolates down and is heated into steam by hot rocks underground. Much more evocative is the short walk to the crater rim at Steaming Bluff, where the magnificent crater view feels infernolike as steam from the cliffs below pours over you.

Cool early mornings or cloudy afternoons showcase the steam best.

Kilauea Caldera & Volcano

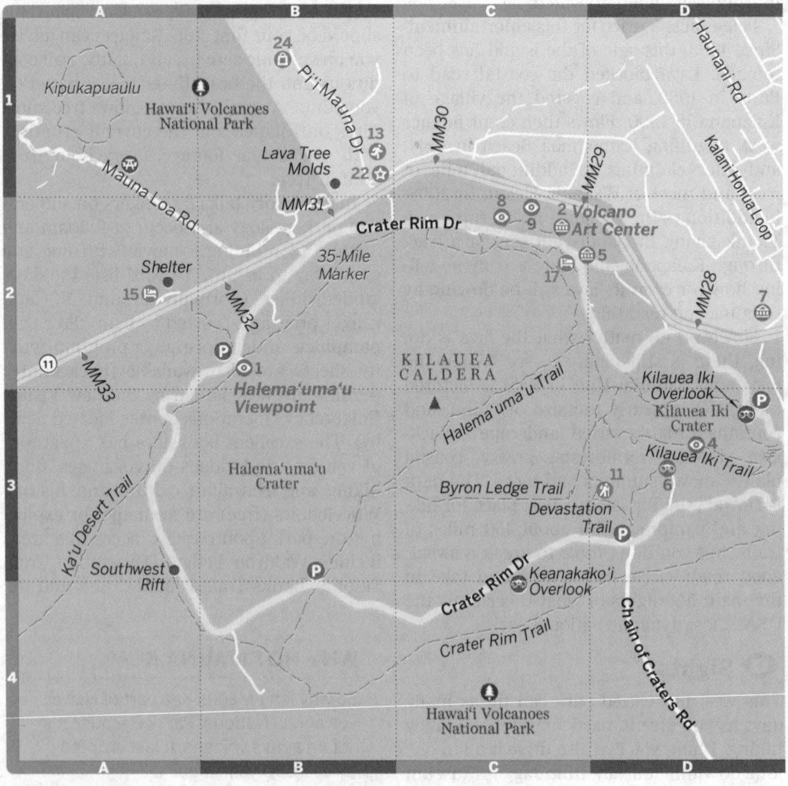

Jaggar Museum MUSEUM

(☎985-6051; ⊙8:30am-7:30pm) FREE The exhibits at this small museum are a nice complement to the visitor center; they introduce the museum's founder, famous volcanologist Dr Thomas A Jaggar, overview the Hawaiian pantheon, and provide a deeper understanding of volcanic geology. A bank of real-time seismographs monitor the park's daily quota of earthquakes, which number from the tens to the hundreds.

Just before you reach the museum, the Kilauea Overlook provides a fine panorama, including the Southwest Rift a few miles to the south. This rocky fissure is more massive and longer than it looks; it slices from the caldera summit all the way to the coast.

★ **Halema'uma'u Viewpoint** VIEWPOINT

(Crater Rim Dr, behind Jaggar Museum) The original Halema'uma'u Overlook was accessed from a parking area off Crater Rim Drive. That section of road has now been closed since 2008. Consequently, the patio behind the Jaggar Museum, which offers the next best vantage point, has become the new viewpoint. Don't worry, it is still extraordinary. Indeed, while there are lots of great sights in HAVO, this is the one that will stay with you the longest. There is really nothing quite like watching a huge smoking crater. It's mesmerizing.

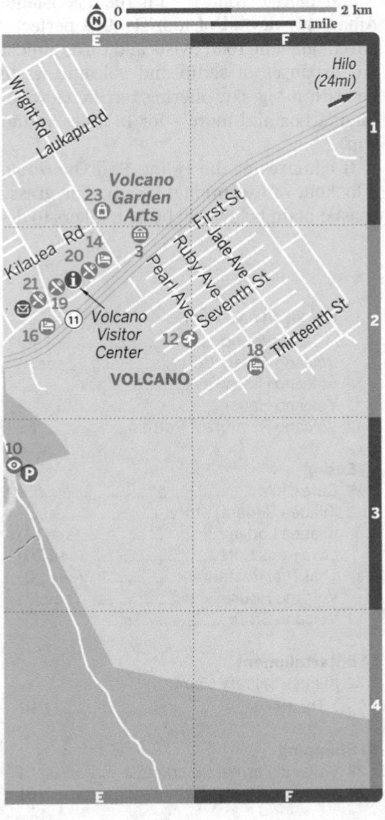

Halema'uma'u is really a crater within a crater, the Kilauea Caldera. About 3000ft across and nearly 300ft deep, it is spewing out about 3000 metric tons of ash per day, a rising column that emerges from the great hole and billows into the sky, partly creating the vog that increasingly carpets the island (Kilauea's Pu'u 'O'o vent adds the rest). You should come here twice, once during the day and once at night, to watch 'the glow,' as it is known locally. The latter has become a kind of pilgrimage, and you won't understand why until you make it: standing there, watching the light flickering from the bowels of the Earth, finally explains the idea of Pele. It is as if there is something alive in that hole. Honest.

On the scientific side, you'll be watching the longest continuous eruption in the crater since 1924. It began on March 18, 2008, when a huge steam-driven explosion shattered a quarter-century of silence, scattering rocks and Pele's hair (strands of volcanic glass) over 75 acres. A series of explosions followed, widening the vent, which has continued to spew a muscular column of smoke ever since. Today the lava bubbles are pretty tame, but it was not always thus, and could easily change again – for better or worse.

All of the Big Island is Pele's territory, but Halema'uma'u is her home. Ceremonial hula is performed in her honor on the crater rim, and you'll see flower lei and other offerings as you venture through the park, although this practice is widely frowned upon. Then again, perhaps that's why the vog persists...

For another great view of the crater, visit the bar at **Volcano House** (www.volcanohouse-hotel.com).

Kilauea Iki Crater VIEWPOINT

(Little Kilauea) When Kilauea Iki burst open in a fiery inferno in November 1959, the whole crater floor turned into a bubbling lake of molten lava. Its fountains reached record heights of 1900ft, lighting the evening sky with a bright orange glow for miles around.

At its peak it gushed out 2 million tons of lava per hour.

An overlook provides an awesome view of the mile-wide crater, and the hike across its hardened surface is the park's most popular. One good strategy for visiting this often crowded but scenic portion of Crater Rim Dr is to park at the **Kilauea Iki Overlook** and walk the Crater Rim Trail to Thurston Lava Tube and back; it's about a mile all told and easy as pie.

Thurston Lava Tube LAVA TUBE

You'll feel like lava yourself as you move through this immense underground tube big enough for a bus, the end point of an enjoyable short walk through lovely, bird-filled ohia forest. Often crowded to the extreme, it's best to come before 10am or after 2pm. The tube's unlit extension was closed at time of research.

Chain of Craters Road

Continuing on from lower Crater Rim Dr, you'll head down the great southern slope of Kilauea Volcano all the way to the sea. While it has shrunk several times (most recently in 2003), Chain of Craters Rd currently winds about 19 miles, ending abruptly at the latest East Rift Zone lava flow on the Puna Coast. Allow 90 minutes round trip without stops.

For visual drama, the road is every bit the equal of Crater Rim Dr. As you descend toward the sea, panoramic coastal vistas open before you, revealing slopes covered in frozen fingers of blackened lava. Then, at the coast, you get to stare at those same flows from below, looking up to where they crested the cliffs and plunged across the land to meet the sea.

The road takes its name from a series of small, drive-up craters that lie along the first few miles. In addition, the road provides access to several trails, a campground, petroglyphs and sometimes to the active flow itself.

Chain of Craters Rd connected to Hwys 130 and 137 in Puna until a 10-mile stretch was overrun by lava. The 'Road Closed' sign here, almost entirely buried in lava, is a classic Big Island photo op; before 9am or after 3pm is best for photography.

★ **Hilina Pali Road** SCENIC DRIVE

The first major intersection off Chain of Craters Rd takes you to one of the best drives – and bicycle routes – on the Big Island. Amazingly devoid of tourists, this perfectly paved one-lane road twists and turns amidst flat expanses of scrub and volcanic waste beneath a big sky, offering terrific views of Mauna Loa and more – for 18 miles 'round trip'.

It climaxes at the **Hilina Pali Overlook**, a lookout of exceptional beauty. The grassy coastal plain below will beckon hikers to de-

Kilauea Caldera & Volcano

Top Sights
- 1 Halema'uma'u Viewpoint ... B2
- 2 Volcano Art Center ... C2
- 3 Volcano Garden Arts ... E2

Sights
- Jaggar Museum ... (see 1)
- 4 Kilauea Iki Crater ... D3
- 5 Kilauea Visitor Center & Museum ... C2
- 6 Pu'u Pua'i Overlook ... D3
- 7 Rainforest Gallery ... D2
- 8 Steam Vents & Steaming Bluff ... C2
- 9 Sulphur Banks ... C2
- 10 Thurston Lava Tube ... E3

Activities, Courses & Tours
- 11 Devastation Trail ... D3
- 12 Hale Ho'ola Hawaiian Healing Arts Center & Spa ... E2
- 13 Volcano Golf & Country Club ... B1

Sleeping
- 14 Kilauea Lodge ... E2
- 15 Namakanipaio Cabins & Campground ... A2
- Volcano Artists Cottage ... (see 3)
- 16 Volcano Hideaways ... E2
- 17 Volcano House ... C2
- 18 Volcano Rainforest Retreat ... F2

Eating
- 19 Café Ohi'a ... E2
- 20 Kilauea General Store ... E2
- Kilauea Lodge ... (see 14)
- Lava Rock Café ... (see 20)
- Thai Thai Restaurant ... (see 20)
- Volcano House ... (see 17)
- 21 Volcano Store ... E2

Entertainment
- 22 Kilauea Military Camp Theater ... B1

Shopping
- 23 Volcano Farmers Market ... E1
- 24 Volcano Winery ... B1

GO TO THE FLOW

Lucky travelers can view **live lava** making the 64-mile journey from the Pu'u 'O'o vent to the ocean. Where the lava will be flowing when you arrive and the effort required to reach it are impossible to predict, but at the time of writing, the lava was visible from the base of the Pulama Pali to the shoreline (over a mile). The eastern edge was about three miles from Kalapana Gardens in Puna. Sometimes it's possible to hike to flowing lava from the park side, at the end of Chain of Craters Rd. Usually this involves covering one to several miles of wracked lava landscape. Inquire at the Visitors Center.

While it is outside park boundaries, a **lava flow viewing area** (⌚4-10pm, last car in 8pm) is maintained by the county at the end of Hwy 130. Visitors park and walk less than a mile on a narrow paved strip and are corralled into a small area to behold the sights. If the show is really on, there will be surface flows, lava 'skylights' and a giant smoke plume where the lava enters the ocean. Otherwise, you'll be a mile or more from the sea entry and see little more than a red glow and lots of smoke. For current information call the Civil Defense **hotline** (☎961-8093) or visit **Hawaiian Lava Daily** (http://hawaiianlavadaily.blogspot.com).

For best viewing, visit at sunset when the coast is bathed in a crepuscular glow and the lava brightens in the growing darkness. You can get closer by joining a lava walk: visitors give high marks to **Kalapana Cultural Tours** (☎936-0456; http://www.kalapanaculturaltours.com; 12-5038 Kalapana-Kapoho Rd; $100). The best option is to walk out at the end of the day, view the flow by night, and hike back by flashlight. But it takes some doing: about three hours of walking, round trip. Another option is jumping on a lava boat tour, of which Lava Ocean Adventures (p284) gets high marks. If it's rough seas, and you lack an iron stomach, avoid inflatables. However you do it, come prepared with rain gear, wear sturdy shoes, pants and a hat, and bring water and one flashlight per person.

Note that lava entering the sea can be dangerous. The explosive clash between water and molten 2100°F rock can spray scalding water hundreds of feet into the air, fill the air with silicate particles, and throw flaming lava chunks well inland. New ledges or benches of lava that form over time can also collapse without warning. Several observers have been killed over the past decade. Always stay at least 500yd inland.

scend the steep **Hilina Pali Trail** here, but the water isn't as close as it looks and only those prepared for a backcountry trek can reach it.

Mauna Ulu — LANDMARK

In 1969 eruptions from Kilauea's east rift began building a new **lava shield**, which eventually rose 400ft above its surroundings; it was named Mauna Ulu (Growing Mountain). By the time the flow stopped in 1974, it had covered 10,000 acres of parkland and added 200 acres of new land to the coast.

It also buried a 12-mile section of Chain of Craters Rd in lava up to 300ft deep. A half-mile portion of the old road survives, and you can follow it to the lava flow by taking the turnoff on the left, 3.5 miles down Chain of Craters Rd. Just beyond this is Mauna Ulu itself.

The easy Pu'u Huluhulu Overlook Trail, an easy 2.5-mile round-trip hike, begins at the parking area (which is also the trailhead for Napau Crater Trail). The overlook trail ends at the top of a 150ft cinder cone, **Pu'u Huluhulu**, which is like a crow's nest on a clear day: the vista nets Mauna Loa, Mauna Kea, Pu'u 'O'o vent, Kilauea, the East Rift Zone and the ocean beyond. Just before you is the steamy teacup of Mauna Ulu crater. To venture beyond the overlook and on to **Napau Crater** requires a free backcountry permit from the Visitor Emergency Operations Center.

Kealakomo — VIEWPOINT

About halfway along the road is this coastal lookout with picnic tables and commanding views. The alternative trailhead for the Naulu Trail is across the road. After Kealakomo the road descends in long, sweeping switchbacks, some deeply cut through lava flows.

Pu'u Loa Petroglyphs — HISTORICAL SITE

The gentle Pu'u Loa Trail leads, after less than a mile, to the largest concentration of ancient petroglyphs in the state. Here early

Hawaiians chiseled more than 23,000 drawings into *pahoehoe* lava with adze tools quarried from Keanakāko'i.

There are abstract designs and animal and human figures, as well as thousands of dimpled depressions (or cupules) that were receptacles for umbilical cords. The practice was meant to bestow health and longevity on a child. The parking area and trailhead are signed between mile markers 16 and 17. At the site, stay on the boardwalk at all times – not all of the petroglyphs are obvious, and you are likely to trample (and damage) some if you walk over the rocks.

Holei Sea Arch LANDMARK

Near the end of the road, across from the ranger station, is this sea arch. This rugged section of the coast has sharply eroded lava cliffs, called Holei Pali, which are constantly being pounded by the crashing surf. The high rock arch, carved out of one of the cliffs, is impressive.

End of the Road LANDMARK

Quite. Chain of Craters Rd ends where the lava says it ends, having swamped this coastal section repeatedly over the past three decades. In years past, this was the starting point for hikes to the active flow. There's a simple information board and portable toilets here, plus a ranger outpost and snack shack that are usually only staffed when the lava is flowing nearby.

When there's no molten lava, this becomes one of the quietest, most dramatic day hikes in the park. There's no trail per se, just wander into the Mordor-like terrain until the surging, frozen, oily veins surround you, looking as if they cooled only yesterday.

Mauna Loa Rd

If you really want to escape the crowds, explore the 11.5-mile Mauna Loa Rd, which begins off Hwy 11 west of the park entrance. The first turnoff leads to some neglected **lava tree molds**, deep tube-like apertures formed when a lava flow engulfed the rainforest. Then, after a mile, there is a picnic area (with toilets) and just beyond this is Kipukapuaulu (p297), known as Bird Park. This unique 100-acre sanctuary protects an island of ancient forest containing rare endemic plants, insects and birds. About 400 years ago a major Mauna Loa lava flow buried the land here, but Pele split the flow and saved this small island of vegetation; in Hawaiian these are known as *kipuka*.

An easy 1-mile loop **trail** through the forest makes a very meditative walk, particularly in the morning, surrounded by birdsong. You'll see lots of koa trees and pass a lava tube where a unique species of big-eyed spider was discovered in 1973.

About 1.5 miles past Bird Park, Mauna Loa Rd passes another *kipuka* (Kipuka Ki), and 2 miles later the road narrows to one lane. Go slow; it's winding, with potholes and lots of blind curves. Along the way are several places to pull over and admire the views, and trails to explore – it's a wonderful diversion. By the end of the road, you've ascended to 6662ft; this is the start of the extremely difficult Mauna Loa Trail (p299) to the summit. Wander down the trail a few dozen yards for expansive southern vistas that include the smoking Kilauea Crater far below.

Activities

Hiking is the park's main activity, and there are trails to suit all abilities. Once you've taken it all in, you might also want to consider the park's vast Kahuku Unit (p309) in Ka'u, which offers excellent hiking of its own, including guided hikes and junior ranger programs.

Cyclists can enjoy circumnavigating Kilauea Caldera along Crater Rim Dr, and mountain bikes are allowed on a few firebreak roads, such as Escape Rd past Thurston Lava Tube. For helicopter tours, see p271.

Hiking

If variety is the spice of life, park trails are a feast. You can hike to secluded beaches or the snowcapped 13,677ft summit of Mauna Loa, through lush native rainforests or barren lava wastelands, across the hardened top of the world's most active volcano or, sometimes, to the glowing flow itself. There are excellent trails of every length and level of difficulty. Plus, many trails intersect, allowing the flexibility to design your own routes (many one-way hikers choose to leave their vehicle at the trail's end, then hitch to the trailhead). Most of the park is accessible to day hikers, while most backcountry destinations require only a single overnight. However, if you wish, you can wander backcountry trails for days. Whatever you choose, prepare for variable weather.

If you're interested in overnight backpacking, note that **backcountry camping** is limited and entirely first come, first served; backcountry trails contain hiking shelters, simple cabins or primitive campgrounds. All have pit toilets. Bring a stove, as open fires are prohibited. Almost no freshwater is available anywhere; some campgrounds have catchment water (always treat before drinking), and the visitor center posts a daily log of water levels. Overnight hikers must get a free permit (and register) at the Visitor Emergency Operations Center (p298) no sooner than the day before their hike; each site has a three-day limit.

Following are some of the most popular and/or recommended day hikes, along with a few backcountry possibilities and variations. Some of the park's shortest hikes are mentioned in the descriptions of the park's main roads.

Kipukapuaulu HIKING

(Bird Park) Kipukapuaulu is a *kipuka*, an island of ancient forest amidst a 400-year-old sea of lava. It is also a 100-acre sanctuary for rare endemic plants, insects and birds. An easy 1-mile loop trail makes for a meditative walk, particularly in the morning, when you are surrounded by birdsong.

Common native forest birds like apapane are high in the canopy; 'elepaio can be spotted closer to eye level chasing insects. Many introduced Kalij pheasants in the grass below will almost walk up to you. You'll also see lots of koa and ohia trees and pass a lava tube where a unique species of big-eyed spider was discovered in 1973. Be aware that at this elevation the weather can change quickly, so your sunny warm hike can quickly become densely foggy and wet. To get there, turn off Crater Rim Dr onto Mauna Loa Rd and it's signed to your right.

★Kilauea Iki Trail HIKING

If you have time for only one hike, choose this one. It's the park's most popular trail for good reason – it captures all the summit's drama and beauty in one manageable, moderate 4-mile package, which can be done in an hour if you walk steadily. The trail's glossy brochure ($2) is a good investment.

The loop trail has multiple start points and trail junctions (making the hike easy to expand). Park at Kilauea Iki Overlook (p294) (avoiding the Thurston Lava Tube madness) and proceed counterclockwise along the crater rim. Passing through an ohia forest, you can admire the mile-long lava bathtub below before descending into it.

After almost a mile you descend onto Waldron Ledge; multiple trail junctions allow for quick explorations of the main caldera rim (highly recommended), or extend your loop by connecting with the Halema'uma'u and Byron Ledge Trails for an all-day adventure. Either way, once you reach the west end of the crater, descend 400ft to the crater floor.

Across the *pahoehoe* crust the trail is easy to follow, and *ahu* (rock cairns) aid navigation. It's possible to enter the vent beneath the Pu'u Pua'i cinder cone, where ohia trees now bloom. As you continue over the surface, consider that molten magma is a mere 230ft below (less than a football field). Once you reach the crater's east end, ascend 400ft up switchbacks to the rim, and explore Thurston Lava Tube on your return to the Kilauea Iki Overlook.

Devastation Trail HIKING

One end of this trail is accessible from the lower terminus of Chain of Craters Rd, the other from the **Pu'u Pua'i Overlook** further east. The trail is paved and passes through the fallout area of the 1959 eruption of Kilauea Iki Crater, which decimated this portion of the rainforest. This is a great trail to do on a guided ranger walk since, at first glance, it's not half as dramatic as its name.

The overlook provides a fantastic vantage into the crater, and it's a quick walk to see Pu'u Pua'i, which formed during the eruption.

Halema'uma'u Trail HIKING

This trail has been closed since 2008, except for short portions along the rim, noted for their ohia forest. Too bad, as it is an extremely rewarding 7-mile loop. Unfortunately Pele is going to have to calm down quite a bit before the trail reopens.

Crater Rim Trail HIKING

(Keanakāko'i Trail) This 11.5-mile trek circles the summit, running roughly parallel to Crater Rim Drive, but large portions of the trail have been closed since 2008. An exception is a 0.7mi section from Chain of Craters Rd just north of Lua Manu Crater, which culminates at the south side of Keanakako'i Crater (hence its informal name, Keanakako'i Trail).

It's short, but winds through native forest along the flows of 1974, where you'll find lava molds, and offers an abundance of views, including the great plume of Halema'uma'u rising in the distance.

Mauna Iki Trail HIKING

For solitude in a mesmerizing lava landscape, take this trail into the **Ka'u Desert**, but start from the north, along what is sometimes labeled the Footprints Trail. From this approach the trailhead access is easier, your initial commitment is low and variations allow great extensions of your route.

This hike can be an easy 3.5-mile sampling, a moderate 7- to 8-mile afternoon or an 18-mile overnight backpack. However, the trail from the Jaggar Museum to the trailhead at Hwy 11 was closed at the time of research due to Halema'uma'u's current eruption.

On Hwy 11 between mile markers 37 and 38, look for the Ka'u Desert Trailhead parking area. Start early, as midday can be brutally hot and dry. Initially the trail is very clear, level and partly paved, threading through sand-covered *pahoehoe* flows. In 20 minutes you reach a structure protecting ancient footprints preserved in hardened ash; more footprints exist in the surrounding rock. As the story goes, in 1790 the army of Hawaiian chief Keoua was retreating from a battle against Kamehameha when a rare explosive eruption buried a group of his soldiers, changing the course of island history.

Past here, the trail is marked by easy-to-follow cairns. As you gradually ascend, views expand, with gentle giant Mauna Loa behind and the immense Ka'u Desert in front. After 1.8 miles you crest the rise at Mauna Iki (and the trail junction) and stand likely alone in the middle of a vast lava field.

From here, backpackers will turn right, following the Ka'u Desert Trail over 7 miles to Pepeiao Cabin. Day hikers can turn left, following the Ka'u Desert Trail for 0.7 miles to the junction with the official Mauna Iki Trail, which runs another 6.3 miles to Hilina Pali Rd (the other starting point). Hiking about halfway along the Mauna Iki Trail, to Pu'u Koa'e, makes a good end point.

The lava terrain is noticeably more intense and wild as you continue, with vivid colorful rents, collapsed tubes and splatter cones; in cracks you can find piles of Pele's golden hair.

Napau Crater Trail HIKING

This trail is one of the park's most varied and satisfying all-day hikes. It passes lava fields, immense craters and thick forest, and ends with distant views of Pu'u 'O'o, the source of Kilauea's ongoing eruption. For a more leisurely experience, consider backcountry camping here.

The distance to the campground (the current end of the trail) is 7 miles (or 5 miles from the Kealakoma starting point), making it a 10- to 14-mile adventure (about six to eight hours round-trip). Note that this is the only day hike that requires a permit; all hikers should register at the **Visitor Emergency Operations Center** ((VEOC); ⌚8am-4pm) before heading out. Rather than taking the Napau Crater Trail from its trailhead (the same one as for Pu'u Huluhulu Overlook Trail), you'll save about 4 miles and several hours if you begin on the Naulu Trail, which leaves from Kealakomo on Chain of Craters Rd. What you miss on this abbreviated version of the trail are the grandest Makaopuhi Crater and Mauna Loa views, plus the huffing vents and cracks peppering the active rift. The Kealakomo route is described here.

For the first hour, you hike mostly sinuous, leathery *pahoehoe* lava, following sometimes-difficult-to-see cairns. Then you enter some trees and (surprise!) stumble across paved portions of the old Chain of Craters Rd, which was buried in a 1972 eruption. Follow the pavement (complete with dashed white line) past the junction with the unmaintained Kalapana Trail.

After a quick sprint across some *'a'a*, you enter moody fern-and-ohia forest; in less than a mile is the Napau Crater Trail junction – turn right.

Keep an eye on your left for openings to view the mile-wide **Makaopuhi Crater**. About 30 minutes later, low lava rock walls indicate the site of an old 'pulu factory.' The golden, silky 'hair' found at the base of fiddlehead stems, *pulu* was exported as mattress and pillow stuffing in the late 1800s. This stretch is often festooned with cheery orchids.

You may think you're near the airport – considering the helicopter traffic – but in fact you're 10 minutes from the primitive **campground** (with pit toilet), closed during research due to fumes. Definitely take the spur to the Napau Crater overlook (to see steaming Pu'u 'O'o) – a picnic spot with a view. At the time of research, the rest of this trail was closed due to a Pu'u 'O'o vent collapse and shifts in the eruption. When open, the trail continues through Napau Crater and on to gaping **Pu'u 'O'o**, a dangerous and volatile area.

Mauna Loa Trail HIKING

For serious hikers, this is your trail to the 13,677ft summit (weekend hikers should opt for the 6.5-mile **Observatory Trail**). Beginning at the end of Mauna Loa Rd, it traverses 19 miles and ascends about 7000ft. While it is not technically challenging, due to the high elevation and frequent subarctic conditions it takes at least three, and usually four, days.

Two simple cabins with foam pad-covered bunks, pit toilets and catchment water (which must be treated before drinking) are located on the route; the first cabin sleeps eight and the second 12, and they are available on a first-come, first-served basis. Get a free backcountry permit, advice and water-level updates at the Visitor Emergency Operations Center (p298) the day before your hike.

Typically, the first day is spent hiking 7.5 miles to **Pu'u 'Ula'ula** at 10,035ft, where Red Hill Cabin is located. The next day is spent hiking 9.5 miles to **Moku'aweoweo Caldera**, and another 2 miles to Mauna Loa Cabin at 13,250ft; from here you can admire the summit directly across the caldera. On the third day you hike nearly 5 miles around the caldera to reach the summit and return for a second night at Mauna Loa Cabin. On the fourth day you descend.

Altitude sickness is common, even expected; going slowly aids acclimatization. Nighttime temperatures are below freezing, and storms may bring snow, blizzards, whiteouts, rain and fog, all of which can obscure the *ahu* that mark the trail, making it difficult to follow.

Puna Coast Trails HIKING

Three main trails take hikers down to the Puna Coast: the Hilina Pali, Keauhou and Puna Coast Trails. These trails start from vastly different places, but they each eventually intersect (with each other and even more trails), and they lead to four separate **backcountry campgrounds** or shelters. Because of steep elevation changes and distance, these trails are most commonly done as overnight backpacks.

This is also because once you see the grassy, wind-swept coast you won't want to leave. Talk to rangers about routes and water-catchment levels at the shelters – low water levels can close some trails to campers (such was the case of the Halape campground at time of research). With lovely swimming and snorkeling, the Halape site is the most popular, with Keauhou a great second choice.

For day hikers, the **Hilina Pali Trail** looks easiest on the map (it's only 3.5 miles to snorkeling at Ka'aha), but it's actually the hardest, with a brutal initial cliff descent; the trailhead is at the end of Hilina Pali Rd. Far gentler on the knees is the 6.8-mile **Keauhou Trail**, which takes about four hours to the stunning coast; the trailhead is past mile marder 6 on Chain of Craters Rd.

Tours

Not everyone grooves to guided hikes, but the geology, flora, fauna, lore and lure of this unique park pops vividly when described by the experts. In addition to daily ranger-led walks listed at the visitor center, these outfits are recommended.

Friends of Hawai'i Volcanoes National Park HIKING

(☎985-7373; www.fhvnp.org) Leads weekend hikes and organizes volunteer activities like trail clearing and tree planting. Ask about their occasional field seminars.

Hawaii Forest & Trail HIKING, TOUR

(☎800-464-1993, 331-8505; www.hawaii-forest.com; adult/child $179/159) Choose from day hikes and a twilight lava tour.

Hawaiian Walkways HIKING, TOUR

(☎800-457-7759, 775-0372; www.hawaiianwalkways.com; adult/child $169/119) Morning and afternoon departures with a Certified Volcano Guide.

Volcano Bike Tours CYCLING

(☎934-9199; www.bikevolcano.com; 5hr tour $129) This is a rare opportunity to take advantage of one of the better (mostly) downhill slopes you'll ever ride on. Volcano Bike Tours will take you on a 5-hour (10am to 3pm) bike tour, including the bike, a guide, lunch and van transportation, for $129. A very good deal.

The tour is aimed at a general audience, hence it's very gentle with lots of stops at park highlights. Other options available.

Festivals & Events

Cultural Festival NATIVE HAWAIIAN

Now in its third decade, this annual Hawaiian cultural festival features native arts, crafts, music and hula performances. Held end of June/early July.

Sleeping

Accommodation options within the national park are limited. Most visitors stay in the nearby village of Volcano, about a mile from the entrance.

★**Volcano House** LODGE $$
(☎866-536-7972, 756-9625; www.hawaiivolcanohouse.com; 1 Crater Rim Dr; r from $200) This is the rare property that earns a Top Choice listing even before it fully reopens. The reason is its unforgettable location, location, location, although a venerable history (c1846), new management and scale of renovation also weigh in. Reserve far in advance.

Perched on the rim of Kilauea Caldera, Volcano House has long enjoyed a unique status as the only hotel in the park, and perhaps that is why attention to detail previously suffered. Now the hotel is slated to reopen sometime in 2013 after a three-year hiatus. Upgrades include the restaurant, lobby areas, and 34 guest rooms. At time of research it was already offering snacks and some shopping from 7:45am to 6:30pm. But to the bar: the new bar will have an enormous window with an absolutely staggering view of Kilauea Caldera (as will certain guest rooms). Watching that enormous steaming hole silently hissing in the distance, you'd swear that you just missed an asteroid strike. So if you can't spring for the room, just sip a beer. Slowly.

Namakanipaio Cabins & Campground CABINS, CAMPGROUND $
(☎866-536-7972, 756-9625; www.hawaiivolcanohouse.com; cabin $55, campsites $10-15) Three miles west of the visitor center, between mile markers 32 and 33 off Hwy 11, this campground offers 10 simple A-frame cabins that sleep four, with a full bed and bunk beds, picnic table and BBQ pit. The one small window makes them a bit claustrophic, and there is no heat or outlets. Towels and linens supplied.

There are also two pleasant grassy meadows that fill with as many tents as they will hold on a first-come, first-served basis. Privacy is lacking, but nice facilities include rest rooms, water, fireplaces, picnic tables and a covered pavilion, although there are no showers. Cabins check in at Volcano House, campers pay the 'iron ranger' on site.

Kulanaokuaiki Campground CAMPGROUND
(www.nps.gov/havo; Hilina Pali Rd) FREE About 4 miles along Hilina Pali Rd, this secluded, quiet eight-site campground has pit toilets and picnic tables, but no water. No registration required.

Eating & Drinking

The restaurant at Volcano House (p293) had just opened for snacks at time of research, but the bar had not. You will also find some sandwiches at the nearby visitor center shop. For more than that you should head to Volcano village.

Entertainment

Regular park programs include **After Dark in the Park** (Kilauea Visitor Center Auditorium; suggested donation $2; ⏲7pm Tue), a series of free talks by experts on cultural, historic and geological matters.

The Volcano Art Center (p292) hosts a full slate of events year-round, including **craft demonstrations** and **hula performances** by the center itself, and various concert, dance and theater performances at the **Kilauea Military Camp Theater** (☎967-8333; tickets adult $25-40, student $10) (accessed via Crater Rim Dr). For information see the events calendar at www.volcanoartcenter.org.

Information

The park never closes. The toll station at the park entrance also sells two annual passes: a three-park Hawaii pass ($25, including HAVO, Pu'uhonua o Honaunau, and Haleakalā on Maui) and one for all national parks ($80). Peak visitation is 10am to 2pm, so it is best to visit popular spots (like Thurston Lava Tube) outside these hours.

The park's **hotline** (☎985-6000; ⏲24hr) provides daily recorded updates on park weather, road closures and lava-viewing conditions. The **USGS** (http://hvo.wr.usgs.gov) also has eruption updates on its website. Note that the nearest gas station is in Volcano village – 25 miles from the end of Chain of Craters Rd.

At 4000ft above sea level, the Kilauea Caldera area is generally 10°F to 15°F cooler than Hilo or Kona, but weather is unpredictable and microclimates can vary dramatically within the park. Plan and prepare for hot sun, dry wind, fog, chilly rain and soaking downpours, all in a day. At a minimum bring long pants, a jacket or sweater and a rain slicker.

DANGERS & ANNOYANCES

Active volcanoes create a few unusual hazards. Though extremely rare and highly unlikely, deaths have occurred on park visits. Molten lava isn't the most threatening personal danger.

Instead, deaths and injuries tend to occur when people venture too close to the active flow – and wind up on unstable 'benches' of new land that collapse, or get caught in steam explosions when lava enters the ocean.

If you plan to walk or hike about, come prepared: bring hiking shoes or sneakers, long pants, a hat, sunscreen, water (and snacks), and a flashlight with extra batteries. For more information see the Visitor Center's excellent safety film.

Lava

As for less mortal dangers, remember that hardened lava is uneven and brittle; rocks can be glass-sharp. Thin crusts can give way over unseen hollows and lava tubes; the edges of craters and rifts crumble easily. Deep earth cracks may be hidden by plants. When hiking, abrasions, deep cuts and broken limbs are all possible. So, it's even more important than most places to stay on marked trails and take park warning signs seriously. Blazing paths into unknown terrain can damage fragile areas, lead to injuries and leave tracks that encourage others to follow.

Vog & Sulfuric Fumes

Another major, constant concern is air quality. Halema'uma'u Crater and Pu'u 'O'o vent belch thousands of tons of sulfur dioxide daily. Where lava meets the sea it also creates a 'steam plume,' where sulfuric and hydrochloric acid mixes with airborne silica (or glass particles). All this combines to create 'vog,' which depending on the winds can settle over the park. Given all this, people with respiratory and heart conditions, pregnant women, infants and young children should take care when visiting.

Dehydration

Vast areas of the park qualify as desert, and dehydration is common. Carrying two quarts of water per person is the standard advice, but bring more and keep a gallon in the trunk: you'll drink it.

EMERGENCIES

- **Park Dispatch** ☎985-6170
- **Emergency services** ☎911

MAPS

The free color map given at the park's entrance is fine for driving around, seeing the main sights and hiking a few short and/or popular trails. The visitor center has some backcountry trail maps if you're headed into the wild blue yonder.

If you'll be backpacking or hiking extensively, consider purchasing National Geographic's Trails Illustrated map, *Hawai'i Volcanoes National Park*. It's a comprehensive, waterproof and rip-resistant large-format topographic hiking map that identifies most terrain features, including campgrounds. For specific hikes, the USGS 1:24,000 maps *Kilauea, Volcano* and *Ka'u Desert* are also helpful.

> **PLAN YOUR VISIT**
>
> Technology and new media helps visitors keep abreast of Pele's antics and how they may affect plans. Here are some top resources:
>
> - **Trail & road closures** (www.nps.gov/havo/closed_areas.htm)
> - **Air quality** (www.hawaiiso2network.com)
> - **Kilauea status** (http://volcano.wr.usgs.gov/kilaueastatus.php)
> - **Hawaiian Volcano Observatory Webcams** (http://volcanoes.usgs.gov/hvo/cams)
> - **Hawai'i Volcanoes National Park iApp** (search for it at iTunes: itunes.apple.com)

Getting There & Around

The national park is 29 miles (about 40 minutes) from Hilo and 97 miles (2½ hours) from Kailua-Kona. From either direction you'll drive on Hwy 11. Volcano village is a mile east of the park entrance.

The Hele-On Bus (p280) connects the park with Hilo (one hour, five daily Monday to Saturday).

Volcano

POP 2600

Like so many aspects of the Big Island, the small village of Volcano is a unique little gem. Most of the town is actually hidden in a remarkable forest of giant ferns, *sugi* (Japanese evergreen), and ohia trees, the main drag being an exception. It is also a magnet for artists and writers, who find inspiration in its quiet and remote setting on the edge of Hawai'i Volcanoes National Park. Their annual coming-out party is the Volcano Village Artists' Hui, an open-studios extravaganza held the three days after Thanksgiving. There's no better time to visit.

Sights & Activities

Rainforest Gallery GALLERY

(☎967-8222; www.volcanoartcenter.org; 19-4074 Old Volcano Rd; ⏲9am-4pm Mon-Sat) A satellite of the Volcano Art Center in Hawai'i Volcanoes National Park, this new gallery showcases local artists (unencumbered by the park's thematic requirements), while the adjacent shop offers some truly remarkable works for sale.

Hale Hoʻola Hawaiian Healing Arts Center & Spa SPA
(☎756-2421; www.halehoola.net; 11-3913 7th St; massage 60/90min $75/100, treatments $45-120) This is a professional Hawaiian massage center with a full menu of body and skin treatments: the perfect complement to a long day's hike. Located in the wing of a private home in the fern forest, it combines indigenous ingredients, traditional methods, and holistic spirituality for therepeutic ends. A perfect place to experience authentic *lomilomi*. Appointments required.

Volcano Golf & Country Club GOLF
(☎967-7331; www.volcanogolfshop.com; Piʻi Mauna Dr; greens fee before/after noon $73/59) A local favorite, the 18-hole course here has majestic links with views of Mauna Kea and Mauna Loa. Restaurant gets mixed reviews.

Tours & Courses

Niaulani Rain Forest Tour WALKING TOUR
(☎967-8222; www.volcanoartcenter.org; 19-4074 Old Volcano Rd; ⏲9-10:30am Mon, 11am-noon Sat)  FREE A free half-mile guided nature walk through the Niaulani rainforest in Volcano. Covers the ecological importance and protection of one of the last old-growth koa and ohia forests, traditional uses of plants, and the role of birds in the forest. Great for families. Run by the Niaulani campus of the Volcano Art Center.

Hawaii Photo Retreat PHOTOGRAPHY
(☎985-7487; www.hawaiiphotoretreat.com; Haunani St; 1-/2-/3-day tour $345/690/1035) One minute looking at Ken and Mary Goodrich's work reveals two world-class photographers. So the opportunity to see the Big Island through their eyes – and lens – is a rare treat. These one- to three-day retreats take participants into the field to photograph some of the island's finest subjects.

Personal instruction in camera skills, composition, Photoshop and Lightroom provided. Involves moderate hiking. Meals and transportation not included.

Festivals & Events

★**Volcano Village Artists Hui** ARTS
(☎987-3472; www.volcanovillageartistshui.com) FREE The best time to visit Volcano is during this annual *hui*, or gathering, a seven-studio tour on Thanksgiving weekend that attracts people from around the island and beyond. It's a delightful and eclectic smorgasbord of fiber work, wood scupture, ceramics, woodblock prints, glass blowing, photography and more.

Rain Forest Runs HALF-MARATHON
Held in early August, this popular half-marathon, 10km run and 5km run/walk passes through Volcano village and nearby subdivisions. Kids can compete, too.

Sleeping

Volcano has more accommodations than a fern has branches and many are excellent.

DON'T MISS

VOLCANO GARDEN ARTS

★**Volcano Garden Arts** (www.volcanogardenarts.com; 19-3834 Old Volcano Rd; ⏲10am-4pm Tue-Sun), set on a restored farm of 2.7 acres in the fern forest, is central to Volcano's creative scene, and a magnet for locals and visitors alike, at once gallery, cafe, garden, studio, B&B and informal community center.

The central gallery represents 80 local artists working in various media at a wide range of prices; the vegetarian Cafe Ono offers homemade and affordable organic cuisine, some of it grown on the property, in a lovely setting; the studio indulges in painting, collage and ceramics; and the *sugi* grove hosts weddings.

Seeking to spark your muse? The simple **Artists Cottage** (☎967-7261; www.volcanoartistcottage.com; 19-3834 Old Volcano Rd; cottage incl breakfast $129; Wi-Fi) has a full kitchen, dining area, queen bed and an inspirational step-down, sea-green tile bathroom as big as the living area; outdoors is a hot tub.

Both savvy entrepeneur and charming host, owner/artist Ira Ono (www.iraono.com) is everywhere, yet always available for a chat. His mascot, Ernest, may be the only goat with his own Facebook page. Your first stop in town.

Almost all properties have a two-night minimum stay or a one-night surcharge. For more listings see Vacation Rentals by Owner (www.vrbo.com).

★Volcano Inn INN $
(☎800-628-3876, 967-7773; www.volcanoinnhawaii.com; 19-3820 Old Volcano Rd; r $89-139; 📶) This inn consists of two properties. Apart from some minor aesthetic blunders (glaring signage, photos tacked to walls), it offers outstanding value. The main building contains immaculate rooms with bright varnished wooden floors and ceilings, and a cooked breakfast, in a positive community atmosphere. The restaurant has also started cooking dinner for guests (mains $8 to $10).

This definitely helps, given limited options elsewhere. A separate site has nine cottages that are also great value, particularly for families. The corner window rooms here have great views of the fern forest. This is a solid mid-range hotel at budget prices. Prices fall significantly for longer stays.

Holo Holo In HOSTEL $
(☎808-967-7950; www.volcanohostel.com; 19-4036 Kalani Honua Rd; dm $24, r $60-75; @📶) While the exterior could use a cleanup, the two six-bed dorms and four private rooms are sizable and feel like a lodge. Well-equipped kitchen and laundry.

★Volcano Rainforest Retreat COTTAGE $$
(☎800-550-8696, 985-8696; www.volcanoretreat.com; 11-3832 12th St, at Ruby Ave; cottage d incl breakfast $155-275; @📶) Serenity abounds within these four luxurious, individually designed cedar cottages embedded in the fern forest. Artfully positioned among giant *hapu'u* (ferns), all have huge windows and either outdoor hot tubs or Japanese-style soaking tubs to maximize your experience of nature.

In-cottage massage, candlelit dinners and champagne service make this property off-the-charts romantic. The Bamboo Guest House, which sleeps six, is great for families too (and to die for). Reserve well ahead.

★Enchanted Rainforest Cottages COTTAGE $$
(☎443-4930; http://erc-volcano.com; 19-4176 Kekoa Nui (B St); cottage $85-140 ; 📶) These two beautiful cottages capture what Volcano is all about. Private, well-designed, and impeccably kept, they are embedded in a remarkable fern forest landscaped with paths and koi ponds.

HOW BAD IS THE VOG?

Volcanic smog – vog as it's known in these parts – is a toxic cocktail of sulfur dioxide and other airborne nasties, including glass particles. Since Kilauea changed its eruption pattern in 2008, vog has affected the island much more seriously; according to park rangers, Kilauea's vog output has more than doubled. When you're downwind it can be hard to breathe, especially for those with respiratory problems. A handy daily sulfur dioxide meter for the island is available at SO2 Alert Index (www.hiso2index.info).

The one-bedroom Apapane Guesthouse ($140) is full of light, bringing nature indoors. Details include a vaulted ceiling, a slate bath, a gas stove, and ohia wood floors. The 'Alalā Hiker's Retreat is smaller, with no cooking facilities, but offers the same attention to detail at a bargain price ($85). Each has an extraordinarily peaceful lanai, which immerses you in a leafy world of bird calls.

Chalet Kilauea Collection HOTEL $$
(☎967-7786; www.volcano-hawaii.com; 19-4178 Wright Rd; r $45-190) This hotel is really three properties targeting different markets. Volcano Hale is group hiker territory, with nine rooms, three baths and shared kitchen. Lokahi Lodge ($95-130), while a bit motel-ish, is perfect for families, particularly the private loft (sleeps six). And romantic Chalet Kilauea has a cozy country-cottage feel, with 25 unique rooms, including a nice honeymoon suite.

While there have been issues with this property in the past, most notably at the front desk, attentive new management ensures that all grounds are well-kept and steady improvements are underway.

Volcano Country Cottages COTTAGE $$
(☎967-7960; www.volcanocountrycottages.com; 19-3990 Old Volcano Rd; r $105-132; 📶) Four one- and two-bed cottages in a nice and quiet fern forest setting define this quality property. The studio and the artist's house are the most charming, the latter offering a full kitchen. Hot tub too. Additional cleaning fee around $25.

Volcano Hideaways COTTAGE $$

(☎985-8959; www.volcanovillage.net; Hale Ohia Rd; cottages $140-160;) The three fully-renovated cottages located on this quiet side street (a designated Historic District) are all spotless, expertly outfitted and tastefully decorated by hosts who put great care into what they do.

The one-bedroom and two three-bedroom houses come fully equipped – from robes and quality DVDs to laundry facilities and freshly roasted coffee from the owners' Laupahoehoe farm. Rain showers, whirlpool tubs and luxurious linens are other perks. The one-bedroom also has a hot tub.

Kilauea Lodge B&B $$

(☎967-7366; www.kilauealodge.com; 19-3948 Old Volcano Rd; r $180-290, cottages $210-290;) This ever-popular lodge sleeps like a B&B with hotel services. The 12 rooms vary their offerings, but all embody upscale country romance with gas fireplaces, Hawaiian quilts, artistic stained glass, vaulted ceilings and bathroom skylights. A relaxing common room has a wood fireplace, and the manicured gardens hold a gorgeous hot tub. Rates include breakfast.

Four one- and two-bedroom cottages of equally high quality are also available off-property; the Ola'a Plantation House is particularly charming. Also contains Volcano's best restaurant.

Hawaii Volcano Tree House TREE HOUSE $$

(☎785-7060; volcanotreehouse.net; Nalehua Rd; tree house $195) Longstanding resident and noted character Skye has constructed two utterly unique tree houses with his own hands in the forest canopy. Made from entirely recycled materials, they bring the Swiss Family Robinson to life. The better of the two is Nancy's tree house, which is totally private, offers great views, and has a cozy interior that must be seen to be believed.

The wood stove should be avoided, but a glass of wine in the treetops is a fine way to end the day. Call for directions.

Eating

Oddly, Volcano has very few restaurants compared with the large number of accommodations; see also Volcano Garden Arts (p302). For groceries, try your luck at **Volcano Store** (Upper Store, cnr Old Volcano & Haunani Rds; 5am-6:45pm) and **Kilauea General Store** (Old Volcano Rd, Lower Store; 7am-7:30pm Mon-Sat, to 7pm Sun).

★ **Café Ohi'a** CAFE $

(19-4005 Haunani Rd; sandwiches $8.50; 7am-5pm) The enormous sandwiches here may well be the very best on the island. Try a pastrami on cranberry mac nut bread – then split it with someone else. The place to pack for a picnic.

Lava Rock Café DINER $

(19-3972 Old Volcano Rd; mains $11-20; 7:30am-9pm Tue-Sat, to 5pm Mon, to 4pm Sun;) Somewhere between a restaurant and a diner, this family-run roadhouse pit-stop has spruced itself up with live music, local drafts, and an expanded menu of burgers, steak, pasta, ribs and more.

Thai Thai Restaurant THAI $$

(☎808-967-7969; 19-4084 Old Volcano Rd; mains $15-26; noon-9pm Thu-Tue, Wed 4-9pm;) Good Thai food doesn't come cheaply anymore, at least not in Volcano. Avoid the tables in the kitschy gift shop or do takeout.

★ **Kilauea Lodge** ECLECTIC $$$

(☎967-7366; www.kilauealodge.com; Old Volcano Rd; breakfast $7-13, mains $22-36; 7:30am-10am & 5-9pm) Volcano's splurge is the only high-end kitchen around, with a menu that seeks to hit all the major categories (plus antelope). The vaulted beamed ceiling, historic stone fireplace and eye-catching paintings of Hawaiian mythology create an upscale rustic atmosphere here. The wine list is extensive and service is attentive. Check out Sunday brunch before your big hike, and definitely reserve ahead.

Shopping

★ **Volcano Farmers Market** MARKET

(1000 Wright Rd, Cooper Community Center; 7-9am Sun) This weekly farmers market – when the whole town comes to socialize and buy local organic produce, hot food and unique crafts – is one of the warmest community events on the island. A bright play structure teems with children, and there's even a second-hand bookstore.

Volcano Winery WINE

(www.volcanowinery.com; 35 Pi'i Mauna Dr; 10am-5:30pm) Drawing on six types of grapes and other infusions of flavor, and planting in volcanic soil, the unique Volcano Winery moves beyond traditional vineyards to offer a suitably creative approach to its subject. Tea wine, mac-nut honey wine, and guava-grape wine are all offered.

The jaboticaba berry (which grows directly on the branches of the tree and takes 12 years to mature) forms 25% of Volcano Red and 50% of Volcano Blush. Whether or not such blends are successful, they make this attractive tasting room and shop a magnet for oenophiles and the layperson alike. There is also a free tour at 10am daily.

★2400° Fahrenheit GLASS
(www.2400F.com; Old Volcano Rd; ⏲10am-4pm Thu-Mon) Watch artists Michael and Misato Mortara create their mind-boggling bowls and vases at this glass blowing studio. A tiny gallery displays finished pieces (here the old saying holds: 'if you need to ask how much, you probably can't afford it'). On Hwy 11, near mile marker 24.

Akatsuka Orchid Gardens GARDENING
(☎888-967-6669; www.akatsukaorchid.com; Hwy 11; ⏲9am-5pm) FREE Famous for its unique hybrid orchids, this warehouse stuffed with 200,000 blooming plants ships all over the world. A visit is an olfactory awakening. Close to mile marker 22.

Information

A laundromat (open daily) and the **Volcano Visitor Center** (☎985-7422; Old Volcano Rd; ⏲7am-7pm) – a teeny unstaffed hut with brochures aplenty – are located next to Thai Thai Restaurant (p304), as is an ATM (at True Value hardware store).

The **post office** (19-4030 Old Volcano Rd) is down the street from the Volcano Store (p304).

KA'U

Mother Nature hasn't been good to Ka'u lately. First the ongoing eruption of Halema'uma'u has meant the vog factory is working overtime. Some farms have packed it in, their crops refusing to grow, and even fence posts are rusting early amidst the sulfurous air. Then came a change in weather patterns. Annual rainfall in the west of this already-bone-dry region has fallen from 30in to 3in. Add global economic problems and you have a recipe for hard times. But they're used to that here. While offering a handful of sights, including the Kahuku Unit of Hawai'i Volcanoes National Park, Ka'u has never been about tourism. Here at the under-tip, locals fiercely protect their rural, stay-away-from-it-all culture, squashing coastal resorts, lobbying for protected land, pioneering off-the-grid living, and speaking lots of pidgin. In many ways this is an island within an island, adding intrigue to any itinerary.

Pahala

POP 1600

A former sugar town muddling through hard times, Pahala hangs on via small-farm agriculture, particularly macadamia nuts and coffee. This quiet town's main streets are lined with unrestored early-20th-century plantation homes, many now rentals; squint and imagine the past.

Between mile markers 51 and 52 on Hwy 11, take the signed turnoff on Kamani St to Pikake St, where you'll find Pahala's post office, bank and gas station. Nearby is the **Ka'u Hospital** (☎928-2050; www.kau.hhsc.org; 1 Kamani St).

Activities

★Ka'u Coffee Mill FARM TOUR
(☎928-0550; www.kaucoffeemill.com; 96-2694 Wood Valley Rd; 8:30am-5:30pm) FREE This well-done, down-to-earth coffee farm tour walks you through the entire process from tree to bag, yet unlike other agricultural tours of this kind, it's free! So load up on a few bags from the nice gift shop on the way out.

Festivals & Events

Ka'u Coffee Festival FESTIVAL
(www.kaucoffeefest.com) In early May, Pahala comes alive with music, coffee, hula, more coffee, farm tours and, ultimately, the Miss Ka'u Coffee Pageant. No decaf there.

LOCAL KNOWLEDGE

KA'ALAIKI ROAD

If travelling between Pahala and Na'alehu, get of Hwy 11 and take the *mauka* backroad. Freshly-paved Ka'alaiki Rd (also called Old Cane Haul Rd) is a beautiful drive that loops through green hills with distant sea views, and you'll have it to yourself. In Na'alehu turn near Punalu'u Bakeshop; in Pahala take Pikake St to Huapala St, turn right and follow out of town.

Ka'u

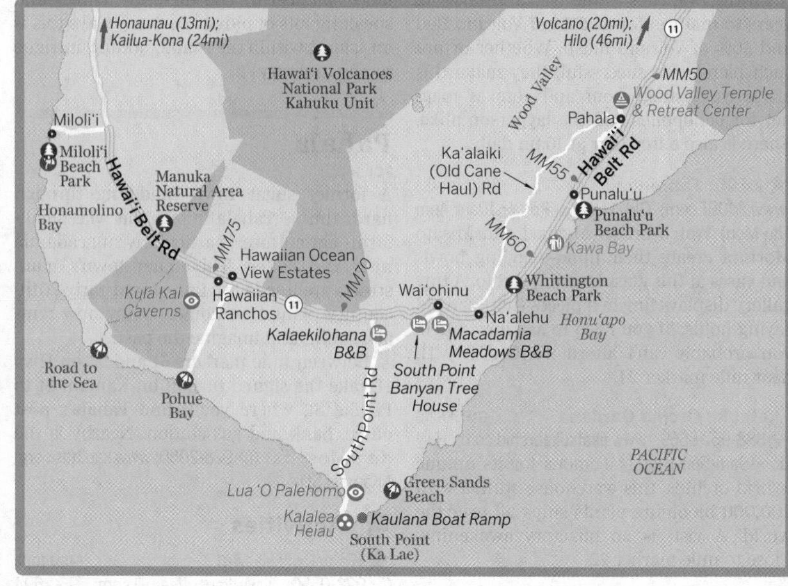

Sleeping

Pahala Plantation Cottages COTTAGES
(www.pahalaplantationcottages.com; 96-3208 Maile St; 2-/3-bed $155/225, cleaning fee $45) Offers 12 plantation cottages scattered around town, from one-bedroom to the huge seven-bedroom 1930s plantation manager's house on 3.5 acres (per night $750). Quality varies between properties, with some a bit worn and full of old furniture, but there is no lack of authenticity: this is what is left when the sugar business goes away. Management open to offers.

Wood Valley

Near Pahala, the 25-acre Tibetan Buddhist **Wood Valley Temple & Retreat Center** (Nechung Dorje Drayang Ling; ☎928-8539; www.nechung.org; requested donation $5; ⏲10am-5pm) makes a lovely escape. The huge, cheerfully painted guesthouse has a full kitchen and screened-in dining hall with lush views. The simple rooms are clean and nicely furnished, with colorful details and new bamboo floors; bathrooms are shared. Next door a colorful, century-old temple welcomes visitors for daily **chanting and meditation** (⏲8am & 6pm) and has a gift shop. Its name, Nechung Dorje Drayang Ling, means Immutable Island of Melodious Sound.

To get here take Maile St from Hwy 11, until it turns into Pikake St, and then Route 151 (Wood Valley Rd); the retreat is about 4.5 miles inland. The meander up into Wood Valley is a great drive with farms and forest and one-lane bridges crossing babbling creeks.

Punalu'u & Around

POP 900

Once a major Hawaiian settlement, today Punalu'u is home to a popular black-sand beach and the nearby Sea Mountain condo development, the only one of its kind on this coast – and perhaps the last.

Beaches

Punalu'u Beach Park BEACH
Punalu'u Beach Park provides easy access to a pretty little bay with a black-sand beach famous for feeding and basking green sea turtles; snorkeling is a real treat here. It's also one of the few beaches where rare hawksbill turtles lay their eggs, so be careful not to disturb their sandy nests.

The northern part of the beach is backed by a duck pond and the remains of an old resort, rotting away in testimony to local economics, the anti-development movement, or both. Most days the rough waters are not good for swimming as there are forceful undertows – a lifeguard is posted. The ruins of the Pahala Sugar Company's old warehouse and pier lie slightly to the north. Follow a trail up the hill past the cement pier to find the unreconstructed ruins of Kane'ele'ele Heiau in a vast field; the trail continues all the way to Kawa Bay via some secluded coves.

The park has picnic pavilions, rest rooms, showers and drinking water. A concession stand is run by local aunties who happily talk story, and camping is allowed (with a county permit). Come morning, the park quickly fills with picnickers and tour buses. There are two signed turnoffs for Punalu'u between mile markers 56 and 57.

★Kawa Bay BEACH

Reached via a dirt road between mile markers 58 and 59 (stay straight rather than taking any lefts), this is Ka'u's best surfable break (known locally as Windmills; competitions are held here occasionally). Paddle out on the northernmost end of the beach. Give locals their space here.

Sleeping

★Kawohi Lani VACATION RENTAL $$

(Precious Heaven; ☎877-526-8352; www.blacksandsbeach.com; Punalu'u Beach Park; 3-bed house per night/week $275/1750) This unique property is the only vacation rental on Punalu'u Beach Park. Just steps from the water in the shelter of coconut trees, it comprises one three-bedroom, two-bathroom house on stilts with a large deck, and a one-bed cottage (per night $175). One of the nicest situations in Ka'u.

Na'alehu & Around

POP 1070

Tiny, low-key Na'alehu is the southernmost town in the USA – a title it milks for all it's worth. The most prominent landmark is the abandoned historic theater with a giant *honu* painted on the roof. Along with its towering banyan trees and pastel plantation homes, Na'alehu has a lost-in-time rural feel.

This is Ka'u's commercial center, and it has a grocery store, laundromat, library, gas station, ATM, post office, police station and a half-dozen churches.

Beaches

Whittington Beach Park BEACH

This small beach park has tide pools to explore, a bird-festooned fishpond and the cement pilings of an old pier that was used for shipping sugar and hemp until the 1930s. The ocean is usually too rough for swimming and, despite the name, there is no beach. Green sea turtles can sometimes be seen offshore.

Bathrooms, with no potable water, and sheltered picnic pavilions are grouped together near a pretty, pondlike inlet. Camping on the grass is allowed with a county permit. The turnoff for the park is between mile markers 60 and 61. Look for it at a stop sign on the *makai* (seaward) side of Hwy 11, just below the rise to the Honu'apo Bay lookout.

Sleeping & Eating

★Ka'u Coffee House & Hostel HOSTEL $

(☎747-4142, 896-9272; 95-5587 Hwy 11; r $35; ⏲cafe 10am-6pm Mon-Sat; 📶) This new hostel is doing everything right. The downstairs cafe makes good sandwiches ($8) and a tasty evening plate dinner ($10), while the upstairs hostel offers clean and tidy rooms and a relaxing community space. Hostel guests also get a cooked breakfast for $5 and free wi-fi all around. For Hawaii you cannot beat these prices. Faces Hwy 11.

★Punalu'u Bakeshop & Visitor Center BAKERY

(www.bakeshophawaii.com; Hwy 11, near Ka'alaiki Rd; sandwiches $6-8, plate lunches $8) An oasis in the desert of Punalu'u, this bakery packs them in from all around. Known for its sandwiches and variety of flavored sweetbreads, such as the colorful 'kalakoa', it offers free samples to aid in decision-making. There's an excellent picnic area out back.

Hana Hou Restaurant DINER $$

(☎929-9717; Spur Rd; mains $10-16; ⏲8am-7pm Sun-Thu, to 8pm Fri & Sat; 📶👪) A community fixture, this friendly, homespun diner offers 'the best of everything…and plenty of it.' Portions *are* generous and dishes, though not fancy, rarely disappoint. A new 'to go' section features fresh sandwiches and wraps for picnicking, and there's live music on Friday and Saturday. Bring your own bottle. If you're stuck there are two overpriced but comfy rooms out back ($65/95).

Shaka Restaurant DINER $$

(☎929-7464; www.shakarestaurant.com; breakfast & lunch $8-14, dinner $12-22; ⏰7am-9pm) Na'alehu's other eatery serves mainly fryer and grill fare and has a hardworking bar with *pupu* that just keep on coming. Live music most Fridays.

Island Market GROCERIES

(⏰8am-7pm Mon-Sat, 9am-6pm Sun) This well-stocked market is the best between Hilo and Captain Cook.

Na'alehu Farmers Market MARKET

(95-5656 Hwy 11; ⏰7am-noon Wed & Sat) A small but quality farmers market is held in front of Ace Hardware.

South Point

South Point is the southernmost point in the USA and a national historic landmark. It is widely believed this is where the first Polynesians landed. In Hawaiian it's known as **Ka Lae**, which means simply the Point, and is revered as a sacred site.

To get here take South Point Rd between mile markers 69 and 70. The 12-mile road is mostly one lane; people edge over for each other and give a *shaka* (Hawaiian hand greeting sign) as they pass. The road forks a few miles south of a wind farm. Veer right for Ka Lae and left for Green Sands Beach.

For a picturesque alternative, take the backdoor route from Kama'oa Rd in Wai'ohinu to South Point Rd, an 8-mile country ramble that deposits you out just north of the wind farm.

Beaches & Sights

★Ka Lae HISTORICAL SITE

The southernmost tip of the Big Island, and of the USA, Ka Lae does feel like the end of the Earth, inspiring reflection. Even with the rushing wind filling your ears, an odd stillness and silence steals over you. From the parking area, a short walk leads down to the tip itself.

You won't be alone, however. The confluence of ocean currents here makes this one of Hawai'i's most bountiful fishing grounds, and locals fish off the craggy cliff, some bracing themselves on tiny ledges partway down. The wooden platforms built on the cliff have hoists and ladders for small boats anchored below. Locals like to cliff jump into the surging waters here, though you may want to peek over the edge and just imagine executing that heart-thumping trick. Behind the platforms, inside a large *puka* (hole), you can watch water rage up and recede with incoming waves. The only facilities are two portable toilets.

Near the parking area is **Kalalea Heiau**, classified as a *ko'a* (a small stone pen designed to encourage fish and birds to multiply). Inside is a fishing shrine where ancient Hawaiians left offerings to Ku'ula, the god of fishermen. A standing rock below the heiau has several canoe mooring holes. Ancient Hawaiians would tether their canoes with ropes to these handles, then let the strong currents pull their canoes into the deep waters to fish.

Green Sands Beach BEACH

(Papakolea) This legendary green sand beach on Mahana Bay is made of semiprecious olivine (a type of volcanic basalt), which erodes from the ancient cone towering over it. The olivine sand mixes with black sand to create an unusual olive green that brightly sparkles in the sun, making this a fun and unique destination.

As a beach, it's wanting. The tiny strand is pounded by strong waves even on calm days, making swimming dubious; high surf can flood it completely and wind howls through here.

To get here take the road to South Point, turning left after 10 miles. Follow this road around until it dead ends at a grassy parking area; don't leave valuables in your car. At this point you can either walk or hire one of the many local 4WD 'taxis' waiting there ($5 to $15 return). It is a dusty, hot and long 2.5-mile hike, so the latter makes sense. If you do choose to walk, head toward the water, past the Kaulana boat ramp, and follow the rutted dirt road left through the metal gate. Now just keep going, enjoying the gorgeous undulating coastline and aiming for the curvaceous cliff-face in the distance. Once there, a good scramble down the cliff is required to reach the beach. In any case, start before 8am to beat the crowds, and bring plenty of water.

Sleeping

★South Point Banyan Tree House VACATION RENTAL $

(☎217-2504; www.southpointbth.com; cnr Pinao St & Hwy 11; house $100; 📶) Nestled high in the limbs of a huge banyan tree off Hwy 11, this fun octagonal vacation rental offers the visually arresting illusion of a jungle escape, and is a bargain at this price. Fully equipped and flooded with light, it has a great kitchen, relaxed living room (with TV) and a hot tub on a hidden deck. Honeymoon, anyone?

★ Kalaekilohana B&B $$$

(☎888-584-7071, 939-8052; www.kau-hawaii.com; 94-2152 South Point Rd; r incl breakfast $249; 📶) There's no doubt about it: this is *the* place to stay in Ka'u. Rising like Tara at the end of a long driveway, this outpost of refinement offers the quality accommodations and hospitality one expects of a fine inn. The impeccable owners lead fine conversation on the veranda and, if you're lucky, cook an amazing dinner ($35).

Upstairs you'll find spacious, private and well-appointed rooms with rainfall showers that make you late for the gourmet breakfast. And out back there is ever-reliable Rusty, a third host offering an endless source of complimentary aperitifs. Shaka!

Hawai'i Volcanoes National Park Kahuku Unit

This massive 2003 addition to Hawai'i Volcanoes National Park is only accessed from Ka'u. Once part of the island's largest *ahupua'a*, a traditional land district running from mountain to sea, its 116,000 acres later served as ranchland. The park is in the process of slowly developing visitor infrastructure, and a lower section is accessible, with portable toilets at trailheads. Current options include a scenic drive (12-mile round trip), four hiking trails, weekly guided hikes, monthly reforestation projects, and occasional junior ranger days. Check www.nps.gov/havo/planyourvisit/events.htm for the latest schedule.

As you might expect, this is a real get-away-from-it-all adventure. You'll have a huge and wild piece of the Big Island to yourself. The walking area was once a ranch, but trees were retained at intervals, so it feels like a vast sloping park. There's a grab bag of sights, including cinder cones, tree molds, spatter ramparts (from lava fountains), lav flows, a quarry, an abandoned airstrip, an old radar station and, best of all, a forested pit crater. You also have a good chance of spotting wild turkeys and big-horned moufflon sheep, which were introduced during the ranching era. Having said all that, the Kahuku Unit is no replacement for the main park.

The Kahuku Unit is open to the public every Saturday and Sunday (except the first Saturday of the month) from 9am to 3pm (the gate is locked at 3pm). The entrance to the park is located 4 miles west of Wai'ohinu; turn right after mile marker 70. At time of research the park's sign was missing.

Activities

Kahuku Road SCENIC DRIVE

This 12-mile round-trip drive ascends the full length of the publicly accessible area, rising 2,145ft. The first 2.5 miles is a leisurely journey along a graded gravel road past open pastures and the remains of the epic 1868 eruption. Past the Upper Palm trailhead the road climbs steeply and requires 4WD.

The landscape becomes more wooded and abandoned water tanks and corrals recall former ranching days. Views stretch to South Point. Look for rare, yellow-flowering ohia lehua trees. All the trailheads are on this main road.

Pu'u o Lokuana Trail HIKING

This easy 2-mile loop follows historic ranch roads that lead into a hidden pasture surrounded by trees. After passing some lava tree molds the route wanders around spatter ramparts from the 1868 eruption. Follow the old airstrip back to the road and climb the cinder cone for great views.

You'll find the route to the top on the uphill side, through a historic cinder quarry. Trailhead located about half a mile from entrance on right.

★ Palm Trail HIKING

An easy 2.6-mile loop traversing scenic pasture along an ancient cinder cone with some of the best panoramic views Kahuku has to offer. Highlights include relics of the ranching era, sections of remnant native forest and striking volcanic features from the 1868 eruptive fissures.

Lower Palm trailhead begins to the left 2 miles from Pu'u o Lokuana trailhead. Loop back to main road at Upper Palm trailhead and walk back down to your car. You can't drive beyond this point without a 4WD.

Kona Trail HIKING

The highlight here is a huge forested pit crater, a deep bowl full of trees which looks like the entrance to the underworld.

Confusingly, the two trailheads are referred to as Glover, not Kona. Lower Glover trailhead is on the right about 2.5 miles from Upper Palm trailhead (4WD only).

Head right 1.1 miles to find the pit crater. The trail loops back to the end of Kahuku Rd at Upper Glover trailhead.

Kahuku Ranger Hikes HIKING TOUR
(www.nps.gov/havo/planyourvisit/events.htm) These ranger-led hikes are a great way to get to know Kahuku. The popular People & Land hike is a 2-mile, three-hour expedition that explores the pastures, quarry, airstrip and 1868 lava fields. Ranch history, land use, invasives and cinder-cone geology are all discussed. Offered most Sundays from 9:30am to 12:30pm (check schedule).

There is also a monthly reforestation hike that combines learning with volunteer work (removing invasives). See online schedule.

Ocean View & Around

POP 2530

When Captain James Cook first saw Ka'u's extensive lava flows, he thought them 'as barren a waste as can be conceived to exist.' Today he might be surprised to find Ocean View, the largest subdivision in the USA, sitting on top. Comprised of Hawaiian Ocean View Estates (inland) and Hawaiian Ranchos (seaward), Ocean View was bulldozed into desolate black lava in the 1950s. Despite their $1500 price tag, the lots were never fully settled, and remain so for a variety of reasons, including lack of jobs, blankets of vog and a reputation for substance abuse. Too bad, because one of the island's most interesting volcanic sights lies buried here.

Across the highway from each other, two shopping centers – Pohue Plaza and Ocean View Town Center – make up the commercial center of Ocean View, offering gas, food, ATM and laundry.

Sights & Activities

Road to the Sea BEACH
The Road to the Sea has a name that calls adventurers, but it's not the human-free destination it once was, despite being at the end of an extremely rugged 4WD-only road. It's a rough, windy piece of shoreline, but well worth the trip.

To get here, turn *makai* (seaward) at the row of mailboxes (near the Ka Ulu Malu Shady Grove Farm) between mile markers 79 and 80 and set your odometer. From here you cross 6 miles over a rudimentary, seemingly never-ending lava road. The first and smaller of the two beaches is at the end of this road; it takes 45 minutes or so, depending on your comfort level driving on rough terrain.

To reach the second beach, drive a half-mile back inland. Skip the first left fork that appears (it's a dead end) and take the second left fork. Look for arrows that are painted on the lava rock. The road heads inland before heading toward the shore again, and the course isn't always apparent. There are many places where you can lose traction or get lost. Almost a mile from the fork you'll reach a red *pu'u*. Park here and walk down to the ocean. If you decide to walk the whole distance, it's about 1.5 miles. Bring as much water as you can carry; it's hot and shadeless. These waters have excellent fishing.

Neither beach is named, but both have exquisite black-and-green sand, backed by looming cliffs. Low tide presents intriguing beach-trekking possibilities. Plan on an all-day adventure.

★ **Kula Kai Caverns** CAVE TOUR
(☎929-9725; www.kulakaicaverns.com; tours adult/child 6-12yr from $20/10) Who knows what lurks under the average Ka'u house? When the ongoing survey is complete, this one will offer the largest lava tube in the world, a vast underground complex stretching back into the bowels of Mauna Loa. With 34 miles of passageways intertwining under 400 acres of earth, it is more than enough to satisfy the most ardent spelunker.

The 30-minute Lighted Trail tour is the gentlest option, an easy walk covering everything you'll want to see and know about lava tubes. The Crawl takes you through a smooth braided passage requiring caving gear ($60), while the Two Hour tour is even more hardcore exploration (adult/child $95/65). Reservations required.

Manuka Natural Area Reserve HIKING
This 13.5-acre reserve offers a very well-done nature trail. Proceeding through forest on a lava rock path, and assisted by a nice trail guide, you'll identify 30 species of plants, and see a pit crater and lava flows. The entrance is off Hwy 11, just north of mile marker 81. There's also a picnic area.

Sleeping & Eating

Leilani Bed & Breakfast B&B $
(☎929-7101; www.leilanibedandbreakfast.com; 92-8822 Leilani Pkwy, Hawaiian Ocean View Estates; r $99, tr $124; wi-fi) Tucked away on a tropical lot in Hawaiian Ocean View Estates, this well-managed property offers a private guest wing with three rooms and a lovely lanai, along with some amazing lava tubes nearby. A perfect stopover between Hilo and Kona.

Lova Lava Land ECORESORT $
(www.lovalavaland.com; Hawaiian Ranchos; yurt/VW buses $65/35; wi-fi) This off-the-grid 'ecoresort' (solar power, catchment water, nifty low-flush toilet) epitomizes Ocean View pluck and ingenuity. Guests sleep in VW campers set on an old lava flow, and share a central compound with fully equipped kitchen, herb garden, wi-fi and lava rock shower. There's also a cozy yurt, with double bed, hardwood floors and moon roof.

It's fun, well-planned DIY living. Reservations required, use website.

Grinds CAFE $
(Pohue Plaza; mains $7-10; 6am-4pm Mon-Sat, 7am-1pm Sun) A very simple cafe with a growing reputation and no competition. Two doors down from the post office.

Ocean View Pizzeria PIZZA $
(☎929-9677; Ocean View Town Center; pizza $13-15, sandwiches $7-12; 11am-7pm, till 8pm Fri & Sat) The submarine sandwiches are great, the pizza good. A place to eat, not linger.

Maui

Includes ➡

Best Places to Eat

- ➡ Lahaina Grill (p329)
- ➡ Mama's Fish House (p385)
- ➡ Alan Wong's Amasia (p377)
- ➡ Geste Shrimp Truck (p354)
- ➡ NorthShore Cafe (p391)

Best Snorkel Spots

- ➡ Malu'aka Beach (p378)
- ➡ Molokini Crater (p363)
- ➡ Honolua Bay (p345)
- ➡ 'Ahihi-Kina'u Natural Area Reserve (p380)
- ➡ Ulua Beach (p374)

Why Go?

Maui is the postcard island. Where snorkelers pause for green turtles. Zipliners swoop over jungles. Couples exchange vows on the beach. And early risers watch the sun punch through morning clouds from the top of a lofty volcano.

The most visited of the Neighbor Islands, Maui lures travelers who are revitalized by outdoor adventure and gorgeous scenery. Nature watching is at its most glorious in winter when humpback whales return to mate and raise their young.

Maui's natural charms are enhanced by top-notch restaurants and lodging. From scrappy food trucks to white-linen dining rooms, eateries embrace local food and its traditions. Resorts wow guests with impeccable service and prime seaside locations, with B&Bs providing more personal alohas.

When to Go

Lahaina

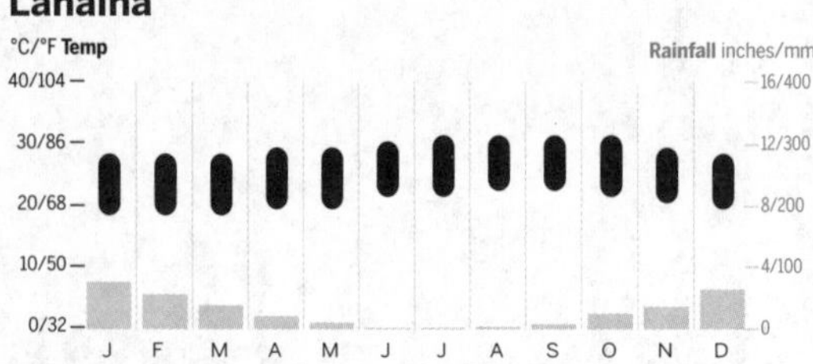

Jan–Mar Humpback whales frolic along Maui's shores during the winter months.

July Maui celebrates July 4 with a big rodeo and *paniolo* (cowboy) parade.

Oct–Nov A quiet season with good weather and lower hotel prices.

History

Maui's early history mirrors the rest of Hawaii's, with warring chiefs, periods of peace, missionaries, whalers and sugarcane. At the time of statehood in 1959, Maui's population was a mere 35,000. In 1961 Maui retained such a backwater appearance that director Mervyn LeRoy filmed his classic *The Devil at 4 O'Clock* in Lahaina, where the dirt roads and untouristed waterfront doubled for the sleepy South Pacific isle depicted in his adventure movie. Spencer Tracy and Frank Sinatra not only shot many of their scenes at Lahaina's Pioneer Inn, but stayed there too.

Enter sugar giant Amfac in 1962, which sweetened its pot by transforming 600 acres of canefields in Ka'anapali into Hawaii's first resort destination outside Waikiki. Things really took off in 1974 with the first nonstop flight between mainland USA and Kahului. Maui soon blossomed into the darling of Hawaii's tourism industry.

Its growth spurt hasn't always been pretty. In the mid-1970s developers pounced on the beachside village of Kihei with such intensity it became a rallying call for anti-development forces throughout Hawaii. Recent years have been spent catching up with Kihei's rampant growth, mitigating traffic and creating plans intent on sparing the rest of Maui from willy-nilly building sprees.

In the 21st century Maui has been a leader in eco-activism. Parks, forest reserves and watersheds cover nearly half of the island. Maui was the first island to approve a ban on single-use plastic bags, which went into effect in 2011. Thirty-four wind turbines line the slopes above wind-whipped Ma'alaea Harbor, enough to power more than 18,000 homes annually. In 2012, eight more windmills went online in east Maui on land leased from 'Ulupalakua Ranch.

Climate

Maui's west coast typically boasts dry, sunny weather, with conditions improving as you approach Kihei and Makena in the south. Hana and the jungle-covered east Maui offer rainforests and gushing waterfalls. The Upcountry slopes, beneath Haleakalā, commonly have intermittent clouds, making for a cooler, greener respite and ideal conditions for land-based activities like hiking and horseback riding. For an islandwide recorded weather forecast, call ☎866-944-5025.

National, State & County Parks

Maui's marquee park is Haleakalā National Park, its lofty volcanic peaks giving rise to east Maui. The park has two distinct faces. The main section encompasses Haleakalā's volcanic summit with its breathtaking crater-rim lookouts and lunarlike hiking trails. In the park's rainforested Kipahulu section you're in the midst of towering waterfalls, swimming holes and ancient Hawaiian archaeological sites.

Top among Maui's state parks is 'Iao Valley State Park, whose towering emerald pinnacle rises picture-perfect from the valley floor. For the ultimate stretch of unspoiled beach, head to Makena State Park. On the east side of Maui, Wai'anapanapa State Park sits on a sparkling black-sand beach.

Maui's county parks center on beaches and include the windsurfing meccas of Kanaha Beach Park and Ho'okipa Beach Park. Details about county parks and beaches, including contact information and lifeguard availability, can be found on the Maui County government website: www.mauicounty.gov.

Camping

On Maui there's a clear pecking order in camping. At the top, offering the best and safest options, are the campgrounds at Haleakalā National Park. After that, the state parks – most notably Wai'anapanapa State Park – are a better option than the county parks.

National Parks Haleakalā National Park has excellent drive-up camping at the summit area and in the seaside Kipahulu

WIND RIDING WEBSITES

Maui is known for its consistent winds. Windsurfers can find action in any month, but as a general rule the best wind is from June to September and the flattest spells are from December to February.

Get the inside scoop on kiteboarding and windsurfing from the following:

➡ **Maui Kiteboarding Association** (www.mauikiteboardingassociation.com)

➡ **Maui Windsurfing** (www.mauiwindsurfing.net)

➡ **Maui Kitesurfing Community** (www.mauikitesurf.org)

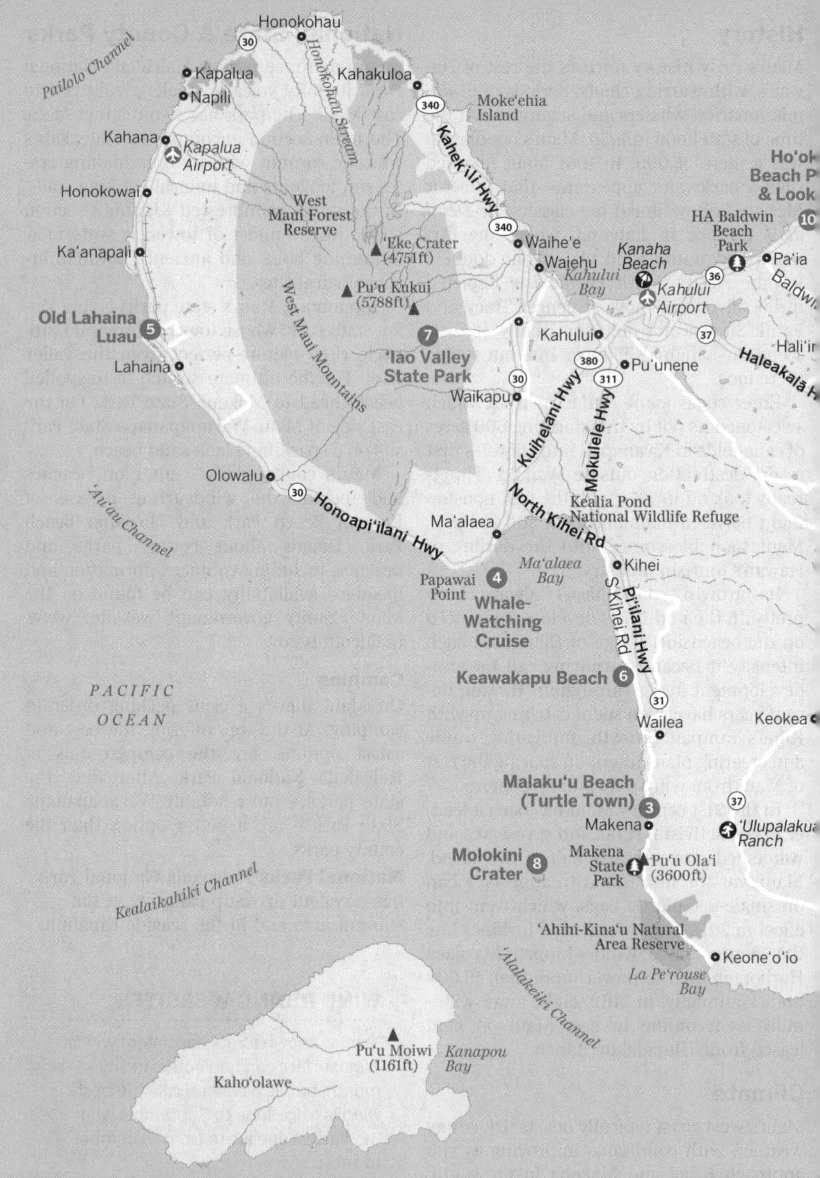

Maui Highlights

1. Wind across 54 one-lane bridges on the dramatic **Road to Hana** (p395)
2. Catch a soulful crater-rim sunrise at **Haleakalā National Park** (p410)
3. Snorkel the turtle-town waters of **Malu'aka Beach** (p378)
4. Sail among breaching humpbacks on a **whale-watching cruise** (p362)
5. Savor a traditional feast at **Old Lahaina Luau** (p330)
6. Photograph Maui's favorite green landmark at **'Iao Valley State Park** (p359)

7 Behold the sunset from glimmering **Keawakapu Beach** (p364)

8 Dive the crystal-clear waters of **Molokini Crater** (p363)

9 Hike through a bamboo forest on the **Pipiwai Trail** (p420)

10 Watch windboarders skim across waves at **Ho'okipa Beach Park & Lookout** (p381)

section. No fees, reservations or permits are required for drive-up camping. Haleakalā also offers free backcountry camping on the crater floor with a permit, as well as $75 cabin rentals, though the cabins are in high demand and difficult to score.

State Parks Maui has campgrounds and cabins at Wai'anapanapa State Park and Polipoli Spring State Recreation Area. Each park allows a maximum stay of five consecutive nights. Tent camping is $18 per night per site. Cabins cost $90. For reservations, contact the **Division of State Parks** (☎984-8109; www.hawaiistateparks.org; 54 S High St, Wailuku; ⌚8am-noon Mon-Fri) in person or online.

County Parks Maui County permits camping at Kanaha Beach Park in Kahului (closed Monday and Tuesday) and at Papalaua Wayside Park south of Lahaina (closed Wednesday and Thursday). Camping is allowed for three consecutive nights and costs $5 to $8 per day ($2 to $3 for children under 18). For reservations at either site, contact the **Department of Parks & Recreation – Central District** (☎270-7389; www.mauicounty.gov; 700 Halia Nakoa St, Wailuku; ⌚8am-1pm & 2:30-4pm Mon-Fri) or the **Department of Parks & Recreation – West District** (☎661-4685; www.mauicounty.gov; 1840 Honoapi'ilani Hwy; ⌚8am-4pm Mon-Fri, sometimes closed noon-1pm).

Getting There & Away

AIR

Most mainland flights to Maui involve at least one stopover, but direct flights to Maui are offered from some cities, including San Diego, Los Angeles, San Francisco, Seattle, Dallas, Phoenix, Denver, Las Vegas and Vancouver BC.

Kahului International Airport (OGG; ☎872-3830; www.hawaii.gov/ogg; 1 Kahului Airport Rd) All trans-Pacific flights to Maui arrive in Kahului, the island's main airport.

Kapalua Airport (JHM; www.hawaii.gov/jhm) Off Hwy 30, south of Kapalua, this regional airport has flights to other Hawaiian islands on small carriers and chartered planes. Regional airlines are **Island Air** (www.islandair.com) and **Mokulele Airlines** (www.mokuleleairlines.com).

Hana Airport (HNM; www.hawaii.gov/hnm) **Mokulele Airlines** (wwww.mokuleleairlines.com) offers twice daily flights from Kahului to this small airport, cutting a two-hour drive to a 20-minute flight.

SEA

Interisland ferries connect Lahaina with its sister islands of Moloka'i and Lana'i. For information on these ferries, see Lana'i and Moloka'i.

Getting Around

To explore Maui thoroughly and reach off-the-beaten-path sights, you'll need your own wheels. Public transportation, while improving, is still limited to the main towns and tourist resorts.

The most comprehensive road atlas available is *Ready Mapbook of Maui County*, which shows every road on the island; it's sold in bookstores.

TO/FROM THE AIRPORTS

With either of the following Kahului Airport transfer services you can make advance reservations for your arrival to speed things along. Speedi Shuttle has a desk and Executive Shuttle has a courtesy phone in the baggage-claim area. Keep in mind you must reserve in advance for your return to the airport – and don't wait till the last minute.

MAUI'S TOP OUTDOOR ACTIVITIES

ACTIVITY	DESTINATION
Hiking	Haleakalā National Park (p410); Waihe'e Ridge Trail (p349); Kapalua Resort (p346)
Horseback Riding	Pony Express (p393); Maui Stables (p409); Piiholo Ranch (p389); Mendes Ranch (p348); Thompson Ranch (p394)
Kayaking	Makena (p378); Honolua-Mokule'ia Bay Marine Life Conservation District (p345)
Kitesurfing	Kite Beach (Kanaha Beach Park, p349)
Scuba Diving	Molokini Crater (p363); Makena Landing (p378)
Snorkeling	Molokini Crater (p363); Malu'aka Beach (p378); Ulua Beach (p374); 'Ahihi-Kina'u Natural Area Reserve (p380); Pu'u Keka'a (Black Rock) (p335)
Surfing	Lahaina (p323); Ma'alaea Pipeline (p362); Honolua Bay (p345)
Windsurfing	Kanaha Beach (p349); Ho'okipa Beach (p381)
Ziplining	Piiholo Ranch Zipline (p388); Skyline Eco-Adventures (p337)

SURFING ONLINE

➡ **Art Guide Maui** (www.artguidemaui.com) For the art scene.

➡ **OMaui Surf Report** (www.omaui.com) For surf conditions.

➡ **Maui News** (www.mauinews.com) For local issues.

➡ **Maui on TV** (http://hawaiiontv.com/hawaiiontv/mauiontv) For lots of cool stuff.

➡ **Both Sides Now** (www.mauigayinfo.com) For the gay community.

➡ **Sierra Club** (www.hi.sierraclub.org/maui) For the environmental scene.

➡ **Maui Time Weekly** (www.mauitime.com/food) For the latest news about Maui dining.

The Maui Visitors Bureau (p355) runs a staffed Visitor Information Desk in the baggage claim area that's open 8am to 9:30pm daily. There are racks of local travel brochures beside the desk.

Speedi Shuttle (☎877-242-5777; www.speedishuttle.com; ⏲reservations 7am-10pm) A big Speedi plus is that they've converted to bio-diesel, using recycled vegetable oil to fuel their vehicles, so if you take them you'll be traveling green-friendly. Fares for one person from Kahului Airport cost $50 to Lahaina, $54 to Ka'anapali, $74 to Kapalua, $33 to Kihei and $39 to Wailea. Add $4 to $6 more per additional person.

Executive Shuttle (☎800-833-2303, 669-2300; www.mauishuttle.com; ⏲reservations 7am-11pm) More conventional vehicles, but usually has lower rates. Like Speedi, the price depends on the destination and the size of the group.

BUS

The **Maui Bus** (☎871-4838; www.mauicounty.gov) offers the most extensive public bus system of any Hawaiian island, except O'ahu. But don't get too excited – the buses can take you between the main towns, but they don't run to prime out-of-the-way places, such as Haleakalā National Park or Hana. Buses come with front-load bike racks.

The main routes run once hourly, every day of the week.

Routes The handiest buses for visitors are the Lahaina Islander (Kahului–Lahaina), Kihei Islander (Kahului–Wailea), Wailuku Loop (Kahului–Wailuku), Haiku Islander (Kahului–Pa'ia), Kihei Villager (Ma'alaea–Kihei), Ka'anapali Islander (Lahaina–Ka'anapali) and Napili Islander (Ka'anapali–Napili) routes.

The Upcountry Islander and Haiku Islander routes stop at Kahului Airport.

Costs Fares are $2 per ride, regardless of distance. There are no transfers; if your journey requires two separate buses, you'll have to buy a new ticket when boarding the second bus. Best deal is a daily pass for just $4.

Carry-on All buses allow you to carry on only what fits under your seat or on your lap, so forget the surfboard.

Resort Shuttle

Free Routes The Ka'anapali Resort Shuttle runs complimentary service between Whalers Village and the major resorts in Ka'anapali.

CAR & MOTORCYCLE

Alamo, Avis, Budget, Dollar, Enterprise, Hertz, National and Thrifty all have operations at Kahului Airport. Most of these rental companies also have branches in Ka'anapali and will pick you up at the nearby Kapalua Airport. For a green option, consider Bio-Beetle (p356) in Kahului. Also check out Kihei Rent A Car (p374).

Be sure to check for any road restrictions on your vehicle rental contract. Some car rental agencies, for instance, prohibit driving on the Kahekili Hwy between Honokohau and Waihe'e and in the Kaupo district of the Pi'ilani Hwy.

Average driving times and distances from Kahului are as follows. Allow more time in the morning and late-afternoon rush hours.

DESTINATION	MILES	TIME
Haleakalā Summit	36	1½hr
Hana	51	2hr
Ka'anapali	26	50min
Kapalua	32	1hr
Kihei	12	25min
Lahaina	23	45min
Makawao	14	30min
Makena	19	40min
'Ohe'o Gulch	61	2¾hr
Pa'ia	7	15min
Wailuku	3	15min

The following are contacts for car rentals serving Maui:

Alamo (☎826-6893, 800-462-5266; www.alamo.com; ⏲5am-11:30pm)

Avis (☎871-7575, 800-331-1212; www.avis.com; ⏲5:30am-11pm)

Budget (☎871-8811, 800-527-0700; www.budget.com; ⏲5:30am-11pm)

Dollar (☎877-7227, 866-434-2226; www.dollar.com; ⏲5am-11:30pm)

Enterprise (☎871-6982, 800-261-7331; www.enterprise.com; ⏰6am-11pm)

Hertz (☎893-5200, 800-654-3131; www.hertz.com; ⏰5am-11:30pm)

National (☎826-6890, 800-227-7368; www.nationalcar.com; ⏰5am-11:30pm)

Thrifty (☎877-283-0898; www.thrifty.com)

TAXI

The following companies offer service throughout Maui.

Kihei Taxi (☎298-1877)

Maui Airport Taxi (☎281-9533; www.nokaoitaxi.com)

TOURS

A number of tour bus companies operate half-day and full-day sightseeing tours on Maui, covering the most visited island destinations. Popular routes include daylong jaunts to Hana, and Haleakalā trips that take in the major Upcountry sights.

Polynesian Adventure Tours (☎833-3000; www.polyad.com; tours $93-159) Part of Gray Line Hawaii, it's a big player among Hawaiian tour companies; offers tours to Haleakalā National Park, Central Maui and 'Iao Valley State Park, and the Road to Hana.

Roberts Hawaii (☎800-831-5541; www.robertshawaii.com; tours $64-124) Another biggie; more limited options but usually better prices.

Valley Isle Excursions (☎661-8687; www.tourmaui.com; tours $132) Costs a bit more but hands-down the best Road to Hana tour. Vans take just 12 passengers and guides offer more local flavor and less canned commentary. Includes continental breakfast and, in Hana, a buffet lunch.

LAHAINA

POP 11,700

The hustle and bustle of Lahaina is tempered by the proximity of the sea, which stretches lazily west from Front St toward Lana'i. This one-time whaling village becomes downright picturesque at sunset, when you're likely to see a rainbow shimmering over the adjacent mountains. Downtown, you can spend an afternoon browsing art galleries, trendy shops and whaling-era sights on Front St. For a bit more excitement, stroll to the harbor and hop aboard a catamaran for a whale-watching cruise. Hungry? After a hard day of exploring, there's no better reward than a savory meal at one of the chef-driven restaurants on the Lahaina shoreline. As for nightlife, it's not exactly ripping, but it is among Maui's best, and a nightcap in a scruffy harborside pub just feels right in this history-filled town.

History

In ancient times Lahaina – known as Lele – housed a royal court for high chiefs, and its lands were the fertile breadbasket of West Maui. After Kamehameha the Great unified the islands he chose Lahaina as his base, and the capital remained there until 1845. The first Christian missionaries arrived in the 1820s and within a decade Hawaii's first stone church, first missionary school and first printing press were all in place in Lahaina.

Lahaina became the dominant port for whalers, not only in Hawaii but also for the

MAUI IN...

Three Days

Plunge into Maui with a dip into the sea at **Ka'anapali**, followed by a sunset cruise. On day two, stroll the historic whaling town of **Lahaina** then treat yourself to the Old Lahaina Luau. Still got jet lag? Good. Set the alarm early for the drive to **Haleakalā National Park** to catch a breathtaking sunrise and hike into the crater. On the way back, stop in **Pa'ia** for Maui's hippest cafe scene and to check the surf action at **Ho'okipa Beach Park**.

Six Days

For your first three days, follow the three day itinerary. Day four is all about those gorgeous beaches. Begin by snorkeling with turtles at **Malu'aka Beach**, followed by a picnic at magnificent **Big Beach**. In the afternoon pop by **'Iao Valley State Park** to ogle central Maui's emerald gem, and then head to **Kanaha Beach** for the sailboarding scene. Day five winds past waterfalls galore on the most legendary drive in Hawaii, the wildly beautiful **Road to Hana**. It's going to be a big day – start early, bring a bathing suit and a sense of adventure. On your last day enjoy Maui's splashiest highlight: a **whale-watching cruise**..

MAUI SURF BEACHES & BREAKS

For action sports, head to Maui's beaches. On the north shore, near the town of Ha'iku, is the infamous big-wave spot known as **Pe'ahi**, or 'Jaws' (see box on p387). Determined pro surfers, such as Laird Hamilton, Dave Kalama and Derrick Doerner, helped put the planet's largest, most perfect wave on the international map. Jaws' waves are so high that surfers must be towed into them by wave runners.

Not into risking your life? No worries, there are plenty of other waves to ride. Maui's west side, especially around **Lahaina**, offers a wider variety of surf. The fun reef breaks at **Lahaina Breakwall and Harbor** (p323) cater to both beginner and intermediate surfers. To the south is **Ma'alaea Pipeline** (p362), a fickle right-hand reef break that is often considered one of the fastest waves in the world. On the island's northwest corner is majestic **Honolua Bay** (p345). Its right point break works best on winter swells and is considered one of the premier points not just in Hawaii, but around the world.

Gentler shorebreaks good for bodysurfing can be found around **Pa'ia**, **Kapalua** and the beaches between **Kihei** and **Makena**.

entire Pacific. The whaling years reached a peak in the 1840s, with hundreds of ships pulling into port each year. The town took on the whalers' boisterous nature, opening dance halls, bars and brothels. The whaling industry fizzled in the 1860s, followed a decade later by the arrival of sugarcane, which remained the backbone of the economy until tourism took over in the 1960s.

The focal point of Lahaina is its harbor and the adjacent Banyan Tree Sq. The main drag and tourist strip is Front St, which runs along the shoreline, offering views of Lana'i. The city is flanked to the east by Honoapi'ilani Hwy and the West Maui mountains.

Sights

Historic attractions in Lahaina reflect the influence of missionaries, whalers and Hawaiian royalty. Most sites are within a few blocks of the harbor.

Old Lahaina Courthouse MUSEUM

(☎667-9193; www.visitlahaina.com; 648 Wharf St; ⏰9am-5pm) FREE Tucked between a landmark banyan tree and the harbor, Lahaina's 1859 courthouse is a repository of history and art. During the whaling era, smuggling was so rampant that officials deemed this the ideal spot for customs operations, the courthouse and the jail. It also held the governor's office, and in 1898 the US annexation of Hawaii was formally concluded here.

The visitor center, where you can pick up a downtown map, is on the first floor. A small museum on the second floor presents the history of Lahaina, with a focus on Native Hawaiians. There are also two art galleries in the building, both operated by the Lahaina Arts Society.

The Banyan Tree Gallery is on the first floor, in the former post office. The Old Jail Gallery can be found in the basement, and cells that once held drunken sailors now display artwork. The paintings, jewelry and woodwork are creations of island artists who operate the galleries as a cooperative. The entrance to the jail is outside, on the north side of the building. Both galleries are open 9am to 5pm daily.

★**Banyan Tree Square** PARK

(cnr Front & Hotel Sts) Marking the center of town, this leafy landmark sprawls across the entire square and ranks as the largest banyan tree in the USA. Planted as a seedling on April 24, 1873, to commemorate the 50th anniversary of missionaries in Lahaina, the tree has become a forest unto itself, with 16 major trunks reaching across the better part of an acre.

Most weekends artists and craftsmen set up booths beneath the tree's shady canopy.

Baldwin House MUSEUM

(www.lahainarestoration.org/baldwin.html; 120 Dickenson St; adult/child 12 & under $7/free, incl admission to Wo Hing Museum; ⏰10am-4pm) Reverend Dwight Baldwin, a missionary doctor, built this house in 1834, making it the oldest surviving Western-style building in Lahaina. It served as his home and the community's first medical clinic. The coral-and-lava rock walls are 24in thick, which keeps the house cool year-round. The exterior walls are now plastered over, but you can get a sense of their original appearance by looking at the Masters' Reading Room next door.

It took the Baldwins 161 days to get here from their native Connecticut, sailing around Cape Horn at the southern tip of South America. Dr Baldwin's passport and a Baldwin family bible are displayed as well as period furniture. A doctor's 'scale of fees' states that $50 was the price for treating a 'very great sickness' while a 'very small sickness' cost $10. It's only a cold, Doc, I swear. Candelight tours are offered on Friday evenings (6pm to 8pm).

★ Wo Hing Museum MUSEUM

(www.lahainarestoration.org/wohing.html; 858 Front St; admission adult/child 12 & under $7/free, incl admission to Baldwin House; ⏲10am-4pm Sat-Thu, 1-8pm Fri) Built in the early 1900s as a meeting hall for the benevolent society Chee Kung Tong, this two-story temple provided Chinese immigrants with a place to preserve their cultural identity, celebrate festivities and socialize in their native tongue. After WWII Lahaina's ethnic Chinese population scattered and the temple fell into decline. Now restored as a cultural museum, it houses period photos, ceremonial instruments, a teak medicine cabinet circa 1900 and a Taoist shrine.

Be sure to step inside the tin-roof cookhouse out back. It holds a tiny theater showing films of Hawaii shot by Thomas Edison in 1898 and 1906, soon after he invented the motion-picture camera. These grainy black-and-white shots capture poignant images of old Hawaii, with *paniolo* (cowboys) herding cattle, cane workers in the fields and everyday street scenes.

Hale Pa'ahao MUSEUM

(www.lahainarestoration.org/paahao.html; 187 Prison St; ⏲8am-3pm Mon-Fri) FREE As far as prisons go, this stone-walled calaboose doesn't look too intimidating. A remnant of the whaling era, Hale Pa'ahao (Stuck-in-Irons

Lahaina

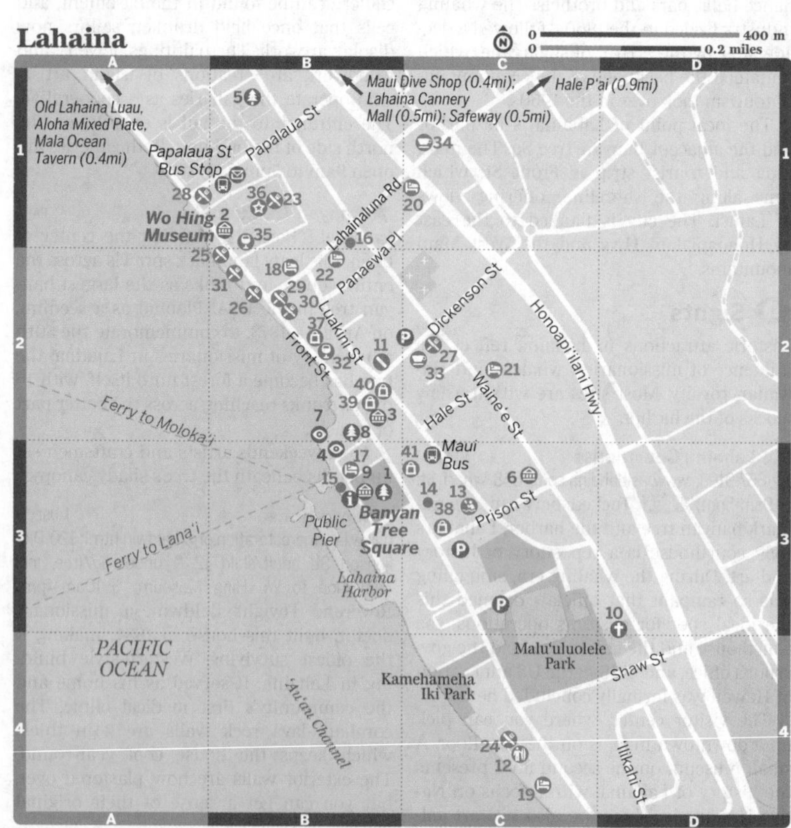

House) was built in 1852 by convicts who dismantled an old fort beside the harbor. The prison looks much as it did 150 years ago.

One of the tiny cells displays a list of arrests in 1855. The top three offenses were drunkenness (330 arrests), 'furious riding' (89) and lascivious conduct (20).

Waine'e (Waiola) Church CHURCH
(535 Waine'e St) The first stone church in Hawaii, Waine'e Church was built in 1832. It has been rebuilt three times over the centuries. The fourth version, renamed Waiola Church, has stood its ground since 1953 and still holds Sunday services. The adjacent **cemetery** is the resting place for Governor Hoapili, who ordered the original church built; Reverend William Richards, Lahaina's first missionary; and Queen Ke'opuolani, wife of Kamehameha the Great and mother of kings Kamehameha II and III.

What calamities did the church face over the years? In 1858 the belfry collapsed. In 1894 royalists, enraged that the minister supported Hawaii's annexation, torched the church to the ground. A second church, built to replace the original, burned in 1947, and the third blew away in a storm a few years later.

Library Grounds HISTORICAL SITE
(680 Wharf St) A cluster of historical sites – the foundations of Kamehameha I's 'palace,' a birthing stone, and a historic lighthouse – surround the Lahaina library. The yard itself was once a royal taro field where Kamehameha III toiled in the mud to instill in his subjects the dignity of labor.

The first Western-style building in Hawaii, the **Brick Palace**, was erected by Kamehameha I around 1800 so he could keep watch on arriving ships. Despite the name, this 'palace' was a simple two-story structure built by a pair of ex-convicts from Botany Bay. All that remains is the excavated foundation, which can be found behind the library.

Lahaina

Top Sights
1 Banyan Tree Square ... B3
2 Wo Hing Museum ... B1

Sights
3 Baldwin House ... B2
4 Brick Palace ... B3
5 Hale Kahiko ... B1
6 Hale Pa'ahao ... C3
7 Hauola Stone ... B2
8 Library Grounds ... B2
9 Old Lahaina Courthouse ... B3
10 Waine'e (Waiola) Church ... D3

Activities, Courses & Tours
Atlantis Submarine ... (see 17)
Goofy Foot Surf School ... (see 12)
11 Lahaina Divers ... B2
12 Maui Surf Clinics ... C4
13 Maui Wave Riders ... C3
14 Pacific Whale Foundation ... C3
15 Reefdancer ... B3
16 Trilogy Excursions ... B1

Sleeping
17 Best Western Pioneer Inn ... B3
18 Lahaina Inn ... B2
19 Lahaina Shores ... C4
20 Lahaina's Last Resort ... C1
21 Outrigger Aina Nalu ... C2
22 Plantation Inn ... B2

Eating
Cool Cat Cafe ... (see 41)
23 Foodland ... B1
Gerard's ... (see 22)
24 I'O ... C4
25 Kimo's ... B2
Lahaina Grill ... (see 18)
26 Ono Gelato Co. ... B2
Pacific'O ... (see 12)
27 Penne Pasta Café ... C2
28 Scoops ... A1
29 Sure Thing Burger ... B2
30 Ululani's Hawaiian Shave Ice ... B2
31 Ululani's Hawaiian Shave Ice ... B2

Drinking & Nightlife
Best Western Pioneer Inn ... (see 17)
32 Fleetwood's on Front St ... B2
33 Lahaina Coolers ... C2
34 MauiGrown Coffee ... C1
35 Moose McGillycuddy's ... B1

Entertainment
Feast at Lele ... (see 24)
36 'Ulalena ... B1

Shopping
Hale Zen Home Décor & More ... (see 27)
Lahaina Arts Society ... (see 9)
37 Lahaina Printsellers ... B2
Lahaina Scrimshaw ... (see 25)
38 Maui Hands Center ... C3
39 Village Gallery ... B2
40 Village Gifts & Fine Arts ... B2
41 Wharf Cinema Center ... C3

MAUI FOR CHILDREN

➡ Peer at mammoth humpbacks on a whale-watching cruise (p324)

➡ Learn to surf on Lahaina's gentle waves (p324)

➡ Walk through the awesome shark tank at Maui Ocean Center (p361)

➡ Tramp the moonlike surface of Haleakalā (p410)

➡ Fly Tarzan-style on a zipline (p337)

➡ Let your kids play with the kids at Surfing Goat Dairy (p392)

From the foundation, walk to the northern shoreline and look down. There lies the **Hauola Stone**, a chair-shaped rock that the ancient Hawaiians believed emitted healing powers to those who sat upon it. It sits just above the water's surface, the middle of three lava stones. In the 14th and 15th centuries royal women sat here while giving birth to the next generation of chiefs and royalty.

About 100ft to the south is the **Lahaina Lighthouse**, the site of the first lighthouse in the Pacific. It was commissioned in 1840 to aid whaling ships pulling into the harbor. The current structure dates from 1916.

Hale Kahiko CULTURAL PARK

(Lahaina Center, 900 Front St; ⌚9am-6pm) FREE They paved paradise and put up a parking lot at Lahaina Center Mall. Fortunately, a patch of earth was reserved for this authentic replication of thatched *hale* (houses) found in ancient, pre-Western Hawaiian villages. The three houses - each with a different function - were hand-constructed true to the period using ohia-wood posts, native *pili* grass and coconut-fiber lashings.

The grounds are planted in native plants that Hawaiians relied upon for food and medicine. Near the entrance, look for copies of John Webber's drawings of native sites. Webber was an official artist on Captain James Cook's third expedition to the Pacific, which lasted from 1776 to 1780. The cultural park is located in the mall parking lot, near Waine'e St.

Lahaina Jodo Mission MISSION

(Map p334; www.lahainajodomission.org; 12 Ala Moana St; ⌚sunrise-sunset) FREE A 12ft-high bronze Buddha sits serenely in the courtyard at this Buddhist mission and looks across the Pacific toward its Japanese homeland. Cast in Kyoto, the Buddha is the largest of its kind outside Japan and was installed here in 1968 to celebrate the centennial of Japanese immigration to the Hawaii islands.

The mission grounds also hold a 90ft pagoda and a whopping 3.5-ton temple bell, which is rung 11 times each evening at 8pm. Inside the temple you can see priceless Buddhist paintings by Haijin Iwasaki.

Hale Pa'i HISTORICAL SITE

(Map p334; ☎667-7040; www.lahainarestoration.org; 980 Lahainaluna Rd; donations appreciated; ⌚10am-4pm Mon-Wed) This small white cottage on the grounds of Lahainaluna High School housed Hawaii's first printing press. Although its primary mission was making the bible available to Hawaiians, the press also produced Hawaii's first newspaper in 1834. Named *Ka Lama* (The Torch), it held the distinction of being the first newspaper west of the Rockies. The adjacent school was founded in 1831, and students operated the press.

The original Rampage Press was so heavily used that it wore out in the 1850s, but several items it printed are on display. There's also an exhibit explaining the history of Hawaii's 12-letter alphabet and a reprint of an amusing 'Temperance Map' ($5), drawn by an early missionary to illustrate the perils of drunkenness.

It's wise to call in advance. Hale Pa'i is staffed by volunteers so opening hours can be iffy. To get there, just follow Lahainaluna Rd two miles northeast from downtown Lahaina.

Activities

Lahaina is not known for its beaches, which are generally shallow and rocky. For swimming and snorkeling, head up the coast to neighboring Ka'anapali.

Cycling

West Maui Cycles BICYCLE RENTAL

(Map p334; ☎661-9005; www.westmauicycles.com; 1087 Limahana Pl; per day $15-60; ⌚9am-5pm Mon-Sat, 10am-4pm Sun) Rents quality hybrid and mountain bikes, as well as cheaper cruisers.

Diving & Snorkeling

Dive boats leave from Lahaina Harbor, offering dives geared for all levels. For the best snorkeling from shore, head north to Ka'anapali or south to some of the beach parks just outside downtown.

Snorkel Bob's SNORKELING

(Map p334; ☎661-4421; www.snorkelbob.com; 1217 Front St; ⏲8am-5pm) For cheap snorkel rentals, try this branch of the local Snorkel Bob chain just north of downtown Lahaina. Snorkel sets begin at $2.50 per day or $9 per week.

Lahaina Divers DIVING

(☎800-998-3483, 667-7496; www.lahainadivers.com; 143 Dickenson St; 2-tank dives from $109; ⏲8am-8pm) Maui's first PADI five-star center offers a full range of dives, from advanced night dives to 'discover scuba' dives for newbies. The latter go to a reef thick with green sea turtles – a great intro to diving.

Maui Dive Shop DIVING, SNORKELING

(Map p334; ☎800-542-3483, 661-5388; www.mauidiveshop.com; 315 Keawe St; 2-tank dives from $120, excursions snorkel/sunset $139/109; ⏲7am-9pm) This full-service operation offers daily scuba and snorkeling trips. Locals recommend the custom-built *Alii Nui,* a 65ft catamaran available for small-group scuba and sunset excursions. Maui Dive Shop has seven locations across Maui; the Lahaina branch is located in Lahaina Gateway Mall. Come to this branch for scuba lessons.

Stand Up Paddleboarding (SUP)

This graceful sport is easy to learn, but Maui's currents can be tricky for newcomers. Beginners should consider a lesson.

Maui Wave Riders STAND UP PADDLEBOARDING

(☎875-4761; www.mauiwaveriders.com; 133 Prison St; ⏲7am-3pm) Limits class size to six students per instructor. Classes last for 90 minutes and start at $60 per person. The company also offers surfing lessons and rents SUP and surf boards. You can call to make reservations until 9pm.

Surfing

Never surfed before? Lahaina is a great place to learn, with first-class instructors, gentle waves and ideal conditions for beginners. The section of shoreline known as

WHALE WATCHING IN MAUI

It's not just honeymooners that converge here – turns out humpback whales prefer Maui too. In winter they can be spotted throughout Hawaii, but the waters off western Maui are the favored haunt for mating and birthing.

Fortunately, humpbacks are coast-huggers, preferring shallow waters to protect their newborn calves. This makes for terrific whale-watching opportunities whether you're on land or on water.

Whale-watching cruises are the easiest way to get close to the action, as the boats know all the best spots and offer a close-up view of humpbacks demonstrating their hulking presence in leaps and bounds. You can readily join a cruise from a green operator like Pacific Whale Foundation (p324) from either Lahaina or Ma'alaea Harbor.

Not that you need a whale-watching cruise to see these 40-ton leviathans. If you're taking the Lana'i ferry in winter, a glimpse of breaching whales is a common bonus; snorkeling tours to Molokini sometimes have sightings en route; and ocean kayaking in south Maui packs good odds of seeing these colossals up close.

From the shore, whale spotting abounds – cliffside lookouts, west-facing beaches, the lanai of your oceanfront condo, most anywhere from Kapalua in the north to Makena in the south. Two particularly rewarding lookouts are Papawai Point, about three miles northwest west of Ma'alaea on the way to Lahaina, and the Wailea Beach walk in Wailea.

Of course, binoculars will bring the action closer. If you're not carrying a pair, stop by the Hawaiian Islands Humpback Whale National Marine Sanctuary headquarters in Kihei where there's a seaside scope. While you're at it, check out the whale displays and discover the difference between a full breach, a spy hop and a peduncle slap. From mid-December through April, the Pacific Whale Foundation posts volunteers at Papawai Point (8am to 2pm daily) to share binoculars and point out whales.

The Whalesong Project maintains an underwater hydrophone off Kihei – visit www.whalesong.net and listen to whales singing in real time. Lucky snorkelers and divers who are in the water at the right time can hear them singing as well – Ulua Beach in Wailea is a top spot for eavesdropping on their haunting music.

World Whale Day festivities are held the third Saturday of February in Kihei (www.mauiwhalefestival.org).

DON'T MISS

FRIDAY TOWN PARTIES

If it's Friday night, suit up for a party in the streets. Created in 2011, the **Maui Town Parties** celebrate local art, food and musicians. On the first Friday of the month the party is held in downtown Wailuku. It moves to Lahaina the second Friday, followed by Makawao and Kihei on the 3rd and 4th Fridays respectively. For exact locations, check www.MauiFridays.com. Festivities start at 6pm.

Lahaina Breakwall, north of Kamehameha Iki Park, is a favorite spot for novices. Surfers also take to the waters just offshore from Launiupoko Beach Park.

Several companies in Lahaina offer surfing lessons. Some guarantee you'll be able to ride a wave after a two-hour lesson or the class is free. Rates vary depending upon the number of people in the group and the length of the lesson, but for a two-hour class expect to pay about $65 in a small group or $150 for private instruction.

Maui Surf Clinics SURFING
(☎244-7873; www.mauisurfclinics.com; Suite 224B, 505 Front St; ⏲8am-5pm; 👪) The oldest surfing school on the island is owned by Nancy Emerson, who was winning international surfing contests by the time she was 14. Maui Surf offers one-, two- and five-hour lessons as well as three-day clinics. The office is available by phone until 8pm.

Goofy Foot Surf School SURFING
(☎244-9283; www.goofyfootsurfschool.com; Suite 123, 505 Front St; ⏲7am-9pm Mon-Sat, 8am-8pm Sun; 👪) This top surf school combines fundamentals with fun. In addition to lessons, it runs daylong surf camps and rents boards to experienced surfers ($20 for two hours).

Tours

Catamarans and other vessels fill the slips in Lahaina Harbor. Catering to the tourist trade, they offer everything from whale-watching trips and glass-bottom boat tours to daylong sails to Lana'i.

★Pacific Whale Foundation ECOTOUR
(☎800-942-5311, 808-249-8811; www.pacificwhale.org; 612 Front St; adult/child 7-12yr from $25/18; ⏲reservations 6am-8pm, snorkel tours from 7am; 👪) The naturalists know their stuff on this nonprofit foundation's cruises – one of the island's best. Several types of trips, all focusing on Maui's spectacular marine environment, leave from Lahaina Harbor. Immensely popular are the whale-watching cruises, which depart several times daily in winter. For a small-group experience, try the new Raft Whalewatch Cruise (adult/child $45/32) on a smooth, anti-slamming raft.

In the unlikely event you don't spot whales on a whale watching trip, your next trip is free. One child under six is free for every one adult.

The company also offers half-day volunteering opportunities in Maui through its popular Volunteering on Vacation program (p418), which has attracted more than 3000 participants. Visit the website for a calendar of their volunteer programs.

★Trilogy Excursions BOAT TOUR
(☎888-225-6284, 874-5649; www.sailtrilogy.com; 180 Lahainaluna Rd; adult/teen 13-18yr/child 3-12yr $199/149/99; ⏲8:30am-4:30pm Mon-Thu, 8:30am-4pm Fri, noon-3pm Sun) This family-run operation specializes in personable ecofriendly catamaran tours that let you get your feet wet. The 10am trip from Lahaina to Lana'i's Hulopo'e Beach includes a cinnamon roll with fruit for breakfast, a BBQ lunch and snorkeling. In winter there's whale watching along the way and you can spot spinner dolphins year-round. Check the website for reduced rates for early and online bookings.

Atlantis Submarine BOAT TOUR
(☎800-381-0237, 661-7827; www.atlantisadventures.com; Pioneer Inn; adult/child under 13yr $109/45; ⏲reservations 7:30am-6pm; 👪) Visit a world usually reserved for divers aboard this 65ft sub that dives to a depth of 130ft to see coral, tropical fish and the sunken *Carthaginian,* a sailing brig that played a leading role in the 1965 movie *Hawaii.* Tours depart from 9am to 2pm from Lahaina Harbor. The reservation office is on Front St at the Pioneer Inn.

Reefdancer BOAT TOUR
(☎800-979-3370, 667-2133; www.mauiglassbottomboat.com; Lahaina Harbor, Slip 6; adult/child 6-12yr per 1hr $35/19, 1½hr $45/25; ⏲reservations 7am-10pm, departures 10am-2:15pm; 👪) A good option for younger kids, this glass-bottom boat has a submerged lower deck lined with viewing windows.

Festivals & Events

Lahaina's top festivals draw huge crowds, with Front St closed to traffic during these events. On Friday nights many Front St galleries are open from 7pm until 10pm for the weekly **Art Night**. Enjoy wine, entertainment and hors d'oeuvres. The Maui Friday Town Party is held in Lahaina on the 2nd Friday of the month (see box on opposite page).

For updated details on Lahaina festivities, contact the **Lahaina Town Action Committee** (event hotline 667-9194; www.visitlahaina.com) or visit the website.

Whale & Ocean Arts Festival ART
Fete the annual humpback whale migration in mid-March at Banyan Tree Sq during this weekend-long celebration with Hawaiian music, hula, games and marine-minded art.

Banyan Tree Birthday Party FESTIVAL
Lahaina celebrates its favorite tree with a two-day birthday party, complete with a birthday cake and nature-inspired art plus games for the *na keiki* (children). It's held on the weekend closest to April 24.

King Kamehameha Celebration PARADE
A parade down Front St and a crafts fair in Banyan Tree Sq, held on different days, honor Kamehameha the Great in mid-June.

Fourth of July PUBLIC HOLIDAY
Bands perform tunes on the lawn of the public library from 5:30pm and fireworks light up the sky over the harbor at 8pm.

Halloween in Lahaina FESTIVAL
Costumed revelers parade up and down Front St on Halloween night. The atmosphere is family friendly in the early evening, but things gets more risqué as the night goes on. There are plenty of police officers, however, to keep things from getting too out of hand. Forget parking; take a bus or taxi to this one or ask your hotel about shuttle service.

Holiday Lighting of the Banyan Tree CHRISTMAS
Lahaina lights Hawaii's biggest tree on the first weekend in December with thousands of colorful lights, accompanied by music, face painting and a craft show. And, of course, Santa shows up for the *na keiki*.

Sleeping

Despite the throngs of tourists filling its streets, Lahaina is surprisingly sparse on places to stay. West Maui's large resort hotels are to the north, where the beaches are better, while Lahaina's accommodations tend to be small and cozy. Between Lahaina and Ma'alaea Harbor to the south are an oceanfront campground and a stylish hillside B&B. Read cancellation policies carefully.

Lahaina's Last Resort HOSTEL $
(808-667-4663, 800-847-0761; www.lahaina-accommodations.com; 252 Lahainaluna Rd; dm from $39; P ❄) Space is tight at this busy hostel that sits beside one of Lahaina's most congested intersections. Figure out what's important to you before booking. The staff is outgoing and super-helpful, and the hostel is just two blocks from Front St. If you're impatient or need a lot of space, however, the small coed bathroom and tight quarters may be a turnoff. No TVs.

MAUI'S BEST BEACHES

Big Beach (p379) For long strolls and bodysurfing.

Charley Young Beach (p364) A secret gem in the heart of Kihei.

Ho'okipa Beach (p381) Where the pros surf and windsurf.

Ka'anapali Beach (p335) A happening resort beach with all the amenities.

Kapalua Beach (p343) Calm-as-a-lake swimming and snorkeling.

Keawakapu Beach (p364) The perfect place for a sunset swim.

Little Beach (p379) A hangout of the clothing-optional crowd.

Malu'aka Beach (p378) The best place to snorkel with turtles.

Pa'iloa Beach (p403) Maui's most stunning black-sand beach.

Ulua Beach (p374) A favorite for morning snorkeling and diving.

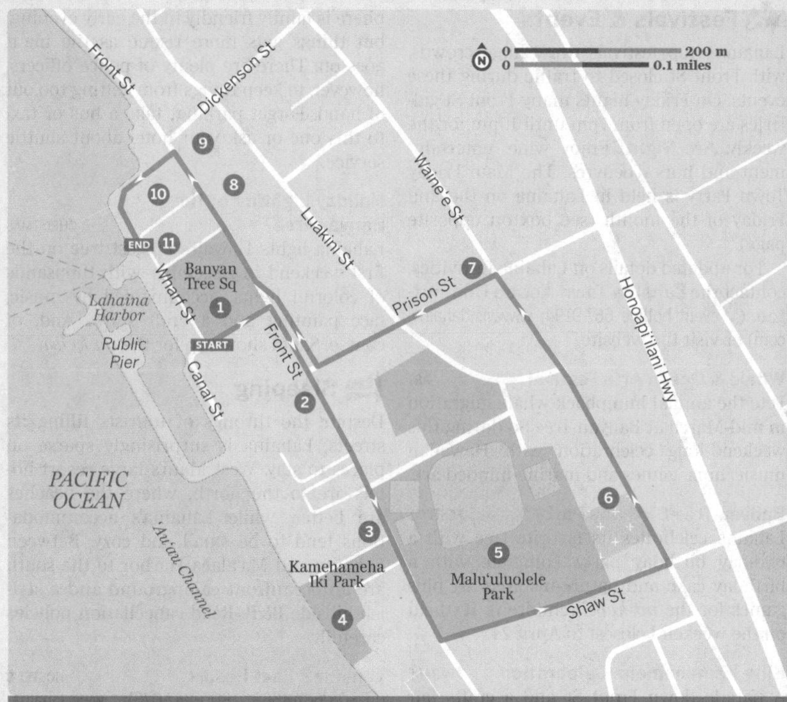

City Walk Lahaina

START BANYAN TREE SQ
FINISH PIONEER INN
LENGTH 1.5 MILES; 2–3 HOURS

Downtown Lahaina is packed with historic sights. Stop by the visitor center (p331) for a free map of Lahaina's Historic Trail. Informative brochures are available at the Baldwin House.

Begin at 1 **Banyan Tree Sq** (p319) with its landmark banyan, the Old Lahaina Courthouse and a coral-block wall just south – ruins from an 1832 fort. Turn right onto Front St to reach 2 **Holy Innocents' Episcopal Church**, at No 561, which has a colorful interior depicting a Hawaiian Madonna, an outrigger canoe and Hawaiian farmers harvesting taro. The site was once a summer home of Hawaii's last monarch, Queen Lili'uokalani.

Just south is the foundation of 3 **Hale Piula**, Lahaina's attempt at a royal palace. It was abandoned in mid-construction because Kamehameha III preferred sleeping in a Hawaiian-style thatched house. Fronted by 4 **Kamehameha Iki Park**, the site is now used by local woodcarvers to build traditional outrigger canoes.

Across the street is 5 **Malu'uluolele Park**, which once held a pond-encircled island, Moku'ula, home to ancient kings and site of an ornate burial chamber. In 1918 it was landfilled to make a county park.

Pivotal figures in 19th-century Maui are buried in the cemetery beside 6 **Waine'e Church** (p321). Evocative inscriptions and cameos adorn many of the old tombstones. Just north, old prison cells at 7 **Hale Pa'ahao** (p320) held drunken whalers serving time.

Back on Front St, 8 **Baldwin House** (p319) is the oldest surviving Western-style building on Maui. The adjacent coral-block 9 **Masters' Reading Room** was an officers' club during whaling days.

Back at the harbor, stop by the 10 **Library Grounds** (p321) for a look at the Brick Palace and Hauola Stone. End with a drink at the 11 **Pioneer Inn** (p330). For many years this was Lahaina's only hotel; Jack London slept here.

★**Plantation Inn** BOUTIQUE HOTEL **$$**
(☎800-433-6815, 667-9225; www.theplantationinn.com; 174 Lahainaluna Rd; r/ste incl breakfast from $158/$248; P ❄ 📶 🏊) The columns and porches at this genteel oasis evoke an earlier era, when sugar cane and pineapples were the island's cash crops. Inside this welcoming retreat, which is set back from the bustle of the waterfront, stylish lanai (porch) rooms, flat-screen TVs and DVD players blend seamlessly with plantation-era decor. Victorian-style standard rooms come with four-poster beds.

A highlight is the complimentary breakfast from on-site Gerard's – try the eggs Florentine – served piping-hot beside the pool. The 18-room property is not on the beach, but guest privileges are provided at sister property Ka'anapali Beach Hotel.

Best Western Pioneer Inn HOTEL **$$**
(☎800-457-5457, 661-3636; www.pioneerinnmaui.com; 658 Wharf St; r $160-190; P ❄ @ 📶 🏊) The Pioneer Inn looks salty and sea-battered on the outside, but step over the threshold of this historic inn for a pleasant surprise. All of the rooms have undergone a stylish revamp, which includes new flat screen TVs, and the accommodating staff keeps the sailing smooth. Ship figureheads and the saloon's swinging doors give a nod to Lahaina's whaling past.

To avoid the chatter of mynah birds in Banyan Park as well as noise from the lively bar, ask for a courtyard room. All rooms are on the second floor, with no elevators.

Outrigger Aina Nalu CONDO **$$**
(☎800-688-7444, 667-9766; www.outrigger.com; 660 Waine'e St; studio/1br/2br from $169/199/225; P ❄ 📶 🏊) Tropical trees shoot through 2nd-floor walkways, giving this complex a Kipling-esque ambience. Though not on the beach, it's just one block from the Wharf Cinema Center. Hotel-style guest services are available in the lobby. Wi-fi is complimentary, but its available in the pool area only. Parking is $15 per day. Check the website for a variety of packages and specials.

Lahaina Inn BOUTIQUE HOTEL **$$**
(☎800-222-5642, 661-0577; www.lahainainn.com; 127 Lahainaluna Rd; r $170-199, ste $222; P 📶) Rooms are tiny but strut their stuff like the chicest of boutique hotels. Think artsy prints, hardwood floors and a touch of greenery. And there's always the balcony if you need more space. The 12-room inn is perched above the highly recommended Lahaina Grill. Per day, parking is $15 and wi-fi is $10. Check the website for seasonal supersaver rates.

★**Lahaina Shores** CONDO **$$$**
(☎661-4835, 866-934-9176; www.lahainashores.com; 475 Front St; studio/1br from $225/305; P ❄ 📶 🏊) They'll have you at aloha at Lahaina Shores, where the staff seems genuinely happy that you're visiting. The seven-story property is the only oceanfront condo complex in central Lahaina operated hotel-style with a front desk and full services. The adjacent beach is a good place for beginner surfers and a small shopping village next door is a convenient venue for nighttime entertainment.

Units are roomy, and even the studios have full kitchen and lanai. Parking is $8 per day and wi-fi is $10 per day.

Eating

Juicy burgers. Macadamia nut–crusted fish. *Kalua* pork (cooked in an underground pit). Spicy ahi poke (cubed, marinated raw fish). And triple berry pie. Need we continue? Lahaina has the finest dining scene on Maui. But fine food draws hungry hordes. Many folks staying in Ka'anapali pour into Lahaina at dinnertime and traffic jams up. Allow extra time and make reservations for the nicer restaurants. For breakfast, consider Aloha Mixed Plate (p328) or Lahaina Coolers (p330).

For groceries, **Foodland** (☎661-0975; www.foodland.com; Old Lahaina Center, 878 Front St; ⏰6am-midnight) and **Safeway** (☎667-4392; www.safeway.com; Lahaina Cannery Mall, 1221 Honoapi'ilani Hwy; ⏰24hr) have everything you need for self-catering, as well as good delis.

LOCAL KNOWLEDGE

FOODLAND POKE

The ahi *poke* (raw tuna) is served fresh, cheap and in endless combinations at the Foodland grocery store seafood counter (www.foodland.com). It's one of the best culinary deals on the island. Our favorite part? The free samples! If you're after a meal to-go, ask for a *poke* bowl, which comes with a hefty helping of rice. The spiced ahi *poke* is outstanding.

CUSTOMER CARDS

To save money on groceries, give the cashier at Foodland your phone number. The store saves your number and you can use it in place of a customer card for discounts on your visits. Safeway accepts customer club cards from the mainland.

Aloha Mixed Plate HAWAII REGIONAL $

(Map p334; ☎661-3322; www.alohamixedplate.com; 1285 Front St; breakfast $7-12, lunch & dinner $6-17; ⏲8am-10pm) This is the Hawaii you came to find: friendly, open-air and on the beach. For a thoroughly Hawaiian experience, order the Ali'i Plate, packed with *laulau* (a steamed bundle of meat and salted butterfish, wrapped in taro and *ti* leaves), *kalua* pig, *lomilomi* salmon (minced and salted with diced tomato and green onion), poi (steamed, mashed taro) and *haupia* (coconut pudding) and, of course, macaroni salad and rice.

The restaurant now serves breakfast, which sticks to the Hawaiian theme – not to mention your ribs – with dishes like loco moco and *kalua* pig omelets.

MauiGrown Coffee CAFE

(☎661-2728; www.mauigrowncoffee.com; 277 Lahainaluna Rd; ⏲6:30am-5pm Mon-Sat) Your view from the porch includes a sugar plantation smokestack and the cloud-capped West Maui Mountains. With 100% Maui-grown coffee, life can be good at 7am.

Sure Thing Burger BURGERS $

(☎214-6982; www.surethingburger.net; Lahaina Marketplace, 790 Front St burgers under $9; ⏲11am-5pm) The folks at this open-air burger shack keep the menu short and the quality high. Choose from one of three burgers: grass-fed Maui beef, fresh ground turkey or veggie (garbanzo beans, lentils, brown rice, spices). Fries, salad and decadent toppings round out the sides. The $4 burger special, from 3pm to 5pm, is one of the best deals going.

One quibble? Make 'em bigger! Find them in the courtyard off Front St just south of Lahainaluna Rd. Cash only.

Honu Seafood & Pizza SEAFOOD, PIZZA $$

(Map p334; ☎667-9390; www.honumaui.com; 1295 Front St; mains $7-29; ⏲lunch 11am-3:30pm, happy hour menu 3:30-4:30pm, dinner 4:30-9:30pm) Named for Maui's famous green turtles, this stylish new venture from restaurateur Mark Ellman is wowing crowds with expansive ocean views and a savory array of wood-fired pizzas, out-of-this world salads and comfort-food dishes. And we haven't even mentioned the fish (from Hawaii, the Pacific Northwest and East Coast). Beer connoisseurs can choose from more than 50 brews.

As you dine, scan the water beside the rocky coast – you might just glimpse a green turtle.

Star Noodle ASIAN $$

(Map p334; ☎667-5400; www.starnoodle.com; 286 Kupuohi St; tapas $3-30, noodle dishes $7-15; ⏲10:30am-10pm) Star Noodle has quickly become one of Lahaina's most popular restaurants, and it's garnering national exposure after chef Sheldon Simeon's appearance on Season 10 of *Top Chef,* in which he was one of three finalists. Inside this sleek noodle shop, diners can nibble from an eclectic array of Asian-fusion share plates. Those seeking heartier fare can dive into the exquisitely flavored noodle dishes, which include garlic noodles, kim chee ramen and a local saimin (Spam included).

A central communal table keeps the ambiance lively.

Kimo's HAWAII REGIONAL $$

(☎661-4811; www.kimosmaui.com; 845 Front St; mains lunch $8-16, dinner $23-36; ⏲11am-10:30pm; 👪) Oh goodness, where to start? The grilled shrimp beet salad? The fresh island fish? The towering hula pie? A locally beloved standby, Hawaiian-style Kimo's keeps everyone happy with reliably good food, a superb water view and a family-friendly setting. Lunch entrées include salads, fresh fish and sandwiches; the dinner menu offers an expanded fish and steak menu.

The delicious Caesar salad is a longtime island fave.

★Mala Ocean Tavern ECLECTIC $$

(Map p334; ☎667-9394; www.malaoceantavern.com; 1307 Front St; mains lunch $12-26, dinner $19-45, brunch $8-15; ⏲11am-9:30pm Mon-Fri, 9am-9:30pm Sat, 9am-9pm Sun) This stylish bistro fuses Mediterranean and Pacific influences with sophisticated flair. Recommended tapas include the kobe beef cheeseburger slathered with caramelized onions and smoked apple bacon, and the 'adult' mac and cheese with mushroom cream and three fancy *fromages*. For entrées, anything with fish is a sure pleaser. And everyone raves over the decadent 'caramel miranda' dessert.

At sunset, tiki torches on the waterfront lanai add a romantic touch.

Cool Cat Cafe DINER $$

(☎667-0908; www.coolcatcafe.com; Wharf Cinema Center, 658 Front St; mains $9-22; ⏲10:30am-10:30pm; 👪) Burgers and sandwiches at this upbeat diner are named for 1950s icons, honoring the likes of Marilyn Monroe, Buddy Holly and Elvis Presley. The 6½-ounce burgers are made with 100% Angus beef and consistently rank as Maui's best.

Penne Pasta Café ITALIAN $$

(☎661-6633; www.pennepastacafe.com; 180 Dickenson St; mains $8-19; ⏲11am-9:30pm) Just off of Front St, this low-key Italian cafe offers a streamlined menu of pastas, pizzas, sandwiches and salads. That said, the food's anything but boring: garlic ahi atop a bed of pesto linguine, roasted squash with almonds, and warm focaccia.

★Lahaina Grill HAWAII REGIONAL $$$

(☎667-5117; www.lahainagrill.com; 127 Lahainaluna Rd; mains $31-79; ⏲6-10pm) The windows at the Lahaina Grill frame a simple but captivating tableau: beautiful people enjoying beautiful food. Trust the crowd gazing in from the sidewalk – there's something special about this restaurant. Once inside, expectations are confirmed by the service and the food. The menu relies on fresh local ingredients given innovative twists and presented with artistic style. A seafood standout is the Maui-onion seared ahi with vanilla-bean jasmine rice. The finishing brush stroke? Always the triple berry pie.

I'O HAWAII REGIONAL $$$

(☎661-8422; www.iomaui.com; 505 Front St; mains $26-44; ⏲5:30-9pm) 🍃 Oceanfront I'O is the handiwork of Maui's most acclaimed chef, James McDonald. The nouveau Hawaii cuisine includes scrumptious creations such as seared, fresh catch in lobster curry and slow-braised short ribs from Maui Cattle. McDonald is so obsessed with fresh produce that he started the O'o Farm (p393) in Kula to grow his own veggies.

Pacific'O ASIAN FUSION, SEAFOOD $$$

(☎667-4341; www.pacificomaui.com; 505 Front St; lunch $13-17, dinner $29-42; ⏲11:30am-9:30pm) 🍃 The entrée descriptions include so much pizzazz at chef James McDonald's chic seaside restaurant that you expect your dinner to arrive high-kicking across the plate. Where else can you enjoy the Bling Bling – an exuberant performance starring pan-roasted lobster tail, filet mignon and tobiko caviar?

Lunch is a tamer affair, with sandwiches and a fish salad, but with the same up-close ocean view.

Gerard's FRENCH $$$

(☎661-8939; www.gerardsmaui.com; 174 Lahainaluna Rd; mains $39-95; ⏲seatings 6-8:30pm) Chef Gerard Reversade takes fresh Lahaina-caught seafood and infuses it with flavors from the French countryside in savory dishes such as the seafood au gratin with shrimp, scallop and lobster sauce and, for dessert, cream puff filled with chocolate mousse and raspberry sauce. Add a candlelit porch, and it makes for a romantic evening.

Drinking & Nightlife

Front St is the center of the action.

★Fleetwood's on Front St BAR

(☎669-6425; www.fleetwoodsonfrontst.com; 744 Front St; ⏲8am-11pm Sun-Thu, 8am-midnight Fri & Sat) With its comfy pillows, cush lounges and ornate accents, this stunning rooftop oasis – owned by Fleetwood Mac drummer

DON'T MISS

LAHAINA'S BEST CHILLY TREATS

I scream, you scream, we all scream for...shave ice. And gelato. And yes, even ice cream. Downtown Lahaina whips up delectable versions of all three. For over-the-top (literally) shave ice, step up to the counter at **Ululani's Hawaiian Shave Ice** (www.ululanisshaveice.com; 819 Front St; ⏲11am-10pm) and pick your tropical flavors. A second location opened in the **Lahaina Marketplace** (790 Front St; ⏲11am-9pm). At **Ono Gelato Co** (☎495-0203; www.onogelatocompany.com; 815 Front St; ⏲8:30am-10:30pm) there's always a crowd gazing at the sinful array of silky gelatos, all prepared with Maui cane sugar. **Scoops** (☎661-5632; 888 Front St; ⏲9am-10pm) serves locally made Lappert's ice cream, but we'll make the choice easy: Kauai Pie, a luscious mix of Kona coffee ice cream, coconut, macadamia nuts and fudge.

Mick Fleetwood – looks a bit Moroccan. But the big views of Lanai and the rippling mountains keep you firmly rooted in Maui. At sunset, a conch-shell blast announces a tiki-lighting ceremony that's followed by a bagpipe serenade – complete with a kilt-wearing Scot! It's all great fun, and it works.

Supplement the sunset ceremony with a Lime in the Coconut cocktail then stick around for some island jazz. If you see the red flag flying, it means Mick is on the island.

Aloha Mixed Plate BAR

(Map p334; ☎661-3322; 1285 Front St; ⌚10:30am-10pm; 📶) Let the sea breeze whip through your hair while lingering over a heady mai tai – come between 2pm and 6pm and they're $3.50. After sunset, listen to Old Lahaina Luau's music beating next door.

Best Western Pioneer Inn PUB

(☎661-3636; 658 Wharf St; ⌚7am-10pm) If Captain Ahab himself strolled through the swinging doors, no one would look up from their grog. With its whaling-era atmosphere, squawking parrot and harborfront veranda, the captain would blend right in at this century-old landmark. For landlubbers, the afternoon happy hour (3pm to 6pm most days) keeps it light on the wallet.

Lahaina Coolers CAFE, BAR

(☎661-7082; www.lahainacoolers.com; 180 Dickenson St; ⌚8am-1am) This eclectic open-air cafe attracts thirtysomethings who come to mingle, munch *pupu* (snacks) and sip wine coolers. As the town's late-night bar, it's the place to head after the dance floor has emptied. Hungover? Come here in the morning for awesome *kalua* pork huevos rancheros.

Moose McGillycuddy's BAR

(☎667-7758; www.moosemcgillycuddys.com; 844 Front St; ⌚7:30am-2am) College kids? Bachelorettes? Dancing fools? Here's your party. This vibrant bar and restaurant attracts a convivial crowd out to party till it drops. With two dance floors, McGillycuddy's jams with live music or DJs most nights of the week. Draft beers are $1 on Tuesdays and Saturdays from 9pm to 1am.

☆ Entertainment

Check the entertainment listings in the free weeklies *Lahaina News* and *MauiTime Weekly*, or just stroll the streets.

Hula & Luau

When it comes to hula and luau (Hawaiian feast), Lahaina offers the real deal. Catching a show is a sure vacation highlight.

Lahaina Cannery Mall HULA

(Map p334; www.lahainacannery.com; 1221 Honoapi'ilani Hwy; ⌚9:30am-9pm Mon-Sat, 9:30am-7pm Sun; 👪) Enjoy free hula shows at Lahaina Cannery Mall at 7pm Tuesday and Thursday, and hula shows for the *na keiki* at 1pm Saturday and Sunday.

★Old Lahaina Luau LUAU

(Map p334; ☎800-248-5828, 667-1998; www.oldlahainaluau.com; 1251 Front St; adult/child 3-12yr $98/68; ⌚5:15-8:15pm Oct-Mar, 5:45-8:45pm Apr-Sep; 👪) From the warm aloha greeting to the extravagant feast and the mesmerizing hula dances, everything is first-rate. No other luau on Maui comes close to matching this one for its authenticity, presentation and all-around aloha. The feast is outstanding, with high-quality Hawaiian fare that includes *kalua* pork, ahi *poke, pulehu* (broiled) steak and an array of salads and sides.

Be sure to stick around for your take-home gift – tasty banana bread. One caveat: the luau often sells out a month in advance, so book ahead.

Feast at Lele LUAU

(☎866-244-5353, 667-5353; www.feastatlele.com; 505 Front St; adult/child 2-12yr $115/85; ⌚5:30-8:30pm Oct-Jan, 6-9pm Feb-Apr & Sep, 6:30-9:30pm May-Aug) 🌿 Food takes center stage at this intimate Polynesian luau held on the beach in front of I'O restaurant. Dance performances in Hawaiian, Maori, Tahitian and Samoan styles are each matched to a food course. With the Hawaiian music, you're served *kalua* pork and *pohole* ferns, with the Maori, duck salad with *poha* (cape gooseberry) dressing and so on. A true gourmet feast.

'Ulalena MODERN DANCE

(☎856-7900; www.mauitheatre.com; Old Lahaina Center, 878 Front St; adult/child from $40/15; ⌚6:30-8pm Mon-Fri) This Cirque du Soleil-style extravaganza has its home at the 680-seat Maui Theatre. The theme is Hawaiian history and storytelling; the medium is modern dance, brilliant stage sets, acrobatics and elaborate costumes. All in all, an entertaining, high-energy performance.

Shopping

Classy boutiques, tacky souvenir shops and flashy art galleries run thick along Front St. You'll find lots of shops under one roof at the **Wharf Cinema Center** (☎661-8748; www.thewharfcinemacenter.com; 658 Front St) and **Lahaina Cannery Mall** (☎661-5304; www.lahainacannery.com; 1221 Honoapi'ilani Hwy).

★**Lahaina Arts Society** ARTS & CRAFTS
(☎661-0111; www.lahaina-arts.com; 648 Wharf St; ⏲9am-5pm) A nonprofit collective representing more than 70 island artists, this extensive gallery covers two floors in the Old Lahaina Courthouse. Works range from avant-garde paintings to traditional weavings.

Lahaina Printsellers ART, MAPS
(☎667-5815; www.printsellers.com; 764 Front St; ⏲9am-10pm) Hawaii's largest purveyor of antique maps, including fascinating originals dating back to the voyages of Captain Cook. The shop also sells affordable reproductions. This location shares space with **Lahaina Giclee**, a gallery selling a wide range of fine quality Hawaiian *giclee* (zhee-clay) digital prints.

Village Gifts & Fine Arts ARTS & CRAFTS
(☎661-5199; www.villagegalleriesmaui.com; cnr Front & Dickenson Sts; ⏲10am-6pm, to 9pm Fri) This one-room shop in the Masters' Reading Room sells prints, wooden bowls, glasswork and other crafts, with a portion of the proceeds supporting the Lahaina Restoration Foundation. The shop's sister property, **Village Gallery** (120 Dickenson St; ⏲9am-9pm), sits behind the store, across the parking lot.

Lahaina Scrimshaw ARTS & CRAFTS
(☎667-9232; www.lahainscrimshawmaui.com; 845 Front St; ⏲9:30am-9:30pm) Contemporary and antique artwork on fossil walrus teeth, mammoth ivory and bone.

Maui Hands Center ARTS & CRAFTS
(☎667-9898; www.mauihands.com; 612 Front St; ⏲10am-7:30pm, to 7pm Sun) Excellent selection of island-made crafts from more than 300 fine artists, jewelers and craftsmen.

Hale Zen Home Décor & More HOMEWARES
(☎661-4802; www.halezen.com; 180 Dickenson St; ⏲10am-8pm Mon-Fri, 10am-9pm Sat, 10am-5pm Sun) The zen is more Balinese than Hawaiian, but this welcoming shop is well-stocked with candles, lotions and gifts.

Information

EMERGENCY

Police (☎244-6400) For non-emergencies.

Police, Fire and Ambulance (☎911)

MEDICAL SERVICES

In an emergency, the hospital (p359) in Wailuku is the nearest facility. For serious accidents, you may want to ask to be transported to Oahu.

Longs Drugs (☎667-4384; www.cvs.com; Lahaina Cannery Mall, 1221 Honoapi'ilani Hwy; ⏲store 7am-midnight, pharmacy 8am-8pm Mon-Fri, 8am-5pm Sat & Sun) Lahaina's largest pharmacy.

Maui Medical Group (☎661-0051; www.mauimedical.com; 130 Prison St; ⏲8am-7pm Mon-Fri, 8am-5pm Sat & Sun) This clinic handles non-emergencies.

MONEY

Bank of Hawaii – Lahaina (www.boh.com; Old Lahaina Center, 130 Papalaua St; ⏲8:30am-4pm Mon-Thu, to 6pm Fri)

POST

Downtown Post Office Station (Old Lahaina Center, 132 Papalaua St; ⏲9am-4pm Mon-Fri)

TOURIST INFORMATION

Lahaina Visitor Center (☎667-9193; www.visitlahaina.com; Old Lahaina Courthouse, 648 Wharf St; ⏲9am-5pm) Inside the old courthouse.

Getting There & Away

The Honoapi'ilani Hwy (Hwy 30) connects Lahaina with Ka'anapali and points north, with Ma'alaea to the south and with Wailuku to the east. Ferries to Lana'i and Moloka'i dock at Lahaina Harbor.

Getting Around

TO/FROM THE AIRPORT

To get to Lahaina from the airport in Kahului, take Hwy 380 south to Hwy 30; the drive takes about 45 minutes. If you're not renting a car, **Executive Shuttle** (☎800-833-2303, 669-2300; www.mauishuttle.com) provides service between Lahaina and the airport, charging $47 for one person and $54 for two.

BICYCLE

For bike rentals head to West Maui Cycles (p322). Check the website for route maps.

BUS

The **Maui Bus** (☎878-4838; www.mauicounty.gov) connects Kahului and Lahaina ($2, one hour) on the Lahaina Islander route, with a stop at Ma'alaea Harbor. At Ma'alaea Harbor, a connection can be made to Kihei via the Kihei Villager. Another route, the Ka'anapali Islander, connects Lahaina and Ka'anapali ($2, 30 minutes). The Kahului and Ka'anapali buses depart from behind the Wharf Cinema Center, on Luakini St, hourly from 6:30am to 8:30pm.

CAR & MOTORCYCLE

Most visitors rent cars upon arrival at Kahului Airport. Motorcycles can be rented at **Lahaina Harley Davidson Rentals** (☎ 667-2800; www.hawaiiharleyrental.com; 602 Front St) for $139 per day, helmet included.

PARKING

Front St has free on-street parking, but there's always a line of cruising cars competing for spots. There's one free lot on tiny Luakini St between Lahainaluna Rd and Dickenson – but get there early, it fills fast. Your best bet is the large parking lot at the corner of Front and Prison Sts where there's free public parking with a three-hour limit. There are also several private parking lots, with the biggest one being Republic Parking on Dickenson St ($10 per day). Otherwise, park at one of the shopping centers and get your parking ticket validated for free by making a purchase.

TAXI

For a taxi in Lahaina, call **Ali'i Cab** (☎ 661-3688) or **LA Taxi** (☎ 661-4545). It's about $17 one-way between Lahaina and Ka'anapali.

WEST MAUI

Simply put, West Maui is where all the action is. Whether your preference is to snorkel beside lava rocks, zipline down the mountains, thwack a golf ball, hike through the jungle or sail beneath the setting sun, West Maui has it all. Ka'anapali is the splashy center, a look-at-me town luring travelers with world-class golf courses, stylish resorts, oceanfront dining and a dazzling, mile-long crescent of beach.

To escape any semblance of a tourist scene, hunker down in Kahana or Napili, lovely seaside communities that are known for their condos and budget-friendly prices. Further north, Hawaiian history and swanky exclusivity have formed an intriguing, and sometimes uneasy, alliance in breezy Kapalua. And for off-the-grid excitement, there's always the wild drive around the untamed northern coast on the Kahekili Hwy.

Lahaina to Ma'alaea

The drive between Lahaina and Ma'alaea offers fine mountain scenery, but in winter everyone is craning seaward to spot humpback whales cruising just offshore. For good whale watching, pull over at Papawai Point midway between mile markers 8 and 9. Note that the road sign reads simply 'scenic point,' but there's a turning lane into it, so slow down and you won't miss it.

Launiupoko Beach Park

Beginner and intermediate surfers head to this **beach park**, a popular surf spot three miles south of Lahaina. The south side of the beach has small waves ideal for beginner surfers, while the north side ratchets it up a notch for those who have honed their skills. These days, you're also likely to see paddle surfers plying through the surf. The park is ideal for families – *na keiki* have a blast wading in the large rock-enclosed shoreline pool and good picnic facilities invite you to linger. Launiupoko is at the traffic lights at mile marker 18.

Sleeping

For B&Bs in Maui, remember to book a room ahead of time. Showing up late at night, unannounced and without reservations, is strongly discouraged.

★Ho'oilo House B&B **$$$**
(Map p334; ☎ 667-6669; www.hooilohouse.com; 138 Awaiku St; r $309;) At this 'zenful' retreat, six Asian- and Maui-themed rooms hug an A-framed community area with a sweeping view of Lana'i. Stylish furnishings differ by room – many contain Balinese imports – but all have a private lanai and an eclectically designed outdoor shower. Breakfast includes fresh muffins and bread, cereal, granola and fruit – often plucked from the property's two-acre organic orchard.

Solar panels installed in 2011 generate 90% of the house's power. There are refrigerators in all rooms.

Olowalu

The West Maui Mountains form a scenic backdrop, giving Olowalu its name, which means 'many hills.' For the moment, the tiny village is marked by the Olowalu General Store, Leoda's Kitchen & Pie Shop and a juice and fruit stand. Construction preparations for the controversial Olowalu Town Project, which calls for the development of 1500 housing units on land just south of the village, were visible from the highway in 2012. The good news? Half of the units will be set aside as affordable housing. The bad? The coral reef at mile marker 14 at Olowalu is a popular snorkeling spot, and environmental groups are concerned that the project will harm the reef.

Sights & Activities

You'll notice snorkelers taking to the water near mile marker 14. Note that the coral reef is shallow and silty, and the 'Sharks May Be Present' signs are the real thing. There were three shark attacks off Olowalu between 1993 and 2002.

Olowalu Petroglyphs ARCHAEOLOGICAL SITE
(Map p334) A short walk behind the general store leads to ancient Hawaiian stone carvings. Park just beyond the water tower at the back of the store. From here, it's a quarter-mile walk up an open road to the petroglyph site. The path is easy to follow; just keep the cinder cone straight ahead of you. As with most of Maui's petroglyphs, these figures are carved into the vertical sides of cliffs rather than on horizontal lava like on the Big Island.

Most of the Olowalu figures have been damaged, but you can still make some out. If you have mobility issues, it's OK to drive to the site, but please be respectful of neighboring landowners.

Sleeping & Eating

Camp Olowalu CAMPING $
(Map p334; ☎661-4303; www.campolowalu.com; 800 Olowalu Village Rd; campsites per adult/child 6-12yr $10/5; P 📶) Bordered by the ocean on one side and a dense thicket of gnarled trees on the other, the setting is pure *Survivor*. But the location, ocean view and simple amenities (cold-water showers, outhouses, picnic tables, drinking water) kick things up a notch. A-frame cabins with six cots are also available for groups for $600 per night.

If you're used to KOAs, then this campground – with its tightly packed sites and what are probably long-term campers – may not be your place. Enter across the highway from the Olowalu General Store then drive southeast beside Hwy 30 to the campground.

Leoda's Kitchen & Pie Shop COMFORT FOOD $
(Map p334; ☎662-3600; www.leodas.com; 820 Olowalu Village Rd, near Honoapi'ilani Hwy, MM 15; mains $6-13, dessert pies $4-9; ⏲10am-8pm) You may want your fat pants for Leoda's, a simple-but-stylish new restaurant from Chef Sheldon Simeon of Star Noodle (p328) and *Top Chef* fame. At the glass-covered counter, which is loaded up with dessert pies, you can order savory pot pies, topping-laden burgers or a rich sandwich like the 'pork, pork...mmm pork.' Prices are a bit steep, but hey, you won't leave hungry – or skinny.

Ukumehame Beach Park & Around

Midway between mile markers 11 and 12 is **Papalaua Wayside Park** (☎661-4685; www.co.maui.hi.us; between MP 11 & 12 Honoapi'ilani Hwy; permit & $5–8 fee required; ⏲no camping on Wed & Thu), a lackluster county park squeezed between the road and the ocean, though it does have firepits, toilets and tent camping under thorny kiawe trees. For more details about obtaining a camping permit, visit the Maui County government website at www.mauicounty.gov. Note that the place buzzes all night with traffic noise.

At mile marker 12 is **Ukumehame Beach Park**. Shaded by ironwood trees, this sandy beach is OK for a quick dip, but because of the rocky conditions most locals stick with picnicking and fishing. Dive and snorkel boats anchor offshore at **Coral Gardens**. This reef also creates **Thousand Peaks** toward its west end, with breaks favored by long-boarders and beginner surfers.

The pull-off for the western end of the **Lahaina Pali Trail** is just south of mile marker 11, on the inland side of the road.

Lahaina to Ka'anapali

The stretch between Lahaina and Ka'anapali offers a couple of roadside beach parks plus two good B&Bs.

Wahikuli Wayside Park

Two miles north of Lahaina, **Wahikuli Wayside Park** occupies a narrow strip of beach flanked by the busy highway. Although the beach is mostly backed by a black-rock retaining wall, there's also a small sandy area. Swimming conditions are usually fine, and when the water is calm you can snorkel near

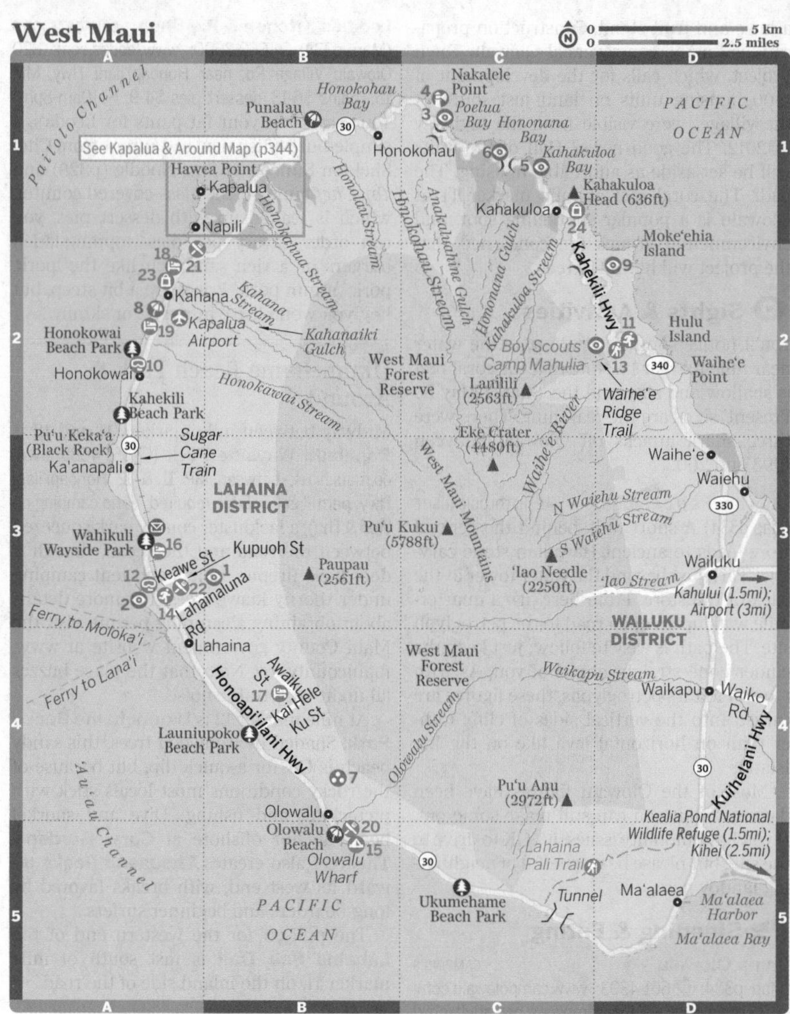

the lava outcrops at the park's south end. The park also has picnic tables, showers and restrooms.

Sleeping

The listed B&B is located in a residential neighborhood between Lahaina and Ka'anapali, inland of Hwy 30. It's just a five-minute drive from the beach.

Guest House B&B $$
(Map p334; ☎800-621-8942, 661-8085; www.mauiguesthouse.com; 1620 A'inakea Rd; s/d incl breakfast $169/189; P ❄ @ 🛜 ≋) Fronted by a saltwater pool, the welcoming Guest House provides amenities that put nearby resorts to shame. Every room has its own hot tub and 42in plasma TV. Stained-glass windows and rattan furnishings reflect a tropical motif. Free perks include beach towels and snorkel gear, a stocked community kitchen and a guest shower you can use before your midnight flight.

In 2012 this eco-minded B&B went 100% solar after installing a 113-panel photovoltaic solar system. The B&B also switched to all LED lighting and is using biodegradable detergents and cleaning products.

West Maui

Sights

1 Hale Pa'i B3
2 Lahaina Jodo Mission A3
3 Nakalele Blowhole C1
4 Nakalele Point Light Station C1
5 Natural Ocean Baths C1
6 Ohai Viewpoint C1
7 Olowalu Petroglyphs B4
Pohaku Kani .... (see 5)
8 Pohaku Park A2
9 Turnbull Studios & Sculpture Garden D2

Activities, Courses & Tours

10 Boss Frog A2
Maui Dive Shop .... (see 23)
Maui Dive Shop .... (see 12)
11 Mendes Ranch D2
12 Snorkel Bob's A3
13 Waihe'e Ridge Trailhead D2
14 West Maui Cycles A3

Sleeping

15 Camp Olowalu B5
16 Guest House A3
17 Ho'oilo House B4
18 Kahana Village A2
19 Noelani A2

Eating

Aloha Mixed Plate .... (see 12)
Farmers Market Deli .... (see 10)
Honu Seafood & Pizza .... (see 12)
20 Leoda's Kitchen & Pie Shop B5
Mala Ocean Tavern .... (see 12)
21 Maui Tacos A2
22 Star Noodle A3

Drinking & Nightlife

Aloha Mixed Plate .... (see 12)
Hawaiian Village Coffee .... (see 23)
Maui Brewing Company .... (see 23)
Napili Coffee Store .... (see 21)

Entertainment

Lahaina Cannery Mall .... (see 12)
Old Lahaina Luau .... (see 12)

Shopping

23 Kahana Gateway A2
24 Kaukini Gallery & Gift Shop C1

Hanaka'o'o Beach Park

This long **beach**, extending south from Ka'anapali Beach Resort, has a sandy bottom and water conditions that are usually safe for swimming. However, southerly swells, which sometimes develop in summer, can create powerful waves and shorebreaks, while the occasional *kona* (leeward side) storm can kick up rough water conditions in winter. Snorkelers head down to the second clump of rocks on the south side of the park, but it really doesn't compare with sites further north. The park has full facilities and is one of only two beaches on the entire West Maui coast that has a lifeguard. Hanaka'o'o Beach is also called 'Canoe Beach,' because West Maui outrigger canoe clubs practice here in the late afternoon. A small immigrant cemetery dating from the 1850s marks the entrance.

Ka'anapali

POP 1045

Whether it's your honeymoon, your birthday, a bachelor party or a girlfriend getaway, Ka'anapali is the place to celebrate – and strut your stuff. Maui's flashiest resort destination boasts three miles of sandy beach, a dozen oceanfront hotels, two 18-hole golf courses and an ocean full of water activities. Here you can sit at a beachfront bar with a tropical drink, soak up the gorgeous views of Lana'i and Moloka'i across the channel and listen to guitarists strum their wiki-wacky-woo.

Beaches

★Ka'anapali Beach BEACH

Home to West Maui's liveliest beach scene, this gorgeous stretch of sand unfurls alongside Ka'anapali's resort hotels, linking the Hyatt Regency Maui with the Sheraton Maui one mile north. Dubbed 'Dig-Me Beach' for all the preening, it's a vibrant spot. Surfers, boogie boarders and parasailers rip across the water while sailboats pull up on shore. Check with the hotel beach huts before jumping in, however, as water conditions vary seasonally and currents are sometimes strong.

For the best snorkeling, try the underwater sights off **Pu'u Keka'a**, also known as Black Rock. This lava promontory protects the beach in front of the Sheraton. Novices stick to the sheltered southern side of the landmark rock – where there's still a lot to see – but the shallow coral here has been stomped to death. If you're a confident swimmer, the less-frequented horseshoe cove cut into the tip of the rock is the real prize, teeming with tropical fish, colorful coral and sea turtles. There's often a current to contend with off the point, which can make getting to the horseshoe tricky, but when it's calm you can swim right in. Pu'u Keka'a is also a popular shore-dive spot; any of the beach huts can set you up.

Kahekili Beach Park BEACH

To escape the look-at-me crowds clustered in front of the resorts, head to this idyllic golden-sand beach at Ka'anapali's less-frequented northern end. The swimming's better, the snorkeling's good and you'll find plenty of room to stretch without bumping into anyone else's beach towel. The park has showers, restrooms, a covered picnic pavilion and BBQ grills.

Access is easy, and there's lots of free parking. Snorkelers will find plenty of coral and marine life right in front of the beach. Sea turtle sightings are common.

From the Honoapi'ilani Hwy, turn *makai* (toward the ocean) 0.2 miles north of mile marker 25 onto Kai Ala Dr, then bear right.

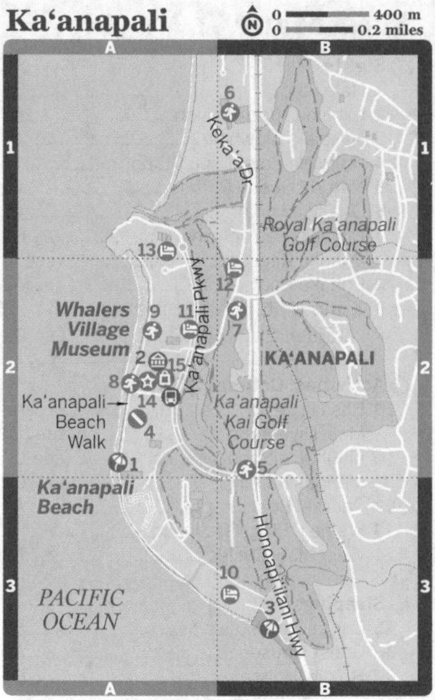

Sights

★Whalers Village Museum MUSEUM

(☎661-5992; www.whalersvillage.com/museum.htm; Level 3, Whalers Village, 2435 Ka'anapali Pkwy; adult/child 6-18yr $3/1; ⏱10am-6pm) Lahaina was a popular stop for whaling ships traveling between Japan and the Arctic in the mid-1800s. This fascinating museum reveals the hardships and routines of the whaler's life. Authentic period photographs, ship logs, harpoons, 19th-century scrimshaw and intriguing interpretive plaques sound the depths of whaling history. Particularly eye-opening is the life-size forecastle. How 20 crewmen could live for weeks in this tiny room – without coming to blows or losing their minds – is a mystery. Also impressive is the intricate rigging on the built-to-scale replica of an 1850s-era whaling ship.

Interest piqued? Stick around for a humpback whale talk offered Thursday to Saturday at 11am and 2pm. Also look for the full-size sperm whale skeleton at the front entrance of the shopping center.

Ka'anapali Beach Walk WALKING TRAIL

Smell the salt air, take in the opulent resort sights and check out the lively beach scene along the mile-long walk between the Sheraton and Hyatt hotels. Both the Hyatt and the Westin are worth a detour for their dazzling garden statuary and landscaping replete with free-form pools and rushing waterfalls. The Hyatt's rambling lobbies are hung with heirloom Hawaiian quilts and meditative Buddhas. Don't miss the pampered black African penguins who love to waddle around their four-star penguin cave.

At the southern end of the walk the graceful 17ft-high bronze sculpture *The Acrobats*, by Australian John Robinson, makes a dramatic silhouette at sunset. In the early evening, you'll often be treated to entertainment from the beachside restaurants.

Ka'anapali

Activities

At Sea

★Teralani Sailing SAILING

(☎661-0365; www.teralani.net; Whalers Village, 2435 Ka'anapali Pkwy; outings adult/teen 13-20yr/child 3-12yr from $53/42/31; ⏱hours vary; 👪) This friendly outfit offers a variety of sails on two custom-built catamarans that depart from the beach beside Whalers Village. The easygoing sunset sail is an inspiring introduction to the gorgeous West Maui coast. Snorkel sails and whale-watching outings are additional options, but no matter which you choose, you'll find a congenial crew, an open bar/morning cocktail and decent food.

Ka'anapali

Note the cancellation policy and $5-per-person fuel charge.

Ka'anapali Dive Company DIVING
(☎800-897-2607; www.goscubamaui.com; Westin Maui Resort & Spa; 1-tank dives $69; ⏰7am-5pm) Want an easy introduction to diving? These are the people to see. The introductory dive ($99) for novices starts with instruction in a pool and moves to a guided dive from the beach. It also offers guided beach dives for certified divers. No rentals. Walk up or make reservations through the 800 number, which is the American Express Tours and Activities line.

Trilogy Ocean Sports WATER SPORTS
(☎661-7789; www.sailtrilogy.com; Ka'anapali Beach Walk; ⏰7:45am-sunset) From a beach hut in front of the Ka'anapali Beach Hotel, these folks can get you up and riding a board with a two-hour surfing lesson ($70). Snorkel sets rent for $20 per day and boogie boards rent for $18 a day. Stand-up paddleboards cost $25 for the first hour then $15 for each additional hour.

On Land

Skyline Eco-Adventures ZIPLINING
(☎878-8400; www.zipline.com; 2580 Keka'a Dr, Fairway Shops; 4hr outing incl breakfast/lunch $150; ⏰departs on the hour 7am-2pm) Got a need for speed? The Ka'anapali course takes you two miles up the wooded cliffsides of the West Maui mountains and sets you off on a free-glide along eight separate lines above waterfalls, stream beds and green valleys. Eco-stewardship is a mission of the company and guides discuss local flora and fauna. If it's drizzly and breezy? Hold on tight and no cannonballs!

Ka'anapali Golf Courses GOLF
(☎661-3691; www.kaanapaligolfcourses.com; 2290 Ka'anapali Pkwy; greens fee $205-249, after 1pm $99-129; ⏰hours vary seasonally, opens about 6:45am) Of the two courses, the more demanding is the **Royal Ka'anapali Golf Course**, designed by Robert Trent Jones. It's tournament grade with greens that emphasize putting skills. The **Ka'anapali Kai Golf Course** is shorter and more of a resort course. The setting isn't as spectacular as the courses in Kapalua, but it tends to be less windy and the greens fees are lower.

If you're a guest at a hotel or condo in the Ka'anapali Resort, ask for the guest rate, which will save you about $50.

Tour of the Stars STARGAZING
(☎667-4727; 200 Nohea Kai Dr; adult/child $25/15) Enjoy stellar stargazing atop the Hyatt resort. These 50-minute viewings, which are open to non-guests, are limited to 14 people, use a 16in-diameter telescope and are held at 8pm and 9pm on clear nights. Romantic types should opt for the couples-only viewing at 10pm Friday and Saturday, which rolls out champagne and chocolate-covered strawberries ($45 per person).

SPIRITS' LEAP

According to traditional Hawaiian beliefs, Pu'u Keka'a (Black Rock, p335), the westernmost point of Maui, is a place where the spirits of the dead leap into the unknown to be carried to their ancestral homeland. The rock is said to have been created during a scuffle between the demigod Maui and a commoner who questioned Maui's superiority. Maui chased the man to this point, froze his body into stone then cast his soul out to sea. Today, daring teens wait their turn to leap off the rock for a resounding splash into the cove below.

Royal Lahaina Tennis Ranch TENNIS
(☎667-5200; www.royallahaina.com/actvities.cfm; 2780 Keka'a Dr; per person per day $15; ⊙pro shop 8am-noon daily & 2-6pm Mon-Fri, 2-5pm Sat & Sun) Named the '2010 Facility of the Year' by the USTA, this is the largest tennis complex in West Maui, with four courts lit for night play. Rackets and shoes can be rented. Private lessons and group clinics are available.

Festivals & Events

Maui Onion Festival FOOD
(www.whalersvillage.com) Held at Whalers Village in late April or early May, this popular celebration highlights everything that can be done with Maui's famed Kula onions.

Hula O Na Keiki HULA
(www.kbhmaui.com; adult/child 12 & under $12/6) Children take center stage at this hula dance competition in early to mid-November, which features some of the best *na keiki* dancers in Hawaii. Held at the Ka'anapali Beach Hotel.

Sleeping

The following accommodations are on the beach or within walking distance of it.

★**Ka'anapali Beach Hotel** RESORT $$
(☎800-262-8450, 661-0011; www.kbhmaui.com; 2525 Ka'anapali Pkwy; r $169-289; P❄@🛜🏊) This welcoming property feels like summer camp – in a good way. The hotel is older than its neighbors and the style is far from posh, but it has its own special charms: warm staff, nightly hula shows, an outdoor tiki bar, tidy grounds framed by palm trees, and an enviable location on a gorgeous stretch of beach. Family-friendly activities, from lei-making to ukulele singalongs, assure that the *na keiki* will never be bored.

For churchgoers, there's a non-denominational outdoor service on Sundays. On your last day, bring a camera and a hankie to your farewell lei ceremony. Parking and wi-fi are each $10 per day.

Outrigger Maui Eldorado CONDO $$
(☎888-339-8585, 661-0021; www.outrigger.com; 2661 Keka'a Dr; studio/1br/2br from $155/215/375; P❄@🛜🏊) Have a golfer in your family? Then consider this quiet condo development, which borders the Royal Ka'anapali Golf Course. How close are units to the fairways? The in-room warning sign says it all: 'Beware of flying golf balls in the lanai areas.' Units are not on the beach, but the complex isn't far from the ocean and the resort shuttle stops out front.

The best rooms are the large studios which have kitchens set apart from the bedroom area. All units have washers and dryers. Parking is $8 per day.

Sheraton Maui RESORT $$$
(☎866-716-8109, 661-0031; www.sheraton-maui.com; 2605 Ka'anapali Pkwy; r/ste from $389/649; P❄@🛜🏊) Hmm, darling. Shall we snorkel beside turtles? Or watch whales breach from the room? Or catch the sunset cliff dive? The choices are many at this sleek hotel, which sprawls across 23 acres at the north end of the Ka'anapali Beach Walk. The beach itself bumps against Pu'u Keka'a (Black Rock), renowned for its snorkeling and silhouette.

Rooms have rich wood tones and Hawaiian prints; grounds have night-lit tennis courts, a fitness center, a lava-rock swimming pool and the spa at Pu'u Keka'a. The resort celebrated its 50th anniversary in 2013. The $30 daily resort fee includes parking, Lahaina shuttle service and wi-fi.

Hyatt Regency Maui Resort & Spa RESORT $$$
(☎800-492-1234, 661-1234; www.maui.hyatt.com; 200 Nohea Kai Dr; r/ste from $449/769; P❄@🛜🏊) The airy atrium is tricked out with cockatoos in palm trees and extravagant artwork, the grounds given over to gardens and swan ponds. Kids of all ages will thrill in the water world of meandering pools, swim-through grottos and towering water slides. As part of a $21 million renovation project, the lobby was modernized and guest rooms 'refreshed' – picture monochromatic walls

and furnishings accented with bold splashes of color and flat screen TVs.

The $25 daily resort fee includes wi-fi, but parking is a separate $14 per day.

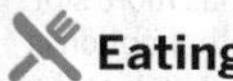

Eating

Don't limit yourself to Ka'anapali's restaurants. Many of Maui's top chefs are just a skip down the road in Lahaina.

★Hula Grill & Barefoot Bar — HAWAII REGIONAL **$$**

(☎667-6636; www.hulagrillkaanapali.com; Whalers Village, 2435 Ka'anapali Pkwy; bar lunch $11-19, bar dinner $13-20, dining room mains $19-32; ⊙bar 10:45am-11pm, dining room 4:45-9:30pm) The Barefoot Bar is your quintessential Maui scene: coconut-frond umbrellas, the sand beneath your sandals and the guy strumming the guitar. The ambience impresses most, and there's no better place on the beach walk to sip mai tai and nibble *pupu*. The Kapulu Joe pork sandwich with macnut slaw – add a dash of chili water – is reliably good. Dinner inside at the restaurant kicks it up a notch with spicy kiawe-grilled seafood.

Live music is offered all day at the Barefoot Bar.

Roy's Kaanapali — HAWAII REGIONAL **$$$**

(☎669-6999; www.royshawaii.com; Ka'anapali Resort, 2290 Ka'an-apali Parkway; lunch $13-19, dinner $16-42; ⊙lunch 11am-2pm, bar pupus 2-5:30pm, dinner from 5:30pm) In 2012 the Maui outpost of chef Roy Yamaguchi's upscale dining empire moved from Kahana to the golf course clubhouse at the Ka'anapali Resort. Here, big-windowed views of the greens are a pleasant backdrop for the exquisitely prepared island and regional fare. Savory entrées include the sashimi-like blackened ahi with Chinese mustard and Yama Mama's meatloaf with shitake gravy.

Son'z at Swan Court — ECLECTIC **$$$**

(☎667-4506; www.sonzrestaurant.com; Hyatt Regency Maui Resort & Spa, 200 Nohea Kai Dr; mains $31-50; ⊙5:30-9:30pm Mon-Sat) Between the water-falls, the swan pond and the tiki torches, this is Ka'anapali's most romantic night out. The award-winning cuisine includes the expected fine-dining steak and lobster, but many appetizers and entrées highlight the best of Maui, from the kula vegetables to ravioli with Surfing Dairy goat cheese and the tenderloin with local coffee marinade. Incredible wine list, too.

Drinking & Entertainment

Most seaside bars offer live music in the evening. Luau and hula shows are also popular. Check www.mauitime.com for performers and schedules.

Live Music

The two places listed here, as well as the Hula Grill & Barefoot Bar, have live music throughout the afternoon and evening. It's typically Jimmy Buffett–style guitar tunes, but it's occasionally spiced up with some ukulele strumming.

Leilani's — LIVE MUSIC

(☎661-4495; www.leilanis.com; Whalers Village, 2435 Ka'anapali Pkwy; ⊙outdoor grill 10:30am-10:30pm, dining room 4:45-9:30pm) This open-air bar and restaurant beside the beach is the place to linger over a cool drink while catching a few rays. It also has a good grill and *pupu* menu. Live music Thursday through Sunday from 3pm to 5pm.

Hyatt Regency Maui Resort & Spa — LIVE MUSIC

(☎661-1234; www.maui.hyatt.com; 200 Nohea Kai Dr) There's live music poolside at Umalu from 6pm to 8pm nightly.

Hula, Luau & Theater

Ka'anapali Beach Hotel — HULA

(☎661-0011; www.kbhmaui.com; 2525 Ka'anapali Pkwy; ⊙6-9pm; 👪) Maui's most Hawaiian hotel cheerfully entertains anyone who chances by between 6pm and 9pm, beginning with a free hula show and Hawaiian music. Enjoy mai tai and brews at the adjacent Tiki Bar, with music and dancing nightly in the Tiki Courtyard.

Sheraton Maui — CLIFF DIVE

(☎661-0031; www.sheraton-maui.com; 2605 Ka'anapali Pkwy; ⊙sunset) Everybody swings by to watch the torch-lighting and cliff-diving ceremony from Pu'u Keka'a that takes place at sunset. There's also live music afterwards at the Cliff Dive Bar until about 8pm.

Drums of the Pacific — LUAU

(☎667-4727; www.maui.hyatt.com; Hyatt Regency Maui Resort & Spa, 200 Nohea Kai Dr; adult/teen 13-20yr/child 6-12yr $105/61/49; ⊙from 5pm Oct-Mar, from 5:30pm Apr-Sep; 👪) Ka'anapali's best luau includes an *imu* ceremony (unearthing of a roasted pig from an underground oven), an open bar, a Hawaiian-style buffet dinner and a flashy South Pacific dance and music show.

Whalers Village HULA, DANCE
(☎661-4567; www.whalersvillage.com; 2435 Ka'anapali Pkwy; ⊙7-8pm Mon, Wed & Sat) Ka'anapali's shopping center hosts free hula and Polynesian dance performances from 7pm to 8pm on Monday, Wednesday and Saturday. Check the website for a monthly calendar of events and classes.

Shopping

Whalers Village MALL
(☎661-4567; www.whalersvillage.com; 2435 Ka'anapali Pkwy; ⊙9:30am-10pm) You'll find more than 70 shops at the Whalers Village shopping center.

ABC Store ACCESSORIES
(☎667-9700; www.abcstores.com; Whalers Village; ⊙7am-11pm) Stop here for sunblock and great beach totes.

Honolua Surf CLOTHING
(☎661-5455; www.honoluasurf.com; Whalers Village; ⊙9am-10pm) This is the place to pick up Maui-style board shorts and other casual beachwear.

Honolua Wahine WOMEN'S CLOTHING
(☎661-3253; www.honoluasurf.com; Whalers Village; ⊙9am-10pm) Get your bikinis here.

Lahaina Printsellers ART, MAPS
(☎661-7617; www.printsellers.com; Whalers Village; ⊙9am-10pm) Packable Hawaiian prints and maps.

Martin & MacArthur ARTS & CRAFTS
(☎667-7422; www.martinandmacarthur.com; Whalers Village; ⊙9:30am-10pm) Head to Martin & MacArthur for museum-quality Hawaiian-made wood carvings, paintings and other crafts.

Getting Around

The **Maui Bus** (☎871-4838; www.mauicounty.gov; $2 per ride; ⊙most routes 6am-8pm) connects Whalers Village Shopping Center in Ka'anapali with the Wharf Cinema Center in Lahaina hourly from 6am to 9pm (and on the half hour between 2pm and 6pm), and runs north up the coast to Kahana and Napili hourly from 6am to 8pm.

The free Ka'anapali Trolley shuttles between the Ka'anapali hotels, Whalers Village and the golf courses about every 30 minutes between 10am and 10pm. The trolley schedule is posted at the Whalers Village stop.

Cabs often line up beside the trolley and Maui Bus stop in front of Whalers Village on Ka'anapali Pkwy.

Ka'anapali's resort hotels offer free beach parking for non-guests, but the spaces allotted are so limited that they commonly fill up by mid-morning. Your best bet for beach parking is at the south end of the Hyatt, which has more slots on offer than the other hotels. Another option is the pay parking at Whalers Village, which costs $3 per half-hour (parking validation varies by merchant).

Honokowai

POP HONOKOWAI-NAPILI 7261

Honokowai and its condos may not have the glamour and pizzazz of pricier Ka'anapali to the south, but it has its virtues. It's convenient, affordable and low-rise, and the ocean views are as fine as in the upscale resorts. Another perk: in winter this is the best place in West Maui to spot passing whales right from your room lanai.

The main road, which bypasses the condos, is Honoapi'ilani Hwy (Hwy 30). The parallel shoreline road is Lower Honoapi'ilani Rd, which leads into Honokowai.

Beaches

Honokowai Beach Park BEACH
(🚻) The real thrills here are on land, not in the water. This family-friendly park in the center of town has cool playground facilities for kids and makes a nice spot for a picnic. Forget swimming, though. The water is shallow and the beach is lined with a submerged rock shelf. Water conditions improve at the south side of town, and you could continue walking along the shore down to lovely Kahekili Beach Park at the northern end of Ka'anapali.

Activities

Boss Frog SNORKELING
(Map p334; ☎665-1200; www.bossfrog.com; 3636 Lower Honoapi'ilani Rd; per day from $1.50; ⊙8am-5pm) Offers great rental prices for a mask, snorkel and fins.

Sleeping

Noelani CONDO $$
(Map p334; ☎800-367-6030, 669-8374; www.noelani-condo-resort.com; 4095 Lower Honoapi'ilani Rd; studios from $157, 1/2/3br from $197/290/357; 📶🏊) This small condo complex is so close to the water you can sit on your lanai and watch turtles swimming in the ocean. The 43 rentable units cover a wide range, from cozy studios to three-bedroom suites, but all have

ocean views. Two heated pools, a Jacuzzi, a small exercise room and concierge services are additional perks.

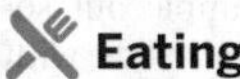

Eating

Farmers Market Deli DELI $

(Map p334; ☎669-7004; 3636 Lower Honoapi'ilani Rd; sandwiches under $6; ⏰7am-7pm; ✎) Stop here for healthy takeout fare. The salad bar (with free samples) includes organic goodies and hot veggie dishes. The smoothies and sandwiches are first-rate and Maui-made ice cream is sold by the scoop. On Monday, Wednesday and Friday mornings vendors sell locally grown produce in the parking lot from 7am to 11pm.

★Honokowai Okazuya INTERNATIONAL $$

(☎665-0512; 3600 Lower Honoapi'ilani Rd; mains $10-18; ⏰11am-2:30pm & 4:30pm-8:30pm Mon-Sat) At this place, plate lunch specialties take a gourmet turn. But the appeal is not immediately apparent: the place is tiny, prices are high and the choices seem weird (kung pao chicken *and* spaghetti with meatballs?). Then you nibble the piping-hot Mongolian beef. Hmm. Chomp chomp. That's pretty interesting. Gulp gulp. Mmm, spicy.

And then...the whole darn container is empty. Cash only.

Java Jazz & Soup Nutz ECLECTIC $$

(☎667-0787; www.javajazz.net; Honokowai Marketplace, 3350 Lower Honoapi'ilani Rd; breakfast $3-15, lunch $10-15, dinner $10-55; ⏰6am-9pm Mon-Sat, to 5pm Sun) With a menu as eclectic as its decor, this arty cafe never disappoints. Breakfast packs 'em in with everything from pancakes to frittata; lunch revolves around Greek salads and innovative sandwiches. Dinner gets downright meaty with tasty flame-grilled filet mignon.

Kahana

Trendy Kahana, the village north of Honokowai, boasts million-dollar homes, upscale beachfront condominiums and Maui's only microbrewery.

Sights & Activities

The sandy **beach** fronting the village offers reasonable swimming. Park at seaside **Pohaku Park** (Map p334) and walk north a couple of minutes to reach the beach. Pohaku Park itself has an offshore break called **S-Turns** that attracts surfers.

Maui Dive Shop DIVING, SNORKELING

(Map p334; ☎669-3800; www.mauidiveshop.com; Kahana Gateway, 4405 Honoapi'ilani Hwy; 2-tank dives from $120, snorkel sets per day $8; ⏰8am-9pm) Come here for information about a full range of dives and to rent snorkel gear.

Sleeping

Kahana Village CONDO $$$

(Mapp334; ☎800-824-3065,669-5111; www.kahanavillage.com; 4531 Lower Honoapi'ilani Rd; 2/3br from $300/510;) With their A-frame ceilings, airy lofts and oceanfront views, the 2nd-story units here have a fun 'vacation' vibe. The breezy appeal of the interior is well-matched outside with lush tropical flora and weekly mai tai parties with live Hawaiian music. Some condos have views of Lana'i while others face Moloka'i. Every unit has a lanai, full kitchen and washer and dryer. Five night minumum stay.

Eating & Drinking

Hawaiian Village Coffee CAFE $

(Map p334; ☎665-1114; www.hawaiianvillagecoffee.com; Kahana Gateway, 4405 Honoapi'ilani Hwy; snacks & sandwiches under $8; ⏰6am-6pm) Off-duty surfers shoot the breeze at this easy-going coffee shop that sells pastries and grab-and-go sandwiches. Surf the net on one of five computers in back (20 minutes for $3).

Maui Brewing Company BREWERY

(Map p334; ☎669-3474; www.mauibrewingco.com; Kahana Gateway, 4405 Honoapi'ilani Hwy; mains $12-25; ⏰11am-midnight) From the seafood burger to the *kalua* pork pizza, pub grub takes a Hawaiian twist at this cavernous brewpub. The company, honored as one of Hawaii's top green businesses in 2008, implements sustainable practices where it can. The Bikini Blonde lager, Big Swell IPA, Mana Wheat and Coconut Porter are always on tap, supplemented by eight to 10 seasonal and specialty brews.

Napili

Napili is a tranquil bayside community tucked between the posh grounds of Kapalua to the north and the hustle and bustle of Ka'anapali to the south. For an oceanfront retreat that's a bit more affordable – but not too far from the action – we highly recommend this sun-kissed center of calm.

Sights

The deep golden sands and gentle curves of **Napili Beach** offer good beachcombing at any time and excellent swimming and snorkeling when it's calm. Look for green turtles hanging out by the rocky southern shore. Big waves occasionally make it into the bay in winter, and when they do it's time to break out the skimboards – the steep drop at the beach provides a perfect run into the surf.

Sleeping

Napili Bay is surrounded by older condos and small, mellow resorts.

Outrigger Napili Shores CONDO $$
(Map p344; ☎800-688-7444, 669-8061; www.outrigger.com; 5315 Lower Honoapi'ilani Rd; studio/1br from $205/249;) This palm-lined condo complex with solar-heated pools, a hot tub and croquet sits at the southern tip of Napili Bay. Grounds are well-maintained, and the long central lawn unfurls toward the Gazebo, one of Maui's top breakfast spots. Prices are reasonable, and you can often find fantastic discounts on its website. Wi-fi available in the lobby and near the pool.

★ **Hale Napili** CONDO $$
(Map p344; ☎800-245-2266, 669-6184; www.halenapili.com; 65 Hui Dr; studios $185-275, 1br $320;) The aloha of the Hawaiian manager ensures lots of repeat guests at these tidy condos smack on the beach. The place is a welcome throwback to an earlier era, when everything in Maui was small and personable. The 18 neat-as-a-pin units have tropical decor, full kitchens and oceanfront lanai. There's a Keurig coffeemaker at the reception desk.

Mauian CONDO, HOTEL $$
(Map p344; ☎800-367-5034, 669-6205; www.mauian.com; 5441 Lower Honoapi'ilani Rd; studios with kitchens from $218, r $196; @) Most condos in Napili wear their age gracefully, but not the sassy Mauian, a 44-room condo/hotel hybrid kicking up her heels like a teenager. Bamboo ceilings, frond prints, crisp whites and browns, Tempur-Pedic mattresses – rooms are sharp, stylish and comfortable, and come with a lanai with big views. Units do not have TVs or phones, but both are available in the common area.

Napili Kai Beach Resort CONDO, HOTEL $$$
(Map p344; ☎800-367-5030, 669-6271; www.napilikai.com; 5900 Lower Honoapi'ilani Rd; r/studios from $305/380; @) The simple but sophisticated lobby lures visitors inside with an open-air view of the ocean. It's the perfect calling card for this pampering resort, which covers 10 acres at the northern end of Napili Bay. The units, which tastefully blend Polynesian decor with Asian touches, have a lanai and, in most cases, kitchenettes.

For modern-style rooms with oceanfront views, stay in the Puna Point, Puna 2 or Lani 1 buildings. Some units have air-con, so ask when booking.

Eating

★ **Gazebo** CAFE $
(Map p344; ☎669-5621; Outrigger Napili Shores, 5315 Lower Honoapi'ilani Rd; meals $8-12; ⏲7:30am-2pm) Locals aren't kidding when they tell you to get here early to beat the crowds. But a 7:10am arrival is worth it for this beloved open-air restaurant – a gazebo on the beach – with a gorgeous waterfront setting. The tiny cafe is known for its breakfasts, and sweet tooths love the white chocolate mac-nut pancakes.

Meal-size salads, hearty sandwiches and the kalua pig steal the scene at lunch. Be warned, the popular fried rice plate will last you for days. The restaurant is behind Outrigger Napili Shores.

Napili Coffee Store CAFE
(Map p334; ☎669-4170; www.coffeestorenapili.com; Napili Plaza, 5095 Napilihau St; pastries & sandwiches $2-10; ⏲6am-6pm;) Having a bad morning? Then try the smooth, ice-blended mocha at Napili's favorite coffee shop. It will set things right. Locals also line up for the pleasant service and the pastries, from banana bread to pumpkin-cranberry muffins and chocolate peanut butter bars. For heartier fare try a slice of quiche or a turkey sandwich with basil pesto.

No laptop? Check the internet on their computers ($1 for every 20 minutes).

Maui Tacos MEXICAN $
(Map p334; ☎665-0222; www.mauitacos.com; Napili Plaza, 5095 Napilihau St; mains under $10; ⏲9am-9pm) Mexican fare can be island-style healthy. The salsas and beans are prepared fresh daily, transfat-free oil replaces lard, and fresh veggies and local fish highlight the menu.

Sea House Restaurant HAWAII REGIONAL $$
(Map p344; ☎669-1500; www.seahousemaui.com; Napili Kai Beach Resort, 5900 Lower Honoapi'ilani Rd; breakfast $10-12, lunch $9-16, dinner $24-38; ⏰7am-9pm, cocktails to 10pm) Pssst. Want a $7 meal with a million dollar view? Sidle up to the bar at this tiki-lit favorite, order a bowl of the smoky seafood chowder then watch the perfectly framed sun drop below the horizon in front of you. Bravo! If you stick around, and you should, seafood and steak dishes are menu highlights. Happy hour (2pm to 5pm) draws crowds for $5 to $6 *pupus* and $5 to $8 cocktails.

☆ Entertainment

★Masters of Hawaiian Slack Key Guitar Concert Series LIVE MUSIC
(Map p344; ☎669-3858; www.slackkey.com; Napili Kai Beach Resort, 5900 Lower Honoapi'ilani Rd; admission $38; ⏰7:30pm Wed) Top slack key guitarists appear regularly at this exceptional concert series, and George Kahumoku Jr, a slack key legend in his own right, is the weekly host. As much a jam session as a concert, this is a true Hawaiian cultural gem that's worth going out of your way to experience. Reservations recommended.

Kapalua & Around

POP 353

Kapalua is a posh resort sprung from the soil of a onetime pineapple plantation. Long known as a world-class golf destination, Kapalua is now making an effort to broaden its appeal. Tennis and golf classes are offered, trails in a once-restricted forest are open to the public and the dining scene is among the island's best. The nightlife doesn't exactly sizzle, but the beaches – all with public access – sure do.

To avoid well-manicured glitz altogether, swoop past the resort and drive the rugged northern coast. The untamed views are guaranteed to replenish your soul.

If uninterrupted sunshine is your goal, note that Kapalua can be a bit rainier and windier than points south.

Beaches & Sights

DT Fleming Beach Park BEACH
(Hwy 30) Surrounded by ironwood trees and backed by an old one-room schoolhouse, this sandy crescent appears like an outpost from another era. In keeping with its Hawaiian nature, the beach is the domain of wave riders. Experienced surfers and bodysurfers find good action here, especially in winter. The shorebreaks can be brutal, however, and this beach is second only to Ho'okipa for injuries. The reef on the right is good for snorkeling in summer when it's very calm.

Fleming has restrooms, showers, grills, picnic tables and a lifeguard. The access road is off Honoapi'ilani Hwy, immediately north of mile marker 31.

The Coastal Trail and Mahana Ridge Trail connect here.

Oneloa Beach BEACH
(Map p344) Also on the Coastal Trail, this white-sand jewel is worth seeking out. Fringed by low sand dunes, it's a fine place to soak up rays. On calm days swimming is good close to shore, as is snorkeling in the protected area along the rocky point at the north side of the beach. When there's any sizable surf, strong rip currents can be present.

The half-mile strand – Oneloa means 'long sand' – is backed by gated resort condos and restricted golf greens, and beach access requires a sharp eye. Turn onto Ironwood Lane, then left into the parking lot. Arrive early or around lunchtime, when people are heading out.

Kapalua Beach BEACH
(Map p344) For a long day at the beach, it's hard to do much better than this crescent-shaped strip at the southwestern tip of Kapula. Snorkel in the morning, grab lunch at the Sea House, try stand-up paddlesurfing, then sip cocktails at Merriman's next door. Or simply sit on the sand and gaze across the channel at Moloka'i.

Long rocky outcrops at both ends of the bay make Kapalua Beach the safest year-round swimming spot on this coast. You'll find colorful snorkeling on the right side of the beach, with abundant tropical fish.

Take the drive immediately north of Napili Kai Beach Resort to get to the beach parking area, where there are restrooms and showers. A tunnel leads from the parking lot north to the beach. The beach is also a starting point for the Coastal Trail.

Dragon's Teeth CULTURAL SITE
(Map p344) Razor-sharp spikes crown rocky Makaluapuna Point, looking uncannily like the mouth of an imaginary dragon. The 3ft-high spikes are the work of pounding winter waves that have ripped into the lava rock point, leaving the pointy 'teeth' behind.

Kapalua & Around

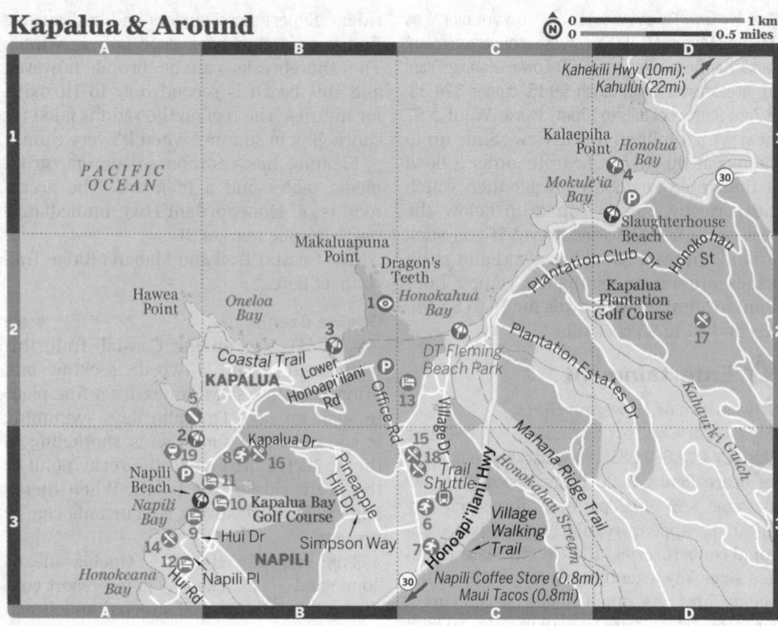

Kapalua & Around

Sights
1 Dragon's Teeth....B2
2 Kapalua Beach....A3
3 Oneloa Beach....B2
4 Slaughterhouse Beach & Honolua Bay....D1

Activities, Courses & Tours
5 Kapalua Dive Company....A2
6 Kapalua Golf....C3
7 Kapalua Golf Academy....C3
8 Kapalua Tennis Garden....B3

Sleeping
9 Hale Napili....A3
Kapalua Villas....(see 6)
10 Mauian....B3
11 Napili Kai Beach Resort....B3
12 Outrigger Napili Shores....A3
13 Ritz-Carlton Kapalua....C2

Eating
14 Gazebo....A3
15 Honolua Store....C3
16 Pineapple Grill....B3
17 Plantation House....D2
18 Sansei Seafood Restaurant & Sushi Bar....C3
Sea House Restaurant....(see 11)

Drinking & Nightlife
19 Point Bar at Merriman's Kapalua....A3

Entertainment
Masters of Hawaiian Slack Key Guitar Concert Series....(see 11)

Signage states that the outcropping is sacred to native Hawaiians. Visitors are strongly discouraged from walking onto the formation, as well as the adjacent **Honokua burial site**, out of respect for native customs. The point is also potentially hazardous, subject to powerful waves and covered by uneven, sometimes sharp, rocks.

You can skirt along the outside of the 13-acre burial area, which is en route to Dragon's Teeth, but don't enter sites marked 'Please Kokua,' which are easily visible islets of stones bordering the Ritz's manicured golf greens.

Get here by driving north to the very end of Lower Honoapi'ilani Rd, where you'll find parking and a plaque detailing the burial site. The path to the Dragon's Teeth leads down from the plaque along the north edge of the Kapalua Bay Golf Course.

Slaughterhouse Beach & Honolua Bay BEACH

(Map p344) This gorgeous spot is a favorite of snorkelers and surfers. Kalaepiha Point separates Slaughterhouse Beach (Mokule'ia Bay) and Honolua Bay. Together the three form the Honolua–Mokule'ia Bay Marine Life Conservation District. Honolua Bay faces northwest and when it catches the winter swells it has some of the gnarliest surfing in the world. In summer, snorkeling is excellent in both bays, thanks in part to prohibitions on fishing in the preserve. Honolua Bay is the favorite, with thriving reefs and abundant coral along its rocky edges.

Spinner dolphins sometimes hang near the mouth of the bays, swimming just beyond snorkelers. When it's calm, you can snorkel around Kalaepiha Point from one bay to the other, but forget it after heavy rains: Honolua Stream empties into Honolua Bay and the runoff clouds the water.

The land fronting Honolua Bay is owned by Maui Land & Pineapple. The company allows recreational access to the bay for no fee. A few families have the right to live on this land, but they cannot charge an access fee or restrict visiting hours. Once you reach the bay, enter via the rocky coastline. Do not use the concrete boat ramp, which is very slippery and potentially hazardous.

When the waters are calm the bays offer superb kayaking. Slaughterhouse Beach is also a top-rated bodysurfing spot during the summer. Its attractive white-sand crescent is good for sunbathing and beachcombing – look for glittering green olivine crystals in the rocks at the south end of the beach.

Just north of mile marker 32, there's public parking and a concrete stairway leading down the cliffs to Slaughterhouse Beach. A half-mile past mile marker 32 there's room for about six cars to park adjacent to the path down to Honolua Bay.

Activities

Kapalua Golf GOLF

(Map p344; 669-8044, 877-527-2582; www.golfatkapalua.com; Bay/Plantation greens fee $208/268, late afternon $98/128, twilight $138/168; 1st tee around 6:40am) Kapalua boasts two of the island's top championship golf courses, both certified by Audubon International as sanctuaries for native plants and animals. How's that for green greens? The **Bay course** (300 Kapalua Dr) is the tropical ocean course, meandering across a lava peninsula. The challenging **Plantation course** (2000 Plantation Club Dr) sweeps over a rugged landscape of hills and deep gorges.

Kapalua Golf Academy GOLF

(Map p344; 662-7740; www.golfatkapalua.com; 1000 Office Rd; 1hr private lesson $180, half-day school $275; 7am-5pm) Hawaii's top golf academy is staffed by PGA pros.

Kapalua Dive Company DIVING

(Map p344; 669-3448; www.kapaluadive.com; Kapalua Bay; beach dive from $85, kayak-snorkel tour $85; 8am-5pm) Offers a range of water activities, including kayak-snorkel tours and a variety of dives. Rent a basic snorkel set for $15 per day (8am to 4:30pm) and a stand-up paddleboard for $40 per hour (9am to 4pm). Look for its beach shack on Kapalua Beach. Will hold credit card, driver's license or car keys for rental deposit.

Kapalua Tennis Garden TENNIS

(Map p344; 662-7730; www.golfatkapalua.com/tennis.html; 100 Kapalua Dr; per person per day $12, racket rental $6; 8am-6pm) Maui's premier full-service tennis club has 10 Plexipave courts and an array of clinics. If you're solo, give the club a ring and they'll match you with other players for singles or doubles games.

Festivals & Events

Hyundai Tournament of Champions GOLF

(www.pgatour.com) Watch the likes of Tiger and friends tee off at the PGA Tour's season opener in early January at the Plantation course, vying for a multimillion-dollar purse.

Celebration of the Arts ART

(www.celebrationofthearts.org) This festival in April at the Ritz-Carlton celebrates traditional Hawaiian culture with art instruction, hula demonstrations, nature walks, panels, films and music.

Kapalua Wine & Food Festival FOOD & WINE

(www.kapaluawineandfoodfestival.com) A culinary extravaganza held over four days in June at the Ritz-Carlton, the festival features renowned winemakers and Hawaii's hottest chefs, with cooking demonstrations and wine tastings.

KAPALUA HIKING TRAILS

Whether you're after an easy coastal stroll or a hard-core trek through thick tropical flora, Kapalua has a trail for you. The remarkable **Maunalei Arboretum Trail** cuts through a forest planted by DT Fleming, the arborist who developed Maui's pineapple industry. This previously inaccessible forest sits above a gated development and access is strictly via a free **shuttle** (☎665-9110; ⏲7am-sunset) that departs from the Kapalua Resort Center at 9:30am, 11:30am and 1:30pm, and returns from the trailhead at 11:50am and 1:50pm. Reservations are required to ride the shuttle van to the trailhead. Call a day or two before your planned hike to secure a spot – the shuttle holds only 14 people. You do not have to be a guest at the resort to ride the hiking shuttle.

For a fantastic one-way hike that ends at the resort, pick up the biologically diverse **Honolua Ridge Trail** (1.25 miles) from the Maunalei Arboretum Trail. You'll enjoy spectacular ridgeline views before dipping back into the junglelike forest for a glimpse of 5788ft Pu'u Kukui, one of the wettest spots in the world, averaging 325in of rainfall annually. Pass through a stand of towering Sugi trees, then pick up the easy **Mahana Ridge Trail** (5.75 miles). At the golf course restrooms, the trail continues on the hill behind the restroom building. When you reach the sharp roadside bend just after the telephone poles, turn right onto the dirt path to descend to DT Fleming Beach (look for the small sign) or follow the road left to return to the Kapalua Resort Center.

The old Village Golf Course, reincarnated as the **Village Walking Trail**, offers stunning scenery as it rises up the mountain slopes. For the best views, follow it all the way to the end, where there's a lake loop. The easy **Coastal Trail** (1.76 miles) links Kapalua Beach with Oneloa Beach then crosses below the Ritz-Carlton to end at DT Fleming Beach. Stay on the designated path to avoid disturbing nesting birds. The Coastal Trail passes ancient burial grounds and the jagged Dragon's Teeth formation, both located north of the Ritz-Carlton and the trail. These sites are of cultural significance to native Hawaiians and should not be inspected up close. Respect the signage.

Free trail maps can be found on the resort website and may be available at the resort center. Note that the trails can be closed at any time by the resort without notice. The Coastal Trail is open sunrise to sunset; all others are open 7am to sunset.

Sleeping

Kapalua Villas CONDO **$$$**

(Map p344; ☎800-545-0018, 665-5400; www.outrigger.com; 2000 Village Rd; 1/2br from $229/309; P❄📶🏊) These swank condos are clustered into three separate compounds. The Golf Villas line the Bay Golf Course while the Bay and Ridge Villas overlook the beach. The one-bedroom units sleep up to four; the two-bedroom units sleep six. For up-close whale watching, try the spacious Bay Villas. The $25 daily resort fee includes parking, wi-fi and use of the resort shuttle.

Ritz-Carlton Kapalua RESORT HOTEL **$$$**

(Map p344; ☎800-262-8440, 669-6200; www.ritzcarlton.com; 1 Ritz-Carlton Dr; r from $349; P❄@📶🏊) This luxe hotel's understated elegance attracts the exclusive golf crowd. On a hillside fronting the greens and the sea, the resort has a heated multilevel swimming pool shaded by palm trees, a spa and a fitness club. Rooms preen with island-chic style, boasting dark wood floors, low-key Hawaiiana and oversize marble bathrooms. The $25 daily resort fees covers wi-fi and use of the fitness center and resort shuttle. Parking is $10 per day.

Eating & Drinking

★**Honolua Store** PLATE LUNCH **$**

(Map p344; ☎665-9105; www.kapalua.com; 502 Office Rd; breakfast $4-9, lunch $6-15; ⏲store 6am-8pm, hot meals to 3pm) The exterior of this porch-wrapped bungalow looks much as it did when it opened in 1929 as the general store for the Honolua Pineapple Plantation. Today, the store is a nod to normalcy in the midst of lavish exclusiveness. The deli is known for its reasonable prices and fantastic plate lunches. The $5.75 hobo lunch (one main and a scoop of rice) is one of Maui's best lunch deals.

There's also a coffee bar with pastries, and grab-and-go sandwiches and bentos in the deli case.

Plantation House HAWAII REGIONAL $$$
(Map p344; ☎669-6299; www.theplantationhouse.com; Plantation Golf Course Clubhouse, 2000 Plantation Club Dr; breakfast & lunch $9-18, dinner $27-46; ⏰8am-3pm, dinner 5:30am-9pm mid-Sep–mid-Apr, 6-9pm rest of year) Breakfast at this open-air eatery is the stuff of which memories and poems are made. The crab cake Benedict? A fluffy, hollandaise-splashed affair that will have you kissing your plate. Stellar views of the coast and Moloka'i, as well as the world-famous golf course, add to the allure. For dinner, fresh fish is prepared with Mediterranean flair and a Mauian finish – think Hawaiian fish with couscous and roasted Maui onions.

Sansei Seafood Restaurant & Sushi Bar JAPANESE $$$
(Map p344; ☎669-6286; www.sanseihawaii.com; 600 Office Rd; sushi $3-16, mains $17-44; ⏰5:30-10pm Sat-Wed, to 1am Thu & Fri) The innovative sushi menu is the draw, but the non-sushi house specials, which often blend Japanese and French flavors, shouldn't be overlooked. The spicy Dungeness crab ramen with truffle broth is a noteworthy prize. Order before 6pm and all food is discounted by 25%. No reservation? Queue up for one of the 12 seats at the sushi bar – folks start gathering outside about 4:50pm!

Pineapple Grill HAWAII REGIONAL $$$
(Map p344; ☎669-9600; www.cohnrestaurants.com; 200 Kapalua Dr, Kapalua Bay Golf Course Clubhouse; breakfast $7-15, lunch $10-16, dinner $25-40; ⏰8am-late) This beauty's got it all, from a sweeping hilltop view to a sleek exhibition kitchen that whips up creative fusion fare. Treat your taste buds with the likes of lobster-coconut bisque, wasabi-seared fish, and truffle mac and cheese with *kalua* pork.

Point Bar at Merriman's Kapalua COCKTAIL BAR
(Map p344; ☎669-6400; www.merrimanshawaii.com; 1 Bay Club Pl; ⏰happy hour 3-5pm) Perched on a scenic point between Kapalua Bay and Napili Bay, this tiki- and palm-dotted spot is a beautiful place to unwind and enjoy a sunset cocktail after braving the Kahekili Hwy.

Kahekili Highway

They call this narrow, serpentine thread of pavement a highway? That's some optimistic labeling, for sure. This challenging road, which hugs the rugged northern tip of Maui, charges around hairpin turns, careens over one-lane bridges and teeters beside treacherous cliffs. It's one of Maui's most adventurous and challenging drives.

Not for the faint of heart, sections slow to just 5mph as the road wraps around blind curves; a lengthy stretch around the village of Kahakuloa is a mere one lane with cliffs on one side and a sheer drop on the other – if you hit oncoming traffic here you may be doing your traveling in reverse! But heck, if you can handle that, this largely overlooked route offers all sorts of adventures, with horse and hiking trails, mighty blowholes and delicious banana bread.

Don't be fooled by car rental maps that show the road as a dotted line – it's paved and open to the public the entire way – although you may want to check with your rental company to see if driving here is permitted under your agreement. There are no services, so gas up beforehand. Give yourself a good two hours' driving time, not counting stops.

Property between the highway and the coast is part privately and part publicly owned; trails to the shore are often uneven, rocky and slippery, and the shoreline is subject to dangerous waves. If you decide to explore, take appropriate precautions and get access permission when possible.

Punalau Beach

Manicured golf courses and ritzy enclaves drop away and the scenery gets wilder as you drive toward the island's northernmost point. Ironwood-lined Punalau Beach, 0.7 miles after mile marker 34, makes a worthy stop if you're up for a solitary stroll. Swimming is a no-go though, as a rocky shelf creates unfavorable conditions for water activities.

Nakalele Point

Continuing on, the terrain is hilly, with rocky cattle pastures punctuated by tall sisal plants. At mile marker 38, a mile-long trail leads out to a **light station** (Map p334) at the end of windswept Nakalele Point. Here you'll find a coastline of arches and other formations worn out of the rocks by the pounding surf.

The **Nakalele Blowhole** (Map p334) roars when the surf is up but is a sleeper when the seas are calm. To check on its mood, park at the boulder-lined pull-off 0.6 miles beyond mile marker 38. Glimpse the action, if there is any, a few hundred yards beyond the parking lot. Keep a safe distance; in 2011 a visitor was killed when he was knocked over by a wave and carried into the blowhole. And it probably goes without saying, but DO NOT sit on the blowhole.

Eight-tenths of a mile after mile marker 40, look for the **Ohai Viewpoint** (Map p334), on the *makai* side of the road. The viewpoint isn't marked but a sign announces the start of the Ohai Trail, a 1.2-mile loop with interpretative signage and views off the coast. For the best views, bear left from the trailhead and walk to the top of the point for a jaw-dropping coastal view that includes a glimpse of the Nakalele Blowhole. If you have kids, be careful – the crumbly cliff has a sudden drop of nearly 800ft!

Ocean Baths & Bellstone

After mile marker 42, the markers change; the next marker is 16 and the numbers go down as you continue on from here.

One-tenth of a mile before mile marker 16, look seaward for a large dirt pull-off and a well-beaten path that leads 15 minutes down lava cliffs to **natural ocean baths** (Map p334) on the ocean's edge. Cut out of slippery lava rock and encrusted with olivine minerals, these incredibly clear pools sit in the midst of roaring surf. If you're tempted to go in, size it up carefully – people unfamiliar with the water conditions here have been swept into the sea and drowned. If the rocks are covered in silt from recent storm runoffs, or the waves look high, forget about it – it's dangerous. Although the baths are on public land, state officials do not recommend accessing them due to the hazardous conditions, including slippery rocks, large and powerful surf, waves on ledges and strong currents.

That huge boulder with concave marks on the inland side of the road just before the pull-off is a bellstone, **Pohaku Kani** (Map p334). If you hit it with a rock on the Kahakuloa side, where the deepest indentations are, you might get a hollow sound. It's a bit resonant if you hit it just right, though it takes some imagination to hear it ring like a bell.

Kahakuloa

An imposing 636ft-tall volcanic dome guards the entrance to Kahakuloa Bay like a lurking, watchful dragon. They say this photogenic landmark, known as **Kahakuloa Head**, was a favorite cliff-diving spot of Chief Kahekili. Before the road drops into the valley, there's a pull-off above town providing a bird's-eye view.

The bayside village of Kahakuloa, tucked at the bottom of a lush valley and embraced by towering sea cliffs, retains a solidly Hawaiian character. Kahakuloa's isolation (population about 100) has protected it from the rampant development found elsewhere on Maui. Farmers tend taro patches, poi dogs wander across the road and a missionary-era **Protestant church** marks the village center. One of Hawaii's most accomplished ukulele players, Richard Hoʻopiʻi, is the church minister.

You won't find stores, but villagers set up hard-to-miss roadside stands selling fruit and snacks to day-trippers. For shave ice ($3), try Ululani's hot-pink stand. For free samples of *'ono* (delicious) banana bread, stop at Julia's lime-green **shack** (www.juliasbananabread.com) where a loaf costs $6 – and tastes fresh for days.

Kahakuloa to Waiheʻe

On the outskirts of Kahakuloa, after a harrowing, narrow climb, you'll reach the hilltop **Kaukini Gallery & Gift Shop** (Map p334; ☎244-3371; www.kaukinigallery.com; ⏲10am-5pm), near mile marker 14. The gallery sells works by more than 100 island artists, with watercolors, jewelry, native-fiber baskets, pottery and more. A locator map on the front porch tells you how many more twisty miles you'll need to drive in either direction to reach relative safety.

Past mile marker 10 look for **Turnbull Studios & Sculpture Garden** (Map p334; ☎244-0101; www.turnbullstudios.org; 5030 Kahekili Hwy; ⏲10am-5pm Mon-Fri), where you can view Bruce Turnbull's ambitious bronze and wood creations, as well as the works of other area artists…very cool stuff.

Continuing around beep-as-you-go blind turns, the highway gradually levels out atop sea cliffs. For an Edenlike scene, stop at the pull-off 0.1 miles north of mile marker 8 and look down into the ravine below, where you'll see a cascading **waterfall** framed by double pools.

Mendes Ranch RANCH
(Map p334; ☎871-5222; www.mendesranch.com; 3530 Kahekili Hwy; 1½hr rides $110; ⏲rides 8:45am

& 11:30pm) For a real *paniolo* experience, saddle up at Mendes Ranch, a working cattle ranch near mile marker 7. The picture-perfect scenery on these rides includes everything from jungle valleys to lofty sea cliffs and waterfalls.

Waihe'e Ridge Trail

This fabulous trail has it all: tropical flora, breezy ridgelines, lush valley landscapes and lofty views of Maui's wild northern coast and the central valley. The best part? The well-defined trail is less than 5 miles roundtrip and only takes about three hours to complete.

The path is a bit steep, but it's a fairly steady climb and not overly strenuous. It's best to start this one before 8am in order to beat the clouds, which can obscure the view from the top later in the morning.

Starting at an elevation of 1000ft, the trail, which crosses reserve land, climbs a ridge, passing from pasture to cool forest. Guava trees and groves of rainbow eucalyptus are prominent along the way, and the pungent aroma of fallen fruit may accompany you after a rainstorm. From the 0.75-mile post, panoramic views open up, with a scene that sweeps clear down to the ocean along the **Waihe'e Gorge** and deep into pleated valleys.

As you continue on, you'll enter ohia forest with native birds and get distant views of waterfalls cascading down the mountains. The path ends at a small clearing on the 2563ft peak of **Lanilili**. When it's clear, you'll find awesome views in all directions as well as a picnic table.

Solos, seniors and in-shape kids should be fine on this hike. If you have access to hiking poles, bring them. The trail gets muddy and steep in spots.

For the **trailhead** (Map p334), take the one-lane paved road that starts on the inland side of the highway just south of mile marker 7. It's almost directly across the road from the big gate at Mendes Ranch. The road (open 7am to 6pm) climbs to the **Boy Scouts' Camp Mahulia** and winds through open pasture, so watch for cattle. The trailhead, marked with a Na Ala Hele sign, is a mile up on the left just before the camp.

For complete details visit http://hawaiitrails.ehawaii.gov, the state's trail and access website.

Waihe'e to Wailuku

Soon after the Waihe'e Ridge Trail, the Kahekili Hwy runs through the sleeper towns of Waihe'e and Waiehu before arriving in **Wailuku**, in Central Maui. There's not much to do here, but if you're up for a round of golf, the county-run **Waiehu Municipal Golf Course** (☎243-7400; www.mauicounty.gov; 200 Halewaiu Rd; greens fee $55, optional cart $20; ⏲6:45am-5pm Mon-Fri, 6am-5pm Sat & Sun) offers an affordable and easily walkable 18 holes on the coast. On-site are a small cafe, a pro shop and public restrooms.

'IAO VALLEY & CENTRAL MAUI

This wind-whipped region is action-central for anything with a sail. Kanaha Beach takes home gold for kitesurfing and windsurfing, bursting into color each day in a glorious mile-long sea of sails. But you don't have to get all your thrills on the water. Central Maui has exceptional green treats, most notably lush 'Iao Valley, a sight so spectacular it was once reserved for royalty; two rare waterbird sanctuaries; and the most dazzling tropical aquarium you'll ever see. History makes an appearance too, with tours through a missionary's home and a sugar museum.

Kahului

POP 26,337

Kahului is the commercial heart of Maui. It's home to the island's gateway airport and cruise-ship harbor. Just about everything that enters Maui comes through this workaday town thick with warehouses and shopping centers. Hardly a vacation scene, you say. True, but if you dig a little deeper you'll find more to your liking. You have to go island-style to have fun here: talk story with the locals at the Saturday swap meet, take in a concert on the lawn of the cultural center or join the wave-riding action at Kanaha Beach.

Beaches

Kanaha Beach Park BEACH

When the wind picks up in the afternoon, this mile-long beach becomes surf city, with hundreds of brilliant sails whipping back and forth across the bay.

Central Maui

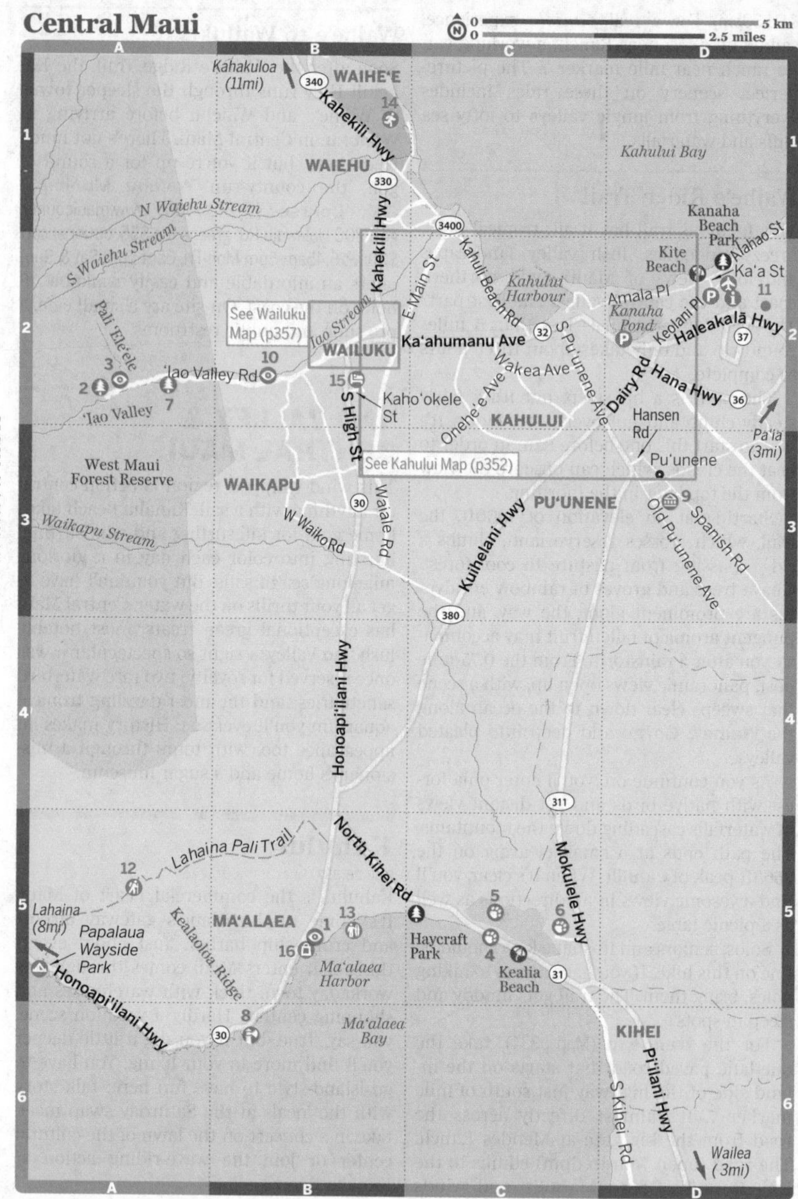

Both windsurfing and kitesurfing are so hot here that the beach is divvied up, with kitesurfers converging at the southwestern end, known as **Kite Beach**, and windsurfers strutting their stuff at the northeastern end. It's mind-blowing to watch, and there are instructors waiting right on the beach if *you're* ready to fly.

A section in the middle of the beach is roped off for swimmers, but this place is really all about wind power. Facilities include restrooms, showers and shaded picnic tables.

Central Maui

Top Sights
1 Maui Ocean Center B5

Sights
2 'Iao Valley State Park A2
3 JFK Profile A2
4 Kealia Pond Boardwalk C5
5 Kealia Pond National Wildlife Refuge ... C5
6 Kealia Pond National Wildlife Refuge Visitor Center C5
7 Kepaniwai Park & Heritage Gardens A2
8 McGregor Point B6
9 Old Pu'unene Bookstore D3
Story of Hawaii Museum .... (see 16)
10 Tropical Gardens of Maui B2

Activities, Courses & Tours
11 Kahului Heliport D2
12 Lahaina Pali Trail A5
13 Ma'alaea Pipeline B5
Pacific Whale Foundation - Ma'alaea .... (see 16)
Shark Dive Maui .... (see 1)
14 Waiehu Municipal Golf Course B1

Sleeping
15 Old Wailuku Inn B2

Eating
Beach Bums Bar & Grill .... (see 16)
Waterfront Restaurant .... (see 16)

Shopping
16 Ma'alaea Harbor Shops B5

Sights

★ Kanaha Pond Bird Sanctuary PRESERVE
(Hwy 37; sunrise-sunset) FREE Tucked between the airport, a highway and a Krispy Kreme, this roadside wetlands seems an unlikely sanctuary for rare Hawaiian birds. But the *ae'o* (black-necked stilt), native coots and black-crowned night herons that flock here don't seem to mind the nearby bustle. You should make several sightings right along the shoreline as you approach the stone **observation deck** a short walk beyond the parking lot.

The estimated population of the *ae'o*, an elegant wading bird with long orange legs, is between 800 and 1100 across the entire state. Fortunately, you'll likely spot one of them here. The parking area is just west of the intersection of Hwy 37 and Dairy Rd.

Maui Nui Botanical Gardens GARDENS
(249-2798; www.mnbg.org; 150 Kanaloa Ave; 8am-4pm Mon-Sat) FREE If you're interested in the subtle beauty of native Hawaiian plants, this garden is a gem. Come here to view rare species and to identify plants you've heard about but haven't yet seen, such as *wauke* (paper mulberry, used to make tapa), *'ulu* (breadfruit) and *'iliahi* (sandalwood). Don't expect it to be overly flowery, however. You won't see the riotous colors of exotic tropicals that dominate most Hawaiian gardens.

To delve even deeper into the key role of native plants in Hawaiian culture, join one of the guided tours (suggested donation $5) that are given between 10am and 11:30am on Mondays, Tuesdays, Fridays and Saturdays.

If you buy lunch from one of the food trucks near the harbor, the picnic tables here are a nice spot to enjoy it.

Schaefer International Gallery MUSEUM
(242-2787; www.mauiarts.org; 1 Cameron Way; 11am-5pm Wed-Sun) This easy-to-reach gallery at the Maui Arts & Cultural Center features fascinating exhibits on Hawaiian culture, hula and art. If you're in the area, it's worth a stop to see what's currently displayed.

Kahului Harbor HARBOR
Kahului's large protected harbor is the island's only deepwater port, so all boat traffic, from cruise ships to cargo vessels, dock here. But it's not all business. You'll find one of the harbor's most attractive faces at **Ho'aloha Park**, where you can watch outrigger canoe clubs practice on weekday afternoons.

Activities

Windsurfing

Windswept Kahului is the base for Maui's main windsurfing operations. Board-and-rig rentals cost around $55/365 per day/week. If you're new to the sport, introductory classes are readily available, last a couple of hours, and cost $90. The business is competitive, so ask about discounts.

Reliable shops that rent out gear and arrange lessons include the following:

Second Wind WINDSURFING
(877-7467; www.secondwindmaui.com; 111 Hana Hwy; 9am-6pm)

Kahului

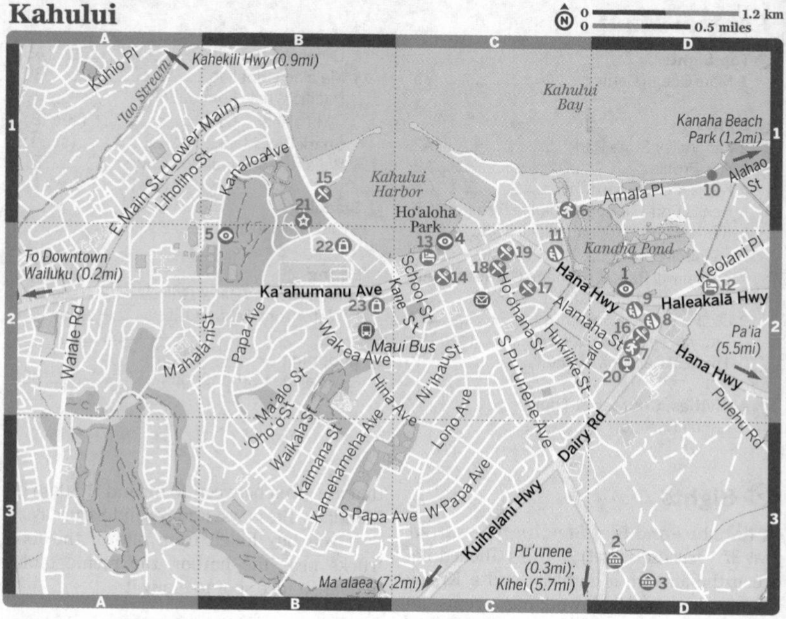

Hawaiian Island Surf & Sport WINDSURFING
(☎871-4981; www.hawaiianisland.com; 415 Dairy Rd; ⏲8:30am-6pm)

Hi-Tech Surf Sports WINDSURFING
(☎877-2111; www.htmaui.com; 425 Koloa St; ⏲9am-6pm)

Kitesurfing

Kitesurfing, also known as kiteboarding, has taken off big-time in Kahului. The action centers on Kite Beach, the southwest end of Kanaha Beach Park. If you've never tried it before, you can learn the ropes from some of the very pros who've made kitesurfing such a hot wave ride. Vans for the companies listed below set up right at Kite Beach to offer lessons, typically after 10:30am. This is the easiest way to check out the scene, instead of locating their various headquarters. Expect to pay about $275 for a half-day intro course. From Amala Pl, look for the vans about ¼ mile west of Ka'a St. Watch the action live at http://kitebeachcam.com.

Some recommended operators include the following:

Kiteboarding School Maui KITESURFING
(☎873-0015; www.ksmaui.com)

Aqua Sports Maui KITESURFING
(☎242-8015; www.mauikiteboardinglessons.com)

Action Sports Maui KITESURFING
(☎871-5857; www.actionsportsmaui.com; 96 Amala Pl; ⏲10am-5pm) Lesson center and retail store in the big red barn on Amala Pl near Kanaha Pond, west of Kite Beach.

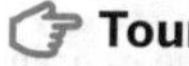

Tours

Helicopter Tours

Several companies, including **Sunshine** (☎270-3999; www.sunshinehelicopters.com), **Blue Hawaiian** (☎871-8844; www.bluehawaiian.com) and **AlexAir** (☎871-0792; www.helitour.com) offer helicopter tours of Maui. All operate out of the **Kahului Heliport** (1 Kahului Airport Rd), at the southeast side of Kahului Airport. Thirty-minute tours of the jungly West Maui Mountains cost around $190 and one-hour circle-island tours about $320. Discounts abound. Companies advertise in the free tourist magazines, with all sorts of deals.

Festivals & Events

★Ki Ho'alu Slack Key Guitar Festival MUSIC
(www.mauiarts.org; 1 Cameron Way) Top slack key guitarists from throughout the state take the stage at this quintessentially Hawaiian festival, which celebrated its 30th anniversary in

Kahului

Top Sights
1 Kanaha Pond Bird Sanctuary D2

Sights
2 Alexander & Baldwin Sugar Museum D3
3 Hawaiian Commercial & Sugar Company Mill D3
4 Kahului Harbor C2
5 Maui Nui Botanical Gardens B2
Schaefer International Gallery .. (see 21)

Activities, Courses & Tours
6 Action Sports Maui C1
Aqua Sports Maui ....(see 11)
7 Crater Cycles Hawaii D2
8 Hawaiian Island Surf & Sport D2
9 Hi-Tech Surf Sports D2
10 Kiteboarding School Maui D1
11 Second Wind C2

Sleeping
12 Courtyard Marriott Kahului Airport D2
13 Maui Seaside Hotel C2

Eating
14 Bistro Casanova C2
Campus Food Court ....(see 22)
Da Kitchen ....(see 8)
15 Geste Shrimp Truck B1
16 Maui Coffee Roasters D2
17 Safeway Kahului C2
18 Tasaka Guri-Guri C2
19 Whole Foods C2

Drinking & Nightlife
20 Wow-Wee Maui's Kava Bar & Grill D2

Entertainment
21 Maui Arts & Cultural Center B1

Shopping
Bounty Music ....(see 11)
22 Maui Swap Meet B2
23 Queen Ka'ahumanu Center B2

2012. It's held on the lawn of the Maui Arts & Cultural Center in June.

Maui Marathon SPORTS
(www.mauimarathonhawaii.com) West Maui's marathon, half-marathon, 10K and 5K races – and a mile-long fun run along Lahaina's Front St – in September.

★ **Maui Ukulele Festival** MUSIC
(www.ukulelefestivalhawaii.org; 1 Cameron Way) A big *'ohana* (family) event, everybody from *na keiki* to elders shows up at the Maui Arts & Cultural Center on a Sunday in mid-October for this outdoor music fest showcasing uke masters from Maui and beyond.

Na Mele OMaui MUSIC
(www.kaanapaliresort.com) The 'Song of Maui' features children's choral groups singing Native Hawaiian music honoring Hawaii's last monarch, Queen Lili'uokalani, who was a renowned music composer and cultural revivalist. Sponsored by the Ka'anapali Beach Resort, this aloha-rich event is held in early December at the Maui Arts & Cultural Center. Donations appreciated at the door.

Sleeping

Maui Seaside Hotel HOTEL $$
(☎877-3311; www.seasidehotelshawaii.com; 100 W Ka'ahumanu Ave; r from $129; ❄@📶🏊) If you want to stay near the airport or the Maui Arts & Cultural Center, this is the better of the two aging hotels on Ka'ahumanu Ave. It's a plain Jane, but the rooms are clean.

Courtyard Marriott Kahului Airport HOTEL $$
(☎871-1800; www.marriott.com; 532 Keolani Pl; r/ste $179/249; P❄@📶🏊) Finally – a modern, stylish hotel near the Kahului airport (p316). At this four-story property, which opened in 2012, guests whisk into a sleek lobby area, best described as Aloha Modern. The breezy bistro, complete with media booths, serves breakfast, dinner and appletinis. Bright murals with beach scenes surround the adjacent lounge. Rooms are bigger than average, with crisp white bedding, large windows and deep brown accents – a hint of solemnity for the business traveler?

The property is not on the beach, but the pool and nearby fire pit are nice places to relax. Parking is $10 per day.

Eating

If you need to stock up the condo on the way in from the airport, the **Safeway** (☎877-3377; www.safeway.com; 170 E Kamehameha Ave; ⏰24hr) in the town center never closes. Like it greener? **Whole Foods** (☎872-3310; www.wholefoodsmarket.com; 70 Ka'ahumanu Ave, Maui Mall; ⏰7am-9pm) carries island-grown produce, fish and beef, and is a good place to pick up lei.

Campus Food Court FOOD COURT $
(www.mauiculinary-campusdining.com; Maui College, 310 W Ka'ahumanu Ave; mains under $10; ⏲ hours vary by station, typically 11am-1pm Mon-Fri) With names such as Farm to Table and the Raw Fish Camp, this isn't your average campus fare. This food court, run by students in Maui College's acclaimed culinary arts program, is well worth a detour. The food court is in the Pa'ina Building, which borders the parking lot used for the Maui Swap Meet (p355). From Kahului Beach Rd turn onto Wahinepio Ave.

For some fine dining, check out **The Class Act** (☎984-3280; ⏲11am-12:30pm Wed & Fri), where students create a multicourse meal made from locally grown food for $32 per person.

Tasaka Guri-Guri DESSERT $
(Maui Mall, 70 E Ka'ahumanu Ave; 2 scoops/quart $1.20/5.50; ⏲9am-6pm Mon-Thu, 9am-8pm Fri, 9am-6pm Sat, 10am-4pm Sun) For the coolest treat in town, queue up at this hole-in-the-wall shop dishing up homemade pineapple sherbet. The *guri-guri,* as it's called, is so popular that locals pick up quarts on the way to the airport to take to friends on neighboring islands.

Maui Coffee Roasters CAFE $
(☎800-645-2877; www.mauicoffeeroasters.com; 444 Hana Hwy; ⏲7am-6pm Mon-Fri, 8am-5pm Sat, 8am-2:30pm Sun; 📶) Good vibes and good java at this coffee shop, where locals linger over lattes while surfing free wi-fi. To jump-start your day, order a Sledge Hammer – a quadruple espresso with steamed half and half. Located in the strip mall at the intersection of Dairy Rd and the Hana Hwy.

★**Geste Shrimp Truck** FOOD TRUCK $$
(☎298-7109; www.gesteshrimp.com; Kahului Beach Rd, beside Kahului Harbor; meals $5-14; ⏲10:30am-5:30pm Tue-Sat) Baby, this is where the magic happens. Inside a small white food truck, emblazoned with a giant shrimp, a hardworking cook sizzles up the tastiest shrimp on Maui. Maybe even the world. We are so not kidding. The $12 shrimp plate – try the hot and spicy – includes 12 seasoned shrimp (they're big, and you gotta peel 'em), a scoop of creamy delicious crab macaroni salad, and one scoop of rice.

A few words to the wise: bring handi-wipes, don't wear white and don't eat the meal in your car. The nearby Maui Nui Botanical Gardens (p351) has picnic tables. Dig in. Die happy.

MAUI FOOD TRUCKS

The food truck phenomenon has finally made its way to Maui. From Lahaina to the Upcountry, these four-wheeled eateries are serving a global array of tasty *grinds*. Most meals are $12 or less. Bring cash. These are a few of our favorites:

Kahului

➡ **Geste Shrimp** (p354) Savor 12 plump and juicy shrimp with crab mac and rice on the side. It's a top island choice.

➡ **Gogi Korean Taco Truck** (www.eatgogi.com) Nosh on tacos and bibim burritos.

Kihei

➡ **Kina'ole Grill** (11 Alanui Keali'i Dr) Fish and shrimp platters are specialties. The truck typically parks on Alanui Ke Ali'i Rd, not far from Kamaole Beach Park 1. Visit its Facebook page for updates.

Kula

➡ **Da Puerto Rican Food Truck** (55 Kiopaa St, Pukalani, Longs Drugs parking lot) Cuban sandwiches, pork plates and plaintains are served on Thursdays from 11:30am until sold out. Check the Facebook page for more details.

Lahaina

➡ **Outrigger Pizzas** (www.outriggerpizzas.com) Woodfired pizzas, from pepperoni to pesto to lilikoi pork, are the draw. Also in Kihei and Kula.

Check online to confirm hours and daily locations.

Da Kitchen LOCAL $$
(☎871-7782; www.da-kitchen.com; Suite 104, Triangle Square, 425 Koloa St; mains $10-25; ⊙11am-9pm Mon-Sat) Hawaiian decor and unbeatable island *grinds* make this a favorite stop. The *kalua* pork is, as they say, 'so tender it falls off da bone,' and the more expensive plate lunches are big enough to feed two. Expect a crowd at lunch but don't be deterred, as the service is quick.

Bistro Casanova MEDITERRANEAN $$
(☎873-3650; www.casanovamaui.com; 33 Lono Ave; lunch $8-20, dinner $14-38; ⊙11am-9:30pm Mon-Sat) An offshoot of the popular Italian restaurant Casanova in Makawao, this is Kahului's classiest dining option, offering a solid tapas menu, Maui-caught fish and plenty of organic Kula veggies. The setting is upscale and urban. Reservations are recommended at dinner, when the bistro can fill solid with a pre-theater crowd en route to a show at the MACC (p355).

Drinking

Wow-Wee Maui's Kava Bar & Grill BAR
(www.wowweemaui.com; 333 Dairy Rd; kava $6; ⊙11am-9pm Mon-Wed, 9am-11pm Thu-Sat, 11am-5pm Sun) This low-key cafe is *the* place to try kava served in a coconut shell. A ceremonial drink in old Hawaii, this spicy elixir made from the *Piper methysticum* plant is a mild relaxant. Wow-Wee Maui's chocolate bars, some spiked with kava, will also make you swoon.

☆ Entertainment

Maui Arts & Cultural Center CONCERT HALL
(MACC; ☎242-7469; www.mauiarts.org; 1 Cameron Way) There's always something happening at this snazzy performance complex, which boasts two indoor theaters and an outdoor amphitheater, all with excellent acoustics. As Maui's main venue for music, theater and dance, it hosts everything from ukulele jams to touring rock bands. Check the online calendar to see if you can catch one of the exceptional Slack Key Masters shows hosted by Grammy award winner George Kahumoku Jr ($25 per person).

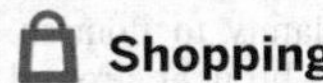

Shopping

Kahului hosts Maui's big-box discount chains of the Wal-Mart and Costco variety, as well as its biggest shopping malls.

★ **Maui Swap Meet** MARKET
(☎244-3100; www.mauiexposition.com; Maui College, 310 Ka'ahumanu Ave; adult/child 11yr & under 50¢/free; ⊙7am-1pm Sat) For a scene that glows with aloha, spend a Saturday morning chatting with local farmers and craftspeople at Maui's largest outdoor market. You'll not only find fresh organic Hana fruits, Kula veggies and homemade banana bread, but it's also a fun place to souvenir shop for everything from jewelry and wood carvings to handpainted coconuts and Maui-designed T-shirts. And hats. Lots of hats.

Make sure you're not misled by the term 'swap meet' – most stands sell quality local goods and every dollar you spend stays right here in the local community. The swap meet is held directly behind the college campus, off Kahului Harbor Rd.

Bounty Music MUSIC
(☎214-1591; www.bountymusicmaui.com; 111 Hana Hwy; ⊙9am-6pm Mon-Sat, 10am-4pm Sun) Hawaiian music lovers, take note. This is where you'll find all sorts of ukuleles, from inexpensive imported models to handcrafted masterpieces.

Queen Ka'ahumanu Center MALL
(☎877-3369; www.queenkaahumanucenter.com; 275 W Ka'ahumanu Ave; ⊙9:30am-9pm Mon-Sat, 10am-5pm Sun) Come here for your standard-issue mall stores, from Macy's to Forever 21 and Footlocker. There are also several swimwear shops and cellphone carriers. Stop by on Monday from 10:30am to 11:30am for a lively hula show.

This is a hub for Maui buses, which stop in back of the mall near Macy's men's department.

ℹ Information

Bank of Hawaii – Kahului (☎871-8250; www.boh.com; 27 S Pu'unene Ave; ⊙8:30am-4pm Mon-Fri)

Longs Drugs – Kahului (☎877-0041; Maui Mall, 70 E Ka'ahumanu Ave; ⊙7am-midnight) The town's largest pharmacy.

Maui Visitors Bureau (☎872-3893; www.gohawaii.com/maui; Kahului Airport; ⊙8am-9:30pm) There are tons of tourist brochures beside this staffed booth in the airport's arrivals area.

Post Office – Kahului (138 S Pu'unene Ave; ⊙8am-4:30pm Mon-Fri, 9am-noon Sat)

Getting There & Around

TO/FROM THE AIRPORT

Kahului airport (p316) is at the east side of town. Most visitors pick up rental cars at the airport. Kihei Rent a Car (p374) will shuttle you from the airport to their office.

BICYCLE

Island Biker (☎877-7744; www.islandbikermaui.com; 415 Dairy Rd; per day/week $50/200; ⏲9am-5pm Mon-Fri, to 3pm Sat) Rents quality mountain bikes and road bikes well suited for touring Maui.

BUS

The **Maui Bus** (www.mauicounty.gov) connects Kahului with Ma'alaea, Kihei, Wailea and Lahaina; each ride costs $2 and runs hourly. Queen Ka'ahumanu Center is a major hub.

CAR

Bio-Beetle (☎873-6121; www.bio-beetle.com; 55 Amala Pl; per day $50-90, per week $229-359) Offers an eco-friendly alternative to the usual car rental scene, renting cars that run on cooking oil from local restaurants. Also available are hybrids, plug-in hybrid-electrics and a 100% electric Nissan Leaf. Rates fluctuate, sometimes a great deal, during the year.

Wailuku

POP 15,313

The lush land surrounding Wailuku is fed by four streams, which made the area an important food source and land holding for Maui chieftains. Missionaries took up residence here in the 1800s. Today, Wailuku boasts more sights on the National Register of Historic Places than any other town on Maui but sees the fewest tourists. As the county capital, its central area wears a modern facade of midrise office buildings, while its age-old backstreets hold an earthy mishmash of curio shops, galleries and mom-and-pop stores that beg to be browsed. At lunchtime, thanks to a combination of low rent and hungry government employees, Wailuku dishes up tasty eats at prices that shame Maui's more touristed towns.

Sights

A cluster of historical buildings anchor the small downtown. Many of them are still in use today as government offices. Hawaii's best-known architect, Maui-born CW Dickey, left his mark on downtown before moving on to fame in Honolulu. The **Wailuku Public Library** (cnr High & Aupuni Sts; ⏲9am-5pm Mon-Wed & Fri, 1-8pm Thu), built c 1928, is a classic example of Dickey's distinctive Hawaii regional design. Another Dickey creation, the **Territorial Building**, lies right across Aupuni St. Within a short walk are four more buildings on the National Register of Historic Places.

To discover all the gems in town, pick up a copy of the Wailuku Historic District walking map (free, but donations appreciated) at the Bailey House Museum. Also be aware that parking enforcement officers are very strict about posted parking times downtown – according to local lore, one officer ticketed his own mother's car!

★ Bailey House Museum MUSEUM

(☎244-3326; www.mauimuseum.org; 2375 W Main St; adult/child 7-12yr $7/2; ⏲10am-4pm Mon-Sat) This evocative museum occupies the 1833 home of Christian missionary Edward Bailey. Bailey was the second missionary to occupy the house, and he lived in the home nearly 50 years. The residence sits on the former compound of Chief Kahekili, who ruled Maui from 1736 to 1795. On the ground floor, the Hawaiian section displays spears, ancient fishing tools and shark-tooth daggers (ouch!). There's also a notable collection of native wood bowls and stone adzes. Period furnishings and photos of the resident missionary families are displayed on the 2nd floor.

The link between ancient Hawaiian wave riders and modern-day surfers comes alive in a low-key exhibit beside the museum parking lot. There you'll find the Duke's Surfboard, a 10ft redwood surfboard that surfing legend Duke Kahanamoku (1890–1968) rode. The Duke not only won Olympian gold in swimming for the US but more importantly he revived the ancient art of surfing. A full-blooded Hawaiian, he traveled the world with his hefty surfboard in hand, introducing the sport to wannabe wave riders in Australia, Europe and the US mainland. Today, he's considered the father of modern surfing.

Ka'ahumanu Church CHURCH

(103 S High St, cnr W Main & S High Sts) This handsome missionary church is named for Queen Ka'ahumanu, who cast aside the old gods and allowed Christianity to flourish. The clock in the steeple, brought around the Horn in the 19th century, still keeps accurate time. Hymns ring out in Hawaiian at Sunday morning services, but at other times it's a look-from-outside site, as the church is usually locked.

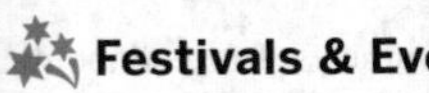

Festivals & Events

E Ho'oulu Aloha FESTIVAL
(www.mauimuseum.org) This old-Hawaii-style festival, held in November at the Bailey House Museum, features hula, ukulele masters, crafts, food and more. You won't find a friendlier community scene.

Maui County Fair FAIR
(www.mauifair.com) Get a feel for Maui's agricultural roots at this venerable fair held in late September, with farm exhibits, tasty island *grinds*, carnival rides, skill games and dazzling orchids.

Wailuku First Friday STREET FAIR
(www.mauifridays.com; 6-9pm 1st Fri of the month) Wailuku turns Market St into a street party complete with live music, poetry slams and a beer garden on the first Friday evening of the month as part of the island-wide Friday Town Parties series (see box on p324).

Sleeping

Wailuku Guesthouse GUESTHOUSE $
(986-8270; www.wailukuhouse.com; 210 S Market St; 1br $89-99, ste/2br $119/189;) This affordable family-run guesthouse has simple, clean rooms, each with its own bathroom, private entrance, refrigerator

Wailuku

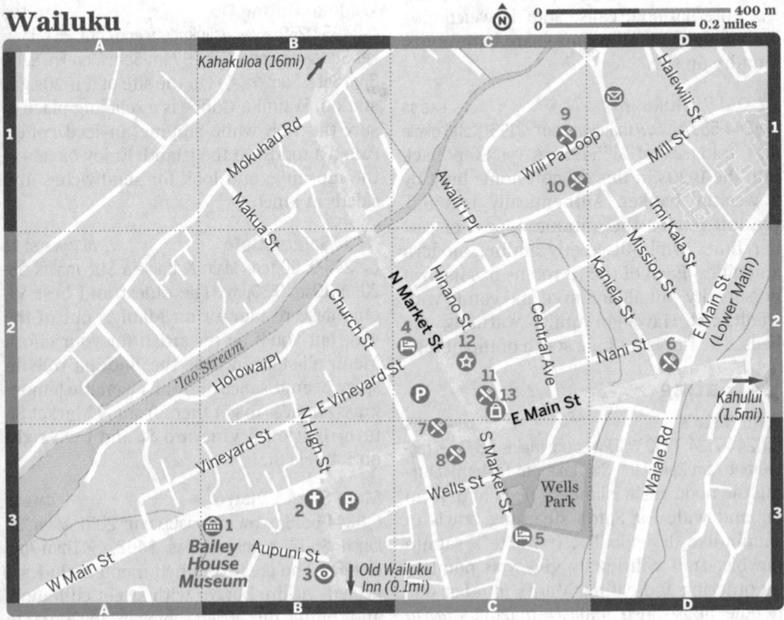

Wailuku

Top Sights
1 Bailey House Museum B3

Sights
2 Ka'ahumanu Church B3
3 Wailuku Public Library B3

Sleeping
4 Northshore Hostel C2
5 Wailuku Guesthouse C3

Eating
6 A Saigon Café D2
7 Giannotto's Pizza C3
8 Main Street Bistro C3
9 Sam Sato's C1
10 Tasty Crust C1
11 Wailuku Coffee Co C2

Entertainment
12 'Iao Theater C2

Shopping
13 Native Intelligence C2

and coffeemaker. There's a park with tennis courts across the street. Two parrots, Ruby and Phoenix, squawk-the-squawk in a small aviary near the central saltwater pool. Complimentary use of beach chairs, towels and coolers. All rooms except the Hibiscus Room have air-con.

Northshore Hostel HOSTEL $
(☎866-946-8095, 986-8095; www.northshorehostel.com; 2080 W Vineyard St; dm $29, semi-private r $35, private r $69-79; ❄@🛜) The smaller and spiffier of Wailuku's two hostels occupies an old building with a fresh coat of paint. Popular with European travelers, it has separate male and female dorms as well as private rooms, a full kitchen and little perks like free international calls. Staff is welcoming and on the ball. All rooms share bathrooms; laundry on site.

★**Old Wailuku Inn** B&B $$
(☎244-5897; www.mauiinn.com; 2199 Kaho'okele St; r incl breakfast $165-195; ❄🛜) Step back into the 1920s in this elegant home built by a wealthy banker. Authentically restored, the inn retains the antique appeal of earlier times while discreetly adding modern amenities. Each of the 10 rooms has its own personality, but all are large and comfy with traditional Hawaiian quilts warming the beds. The inn is 0.1 mile south of the library.

Eating

Sam Sato's JAPANESE $
(☎244-7124; 1750 Wili Pa Loop; mains $8-9; ⏲restaurant 7am-2pm Mon-Sat, take-out to 4pm) During the noon rush, islanders flock here from far and wide for Sato's steaming bowls of saimin-like dry noodles. If you're a saimin newbie, staff will gladly give you pointers on ordering and eating. Maui's number one noodle house also makes amazing *manju* (Japanese cakes filled with sweet bean paste), which are sold for takeout at the counter until 4pm.

To get there take E Vineyard St, go left on Central, right on Mill, left on Imi Kala and left on Wili Pa Loop.

Giannotto's Pizza ITALIAN $
(☎244-8282; www.giannottospizza.com; 2050 Main St; pizza slice $2-4, mains $7-26; ⏲11am-9pm Mon-Sat, 11am-8pm Sun) Brando, Sinatra and the Sopranos look down in approval from the cluttered walls of Giannotto's, a pizza joint where the slices are served super thin and piping hot. If it's 3pm, and you're worried about finding lunch – fuhgeddaboutit. Stop here and the boys will hook you up.

Tasty Crust DINER $
(☎244-0845; www.tastycrust.com; 1770 Mill St; breakfast $5-17, lunch & dinner $6-17; ⏲6am-3pm Mon, 6am-10pm Tue-Thu, 6am-11pm Fri-Sun) The old-school American diner gets a Hawaiian twist at Tasty Crust, a low-frills locals' joint where breakfast standbys like Denver omelets and banana pancakes jostle for attention on the menu beside *loco moco*, Spam, and fried rice with egg. Settle in among the aunties, crying babies and breakfast-steak-eating businessmen for a solid budget meal on your way to the 'Iao Valley.

Wailuku Coffee Co CAFE $
(☎495-0259; www.wailukucoffeeco.com; 26 N Market St; mains under $9; ⏲7am-5pm Mon-Fri, 8am-3pm Sat & Sun; 🛜✎) On the site of a 1920s gas station, Wailuku Coffee is a relaxing place to surf the web while sipping an iced coffee, called a toddy on the island. Enjoy bagels in the morning, and look for sandwiches and salads at lunch.

★**A Saigon Café** VIETNAMESE $$
(☎248-9560; cnr Main & Kaniela Sts; mains $8-20; ⏲10am-9:30pm) The oldest and best Vietnamese restaurant on Maui is out of the way, but you'll be rewarded for your effort. Menu all-stars include the Buddha rolls in spicy peanut sauce and the aromatic lemongrass curries. To get there from N Market St, turn right on E Vineyard St and then right on Kaniela St.

Main Street Bistro CAFE $$
(☎244-6816; www.msbmaui.com; 2051 Main St; lunch $6-12, evening tapas $4-18; ⏲11am-7pm Mon-Fri) The creative lunch menu includes a grilled shrimp burger with sweet chili aioli, and buttermilk fried chicken with white BBQ sauce. The tapas menu, available from 3pm to 7pm, features a grits-and-chorizo stuffed poblano pepper, flat iron steak salad with bleu crumbles and 12-hour-smoked beef brisket, with reasonably priced wines to wash it all down.

Entertainment

'Iao Theater THEATER
(☎242-6969; www.mauionstage.com; 68 N Market St) Beautifully restored after years of neglect, this 1928 Spanish Mission–style theater, which once hosted big names such as Frank Sinatra, is now the venue for community

theater productions. The theater, supposedly haunted by a friendly female spirit, was the ghost-hunting site for the season finale of the SyFy Channel's Ghost Collector series.

Shopping

Head to N Market St and nearby Main St for fun browsing, with inviting antique stores between the 'Iao Theater and Wailuku Coffee on N Market St.

Native Intelligence GIFTS
(☎249-2421; www.native-intel.com; 19890 Main St; ⏰10am-5pm Mon-Fri, 10am-4pm Sat) This welcoming shop sells hula instruments, koa bowls and finely handcrafted items.

Information

First Hawaiian Bank (www.fhb.com; 27 N Market St)

Maui Memorial Medical Center (☎244-9056; www.mmmc.hhsc.org; 221 Mahalani St; ⏰24hr) The island's main hospital. For extreme emergencies flying to Queen's Medical Center in Honolulu may be preferable.

Post Office (☎244-1653; www.usps.com; 250 Imi Kala St; ⏰9am-4pm Mon-Fri, 9am-noon Sat)

DANGERS & ANNOYANCES

One caution: the town can get rough at night. The public parking lot on W Main St is an after-dark hangout rife with drug dealing and fights that gets more police calls than any other spot on Maui.

Getting There & Around

The Maui Bus (p356) loops beween the Queen Ka'ahumanu Center (Kahului) and various stops in Wailuku, including the state office building and the post office, between 6:30am and 8:30pm. The cost is $2 per boarding.

Wailuku to 'Iao Valley State Park

'Iao Valley is such a sumptuous sight that in ancient times it was reserved for royalty. Today much of the upper valley's natural beauty is preserved as parkland, all reached via 'Iao Valley Rd, which ends at misty 'Iao Valley State Park.

Sights

Tropical Gardens of Maui GARDENS
(☎244-3085; www.tropicalgardensofmaui.com; 200 'Iao Valley Rd; adult/child under 8yr $5/free; ⏰9am-4:30pm Mon-Sat) These fragrant gardens, which straddle both sides of 'Iao Stream, showcase a superb orchid collection, endemic Hawaiian plants, brilliant bromeliads and a meditative bamboo grove with a trickling waterfall. See if you can find the world's largest orchid! Visitors are given a numbered plant list, with descriptions, for their walk.

After your tour, explore the greenhouse. If you live on the mainland (and a few foreign countries), they'll ship your favorite exotic flower home.

Kepaniwai Park & Heritage Gardens PARK
(www.mauicounty.gov; 870 'Iao Valley Rd; ⏰7am-7pm; 👪) Two miles west of Wailuku, this family-oriented park pays tribute to Hawaii's ethnic heritage. Sharing the grounds are a traditional Hawaiian *hale,* a Filipino farmer's hut, Japanese gardens and a Chinese pavilion with a statue of revolutionary hero Sun Yat-sen (who, incidentally, briefly lived on Maui). 'Iao Stream runs through the park, bordered by picnic shelters with BBQ pits.

A lone pine tree, or *matsu,* was planted atop the small hill overlooking the gardens. A symbol of longevity and perservance, it honors the victims of the devastating Japanese earthquake and tsunami in 2011.

JFK Profile LANDMARK
('Iao Valley Rd) At a bend in the road a half-mile after Kepaniwai Park, you may see a few cars parked and their occupants staring off into Pali 'Ele'ele, a gorge on the right where a rock formation has eroded into the shape of a profile. Some legends associate it with a powerful kahuna (priest) who lived here during the 1500s; today it bears an uncanny resemblance to former US president John F Kennedy.

If parking is difficult, continue to 'Iao Valley State Park, a short walk away.

'Iao Valley State Park

The 'Iao Needle, rising above a mountain stream in Maui's lush interior, is a landmark scene of singular beauty. This sensuous rock pinnacle is the focal point of **'Iao Valley State Park** (www.hawaiistateparks.org; admission per car $5; ⏰7am-7pm), which starts 3 miles west of central Wailuku. This rainforest park extends up to Pu'u Kukui (5788ft), Maui's highest and wettest point.

History

The park's breathtaking beauty hides a tragic past. In 1790, Kamehameha I, who sought control over all of the Hawaiian islands, battled Mauian warriors who had retreated here following a barrage from his cannons, which were provided by westerners. The conflict was called the Battle of Kepewani, or the 'damming of the waters.' According to legend, the streams were clogged with the bodies of warriors killed during the final fight.

'Iao Needle

The velvety green pinnacle that rises straight up 2250ft takes its name from 'Iao, the daughter of Maui. 'Iao Needle is said to be 'Iao's clandestine lover, captured by an angry Maui and turned to stone. A monument to love, this is the big kahuna, the ultimate phallic symbol.

Whether you believe in legends or not, this place looks like it was torn from the pages of a fairy tale. Clouds rising up the valley form an ethereal shroud around the top of 'Iao Needle. With a stream meandering beneath and the steep cliffs of the West Maui Mountains as the backdrop, it's a prime photo-op.

Just a few minutes walk from the parking lot, you'll reach a bridge where most people shoot their photos of the needle. A better idea is to take the walkway just before the bridge that loops downhill by the stream; this leads to the nicest photo angle, one that captures the bridge and 'Iao Needle together.

If the water is high you'll see local kids taking bravado jumps from the bridge to the rocky stream below. You might be tempted to join them, but expect to get the stink-eye – not to mention that the rocks below are potentially spine-crushing for unfamiliar divers. Instead, take your dip in the swimming holes along the streamside path. Even there, however, be aware of potential dangers – the rocks in the stream are slippery and there can be flash floods.

WALKING TRAILS

After you cross the bridge you'll come to two short trails that start opposite each other. Both take just 10 minutes to walk and shouldn't be missed. The upper path leads skyward up a series of steps (133 to the top), ending at a sheltered lookout with a close-up view of 'Iao Needle. The lower path leads down along 'Iao Stream, skirting the rock-strewn stream-bed past native hau trees with their hibiscus-like flowers. Look around and you'll be able to spot fruiting guava trees as well. The lower path returns to the bridge by way of a garden of native Hawaiian plants, including patches of taro.

Pu'unene

Sugar is the lifeblood of Pu'unene. Endless fields of sugarcane expand out from the **Hawaiian Commercial & Sugar (C&S) Company's mill**, which sits smack in the center of the village. If you swing by when the mill is boiling down the sugarcane, the air is heavy with the sweet smell of molasses.

Sights

Alexander & Baldwin Sugar Museum MUSEUM

(☎871-8058; www.sugarmuseum.com; 3957 Hansen Rd, cnr Pu'unene Ave & Hansen Rd; adult/child 6-12yr $7/2; ⏲9:30am-4:30pm) The former home of the sugar mill's superintendent now houses this informative museum, which gives the skinny on the Maui sugarcane biz. Exhibit panels trace how the privileged sons of missionaries wrested control over Maui's fertile valleys and dug the amazing irrigation system that made large-scale plantations viable. Displays and photographs delve into immigration, work policies and plantation recreation. There's also a 10-minute video about sugar cane production. Last admission at 4pm.

Unique artifacts include a working scale model of a cane-crushing plant, an early-20th-century labor contract from the Japanese Emigration Company committing laborers to work the canefields 10 hours a day, 26 days a month for a mere $15, and a rubbing of the tombstone of founder Samuel Alexander, who was killed at Victoria Falls.

Old Pu'unene HISTORICAL SITE

A little slice of a bygone plantation village lies hidden behind the Hawaiian Commercial & Sugar Company's sugar mill. There, a long-forgotten church lies abandoned in a field of waving cane, across from the village's old schoolhouse. Still, the place isn't a ghost town. Out back, just beyond the school, is an old shack that has served as a used bookstore since 1913. Now managed by **Maui Friends of the Library** (www.users.

maui.net/~mfol; ⏲9am-4pm Tue-Sat), it's a bit musty and dusty, but the volunteers are super nice, the selection is wide and books sell for a mere quarter.

To get there turn off Mokulele Hwy (Hwy 311) onto Hansen Rd and take the first right onto Old Pu'unene Ave, continuing past the old Pu'unene Meat Market building (c 1926) and the mill. Turn left after 0.6 miles, just past a little bridge. Just before the pavement ends, turn right and drive behind the school to reach the bookstore.

Kealia Pond National Wildlife Refuge

A magnet for both birds and birdwatchers, this **refuge** (☎875-1582; www.fws.gov/kealiapond; Mokulele Hwy, MP 6; ⏲7:30am-4pm Mon-Fri) **FREE** harbors native waterbirds year-round and migratory birds from October to April. In the rainy winter months Kealia Pond swells to 400 acres, making it one of the largest natural ponds in Hawaii. In summer it shrinks to half that size, creating the skirt of crystalline salt that gives Kealia (meaning 'salt-encrusted place') its name.

Birding is excellent from the Kealia Pond Boardwalk, as well as from the refuge's **visitor center** off Mokulele Hwy (Hwy 311) at mile marker 6. In both places, you're almost certain to spot wading Hawaiian black-necked stilts and Hawaiian coots, two endangered species that thrive in this sanctuary.

Kealia Pond Boardwalk

The coastal marsh and dunes nestling Kealia Pond not only provide feeding grounds for native waterbirds but are also a nesting site for the endangered hawksbill sea turtle. On N Kihei Rd, just north of mile marker 2, interpretive plaques and benches along a 2200ft elevated **boardwalk** offer opportunities to stop and enjoy the seaside splendor. In winter you might be able to spot passing humpback whales. You'll even find a turtle laying eggs at the end of the boardwalk. Say what? Go take a look…

Ma'alaea

POP 352

Ma'alaea literally means 'beginning of red dirt,' but once you're there you'll swear it means 'windy.' Prevailing trade winds funneling between Maui's two great rises, Haleakalā and the West Maui Mountains, whip down upon the region. By midday you'll need to hold on to your hat. It's no coincidence that Maui's first windmill farm marches up the slopes above Ma'alaea.

Beaches

Ma'alaea Bay BEACH

Ma'alaea Bay is fronted by a 3-mile stretch of sandy beach, running from Ma'alaea Harbor south to Kihei. It can be accessed from **Haycraft Park** (http://www.co.maui.hi.us; 399 Hauoili St) at the end of Hauoli St in Ma'alaea and from several places along N Kihei Rd including **Kealia Beach** in front of the Kealia Pond Boardwalk.

Sights

★**Maui Ocean Center** AQUARIUM

(☎270-7000; www.mauioceancenter.com; 192 Ma'alaea Rd; adult/child 3-12yr $26/19; ⏲9am-5pm Sep-Jun, to 6pm Jul & Aug; 👪) The largest tropical aquarium in the USA showcases Hawaii's dazzling marine life with award-winning style. The exhibits lead you on an ocean journey, beginning with nearshore reefs teeming with colorful tropical fish and ending with deep-ocean sealife. For the spectacular grand finale, you walk along a 54ft clear acrylic tunnel right through the center of a 750,000 gallon tank as stingrays and sharks encircle you.

Kid-friendly features abound, including interactive displays about whales in the Marine Mammal Discovery Center, a cool touch pool and, best of all, *na keiki*–level viewing ports that allow the wee ones to peer into

> **SWIM WITH THE FISHES**
>
> The sharks are circling. Some 20 of them, to be exact. Blacktip reef sharks, hammerheads and, gasp, a tiger shark. And you can jump in and join them. **Shark Dive Maui** (☎270-7075; www.mauioceancenter.com; 2hr dive $199; ⏲8:15am Mon, Wed & Fri) takes intrepid divers on a daredevil's plunge into Maui Ocean Center's 750,000-gallon deep-ocean tank to swim with the toothy beasts as aquarium visitors gaze on in disbelief. You do need to be a certified diver and because it's limited to four divers per outing, advance reservations are essential.

everything on their own. While the kids explore, mom and dad might enjoy a quiet moment listening to whale songs or gazing at the graceful sea jellies.

Story of Hawaii Museum MUSEUM

(☎242-6938; www.storyofhawaiimuseum.com; Ma'alaea Harbor Shops, 300 Ma'alaea Rd; tour per person $10; ⏰10am-5pm) For a concise but illuminating history of the Hawaiian Islands, step inside this small museum and map gallery, which opened in 2012. If you have 30 minutes, take the docent-led tour, which stops beside original and reproduced historic maps. These cartographic wonders – check out the 1785 chart from Captain James Cook's explorations – are a fascinating backdrop for stories about the settlement and development of the islands.

Vintage Hawaiiana adds a retro kick to Hawaii's modern history. A donation of $7 per adult and $5 per child is requested for admission, but not required.

Giclee prints of the maps, as well as local arts and crafts, are also for sale. Check online for details about the monthly Hawaiian history talks. The museum is beside the Pacific Whale Foundation.

Activities

Snorkel & Whale-Watching Cruises

Many of the boats going to Molokini leave from Ma'alaea. Go in the morning. Afternoon trips are typically cheaper, but that's when the wind picks up so it's also rougher and murkier. Snorkel gear is included in the snorkeling cruises; bring your own towels and sunscreen.

★Pacific Whale Foundation - Ma'alaea BOAT TOUR

(☎249-8811; www.pacificwhale.org; Ma'alaea Harbor Shops; adult/child 7-12yr $55/35; 👪) Led by naturalists, these Molokini tours do it right, with onboard snorkeling lessons and wildlife talks. Snacks are provided and kids under six are free. Half-day tours concentrate on Molokini. Full-day tours combine snorkeling at Molokini and Lana'i, or Molokini and Turtle Arches. Also recommended are the whale-watching cruises (adult/child $34/18) that operate several times a day in the winter season.

Windsurfing & Surfing

Wicked winds from the north shoot straight out toward Kaho'olawe, creating some of the best windsurfing conditions on Maui. In winter, when the wind dies down elsewhere, windsurfers still fly along Ma'alaea Bay.

The bay has a couple of hot surfing spots. The **Ma'alaea Pipeline**, south of the harbor, freight-trains right and is the fastest surf break in all Hawaii. Summer's southerly swells produce huge tubes.

Hiking

Lahaina Pali Trail HIKING

Fine hilltop views of Kaho'olawe and Lana'i are in store along this trail, which follows an ancient footpath as it zigzags steeply up through native dryland. From the Hwy 30 trailhead, after the first mile, the trail passes into open, sun-baked scrub, from where you can see Haleakalā and the fertile central plains.

Ironwood trees precede the crossing of Kealaoloa Ridge (1600ft), after which you descend through Ukumehame Gulch. Look for stray petroglyphs and *paniolo* graffiti. Stay on the footpath all the way down to Papalaua Beach and don't detour onto 4WD roads. The 5.5-mile trail should take about 2½ hours each way.

You can hike in either direction, but starting off early from the east side of the mountains keeps you ahead of the blistering sun. Be aware of the risk of dehydration and heatstroke on this trail – bring plenty of water and a hat that provides shade. The trailhead access road, marked by a Na Ala Hele sign, is on Hwy 30, just south of its intersection with N Kihei Rd. If you prefer to start at the west end, the trailhead is 200 yards south of mile marker 11 on Hwy 30.

For a basic map and more details visit http://hawaiitrails.ehawaii.gov.

Eating

Beach Bums Bar & Grill BBQ $$

(☎243-2286; Ma'alaea Harbor Shops; lunch $7-12, dinner $9-24; ⏰8am-10pm) This harborfront eatery uses a wood-burning rotisserie smoker to grill up everything from burgers and ribs to turkey, mahi-mahi and Spam. Come between 3pm and 6pm for $3.25 drafts of Kona-brewed Longboard Lager.

★Waterfront Restaurant SEAFOOD $$$

(☎244-9028; www.waterfrontrestaurant.net; Ma'alaea Harbor Shops, 300 Ma'alaea Rd; lunch mains $10-19, dinner mains $25-47; ⏰11am-9pm) Savor the good life and fresh-off-the-boat seafood at this sparkling restaurant above Ma'alaea Harbor. A longtime favorite for fine dining, the Waterfront re-opened in this new, picturesque spot in 2012. At dinner, the fish depends on the daily catch, but the method of preparation – six tempting options – is yours.

For lunch, try the fish, a kiawe-grilled burger, or a globally inspired array of sandwiches. Food, service and wine selection are among Maui's best.

Getting There & Away

Located at a crossroads, Ma'alaea has good connections to the rest of Maui's public bus system. The **Maui Bus** (www.mauicounty.gov) connects the Harbor Shops at Ma'alaea with Lahaina, Kahului and Kihei. Service depends on the route, but buses operate hourly from around 6am to 8pm.

Molokini Crater

Molokini (per person $140) is a volcanic crater sitting midway between the islands of Maui and Kaho'olawe. The underwater sites within the crater often draw more than 1000 visitors per day.

Half of the crater rim has eroded away, leaving a pretty crescent moon that rises 160ft above the ocean surface, with a mere 18 acres of rocky land that's high and dry. But it's what's beneath the surface that draws the crowds. Snorkelers and divers will be thrilled by steep walls, ledges, white-tipped reef sharks, manta rays, turtles and abundant fish.

The legends about Molokini are myriad. One says Molokini was a beautiful woman who was turned to stone by jealous Pele, goddess of volcanoes. Another claims one of Pele's lovers angered her by secretly marrying a *mo'o* (shape-shifting water lizard). Pele chopped the sacred lizard in half, leaving Molokini as its tail and Pu'u Ola'i in Makena as its head. Yet another tale alleges that Molokini, which means 'many ties' in Hawaiian, is the umbilical cord left over from the birth of Kaho'olawe.

The coral reef that extends outward from Molokini is extraordinary, though it has lost some of its variety over the years. Most of the black coral that was once prolific in Molokini's deeper waters made its way into Lahaina jewelry stores before the island was declared a marine conservation district in 1977. During WWII the US Navy shelled Molokini for target practice, and live bombs are still occasionally spotted on the crater floor.

Be sure to consider the following when planning your excursion to Molokini: the water is calmest and clearest in the morning. Don't fall for discounted afternoon tours – get out there early for the smoothest sailing and best conditions. For snorkelers, there's simply not much to see when the water's choppy. The main departure point for outings to Molokini is Ma'alaea, but you can also get there from other ports, including Kihei.

KIHEI & SOUTH MAUI

Dubbed Haole-wood for its LA-style strip malls and white-bread resorts, South Maui *is* a bit shiny and overbuilt. But dig deeper and you'll find mixed plate of scenery and adventure – from Kihei to Wailea, Makena, and beyond – that's truly unique.

You can snorkel reefs teeming with turtles, kayak to remote bays or sail in an outrigger canoe. The coral gardens are so rich you can dive from the shore. And the beaches are undeniably glorious, whether you're looking to relax beneath a resort cabana or discover your own little pocket of sand. Add reliably sunny weather and a diverse dining scene, and South Maui is a pretty irresistible place to strand yourself.

Kihei

POP 20,881

This energetic community is a good choice for short-trip vacationers who want to maximize their beach time and their budgets – and throw in an adventure or two. Yes, it's overrun with strip malls, but with 6 miles of sun-kissed beaches, loads of affordable accommodations and a variety of dining options, it offers everything you need for an enjoyable seaside vacation.

To zip from one end of Kihei to the other, take the Pi'ilani Hwy (Hwy 31). It runs parallel to and bypasses the stop-start traffic of S Kihei Rd. Well-marked crossroads connect these two routes.

Beaches

The further south you go, the better the beaches. At the northern end of Kihei, swimming is not advised, but kayaking is good in the morning and windsurfers set off in the afternoon.

★**Keawakapu Beach** BEACH

(Map p366) From break of day to twilight, this sparkling stretch of sand is a showstopper. Extending from southern Kihei to Wailea's Mokapu Beach, Keawakapu is set back from the main road and less visible than Kihei's main roadside beaches just north. Also less crowded, it's a relaxing place to sunbathe, read and watch the sun go down.

With its cushiony soft sand, Keawakapu is also a favorite for sunrise yoga and wake-up strolls and is the perfect spot for an end-of-day swim. Mornings are the best time for snorkeling: head to the rocky outcrops that form the northern and southern ends of the beach. During winter keep an eye out for humpback whales, which come remarkably close to shore here.

There are three beach access points, all with outdoor showers. To get to the southern end, go south on S Kihei Rd until it dead-ends at a beach parking lot. Near the middle of the beach, there's a parking lot at the corner of Kilohana Dr and S Kihei Rd; from the parking lot, look across S Kihei Rd for a blue shoreline access sign. At the northern end, use the large unpaved access lot north of the Days Inn.

Kama'ole Beach Parks BEACH

Kama'ole Beach is having so much fun, it just keeps rolling along. And along. And along. Divided into three sections by rocky points, these popular strands are known locally as **Kam I** (Map p366; 2400 S Kihei Rd), **Kam II** (Map p366; 2550 S Kihei Rd) and **Kam III** (Map p366; 2800 S Kihei Rd). All three are pretty, golden-sand beaches with full facilities, lifeguards included. There's a volleyball court at Kam I while Kam I and III both have parking lots.

Water conditions vary with the weather, but swimming is usually good. For the most part, these beaches have sandy bottoms with a fairly steep drop, which tends to create good conditions for bodysurfing, especially in winter.

For snorkeling, the south end of Kama'ole Beach Park III has some nearshore rocks harboring a bit of coral and a few colorful fish, though it pales in comparison to the snorkeling at beaches further south.

Charley Young Beach BEACH

(Map p366) Out of sight from sightseers cruising the main drag, this side-street neighborhood beach is the least-touristed strand in Kihei. It's a real jewel in the rough: broad and sandy, and backed by swaying coconut palms. You're apt to find fishers casting their lines, families playing volleyball and someone strumming a guitar. It also has some of the better bodysurfing waves in Kihei.

Beach parking is on the corner of S Kihei Rd and Kaia'u Pl. To get to the beach, simply walk to the end of Kaia'u Pl and follow the steps down the cliff.

North Kihei

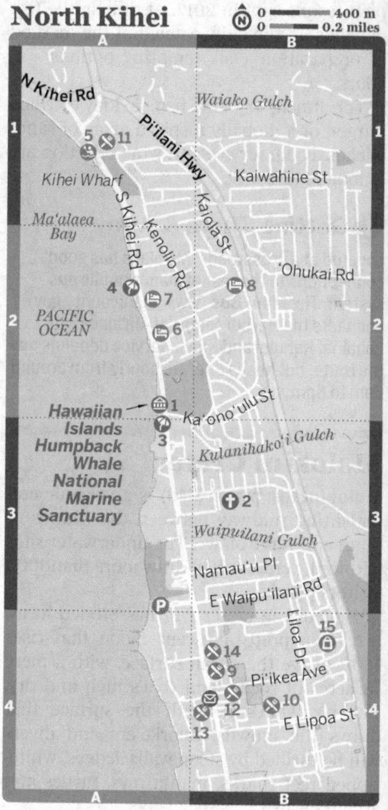

Kalepolepo Beach Park BEACH

(Map p364; 👪) Adjacent to the headquarters for the Humpback Whale National Marine Sanctuary, this compact park is a nice spot for families with younger kids. A grassy lawn is fronted by the ancient Ko'ie'ie Fishpond, whose stone walls create a shallow swimming pool with calm waters perfect for wading. There are also picnic tables, a grill and an outdoor shower.

North Kihei

Top Sights
1 Hawaiian Islands Humpback Whale National Marine Sanctuary ... A2

Sights
2 David Malo's Church ... B3
3 Kalepolepo Beach Park ... A3
Ko'ie'ie Fishpond ... (see 3)
4 Mai Poina 'Oe Ia'u Beach Park ... A2

Activities, Courses & Tours
5 Kihei Canoe Club ... A1

Sleeping
6 Maui Sunseeker ... A2
7 Nona Lani Cottages ... A2
8 Ocean Breeze Hideaway ... B2

Eating
9 Amigo's ... B4
Coconut's Fish Cafe ... (see 12)
10 Fabiani's Bakery & Pizza ... B4
11 Kihei Farmers Market ... A1
Safeway - Kihei ... (see 15)
12 Stella Blues ... B4
13 Vietnamese Cuisine ... B4
14 Yee's Orchard ... B4

Drinking & Nightlife
Diamonds Ice Bar ... (see 12)

Shopping
15 Pi'ilani Village ... B4

Mai Poina 'Oe Ia'u Beach Park BEACH
(Map p364) This long sandy beach at the northern end of Kihei is a popular morning launch for outrigger canoes and kayaks. After the wind picks up in the afternoon, it's South Maui's main venue for windsurfing.

Kalama Park PARK
(Map p366;) Athletes and fidgety kids will appreciate this expansive park which has tennis and basketball courts, ball fields and a skate park. Also on-site are a playground, picnic pavilions, restrooms and showers. There is a small beach behind a whale statue, but a runoff ditch carries waste water here after heavy rains so best swim elsewhere.

Sights

★Hawaiian Islands Humpback Whale National Marine Sanctuary MUSEUM
(Map p364; 800-831-4888, 879-2818; www.hawaiihumpbackwhale.noaa.gov; 726 S Kihei Rd; 10am-3pm Mon-Fri, also 10am-1pm Sat Dec-Mar;) FREE If you're curious about Maui's most famous annual visitors, stop by the marine sanctuary headquarters. The center overlooks an ancient fishpond, and its oceanfront lookout is ideal for sighting the humpback whales that frequent the bay during winter. There are even free scopes set up for viewing. Displays about whales and sea turtles provide background, and you'll find informative brochures about Hawaiian wildlife.

Swing by at 11am on Tuesday and Thursday (and on Saturday December to March) for free '45-Ton Talks' about whales.

Ko'ie'ie Fishpond HISTORICAL SITE
(Map p364) FREE In ancient Hawaii, coastal fishponds were built to provide a ready source of fish for royal families. The most intact fishpond remaining on Maui is the 3-acre Ko'ie'ie Fishpond, now on the National Register of Historic Places; it borders both Kalepolepo Beach Park and the Hawaiian Islands Humpback Whale National Marine Sanctuary headquarters.

David Malo's Church CHURCH
(Map p364; www.trinitybts.org; 100 Kulanihako'i St) Philosopher David Malo, who built this church in 1852, was the third Hawaiian ordained to the Christian ministry. He was also co-author of Hawaii's first constitution and an early spokesperson for Hawaiian rights. While most of Malo's original church has been dismantled, a 3ft-high section of the walls still stands beside a palm grove. Pews are lined up inside the stone walls.

Open-air services are held here at 9am Sunday by Trinity Episcopal Church-by-the-Sea. It's really quite beautiful.

Activities

Canoeing & Kayaking

★South Pacific Kayaks & Outfitters KAYAKING
(875-4848; www.southpacifickayaks.com; single/double kayak rental per day $45/65, tours from $69; rentals 6:45-11am, reservations 6am-8pm) This top-notch operation leads kayak-and-snorkel tours. It also rents kayaks, by reservation, and will deliver them to Makena Landing. The company recently started renting stand-up paddleboards, surfboards,

and kayaks (reservations strongly recommended) at Kalama Park, across from Kihei Caffe, from 7am to noon Monday to Saturday.

Kihei Canoe Club CANOEING
(Map p364; ☎879-5505; www.kiheicanoeclub.com; donation $30) As part of their Visitor Paddling Program, this canoe club invites travelers to share in the mana by joining members in paddling their outrigger canoes on Tuesday and Thursday mornings from about 7:30am to 9am. No reservations are necessary; show up just north of the junction of Uwapo and S Kihei Rd at 7am. It's first-come, first-served, and spots fill quickly. The $30 donation helps offset the cost of maintaining the canoes.

Diving & Snorkeling

Maui Dreams Dive Co DIVING, SNORKELING
(Map p366; ☎874-5332; www.mauidreamsdiveco.com; 1993 S Kihei Rd; 1-/2-tank shore dives from $69/99, 2-tank boat dive $129; 7am-6pm) Maui Dreams is a first-rate, five-star PADI operation specialising in shore dives. With this family-run outfit, a dive trip is like going out with friends. Nondivers, ask about the introductory dive ($89); to zoom around underwater, check out their scooter dive ($99 to $129).

Maui Dive Shop DIVING, SNORKELING
(Map p366; ☎879-3388; www.mauidiveshop.com; 1455 S Kihei Rd; 2-tank dives $140-150, snorkel rentals per day $6-8; 6am-9pm) This is a good spot to rent or buy watersports gear, including boogie boards, snorkels and wetsuits.

Blue Water Rafting BOAT TOUR
(Map p366; ☎879-7238; www.bluewaterrafting.com; Kihei Boat Ramp; Molokini Express/Kanaio Coast $50/100; departure times vary) In a hurry? Try the Molokini Express trip if you want to zip out to the crater, snorkel and be back within two hours. An adventurous half-day trip heads southward on a motorized raft to snorkel among sea turtles and dolphins at remote coves along the Kanaio coast. The Kihei Boat Ramp is south of Kam III.

Stand Up Paddleboarding

Stand Up Paddle Surf School SUP
(☎579-9231; www.standuppaddlesurfschool.com; 90min lesson $159; 9am & 11am) This SUP school is owned by Maria Souza, a champion paddle boarder who was also the first woman surfer to tow into the monster waves at Jaws. Small classes and safety are priorities, and the paddling location is determined by water conditions. Classes fill quickly, so call a few days – or a week – ahead.

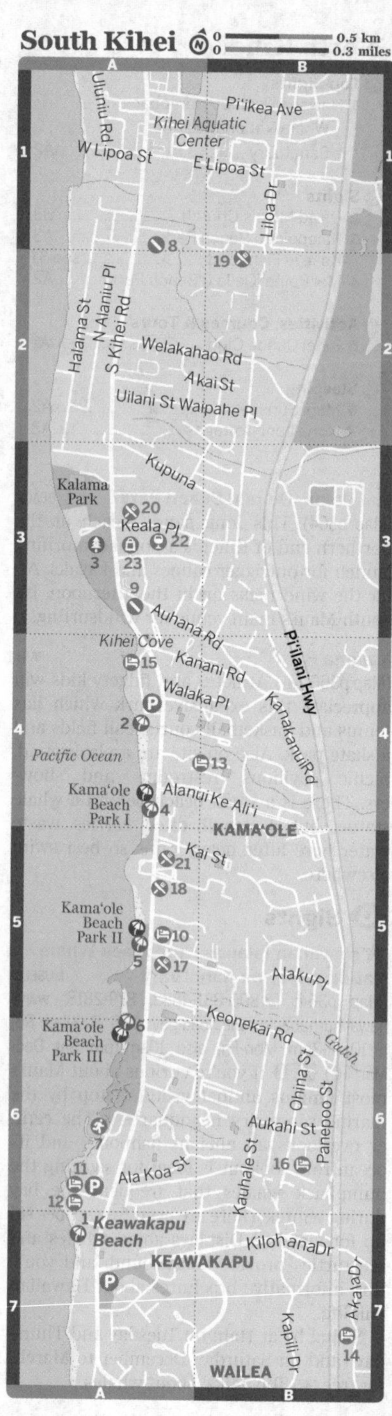

South Kihei

Top Sights
1 Keawakapu Beach...A7

Sights
2 Charley Young Beach...A4
3 Kalama Park...A3
4 Kama'ole Beach Park I...A4
5 Kama'ole Beach Park II...A5
6 Kama'ole Beach Park III...A6

Activities, Courses & Tours
7 Blue Water Rafting...A6
8 Maui Dive Shop...A1
9 Maui Dreams Dive Co...A3

Sleeping
10 Kihei Kai Nani...A5
11 Kihei Surfside Resort...A6
12 Mana Kai Maui...A6
13 Maui Coast Hotel...B4
14 Pineapple Inn Maui...B7
15 Punahoa...A4
16 Tutu Mermaids on Maui B&B...B6

Eating
808 Bistro...(see 17)
17 808 Deli...A5
18 Café O'Lei...A5
Da Kitchen Express...(see 18)
19 Eskimo Candy...B2
20 Foodland...A3
21 Hawaiian Moons Natural Foods...A5
Joy's Place...(see 9)
Kihei Caffe...(see 23)
Local Boys Shave Ice...(see 23)
Pita Paradise...(see 23)
Sansei Seafood Restaurant & Sushi Bar...(see 20)

Drinking & Nightlife
Five Palms...(see 12)
Lava Java...(see 23)
South Shore Tiki Lounge...(see 23)
22 The Dog and Duck...A3

Shopping
23 Kihei Kalama Village...A3

Festivals & Events

World Whale Day Celebration OUTDOOR FESTIVAL
(www.mauiwhalefestival.org; 9am-8pm;) Organized by the Pacific Whale Foundation, this family-friendly bash honors Maui's humpback whales with crafts, live music and food booths. It's held at Kalama Park, next to the big whale statue, on a Saturday in mid-February. The day kicks off with the Parade of Whales down S Kihei Rd at 9am.

Sleeping

Condos are plentiful in Kihei, whereas hotels and B&Bs are scarce. Some condominium complexes maintain a front desk that handles bookings, but others are booked via rental agents. When making a reservation, be sure to ask about reservation fees, cleaning fees and cancellation policies.

★Pineapple Inn Maui INN $$
(Map p366; 877-212-6284, 298-4403; www.pineappleinnmaui.com; 3170 Akala Dr; r $159-169, cottages $255;) If you're an active traveler who likes to unwind in an attractive, low-key setting, consider this inviting boutique inn overlooking Wailea, less than a mile from the beach. Rooms, which have ocean-view lanai and private entrances, are as nice as those at the exclusive resorts, but at a fraction of the cost. You can watch the sunset from the pool.

Rooms have kitchenettes, and the two-bedroom cottage comes with a full kitchen.

Maui Sunseeker BOUTIQUE HOTEL $$
(Map p364; 800-532-6284, 879-1261; www.mauisunseeker.com; 551 S Kihei Rd; r $175, ste $260-295, studio $185;) After a no-holds-barred makeover on the Travel Channel's reality show *Hotel Impossible,* the Maui Sunseeker emerged sleeker, smarter and, dare we say, a bit more fun. Catering to gays and lesbians, this breezy, 23-room property sprawls across five buildings in north Kihei, just across the street from Mai Poina 'Oela'u Beach.

Rooms beam with tasteful decor that outshines other places in this price range; all come with refrigerator, microwave and lanai. The hotel's revamp is ongoing, but watch for a new reception area and cafe. And the clothing-optional rooftop deck? The buns may have changed, but the deck's still there. The property is adults only.

Tutu Mermaids on Maui B&B B&B $$
(Map p366; 800-598-9550, 874-8687; www.twomermaids.com; 2840 Umalu Pl; studio/1br incl breakfast $140/170;) I'd like to be, under the sea…yep, the happy-go-lucky Beatles tune springs to mind inside the Ocean Ohana suite, a bright space swirling with whimsical maritime imagery. The Poolside Sweet,

with its sunset colors and in-room guitar, might inspire your own inner songwriter. Organic island fruit is provided for breakfast, and owner/mermaid Juddee bakes delicious banana bread.

Both units have kitchenettes, and the Ocean Ohana suite has air-con. Families are welcome. Formerly known as Two Mermaids, the new name reflects the owners status as *tutu* – or grandmothers.

Kihei Surfside Resort CONDO **$$**
(Map p366; www.kiheisurfsideresort.com; 2936 S Kihei Rd; 1br/2br from $180/360;) Tucked between the Kihei Coastal Trail and Keawakapu Beach, this six-story condo complex sports a bit of natty style – just look at that crisp, green lawn. Units are managed by a variety of management companies, and some individual owners. Photos, rates, and contact information for each unit can be found on the Kihei Surfside website. All have full kitchens, and the grounds include a heated oceanside pool and a putting green.

Nona Lani Cottages COTTAGES **$$**
(Map p364; 879-2497; www.nonalanicottages.com; 455 S Kihei Rd; cottages/suites $175/128;) Wooden cottages, lazy hammocks, picnic tables, swaying palms – this place looks like the tropical version of Camp Minnehaha. The eight retro cottages are compact, but squeeze in a full kitchen, a private lanai, a living room with daybed and a bedroom with a queen bed, plus cable TV. Wi-fi available in the lobby area.

Ocean Breeze Hideaway B&B **$$**
(Map p364; 888-463-6687, 879-0657; www.hawaiibednbreakfast.com; 435 Kalalau Pl; r incl breakfast from $99;) Bob and Sande have run this welcoming B&B for more than 12 years and, with their licensed activity desk certification, the couple is a treasure trove of insider tips. Their home has two comfortable guest rooms, one with a queen bed and ceiling fans and the other with a king bed and air-con. Both have a private entrance and a refrigerator. Children 12 and older OK.

Kihei Kai Nani CONDOS **$$**
(Map p366; 800-473-1493, 879-9088; www.kiheikainani.com; 2495 S Kihei Rd; 1br from $140;) Rooms and decor may be a little on the old side, but when it comes to amenities this inviting low-rise condo is on par with more expensive properties. On site are a large pool, a laundry room, shuffleboard, gas BBQ grills and picnic tables – all fringed by colorful tropical landscaping. Kam II is across the street.

With 150-rentable units, give these folks a call if you've landed in Maui without reservations. Wi-fi available in some units and by the pool.

Maui Coast Hotel HOTEL **$$$**
(Map p366; 800-895-6284, 874-6284; www.mauicoasthotel.com; 2259 S Kihei Rd; r $279-325, ste $319-365;) We're not swooning, but among Kihei's few hotels, this is the best. It's clean and comfortable, and the set-back-from-the-road location makes it quieter than other places on the strip. The $18 daily resort fee – a bit presumptuous for a compact property that's not on the beach – includes wi-fi, parking and use of bicycles and local shuttle service.

★ **Punahoa** CONDO **$$$**
(Map p366; 800-564-4380, 879-2720; www.punahoabeach.com; 2142 Ili'ili Rd; studio/1br/2br $189/269/299;) Sip coffee, scan for whales, savor sunsets – it's hard to leave your lanai at Punahoa, a classy boutique condo where every unit has a clear-on ocean view. This 15-unit complex on a quiet side street offers privacy and warm alohas. It's also next to a gorgeous strand of sand, Punahoa Beach, that's a favorite of turtles and surfers alike. Penthouse units have air-conditioning.

Mana Kai Maui CONDO **$$$**
(Map p366; 800-525-2025, 879-1561; www.manakaimaui.com; 2960 S Kihei Rd; r/1br/2br from $205/345/405;) On a point overlooking Keawakapu Beach, this complex offers great sunset views. You can swim and snorkel from the beach right outside the door or stay inside and take a class at the yoga studio. The on-site rental company manages 50 units, offering a mix of hotel rooms and one- and two-bedroom condos, with a front desk. There's also a full-service restaurant.

Request an upper floor for the best views.

Eating

Kihei has two 24-hour supermarkets: **Foodland** (Map p366; 879-9350; www.foodland.com; Kihei Town Center, 1881 S Kihei Rd; 24hr) and **Safeway** (Map p364; 891-9120; www.safeway.com; Pi'ilani Village, 277 Pi'ikea Ave; 24hr). **Hawaiian Moons Natural Foods** (Map p366; 875-4356; www.hawaiianmoons.com; Kama'ole Beach Center, 2411 S Kihei Rd; 8am-9pm;) is a good place to pack a healthy picnic lunch. **Kihei Farmers Market** (Map p364; 61 S Kihei

Rd; ⏲ 8am-4pm Mon-Thu, to 5pm Fri) sells island-grown fruits and vegetables – a bit pricey but fresh. For out-of-this-world mangoes from May through summer, try the fruit stand at 60-year-old **Yee's Orchard** (Map p364; 1165 S Kihei Rd; ⏲ 11am-5pm Tue-Thu, Sat & Sun) just north of Longs Drugs.

808 Deli CAFE $
(Map p366; ☎ 879-1111; www.808deli.com; #102, 2511 S Kihei Rd; breakfast $5-7, lunch $6-8; ⏲ 7am-5pm) As Subway wept and Quizno's cried, 808 Deli tap-danced its way into our sandwich-loving hearts. With fresh breads, gourmet spreads and 22 different sandwiches and paninis, this tiny gourmet sandwich shop across from Kam II is the place to grab a picnic lunch. For a spicy kick, try the roast beef with pepper jack and wasabi aioli.

Kihei Caffe CAFE $
(Map p366; 1945 S Kihei Rd; mains $8-15; ⏲ 5am-2pm) Advice for newbies and the indecisive: step to the side and review the menu before joining the queue. The cashier is chatty, but he keeps that long line moving. Next, fill your coffee cup at the thermos, snag a table on the patio, then watch the breakfast burritos, veggie scrambles and *loco mocos* flash by. And keep an eye on those sneaky birds. Cash only.

Solos, couples, families – everybody's here or on the way.

Eskimo Candy SEAFOOD $
(Map p366; ☎ 891-8898; www.eskimocandy.com; 2665 Wai Wai Place; mains $8-17; ⏲ 10:30am-7pm Mon-Fri) On a side street, Eskimo Candy is a fish market with a takeout counter and a few tables. Fresh-fish fanatics should zero in on the *poke,* ahi wraps and fish tacos.

Amigo's MEXICAN $
(Map p364; ☎ 879-9952; www.amigosmaui.com; Azeka Mauka II, 1215 S Kihei Rd; breakfast $6-11, lunch $8-15, dinner $10-15; ⏲ 10am-9pm Mon-Fri, 9am-9pm Sat & Sun) On Tuesdays burritos are only $7 at this family-run Mexican restaurant that's part of a small island-wide chain. Come here for *huevos rancheros,* sizzling fajitas and combo plates. Staff is attentive, and the salsa bar is can't miss if you like to spice it up.

Lava Java CAFE $
(Map p366; ☎ 879-1919; www.lavajavamaui.com; Kihei Kalama Village, 1941 S Kihei Rd; ⏲ 6am-8pm; 📶) Counter service can be slow in the morning but that might be due to the drink special: buy-one-get-the-second-half-price (6am to 9am). The super-nice owner regularly serves free samples of iced mocha. Computers with internet access (20¢ per minute) are in the back. Scaly gecko balls – a chocolate-and-macdamia-nut treat – are in the middle.

Local Boys Shave Ice SHAVE ICE $
(Map p366; www.localboysshaveice.com; Kihei Kalama Village, 1941 S Kihei Rd; shave ice $4-6; ⏲ 10am-9pm) Local Boys dishes up soft shave ice in a dazzling rainbow of sweet syrups. Try it tropical (banana, mango and 'shark's blood') with ice cream, *kauai* cream and azuki beans. Load up on napkins; these babies are messy!

★ **Café O'Lei** HAWAII REGIONAL $$
(Map p366; ☎ 891-1368; www.cafeoleicatering.com/restaurants; Rainbow Mall, 2439 S Kihei Rd; lunch $7-15, dinner $19-49; ⏲ 10:30am-3:30pm & 4:30-9:30pm) With its strip-mall setting, this bistro looks ho-hum at first blush. But step inside. The sophisticated atmosphere, innovative Hawaii regional cuisine, honest prices and excellent service knock Café O'Lei into the fine-dining big leagues. For a tangy treat, order the blackened mahimahi with fresh papaya salsa. Unbeatable lunch entrées, with salads, are available for under $10. Famous martinis, too.

★ **Da Kitchen Express** HAWAII REGIONAL $$
(Map p366; www.da-kitchen.com; Rainbow Mall, 2439 S Kihei Rd; breakfast $9-13, lunch & dinner $9-19; ⏲ 9am-9pm) Da kitchen is da bomb. Congenial service, heaping portions, loads of flavor – come here to eat like a king. Tucked in the back of anvil-shaped Rainbow Mall, this low-frills eatery is all about Hawaiian plate lunches. The local favorite is Da Lau Lau Plate (steamed pork wrapped in taro leaves), but you won't go wrong with any choice. We particularly liked the spicy *kalua* pork.

Sansei Seafood Restaurant & Sushi Bar JAPANESE $$
(Map p366; ☎ 879-0004; www.sanseihawaii.com; Kihei Town Center, 1881 S Kihei Rd; appetizers $3-15, mains $17-32; ⏲ 5:30-10pm, to 1am Thu-Sat) Maui is laid back, but sometimes you've got to plan ahead. Dinner at Sansei is one of those times – make a reservation or queue early for the sushi bar. Sansei's creative appetizer menu includes everything from a shrimp cake with ginger-lime chili butter to lobster and blue-crab ravioli. Hot Eurasian fusion dishes include ginger hoisin smoke duck in a soy demi.

Maui

There's a thrill for every adventurer on the Valley Isle. Adrenaline junkies surf and soar while take-it-easy explorers snorkel the coast or drive past waterfalls. Armchair adventurers might glimpse a whale from the comforts of their cushy lounge chair. And for culinary explorers? From food truck to four-star, Maui has it all.

1

2

GREG ELMS / GETTY IMAGES ©

4

JOHN ELK / GETTY IMAGES ©

1. Molokini Crater (p363)
Marine wildlife is on display at this crater located between the islands of Maui and Kaho'olawe.

2. Pipiwai Trail (p420)
This trail in 'Ohe'o Gulch, with its bamboo forest and waterfalls, offers something for every hiker.

3. Big Beach (p379)
Makena's Big Beach (aka Oneloa Beach) offers perfect, glassy waves for boogie boarding.

4. 'Iao Needle (p360)
This startling pinnacle rises 2250ft above the greenery of 'Iao Valley State Park.

3

QUINCY DEIN / GETTY IMAGES ©

Between 5:30pm and 6pm all food is discounted 25%; sushi and appetizers are discounted 50% from 10pm to 1am Thursday through Saturday.

Fabiani's Bakery & Pizza ITALIAN, BAKERY $$
(Map p364; ☎874-0888; www.fabianis.com; 95 E Lipoa St; breakfast $3-9, lunch $7-13, dinner $8-15; ⊙8am-10pm) What puts the fab in Fabiani's? Definitely the prosciutto, mozzarella and arugula pizza with truffle oil. Or wait, maybe it's the linguini with sauteed clams. Or the chef-made pastries – the macaroons, cinnamon rolls and croissants preening like celebrities as you walk in the door.

Whatever your choice, you'll surely feel fabulous nibbling your meal inside this sparkling new Italian eatery and pastry shop that's the talk of south Maui. There's also a rather nice bar.

Coconut's Fish Cafe SEAFOOD $$
(Map p364; ☎875-9979; www.coconutsfishcafe.com; Azeka Mauka II, 1279 S Kihei Rd; mains $10-16; ⊙11am-9pm;) This breezy spot is Kihei's go-to spot for fresh, healthily prepared seafood. Order at the counter – we recommend the fish tacos – then settle in at one of the seven surfboard tables. All the fish is grilled, all ingredients are homemade (except the catsup), and the staff is welcoming.

With its quick service, simple entrées and low-fuss decor, Coconut's is a great choice for families with younger kids.

808 Bistro BISTRO $$
(Map p366; ☎879-8008; www.808bistro.com; 2511-A S Kihei Rd; breakfast $7-15, dinner $15-24; ⊙7am-noon & 5-9pm) The menu at this open-air bistro showcases comfort foods prepared with a gourmet spin – think short rib pot pie and Gorgonzola alfredo. Give up your diet at breakfast with banana bread French toast or the decadent whale pie with ham, hash browns, eggs, cheese and brown gravy.

The eatery, which is owned by the folks running the ever-popular 808 Deli, is BYOB with a $5 corkage fee.

Joy's Place CAFE $$
(Map p366; www.joysplacemaui.com; Island Surf Bldg, 1993 S Kihei Rd; breakfast $3-9, sandwiches $11-13; ⊙8am-4pm Mon-Sat;) The operative words here are organic, free range, locally harvested. The overstuffed sandwiches and daily specials like fresh fish tacos attract a loyal following. In fact, Joy's sandwiches have proven so popular that they're now also sold at Whole Foods (p353) in Kahului.

Stella Blues ECLECTIC $$
(Map p364; ☎874-3779; www.stellablues.com; Azeka Mauka II, 1279 S Kihei Rd; breakfast $6-15, lunch $9-13, dinner $12-29; ⊙7:30am-11pm;) Named for the owners' favorite Grateful Dead song, this local stand-by never skimps, and the eclectic menu offers something for every mood, from Hawaiian-style banana macadamia-nut pancakes to pan-seared fresh fish and Maui Cattle Co burgers. Stella Blues is also a great place to catch live music. Check its Facebook page for the schedule.

Vietnamese Cuisine VIETNAMESE $$
(Map p364; ☎875-2088; www.mauivietnameserestaurant.com; Azeka Makai, 1280 S Kihei Rd; mains $10-19; ⊙10am-9:30pm) The restaurant's name and the strip-mall location may be ho hum, but the curried lemongrass chicken with jasmine rice awakens the senses. Or take a trip around the world with the *banh hoi,* a roll-your-own Vietnamese version of a burrito that come with mint leaves, assorted veggies and grilled shrimp.

Pita Paradise MEDITERRANEAN $$
(Map p366; ☎875-7679; www.pitaparadisehawaii.com; Kihei Kalama Village, 1913 S Kihei Rd; mains $8-20; ⊙11am-9:30pm) Aloha. Yassou. Dig in. Enjoy gyros and kebabs inside or on the deck at this low-key Greek favorite in the Triangle.

Drinking & Nightlife

Most bars in Kihei are across the street from the beach and have nightly entertainment. Kihei Kalama Village, aka the Bar-muda Triangle (or just the Triangle), is crammed tight with buzzy watering holes.

South Shore Tiki Lounge BAR
(Map p366; ☎874-6444; www.southshoretikilounge.com; Kihei Kalama Village, 1913 S Kihei Rd; ⊙11am-2am;) This cozy tropical shack has a heart as big as its lanai. The drink maestros here regularly win annual *Maui Time Weekly* awards for best female and male bartenders. Good for dancing too.

Dog and Duck PUB
(Map p366; ☎875-9669; 1913 S Kihei Rd, Kihei Kalama Village; ⊙11am-2am Mon-Fri, 8am-2am Sat & Sun) This cheery Irish pub with a welcoming vibe attracts a younger crowd. And yes, it has sports on TV, but it's not blaring from every corner. Decent spuds and pub grub go along with that heady Guinness draft, and there's music most nights of the week.

Five Palms COCKTAIL BAR
(Map p366; www.manakaimaui.com; 2960 S Kihei Rd; ⌚8am-11pm, happy hour 3-7pm & 9-11pm) For a sunset mai tai beside the beach, this is the place. Arrive an hour before the sun goes down because the patio, just steps from stunning Keawakapu Beach, fills quickly. Sushi and *pupus* are half-price during happy hour.

Diamonds Ice Bar BAR
(Map p364; ☎874-9299; www.diamondsicebar.com; Azeka Mauka II, 1279 S Kihei Rd; ⌚11am-2am Mon-Sat, 7am-2am Sun) We're not sure where the cheesy name orginated, but we can tell you this – Diamonds Ice sells more jagermaester than any other watering hole on the island. So get your woozy shot, play a little pool then sit and watch who's lured in by the bright neon lights. Check the Facebook page to see who's playing or spinning on the weekends.

Shopping

Pi'ilani Village SHOPPING CENTER
(Map p364; 225 Pi'ikea Ave) Kihei's largest shopping center has a variety of stores, perfect for stocking up on everything from gifts to beachwear.

Kihei Kalama Village MARKET
(Map p366; ☎879-6610; 1913 S Kihei Rd; ⌚pavilion shops 10am-7:30pm) More than 40 shops and stalls cluster at this shopping arcade. Ladies, for fashionable beachwear pop into **Mahina**. Looking for unique T-shirts? Check out the T-shirts, hoodies and hats, with original Maui designs, inside **808 Clothing Company** which has two locations at Kalama Village. For made-in-Hawaii jams and seasonings, step into **Tutu's Pantry**. Hours may vary slighty from store to store.

Information

Bank of Hawaii – Kihei (☎879-5844; www.boh.com; Azeka Mauka II, 1279 S Kihei Rd; ⌚8:30am-4pm Mon-Thu, to 6pm Fri)

Kihei Police District Station (☎244-6400; Kihei Town Center, 1881 S Kihei Rd; ⌚7:45am-4:30pm Mon-Fri)

Longs Drugs (☎879-2033; www.cvs.com; 1215 S Kihei Rd; ⌚24hr) Kihei's largest pharmacy, with one aisle stocked totally with slippers (flip flops, yo).

Post Office (☎879-1987; www; 1254 S Kihei Rd; ⌚8:30am-4:30pm Mon-Fri, 9am-1pm Sun)

Urgent Care Maui Physicians (☎879-7781; 1325 S Kihei Rd; ⌚7am-9pm) This clinic accepts walk-in patients.

Getting There & Around

TO/FROM THE AIRPORT

Almost everyone rents a car at the airport in Kahului. Otherwise, expect to pay about $29 to $33 for a shuttle service or $30 to $45 for a taxi depending on your location in Kihei.

BICYCLE

Bike lanes run along both the Pi'ilani Hwy and S Kihei Rd, but cyclists need to be cautious of inattentive drivers making sudden turns across the lanes.

South Maui Bicycles (☎874-0068; www.southmauibicycles.com; Island Surf Bldg, 1993 S Kihei Rd; per day $22-60, per week $99-250; ⌚10am-6pm Mon-Sat) This shop rents top-of-the-line Trek road bicycles as well as basic around-town bikes.

BUS

The **Maui Bus** (www.mauicounty.gov) serves Kihei with two routes. One route, the Kihei Islander, connects Kihei with Wailea and Kahului; stops include Kama'ole Beach Park III, Pi'ilani Village shopping center, and northern Wailea. The other route, the Kihei Villager, primarily serves the northern half of Kihei, with a half-dozen stops

CYCLING ON MAUI

Maui's stunning scenery will entice hard-core cyclists, but casual riders hoping to use a bike as a primary source of transportation around the island may well find the island's steep topography and narrow roads daunting. A cyclist was killed on the narrow Kahekili Hwy in 2013.

Getting around by bicycle within a small area can be a reasonable option for the average rider, however. For example, the tourist enclave of Kihei is largely level and has cycle lanes on its two main drags, S Kihei Rd and the Pi'ilani Hwy.

The full-color *Maui County Bicycle Map* ($6), available from bicycle shops, shows all the roads on Maui that have cycle lanes and gives other nitty-gritty details. Consider it essential if you intend to do your exploring by pedal power. You can also peruse it online at the West Maui Cycles and South Maui Cycles websites.

along S Kihei Rd and a stop in Ma'alaea. From Ma'alaea you can connect with buses bound for Lahaina. Both routes operate hourly from around 5:30am to 8:30pm and cost $2.

CAR

Kihei Rent A Car (800-251-5288, 879-7257; www.kiheirentacar.com; 96 Kio Loop; per day/week from $35/175) This family-owned company rents cars and jeeps to those aged 21 and over, and includes free mileage. For lower rental rates, consider one of the older model cars (which can be well-worn!). Provides Kahului Airport shuttle pickup for rentals over five days.

Wailea

POP 5938

With its tidy golf courses, protective privacy walls and discreet signage, Wailea looks like a members-only country club. It is South Maui's most elite haunt, standing in sharp contrast to Kihei. Don't bother looking for gas stations or fast-food joints; this exclusive community is all about swank beachfront resorts and low-rise condo villas, with all the glitzy accessories.

One look at the beaches and it's easy to see why it has become such hot real estate. The golden-sand jewels sparkling along the Wailea coast are postcard material, offering phenomenal swimming, snorkeling and sunbathing. If you're not staying here, say a loud *mahalo* for Hawaii's beach access laws that allow you to visit anyway.

From Lahaina or Kahului, take the Pi'ilani Hwy (Hwy 31) to Wailea instead of S Kihei Rd, which is Kihei's stop-and-go main road. Once in Wailea, Wailea Alanui Dr turns into Makena Alanui Dr after Polo Beach and continues into Makena.

Beaches

Wailea's fabulous beaches begin with the southern end of Keawakapu Beach in Kihei and continue south toward Makena. All of the beaches that are backed by resorts have public access, with free parking, showers and restrooms. The beaches in this section are listed from north to south.

Mokapu & Ulua Beaches — BEACH

Ulua Beach offers Wailea's best easy-access snorkeling. It's teeming with brilliant tropical fish, and it's also one of the best spots for hearing humpbacks sing as they pass offshore. Snorkelers should head straight for the coral at the rocky outcrop on the right side of Ulua Beach, which separates it from **Mokapu Beach** just north.

Snorkeling is best in the morning before the winds pick up. When the surf's up, forget snorkeling – go bodysurfing instead. The beach access road is just north of the Wailea Marriott Resort.

Snorkelers will be glad to learn that the tiny parking lot here recently added more spaces, so you don't have to rise at dawn to find a spot. The bad news? The lot straddles the massive Andaz Maui at Wailea, set to open in the summer of 2013. The reef is about to get a lot more company.

★Wailea Beach — BEACH

Strut your stuff celebrity-style on this popular, crescent-shaped beach, which fronts the Grand Wailea and the Four Seasons. The shore slopes gradually here, making it a good swimming spot. When it's calm, there's decent snorkeling around the rocky point on the southern end. Most afternoons there's a gentle shorebreak suitable for bodysurfing. Divers entering the water at Wailea Beach can follow an offshore reef that runs down to Polo Beach.

The beach access road is between the Grand Wailea and Four Seasons resorts, and there is plenty of free parking.

Polo Beach — BEACH

In front of the Fairmont Kea Lani, Polo Beach is seldom crowded. When there's wave action, boogie boarders and bodysurfers usually find good shorebreaks here. When calm, the rocks at the northern end of the beach provide good snorkeling. At low tide, the lava outcropping at the southern end holds tide pools harboring spiny sea urchins and small fish.

To find it, turn down Kaukahi St after the Fairmont Kea Lani and look for the beach parking lot on the right.

Palauea Beach — BEACH

This untouristed sandy stretch to the south of Polo Beach attracts local surfers and boogie boarders. Kiawe trees block the view of the beach from the roadside, but you can find it easily by spotting the line of cars parked along Makena Rd.

Po'olenalena Beach — BEACH

To avoid the resorts, drive south to this long and lovely crescent favored by local families on weekends. It's rarely crowded and the shallow, sandy bottom and calm waters make for excellent swimming. There's good

LOCAL KNOWLEDGE

WAILEA BEACH WALK

For the perfect sunset stroll, take the 1.3-mile shoreline path that connects Wailea's beaches and the resort hotels that front them. The undulating path winds above jagged lava points and back down to the sandy shore. In winter this is one of the best places in all of Maui for spotting humpback whales. On a good day you may be able to see more than a dozen of them frolicking offshore.

Some of the luxury hotels along the walk are worth a stroll, most notably the Grand Wailea Resort, which is adorned with $30 million worth of artwork. In front of the Wailea Point condos you'll find the foundations of three Hawaiian house sites dating to AD 1300 – it's also a fine spot to watch the sunset.

snorkeling off both the southern and northern lava points. The parking lot is on Makena Alanui Rd.

Activities

Hawaiian Sailing Canoe Adventures CANOEING
(281-9301; www.mauisailingcanoe.com; adult/child 5-12yr $99/79; tours 8am & 10am) Learn about native traditions on two-hour sails aboard a Hawaiian-style outrigger canoe. With a max of six passengers, they're able to accommodate requests – including stopping to snorkel with turtles. Tours depart from Polo Beach.

Maui Ocean Activities WATER SPORTS
(357-8989; www.mauioceanactivities.com; Grand Wailea Resort, 3850 Wailea Alanui Dr; snorkel/boogie boards/kayak/stand up paddleboard per hr $10/10/30/40; 8am-3pm) On the beach behind the Grand Wailea, Maui Ocean rents what you need for watery fun.

Wailea Golf Club GOLF
(875-7450; www.waileagolf.com; 100 Wailea Golf Club Dr; greens fee $160-235; 1st tee around 7am) There are three championship courses in Wailea: the **Emerald** is a tropical garden that consistently ranks at the top; the rugged **Gold** course takes advantage of volcanic landscapes; and the **Old Blue** course (120 Kaukahi St) is marked by an open fairway and challenging greens.

Wailea Tennis Club TENNIS
(879-1958; www.waileatennis.com; 131 Wailea Ike Pl; per person opening-noon $15, noon-close $20; 7am-noon & 3-6pm Mon-Fri, 8am-4pm Sat & Sun) Nicknamed 'Wimbledon West,' this award-winning complex has 11 Plexi-pave courts and equipment rentals. Ninety-minute lessons are also available (clinic/private $35/140).

Festivals & Events

Maui Film Festival FILM
(www.mauifilmfestival.com) Hollywood celebs swoop in for this five-day extravaganza in mid-June. Join the stars under the stars at various Wailea locations, including the open-air 'Celestial Theater' on a nearby golf course.

Sleeping

★Four Seasons Maui at Wailea RESORT HOTEL $$$
(800-311-0630, 874-8000; www.fourseasons.com/maui; 3900 Wailea Alanui Dr; r/ste from $525/995; P ❄ @ 🛜 ≋) As you sip your complimentary ginger-mint lemonade in the lobby, it's hard not to be impressed by the Four Season's sophisticated charm. From the plush lobby lounge with its framed ocean views to the accommodating staff to the inclusive pricing (no resort fee), the joy is in the details and the warm aloha spirit. Standard rooms are midsized and furnished with understated tropical elegance, slightly more comfy than sophisticated. Marble bathrooms have loads of counter space and a choice of piped-in music.

Children are welcome – there are fun pools plus the Kids for All Seasons program – but the resort feels more low-key than its neighbors. Relaxing is easy; float in the adults-only serenity pool or enjoy a Hawaiian hot stone massage with cocoa butter slathering in a seaside hale. Parking is $20 per day.

Grand Wailea Resort Hotel & Spa RESORT HOTEL $$$
(800-888-6100, 875-1234; www.grandwailea.com; 3850 Wailea Alanui Dr; r /ste from $609/1200; ❄ @ 🛜 ≋) We planned to make this posh, fun-loving resort a Top Choice, but when Paris Hilton, Jennifer Aniston and Oprah Winfrey

have already given their stamp of approval, why bother? We jest, but it's OK to tease an icon you love. The Grand Wailea's unbridled extravagance, from the million-dollar artwork in the lobby to the guest rooms decked out in Italian marble, is a wonder.

But it's not all highbrow. The resort, part of the Hilton's Waldorf-Astoria line, boasts the most elaborate water-world wonders in Hawaii, an awesome series of interconnected pools with swim-through grottos, towering water slides and a swim-up bar. The $25 resort fee includes wi-fi.

Hotel Wailea HOTEL **$$$**
(874-0500, 866-970-4167; www.hotelwailea.com; 555 Kaukahi St; ste $264;) Want to sleep inside a landscape painting? The Hotel Wailea, with its hilltop perch, lush grounds and stove-pipe lobby, just needs a frame for artistic completion. The all-suites hotel, which formerly catered to Japanese businessmen, is under new ownership. Rooms come with microwaves and mini-fridges, and are in the process of a stylish revamp.

The hotel is not on the ocean, but the $25 resort fee includes a shuttle to Wailea Beach. On-site yoga classes offered daily. Wi-fi available in the lobby and by the pool.

Eating

Waterfront Deli DELI **$**
(891-2039; Shops at Wailea, 3750 Wailea Alanui Dr; mains under $7; 7am-8pm) For a quick, inexpensive meal to-go, head to this deli inside the Whalers General Store at the back of the Shops at Wailea.

Monkeypod Kitchen PUB **$$**
(891-2322; www.monkeypodkitchen.com; Wailea Gateway, 10 Wailea Gateway Pl; lunch $11-21, dinner $14-33; 11:30am-11pm, happy hour 3-5:30pm & 9-11pm) At first glance this new eatery seems a little too hip and a little too glossy for laid back Maui. But then you take a seat at the chattering bar. There, the staff and your fellow drinkers keep the alohas real. The restaurant strives to maintain an organic and sustainable menu, evidenced by the Maui Cattle burgers and Upcountry veggies.

Woodfired pizzas are $9 during happy hour – mmm, Hamakua wild mushroom – and there are 36 beers on tap.

Pita Paradise MEDITERRANEAN **$$**
(879-7177; www.pitaparadisehawaii.com; Wailea Gateway Center, 34 Wailea Gateway Pl; lunch $9-18, dinner $16-30; 11am-9:30pm) Although this

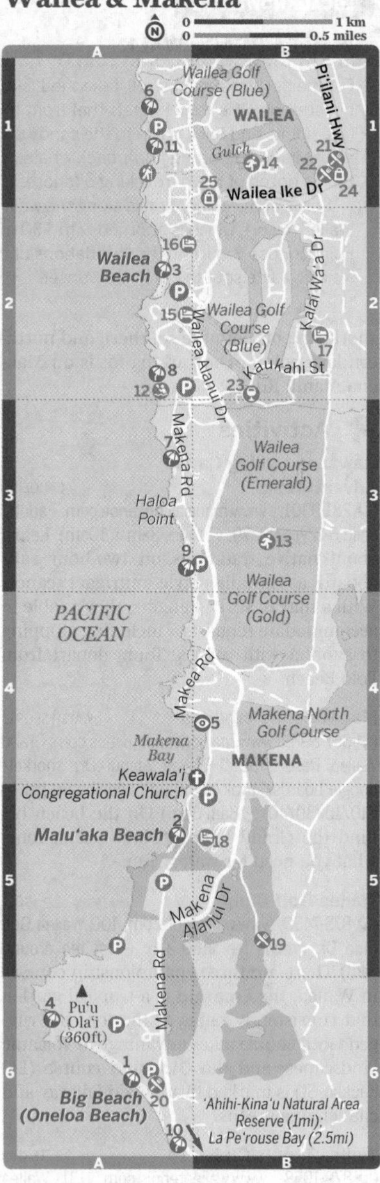

Greek taverna sits in a cookie-cutter strip mall lacking ocean views, the inviting patio, townscape mural and tiny white lights – not to mention the succulent Mediterranean chicken pita – banish any locational regrets. Owner John Arabatzis Jr catches his own

Wailea & Makena

fish, which is served in everything from pita sandwiches at lunch to grilled kabobs at dinner.

★ **Alan Wong's Amasia** FUSION, TAPAS $$$
(☎891-3954; www.wailearesortdining.com; Grand Wailea, 3850 Wailea Alanui Dr; small plates $11-40, sushi $8-50; ⏲5-10pm) The Whole Tomato Salad looks like art – a bright red orb balanced on a delicate layer of cucumber, all framed by a circle of plummy-orange dressing. One bite and the distinct but complementary flavors lift the meal to masterpiece. It's a skill that owner and chef Alan Wong brings to an enticing array of international small plates at his latest venture, Amasia, inside the Grand Wailea.

To find the tucked-away restaurant, once the lair of the resort's Japanese owner, descend from the lobby to the koi pond; it's surrounded by rocks from Mt Fuji. And the restaurant's name? It's pronounced, appropriately, amaze-ya.

Ferraro's ITALIAN $$$
(☎874-8000; www.fourseasons.com/maui; Four Seasons Maui at Wailea, 3900 Wailea Alanui Dr; lunch $19-28, dinner $29-47; ⏲11:30am-9pm) No other place in Wailea comes close to this breezy restaurant for romantic seaside dining. Lunch strays into fun selections like a gorgonzola pizza with roasted pear and a lobster salad sandwich with garlic aioli. Dinner gets more serious, showcasing a rustic Italian menu.

Drinking & Entertainment

All of the Wailea hotels have live music, most often jazz or Hawaiian, in the evening.

Red Bar at Gannon's COCKTAIL BAR
(☎875-8080; www.gannonsrestaurant.com; 100 Wailea Golf Club Dr; ⏲8:30am-9pm) Everyone looks sexier when they're swathed in a sultry red glow. Come to this chic spot at happy hour for impressive food (3pm to 6pm) and drink specials (3pm to 7pm), attentive bartenders and stellar sunsets. The bar is located inside Gannon's, Bev Gannon's restaurant at the Gold and Emerald courses' clubhouse.

Mulligan's on the Blue PUB
(☎874-1131; www.mulligansontheblue.com; 100 Kaukahi St; ⏲11am-1am Mon-Fri, 7am-1am Sat & Sun) Rising above the golf course, Mulligan's offers entertainment nightly, from Irish folk music to European jazz. It's also a good place to quaff an ale while enjoying the distant ocean view – or catching a game on one of the 10 TVs.

Lobby Lounge at Four Seasons Maui LIVE MUSIC
(☎874-8000; www.fourseasons.com/maui; 3900 Wailea Alanui Dr; ⊙5-11:30pm) The lobby lounge has Hawaiian music and hula performances from 5:30pm to 7:30pm nightly, and jazz or slack key guitar later in the evening.

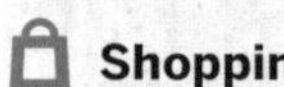

Shopping

Shops at Wailea MALL
(☎891-6770; www.shopsatwailea.com; 3750 Wailea Alanui Dr; ⊙9:30am-9pm) This outdoor mall has dozens of stores, most flashing designer labels like Prada and Louis Vuitton, but there are some solid island choices, too. Store hours may vary slightly from the mall's hours.

Blue Ginger WOMEN'S CLOTHING
(☎891-0772; www.blueginger.com; Shops at Wailea, 3750 Wailea Alanui Dr) Women's clothing in cheery colors and tropical motifs.

Honolua Surf Co CLOTHING
(☎891-8229; www.honoluasurf.com; Shops at Wailea, 3750 Wailea Alanui Dr) Hip surfer-motif T-shirts, board shorts and aloha shirts.

Martin & MacArthur ARTS & CRAFTS
(☎891-8844; www.martinandmacarthur.com; Shops at Wailea, 3750 Wailea Alanui Dr) Museum-quality Hawaiian-made woodwork and other crafts.

Maui Waterwear SWIMWEAR
(☎891-8669; www.mauiclothingcompany.com; Shops at Wailea, 3750 Wailea Alanui Dr) Tropical swimwear you'll love to flaunt.

Aloha Shirt Museum & Boutique CLOTHING
(☎875-1308; www.the-aloha-shirt-museum.com; Wailea Gateway Place, A-208; ⊙10:30am-9:30pm) Quality new and vintage aloha shirts for sale and on display. We like the 100% silk Elvis Aloha, aka the King's shirt, in blue ($98). The musuem recently moved from the Shops at Wailea to new digs in Wailea Gateway. Also open by appointment after hours.

Getting There & Around

The **Maui Bus** (www.mauicounty.gov) operates the Kihei Islander 10 between Wailea and Kahului hourly until 8:27pm. The first bus leaves the Shops at Wailea at 6:27am and runs along S Kihei Rd before heading to the Pi'ilani Village shopping center and then into Kahului, with a final stop at Queen Ka'ahumanu Center. For Lahaina, pick up the Kihei Villager 15 at Pi'ilani Village, which travels to Ma'alaea Harbor. There, transfer to the Lahaina Islander 20.

Makena

POP 99

Makena may be home to an oceanfront resort and a well-manicured golf course, but the region still feels wild, like a territorial outpost that hasn't been tamed. It's also a perfect setting for aquatic adventurers who want to escape the crowds, offering primo snorkeling, kayaking and bodysurfing, plus pristine coral, reef sharks, dolphins and sea turtles galore.

The beaches are magnificent. The king of them all, Big Beach, is an immense sweep of glistening sand and a prime sunset-viewing locale. The secluded cove at neighboring Little Beach is Maui's most popular nude beach – you *will* see bare buns. Together these beaches form **Makena State Park**, but don't be misled by the term 'park,' as they remain in a natural state, with no facilities except for a couple of pit toilets and picnic tables. No one on Maui would have it otherwise.

Beaches

Beaches are listed from north to south.

Makena Bay BEACH
Paniolo used to herd cattle onto boats bound for Honolulu at this low-key bay, once a busy port for livestock, pineapples and people. Today, there's no better place on Maui for kayaking. And when seas are calm, snorkeling is good along the rocks at the south side of **Makena Landing**, the boat launch that's the center of the action. Makena Bay is also good for shore dives; divers should head to the north side of the bay.

Kayakers should paddle south along the lava coastline to Malu'aka Beach, where green sea turtles abound. Kayak-rental companies deliver kayaks to Makena Landing – you can either head off on your own or join a tour (there are no shops here). If there's an extra kayak on the trailer, you might be able to arrange something on the spot, although reservations are highly recommended.

★Malu'aka Beach BEACH
Dubbed 'Turtle Beach,' this golden swath of sand in front of the Makena Beach & Golf Resort is popular with snorkelers and kayakers hoping to glimpse the green turtles that feed along the coral here. These graceful beauties often swim within a few feet of snorkelers. There's terrific coral about 100 yards out, and the best action is at the south end of the beach.

Come on a calm day – this one kicks up with even a little wind and when it's choppy you won't see anything. Parking lots, restrooms and showers are at both ends of the beach. At the north side, park at the lot opposite Keawala'i Congregational Church then walk along the road a short distance south. If the lot's full, take the first right after the resort, where there's additional parking for about 60 cars.

Little Beach BEACH
Ready to even out those tan lines? Also known as Pu'u Ola'i Beach, this cozy strand is South Maui's *au naturel* beach. Mind you, nudity is officially illegal, though enforcement is at the political whim of the day.

The beach is hidden by a rocky outcrop that juts from Pu'u Ola'i, the cinder hill that marks the north end of Big Beach (below). Take the short trail over the outcrop and bam, there it is, bare buns city. The crowd is mixed, about half gay and half straight.

Little Beach fronts a sandy cove that usually has a gentle shorebreak ideal for bodysurfing and boogie boarding. When the surf's up, you'll find plenty of local surfers here as well. When the water's calm, snorkeling is good along the rocky point. For parking, use the northern lot at Big Beach.

★Big Beach (Oneloa Beach) BEACH
The crowning glory of Makena State Park, this untouched beach is arguably the finest on Maui. In Hawaiian it's called 'Long Sand.' And indeed the broad golden sands stretch for the better part of a mile. The waters are a beautiful turquoise. When they're calm you'll find kids boogie boarding, but at other times the breaks belong to experienced bodysurfers, who get tossed wildly in the transparent waves.

There is a lifeguard station here. For a sweeping photograph of the coast, climb the short trail to the rocky outcropping just north, which divides Big Beach from Little Beach.

The turnoff to the main parking area is a mile beyond the Makena Beach & Golf Resort. A second parking area lies a quarter of a mile to the south. Thefts and broken windshields are a possibility, so don't leave valuables in your car in either lot.

Secret Cove BEACH
This lovely, postcard-size swath of golden sand, with a straight-on view of Kaho'olawe, is worth a peek – although it's no longer much of a secret. The cove is a quarter-mile after the southernmost Makena State Park parking lot. The entrance is through an opening in a lava-rock wall just south of house No 6900.

Activities

Aloha Kayaks KAYAKING
(270-3318; www.alohakayaksmaui.com; adult/child 5-9yr $75/45; tours 7:15am) For an ecominded snorkel-kayak trip from an enthusiastic team of owner-operators, take a paddle with Aloha Kayaks. The owners of this new outfit, Griff and Peter, have about 10 years of guiding experience apiece. Their mission? To educate guests about the environment and to keep their operations sustainable. Tours also available at Olawalu.

Check the website for details about the company's Green Paddling Blue Water Campaign, which describes how Aloha Kayaks keeps things green.

Sleeping & Eating

Makena Beach & Golf Resort RESORT $$$
(800-321-6284, 874-1111; www.makenaresortmaui.com; 5400 Makena Alanui Dr; r from $300; P❄@🛜🏊) Under new management following a foreclosure auction in 2010, this striking, fortresslike resort has revamped all of its rooms, which shine with simple but sophisticated island style: white bedspreads, tropical green throws, granite countertops and cherrywood furniture. The resort's 1800-acre perch beside Makena Beach is beautiful, not to mention a top launch pad for snorkelers and kayakers hoping to spy a sea turtle.

Management has also gone on a hiring spree, picking up chefs as well as golf and tennis pros from top Maui resorts. Best of all? No resort fee or parking fee.

Café on the Green CAFE $
(875-5888; www.makenaresortmaui.com; Makena Alanui, golf couse clubhouse; lunch $8-16, happy hour menu under $7; 11am-6:30pm) The view and the food are both top notch at this cafe overlooking the Makena golf course. For the best experience, settle in on the hilltop patio at happy hour (3pm to 6:30pm) to savor one of the half dozen or so appetizers – from the chicken quesadilla to beef sliders – with a $4 Maui Brewing beer. Then 'ooh' and 'ahh' as the sun sets.

Jawz Fish Tacos FOOD TRUCK $
(www.jawzfishtacos.com; Makena State Park; snacks $6-11; 11am-3pm) Get tacos, burritos and shave ice at this food truck at the northernmost Big Beach parking lot. Hours vary, depending on the weather. Look for a second truck on Makena Alanui Rd just north.

Beyond Makena

Makena Rd turns adventurous after Makena State Park, continuing for three narrow miles through the lava flows of 'Ahihi-Kina'u Natural Area Reserve before dead-ending at La Pe'rouse Bay.

'Ahihi-Kina'u Natural Area Reserve

Scientists haven't been able to pinpoint the exact date, but it is believed that Maui's last lava flow spilled down to the sea here between AD 1480 and 1600, shaping 'Ahihi Bay and Cape Kina'u. The jagged lava coastline and the pristine waters fringing it have been designated a reserve because of its unique marine habitat.

Thanks in part to the prohibition on fishing, snorkeling is incredible. Just about everyone heads to the little roadside cove 0.1 miles south of the first reserve sign – granted, it offers good snorkeling, but there are better (and less-crowded) options. Instead, drive 0.2 miles past the cove and look for a large clearing on the right. Park here and follow the coastal footpath south for five minutes to a black-sand beach with fantastic coral, clear water and few visitors. Enter the water from the left side of the beach where access is easy, snorkel in a northerly direction and you'll immediately be over coral gardens teeming with an amazing variety of fish. Huge rainbow parrotfish abound here, and it's not unusual to see turtles and the occasional reef shark.

Large sections of the 1238-acre reserve (http://hawaii.gov/dlnr/dofaw) are closed to visitors until July 31, 2014, which will allow the Department of Land and Resource Management to protect the fragile environment from tourist wear-and-tear and to develop a long-term protection plan. Visitation in the north is still permitted between 5:30am and 7:30pm.

La Pérouse Bay

Earth and ocean merge at La Pérouse Bay with a raw desolate beauty that's almost eerie. Historians originally thought that the blast occurred in 1790, but more recent analysis indicates that the lava flow occurred about 200 to 300 years earlier. Before the blast the ancient Hawaiian village of Keone'o'io flourished here, and its remains – mainly house and heiau platforms – can be seen scattered among the lava patches. From the volcanic shoreline look for pods of spinner dolphins, which commonly come into the bay during the early part of the day. The combination of strong offshore winds and rough waters rule out swimming, but it's an interesting place to explore on land.

Activities

Makena Stables HORSEBACK RIDING
(Map p398; ☎879-0244; www.makenastables.com; Makena Rd; 3hr trail rides $145-170; ⏰8am-6pm) Located just before the road ends, Makena Stables offers morning and sunset horseback rides across the lava flows and up the scenic slopes of 'Ulupalakua Ranch.

Hoapili (King's Highway) Trail HIKING
From La Pérouse Bay, this trail follows an ancient path along the coastline across jagged lava flows. Be prepared: wear hiking boots, bring plenty to drink, start early and tell someone where you're going. It's a dry area with no water and little vegetation, so it can get very hot.

The first part of the trail is along the sandy beach at La Pérouse Bay. Right after the trail emerges onto the lava fields, it's possible to take a spur trail for three-quarters of a mile down to the light beacon at the tip of Cape Hanamanioa. Alternatively, walk inland to the Na Ala Hele sign and turn right onto the King's Hwy as it climbs through *'a'a* (rough, jagged lava) inland for the next 2 miles before coming back to the coast to an older lava flow at Kanaio Beach. Although the trail continues, it becomes harder to follow and Kanaio Beach is the recommended turn-around point. If you don't include the lighthouse spur, the roundtrip distance to Kanaio Beach is about 4 miles.

For more details and a very basic map, visit http://hawaiitrails.ehawaii.gov, the state's trail and access website.

NORTH SHORE & UPCOUNTRY

The surf-sculpted North Shore stands in sharp contrast to the gently rolling pastures carpeting the Upcountry slopes nearby. The towns – beachy Pa'ia, artsy Makawao and mud-on-your-boots Keokea – boast as much weathered personality as their proud residents.

Green and fragrant, the Upcountry simply begs a country drive. The possibilities for exploring are nothing short of breathtaking. Zipline over deep gorges, paraglide down the hillsides or ride a horse through a lofty cloud forest.

Everyone passes through a slice of the Upcountry on the way to Haleakalā National Park, but don't settle for a fly-by. Look around the showy gardens, lightly trodden trails and rambling back roads. They alone are worth the trip.

Pa'ia

POP 2668

The intersection of Baldwin Ave and the Hana Hwy is surely the hippest spot in all of Maui. Surfers grab coffee at Anthony's, yoga ladies peer in the window at Lululemon and Willie Nelson might just be checking out the scene at Charley's. Everyone else? They're bumping into each while navigating the aisles at impossibly tight Mana Foods.

Once a thriving sugar town, a century ago Pa'ia boasted 10,000 residents living in plantation camps above the now-defunct sugar mill. During the 1950s there was an exodus to Kahului, shops were shuttered and Pa'ia began to collect cobwebs.

Attracted by low rents, hippies seeking paradise landed in Pa'ia in the 1970s. A decade later, windsurfers discovered Ho'okipa Beach, and Pa'ia broke onto the map bigtime. Its aging wooden storefronts, now splashed in sunshine yellows and sky blues, house a wild array of shops geared to visitors. And the dining scene? Any excuse to be here at mealtime will do.

Parking is notoriously tight in Pa'ia, doubly so at mealtimes. Try the public parking lot on the west side of town just before the Shell gas station. If that's full, try the dirt lot on Baldwin Ave between the post office and downtown.

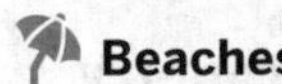

Beaches

Ho'okipa Beach Park & Lookout BEACH

Ho'okipa is to daredevil windsurfers what Everest is to climbers. The world's premier windsurfing beach, it has strong currents, dangerous shorebreaks and razor-sharp coral to offer the ultimate challenge.

Ho'okipa is also one of Maui's prime surfing spots. Winter sees the biggest waves for board surfers, and summer has the most consistent winds for windsurfers. To prevent intersport beefs, surfers typically hit the waves in the morning and the windsurfers take over during the afternoon.

The action in the water is suitable for pros only. But a hilltop perch overlooking the beach offers spectators a bird's-eye view of the world's top windsurfers doing their death-defying stuff. Ho'okipa is just before mile marker 9 on the Hana Hwy; to reach the lookout above the beach take the driveway at the east side of the park.

HA Baldwin Beach Park BEACH

Grab a table at this palm-lined park to enjoy a picnic from Mana Foods. About one mile west of Pa'ia, at mile marker 6 on the Hana Hwy, the park also attracts bodyboarders and bodysurfers. The wide sandy beach drops off quickly, however, and when the shorebreak is big, unsuspecting swimmers can get slammed soundly.

Calmer waters, better suited for swimming, can be found at the northeast end of the beach where there's a little cove shaded by ironwood trees. Showers, restrooms, picnic tables, and a well-used baseball and soccer field round out the facilities. The park has a reputation for drunken nastiness after the sun sets, but it's fine in the daytime when there's a lifeguard on duty.

Spreckelsville Beach BEACH

(Map p382;) Extending west from HA Baldwin Beach, this 2-mile stretch of sand punctuated by lava outcrops is a good walking beach, but its near-shore lava shelf makes it less than ideal for swimming for adults. The rocks do, however, provide protection for young kids. If you walk toward the center of the beach, you'll soon come to a section dubbed 'baby beach,' where local families take the little ones to splash.

There are no facilities. To get here, turn toward the ocean on Nonohe Pl at mile marker 5, then turn left on Kealakai Pl just before the Maui Country Club.

North Shore & Upcountry

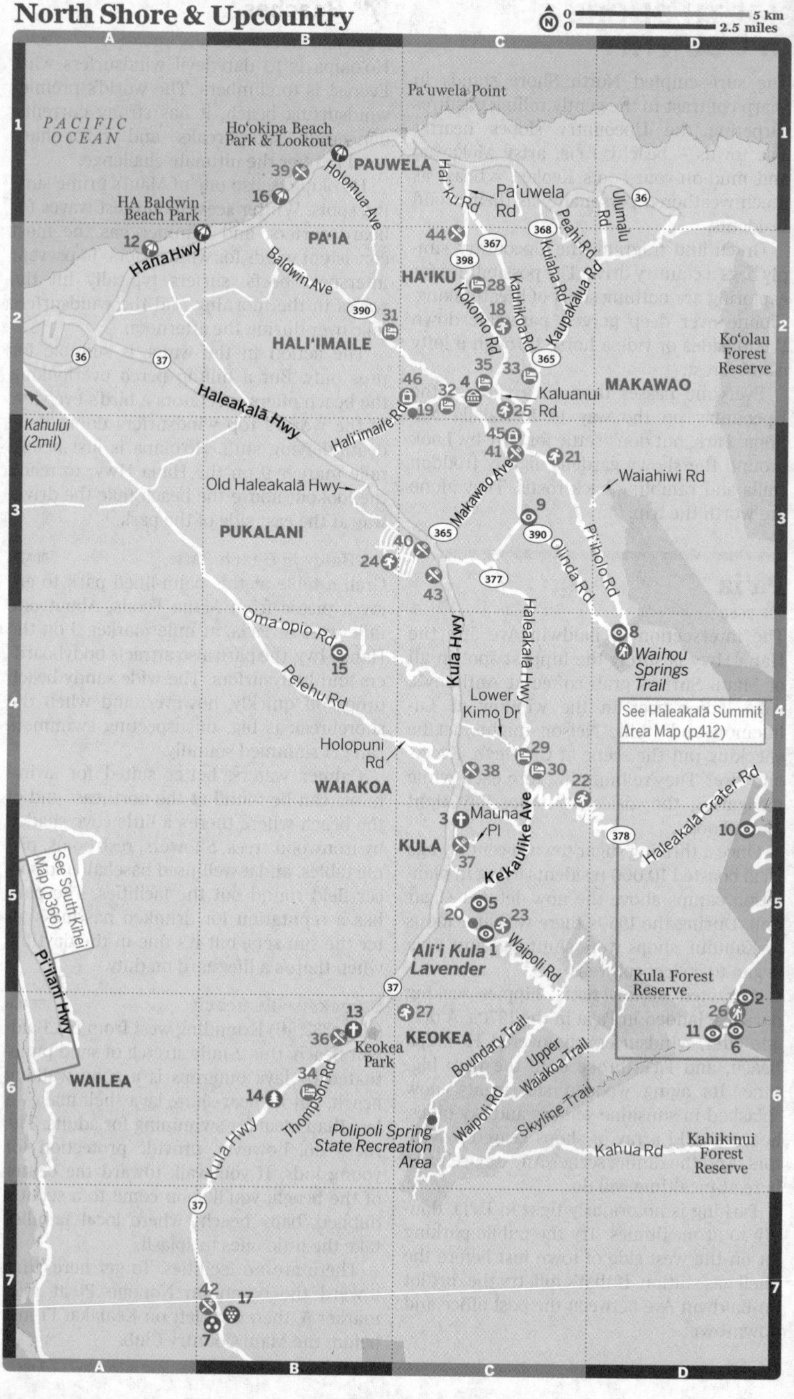

0 — 5 km
0 — 2.5 miles

PACIFIC OCEAN
Pa'uwela Point
Ho'okipa Beach Park & Lookout
PAUWELA
HA Baldwin Beach Park
Hana Hwy
PA'IA
Holomua Ave
Baldwin Ave
Hai'ku Rd
Pa'uwela Rd
Peahi Rd
Ulumalu Rd
Kuiaha Rd
Kaupakalua Rd
HA'IKU
Kokomo Rd
Kauhikoa Rd
HALI'IMAILE
Ko'olau Forest Reserve
Haleakalā Hwy
Kahului (2mil)
Hali'imaile Rd
Kaluanui Rd
MAKAWAO
Makawao Ave
Waiahiwi Rd
Old Haleakalā Hwy
PUKALANI
Olinda Rd
Pi'iholo Rd
Oma'opio Rd
Pelehu Rd
Kula Hwy
Haleakalā Hwy
Waihou Springs Trail
Lower Kimo Dr
Holopuni Rd
See Haleakalā Summit Area Map (p412)
WAIAKOA
Haleakalā Crater Rd
Mauna Pl
KULA
Kekaulike Ave
See South Kihei Map (p366)
Pi'ilani Hwy
Ali'i Kula Lavender
Waipoli Rd
Kula Forest Reserve
KEOKEA
Keokea Park
Boundary Trail
Upper Waiakoa Trail
WAILEA
Thompson Rd
Skyline Trail
Waipoli Rd
Polipoli Spring State Recreation Area
Kula Hwy
Kahua Rd
Kahikinui Forest Reserve

North Shore & Upcountry

Top Sights
1 Ali'i Kula Lavender C5

Sights
2 Haleakalā Visitor Center D5
3 Holy Ghost Church C5
4 Hui No'eau Visual Arts Center C2
5 Kula Botanical Garden C5
6 Magnetic Peak D6
7 Makee Sugar Mill Ruins B7
8 Maui Bird Conservation Center D4
9 Oskie Rice Arena C3
10 Park Headquarters Visitor Center D5
Pu'u'ula'ula (Red Hill) Overlook .....(see 6)
11 Science City D6
12 Spreckelsville Beach A2
13 St John's Episcopal Church B6
14 Sun Yat-sen Park B6
15 Surfing Goat Dairy B4
16 Tavares Beach B1
17 Tedeschi Vineyards B7

Activities, Courses & Tours
18 Fourth Marine Division Memorial Park C2
19 Maui Gold Pineapple Tour C2
20 O'o Farm C5
Piiholo Ranch .... (see 21)
21 Piiholo Ranch Zipline C3
22 Pony Express C4
23 Proflyght Paragliding C5
24 Pukalani Country Club B3
25 Sacred Garden of Maliko C2
Skyline Eco-Adventures .... (see 22)
26 Sliding Sands (Keonehe'ehe'e) D6
27 Thompson Ranch C6

Sleeping
Blue Tile Beach House .... (see 16)
28 Haiku Cannery Inn B&B C2
Inn at Mama's .... (see 39)
29 Kula Lodge C4
30 Kula Sandalwoods Cottages C4
31 Lumeria Maui B2
32 Peace of Maui C2
33 Pilialoha C2
34 Star Lookout B6
35 Wild Ginger Falls C2

Eating
Casanova Deli .... (see 41)
Casanova Restaurant .... (see 41)
Colleen's .... (see 44)
36 Grandma's Coffee House B6
Hali'imaile General Store .... (see 19)
Komoda Store & Bakery .... (see 41)
37 Kula Bistro C5
Kula Marketplace .... (see 29)
38 La Provence C4
Makawao Farmers Market .... (see 41)
Makawao Garden Café .... (see 41)
39 Mama's Fish House B1
NorthShore Cafe .... (see 44)
Polli's .... (see 41)
40 Pukalani Superette C3
41 Rodeo General Store C3
42 'Ulupalakua Ranch Store B7
43 Upcountry Farmers Market C3
44 Veg Out C2

Drinking & Nightlife
Crater Coffee .... (see 29)
Maui Kombucha .... (see 44)

Shopping
45 Aloha Cowboy C3
Designing Wahine .... (see 45)
46 Makai Glass Creations C2
Viewpoints Gallery .... (see 45)
Volcano Spice .... (see 45)

Tavares Beach BEACH

(Map p382) This unmarked sandy beach is quiet and relatively deserted during the week but livens up on weekends when local families arrive toting picnics, guitars, dogs and kids. A submerged lava shelf runs parallel to the beach about 25ft from the shore and is shallow enough for swimmers to scrape over. Once you know it's there, the rocks are easy to avoid, so make sure you take a look before jumping in.

The beach parking lot is at the first shoreline access sign on the Hana side of mile marker 7, just before the Blue Tile beach House. There are no facilities.

Activities

Simmer WINDSURFING

(579-8484; www.simmerhawaii.com; 137 Hana Hwy; sailboards per day $50; 10am-7pm) Simmer is all about windsurfing and handles everything from repairs to top-of-the-line gear rentals and windsurfer lifestyle apparel.

Maui Dharma Center MEDITATION

(579-8076; www.mauidharmacenter.com; 81 Baldwin Ave; 6:30am-6:30pm) This Tibetan Buddhist temple shares good karma, inviting visitors to join in morning meditation. Or just swing by to take a meditative stroll around the gardens and the stupa on your own. There's also a gift shop.

Sleeping

Blue Tile Beach House

B&B $$

(Map p382; ☎579-6446; www.beachvacationmaui.com; 459 Hana Hwy; r $110-165, ste $250; 📶) Step out the door of this oceanfront estate and you're literally on Tavares Beach. Sleeping options range from a small straightforward room to a spacious honeymoon suite with wraparound ocean-view windows and a four-poster bed. All six rooms share a living room and a kitchen. Reservations strongly recommended – don't show up at midnight unannounced. Note cancellation policies carefully before booking.

★ Pa'ia Inn

INN $$$

(☎579-6000; www.paiainn.com; 93 Hana Hwy; r $259-329, ste $359-899; ❄@📶) For a hip hotel, the Pa'ia Inn has a surprisingly hospitable heart. Spread across three buildings in downtown Pa'ia, this friendly boutique inn is anchored by a classic century-old building that's been spruced up with bamboo floors, travertine bathrooms and original artwork. In the back, a private walkway leads to a stunning stretch of sand.Out front, Pa'ia's restaurants and shops await on the doorstep. It's the ultimate Pa'ia immersion.

Pa'ia

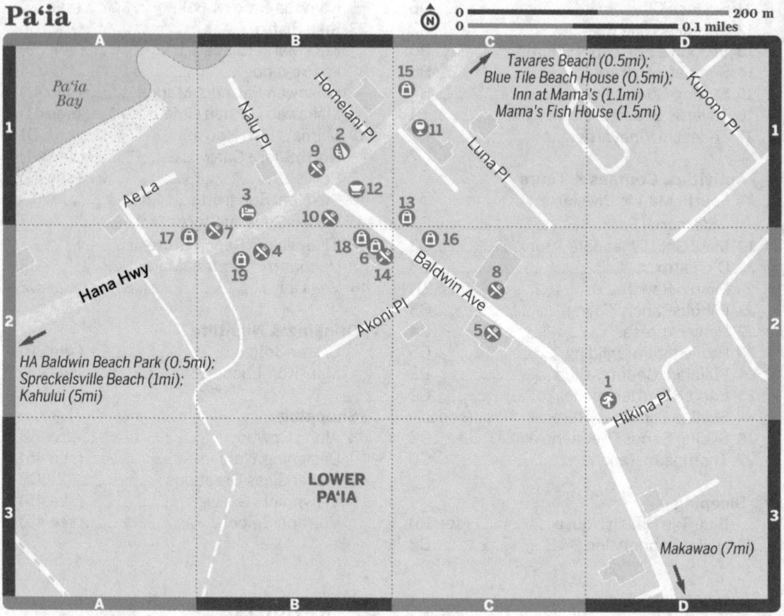

Pa'ia

Activities, Courses & Tours

1 Maui Dharma Center D2
2 Simmer B1

Sleeping

3 Pa'ia Inn B1

Eating

4 Anthony's Coffee Company B2
5 Café des Amis C2
6 Café Mambo B2
7 Flatbread Company B2
8 Mana Foods C2
9 Ono Gelato B1
10 Pa'ia Fish Market Restaurant B1

Drinking & Nightlife

11 Charley's C1
12 Milagros B1

Shopping

13 Alice in Hulaland C1
14 Hemp House B2
15 Indigo C1
16 Mandala Ethnic Arts C2
17 Maui Crafts Guild A2
18 Maui Girl B2
19 Maui Hands - Pa'ia B2

Inn at Mama's COTTAGE $$$
(Map p382; ☎579-9764; www.mamasfishhouse.com; 799 Poho Pl; cottage $175-575, ste $325; ❄ 📶) There's more to Mama's Fish House than fabulous food. Tucked behind Maui's most famous seafood restaurant are a dozen pretty cottages, some with ocean views, others with garden settings. Think retro Hawaiian decor, rattan and bamboo, and an airy, clean simplicity that you'd expect at a high-end operation. One caveat: there's a lot of activity nearby and Mama's is not always the quietest of places. But guests do receive a 15% discount at the restaurant.

Eating

Most of Pa'ia's eateries cluster around the intersection of Baldwin Ave and the Hana Hwy. Poke your head in a few places and see what's cookin'. Nothing better awaits in Hana, so grab your picnic supplies before heading onward.

Ono Gelato DESSERT $
(www.onogelatocompany.com; 115 Hana Hwy; cones $5; ⏰11am-10pm) This little shop dishes up Maui-made organic gelato in island flavors like guava, mango and Kula strawberry. For the ultimate treat, order the *liliko'i* (passion fruit) quark, combining passion fruit and goat's cheese – it's awesome...really.

Mana Foods TAKEOUT $
(☎579-8078; www.manafoodsmaui.com; 49 Baldwin Ave; deli items under $10; ⏰8am-8:30pm; 🖉) Dreadlocked, Birkenstocked or just needing to stock up – everyone rubs shoulders at Mana, a health food store, bakery and deli wrapped in one. Don't miss the walnut cinnamon buns made fresh every morning. Then look for the hot rosemary-grilled chicken and organic salad bar. It's gonna be a *g-o-o-d* picnic!

Anthony's Coffee Company CAFE $
(☎579-8340; www.anthonyscoffee.com; 90 Hana Hwy; breakfast $5-13, lunch $7-12; ⏰5:30am-6pm; 📶) The best cup of joe on this side of the island. Fresh-ground organic coffee and a delish variety of goodies from pastries to lox Benedict. Staff even pack picnic boxes ($12) for the drive to Hana. You know everything's done right – you'll find the owner himself on the other side of the counter grinding away.

★**Café des Amis** CAFE $$
(☎579-6323; www.cdamaui.com; 42 Baldwin Ave; breakfast $5-11, lunch & dinner $9-18; ⏰8:30am-8:30pm) Grab a seat in the breezy courtyard to dine on the best cafe fare in Pa'ia. It's not always fast, but it's done right. The savory options include spicy Indian curry wraps with mango chutney and mouthwatering crepes. You'll also find vegetarian offerings, creative breakfasts and tempting drinks from fruit smoothies to fine wines.

Pa'ia Fish Market Restaurant SEAFOOD $$
(☎579-8030; www.paiafishmarket.com; 110 Baldwin Ave; mains $9-19; ⏰11am-9:30pm) The Pa'ia Fish Market has been open 20 years, but the place knows how to run with the times. A recent addition to the menu is the Obama burger: a fresh, cajun-style *ono* fish topped with wasabi butter. Like all of the fish served here, it's fresh, local and affordable. Little wonder people are packed in like sardines. But don't worry, the tables turn over quickly.

Flatbread Company PIZZA $$
(☎579-8989; www.flatbreadcompany.com; 89 Hana Hwy; pizzas $12-22; ⏰11am-10pm) 🍃 Wood-fired pizzas made with organic sauces, nitrate-free pepperoni, local veggies – you'll never stop at a chain pizza house again. Lots of fun combinations, from pure vegan to *kalua* pork.

Café Mambo CAFE $$
(☎579-8021; www.cafemambomaui.com; 30 Baldwin Ave; breakfast under $10, mains lunch & dinner $10-21; ⏰8am-9pm) This upbeat, arty cafe adds a splash of innovation to its dishes. Breakfast features burritos and create-your-own omelets. At other times choose from fragrant Moroccan stews, mouthwatering *kalua* duck fajitas and a varity of burgers, from ahi fish to Maui cattle. On Thursday nights settle in for Cafe Mambo Cinema, when the restaurant shows a classic movie at 9pm.

★**Mama's Fish House** SEAFOOD $$$
(Map p382; ☎579-8488; www.mamasfishhouse.com; 799 Poho Pl; mains $34-50; ⏰11am-2:30pm & 4:15-9pm) Mama's is where you go when you want to propose or celebrate a big anniversary. Not only is the seafood as good as it gets, but when the beachside tiki torches are lit at dinnertime, the scene's achingly romantic. The island-caught fish is so fresh your server tells you who caught it, and where! Mama's is at Ku'au Cove, along the Hana Hwy, 2 miles east of Pa'ia center. Reservations are essential.

BEST UPCOUNTRY-GROWN TREATS

- ➡ Maui Splash wine at Tedeschi Vineyards (p395)
- ➡ Olé chèvre at Surfing Goat Dairy (p392)
- ➡ Maui coffee at Grandma's (p394)
- ➡ Lunch tour at O'o Farm (p393)
- ➡ Lavender scones at Ali'i Kula Lavender (p392)
- ➡ Black and Blue burger at Bully's Burgers (p395)

Drinking & Entertainment

Charley's BAR
(579-8085; www.charleysmaui.com; 142 Hana Hwy; 7am-10pm Sun-Thu, to 2am Fri & Sat) Don't be surprised to find country-singer legend Willie Nelson at the next table or on stage. He's a part-time Pa'ia resident, and this cowboy-centric place is his favorite hang. Charley's has live music most nights.

Milagros CAFE
(579-8755; www.milagrosfoodcompany.com; 3 Baldwin Ave; 11am-10pm) *The* spot for a late-afternoon beer or a tasty margarita. The sidewalk tables are perched perfectly for watching the action on Pa'ia's busiest corner. Good southwestern grub too. Inside, enjoy $3 draft beers and house margaritas during happy hour (1pm to 6pm).

Shopping

This is a fun town for browsing, with owner-run shops and boutiques selling Maui-made goodies of all sorts.

★Maui Crafts Guild ARTS & CRAFTS
(579-9697; www.mauicraftsguild.com; 69 Hana Hwy; 10am-6pm) In a freestanding cottage on the Hana Hwy, this longstanding collective of Maui artists and craftspeople sells everything from pottery and jewelry to handpainted silks and natural-fiber baskets at reasonable prices.

Maui Hands – Pa'ia ARTS & CRAFTS
(579-9245; www.mauihands.com; 84 Hana Hwy; 10am-7pm Mon-Sat, to 6pm Sun) Head here for top-end koa bowls, pottery and Maui-themed paintings.

★Indigo CARPETS, CRAFTS
(579-9199; www.indigopaia.com; 149 Hana Hwy; 10am-6pm) Step into this inviting boutique for a shopping trip through Central and Southwest Asia. The handcrafted rugs, one-of-a-kind furnishings and traditional crafts were collected by owner Daniel Sullivan and wife Caramiya Davies-Reid. Sullivan also sells vibrant photographs taken during his travels. Davies-Reid designs breezy dresses for the island lifestyle.

The couple lived in Afghanistan before moving to Maui. Pop-in if you have questions about Pa'ia; Daniel is on the Pa'ia merchant's association board and knows the town well.

Maui Girl CLOTHING
(579-9266; www.maui-girl.com; 12 Baldwin Ave; 9am-6pm) Get your itty-bitty bikinis here.

Alice in Hulaland GIFTS
(579-9922; www.aliceinhulaland.com; 19 Baldwin Ave; 9am-8pm) Kitschy but fun clothing and souvenirs.

Hemp House HEMP
(579-8880; www.hemphousemaui.com; 16 Baldwin Ave; 9:30am-7pm) Sells all things hemp – well, almost all.

Mandala Ethnic Arts CLOTHING, CRAFTS
(579-9555; 29 Baldwin Ave; 10am-7:30pm) Lightweight cotton and silk clothing, Buddhas and Asian handicrafts.

Information

Bank of Hawaii – Pa'ia (www.boh.com; 35 Baldwin Ave; 8:30am-4pm Mon-Thu, to 6pm Fri)

Getting There & Around

BICYCLE

Rent bicycles at **Maui Sunriders** (579-8970; www.mauibikeride.com; 71 Baldwin Ave; per day $30; 8am-5pm). Includes a bike rack, so a companion could drop you off on Haleakalā, or anywhere else, to cycle a one-way route.

BUS

The Maui Bus runs from the Queen Ka'ahumanu Center to Pa'ia ($2) and back every 90 minutes from 5:30am to 8:30pm on the Haiku Islander 35.

Hali'imaile

The little pineapple town of Hali'imaile ('fragrant twining shrub') is named after the sweet-scented maile plants used in lei-making that covered the area before pineapple took over. The heart of town is the old general store (c 1918), which has been turned into Upcountry's best restaurant. Hali'imaile Rd runs through the town, connecting Baldwin Ave (Hwy 390) with the Haleakalā Hwy (Hwy 37).

Activities

Maui Gold Pineapple Tour FARM TOUR
(Map p382; 665-5491; www.mauipineappletour.com; 875 Hali'imaile Rd; tour adult/child 5-12yr $65/55, incl lunch $80/70; tours 9:30am & 11:45am) On the only pineapple tour in the US, you pick your own fruit on a working pineapple farm. You'll also learn about the history and culture of Maui's pineapple-growing past. For an extra $15 enjoy a lunch prepared by Hali'imaile General Store. The tour lasts about one hour and 15 minutes.

Sleeping & Eating

Peace of Maui GUESTHOUSE $
(Map p382; 572-5045; www.peaceofmaui.com; 1290 Hali'imaile Rd; r with shared bathroom from $70;) This easygoing guesthouse is Upcountry's top budget sleep. In the middle of nowhere yet within an hour's drive of nearly everywhere, it's a good central base for exploring the whole island, and works well for catching the sunrise at Haleakalā. Rooms, spotlessly clean, are small but comfortable, each with refrigerator and TV. There's a guest kitchen and a hot tub.

If you need more space, there's a two-bedroom cottage (from $150).

★Hali'imaile General Store HAWAII REGIONAL CUISINE $$$
(Map p382; 572-2666; www.bevgannonrestaurants.com; 900 Hali'imaile Rd; lunch $12-20, dinner $26-42; 11am-2:30pm Mon-Fri, 5:30-9:30pm daily;) Chef Bev Gannon was one of the original forces behind the Hawaii Regional Cuisine movement and a steady flow of in-the-know diners beats a track to this tiny village to feast on her inspired creations. Tantalize your taste buds with fusion fare like sashimi pizza or Kahlua pork enchilada pie. The atmospheric plantation-era decor sets the mood.

Vegetarian menu is available at dinner.

Shopping

Makai Glass Creations ARTS & CRAFTS
(Map p382; 269-8255; www.makaiglass.com; 903 Hali'imaile Rd; 10am-7pm most days) For fine glass creations inspired by Hawaii's unique natural beauty, step inside this new gallery and glass blowing studio, which spotlights the work of artists Justin Brown and Randy Schaffer. Although open most days of the week, call first to confirm and to check the status of glass-blowing demos. The studio and gallery are located inside a warehouse across the street from Hali'imaile General Store.

THE ULTIMATE WAVE

When this monster rears its powerful head, it's big, fast and mean enough to crunch bones. What is it? **Jaws**, Maui's famous big-wave surf spot near Ha'iku (p390). A few times a year, strong winter storms off the coast of Japan generate an abundance of energy that races unimpeded across the Pacific Ocean to Hawaii's shores, translating into the planet's biggest rideable waves.

News of the mammoth swells, which reach as high as a seven-story building, attracts gutsy surfers from all over the state and beyond. Unfortunately, there's no legitimate public access to the cliffs that look out toward Jaws, as getting to them requires crossing privately owned agricultural land.

When Jaws (also known locally as Pe'ahi) is up, it's impossible for surfers to paddle through the break to catch a ride. But where there's a thrill, there's a way. Tow-in surfers work in pairs, using wave runners to get people and their boards beyond the break. When a wave runner is outmatched, surfers get dropped into the ocean from a helicopter.

There are myriad opportunities for big-wave surfers to get hurt or killed. The insanely powerful waves can wash surfers into rocks, throw them into their wave runners, knock them against their surfboards or simply pummel them with the force of all that moving water. That said, these guys are pros and are very good at skirting the perils.

Makawao

POP 7184

Aloha Cowboy! That's the name of Makawao's most eclectic store, and it perfectly captures the essence of this quirky art town that refuses to remove its boots and spurs.

Started as a ranching town in the 1800s, Makawao wears its *paniolo* history in the Old West–style wooden buildings lining Baldwin Ave. And the cattle pastures surrounding town remind you it's more than just history.

But that's only one side of Makawao. Many of the old shops that once sold saddles and stirrups now have artsy new tenants who have turned Makawao into the most happening art center on Maui. Its galleries display the works of painters and sculptors who have escaped frenzied scenes elsewhere to set up shop in these inspirational hills.

All of the shops and restaurants that follow are within a few minutes' walk of Makawao's main intersection, where Baldwin Ave (Hwy 390) meets Makawao Ave (Hwy 365).

Sights

Hui No'eau Visual Arts Center ART GALLERY
(Map p382; ☎572-6560; www.huinoeau.com; 2841 Baldwin Ave; ⏰10am-4pm Mon-Sat) FREE Occupying the former estate of sugar magnates Harry and Ethel Baldwin, the Hui No'eau center showcases local art and encourages artistic expression through its workshops and studio spaces. The plantation house, where the main galleries and gift shop are found, was designed by famed architect CW Dickey in 1917 and displays the Hawaiian Regional style architectural features he pioneered.

The prestigious arts club founded here in the 1930s still offers classes in printmaking, pottery, woodcarving and other visual arts. Galleries exhibit the diverse works of island artists, and you can walk around the grounds to check out artists at work in one-time stables converted into art studios. The gift shop sells quality ceramics, glassware and prints created on-site. Pick up a walking-tour map at the front desk; there's a small historical exhibition room beside the entrance. The center is just north of mile marker 5.

WORTH A TRIP

LABYRINTH WALKS

Up for a meditative moment? The **Sacred Garden of Maliko** (Map p382; ☎573-7700; www.sacredgardenmaui.com; 460 Kaluanui Rd, Makawao; ⏰10am-5pm) FREE, a self-described healing sanctuary, has a pair of rock-garden labyrinth walks guaranteed to reset the harmony gauge. One's in an orchid greenhouse facing a contemplative Buddha statue; the other's in a *kukui* (candlenut tree) grove beside Maliko Stream. Check the website for details about the monthly full-moon labyrinth walks (7:30pm to 9pm)To get there, turn east off Baldwin Ave onto Kaluanui Rd. After 0.8 miles cross a one-lane bridge; 0.2 miles further on, look for a low stone wall – the garden is on the right just before a sharp S-curve in the road.

Activities

Piiholo Ranch Zipline ZIPLINING
(Map p382; ☎572-1717; www.piiholozipline.com; zip-line course Piiholoi Rd, canopy tour Makawao Rd; zip tours $146-198, canopy tours $94-172; ⏰reservations 7am-8pm, tour times vary) This top-rate operation takes care to orient zipriders before they jump. The first zip is a warm-up, with a glide over a gentle sloping meadow. It gets progressively more interesting, with the last zip ripping more than half a mile at an eagle's height of 600ft above the tree canopy. Dual lines let you zip side by side with a buddy. The company's canopy tour spends more time in the trees, with guests hiking on lofty bridges between towering platforms then zipping through the forest.

Olinda Road SCENIC DRIVE
For the ultimate country drive, head high into the hills above Makawao along Olinda Rd then loop back to town on Pi'iholo Rd. The route, which picks up where Baldwin Ave ends, twists and turns through a lush residential area on the slopes of Haleakala, offering tantalizing glimpses of coastal landscapes far below.

The scenic drive drifts up past the **Oskie Rice Arena** (Map p382), where rodeos are held, and the Maui Polo Club, which hosts matches on Sunday afternoons in the fall. From here the winding road is little more than a path through the forest, with knotty tree roots as high as your car caressing the roadsides. The air is rich with the spicy fragrance of eucalyptus trees and occasionally there's a clearing with an ocean vista.

Four miles up from town, past mile marker 11, is the **Maui Bird Conservation Center** (Map p382), which breeds nene (native Hawaiian geese) and other endangered birds. To make a loop, pass the parking area for the Waihou Springs Trail then turn left onto Pi'iholo Rd and wind back down into town.

Waihou Springs Trail HIKING
(http://hawaiitrails.ehawaii.gov) The trailhead for this peaceful woodland path is 4.75 miles up Olinda Rd from central Makawao. The trail, which starts on a soft carpet of pine needles, passes Monterey cypress, eucalyptus and orderly rows of pine trees. After 0.7 easy miles, enjoy a view clear out to the ocean.

You can continue steeply downhill for another 0.25 miles to reach Waihou Springs, but that section of trail can be a muddy mess. The forest is amazingly varied, having been planted by the US Forest Service in an effort to determine which trees would produce the best quality lumber in Hawaii.

Piiholo Ranch HORSEBACK RIDING
(Map p382; reservations 270-8750, ranch 357-1755; www.piiholo.com; 325 Waiahiwi Rd; 2hr ride $120; rides 9:30am & 11am Mon-Sat) Ride with real *paniolo* across the open range of this cattle ranch that's been worked by the same family for six generations. Mountain, valley and pasture views galore. Check-in is 30 minutes before start of tour. Families can also book riding lessons for children as young as three (half-/full hour $45/75).

Festivals & Events

Makawao's Friday town party (see box on p324) is held on Baldwin Ave on the third Friday of the month.

Upcountry Ag & Farm Fair AGRICULTURAL FAIR
(572-3545; 8am-4pm Sat & Sun) Traditional agricultural fair with a farmers market, arts and crafts, rodeo, *na keiki* games and good ol' country music; held on the second weekend in June at the Oskie Rice Arena (opposite).

Makawao Rodeo RODEO
More than 350 *paniolo* show up at the Oskie Rice Arena on the weekend closest to Independence Day (July 4) for Hawaii's premier rodeo. Qualifying roping and riding events occur all day on Thursday and Friday to determine who gets to compete for the big prizes over the weekend. For thrills on Friday night, head up to the arena to see the bull-riding bash.

Paniolo Parade PARADE
Held on the Saturday morning closest to July 4, this festive parade goes right through the heart of Makawao; park at the rodeo grounds and take the free shuttle to the town center.

Sleeping

★Wild Ginger Falls COTTAGE $$
(Map p382; 573-1173; www.wildgingerfalls.com; 355 Kaluanui Rd; d $165) This stylish studio cottage overlooks a stone gorge and streambed that spouts a waterfall after it rains. Banana and coffee trees dot the lush garden surrounding the cottage and you can soak up the scenery from an outdoor hot tub. Owned by one of Hawaii's top contemporary ceramic artists, the cottage has an engaging retro '40s Hawaiiana decor. Breakfast items are provided your first morning and coffee your entire stay.

Full kitchen and washer and dryer. Books up early.

Lumeria Maui YOGA RETREAT $$$
(Map p382; 855-579-8877; www.lumeriamaui.com; 1813 Baldwin Ave; r/ste incl breakfast $349/429) This summer camp for the soul starts working its magic the moment you pull into the hibiscus-lined drive. Set on tidy, garden-filled grounds on an upcountry slope above Pa'ia, Lumeria is a gorgeous place to nourish your mind and body. Organic, locally sourced breakfasts prime the spirit before days filled with yoga, garden strolls, hot stone massages and reiki treatments.

At night guests retreat to minimalist, Asian-inspired cottages that once served as dorms for workers on the pineapple plantation. The $25 daily resort fee covers wi-fi, light breakfast and on-campus classes.

Eating

Komoda Store & Bakery BAKERY $
(Map p382; 3674 Baldwin Ave; 7am-5pm Mon, Wed, Thu & Fri, to 2pm Sat) In an aging building that looks abandoned, this homespun bakery is a must-stop. Legendary for its mouthwatering cream puffs and guava-filled *malasadas* (Portuguese donut), it's been a Makawao landmark since Tazeko Komoda first stoked up the oven in 1916. His offspring, using the same time-honored recipes, have been at it ever since. Arrive early – it often sells out by noon.

Makawao Garden Café CAFE $
(Map p382; ☎573-9065; www.makawaogarden-cafe.com; 3669 Baldwin Ave; mains under $10; ⏲11am-3pm Mon-Sat) This sunny outdoor cafe is tucked into a courtyard at the north end of Baldwin Ave – and it's worth seeking out. The menu is strictly sandwiches and salads, but everything's fresh, generous and made to order by the owner herself. The mahimahi on homemade focaccia is killer.

Casanova Deli DELI $
(Map p382; ☎572-0220; www.casanovamaui.com/deli; 1188 Makawao Ave; breakfast $2-9, sandwiches $7-13; ⏲7:30am-5:30pm Mon-Sat, 8:30am-5:30pm Sun) Makawao's hippest haunt brews heady espressos and buzzes all day with folks savoring buttery croissants, thick Italian sandwiches and hearty Greek salads. Take it all out to the roadside deck for the town's best people-watching.

Rodeo General Store TAKEOUT $
(Map p382; 3661 Baldwin Ave; meals under $8; ⏲6:30am-10pm Mon-Sat, to 9pm Sun) This is one-stop shopping at its best. Grab a tasty takeout meal from the central warmer – mmm, mac and cheese – or step up to the deli counter, which sells everything from fresh salads and Hawaiian *poke* to hot teriyaki chicken and plate lunches. Everything is made from scratch. There's also wine, beer and an ATM.

Makawao Farmers Market MARKET $
(Map p382; ☎280-5516; www.makawaofarmersmarket.com; 3654 Baldwin Ave; ⏲10am-4pm Wed, 10am-2pm Sat) Upcountry gardeners gather to sell their homegrown veggies and fruit twice a week at this small open-air market opposite Rodeo General Store.

★Casanova Restaurant ITALIAN $$
(Map p382; ☎572-0220; www.casanovamaui.com; 1188 Makawao Ave; lunch $9-20, dinner $10-38; ⏲11:30am-2pm Mon-Sat, 5-9pm daily) Casanova lures diners up the mountain with its reliably good Italian fare. The crispy innovative pizzas cooked in a kiawe-fired oven are as good as they get. Juicy Maui-raised steaks and classic Italian dishes like the spicy seafood *fra diavola* shore up the rest of the menu. Casanova also has a happening dance floor with music Wednesday, Friday and Saturday nights.

Polli's MEXICAN $$
(Map p382; ☎572-7808; www.pollismexicanrestaurant.com; 1202 Makawao Ave; mains $11-23; ⏲11am-10pm) Locals and visitors alike flock to this old standby Tex-Mex restaurant to down a few *cervezas* (beers) while munching away on nachos, tacos and sizzling fajitas. The food's average, but surf videos and plenty of spirited chatter keep the scene high energy.

Shopping

Start your exploration by wandering down Baldwin Ave, beginning at its intersection with Makawao Ave.

★Aloha Cowboy CLOTHING
(Map p382; ☎573-8190; www.alohacowboy.net; 3643 Baldwin Ave; ⏲9:30am-6pm Mon-Sat, 10am-5pm Sun) This welcoming store captures what's cool about Makawao – cowboys and island spirit. Get your cowboy-themed retro lunch pails, Cowgirl-Up hoodies and rhinestone-studded leather bags here.

Volcano Spice SPICES
(Map p382; ☎572-7729; www.volcanospicecompany.com; 3623 Baldwin Ave; ⏲10am-4:30pm) An enticing array of spicy rubs and hot sauces are sold in this tiny shop on Baldwin Ave. Stroll by at the right time and you might hear someone tickling the ivories on the shop's piano.

Designing Wahine GIFTS
(Map p382; ☎573-0990; 3640 Baldwin Ave; ⏲10am-6pm Mon-Sat, 11am-5pm Sun) Quality gifts, classic aloha shirts and hand-dyed tees with *paniolo* themes.

Viewpoints Gallery ART GALLERY
(Map p382; ☎572-5979; www.viewpointsgallerymaui.com; 3620 Baldwin Ave; ⏲10:30am-5pm) It feels like a museum inside this classy gallery, where a dozen of the island's finest artists hang their works.

Information

Post Office – Makawao (☎572-0019; www.usps.com; 1075 Makawao Ave; ⏲9am-4:30pm Mon-Fri, 9-11am Sat)

Ha'iku

HAIKU-PAUWELA POP 8118

Ha'iku, like Pa'ia, has its roots in sugarcane. Maui's first 12 acres of the sweet stuff were planted here in 1869, and the village once had both a sugar mill and pineapple canneries. Thanks to its affordability and proximity to Ho'okipa Beach, it's a haunt of pro surfers who have rejuvenated the town. Today the old cannery buildings are once again the heart of the community, housing a market, a Haleakalā bike tour company and detour-worthy eateries.

Sights

Fourth Marine Division Memorial Park PARK

(Map p382; www.mauicounty.gov; MM 2, Kokomo Rd;) The jungle gym at this county park – complete with turrets, boardwalks and slides – is awesome. On the grounds of a WWII marine camp, the park is a great place to come if the kids are wound-up after a morning of shopping in Makawao.

Sleeping

Haiku Cannery Inn B&B B&B $$

(Map p382; 283-1274; www.haikucanneryinn.com; 1061 Kokomo Rd; r incl breakfast $105-135) Solo travelers, the Malia Room is for you. One of three units in a 1920s plantation manager's house, the room is bright, comfy and, with its bay window, well-suited for reading and relaxing. The house, which sits down a winding dirt road, is surrounded by banana and breadfruit trees. High ceilings, hardwood floors and period decor reflect the century-old history, and there's a fabulous view of the ocean from the porch.

Breakfast includes island fruit, baked goods, yogurt and wonderful island-made granola. In addition to the rooms in the main house, there's a roomy two-bedroom detached cottage for $200.

Pilialoha COTTAGE $$

(Map p382; 572-1440; www.pilialoha.com; 2512 Kaupakalua Rd; d $145;) This sunny split-level cottage is nestled in a pretty eucalyptus grove in the countryside. Everything inside is pretty, too. But it's the warm hospitality and attention to detail – from the fresh-cut roses on the table to the Hawaiian music collection and cozy quilts on the beds – that shines brightest. Breakfast goodies for your first morning and coffee for the entire stay are provided. Washer and dryer on-site.

Eating & Drinking

★NorthShore Cafe CAFE $

(Map p382; 575-2770; www.northshorecafe.net; 824 Kokomo Rd; mains $6-8; 7am-2pm) It's got a funky little interior with chairs that look like they were hauled out of a 1950s attic, but this homespun eatery dishes up unbeatable value and great service. For both breakfast and lunch there are $5.75 and $8.08 menus; breakfast options include a knockout eggs Benedict. Enjoy burgers and sandwiches at lunch. The cafe is hidden behind the power station opposite Colleen's.

Veg Out VEGETARIAN $

(Map p382; 575-5320; www.veg-out.com; Ha'iku Town Center, 810 Kokomo Rd; mains $6-10, pizza $7-17; 10:30am-7:30pm Mon-Fri, 11:30am-7:30pm Sat & Sun;) This rasta-casual vegetarian eatery serves a dynamite burrito loaded with beans, hot tofu and jalapenos. Also on the mark are the taro cheeseburgers and pesto-chèvre pizza.

Colleen's AMERICAN $$

(Map p382; 575-9211; www.colleensinhaiku.com; Ha'iku Marketplace, 810 Ha'iku Rd; breakfast $8-13, lunch $6-15, dinner $11-30; 6am-10pm) If Ha'iku had a 'scene,' Colleen's is where you'd find it. Surfers get their pre-sunrise espresso jolt here in the morning and return in the evening to cap things off with a pint of Big Swell Ale. Colleen's is pure locavore. The burgers are made with hormone-free Maui cattle, the salads with organic Kula greens and the beers Colleen pours are Hawaiian microbrews.

★Maui Kombucha TEA, VEGAN

(Map p382; 575-5233; www.mauikombucha.com; Ha'iku Town Center, 810 Kokomo Rd; 8am-8pm Mon-Fri, 10am-5pm Sat & Sun;) Yoga lads and ladies gather at 'The Booch' for invigorating probiotic teas. Never had kombucha tea? Then step up to the welcoming front counter where you can sample the three daily flavors. Trust us – you'll be hooked by at least one of these cold, bubbly tonics. Also sells tasty raw and cooked vegan meals.

Maui Kombucha is in the back of the Ha'iku Town Center.

Pukalani & Around

POP 7574

True to its name, which means Heavenly Gate, Pukalani is the gateway to the lush Upcountry. Most visitors just drive past Pukalani on the way to Kula and Haleakalā, but there are a few worthwhile stops off the bypass road. To reach the business part of town, get off Haleakalā Hwy (Hwy 37) at the Old Haleakalā Hwy exit, which becomes Pukalani's main street. There are a couple of gas stations along this street – the last place to fill up before Haleakalā National Park.

Sights & Activities

Surfing Goat Dairy FARM

(Map p382; ☎878-2870; www.surfinggoatdairy.com; 3651 Oma'opio Rd; tours adult/child 11yr and over/child under 11yr from $10/7/free; ⏲dairy store 9am-5pm Mon-Sat, 9am-2pm Sun, tours 10am-3:30pm Mon-Sat, 10am-1pm Sun;) 'Da Feta mo betta' is the motto at this 42-acre farm, the source of all that luscious chèvre adorning the menus of Maui's top restaurants. The shop here carries an amazing variety of creamy goat cheeses; stop by with a bottle of Tedeschi wine to enjoy with some of the cheeses at one of the dairy's picnic tables.

Your kids can meet the goat kids in a fun 20-minute dairy tour, or they can milk a goat on the Evening Chores tour.

Pukalani Country Club GOLF

(Map p382; ☎572-1314; www.pukalanigolf.com; 360 Pukalani St; greens fee with cart $88; ⏲7am-dusk) A mile west of Old Haleakalā Hwy, this golf course has 18 holes of smooth greens with sweeping views. Come after 2:30pm and golf the rest of the day for just $28 – cart included!

Eating

Upcountry Farmers Market MARKET

(Map p382; www.upcountryfarmersmarket.com; 55 Kiopaa St; ⏲7am-noon Sat) More than 40 local farmers – and a food truck or two – share fruit, vegetables and locally prepared fare at this market in the parking lot of Longs Drugs at the Kulamalu Shopping Center. Get here by 9:30am for the best choice.

Pukalani Superette SUPERMARKET

(Map p382; ☎572-7616; www.pukalanisuperette.com; 15 Makawao Ave; prepared meals $5-10; ⏲5:30am-9pm Mon-Fri, 6:30am-9pm Sat, 7am-8pm Sun) If you're on your way home from Haleakalā National Park and don't feel like cooking, pick up a prepared hot meal – *kalua* pork, chicken long rice, Spam musubi – at this popular market. In a bad mood? Just listen to the store's catchy jingle on its website, 'Pukalani Superette, welcome to Upcountry...'

Kula

POP 6,452

Kula is Maui's gardenland. The very name 'Kula' is synonymous with the fresh veggies on the best Maui menus, and the region, with its rich vocanic soil, produces most of the onions, lettuce and strawberries grown in Hawaii. Even Oprah is set to get in on the action, with plans to start her own line of Kula-grown produce, 'Oprah's Organics.' The key to these bountiful harvests is the elevation. At 3000ft, Kula's cool nights and sunny days are ideal for growing all sorts of crops.

Kula's farmers first gained fame during the California gold rush of the 1850s, when they shipped so many potatoes to West Coast miners that Kula became known as 'Nu Kaleponi,' the Hawaiian pronunciation for New California. In the late 19th century Portuguese and Chinese immigrants who had worked off their contracts on the sugar plantations also moved up to Kula and started small farms, giving Kula the multicultural face it wears today.

Sights

Stop and smell the roses...and the lavender and all those other sweet-scented blossoms. No two gardens in Kula are alike, and each has its own special charms.

★ **Ali'i Kula Lavender** GARDENS

(Map p382; ☎878-3004; www.aklmaui.com; 1100 Waipoli Rd; adult/12yr and under $3/free; ⏲9am-4pm) Immerse yourself in a sea of purple. Start by strolling along the garden paths where dozens of varieties of these fragrant plants blanket the hillside. Then sit on the veranda with its sweeping views and enjoy a lavender scone with a cup of lavender tea. Browse the gift shop, sample the lavender-scented oils and lotions. To really dig in, take the 30 minute garden tour ($12 per person).

Kula Botanical Garden GARDENS

(Map p382; ☎878-1715; www.kulabotanicalgarden.com; 638 Kekaulike Ave; adult/child 6-12yr $10/3; ⏲9am-4pm) Pleasantly overgrown and shady, this mature garden has walking paths that wind through acres of theme plantings, including native Hawaiian specimens and a 'taboo garden' of poisonous plants. Because a stream runs through it, the garden supports water-thirsty plants that you won't find in other Kula gardens. When the rain gods have been generous the whole place is an explosion of color.

Holy Ghost Church CHURCH

(Map p382; 4300 Lower Kula Rd; ⏲8am-6pm) FREE On the National Register of Historic Places, the octagonal Holy Ghost Church was built in 1895 by Portuguese immigrants. The church features a beautifully ornate interior that looks like it came right out of the Old World, and indeed much of it did. The gilded altar was carved by renowned Austrian woodcarver Ferdinand Stuflesser and shipped in pieces around the Cape of Good Hope.

Activities

Pony Express HORSEBACK RIDING
(Map p382; ☎667-2200; www.ponyexpresstours.com; Haleakalā Crater Rd; trail rides $95-182; ⏲7am-9pm) Several horseback rides are offered, beginning with easy nose-to-tail walks across pastures and woods on Haleakalā Ranch. But the real prize is the ride into the national park's Haleakalā crater that starts at the crater summit and leads down Sliding Sands Trail to the floor of this lunarlike wonder.

Skyline Eco-Adventures ZIPLINING
(Map p382; ☎878-8400; www.zipline.com; Haleakalā Crater Rd; zipline tour $95; ⏲8:30am-3:30pm) Maui's first zipline scored a prime location on the slopes of Haleakalā. Even though the zips are relatively short compared with the new competition, there's plenty of adrenaline rush as you soar above the treetops over a series of five gulches. A half-mile hike and a suspension bridge are tossed in for good measure.

Proflyght Paragliding PARAGLIDING
(Map p382; ☎874-5433; www.paraglidemaui.com; Waipoli Rd; paraglide $95-185; ⏲office 7am-7pm, flights 2hrs after sunrise) Strap into a tandem paraglider with a certified instructor and take a running leap from a Haleakalā incline near the Ali'i Kula Lavender Farm. After a lesson, soar on a 1000ft descent or a 3000ft descent. Reserve your spot a few days to a week in advance. The term 'bird's-eye view' will never be the same.

Tours

★O'o Farm FARM TOUR
(Map p382; ☎667-4341; www.oofarm.com; Waipoli Rd; lunch tour adult/child 5-12yr $50/25; ⏲10:30am-2pm Mon-Thu) Whether you're a gardener or a gourmet you're going to love a tour of famed Lahaina chef James McDonald's organic Upcountry farm. Where else can you help harvest your own meal, turn the goodies over to a gourmet chef and feast on the bounty? Bring your own wine and suntan lotion, and wear your walking shoes.

Festivals & Events

Holy Ghost Feast PORTUGUESE FESTIVAL
(www.kulacatholiccommunity.org) Dating back to the 1890s, this festival celebrates Kula's Portuguese heritage. Held at the Holy Ghost Church on the fourth Saturday and Sunday in May, it's a family event with games, craft vendors, a farmers market and a free Hawaiian-Portuguese lunch on Sunday.

Sleeping

Kula Sandalwoods Cottages COTTAGE $$
(Map p382; ☎878-3523; www.kulasandalwoods.com; 15427 Haleakalā Hwy; r $139; 📶) A half-dozen freestanding cottages dot the hillside above Kula Sandalwoods Restaurant. Think rustic, but rooms do have flat screen TVs and wi-fi. The sweeping view from the lanai is top rate and the price is a bargain for being on the doorstep of the national park. It's about 45 minutes to Haleakalā's summit. On-site restaurant serves breakfast and lunch Monday to Saturday and breakfast only on Sunday.

Kula Lodge CABINS $$
(Map p382; ☎878-1535; www.kulalodge.com; 15200 Haleakala Hwy; cabins $150-220; 📶) The word 'chalet' might be a stretch for the five rustic cabins that comprise Kula Lodge, but hey, who are we to knock a little can-do optimism? The cabins sit on the slopes of Haleakalā about 45 minutes from the volcano's summit. All units come with lanai, coffeemakers and extra blankets. Four have lofts, which are great for kids. There are no TVs, telephones or kitchenettes. Wi-fi available at the on-site restaurant.

Eating & Drinking

Kula Marketplace AMERICAN $
(Map p382; ☎878-2135; www.kulamarketplace.com; 15200 Haleakala Hwy; sandwiches $7, slice of pizza $3; ⏲7am-7pm) Enjoy the view as well as a pre-made sandwich or a slice of pizza at this gourmet market perched on the side of the volcano. You'll also find wine, chocolate, homemade jams and arts and crafts. It's the last stop for supplies on the way to the summit.

La Provence CAFE $$
(Map p382; ☎878-1313; www.laprovencekula.com; 3158 Lower Kula Rd, Waiakoa; pastries $3, lunch $10-12, crepes $4-13; ⏲7am-9pm Wed-Sun) One of Maui's top pastry chefs hangs his shingle here. Even if you're not hungry, swing by

to pick up a ham-and-cheese croissant or some flaky chocolate-filled pastries for that Haleakala picnic. The chèvre green salads are a Kula treat to savor. Coming from Pukulania, turn left off Hwy 37 onto Kaa St then turn right onto Lower Kula Rd and drive ¼ mile.

Kula Bistro ECLECTIC **$$**
(Map p382; ☎871-2960; www.kulabistro.com; 4566 Lower Kula Rd; breakfast $7-15, lunch & dinner $9-25; ⌚breakfast, lunch, dinner) The airy and welcoming Kula Bistro offers a globally inspired menu, with an emphasis on pasta and Hawaiian favorites. The menu is a bit too eclectic – from Chinese chicken salad to Cajun-style mahimahi on focaccia to dry mein to shrimp scampi – but the food is solid and filling after a day of exploring the national park.

Crater Coffee COFFEE CART
(Map p382; ☎757-1342; www.cratercoffee.com; 15200 Haleakala Hwy; coffee $4; ⌚3am-7pm) On the early morning climb to see the Haleakalā sunrise, it's nice to see a smiling face. Especially if that smiling face is selling a hot cup of Maui Coffee Roasters java. This friendly coffee cart parks in front of Kula Marketplace on Hwy 377. There's a bathroom in the building behind the kiosk.

Keokea

Property owner Oprah Winfrey has brought low-key star power to tiny Keokea, the last real town before Hana if you're swinging around the southern part of the island. The sum total of the town center consists of a coffee shop, an art gallery, a gas station and two small stores, the Ching Store and the Fong Store. As for Oprah, her presence might be less low-key in coming years; if news reports are true, she plans to sell organic vegetables and food products sourced from her Upcountry land.

Sights

Drawn by rich soil, Hakka Chinese farmers migrated to this remote corner of Kula at the turn of the 20th century. Their influence is readily visible throughout the village. Keokea's c 1907 landmark **St John's Episcopal Church** (Map p382) still bears its name in Chinese characters. For a time Sun Yat-sen, father of the Chinese nationalist movement, lived on the outskirts of Keokea. He's honored at **Sun Yat-sen Park** (Map p382), found along the Kula Hwy (Hwy 37) 1.7 miles beyond Grandma's Coffee House. The park has picnic tables and is a great place to soak up the broad vistas that stretch across to West Maui.

Activities

Thompson Ranch HORSEBACK RIDING
(Map p382; ☎878-1910; www.thompsonranchmaui.com; cnr Middle & Polipoli Rds; 2hr ride $100; ⌚tour 10am) Join these folks for horseback rides across ranch land in the cool Upcountry bordering Polipoli Spring State Recreation Area. At elevations of 4000ft to 6000ft, it's a memorable ride for those who enjoy mountain scenery. By reservation only; 200lb weight limit.

Sleeping

★Star Lookout COTTAGE **$$**
(Map p382; ☎907-250-2364; www.starlookout.com; 622 Thompson Rd; cottage $200; 📶) A fabulous ocean view, outdoor hot tub and grounds so quiet you can hear the flowers bloom. Half a mile up a one-lane road from Keokea center, this two-bedroom cottage with a loft sleeps four people comfortably, six in a pinch. But what makes it spectacular is the setting, which overlooks a thousand acres of green pastureland that's now owned by Oprah Winfrey and set aside for preservation. Book early.

Eating

Grandma's Coffee House CAFE **$**
(Map p382; ☎878-2140; www.grandmascoffee.com; 9232 Kula Hwy; pastries $3, breakfast $6-15, sandwiches $8-10; ⌚7am-5pm) 🌿 Saturday and Sunday mornings on Grandma's patio are hard to beat. Heaping portions, a guy on a guitar and Grandma's Hawaii-grown coffee. This earthy cafe also dishes up homemade pastries, hearty sandwiches and deli salads. Grandma's family has been growing coffee in Keokea for generations. On the patio, you're eating right under their coffee trees.

'Ulupalakua Ranch & Beyond

This sprawling 20,000-acre ranch was established in the mid-19th century by James Makee, a whaling captain who jumped ship and befriended Hawaiian royalty. King David Kalakaua, the 'Merrie Monarch,' became a frequent visitor who loved to indulge in late-night rounds of poker and champagne. The ranch is still worked by *paniolo,* who have been herding cattle here for generations. More than 2000 head of cattle, as well as a small herd of Rocky Mountain elk, dot the hillside pastures.

The ranch is green in more ways than one. The owners restored a rare native dry-land forest on the upper slopes of the ranch's property and also set aside more than 11,000 acres to be preserved as perpetual agricultural land. In December 2012, the ranch began hosting the Upcountry's first wind energy farm.

Today most people come to visit Tedeschi Vineyards, Maui's sole winery, which is on 'Ulupalakua Ranch land, about 6 miles beyond Keokea. After the winery, it's another 25 undulating miles to Kipahulu along the remote Pi'ilani Hwy.

Sights

Tedeschi Vineyards WINERY

(Map p382; ☎878-6058; www.mauiwine.com; Kula Hwy; ⏲10am-5pm, tours 10:30am & 1:30pm) Enjoy free tours and wine tastings in the historic stone cottage where King David Kalakaua once slept. In the 1970s, while awaiting their first grape harvest, the owners decided to take advantage of Maui's prickly fruit – today the biggest hit is the sweet Maui Splash, a light blend of pineapple and passion fruit. Other pineapple novelties worth a taste: the dry Maui Blanc and the sparkling Hula O'Maui.

This is no Napa Valley, however, and the grape wines are less of a splash. Reservations are necessary for groups of 10 or more.

Don't miss the fascinating exhibit at the side of the tasting room that features Kalakaua lore, ranch history and ecological goings-on. Opposite the winery, see the stack remains of the **Makee Sugar Mill** (Map p382), built in 1878.

Check the website for details about the ranch's quarterly Sunday Drive Event (March, June, September, December) featuring live slack key guitar music, glassblowing demonstrations and cowboy-centric food.

Eating

★**Bully's Burgers** BURGERS $

(Map p398; ☎878-3272; www.triplelranchmaui.com; 15900 Pi'ilani Hwy; burgers $9-12; ⏲11am-7pm winter, to 8pm summer) A hut plunked in the midst of cow skulls, Bully's has no gourmet pretensions – other than the blue cheese on the bacon-topped Black and Blue burger. The organic beef, fresh from the adjoining Triple L Ranch, is grilled while you wait and served with a chatyote pickle. Try the spicy chipotle sauce. Bully's is in Kanaio, about 4 miles beyond Tedeschi Vineyards. If you're coming from Hana, this is where you reward yourself for surviving the drive.

'Ulupalakua Ranch Store DELI $

(Map p382; www.ulupalakuaranch.com; burgers $9-11; ⏲grill 11am-2:30pm, store 9:30am-5pm) Sidle up to the life-size wooden cowboys on the front porch and say howdy. Then pop inside and check out the cowboy hats and souvenir T-shirts. If it's lunchtime, mosey over to the grill and treat yourself to an organic ranch-raised elk burger. Can't beat that for local. The store is 5.5 miles south of Keokea, opposite the winery.

THE ROAD TO HANA

The Road to Hana is ravishingly beautiful, but it's not just the gorgeous views that make it special. There's also the thrill of expectation – what lies beyond the next jungly curve? Fortunately, the serpentine Hana Hwy delivers one jaw-dropping view after another as it winds between tropical valleys and towering cliffs.

Along the way 54 one-lane bridges mark nearly as many waterfalls, some tranquil and inviting, others so sheer they kiss you with spray as you drive past. When you're ready to get out and stretch your legs the real adventure begins: hiking trails climb into cool forests, short paths lead to Eden-like swimming holes, side roads wind down to sleepy seaside villages. If you've never tried smoked breadfruit, taken a dip in a spring-fed cave or gazed upon an ancient Hawaiian temple, set the alarm early – you've got a big day. And as far as rental cars go, Jeeps and Mustangs are the ride of choice on the Hana Hwy.

As for the waterfalls, whether you see torrents or trickles depends on recent rainfall up in the mountains. And if it really starts to pour, watch out for sudden rockslides and muddy debris on the road.

Heading east from Pa'ia, houses give way to fields of sugarcane and the scenery gets more dramatic with each mile. After mile marker 16 on Hwy 36 the Hana Hwy changes numbers and becomes Hwy 360 and the mile markers begin again at zero.

HANA TRIP TIPS

- Beat the crowd – get a sunrise start.
- Fill up the tank in Pa'ia; the next gas station isn't until Hana.
- Bring snacks and plenty to drink.
- Wear a bathing suit under your clothes so you're ready for impromptu swims.
- Pull over to let local drivers pass – they're moving at a different pace.
- Bring cash for small roadside purchases.
- Wear shoes that are good for hiking, as well as scrambling over slick rocks.
- Leave valuables at your hotel or condo. Electronics left on car seats may lead to smashed windows.

Twin Falls

Just after mile marker 2 on Hwy 360, a wide parking area with a fruit stand marks the start of the 1.1 mile trail (one-way) to Twin Falls. The pleasant, mostly level trail unfurls through a lush strand of tropical trees, passing one small waterfall before ending at Twin Falls and a swimming hole. Not quite half a mile in, follow a short path to your left to the stream's edge then down to a small cascade. On the main trail, cross a stream then turn left at the unmarked trail junction just ahead. Continue a short distance then climb over the aqueduct. Look straight ahead for the twin falls. It's a beauty. You will have to wade through the stream to reach the pool. Turn around if the water is too high.

We saw smashed glass in the overflow parking lot, just beyond the juice stand. Take valuables with you as a precaution. Obey all signs on the gated trailhead. The area can be hit by flash floods. Arrive before 9:30am to nab a spot in the main lot.

Huelo

With its abundant rain and fertile soil Huelo once supported more than 50,000 Hawaiians, but today it's a sleepy, scattered community of farms and enviable cliffside homes.

The double row of mailboxes and green bus shelter that come up after a blind curve 0.5 miles past mile marker 3 marks the start of the narrow road that leads into the village. The only sight, Kaulanapueo Church, is a half-mile down.

It's tempting to continue driving past the church, but don't bother – it's not rewarding, as the road shortly turns to dirt and dead-ends at gated homes. There's no public beach access.

Sights

Kaulanapueo Church CHURCH

(Map p398) Constructed in 1853 of coral blocks and surrounded by a manicured green lawn, this tidy church remains the heart of the village. It's in early Hawaiian missionary style with a spare interior and a tin roof topped with a green steeple. Swaying palm trees add a tropical backdrop.

Sleeping & Eating

Tea House COTTAGE $$

(Map p398; ☎572-8596; www.mauiteahouse.com; Hoolawa Rd; s/d $135/150; wi-fi) Off-the-grid doesn't mean you have to sacrifice wi-fi or Direct TV. Built with walls recycled from a Zen temple, this secluded, one-of-a-kind cottage, now under new ownership, is completely self-sustaining and uses its own solar power to stoke up the lights. It also has everything you'll need, from a kitchen with gas burners to an open-air shower in a redwood gazebo.

The grounds also contain a Tibetan-style stupa with a spectacular clifftop ocean view and a second unit, the Tiare Cottage, that rents by the week ($500).

★**Huelo Lookout** LOOKOUT, FRUIT STAND $

(Map p398; ☎280-4791; www.huelolookout.coconutprotectors.com; 7600 Hana Hwy; snacks $5-7; ⏲7:30am-5:30pm) The fruit stand itself is tempting enough: drinking coconuts, smoothies, even French crepes...ooh la la. And everything's organic from their own 12-acre farm. But it doesn't stop there. Take your goodies down the steps, where there's a table with a wide-open panorama clear out to the coast. The lookout is located at mile marker 4.5 on Hwy 360.

Ko'olau Forest Reserve

This is where it starts to get wild! As the highway snakes along the edge of the Ko'olau Forest Reserve, the jungle takes over and one-lane bridges appear around every other bend. Ko'olau means 'windward,' and the upper slopes of these mountains squeeze passing clouds of a mighty 200in to 300in of rain annually. No surprise – that makes for awesome waterfalls as the rainwater rushes down the reserve's abundant gulches and streams.

After mile marker 5 you'll pass through the village of **Kailua**. This little community of tin-roofed houses is the home base for the employees of the East Maui Irrigation (EMI) company. These workers maintain the extensive irrigation system that carries water from the rainforest to thirsty sugarcane fields in Central Maui.

After leaving the village, just past mile marker 6, you'll be treated to a splash of color as you pass planted groves of **painted eucalyptus** with brilliant rainbow-colored bark. Roll down the windows and inhale the sweet scent given off by these majestic trees introduced from Australia.

Waikamoi Nature Trail

Sturdy sandals – and maybe a rain slicker – come in handy on this 30-minute **nature trail** (Map p398) that's filled with majestic sights and spicy scents. A covered table at the top offers one pretty spot to break out that picnic lunch. Look for the signposted trailhead 0.5 miles past mile marker 9, where there's a wide dirt pull-off with space for several cars to park.

At the start of this 0.8-mile trail you're welcomed by a sign that reads 'Quiet. Trees at Work' and a strand of grand reddish *Eucalyptus robusta*, one of several types of towering eucalyptus trees that grow along the path. Once you reach the ridge at the top of the loop, you'll be treated to fine views of the winding Hana Hwy.

Waikamoi Falls

Just a handful of cars can squeeze in before the bridge at mile marker 10, but unless it's been raining recently don't worry about missing this one. The East Maui Irrigation Company diverts water from the stream, and as a result the falls are usually just a trickle. After you drive past the bridge, bamboo grows almost horizontally out from the cliffs, creating a green canopy over the road.

Garden of Eden Arboretum

Why pay $15 per person to visit an arboretum when the entire road to Hana is a garden? Because the **Garden of Eden** (Map p398; www.mauigardenofeden.com; 10600 Hana Hwy; admission $15; ⏲8am-3pm) offers a tamer version of paradise. The winding paths are neatly maintained, about 700 plants are labeled and the hilltop picnic tables sport gorgeous views, including ones of Puohokamoa Falls and of Keopuka Rock, which was featured in the opening shot of the 1993 film *Jurassic Park*. A small gallery and gourmet food truck are also on site. Expect to spend at least an hour wandering the grounds. The arboretum is 0.5 miles past mile marker 10. Cash only.

Puohokamaka Falls

Immediately after mile marker 11 you'll pass Puohokamoa Falls. This waterfall no longer has public access, but you can get a glimpse of it from the bridge, or a bird's-eye view of the falls from the Garden of Eden Arboretum.

Haipua'ena Falls

If you're ready for a dip, Haipua'ena Falls, 0.5 miles past mile marker 11, provides a gentle waterfall with a zenlike pool deep enough for swimming. Since you can't see the pool from the road, few people know this one's here. There's space for just a couple of cars on the Hana side of the bridge. To reach the falls, simply walk 100 yards upstream. Wild ginger grows along the path, and ferns hang from the rock wall behind the waterfall, making an idyllic setting. Be aware of VERY slippery rocks and flash floods.

Kaumahina State Wayside Park

Clean restrooms and a grassy lawn with picnic tables make this roadside **park** a perfect choice for a family picnic stop (although some might find the gaze of the feral cats

East Maui

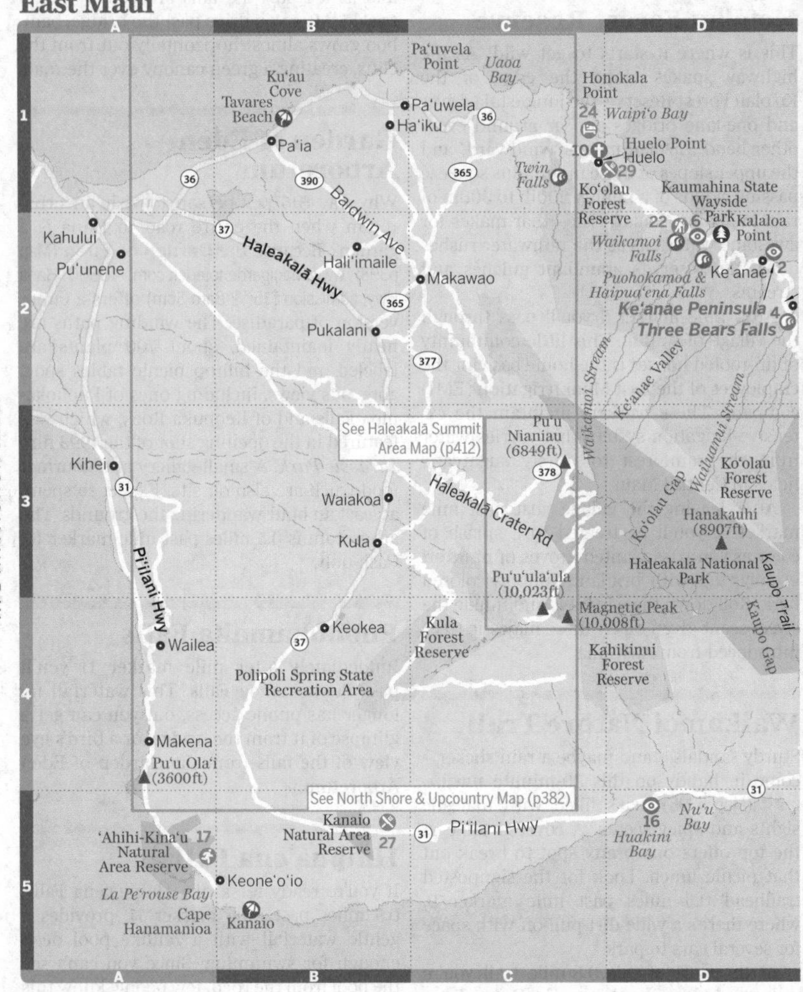

just a little unsettling). The park comes up around 0.2 miles after mile marker 12. Be sure to make the effort and take the short walk up the hill past the restrooms for an eye-popping panoramic view of the coastal scenery that awaits to the south.

For the next several miles, the scenery is absolutely stunning, opening up to a breathtaking new vista as you turn round each bend. If it happens to have been raining recently, you can expect to see waterfalls galore crashing and cascading down the mountains.

Honomanu Bay

Your first view of this striking stream-fed bay comes at mile marker 13, where there's a roadside pull-off that invites you to pause and take in the scene.

The rocky black-sand beach is used mostly by local surfers and fishers. Surfable waves form during big swells, but the rocky bottom and strong rips make it dangerous if you're not familiar with the spot. Honomanu Stream, which empties into the bay, forms a pool just inland of the beach that's

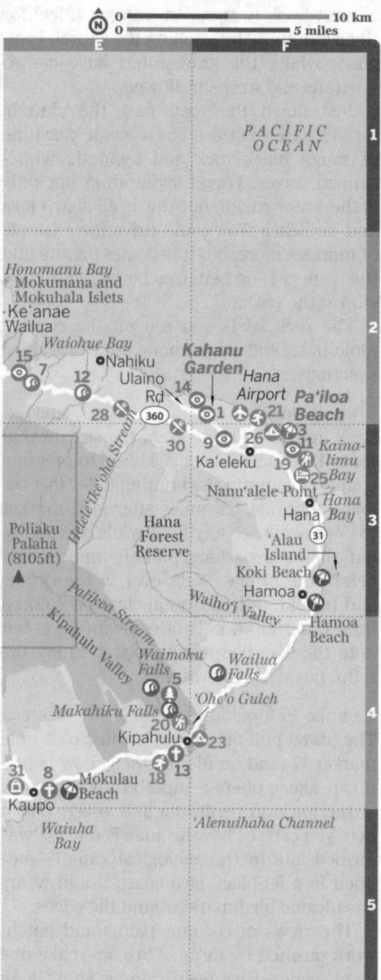

East Maui

Top Sights

1 Kahanu Garden F2
2 Ke'anae Peninsula D2
3 Pa'iloa Beach F3
4 Three Bears Falls D2

Sights

5 Bamboo Forest E4
Charles Lindbergh's Grave .... (see 13)
6 Garden of Eden Arboretum D2
7 Hanawi Falls E2
8 Hui Aloha Church E4
9 Ka'eleku Caverns F3
10 Kaulanapueo Church C1
11 Lava Caves F3
12 Makapipi Falls E2
13 Palapala Ho'omau Congregational Church E4
14 Pi'ilanihale Heiau F2
15 Pua'a Ka'a State Wayside Park E2
16 Sea Arch D5

Activities, Courses & Tours

Hana Lava Tube .... (see 9)
Kipahulu 'Ohana .... (see 23)
Lower Pools .... (see 23)
17 Makena Stables A5
18 Maui Stables E4
19 Pi'ilani Trail F3
20 Pipiwai Trail E4
21 Skyview Soaring F2
22 Waikamoi Nature Trail D2

Sleeping

23 Kipahulu Campground F4
24 Tea House C1
25 Wai'anapanapa Cabins F3
26 Wai'anapanapa Campground F3

Eating

27 Bully's Burgers B5
28 Coconut Glen's E2
29 Huelo Lookout D1
30 Up In Smoke E3

Shopping

31 Kaupo Store E4

good for splashing in; on weekends local families take the kids here to wade in its shallow water.

Just after mile marker 14, an inconspicuous road plunges straight down to Honomanu Bay. But the road can be shockingly bad – if you're not in a high-clearance vehicle, send a scout before driving down.

Kalaloa Point

For a fascinating view of the coast, stop at the wide pull-off on the ocean side of the highway 0.4 miles past mile marker 14. From here you can look clear across Honomanu Bay and watch ant-size cars snaking down the mountain cliffs on the other side. If there's no place to park, there's another pull-off with the same view 0.2 miles further on.

Ke'anae

Congratulations – you're halfway to Hana! Your reward? Dramatic landscapes and the friendliest seaside village on the route.

The sweeping Ke'anae Valley starts way up at the Ko'olau Gap in the rim of Haleakalā Crater and stretches clear down to the coast. The land radiates green, thanks to the 150in of rainfall that drenches it each year.

At the foot of the valley lies Ke'anae Peninsula, created by a late eruption of Haleakalā that sent lava gushing all the way down Ke'anae Valley and into the sea. Unlike its rugged surroundings, the volcanic peninsula is perfectly flat, like a leaf floating on the water.

You'll want to see Ke'anae up close. But keep an eye peeled, as sights come up in quick succession. After passing the YMCA camp 0.5 miles past mile marker 16, the arboretum pops up on the right and the road to Ke'anae Peninsula heads off to the left around the next bend.

Sights & Activities

Ke'anae Arboretum HIKING

A short walk offers big rewards inside the Ke'anae Arboretum, 0.6 miles past mile marker 16. The 0.6-mile trail, which is fairly level, follows the Pi'ina'au Stream past an array of shady trees. Most eye-catching are the painted eucalyptus trees and the golden-stemmed bamboo, whose green stripes look like the strokes of a Japanese *shodo* (calligraphy) artist.

The 6-acre arboretum is divided into two sections, with exotic timber and ornamental trees in one area and Hawaiian food and medicinal plants in the upper section.

The path, which starts on a paved road and then turns to dirt, takes about 30 minutes to walk. Expect some mosquitoes on the way.

★Ke'anae Peninsula VILLAGE

(Map p397) A jagged, wave-pounded coastline embraces a village so quiet you can hear the grass grow. This rare slice of 'Old Hawaii' is reached by taking the unmarked Ke'anae Rd on the *makai* side of the highway just beyond Ke'anae Arboretum. Here, families who have had roots to the land for generations still tend stream-fed taro patches.

Marking the heart of the village is **Lanakila 'Ihi'ihi o Iehova Ona Kaua (Ke'anae Congregational Church)**, built in 1860. This is one church made of lava rocks and coral mortar whose exterior hasn't been covered over with layers of whitewash. It's a welcoming place with open doors and a guest book to sign. You can get a feel for the community by strolling the church cemetery, where the gravestones have cameo portraits and fresh-cut flowers.

Just down the road past the church, **Ke'anae Beach Park** has a scenic coastline of rough black rock and hypnotic white-capped waves. Forget swimming: not only is the water rough, but this is all sharp lava and no beach. You could drive for a couple of minutes more, but it becomes private and the scenery is no better, so be respectful and stop at the park.

The rock islets you see off the coast – Mokuhala and Mokumana – are seabird sanctuaries.

Ching's Pond OUTDOORS

Back up on the Hana Hwy, the stream that feeds Ke'anae Peninsula pauses to create a couple of tempting swimming holes just below the bridge, 0.9 miles after mile marker 16. You won't see anything while driving by, but there's a parking pull-off immediately before the bridge. Walk over to the bridge and behold: a deep crystal-clear pool and a little waterfall. Locals often swim here, but note the 'No Trespassing' signs. Enjoy the sight, but swim elsewhere.

Ke'anae Peninsula Lookout VIEWPOINT

The paved pull-off, on the left just past mile marker 17 (and beside the the yellow tsunami speaker), offers a superb bird's-eye view of the lowland peninsula and village. From here you can see how Ke'anae Peninsula was formed late in the geological game – outlined in a jet-black lava coast, it still wears its volcanic birthmark around the edges.

The views of coconut palms and patchwork taro fed by Ke'anae Stream make one tasty scene. If it's been raining lately, look to the far left to spot a series of cascading waterfalls.

Sleeping & Eating

YMCA Camp Ke'anae CABINS $

(☎248-8355; www.ymcacampkeanae.org; 13375 Hana Hwy; campsite or VW van site s/family $20/35, cabins per person $20, cottages $150) When they're not tied up by groups, the Y's cabins, on a knoll overlooking the coast, are available to individuals as hostel-style dorms. You'll need your own sleeping bag, and cooking facilities are limited to simple outdoor grills. Another option is to pitch your tent on the grounds. The Y also has two cottages, each with full facilities, two bedrooms and a lanai. The camp is located at mile marker 16.5. Advance reservations are required.

★Ke'anae Landing Fruit Stand FRUIT STAND $

(248-7448; 210 Keanae Rd, Ke'anae Peninsula; banana bread $6, snacks $4-6; 8:30am-2:30pm) Also known as Aunty Sandy's Banana Bread, this roadside eatery serves 'da best' banana bread on the entire road to Hana. It's baked fresh every morning and is so good you'll find as many locals as tourists pulling up here. You can also get fresh fruit and drinks at this stand in the village center just before Ke'anae Beach Park. Cash only.

Wailua

After the Ke'anae Peninsula Lookout, you'll pass a couple of roadside fruit stands. A quarter-mile after mile marker 18, the unmarked Wailua Rd leads to the left into the village of Wailua. There's little to see other than a small church, and the village doesn't exactly welcome visitors, so you might as well stick to the highway where the real sights are.

Sights

Wailua Valley State Wayside VIEWPOINT

Just before mile marker 19, Wailua Valley State Wayside lookout comes up on the right. The sign is just PAST the entrance, which appears quickly after turning round a bend. The lookout provides a broad view into verdant Ke'anae Valley, which appears to be a hundred shades of green.

You can see a couple of waterfalls, and on a clear day you can steal a view of Ko'olau Gap, the break in the rim of Haleakalā Crater. Up the steps to the right, you'll find a good view of Wailua Peninsula. If you miss the entrance, turn around at the Wailua Peninsula Lookout just ahead on the left.

Wailua Peninsula Lookout VIEWPOINT

For the most spectacular view of Wailua Peninsula, stop at the large paved pull-off on the ocean side of the road 0.25 miles past mile marker 19. There's no sign but it's not hard to find, as two concrete picnic tables mark the spot. Grab a seat, break out your snack pack and ogle the taro fields and jungly vistas unfolding below.

Wailua to Nahiku

Keep your camera handy for the magnificent run of roadside cascades popping up between mile markers 19 through 25.

Sights

★Three Bears Falls WATERFALL

(Map p398) Three Bears, 0.5 miles past mile marker 19, is a real beauty. It takes its name from the triple cascade that flows down a steep rockface on the inland side of the road. Catch it after a rainstorm and the cascades come together and roar as one mighty waterfall.

There's a small turnout with parking for a few cars right before crossing the bridge. You can scramble down to the falls via a steep ill-defined path that begins on the Hana side of the bridge. The stones are moss-covered and slippery, so either proceed with caution or simply enjoy the view from the road.

Pua'a Ka'a State Wayside Park SWIMMING

(Map p398) This delightful park with an odd name, Pua'a Ka'a (Rolling Pig), rolls along both sides of the highway 0.5 miles after mile marker 22. From the restrooms and parking lot on the ocean side of the road, cross the highway and head inland to find a pair of delciious waterfalls cascading into pools.

The best for swimming is the upper pool, which is visible just beyond the picnic tables. To reach it, cross the stream, skipping across a few rocks. (Be aware of the possibility of falling rocks beneath the waterfall, and flash floods.) To get to the lower falls, which drop into a shallow pool, walk back to the south side of the bridge and then follow the trail upstream. And while you're at it, be sure to catch the scene from the bridge. Just don't hog the view.

Hanawi Falls WATERFALL

(Map p398) Another waterfall with a split personality, Hanawi sometimes flows gently into a quiet pool and sometimes gushes wildly across a broad rockface. No matter the mood, it always invites snapping a pic. The falls are 0.1 miles after mile marker 24. There are small pull-offs before and after the bridge.

Makapipi Falls WATERFALL

(Map p398) Look down, not up, to see the cascades at Makapipi Falls. The falls make a sheer plunge right beneath your feet as you stand on the ocean side of the Makapipi Bridge. You don't see anything from your car so if you didn't know about it, you'd never even imagine this one was here. It's 0.1 miles after mile marker 25; you'll find pull-offs before and after the bridge.

Nahiku

While the village of Nahiku is down on the coast, its tiny 'commercial' center – such as it is – is on the ocean side of the Hana Hwy, just before mile marker 29. Here you'll find the Nahiku Marketplace, home to a little coffee shop, and arts and crafts store and several eateries clustered together.

If you're hungry, stop here. The food's tempting and this is the last place for a meal between here and Hana. Be aware that hours are island-style flexible and a kiosk may be closed when you think it would likely be open. Gone fishin'?

Eating

★Coconut Glen's ICE CREAM $

(Map p398; 979-1168; www.coconutglens.com; MM 27.5 Hana Hwy; scoop of ice cream $5;) We have a crush on Coconut Glen. Trained at the New England Culinary Institute, eco-minded Glen Simkins whips up some mighty delicious organic, vegan ice cream, which is served in a coconut shell with a coconut-shard for a spoon. The ice cream comes in five flavors – we're partial to the chili chocolate – and is so darn tasty you won't even notice it's made from coconut milk, not cream.

The coconuts come from Glen's organic farm, and his roadside stand is made from 90% recycled materials.

Up In Smoke HAWAII REGIONAL $

(Map p398; Hana Hwy, Nahiku Marketplace; mains under $9) The *kalua* pig tacos rock the house at this bustling BBQ stand. It's also *the* place to try kiawe-smoked breadfruit. Closed Thursdays.

'Ula'ino Road

'Ula'ino Rd begins at the Hana Hwy just south of mile marker 31. Hana Lava Tube is half a mile from the highway and Kahanu Garden a mile further.

Sights & Activities

★Kahanu Garden HISTORICAL SITE

(Map p398; 248-8912; www.ntbg.org; 650 'Ula'ino Rd; adult/child 12yr and under $10/free; 9am-2pm Mon-Sat) This one-of-a-kind place delivers a double blast of mana: Hawaii's largest temple and one of its most important ethnobotanical gardens share the 294-acre site. The National Tropical Botanical Garden, which is dedicated to the conservation of rare and medicinal plants from the tropical Pacific, maintains Kahanu. Guided tours ($25) are offered at 10am on Saturdays and require advance reservations.

Of the gardens, the most interesting is the canoe garden, landscaped with taro and other plants brought to Hawaii by early Polynesian settlers. The scope is amazing, as the garden holds the world's largest breadfruit tree collection and a remarkable variety of coconut palms.

The garden paths also skirt **Pi'ilanihale Heiau** (Map p398), an immense lava-stone

TREAD GENTLY

Travelers wanting to explore every nook and cranny of the island sometimes come into conflict with Maui residents who feel their quality of life is being encroached upon. At no place has this come more to a head than at **Blue Pool**, a coastal waterfall and swimming hole off 'Ula'ino Rd. Access to this slice of paradise leads across private property and the rural landowners who cherish their privacy are increasingly at odds with day-trippers cutting across their backyards.

A signboard posted opposite Hana Lava Tube, which explains how the Blue Pool is of spiritual significance to Native Hawaiians and encourages tourists not to visit, has been overlaid with a 'Closed to the Public. Trespassers will be Prosecuted' sign. For those who fail to heed the message, heated confrontations are common. If you don't want to chance getting bopped by a coconut, swim at one of the many other waterfall pools along the Hana Hwy.

platform reaching 450ft in length. The history of this astounding heiau is shrouded in mystery, but there's no doubt that it was an important religious site for Hawaiians. Archaeologists believe construction began as early as AD 1200 and the heiau was built in sequences. The final grand scale was the work of Pi'ilani (the heiau's name means House of Pi'ilani), the 14th-century Maui chief who is also credited with the construction of many of the coastal fishponds in the Hana area. It's a memorable place to bring the entire family and children 12 years and under are admitted free.

Visiting Kahanu Garden takes a couple of hours, so few day-trippers come this way and you may have the place to yourself. The site, on Kalahu Point, is 1.5 miles down 'Ula'ino Rd from the Hana Hwy. The road is crossed by a streambed immediately before reaching the gardens; if it's dry you should be able to drive over it OK, but if it's been raining heavily don't even try.

Hana Lava Tube CAVE

(Map p398; ☎248-7308; www.mauicave.com; 'Ula'ino Rd; admission $12.50; ⏰10:30am-4pm; 👪) Who's afraid of the dark? See for yourself at the end of this fascinating underground walk by flipping off your flashlights. Eerie! The lava tubes, which reach heights of up to 40ft, contain a unique ecosystem of dripping stalactites and stalagmites. A hand railing runs beside the main path, which is dotted with explanatory markers. Admission for the self-guided tour includes two flashlights and optional hard hats.

These caves are so formidable that they once served as a slaughterhouse – 17,000lb of cow bones had to be removed before they were opened to visitors! The tubes, which are on 'Ula'ino Rd at mile marker 31, take about one hour to explore.

Wai'anapanapa State Park

Swim in a cave, sun on a black-sand beach, explore ancient Hawaiian sites, use the public restrooms – yep, this is one cool park. A sunny coastal trail and a seaside campground make it a tempting place to dig in for awhile. Honokalani Rd, which leads into Wai'anapanapa State Park (www.hawaiistateparks.org), is just after mile marker 32. The road ends overlooking the park's centerpiece, the jet-black sands at Pa'iloa Bay.

RED WATERS

On certain nights of the year, the waters in Wai'anapanapa State Park's lava-tube caves take on a red hue. Legend says it's the blood of a princess and her lover who were killed in a fit of rage by the princess's jealous husband after he found them hiding together here. Less romantic types attribute the phenomenon to swarms of tiny bright-red shrimp called *'opaeula,* which occasionally emerge from subterranean cracks in the lava.

Beaches

★Pa'iloa Beach BEACH

(Map p398) The park's beach is a stunner – hands-down the prettiest black-sand beach on Maui. Walk on down, sunbathe, enjoy. But if you're thinking about jumping in, be cautious. It's open ocean with a bottom that drops quickly and water conditions that are challenging, even for strong swimmers. Powerful rips are the norm (Pa'iloa means 'always splashing') and there have been several drownings here.

Sights & Activities

Wai'anapanapa Lava Caves CAVES

(Map p398) A 10-minute loop path north from the beach parking lot leads to a pair of impressive lava-tube caves. Their gardenlike exteriors are draped with ferns and colorful impatiens, while their interiors harbor deep spring-fed pools. Wai'anapanapa means 'glistening waters' and the pools' crystal-clear mineral waters reputedly rejuvenate the skin. They certainly will invigorate – these sunless pools are refreshingly brisk!

Pi'ilani Trail HIKING

(Map p398) This gem of a coastal trail leads 3 miles south from the park to Kainalimu Bay, just north of Hana Bay, offering splendid views along the way. The route follows an ancient footpath known as the King's Highway that was the main land route between Hana and villages to the north. Some of the worn stepping stones along the path date from the time of Pi'ilani, the king who ruled Maui in the 14th century.

The trail packs a lot up front, so even if you just have time to do the first mile, you won't regret it. If you plan to hike the whole trail be sure to bring water (it's unshaded the entire way) and good hiking shoes (it gets rougher as you go along).

The trail begins along the coast just below the camping area and parallels the ocean along lava sea cliffs. After just a few minutes you'll pass a burial ground, a natural sea arch and a blowhole that roars to life whenever there's pounding surf. This is also the area where you're most likely to see endangered Hawaiian monk seals basking onshore.

Perched above the sea at 0.7 miles are the remains of **'Ohala Heiau**, a place of worship to the harvest god Lono. A fishing shrine ahead on the left affords a good view south of basalt cliffs lined up all the way to Hana. Hala and ironwood encroaches the shoreline past the heiau. Round stones continue to mark the way across lava and a grassy clearing, fading briefly on the way over a rugged sea cliff. A dirt road comes in from the right as the trail arrives at Luahaloa, a ledge with a small fishing shack. Inland, stands of ironwood heighten the beauty of the scenic last mile of clifftop walking to Kainalimu Bay.

Stepping stones hasten the approach to the bay ahead, as the trail dips down a shrubby ravine to a quiet black cobble beach. Dirt roads lead another mile from here south to Hana, but if you're up for more adventure you could continue walking along the beach all the way to Hana Bay.

For a basic map and more details visit http://hawaiitrails.ehawaii.gov.

Sleeping

Fall asleep to the lullaby of the surf at one of the park's **campsites** (Map p398) on a shady lawn near the beach. It's a great place to camp but there is one caveat – this is the rainy side of the island. Plan accordingly. The park also has a dozen rustic **cabins** (Map p398) that are extremely popular and usually book up months in advance. To make a cabin reservation online, visit www.hawaiistateparks.org. Undesignated campsites are $18 per night and cabins are $90 per night. Call ☎808-984-8109 if you have questions.

HANA & EAST MAUI

Where do Mauians go when they want to get away? Raw and rugged East Maui, the most isolated side of the island. Instead of golf courses and beach resorts, you'll see a place that's barely changed a speck for tourism. In time-honored Hana, you'll relearn the meaning of s-l-o-w, and talk story with people who actually take the time. Beyond Hana lie fantastical waterfalls, stop-for-a-dip swimming holes and off-the-grid farms. Don't miss an adventurous romp through the cowboy village of Kaupo.

Hana

POP 1235

When you reach Travaasa Hana, hit the brakes. If you continue another block or two, you'll already be leaving town. That's the biggest surprise about Hana – after the spectacular drive to get here, the place is actually a bit of a sleeper. Cows graze lazily in green pastures stretching up the hillsides. Neighbors chat over plate lunches at the beach. Even at Hana's legendary hotel, the emphasis is on relaxation.

Isolated as it is by that long and winding road, Hana stands as one of the most Hawaiian communities in the state. Folks share a strong sense of *'ohana,* and if you listen closely you'll hear the words 'auntie' and 'uncle' a lot. There's a timeless rural character, and though 'Old Hawaii' is an oft-used cliché elsewhere, it's hard not to think of Hana in such terms. What Hana has to offer is best appreciated by those who stop and unwind.

For those who don't want to rent a car, there are now twice-daily daily flights to Hana from Kahului Airport (p316).

History

Believe it or not, little Hana was once the epicenter of Maui, producing many of ancient Hawaii's most influential *ali'i* (chiefs). Hana's great 14th-century chief Pi'ilani marched from here to conquer rivals in Wailuku and Lahaina, and became the first leader of unified Maui. The paths he took became such vital routes that even today half of Maui's highways bear his name.

The landscape changed dramatically in 1849 when ex-whaler George Wilfong bought 60 acres of land to plant sugarcane. Hana became a booming plantation town, complete with a narrow-gauge railroad connecting the fields to the Hana Mill. Artist Georgia O'Keeffe paid a visit in 1939 when she was hired by the Dole Pineapple Company to paint canvases for an ad campaign. At that time there were six sugar plantations in Hana. Later, in the 1940s, Hana could no longer compete with larger sugar operations in Central Maui. All the plantations closed by the end of the decade.

Enter San Francisco businessman Paul Fagan, who purchased 14,000 acres in Hana in 1943. Starting with 300 Herefords, Fagan converted the canefields to ranch land. A few years later he opened a six-room hotel as a getaway resort for well-to-do friends and brought his minor-league baseball team, the San Francisco Seals, to Hana for spring training. That's when visiting sports journalists gave the town its moniker, 'Heavenly Hana.'

Today, Hana Ranch, along with the Travaasa Hana, remains an important part of Hana's economy and its hillside pastures graze some 1200 head of cattle worked by Hawaiian *paniolo*. Bio-Logical Capital bought the ranch in 2012 and plans to continue raising cattle while also exploring sustainable farming projects.

Beaches

Hana Beach Park BEACH

Some towns have a central plaza. Hana's pulse beats from this bayside park. Families come here to take the kids for a splash, to picnic on the black-sand beach and to strum their ukuleles with friends.

When water conditions are very calm, snorkeling and diving are good out in the direction of the light beacon. Currents can be strong, and snorkelers shouldn't venture beyond the beacon. Surfers head to **Waikoloa Beach**, at the northern end of the bay.

Sights

Hana Cultural Center MUSEUM

(☎248-8622; www.hanaculturalcenter.org; 4974 Uakea Rd; adult/child under 12yr $3/free; ⏲10am-4pm Mon-Fri) This down-home museum displays Hawaiian artifacts, woodcarvings and hand-stitched quilts. On the grounds are several authentically reconstructed **thatched hale**, which can be admired outside opening hours. Here, too, is a tiny, three-bench **courthouse** (c 1871) that is still used on the first Tuesday of each month when a judge shows up to hear minor cases.

Inside is an interesting exhibit about the devastating tsunami that hit Hana in 1946.

Hasegawa General Store HISTORICAL SITE

(☎248-8231; www.hanamaui.com; 5165 Hana Hwy; ⏲7am-7pm Mon-Sat, 8am-6pm Sun) The Hasegawa family has operated a general store in Hana since 1910. The narrow aisles inside the tin-roof store are jam-packed with fishing poles, machetes, soda pop and bags of poi. This icon of mom-and-pop shops is always crowded with locals picking up supplies, travelers stopping for snacks and the ATM, and sightseers buying 'I Survived the Hana Highway' T-shirts.

The store produces the helpful (and free) Hana Visitors guide that includes history about the store, a town map and listings for sights and activities.

Wananalua Congregational Church CHURCH

(cnr Hana Hwy & Hau'oli St) This c 1838 building, which is on the National Register of Historic Places, has such hefty walls it resembles an ancient Norman church. Also noteworthy is the little **cemetery** at the side, where the graves are randomly laid out rather than lined up in rows. Even at rest, Hana folks like things casual.

Hana Coast Gallery GALLERY

(☎248-8636; www.hanacoast.com; 5031 Hana Hwy; ⏲9am-5pm) Even if you're not shopping, visit this gallery at the north side of Travaasa Hana to browse the museum-quality wooden bowls, paintings and Hawaiian featherwork.

Activities

In addition to what follows, Travaasa Hana organises activities, including stand up paddling and snorkeling, for their guests.

Lyon's Hill HIKING

Former Hana Ranch owner Paul Fagan often ended his day with a walk up Lyon's Hill to enjoy the view at sunset – and if you've got time you can follow in his footsteps. The big cross topping the hill, a memorial to Fagan, is Hana's most dominant landmark. The 25-minute trail up Lyon's Hill starts opposite Travaasa Hana.

At the junction with the trail from the Hana Store area, bear right on the road to ascend the hill.

Skyview Soaring GLIDER

(Map p398; ☎344-9663; www.skyviewsoaring.com; 30min/1hr $165/300; ⏲by reservation) Climb up the side of Haleakalā from Hana Airport inside a sleek glider then catch your breath. Weather permitting, owner-pilot Hans Pieters, after reaching sufficient altitude, will

Hana

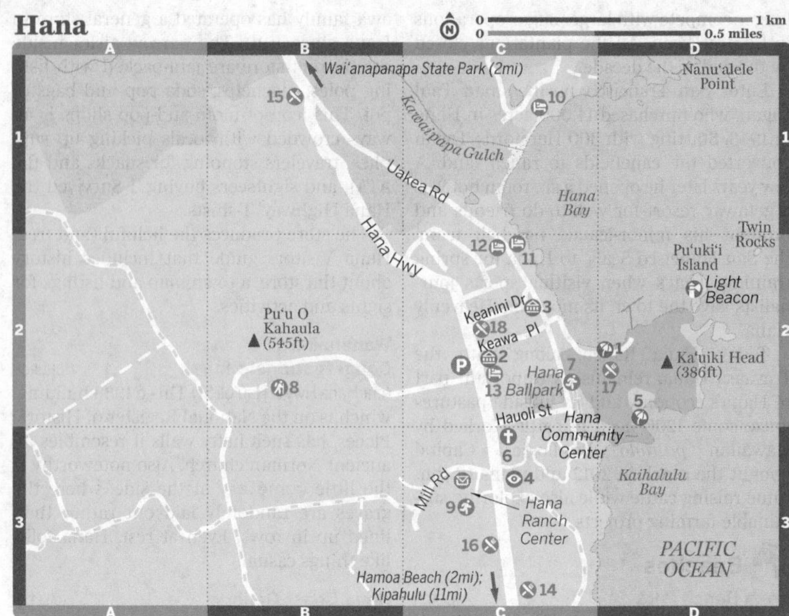

fly over the crater. After he cuts the engine, enjoy a silent soar near the top of the world followed by a no-engine glide back down the volcano's lush slopes.

Call a week in advance for a reservation. Otherwise, try your luck and see if Hans is at the airport and ready to soar.

Travaasa Stables HORSEBACK RIDING
(☎270-5276; www.travaasa.com; Mill Rd; 1hr ride $60) These stables, which book through Travaasa Hana, give horseback riders the chance to trot along cattle pastures to Hana's black-lava coastline. Open to non-guests.

Spa at Travaasa Hana DAY SPA
(☎270-5290; www.travaasa.com; Travaasa Hana, 5031 Hana Hwy; treatments $130-285) If the long drive to Hana has tightened you up, the posh Spa at Travaasa Hana can work off the kinks with *lomilomi* (traditional Hawaiian massage) and a soak in the lava-rock whirlpool.

Luana Spa DAY SPA
(☎248-8855; www.luanaspa.com; 5050 Uakea Rd; treatments $45-160) Massages, body treatments and skin care in a cozy yurt or a Hawaiian-style open-air hale with a view of Hana Bay. Ahhh...

Festivals & Events

★East Maui Taro Festival FESTIVAL
(www.tarofestival.org) Maui's most Hawaiian town throws its most Hawaiian party. If it's native, it's here – a taro pancake breakfast, poi pounding, hula dancing and a big jamfest of Hawaiian music, and loads and loads of Hawaiian food. Held on the last weekend in April, it's Hana at its finest; book accommodations well in advance.

Sleeping

In addition to the following accommodation options, there are cabins and tent camping at Wai'anapanapa State Park, just to the north of Hana, and camping at 'Ohe'o Gulch, about 10 miles south.

Joe's Place HOTEL $
(☎248-7033; www.joesrentals.com; 4870 Uakea Rd; r with shared/private bathroom $50/60) At Hana's only nod to the budget traveler, the decor is dated and the furniture tired (and we saw a moldy bathmat), but the shared BBQ, den and kitchen do provide homey opportunities to exchange tips with fellow explorers. The property is within walking distance of the beach and town.

Hana

Luana Spa Retreat YURT $$
(248-8855; www.luanaspa.com; 5050 Uakea Rd; d $150;) On a secluded hill overlooking Hana Bay, this back-to-nature charmer fuses outdoor living with indoor comforts. The yurt sports a well-equipped kitchenette and a stereo with Hawaiian music. Shower outdoors in a bamboo enclosure, enjoy spectacular star-gazing over the bay and eat incredibe lunches at the on-property eatery Pranee's & Nutcharee's Thai.

Hana Kai-Maui CONDO $$
(248-8426; www.hanakaimaui.com; 4865 Uakea Rd; studio/1br from $205/215;) Hana's only condo complex is just a stone's throw from Hana's hottest surfing beach. The units are nicely fitted and although the walls are thin, the sound of the surf drowns out neighboring chatter. For primo ocean views request a top-floor corner unit. With the exception of the oceanfront condos, Hana Kai-Maui has no minimum stay. The two-bedroom unit rents for $450 per night.

Hale Waikoloa COTTAGE $$
(248-8980; www.halewaikoloa.com; Waikoloa Rd; 1br $200) This pleasant, deck-wrapped cottage is just a few steps from Waikoloa Beach at Hana Bay. Although it contains three units, only the two-bedroom ground floor unit, with kitchen and living area, was available for rent at press time. The property is fronted by a rock outcropping which served as a fishing *heiau*, or holy place. It may date from the 1500s.

Travaasa Hana BOUTIQUE HOTEL $$$
(855-868-7282, 359-2401; www.travaasa.com; 5031 Hana Hwy; ste/cottage from $400/550;) This landmark resort is under new ownership, but it's just as appealing as ever. Known for decades as Hotel Hana-Maui, this new incarnation retains the property's tranquil, get-away-from-it-all charm. The decor is rich with Hawaiian accents, from island art in the lobby to made in Maui bath products. Rooms have a subdued elegance with bleached hardwood floors, ceiling fans and French doors opening to trellised patios – but no TVs.

Travaasa properties tout their 'experiental' getaways; in Hana, guests can enjoy an an assortment of adventures, from coconut husking and lei making to yoga and snorkeling. One quibble? The $72 daily resort fee! Wi-fi is available in the lobby only.

Eating

Hana has just a couple of stores with limited grocery selections, so if you're staying awhile stock up in Kahului beforehand. Many 'restaurants' are simple open-air eateries that are only open during the day. Bring cash for these. Dinner is served at Travaasa Hana and the Hana Ranch restaurant.

★ **Pranee's & Nutcharee's Thai Food** THAI $
(248-8855; 5050 Uakea Rd; meals $10-12; 10:30am-4pm) It's just a simple outdoor cafe, but chefs Pranee and Nutcharee, who rotate cooking duties during the week, are famous in these parts for their curries and stir-fries. Dishes come with white or brown rice and salad. If the special is panang curry with ahi, order it without hesitation. The restaurant is set back from the road opposite Hana Ballpark, and it fronts Luana Spa.

Braddah Hutt's BBQ BBQ $
(Hana Hwy; meals $8-13; 11am-3:30pm) This joint's a bit like a neighborhood BBQ, with

diners sitting on folding chairs under a canvas awning and an extended family cooking away over sizzling gas grills. Favorites are the barbecued chicken and the fish tacos. Expect a crowd at noon, and don't take the closing time too seriously as it shuts down when the food runs out. Braddah Hutt's is just a short distance south of Hasegawa General Store.

Hana Fresh Market FARM STAND $
(248-7515; www.hanahealth.org; 4590 Hana Hwy; lunch $7-8; 10am-4pm Mon-Fri, 10am-3pm Sat & Sun) This roadside stand in front of the Hana Health Center sells organic produce grown right on-site. Lunches include salads, wraps and healthy takeout plates.

Ono Farmers Market MARKET $
(www.onofarms.com; Hana Hwy; 10am-6pm) Stop here for Kipahulu-grown coffee, jams and the most incredible array of fruit from papaya to rambutan.

Uncle Bill's AMERICAN $
(cnr Hana Hwy & Keanini Dr; sandwiches $8-10; 6am-1pm) We're not sure what's going on here. Is it really open? Why is there a sink in the yard? Am I sitting in someone's driveway? And where's Bill? Who knows, just grab a coffee mug, order at the counter – which is surrounded by an old portrait frame – and enjoy the show starring Phyllis the cook. Come in the morning for waffle sandwiches, bagel sandwiches, or eggs and bacon with rice and toast.

Tutu's SNACK BAR $
(248-8224; Hana Beach Park; snacks $4-10; 9am-4pm) Hana Beach Park's fast-food grill serves shave ice, burgers and plate lunches. Grab a table on the beach for a picnic.

Clay Oven at Hana Farms PIZZA $$
(248-7371; www.facebook.com/hanafarms; Hana Hwy; pizza $12-17; market 6:30am-6:30pm, pizza 4-8pm Fri & Sat) On Friday and Saturday nights the folks at the Hana Farms roadside stand – next to the Welcome to Hana sign – fire up the clay oven for gourmet pies with toppings sourced from their fields and other local purveyors. Hana Farms is a 7-acre chemical-free farm using sustainable growing practices. To volunteer on the farm, see the blog for information about its work-trade program (http://hanafarmsonline.com/work-trade).

Drinking & Entertainment

Paniolo Bar BAR
(248-8211; Travaasa Hana, 5031 Hana Hwy; 11am-9pm) A classy place to enjoy a drink. This open-air bar at Travaasa Hana has live Hawaiian music Thursdays and Fridays.

Information

Hana closes up early. The sole gas station in all of East Maui is **Hana Gas** (248-7671; cnr Mill Rd & Hana Hwy; 7am-8:30pm Mon-Sat, 7am-6pm Sun), so plan accordingly.

Hana Ranch Center (Mill Rd) is the commercial center of town. It has a **post office** (Hana Ranch Center, 1 Mill Rd; 8am-4:30pm Mon-Fri), a tiny **Bank of Hawaii** (248-8015; www.boh.com; Mill Rd; 3-4:30pm Mon-Thu, 3-6pm Fri) and **Hana Ranch Store** (248-8261; Mill Rd; 7am-7:30pm), which sells groceries and liquor. There's no ATM at the bank, but **Hasegawa General Store** (248-8231; 5165 Hana Hwy; 7am-7pm Mon-Sat, 8am-6pm Sun) has one. For medical needs, **Hana Health** (248-8294; www.hanahealth.org; 4590 Hana Hwy; 8:30am-5pm Mon-Fri) is at the north side of town.

Hana to Kipahulu

The question on every day-tripper's mind: should we keep going beyond Hana? The answer: absolutely! The stretch ahead is arguably the most beautiful part of the entire drive. Less than an hour away lies magical 'Ohe'o Gulch, with its cascading waterfalls, swimming holes and awesome trails. Between the hairpin turns, one-lane bridges and drivers trying to take in all the sights, it's a slow-moving 10 miles, so sit back and enjoy the ride.

Haneo'o Road Loop

It's well worth a detour off the highway to take this 1.5-mile loop, which skirts a scenic coastline. The turnoff onto Haneo'o Rd is just before mile marker 50.

At the base of a red cinder hill, less than 0.5 miles from the start of the loop, the chocolate-brown sands of **Koki Beach** attract local surfers. The offshore isle topped by a few coconut palms is 'Alau Island, a seabird sanctuary. Incidentally, those trees are a green refreshment stand of sorts, planted by Hana residents to provide themselves with drinking coconuts while fishing from the island.

A little further along is **Hamoa Beach**; its lovely gray sands are maintained by Travaasa Hana, but it's open to all. Author James Michener once called it the only beach in the North Pacific that actually looked as if it belonged in the South Pacific. When the surf's up, surfers and boogie boarders flock to the waters, though be aware of rips. When seas are calm, swimming is good in the cove. Public access is down the steps just north of the hotel's bus-stop sign. Facilities include showers and restrooms.

Wailua Falls

As you continue south, you will see waterfalls cascading down the cliffs, orchids growing out of the rocks, and jungles of breadfruit and coconut trees. Hands-down the most spectacular sight along the way is Wailua Falls, which plunges a mighty 100ft just beyond the road. It appears 0.3 miles after mile marker 45, but you won't need anyone to point this one out, as folks are always lined up along the roadside snapping photos.

'Ohe'o Gulch

Fantastic falls, cool pools, paths galore. The indisputable highlight of the drive past Hana is 'Ohe'o Gulch, aka the Kipahulu section of Haleakalā National Park. You'll also hear the area referred to (inaccurately) as the Seven Sacred Pools.

Kipahulu

Less than a mile south of 'Ohe'o Gulch lies the little village of Kipahulu. It's hard to imagine, but this sedate community was once a bustling sugar-plantation town. After the mill shut down in 1922, most people left for jobs elsewhere. Today mixed among modest homes, organic farms and back-to-the-landers living off the grid are a scattering of exclusive estates, including the former home of famed aviator Charles Lindbergh.

Kipahulu is also the site of the east entrance to Haleakalā National Park (p410).

Sights

Charles Lindbergh's Grave GRAVESITE

(Map p398) Charles Lindbergh moved to remote Kipahulu in 1968. Although he relished the privacy he found here, he did occasionally emerge as a spokesperson for conservation issues. When he learned he had terminal cancer, he decided to forgo treatment on the mainland and came home to Maui to live out his final days.

Following his death in 1974, Lindbergh was buried in the graveyard of **Palapala Ho'omau Congregational Church** (Map p398). The church (c 1864) is also notable for its window painting of a Polynesian Christ draped in the red-and-yellow feather capes that were reserved for Hawaii's highest chiefs.

Lindbergh's desire to be out of the public eye may still be at play; many visitors fail to find his grave. To get there, turn left at the sign for Maui Stables, which is 0.2 miles south of mile marker 41, then veer left after the stables. The church is 0.2 miles further. Lindbergh's grave, a simple granite slate laid upon lava stones, is in the yard behind the church. The inscription reads simply, '...If I take the wings of the morning, and dwell in the uttermost parts of the sea...C.A.L.'

Activities

★Maui Stables HORSEBACK RIDING

(Map p398; 248-7799; www.mauistables.com; 3hr ride $160; departures 10am) Ride off into the wilderness on horseback trips that mix breathtaking views with Hawaiian storytelling and chanting – a real cultural immersion experience led by Native Hawaiian cowboys. Along the way you'll see thundering waterfalls in the national park. The stable is between mile markers 40 and 41. Check-in is 9:45am. With only one trip per day and 10 people per tour, these trips fill fast. Book one month ahead if possible.

Ono Organic Farms FARM TOUR

(248-7779; www.onofarms.com; 90min tours adult/child 9yr & under $35/free; 1:30pm Mon-Fri) The variety at this exotic farm is amazing – scores of tropical fruits the likes of which you've never seen, spices, cocoa and coffee – all of it top rate and grown organically. The tour ends with a generous spread of seasonal tastings. Advance reservations required. The farm is on the inland side of the road just south of the national park.

Pi'ilani Highway

Secure your seat belt – and maybe offer up a prayer – if you decide to return to civilization on the bumpy and untamed Pi'ilani Hwy. This narrow roadway romps across the far southeastern Maui coast, skirting the southern flank of Haleakalā for 25 ruggedly scenic miles between Kipahulu and 'Ulupalakua Ranch.

The tight hairpin curves will have you clenching your teeth – and the wheel – while signs such as 'Motorists assume risk of damage due to presence of cattle' and 'Safe speed 10mph' remind you that this is not your typical highway.

The road winds like a drunken cowboy through these lonesome boonies but most of it is paved. The trickiest section is around Kaupo, where the road is rutted. Depending on when it was last graded, you can usually make it in a regular car, though it may rattle your bones. But after hard rains, streams flow over the road, making passage difficult, if not dangerous.

Flash floods occasionally wash away portions of the road, closing down the highway until it's repaired. The Kipahulu Visitor Center (p421) at 'Ohe'o Gulch can tell you whether or not the road is open.

The best way to approach the drive is to be sure and get an early morning start, when the road is so quiet you'll feel like the last soul on earth. Pack something to eat and plenty to drink, and take care to check your oil and spare tire before setting out. It's a long haul to civilization if you break down or get stranded with a flat – gas stations are nonexistent between Hana and the Upcountry.

Kaupo

Near mile marker 35 is Kaupo, a scattered community of *paniolo,* many of them fourth-generation ranch hands working at Kaupo Ranch. As the only lowlands on this section of coast, Kaupo was once heavily settled and is home to a number of ancient heiau and two 19th-century churches. However, don't arrive expecting a developed village in any sense of the word. The sole commercial venture on the entire road is **Kaupo Store** (Map p398; ☎248-8054; ⏰10am-5pm Mon-Sat), which sells snacks and drinks and is worth popping inside just to see the antique displays – from old bottles to paintings to vintage cameras – lining the shelves.

Kaupo's prettiest sight, the whitewashed 1859 **Hui Aloha Church** (Map p398), sits perched above the striking black-sand **Mokulau Beach**, an ancient surfing site.

Kaupo to 'Ulupalakua Ranch

Past Kaupo village, you'll be rewarded with striking views of **Kaupo Gap**, the southern opening in the rim of majestic Haleakalā. Near mile marker 31 a short 4WD road runs down to **Nu'u Bay**, favored by locals for fishing and swimming; if you're tempted to hit the water, stay close to shore, as riptides inhabit the open ocean beyond.

Just east of mile marker 30 are two gateposts marking the path to dramatic **Huakini Bay**. Park at the side of the highway and walk down the rutted dirt drive. It takes just a couple of minutes to reach this rock-strewn beach whipped by violent surf. After mile marker 29, watch for a natural lava **sea arch** (Map p398) that's visible from the road. Near this point, the quality of the road vastly improves.

At mile marker 19 the road crosses a vast **lava flow** dating from Haleakalā's last-gasp eruption. This flow, part of the Kanaio Natural Area Reserve, is the same one that covers the La Pe'rouse Bay area. It's still black and barren all the way down to the sea.

Just offshore is Kaho'olawe and on a clear day you can even see the Big Island popping its head up above the clouds. It's such a wide-angle view that the ocean horizon is noticeably curved. You'll wonder how anyone could ever have thought the world was flat!

As you approach 'Ulupalakua Ranch, groves of fragrant eucalyptus trees replace the drier, scrubbier terrain. New on the horizon are eight towering windmills. The turbines are part of the **Auwahi Wind Farm**, which is managed by Sempra US Gas & Oil on acreage leased from the ranch. The wind farm started producing electricity in 2012 and should produce enough to power 10,000 Maui homes.

A few miles ahead is Bully's Burgers (p395), a rugged burger outpost, soon followed by Tedeschi Vineyards (p395). Cheers!

HALEAKALĀ NATIONAL PARK

Haleakalā is not a park that you simply 'see.' With its serpentine entrance road, breezy view points, quiet trails and dusty moonscapes, it's a place that you experience. Throw in the vivid sunrises, and you've got a

KNOW BEFORE YOU GO

The park is divided into two distinct sections that must be accessed separately. The **summit area** surrounds the volcano's lofty crater. The **Kipahulu area**, also known as 'Ohe'o Gulch, extends up the southeastern flank of the volcano from the coast, not far from Hana. The entrance fee, valid for three days at both sections of the park, is $10 per car or $5 per person on foot, bicycle or motorcycle.

place like no other in the national park system. Its appeal is magnetic: ancient Hawaiians came to the summit to worship, Mark Twain praised its healing solitude and visitors of all walks still find it mystical. Trek to Haleakalā to look into the soul of Maui.

Lookouts on the crater's rim provide breathtaking views of Haleakalā's volcanic surface. But there's more to Haleakalā than just peering down from on high. With a pair of hiking boots you can walk down into the crater on crunchy trails that meander around cinder cones. Or saddle up and mosey across the crater floor on horseback. For the ultimate adventure, bring a sleeping bag and spend the night.

No food or drinks are sold anywhere in the park, though there are drinking fountains at the visitor centers. Bring something to eat if you're going up for the sunrise; you don't want hunger pangs to send you back down the mountain before you've explored the sights.

Summit Area

Haleakalā's astonishing volcanic landscape so resembles a lunar surface that astronauts practiced mock lunar walks here before landing on the moon.

Often referred to as the world's largest dormant volcano, the floor of Haleakalā measures a colossal 7.5 miles wide, 2.5 miles long and 3000ft deep – large enough to swallow the island of Manhattan. In its prime, Haleakalā reached a height of 12,000ft before water erosion carved out two large river valleys that eventually eroded into each other to form Haleakalā crater. Technically, as geologists like to point out, it's not a true 'crater,' but to sightseers that's all nitpicking. Valley or crater, it's a phenomenal sight like no other in the US National Park system.

For a real-time view of the summit check out the crater webcam at **Haleakalā Crater Live Camera** (http://www.ifa.hawaii.edu/haleakalanew/webcams.shtml).

Sights

Hosmer Grove FOREST

Hosmer Grove, off a side road just after the park's entrance booth, is worth a stop for a pleasant half-mile loop trail that winds through a small pine- and cedar-filled forest, as well as native scrubland. The whole area is sweetened with the scent of eucalyptus and alive with the red flashes and calls of native birds.

There's a campground here as well as picnic tables and restrooms; the trail begins at the edge of the campground. Drive slowly on the road in, as this is one of the top places to spot nene.

Waikamoi Preserve PRESERVE

(☎572-4459; www.nature.org) This windswept native cloud forest supports one of the rarest ecosystems on earth. Managed by the Nature Conservancy, the 5230-acre Waikamoi Preserve provides the last stronghold for 76 species of native plants and forest birds. The only way to see the preserve is to join a guided hike.

You're apt to spot the 'i'iwi (scarlet Hawaiian honeycreeper), the 'apapane (bright red Hawaiian honeycreeper) and the yellow-green 'amakihi (yellow-green Hawaiian honeycreeper) flying among the preserve's koa and ohia trees. You might also glimpse the yellow-green 'alauahio (Maui creeper) or the 'akohekohe (Maui parrotbill), both endangered species found nowhere else on earth.

The National Park Service offers free 3½-hour, 3-mile guided hikes that enter the preserve from Hosmer Grove campground at 8:45am on Monday and Thursday. On the third Sunday of the month hike deep into the native forest on a five-hour, 5-mile hike which starts at 11:45am. Make reservations for both hikes up to one week in advance. Expect wet conditions and bring rain gear. Both hikes are rated moderately strenuous.

Park Headquarters Visitor Center TOURIST INFORMATION

(Map p382; ☎572-4400; www.nps.gov/hale; 3-day pass car/individual on foot, bicycle or motorcycle $10/5; 7am-3:45pm) This is the place for brochures, camping permits and the skinny

Haleakalā Summit Area

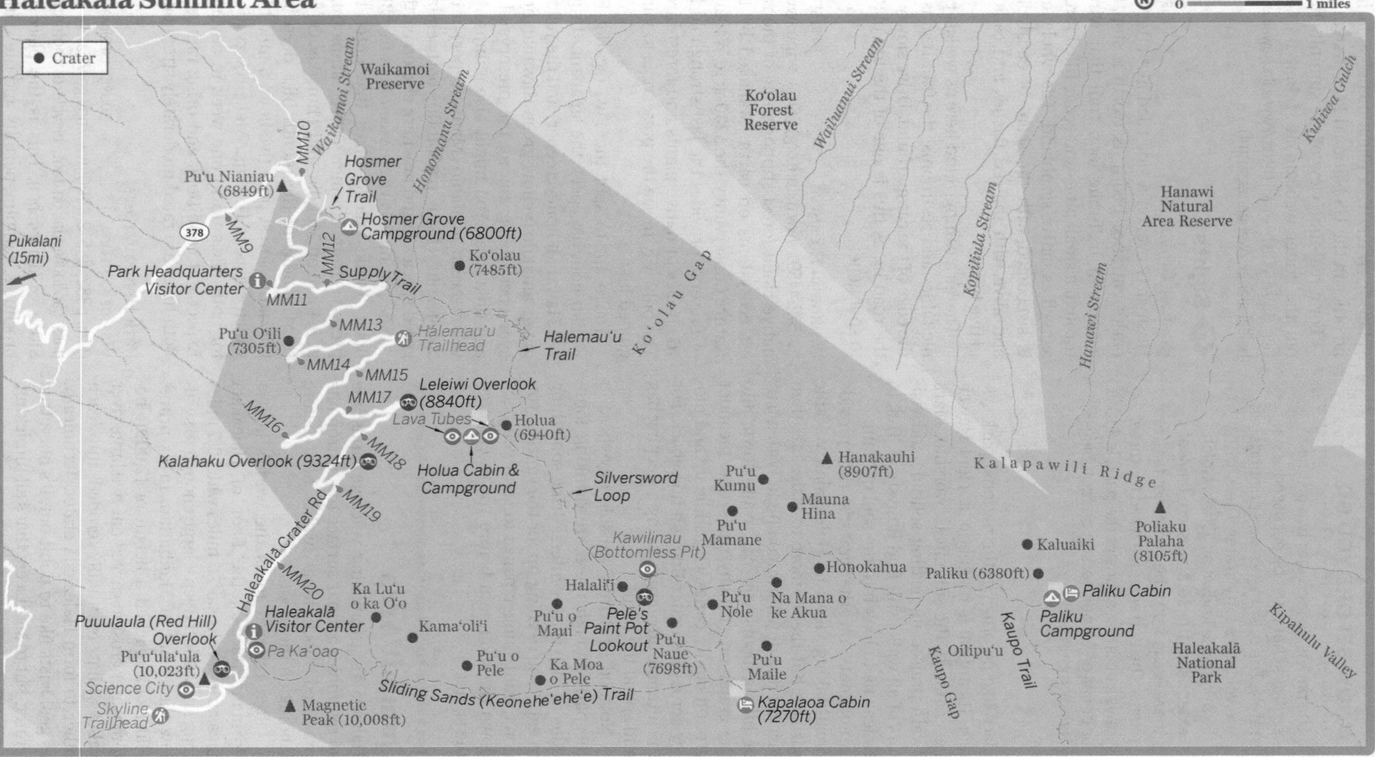

on ranger talks and activities. This is also a convenient stop for restrooms and one of only two places in the park where you'll find drinking fountains. If you're going hiking, fill your water bottles here.

Keep an eye out for nene wandering the grounds, as they're frequent visitors here. Also note that these endangered birds are too friendly for their own good; do not feed them, and be careful when driving out of the parking lot – most nene deaths are the result of being hit by cars.

Leleiwi Overlook — VIEWPOINT

A stop at Leleiwi Overlook (8840ft), midway between the Park Headquarters Visitor Center and the summit, offers your first look into the crater, and gives you a unique angle on the ever-changing clouds climbing up the mountain. You can literally watch the weather form at your feet. From the parking lot, it's a five-minute walk across a gravel trail to the overlook.

En route you'll see an 1880s stone wall built by ranchers and get a fine view of the West Maui Mountains and the isthmus connecting the two sides of Maui.

Kalahaku Overlook — VIEWPOINT

Time your visit for late-morning, after the the sunrise crowds have gone home, and you might have this above-the-clouds overlook to yourself. Perched on the crater rim 0.8 miles beyond Leleiwi Overlook, the stunning Kalahaku Overlook (9324ft) offers a bird's-eye view of the crater floor and the ant-size hikers on the trails snaking around the cinder cones.

The observation deck also provides an ideal angle for viewing both the Ko'olau Gap and the Kaupo Gap on Haleakalā's crater rim. On a clear day you'll be able to see the Big Island's Mauna Loa and Mauna Kea, Hawaii's highest mountaintops.

Between May and October the 'ua'u (Hawaiian dark-rumped petrel) nests in burrows in the cliff face. Even if you don't spot the birds, you can often hear the parents and chicks making their unique clucking sounds. Of the 6000 to 11,000 'ua'u remaining today, more than 1000 nest at Haleakalā, where they lay just one egg a year. These seabirds were thought to be extinct until re-sighted here in the 1970s.

A short trail below the parking lot leads to a field of native silversword *('ahinahina)*, ranging from seedlings to mature plants. On a dangerous curve, the overlook can only be accessed while descending the mountain.

Haleakalā Visitor Center — TOURIST INFORMATION

(Map p382; www.nps.gov/hale; ⌚6am-3pm) Perched on the rim of the crater, at a 9745ft elevation, this small visitor center is the park's main viewing spot. The ever-changing interplay of sun, shadow and clouds reflecting on the crater's interior creates a mesmerizing dance of light and color. The center has displays on Haleakalā's volcanic origins and details about the crater floor 3000ft below. Nature talks are given, and books on Hawaiian culture and the environment are for sale. You can also buy a copy of the National Geographic Haleakalā trail map here for $11.95.

By dawn the parking lot fills with people coming to see the sunrise show, and it pretty much stays packed all day. There are drinking fountains and restrooms here.

Leave the crowds behind by taking the 10-minute hike up Pa Ka'oao (White Hill), which begins at the east side of the visitor center and provides stunning crater views.

Pu'u'ula'ula (Red Hill) Overlook — VIEWPOINT

(Map p382) Congratulations! The 37-mile drive from sea level to the 10,023ft summit of Haleakalā you've just completed is the highest elevation gain in the shortest distance anywhere in the world. You've passed through as many ecological zones as you would have on a drive from central Mexico to Alaska.

Perched atop Pu'u'ula'ula, Maui's highest point, the **summit building** provides a top-of-the-world panorama from its wraparound windows. On a clear day you can see the Big Island, Lana'i, Moloka'i and even O'ahu. When the light's right, the colors of the crater from the summit are nothing short of spectacular, with an array of grays, greens, reds and browns. A **silversword garden** has been planted at the overlook, making this the best place to see these luminous silver-leafed plants in various stages of growth.

Magnetic Peak — MOUNTAIN

(Map p382) The iron-rich cinders in this flattop hill, which lies immediately southeast of the summit building, in the direction of the Big Island, pack enough magnetism to play havoc with your compass. Modest looking as it is, it's also 10,008ft and the second-highest point on Maui.

Science City LANDMARK
(Map p382) On the Big Island's Mauna Kea, scientists study the night sky. Here at Haleakalā, appropriately enough, they study the sun. The 18-acre Science City, just beyond the summit, is off-limits to visitors. It's under the jurisdiction of the University of Hawai'i, which owns some of the domes and leases other land for a variety of private and government research projects.

US Department of Defense–related projects here include laser technology associated with the 'Star Wars' project, satellite tracking and identification, and a deep-space surveillance system. The Air Force's Maui Space Surveillance System (MSSS), an electro-optical state-of-the-art facility used for satellite tracking, contains the largest telescope anywhere in use by the Department of Defense. The system is capable of identifying a basketball-size object in space 22,000 miles away.

In 2012 the Hawaii Board of Land and Natural Resources approved a use permit for the construction of a 143ft solar telescope on a half-acre site here. Although it will be the world's largest optical solar telescope and a powerful tool for research, the large-scale project has met resistance from native Hawaiian groups concerned about desecrating a sacred site. According to Hawaiiain lore, the ancient demigod Maui roped the sun from Haleakalā in order to slow its movement. There are also concerns about the project's environmental impact.

 Activities

Hiking trails ribbon across an amazing variety of landscapes in Haleakalā. To ride a horse across the floor of the crater, consider a tour with Pony Express (p393).

Ranger Programs

Stop at the Park Headquarters Visitor Center to see what talks and programs are on the

THE SUNRISE EXPERIENCE

'Haleakalā' means 'House of the Sun.' So it's no surprise that since the time of the first Hawaiians, people have been making pilgrimages up Haleakalā to watch the sun rise. It's an experience that borders on the mystical. Mark Twain called it the 'sublimest spectacle' he'd ever seen.

Plan to arrive at the summit an hour before the actual sunrise; that will guarantee you a parking space and time to see the world shake off the night. Have cash handy to feed into the automated fee machine in the wee hours, when the entry booth may be unattended. For the loftiest sunrise views, drive past the Haleakalā Visitor Center and climb a short distance to the Pu'u'ula'ula (Red Hill) summit parking lot where there are about 40 parking spots. For views of the crater, return to the larger visitor center lot just below.

Soon, the night sky will lighten and turn purple-blue, and the stars fade away. Ethereal silhouettes of the mountain ridges appear. The gentlest colors show up in the fragile moments just before dawn. The undersides of the clouds lighten first, accenting the night sky with pale silvery slivers and streaks of pink.

About 20 minutes before sunrise, the light intensifies on the horizon in bright oranges and reds. Turn to look at Science City, whose domes turn a blazing pink. For the grand finale, when the disk of the sun appears, all of Haleakalā takes on a fiery glow. It feels like you're watching the earth awaken.

Come prepared – it's going to be c-o-l-d! Temperatures hovering around freezing and a biting wind are the norm at dawn and there's often a frosty ice on the top layer of cinders. If you don't have a winter jacket or sleeping bag to wrap yourself in, bring a warm blanket from your hotel. However many layers of clothes you can muster, it won't be too many. Also bring a headlamp or flashlight. These will help you follow the short trail to the summit shelter.

The best photo opportunities occur before the sun rises. Every morning is different, but once the sun is up, the silvery lines and the subtleties disappear.

One caveat: a rained-out sunrise is anticlimactic after tearing yourself out of bed to drive up a pitch-dark mountain. So check the **weather report** (☎866-944-5025) the night before to calculate your odds of having clear skies. If you can't get up that early, come for the sunset which is also beautiful.

GOING DOWNHILL

For years downhill bike tours were heavily promoted. A van ride to Haleakalā summit for the sunrise was followed by a bicycle cruise 38 miles down the 10,000ft mountain, snaking along winding roads clear to the coast. What a rush. And no need to be in shape, since there's no pedaling involved.

But it became *too* popular. Some mornings as many as 1000 cyclists huddled at the crater overlooks jostling for space to watch the sun rise. Then, group by group, they'd mount their bikes and take off.

Residents using Upcountry roads were forced to slow to a crawl, waiting for a gaggle of cyclists and their support van to pull over to let them pass. The narrow roads have few shoulders, so the wait was often a long one.

Then there were the accidents. Sometimes the weather was bad, with fog cutting visibility to near zero. Ambulance calls for injured cyclists became weekly occurrences. After two cyclist fatalities in 2007, Haleakalā National Park suspended all bicycle tour operations. A compromise now lets the van tours come up for the sunrise then drive back down to the park's boundary, where the trailers are unpacked and riders begin a 27-mile cycle to the coast. However, another fatality in 2010 spurred the county to consider restrictions of its own. So, for downhill bike tours, the road ahead remains a bumpy one.

For a list of park-approved bicycle tour companies offering vehicle tours within the park and bike rides outside the park, visit the park website (www.nps.gov/hale).

day's schedule. All park programs offered by the National Park Service are free. **Ranger talks** on Haleakalā's unique natural history and Hawaiian culture are given at the Haleakalā Visitor Center and the Pu'u'ula'ula (Red Hill) Overlook; the schedule varies, but they typically take place between 7am and 1pm, and there are usually half a dozen daily. On clear nights, stargazing is phenomenal on the mountain. Hour-long evening **stargazing programs** are offered in the summer at Hosmer Grove, typically on Friday nights, depending on staff availability.

A seasonal program schedule can be accessed at the park's website.

Hiking

To really experience this amazing place, lace up your hiking boots and step into the belly of the beast. There's something for everyone, from short nature walks ideal for families to hardy multiday treks. Those who hike the crater will discover a completely different angle on Haleakalā's lunar landscape. Instead of peering down from the rim, you'll be craning skyward at the walls and towering cinder cones. It's a world away from anyplace else. The crater is remarkably still. Cinders crunching underfoot are the only sound, except for the occasional bark of a Hawaiian owl or honking of a friendly nene. Whatever trail you take, allow extra time to absorb the wonder of it all.

To protect Haleakalā's fragile environment, keep to established trails and don't be tempted off them, even for well-beaten shortcuts through switchbacks.

Be prepared. Hikers without proper clothing risk hypothermia. The climate changes radically as you cross the crater floor – in the 4 miles between Kapalaoa and Paliku cabins, rainfall varies from an annual average of 12in to 300in! Take warm clothing in layers, sunscreen, rain gear, a first-aid kit and lots of water.

★**Sliding Sands (Keonehe'ehe'e)** HIKING

(Map p382) Sliding Sands (Keonehe'ehe'e) Trail starts at the south side of the Haleakalā Visitor Center at 9740ft and winds down to the crater floor. If you take this hike after catching the sunrise, you'll walk directly into a gentle warmish wind and the rays of the sunshine.

Even if you're just coming to the summit for a peek at the incredible view, consider taking a short hike down Sliding Sands Trail. Just walking down 20 to 30 minutes will reward you with an into-the-crater experience and fab photo opportunities; but remember that the climb out takes nearly twice as long as the walk down.

The full trail leads 9.2 miles to the Paliku cabin and Paliku campground, passing the Kapalaoa cabin at 5.6 miles after roughly four hours.

The first 6 miles of the trail follow the south wall. There are great views on the way down, but almost no vegetation. About 2 miles down, a steep spur trail leads past silversword plants to Ka Lu'u o ka O'o cinder cone, about 0.5 miles north. Four miles down, after an elevation drop of 2500ft, Sliding Sands Trail intersects with a spur trail that leads north into the cinder desert; that spur connects with the Halemau'u Trail after 1.5 miles.

Continuing on the Sliding Sands Trail, as you head across the crater floor for 2 miles to Kapalaoa, verdant ridges rise on your right, giving way to ropy *pahoehoe* (smooth-flowing lava). From Kapalaoa cabin to Paliku, the descent is gentle and the vegetation gradually increases. Paliku (6380ft) is beneath a sheer cliff at the eastern end of the crater. In contrast to the crater's barren western end, this area receives heavy rainfall, with ohia forests climbing the slopes.

Halemau'u Trail HIKING

Hiking the Halemau'u Trail down to the Holua campground and back – 7.4 miles round-trip – can make a memorable day hike. Just be sure to start early before the afternoon clouds roll in and visibility vanishes. The first mile of this trail is fairly level and offers a fine view of the crater with Ko'olau Gap to the east. It then descends 1400ft along 2 miles of switchbacks to the crater floor and on to the Holua campground.

At 6940ft, Holua is one of the lowest areas along this trail, and you'll see impressive views of the crater walls rising a few thousand feet to the west. Large lava tubes here are worth exploring: one's up a short, steep cliff behind the Holua cabin, and another's a 15-minute detour further along the trail. According to legend, the latter tube was a spiritual place where mothers brought the *piko* (umbilical cords) of their newborns to gather mana for the child.

If you have the energy, push on another mile to reach colorful cinder cones, and make a short detour onto the **Silversword Loop**, where you'll see these unique plants in various stages of growth. In summer, you might even see silverswords in flower, their tall stalks ablaze with hundreds of maroon and yellow blossoms. But be careful – half of all silverswords today are trampled to death as seedlings, mostly by hikers who wander off trails and unknowingly step on their shallow roots. The trail continues another 6.3 miles to the Paliku cabin.

The trailhead to Halemau'u is 3.5 miles above the Park Headquarters Visitor Center and about 6 miles below the Haleakalā Visitor Center. There's a fair chance you'll see nene in the parking lot. If you're camping at Hosmer Grove, you can take the little-known, unexciting Supply Trail instead, joining the Halemau'u Trail at the crater rim after 2.5 miles.

Cinder Desert HIKING

A spur trail connects Sliding Sands Trail, just west of Kapalaoa cabin, with the Halemau'u Trail, about midway between the Paliku and Holua campgrounds. This spur trail takes in many of the crater's most kaleidoscopic cinder cones, and the viewing angle changes with every step.

The trail ends up on the north side of the cinder desert near Kawilinau, also known as the **Bottomless Pit**. Legends say the pit leads down to the sea, though the National Park Service says it's just 65ft deep. Truth be told, there's not much to see, as you can't really get a good look down the narrow shaft. The real prize is the nearby short loop trail, where you can sit for awhile in the saddle of **Pele's Paint Pot Lookout**, the crater's most brilliant vantage point.

Kaupo Trail HIKING

The most extreme of Haleakalā's hikes is the Kaupo Trail, which starts at the Paliku campground and drops to Kaupo on the southern coast. Be prepared for ankle-twisting conditions, blistered feet, intense tropical sun and torrential showers. Your knees will take a pounding as you descend more than 6100ft over 8.6 miles, but you'll be rewarded with spectacular ocean views.

The first 3.7 miles of the trail drop 2500ft in elevation before reaching the park boundary. It's a steep rocky trail through rough lava and brushland, with short switchbacks alternating with level stretches. From here, the great ocean views begin.

The last 4.9 miles pass through Kaupo Ranch property on a rough jeep trail as it descends to the bottom of Kaupo Gap, exiting into a forest where feral pigs snuffle about. Here trail markings become vague, but once you reach the dirt road, it's another 1.5 miles to the end at the east side of the Kaupo Store.

The 'village' of Kaupo is a long way from anywhere, with light traffic. Still, what traffic there is – sightseers braving the circle-island road and locals in pickup trucks –

moves slowly enough along Kaupo's rough road to start conversation, so you'll probably manage a lift. If you have to walk the final stretch, it's 8 miles to the 'Ohe'o Gulch campground.

Because this is such a strenuous and remote trail, it's not advisable to hike it alone. No camping is allowed on Kaupo Ranch property, so most hikers spend the night at the Paliku campground and then get an early start.

★Hosmer Grove Trail HIKING

For an easy leg-stretcher – and a little greenery – after hiking the crater, try this mostly shaded woodland walk. Birders should wing it here as well. The half-mile loop trail starts at Hosmer Grove campground, 0.75 miles south of Park Headquarters Visitor Center, in a forest of lofty trees.

The exotics in Hosmer Grove were introduced in 1910 in an effort to develop a lumber industry in Hawaii. Species include fragrant incense cedar, Norway spruce, Douglas fir, eucalyptus and various pines. Although the trees adapted well enough to grow, they didn't grow fast enough at these elevations to make tree harvesting practical. Thanks to this failure, today there's a park here instead.

After the forest, the trail moves into native shrubland, with *'akala* (Hawaiian raspberry), kilau ferns and sandalwood. The *'ohelo,* a berry sacred to the volcano goddess Pele, and the pukiawe, which has red and white berries and evergreen leaves, are favored by nene.

Listen for the calls of the native *'i'iwi* and *'apapane,* both sparrow-size birds with bright red feathers that are fairly common here. The *'i'iwi* has a loud, squeaking call, orange legs and a curved salmon-colored bill. The *'apapane,* a fast-moving bird with a black bill, black legs and a white undertail, feeds on the nectar of ohia flowers, and its wings make a distinctive whirring sound.

Cycling & Mountain Biking

For experienced mountain bikers, Haleakalā's **Skyline Trail**, which starts near Science City, is the ultimate wild ride, plunging some 3000ft in the first 6 miles with a breathtaking 10% grade. The trail starts out looking like the moon and ends up in a cloud forest of redwood and cypress trees that resembles California's northern coast. The route follows a rough 4WD road that's used to maintain Polipoli Spring State Recreation Area. At press time, a new fence was going up below Science City; open the gate to continue on the trail then close it behind you. Equip yourself with full pads, use a proper downhill bike and watch that you don't run any hikers down. **Crater Cycles Hawaii** (☎893-2020; www.cratercycleshawaii.com; 358 Papa Pl, Kahului; downhill bikes per day $85, road bike per day $65; ⏰9am-5pm Mon-Sat) rents out quality full-suspension downhill bikes, complete with helmet, pads and a map, for the Skyline ride. A roof rack is $5. Check the Crater Cycle website for more details.

One-way downhill group cycle tours are no longer allowed to cycle within the park, though they do offer tours that begin pedaling just below park boundaries. Another option? Rent a bicycle and head here on your own. Individual cyclists are allowed to pedal their way up and down the mountain without restriction. Up is a real quad buster. If you prefer to do it just downhill, most bicycle rental companies also rent out racks for transporting the bike.

Sleeping

To spend the night at Haleakalā is to commune with nature. The camping options are primitive: no electricity or showers. Backcountry campgrounds have pit toilets and limited nonpotable water supplies that are shared with the crater cabins. Water needs to be filtered or chemically treated before drinking; conserve it, as water tanks occasionally run dry. Fires are allowed only in grills, and in times of drought are prohibited entirely. You must pack in all your food and supplies and pack out all your trash. And remember, sleeping at an elevation of 7000ft isn't like camping on the beach. You need to be well equipped – without a waterproof tent and a winter-rated sleeping bag, forget it.

Camping

Hosmer Grove Campground CAMPGROUND

FREE Hosmer Grove is the only drive-up campground in the summit area of the park. Surrounded by lofty trees and adjacent to one of Maui's best birding trails, this campground at an elevation of 6800ft tends to be cloudy but a covered picnic pavilion offers shelter if it starts to rain. Facilities include grills, toilets and running water.

Camping is free on a first-come, first-served basis. No permit is required, though there's a three-day camping limit per month. The campground is just a small field, with no individual campsites, so it can get supercrowded. It's busier in summer than in winter and is often full on holiday weekends. The campground is just after the park entrance booth. And here's a bonus: you're close to the summit, so it's a cinch getting up for the sunrise.

Backcountry Camping CAMPGROUND $

FREE For hikers, two backcountry campgrounds lie on the floor of Haleakalā Crater. The easiest to reach is at **Holua**, 3.7 miles down the Halemau'u Trail. The other is at **Paliku**, below a rainforest ridge at the end of Halemau'u Trail. Weather can be unpredictable at both.

Holua is typically dry with clouds rolling in during the late afternoon. Paliku is in a grassy meadow, with skies overhead alternating between stormy and sunny. Wasps are present at both campsites, so take precautions if you're allergic to stings.

Permits (free) are required for crater camping. They're issued at the Park Headquarters Visitor Center on a first-come, first-served basis from 7am until 3pm on the day of the hike. Photo identification is required for the permittee, and an 8-minute video orientation is required for everyone in the group. Camping is limited to three nights in the crater each month, with no more than two consecutive nights at either campground. Only 25 campers are allowed at each site, so permits can go quickly when large parties show up, a situation more likely to occur in summer.

Rustic Cabins CABIN $

(☎572-4400; https://fhnp.org/wcr; per cabin with 1-12 people $75) Three charming rustic cabins dating from the 1930s lie along trails on the crater floor at Holua, **Kapalaoa** and Paliku. Each has a wood-burning stove, two propane burners, 12 bunks with sleeping pads (but no bedding), pit toilets and a limited supply of water and firewood. There is no electricty.

Hiking distances to the cabins from the crater rim range from 4 to 9 miles. The driest conditions are at Kapalaoa, in the middle of the cinder desert off Sliding Sands Trail. Those craving lush rainforest will find Paliku serene. Holua has unparalleled sunrise views. There's a three-day limit per month, with no more than two consecutive nights in

LOCAL KNOWLEDGE

HALEAKALĀ: VOLUNTEERING & TOP DAY HIKE

Melissa Chimera, Volunteer Manager at Haleakalā National Park and a local artist, details volunteer opportunities and shares her favorite park day hike.

Volunteer Opportunities

We currently have two types of drop-in opportunities. One is an overnight service trip in the wilderness that requires hiking and a couple of nights in our wilderness cabins. Then there is a day trip into Haleakalā National Park to help restore native ecosystems and endangered species.

The first type of overnight service trip is sponsored by the **Friends of Haleakalā** (www.fnhp.org); it's a totally volunteer-led and -run operation. They take up to 12 visitors. Largely they work on weeding sensitive ecosystems which are habitat for some of our endangered wildlife.

The **Pacific Whale Foundation** (www.pacificwhale.org) has a program called Volunteers on Vacation. They come up on the first and third Saturday of every month. And they provide transportation into the park. They come up to do projects for maybe three hours or so. People bring ther own lunch up here. They go for a very short guided hike and interact with some of the park staff or alternately the Pacific Whale Foundation staff.

Both programs include free entry into the park.

Top Day Hike

Going from the summit down Sliding Sands Trail and up Halemau'u switchback is probably one of my favorite hikes. It requires a little bit of coordination because the exit point is actually well below the summit, so somebody's got to be there or else you've got to leave a car and hitch a ride up with some other visitor. I think it's one of the most rewarding things you can do in a single day.

any cabin. Each cabin is rented to only one group at a time.

The cabins can be reserved up to 90 days in advance, either online or by phone between 1pm and 3pm Monday to Friday. A photo ID is required for the permittee, and all of those staying in the cabin must watch an 8-minute wilderness orientation video.

Even those without reservations have a shot, as cancellations sometimes occur at the last minute. You can check for vacancies in person at the Park Headquarters Visitor Center between 7am and 3pm. As an added boon, if you get a vacancy within three weeks of your camping date, the cabin fee drops to $60 a day.

Information

ENTRANCE FEES & PASSES

Haleakalā National Park (www.nps.gov/hale; 3-day entry pass per car $10, per person on foot, bicycle or motorcycle $5) The park never closes, although you may have to feed cash into the payment kiosk at the summit pay booth for your admission permit if you arrive well before sunrise. If you're planning several trips, or are going on to the Big Island, consider buying an annual pass ($25), which covers all of Hawaii's national parks.

DANGERS & ANNOYANCES

The weather at Haleakalā can change suddenly from dry, hot conditions to cold, windswept rain. Although the general rule is sunny in the morning and cloudy in the afternoon, fog and clouds can blow in at any time, and the windchill can quickly drop below freezing. Dress in layers and bring extra clothing; don't even think of coming up without a jacket.

At 10,000ft the air is relatively thin, so expect to tire more quickly, particularly if you're hiking. The higher elevation also means that sunburn is more likely.

MAPS

National Geographic's *Haleakalā National Park Trails Illustrated Map* shows elevations and other useful features on the hiking routes. It's waterproof and can be purchased at Haleakalā Visitor Center for $12.

Getting There & Around

Getting to Haleakalā is half the fun. Snaking up the mountain it's sometimes hard to tell if you're in an airplane or a car – all of Maui opens up below you, with sugarcane and pineapple fields creating a patchwork of green on the valley floor. The highway ribbons back and forth, and in some places as many as four or five switchbacks are in view all at once.

Haleakalā Crater Rd (Hwy 378) climbs 11 miles from Hwy 377 near Kula up to the park entrance, then another 10 miles to Haleakalā summit. It's a good paved road all the way, but it's steep and winding. You don't want to rush it, especially when it's dark or foggy. And watch out for cattle wandering across the road.

The drive to the summit takes about 1½ hours from Pa'ia or Kahului, two hours from Kihei. If you need gas, fill up the night before, as there are no services on Haleakalā Crater Rd. On your way back downhill, be sure to put your car in low gear to avoid burning out your brakes.

DIVINE, YES. SACRED, NO.

Back in the 1970s 'Ohe'o Gulch was dubbed the 'Seven Sacred Pools' as part of a tourism promotion and the term lives on today, still floating around freely, much to the chagrin of park officials. It's a complete misnomer since there are 24 pools in all, extending from the ocean to Waimoku Falls, and they were never sacred – but they certainly are divine.

The waters once supported a large Hawaiian settlement that cultivated sweet potatoes and taro in terraced gardens beside the stream. Archaeologists have identified the stone remains of more than 700 ancient structures at 'Ohe'o.

Kipahulu Area ('Ohe'o Gulch)

There's more to Haleakalā National Park than the cindery summit. The park extends down the southeast face of the volcano all the way to the sea. The crowning glory of its Kipahulu section is 'Ohe'o Gulch with its magnificent waterfalls and wide pools, each one tumbling into the next one below. When the sun shines, these cool glistening pools make the most inviting swimming holes on Maui.

Because there's no access between the Kipahulu section of the park and the main Haleakalā summit area, you'll be visiting the two sections of the park on different days. So hold on to your ticket – it's good for both sections of the park.

Sights & Activities

Lower Pools HIKING, SWIMMING

(Map p398) First on your agenda should be the **Kuloa Point Trail**, a half-mile loop from the visitor center down along the lower pools and back. These large freshwater pools are terraced one atop the other and connected by gentle cascades. They're usually calm and great for swimming, their cool waters refreshingly brisk. The second big pool below the bridge is a favorite swimming hole.

However, be aware: conditions can change in a heartbeat. Heavy rains falling far away on the upper slopes can bring a sudden torrent through the pools at any time. If the water starts to rise, get out immediately; several people have been swept out to sea by flash floods. Slippery rocks and unseen submerged ledges are other potential hazards, so check carefully before jumping in. Heed all park warning signs, including temporary ones based on weather conditions.

At the path's junction with Pipiwai Trail, go right. A few minutes down, you'll come to a broad grassy knoll with a gorgeous view of the Hana coast. On a clear day you can see the Big Island, 30 miles away across 'Alenuihaha Channel.

Waterfall Trails HIKING

The **Pipiwai Trail** (Map p398) is a fantastic day hike, rewarding hikers with picture-perfect views of waterfalls and a spellbinding stroll through a bamboo forest. The trail, which runs up the 'Ohe'o streambed, starts on the *mauka* side of the visitor center. It passes Makahiku Falls and ends at Waimoku Falls (2 miles). To see both falls, allow about two hours.

Along the path, you'll pass large mango trees and patches of guava before coming to an overlook after about 10 minutes. Makahiku Falls, a long bridal-veil waterfall that drops into a deep gorge, is just off to the right. Thick green ferns cover the sides of basalt cliffs where the fall cascades – a very rewarding scene for such a short walk.

Continuing along the main trail, you'll walk beneath old banyan trees, cross Palikea Stream (killer mosquitoes thrive here) and enter the wonderland of the **Bamboo Forest** (Map p398), where thick groves of bamboo bang together musically in the wind. The trail here is muddy, but boardwalks cover some of the worst bits. Beyond the bamboo grove is **Waimoku Falls**, a thin, lacy 400ft waterfall dropping down a sheer rock face. When you come out of the first grove, you'll see the waterfall in the distance. Forget about swimming under Waimoku Falls – its pool is shallow and there's a danger of falling rocks.

If you want to take a dip, you'll find better pools along the way. About 100yd before Waimoku Falls, you'll cross a little stream. If you go left and work your way upstream for 10 minutes, you'll come to an attractive waterfall and a little pool about neck deep. There's also an inviting pool in the stream about halfway between Makahiku and Waimoku Falls.

Ranger Programs NATURE TALKS

(www.nps.gov/hale) Stop by the visitor center or check the park website to find out what programs are on the schedule. In the morning, look for guided hikes on the Kuloa Point and Pipiwai Trails. In the early afternoon, head to the visitor center for nature talks and cultural demonstrations.

Tours

For fascinating insights into the area's past, join one of the ethnobotanical tours that are led by **Kipahulu 'Ohana** (Map p398; ☎248-8558; www.kipahulu.org), a collective of Native Hawaiian farmers who have restored ancient taro patches within the park. Tours include a two-hour morning outing ($49) that concentrates on the farm and a 3½-hour afternoon tour ($79) that adds on a hike to Waimoku Falls. Both tours leave from the thatched hala near the Kipahulu Visitor Center; advance reservations are advised.

Sleeping

At the national park's **Kipahulu Campground** (Map p398), there's so much mana you can almost hear the whispers of the ancient Hawaiians. The facilities are minimal: pit toilets, picnic tables, grills. But the setting – oceanside cliffs amid the stone ruins of an ancient village – is simply incredible. There's no water at the campsite, so bring your own or walk over to the restrooms at the visitor center. Mosquito repellent and gear suitable for rainy conditions are also a must.

Permits aren't required. Camping is free but limited to three nights per month. In winter you'll probably have the place to yourself, and even in summer there's typically enough space for everyone who shows up.

Information

Kipahulu Visitor Center (248-7375; www.nps.gov/hale; 3-day pass per car $10, per person on foot, bicycle or motorcyle $5; park 24hr, visitor center 9am-5pm) Staffed by rangers who can give you an orientation to the park.

Getting There & Around

The Kipahulu section of Haleakalā National Park is on Hwy 31, 10 miles south of Hana. The most famous route from Kahului to Hana, and the one that's fully paved, is the stunning Road to Hana.

KAHO'OLAWE

Seven miles southwest of Maui, the sacred but uninhabited island of Kaho'olawe has long been central to the Hawaiian-rights movement. Many consider the island a living spiritual entity, a *pu'uhonua* (refuge) and *wahi pana* (sacred place).

Yet for nearly 50 years, from WWII to 1990, the US military used Kaho'olawe as a bombing range. Beginning in the 1970s, liberating the island from the military became a rallying point for a larger resurgence of Native Hawaiian pride. Today, the bombing has stopped, the navy is gone and healing the island is considered both a symbolic act and a concrete expression of Native Hawaiian sovereignty.

The island (11 miles long and 6 miles wide) and its surrounding waters are now a reserve that is off-limits to the general public because of the unexploded ordnance that remains on land and in the sea.

Pathway to Tahiti

The channel between Lana'i and Kaho'olawe, as well as the westernmost point of Kaho'olawe itself, is named Kealaikahiki, meaning 'pathway to Tahiti.' When early Polynesian voyagers made the journey between Hawaii and Tahiti, they lined up their canoes at this departure point.

However, Kaho'olawe was much more than an early navigational tool. Over 540 archaeological and cultural sites have been identified. They include several heiau (stone temples) and *ku'ula* (fishing shrines) dedicated to the gods of fishers. Pu'umoiwi, a large cinder cone in the center of the island, contains one of Hawaii's largest ancient adze quarries.

A Penal Colony

In 1829, Ka'ahumanu, the Hawaiian prime minister, put forth an edict to banish Catholics to Kaho'olawe. Beginning in 1830, Kaulana Bay, on the island's northern side, served as a penal colony for men accused of such crimes as rebellion, theft, divorce, murder and prostitution. History does not say if Catholics were included, and the penal colony was shut down in 1853.

Into the Dust Bowl

Kaho'olawe, now nearly barren, was once a lush, forested island.

The territorial Hawaiian government leased the entire island to ranchers in 1858. None were successful, and sheep, goats and cattle were left to run wild. By the early 1900s, tens of thousands of sheep and goats had denuded most of the island, turning it into an eroded dusty wasteland (even today, Kaho'olawe looks hazy from dust when seen from Maui).

From 1918 to 1941, Angus MacPhee ran Kaho'olawe's most successful ranching operation. Granted a lease on the grounds to get rid of the goats, MacPhee rounded up and sold 13,000 goats, and then built a fence across the width of the entire island to keep the remaining goats at one end. He planted grasses and ground cover and started raising cattle. It wasn't easy, but MacPhee, unlike his predecessors, was able to turn a profit.

Target Practice

The US military had long felt that Kaho'olawe had strategic importance. In early 1941, it subleased part of the island from MacPhee for bombing practice. Following the Pearl Harbor attack (December 7, 1941), the military took control of Kaho'olawe entirely. Until the war's end, it used the island to practice for invasions in the Pacific theater; in addition to ship-to-shore and aerial bombing, it tested submarine torpedoes by firing them at shoreline cliffs. It is estimated that of all the fighting that took place during WWII, Kaho'olawe was the most bombed island in the Pacific.

After the war, bombing practice continued. In 1953, President Eisenhower signed a decree giving the US Navy official jurisdiction over Kaho'olawe, with the stipulation that when Kaho'olawe was no longer 'needed,' the unexploded ordnance would be removed and the island would be returned to Hawaiian control 'reasonably safe for human habitation.'

The Kaho'olawe Movement

In the mid-1960s Hawaii politicians began petitioning the federal government to cease its military activities and return Kaho'olawe to the state of Hawaii. In 1976, a suit was filed against the navy, and in an attempt to attract greater attention to the bombings, nine Native Hawaiian activists sailed across and occupied the island. Despite their arrests, more occupations followed.

During one of the 1977 crossings, group members George Helm and Kimo Mitchell mysteriously disappeared in the waters off Kaho'olawe. Helm had been an inspirational Hawaiian-rights activist, and with his death the Protect Kaho'olawe 'Ohana movement arose. Helm's vision of turning Kaho'olawe into a sanctuary of Hawaiian culture became widespread among islanders.

In 1980, in a court-sanctioned decree, the navy reached an agreement with Protect Kaho'olawe 'Ohana that allowed them regular access to the island. The decree restricted the navy from bombing archaeological sites. In 1981 Kaho'olawe was added to the National Register of Historic Places as a significant archaeological area. For nearly a decade, the island had the ironic distinction of being the only such historic place that was bombed by its government.

In 1982 the 'Ohana began going to Kaho'olawe to celebrate *makahiki*, the annual observance to honor Lono, god of agriculture and peace. That same year – in what many Hawaiians felt was the ultimate insult to their heritage – the US military offered Kaho'olawe as a bombing target to foreign nations during the biennial Pacific Rim exercises.

The exercises brought what was happening to Kaho'olawe to worldwide attention. International protests grew, and New Zealand, Australia, Japan and the UK withdrew from the Kaho'olawe exercises. The plan was scrapped. In the late 1980s, Hawaii's politicians became more outspoken in their demands that Kaho'olawe be returned to Hawaii. Then in October 1990, as Hawaii's two US senators, Daniel Inouye and Daniel Akaka, were preparing a congressional bill to stop the bombing, President George Bush issued an order to immediately halt military activities.

The Navy Sets Sail

In 1994, the US Navy finally agreed to clean up and return Kaho'olawe to Hawaii. The navy promised to work until 100% of surface munitions and 30% of subsurface munitions were cleared. However, the catch was that the federally authorized cleanup would end in 10 years, regardless of the results.

Ten years later, after spending over $400 million, the navy's cleanup ended, and Kaho'olawe was transferred to the state. The government estimated that only 70% of surface ordnance and a mere 9% of subsurface ordnance had been removed.

The same year, in 2004, Hawaii established the Kaho'olawe Island Reserve Commission to manage access and use of the island, preserve its archaeological areas and restore its habitats. As of 2004, nearly 3000 archaeological and historical sites had been inventoried. KIRC's mandate calls for the island to be 'managed in trust until such time and circumstances as a sovereign Native Hawaiian entity is recognized by the federal and state governments.' This mandate came one step closer to fulfillment in 2011 when Governor Neil Abercrombie signed into law a bill recognizing Native Hawaiians as the state's only indigenous people.

Helping the 'Ohana

KIRC runs volunteer trips to the island every other week for restoration work, which includes pulling weeds, planting native foliage, cleaning up historic sights and honoring the spirits of the land. It welcomes respectful volunteers who are ready to work (not just sightsee). Visits last four days, from Tuesday through Friday; volunteers pay a $125 fee, which covers food, lodging and transportation to the island. The KIRC website lists full details and contact information. As of January 2013, there was more than a year-long wait list, possibly up to two years. Plan ahead!

Lana'i

Best Places to Eat

- Lana'i City Grille (p433)
- Blue Ginger Café (p432)
- Pele's Other Garden (p433)
- Nobu (p436)

Best Adventures

- Munro Trail (p434)
- Keomuku Road (p437)
- Road to Garden of the Gods (p438)
- Kaunolu (p439)

Why Go?

Although Lana'i is the most central of the Hawaii islands – on a clear day you can see five islands from here – it is also the least 'Hawaiian' of the islands. Now-closed pineapple plantations are its main historic legacy, and the locals are a mix of people descended from immigrant field workers from around the world. The relatively few buildings mostly hew to a corporate plantation style and the miles of red-dirt roads see few tourists.

Its signature (imported) Norfolk and Cook Island pines give the island a feel that could just as well come from a remote corner of the South Pacific. And therein lies the charm of Lana'i, an entire island that's an off-the-beaten-path destination (albeit with a billionaire owner, Larry Ellison). Hidden beaches, archaeological sites, oddball geology and a sense of isolation are perfect for those who don't want to go far to get away from it all.

When to Go

Lana'i City

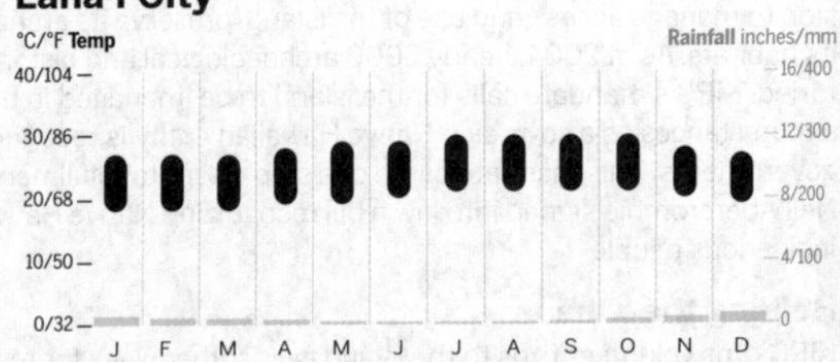

Nov–Mar Jackets are needed at night in lofty, temperate Lana'i City, while the beaches stay balmy.

Apr–Aug Winter rains have stopped and the entire island enjoys breezy tropical comfort.

Sep–Oct Lana'i City stays in the sunny 70s (°F), while Hulopo'e Beach is in the lovely low 80s.

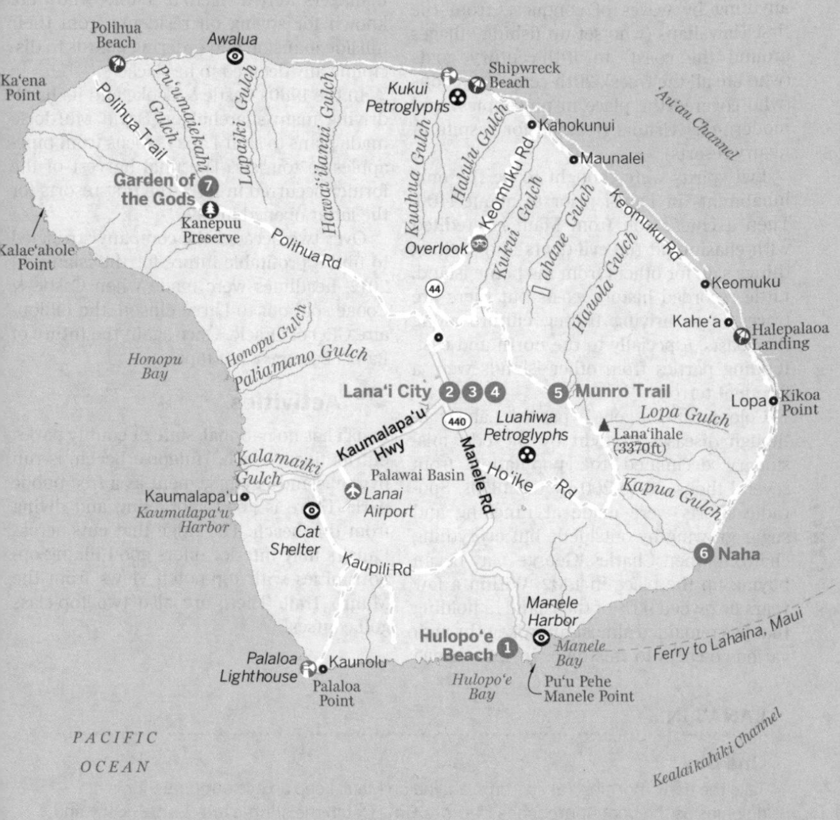

Lana'i Highlights

1. Snorkel the protected reef at the island's best beach, **Hulopo'e Beach** (p435)
2. Browse the choices, then enjoy simple but good food and drink at any of Lana'i City's many **cafes** (p432)
3. Stroll the square picking up local gossip, flavor and even artwork at **Dole Park** (p428)
4. Get into local rhythms by renting a vacation house in **Lana'i City** (p428)
5. Hike the **Munro Trail** (p434) through the island's small but lush heart, stretching just above Lana'i City
6. Get lost on the unpaved Keomuku Road to **Naha** (p438), where ancient fishponds lie offshore
7. Count the other islands from the otherworldly heights of the **Garden of the Gods** (p438), then ponder its weird rocks

History

Among its translations, Lana'i is thought to mean 'day of conquest,' and although there is debate about this, it seems appropriate. This small island (at its widest point only 18 miles across) has been affected more than anything by waves of conquest, from the first Hawaiians (who set up fishing villages around the coast) to 19th-century goats (who ate all the trees), 20th-century tycoons (who covered the place in pineapples) and modern-day visitors (looking for respite at luxury resorts).

Evil spirits were thought to be the only inhabitants of Lana'i prior to about 1400. Then a chief's son from Maui is credited with chasing off the evil-doers and making things safe for others from his home island. Little recorded history exists but there are traces of a thriving fishing culture along the coasts, especially to the north and east. Raiding parties from other islands were a frequent terror.

Colonialism largely bypassed Lana'i, although diseases brought by the odd missionary decimated the population from several thousand to 200 by the 1850s. Sporadic efforts were made at ranching and sugar growing by outsiders, but everything changed when Charles 'George' Gay began buying up the place in 1902. Within a few years he owned 98% of the island (a holding that has remained almost unbroken through various owners to this day). In 1922 Lana'i passed into the hands of Jim Dole, who fatefully started a pineapple plantation that was soon the world's largest.

Under Dole (and later its corporate successor, Castle & Cooke), Lana'i was not just a company town but a company island. Early managers were de facto dictators, who were known for spying on residents from their hillside mansion and ordering guards to discipline any deemed to be slackers.

In the 1980s Castle & Cooke and its hard-driving main shareholder, David Murdock, made plans to shift Lana'i's focus from pineapples to tourists. The final harvest of the former occurred in 1992, the first resorts for the latter opened in 1990.

Over two decades the company struggled to find a profitable future for the island. In 2012, headlines were made when Castle & Cooke sold out to Larry Ellison, the billionaire CEO of Oracle. Once again the future of Lana'i became a hot topic.

Activities

Lana'i has no national, state or county parks, but its finest beach, Hulopo'e Beach, is run by the island's management as a free public park. There is good snorkeling and diving from this beach. The ridge that cuts across Lana'i's hilly interior offers good hiking opportunities with top-notch views from the Munro Trail. There are also two top-class golf courses.

LANA'I IN...

One Day

Take the early morning **ferry** from Lahaina on Maui; keep an eye out for schools of dolphins as the boat approaches **Manele Bay**. Catch the shuttle into **Lana'i City** and pour your own coffee for breakfast at **Blue Ginger Café** before strolling the town's shops and superb **Culture & Heritage Centre**. In the afternoon, snorkel at **Hulopo'e Beach** or dive at **Manele Bay** before heading back to Maui on the sunset ferry.

Two Days

If you have an extra day, rather than heading back to Maui, wander back into town and watch the sun set over the majestic Norfolk Island pines at **Dole Park**. On the second day rent a mountain bike or put on your hiking boots and head up the **Munro Trail** for a sweeping view of everything Lana'i has to offer.

Four Days

With another couple of days, get a jeep and do some beachcombing along **Shipwreck Beach** and then explore the road to **Naha**. That night enjoy a superb meal at **Lana'i City Grille**. On day four choose from one of the old-time **eateries** on Dole Park before a day exploring the **Garden of the Gods**, the **Luahiwa Petroglyphs** and the ancient village of **Kaunolu**.

Guests at the island's two resorts tend to book their activities through the hotels. However, there are also excellent independent operators.

Lana'i Surf Safari SURFING

(☎306-9837; www.lanaisurfsafari.com; surf lessons $200) Lana'i native Nick Palumbo offers half-day surfing lessons at secluded spots. Surfboard/paddleboard rentals from $60/50 per hour including delivery.

Trilogy Lana'i Ocean Sports DIVING, SNORKELING

(☎888-874-5649; www.scubalanai.com; boat dives from $190) Runs diving and snorkeling trips around Manele Bay, including to the excellent Cathedrals dive site. It also runs diving and snorkeling day trips (packages from adult/child $180/100) to Lana'i from Maui aboard a catamaran.

Getting There & Away

AIR

Lana'i airport (LNY; ☎565-7942; http://hawaii.gov/lny; Lana'i Ave, Lana'i City) is about 3.5 miles southwest of Lana'i City. There are no direct flights to Lana'i from the mainland. Service is by small planes; because of weight limits for individual bags (40lb), take a small duffel bag in case you have to redistribute your possessions.

Island Air (☎800-652-6541; www.islandair.com) Flies several times daily to/from Honolulu; partners with Hawaiian Airlines and United. Bought by Larry Ellison in 2013.

Mokulele Airlines (☎426-7070; www.mokuleleairlines.com) Flies several times daily to/from Honolulu and Kahului; codeshares with intra-island carrier Go!.

SEA

Worth it just for the ride, the **Expeditions Maui–Lana'i Ferry** (☎800-695-2624, 661-3756; www.go-lanai.com; adult/child one way $30/20) links Lahaina Harbor (Maui) with Manele Bay Harbor on Lana'i (one hour) several times daily. In winter there's a fair chance of seeing humpback whales; spinner dolphins are a common sight all year, especially on morning sails. Hulopo'e Beach is near the dock; Lana'i tour and activity operators will meet the ferries if you call ahead. Day-trip packages from Maui are popular.

Getting Around

Outside Lana'i City there are only three paved roads: Keomuku Rd (Hwy 44), which extends northeast to Shipwreck Beach; Kaumalapa'u Hwy (Hwy 440), which extends west past the airport to Kaumalapa'u Harbor; and Manele Rd (also Hwy 440), which flows south to Manele and Hulopo'e Bays. To really see the island, you'll need to rent a 4WD vehicle; Lana'i's dirt roads vary from good to impassable, largely depending on the weather. Rain can turn them into scarlet-hued bogs.

TO/FROM THE AIRPORT

The resorts provide a shuttle-van service that meets guests at the airport and ferry dock. Nonguests can use the shuttle for a fee ($10), or call a taxi (about $10 per person) in advance of your arrival.

CAR

The only car-rental company on the island, **Lana'i City Service** (☎800-533-7808, 565-7227; 1036 Lana'i Ave, Lana'i City; ⏲rentals 7am-7pm, gas station 6:30am-10pm), is an affiliate of Dollar Rent A Car. Having a monopoly on Lana'i translates into steep prices: heavily used 4WD Jeep Wranglers cost from $125 to $150 per day (the only other type of car available is a minivan, which rent out at similar prices, but won't give you much freedom on the bad roads). Note that Lana'i City Service limits where you can drive. Check in advance, as a tow from a restricted area incurs fines, fees and possible financial ruin.

Gas is also pricey (sold at, you guessed it, Lana'i City Service): it can cost up to $6 per gallon – a hefty charge for the gas-guzzling Jeeps.

Driving Distances & Times From Lana'i City

DESTINATION	MILES	TIME
Garden of the Gods	6	20min
Hulopo'e Beach	8	20min
Kaumalapa'u Harbor	7	20min
Keomuku	15	1hr
Lana'i Airport	3.5	10min

SHUTTLE

The resorts run a shuttle that links the Four Seasons Resort Lana'i at Manele Bay, Hotel Lana'i and the Lodge at Koele, as well as the airport and ferry dock. Shuttles run about every 30 minutes throughout the day in peak season, hourly in the slower months. The first usually heads out about 7am, the last around 11pm. Fares may be included in the tariff for guests ($35 for unlimited use during your stay); others pay from $10 for a round-trip from the airport or ferry dock (credit cards only).

Lana'i City

POP 3000

Have you been you transported back in time, to another place in the Pacific, or both? Pausing to get your bearings is perfectly alright in cute little Lana'i City. In fact, you may need to pause to understand that it's really just a village, albeit one with irrepressible charm.

Lana'i City's main square, Dole Park, is surrounded by tin-roofed houses and shops, with not a chain in sight. It looks much the same as it did during its plantation days dating back to the 1920s. If you're not staying at one of the island's two resorts, you're probably staying here and that's all the better as you can wander between the surprisingly rich collection of eateries and shops, all with an authenticity not found in more touristed places. At night stroll the quiet streets and watch the moon rise through the pine trees.

History

Lana'i is the only Hawaii island where the largest town is in the highlands and not on the coast. Lana'i City is, in fact, the only town on the island – as has been the case for the last eight decades.

The village was built in the 1920s as a plantation town for the field workers and staff of Dole's Hawaiian Pineapple Company. The first planned city in Hawaii, Lana'i City was built in the midst of the pineapple fields, with shops and a theater surrounding the central park, rows of plantation houses lined up beyond that and a pineapple-processing plant on the edge of it all. Fortunately it was done with a little pizzazz. Dole hired New Zealander George Munro, a naturalist and former ranch manager, to oversee much of the work. Munro planted the now-tall Norfolk and Cook Island pines that give the town its green character and help suck some moisture from passing clouds.

LANA'I'S TOP ACTIVITIES

ACTIVITY	DESTINATION
Diving	Cathedrals (p435)
Hiking	Koloiki Ridge Trail (p428)
Snorkeling	Hulopo'e Bay (p435)
Swimming	Hulopo'e Bay (p435)
	Halepalaoa Beach (p438)

Sights

Lana'i City is a charming place for a stroll. The town is laid out in a simple grid pattern, and almost all of the shops and services border **Dole Park**. The vaguely alien-looking pine trees provide plenty of shade and you can enjoy the comings and goings of the locals. On Sunday mornings, listen for choir music spilling out of the **Hawaiian church** on Fraser Ave.

★ Lana'i Culture & Heritage Center — MUSEUM

(www.lanaichc.org; 111 Lana'i Ave; ⌚8:30am-3:30pm Mon-Fri, 9am-1pm Sat) FREE This is one of the most engaging small museums in the islands. Displays cover Lana'i's often mysterious history; photos and a timeline show its transformation into the world's pineapple supplier. The lives of the workers are shown in detail and facts such as this jaw-dropper abound: each worker was expected to plant up to 10,000 new pineapple plants per day!

Note also the shots of Lana'i City in the 1920s when it sat on bald plains before the trademark pines had taken root. The museum runs several preservation projects.

Activities

Most tourist activities take place about a mile north of Dole Park at or near the Lodge at Koele (officially the 'Four Seasons Resort at Lana'i, the Lodge at Koele').

Koloiki Ridge Trail — HIKING

This 5-mile hike, leads up to one of the most scenic parts of the Munro Trail. It takes about three hours (return) and offers sweeping views of remote valleys (where taro was once grown), Maui and Moloka'i.

The trail begins at the rear of the Lodge at Koele on the paved path that leads to the golf clubhouse. From there, follow the signposted path uphill past Norfolk Island pines until you reach a hilltop bench with a plaque bearing the poem 'If' by Rudyard Kipling. Enjoy the view and then continue through the trees until you reach a chain-link fence. Go around the right side of the fence and continue up the hillside towards the power lines. At the top of the pass, follow the trail down through a thicket of guava trees until you reach an abandoned dirt service road, which you'll turn left on. You'll soon intersect with the Munro Trail; turn right on it and after a few minutes you'll pass Kukui Gulch, named for the *kukui* (candlenut trees) that grow there. Continue along

Lana'i City

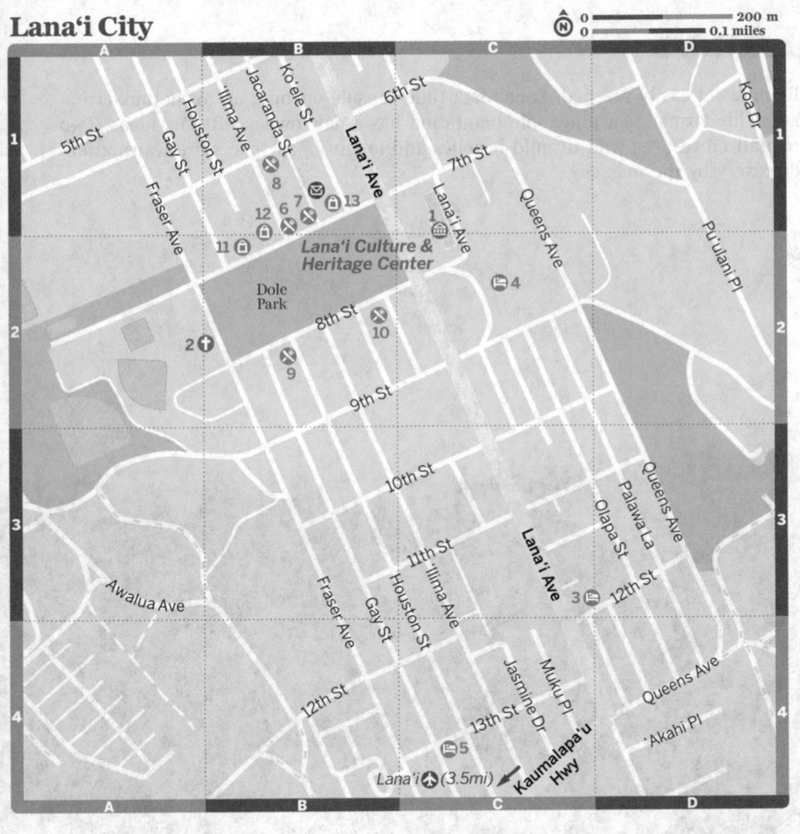

Lana'i City

Top Sights
1 Lana'i Culture & Heritage Center C1

Sights
2 Hawaiian Church B2

Sleeping
3 Dreams Come True C3
4 Hotel Lana'i C2
5 Plantation Home C4

Eating
6 Blue Ginger Café B1
7 Canoes Lana'i B1
8 Coffee Works B1
Lana'i City Grille ..... (see 4)
9 Pele's Other Garden B2
10 Richard's Market B2

Shopping
11 Lana'i Arts & Cultural Center B2
12 Local Gentry B1
13 Mike Carroll Gallery B1

the trail until you reach a thicket of tall sisal plants; about 50yd after that bear right to reach Koloiki Ridge, where you'll be rewarded with panoramic views of much of the island.

Stables at Koele HORSEBACK RIDING
(☎563-9385; www.lanaigrandadventures.com; rides from $130; ⏲7am-5pm) If you would prefer to see Lana'i from a saddle, this 25-horse operation, just west of the Lodge at Koele resort (within eyeshot), offers everything from a 1½-hour trail ride that takes in sweeping views of Maui to a four-hour private ride catered to your particular interest. There are also pony rides for kids ($25). You can even get lessons in roping.

Lana'i

Remote yet easily reached, Lana'i is a time capsule opening up to the modern age. This former vast pineapple plantation has a new owner with big ideas. Two revitalized resorts, wild to mild beaches and lots of open spaces are waiting for discovery by the masses.

2

ANN CECIL / GETTY IMAGES ©

4

WALTER BIBIKOW / GETTY IMAGES ©

1. Highway to Lana'i City (p428)
Lana'i's signature Cook Island pines line the Kaumalapa'u Highway.

2. Pu'u Pehe Cove (p435)
This cove and its 'Sweetheart's Rock' feature in the ancient Hawaiian legend of Pele.

3. Hulopo'e Bay (p435)
Swim or snorkel in this family-friendly bay and catch a glimpse of Hawaii's incredible marine life.

4. Garden of the Gods (p438)
Boulders punctuate this silent martian landscape that offers views of four other islands.

3

PERSPECTIVES / GETTY IMAGES ©

LANA'I FOR CHILDREN

The kids will love **Hulopo'e Beach** (p435), where there are some cool tide pools filled with colorful little critters that will thrill the little ones; older kids will enjoy the great snorkeling. Other activities for children are based at the resorts; the **Stables at Koele** (p429) has pony rides open to guests and nonguests.

Experience at Koele GOLF
(☎565-4653; www.golfonlanai.com; guests/nonguests $125/185; ⊙8am-6:30pm) Curving around Four Seasons Resort Lana'i, Lodge at Koele, this Greg Norman-branded course offers world-class golfing with knockout vistas along the way. The front nine meanders through park-like settings; the signature 17th hole drops 200ft to a tree-shrouded gorge.

Festivals & Events

Lana'i's main bash, the **Pineapple Festival** (www.visitlanai.net), is held on or near July 4 and celebrates the island's pineapple past with games and live music at Dole Park (any pineapple you see is imported!).

Sleeping

Most people stay at the resorts or Hotel Lana'i, but there are several rental houses and B&Bs right in town and an easy walk to restaurants. There are several choices at www.vrbo.com.

★**Hotel Lana'i** HOTEL $$
(☎565-7211; www.hotellanai.com; 828 Lan'i Ave; r $100-170, cottage $200;) From 1923 to 1990 the Hotel Lana'i was the only hotel on the island. It seems little has changed here over the decades, other than the conversations that echo through the thin walls. The 10 renovated rooms have hardwood floors, antiques, pedestal sinks, patchwork quilts and more period pieces.

Go for a room with – appropriately – a lanai (a small porch) for viewing town, or opt for privacy and quiet in the detached cottage out back. A modest continental breakfast is provided.

Dreams Come True VACATION RENTAL $$
(☎800-566-6961, 565-6961; www.dreamscometruelanai.com; 1168 Lana'i Ave; r daily/weekly $130/905; @) This spiffy plantation-style house was one of the first built in Lana'i City (1925) and has a long porch. Rooms have hardwood floors, and are furnished with a mixture of comfy antique and modern pieces. There are numerous amenities, including laundry, DVD, internet access and private marble baths. You can arrange vehicle rentals here through the owner. Ask about breakfast options.

Plantation Home VACATION RENTAL $$
(☎276-1528; craige@maui.net; cnr Gay & 13th Sts; per night $135) A small, renovated two-bedroom plantation-style house, this option comes with an amazing bonus: a free Jeep (which means the house rental with the Jeep costs less than renting just a Jeep from the local monopoly). Rooms are basic in decor, but there is a long list of included sports equipment plus DVD and full kitchen, laundry and a friendly neighborhood cat.

Four Seasons Resort Lana'i, the Lodge at Koele RESORT $$$
(☎800-321-4666, 565-4000; www.fourseasons.com/koele; 1 Keomuku Hwy; r from $250; @) Pondering a sticky wicket on the croquet lawn amidst the manicured gardens, you'd be forgiven for thinking you had been transported to an English estate. Inside the soaring central building, however, there are just enough local touches to remind you you're in Hawaii. Guests in the 102 rooms and suites enjoy a small pool, a library, lawn bowls and misty mountain air.

Activities are shared with the companion Four Seasons Resort Lana'i at Manele Bay. During much of the year this resort is almost somnolent and rarely busy. Find it about a half-mile north of the Dole Park on Keomuku Hwy.

Eating & Drinking

The old-time feel of Lana'i City extends to eating hours: kitchens close by 8pm. Of the two main supermarkets, **Richard's Market** (434 8th St; ⊙8:30am-7pm Mon-Sat, 10am-5pm Sun) (now owned by Larry Ellison) has the better wine selection. All the places to eat offer take-out service – good for picnics.

★**Blue Ginger Café** CAFE $
(409 7th St; breakfast & lunch $5-8, dinner $8-15; ⊙6am-8pm Thu-Mon, till 2pm Tue & Wed) Don't worry, all the care goes into the food, not the decor at this bare-bones diner, where you can serve yourself a cup of coffee, grab a

newspaper and settle back at a table outside. Muffins are some of the excellent items that arrive warm from the bakery.

The long menu ranges from omelets and salads to burgers, delectable chicken katsu and more. It's been run by the same family for decades.

Canoes Lana'i LOCAL $

(419 7th St; meals $5-12; ⏲6:30am-1pm Sun-Thu, to 8pm Fri & Sat) Breakfast is always on the menu at this old-time Hawaii cafe that is little changed since pineapple pickers filled the tables. The best-seller? *Loco moco* (rice, fried egg and hamburger topped with gravy). Teriyaki figures prominently on the dinner menu. Look for *laulau* – pungent, marinated pork cooked in taro leaves – on special.

Coffee Works CAFE $

(604 'Ilima Ave; snacks $2-5; ⏲7am-3pm Mon-Sat, 8am-noon Sun) Settle back on the vast deck at this long-running java-jiving caffeine house and soon most of the locals will pass by.

Pele's Other Garden ITALIAN $$

(cnr 8th & Houston Sts; lunch $5-9, dinner $10-20; ⏲11am-3pm & 5-8pm Mon-Sat) More bistro than deli, this restored plantation house has tables inside and out. The kitchen leans Italian and serves up classic spaghetti and meatballs, crispy thin-crust pizza and some first-rate pesto. Salads are made with organic local greens; desserts are large but not extraordinary.

There's a fine beer list with 12 brews on tap. Last call in the tiny bar area and outside is 9pm. Watch for William Shatner, a regular when he beams down on holiday.

★ **Lana'i City Grille** FUSION $$$

(☎565-7211; 828 Lana'i Ave, Hotel Lana'i; mains $28-42; ⏲5-9pm Wed-Sun) Famed Maui chef Bev Gannon is the brains behind the charming restaurant within the Hotel Lana'i. Sturdy 1930s schoolhouse furnishings give the wood-floored dining room a vintage air, while the menu combines fresh seafood with various meats in ways both familiar (a perfect rib-eye) and surprising (ahi *poke* tacos).

Specials are, well, special. The small bar, which draws local movers and shakers (trust us, there are some), pours a fine highball, has a great wine list and is often open until 11pm! On Friday nights there's live Hawaiian music).

Dining Room HAWAII REGIONAL CUISINE $$$

(☎565-7300; www.fourseasons.com/koele; 1 Keomuku Hwy; mains $45-65; ⏲6-9:30pm Fri-Tue) Leave your sandals in the room but bring your wallet to this very high-end Lodge at Koele restaurant with a name that will remind you where you are. Locally sourced Hawaiian foods populate a menu of expertly prepared creations. But really, this is Lana'i and we'll take the fun and food of any of the places ringing Dole Park, first.

Shopping

Shops and galleries encircle Dole Park selling everything from flip-flops for locals to fine art for connoisseurs. You can spend an hour or much longer wandering.

Mike Carroll Gallery ART, BOOKS

(www.mikecarrollgallery.com; cnr 7th & Ko'ele Sts; ⏲10am-5pm Mon-Sat) Art lovers enjoy Mike Carroll Gallery, where you can find

LANA'I SURF BEACHES & BREAKS

When it comes to surfing, Lana'i doesn't enjoy quite the bounty of waves as some of the other islands. Because rain clouds get trapped in the high peaks of Maui and Moloka'i there's very little rain on Lana'i, and therefore far fewer reef passes have been carved out by runoff.

Yet on the south shore the most consistent surf comes in around the **Manele Point** area, where the main break peels off the tip of Manele and into Hulopo'e Bay. Shallow reef and submerged rocks make this a dangerous spot at low tide or in smaller surf conditions (you're more likely to get ideal conditions on a double overhead swell, but check with locals to be safe). Over at the ancient fishponds of **Naha** (p438) (also known as Stone Shack) there is a fun two-way peak, but it does close out when it gets bigger.

On the island's north shore is **Polihua Beach** (p438), the longest and widest sandy beach on Lana'i. Be careful of the current here, dubbed 'the Tahitian Express.' The water flowing between Moloka'i and Lana'i in the Kalohi Channel has driven many a ship into the reef, and it could easily take you on a trip to Tahiti if you're not careful.

LUAHIWA PETROGLYPHS

Lana'i's highest concentration of petroglyphs (over 400, both ancient and modern) are carved into three-dozen boulders spread over a remote slope overlooking the Palawai Basin.

To get to this seldom-visited site, head south from Lana'i City along tree-lined Manele Rd. After 2 miles, look for a cluster of six trees on the left and turn on the wide dirt road. Stay on this for 1.2 miles as you head toward the hills. When you see a house and gate, take a very sharp turn left onto a grass and dirt track for 0.3 miles. The large boulders will be on your right up the hill and there will be a turnout and small stone marker.

Many of the rock carvings are quite weathered, but you can still make out linear and triangular human figures, dogs and a canoe. Other than gusts of wind, the place is eerily quiet. You can almost feel the presence of the ancients here – honor their spirits and don't touch the fragile carvings.

the eponymous owner either creating a new work or busy displaying the work of another artist. It's also a good source for local books.

Lana'i Arts & Cultural Center ART
(cnr 7th & Houston Sts; ⏲10am-4pm Mon-Sat) Staffed by local artist volunteers (so never assume it's closed), you can choose from works in many mediums or learn how to create your own from the artists themselves. A great place to get *very* local recommendations.

Local Gentry CLOTHING
(363 7th St; ⏲10am-5pm Mon-Sat) Lovers of artful clothing flock to Local Gentry, a clothing store with color and flair that caters to visitors and locals alike. There's no polyester schlock here.

Information

There's no local daily newspaper, but community notices, including rental-housing ads, are posted on bulletin boards outside the grocery stores. The monthly *Lana'i Today* covers local events.

Bank of Hawaii (460 8th St) Has one of the island's two 24-hour ATMs.

Lana'i Community Hospital (☎565-6411; 628 7th St) Offers 24-hour emergency medical services.

Lana'i Public Library (555 Fraser Ave; ⏲10am-5pm Mon-Fri, noon-8pm Wed) Has internet access.

Post Office (620 Jacaranda St)

Getting There & Around

The resort shuttle stops at Hotel Lana'i, the Lodge at Koele and pretty much anywhere else you ask. Lana'i's only car-rental office is Lana'i City Service (the shuttle stops there as well).

Munro Trail

This exhilarating 12-mile adventure through verdant forest can be hiked, mountain biked or negotiated in a 4WD vehicle. For the best views, get an early start. Those hiking or biking should be prepared for steep grades and allow a whole day. If you're driving give yourself at least two to three hours. However, be aware that rains turn the dirt into a red swamp and the road may be off-limits to rental jeeps. Watch out for sheer drop-offs.

To start, head north on Hwy 44 from Lana'i City. About a mile past the Lodge at Koele, turn right onto the paved road that ends in half a mile at the island's **cemetery**. The Munro Trail starts left of the cemetery; passing through eucalyptus groves, it climbs the ridge and the path is studded with Norfolk Island pines. These trees, a species that draws moisture from the afternoon clouds and fog, were planted in the 1920s as a watershed by naturalist George Munro, after whom the trail is named.

The trail looks down on deep ravines cutting across the east flank of the mountain, and passes **Lana'ihale** (3370ft), Lana'i's highest point. On a clear day you can see all the inhabited Hawaii islands except for distant Kaua'i and Ni'ihau along the route. Stay on the main trail, which descends 6 miles to the central plateau. Keep the hills to your left and turn right at the big fork in the road. The trail ends back on Manele Rd (Hwy 440) between Lana'i City and Manele Bay.

Ask at the Stables at Koele (p429) about ATV tours of the trail (from $200), which may be the best recourse for non-hikers.

Hulopo'e & Manele Bays

Lana'i's finest beach (and one of the best in Hawaii) is the golden crescent of sand at Hulopo'e Bay. Enjoy snorkeling in a marine preserve, walking to a fabled archaeological site or just relaxing in the shade of palms. Nearby, Manele Harbor provides a protected anchorage for sailboats and other small craft, just a 10-minute walk from Hulopo'e Beach.

Manele and Hulopo'e Bays are part of a marine-life conservation district that prohibits the removal of coral and restricts many fishing activities, all of which makes for great snorkeling and diving. Spinner dolphins seem to enjoy the place as much as humans. During wintertime *kona* (leeward) storms, strong currents and swells enliven the calm and imperil swimmers.

Beaches

★Hulopo'e Beach BEACH

One good thing about being the main beach on company-run Lana'i is that the same gardeners who manicure the Four Seasons keep things looking lovely in this free, public park. Everybody loves it – locals taking the kids for a swim, tourists on day trips from Maui and the many visitors who end up losing track of time here.

This gently curving golden-sand beach is long, broad and protected by a rocky point to the south. The Four Seasons Resort Lana'i at Manele Bay sits on a low seaside terrace on the north side. But the beach is big enough that even with the hotel presence it never gets crowded. Generally, the most action occurs when the tour boats pull in from Maui late-morning. Picnic tables shelter under palms and there are public restrooms with solar-heated showers.

For the best snorkeling, head to the left side of the bay, where there's an abundance of coral and reef fish. To the left, just beyond the sandy beach, you'll find a low lava shelf with tide pools worth exploring. Look for the protected shoreline splash pool, ideal for children.

Sights & Activities

Pu'u Pehe NATURAL FEATURE

From Hulopo'e Beach, a path (of around 0.75 miles) leads south to the end of **Manele Point**, which separates Hulopo'e and Manele Bays. The point is actually a volcanic cinder cone that's sharply eroded on its seaward edge. The lava here has rich rust red colors with swirls of gray and black, and its texture is bubbly and brittle – so brittle that huge chunks of the point have broken off and fallen onto the coastal shelf below.

Pu'u Pehe is the name of the cove to the left of the point, as well as the rocky islet just offshore. This islet, which is also known as Sweetheart's Rock, has a tomblike formation on top that features in the Hawaiian legend of Pehe. According to the legend, Pehe was a beautiful maiden who was stashed away in a cave by her lover, lest any other young men on Lana'i set eyes upon her. One day when her lover was up in the mountains, a storm suddenly blew in and powerful waves drowned Pehe. The grief-stricken boy carried Pehe's body to the top of Pu'u Pehe, where he erected a tomb and laid her to rest. He then jumped to his death in the surging waters.

Manele Harbor HARBOR

During the early 20th century, cattle were herded down to Manele Bay for shipment to Honolulu. These days the herds start in Maui, traveling on day trips to Lana'i on the ferry. There's a few picnic tables under a shelter and bathrooms.

Cathedrals DIVING

Diving in and around the bay is excellent. Coral is abundant near the cliff sides, where the bottom quickly slopes off to about 40ft. Beyond the bay's western edge, near Pu'u Pehe rock, is Cathedrals, the island's most spectacular dive site, featuring arches and grottoes amidst a large lava tube that is 100ft in length.

Trilogy Lana'i Ocean Sports (p427) runs diving and snorkeling trips in the area.

Challenge at Manele GOLF

(☎565-2222; www.golfonlanai.com; guests/non-guests $210/225; ⏲7am-6:30pm) This Jack Nicklaus–branded course at the Four Seasons resort offers spectacular play along

> **CARRY WATER**
>
> Outside of Lana'i City there is nowhere to buy refreshments. So if you have a day planned on the various rural roads to places like Naha or the Garden of the Gods, be sure to bring plenty of water. This is especially important if you're embarking on hikes such as the Munro Trail.

seaside cliffs. The 12th hole challenges golfers to hit across a fairway that is really the ocean's surf.

Sleeping

Note that owners of the condos around Manele Bay are prevented from renting out their units to visitors.

Hulopo'e Beach Camping CAMPGROUND $
(permit $30 plus $15 per person per night) Camping is allowed on the grassy expanse above Hulopo'e Beach. The pricey permits are issued by staff in the park.

★ **Four Seasons Resort Lana'i at Manele Bay** RESORT $$$
(800-321-4666, 565-2000; www.fourseasons.com/manelebay; 1 Manele Bay Rd; r from $400;) Of the two island resorts on offer, this is the one that screams – well, stage-whispers – Hawaii vacation! The decor of the 236 rooms is newly minimalist, in line with Larry Ellison's aesthetics. He's also had the Asian-themed art collection replaced with Hawaiian works.

The views of the azure waters (often featuring cavorting porpoises), the surrounds of the vast pool and the soaring public rooms are impressive. Given a choice, we'll take this resort first as it most says 'Hawaii.'

Eating & Drinking

The resort has many tables well-placed for watching the orange glint of the waters at sunset. The bar area now features huge TVs for sporting events.

Other than the Four Seasons, the closest sources for food, drinks and picnics on Hulopo'e Beach are in Lana'i City.

Nobu JAPANESE $$$
(565-2000; Four Seasons Resort Lana'i at Manele Bay; meals from $50; 6-9:30pm) One of the

LANA'I'S BILLIONAIRE OWNER

Decades of sleepy seclusion for Lana'i were interrupted in 2012 when the fabulously wealthy co-founder of Oracle Software, Larry Ellison, bought out the island's long-time owner Castle & Cooke (which once ran the ubiquitous pineapple plantations under the Dole name).

It's the biggest change to the island since Castle & Cooke stopped farming and built the Four Seasons resorts in the early 1990s. That the new owner is Ellison, a legendary hard-driving Silicon Valley entrepreneur known for, among other dramatics, winning the America's Cup yacht race in 2010, only added to the interest.

For his estimated $600 million purchase price, Ellison got 98% of Lana'i (the rest is private homes or government land) and a bevy of businesses, such as the resorts. Given that the island has struggled economically since the glory days of pineapples, Ellison's potential plans for his trophy are generating intense interest.

Locals have noted an uptick in the number of private jets parked at the airport and he has docked a racing yacht in the small harbor at times. He also has gone about remodeling the resorts to reflect his design ethos (white, lots of white) and he's snapped up a few local businesses such as the town's main supermarket (it promptly instituted a dress code, eg no bare feet). Ellison also made efforts to show he was going to spruce up the somewhat dilapidated island by literally mending fences and making gestures such as reopening the community pool which David Murdock, the much-unloved billionaire head of Castle & Cooke, had closed to save money.

Meanwhile after a half year of ownership, Ellison began making clear some of his plans for the island. The airport will get a second runway to better accommodate large business jets, a reverse osmosis plant will supply water to a revitalized local farming community (meaning that for the first time in more than 20 years pineapple served on the pineapple island may actually have been grown there) and a new solar farm will help make the island energy independent. Besides continuing renovations of the existing Four Seasons resorts, a new low-rise luxury resort will be built on the sight of the old Club Lana'i at lovely Halepalaoa Beach. Also in the works are improvements to the medical and education infrastructure. It's a heady time indeed on Lana'i.

There's one echo of the old owners, however, that still needs resolution: Murdock holds an option to build an enormous wind farm that would supply electricity to O'ahu and likely be sited atop – and destroy – the Garden of the Gods.

most visible changes wrought by Larry Ellison has been this branch of the worldwide chain of very high-end Japanese sushi restaurants. Created by Chef Nobuyuki Matsuhisa, Nobu is known for ultra-fresh and creative sushi and other Japanese dishes, in this case with Hawaiian elements.

At lunch you can enjoy a few items off the Nobu menu along with the more casual fare at Kailani, the poolside cafe. Get a table with a view of dolphins in Manele Bay.

Keomuku Road

The best drive on Lana'i, Keomuku Road (Hwy 44), heads north from Lana'i City into cool upland hills, where fog drifts above grassy pastures. Along the way, impromptu overlooks offer straight-on views of the undeveloped southeast shore of Moloka'i and its tiny islet Mokuho'oniki, in marked contrast to Maui's sawtooth high-rises in Ka'anapali off to your right.

The surprisingly short 8-mile road gently slopes down to the coast in a series of switchbacks through a mostly barren landscape punctuated by eccentrically shaped rocks. The paved road ends near the coast and you are in 4WD country. To the left, a dirt road leads to Shipwreck Beach, while turning right onto Keomuku Road takes the adventurous to Keomuku Beach or all the way to Naha.

Shipwreck Beach

Unlike many worldwide places named Shipwreck Beach, where the name seems fanciful at best, you can't miss the namesake wreck here. A fairly large **WWII tanker** sits perched atop rocks just offshore. Unlike a metal ship (which would have dissolved decades ago), this one was part of a series made from concrete. It was dumped here by the navy after the war.

Start your beach exploration by taking the dirt road that runs 1.4 miles north from the end of Hwy 44, past some beach shacks. Often there seems to be more sand on the road than the beach. Park in the large clearing overlooking a rocky cove, which is known locally as Po'aiwa and has good **snorkeling** among the rocks and reef, as well as protected **swimming** over the sandy bottom. The wreck is about 440yd to the north, and you can stroll for at least 9 miles along the shore while looking for flotsam and taking in the Moloka'i and Maui views. Close to the parking area is the site of a former lighthouse on a lava-rock point, though only the cement foundation remains.

Sights & Activities

Kukui Petroglyphs HISTORICAL SITE

From the lighthouse foundation, trail markings lead directly inland about 100yd to the Kukui petroglyphs, a cluster of fragile carvings marked by a sign reading 'Do Not Deface.' The simple figures are etched onto large boulders on the right side of the path.

Keep your eyes open here – sightings of wild mouflon sheep on the inland hills are not uncommon. Males have curled-back horns, and dominant ones travel with a harem.

Shipwreck in Awalua HIKING

The lighthouse site is the turn-around point for most people, but it's possible to walk another 6 miles all the way to Awalua, where there's another shipwreck, the WWII tender YO-21. The hike is windy, hot and dry (bring water); the further down the beach you go, the prettier it gets.

You'll pass the scant remains of more than a dozen other ships along the way (timbers and machinery).

Kahokunui to Naha

The stretch of Keomuku Road running from Kahokunui to Naha is just the journey for those looking for real adventure on Lana'i. From the hillsides it looks barren, but once you are on it you are shaded by overhanging kiawe trees. The dirt course varies from smooth to deeply cratered (and impossibly soupy after storms). This is where your 4WD will justify its daily fee, as you explore the ruins of failed dreams and discover magical beaches. If the road is passable, driving the entire length should take about an hour. The reef-protected shore is close to the road but usually not quite visible.

Sights

Maunalei HISTORICAL SITE

Less than a mile from the end of paved Hwy 44 is Maunalei. An ancient heiau (stone temple) sat there until 1890, when the Maunalei Sugar Company dismantled it and used the stones to build a fence and railroad. Shortly after the temple desecration, the company was beset by misfortune, as saltwater filled the wells and disease decimated the workforce.

★ Keomuku HISTORICAL SITE

The center of the short-lived sugarcane plantation, Keomuku is 6 miles southeast of Maunalei. The highlight is the beautifully reconstructed **Ka Lanakila o Ka Malamalama Church**, which was originally built in 1903.

Under the dense tropical vegetation other ruins can be found, including a steam locomotive and buildings and an old boat towards the water.

Halepalaoa Landing HISTORICAL SITE

Just under 2 miles southeast along the road from Keomuku, you reach Halepalaoa Landing, which was where the sugar company planned to ship out its product from. But little was accomplished during its short life (1899–1901), other than to shorten the lives of scores of Japanese workers, who are buried in a small **cemetery**.

Nearby, look for the ruins of an 1830s **school**. On the ocean side, you'll see the remains of Club Lana'i, a 1970s failed recreation spot. There's a **pier** here that's maintained and which provides a good stroll out from the shore. Note that Larry Ellison announced plans in 2013 to build a new resort here.

★ Halepalaoa Beach BEACH

Running southeast from the pier is the reef-protected and shaded Halepalaoa Beach, which seems to have come from desert-island central casting and runs to Lopa. There's rarely many people here. In season you may see whales breaching just offshore.

Naha HISTORICAL SITE

Four miles southeast of Halepalaoa brings you to Naha, which is both the end of the road and the site of ancient fishponds just offshore. With the wind whistling in your ears, this is a dramatic and desolate setting where the rest of Hawaii feels a thousand miles away.

It's an otherworldly place that seems utterly incongruous, given the view of developed Maui just across the waters. Look for traces of a flagstone path that ran from here right up and over the hills to the Palawai Basin.

Road to Garden of the Gods

Strange rock formations, views that would overexcite a condo developer and more deserted beaches are the highlights of northwestern Lana'i.

It's all reached via the unpaved Polihua Rd, which starts near the Lodge at Koele's stables. The stretch of road leading to Kanepu'u Preserve and the Garden of the Gods is a fairly good, albeit often dusty, route that generally takes about 30 minutes from town. To travel onward to Polihua Beach, though, is another story: depending on when the road was last graded, the trip could take anywhere from 20 minutes to an hour, as you head 1800ft down to the coast.

Beaches & Sights

Kanepu'u Preserve NATURE RESERVE

The 590-acre Kanepu'u Preserve is the last native dryland forest of its kind across all Hawaii. Just 5 miles northwest of Lana'i City, the forest is home to 49 species of rare native plants, including the endangered *'iliahi* (Hawaiian sandalwood) and *na'u* (fragrant Hawaiian gardenia).

★ Garden Of The Gods NATURAL FEATURE

The only fertilizer that might work in this garden is cement. Often weirdly shaped volcanic rocks are strewn about this seemingly martian landscape. Multihued rocks and earth, with a palette from amber to rust to sienna, are stunning.

It's utterly silent up here and you can see up to four other islands across the white-capped waters. The colors change with the light – pastel in the early morning, rich hues in the late afternoon. Look for rocks oddly perched atop others.

Polihua Beach BEACH

This broad, 1.5-mile-long white-sand beach at the northwestern tip of the island takes its name from the green sea turtles that nest here (*polihua* means 'eggs in the bosom'). Although the beach itself is gorgeous, strong winds kicking up the sand and tiny shells often make it stingingly unpleasant; water conditions are treacherous.

Kaumalapa'u Highway

Kaumalapa'u Hwy (Hwy 440) connects Lana'i City to the airport before ending at Kaumalapa'u Harbor, the island's deep-water barge dock. The road itself is about as exciting as a can of pineapple chunks in heavy syrup, but it runs close to Lana'i's best archaeological site, at Kaunolu. Just off Hwy 440 on the Kaunolu road, look for a large open-air **cat shelter**, run by local volunteers. Feral cats enjoy a life of leisure and a few even welcome your visit.

Kaunolu

Perched on a majestic bluff at the island's southwestern tip, the ancient fishing village of Kaunolu thrived until its abandonment in the mid-19th century after missionary-transmitted disease had decimated the island. The waters of Kaunolu Bay were so prolific that royalty came here to cast their nets.

Now overgrown and visited by few, Kaunolu boasts the largest concentration of stone ruins on Lana'i. A gulch separates the two sides of the bay, with remnants of former house sites on the eastern side, obscured by thorny kiawe. The stone walls of **Halulu Heiau** at the western side of the gulch still dominate the scene. The temple once served as a *pu'uhonua* (place of refuge), where taboo-breakers fled to elude their death sentences. There are over 100 building sites here.

Northwest of the heiau, a natural stone wall runs along the perimeter of the sea cliff. Look for a break in the wall at the cliff's edge, where there's a sheer 80ft drop known as **Kahekili's Jump**. The ledge below makes diving into the ocean a death-defying thrill, but is recommended for professionals only. It's said that Kamehameha the Great would test the courage of upstart warriors by having them leap from this spot. More recently, it has been the site of cliff-diving championships.

To get to Kaunolu, follow Kaumalapa'u Hwy (Hwy 440) 0.6 miles past the airport, and turn left onto a partial gravel and dirt road that runs south through abandoned pineapple fields for 2.2 miles. A carved stone marks the turn onto a much rougher but still 4WD-capable road down to the sea. After a further 2.5 miles you'll see a sign for a short **interpretive trail**, which has well-weathered signs explaining the history of Kaunolu. Another 0.3 miles brings you to a parking area amid the ruins. One complication of a visit to this spot is that your rental firm may not allow you to drive here. Check first.

Moloka'i

Includes ➡

Best Beaches

- ➡ Papohaku Beach (p472)
- ➡ Mo'omomi Beach (p465)
- ➡ Twenty Mile Beach (p455)
- ➡ Halawa Beach (p458)

Best Adventures

- ➡ Kalaupapa by mule (p468)
- ➡ Halawa Valley hike (p457)
- ➡ Pepe'opae Trail (p462)
- ➡ Kayaking the coast (p443)

Why Go?

The popular local T-shirt proclaiming 'Moloka'i time is when I want to show up' sums up this idiosyncratic island perfectly: feisty and independent while not taking life too seriously.

Moloka'i is often cited as the 'most Hawaiian' of the islands, and in terms of bloodlines this is true – more than 50% of the residents are at least part Native Hawaiian. But whether the island fits your idea of 'most Hawaiian' depends on your definition. If your idea of Hawaii includes great tourist facilities, forget it.

But if you're after a place that best celebrates the islands' geography and indigenous culture, then Moloka'i is for you. It regularly ranks as one of the least spoiled islands worldwide; ancient Hawaiian sites in the island's beautiful, tropical east are jealously protected and restored, and island-wide consensus eschews development of the often sacred west.

When to Go

Kaunakaka

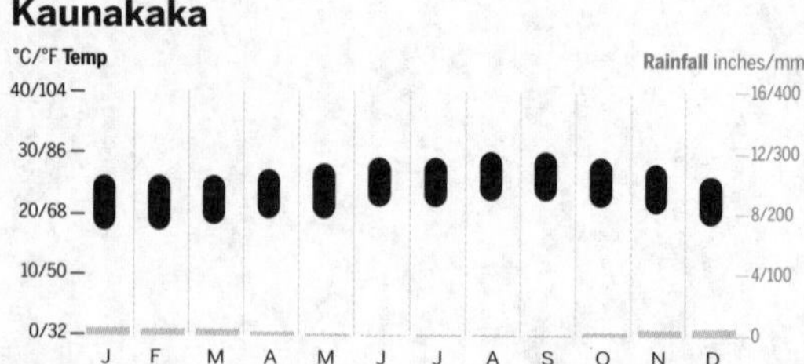

Nov–Mar Rain gear is needed in Kaunakakai and any place east, but it's otherwise balmy.

Apr–Aug Winter rains have stopped and the entire island enjoys breezy tropical comfort.

Sep–Oct Moloka'i enjoys lovely low 80s (°F) daytime temps; conditions a little cooler up high.

Moloka'i Highlights

1. Hear echoes of Hawaii's past while hiking in the pristine and deeply spiritual **Halawa Valley** (p457)
2. Discover underwater delights, or just laze the day away, at **Twenty Mile Beach** (p455)
3. Kick back at a picnic table with a superb plate lunch at **Puko'o** (p455)
4. Follow in the footsteps of America's first saint on the **Kalaupapa Peninsula** (p466)
5. Make friends bust a nut by sending a **Post-a-nut** from Ho'olehua (p464)
6. Kayak past the world's tallest sea cliffs on the remote **Pali Coast** (p458)
7. Get your skin blasted clean on windswept and untrammeled **Papohaku Beach** (p472), on the west coast
8. Relive plantation Hawaii wandering unrefined **Kaunakakai** (p447), the intriguing main town

History

Moloka'i was possibly inhabited by the 7th century. Over the following years it was a vital locale within the Hawaiian Islands and played a key role in local culture. It was known for its warriors, and its chiefs held great sway in the ever-shifting alliances between O'ahu and Maui. Much of the population lived in the east, where regular rainfalls, fertile soil and rich waters ensured abundant food.

Some of the most amazing historical sites in the islands can be found here, including the enormous 'Ili'ili'opae Heiau and the series of fishponds just offshore.

At first European contact in 1786, the population was about 8000, close to today's total. Missionaries turned up in the east in the 1830s. Meanwhile the possibilities of the vast western plains drew the interest of early capitalists and colonists. By the 1900s there were large plantations of sugarcane and pineapples as well as cattle ranches. All the big pineapple players – Libby, Dole and Del Monte – had operations here but had ceased all production by 1990. Given the large local population, relatively few immigrant laborers were brought to Moloka'i, one of the reasons the island population includes such a high proportion (50%) of Native Hawaiians.

Cattle was an important commodity throughout the 20th century. The Moloka'i Ranch owns much of the western third of the island, but changing investors coupled with some unsuccessful dabbles in tourism caused the ranch to shut down in 2008, throwing hundreds out of work.

Tourism plays a minor role in the local economy and, besides small-scale farming, the main employer now is Monsanto, which keeps a low profile at its experimental farms growing genetically modified (GM) seeds.

UNFORGIVING TRESPASSES

Exploring unmarked roads is not advisable. Folks aren't too keen on strangers cruising around on their private turf, and fair enough – trespassing is illegal. On the other hand, if there's a fishpond you want to see, and someone's house is between the road and the water, it's usually easy to strike up a conversation and get permission to cross. If you're lucky they might even share some local lore and history with you, particularly the old-timers.

National, State & County Parks

The stunning Kalaupapa Peninsula, within Kalaupapa National Historical Park, and a tour of the leprosy settlement there are reason enough to visit Moloka'i. Verdant Pala'au State Park has views down to Kalaupapa and a range of attractions, from woodsy hikes to erotic rock formations.

The county's Papohaku Beach Park, which fronts one of Hawaii's longest and best beaches, is incentive enough to make the trek out west.

Camping

Moloka'i's most interesting place to camp, in terms of setting and set-up, is the county's **Papohaku Beach Park** on the untrammeled West End. Camping at the county's One Ali'i Beach Park is not recommended.

County permits (adult/child Monday to Thursday $5/3, Friday to Sunday $8/5) are issued by the **Department of Parks & Recreation** (☎553-3204; www.co.maui.hi.us; 90 Ainoa St, Mitchell Pauole Center, Kaunakakai; ⏰8am-1pm & 2:30am-4pm Mon-Fri), either by phone or in person. Permits are limited to three consecutive days in one park, with a yearly maximum of 15 days.

You can enjoy the views from Pala'au State Park and be ready for an early start on a visit to Kalaupapa from a peaceful **camping area** near the trailhead. For a true wilderness experience, consider the remote camping at Waikolu Lookout (p459). State permits (resident/non-resident $12/18 per campsite per night) are obtained from the **Division of State Parks** (☎587-0300; www.hawaiistateparks.org) via the website. Permits cannot be obtained on Moloka'i.

None of the campgrounds listed are near sources of food or drink. If you forget a piece of camping equipment, Moloka'i Fish & Dive (p443) has supplies.

Activities

Moloka'i has wild ocean waters, rough trails, remote rainforests and the most dramatic oceanside cliffs in Hawaii. It's a perfect destination for adventure – just don't expect to be spoon-fed.

If you're considering action at sea, note that conditions are seasonal. During the summer you'll find waters are calm on the north and west shores, and made rough by the persistent trade winds on the south shore outside of the Pala'au barrier reef. Plan on getting out early, before the winds pick up. Winter storms make waters rough all around the island (outside of the reef, which runs the length of the south side of the island) but, even so, the calm days between winter storms can be the best times to get out on the water.

Moloka'i has plenty of wind – advanced windsurfers can harness it in the Pailolo and Ka'iwi Channels; however, you'll need your own gear.

ACTIVITY	BEST PLACES
Fishing	Penguin Banks (p443)
Kayaking	Northeast Coast (p457)
	South Coast
Scuba Diving	Pala'au Barrier Reef
Snorkeling	Dixie Maru Beach (p473)
	Kawakiu Beach (p470)
	Twenty Mile Beach (p455)
Swimming	Dixie Maru Beach (p473)
	Twenty Mile Beach (p455)
Biking	Island-wide (p449)
Hiking	Halawa Valley (p457)
	Kalaupapa Peninsula (p466)
	Kamakou Preserve (p459)

There are two main activities operators and outfitters who pretty much handle every activity on the island and often work together:

➡ **Moloka'i Fish & Dive** (Map p450; ☎553-5926; www.molokaifishanddive.com; Ala Malama Ave, Kaunakakai; ⏲8am-6pm Mon-Sat, to 2pm Sun)

➡ **Moloka'i Outdoors** (☎877-553-4477, 553-4477; www.molokai-outdoors.com; Hio Pl, Kaunakakai; ⏲hours erratic)

Cycling & Mountain Biking

There are more than 40 miles of trails on Moloka'i that are good for mountain biking: the roads of the thick Moloka'i Forest Reserve (p459) are prime, as are trails on the arid West End, many with ocean views. As for cycling, pretty much all of Moloka'i's paved highways would make for a scenic ride, especially the trip to the Halawa Valley.

Moloka'i Bicycle (p449), located in Kaunakakai, is the best place to go for all things cycling.

Fishing

The sportfishing is excellent in the waters off Moloka'i, especially around the fish-filled Penguin Banks off the southwestern tip. Bait casting is good on the southern and western shores. Boats dock and leave from the Kaunakakai Wharf. Rates run at about $25 per person per hour with various time and passenger minimums (eg six-person, four-hour minimum would be $600). Close to shore expect to find large fish including *'omilu,* a type of trevally. Further out you'll find *a'u* (marlin) and the popular various species of ahi (yellowfin tuna).

Kayaking

Moloka'i Fish & Dive (p443) runs a guided five-hour trip ($70) that paddles the south coast with the wind, finishing with a boat tow back to the dock.

Scuba Diving

Moloka'i's 32-mile Pala'au barrier reef – Hawaii's longest – lies along the south side of the island, promising top-notch snorkeling and excellent diving in uncrowded waters all year long, when conditions allow. Note that in order to reach the good spots you will need a boat.

Check the boat charters, or go with one of the activity operators (from $140, three to four hours).

Whale Watching

Witness the sudden drama of humpback whales breaching from December to April. Moloka'i Fish & Dive (p443), Moloka'i Outdoors (p443) and the boat charter operators all offer trips. Rates start at $70.

 Tours

Tours on Moloka'i mirror the island's personality. Don't expect little buses to take you around with canned commentary and a stop for souvenirs. Rather, local tours concentrate on experiences you wouldn't be able to enjoy on your own, such as a trek up the Halawa Valley, Kalaupapa or the guided tours of the Nature Conservancy's Kamakou Preserve and Mo'omomi Beach.

The two main activity operators offer various tours, including custom drives to pretty much any place on the island.

Much of Moloka'i's coastline is only accessible by boat. The wild beauty of the impenetrable Pali Coast, home to the world's tallest sea cliffs, is unforgettable. The activity operators and boat charters all arrange trips that take the better part of a day, often including a stop for snorkeling, and don't run in the winter, lest storms send you to Gilligan's Island.

Boat charters generally leave from Kaunakakai Wharf and, if you're traveling in a group, can be tailored to your desires. Rates start at about $100 per hour for whole-boat charters, with a four-hour minimum. Try one of these personable outfits:

Alyce C Sportfishing Charters BOAT TOUR, FISHING
(☎558-8377; www.alycecsportfishing.com) Joe Reich has over 30 years of experience and, in addition to sportfishing charters, also does whale-watching jaunts and round-island runs on his 31ft boat.

Fun Hogs Sport Fishing FISHING
(☎567-6789; www.molokaifishing.com) Fish your heart out on the *Ahi,* a 27ft sportfishing boat. Snorkeling and whale watching are also offered. Mike Holmes is a legendary local long-distance canoeist.

Hallelujah Hou Fishing BOAT TOUR, FISHING
(☎336-1870; www.hallelujahhoufishing.com) Captain Clayton Ching runs all types of fishing trips, plus he's a real captain in the sense that he can marry you on ship *or* shore. He also organizes fly-fishing trips.

Walter Naki CULTURAL TOURS, BOAT TOURS
(☎558-8184) Walter Naki, who is also known for his cultural tours and treks, offers deep-sea fishing, whale watching and North Shore tours.

Festivals & Events

If you're planning a visit during the island's culture-rich festivals, make sleeping reservations many months in advance. See www.visitmolokai.com for more details.

Ka Moloka'i Makahiki TRADITIONAL FESTIVAL
(☎553-3673) Moloka'i is the only island still holding the ancient *makahiki* festival. It is celebrated in late January with a traditional ceremony, an Olympics-esque competition of ancient Hawaiian sports, crafts and activities held in Kaunakakai.

Moloka'i Ka Hula Piko HULA
(☎553-3673; www.kahulapiko.com) As Moloka'i is known as the birthplace of hula, its hula festival in early May has some profound roots. It opens with a solemn ceremony at 3am at Pu'u Nana (the site of Hawaii's first hula school), followed by a day-long festival including performance, food and crafts.

St Damien's Feast Day RELIGIOUS FESTIVAL
(☎553-5112) There are various events held in honor of Moloka'i's first saint on his feast day May 10. Plans call for a walk between the churches in the east that he built: St Joseph's (p453) and Our Lady of Seven Sorrows (p454).

Na Wahine O Ke Kai CANOE RACE
(www.nawahineokekai.com) Much the same as the Moloka'i Hoe (see below), but with all-female teams. Best time (2008): five hours, 22 minutes, five seconds. Held in September.

Moloka'i Hoe CANOE RACE
(www.molokaihoe.com) This grueling outrigger canoe race from remote Hale O Lono Point has close to 200 six-person teams paddling

MOLOKA'I SURF BEACHES & BREAKS

What Moloka'i – one of the most breathtaking islands in Hawaii, if not the entire Pacific – possesses in beauty, it lacks in waves. Unfortunately, due to shadowing from the other islands, there just isn't much in the way of consistent surf. Yet when the surf's up, keep in mind that the Friendly Isle encompasses the ideals of 'old Hawaii' in which family remains the priority, so remember to smile a lot and let the locals have the set waves.

On the western end of Moloka'i, winter swells bring surf anywhere between 2ft and 10ft (and, very rarely, 15ft). The break known as **Hale O Lono** (p469) is one such exposed area. It comprises several fun peaks and is the starting point for the annual 32-mile Moloka'i-to-O'ahu outrigger and paddleboard races.

When it's breaking, the stretch from **Rock Point** (p456) to **Halawa Beach** (p458) on the east end and **Kepuhi Beach** (p472) on the West End are reliable spots. Leave Kawakiu Beach's (p470) winter waves to the experts.

Moloka'i Fish & Dive (p443) and **Moloka'i Outdoors** (p443) charge from $25 to $40 per day for surfboard rentals.

MOLOKA'I IN...

Two Days

After checking out **Kaunakakai**, drive the gorgeous 27 miles east to the **Halawa Valley** and hike out to the waterfall. Head down to Puko'o for some lunch and kicking back at **Mana'e Goods & Grindz** and a snorkel at **Twenty Mile Beach**. Wander along to **Kaunakakai** to gather vittles for a dinner under the stars at your rental pad. On your last day let the sure-footed mules give you the ride of your life to the **Kalaupapa Peninsula** and crack open some fun at **Purdy's Macadamia Nut Farm**.

Four Days

After the two days above, spend your third day in the ancient rainforests of **Kamakou Preserve**, followed by the island's best dinner at **Kualapu'u Cookhouse**. On the morning of day four, stop by Kaunakakai and pick up some island books at **Kalele Bookstore**, then head northwest to the culturally significant beaches of **Mo'omomi**, before finding the ultimate souvenirs at Maunaloa's **Big Wind Kite Factory**.

One Week

As above, but add in lots of time to do nothing at all. You're on Moloka'i time.

furiously across the 41-mile Ka'iwi Channel to O'ahu. Best time (2011): four hours, 30 minutes, 54 seconds by the legendary Shell Va'a team. Considered the world championship of men's long-distance outrigger canoe racing. Held in October.

Sleeping

Moloka'i's hotel choices are limited to one, in Kaunakakai. Almost everybody stays in a B&B, cottage, condo or house. Quality ranges from rustic to swank, with the best places having private grounds located right on the ocean. Listings are found throughout this chapter, although the nicest properties are usually in the verdant and coastal east. (With the closure of Moloka'i Ranch, condos in the west can seem desolate.) There are no hostels on the island; camping is limited to state and county parks.

Maui County (which comprises the islands of Maui, Moloka'i, Lana'i and Kaho'olawe) has relaxed the rules somewhat that once made renting private homes complicated or even illegal. Condos have always been in the clear and now private houses in an approved zoning district (hotel, business, historic etc) may be rented. Those that are not in approved districts can operate legally if they have received a conditional permit. The situation on Moloka'i is relaxed and there should be no problems.

Good local sources of rental and accommodation information and reservations include the following:

Friendly Isle Realty ACCOMMODATION SERVICES
(Map p450; ☎800-600-4158, 553-3666; www.molokairesorts.com; 75 Ala Malama Ave, Kaunakakai) Books for more than 70 condos island-wide. Rates average from $550 to $800 per week.

Moloka'i Vacation Properties ACCOMMODATION SERVICES
(☎800-367-2984, 553-8334; www.molokai-vacation-rental.com) Well-respected local agent with houses and condos. The former cost an average of $175 to $300 per night.

Vacation Rentals By Owner WEBSITE
(www.vrbo.com) More than 100 online listings of condos and houses Moloka'i-wide, from $100 to $1500 per night (average $200). An excellent source.

Eating

Foodie sensations have mostly passed by Moloka'i by. But there are glimmers of change here, with a few interesting options (including a great place in Kualapu'u and a fine lunch counter on the way to the Halawa Valley). But your best bet is to cook for yourself – the markets in Kaunakakai are well stocked and Moloka'i has some unique foods.

Getting There & Away

If you have time, taking the ferry from Maui is a more sociable and scenic experience than flying – the afternoon boat catches the sunset

Moloka'i

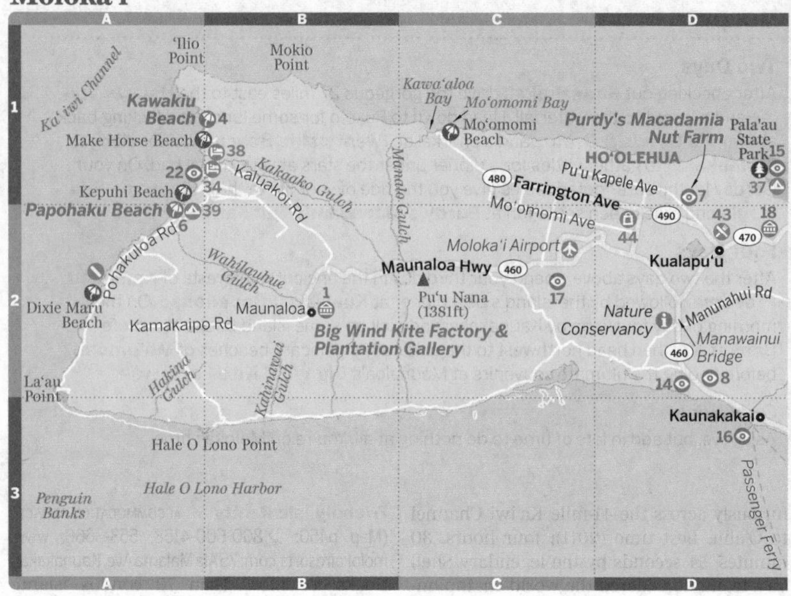

almost year-round, and in winter breaching whales glorify the scene.

AIR

Moloka'i (Ho'olehua) Airport (MKK; ☎567-9660; http://hawaii.gov/mkk; Ho'olehua) is small: you claim your baggage on a long bench. Single-engine planes are the norm; sit right behind the cockpit area for spectacular views forward. Because of weight limits for individual bags (40lb), pack a small duffel bag in case you have to redistribute your belongings.

The main airlines servicing Moloka'i have frequent service to Honolulu plus flights to Kahului on Maui. Unless you have a through ticket from the mainland, it's usually much cheaper to buy from the carriers listed here, rather than their larger airline partners. Hawaiian Airlines has announced plans to start its own Moloka'i service.

Island Air (☎800-652-6541; www.islandair.com) Codeshares with Hawaiian Airlines; flies planes with two, yes two!, engines.

Mokulele Airlines (☎866-260-7070; www.mokuleleairlines.com) Partner with go! airlines.

SEA

Moloka'i Ferry (☎877-500-6284, 667-9266; www.molokaiferry.com; adult/child one way from $70/35) runs a morning and late-afternoon ferry between Lahaina on Maui (across from the Pioneer Inn) and Moloka'i's Kaunakakai Wharf. The 90-minute crossing through the Pailolo Channel (aka Pakalolo Channel for all the pot smuggling) can get choppy; in fact, you can enjoy the thrill of a water park just by sitting on the top deck and getting drenched. Buy tickets online, by phone or on the *Moloka'i Princess* a half-hour before departure. Fares fluctuate with the price of gas.

Getting Around

Renting a car is essential if you intend to fully explore the island or if you are renting a house or condo and will need to shop. All of Moloka'i's highways and primary routes are good, paved roads. The free tourist map, widely available on the island, is good; *Franko's Moloka'i Guide Map* is massively detailed but has out-of-date information even in the current edition. James A Bier's *Map of Moloka'i & Lana'i* has an excellent index. Both fold up small, cost under $6 and are easily found on the island.

TO/FROM THE AIRPORT & FERRY

If you arrive by ferry, you'll likely need to arrange a taxi ($30) to reach the car rental counter (p447) at the airport.

A taxi from the airport costs around $30 to Kaunakakai and $60 to the West End.

One of Moloka'i's trademarks is the sign you see leaving the airport: 'Aloha. Slow down, this is Moloka'i. Mahalo.'

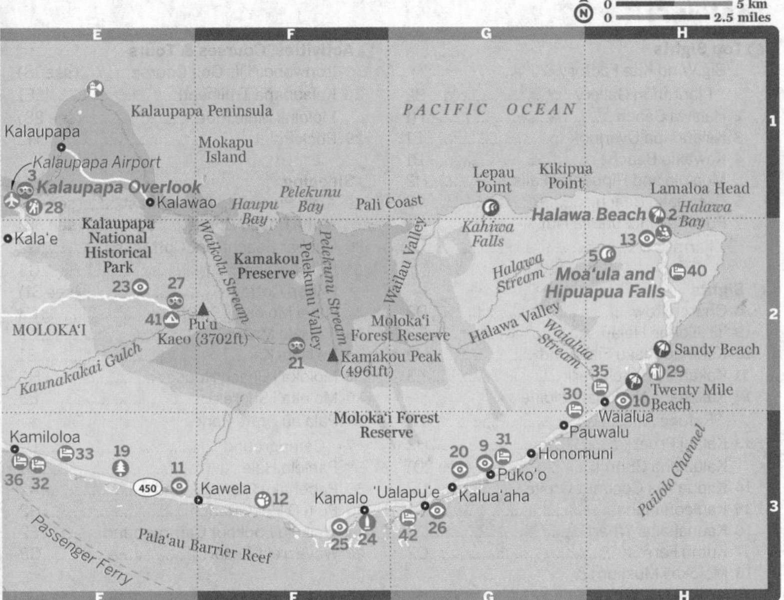

BICYCLE

Moloka'i is a good place for cycling. The local bike shop, Molokai Bicycle (p449) in Kaunakakai, is a treasure.

BUS

MEO Bus (p651), a government economic development service, runs a free shuttle bus around Moloka'i, roughly from 6am to 4pm. From a stop by Misaki's market in Kaunakakai routes go east past the Hotel Moloka'i to Puko'o at mile marker 16 and west to Maunaloa via the airport. The buses run roughly every two hours but it is essential that you confirm all details in advance and with the driver if you are hoping to make a round-trip. Stops are not marked.

CAR

Keep in mind that rental cars are technically not allowed on unpaved roads and there can also be restrictions on camping. If you intend to explore remote parts of the island, such as Mo'omomi Bay, you'll at least need a vehicle with high clearance, probably a 4WD. Book well in advance, especially if planning a weekend visit. But if you're feeling lucky in low season, walk-up rates at the airport can be half that found online.

There are gas stations in Kaunakakai. Expect sticker shock at the pump.

Average driving times and distances from Kaunakakai:

DESTINATION	MILES	TIME
Halawa Valley	27	1¼hr
Ho'olehua Airport	6.5	10min
Kalaupapa Trailhead	10	20min
Maunaloa	17	30min
Papohaku Beach	21.5	45min
Puko'o	16	20min
Twenty Mile Beach	20	40min

Alamo Rental Car (www.alamo.com) The sole operator at the airport. Reserve well in advance.

TAXI

Hele Mai Taxi (☎ 646-9060, 336-0967; www.molokaitaxi.com) Services Moloka'i.

KAUNAKAKAI

POP 2700

View a photo of Moloka'i's main town from 50 years ago and the main drag won't look that much different than it does today. Worn wood-fronted buildings with tin roofs that

Moloka'i

roar in the rain seem like refugees from a Clint Eastwood western. But there's no artifice to Kaunakakai – it's the real deal. All of the island's commercial activities are based here and you'll visit often during your time on the island – if nothing else, for its shops and services.

Walking around the town can occupy a couple of hours if you take time to get into the rhythm of things and do a little exploring. Another popular local T-shirt reads 'Moloka'i Traffic Jam: Two Drivers Stopped in the Middle of the Road Talking Story.' And while there are stop signs, there are no stoplights.

If possible, stop by on Saturday morning when the street market draws crowds.

Sights

Kaunakakai is an attraction in itself. Specifically look for gems of old buildings such as the **Moloka'i Library** (Map p450; Ala Malama Ave; 9:30am-5pm Mon-Fri, Wed noon-8pm), which dates from 1937. **Kaunakakai Wharf** is the busy commercial lifeline for Moloka'i. OK, it's not that busy... A freight barge chugs in, skippers unload catches of mahimahi (white-fleshed fish also called 'dolphin') and a buff gal practices for a canoe race. A roped-off area with a floating dock provides a kiddie swim area. On the west side of the wharf, near the canoe shed, are the stone foundations of oceanfront **Kamehameha V house**, now overgrown. The house was once called 'Malama,' which today is the name of Kaunakakai's main street.

Kapua'iwa Coconut Grove HISTORICAL SITE
(Maunaloa Hwy) As Moloka'i was the favorite island playground of King Kamehameha V, he had the royal 10-acre Kapua'iwa Coconut Grove planted near his sacred bathing pools in the 1860s. Standing tall, about a mile west of downtown, its name means 'mysterious taboo.' Be careful where you walk (or park) when you visit, because coconuts frequently plunge silently to the ground, landing with a deadly thump.

Church Row HISTORICAL SITE
(Maunaloa Hwy) Across from the coconut grove is Church Row. Any denomination that attracts a handful of members receives its own little tract of land. Religion in general is very popular on Moloka'i; there are many churches and some denominations – such as Catholicism – have more than one.

One Ali'i Beach Park PARK
(Maunaloa Hwy) Three miles east of town, One Ali'i Beach Park is split into two parks. One side has a coconut palm–lined shore, a playing field, a picnic pavilion and bathrooms, and although not especially attractive it's very popular with local families for huge weekend BBQs. Two memorials commemorate the 19th-century immigration of Japanese citizens to Hawaii. The other side is a greener and more attractive picnic area. The water is shallow and silty.

Pacifica Hawai'i CRAFT PRODUCER
(553-8484; www.pacificahawaii.com; Kolapa Pl; by appointment) Moloka'i offers a nascent foodie scene. Some noteworthy sea salt is produced close to the center in the front yard of a house belonging to well-known (among salties) salt-maker Nancy Gove. Her Pacifica Hawai'i salt comes in various flavors – ask for a sample of smoked salt.

Free tours (one hour, by appointment) reveal that there are more mysteries to making salt from ocean water than you'd imagine.

Softball & Baseball Fields PARKS
The downtown softball and baseball fields are often the most active spot on the island. For some local flavor, go down there and cheer on the Moloka'i Farmers as they compete against their high-school rivals, the Lana'i Pinelads.

Activities

While activities in Kaunakakai proper are limited, it is *the* place to rent gear or arrange tours for island activities. See the listings for the two main operators, Moloka'i Fish & Dive (p443) and Moloka'i Outdoors (p443).

Moloka'i Bicycle BICYCLE RENTAL
(Map p450; 800-709-2453, 553-3931; www.mauimolokaibicycle.com; 80 Mohala St; 3-6pm Wed, 9am-2pm Sat & by appointment) This shop's owner, Phillip Kikukawa, has a great depth of knowledge about biking across the breadth of the island. He'll do pick-ups and drop-offs outside his opening hours. As well as offering repairs, parts and sales, there is a full range of bike rentals starting at $25/75 per day/week; glam models go for more. Prices include helmet, lock, pump, maps and much more.

Molokai Acupuncture & Massage SPA
(553-3930; www.molokai-wellness.com; 40 Ala Malama Ave, suite 206; prices vary) Popular local place for yoga, massage and acupuncture. Drop-ins accepted.

Sleeping

Few travelers actually stay in Kaunakakai. The best places are further along the scenic east coast near the beaches and ocean.

Ka Hale Mala B&B $
(553-9009; www.molokai-bnb.com; apt $90, incl breakfast $100;) Enjoy the spaciousness of a 900-sq-ft, one-bedroom apartment with a fully equipped kitchen and living room with an exposed-beam ceiling. The two-story house is secluded by lush plantings, including trees laden with low-hanging fruit. The owners add to the bounty with organic vegetables and healthy breakfasts. Rates are for two people; extras (up to two) are $20 each.

It's about 5 miles east of Kaunakakai; the charming owners do airport and ferry pick-ups.

A'ahi Place Bed & Breakfast COTTAGE $
(553-8033; www.molokai.com/aahi; main cabin from $75) This very simple, clean cedar cottage is in a small subdivision, 1 mile east

MOLOKA'I FOR CHILDREN

- Take a free sport kite-flying lesson at the Big Wind Kite Factory (p470)
- Rent a house for running-around room, plus usually a TV, DVD and often games
- Explore under the sea in the calm, shallow waters of Twenty Mile Beach (p455)

Kaunakakai

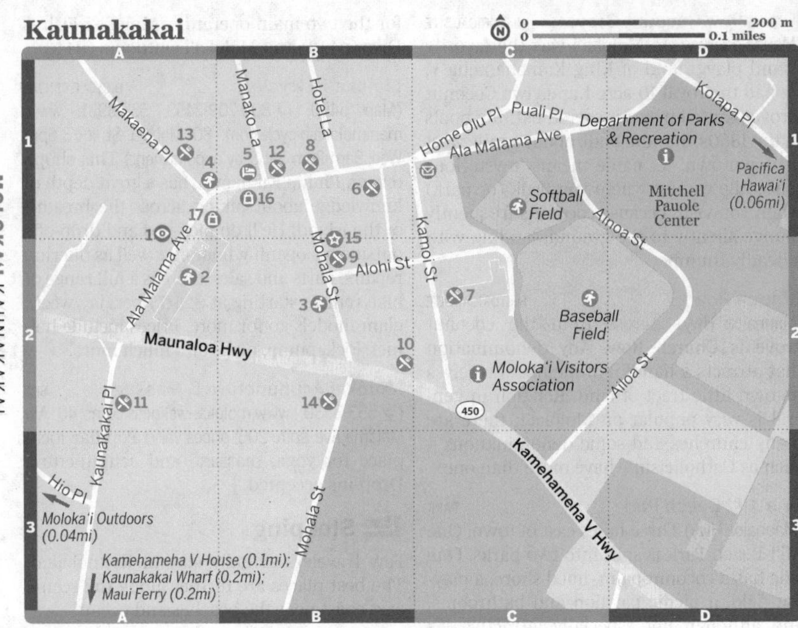

of Kaunakakai. Kind of like a camp cabin (with lots of wood paneling), this place has a kitchen area, washing machine and garden lanai (veranda). More than two people will feel crowded, whether in the bare-bones 'backpackers cabin' ($35) or the somewhat more swank main cabin. Breakfast is $10.

Hotel Moloka'i HOTEL $$$
(800-535-0085, 553-5347; www.hotelmolokai.com; Kamehameha V Hwy; r $150-270;) Moloka'i's only hotel has a certain veteran feel about it and it's not especially alluring. It has quirky rooms with a faux-native design that gives them tunnel-like qualities, and compact grounds with a small pool and hammocks along the reef-protected limpid, silty shore. Upstairs rooms are slightly larger and brighter; some units have fridges and microwaves. It should have a new restaurant later in 2013.

Moloka'i Shores CONDO $$
(553-5954, reservations 800-535-0085; www.castleresorts.com; Kamehameha V Hwy; condos from $185;) This 1970s condo development has units ranging from atrocious to charming, depending on the whims of the individual owners. If you decide to stay here, choose your unit carefully. All have full kitchens, cable TV, lanai (veranda) and ceiling fans.

The grounds are the best feature and have a large pool, shuffleboard, BBQ areas and more. Like elsewhere on this stretch of coast, the water is shallow and muddy.

Eating & Drinking

The Saturday morning market along Ala Malama Ave is a good source for local produce and prepared foods.

Maka's Korner CAFE $
(Map p450; cnr Mohala & Alohi Sts; meals $5-8; 7am-9pm Mon-Fri, to 1pm Sat) A dead-simple corner location belies the fine yet basic fare that hops hot off the grill onto your plate at Maka's. Moloka'i's best burgers come with excellent fries, although many patrons are simply addicted to the teri-beef. Pancakes are served throughout the day and many a long night has been soothed the next day with a fried-egg sandwich. Sit at the counter or at a picnic table outside.

Kanemitsu Bakery BAKERY $
(Map p450; 79 Ala Malama Ave; 5:30am-5pm Wed-Mon) Known for its Moloka'i sweet bread and lavosh crackers (the mac nut ones are extraordinary). Otherwise, you'll be surprised such good stuff can come from such

Kaunakakai

a drab place. Every night but Monday, slip down the alley to the bakery's back door at 8:30pm and buy hot loaves, sliced open and with one of five spreads, from the taciturn baker.

Note: the best stuff is often gone by 1pm each day.

Moloka'i Drive-Inn FAST FOOD $

(Map p450; Kamehameha V Hwy; meals $4-7; 6:30am-9:30pm) Always popular, this timeless fast-food counter is best for classic plate lunches and simple local pleasures like teri-beef sandwiches, omelettes with Spam or Vienna lunch meat, and fried saimin noodles. Serious talking story and gossip entertains while you wait.

Kamo'i Snack-N-Go SWEETS, DESSERTS $

(Map p450; Kamoi St, Moloka'i Professional Bldg; scoops $2; 10am-9pm Mon-Sun) This candy store is loaded with sweets and, more importantly, Honolulu-made Dave's Hawaiian Ice Cream. The banana fudge is truly a treat.

Moloka'i Wines & Spirits MARKET $

(Map p450; Ala Malama Ave; 9am-8pm) Has many Hawaii and mainland microbrews plus inexpensive wines, upscale cheeses and deli items. This is the place to get all you need for silly tropical drinks. Fire up the blender!

Friendly Market SUPERMARKET $

(Map p450; 90 Ala Malama Ave; 8:30am-8:30pm Mon-Fri, to 6:30pm Sat) The best selection of any supermarket on the island. In the afternoon fresh fish from the docks often appears.

Outpost Natural Foods HEALTH FOOD, DELI $

(Map p450; 70 Makaena Pl; 10am-5pm Mon-Thu & Sun, to 4pm Fri;) Organic produce, a selection of packaged and bulk health foods and various local fare sold from a building that might be called a 'shack'. Its deli (meals $5 to $8, open 10am to 3pm weekdays) makes vegetarian burritos, sandwiches, salads and smoothies.

Misaki's MARKET $

(78 Ala Malama Ave; 8:30am-8:30pm Mon-Sat, 9am-noon Sun) The long hours are the key to success at this living museum of grocery retailing.

★ **Paddler's Inn** PUB $$

(Map p450; 10 Mohala St; mains $8-20; 7am-2am) This casual bar with a large outside patio has a long menu that's served until about 9pm. There are few surprises, from the deep-fried pub grub to the burgers, steaks and simple pastas. Service is surprisingly crisp, a quality you may lack after a few runs at the vast cocktail menu.

Moloka'i Pizza Cafe PIZZERIA $$

(Map p450; Kaunakakai Pl; meals $9-15; 10am-10pm Mon-Thu, to 11pm Fri & Sat, 11am-10pm Sun) Order at the counter or have a seat in the unadorned dining area at this pizza joint offering everything from salad and sub sandwiches to burgers and pasta. Divert yourself with a festival of coin-operated games with dubious 'prizes.' Lazy cooks can get their pizza half-baked (it's neither thick, thin, nor even just right) and finish cooking it in their rental unit.

Hula Shores ISLAND CONTEMPORARY $$

(Kamehameha V Hwy, Hotel Moloka'i; bar 4-9pm) You can't beat the oceanfront location of the Hotel Moloka'i's restaurant. After a major fire, the restaurant was due to reopen later in 2013. Although it was the least-casual dining option on the island, its previous incarnation was never noted for its food which was pretty average.

LOCAL KNOWLEDGE

LIVE LIKE A LOCAL

You've probably noticed that most of what there is to do on Moloka'i happens outdoors and often involves group functions. So how do you hook up with the local folks, that is, talk some story and get a feel for local culture? Start by picking up the *Molokai Dispatch* at Kalele Bookstore (p452) in Kaunakakai; it lists events of all kinds, including school benefits, church events and 4-H livestock competitions. Then go buy some crafts, get a taste of some home cooking or cheer on your favorite heifer. Other good sources in Kaunakakai are the bulletin boards outside Friendly Market (p451) and the library. There are inevitably community groups selling goods to raise money along Ala Malama Ave; have a chat with these folk. Ball games at softball and baseball fields are also real community events.

The simple waterfront bar area was untouched by the fire and is a nice place for a sunset drink.

Entertainment

Bring board games, books and a gift for gab as nighttime fun is mostly DIY on Moloka'i.

Paddler's Inn (p451) serves booze until 2am. Friday nights, there is often a live band; otherwise satellite sports prevails.

★Hula Shores HAWAIIAN MUSIC
(Kamehameha V Hwy, Hotel Moloka'i; 4-6pm Fri) The Hotel Moloka'i's simple waterfront bar features local *kapuna* (elders) who gather at a long table to play Hawaiian music on 'Aloha Fridays' from 4pm to 6pm. The music always draws a crowd; the performers range from those with some languid and traditional hula moves to jam sessions with a ukulele.

It's a true community gathering with some of the people who are the heart and soul of local culture and who delight in showing off their traditional talents.

Moloka'i Mini Mart DVD RENTALS
(Map p450; Mohala St; 6am-11pm) DVD rentals for your condo nights.

Shopping

★Kalele Bookstore BOOKS
(Map p450; 567-9094; 64 Ala Malama Ave; 10am-5pm Mon-Fri, 9am-2pm Sat; wi-fi) New and used books, local artworks and loads of local culture and travel advice.

Saturday Morning Market MARKET
(Map p450; Ala Malama Ave; 8am-2pm Sat) This weekly market at the west end of Ala Malama Ave is the place to browse local crafts, try new fruits, stock up on organic produce and pick up some flowers. You'll find much of Moloka'i here before noon.

Moloka'i Art from the Heart ART
(Map p450; 64 Ala Malama Ave; 9:30am-5pm Mon-Fri, 9am-2:30pm Sat) Run by local artists, this small shop is as packed with art as a Jackson Pollock painting is packed with brushstrokes. Works in all mediums can be found here; quality ranges from the earnest to the superb. The T-shirts with local sayings are the real sleepers in the souvenir department.

Information

Bank of Hawai'i (Ala Malama Ave) One of many locations with 24-hour ATMs.

Kalele Bookstore (567-9094; 64 Ala Malama Ave; 10am-5pm Mon-Fri, 9am-2pm Sat; wi-fi) A community treasure. Besides books, get free maps or enjoy a coffee and meet some locals out back on the shady terrace. Owner Teri Waros is a fount of local knowledge.

Molokai Dispatch (www.themolokaidispatch.com) Free weekly published each Thursday; watch the events calendar for local happenings.

Moloka'i Drugs (Kamoi St, Moloka'i Professional Bldg; 9am-5:45pm Mon-Fri, to 2pm Sat) Drugstore fare.

Moloka'i General Hospital (280 Homeolu Pl; 24hr) Emergency services.

Moloka'i Library (Ala Malama Ave; 9:30am-5pm Mon, Tue, Thu & Fri, noon-8pm Wed; wi-fi) Buy a library card for three months ($10) or five years ($25) and enjoy internet use (including wi-fi) and library privileges here and at 50 other branches statewide.

Moloka'i Mini Mart (Mohala St; 6am-11pm) Convenience store with internet access (per min 8¢) plus printing, and espresso in the morning.

Moloka'i Visitor Center (www.visitmolokai.com) A website with excellent links.

Moloka'i Visitors Association (MVA; 800-800-6367, 553-3876; www.molokai-hawaii.com; 2 Kamoi St; 9am-noon Mon-Fri) This simple office can help with information about member businesses.

Post Office (Ala Malama Ave) The one out west is more fun.

Getting There & Around

Kaunakakai is a walking town. **Rawlin's Chevron** (cnr Maunaloa Hwy [Hwy 460] & Ala Malama Ave; 6:30am-8:30pm Mon-Sat, 7am-6pm Sun) has credit card–operated pumps, making it the only round-the-clock gas station on the island.

EAST MOLOKA'I

The oft-quoted road sign 'Slow down, this is Moloka'i' really applies as you head east. Whether you are on the island for a day or a week, the 27-mile drive on Hwy 450 (aka Kamehameha V Hwy) from Kaunakakai to the Halawa Valley is simply a must.

Unlike the arid west, this is tropical Moloka'i, with palm trees arching over the road, and banana, papaya, guava and passion fruits hanging from the lush foliage, ripe for the picking. As you drive you'll catch glimpses of ancient fishponds, the neighboring islands of Lana'i and Maui, stoic old wooden churches, modest family homes, beaches and much more. But don't take your eye off the road for long or you'll run over a dog sleeping on the yellow line.

This being Moloka'i, the intoxicating drive is rarely crowded and cars tend to mosey. Of course for the final third, when the smoothly paved road narrows down to one sinuous lane, you have little choice but to slow down. But that's just as well, as each curve yields a new vista. The final climb up and over into the remote Halawa Valley is breathtaking.

On the practical side, bring gear so you can swim and snorkel at beaches that catch your fancy along the way. There's no gas east of Kaunakakai but there is an excellent small grocery and lunch counter about halfway, in Puko'o. Most of the choicest rentals are also found along this drive. Mile markers simplify finding things.

Kawela

Kakahaia Beach Park is a grassy strip wedged between the road and sea in Kawela, shortly before the 6-mile marker. It has a couple of picnic tables and is always popular for that high point in the locals' weekend calendar: the family picnic. This park is the only part of the **Kakahai'a National Wildlife Refuge** (www.fws.gov/kakahaia) that is open to the public. Most of the 20-acre refuge is inland from the road. It includes freshwater marshland, with a dense growth of bulrushes and an inland freshwater fishpond that has been expanded to provide a home for endangered birds, including the Hawaiian stilt and coot. Look for the nene, the goose-like Hawaiian state bird.

Kamalo

You can't help but be swept away by the quaint charm of little **St Joseph's Church**. It's one of only two still standing of the four island churches that missionary and saint Father Damien built outside of the Kalaupapa Peninsula. (The other, Our Lady of Seven Sorrows, is 4 miles further on). This simple, one-room wooden church, dating from 1876, has a steeple and a bell, five rows of pews and some of the original wavy glass panes. There is also a lei-draped statue of Father Damien and a little cemetery beside the church. It is just past mile marker 10, where the road – like the snakes St Patrick chased out of Ireland – becomes sinuous.

Just over three-quarters of a mile after mile marker 11, a small sign on the *makai* (seaward) side of the road notes the **Smith-Bronte Landing**, the site where pilot Ernest Smith and navigator Emory Bronte safely crash-landed their plane at the completion of the world's first civilian flight from the US mainland to Hawaii. The pair left California on July 14, 1927, destined for O'ahu and came down on Moloka'i 25 hours and two minutes later. A little memorial plaque is set among the kiawe trees and grasses.

WHAT FRIENDLY MEANS LOCALLY

In a cynical world, people don't realize that Moloka'i's moniker, 'the friendly isle,' is exactly right. There are the waves you get as you explore the uncrowded corners, and the advice about which fresh fish is best when you're buying food for your holiday rental. More importantly, you'll start to slow your pace and understand that 'friendly' locally means slowing waaay down and taking your sense of rhythm from others. Don't expect smiles that come your way first, but do expect your smiles to be returned.

FISHPONDS

Starting just east of Kaunakakai and continuing past mile marker 20 are dozens of *loko i'a* (fishponds), huge circular walls of rocks that are part of one of the world's most advanced forms of aquaculture. Monumental in size, backbreaking in creation, the fishponds operate on a simple principle: little fish swim in, big fish can't swim out. Some of the ponds are obscured and overgrown by mangroves, but others have been restored by locals anxious to preserve this link to their past. The **Kahinapohaku Fishpond**, about half a mile past mile marker 19, is in excellent shape and is tended to by *konohiki* (caretakers) who live simply on site. Another good one is at mile marker 13 in 'Ualapu'e (see below).

'Ualapu'e

A half-mile beyond Wavecrest Resort condo development, at the 13-mile marker, you'll spot **'Ualapu'e Fishpond** on the *makai* side of the road. This fishpond has been restored and restocked with mullet and milkfish, two species that were raised here in ancient times. It's a good place to ponder the labor involved in moving these thousands of large volcanic rocks.

With a striking view of green mountains rising up behind as well as the ocean lapping gently out front, the **Wavecrest Resort** (www.wavecrestaoao.com; per day/week 1br from $100/600, 2br from $150/800;) is just around the bend on a small drive in from the main road. This place is about as low-key as its host island. There is no beach, but the views are sweeping. Each unit is rented (and decorated) by the owner. Find links via agents and websites. All units have full kitchen, sofa bed, lanai or balcony, and use of the tennis court. Some have internet access.

Kalua'aha

The barely perceptible village of Kalua'aha is less than 2 miles past Wavecrest. The ruins of **Kalua'aha Church**, Moloka'i's first Christian church, are a bit off the road and inland but just visible, if you keep an eye peeled. It was built in 1844 by Moloka'i's first missionary, Harvey R Hitchcock. **Our Lady of Seven Sorrows** (service 7am Sun) is found a quarter of a mile past the Kalua'aha Church site. The present Our Lady of Sorrows is a reconstruction from 1966 of the original wood-frame church, constructed in 1874 by the missionary Father Damien.

'Ili'ili'opae Heiau

Where's Unesco when you need it? **'Ili'ili-'opae** (off Hwy 450; car) is Moloka'i's biggest heiau and is thought to be the second largest in Hawaii. It also might possibly be the oldest religious site in the state. Yet this remarkable treasure is barely known, even by many locals.

The dimensions are astonishing: over 300ft long and 100ft wide, and about 22ft high on the eastern side, and 11ft high at the other end. The main platform is strikingly level. Archaeologists believe the original heiau may have been three times its current size, reaching out beyond Mapulehu Stream. Like the fishponds, this heiau represents an extraordinary amount of labor by people with no real tools at their disposal.

Once a *luakini* (temple of human sacrifice), 'Ili'ili'opae is today silent except for the singing of birds. African tulip and mango trees line the trail to the site, a peaceful place filled with mana (spiritual essence), whose stones still seem to emanate vibrations of a mystical past. Remember: it's disrespectful to walk across the top of the heiau.

Visiting this heiau is a little tricky, since it's on private property. Park on the highway (to avoid upsetting the neighbors) or, better yet, up the road near the market and walk back along the main road (about half a mile).

The trail is on the *mauka* (inland) side of the highway, just over half a mile past mile marker 15, immediately after Mapulehu Bridge. Look for the gated dirt track into the trees and a fire hydrant.

Walk up this dirt track off the main road, pass the roundabout around a patch of trees and continue up the rocky road. Soon after, you'll see a trail on the left-hand side, opposite a house, that will take you across a streambed. Head to the steps on the northern side of the heiau.

For more info about crossing the property, call the owner Pearl Hodgins on 336-0378. Alternatively, ask Mischi at **Molokai**

Acupuncture and Massage (p449) for permission, as they have property at the base of Heiau. Talk to either and you are good to go; both are very nice.

Puko'o

Puko'o was once the seat of local government (complete with a courthouse, jail, wharf and post office), but the center of island life shifted to Kaunakakai when the plantation folks built that more centrally located town. Nowadays, Puko'o is a sleepy, slow-paced gathering of a few structures just sitting on a bend on the road (near 'Ili'ili'opae Heiau). But it has some nice surprises in store, such as the cozy **beach** accessible just before the store, near mile marker 16. Take the short, curving path around the small bay, where fish leap out of the water, and you'll come to an inviting stretch of sand with swimmable waters, backed by stands of kiawe and ironwood trees.

Sleeping & Eating

Hilltop Cottage COTTAGE **$$**
(☎357-0139; www.molokaihilltopcottage.com; Kamehameha V Hwy; per night $110-160; @) Instead of sleeping down near the water, put your head in the clouds here. The wraparound lanai is almost as big as the living space and you can savor the views of the neighbor islands by day or the millions of stars (which would be drowned out by light in cities and suburbs) by night.

There's one nicely furnished bedroom, a full kitchen, laundry facilities and a two-night minimum stay.

★**Hale Lei Lani** HOUSE **$$$**
(☎415-457-3037, 415-218-3037; www.tranquilmolokai.com; off Kamehameha V Hwy; $240-325 per night;) The Moloka'i estate you wish you had if you hadn't put all that money in Icelandic banks. Perched partway up a hill near mile marker 16 (and more importantly, Mana'e Goods & Grindz), this contemporary home has sweeping views out to Maui and beyond. Two large bedrooms open off a great room and a kitchen that will inspire you to cook on your holiday.

A walled pool is outside the door and fruit trees drop their bounty in the gardens. There is also a slightly smaller two-bedroom guesthouse available.

★**Mana'e Goods & Grindz** HAWAIIAN **$**
(Kamehameha V Hwy [Hwy 450], MM 16; meals $5-12; kitchen 7am-4pm daily, store 7am-6pm Mon-Fri, to 4pm Sat & Sun;) Even if it wasn't your only option, you'd still want to stop here. The plate lunches are something of a local legend: tender yet crispy chicken katsu (deep-fried fillets), specials such as pork stew, and standards such as excellent teriyaki burgers and fresh fish sandwiches. Sauces are homemade, the potato salad is superb and the mac salad is simply the island's best (it's not too gloopy).

Picnic tables are shaded by trees and there's a little garden. The store manages to pack an amazing amount of groceries, goods and a few DVDs into a small space. The bit of Hwy 450 between the entrance and exit to the parking area is easily the least-used stretch.

Waialua

Waialua is a little roadside community found after a few bends along the increasingly rugged coast, just past the 19-mile marker. The attractive **Waialua Congregational Church** was built of stone in 1855. Onward north from there, the road is wafer-thin, winding its way along an undulating coast that's forlorn, mysterious and fronted by white-flecked turquoise surf. The well-tended **Kahinapohaku Fishpond** (see opposite) is a half-mile past mile marker 19.

There are few prizes for guessing what mile marker is found at **Twenty Mile Beach**, although its alias, Murphy's Beach, might keep you guessing. Well protected by a reef, the curve of fine sand fronts a large lagoon that is great for snorkeling. Near shore there

YOGA RETREAT

Sacred Waters (☎558-8225; www.molokai.com/yoga) offers intimate monthly Ashtanga Vinyasa yoga retreats, run by Karen Noble, on a lush property situated in Honomuni, East Moloka'i. There are weekly classes as well as private retreats, which feature accommodation in simple screened huts, and vegetarian foods. Jump right into the ocean after finishing class in the open-air pavilion. All-inclusive prices for a week (including mud baths and other delights) are $1260.

are rocks and the water can be very shallow, but work your way out and you'll be rewarded with schools of fish, living sponges, octopuses and much more.

The pointy clutch of rocks sticking out as the road swings left before mile marker 21 is called **Rock Point** (aka Pohakuloa Point). This popular surf spot is the site of local competitions and it's the place to go if you're looking for east-end breaks. The recent burst of creativity in place names extends to the fine little swimming cove about 500yd beyond mile marker 21: **Sandy Beach**. Look for a taro farm back in a verdant notch in the coast near here.

Sleeping

Some of Moloka'i's more popular rental houses are here. All offer your own little stretch of reef-protected beach, lots of privacy and nighttime views of the resorts, shops and traffic jams of Ka'anapali (Maui) flickering across the Pailolo Channel.

Dunbar Beachfront Cottages COTTAGE **$$**
(☎800-673-0520, 558-8153; www.molokai-beachfront-cottages.com; Kamehameha V Hwy; 2br cottages from $190; 📶) The layout and furnishings are tidy and functional at these two vacation cottages near the 18-mile marker. Each cottage sleeps four people and comes with a fully equipped kitchen, TV, ceiling fans, laundry, lanai and BBQ grills. The Pu'unana unit sits on stilts, while Pauwalu is more grounded. Both have good views and a three-night minimum.

Moloka'i Beach House HOUSE **$$**
(☎888-575-9400, 261-2500; www.molokaibeachhouse.com; Kamehameha V Hwy; per day/week $250/1600; 📶) Like most of the houses in the east, this simple wooden affair holds a few surprises. Rooms follow one after another until you realize you've got three bedrooms and a huge living/family room. It's not posh but it's very relaxed. There's cable, plus the usual DVD, BBQ etc. The grassy yard backs up to a narrow palm-shaded beach.

Aloha Beach House HOUSE **$$$**
(☎888-828-1008, 828-1100; www.molokaivacation.com; Kamehameha V Hwy; per day/week from $290/2030; @) This modern house built in traditional plantation style has a breezeway linking the two bedrooms. The excellent kitchen flows into the living room, which flows out onto the large covered porch, which flows out onto the lawn and the beach and... There's high-speed internet and lots of beach toys. It's just past mile marker 19, near the church and close to Moloka'i Beach House.

Waialua to Halawa

After mile marker 22 the Kamehameha V Hwy starts to wind upwards. It's a good paved road, albeit narrow. Take it slow and watch for other cars coming around the cliff-hugging corners; there's always a place to pull over so cars can pass.

The terrain is rockier and less verdant here than over the preceding miles. The road levels out just before mile marker 24, where there's a view of the spiky islet of **Mokuho'oniki**, a seabird sanctuary and natural photo spot. If you hear a boom, it's a hapless gull setting off one of the shells left over from WWII target practice.

As you crest the hill, the fenced grassland is part of **Pu'u O Hoku Ranch** (☎558-8109; www.puuohoku.com; 2br cottage $225, 4br house $300; 🏊), which at 14,000 acres is Moloka'i's second-largest ranch. Founded by Paul Fagan of Hana, the name means 'where hills and stars meet.' Guests who stay here can enjoy views across the Pacific, and absolute isolation. A lodge that can sleep you and 21 of your closest friends is available for $165 each per night. (Also, a one-bedroom cottage by 20 Mile Beach is available for $200 per night.)

The ranch is also a certified **organic farm** growing tropical fruits and *'awa* (kava, a native plant used to make an intoxicating drink). If you are staying in one of the east Moloka'i rentals, they will drop off a 10lb box of organic fruits and vegetables ($25) on their way to town on Thursdays; otherwise goods from the ranch can be found at Kaunakakai's Saturday morning market (p452). A small **store** (⏲9am-4pm Mon-Fri) along the road has snacks, drinks, some of the ranch's fine produce and a few locally made gifts.

A hidden grove of sacred *kukui* (candlenut trees) on the ranch property marks the grave of the prophet Lanikaula, a revered 16th-century kahuna (priest, healer). One of the reasons the battling armies of Maui and O'ahu steered clear of Moloka'i for centuries was the powerful reputations of such kahuna, who were said to have been able to pray their enemies to death. Many islanders claim to have seen the night lanterns

DON'T MISS

LOCAL TREATS

Fruit trees grow in profusion in the east end of Moloka'i; if you're lucky you'll have plenty to pick from your rental. Organic farms are sprouting as well and you'll find their produce at Kaunakakai's Saturday morning market (p452) and Outpost Natural Foods (p451). Other local foods to look for include the following:

- **Macadamia nuts** from Purdy's farm (p465) Probably the best you'll have anywhere
- **Coffee** from Coffees of Hawaii (p463) Mostly grown and roasted on the island
- **Macadamia nut pesto** from Kumu Farms (p465) Buy it at the farm shop; superb and bursting with basil goodness
- **Lavosh crackers** from Kanemitsu Bakery (p450) The macadamia nut and taro varieties are crunchy and delicious
- **Sea salt** from Pacifica Hawai'i (p449)

of ghost marchers bobbing along near the grove.

Past mile marker 25, the jungle closes in and the scent of eucalyptus fills the air. About 1.25 miles further on, you round a corner and the fantastic panorama of the Halawa Valley sweeps into view. Stop and enjoy the view for a bit. Depending on recent rains, the Moa'ula and Hipuapua Falls will either be thin strands or gushing white torrents back up the valley. In winter, look across the swirl of waves and volcanic sand below for the spectacle of whales breaching.

The recently paved road descends into the valley at a steep but manageable rate. Cyclists will love the entire ride, with the exception of having to stay alert for errant drivers in rental cars mesmerized by the views.

Halawa Valley

Halawa Valley enjoys end-of-the-road isolation, which residents guard jealously, and stunningly gorgeous scenery. It was an important settlement in precontact Moloka'i, with a population of more than 1000 and a complex irrigation system watering more than 700 taro patches. Little remains of its three heiau sites, two of which are thought to have been *luakini,* but you'll probably still feel the charge down here.

As late as the mid-19th century, the fertile valley still had a population of about 500 and produced most of Moloka'i's taro, as well as many of its melons, gourds and fruits. However, taro production came to an abrupt end in 1946, when a massive tsunami swept up the Halawa Valley, wiping out the farms and much of the community. A second tsunami washed the valley clean in 1957. Only a few families now remain.

Sights & Activities

Sunday services are still occasionally held in Hawaiian at the saintly little 1948 green-and-white **church**, where visitors are welcome anytime (the door remains open).

The northeastern shore, sheltered by the reef, is good for kayaking. At the very tip, Halawa Beach is a good launching point when seas are calm. In the summer, expert paddlers can venture around to the northern shore to witness the grandeur of the world's tallest sea cliffs. Note that the rental-car company does not allow kayaks to be carried atop their vehicles and you'll have to hunt for a source of kayaks locally. Many places stopped renting them after people kept getting into trouble trying to paddle to Lana'i.

★ Moa'ula and Hipuapua Falls WATERFALL

The hike and spectacle of the 250ft, twin Moa'ula and Hipuapua Falls, which cascade down the back of the lush Halawa Valley, are a highlight of many people's Moloka'i visit. They are reached via a straightforward 2-mile trail lined with historical sites. To protect these sites, and because the trail crosses private property, visiting the falls requires a hike with a local guide.

The $80-per-person fee includes a wealth of cultural knowledge; walks can easily take three to five hours. Prepare for muddy conditions and wear stout shoes so you can navigate over river boulders. Some of the river crossings may be especially perilous.

Organize a guide with Moloka'i Fish & Dive (p443) or Kalele Bookstore (p452) in

Kaunakakai. Prepare for voracious mosquitoes, bring water and a lunch and have plenty of sunscreen. Most people thrill to a bracing plunge into the pools at the bottom of the falls.

You'll pass through lush tropical foliage during the walk. Look for the bright orange blossoms of African tulip trees and the brilliant green of beach heliotrope trees. Among the sights are a **burial ground** that may date to 650 AD and a **seven-tiered stone temple**.

★Halawa Beach BEACH

Halawa Beach was a favored surfing spot for Moloka'i chiefs and remains so today for local kids, although often you won't see a soul. The beach has double coves separated by a rocky outcrop, with the north side a bit more protected than the south.

When the water is calm, there's good swimming and folks launch sea kayaks here, but both coves are subject to dangerous rip currents when the surf is heavy.

Up from the beach, Halawa Beach Park has picnic pavilions, restrooms and nondrinkable running water. Throughout the valley, there's an eerie feel that you can't quite shake, as if the generations that came before aren't sure what to make of it all. Some locals aren't entirely welcoming of visitors.

Kalani Pruet FARM

(☎336-1149; www.molokaiflowers.com) Pruet runs a flower farm, offers waterfall hikes and makes a mean smoothie from fruit he gathers at this lush and colorful spread of land.

Pali Coast

The world's tallest sea *pali* (cliffs) rise from the Pacific along an awe-inspiring 14-mile stretch of the Moloka'i coast from the Kalaupapa Peninsula east almost to Halawa Beach. The average drop of these sheer cliffs is 2000ft, with some reaching 3300ft. And these intimidating walls are not monolithic; vast valleys roaring with waterfalls cleave the dark rock faces. It's Moloka'i's most dramatic sight and also the most difficult one to see.

From land you can get an idea of the drama in the valleys from the remote Waikolu Lookout (p459) and the Pelekunu Valley Overlook (p462) in the Kamakou area.

But to really appreciate the cliffs, you won't want to settle for the backsides. From the Pacific you can get a full appreciation of their height. You can organize a boat trip or really earn your adventure cred by paddling yourself here in a kayak. In summer, when conditions allow, you can leave from Halawa Beach, but this is only for expert kayakers and will require a few days plus camping on isolated stone beaches. You can get advice from Moloka'i Fish & Dive (p443).

A visit to Kalaupapa Peninsula also gives you an idea of the spectacle. Or you can appreciate the drama of the cliffs from the air. Many of Maui's helicopter tours include Moloka'i's Pali Coast and some will do pickups on Moloka'i. Moloka'i Fish & Dive offers packages from $160 per person.

CENTRAL MOLOKA'I

Central Moloka'i is really two places. In the west there's the dry and gently rolling Ho'olehua Plains, which stretch from the remote and rare sand dunes of Mo'omomi Beach to the former plantation town and current coffee-growing center of Kualapu'u. To the east, the terrain rises sharply to the misty, ancient forests of Kamakou. Enjoy one of the island's great adventures here by going on a hike that takes you back in evolutionary time.

Moloka'i's second most popular drive (after the Halawa Valley drive in the east) runs from Kualapu'u (with its superb little cafe) up Hwy 470 to Pala'au State Park, site of the Kalaupapa Overlook (p464), where you'll find one of the island's most captivating views.

Kamakou Area

The best reason to rent a 4WD vehicle on Moloka'i is to thrill to the views from the Waikolu Lookout before discovering the verdant mysteries of the Nature Conservancy's Kamakou Preserve, where you'll find the island's highest peaks. Exploring this secret side of Moloka'i is pure adventure. Besides gazing down into two deep valleys on the island's stunning and impenetrable north coast, you'll explore a near-pristine rainforest that is home to more than 250 native plants (more than 200 endemic) and some of Hawaii's rarest birds. Although you can't quite reach the island's highest point, Kamakou Peak (4961ft), you'll still get your head in the clouds.

GETTING THE GOAT & SAVING THE REEF

Nonnative feral goats, pigs and deer have run amok in the highlands of Moloka'i and are voraciously chewing their way through the foliage. This has led to deforestation and greatly increased the runoff from the frequent rains. These flows of mud slop down to the south coast along the east end of Moloka'i, choking the Pala'au barrier reef, which in parts is massively degraded. Some of the old fishponds have been filling with silt at the rate of a foot per year. Talk about Indonesian butterflies and chaos theory! A goat eats a shrub on a remote Moloka'i peak and coral dies off the coast.

Locals have been encouraged to hunt the critters, especially the feral pigs, which often star at family BBQs. Still, amateur efforts are not enough and the Nature Conservancy has ferried hunters by helicopter to remote parts of the mountains.

Orientation

The turnoff for the Kamakou Area is between mile markers 3 and 4 on Hwy 460, immediately south of the Manawainui Bridge. The paved turnoff is marked with a sign for the Homelani Cemetery. The pavement quickly ends and the road deteriorates into 4WD-only conditions.

About 5.5 miles from Hwy 460 and well past the cemetery, you'll cross into the Moloka'i Forest Reserve. After a further 1.5 miles, there's an old water tank and reservoir off to the left. Another 2 miles brings you to the Sandalwood Pit, and 1 mile past that to Waikolu Lookout and the boundary of the Kamakou Preserve.

Moloka'i Forest Reserve

As you climb and enter the Moloka'i Forest Reserve, the landscape starts off shrubby and dusty but then becomes filled with dark, fragrant woods of tall eucalyptus, with patches of cypress and Norfolk pines. Don't bother heading down the roads branching off Maunahui Rd, as the scenery will be exactly the same. Although there's no evidence of it from the road, the Kalamaula area (an old name for this general area) was once heavily settled. It was here that Kamehameha the Great (Kamehameha I) knocked out his two front teeth in grieving the death of a female high chief whom he had come to visit. Local lore says that women once traveled up here to bury their afterbirth in order to ensure that their offspring reached great heights.

Sights

Lua Na Moku 'Iliahi HISTORICAL SITE

A grassy depression on the left side of the road marks the centuries-old Lua Na Moku 'Iliahi (Sandalwood Pit). In the early 19th century, shortly after the lucrative sandalwood trade began, the pit was hand-dug to the exact measurements of a 100ft-long, 40ft-wide and 7ft-deep ship's hold, and filled with fragrant sandalwood logs cleared from the nearby forest.

The *ali'i* (royalty) forced the *maka'ainana* (commoners) to abandon their crops and work the forest. When the pit was full, the wood was strapped onto the backs of the laborers, who hauled it down to the harbor for shipment to China. After all the mature trees were cut down, the *maka'ainana* pulled up every new sapling, sparing their children the misery of forced harvesting.

Waikolu Lookout LOOKOUT

At 3600ft, Waikolu Lookout provides a breathtaking view into the steep Waikolu Valley and out to the ocean beyond. After rains, the white strands of numerous waterfalls accent the sheer cliffs and fill the valley with a dull roar. Morning is best for clear views, but if it's foggy, have a snack at the picnic bench and see if it clears.

The wide, grassy **Waikolu Lookout campground** is directly opposite the lookout. If you can bear the mist and cold winds that sometimes blow up from the canyon, this could make a base camp for hikes into the preserve. The site has a picnic pavilion. Bring water. No open fires are allowed and state camping permits are required.

Kamakou Preserve

Since 1982, the Nature Conservancy has managed the Kamakou Preserve, which includes cloud forest, bogs, shrub land and habitat for many endangered plants and animals. Its 2774 acres of native ecosystems start immediately beyond the Waikolu Lookout and feature over 230 native plant species.

Moloka'i

Fully half of this elongated island's population claim at least some Hawaiian ancestry and that's just part of a local pride that eschews the commercialism that drives the other islands. Sacred valleys, a stunner of a national park and tidy rental beach houses are some of the un-glitzy lures.

2

WALTER BIBIKOW / GETTY IMAGES ©

4

JOHN ELK / GETTY IMAGES ©

1. Pali Coast (p458)
Moloka'i's spectacular north coast features the world's highest sea cliffs.

2. Kalaupapa Beach (p467)
A mule ride will get you to this unspoiled beach and a crucial part of the island's history.

3. Pepe'opae Trail (p462)
Take a hike back through three million years of plant evolution on this trail through a primeval forest.

4. St Joseph's Church (p453)
This simple church was built by Father Damien, who would become the USA's first saint.

3

JONATHAN KINGSTON / GETTY IMAGES ©

Much of the preserve is forested with *'ohi'a lehua*, a native tree with fluffy red blossoms, whose nectar is favored by native birds. It is home to the *'apapane* (bright-red Hawaiian honeycreeper), *'amakihi* (yellow-green honeyeater) and pueo (Hawaiian owl). Other treasures include tree ferns, native orchids and silvery lilies.

Sights & Activities

Pepe'opae Trail HIKING

The hike back through three million years of evolution on the Pepe'opae Trail is the star attraction of the Kamakou area. The trail ends at the **Pelekunu Valley Overlook**, where you'll enjoy a valley view of fantastic depth and, if it's not foggy, the ocean beyond.

You'll pass the **Pepe'opae Bog**, a Hawaiian montane bog that's a miniature primeval forest of stunted trees, dwarfed plants and lichens that feels like it's from the dawn of time. This bog receives about 180in of rain each year, making it one of the wettest regions in the Hawaii Islands.

Almost the entire 1.5-mile-long trail is along an extremely narrow uphill boardwalk that feels at times like tightrope walking. It is covered with a coarse metal grating to prevent hikers from slipping, but you should still wear shoes with a good grip. At one point a trail seems to branch off to the left but ignore this and stay on the metal mesh.

To reach the Pepe'opae Trail from Waikolu Lookout, you walk along a crude 2.2-mile-long access road that is not passable by any vehicles.

Visitors should sign in and out at the preserve's entrance. Look for entries in the logbook from others on everything from car breakdowns to trail conditions and bird sightings. Posted notices announce if any part of the preserve is closed. Bring rain gear, as the trails in Kamakou can be wet and muddy.

Tours

Excellent monthly Saturday hikes with the **Nature Conservancy** (☎553-5236; www.nature.org/hawaii; donation requested) explore the preserve's history and ecology. The hikes have an eight-person maximum and tend to book up several months in advance.

Local tour guide Walter Naki (p444) leads custom hikes in the lush areas outside the preserve.

Getting There & Away

Check driving and hiking conditions with the **Nature Conservancy** (☎553-5236; www.nature.org/hawaii; 23 Pueo Pl, Moloka'i Industrial Park, Kualapu'u; ⌚9am-3pm Mon-Fri). The office has maps and a wealth of good information.

Kamakou is protected in its wilderness state in part because the rutted dirt road leading in makes it hell to reach. A 4WD vehicle is obliga-

LOCAL KNOWLEDGE

AUNTIE JULIA HOE

Local *kupuna* (elder) who sings and dances a much-lauded version of hula.

You're famous for?

I sing every Sunday at Coffees of Hawaii (p463) with a local group of home-spun musicians, fondly known as Na Ohana Hoaloha (Family of Friends). Visitors get to realize that our entertainers are sharing just as much as performing, and this is the key to connecting with the culture of Moloka'i.

What to do first?

Visitors need to take note of the airport welcome sign that encourages them to slow down; right there they should know that they are in a special place. Then they can approach their stay here with an open heart and mind. Greet all that they meet with a smile; doesn't matter if you don't know a person, it is what you give off that is important.

On sharing

Most locals will generously share their aloha with any who come with a true desire to understand the Hawaiian culture, to learn more about living in harmony with nature and with respect for what they find. Return the favor with a sense of gratitude and aloha. We love our island, our way of life, our Hawaiian heritage and culture and we are passionate about protecting it.

tory and even then the narrow, rutted track with its sheer edges and tendency to turn into a bog after rains is a challenge.

The 10 miles from Hwy 460 to Waikolu Lookout takes about an hour to drive. Skilled mountain bikers will enjoy the trip.

Kualapu'u

Kualapu'u is the name of both a 1017ft hill and a nearby village. In a fact that only a booster could love, the world's largest rubber-lined reservoir lies at the base of the hill. Its 1.4 billion gallons of water are piped in from the rainforests of eastern Moloka'i and it is the only source of water for the Ho'olehua Plains and the dry West End. Operations were threatened when its owner, the Moloka'i Ranch, ceased operations in 2008.

In the 1930s the headquarters of the Del Monte pineapple plantation were located here and a company town grew. Pineapples ruled for nearly 50 years, until Del Monte pulled out of Moloka'i in 1982 and the economy crumbled.

While farm equipment rusted in overgrown pineapple fields, small-scale farming developed: watermelons, dryland taro, macadamia nuts, sweet potatoes, seed corn, string beans and onions. The soil is so rich here, some feel Moloka'i has the potential to be Hawaii's 'breadbasket.' In 1991 coffee saplings were planted on formerly fallow pineapple fields and now cover some 600 acres.

Eating & Drinking

★ Kualapu'u Cookhouse HAWAIIAN $$
(Hwy 490; meals $5-25; ⏲8am-8pm Tue-Sat, 9am-2pm Sun, 8am-4pm Mon) Once called the Kamuela Cookhouse, this old roadhouse serves the island's best food. A recent revamp has put a little flair in the traditional charm, but pretension remains off the menu. When your plate lunch of the best and tenderest teriyaki beef you've ever had appears, you'll be hooked.

Breakfasts here are huge and feature the most perfect omelettes you're ever likely to come across. Panko-crusted Monte Cristo sandwiches join the plate lunch brigade, while at dinner inventive fare like ahi in a lime cilantro sauce or lusciously juicy prime rib star. At night locals sometimes serenade with Hawaiian music. Beer and wine can be purchased at the grocery directly across the street.

Coffees of Hawaii CAFE, SHOP
(www.coffeesofhawaii.com; cnr Hwys 470 & 490; snacks from $2; ⏲10am-4pm Mon-Sat, 1-5pm Sun) Coffees of Hawaii grows and roasts its own coffee, although it has been shrinking operations as it sells off land to Monsanto. Still it's an attractive and easily reached setting. You can survey the scene from the verandah and enjoy a cup of the local coffee and a snack or modest lunch.

On Sunday afternoons, the porch is the scene for the lilting tunes of Hawaiian traditional performers. The grande-sized gift shop, Blue Monkey, has an excellent and compelling selection of locally made goods. Besides books there is an intriguing selection of ukuleles.

Kala'e

Rudolph Wilhelm Meyer, a German immigrant who had plans to make it big in the California gold rush, stopped off in Hawaii en route (he was going the long way around) and never left. He married a member of Hawaiian royalty who had huge tracts of land on Moloka'i and busied himself growing potatoes and cattle for export, serving as overseer of the Kalaupapa leprosy settlement and as manager of King Kamehameha V's ranch lands. In 1876, when a new treaty allowed Hawaii sugar planters to export sugar duty-free to the US, Meyer turned his lands over to sugar and built a mill; it operated for only a decade until falling prices rendered it unviable.

Sights & Activities

Moloka'i Museum & Cultural Center MUSEUM
(☎567-6436; adult/child $5/1; ⏲10am-2pm Mon-Sat) The RW Meyer Sugar Mill has enjoyed a series of restorations over time. It now houses a museum and cultural center, which has a small but intriguing display of Moloka'i's history with period photos, cultural relics and a 10-minute video.

Features of the mill include a 100-year-old steam engine, a mule-powered cane crusher and other working artifacts. Meyer and his descendants are buried in a little family plot out back.

Ironwood Hills Golf Course GOLF
(☎567-6000; www.molokaigolfcourse.com; greens fee [9 holes] $25; ⏲8am-5pm) The 'pro shop' in the dilapidated trailer tells you everything

you need to know about this casual nine-hole golf course, which was originally built for plantation managers in the 1920s. Electric cart rental is $10; clubs are $5.

Palaʻau State Park

Soak in the views over the Kalaupapa Peninsula, listen to winds rustle through groves of ironwood and eucalyptus trees and witness sacred rocks that represent human genitals. This misty state park is at the end of Hwy 470, near the Kalaupapa trailhead. It's good for a picnic, some photos and possibly to increase your chances of falling pregnant.

Sights & Activities

★Kalaupapa Overlook LOOKOUT

The Kalaupapa Overlook provides a scenic overview of the Kalaupapa Peninsula from the edge of a 1600ft cliff.

It's easy to get the lay of the land from up here now that vegetation has been cleared. You'll get a good feel for just how far you'll travel if you descend the nearly 1700ft on the trail. Interpretive plaques identify significant landmarks below and explain Kalaupapa's history.

The village where all of Kalaupapa's residents live is visible, but Kalawao, the original settlement and site of Father Damien's church and grave, is not. Kalaupapa means 'flat leaf,' an accurate description of the lava-slab peninsula that was created when a low shield volcano poked up out of the sea, long after the rest of Moloka'i had been formed.

The dormant Kauhako Crater, visible from the overlook, contains a little lake that's more than 800ft deep. At 400ft, the crater is the highest point on the Kalaupapa Peninsula. A lighthouse stands erect near the northern tip of land. It once boasted the most powerful beam in the Pacific but now holds only an electric light beacon. The best light for photography is usually from late morning to mid-afternoon.

There's a vague trail of sorts that continues directly beyond the last plaque at the overlook. The path, on a carpet of soft ironwood needles, passes through diagonal rows of trees planted during a Civil Conservation Corps (CCC) reforestation project in the 1930s. Simply follow this trail for 20 minutes or so until it peters out.

Kauleonanahoa CULTURAL SITE

Kauleonanahoa (the penis of Nanahoa) is Hawaii's premier phallic stone, standing proud in a little clearing inside an ironwood grove, about a five-minute walk from the parking area. The legend goes that Nanahoa hit his wife Kawahuna in a jealous rage and when they were both turned to stone, he came out looking like a dick, literally.

Reputedly, women who come here with offerings of lei and stay overnight will soon get pregnant. There's no mention of what happens to men who might try the same thing with some nearby stones that have been carved into a female counterpart to the main rock.

Before the trees were planted, the stone, which has had some plastic surgery through the years to augment its effect, was a striking pinnacle atop the ridge.

Sleeping

Camping is allowed in a peaceful grassy field a quarter of a mile before the overlook. There's a picnic pavilion and a portable toilet here (although there are good bathrooms near the main parking area). It rains a lot

DON'T MISS

POST-A-NUT

Why settle for a mundane postcard or, worse, an emailed photo of you looking like a tan-lined git, when it comes to taunting folks in the cold climes you've left behind? Instead, send a coconut. Gary Lam, the world-class postmaster of the **Ho'olehua post office** (Pu'u Peelua Ave; ⌚8.30am-4pm Mon-Fri), has baskets of them for free. Choose from the oodles of markers and write the address right on the husk. Add a cartoon or two. Imagine the joy when a loved one waits in a long line for a parcel and is handed a coconut! Depending on the size of your nut, postage costs $8 to $13 and takes three to six days to reach any place in the US; other countries cost more and take longer – and you may run into quarantine issues.

If Lam, who takes the time to apply a panopoly of colored stamps to each coconut, was in charge of the postal service, its current financial woes would likely vanish.

here and outside of the summer dry season, your tent will likely be drenched by evening showers.

Ho'olehua

Ho'olehua is the dry plains area that separates eastern and western Moloka'i. Here, in the 1790s, Kamehameha the Great trained his warriors in a year-long preparation for the invasion of O'ahu.

Ho'olehua was settled as an agricultural community in 1924, as part of the first distribution of land under the Hawaiian Homes Commission Act, which made public lands available to Native Hawaiians. Water was scarce in this part of Moloka'i and Ho'olehua pineapple farms drew settlers as the spiky fruit required little irrigation. But the locals were soon usurped by the pineapple giants Dole, Del Monte and Libby. Most were forced to lease their lands to the plantations.

Today the plantations are gone, but locals continue to plant small crops of fruits, vegetables and herbs. And Hawaiians continue to receive land deeds in Ho'olehua in accordance with the Hawaiian Homes Commission Act.

Sights

★Purdy's Macadamia Nut Farm FARM

(www.molokai-aloha.com/macnuts; Lihi Pali Ave; 9:30am-3:30pm Tue-Fri, 10am-2pm Sat) FREE The nutty tour here lets you poke your pick of macadamia nuts as Tuddie Purdy takes you into his 80-year-old orchard and personally explains how the nuts grow without pesticides, herbicides or fertilizers.

Everything is done in quaint Moloka'i style: you can crack open macadamia nuts on a stone you poke with a hammer and sample macadamia blossom honey scooped up with slices of fresh coconut. Nuts (superb!) and honey are for sale. Linger and Purdy will go into full raconteur mode.

To get to the farm, turn right onto Hwy 490 from Hwy 470. After 1 mile, take a right onto Lihi Pali Ave, just before the high school. The farm is a third of a mile up, on the right.

Kumu Farms FARM

(9am-4pm Tue-Fri) Part of a burgeoning organic farming scene on Moloka'i (in contrast to the GM fields of Monsanto), Kumu Farms grows bananas, papayas, herbs, tomatoes, lettuce and much more. At its very attractive company store you can enjoy various fresh treats at picnic tables and buy produce for your condo or vacation house. The pesto is extraordinary.

The farm store is just south of the airport; look for the signs off Hwy 460.

Mo'omomi Beach

When you think of Hawaii you think of beaches, so it is surprising that the islands have very few sand dunes. One of the few undisturbed, coastal sand-dune areas left in the state is found on remote Mo'omomi Beach. Among its native grasses and shrubs are at least four endangered plant species that exist nowhere else on earth, including a relative of the sunflower. It is one of the few places in the populated islands where green sea turtles still find suitable breeding habitat.

Managed by Hawaiian elders as well as the Nature Conservancy, Mo'omomi is not lushly beautiful, but windswept, lonely and wild. It's a classic Moloka'i sight; alluring and worth the effort to visit. Follow Farrington Ave west, past the intersection with Hwy 480, until the paved road ends. If you are in a regular car and it has been raining, this is where your journey will end as there is often a richly red mud swamp here.

When passable, it's 2.2 miles further along a dirt road that's in some areas quite smooth and in others it's deeply rutted. In places, you may have to skirt the edge of the road and straddle a small gully. It's ordinarily sort of passable in a standard car, although the higher the vehicle the better; it's definitely best to have a 4WD. If you get stuck in a car, you may gift your rental company with a windfall in fees and fines.

Look for the picnic pavilion that announces you've found Mo'omomi Bay, with a little sandy beach used at times by elders teaching the young traditional fishing techniques. The rocky eastern point, which protects the bay, provides a fishing perch and further along the bluffs a sacred ceremony might be underway. There are toilets but no drinking water.

There is a broad, white-sand beach (often mistakenly called Mo'omomi) at **Kawa'aloa Bay**, a 20-minute walk further west. The wind, which picks up steadily each afternoon, blows the dune sand into interesting ripples and waves. Like a voyeur, you're here just to look around. Swimming is dangerous.

The high hills running inland are actually massive sand dunes – part of a mile-long stretch of dunes that back this part of coast. The coastal cliffs, which have been sculptured into jagged abstract designs by wind and water, are made of sand that has petrified due to Mo'omomi's dry conditions.

Because of the fragile ecology of the dunes, visitors should stay along the beach and on trails only.

Tours

Nature Conservancy HIKING

(553-5236; www.nature.org/hawaii; donation requested; 9am-2pm some Sat) Nature Conservancy leads excellent monthly guided hikes of Mo'omomi. Transportation is provided to and from the preserve. Reservations are required and spots fill up far in advance, so get in early.

KALAUPAPA NATIONAL HISTORICAL PARK

The spectacularly beautiful **Kalaupapa Peninsula** is the most remote part of Hawaii's most remote island. The only way to reach this lush green peninsula edged with long, white-sand beaches is on a twisting trail down the steep *pali,* the world's highest sea cliffs, or by plane. This remoteness is the reason it was, for more than a century, where leprosy patients were forced into isolation. From its inception until separation ended in 1969, 8000 patients were forced to come to Kalaupapa. Less than a dozen patients (respectively called 'residents') remain. They have chosen to stay in the only home they have ever known and have resisted efforts to move them away. The peninsula has been designated a national historical park and is managed by the Hawaii Department of Health and the **National Park Service** (www.nps.gov/kala).

State laws dating back to when the settlement was a quarantine zone require all who enter the settlement to have a 'permit' and to be accompanied at all times by a guide. The laws are no longer necessary for health reasons but they continue to be enforced in order to protect the privacy of the residents. You can secure a permit through Damien Tours (p468) or Molokai Mule Ride (p468). Because the exiled patients were not allowed to keep children if they had them, the residents made a rule that no one under the age of 16 is allowed in the settlement – this is strictly enforced, as are the permit requirements. Only guests of Kalaupapa residents are allowed to stay overnight.

The guided tour is Moloka'i's most well-known attraction but, interesting as it is, the tour itself is not the highlight: this is one case where getting there truly is half the fun. Riding a mule or hiking down the steep trail, winding through lush green tropical forest, catching glimpses of the sea far below, is unforgettable.

History

Ancient Hawaiians used Kalaupapa as a refuge when caught in storms at sea. The peninsula held a large settlement at the time of early Western contact and the area is rich in archaeological sites currently under investigation. A major discovery in 2004 indicated that Kalaupapa heiau had major ritual significance, with possible astronomical purposes.

In 1835 doctors in Hawaii diagnosed the state's first case of leprosy, one of many diseases introduced by foreigners. Before modern medicine, leprosy manifested itself in dripping, foul-smelling sores. Eventually patients experienced loss of sensation and tissue degeneration that could lead to small extremities becoming deformed or falling off altogether. Blindness was common. Alarmed by the spread of the disease, King Kamehameha V signed into law an act that banished people with leprosy to Kalaupapa Peninsula, beginning in 1865.

Hawaiians call leprosy *mai ho'oka'awale,* which means 'separating sickness,' a disease all the more dreaded because it tore families apart. Some patients arrived at the peninsula in boats, whose captains were so terrified of the disease and the rough waters they would not land, but instead dropped patients overboard. Those who could, swam to shore; those who couldn't, perished.

Once the afflicted arrived on Kalaupapa Peninsula, there was no way out, not even in a casket. The original settlement was in Kalawao, at the wetter eastern end of the peninsula. Early conditions were unspeakably horrible, with the strong stealing rations from the weak, and women forced into prostitution or worse. Life spans were invariably short and desperate.

Father Damien arrived at Kalaupapa in 1873. He wasn't the first missionary to come, but he was the first to stay. What Damien provided, most of all, was a sense of hope and inspiration to others. Brother Joseph Dutton arrived in 1886 and stayed 44 years. In addition to his work with the sick, he was a prolific writer who kept the outside world informed about what was happening in Moloka'i. Sister Marianne Cope arrived a year before Damien died. She stayed 30 years, helping to establish a girls' home and encouraging patients to live life to the fullest. She is widely considered to be the mother of the hospice movement.

The same year that Father Damien arrived, a Norwegian scientist named Dr Gerhard Hansen discovered *Mycobacterium leprae*, the bacteria that causes leprosy, thus proving that the disease was not hereditary, as was previously thought. Even in Damien's day leprosy was one of the least contagious of all communicable diseases: only 4% of human beings are even susceptible to it.

In 1909 the US Leprosy Investigation Station opened at Kalawao. However, the fancy hospital was so out of touch – requiring the patients to sign themselves in for two years, live in seclusion and give up all Hawaii-grown food – that even in the middle of a leprosy colony, it attracted only a handful of patients. It closed a few years later.

Since the 1940s sulfa antibiotics have successfully treated and controlled leprosy, but the isolation policies in Kalaupapa weren't abandoned until 1969, when there were 300 patients here. The last arrived in 1965 and today the remaining handful of residents are all in their 70s or older.

While the state of Hawaii officially uses the term 'Hansen's disease' for leprosy, many Kalaupapa residents consider that to be a euphemism that fails to reflect the stigma they have suffered, and continue to use the old term 'leprosy.' The degrading appellation 'leper,' however, is offensive to all. 'Resident' is preferred.

Sights & Activities

At the bottom of the park's near-vertical *pali* is a deserted **beach** with stunning views of

MOLOKA'I'S SAINTS

Moloka'i was a key locale for two of the US's first saints in the Roman Catholic Church.

On October 11, 2009, Moloka'i (and the US) got its first saint. The story of Joseph de Veuster (better known as **Father Damien**), the Belgian priest who sacrificed everything to care for leprosy patients, has been the subject of many books and TV movies, few of which rise above the treacly clichés inherent in such a story. And yet Father Damien's story, once learned, makes the honor of sainthood seem like the bare minimum he deserves.

In 1873 the famously strong-willed priest traveled, at age 33, to the Kalaupapa Peninsula, the leprosy settlement he'd heard called 'the living tomb.' Once on this remote place of exile he found scores of people who'd been dumped ashore by a government not quite cruel enough to simply drown them at sea. Soon he had the residents helping him construct more than 300 houses, plant trees and much more. He taught himself medicine and gave his flock the care they desperately needed. In 1888 he installed a water pipeline over to the sunny western side of the peninsula and the settlement moved from Kalawao to where it remains today.

Father Damien contracted Hansen's disease in 1885, 12 years after he arrived, and died four years later at age 49, the only outsider ever to contract leprosy on Kalaupapa. The Vatican has recognized two miracles attributed to him. Both were people diagnosed with terminal illnesses decades after his death, who attributed their recoveries to their prayers and faith in Father Damien.

Meanwhile, in Syracuse, New York, **Sister Marianne Cope** was running a public hospital. In 1883 at age 45 she accepted a plea to treat leprosy patients in Hawaii after 50 other institutions had said no. After establishing hospitals in O'ahu and Maui, she moved to Kalaupapa to care for Father Damien and the other patients. She remained here until her death from natural causes in 1918.

Excitement over Moloka'i's saints is widespread locally, although an expected massive windfall in visitors has failed to materialize. But the number of pilgrims and otherwise interested is growing slowly. Father Damien's feast day, May 10, is sparking festivities. Sister Marianne, whose feast day is January 23, was made a saint in 2012.

the steep cliffs you've just come down. If you've come by mule, the ride ends here and you'll board a small bus for the tour. If you're hiking, wait for the mandatory tour here, for which you should book in advance.

The settlement is very quiet, and residents tend to stay indoors while the tour is going on. With their history of being persecuted and stigmatized, you can't blame them for avoiding curious tourists, but the guide says that residents welcome visitors because it helps prevent their story from being forgotten. Restoration of village buildings is ongoing and the homes that have been restored are small and tidy, with covered lanai, clapboard siding and tin roofs. Other sights are mainly cemeteries, churches and memorials. Buy drinks and snacks at Fuesaina's Bar, which is run by Gloria Marks, the wife of the late Richard Marks, who was something of an ambassador for Kalaupapa for many years. A park **visitor center** doubles as a small museum and bookstore, with displays of items made and used by former residents ('Kalaupapa Patients Adapt & Innovate') and books and films about the settlement for sale.

On the way to the east side of the peninsula is **St Philomena Church** (better known as Father Damien's Church), in **Kalawao**, which was built in 1872. You can see where Damien cut open holes in the floor as a way to welcome the sick, whose disease made them need to spit frequently. The graveyard at the side contains Damien's gravestone and original burial site, although his body was exhumed in 1936 and returned to Belgium. In 1995 his right hand was reinterred here. The large black cross on the revered Father's grave is adorned with shells and lei.

The tour stops for lunch at Kalawao after a short drive through lush greenery dotted with colorful lantana vines. On the way, keep your eyes open for a heiau just past the water wells; the remains of the ancient temple are on the same side as the wells.

The amazing view from Kalawao could be reason enough to visit the peninsula. It gives you a glimpse of Moloka'i's Pali Coast. This impenetrable section of the northern shore contains two majestic valleys and **Kahiwa Falls**, the state's longest waterfall, and is a popular film location for producers needing an almost otherworldly landscape. It served as 'Skull Island' in the second – and less impressive – *King Kong*, from 1976.

HOLY WATER

It's hot walking down the Kalaupapa trail, but it's far hotter walking back up. Instead of lugging a lot of water both ways, or even just bringing it back up with you, take extra containers and stash them behind rocks at the numbered switchbacks on your way down. Remember the numbers and retrieve your water on the way back up.

Tours

★Molokai Mule Ride TOUR

(☎800-567-7550, 567-6088; www.muleride.com; rides $200; ⏲Mon-Sat) A mule ride is the only way down the *pali* besides hiking, but be prepared – this is not an easy ride. You'll be sore afterwards, even if you're an experienced rider, and it's a safe bet that you've never experienced a ride like this one.

At some points the trail is only eight to 10 inches wide, nearly vertical in places, and it's simply amazing how the mules carefully pick their way down. The mule skinners happily announce on the second switchback that it's here that some people just get off and walk back to the barn, not willing to trust their lives to the sure-footed animals. So settle back and enjoy a natural thrill ride.

You'll need to be quick with the camera if you want to get shots of the amazing views, because the mules don't stop for photo ops. (Hiking down would offer better chances for good pictures.) It takes about 45 minutes going down and one hour going up. The ride back is as challenging as the ride down, but it's definitely easier than hiking. Remember your mule's name so that the guides will put you back on the right one for the trip up! Tours include a short riding lesson from real *paniolo* (Hawaiian cowboys), and lunch. Make reservations well in advance. Round-trip airport transfers are $32 per person (two-person minimum).

Damien Tours BUS TOUR

(☎567-6171; tours from $60; ⏲Mon-Sat) Everyone who comes to the Kalapaupa Peninsula is required to visit the settlement with this tour. Reservations must be made in advance (call between 4pm and 8pm). Tours last 3½ hours, are done by bus and are accompanied by lots of stories about life in years past. If you're not on the mule ride, bring your own lunch and a bottle of water. You must be 16 or over.

Getting There & Around

The mule trail down the *pali* is the only land route to the peninsula and can be taken either on foot or by the mule rides. It is possible to combine hiking and flying.

AIR

The beauty of flying in on a small prop plane is the aerial view of the *pali* and towering waterfalls. Passengers need to first book a tour with Damien Tours (p468) before buying air tickets; otherwise you will be stuck at the landing strip if the day's tour is full.

If your flight gets you to the Kalaupapa landing strip before the 10am Damien Tours pick-up, you'll have nothing to do but stand around admiring the view of the surf. If you are coming from another island, you may need to fly to Moloka'i the night before. Return trips 'topside,' as they say locally, to Ho'olehua are more convenient and usually allow for easy connections to Honolulu and Maui.

Makani Kai Air Charters (☎877-255-8532; www.makanikaiair.com) runs regular flights from Ho'olehua on Moloka'i and Oahu which are timed to allow for visits in a day. It offers round-trips; one-way schemes allow you to walk down and fly up. Tours start at $230 and can be booked through the airline. You can also book air packages through Molokai Mule Ride (p468) and Moloka'i Fish & Dive (p443).

LAND

The **Kalaupapa trailhead** is on the east side of Hwy 470, just north of the mule stables, and marked by the Pala'au park sign and parked Kalaupapa employee cars. The 3-mile trail has 26 switchbacks, 1400 steps and drops 1664ft in elevation from start to finish.

It's best to begin hiking by 8am, before the mules start to go down, to avoid walking in fresh dung, though you have no choice on the return trip. Allow an hour and a half to descend comfortably. It can be quite an adventure after a lot of rain, though the rocks keep it from getting impossibly muddy. Many find walking sticks a huge help.

You can also hike down and fly back up.

WEST END

Seemingly deserted and just a couple of missed rainfalls from becoming a desert, Moloka'i's West End occupies a surprisingly significant place in Hawaii's history and culture. Pu'u Nana is the site of Hawaii's first-established hula school and the Maunaloa Range was once a center of sorcery. In recent decades, much of the land has been controlled by the Moloka'i Ranch, and its fortunes – for better and more recently for much worse – have affected the entire island. Hale O Lono Harbor is the launching site for the two long-distance outrigger canoe races, and the island's longest beach, Papohaku Beach, dominates the west coast.

Once you pass the airport, Hwy 460 starts to climb up through dry, grassy rangeland without a building in sight. The mountain range that begins to form on your left past mile marker 10 is Maunaloa, which means 'long mountain.' Its highest point, at 1381ft, is Pu'u Nana.

Given the woes of Moloka'i Ranch the atmosphere out west is a bit bleak. With the exception of one superlative store, Maunaloa might as well hold tumbleweed races, while the Kaluakoi resort area is beset by financial troubles. Still, you can ignore all the earthly turmoil on one of the many fine beaches.

History

During the 1850s Kamehameha V acquired the bulk of Moloka'i's arable land and formed Moloka'i Ranch. Overgrazing eventually led to the widespread destruction of native vegetation and fishponds. Following his death, the ranch became part of the Bishop Estate (a huge estate created in 1884 by the will of Bernice Pauahi Bishop, the great-granddaughter of King Kamehameha the Great), which quickly sold it off to a group of Honolulu businesspeople.

A year later, in 1898, the American Sugar Company, a division of Moloka'i Ranch, attempted to develop a major sugar plantation in central Moloka'i. The company built a railroad system to haul the cane, developed harbor facilities and installed a powerful pumping system to draw water. However, by 1901 the well water used to irrigate the fields had become so saline that the crops failed. The company then moved into honey production on such a large scale that at one point Moloka'i was the world's largest honey exporter, but in the mid-1930s an epidemic wiped out the hives and the industry. Strike two for the industrialists.

Meanwhile the ranch continued its efforts to find *the* crop for Moloka'i. Cotton, rice and numerous grain crops all took their turn biting Moloka'i's red dust. Finally pineapple took root as the crop most suited to the island's dry, windy conditions. Plantation-scale production began in Ho'olehua in 1920. Within 10 years Moloka'i's population tripled, as immigrants arrived to toil in the fields.

During the 1970s, overseas competition brought an end to the pineapple's reign on Moloka'i. Dole closed its operation in 1976; the other island giant, Del Monte, later followed suit. These closures brought hard times and the highest unemployment levels in the state. Cattle raising, long a mainstay industry, was the next to collapse. This was due to a controversial state decision in 1985, pursuant to which every head of cattle on Moloka'i was destroyed after an incidence of bovine tuberculosis. The majority of the 240 smaller cattle owners then called it quits. The Moloka'i Ranch still owns some 64,000 acres – about 40% of the island – and more than half of the island's privately held lands. What will happen with these fallow holdings is the question of the young century.

Maunaloa

POP 200

In the 1990s the Moloka'i Ranch bulldozed the atmospheric old plantation town of Maunaloa, leveling all but a few buildings. New buildings mimicking old, plantation-style homes were erected. This drove up rents and forced out some small businesses, provoking the ire of island residents.

Ironically, the new development is now all but closed; the hotel, luxury beach campsite, cinema and even the local outlet of Kentucky Fried Chicken are all shuttered.

Attractions are few, unless you're an urban planner doing research. The **Maunaloa General Store** (⏲8am-6pm Mon-Sat) is the last retail holdout, and provides the village basics. It has a limited selection of pricey groceries and alcohol, but does much to keep community spirit going. However, there is one excellent reason to visit the quiet streets, one that will literally blow you away...

★Big Wind Kite Factory & Plantation Gallery GALLERY

(☎552-2364; www.bigwindkites.com; 120 Maunaloa Hwy; ⏲8:30am-5pm Mon-Sat, 10am-2pm Sun) Big Wind custom-makes kites for high fliers of all ages. It has hundreds ready to go in stock or you can choose a design and watch production begin. Lessons are available, lest you have a Charlie Brown experience with a kite-eating tree.

There is a range of other goods to browse as well, including an excellent selection of Hawaii-themed books and artworks, clothing and crafts originating from everywhere, from just down the road to Bali.

Kaluakoi Resort Area

You can almost picture this place when times were good: a low-key resort fronted a perfect crescent of sand while upscale condos lined the fairways of an emerald-green championship golf course.

Well, that was then (the 1980s) and the now is rather bleak. The resort was closed years ago and is in a state of advanced decay. The golf course died when Moloka'i Ranch pulled the plug in 2008. The fairways are now a sort of post-apocalyptic-desert spectacle. Meanwhile the condo complexes do their best to put a good face on the situation as the individual owners try to play up the quiet aspects of the complex in their efforts to market their vacation rentals. Surrounding house lots have sold very slowly, although a few large mansions lurk behind walls along the beaches.

As with the rest of the west, you're best off bringing a picnic from Kaunakakai and enjoying the beautiful beaches. Everything is accessed from a good road that branches off Hwy 460 at mile marker 15 and curves its way down to the shore.

Beaches

★Kawakiu Beach BEACH

Kaluakoi's northernmost beach is also the best. Kawakiu Beach is a broad crescent beach of white sand and bright-turquoise waters. It's partially sheltered from the winds that can bedevil the beaches to the south and when seas are calm, usually in summer, Kawakiu is generally safe for swimming.

When the surf is rough, there are still areas where you can at least get wet. On the southern side of the bay, there's a small, sandy-bottomed wading pool in the rocks; the northern side has an area of flat rocks over which water slides to fill up a shallow shoreline pool. Spindly kiawe trees provide shade. Outside of weekends, you may well have the place to yourself.

To get there, turn off Kaluakoi Rd onto the road to the Paniolo Hale condos, but instead of turning left down to the condos, continue straight toward the old golf course. Where the paved road ends there's space to pull over and park. You'll come first to a rocky point at the southern end of the bay. Before descending to the beach, scramble around up here for a scenic view of the coast, south to Papohaku Beach and north to 'Ilio Point.

Make Horse Beach BEACH

Make Horse Beach supposedly takes its name from days past when wild horses were run off the tall, dark cliff on its northern end; *make* (*mah*-kay) means 'dead.' This pretty, tiny white-sand cove is a local favorite and more secluded than Kepuhi further to the south.

It's a sublime spot for sunbathing and sunset, but usually not for swimming as the currents are fierce. On the calmest days, daredevils leap off the giant rock ledge at the beach's southern end.

TOO QUIET ON THE WESTERN FRONT

Even before Moloka'i Ranch began efforts to develop its lands on the West End in the 1970s, local people weren't so fond of the company. They resented the ranch for restricting access to land, which in turn restricted a number of traditional outdoor activities and visitation to sacred cultural and historical sites. And few were impressed by the Kaluakoi Hotel, which was built on Kepuhi Bay.

By 1975 tensions had mounted and people took to the streets, marching from Mo'omomi Beach to Kawakiu Beach to demand access to private, and heretofore forbidden, beaches on the West End. The protest was successful and convinced Moloka'i Ranch to provide public access to Kawakiu. At the same time locals successfully scuttled plans to build an O'ahu suburb here that would have been linked to the neighboring island by a new airport and ferry system.

In the 1990s the ranch operated a small wildlife-safari park, where tourists snapped pictures of exotic animals, and trophy hunters paid $1500 a head to shoot African eland and blackbuck antelope. Rumors abound of how local activists, long resistant to the type of tourist-oriented development that has all but consumed neighboring Maui, made life so difficult for the ranch that the safari park was shut down.

Beginning in 2001, the current owners of Moloka'i Ranch, the Singapore-based Moloka'i Properties, began a campaign to revitalize the holdings. They developed plans to reopen the Kaluakoi Hotel (and did reopen the golf course) and transfer the title to cultural sites and recreational areas amounting to 26,000 acres to a newly created Moloka'i Land Trust, essentially turning it into public land. They would also have given up the right to develop another 24,000 acres of their own lands.

But there was one small detail...what Moloka'i Properties wanted in return: the right to develop 200 one-acre lots on pristine La'au Point into a luxury subdivision marketed to multimillionaires. Most locals had an immediate and negative reaction to this. It was the '70s all over again. Signs saying 'Save La'au Point' sprouted island-wide (and can still be seen).

Despite numerous community meetings and plans, Moloka'i Properties got nowhere, as the residents of the Hawaii island with the highest unemployment thumbed their noses at the promise of hundreds of resort and service jobs.

In 2008 Moloka'i Properties essentially took its toys and went home. It pulled the plug on all its operations, laid off dozens, closed its hotel and golf course and furthered the ghost-town feel of Maunaloa and the Kaluakoi resort area. Only a last-minute intervention by Maui County kept the water running.

With the global economy in the dumps, it's unlikely that Moloka'i Properties will be back anytime soon with new development schemes. Meanwhile, schemes to erect 91 enormous power-generating windmills west of Maunaloa have run afoul of Moloka'i's fractious politics and strong preservation beliefs.

A further example of the local political scene occurred in 2012 when word spread around the island that cruise ships planned to visit Moloka'i. Soon anti-cruise-ship signs sprouted in yards and meetings were held. Eventually it became clear that 'cruise ships' were really a yacht that carried not 3600 passengers, nor 360 passengers but rather 36 passengers. Eventually American Safari Cruises (www.un-cruise.com) defused the protests by promising to only visit the island once a week and to hire lots of local people for its operations.

To get here, turn off Kaluakoi Rd onto the road to the Paniolo Hale condos and then turn left toward the condo complex. You can park just beyond the condos and walk, or follow the dirt road heading off to the right for a quarter of a mile to a parking area. From there, cross the golf course remains to the beach. In some of the distant reaches clothing has been deemed optional.

Kepuhi Beach BEACH

You can see why they built the defunct Kaluakoi Hotel here: the beach is a rocky, white-sand dream. However, swimming here can be a nightmare. Not only can there be a tough shorebreak, but strong currents can be present even on calm days.

During winter, the surf breaks close to shore, crashing in sand-filled waves that can be a brutal exfoliant.

A five-minute hike up to the top of **Pu'u o Kaiaka**, a 110ft-high promontory at the southern end of Kepuhi Beach, is rewarded with a nice view of Papohaku Beach. At the top you'll find the remains of a pulley that was once used to carry cattle down to waiting barges for transport to O'ahu slaughterhouses. There was also a 40ft heiau on the hilltop until 1967, when the US army bulldozed it (and gave the superstitious another reason to ponder the local run of bad luck). There's plenty of parking in the resort's cracked parking lots.

Sleeping & Eating

Units in the condominium complexes are rented either directly from the owners or through various agents. All units are decorated by the owners; facilities such as internet access vary. You'll need to shop in Kaunakakai, 20 miles distant, for all but a few convenience items that you can get up the hill at the Maunaloa General Store (p470). The closest restaurant is the splendid Kualapu'u Cookhouse (p463), 15 miles east in Kualapu'u.

Although the two condo complexes listed here are maintaining their properties well, we need to again note that much of the rest of the area has a run-down and eerie feel. We can't recommend the Kaluakoi Resort, which has rental units in one wing of the failed resort: for one, its cooking facilities are meager and there's nowhere locally to eat.

Paniolo Hale CONDO **$$**

(www.paniolohale.org; studios from $100, 1br/2br from $150/180;) Separated from the environs of the failed resort by the arid expanse of the former golf course, this is an attractive option. Large trees shade this plantation-style complex, giving it a hidden, secluded air. Each unit has a long, screened-in lanai overlooking the quiet grounds; as always with condos, shop around to get one that's been recently renovated. It's a short walk to Make Horse Beach.

Ke Nani Kai CONDO **$$**

(www.kenanikai.com; Kaluakoi Rd; 1br/2br from $140/150;) This tidy operation shames the rest of the resort complex. The 100-plus units are large and well-maintained (though your interior-decor mileage may vary depending on the owner). The pool is big. Note that the ocean is not right outside, so the premium for 'ocean view' units is debatable.

Kepuhi and Papohaku beaches are short walks away and you may have company from the local flock of wild turkeys.

West End Beaches

Windy, isolated and often untrodden, the West End beaches define moody and atmospheric. Together with the beaches in the Kaluakoi Resort area, they can easily occupy a day of beachcombing and beach-hopping.

From this stretch of coast the hazy outline of O'ahu is just 26 miles away. Diamond Head is on the left, Makapu'u Point on the right. You can, reportedly, see the famous 'green flash' (the green color results from atmospheric refraction of the setting or rising sun) during sunset here. Another flash of green worth spotting is the green sea turtles that sometimes pass by.

During summer the West End beaches are easily accessible, magical spots for snorkeling, with clear, flat waters.

To get to the West End beaches, take the turnoff for the Kaluakoi Resort Area at mile marker 15. Pass the former golf course and follow Pohakuloa Rd south.

★Papohaku Beach BEACH

Straight as a toothpick, the light-hued sands of Papohaku Beach run for an astounding 2.5 miles. The sand is soft and you can often stroll from one end to another without seeing another soul.

But just when you think you may have found the ultimate strand, consider a few leveling details. That intoxicating surf is also a viper's nest of undertow and unpredictable currents. And there's no easy shade. You can bring an umbrella, but the often strong winds may send it O'ahu-bound. Those same breezes kick up the fine sand, which can sting on blustery days. So come here for the solitude, but do so with your eyes figuratively, if not literally, wide open.

There are seven turnoffs from Kaluakoi and Pohakuloa Rds that access the beach and have parking. The first leads to **Papohaku Beach Park**, a grassy place with picnic facilities under gnarled ironwood and kiawe trees. Bathroom and shower facilities are rugged. You can camp here to the left of the restrooms as you face them from the parking lot, the 'no camping' sign only applies to the area to the right (be sure to read the signs that explain which areas are soaked by the automatic sprinklers on which days). There are seldom any other campers here and the view of the stars at night and the sound of surf is mesmerizing. However, the park can be popular with rowdy folks young and old and occasionally some try to stay the night. Guards are meant to check permits but you may be happier here if you are not alone.

Dixie Maru Beach — BEACH

South of Papohaku, beach access is to small sandy coves surrounded by rocky outcrops. At the southern end of the paved road there's a parking lot with access to a small, round inlet, which the ancient Hawaiians knew as Kapukahehu.

It is now called Dixie Maru, after a ship that went down in the area long ago. Dixie Maru is the most protected cove on the west shore, and the most popular swimming and snorkeling area. The waters are generally calm, except when it is stormy.

If you're up for just finding your way as you go, it's possible to hike south 3 miles along the coast to La'au Point and see what all the fuss was about (see boxed text on p471). You'll pass the failed luxury camping resort and several utterly untouched beaches. So secluded is this area that the notoriously shy Hawaiian monk seals are often found enjoying the solitude.

NI'IHAU

Nicknamed the 'Forbidden Island,' Ni'ihau remains an intriguing mystery due to its private ownership and unique isolation. Accessible only to its owners, its Native Hawaiian residents, government officials, occasional US Navy personnel and invited guests, Ni'ihau is the last bastion of traditional Native Hawaiian culture.

Captain Cook anchored off Ni'ihau on January 29, 1778, two weeks after 'discovering' Hawaii. Cook noted in his log that the island was lightly populated and largely barren – a description still true today. His visit was short, but it had a lasting impact. Cook introduced two things to Ni'ihau that would quickly change the face of Hawaii: he left two goats, the first of the grazing animals that would devastate the island's native flora and fauna, and his men introduced syphilis, the first of several Western diseases that would strike the Hawaiian people.

In 1864 Elizabeth Sinclair, a Scottish widow who was moving from New Zealand to Vancouver when she got sidetracked in Hawaii, bought Ni'ihau from King Kamehameha V for $10,000 in gold. He originally tried to sell her the 'swampland' of Waikiki, but she passed it up for the 'desert island.' Interestingly no two places in Hawaii could be further apart today, either culturally or in land value. Mrs Sinclair brought the first sheep to Ni'ihau from New Zealand and started the island's longstanding, but now defunct, ranching operation.

Today the island is owned by Mrs Sinclair's great-great-grandsons Keith and Bruce Robinson, brothers who also own a vast expanse of former sugarcane land, which they now lease to big chemical corn-growing operations on Kaua'i, where they live. The Robinsons, an old Kaua'i family that inspired the book and film *The Descendants*, are outdoorsmen and are fluent in Native Hawaiian. Keith, who worked for years in ranching and fishing, is often found in red-dirt-covered jeans, driving a beat-up pickup or doing heavy labor to save endangered plants. Bruce, whose wife is Ni'ihauan, holds top management positions in the family businesses – while also leading hunting tours and efforts to safeguard Ni'ihau's monk seals.

Population & Lifestyle

Ni'ihau's population is predominantly Native Hawaiian. Over the years the population has dropped from 600 in the early 1980s, to 230 in the 1990 census, to 160 a decade later. Today Ni'ihau's population is a mere 130, and it is the only island where the primary language is still Hawaiian. Business is conducted in Hawaiian, as are Sunday church services. In its two-room schoolhouse, three teachers hold classes from kindergarten through 12th grade for the island's 40 students. Although courses are taught solely in Hawaiian up to the fourth grade, students learn English as a second language and most are bilingual.

Residents are known for being humble, generous and mellow, and most live in Pu'uwai (meaning 'heart' in Hawaiian), a settlement on the dry western coast. Their lifestyle is extremely rustic, with no sense of hurry. The island has no paved roads, no airport, no phones and no running water. Rainfall is collected in catchments and toilets are in outhouses. While there is no islandwide electricity, homes have generators and TV. Alcohol and firearms are banned, and a code of ethics advocates monogamy.

Despite the isolation, residents are not unacquainted with the outside world. Ni'ihau residents are free to go to Kaua'i or even Las Vegas to shop, drink a few beers or just hang out. While they are free to visit other islands, however, there are restrictions on Ni'ihauans bringing friends from other islands back home with them. If Ni'ihauans marry people from other islands, or if the Robinsons view particular residents as undesirable, they are rarely allowed to return.

While the Robinsons consider themselves protectors of Ni'ihau's isolation and its people, and most Ni'ihauans seem content with their lifestyle, outsiders have been critical. Some Native Hawaiians living on other islands see the Robinsons as colonialists and believe inhabitants should be granted their own land and self-determination.

Geography & Environment

Ni'ihau is the smallest of the inhabited Hawaiian Islands: 18 miles long and 6 miles at the widest point, with a total land area of about 72 sq miles, including 45 miles of coast. The island is slightly over 17 miles southwest of Kaua'i. The climate is warm, windy and semiarid, with a relatively extreme temperature range, from 42°F to 110°F in the shade. Ni'ihau rainfall averages a scant 12in annually because the island is in Kaua'i's rain shadow. Its highest peak, Paniau, is only 1250ft tall and cannot generate the trade wind–based precipitation that is prevalent throughout the majority of the Hawaiian Island chain, notably on Kaua'i.

Ni'ihau's 865-acre Halali'i Lake is the largest in Hawaii, but even during the rainy winter season it's only a few feet deep. In summer it sometimes dries up to a mud pond.

Almost 50 endangered monk seals live on Ni'ihau, and about half of all Hawaii's endangered *'alae ke'oke'o* (coots) breed here. Introduced creatures proliferate: there are an estimated 6000 feral pigs, plus wild sheep, goats and turkeys. Ni'ihau waters have suffered depletion by outside sport and commercial fishers who sail in to fish and pick *'opihi* (an edible limpet) from the island's shorebreaks.

Economy & Politics

The island economy has long depended on Ni'ihau Ranch, the sheep and cattle business owned by the Robinsons. But it was always a marginal operation on windy Ni'ihau, with droughts devastating herds. In 1999 Ni'ihau Ranch closed, putting most of the island's inhabitants on federal welfare.

Historically the Robinsons diverted funds from their (now defunct) sugar company on Kaua'i to provide Ni'ihauans with proper shelter, food staples, medical care and higher education.

Since then, the Robinsons have focused on two income and employment sources: the military and tourism. Since 1999 military special operations forces have been leasing sites on the uninhabited southern end of the island to stage periodic training maneuvers. The operations are small scale, typically with teams of a dozen soldiers practicing mock rescue operations. The Robinsons have also pushed for Ni'ihau's participation in major Navy missile testing, which they consider less invasive and damaging (both to the physical land and to the preservation of Ni'ihau's culture and privacy) than popular tourism and overgrazing by sheep.

However, based on the minimal income actually derived from said military testing, the only other realistic option is tourism, which is why the Robinsons started offering helicopter and hunting safari tours. Neither is a booming moneymaker, probably due to the steep tour prices and the low-key Robinsons' ambivalence about opening the island to tourists. They publicize the tours mainly by word-of-mouth, with only minimal advertising.

Politically, Ni'ihau falls under the jurisdiction of Kaua'i County.

Visiting Ni'ihau

Although outsiders are not allowed to visit Ni'ihau on their own, the Robinsons offer helicopter flights and hunting excursions, and dive outfits on Kaua'i offer scuba diving tours to the waters around Ni'ihau (a typical three-tank day trip costs around $350).

Ni'ihau Helicopters (☎877-441-3500; www.niihau.us; per person $385, minimum of five guests required) The pilot flies over much of Ni'ihau (but avoids the population center of Pu'uwai) and lands beachside to snorkel. Tours must be arranged well in advance.

Ni'ihau Safaris (☎877-441-3500; www.niihau.us; per hunter/observer $1750/500) Provides everything you'll need (rifle, license, transportation, guide, preparation and shipping of trophies) to hunt Polynesian boar and feral sheep, as well as wild eland, Barbary sheep and wild oryx. Organizers promote this as 'useful harvesting of game' (due to overpopulation and overgrazing) and obey norms of free-chase hunting.

Kaua'i

Includes ➡

Best Places to Eat

- ➡ Josselin's (p551)
- ➡ Kintaro (p499)
- ➡ Tahiti Nui (p527)
- ➡ Hanalei Dolphin Restaurant & Sushi Lounge (p528)
- ➡ Tortilla Republic (p551)

Best Beaches

- ➡ Hanalei Bay (p523)
- ➡ Polihale State Park (p567)
- ➡ Kauapea (Secrets) Beach (p510)
- ➡ Maha'ulepu Beach (p543)
- ➡ Makua (Tunnels) Beach (p533)

Why Go?

On Kaua'i, the mana (life force) of the *'aina* (land) is palpable, and will hit you when you least expect it. It could descend as you round a corner and come face to face with one of her velvety emerald mountain ranges. Or while navigating one of her spectacular trails into an interior blessed with endless rainbows and waterfalls. Or maybe when paddling down a sinuous red river.

For many, it's a side effect from diving, swimming, paddling or riding world-class waves in bays deep blue and life-affirming – where you can mingle with dolphins and whales and contemplate endless Pacific perfection. Yes, on Kaua'i, your heart and mind cannot help but open wide. For some, even a short hop will become an extended stay, which on the flight home may have you debating immediate relocation – if you go home, that is.

When to Go

Lihu'e

°C/°F **Temp** — **Rainfall** inches/mm

40/104 – 30/86 – 20/68 – 10/50 – 0/32 | 16/400 – 12/300 – 8/200 – 4/100 – 0

J F M A M J J A S O N D

Jun–Sep Sunshine abounds; the ocean is calmer, days are longer, sunsets paint-splattering.

Dec–Mar Whale watching, daily rainbows and sudden rain; don't leave unattended car windows open!

Apr–May Least crowds and best deals; also numerous festivals.

History

Like the other Hawaiian Islands, Kaua'i saw a sea change in all aspects of life with the arrival of Captain Cook, sugar plantations, statehood and tourism. While Kaua'i developed as a sugar town through the early 1900s, it became iconic as a tropical paradise after WWII, when Hollywood glamorized Lumaha'i Beach in Mitzi Gaynor's *South Pacific* (1958) and Coco Palms Resort in Elvis Presley's *Blue Hawaii* (1961).

State & County Parks

About 30% of the island is protected by the state as parks, forest reserves and natural-area reserves. Must-see state parks include the adjacent Westside standouts, Waimea Canyon and Koke'e State Parks, for the awesome chasm, steep cliffs and native forests. Hiking trails abound, but most trailheads are accessible only by 4WD. Na Pali Coast State Park is another headliner, as the steep, slippery Kalalau Trail is now practically de rigueur. Most of Kaua'i's best and easiest-to-access beaches are designated as county parks, such as Po'ipu Beach Park on the South Shore; the gorgeous Hanalei Bay Beach Park and serene 'Anini Beach Park, both on the North Shore; and family-friendly Lydgate Beach Park on the Eastside.

Camping

State park campgrounds can be found at Na Pali Coast State Park, Koke'e State Park and Polihale State Park. Permits are required from the **Division of State Parks** (274-3444; www.hawaiistateparks.org; 3060 Eiwa St, State Bldg, Room 306, Lihu'e; 8am-3:30pm Mon-Fri), and are obtainable either in person or by mail. Fees range from $5 to $10 per night and time limits are enforced.

For remote backcountry camping around Waimea Canyon and Koke'e, there is no charge; the **Division of Forestry & Wildlife** (274-3433; www.hawaiitrails.org; 3060 Eiwa St, Department of Land & Natural Resources, State Bldg, Room 306, Lihu'e; 8am-3:30pm Mon-Fri) issues free permits for four sites in Waimea Canyon, two sites (Sugi Grove and Kawaikoi) in and around Koke'e and the Waialae site near the Alaka'i Wilderness Preserve.

Among the seven **county parks** with campgrounds, the most pleasant are Ha'ena Beach Park, Black Pot Beach Park (Hanalei Pier), 'Anini Beach Park and Salt Pond Beach Park on the Westside.

Camping permits cost $3 per night per adult camper (children under 18 years free) and are issued in person or by mail (at least one month in advance) at the **Division of Parks & Recreation** (241-4463; www.kauai.gov; 4444 Rice St, Lihu'e Civic Center, Division of Parks & Recreation, Suite 150, Lihu'e; 8:15am-4pm). Requirements include a signed waiver, application and payment. Permits can also be obtained in person at four satellite locations: **Kaumakani Neighborhood Center** (335-5770; 2301 Kaumakani Rd); **Kalaheo Neighborhood Center** (332-9770; 4480 Papalina Rd); **Kapa'a Neighborhood Center** (822-1931; 4491 Kou St); and **Kilauea Neighborhood Center** (828-1421; 2460 Keneke St). They are open weekdays from 8am to noon, but only cashier's checks or money orders are accepted for payment.

Getting There & Away

All commercial flights land at **Lihu'e airport** (LIH; 274-3800; http://hawaii.gov/lih; 3901 Mokulele Loop, Lihu'e).

The vast majority of incoming flights from overseas and the US mainland arrive on O'ahu at Honolulu International Airport. From there, travellers must catch an interisland flight to Kaua'i. The following airlines fly directly to Lihu'e airport from the US mainland:

Alaska Airlines (800-252-7522; www.alaskaair.com)

American Airlines (800-223-5436; www.aa.com)

KAUA'I'S TOP OUTDOOR ACTIVITIES

ACTIVITY	DESTINATION
Hiking	Na Pali Coast (p536), Waimea Canyon (p567), Koke'e State Park (p569), Nounou Mountain Trail (aka Sleeping Giant) (p497)
Diving	South Shore (p546), Ni'ihau (p474), Makua (Tunnels) Beach (p533)
Kayaking	Wailua River (p496), Na Pali Coast (p536)
Snorkeling	Makua (Tunnels) Beach (p533), Po'ipu Beach Park (p543), Brennecke's Beach (p543)
Surfing	Hanalei Pier (p523), Po'ipu Beach (p544), Kalapaki Beach (p481)

Kaua'i Highlights

1. Test your paddling strength by **kayaking the Na Pali Coast** (p524)
2. Take in vistas from **Waimea Canyon** (p567) and **Koke'e State Park** (p569)
3. Lace up your boots and hike to **Hanakapi'ai Falls** (p538)
4. Hop in a kayak and meander along the **Wailua River Valley** (p496)
5. Cruise the beach or learn to surf in **Hanalei Bay** (p523)
6. Take the plunge and snorkel **Brennecke's Beach** (p543) on the South Shore
7. 'Drink in' a sunset sail (p556) along the **Na Pali Coast**
8. Absorb the stunning manicured beauty of the **National Tropical Botanical Gardens** (p545)
9. Score a bird's-eye view of the Garden Island on a helicopter tour from **Princeville** (p519)
10. Spot countless seabirds and sunbathing monk seals at **Kilauea Point National Wildlife Refuge** (p511)

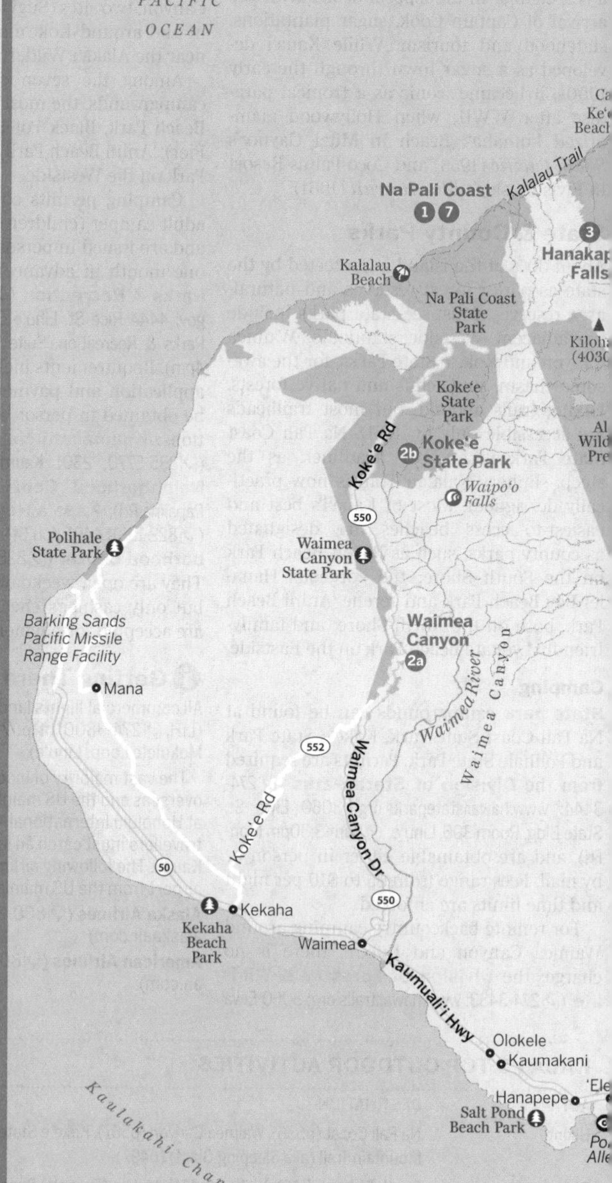

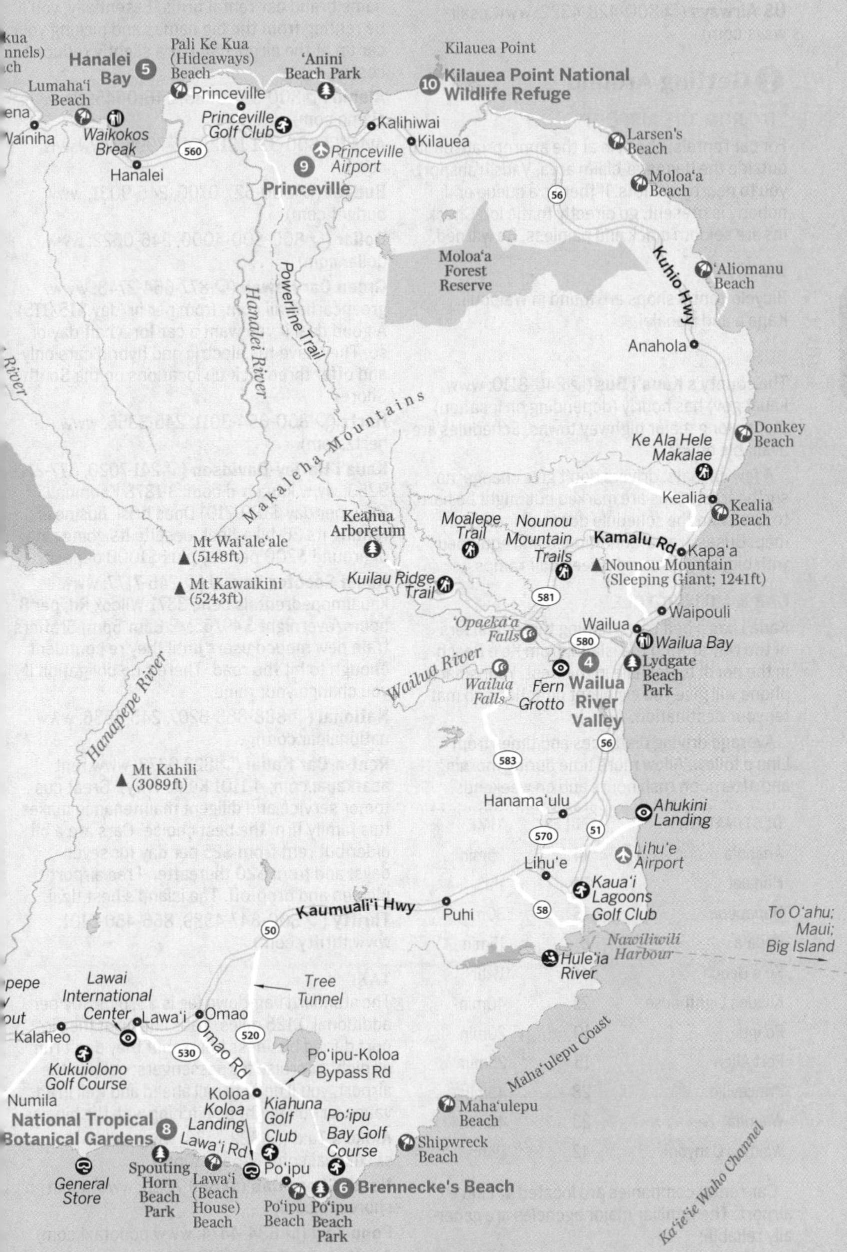

0
10 km
0
5 miles
Kilauea Point
Kilauea Point National Wildlife Refuge
10
Hanalei Bay
5
Pali Ke Kua (Hideaways) Beach
'Anini Beach Park
Lumaha'i Beach
Princeville
Princeville Golf Club
Kalihiwai
Kilauea
Waikokos Break
Wainiha
560
Princeville Airport
9
Hanalei
Princeville
Larsen's Beach
Moloa'a Beach
56
Moloa'a Forest Reserve
Kuhio Hwy
'Aliomanu Beach
Powerline Trail
Hanalei River
Anahola
Makaleha Mountains
Donkey Beach
Ke Ala Hele Makalae
Kealia
Kealia Beach
Keahua Arboretum
Moalepe Trail
Nounou Mountain Trails
Kamalu Rd
Kapa'a
Mt Wai'ale'ale (5148ft)
Nounou Mountain (Sleeping Giant; 1241ft)
Mt Kawaikini (5243ft)
Kuilau Ridge Trail
581
Waipouli
'Opaeka'a Falls
Wailua
580
Wailua Bay
4
Lydgate Beach Park
Wailua River
Wailua Falls
Fern Grotto
Wailua River Valley
Hanapepe River
56
583
Mt Kahili (3089ft)
Hanama'ulu
Ahukini Landing
570
51
Lihu'e Airport
Lihu'e
Kaua'i Lagoons Golf Club
Kaumuali'i Hwy
Puhi
58
To O'ahu; Maui; Big Island
50
Nawiliwili Harbour
Hule'ia River
Tree Tunnel
Lawai International Center
Lawa'i
Omao
Kalaheo
Omao Rd
520
530
Po'ipu-Koloa Bypass Rd
Maha'ulepu Coast
Kukuiolono Golf Course
Numila
Koloa
Koloa Landing
Kiahuna Golf Club
Po'ipu Bay Golf Course
Maha'ulepu Beach
National Tropical Botanical Gardens
8
Lawa'i Rd
Shipwreck Beach
General Store
Spouting Horn Beach Park
Lawa'i (Beach House) Beach
Po'ipu
Po'ipu Beach
Po'ipu Beach Park
6
Brennecke's Beach
Ka'ie'ie Waho Channel

Delta Airlines (800-221-1212; www.delta.com)

United Airlines (800-241-6522; www.united.com)

US Airways (800-428-4322; www.usairways.com)

Getting Around

TO/FROM THE AIRPORT

For car rentals, check in at the appropriate booth outside the baggage-claim area. Vans transport you to nearby car lots. If there's a queue or if nobody is present, go directly to the lot. Check-ins are seldom quick and painless. Be warned.

BICYCLE

Bicycle-rental shops are found in Waipouli, Kapa'a and Hanalei.

BUS

The county's **Kaua'i Bus** (246-8110; www.kauai.gov) has hourly (depending on location) stops along major highway towns. Schedules are available online.

A few caveats: drivers don't give change; no surfboards; stops are marked but might be hard to spot; and the schedule does not include a map. Buses are air-conditioned and equipped with bicycle racks and wheelchair ramps.

CAR & MOTORCYCLE

Kaua'i has a belt road running three-quarters of the way around the island, from Ke'e Beach in the north to Polihale in the west. Your smartphone will give you excellent directions no matter your destination.

Average driving distances and times from Lihu'e follow. Allow more time during morning and afternoon rush hours and on weekends.

DESTINATION	MILES	TIME
Anahola	14	25min
Hanalei	31	1hr
Hanapepe	16	30min
Kapa'a	8	15min
Ke'e Beach	40	1¼hr
Kilauea Lighthouse	25	40min
Po'ipu	10	20min
Port Allen	15	25min
Princeville	28	45min
Waimea	23	40min
Waimea Canyon	42	1½hr

Car-rental companies are located at Lihu'e airport. The familiar major agencies are generally reliable:

Discount Hawaii Car Rental (1-800-292-1930; www.discounthawaiicarrental.com) An aggregator who will guarantee the absolute lowest rate possible for new cars sourced from name brand car rental firms. Essentially, you'll be renting from the big names and picking your car up at the airport, but at a slightly reduced cost.

Alamo (800-327-9633, 246-0645; www.alamo.com)

Avis (800-331-1212, 245-7995; www.avis.com)

Budget (800-527-0700, 245-9031; www.budget.com)

Dollar (800-800-4000, 246-0622; www.dollar.com)

Green Car Hawaii (877-664-2748; www.greencarhawaii.com; from per hr/day $15/115) A good deal if you want a car for a half-day or so. They have full electric and hybrid cars only and offer three pick-up locations on the South Shore.

Hertz (800-654-3011, 245-3356; www.hertz.com)

Kaua'i Harley-Davidson (241-7020, 877-212-9253; www.kauaih-d.com; 3-1878 Kaumuali'i Hwy; per day $189-210) Does brisk business renting its 26-bike fleet, despite its going rate of around $200 per day plus $1000 deposit.

Kauai Scooter Rental (245-7177; www.kauaimopedrentals.com; 3371 Wilcox Rd; per 8 hours/overnight $49/65; 8am-5pm) Staffers train new moped users until they're confident enough to hit the road. There's no obligation if you change your mind.

National (888-868-6207, 245-5636; www.nationalcar.com)

Rent-a-Car Kauai (822-9272; www.rentacarkauai.com; 4-1101 Kuhio Hwy) Great customer service and diligent maintenance makes this family firm the best choice. Cars are a bit older but rent from $25 per day for seven days, and from $20 thereafter. Free airport pick-up and drop-off. The island's best deal.

Thrifty (800-847-4389, 866-450-5101; www.thrifty.com)

TAXI

The standard flag-down fee is $3, plus 30¢ per additional 0.125 miles. Cabs line up at the airport during business hours, but they don't run all night or cruise for passengers; outside the airport, you'll need to call ahead and well in advance, or you might be hitching with the hippies.

Akiko's Taxi (822-7588; www.akikostaxikauai.com; 5am-10pm)

North Shore Cab (639-7829; www.northshorecab.com)

Pono Taxi (634-4474; www.ponotaxi.com)

Southshore Cab (742-1525; www.southshoretaxi.com)

KAUA'I IN...

Two Days

Head directly to the North Shore, where you will be embraced by lush mountains and can dip your toes in legendary **Hanalei Bay**. Grab sushi rolls at **Dolphin Fish Market**, go for a stand up paddle on **Hanalei River**, take in the sunset on the beach and dine at **Tahiti Nui**. The next morning, drive to the end of the road in **Ha'ena**, test your sure-footedness on the first leg of the **Kalalau Trail**, and if you have the energy, hike all the way to **Hanakapi'ai Falls**. After, meet native flora at **Limahuli Garden** and then soak up that surf-town vibe in **Hanalei**, dining at **BarAcuda**.

Four Days

Day three, head to South Shore and spend the day at **Po'ipu Beach Park**, making time for the glorious South Shore sunset. That night, dine at **Josselin's**, the finest kitchen on the island. Day four, splash yourself awake with a **surf lesson**, grab a quick snack at **Living Foods Market** and end your trip with a bike ride along the **Eastside coastal path** before dinner at **Kintaro**.

A Week

Make the remaining three days count. Join **Captain Don's Sportfishing** for a half-day excursion on Kaua'i's plentiful waters, then get away from it all by booking a cabin via the Koke'e Lodge in **Koke'e State Park**, where you can choose from dozens of trails and glimpse the 'Grand Canyon of the Pacific', then camp for a night at **Polihale State Park**. Spend your final evening on a sunset cruise up the Na Pali Coast with **Captain Andy's Sailing Adventures**.

LIHU'E

POP 6455

Lihu'e won't wow you. However, within its rather scattered, vaguely industrial center, there's a plethora of economical eateries and shops along with a down-to-earth, workaday quality that's missing in the major resort areas. And while Lihu'e's very own Kalapaki beach is a versatile charmer, this is more a place to stock up at the big box stores and catch a flick before heading out on your next adventure.

Lihu'e arose as a plantation town back when sugar was king and the massive Lihu'e Plantation sugar mill was Kaua'i's largest. The plantation closed in 2001, ending more than a century of operation, but it left behind an ethnic melting pot, flecked with Japanese and Filipino ancestry along with a splash of European and native Hawaiian spice too.

Sights

Kalapaki Beach BEACH

(👪) This sandy beach and sheltered bay is tucked between a marina and mountainous spine, and overlooked by an enviable collection of houses on the rocky ridge to the east. The easy-access location and remarkable versatility makes it popular among families. The calmer waters toward the east are good for swimming, while the swells toward the west draw bodyboarders and surfers.

It's a good place for beginners, as surfers of all skill levels can enjoy the spot. You have to paddle out about 50yd to get to the reef, and it's an easy paddle. There's no pounding shorebreak to get through. Most go right – that's a mellow and predictable wave, but there are more aggressive lefts here too.

Kilohana Plantation HISTORIC SITE

(Map p482; www.kilohanakauai.com; 3-2087 Kaumuali'i Hwy; 9:30am-6:30pm Mon-Sat, to 5pm Sun; 👪) FREE If you're curious about how Kaua'i's powerful sugar barons lived, visit this handsome plantation estate turned shopping complex, which also hosts a stellar luau show. Plantation owner Gaylord Parke Wilcox built the house in 1936. The 15,000-sq-ft Tudor-style mansion has been painstakingly restored and its legacy as one of Kaua'i's distinguished historic houses is unquestioned.

Antique-filled rooms and ornate carpets on hardwood floors lead you past cases of poi (fermented taro) pounders, koa bowls and other Hawaiiana to a row of gallery shops. Our favorite attraction is the Kauai

Lihu'e Area

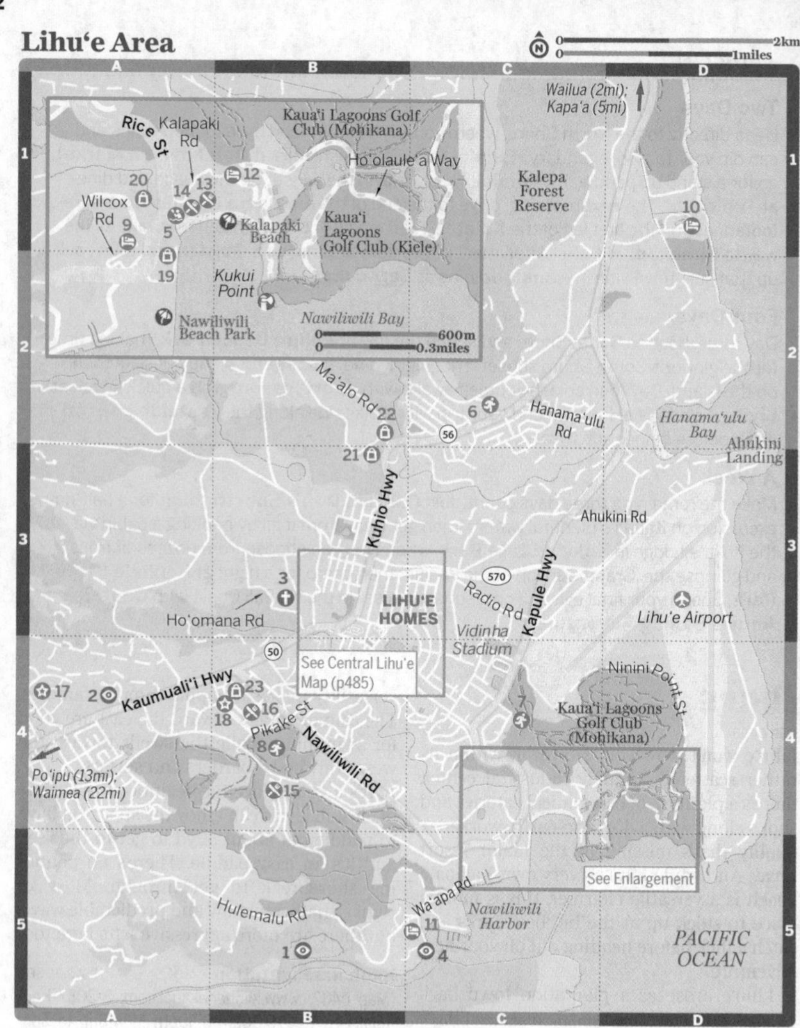

Plantation Railway (p486), which features open-air replica cars and a restored historic train that passes fields of tropical crops and modest pastures with cattle and horses. The big thrill for city-slicker kids is stopping to feed an eager herd of pigs.

Kaua'i Museum MUSEUM

(Map p485; ☎245-6931; www.kauaimuseum.org; 4428 Rice St; adult/senior/student 12-17yr/child 6-11yr $10/8/6/2; ⏰10am-5pm Mon-Sat, live music 1-2pm Sat) The island's largest museum is set in two buildings – one of which was built with lava rock in 1960. This is where you can get a quick grounding in Kaua'i's history specifically, and Hawaiian history in general, especially if you catch a free **guided tour** (10:30am Monday to Friday; call for reservations). There is a smattering of Asian art here too.

The first Saturday of the month is free.

Wailua Falls WATERFALL

Made famous in the opening credits of *Fantasy Island,* these falls appear at a distance, but when they are in full bloom and misting the surrounding tropical foliage, it's a fantastic photo op. While officially listed as

Lihu'e Area

Sights
1 Alekoko (Menehune) Fishpond............ B5
2 Kilohana Plantation A4
3 Lihu'e Lutheran Church B3
4 Nawiliwili Small Boat Harbor................ C5

Activities, Courses & Tours
Blue Hawaiian Helicopters .... (see 20)
5 Island Adventures................................... A1
6 Kaua'i Backcountry Adventures........... C2
7 Kaua'i Lagoons Golf Club...................... C4
Kauai Plantation Railway ....(see 2)
8 Puakea Golf Course................................ B4

Sleeping
9 Garden Island Inn.................................. A1
10 Kaua'i Beach Resort............................... D1
11 Kaua'i Inn C5
12 Kaua'i Marriott B1

Eating
13 Café Portofino A1
14 Duke's.. A1
Feral Pig .... (see 20)
15 The Right Slice....................................... B4
16 Times Market.. B4

Drinking & Nightlife
Café Portofino.................................(see 13)
Koloa Rum Tasting Room .... (see 2)

Entertainment
17 Kaua'i Community College Performing Arts Center....................... A4
18 Kukui Grove Cinemas B4
Luau Kalamaku .... (see 2)

Shopping
19 Anchor Cove Shopping Center A2
Clayworks....................................... (see 2)
Da Life... (see 5)
20 Harbor Mall... A1
21 Kapaia Stitchery...................................... B3
Kilohana Plantation......................... (see 2)
22 Koa Store.. B2
23 Kukui Grove Shopping Center............... B4

80ft, the falls have been repeatedly measured at between 125ft and 175ft.

At the lookout spot, a sign reads: 'Slippery rocks at top of falls. People have been killed.' Heed it. Many have slipped while trying to scramble down the steep, untamed path. To get here from Lihu'e, follow Kuhio Hwy north and turn left onto Ma'alo Rd (Hwy 583), which ends at the falls after 4 miles. Be sure to lock your car if venturing down the trail.

Alekoko (Menehune) Fishpond RESERVE

(Map p482) Don't expect a dip – only a distant view of this tranquil 39-acre pond, an ancient *loko wai* (freshwater fishpond), proof of ancient Hawaiian's reliance on aquaculture. According to legend, Kaua'i's *menehune* (the legendary 'little people') built the 900ft stone dam across a bend in the Hule'ia River and created the pond overnight. To get to the overlook, drive up Hulemalu Rd for 0.5 miles.

Holes in the structure allowed young fish to enter the pond but not to escape once grown. The pond was productive with mullet until 1824, when Kaua'i's leader Kaumuali'i died and *ali'i* (chiefs) from O'ahu and Maui ruled the island as absentee landlords. With no *ali'i* to feed and maintain the pond, it sorely declined. Later the surrounding area was planted with taro and rice. Today it is privately owned and not in use.

The US Fish & Wildlife Service owns the lands surrounding the fishpond (about 240 acres of river basin and steep forested slopes along the north side of Hule'ia River). In 1973 the area was designated the Hule'ia National Wildlife Refuge and now provides breeding and feeding grounds for endemic water birds. The refuge is closed to the public, but kayak tours (p484) along Hule'ia River drift through it.

Lihu'e Lutheran Church CHURCH

(Map p482; 4602 Ho'omana Rd; services 8am & 10:30am Sun) Hawaii's oldest Lutheran church is a quaint clapboard house, with an incongruously slanted floor that resembles a ship's deck and a balcony akin to a captain's bridge. The building is actually a faithful 1983 reconstruction of the 1885 original (built by German immigrants), leveled by Hurricane 'Iwa. It's located just off Kaumuali'i Hwy (Hwy 50).

Activities

The only way to navigate the Hule'ia River and see the Hule'ia National Wildlife Refuge is on a commercial tour. Most fishing charters depart from Nawiliwili Small Boat Harbor.

★Island Adventures KAYAKING
(Map p482; ☎246-6333; www.islandadventureskauai.com; Da Life, 3500 Rice St, Kalapaki Beach; tour incl lunch adult/child $99/77; ⏲8:30am Mon-Wed & Sat, 11:30am Fri) Offers a 4½-hour tour in the Hule'ia National Wildlife Refuge, where you'll paddle 2.5 miles into the wildlife refuge, hike to two private waterfalls, swim and picnic. If you can't hike eight to 10 flights of uneven steps, take a pass. Check-in for this tour on Kalapaki Beach at Da Life (p490) next to Duke's (p489).

Captain Don's Sportfishing BOAT TOUR
(☎639-3012; www.captaindonsfishing.com; 4hr shared charter per person $140, 4hr private charter per 6 passengers $595) Giving guests creative freedom to design their own trip (fishing, whale watching, snorkeling, a Na Pali coast cruise) on the 34ft *June Louise*, Captain Don serves with decades of experience on Kaua'i waters.

Just Live ZIPLINING
(☎482-1295; www.justlive.org; Kuhio Hwy; tours $79-125; ⏲tours depart at 8am & 1pm) This outfit offers canopy-based zipping, meaning you never touch ground after your first zip. The 3½-hour zip tour includes seven ziplines and five bridge crossings, 60ft to 80ft off the ground in 200ft Norfolk Island pines. Minimum age is nine.

Kaua'i Backcountry Adventures ZIPLINING
(Map p482; ☎888-270-0555, 245-2506; www.kauaibackcountry.com; 3-4131 Kuhio Hwy; zipline/tubing tour incl lunch $130/102; 👪) Offers a 3½-hour zipline tour with seven lines, elevated as high as 200ft above the ground and running as far as 900ft (three football fields). Afterward, refuel on a picnic lunch at a swimming pond. They also run a tubing tour through remnant forest. Groups run as large as 11. Minimum age is 12.

Outfitters Kaua'i ADVENTURE TOUR
(☎888-742-9887, 742-9667; www.outfitterskauai.com; 2827A Po'ipu Rd, Po'ipu Plaza; 4hr tour adult/child $114/104, 7hr tour incl lunch $184/144; 👪) Offers two multi-activity tours at Kipu Ranch (just outside Lihu'e) that combine aspects of zipping, hiking, and kayaking. Half-day tour includes six zips. Minimum zipping age is seven. Book in Po'ipu.

> **ℹ KIPU FALLS**
>
> Once famous for its cliff jump and rope swing involving slippery rocks and dirty water that is likely to carry Leptospirosis, these falls are no longer legally accessible, let alone advisable to explore.

Kaua'i Lagoons Golf Club GOLF
(Map p482; ☎241-6000, 800-634-6400; www.kauailagoonsgolf.com; 3351 Ho'olaule'a Way, Kaua'i Marriott; greens fee morning $150-205, afternoon $115-135, club rental $35-50) Once 36 holes, there are now but 27 holes, including the original – and recently renovated – Jack Nicklaus – designed 18-hole par-72 course. That one is called **Kiele** with nine holes each tucked into the mountains and the coast. There are nine additional inland holes here too. They call that the **Waikahe Nine**.

Puakea Golf Course GOLF
(Map p482; ☎866-773-5554, 245-8756; www.puakeagolf.com; 4150 Nuhou St; greens fee incl cart before 11am $99, 11am-2pm $85, after 2pm $59, club rental $40, after 2pm $25; ⏲6:30am-6pm) The lush cliffs of Mt Ha'upu serve as a backdrop to this Robin Nelson-designed course, which first opened in 1997 (with an odd 10 holes) and became an 18-hole course in 2003. It's near Kukui Grove Shopping Center.

Lahela Ocean Adventures FISHING
(☎635-4020; www.sport-fishing-kauai.com; 4hr shared charter per person $219, 4hr private charter per 6 passengers $595) Captain Scott Akana is named by other fishermen as the island's 'best' and a real 'pro.' Spectators ride at half-price. Its detailed website answers all your questions and more.

Happy Hunter Sport Fishing FISHING
(☎639-4351; www.happyhuntersportfishing.com; 4hr private charter per 6 passengers $625) Captain Harry Shigekane has 30 years' experience and sails a fantastic 41ft Pacifica. Private charters only.

☞ Tours

★Safari Helicopters HELICOPTER TOUR
(Map p485; ☎246-0136, 800-326-3356; www.safarihelicopters.com; Akahi St; 55/90min tours from $229/279) Besides fair prices, this outfit offers a fascinating tour that lands on a cliff overlooking Olokele Valley in Waimea. The landowner, Keith Robinson (whose family owns Ni'ihau and 2000 Kaua'i acres), occasionally meets the tour and chats with passengers about his conservation work with endangered species. They offer significant discounts for web bookings.

Central Lihu'e

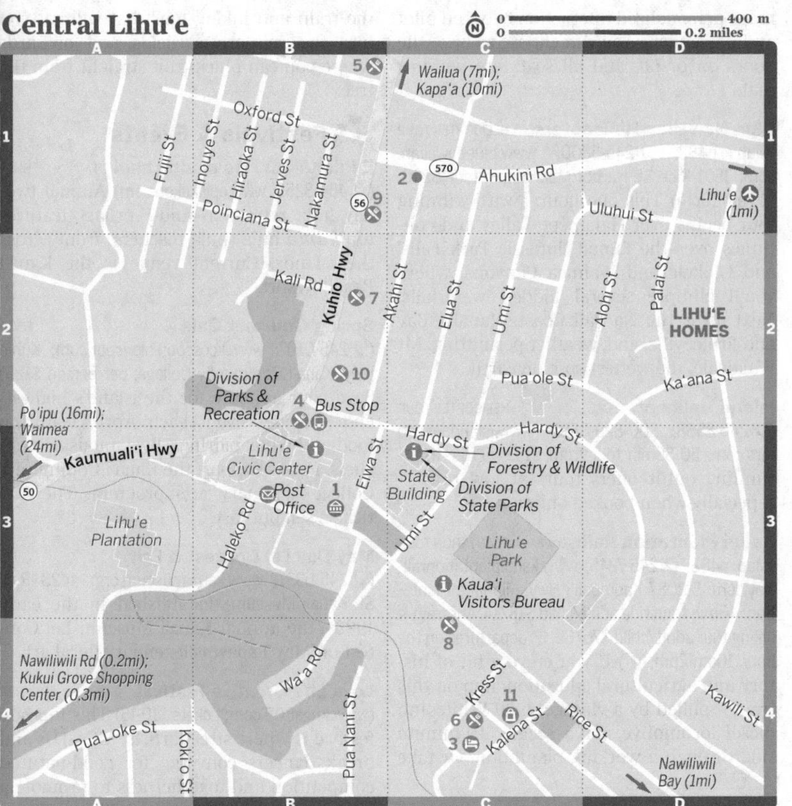

Central Lihu'e

Sights
1 Kaua'i Museum B3

Activities, Courses & Tours
2 Safari Helicopters C1

Sleeping
3 Kaua'i Palms Hotel C4

Eating
4 Big Save B2
5 Fish Express B1
6 Hamura Saimin C4
7 Kaua'i Pasta B2
8 Pho Kauai C4
9 Sweet Marie's Hawaii B1
10 Vim 'n Vigor B2

Drinking & Nightlife
Rob's Good Times Grill .... (see 8)

Shopping
Edith King Wilcox Gift Shop .... (see 1)
11 Flowers Forever C4

Jack Harter Helicopters HELICOPTER TOUR
(☎245-3774, 888-245-2001; www.helicopters-kauai.com; 60-65min tour $239-269) Choose from standard enclosed, six-passenger AStars ($229) or doors-off, four-passenger Hughes 500s ($259). Longer 90-minute to 95-minute tours offered. Widely considered the best helicopter tour company among locals. Book online for the lowest rates.

Mauna Loa Helicopters HELICOPTER TOUR
(☎245-4006; www.maunaloahelicoptertours.com; 1hr tour $259) Highly qualified pilots don't skimp on full 60-minute private tours for up to three passengers. Small groups allow for

more-personalized interaction between pilot and passengers. You can choose to have the doors on or off, and all seats are window seats.

Blue Hawaiian Helicopters HELICOPTER TOUR
(Map p482; ☎245-5800; www.bluehawaiian.com; 3501 Rice St, Harbor Mall; 55min tour $240; ⏰7am-10pm) This one hour, award-winning tour begins over Hanapepe Valley and continues over the famed 'Jurassic Park Falls' and Olokele and Waimea Canyons, where you'll glimpse several hidden waterfalls. Next up is the Na Pali Coast, Hanalei Bay and Princeville, and, weather permitting, Mt Waialeale, the wettest spot on earth.

Island Helicopters HELICOPTER TOUR
(☎245-8588, 800-829-8588; www.islandhelicopters.com; 50-55min tour from $153) This long-running outfit offers tours at low rates – especially when booked online.

Kauai Plantation Railway PLANTATION TOUR
(Map p482; ☎245-7245; www.kauaiplantationrailway.com; 3-2087 Kaumuali'i Hwy, Kilohana Plantation; 40min train ride adult/child $18/14, 4hr train & hiking tour adult/child $75/65; ⏰departures on the hour, 10am-2pm;) If you crave a bit of history and agricultural education, hop on this train – pulled by a vintage, 1939 Whitcomb diesel locomotive, for a scenic, 40-minute ride through a working plantation. Or take the train and hiking tour that will get you into the rainforests, fields and orchards where you can pluck fruit straight from the tree.

WHY FLY?

For many, getting a bird's-eye view of the verdant majesty of the Garden Island is a once-in-a-lifetime opportunity. The chance to take a breath from above and witness aggressive earth at its finest is worth the risk of a chopper flight and the dough the journey requires. And let's be clear… this is a magnificent ride and one even many locals rave about. Still, some consider it an audible thorn in their side.

The Sierra Club and other island advocacy groups have long pushed for limits on the freedom of commercial aircrafts to fly over residential neighborhoods and Federal Aviation Administration–designated noise-abatement areas. For now it's a voluntary system, however, so local activists recommend that passengers ask pilots to avoid sensitive areas, such as the Kalalau Trail and popular beaches.

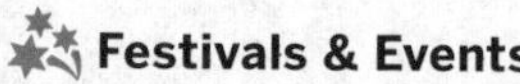

Festivals & Events

E Pili Kakou I Ho'okahi Lahui HULA
(☎454-3256; www.epilikakou.com) Annual two-day hula retreat in mid-February features top *kumu* hula (hula teachers) from across the islands. Current venue is the Kaua'i Beach Resort.

Spring Gourmet Gala FOOD
(☎245-0107; www.kccscoop.blogspot.com; Kuhio Hwy, Kaua'i Community College; per person $125) Save your appetite for the island's highest-end gourmet event each April, featuring food-and-wine pairings by famous Hawaii chefs. Funds support the Kaua'i Community College's culinary arts program. The 300 tickets sell out fast.

May Day Lei Contest & Fair LEI
(☎245-6931; www.kauaimuseum.org; 4428 Rice St, Kaua'i Museum) Established in the early 1980s, the annual Kaua'i Museum Lei Contest on May 1 spawns legendary floral art.

Love Life Creative Festival HIP-HOP
(www.kuga808.com; tickets $10-15) This hip-hop festival is where street artists, MCs, DJs and break dancers converge for good-natured competition and togetherness to promote a drug- and suicide-free Kaua'i. It's sponsored by Kuga, a non-profit arts collective in Kalaheo, and held in mid-May at Lihu'e's War Memorial Convention Center.

Kaua'i Polynesian Festival CULTURAL
(☎335-6466; www.kauaipolynesianfestival.org) A four-day event in late May that features rockin' competitions in expert Tahitian, Maori, Samoan and hula dancing, plus food booths and cultural workshops, held at various locations.

Fourth of July Concert in the Sky FIREWORKS
(☎246-2440; www.kauai.com/calendar; Vidinha Stadium; adult/child $15/7; ⏰4-9:30pm;) Enjoy island foods, entertainment and a fireworks show set to music at Vidinha Stadium.

Kaua'i County Farm Bureau Fair FAIR
(☎332-8189; www.kauaifarmfair.org; Vidinha Stadium; adult/senior/child $5/4/2;) Have old-fashioned family fun at Vidinha Stadium in

KAUA'I SURF BEACHES & BREAKS

The Garden Isle is one of Hawaii's most challenging islands for surfers. On the North Shore, a heavy local vibe is pervasive. With the St Regis Princeville Resort overlooking the break, residents may be a bit more understanding of out-of-towners in the water at **Hanalei** than at other North Shore spots – but surfing with respect is a must. Between local resistance and the inaccessibility of the Na Pali Coast, not to mention a sizable tiger-shark population, you may want to pass on surfing the North Shore.

As a rule, surf tourism is relegated to the South Shore around Po'ipu. Chances are good that you'll be staying in this popular area anyway, which is perfect, as there are some fun waves to be had. Breaking best in the summer on south swells, spots like **PK's**, **Acid Drop's** and **Center's** challenge even the most experienced surfers. First-timers can get their feet wet at the **Poipu Inside** break near the Sheraton. At nearby **Brennecke's**, only bodyboarding and bodysurfing are permitted – no stand up surfing.

On the Northeast Coast, **Unreals** breaks at Anahola Bay. It's a consistent right point that can work well on an easterly swell, when *kona* (leeward) winds are offshore.

Surfing lessons and board hire are available mainly in Hanalei and in Po'ipu. To find the swells, log onto the Kauai Explorer (p537) website, which offers updated reports to even the island's lesser-known beaches and breaks.

late August, with carnival rides and games, a livestock show, petting zoo, hula performances and lots of local-food booths.

Aloha Festivals Ho'olaule'a & Parade CULTURAL
(☎245-8508; www.alohafestivals.com) This statewide event in early September starts on Kaua'i with a parade from Vidinha Stadium to the county building. The ho'olaule'a (celebration) includes an appearance by the royal court.

Kaua'i Mokihana Festival Hula Competition HULA
(☎822-2166; www.maliefoundation.org; ⏲mid-Sep) Three days of serious hula performances at the Kauai Beach Resort (p488) in September. Both *kahiko* (ancient) and *'auana* (modern) styles deliver the goods. At $5 to $10, it's a must-see.

Kaua'i Composers Contest & Concert MUSIC
(☎822-2166; www.maliefoundation.org/composers.html; KCC Performing Arts Center; tickets $20-25) The signature event of the Kaua'i Mokihana Festival, this contest in mid- to late September showcases homegrown musical talent.

'Kaua'i Style' Hawaiian Slack Key Guitar Festival MUSIC
(☎226-2697; www.slackkeyfestival.com; Kauai Beach Resort) FREE Held in mid-November, this opportunity to see master slack key guitarists for free is not to be missed.

Lights on Rice Parade PARADE
(☎246-1004; www.lightsonrice.com; Rice St, Kaua'i Museum) Thanks to the local Rotary Club, Kaua'i hosts this charming parade of illuminated floats in early December. The 2012 version had 60 floats and 2000 performers. It's quite an event.

Garden Island Range & Food Festival FOOD
(www.kauaifoodfestival.com; adult/child $35/18; ⏲late Nov) This annual food fest highlights local chefs, as well as the farmers and ranchers who provide their Kaua'i-grown ingredients. It's held at the Kilohana Luau.

Canoe Surfing Challenge COMPETITION
(www.canoesurfingkauai.com; Kalapaki Beach; ⏲1st weekend in Nov) Seven years running, this outstanding event attracts local paddlers from across Kaua'i into the Kalapaki surf. Whether you watch (recommended) or participate (let's hope you have skills), you will enjoy the action and overall vibe.

Sleeping

Lihu'e's sleeping options range from the high-end Marriott to no-frills motels in the nondescript town center.

Kaua'i Palms Hotel MOTEL $
(Map p485; ☎246-0908; www.kauaipalmshotel.com; 2931 Kalena St; r $96; ⏲office 7am-8pm; 📶) One of two motels in central Lihu'e and easily the more appealing. The 28 rooms are small but tidy and include fridge, cable TV and windows on opposite walls to allow

cooling cross-breezes. It's set at the end of an otherwise industrial road.

★ **Garden Island Inn** HOTEL $$
(Map p482; ☎245-7227, 800-648-0154; www.gardenislandinn.com; 3445 Wilcox Rd; d $100-150; ❄📶🏊) You won't find the Marriott's beachfront cachet and megapool here, but this two-storey inn across the street holds its own for value and friendliness. Rooms are bright and kitschy, with cute murals splashed on the doors, walls and headboards, bamboo and wood furnishings, ceiling fans and a wet bar and kitchenette. Upper floors have fabulous ocean views from the lanai.

Kaua'i Marriott RESORT $$
(Map p482; ☎245-5050, 800-220-2925; www.marriotthotels.com; 3610 Rice St; pool/ocean view r from $229/279; ❄📶🏊) An aging beauty, the Marriott won't disappoint those looking for a classic resort experience, It's got the user-friendly Kalapaki Beach, two top golf courses, the island's liveliest oceanfront restaurant and a gargantuan pool that could provide all-day entertainment. Room decor and amenities are standard and rather staid. If you can afford an oceanfront unit, the view is worth it.

Kaua'i Inn HOTEL $$
(Map p482; ☎245-9000; www.kauai-inn.com; 2430 Hulemalu Rd; r with kitchenette $99-139; ❄@📶🏊) This large inn, tucked into the green hills near the fish pond and just south of the airport, offers a simple home base away from traffic and crowds. While not fancy, the 48 rooms include refrigerator and microwave. Ground-floor rooms have back porches, while 2nd-floor rooms are larger but sans lanai. Rooms vary in decor and bed count.

Kaua'i Beach Resort RESORT $$
(Map p482; ☎866-536-7976; www.kauaibeachresorthawaii.com; 4331 Kaua'i Beach Dr; r from $129; P❄📶🏊) Set on its own thin ribbon of cream-colored sand, this sprawling brick resort has 350 rooms, four pools, two hot tubs and an upscale three-star feel. There's a full spa and service is excellent across the board. You'll pay more for a room with a view, but overall it's a good value.

Eating & Drinking

★ **Fish Express** SEAFOOD $
(Map p485; ☎245-9918; 3343 Kuhio Hwy; mains $7-12; ⏲10am-6pm Mon-Sat, to 5pm Sun, lunch served to 2pm daily) Fish lovers, this is a no-brainer. Order chilled deli items, from fresh ahi *poke* to green seaweed salad, or try a plate lunch of blackened ahi with guava-basil sauce, plus rice and salad. Even better: pack fresh, wild opah, ono, mahi or ahi – sold at the best prices on island – and grill it yourself. Call for takeout orders.

Pho Kauai VIETNAMESE $
(Map p485; ☎245-9858; 4303 Rice St, Rice Shopping Center; mains $7.50-10; ⏲10am-9pm Mon-Sat; ✍) Hidden in a strip mall, this no-frills eatery serves steaming bowls of well-made *pho* (Vietnamese noodle soup). Meat and veggie options include curry chicken, grilled shrimp, snow peas and eggplant. Or ditch the soup in favor of a rice dish topped with shredded and grilled pork, or a plate of stir-fried vermicelli noodles. Cash only.

The Right Slice PIE $
(Map p482; ☎212-8320; www.rightslice.com; 1543 Haleukana St; slices under $5; ⏲11am-6pm) The amazing pie vendor who graces farmers markets across the island has her commercial baking operation with attached shop in a Lihu'e industrial park. Sniff and watch pies shape and rise as you order your savory pot pie to take and bake, or a sweet pie by the slice or whole. Hint: the *liliko'i* (passion fruit) chiffon is heart-achingly glorious.

Hamura Saimin NOODLES $
(Map p485; ☎245-3271; 2956 Kress St; dishes $3-8; ⏲10am-10:30pm Mon-Thu, to midnight Fri & Sat, to 9:30pm Sun) An island institution, Hamura's is a hole-in-the-wall specializing in homemade saimin (local-style noodle soup). Expect crowds at lunchtime, slurping noodles elbow-to-elbow at retro, U-shaped lunch counters, and save room for the other (and much more beloved) specialty, *liliko'i* chiffon pie.

Sweet Marie's Hawaii BAKERY $
(Map p485; ☎823-0227; www.sweetmarieshawaii.com; 3-3204 Kuhio Hwy; mains $6-10; ⏲7am-3pm Tue-Sat) A dedicated gluten-free bakery operating out of a rather cute storefront. Here are macaroons, shortbread cookies, pans of chocolate brownies, a host of muffins and cakes, as well as a few breakfast and lunch mains. It's popular for a reason.

Feral Pig PUB $
(Map p482; ☎246-1100; www.theferalpigkauai.com; 3501 Rice St; mains $8-10; ⏲7:30am-9pm) A Kalapaki pub and diner with a strong local

following. They have 10 local beers and Guinness on tap, and serve popular breakfasts and a massive (and quite delectable) burger made from locally raised beef.

Kaua'i Pasta ITALIAN **$$**
(Map p485; ☎245-2227; www.kauaipasta.com; 3-3142 Kuhio Hwy; mains $9-23; ⊙11am-9pm) This centrally located Italian bistro is your ticket to surprisingly good Italian food. Colorful salads meld diverse flavors, such as peppery arugula, creamy goat cheese and sweet tomatoes. Hot focaccia sandwiches, classic pasta mains and luscious tiramisu would pass muster with mainland foodies. Pasta is homemade and they also serve gluten-free noodles.

Duke's HAWAII REGIONAL **$$$**
(Map p482; ☎246-9599; www.dukeskauai.com; 3610 Rice St, Kaua'i Marriott Resort; appetizers $8-11, mains $16-32; ⊙5-9:30pm) Duke's dominates the Kalapaki Beach dining scene. The steak-and-seafood menu is none too innovative, but the fish tacos (served in their lively and inviting **Barefoot Bar** and priced to move on Taco Tuesdays) are always a winner and the atmosphere is generally lively. Expect a touristy crowd.

Café Portofino ITALIAN **$$$**
(Map p482; ☎245-2121; www.cafeportofino.com; Kaua'i Marriott Resort, Kalapaki Beach; appetizers $8-12, mains $22-36; ⊙5-9:30pm) The Marriott's fine dining offering and a textbook example of 'romantic,' this oceanfront restaurant offers white tablecloths, low lighting and, ahem, the occasional solo harpist. The traditional Italian menu features fine pastas, filet mignon and the house-specialty, osso bucco.

Rob's Good Times Grill SPORTS BAR
(Map p485; ☎246-0311; www.kauaisportsbarandgrill.com; 4303 Rice St, Rice Shopping Center; ⊙11am-2am) Behind these tinted mini-mall windows is a terrific sports bar with a dozen flat screens, two pool tables and live music and DJs on weekends.

Café Portofino BAR, CLUB
(Map p482; ☎245-2121; www.cafeportofino.com; Kaua'i Marriott Resort, Kalapaki Beach; ⊙10pm-2am Thu) From 10pm until late on Thursdays and occasional Saturdays, Portofino sheds its formal skin as guest DJs spin music ranging from swing to hip-hop to salsa, and visiting night owls and socially starved locals mingle, let loose and groove.

Koloa Rum Tasting Room RUM
(Map p482; ☎246-8900; www.koloarum.com; 3-2087 Kaumuali'i Hwy; ⊙9:30am-5 Mon, Wed & Sat, to 9pm Tue & Fri, to 6:30pm Thu, to 3pm Sun) The tasting room of Kaua'i's own upstart Rum label. It's a tasty new brand, which means they don't have a fine aged rum yet, but their white and spiced rums are quite good. Tastings are free, but for the moment there are no factory tours.

Self-Catering

Big Save SELF-CATERING **$**
(Map p485; 4444 Rice St; ⊙7am-11pm) This chain is decent but lacks a deli.

Times Market SUPERMARKET **$**
(Map p482; www.timessupermarkets.com; 3-2600 Kaumuali'i Hwy, Kukui Grove Shopping Center; ⊙6am-11pm) A major supermarket in the Kukui Grove Shopping Center.

Vim 'n Vigor SELF-CATERING **$$**
(Map p485; ☎245-9053; 3-3122 Kuhio Hwy; ⊙9am-7pm Mon-Fri, to 5pm Sat) Carries vitamins, supplements, health food and bulk staples, but not much produce.

☆ Entertainment

★Luau Kalamaku LUAU
(Map p482; ☎877-622-1780; www.luaukalamaku.com; 3-2087 Kaumuali'i Hwy, Kilohana Plantation; adult/teens 12-16yr/child 5-11yr $104/83/57; ⊙luau 5:30pm Tue & Fri; 👪) Skip the same-old commercial luau and catch this mesmerizing dinner theater with a dash of Cirque du Soleil (think lithe dancers, flashy leotards and pyrotechnics) thrown in. The thrilling stage play about one family's epic voyage to Hawaii features hula and Tahitian dancing, and showstopping, nail-biting Samoan fire dancing, and it's the only one of its kind on the island.

The buffet dinner is above average, despite the audience size (typically 550, maximum 1000), and there's little cringe-worthy 'embarrass the tourist' forced dancing.

Kukui Grove Cinemas CINEMA
(Map p482; ☎245-5055; www.kukuigrovecinema.com; 4368 Kukui Grove St; adult/child $8/5, before 5pm $5; 👪) For mainstream first-run movies, this is your standard shopping-mall fourplex. Despite the name, it's actually set across the road from the Kukui Grove Shopping Center and is a wholly separate entity. Call for showtimes.

Kaua'i Concert Association CONCERT VENUE
(245-7464; www.kauai-concert.org; tickets $30-45) The **Kaua'i Community College Performing Arts Center** (Map p482; info.kauai.hawaii.edu/pac/; 3-1901 Kaumuali'i Hwy) offers classical, jazz, world music concerts and dance performances, generally starting at 7pm. Past performers include African singer Angélique Kidjo and banjo shaman Alison Brown. Call or log on for tickets and upcoming performances.

Shopping

Near Nawiliwili Harbor, **Anchor Cove Shopping Center** (Map p482; 246-0634; 3416 Rice St) and **Harbor Mall** (Map p482; 245-6255; www.harbormall.net; 3501 Rice St) draw mainly tourists from cruise ships and the nearby Marriott. The shops at **Kilohana Plantation** (Map p482; www.kilohanakauai.com; 3-2087 Kaumuali'i Hwy; most shops 10am-6pm Mon-Sat, to 4pm Sun) are a step up.

★ **Clayworks** CERAMICS
(Map p482; 246-2529; www.clayworksatkilohana.com; 3-2087 Kaumuali'i Hwy, Kilohana Plantation; 90min lessons $45-75; 10am-6pm Mon-Sat, 11am-3pm Sun, instruction available 10:30am-4pm Mon-Sat only) A lovely pottery studio and gallery, owned and operated by three sisters (Southern California transplants, all) who have lived here since 1986 and create all the gorgeous vases, mugs, bowls, and tiles you'll see on display. They also offer tutelage at the wheel, and you'll get to take home your masterpiece. Call to schedule your tutorial.

Da Life OUTDOOR EQUIPMENT
(Map p482; 246-6333; www.livedalife.com; 3500 Rice St, Kalapaki Beach; 9am-5pm Mon-Fri, 10am-4pm Sat & Sun) An outdoor and adventure outfitter and booking agent, with a terrific retail showroom stuffed with gear for all manner of Kaua'i adventure. If you forgot it, don't worry, they stock it.

> **A WHALE'S TALE**
>
> Every year from November to March, thousands of those large loveable mammals make a 3000-mile oceanic voyage from their feeding grounds in Alaska to mate or give birth in the warm, welcoming waters of Kaua'i. If you're keen eyed, you'll see them spout offshore from Polihale to Po'ipu to Princeville.

Edith King Wilcox Gift Shop SOUVENIRS
(Map p485; 245-6931; www.kauaimuseum.org; 4428 Rice St, Kaua'i Museum; 10am-5pm Mon-Sat) Kaua'i Museum's gem of a gift shop features a variety of genuine Hawaiian crafts, such as Ni'ihau shell jewelry, koa woodwork and *lauhala* (a type of Hawaiian leaf weaving) hats, plus books on Hawaii and collectible ceramics. Enter the shop, free of charge, through the museum lobby.

Koa Store SOUVENIRS
(Map p482; 245-4871; www.thekoastore.com; 3-3601 Kuhio Hwy; 10am-6pm) Other koa galleries carry higher-end masterpieces, but here you'll find lots of affordable souvenirs, such as sleek chopsticks and desk accessories. Many items come in three grades, from the basic straight-grain koa to the rare, almost three-dimensional, premium 'curly' koa. All woodcraft are genuine koa – the prized Hawaiian wood (not the cheap fakes sold at tourist traps).

Flowers Forever FLOWERS
(Map p485; 800-646-7579; www.flowersforeverhawaii.com; Kalena St; 8am-5pm Mon-Thu, to 6pm Fri, to 4pm Sat) Voted 'Best Kaua'i Flower Shop' eight years running, Flowers Forever offers floral arrangements, balloons, fruit and gourmet baskets, champagne and a multitude of flower and maile style ti-leaf lei. They'll ship tropical flowers, plants and lei to the mainland.

Kapaia Stitchery SOUVENIRS, CLOTHING
(Map p482; 3-3551 Kuhio Hwy; 9am-5pm Mon-Sat) A quilter's heaven, this longtime shop features countless cotton fabrics, plus island-made patterns and kits. Stop here also for handmade gifts, such as children's clothing, Japanese kimonos, potholders and an assortment of bags.

Kukui Grove Shopping Center MALL
(Map p482; 245-7784; 3-2600 Kaumuali'i Hwy) Lihu'e's only major mall is an aging complex home to mostly chain stores, a couple of banks and a Starbucks. The cinema is across the street.

Information

EMERGENCY

Police, Fire & Ambulance (911)

Police Station (241-1771; www.kauai.gov; 3990 Kaana St) For non-emergencies, incident reporting and information.

Sexual Assault Crisis Line (245-4144)

INTERNET ACCESS

Lihue Cyber Cafe (245-5277; 3-3100 Kuhio Hwy; per hour $10; 9am-7pm Mon-Fri, noon-7pm Sat)

Kukui Grove Shopping Center (3-2600 Kaumuali'i Hwy, Kukui Grove Shopping Center; 9:30am-7pm Mon-Thu & Sat, to 9pm Fri, to 6pm Sun;) Free wi-fi at Starbucks, near the east entrance.

MEDICAL SERVICES

Longs Drugs (245-7771; 3-2600 Kaumuali'i Hwy, Kukui Grove Shopping Center; 7am-10pm Mon-Sat, 8am-8pm Sun, pharmacy 8am-6pm Mon-Sat, 9am-6pm Sun) Also has photocopying, FedEx, UPS and US Postal Service.

Wilcox Memorial Hospital (245-1010, TTY 245-1103; www.wilcoxhealth.org; 3-3420 Kuhio Hwy) Kaua'i's only major hospital. Emergency services 24 hours.

MONEY

Banks with 24-hour ATMs include the following:

American Savings Bank (246-8844; 3-2600 Kaumuali'i Hwy, Kukui Grove Shopping Center)

Bank of Hawaii (245-6761; 4455 Rice St)

POST

Post Office (800-275-8777; 4441 Rice St; 8am-4pm Mon-Fri, 9am-1pm Sat) Kaua'i's main post office holds poste restante (general delivery) mail for a maximum of 30 days.

TOURIST INFORMATION

Kaua'i Visitors Bureau (245-3971, 800-262-1400; www.kauaidiscovery.com; Suite 101, 4334 Rice St) Offers a monthly calendar of events, bus schedules and list of county-managed Sunshine Markets (farmers markets) for the sale of Kaua'i produce. Order a free 'vacation planning kit' online.

Getting There & Around

Lihu'e's focal points are Nawiliwili Bay, the island's only major harbor, and Lihu'e airport, the island's only major airport. Rice St, considered the town's main drag, runs east–west and passes the government buildings and post office, while Kuhio Hwy (Hwy 56) leads to shops and restaurants toward the north, and Kukui Grove Shopping Center (p490) to the south.

The Kaua'i Bus (241-6410; www.kauai.gov/Government/Departments/TransportationAgency/BusSchedules/tabid/208/Default.aspx) serves Lihu'e hourly from 6am to about 10pm, with stops at major destinations such as Kukui Grove Shopping Center, Lihu'e airport, Vidinha Stadium, Wilcox Memorial Hospital and Big Save. In addition, there is a **lunch shuttle** that runs at 15-minute intervals within central Lihu'e between 10:30am and 2pm on weekdays.

LOCAL KNOWLEDGE

HIGHWAY NICKNAMES

Locals call highways by nickname rather than by number. Here's a cheat sheet:

Hwy 50 Kaumuali'i Hwy

Hwy 51 Kapule Hwy

Hwy 56 Kuhio Hwy

Hwy 58 Nawiliwili Rd

Hwy 520 Maluhia Rd (Tree Tunnel) and Po'ipu Rd

Hwy 530 Koloa Rd

Hwy 540 Halewili Rd

Hwy 550 Waimea Canyon Dr

Hwy 552 Koke'e Rd

Hwy 560 Kuhio Hwy (continuation of Hwy 56)

Hwy 570 Ahukini Rd

Hwy 580 Kuamo'o Rd

Hwy 581 Kamalu Rd and Olohena Rd

Hwy 583 Ma'alo Rd

Kaua'i is car dependent, so most businesses have parking lots, and street parking is relatively easy to find. Metered parking in Lihu'e costs 25¢ for 30 minutes.

KAPA'A & THE EASTSIDE

If you look past the strip malls and highway traffic, the Eastside will fascinate on many levels. Its geography runs the gamut, from mountaintop forests and grassy pasture land to pounding surf and a majestic river. In ancient times, the Wailua River was sacred and royalty lived on its fertile banks. Kapa'a's historic center winks at a more recent, plantation-based era. Today, Kaua'i's population is concentrated here, creating enough critical mass for a variety of restaurants, shops and accommodations. From Wailua to Kapa'a, the Coconut Coast, as it is known, has a busier, more workaday vibe than the swankier resort strongholds in Po'ipu and Princeville – and that's no insult. However, traffic can grind to halt here from time to time. Hidden away from all this, on the northeast coast, is inviting, rootsy Anahola – a fishing and farming enclave where Native Hawaiians constitute 70% of all residents.

Wailua

POP (INCL WAILUA HOMESTEADS) 7442

Wailua has two sides to it. The coast is rather package touristy. Here guests are tucked into neat oceanfront development blocks like happy slices in a pie chart. But if you're after that wild-palm-grove nature magic for which Kaua'i is famous, you can find that here too. Just head to that languid green river – the only navigable one in the state – and follow it up into the Homesteads, where

Eastside

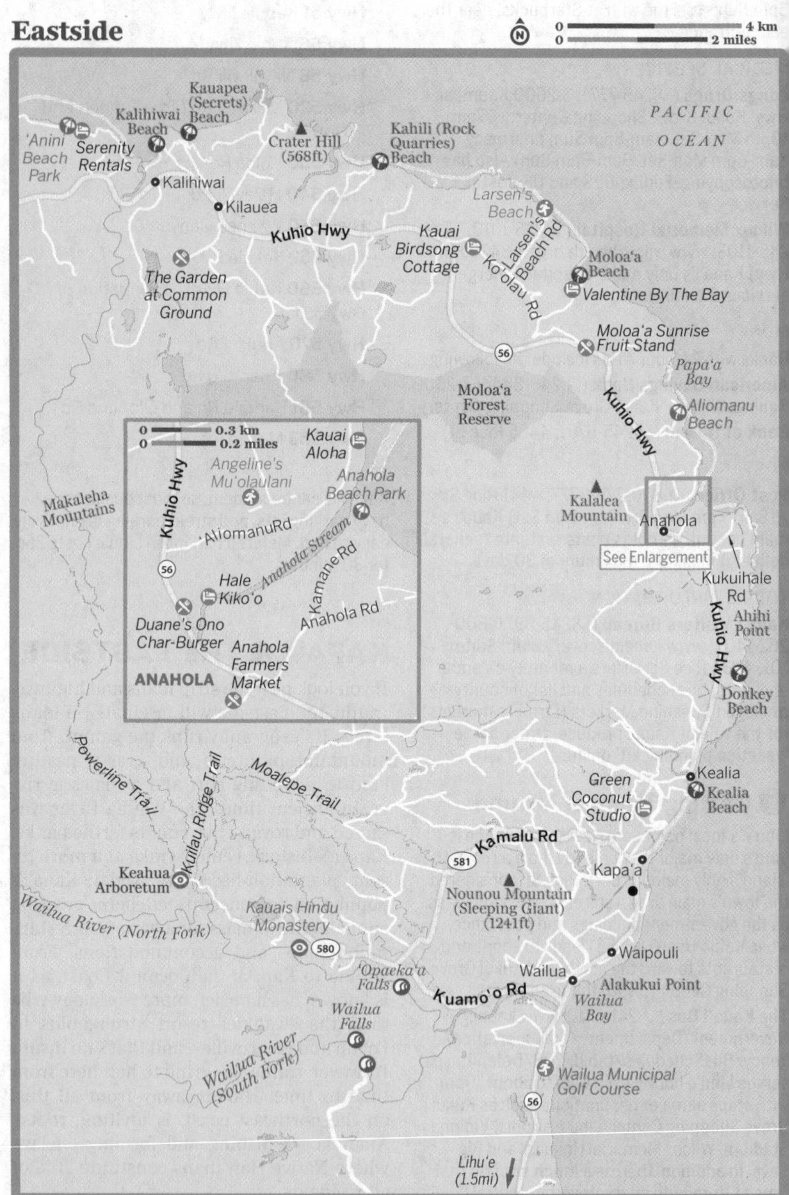

you can access trails that wind high into the mountains and the island's central spine.

Sights

See the **Kaua'i Heritage Trail** (www.wailuaheritagetrail.org) website and map for a more detailed overview of Wailua's major sights.

Lydgate Beach Park BEACH

(www.kamalani.org;) A narrow stretch of windswept blonde sand strewn with driftwood, with safe swimming, beginner snorkelling and two massive kids' playgrounds, this popular beach park can entertain restless kids of all ages, all afternoon. The multifeatured **Kamalani Playground** (at the north end), is a massive 16,000-sq-ft wooden castle with swings, slides, mirror mazes, an epic suspension bridge and other kid-pleasing contraptions.

Or you can opt for the simpler, two-level **Kamalani Kai Bridge** (at the south end). Other amenities include game-sized soccer fields, a 2.5-mile bicycle-pedestrian path, pavilions, picnic tables, restrooms, showers, drinking water and ample parking.

To get here, turn *makai* (seaward) on Kuhio Hwy between mile markers 5 and 6.

Steelgrass Farm FARM

(821-1857; www.steelgrass.org; adult/child under 12 $60/free; 9am-noon Mon, Wed & Fri;) Learn more about diversified agriculture, cacao growing and the owners' intriguing family history at this working farm, which offers a unique chocolate-farm tour. Steelgrass Farm's two other crops are bamboo and vanilla, but these 8 acres feature literally hundreds of thriving tropical species, which you'll also see on the tour. Contact the family for farm location and directions.

Smith's Tropical Paradise GARDEN

(821-6895; www.smithskauai.com; adult/child $6/3; 8:30am-4pm;) Other gardens might have loftier goals, but you can't beat Smith's for value. For $6 you can leisurely stroll a loop trail past a serene pond, grassy lawns and island-themed gardens. The setting can seem Disney-esque, with an Easter Island replica and tour trams, but it's mellow and unpretentious. The Smith's family-run luau is held on the garden grounds.

Kaua'i's Hindu Monastery TEMPLE

(822-3012, 888-735-1619; www.himalayanacademy.com; 107 Kaholalele Rd; 9am-noon) FREE On an island historically devoid of Hinduism, this Hindu monastery welcomes serious pilgrims and curious sightseers. Set on 458 acres of thriving rainforest above the Wailua River, here is an astoundingly glorious green setting with two temples dedicated to Shiva. The **Kadavul Temple**, adorned with dozens of dancing shiva statues, is where you will find the world's largest single-pointed quartz crystal.

This 50-million-year-old, six-sided wonder weighs 700lb and stands over 3ft tall. In the temple, meditating monks have been rotating in three-hour vigils round the clock since it was established in 1973. Most guests are discouraged from entering, but if you wish to pray or meditate here, you will be welcomed. The wall at the end of the path is the so-called **public temple**, and it has a wondrous south facing view onto a gorgeous teal green bend in the river. While visitors can access a limited area from 9am to noon daily, we highly recommend taking a free guided tour offered once a week; call for tour dates and parking reservations.

Keahua Arboretum RESERVE

Sitting pretty at the top of Kuamo'o Rd, this arboretum boasts grassy fields, a gurgling stream and groves of teak, eucalyptus and other towering trees. Hikers descend early to access the Kuilau Ridge Trail (p497), a 1.5 mile trail that becomes the **Moalepe Trail**.

Kamokila Hawaiian Village MUSEUM

(823-0559; www.villagekauai.com; 5443 Kuamo'o Rd; village adult/child 3-12yr/child under 3yr $5/3/free, outrigger canoe tours adult/child $30/20; outrigger canoe tours departures hourly 9:30am-2:30pm;) A pleasant diversion, especially for kids, and set along the Wailua River, it includes reproductions of traditional Hawaiian structures amid thriving gardens of guava, mango and banana trees. Kamokila also offers **outrigger canoe tours**, which include a paddle, hike and waterfall swim. Turn south from Kuamo'o Rd, opposite 'Opaeka'a Falls. The half-mile road leading to the village is steep and narrow.

'Opaeka'a Falls WATERFALL

While not a showstopper, this 40ft waterfall makes an easy roadside stop, less than 2 miles up Kuamo'o Rd. For the best photographic conditions, go in the morning. Don't be tempted to try trailblazing to the falls. The steep, slippery cliffs are perilous and have caused fatalities. Cross the road for a fantastic shot of the Wailua River.

Wailua

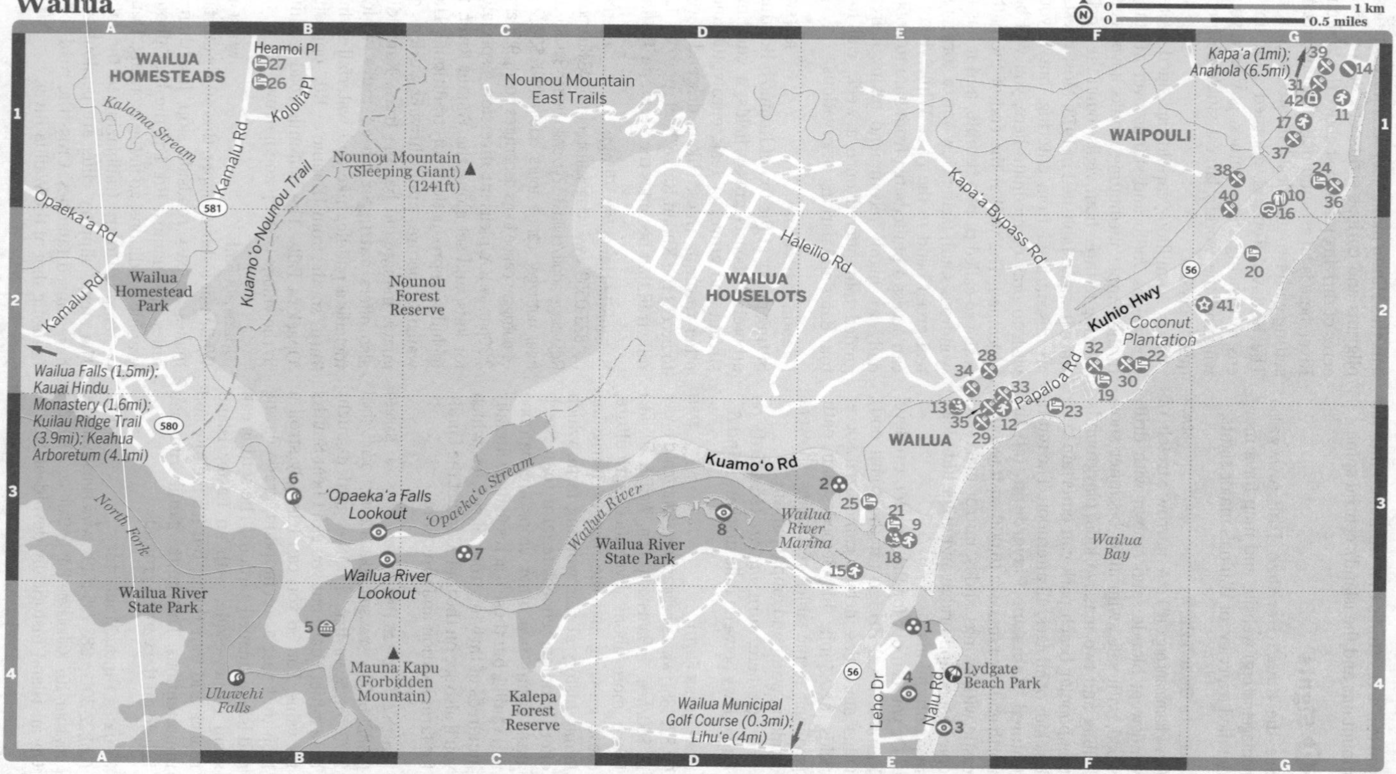

0 — 1 km
0 — 0.5 miles

WAILUA HOMESTEADS
Heamoi Pl
27
26
Kololia Pl
Kalama Stream
Kamalu Rd
581
Nounou Mountain East Trails
Nounou Mountain (Sleeping Giant) (1241ft)
Kuamo'o-Nounou Trail
Opaeka'a Rd
Wailua Homestead Park
Kamalu Rd
Nounou Forest Reserve
Wailua Falls (1.5mi); Kauai Hindu Monastery (1.6mi); Kuilau Ridge Trail (3.9mi); Keahua Arboretum (4.1mi)
580
North Fork
6
'Opaeka'a Falls Lookout
'Opaeka'a Stream
7
Wailua River Lookout
Wailua River State Park
5
Uluwehi Falls
Mauna Kapu (Forbidden Mountain)
Kalepa Forest Reserve
Wailua River
Wailua River State Park
8
Kuamo'o Rd
WAILUA HOUSELOTS
Haleilio Rd
Kapa'a Bypass Rd
WAIPOULI
Kapa'a (1mi); Anahola (6.5mi)
39
14
31
42
11
17
37
38
40
24
36
10
16
20
56
41
Kuhio Hwy
Coconut Plantation
32
22
30
19
28
34
33
Papaloa Rd
23
13
35
12
29
WAILUA
2
25
21
9
18
Wailua River Marina
15
Wailua Bay
1
Lydgate Beach Park
4
Leho Dr
Nalu Rd
3
56
Wailua Municipal Golf Course (0.3mi); Lihu'e (4mi)

Wailua

Sights
1 Hikinaakala Heiau E4
2 Holoholoku Heiau E3
3 Kamalani Kai Bridge E4
4 Kamalani Playground E4
5 Kamokila Hawaiian Village B4
6 'Opaeka'a Falls B3
7 Poli'ahu Heiau C3
8 Smith's Tropical Paradise D3

Activities, Courses & Tours
9 Ali'i Kayaks E3
10 Ambrose's Kapuna G1
11 Kauai Cycle G1
12 Kauai Water Ski & Surf F3
13 Kayak Wailua E3
14 Seasport Divers G1
15 Smith's Motor Boat Service E3
16 Snorkel Bob's G1
17 The Yoga House G1
18 Wailua Kayak & Canoe E3

Sleeping
19 Aston Islander on the Beach F2
20 Courtyard Marriot Kauai G2
21 Fern Grotto Inn E3
22 Kauai Coast Resort F2
23 Kauai Sands Hotel F3
24 Outrigger Waipouli Beach Resort & Spa G1
25 Pineapple House E3
26 Rosewood Kaua'i B1
27 Sleeping Giant Cottage B1

Eating
28 Caffè Coco E2
29 Cakes By Kristin E3
30 Hukilau Lanai F2
31 Kaua'i Pasta G1
32 Kilauea Fish Market F2
33 Kintaro F2
34 Mema's E2
35 Monico's Taqueria E3
36 Oasis on the Beach G1
Papaya's Natural Foods .... (see 37)
37 Safeway G1
38 Shivalik Indian Cuisine G1
39 Tiki Tacos G1
Tropical Dreams .... (see 37)
40 Wahoo G1

Entertainment
41 Coconut Marketplace G2
Smith's Tropical Paradise .... (see 8)
Trees Lounge .... (see 32)

Shopping
Bambulei .... (see 28)
Marta's Boat .... (see 10)
42 Nani Moon G1

Activities

Wailua Municipal Golf Course GOLF

(☎241-6666; 3-5350 Kuhio Hwy; greens fee weekdays/weekends & holidays $48/60, optional cart rental $18, club rental from $32) This 18-hole, par-72 course, designed by former head pro Toyo Shirai, is ranked among the finest municipal golf courses nationally. Plan ahead because morning tee times are sometimes reserved a week in advance. After 2pm, the greens fee drops by half and no reservations are taken.

Kauai Water Ski & Surf WATERSPORTS

(☎822-3574; www.kauaiwaterskiandsurf.com; 4-356 Kuhio Hwy, Kinipopo Shopping Village; per 30/60min $75/140; ⏲9am-5pm Mon-Fri, to noon Sat) The only non-ocean water skiing in the state is found here on the Wailua, allowed only from the Wailua Bridge to the first big bend in the river. They also rent surfboards ($30/90 per day/week, $300 deposit), bodyboards ($5/20, $75 deposit), snorkel gear ($5/15, $75 deposit) and stand up paddle boards ($45/180, $600 deposit).

Powerline Trail MOUNTAIN BIKING

While this trail (which covers 13 miles between Wailua and Princeville) is used mainly by hunters, it's a decent option for die-hard mountain bikers. Hikers might find the trek too long, too exposed and, especially toward the north, too monotonous. Beware of steep drop-offs hidden in the dense foliage. Expect to slog through mud and puddly ruts.

The south end of the trail begins across the stream at the Keahua Arboretum, at the end of Kuamo'o Rd. Consider starting from the Princeville end (p518), where it's less messy. Just south of Princeville, look for the Princeville Ranch Stables turnoff. This is Po'oku Rd. The trail starts about 2 miles down this road, near an obvious water tank. Get creative with a car shuttle and you can hike from Princeville to Wailua.

Smith's Motor Boat Service BOAT TOUR

(☎821-6892; www.smithskauai.com; Wailua Rd; 1½hr tour adult/child $20/10; ⏲departures at 9:30am, 11am, 2pm, 3:30pm) If you're curious to see the legendary **Fern Grotto**, this covered boat ride is your only chance. Bear in mind that since the heavy rains and rockslides of 2006, visitors cannot enter the grotto – which looks a bit parched, frankly – but must stay on the wooden platform quite a distance from the shallow cave.

Kayaking

Majestic and calm, the Wailua River spans 12 miles, fed by two streams originating on Mt Wai'ale'ale. It's the only navigable river across the Hawaiian Islands, and kayaking the Wailua has become a tourist must-do. Fortunately, the paddle is a doable 5 miles for all ages and fitness levels. Tours usually don't pass the Fern Grotto and instead take the river's north fork, which leads to a mile-long hike through dense forest to **Uluwehi Falls** (Secret Falls), a 130ft waterfall. The hike scrambles over rocks and roots, and if muddy it will probably cause some slippin' and slidin'. Tip: wear sturdy, washable, nonslip sandals such as Chacos. Note that at research time the waterfall was no longer flowing due to a prolonged drought, so confirm conditions before signing on, lest you be disappointed.

Most tours last four to five hours and depart around 7am or noon (call for exact check-in times). The maximum group size is 12, with paddlers going out in double kayaks. The pricier tours include lunch, but on budget tours you can store your own food in coolers and waterproof bags. Bring a hat, sunscreen and mosquito repellent.

Experienced paddlers might want to rent individual kayaks and go out on their own. Note that not all tour companies are also licensed to rent individual kayaks.

No kayak tours or rentals are allowed on Sundays. Of course, non-commercial kayaks are always allowed on the river.

Kayak Wailua KAYAKING
(☎822-3388; www.kayakwailua.com; 4565 Haleilio Rd, Wailua; tour per person $48) This small, family-owned outfit specializes in Wailua River tours. It keeps boats and equipment in tip-top shape and provides dry bags for your belongings and a nylon cooler for your BYO snacks.

Wailua Kayak Adventures KAYAKING
(☎822-5795, 639-6332; www.kauaiwailuakayak.com; 4-1596 Kuhio Hwy, Kapa'a; single/double kayak rental per day $25/50, tours from $50; ⏲check-in 7am & 12:30pm) They offer three budget-friendly Wailua River tours (which include

THE SACRED WAILUA RIVER

To ancient Hawaiians, the Wailua River was among the most sacred places in the archipelago. The river basin, near its mouth, was one of the island's two royal centers (the other was Waimea) and home to the high chiefs. Here, you can find the remains of many important heiau (ancient stone temples).

The **Hikina'akala Heiau** ('rising of the sun') sits south of the Wailua River mouth, which is today the north end of Lydgate Beach Park. In its heyday, the long, narrow temple (c AD 1200) was aligned directly north to south, but only a few remaining boulders outline its original massive shape. The neighboring **Hauola Pu'uhonua** ('dew of life,' 'place of refuge') is marked by a bronze plaque. Ancient Hawaiian kapu (taboo) breakers were assured safety from persecution if they made it inside.

Believed to be the oldest *luakini* (temple dedicated to war god Ku, often a place for human sacrifice) on the island, **Holoholoku Heiau** is a quarter-mile up Kuamo'o Rd on the left. Toward the west, against the flat-backed birthstone marked by a plaque reading 'Pohaku Ho'ohanau' ('royal birthstone'), queens gave birth to future kings. Only a male child born here could become king of Kaua'i.

Perched high on a hill overlooking the meandering Wailua River, the well-preserved **Poli'ahu Heiau**, another *luakini*, is named after the snow goddess Poli'ahu, one of the sisters of the volcano goddess Pele. Poli'ahu Heiau is immediately before the **'Opaeka'a Falls lookout**, on the opposite side of the road.

Bear in mind, unmarked Hawaiian heiau might not catch your eye. Although they were originally imposing stone structures, most now lie in ruins, covered with scrub. It takes a leap of imagination for non-Hawaiians to appreciate heiau, but they are still considered powerful vortices of great *mana* (spiritual energy).

Find an excellent brochure on the Wailua complex of heiau at www.hawaiistateparks.org/pdf/brochures/Hikinaakala.pdf. For a compelling history on the Wailua River's meaning to ancient Hawaiians, see Edward Joesting's *Kauai: The Separate Kingdom*.

generous snacks at the waterfall) and rent kayaks too.

Wailua Kayak & Canoe KAYAKING

(☎821-1188; www.wailuariverkayaking.com; 169 Wailua Rd, Wailua River State Park; s/d kayak per 5hr $42.50/85, waterfall tour per person $43; ⊙7am-5pm; 👪) Located at the boat ramp on the north bank, this outfit is most convenient for individual rentals.

Ali'i Kayaks SUP

(☎241-7700; www.aliikayaks.com; 174 Wailua Rd; SUP for 2hr/day $30/45; waterfall tour $50; ⊙7am-5pm) Specializing in SUP and kayak rental. Their usual guided kayaking/hiking tour to the waterfall was suspended at research time, as the waterfall wasn't flowing. Once the falls bloom, they'll be back. Plus, it is always lovely to paddle this river on a SUP board. They rent SUP gear but not kayaks.

Hiking

Most hiking on the Eastside ascends into Kaua'i's tropical-jungle interior. You can expect humid climes, red dirt (or mud) and slippery patches after rains.

Kuilau Ridge & Moalepe Trails HIKING

The **Kuilau Ridge Trail** (2.1 miles; one way) leads to emerald valleys, colorful birds, dewy bushes, thick ferns and glimpses of misty Mt Wai'ale'ale in the distance. After 1 mile, you'll see a grassy clearing with a picnic table; continue east in descending switchbacks until you reach the **Moalepe Trail** (2.25 miles). From here on, you'll see Nounou and the Makaleha Mountains.

While they are independent trails, the two are often mentioned together because they connect and can be hiked in sequence. Both are moderate hikes and among the most visually rewarding on Kaua'i. Remember, the trails don't complete a circuit so you must retrace your steps on a 9-mile out-and-back. Mountain bikers would also enjoy these forestland trails, although they're used mostly by hikers and hunters.

The Kuilau Ridge Trail starts at a marked trailhead on the right just before Kuamo'o Rd crosses the stream at the Keahua Arboretum, 4 miles above the junction of Kuamo'o Rd and Kamalu Rd. The Moalepe Trail trailhead is at the end of Olohena Rd where it bends into Waipouli Rd.

Nounou Mountain Trails HIKING

Summit Nounou Mountain (Sleeping Giant) and you'll ascend over 1000ft, rewarded with panoramic views of Kaua'i's Eastside. Approach the mountain from the east on the **Nounou Mountain East Trail** (1.75 miles), from the west on the **Nounou Mountain West Trail** (1.5 miles) or from the south on the **Kuamo'o-Nounou Trail** (2 miles). The trails meet near the center.

Visitors tend to prefer the exposed East Trail because it offers sweeping views of the ocean and distant mountains. The well-maintained trail is strenuous and steep, climbing through wild thickets of guava, *liliko'i* and ironwood, with switchbacks almost to the ridge. At the three-way junction near the top, take the left fork, which will lead to the summit, marked by a picnic shelter. Now atop the giant's chest, only his head prevents you from a 360-degree view. Climbing further is extremely risky and not recommended. Do this hike early in the morning, when it's relatively cool and you can witness daylight spreading across the valley. The hard-packed dirt trail is exceedingly slippery when wet; look for a walking stick, which hikers sometimes leave near the trailhead. The East Trail starts at a parking lot a mile up Haleilio Rd in the Wailua Houselots neighborhood. When the road curves left, look for telephone pole 38 with the trailhead sign.

The Nounou Mountain West Trail starts higher and is therefore somewhat less strenuous and better if you prefer a cooler forest trail. Much of the hike is shaded by towering Cook Pines. There are two ways to

THE SOURCE: MT WAI'ALE'ALE

Translated as 'rippling water' or 'overflowing water,' and with the earned nickname of the Rain Machine, Mt Wai'ale'ale averages 460 to 500 inches of rainfall annually, with a yearly record of 683 inches in 1982, and is widely regarded as one of the wettest places on earth. Its steep cliffs cause moist air to rise rapidly and focus rainfall in one area. Believed by ancient Hawaiians to be occupied by the god Kane, it's located in the center of the island and is the source of the Wailua, Hanalei and Waimea Rivers, as well as the Alaka'i Wilderness Preserve and almost every visible waterfall on the island.

access the trailhead: from Kamalu Rd, near telephone pole 11, or from the end of Lokelani Rd, off Kamalu Rd. Walk through a metal gate marked as a forestry right-of-way. You'll have a magnificent views of Mt Waialeale to Mt Makaleha as you ascend.

The Kuamo'o-Nounou Trail runs through groves of trees planted in the 1930s by the Civilian Conservation Corps; it connects with the West Trail. The trailhead branches from the middle of a residential community off Kuamo'o Rd between mile markers 2 and 3. Look for the petit brown state park sign and follow it behind the last house on the ridge.

For guided hikes, the gold standard is geologist Chuck Blay's company, **Kaua'i Nature Tours** (742-8305, 888-233-8365; www.kauainaturetours.com; Nounou Mountain tour adult/child $125/90), which offers an all-day tour that includes lunch and transportation.

Festivals & Events

Taste of Hawaii FOOD
(www.tasteofhawaii.com; per person in advance/day of $100/115; 11:30am-3:30pm) On the first Sunday in June, the Rotary Club of Kapa'a hosts the 'Ultimate Sunday Brunch' at Smith's Tropical Paradise, where you can indulge in gourmet samples by 50 distinguished local chefs. With additional booths offering wines, microbrews, ice cream and desserts, you're liable to stuff yourself silly. Dance it off to more than 10 live music acts.

Sleeping

Most condos, B&Bs and inns require a three-night minimum stay and a cleaning fee. Rosewood Kaua'i represents many outstanding vacation rental homes in Wailua and Kapa'a.

★ **Rosewood Kaua'i** HOTEL $
(822-5216; www.rosewoodkauai.com; 872 Kamalu Rd; r with shared bathroom $65-75, cottages from $135;) Set high in the Wailua Homesteads, budgeteers will be forever spoiled by these meticulously tidy private bunkrooms with private entrances, sleeping lofts, sky lights and tasteful built-in furnishings. Expect a cleaning fee ($25). For a step up, inquire about their romantic cottages.

Colleen's Dream ($135) is a wonderful lavender-brushed gem with an outdoor shower, shabby chic furnishings and kitchenette. The Victorian ($145) is a two bedroom with a full kitchen and wood floors throughout. The entire property is landscaped with stunning gardens. It is a family-run operation and not associated with the Rosewood Hotel brand. They also rent private homes throughout Wailua.

Sleeping Giant Cottage COTTAGE $
(505-401-4403; www.wanek.com/sleepinggiant; 5979 Heamoi Pl; cottage $99, 3-night minimum;) A painfully cute shuttered mountainside fantasy nestled under shade trees near the foot of the Sleeping Giant. It's pleasantly appointed with hardwood floors, kitchen, a comfortably sized bedroom and living-dining room, plus a huge screened patio facing a backyard garden. Cleaning fee is $50; discounts for weekly or monthly stays.

Kauai Sands Hotel HOTEL $
(822-4951; www.kauaisandshotel.com; 420 Papaloa Rd; standard/superior/deluxe $79/89/99, wi-fi pass per day $9;) An affordable three-star hotel with a motel feel, a pool and a rather sweet slice of beach front. This is by far the most affordable hotel in the area. Rooms are clean enough, if aging, with fresh paint, carpet and mini fridge.

Fern Grotto Inn INN $$
(821-9836; www.ferngrottoinn.com; 4561 Kuamo'o Rd; cottages $125-195;) Charmingly retro, these remodeled, 1940s plantation-style cottages vary in size, but all feature hardwood floors, tasteful furnishings, TV and DVD, shared laundry, and kitchen or kitchenette. Rates are slightly high, but the location near the Wailua River dock reduces driving. Friendly owners go the extra mile to ensure guests' comfort.

Pineapple House VACATION RENTAL $$
(www.vrbo.con/174696; 4617 Kuamo'o Rd; per week $1495) This humble house with three bedrooms, two bathrooms, a white picket fence and turquoise shutters is just steps from Wailua River. From the Jacuzzi on your back deck you'll enjoy views of a vast and elegant coconut grove. It sleeps up to six people.

Aston Islander on the Beach HOTEL $$
(822-7417; www.astonislander.com; 440 Aleka Pl; r $140-250;) Among midrange hotels, you can't top the Islander. It's not a resort so don't expect frills, but the 186 rooms are relatively modern and upscale, with granite countertops, flat-panel TVs and stainless-steel and teak furnishings. Deep discounts online.

Courtyard Marriot Kauai HOTEL $$
(☎822-3455, 800-760-8555; www.marriotthawaii.com; 650 Aleka Loop; r from garden/ocean view $150/200; ❄ 📶 🏊) For a presentable business-class hotel, look no further. The 300-plus-room beachside hotel is set apart from the rest of the Coconut Plantation development and has a classy, efficient feel, from the soaring lobby full of plush seating to the pleasant pool. Rooms pamper the business traveler with dark woods, black-marble counters and work desk with rolling chair.

Kauai Coast Resort RESORT $$$
(☎822-3441; www.shellhospitality.com; 520 Aleka Loop; r from $285; P ❄ 📶 🏊) A rather splashy condo development that rolls to the beach in the Coconut Plantation swirl. They have 108 units, most of which are one- and two-bedroom condos with full kitchen and washer-dryer among their array of standard amenities. They have six studios, as well. The pool and garden are lovely. It's a good choice for families. Online discounts abound.

Eating

With no commercial center, Wailua is not a hang-out town, but it boasts a handful of notable eateries.

Monico's Taqueria MEXICAN $
(☎822-4300; www.monicostaqueria.com; 4-356 Kuhio Hwy, Kinipopo Shopping Village; mains $8-14; ⏲11am-3pm, 5-9pm Tue-Sun) Everything tastes fresh and authentic, from the generous burritos and taco plates to the freshly made chips, salsa and sauces. Thumbs up for the affordable fish mains.

Cakes By Kristin CAFE $
(☎823-1210; www.cakesbykristin.com; 4-356 Kuhio Hwy, Kinipopo Shopping Center; ⏲9am-9pm Tue-Sat) A corner bite of hip yumminess in the Kinipopo Shopping Center. They do tasty coffee and teas, mango croissants, macadamia honey tarts and cupcakes. Lord, do they do cupcakes!

★ **Kintaro** JAPANESE $$
(☎822-3341; 4-370 Kuhio Hwy; nigir $3.50-8, rolls $6.50-15, mains $11-26; ⏲5:30-9:30pm Mon-Sat) Night after night, this local favorite packs 'em in for melt-in-your-mouth yellow fin sashimi, even creamier hamachi, a stunning spicy tuna roll and assorted cooked mains that all shine in quality and quantity. Another specialty is their sizzling *teppanyaki* service (five such tables are hidden around back), where chefs wow guests tableside on steel grills.

Caffè Coco FUSION $$
(☎822-7990; www.restauranteur.com/caffecoco; 4-369 Kuhio Hwy; mains $10-19; ⏲5-9pm Tue-Sun; P 🌱) At this rustic little hideaway, chefs fuse Asian, Middle Eastern and other flavors into healthy dishes that delight the Om crowd. Just seafood and veggie dishes here. Ahi is a standout, prepared with Moroccan spices and a curried veggie samosa, or seared and rolled in black sesame with wasabi cream. Big positive: live, homegrown music nightly 7pm to 9pm.

Hukilau Lanai HAWAII REGIONAL $$
(☎822-0600; www.hukilaukauai.com; 520 Aleka Loop, Kaua'i Coast Resort at the Beachboy; dinner $18-30; ⏲5-9pm Tue-Sun) To upgrade from the typical T-shirt-casual joint, we recommend this relaxed, elegant favorite. The menu features top local ingredients, from Kilauea goat cheese to Lawa'i Valley *warabi* (fiddlehead fern). Standout selections include feta-and-sweet-potato ravioli and ahi *poke* nachos. For an affordable splurge, arrive between 5pm and 6pm for the early-bird six-course, wine-paired tasting menu ($40; food-only menu $28).

Kilauea Fish Market SEAFOOD $$
(☎822-3474; 440 Aleka Pl #5; mains $10-16; ⏲11am-8pm Mon-Sat) A Wailua-based shingle of the original, with the same exact menu in slightly better-dressed environs. It's still a bit of a secret thanks to their tucked-away location, but there's no place better for *poke*, plate lunches or ahi wraps on the Eastside.

Mema's THAI, CHINESE $$
(☎823-0899; 4-369 Kuhio Hwy; mains $9-18; ⏲11am-2pm Mon-Fri, 5-9pm daily) While not stark-raving awesome, Mema's serves decent pan-Asian dishes that can be tailored to your carnivorous (or other) preferences. The cozy wooden lodge dining room sprinkled with buddhas offers a charming, old-school atmosphere.

Entertainment

For most, the best nightlife in Wailua is curling up in bed before the roosters wake you. While touristy, the **Coconut Marketplace's** (www.coconutmarketplace.com; 4-484 Kuhio Hwy; ⏲free hula show 5pm Wed, 1pm Sat) free hula show is fun and lively, featuring Leilani Rivera Bond and her *halau* (troupe). She's the daughter of famous Coco Palms entertainer

Larry Rivera, who joins the show on the first Wednesday monthly. Or, if the price isn't a deterrent, a commercial luau makes a decent diversion.

★ **Trees Lounge** LIVE MUSIC
(☎823-0600; www.treesloungekauai.com; 440 Aleka Pl, Behind Coconut Marketplace; ⏰5-11pm) For those seeking a live music fix, this is Kaua'i's most impressive musical venue hosting nightly happy hour and headliner acts ranging from melt-your-face-off rock to mellow acoustic, jazz and traditional Hawaiian. Open mic nights are common – guitars are provided. All are welcome to perform.

Smith's Tropical Paradise LUAU
(www.smithskauai.com; Wailua River Marina; luau adult/student 7-13yr/child 6yr & under $78/30/19; ⏰luaus 4:45pm Mon, Wed & Fri) A Kaua'i institution, Smith's Tropical Paradise launched its luau in 1985, attracting droves of tourists. It's a lively affair, run with lots of aloha spirit by four generations at the lovely 30-acre garden. The multicultural show features Hawaiian, Tahitian, Samoan, Filipino, Chinese, Japanese and Maori dances.

Shopping

Bambulei CLOTHING
(www.bambulei.com; 4-369D Kuhio Hwy; ⏰10am-6pm Mon-Fri, to 5pm Sat) This irresistible women's boutique is chock-full of feminine gear made for those who've outgrown the teenage surfer-chick look. The drapey sweaters, platform sandals and kimono-fabric accessories aren't haute couture, but they're affordable and unique. Also find vintage clothing and retro home decor.

KAUA'I FOR CHILDREN

- Float along backcountry waterways on inner tubes (p484)
- Slurp up a rainbow shaved ice with the works at Jo-Jo's Anuenue Shave Ice & Treats (p565)
- Feed a hungry pig herd on Kilohana Plantation's train ride (p481)
- Explore a giant beachfront playground (p493)
- Ride coaster bikes (p503) along the Eastside coastal path
- Introduce tots to the ocean at two baby beaches (p544)
- Learn to surf at Hanalei Bay (p523) or Po'ipu Beach Park (p543)
- Splash in the Grand Hyatt Kaua'i's (p550) river pools

Getting There & Away

Don't look for a town center. Most attractions are scattered along Kuhio Hwy (Hwy 56) or along Kuamo'o Rd (Hwy 580), which leads *mauka* (inland). To get to Kapa'a or beyond, take the Kapa'a Bypass Rd, which runs from Coconut Plantation to north Kapa'a.

Waipouli

Sandwiched between Wailua and Kapa'a, Waipouli is less a town than a cluster of restaurants, grocers, a drugstore and other basic businesses. You're likely to stop here to stock up.

Activities

Bear in mind that though rentals are here, the actual activities are elsewhere.

Ambrose's Kapuna SURFING
(www.ambrosecurry.com; 770 Kuhio Hwy; per hr $35) Don't miss the chance to meet surf guru Ambrose Curry, who offers to 'take people surfing' (or stand up paddling), not to 'give surf lessons.' If you're baffled, then you have much to learn from this longtime surfer-philosopher, once dubbed a tribal elder.

Originally from California, Curry has lived on Kaua'i since 1968 and is also the artist and board shaper behind much of the quirky prints and pieces you'll find at Marta's Boat (p502).

The Yoga House YOGA
(☎823-9642; www.bikramyogakapaa.com; 4-885 Kuhio Hwy; drop-in classes $15; ⏰classes 9:15am daily & 5:15am Mon-Fri) Sweat blissfully in this bikram style studio set in a cute yellow house at the back of a minimall. Offering 12 classes weekly, there's plenty of opportunity to get centered here.

Spa by the Sea SPA
(☎823-1488; www.spabytheseakauai.com; 4-820 Kuhio Hwy, Outrigger Waipouli Beach Resort & Spa; treatments from $140; ⏰9am-6pm Mon-Sat, 10am-6pm Sun) Indulge in a *lomilomi* massage, Noni facial or volcanic clay body treatment.

Snorkel Bob's SNORKELING
(☎823-9433; www.snorkelbob.com; 4-734 Kuhio Hwy; basic snorkel sets per day/week $2.50/9, bet-

ter sets $9/35, bodyboards from $8/32; ⏲8am-5pm Mon-Sat) The cool thing about this place is that if you're island-hopping, you can rent gear on Kaua'i and return it on the Big Island, O'ahu or Maui.

Kauai Cycle CYCLING
(☎821-2115; www.kauaicycle.com; 4-934 Kuhio Hwy, Waipouli; per day/week cruiser $20/110, mountain or road bike $30/165, full-suspension $45/250; ⏲9am-6pm Mon-Fri, to 4pm Sat) Sells, services and rents high quality bikes – including full-suspension mountain bikes and specialized road bikes, maintained by experienced cyclists. Prices include helmet and lock.

Sleeping

Waipouli is sandwiched between Wailua and Kapa'a, both with plenty of options.

Outrigger Waipouli Beach Resort & Spa RESORT $$
(☎800-688-7444, 822-6000; www.outriggerwaipouli.com; 4-820 Kuhio Hwy; 1/2br from $225/275; ❄📶🏊) The surrounding strip malls and traffic belie this condo's cachet as the Eastside's newest and fanciest. Units are law-firm handsome with 37in flat screens, washer-dryers and an 'extra' bathroom per unit. There's no swimmable beach, but a saltwater 'river pool' and sand-bottom hot tubs compensate somewhat. Outrigger represents 100 of the 196 total units, but also check www.vrbo.com.

Eating & Drinking

While most restaurants have a bar-type area, the best 'nightlife' can be found at Trees Lounge (p500) in nearby Wailua.

★ **Tiki Tacos** MEXICAN $
(☎823-8226; 4-961 Kuhio Hwy, Waipouli Complex; tacos $5-8; ⏲11am-8pm) The latest to spark an island-wide taco craze, this new spot offers authentic *taqueria* gravitas right down to their house-made tortillas. It does help when the chef is Mexican. Tacos come with choice of chicken, fish, chorizo, shrimp, beef or pork and are piled with island-grown cabbage, *queso fresco,* sour cream and onion. Call for takeout.

Tropical Dreams ICE CREAM $
(www.tropicaldreamsicecream.com; 4-831 Kuhio Hwy; one scoop $4.50; ⏲noon-9pm Sun-Thu, to 9:30pm Fri & Sat) A tiny drop of ice-cream heaven set in the Kaua'i Village complex. This boutique chain stocks their goods from a rotation of 381 flavors crafted from 85% local ingredients. They do soft serve as well as old-fashioned scoops. Don't miss it.

Shivalik Indian Cuisine INDIAN $$
(☎821-2333; www.shivalikindiancuisine.com; 4-771 Kuhio Hwy; mains $13-19, buffet $14; ⏲11:30am-2:30pm Thu-Tue, 5-9pm daily) Hidden in the corner of the Waipoli shopping center, the steady business is a testament to the quality of its tandoori-style cuisine (cooked in a cylindrical clay oven). The extensive menu covers the gamut of Indian cuisine, from lentil and lamb curry to vegetable samosas and everything in between.

Kaua'i Pasta ITALIAN $$
(☎822-7447; www.kauaipasta.com; 4-939B Kuhio Hwy; mains $9-15, lunch specials $10; ⏲11am-9pm, lounge to midnight) Tricky to find but worth the search, this is a saving grace for pasta lovers. With the list of Italian standards covered after years of perfecting the practice, they're able to focus on creative daily specials, maximizing the use of fresh local ingredients. With steady local clientele as the strongest testament, it's a worthwhile venture.

Oasis on the Beach FUSION $$
(☎822-9332; www.oasiskauai.com; 4-820 Kuhio Hwy, Waipouli Beach Resort; dishes $14-28; ⏲noon-9pm Mon-Sat, 10am-9pm Sun) Excellent breakfasts and tasty lunch and dinner mains are served in this fun boathouse at the Outrigger. Dishes are rather counterintuitive (in a good way), with offerings like shepherd's pie, braised brisket and farmers market curry along with grilled fresh catch. The Sunday brunch is a full-on affair, so come hungry.

Wahoo SEAFOOD $$
(☎822-7833; www.wahoogrill.com; 4-733 Kuhio Hwy; mains $24-28; ⏲4-9:30pm daily) A Hawaiian-themed seafood house where mahi is stuffed with crabmeat and smothered in macadamia butter and pineapple salsa, ahi is broiled then simmered in a clam-and-coconut-milk stock, and opah is broiled and served with a lobster brandy and cream sauce. The dining area opens onto an outdoor patio overlooking the coconut trees.

Self-Catering

Safeway SELF-CATERING $
(☎822-2464; 4-831 Kuhio Hwy, Kaua'i Village; ⏲24hr) Caters to mainland tourists, with familiar brands and an American-style deli and bakery.

Papaya's Natural Foods SELF-CATERING $
(☎823-0190; www.papayasnaturalfoods.com; 4-831 Kuhio Hwy; ⊙8am-8pm Mon-Sat 10am-5pm Sun) Foodies will prefer Papaya's for organic produce, a terrific salad bar, an abundance of health and beauty products, plus other island specialties such as Kilauea honey and goat cheese.

Shopping

Waipouli's two main shopping malls are **Waipouli Town Center** and **Kaua'i Village**. Though there is one gem of a boutique here too.

★**Marta's Boat** BOUTIQUE
(☎822-3926; www.martasboat.com; 4-770 Kuhio Hwy; ⊙10am-6pm Mon-Sat) The whimsical Marta's Boat delights 'princesses of all ages' with an amazing selection of original block and screen prints on silks and other soft and flowing fabrics, some funky lacquered boxes and fabulous jewelry. Not to mention dresses and hats for baby girls. There is a quirky art-love philosophy at work in this jewel box.

Nani Moon MEAD
(www.nanimoonmead.com; 4-939 D Kuhio Hwy; bottles $15-24; ⊙noon-5pm Tue-Sat) Nani Moon is a meadery (and tasting room), meaning they make (and pour) tropical honey wine, arguably the oldest alcoholic beverage on earth. Humans have been drinking it for 6000 years or more. They do five flavors, and all are surprisingly dry and food forward.

Information

There's an ATM inside Safeway (p501) in Kaua'i Village on the *mauka* (inland) side of Kuhio Hwy.

Starbucks (Kaua'i Village Shopping Center; ⊙5am-8:30pm, Sun 5:30am-8pm) Offers free wi-fi.

Longs Drugs (☎822-4915; Kaua'i Village; ⊙store 7am-9pm Mon-Sat, 8am-8pm Sun, pharmacy 8am-8pm Mon-Fri, 9am-5pm Sat & Sun) Pharmacy and general merchandise.

Kapa'a

POP 10,699

Downhill and around the corner from the lush, mountainous north shore, Kapa'a is the only walkable town on the Eastside, and it has its charms. Although this is not Kaua'i at its most beautiful, Kapa'a has a sunnier, less self-satisfied and strangely more down-to-earth disposition than elsewhere on Kaua'i, and the eclectic population of old-timers, new transplants, nouveau hippies and budget tourists coexists smoothly. A bike- and footpath runs along the part-sandy, part-rocky coast, the island's best vantage point for sunrises. Plus, it's still less than 30-minutes to Hanalei. Kapa'a's downfall? It sits right along the highway. Try crossing the road during rush hour!

Sights & Activities

Kapa'a Beach Park BEACH
(☎pool 822-3842; ⊙pool 7:30am-3:45pm Tue-Fri, 10am-4:30pm Sat, noon-4:30pm Sun; 👪) FREE From the highway, you'd think that Kapa'a is beachless. But along the coast is a mile-long ribbon of sand that's very low-key and local. While the whole area is officially a county park called Kapa'a Beach Park, that name is commonly used only for the northern end, where there's a grassy field, picnic tables and a public **swimming pool**.

The south end of the beach is informally called **Lihi Beach**, where you'll find locals hanging out and talking story. It's a scrubby thin slab of beach with grass shoots sprouting here and there. Further down the beach are some cemented rock breakwaters that form shallow natural swimming pools but are a bit of an eyesore. Nevertheless, a good starting point for the paved coastal path is the footbridge just north of Lihi. To get here, turn *makai* (seaward) on Panihi Rd from the highway. Further south is Fuji Beach, nicknamed **Baby Beach** because an offshore reef creates a shallow, placid pool of water that's perfect for toddlers. Located in a modest neighborhood that attracts few tourists, this is a real locals' beach, so be respectful. For swimming, we prefer the beaches north of the river mouth. The water is far cleaner.

A Joy of Movement YOGA
(☎639-2767; www.ajoyofmovementstudio.com; 4504 Kukui St, Dragon Bldg; drop-in classes $15; ⊙1-4 classes daily) Offers a weekly blend of 14 classes such as Hot Yoga, Restorative, Rope Wall Yoga and they even have Mommy & Me and belly dance classes. Visit the website or call for a class schedule.

Seasport Divers DIVING
(☎823-9222, 800-685-5889; www.seasportdivers.com; 4-976 Kuhio Hwy; two tanks and gear rental $165, open water certification $435) Eastside waters are less protected by reefs and choppier due to easterly onshore winds. Therefore diving and snorkeling are very limited here. Still, this small branch of a Po'ipu-

WALK THIS WAY

The Eastside's newest road is a shared-use path reserved for pedestrians and bicyclists. Ten-feet wide and paved in concrete, **Ke Ala Hele Makalae** (The Path that Goes by the Coast) starts at the **Lihi Boat Ramp** at the south end of Kapa'a Beach Park and ends just past Donkey Beach at **Ahihi Point**, a 4-mile stretch. But this constitutes only a small piece of the ambitious facility, which will eventually run over 16 miles all the way from Lihu'e to Anahola Beach Park.

Sunrise walks are brilliant, but for an added kick rent a coaster bike! **Coconut Coasters** (822-7368; www.coconutcoasters.com; 4-1586 Kuhio Hwy; bike rentals per hr/day from $8.50/20, snorkel sets per day $7; 7am-6pm Tue-Sat, 9am-4pm Sun;) specializes in hourly rentals for the path. Classic single-speed coasters are just right for the gentle slope north, but you can upgrade to a three-speed model ($9.75 per hour) for an extra cushy ride. Also try Kauai Cycle (p501) at the south end of the path for daily or weekly rentals of coaster, mountain or road bikes.

A nonprofit community group called **Kaua'i Path** (www.kauaipath.org) is promoting and maintaining the path. The next phase will be the Wailua portion set for construction in early 2013.

based outfit rents diving, snorkeling and other ocean gear and can arrange trips to the north- and south-shore sites.

Kainalu Fishing FISHING
(639-9866; www.kauaifishing.com; Kapa'a Small Boat Harbor; per person $150, private charters $600-800) A recommended Kapa'a-based charter fishing outfit, with half- and full-day itineraries available. Keep and eat what you catch.

Kapa'a New Park TENNIS, SKATEBOARDING
There are free **tennis courts** and a **skateboarding park**, along with a soccer field and baseball diamond.

Tours

Kapa'a Town Walking Tour WALKING TOUR
(822-1651; www.kauaihistoricalsociety.org; adult/child $20/10; by appointment) Andy Bushnell, a retired history professor (he was on the Kaua'i Community College faculty for 37 years, and both he and his father are considered experts on Hawaiian history) offers a wonderful two-hour tour of historic Kapa'a with descriptions of landmarks and Kapa'a's sugar and pineapple boom days.

Festivals & Events

Heiva I Kaua'i Ia Orana Tahiti CULTURAL
(822-9447) In early August, dance troupes from as far away as Tahiti, Japan and Canada join groups from Hawaii at Kapa'a Beach Park for this Tahitian dancing and drumming competition.

Coconut Festival FOOD
(651-3273; www.kbakauai.org; Kapa'a Beach Park; 1st weekend in October) Celebrate all things coconut! Events during this free two-day festival in early October include coconut-pie-eating contests, coconut cook-off, cooking demonstrations, music, hula, crafts and food.

Sleeping

There are a couple of hostels and resorts within walking distance of downtown Kapa'a. Most B&Bs and inns in the area require a vehicle.

★**Honuea Hostel** HOSTEL $
(823-6143; www.kauaihotels.com; 4532 Lehua St; dm $25, r with shared/private bathroom $60/70;) Kaua'i's best hostel is eat-off-the-floor clean. Private rooms are set off from the dorms, share a bathroom and are graced by tasteful murals that add color and character. Bunk beds in the dorms are brand new, and deluxe private rooms have access to the communal kitchen and TV room after hours, as well as a private bathroom.

Kauai Beach House Hostel HOSTEL $
(652-8164; www.kauaibeachhouse.net; 4-1552 Kuhio Hwy; dm $30, r $70;) Not the cleanest of hostels, what with the ramshackle bunks and courtyard. The private rooms are better maintained and sleep two, but they also share bathrooms. Still, there's a communal kitchen and it is well located under the trees and on the beach.

Kapa'a

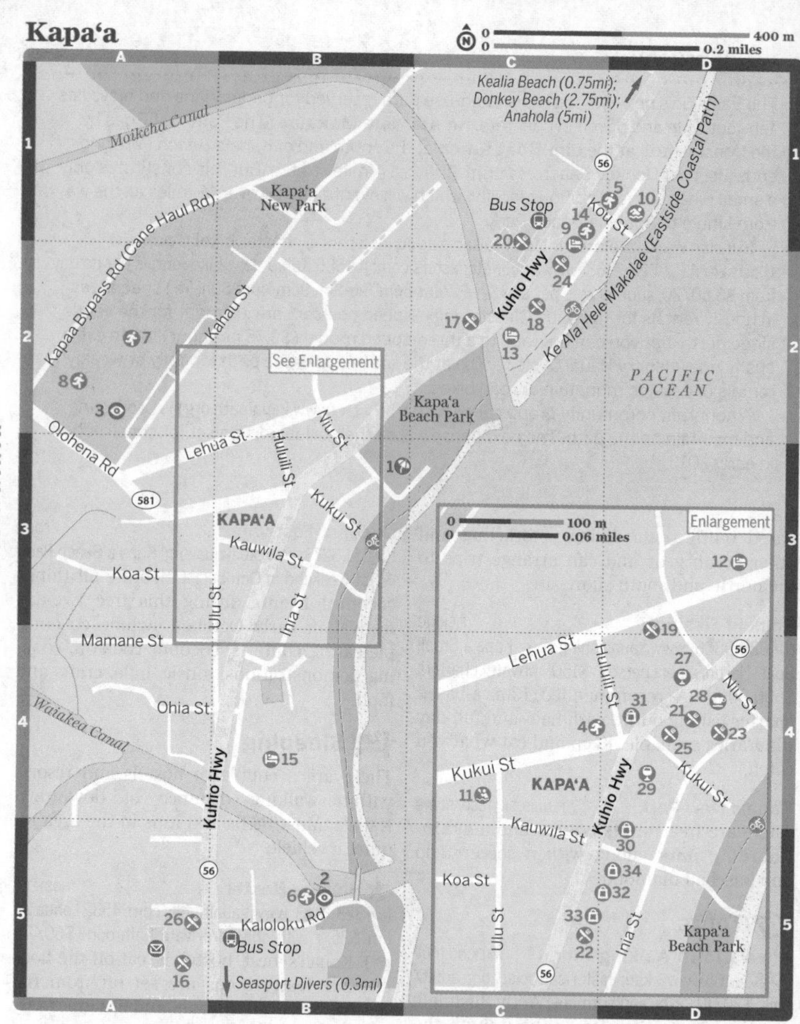

Kaua'i Country Inn

INN $$

(☎821-0207; www.kauaicountryinn.com; 6440 Olohena Rd; 1 & 2br $149-179; ⊙office hours 8am-11am Mon-Fri, 9am-10:30pm Sat & Sun; @ 📶) Still rocking in all its kitsch glory. Think vintage juke box in the foyer, mural-wrapped entry, porch wind-chimes, hardwood floors and upscale furnishings. The four spacious suites include cable TV, DVD, wi-fi and kitchen or kitchenette. The inland location provides serene surroundings and breezy nights.

Green Coconut Studio

INN $$

(☎647-0553; www.greencoconutstudio.com; 4698 Pelehu Rd; studio $110; ❄ 📶) Literally lined with windows (and a wraparound veranda), this fantastically airy studio allows spectacular coastal views and cooling cross-breezes. The layout makes great use of space, allowing for a comfy satellite-TV setup, and a kitchenette with full-sized fridge and the gamut of appliances. There's a $100 cleaning fee for brief stays.

Hotel Coral Reef Resort

HOTEL $$

(☎822-4481, 800-843-4659; www.hotelcoralreefresort.com; 4-1516 Kuhio Hwy; r from $245; ❄ 📶 🏊) A wonderful little family-run resort. Though the exterior gives off a three-star

Kapa'a

vibe, the rooms are much better than that, with shuttered floor-to-ceiling glass doors facing the beach, a granite-topped sink and bar, and queen and king beds with headboards and plush linens. Walk-in rates plummet to as low as $169. Service is warm and impeccable.

Pono Kai Resort RESORT $$
(☎822-9831; www.ponokai.com; 4-1250 Kuhio Hwy; studio/1br/2br from $125/160/179;) An aging, affordable three-star condo complex that dominates the middle stretch of Kapa'a beach. The units are clean and well maintained but offer outdated electronics and bathrooms. Digs are spacious, however.

Eating

Roadside restaurants abound, none too terrible, some terribly touristy.

Verde MEXICAN, FUSION $
(☎821-1400; www.verdehawaii.com; 4-1101 Kuhio Hwy, Kapa'a Shopping Center; mains $7-14; ⊙11am-9pm;) With a stellar local reputation, this new Mexican–Hawaiian fusion taqueria receives island-wide buzz for their inventive fish tacos. The ahi variety are especially righteous, and their one-taco lunch special with rice and beans ($6.95) is a terrific deal. Be sure to save room for the sopaipilla and honey for dessert. Call for takeout.

Pono Market DELI $
(☎822-4581; 4-1300 Kuhio Hwy; plate lunch $6.50; ⊙6am-6pm Mon-Fri, to 4pm Sat) Fill up on local *grinds* (food) at this longtime hole in the wall, now with a fully fledged espresso bar. At lunch, line up for generous plate lunches, homemade sushi rolls, fresh ahi *poke* and savory delicacies such as dried *'opelu* (pan-sized mackerel scad) and smoked marlin.

Cafe Hemingway CAFE $
(☎822-2250; www.artcafehemingway.com; 4-1495 Kuhio Hwy; mains $6-14; ⊙6am-6pm Tue-Fri, from 8am Sat, 8am-2pm Sun) A painfully cute, white-washed art cafe decorated with antiquated furnishings, and serving flakey quiches and breakfast platters named after Hemingway novels. *Sun Also Rises* features scrambled eggs with parmigiano reggiano and smoked ham. *For Whom The Bell Tolls* is a salami and liverwurst omelet with pancetta and cheese. Perhaps the bell tolls for a heart surgeon?

Coconut Cup Juice Bar & Cafe JUICE BAR, CAFE $
(☎823-8630; www.coconutcupjuicebar.com; 4-1516 Kuhio Hwy; juices & smoothies from $6.25, sandwiches $9-10; ⊙8am-5pm;) A juice and natural food takeout stand, this roadside treasure slings generously endowed sandwiches. Wash down your hulking albacore tuna or avocado veggie varietal with a

REDUCE, REUSE, RECYCLE

As eco-conscious as Kauai first appears, and it does have a green soul, there is not a comprehensive recycling program in place island-wide. Some, not all, condo complexes offer recycling bins, so you may need to seek out one of the following recycling centers and get the job done yourself. Here's a list of the island's recycling centers:

North Shore North Shore Transfer Station (across from the Prince Course) in Princeville

Eastside End of Kahau Rd, behind the ball field near the bypass road, in Kapa'a

Lihu'e Back of the Kmart parking lot on the pavilion side of the store

Nawiliwili Harbor Reynolds Recycling (corner of Wilcox and Kanoa Sts)

South Shore Po'ipu in the Brennecke's parking lot

Westside Waimea Canyon Park; Kekaha Landfill

fluorescent shot of wheat grass or fresh-squeezed organic orange, carrot or green juice cocktail (kale, celery and cucumber). They have tasty salads too.

Mermaids Café CAFE **$$**
(☎821-2026; www.mermaidskauai.com; 4-1384 Kuhio Hwy; mains $11-13; ⊙10:30am-9pm; ✎) This walk-up counter offers sizeable burritos, fresh organic salads and homemade wok-fried entrée plates jazzed up with lemongrass and organic herbs. Get the ahi *nori* with brown rice and wasabi cream sauce and you'll dream of it for days.

The Eastside HAWAII REGIONAL **$$**
(☎823-9500; 4-1380 Kuhio Hwy; mains $19-28; ⊙5:30-9:30pm daily) With a bit more style and grace than other Kapa'a haunts, they start with *poke* and steamed pork-belly sticky buns (think *dim sum*) and move on to island-inflected takes on ahi and mahi, prawns and shortrib. They have a stellar wine selection too.

Rainbow Living Foods VEGAN **$$**
(☎821-9759; 4-1384 Kuhio Hwy; mains $13-14; ⊙10am-5pm Mon-Fri, to 3pm Sat; ✎) For those hungry for purity, everything here is gluten-free, vegan and raw. Portions don't match the price, but their vegan integrity – utilizing local organic farms and serving an abundance of superfoods with inventive preparation – justify the expense and will leave your body feeling clean.

Sushi Bushido JAPANESE **$$**
(☎822-0664; www.sushibushido.com; 4504 Kukui St; rolls $8-13, nigiri $5-10, bento boxes $7-10; ⊙noon-close Mon-Fri, 5pm-close Sat & Sun) A locally recommended sushi stop set up in a funky corner of the Dragon Building. They have congas on the bandstand, pop art on the walls and tasty sushi at knifepoint. They do bento box lunches on the cheap too.

Scotty's Beachside BBQ BARBECUE **$$**
(☎823-8480; 4-1546 Kuhio Hwy; mains $13-25; ⊙7-10am & 11am-8:30pm Mon-Sat, 7-11am Sun) Racks of ribs, smoked chicken, that perfect mai tai, fish and brisket sandwiches and an all-you-can-eat daily breakfast buffet are on offer at this beachside grill shack. Get $2 and $3 off drinks and appetizers at happy hour (3pm to 5pm).

Self-Catering

The best place for local produce is the **farmers market** (Kapa'a New Town Park, Kahau Rd & Olohena Rd; ⊙Wed 3-6pm). It's among the island's largest.

Hoku Foods SELF-CATERING **$**
(www.hokufoods.com; 4585 Lehua St; ⊙10am-6pm; ✎) Ideal for the cuisine conscious who seek a wide assortment of organic, gluten-free and raw foods.

Big Save SUPERMARKET **$**
(☎822-4971; 1105 Kuhio Hwy, Kapa'a Shopping Center; ⊙7am-11pm) This local chain has a deli.

Kojima Market MARKET **$**
(☎822-5221; 4-1543 Kuhio Hwy; ⊙8am-7pm Mon-Fri, to 6pm Sat, to 1pm Sun) Rather limited but recommended by locals for its fresh local beef and produce.

Drinking & Entertainment

Kapa'a comes alive on **First Saturdays**, a block party held on the first Saturday of each month featuring live bands and street vendors.

Java Kai CAFE

(www.javakai.com; 4-1384 Kuhio Hwy; ⏲ 6am-5pm Mon-Sat, 7am-1pm Sun; 📶) Always busy, this Kaua'i-based microroaster is best for grabbing a cup to go. The muffins, scones and cookies are baked fresh; keep an eye out for the 'vocab word of the day' so you can *confabulate* with the always pleasant baristas about music and such.

Olympic Cafe BAR

(☎ 822-5825; 1354 Kuhio Hwy; ⏲ 6am-9pm Mon-Thu, Sun to 10pm Fri & Sat, Happy Hour 5-7pm) An all things to all people bar and grill specializing in average tourist fare, it's best enjoyed at happy hour. That's when locals pack this spacious 2nd-floor sports bar. Oh, and on Fridays happy hour includes free fish and meat tacos.

Backyards SPORTS BAR

(☎ 821-1242; 4-1387 Kuhio Hwy; ⏲ 5pm-midnight) Kapa'a's local sports bar serves decent appetizers like kalua pork sliders and wasabi fries. They have three flat screens and occasional live music too.

Shopping

Larry's Music MUSIC

(www.kamoaukes.com; 4-1310 Kuhio Hwy; ⏲ 11am-4pm Mon-Fri, to 2pm Sat) This music shop has been open since the 1940s, but was only recently bought by Kamoa Ukelele, a local manufacturer. Less expensive models are made in China and start from under $100, but vintage and high-end ukes made locally from koa wood range from $1000 to $5000.

Serendipity VINTAGE

(☎ 631-1468; 4-1302 Kuhio Hwy; ⏲ hours vary, call for appointment) A charming treasure chest of 1930s to 1950s collectibles. Everything and anything that may have washed up on these shores is here, from vintage leather suitcases to glass buoys to all manner of furniture and fixtures – yes, including elaborate candelabras. The owner literally has warehouses full of stuff and her shop is a damned fine browse.

Hula Girl CLOTHING

(☎ 822-4422; 4-1340 Kuhio Hwy; ⏲ 9am-6pm Mon-Sat, 10am-5:30pm Sun) Aloha-shirt aficionados will find a wide selection of quality, name-brand shirts ($40 to $125), most of which are reprints of vintage designs.

Vicky's Fabrics SOUVENIRS

(☎ 822-1746; www.vickysfabrics.com; 4-1326 Kuhio Hwy; ⏲ 9am-5pm Mon-Sat) Established in the early 1980s, Vicky's is a gem for quilters and homemakers. Find a wide selection of Hawaiian, Japanese and batik fabrics. Owner and seamstress, Vicky, also offers some handmade quilts, pin cushions and bags.

Island Hemp & Cotton CLOTHING

(☎ 212-7550; www.islandhempclothing.com; 4-1320 Kuhio Hwy) A rather elegant hippie emporium with linen shirts, coconut wood jewelry and some surprisingly slinky dresses, blouses and tailored tees, crafted from hemp, organic cotton and bamboo. They also have (gulp) man purses.

Information

Samuel Mahelona Memorial Hospital (☎ 822-4961; www.smmh.hhsc.org; 4800 Kawaihau Rd) Basic emergency care. Serious cases are transferred to Lihu'e's Wilcox Memorial Hospital.

First Hawaiian Bank (☎ 822-4966; www.fhb.com; 4-1366 Kuhio Hwy) Has a 24-hour ATM.

Getting There & Around

Kapa'a is 8 miles north of the Lihu'e airport. Kaua'i Bus (p480) ($2) runs north and south through Kapa'a once an hour from 6:30am to 10pm. There's also Akiko's Taxi (p480).

To avoid the paralyzing Kapa'a to Wailua crawl, take the **Kapa'a Bypass Rd**. Note that except in the heart of Kapa'a, you will definitely need a car; Rent-a-Car Kauai (p480) is a good choice.

To go ecofriendly, rent a bike from Coconut Coasters (p503) and cruise at your own pace.

Kealia Beach

Blessed with a wild, near-pristine location, a laid-back vibe and easy access via car or the coastal path, scenic Kealia is the best beach on the east coast, bar none. Isolated from residential development, the beach begins at mile marker 10 as you head north and continues for more than a mile. The sandy bottom slopes offshore very gradually, making it possible to walk out far to catch long rides back. But the pounding barrels can be treacherous and are definitely not recommended for novices; it's a crushing shorebreak. A breakwater protects the north end, so swimming and snorkeling are occasionally possible there. Showers, restrooms, picnic tables and ample parking – including disabled – are available. Natural shade is not, so sunscreen is a must.

Anahola

POP 1930

Most don't even stop in sleepy Anahola and what they're missing is an authentic Hawaiian fishing and farming village with rootsy charm and a stunning coastline. Pineapple and sugar plantations once thrived here, but today the area is mainly residential, with subdivisions of Hawaiian Homestead lots sprouting at the southern and northern ends. The few who spend the night will find themselves in rural seclusion among true locals.

Grouped together at the side of Kuhio Hwy, just south of mile marker 14, Anahola's modest commercial center includes a **post office** (10am-1:30pm, 2-3:30pm Mon-Fri, 9:30am-11:30am Sat), burger stand and convenience store.

Sights & Activities

Anahola Beach Park BEACH

() Tucked away with no sign to get here from the highway, backed by pines and palms and blessed with excellent swimming thanks to a wide bay fringed with a J-shaped sweep of sand that curls into a sheltered cove on the south end, this locals' beach makes an easy getaway.

Because this county park sits on Hawaiian Home Lands, you'll probably share the beach with Hawaiian families, especially on weekends. Remember, it's their beach: respect the locals. There are two ways to get here: for the south end, turn off Kuhio Hwy onto Kukuihale Rd at mile marker 13, drive a mile down and then turn onto the dirt beach road. For the north end, take 'Aliomanu Rd at mile marker 14 and park in the sandy lot. Camping is available by permit.

'Aliomanu Beach BEACH

Secluded 'Aliomanu Beach is another spot frequented primarily by locals, who pole- and throw-net fish and gather *limu* (seaweed). It's a gorgeous mile-long stretch of beach, with grittier golden sand, a few rocks in the shallows and crystalline water.

You can get to the pretty north end by turning onto 'Aliomanu Rd (Second), just past mile marker 15 on Kuhio Hwy. Turn left onto Kalalea View Dr and make your first right on the road bisecting the upmarket housing development. Park in the paved area at the bottom of the hill. From here it's a quarter-mile walk down to the sand.

Hole in the Mountain LANDMARK

Ever since a landslide altered this once-obvious landmark, the *puka* (hole) in **Pu'u Konanae** has been a mere sliver. From slightly north of mile marker 15 along Hwy 56, look back at the mountain, down to the right of the tallest pinnacle: on sunny days you'll see a smile of light shining through a slit in the rock face.

Legend has it that the original hole was created when a giant threw his spear through the mountain, causing the water stored within to gush forth as waterfalls.

Angeline's Mu'olaulani SPA

(822-3235; www.angelineslomikauai.com; Kamalomalo'o Pl; massage treatment $150; 9am-2pm Mon-Fri by appointment only) Experience authentic *lomilomi* (traditional Hawaiian massage; literally 'loving hands') at this longstanding bodywork center run by a Native Hawaiian family. With outdoor shower, open-air deck, massage tables separated by curtains and simple sarongs to cover up, Angeline's is a rustic contrast to plush resort spas. Last appointment at noon.

Sleeping & Eating

'Ili Noho Kai O Anahola B&B $

(821-0179, 639-6317; 'Aliomanu Rd; r with shared bathroom incl breakfast $100) This simple guesthouse fronts Anahola Beach and offers three compact but tidy rooms (sharing two bathrooms) surrounding a central lanai, where guests talk story and fill up on home-cooked breakfasts.

★ **Kauai Aloha** VACATION RENTAL $$

(822-3000; www.kauaialoha.com; Aliomanu Rd; per week $900-1100) Set on the north end of the Anahola Beach area, this sprinkling of four romantic, wooden houses is in a lovely quiet neighborhood and right on the beach. It's locally owned, and you'll get tremendous value for the dollar here, but there's no telephone or TV.

Hale Kiko'o INN $$

(822-3922, 639-1734; www.halekikoo.com; 4-4382-B Kuhio Hwy; s $85-89, d $110;) Just off the highway on an unnamed, unpaved road are two charming modern studios, each with full kitchen. The downstairs unit is spacious and features stylish slate floors, lava-rock pillars, garden patio and artsy outdoor shower. The upstairs unit is more ordinary, but brighter, with windows aplenty and a deck. An additional cleaning fee ($100 to $125) is charged.

Duane's Ono Char-Burger FAST FOOD **$**
(4-4350 Kuhio Hwy; mains $5-9; ⏲10am-6pm Mon-Sat, from 11am Sun) If you're a fan of In-N-Out and Dairy Queen, you'll enjoy this drive-in. Try the 'old fashioned' (cheddar, onions and sprouts) or the 'local boy' (cheese, pineapple and teriyaki sauce). Add crispy thin fries and melt-in-your-mouth onion rings. Burgers come smothered in mayo, so you may want to order yours dry. They do fish or shrimp and chips too.

Anahola Farmers Market MARKET
(Kuhio Hwy; ⏲9am-6pm Fri-Sun) More of a permanent weekend market than the traditional farmers market you might be used to. Goods vary but you can usually expect papaya, pineapple, greens, fresh fish and more.

Getting There & Away

The Kaua'i Bus (p480) stops hourly on Kuhio Hwy across from the post office at the bottom of the hill.

Ko'olau Road

Ko'olau Rd is a peaceful, scenic loop drive through rich green pastures, dotted with soaring white egrets, organic permaculture farms and bright wildflowers. It makes a nice diversion and is the way to reach untouristed Moloa'a Beach or Larsen's Beach (no facilities at either). Ko'olau Rd connects with Kuhio Hwy 0.5 miles north of mile marker 16 and again 180 yards south of mile marker 20.

For a quick bite, **Moloa'a Sunrise Fruit Stand** (☎822-1441; cnr Kuhio Hwy & Ko'olau Rd; juices & smoothies $3-6.25, mains $5.50-7; ⏲7:30am-6pm Mon-Sat, 9am-5pm Sun) offers tasty smoothies, fish tacos, burritos and beautiful fresh fruit. It's basically the most appealing roadside stand you can imagine. They even have fresh baked chocolate chip macadamia cookies for sale.

Beaches

Moloa'a Beach BEACH
(👪) Off the tourist radar, there's a shallow protected swimming area good for families at the north end; to the south, the waters are rougher but there's more sand. When the surf's up, stay dry and safe. Follow Ko'olau Rd and turn onto Moloa'a Rd, which ends 0.75 miles down at a few beach houses and a little parking area.

Larsen's Beach BEACH
This long, loamy, golden-sand beach, named after L David Larsen (former manager of C Brewer's Kilauea Sugar Company), is stunning, raw and all-natural with a scrubby backdrop offering plenty of afternoon shade (the sun is usually behind you in the afternoon). Although shallow, snorkeling can be good when the waters are calm, usually only in the summer.

Beware of a vicious current that runs westward along the beach and out through a channel in the reef. The calmest waters are north of the giant buoy sunk in the sand. To get here, turn onto Ko'olau Rd from whichever end (ie where it intersects either Kuhio Hwy or Moloa'a Rd), go just over a mile then turn toward the ocean on a dirt road (easy to miss from the south: look for it just before the cemetery) and take the immediate left. It's 1 mile to the parking area and then a five-minute walk downhill to the beach.

Sleeping

Valentine By The Bay VACATION RENTAL **$$$**
(☎822-5216; www.rosewoodkauai.com/valentine-by-the-bay/; Moloa Rd; per night $545, 3-night minimum) This stunner of a vacation rental offers four bedrooms, four bathrooms, is fully updated and renovated and sleeps up to eight. The gourmet kitchen has granite counter tops, the lanai has mountain, stream and beach views, and it's within walking distance to a gem of a beach.

HANALEI BAY & THE NORTH SHORE

Forget Eden. Arguably the most pristine part of the island, the North Shore's quilted green slopes and valleys are effortlessly fertile. Somewhere between Hanalei Valley and the 'end of the road,' the seemingly untouched landscape makes it easy to imagine what it must have been like for the Hawaiian gods taking it in from above the sand, sea and mountains below. Savor life here: swim through the turquoise sea, bite into juicy fresh-picked fruit and nap away the afternoon on warm sugary sand. To be sure, the sleepy little enclave that is the North Shore is an unassuming treasure; the island within the island.

North Shore (Kauai)

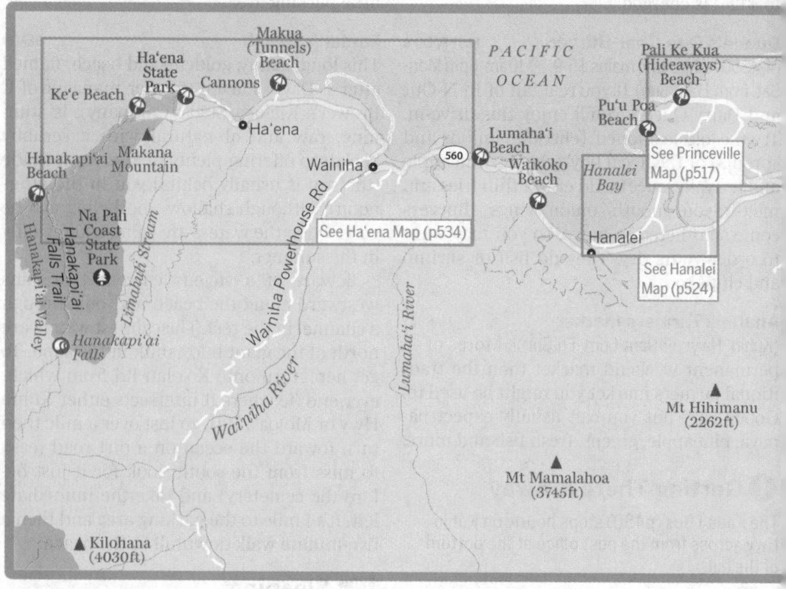

Kilauea

POP 2803

Many North Shore visitors treat Kilauea – a working- and middle-class community that runs far deeper than it first appears – as an ephemeral stop in which to gas up, grab lunch and snap a few photographs on their way north. Perhaps they're a little too hasty.

The most northern point of the island offers lush vegetation, a tasty fish market, a scenic wildlife refuge, two terrific yoga studios, sustainable farms and arguably the island's best beach. A 'secret' no longer, and well-located to reach the end of the highway in one direction and the busier eastside in the other, Kilauea is Kaua'i's undercover sweet spot.

Beaches

★ Kauapea (Secrets) Beach — BEACH

This thick band of powdery white sand extends along massive lava cliffs for more than a mile, wrapping around two rock reefs, all the way to Kilauea point. It offers a sand bar ocean floor and sea shells galore, and boasts crystal clear seas that are the domain of bait balls and (occasionally) marauding dolphins. And the waves are tasty too.

Alas, the swimming here isn't always easy, thanks to that massive shore break, with frequent close outs and tremendously strong currents that flow along the entirety of the beach. Swimming is especially hazardous during big swells (common in winter), which is why it is extremely popular for surfing. It's a local spot, so bring your refined etiquette. Nudists also dig it here. And if you can handle such, ahem, sights, don't mind dirt roads and steep(-ish) trails, adore virginal beaches and typically dig sunsets, you will find Secrets absolutely magical.

However, if the swells are even remotely big or rough, do not go out even knee-high and don't clamber on the rocky outcrops. In January 2013, two San Francisco men drowned here. The first was knocked over and dragged out to sea when he least suspected it. The other went in after him. Respect the waves.

To get here take the southernmost Kalihiwai Rd (there are two), and make the second right on the first dirt road you find. Drive to the end, park and find the trail at the bulb of the cul de sac, which leads 200m or so down a steep path to the beach. If you choose to stroll its entirety (wise choice), be careful as you navigate the rocks, which can be quite slippery, and be mindful of the tides. Be sure

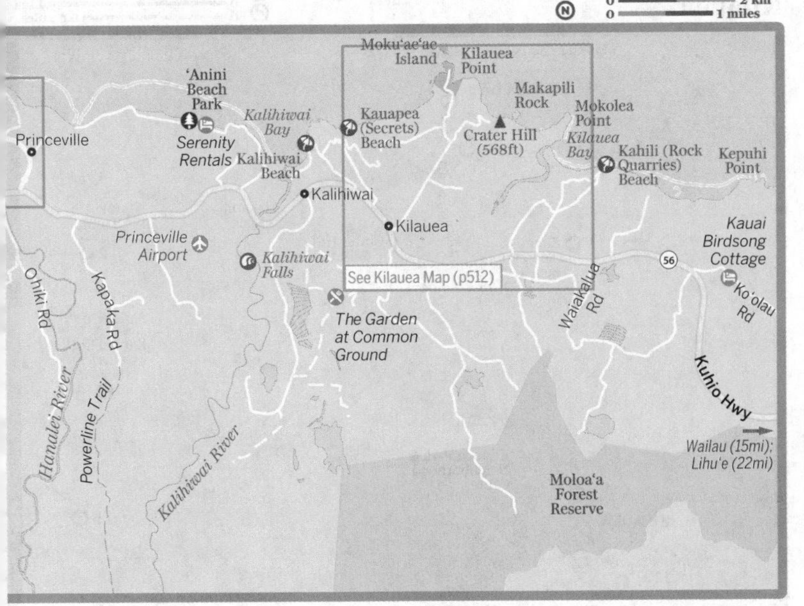

to lock your car and don't leave any visible valuables behind.

Kahili (Rock Quarries) Beach & Pools of Mokolea BEACH

This scenic little stretch of beach, while challenging to find, is tucked away between two densely vegetated cliffs where the Kilauea Stream meets the ocean. There's no protective barrier reef, so when the surf is up, waves can pound. A calm summer day is most suitable for swimming and snorkeling.

The main public access is via Wailapa Rd, which begins midway between mile markers 21 and 22 on Kuhio Hwy. Follow Wailapa Rd north for less than 0.5 miles beyond Kuhio Hwy and then turn left on the unmarked dirt road (4WD recommended) that begins at a bright-yellow water valve. Break-ins are not an uncommon thing around here, so be sure to lock your car.

Sights & Activities

Kilauea Point National Wildlife Refuge WILDLIFE RESERVE

(☎828-1413; www.fws.gov/kilaueapoint; Lighthouse Rd; adult/child under 16yr $5/free; ⏰10am-4pm, closed federal holidays) Home to some of Hawaii's endangered wildlife, this refuge also has sweeping views, as seen from the 216ft sea cliffs where you'll also find the 52ft lighthouse (under renovation at research time). Here you'll find rare birds, glimpse occasional breaching whales (November to March) and spinner dolphins.

You'll also see **Moku'ae'ae Island**, which is teeming with protected wildlife – most often the endangered monk seal can be seen warming itself in the sun.

Na 'Aina Kai Botanical Gardens GARDENS

(☎828-0525; www.naainakai.org; 4101 Wailapa Rd; tours $35-85; ⏰tours depart 9am, 9:30am & 1pm Tue-Thu, and 9am Fri) In a somewhat over-the-top approach, this husband-and-wife operation pays tribute to Hawaiian culture on 240 acres of botanical gardens. Also on the grounds: a beach, a bird-watching marsh and a forest of 60,000 South and East Asian hardwood trees. Turn right onto Wailapa Rd, between mile markers 21 and 22 on Kuhio Hwy and look for their sign.

Christ Memorial Episcopal Church CHURCH

(2518 Kolo Rd) FREE This charming lava built church boasts nine English stained-glass windows, beamed rafters and a wooden ceiling, not to mention a backyard cemetery. Here's proof that the Episcopal church has been on Hawaii for over 150 years.

Kilauea

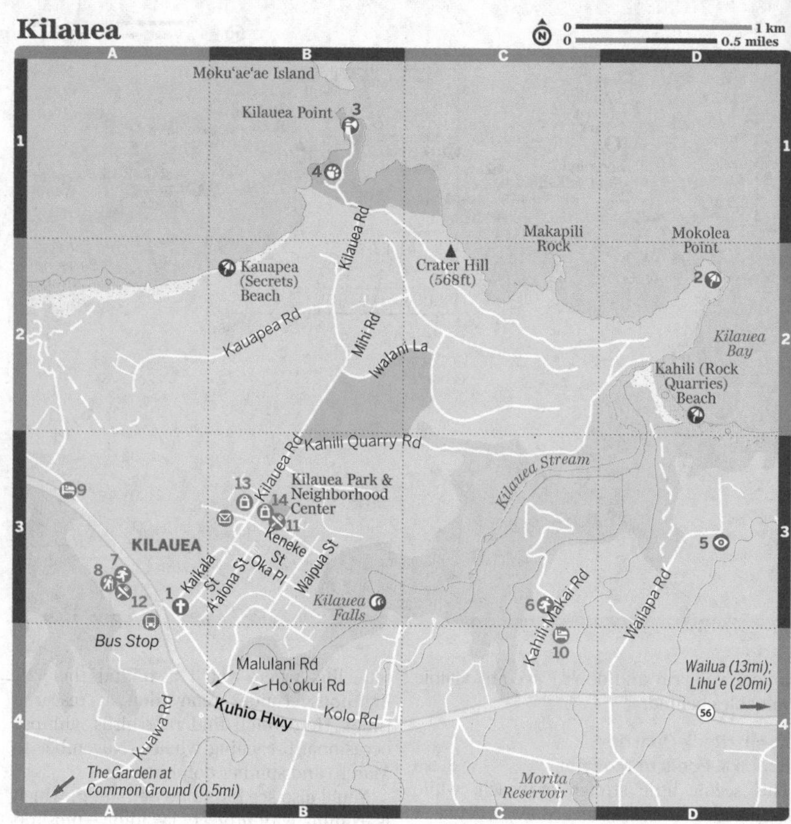

Kilauea

Sights

1 Christ Memorial Episcopal Church A3
2 Kahili (Rock Quarries) Beach & Pools of Mokolea D2
3 Kilauea Lighthouse B1
4 Kilauea Point National Wildlife Refuge B1
5 Na 'Aina Kai Botanical Gardens D3

Activities, Courses & Tours

6 Anahata Spa & Sanctuary C3
Kauai Fresh Farms .... (see 12)
7 Kauai Mini Golf A3
Metamorphose .... (see 13)
Pineapple Yoga .... (see 1)
8 Wai Koa Loop Trail A3

Sleeping

Anahata Spa & Sanctuary .... (see 6)
9 Bamboo A3
10 North Country Farms C4

Eating

Healthy Hut .... (see 13)
11 Kailua Sunshine Market B3
Kilauea Bakery & Pau Hana Pizza .... (see 14)
Kilauea Fish Market .... (see 13)
Kilauea Town Market .... (see 14)
Lighthouse .... (see 14)
12 Namahana Farmers Market A3

Shopping

Cake .... (see 14)
Island Soap & Candle Works .... (see 14)
13 Kilauea Plantation Center B3
14 Kong Lung Shopping Center B3
Kong Lung Trading .... (see 14)
Lotus Gallery .... (see 14)
Oskar's Boutique .... (see 13)

Metamorphose YOGA
(828-6292; www.metamorphoseyoga.com; 4720 Kilauea Rd, Plantation Center; classes $10-20) A new bright and airy yoga studio with a concentration on vinyasa style classes, priced on a sliding scale to suit all budgets. They offer up to five classes per day including qi gong on Tuesday, a gravity defying inversion intensive called Off The Wall once weekly, and a Sunset Restore class at 5:30 pm everyday but Sunday.

Pineapple Yoga YOGA
(652-9009; www.pineappleyoga.com; 2518 Kolo Rd; drop-in classes $20; 7:30am-9:30am Mon-Sat) A long-running Ashtanga style studio set in the parish house of the Christ Memorial Church, across the street from the Menehune Mart gas station.

Anahata Spa & Sanctuary SPA
(652-3698; www.anahatasanctuary.net; Kahili Makai St; sessions $95-125; by appointment) This ain't no ordinary day spa. Taj Jure is fluent in hypnosis, cranial sacral and massage, and she's a gifted energetic healer who does amazing work with crystal bowls and tuning forks that will have your aura tuned, mind calm and body buzzing. Her's is a sound massage that will keep you uplifted for hours if not days. Highly recommended.

Kauai Mini Golf GOLF
(828-2118; www.kauaiminigolf.com; 5-2723 Kuhio Hwy; adult/child 4-10yr/under 4yr $18/10/free; 11am-8pm;) Part mini golf, part botanical gardens, this is one environmentally educational round of putt putt. Separated into five sections (Rare Plants, Polynesian Kunu Plants, Kilauea Town Plantation Heritage, Cultural Influence and Hawaii Today), each hole offers a first-hand experience of exquisite flowering flora.

Kauai Kunana Dairy TOUR
(651-5046; www.kauaikunanadairy.com; 4552 Kapuna Rd; adult/child 2-10yr $40/10; 2-3hr tours by appointment only) For a snapshot of farm bliss, this microdairy offers a tour harkening back to a simpler time, with fruits, vegetables and, of course, goats to milk and feed, and goat cheese to sample.

Wai Koa Loop Trail HIKING, CYCLING
(828-2118; www.kauaiminigolf.com; 5-2723 Kuhio Hwy; 11am-9pm, closed Mon Sep-May) FREE This 5-mile loop trail leads through the greater Namahana Plantation property (the same parcel where you'll find the mini-golf course). Along the way you'll traverse a stream, wind through fruit orchards and take in signage explaining the plantation's history. Hike it for free or rent a mountain bike ($20 for six hours).

Kauai Fresh Farms TOUR
(651-1191; www.kauaifreshfarms.com; 5545 Kahiliholo Rd; per person $50; by reservation) The farm curious might enjoy this sustainable farm tour on the Namahana property. Learn about the hydroponically grown fruits, veggies and herbs, experience the beauty of the world's largest mahogany plantation and enjoy a lunch featuring their produce.

Sleeping

Sleepy Kilauea has some unique B&Bs. What these lack in ocean views, they make up for with lush, tropical farm settings.

Anahata Spa & Sanctuary GUESTHOUSE $
(652-3698; www.anahatasanctuary.net; Kahili Makai St; r with shared bathroom $70-80, with private bathroom $135-145, 2-night minimum; P) Grab a room in this rather uplifting home owned by a charming couple who will dazzle with warmth and wisdom. Their great room features wood floors, an open kitchen and gorgeous leafy views and the outdoor shower is a stunner; all rooms open onto a common lanai and are dressed in plush linens. They even have a bamboo sleeping hale in the garden.

★ **North Country Farms** COTTAGE $$
(828-1513; www.northcountryfarms.com; 4387 Kahili Makai Rd; d $160) These charming cottages are set on a working organic farm. The **Orchard** cottage is a 500-sq-ft studio with a vaulted ceiling and equally large covered lanai (with outside bed), while the more compact **Garden** cottage is a tasteful redwood layout with queen bed and a cornered couch, ideal for couples or families who get along well.

You'll get a basket of breakfast goodies upon check-in and are free to harvest fruit, veggies and herbs from the farm at any time. There's a three-night minimum stay.

Kauai Birdsong Cottage COTTAGE $$
(828-6797, 651-9460; www.kauaibirdsongcottage.com; 7595 Koolau Rd; cottage $160) Secluded, serene, with a hot tub and a rather large hammock under the shelter of Jamaican Lilikoi vines – this spot is worth every penny. The 650-sq-ft studio features a marble-countertopped kitchen, stylish outdoor shower,

queen bed, futon and TV/DVD. Take a few steps outside and pick fresh mangoes, avocados and grapefruit from the tree. There's a $100 cleaning fee.

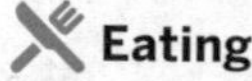

Eating

Kilauea's kitchens are where most locals mix and mingle, and spontaneously so.

★The Garden at Common Ground CAFE $
(828-2192; www.commongroundkauai.net/the-garden; 4900 Kuawa Rd; mains $8-16; 9am-3pm Tue-Sun) This tasty natural food cafe is based on a 42-acre sustainable organic farm, and the kitchen gets creative with seasonal crops. They grill Kilauea lamb burgers and fresh fish, toss kale salads and blend an epic smoothie list. Meals are served in a gorgeous indoor-outdoor dining patio and guests are welcome to roam the property.

Kilauea Fish Market MARKET $$
(828-6244; 4270 Kilauea Rd, Kilauea Plantation Center; plates & wraps $10-20; 11am-8pm Mon-Sat; P) With healthy versions of over-the-counter plate lunches of fresh *opakapaka* or Korean BBQ chicken, *mahi mahi* tacos and aggressively large ahi wraps, consider this Hawaiian-style deli a necessity and build it into the itinerary. Service is speedy and though alcohol is not sold, bringing your own beer or wine for dinner (or lunch) is welcomed. Takeout orders available.

Kilauea Bakery & Pau Hana Pizza BAKERY $$
(828-2020; www.kilaueabakery.wordpress.com; 2484 Keneke St, Kong Lung Center; pizza slices $3-4, pies $15-33; 6am-9pm, pizza from 10:30am; P) Kiluea's go-to comfort spot and social hub, they offer an impressive array of hearty homemade soups, baked goods and popular pizzas (try the Billie Holiday, you won't regret it). The coffee is tasty and people-watching superb. Takeout available.

Lighthouse HAWAII REGIONAL $$
(828-0480; www.lighthousebistro.com; 2484 Keneke St, Kong Lung Center; lunch $12-23; noon-2:30pm Mon-Sat & 4-9pm daily; P) The tasteful, shabby chic ambience works, the wine list is terrific, and they do burgers, fish sandwiches and entrée salads, seafood mains and other carnivorous offerings, but not equally well. The best dish in the house is the fish rockets. Think seared rare ahi wrapped in a lumpia dough, flash fried with furikake and served with wasabi aioli.

Self-Catering

Kailua Sunshine Market MARKET $
(Kilauea Neighborhood Center, Keneke St; 4:30pm-6:30pm Thu) A sweet if modest local farmers market, with ample mangos, papaya, limes, cucumbers, tomatoes, fresh young coconuts and greens available at fair prices. And if you're lucky, a gorgeous string quintet will be strumming silky Hawaiian harmonies until the sun goes down in their front yard across the street. Slide guitar included.

Healthy Hut HEALTH FOOD $
(828-6626; www.healthyhutkauai.com; 4480 Ho'okui Rd; 7:30am-9pm) A great salad, coffee and juice bar, all the very un-gluten, cruelty-free, all-natural vegan supplies you'll need, and some you'll just want, if you too desire a high-end, om-licious, healthy lifestyle. And why wouldn't you?

Kilauea Town Market MARKET $
(2474 Keneke St, Kong Lung Center; 8am-8pm Sun-Thu, to 8:30pm Fri & Sat) An outstanding local corner market filled with a tremendous selection of wines, specialty pastas and sauces, craft beers and local Kilauea grown products. There's a lot of love here.

Namahana Farmers Market MARKET $
(5-2723 Kuhio Hwy; 4pm-dusk Mon, 9am-1pm Sat) Two of Kilauea's three weekly farmers markets are held here.

Shopping

Kilauea Plantation Center, a cute old lava stone complex, sits caddy corner to **Kong Lung Shopping Center**, another historic merchant block. This is where you'll find the bulk of Kilauea's shopping and restaurants. Kong Lung also has the town's only ATM. It's in the Lighthouse (p514).

Lotus Gallery ART
(828-9898; www.jewelofthelotus.com; 2484 Keneke Rd, Kong Lung Center; 9:30am-5:30pm) An absolute gem of a real deal Asian antique art gallery with incredible gold leaf and marble Burmese Buddhas, wood sculpture from Thailand and India and a wonderful collection of jewelry including authentic black pearls.

Oskar's Boutique CLOTHING
(828-6858; 4270 Lighthouse Rd, Kilauea Plantation Center; 10am-6:30pm Mon-Fri, from noon Sat) It skews younger, slightly hipper and slightly cheaper than other Kilauea boutiques with nice bikinis, lace under bless-

ings, jeans, summery dresses and tops, flip flops and more.

Island Soap & Candle Works SOUVENIRS
(☎828-1955; www.islandsoap.com; 2484 Keneke St, Kong Lung Center; ⊙9am-8pm) Though there are several of these shops on Kaua'i, this is the most unique on the island, as the soap is made in-house. It's a great place to pick up gifts for your beloved (and envious) mainlanders.

Kong Lung Trading ART, CLOTHING
(☎828-1822; www.konglung.com; 2484 Keneke St, Kong Lung Center; ⊙10am-6pm Mon-Sat, from noon Sun) Asian-inspired art and clothing boutique with a wide array of tchotchkes, pricey souvenirs, reclaimed kimono quilts and an excellent all-natural children's section featuring clothes, books and toys.

Cake CLOTHING
(☎828-6412; 2484 Keneke St, Kong Lung Center; ⊙10am-6pm) Not particularly fashion forward, but they do offer a nice array of classic tropical dresses. Their collection of elegant jewelry gathered from mostly local designers, however, is impressive and inspired.

Getting There & Around

The Kaua'i Bus (p480) stops hourly along the highway across from the Menehune Mart at the entrance to town. The first bus is scheduled to arrive at 6:34am and the last one leaves at 8:34pm.

Kalihiwai

POP 717

Sandwiched between Kilauea and 'Anini, Kalihiwai ('water's edge' in Hawaiian) is a hidden treasure that is easy to pass by. The main indication that it's on the *mauka* (inland) side is Kalihiwai Bridge, which curves dramatically after an abundance of towering albesia trees. And if you haven't exhaled that deep 'thank God I'm here' breath yet, this is the stretch of road that will inspire sweet ecstasies. Most venture here to discover the remote beach, backed by weeping pines blessed with a sandy bottom and a thick slab of golden sand tucked between two scrubby cliffs. It's an ideal frolicking spot for sunbathing, sandcastle building and, swells permitting, swimming, bodyboarding and surfing along the cliff on the east side.

Kalihiwai Rd was at one point a road that passed through Kalihiwai Beach, connecting the highway at two points. A tidal wave in 1957 washed out the old Kalihiwai Bridge. The bridge was never rebuilt and now there are two Kalihiwai Rds, one on each side of the river. To get here, take the first Kalihiwai Rd, 0.5 miles west of Kilauea.

Overlooking the astonishing Kalihiwai Valley and a 10-minute walk to either 'Anini or Kalihiwai beaches, **Bamboo** (☎828-0811; www.surfsideprop.com; 3281 Kalihiwai Rd; 1br $185, per week $1200;) is a charming getaway attached to a larger house inhabited by the owners. The private entrance stairs are steep to this cozy but well-appointed spot, which works well for two people. It's set in a lush garden with dozens of fruit trees, a koi pond, cascading fountains and outrageous views from the Jacuzzi. Your stay includes complimentary use of kayaks, bikes, snorkel gear and boogie boards. It's accessible from the second Kalihiwai Rd.

'Anini

A popular destination for locals spending the day or weekend camping, fishing, diving or just 'beaching' it, golden sand 'Anini is generally beloved by all. To get here, cross Kalihiwai Bridge, go up the hill and turn onto (the second) Kalihiwai Rd, bearing left onto 'Anini Rd soon thereafter.

Sights & Activities

'Anini Beach Park BEACH
() It may not be the island's best-looking beach, but 'Anini is conveniently located and wears many proverbial hats. It's arguably Kaua'i's best wind- and kitesurfing beach, and is likewise popular for snorkeling, camping and swimming, which makes it a good fit for families. Plus it's protected by one of the longest and widest fringing reefs in the Hawaiian Islands.

At its widest point, the reef extends over 1600ft offshore. Note that the shallows do bottom out at low tide, so timing your snorkel is key or you may have to step awkwardly around exposed corals and sea urchins on your way in. The park is unofficially divided into day-use, camping and windsurfing areas. While weekends might draw crowds, weekdays are low-key. Facilities include restrooms, showers, changing rooms, drinking water, picnic pavilions and BBQ grills. Note there is a second entrance to the beach from Princeville, near the Westin. That path leads to 'Anini's secondary beach, across the tidal inlet.

Windsurf Kaua'i WINDSURFING
(☎828-6838; www.windsurf-kauai.com; 'Anini Beach Park; 3hr lesson $100, board rental per hr $25; ⏲rentals 10am-4pm, lessons 10am Mon-Fri) Learn what it's like to glide on water with teacher Celeste Harvel, who wants nothing more than to stoke you out with her 30 years of windsurf experience. She guarantees you'll be sailing in your first lesson. Lessons by appointment only.

Na Pali Sea Breeze FISHING
(☎828-1285; www.napaliseabreezetours.com; Nawiliwili Harbor; 4-/6-/8-hour charters per person $135/165/195) Based in 'Anini but departing from Nawiliwili Small Boat Harbor, this well-priced fishing charter is an excellent choice. You'll be surprised what you can catch and keep from this 33-footer. Na Pali Coast sightseeing tours are also offered.

Sleeping

High-end vacation rentals abound in 'Anini. **Camping** at the justifiably popular 'Anini Beach Park is another option. The campground hosts a mix of frugal travelers and long-term 'residents.' It's generally very safe. Note all campers must vacate the park from Tuesday to Wednesday for upkeep.

Plumeria Cottage VACATION RENTAL $$
(☎828-0811; www.surfsideprop.com; 3585 'Anini Rd; per night/week $225/1725 ; 📶) A charming and unique spot that's both comfortable, chic and child-friendly, it's worth the splurge for the location (it's a short walk to the beach). With a finely polished wood interior, sweeping views, amicable caretakers and access to any and all land and ocean toys, this is modest luxury Hawaiian style.

Serenity Rentals VACATION RENTAL $$$
(☎828-2815; www.serenity-rentals.com; per week from $1925; P📶) Some of the sweetest rentals on the north shore are the series of rather stylish homes with wide porches fronting the west end of 'Anini Beach. These are bright, airy wooden houses with plenty of windows and porch space, steps from the sand.

QUEEN'S BATH

Kaua'i's deadliest spot, situated near Princeville and formed by a sharp lava-rock shelf, has pools that provide natural and rather inviting swimming holes. But it's often hit by powerful waves, notorious for pulling visitors out to sea, as happens annually. Though the surf at times splashes in softly, what many people don't realize is that waves come in sets, which means a 15-to-20 minute flat period could be followed by a 10ft to 15ft wave, seemingly out of nowhere. People die here every year, most commonly by walking along the ledge used to access it. We highly recommend staying away.

Princeville

POP 2158

Kilauea's rich cousin, Princeville (dubbed 'Haolewood') is a methodically landscaped resort community that is about as carefully controlled – and protected – as a film set, especially when it actually is a film set. Made up of high-end resorts, finely manicured golf courses and a mixture of cookie-cutter residences, vacation rentals and even some working-class condominium complexes, what it may lack in personality it makes up for in convenience, as it's the most centrally located 'community' on the North Shore. The only major commercial area is the **Princeville Center**, with a grocery store, several restaurants and a mix of kiosks and retail stores.

Princeville traces its roots to Robert Wyllie, a Scottish doctor who became foreign minister to King Kamehameha IV. In the mid-19th century Wyllie established a sugar plantation in Hanalei. When Queen Emma and Kamehameha came to visit in 1860, Wyllie named his plantation and the surrounding lands Princeville, to honor their two-year-old son, Prince Albert, who died only two years later. The plantation later became a cattle ranch.

Beaches

Pali Ke Kua (Hideaways) Beach BEACH
(🚻) Pali Ke Kua Beach (Hideaways) is a cove notched in the cliffs with 20m of pale golden sand and idyllic turquoise shallows. It's an ideal snorkel and swim spot (when it's calm) with a teeming reef just steps off the beach. But be wise and don't get caught out when the tide comes in.

Park at the lot after the St Regis (p520) gatehouse, where a path between two fences followed by a steep railing- and rope-assisted scramble leads you to Pali Ke Kua. A path to

Princeville

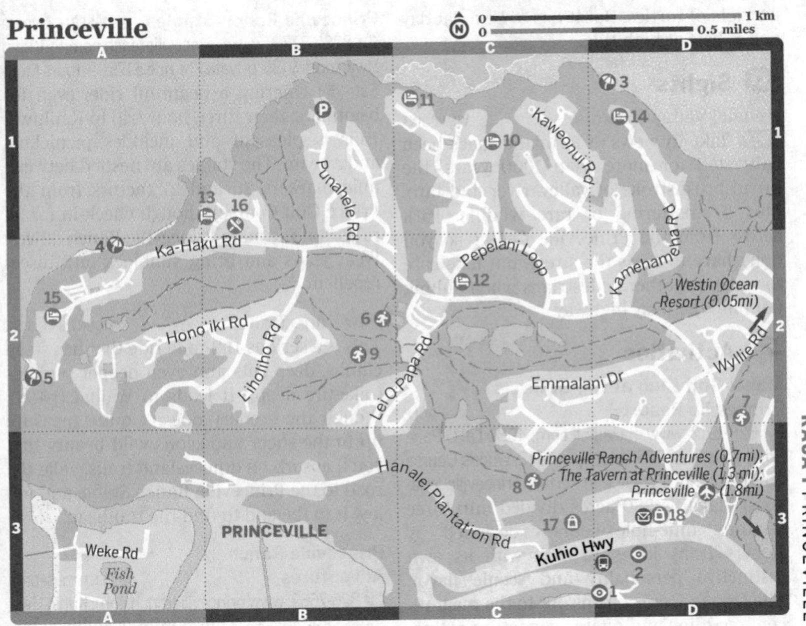

Princeville

Sights
1 Hanalei Bridge D3
2 Hanalei Valley Lookout D3
3 Honu Cove D1
4 Pali Ke Kua (Hideaways) A2
5 Pu'u Poa Beach A2

Activities, Courses & Tours
6 Makai Golf Club at the St Regis Princeville Resort B2
7 Prince Golf Course D2
8 Princeville Trail C3
Princeville Yoga .... (see 17)
9 Tennis at the Makai Club B2

Sleeping
10 Cliffs at Princeville C1
11 Holly's Kauai Condo C1
12 Nihilani C2
13 Pali Ke Kua B1
14 Sealodge D1
15 St Regis Princeville A2

Eating
CJ's Steak & Seafood .... (see 17)
Federico's .... (see 17)
Foodland .... (see 17)
16 Infigo's B1
Lappert's Ice Cream .... (see 17)
Lei Petite Cafe & Bakery .... (see 17)
Lotus Garden .... (see 18)
North Shore General Store .... (see 17)
Paradise Bar & Grill .... (see 17)
The Tavern at Princeville .... (see 7)

Entertainment
Lobby Bar at St Regis Princeville .... (see 15)

Shopping
17 Princeville Center C3
18 Princeville Wine Market D3

the left of the gatehouse leads you to **Pu'u Poa Beach** which, although public, sits below and adjacent to the St Regis Princeville and serves as its on-campus beach.

Honu Cove BEACH

A secret cove beloved by locals and best accessed on calm days only, you'll find it at the end of Kamehameha Rd. Simply take the next right past the Westin, follow it all the way to the end and keep left. At the end of the road you'll see a trail that hugs the cliffs.

At the bottom, stay left along the cliffs and you'll find a beach with good snorkeling and lots of turtles. But it has to be a flat day and is best at high tide.

Sights

Hanalei Valley Lookout VIEWPOINT

FREE Take in views of farmland that's been cultivated for more than 1000 years, the broad brushstroke of valley, river and taro, plus a smattering of rare wildlife. Park across from the Princeville Center so you don't have to cross the street, but take care to watch for other pedestrians when pulling out onto the busy highway.

Activities

Makai Golf Club at the St Regis Princeville Resort GOLF
(826-1912; www.makaigolf.com; 4080 Lei O Papa Rd; greens fee $225, after 1pm $149, Woods Course $55, discounts if staying in certain Princeville locations) Makai is 280 acres divided into three separate nine-hole courses designed by Robert Trent Jones Jr, each with its own distinctive personality and scenic flavor. The **Ocean Course** runs out to the magnificent coastline and offers a signature ravine-contemplating par 3 with an expansive coastal view.

The **Lakes Course** winds its way around several serene lakes, culminating with a par 5 that tempts all those with valor to go for it in two. The **Woods Course** – the cheapest and gentlest – meanders through native woodlands. The Ocean and Lakes link up for a traditional 18 holes.

Prince Golf Course GOLF
(826-5001; www.princeville.com; 5-3900 Kuhio Hwy; greens fees $240, if staying anywhere in Princeville $170; pro shop 7am-6:30am, 1st tee time 7:30am, last tee time 1:30pm) Most call it difficult; Tiger Woods is rumored to have called it 'unfair.' Regularly ranked amongst the world's best golf courses and widely considered the best in the state, this Robert Trent Jones Jr–designed links-style golf course offers some of the most breathtaking vistas in the world. It's as humbling as it can be rewarding – you best bring your A-game.

Tennis at the Makai Club TENNIS
(826-1912, 639-0638; www.makaigolf.com; 4080 Lei O Papa Rd; lessons group/private $18/65, hourly court rental per person $25;) We love the rust-tinted hard courts, which host group and semi-private lessons offered daily by the local pro, pick-up games, junior clinics and round robins. Racket rental available.

Princeville Ranch Stables HORSEBACK RIDING
(826-6777; www.princevilleranch.com; Kuhio Hwy; tours $135, private 2hr ride $175; tours Mon-Sat;) Offering a beautiful ride, even for beginners, their three-hour trip to Kalihiwai Falls is pleasant and includes picnicking and a swim. The stables are nestled between mile markers 26 and 27 (across from the Prince Golf Course), though check-in for all rides is at the main Princeville Ranch offices. Wear jeans and bring sunblock and insect repellent.

Powerline Trail MOUNTAIN BIKING
This is a serious 11.2-mile ride that has steep climbs, deep ruts and even deeper puddles (bike-tire deep). It leads to Wailua (p495), though the scenery doesn't quite measure up to the sheer audacious wild beauty that you'll absorb on other island trails. Take the road to the Princeville Ranch Stable and follow it to the end to find the trailhead.

Princeville Ranch Adventures ADVENTURE SPORTS
(826-7669; www.princevilleranch.com; Kuhio Hwy; tours $89-145;) This family-friendly enterprise can bring out your adventurous side, whether it's for a hike, kayak or a four-hour tour consisting of eight ziplines, a suspension bridge, a swimming hole and a picnic lunch. Minimum requirements are 12 years and 80lb. Check-in here for Princeville Ranch Stables (p518) as well.

Princeville Yoga YOGA
(826-6688; www.princevilleyoga.com; 5-4280 Kuhio Hwy, Princeville Center; classes $15, seniors $10; 9:15am Mon, Wed & Fri, 8am Tue, Thu & Sat, 4:45pm Tue & Thu) Specializing in the beginning Bikram Yoga Hatha series, this skilled team of yogis lead therapeutic classes for any and all willing to endure the steamy climes of a studio usually ranging from 95°F to 100°F.

Mana Yoga YOGA
(826-9230; www.manayoga.com; 3812 Ahonui Pl; classes $20; 8:30am Mon, Wed & Fri) It's no gimmick: Michaelle Edwards created her own version of yoga that has been known to straighten even the most unruly of spines. Combining massage and yoga, her style has proven to help heal via natural poses rather than contortionistic ones.

Halele'a Spa SPA
(877-787-3447; www.stregisprinceville.com; 5520 Ka Haku Rd, St. Regis Princeville Resort; treatments from $165; 9am-7pm) Translated as 'house

of joy,' this 11,000-sq-ft palatial escape offers massages, replete with couples and VIP treatment rooms. The interior incorporates native Hawaiian woods and natural fibers, and the treatments are based upon a foundation of traditional Hawaiian medicine, using both botanical and ocean resources. Think Kaua'i taro clay or seaweed leaf body wraps, and lomi lomi massage.

Princeville Trail RUNNING

Runners would be wise to find the Princeville Trail, and you really can't miss this mostly asphalt path that winds for two miles from Princeville Center to the St Regis. Add mileage by crossing the highway and following the trail's extension for two more miles to the Prince Golf Course.

Sunshine Helicopters HELICOPTER TOUR

(☎270-3999; www.sunshinehelicopters.com; 50min tours $289; first flight of the day $239) Leaving out of both Lihu'e and Princeville airports, Sunshine Helicopters offers convenience if you're on the North Shore. At research time they were the only operation leaving from the Princeville airport.

Sleeping

Princeville, with its abundance of vacation rentals, is devoid of the quaint B&Bs found in neighboring Kilauea and Hanalei, and its overly planned retirement village feel isn't for everyone – though working families do reside here too. Still, its central northshore positioning and elevated tropical milieu is undeniably delicious, and some real steals may be found by searching **Vacation Rentals by Owners** (www.vbro.com), **Craigslist** (www.craigslist.org) or **Airbnb** (www.airbnb.com).

The following companies handle a large portion of condos, homes and resorts in Princeville and offer a variety of units:

Kauai Vacation Rentals VACATION RENTAL $$

(☎866-922-5642; www.kauai-vacations-ahh.com) A nice choice of midrange options.

Princeville Vacations VACATION RENTAL $$

(☎800-800-3637, 828-6530; www.princeville-vacations.com; weekly rates from $700) A decent selection of midrange choices.

★Mana Yoga Vacation Rental VACATION RENTAL $$

(☎826-9230; www.kauainorthshorevacationrentals.com; Ahonui Pl; 2br apt $135; studio $85-100; 3-night minimum; 📶) Situated next to the serene Mana Yoga Center, the larger apartment features all natural wood details, teak cabinets and a tile floor. The lanai offers a vast 180-degree mountain view to contemplate and all the silence you could desire. Though more compact, the studio still boasts a king-size bed and private lanai.

Holly's Kauai Condo CONDO $$

(☎480-831-0061; www.hollyskauaicondo.com; 3830 Edward Rd, Ali'i Kai Resort; 2br $175, 3-night minimum; ❄📶) Perched cliffside with nothing but water between you and Alaska, this 1200-sq-ft two-bedroom two-bathroom unit is a real deal. Winter time (November to March) offers guaranteed whale sightings – basically from your bed – and the recently remodeled interior has HDTV, bamboo furnishings and new bedding and carpets.

Pali Ke Kua CONDO $$

(☎826-6585; www.oceanfrontrealty.com; 5300 Ka Haku Rd; 1/2br per night from 150/$165; 3-night minimum; ❄📶🏊) Situated cliffside, some units offer both ocean and mountain views. Easier alternative access to Pali Ke Kua (Hideaways) Beach is on the property. Listed prices do not include additional $50 reservation and $157 cleaning fees.

Sealodge CONDO $$

(☎800-800-3637, 828-6530; www.princeville-vacations.com; 3700 Kamehameha Rd; 1br per night/weekly $115/$700; ❄📶🏊) Dig that dated shingled-condo funk! Here are wonderfully quaint wooden shingled affairs with a gorgeous cliffside perch. Some are in better shape than others and not all interiors are wonderful, so insist upon pictures prior to online booking; nonetheless, the bones and settings will not disappoint.

Nihilani CONDO $$

(www.nihilanikauai.com; Pepelani Loop; condos $107-219; P❄📶🏊) Our favorite new Princeville condo complex is not cliffside nor does it have sea views, but it is well built with a certain Cape Cod panache (we loved those louvered awnings and shutters), with up-to-date pool area.

Parrish Collection Kaua'i VACATION RENTAL $$$

(☎800-325-5701; www.parrishkauai.com) A more refined, upscale collection of rental options.

Westin Princeville Ocean Resort CONDO RESORT $$$

(☎866-716-8112, 827-8700; www.westinprinceville.com; 3838 Wyllie Rd; studio/1br from $395/550; ❄@📶🏊) A gorgeous cliffside Starwood property with expansive views from nearly every corner. Winter (November to March) whale sightings require merely looking out the closest window. Condo-like 'villas' boast full kitchens, flat-screen TVs and washer-dryers, while the studio units have kitchenettes. The poolside facilities are also marvelous.

St Regis Princeville RESORT $$$

(☎826-9644, 877-787-3447; www.stregisprinceville.com; 5520 Ka Haku Rd; d from $400; P ❄ 📶 ≋) The Oz at the end of the Princeville road overlooks Hanalei Bay, and its 252 rooms range from slightly epic to 'what do I do with myself' extravagant. A 5000-sq-ft infinity pool with three hot tubs sits oceanside, with **Pu'u Poa Beach** just steps away. Even the cheapest rooms are opulent.

Cliffs at Princeville CONDO $$$

(www.cliffsatprinceville.com; 3811 Edward Rd; 1br with garden/ocean view from $300/335; P ❄ 📶 ≋) Another dated but still charming development with sloping roofs, wide verandas and long louvered facade. Amenities include a pool and Jacuzzi, playground for the little ones, tennis courts, shuffleboard and a putting green.

Eating

Federico's MEXICAN $

(☎826-7177; 5-4280 Kuhio Hwy, Princeville Center; tacos $5, burritos & tostadas $10-11; ⏲9am-8pm Mon-Sat; P 👪) A great little taco shop in the Princeville Center. Nachos are piled with beans, meat and veggie goodness. Tostadas are layered with fish and shrimp ceviche. Fish tacos are fresh, breaded and flash fried, and burritos come stuffed with carne asada, carnitas or grilled chicken. All served from a little hole in the mall. Call for takeout.

Lotus Garden CHINESE, THAI $

(☎826-9999; 5-4280 Kuhio Hwy, Princeville Center; mains $7.95-11.95; ⏲10:30am-9pm daily) Thai owned, this pan-Asian store front in the Princeville Center offers relatively cheap eats in large, wok-fried portions. The menu includes spicy garlic fish, Szechuan string beans, tom yam soup, pad thai, pad ka pow and three different Thai curries. Dine in the courtyard or order takeout.

Lei Petite Cafe & Bakery CAFE $

(5-4280 Kuhio Hwy, Princeville Center; lattes $3; ⏲6:30am-4:30pm Mon-Sat, 7am-1pm Sun; P 📶) Princeville's premier caffeine depot offers bagels and bagel sandwiches, fresh baked muffin-tops and sinful cream-cheese-stuffed scones along with fabulous coffee and superb customer service.

Lappert's Ice Cream ICE CREAM $

(5-4280 Kuhio Hwy, Princeville Center; ⏲10am-9pm; P 👪) The sweet, toasty wafflecone scent beckons, and the delectable locally inspired options are sure not to disappoint. Don't miss out.

Foodland SUPERMARKET $

(☎826-9880; 5-4280 Kuhio Hwy, Princeville Center; ⏲6am-11pm; P) The biggest supermarket on the North Shore, Foodland has an abundance of fresh produce, prepared sushi, eight varieties of *poke* (come early in the day) wine, beer and liquor. It has a much better selection than Hanalei's Big Save.

★ **The Tavern at Princeville** HAWAIIAN $$

(☎826-8700; 5-3900 Kuhio Hwy; lunch mains $13-20, dinner mains $19-40; ⏲11am-4pm & 5-9:30pm) While 'tavern' might be a misnomer, revered chef Roy Yamaguchi's newest place is a worthy diversion. They do an ahi nicoise and steamed fish in hot-and-sour broth at lunch, a delicious braised short rib and shrimp and grits at dinner, as well as an addictive macadamia nut pesto flatbread anytime. And don't sleep on the spicy, gingery fish soup.

North Shore General Store AMERICAN $$

(5-4280 Kuhio Hwy, Princeville Center; sandwiches $5-7, pizzas $13-26; ⏲6am-8pm Mon-Sat) Your greasy spoon minimarket is also a fully fledged coffee bar with espresso drinks, bagel sandwiches, breakfast burritos and more. All at decent prices. They do burgers and brick-oven pizzas here too. It's inside the Chevron gas station.

Infigo's TAPAS, FUSION $$

(☎631-7282; www.infigo-experience.net; 5300 Ka Haku Rd, Pali Ke Kua Condo Complex; mains $18-28; ⏲Mon-Wed & Fri-Sun 6-9:30pm; P) Adventurous cuisine served amidst kitschy gold club environs. Dishes range from wasabi prosciutto-wrapped scallops to lobster risotto tapas to herb-baked opah to chorizo-stuffed mahi to house-made gnocchi. And they get rave reviews from the Princeville masses.

Nanea HAWAII REGIONAL $$

(☎827-8808; www.westinprinceville.com/dining/nanea; Westin Princeville Ocean Resort Villas Clubhouse; mains $14-36; brunch $39; ⏲6:30-10:30am & 5:30-9:30pm; P 📶) Nanea presents elegant Hawaii fusion cuisine, and broils some of the best steaks and chops around. They are considered to have the finest burger on Kaua'i (and at $16 it ain't cheap), do a tasty Cubano sandwich and an intriguing short-rib fried rice, while relying heavily on island-grown produce. The poolside brunch is an indulgent classic.

Paradise Bar & Grill AMERICAN $$
(826-1775; www.paradisebarandgrillkauai.com; 5-4280 Kuhio Hwy, Princeville Center; mains $6-24; 7-10:30pm; P) With a surfboard-laden ceiling, photographic testimonials on the walls and an actual surfboard-table in the bar (kids love it), there are some gems amongst its standard burger-and-fries menu. Highlights include macadamia-nut pancakes drizzled with a habit-forming homemade syrup, and a tasty fresh fish sandwich or salad (get it Cajun-style). Two more words: adult milkshakes.

CJ's Steak & Seafood SEAFOOD, STEAKHOUSE $$$
(826-6211; www.cjssteak.com; 5-4280 Kuhio Hwy, Princeville Center; lunch mains $9-15, dinner mains $28-42; 11:30am-2:30pm Mon-Fri & 5:30-9:30pm nightly; P) CJ's is a Princeville standard thanks to its cuisine of prime rib, lobster and fresh fish and to its ability to survive. Hearty dishes are all done well, but without the frills (you won't find any wasabi marinades here). And the induced nostalgia for your favorite late-'70s steakhouse might keep you coming back too.

Drinking & Entertainment

Lobby Bar at St Regis Princeville LIVE MUSIC
(www.princevillehotelhawaii.com; 5520 Ka Haku Rd; 3:30-11pm) Don't let the elegance or the enormous crystal raindrop chandelier intimidate you – the lobby bar is for any and all wanting to cruise and take a load off. The vibe is a step more welcoming than its seemingly chichi surroundings, and if you time it right you can grab a table on the lanai and enjoy the ultimate location for a sunset cocktail.

Shopping

Princeville Wine Market WINE
(826-0040; www.princevillewinemarket.com; 5-4280 Kuhio Hwy, Princeville Center; 10am-7pm) This cozy, life-affirming room trades in a tremendous selection of red and whites from all over the world, spanning in price from the late teens to the hundreds. They also have cigars, fine whiskeys, rums and tequilas at reasonable prices. The cooling barrel out front can chill your bottle in a matter of minutes.

Information

Bank of Hawaii (826-6551; 5-4280 Kuhio Hwy, Princeville Center; 8:30am-4pm Mon-Thu, to 6pm Fri) Has a 24-hour ATM.

Chevron Gas Station (Kuhio Hwy; 6am-10pm Mon-Sat, to 9pm Sun) The last fuel option before the end of the road.

First Hawaiian Bank (826-1560; 5-4280 Kuhio Hwy, Princeville Center; 8:30am-4pm Mon-Thu, to 6pm Fri) Has a 24-hour ATM.

Post Office (800-275-8777; 5-4280 Kuhio Hwy, Princeville Center; 10:30am-3:30pm Mon-Fri, to 12:30pm Sat) In the shopping center.

Getting There & Around

Princeville is great for walking or cruising on bicycle, with one main arterial road (Ka Haku Rd) running through the middle.

The Kaua'i Bus (p480) stops hourly across the street from the Princeville Center on Kuhio Hwy.

Hanalei Valley

A mist hovers above this jade valley, dense with deep *kalo loi* (taro fields), where fertile ground has been the lifeblood of taro for centuries. Exploring Hanalei's interior is to experience native Hawaiian wildlife, gushing waterfalls, stubborn mountains and afternoon rainbows.

The 1912 landmark **Hanalei Bridge** is the first of seven bridges to cross the Hanalei River and lead you to the famed 'end of the road.' The bridge forces you to stop and appreciate the sleepiness of the North Shore. Thanks to this landmark, big trucks, buses and road-ragers can't rampage through this serene little entrance to Hanalei.

From here, an undulating, winding strip of asphalt is canopied by mammoth trees with glimpses here and there of ocean, valley and river. The special **Hanalei Valley Scenic Drive** swerves north on 'the road' to its beautiful end in Ha'ena. Princeville offers some of the first famous North Shore views from its **Hanalei Valley Lookout**. To get here, turn left onto Ohiki Rd immediately after the Hanalei Bridge. Coming from Princeville you can also glimpse miraculous valley views from the **Okolehao Trail**, a rather steep yet rewarding climb. Just take the left at the bridge instead of the right (which leads into Hanalei town) and head

HOMAGE TO KALO

According to Hawaiian cosmology, *Papa* (earth mother) and *Wakea* (sky father, who also gave birth to the Hawaiian Islands) gave birth to *Haloa*, a stillborn and brother to man. Haloa was planted in the earth, and from his body came taro *(kalo)*, a plant that has long sustained the Hawaiian people and been a staple for oceanic cultures around the world.

Kalo is still considered a sacred food, full of tradition and spirituality for Native Hawaiians. The North Shore's Hanalei is home to the largest taro-producing farm in the state, where the purple, starchy potatolike plant is grown in pondfields known as *lo'i kalo* (Hawaiian wet taro fields). After crossing the first of several one-way bridges in Hanalei, you'll notice the *kalo* growing to the left.

Kalo regained the spotlight in the '70s thanks to the 'Hawaiian Renaissance,' a time during which some aspects of the Hawaiian culture enjoyed a modest, long-overdue resurgence and reclaimed practice. Though dismissed by some outsiders as little more than a glorified, garnet-colored potato, *kalo* is rich in nutrients. It is often boiled and pounded into poi, an earthy, starchy and somewhat sweet and sticky pudding-like dish.

Families enjoy poi, defined as the 'staff of life' in the Hawaiian dictionary, a number of ways. Some prefer it fresh, while others prefer sour poi, or poi *'awa 'awa* (bitter), possibly from the method in which poi used to be served – often it sat in a bowl on the table for quite some time.

All traditional Hawaiian households show respect for taro: when the poi bowl sits on the table, one is expected to refrain from arguing or speaking in anger. That's because any bad energy is *'ino* (evil) – and can spoil the poi.

A tip for avoiding offence: because of the spiritual relevance and cultural history of *kalo*, it's quite disrespectful to dismiss it as bland. If you happen upon one of many luaus on the island that include *kalo*-based poi in their smorgasbord, please don't disparage it.

north along Rice Mill Rd for about half a mile. Follow the green river into the **Hanalei Wildlife Refuge** and a parking lot across from the start of the trail.

The Okolehao Trail offers panoramic views of Hanalei taro plots, the Kilauea Lighthouse (on clear days) and the start of the Na Pali Coast. Rumored to be named for 'moonshine,' it refers to the distilled liquor made from the roots of ti plants during Prohibition. The first half-mile is a quad burner which means a fairly quiet hike (except for your heavy breathing). The visual spoils are worth the pain. After the initial vista at the power-line tower, the 2.25-mile trail continues gradually upward, offering numerous photo opportunities and ends 1250ft above the slow shuffle of Hanalei. Bring plenty of water. Most experience the valley by paddle, on the river itself, via kayak or SUP.

You will also get to explore the Hanalei Wildlife Refuge if you join the wonderful Ho'opulapula Haraguchi Rice Mill Tour (see p526).

Hanalei

POP 1001

There are precious few towns on this sweet earth with the majestic natural beauty and barefoot soul of Hanalei. The bay is the thing, of course. And its half-dozen surf breaks swell to well above triple overhead and are the stuff of legend. Partly because local surf gods like the late Andy Irons and Laird Hamilton cut their teeth here. But even if you aren't here for waves, the beach, with its wide sweep of cream colored sand and magnificent jade mountain views, will demand your loving attention. And when beach time is done, stroll into the ubercute downtown, take a yoga class, snack on divine sushi or duck into a dive bar blessed with local tunes and special sustenance. It's true that Hanalei has more than its fair share of adults with Peter Pan syndrome, and you'll see as many men in their 60s waxing their surfboards as you will groms with 'guns' (ie big-wave surfboards). Which begs the query, why grow up at all when you can grow old in Hanalei?

Beaches

Hanalei Bay (👪) is easily Kaua'i's most famous beach and for good reason. Made up of four beaches (really one beach, divided into four sections with four names), there's something for almost everyone here: sunbathing, bodyboarding and surfing. The winter months can make this stretch of water an experts-only spot, though in summer months the water is sometimes so calm it's hard to distinguish between sky and sea.

This is the beach where George Clooney and family stalked the cheeseball realtor who cuckolded him in *The Descendants*.

Hanalei Beach Park BEACH

With its lifeguards and sweeping views, this is a great place for a picnic, sunset or lazy day at the beach. Ideally located, its downside is the parking, which can be a challenge. Park along Weke Rd if you have to, as the lot can get crowded.

Black Pot Beach Park (Hanalei Pier) BEACH

This is one of the most popular beaches within the already popular Hanalei Bay thanks to sweeping mountain views from a bed of powdery sand. Keep an eye out for **Namolokama** looming over the bay, when **Wai'oli Falls** has been rejuvenated by a previous night's rain. The drawback: it's set at the river mouth, and the water does get gritty here.

The break here near the river mouth is dubbed **Grandpas** by surfers, thanks to its unusually mellow wave, ideal for beginners.

Wai'oli (Pine Trees) Beach Park BEACH

A less popular but equally beautiful spot, this beach is dominated by locals. The shorebreak is harder here than any other spot on Hanalei Bay and swimming can be dangerous, except during the calmest summer surf. The park has restrooms and showers.

Waikokos BEACH

Catch rights and lefts at Waikokos break, protected by a reef on the western bend of Hanalei Bay. To get there, park on the side of the main highway and find the short path between mile markers 4 and 5.

Middles SURFING

The surf break known as Middles is set between two more prominent breaks: Waikokos and Pine Trees, but outside (as in 'outside the reef') and to the left.

The Bowl & The Point SURFING

The two most famous surf spots on Hanalei Bay, cum Kaua'i, cum planet earth. The trade winds circle around Princeville and almost always blow offshore here, so it's a prime set up and you can surf whether the swell is small or large. And it does get large here.

The Bowl is the inside break, and it's generally for beginners and intermediates. **The Point** is for advanced surfers only and can get up to 20ft to 30ft. When it's that big, bring binoculars and watch fearless surfers shred from the pier.

Sights & Activities

Though not the largest or most sacred river in the state (the Wailua River holds that honor) the **Hanalei River's** 6 miles are scenic, calm, safe and ideal for novice kayakers and stand up paddlers (SUP). This is how most folks experience Hanalei's interior.

Wai'oli Hui'ia Church & Mission Hall CHURCH

A popular site for quaint church weddings, Wai'oli Hui'ia Church was built in 1912 by Hanalei's first missionaries, Reverend and Mrs William Alexander, who arrived in a double-hulled canoe. Their church, hall and mission house remain in the middle of town, set on a huge manicured lawn with a beautiful mountain backdrop.

North Shore Divers DIVING

(☎828-1223; www.northshoredivers.com; 1-/2-tank dives $79/119; night dives $99; equipment rental $40-50; ⏰dives 8am, 11am, 1pm Mon-Fri, North Shore dives Mar-Oct) A dive shop without a, well, shop. Still, we dove with them at Tunnels – where swim throughs and snoozing sharks are the rule – and their gear and divemasters were top notch. For an unforgettable experience, try night diving (summer only). An open-water certification course is $450.

Ocean Quest Fathom Five Divers DIVING

(☎742-6991, 800-972-3078; www.fathomfive.com; two tanks from $110, plus $40 for gear; ⏰dives 7am, 7:30am & 1pm Mon-Fri, North Shore dives Mar-Oct) Fathom Five is based in Koloa but during the summer they do dive at Tunnels in Ha'ena. Theirs is a PADI-certified shop and will meet you at Tunnels with all the gear you'll need. You must book at least 48 hours ahead.

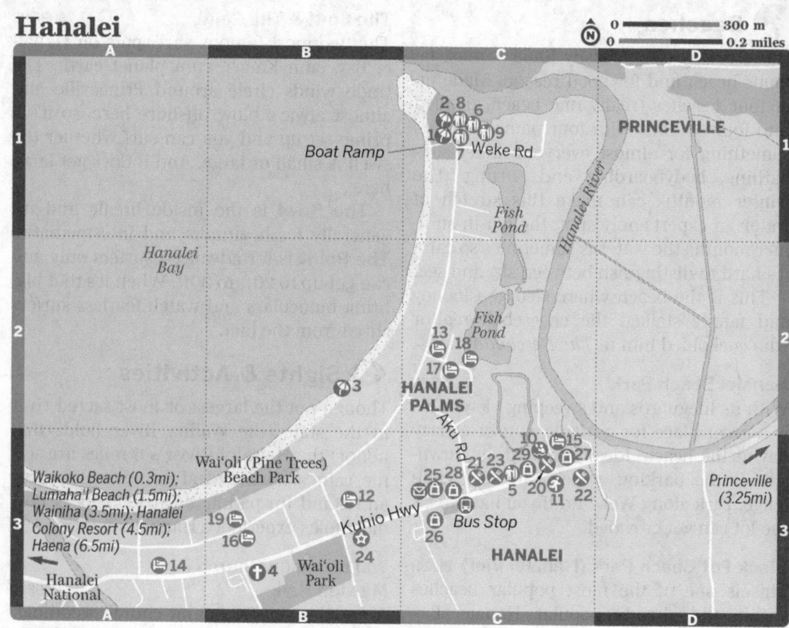

Kayak Kaua'i KAYAKING, SUP

(☎800-437-3507; www.kayakkauai.com; Suite A, 5-5070 Kuhio Hwy; s/d rental per 24hr $29/54, paddle boards per 24hr $45, snorkeling gear per 24hr $8, Na Pali kayak treks $214; ⊙8am-5pm, to 8pm summer) Famous for pioneering sea kayaking in Kaua'i and the first to offer the famed Na Pali kayak trek and the Wailua River waterfall tour, they offer a variety of hiking and paddling tours, as well as kayak, SUP and snorkeling rental. There's a convenient river-launch sight on the property.

Kauai Outrigger Adventures SURFING, SUP

(☎651-2636; www.kauaioutriggeradventures.com; Hanalei Pier; SUP & kayak rental for 2hr $30-40, surf board rental per day $20, SUP & surf lessons $60-70, Outrigger surf lesson $70) The only company on the North Shore offering proper outrigger canoe surf lessons (1½ hours) – it's one of Polynesia's most beloved sports. They offer surf and SUP lessons and rental too, as well as kayak rental. They're near the pier with a Hanalei River put-in.

Na Pali Explorer SNORKELING

(☎338-9999, 877-335-9909; www.napali-explorer.com; Kaumuali'i Hwy; 5hr tour adult/child $125/85; 👪) They do snorkeling trips on rigid-hull inflatable rafts (hard bottom, inflatable sides), which are smoother than the all-inflatable Zodiacs. Expect between 16 and 35 passengers. The 48ft raft includes a restroom and canopy for shade, and runs out of Hanalei Bay from April to October.

Bali Hai Tours BOAT TOUR

(☎634-2317; www.balihaitours.com; adult/child $160/90; 👪) Explore the Na Pali Coast in a 20ft Zodaic and splash your way to pure nature bliss. Cruise for up to four hours among humpbacks, dolphins and flying fish, explore sea caves and pristine beaches. Life doesn't get much more exhilarating.

Na Pali Catamaran BOAT TOUR

(☎826-6853, 866-255-6853; www.napalicatamaran.com; 5-5190 Kuhio Hwy; 4hr tours per person $160; ⊙morning & afternoon May-Oct) This exceptional tour has been running for 35 years and offers comfy cruises along the Na Pali Coast from Hanalei Bay. Depending on the waves, you might venture into some sea caves. Remember though, the surf can pound and there's no reprieve from the elements, sea sickness tablets notwithstanding.

Hanalei Surf Company SURFING

(☎826-9000; www.hanaleisurf.com; 5-5161 Kuhio Hwy, Hanalei Center; 2½hr lesson $65-150, surfboards per day/week $20/90, bodyboards $5/20; ⊙8am-9pm) Surf instructors here have an ex-

Hanalei

Sights

1 Black Pot Beach Park (Hanalei Pier) ... C1
2 Hanalei Beach Park ... C1
3 Waikokos ... B2
4 Wai'oli Hui'ia Church & Mission Hall ... B3

Activities, Courses & Tours

5 Hanalei Beach Boys Surf Shack ... C3
Hanalei Surf Company ... (see 26)
6 Hanalei Surf School ... C1
7 Hawaiian School of Surfing ... C1
8 Hawaiian Surfing Adventures ... C1
9 Kauai Outrigger Adventures ... C1
10 Kayak Kaua'i ... C3
11 Na Pali Kayak ... C3
Pedal'n Paddle ... (see 25)
Yoga Hanalei ... (see 26)

Sleeping

12 Garden Cottage ... B3
13 Hale Reed ... C2
14 Hanalei Inn ... A3
15 Hanalei Riverside Cottages ... C3
16 Hanalei Surfboard House ... B3
17 Miller House at Hanalei ... C2
18 Ohana Hanalei ... C2
19 Pine Trees Beach House ... B3

Eating

BarAcuda Tapas & Wine ... (see 26)
Big Save ... (see 25)
Hanalei Coffee Roasters ... (see 26)
Hanalei Dolphin Fish Market ... (see 27)
Hanalei Dolphin Restaurant & Sushi Lounge ... (see 27)
Hanalei Pizza ... (see 25)
20 Hanalei Taro & Juice Co ... C3
Harvest Market ... (see 26)
Neide's Salsa Samba ... (see 26)
21 Pink's ... C3
22 Postcards Café ... C3
23 Tahiti Nui ... C3

Drinking & Nightlife

Iti Wine Bar ... (see 23)
Tahiti Nui ... (see 23)

Entertainment

24 Hawaiian Slack Key Guitar Concerts ... B3

Shopping

aFeinPhoto Gallery ... (see 28)
25 Ching Young Village ... C3
26 Hanalei Center ... C3
Hanalei Strings ... (see 25)
Hanalei Surf Company ... (see 26)
27 I Heart Hanalei ... C3
28 Kauai Nut Roasters ... C3
Sand People ... (see 26)
29 Titus Kinimaka Surf Shop ... C3

cellent reputation and are especially suited to teaching advanced surfers.

Hawaiian School of Surfing SURFING

(☎652-1116; www.hawaiianschoolofsurfing.com; 5-5088 Kuhio Hwy; 1½hr lesson $65; board rental per day $25; ⊙8am-3pm) Stop by or call in advance for a lesson with legendary pro big-wave surfer Titus Kinimaka or, more likely, one of his minions, who line up the boards and red rashguards daily at the pier. No more than three students per instructor.

Hawaiian Surfing Adventures SURFING

(☎482-0749; www.hawaiiansurfingadventures.com; 2hr group/private lesson $65/225, surfboards per day/week $20/75; SUP for 2½ hours $35; ⊙8am-2pm) The generous lessons offered by this organization include a half-hour on land, one hour in the water and another hour of solo practice. They also have a rack of SUP boards at the river mouth just begging to be ridden. Park at the first lot next to the pier.

Hanalei Surf School SURFING, SUP

(☎826-9283; group/private lessons $75/160) Learn how to surf and/or SUP from a pro. Evan Valiere is a Kaua'i-raised pro surfer who competes regularly on the World Qualifying Tour and in Hawaii's Triple Crown of surfing, including the Pipeline Masters, yet makes even beginners feel comfortable on the board.

Group lessons are led by one of Valiere's seasoned instructors. Private lessons with Valiere can be arranged in advance as well.

Kayak Kaua'i SURFING

(☎826-9844; www.kayakkauai.com; Kuhio Hwy; 1hr lesson $50, surfboards/bodyboards per day $20/6; ⊙10am & 2pm) If you rent gear for four days you get an additional three days free.

Hanalei Beach Boys Surf Shack SURFING, SUP

(☎482-0749; www.hawaiiansurfingadventures.com; Kuhio Hwy; surf boards per day $15-20, SUP rental for 2½hr $30, surf/SUP lessons $65/75;

⏲8am-3pm) A terrific new surf school with an array of surf and paddle boards in good condition. First lessons launch at 8am. Boards must be in by 5pm.

Island Sails SAILING
(☎212-6053; www.islandsailskauai.com; 1½hr tours, morning snorkel trip adult/child $125/85; ⏲9-10:30am, 3:30am-5pm, 5:30pm-sunset) Whether snorkeling in the morning, cruising in the afternoon or taking in a sunset on the water, here's your chance to get a taste of the traditional Polynesian sailing canoe.

Yoga Hanalei YOGA
(☎826-9642; www.yogahanalei.com; 5-5161E Kuhio Hwy, Hanalei Center, 2nd fl; classes $15) Local Ashtanga luminary Bhavani Maki teaches the uberpopular first class of the day, which is primarily a local scene. Mid-morning classes can also get pretty packed. If you're looking for something more mellow, come later in the day. All classes tend to flow vinyasa style, except the ropes class, which is for dangling.

Snorkel Depot SNORKELING, SUP
(☎826-9983; 5-5075 Kuhio Hwy; SUP half/full-day $25/45, snorkel gear per 24hr $5; ⏲8am-5pm) This little stand in the Hanalei Trading Company building offers the best deal on snorkel gear and SUP boards in town.

Pedal'n Paddle CYCLING, WATERSPORTS
(☎826-9069; www.pedalnpaddle.com; Ching Young Village; snorkel gear per day $5, boogie board per day $5, kayaks s/d $20/40, bikes per day $15-20, per week $60-80; ⏲9am-6pm) This full-service rental shop is conveniently located and offers some of the best rates in town.

Tours

Ho'opulapula Haraguchi Rice Mill TOUR
(☎651-3399; Kuhio Hwy; 3hr tour incl lunch per person $87; ⏲tours 10am Wed) The Haraguchi family offers tours (by appointment only) of its historic rice mill and wetland taro farm. See the otherwise inaccessible Hanalei National Wildlife Refuge and learn about Hawaii's immigrant history.

Sleeping

In addition to the nests listed here, some tourists scope out an underground B&B from area homeowners who rent out their guest cottage/rooms privately.

★**Garden Cottage** VACATION RENTAL **$$**
(☎346-4371; 5278 Malolo Pl; per night $150; 📶) A painfully cute, if rustic, wooden surf shack with terracotta floors, an old school stove top, flat-screen TV, wi-fi and a grill on the patio next to the hammock. The location is quiet, yet right in the center of the action. From here you can stroll to downtown in one direction and the beach in the other. Price does not include the $80 cleaning fee.

Ohana Hanalei STUDIO **$$**
(☎826-4116; www.hanalei-kauai.com; Pilikoa Rd; r $125, cleaning fee $65) It's amazing how cheap this studio is given the location, a mere

BUY LOCAL: KAUA'I'S FARMERS MARKETS

You are what you eat. While on Kaua'i, take the opportunity to let part of the Garden Island become part of you. Check online for a full up-to-the-minute schedule (www.realkauai.com/FarmersMarkets).

DAY	TIME	LOCATION
Monday	noon-2pm	Koloa Knudsen Ball Park, Koloa
	3-5pm	Kukui Grove Shopping Center, Lihu'e
Tuesday	2-4pm	Waipa Ahupua'a Field, Hanalei
	3:30-5:30pm	Kalaheo Neighborhood Center, Kalaheo
Wednesday	3-6pm	Kapa'a New Town Ball Park, Kapa'a
	4:30-6:30pm	Shops at Kukuiula, Po'ipu
Thursday	4:30-6:30pm	Kilauea Neighborhood Center, Kilauea
	3-4pm	Hanapepe Rd, Hanapepe
Friday	3-5pm	Vidinha Stadium, Lihu'e
Saturday	9am-noon	Hanalei Neighborhood Center, Hanalei
	9am-noon	Kekaha Neighborhood Center, Kekaha
	11am-2pm	Kilauea Mini-Golf, Kilauea

half-block from the beach. It has its own kitchenette, private entrance, phone, cable TV and convenient parking. A cozy porch table allows for pleasant (or romantic) meals and the bikes and beach chairs have you beach-ready from the get-go. A three-night minimum is required.

Hanalei Inn INN $$
(826-9333; www.hanaleiinn.com; 5-5468 Kuhio Hwy; r $159;) The four studios here – each with a kitchen, HDTV and simple yet classic retro furnishings from the famed but now dilapidated Coco Palms resort – are in an ideal locale. Stay for a week, pay no taxes.

Miller House at Hanalei VACATION RENTAL $$
(828-1427; 4456 Pilikoa Rd; per week $1500-1900) It won't win any design awards, but this all-wood, four-bedroom/two-bathroom home is steps from the sand and sleeps up to six with ceiling fans in every room. Solid value.

Pine Trees Beach House INN $$
(888-773-4730, 826-9333; www.hanaleibayinn.com; 5404 Weke Rd; r/studio/apt $88/$191/$237;) Managed by the Hanalei Inn and set on the frontage road of Hanalei Bay, options here include an embellished closet with a twin bed, a downstairs studio apartment with queen bed and pull-out couch, and an airy 1200-sq-ft loft, with Italian marble floor, snazzy kitchen and, um, a stripper pole (bought from Larry Flynt). Weird is good sometimes.

Hanalei Riverside Cottages COTTAGE $$
(826-1675; www.hanaleicottages.com; 5-5016 Kuhio Hwy; 2br per night $200-240, per week $1440;) Staying here, you can launch a canoe, kayak or stand up paddleboard right from your backyard on the Hanalei River. A stone's throw from the heart of Hanalei town, each cottage is styled in a similar fashion, with bamboo furniture, full kitchens, outdoor (and indoor) showers, front-of-house bedrooms and airy quasi-lounge areas facing the river, some of which could be used as a third bedroom.

Hale Reed VACATION RENTAL $$
(415-662-1086; www.hanalei-vacation.com; 4441 Pilikoa Rd; house per week from $1200;) This ground floor apartment has a full kitchen, one queen bed and two twins (that could be made into a king), and can sleep up to four people. The upstairs unit has three bedrooms, two bathrooms and a loft, along with a wrap-around lanai. It sleeps up to 10. Boards and beach gear come with the territory.

Hanalei Surfboard House INN $$$
(651-1039; www.hanaleisurfboardhouse.com; 5459 Weke Rd; ste $295, plus $95 cleaning fee;) A work of art and just a one-minute walk to the beach, this uberstylish property is an upmarket surfer's haven. Two of the 400-sq-ft rooms (the Elvis and Cowgirl rooms to be precise) feature unique vintage Americana decor, as well as a lanai with a BBQ grill. The ever-mellow owner sets the pace for this enchanting house. No children allowed.

Eating

With no shortage of choices, there's something in town for everyone.

Hanalei Taro & Juice Co LOCAL $
(826-1059; Kuhio Hwy; snacks from $3, meals $8-10; 11am-3pm Mon-Sat;) Find this roadside trailer for a taste of taro, the traditional Hawaiian staple food. They have tropical taro smoothies, taro hummus, taro burgers and Hawaiian plate lunches too.

Hanalei Coffee Roasters CAFE $
(www.hanaleicoffeeroasters.com; Hanalei Center; mains $6-10; 6:30am-6pm;) You gotta love a coffee joint with a working mega vintage roaster in the building! Choose from a selection of waffles, bagel sandwiches or a granola and yogurt stuffed half papaya in the morn, paninis at lunch, and the coffee is best paired with decadent lemon or aloha bars (shortbread, chocolate, coconut and macadamia) all damn day.

Pink's ICE CREAM $
(826-1257; 4484 Aku Rd; dishes $5-9; 11am-5pm;) A fabulous little ice-cream shop scooping tropical flavors like mango guava and an unreal *haupia* (coconut custard). They can also whip up organic smoothies, personal soft-serve flavors and feature an absurdly tasty Hawaiian grilled cheese sandwich: Hawaiian sweet bread, Kalua pork, muenster cheese and pineapple.

★Tahiti Nui HAWAII REGIONAL $$
(826-6277; www.thenui.com; 5-5134 Kuhio Hwy; mains $20-32; 11:30am-midnight Mon-Sat, 2pm-midnight Sun) It looks like a dive. And it is. But it's a dive with a sneaky good kitchen. Everything, from the baby backs to the pizzas, is fabulous. Salads are huge and the seafood

dishes – especially that thick wedge of fresh ahi seared perfectly and served in a wasabi cream – are simple and life affirming.

Hanalei Dolphin Restaurant & Sushi Lounge SEAFOOD, SUSHI **$$**
(826-6113; www.hanaleidolphin.com; 5-5016 Kuhio Hwy; lunch/dinner mains $14/21, sushi $11-20; 11:30am-3pm, 5:30-9:30pm) One of the oldest establishments in Hanalei (over 30 years), the slow-roasted menu is tasty, but it really is all about the sushi. The Next Best Thing wraps shrimp tempura, avocado, white onion and asparagus in seaweed and hamachi, and is drizzled with miso-chile-sake sauce. The Best Thing does the same with lobster tempura, but only on Fridays.

BarAcuda Tapas & Wine TAPAS **$$**
(826-7081; www.restaurantbaracuda.com; 5-5161 Kuhio Hwy, Hanalei Center; tapas $7-16; 5:30am-9pm) Hanalei's hotspot, this deluxe tapas bar crafts gourmet flavors from sustainable produce like North Shore honeycomb, Kunana Farms goat cheese and Mizuna greens and apples. Think seared mahi with macadamia nut pesto, slow braised pork shoulder with apple cider reduction and house-made chorizo. The decor (and crowd) are rather alluring too.

Hanalei Pizza PIZZA **$$**
(826-1300; www.hanaleipizza.com; 5190 Kuhio Hwy, Chin Young Village; slices $5, pies $15-35; 11:30am-8:30pm) The sauce has a kiss of Shiraz and the dough is made with hemp oil, coconut water and hemp, flax and chia seed. Pizzas come loaded with cheese, the pesto sauce is remarkable and the Wild Pig Pie with Kalua pork and Maui onion is a local favorite. BYOB and dine in the courtyard. This pizza is love.

Postcards Café HAWAII REGIONAL **$$**
(826-1191; www.postcardscafe.com; 5-5075 Kuhio Hwy; mains $18-27; 6-9pm;) A refined cottage restaurant with hit or miss culinary chops. Creations range into the veg-head fanciful (seared polenta cakes with a hemp seed crust) and back into the tasty range of island classics (wasabi-crusted ahi). And though some dishes come up short, know that the grilled ono with macadamia and honey butter is a revelation, and that they don't take reservations.

Neide's Salsa Samba BRAZILIAN **$$**
(826-1851; www.neidesalsaandsamba.com; 5-5161 Kuhio Hwy, Hanalei Center; dishes $12-17; 11am-9pm) Hidden in the back of the Hanalei Center, the food platters are abundant and the margaritas flow almost too quickly at this Brazilian-Mexican kitchen. The more authentic items on the menu come from Brazil and include *muqueca* (fresh fish with coconut sauce), *ensopado* (baked chicken and vegetables) and *bife acebolado* (beefsteak with onions).

Harvest Market MARKET **$$**
(826-0089; www.harvestmarkethanalei.com; 5-5161 Kuhio Hwy, Hanalei Center; smoothies $7, salads by weight; 9am-7pm Mon-Sat, to 6pm Sun;) If you like to treat your body well, there's a decent selection of organic snacks and products here. Be frugal if you approach the salad bar, smoothie station or weighable-snack section (dried fruit, nuts and such), as prices can sneak up on you.

Self-Catering

Hanalei Farmers Markets (Saturday) MARKET **$**
(Kuhio Hwy; 9am-noon) One of the island's more popular farmers markets. It's held on the soccer fields in front of the Teen Center.

Hanalei Farmers Markets (Tuesday) MARKET **$**
(Kuhio Hwy, Waipa; 2-4pm) Set at the Waipa Foundation, an old land grant just over the one lane bridge from Hanalei proper on the way to Ha'ena, this market is small but still ample.

Big Save SUPERMARKET **$**
(5-5172 Kuhio Hwy, Ching Young Village; 7am-9pm) Has an ATM and any necessary basic grocery items you might need.

Hanalei Dolphin Fish Market MARKET **$$**
(826-6113; www.hanaleidolphin.com; 5-5016 Kuhio Hwy; handrolls $12, soup $3-9; 10am-7pm; P) If you're hungry for raw flavor on the cheap, wander around the back of the Dolphin proper to the fish market where you can grab assorted sushi rolls, a daily fish-salad sandwich and a chunky seafood chowder. They serve fresh fish by the pound too.

Drinking & Entertainment

Tahiti Nui BAR
(826-6277; www.thenui.com; 5-5134 Kuhio Hwy, Tahiti Nui Bldg; lunch noon-3pm, dinner 5-9pm, bar week/weekends to 10/11pm) Where Clooney and Beau Bridges had their lubricated, lukewarm encounter in *The Descendants*. With its carved tiki bar stools, bamboo-mat ceil-

TAHITI NUI'S GLORY DAYS

The Tahiti Nui (p528) has changed hands and menus, and seen its fair share of dated hairdos, barflies and beer bellies. But there's a part of 'the Nui' that always seems to remain the same. It's the liveliest spot in little Hanalei, and, though certainly a dive, it remains *the* North Shore joint par excellence for regulars and visitors alike.

In 1964, Louise Hauata, a Tahitian woman, and her husband, Bruce Marston, founded the now iconic Tahiti Nui, a classic South Seas–style restaurant and bar. Its popularity grew and so did its draw – luring such names as Jacqueline Kennedy, who legendarily arrived unexpectedly, preceded by secret service agents. Yet despite the fact that it's seen its share of A-listers (most recently it was the setting for the fateful meeting between George Clooney and Beau Bridges in *The Descendants*), you'd never guess it at first glance.

Bruce died in 1975, but Louise continued the spot's luau tradition, augmenting it with renditions of Tahitian songs in English, French or their original language. She was also well known for giving much aloha to her community in times of need.

Louise died in 2003, and until recently Tahiti Nui was run by her son Christian Marston, her nephew William Marston, and the president and CEO, John Austin, who is married to celebrated singer Amy Hanaiali'i Gilliom. These days an entirely new generation of the family has gotten involved and is beginning to take over. Proving that the Nui will endure and remain a lively hangout long after happy hour (from 4pm to 6pm Monday to Saturday and all day Sunday).

ing and occasional live Hawaiian slack key guitar, this joint is replete with dive bar gravitas.

Iti Wine Bar WINE BAR
(www.itiwinebar.com; 5-5134 Kuhio Hwy; ⌚6-11pm) Next door to Tahiti Nui with a slightly more, ahem, upscale approach to revelry. Point is, there are wine snobs hidden in this barefoot beach community. Not that there's anything wrong with that. They generally stay open latest.

Hawaiian Slack Key Guitar Concerts LIVE MUSIC
(www.hawaiianslackkeyguitar.com; Kuhio Hwy, Hanalei Community Center; adult/senior & child $20/15; ⌚4pm Fri & 3pm Sun) You'll find slack key guitar and ukulele concerts performed by longtime musicians Doug and Sandy McMaster year-round here, in a refreshingly informal atmosphere.

Shopping

Hanalei offers a smattering of boutiques that range from tourist kitsch to beach chic. Most of the options center around the old guard, **Ching Young Village** and the more discerning (and upscale) **Hanalei Center**.

★ **Kauai Nut Roasters** FOOD
(www.kauainutroasters.com; 5-5190 Kuhio Hwy Bldg E; packages $4-9; ⌚10am-6pm Mon-Sat, from 11am Sun) Some of the most delicious treats you can find are in these unassuming little packages, bursting with sweetness. Coconut, wasabi, lavender, sesame, butterscotch and praline flavors earn top ranking. Be sure to wash down the free samples with the alkaline-heavy ionized water, said to have great health benefits.

I Heart Hanalei BOUTIQUE
(☎826-5560; www.shopihearthanalei.com; 5-5106 Kuhio Hwy; ⌚11am-9pm Mon-Fri, from 10am Sat & Sun) Easily the most popular and cutest of Hanalei's beachy boutiques, with racks of stylish bikinis, comfy and chic beach wear, sun hats, shorts and cute handmade jewelry too. Favored by local ladies aged 13 to 99.

Hanalei Strings MUSIC
(☎826-9633;www.hanaleistringskauai.com;5-5190 Kuhio Hwy, Ching Young Village; ⌚10am-6pm) If you've ever been struck by the mood to strum and sing in the sunshine, come here for your mini-axe and book lessons too. They can get you into an entry-level ukulele for $70 and have pro-grade varietals that range up to $1200. Those are manufactured by hand on Kaua'i from local koa wood with oyster shell inlay.

Titus Kinimaka Surf Shop SURF SHOP
(5-5088 Kuhio Hwy; ⌚9am-8pm) Hanalei's best surf shop, where you can get everything from board shirts to long and short boards to sunglasses and Go Pros.

Kaua'i

From the legendary surf swells of Hanalei to the Na Pali Coast's stunning treks, this island offers laidback adventures for all. Kayak in Wailua, then snorkel off Po'ipu; venture to the rim of magnificent Waimea Canyon, dripping with waterfalls, and hit the trail in Koke'e State Park – it's all here waiting.

JOHN ELK / GETTY IMAGES ©

rf Beaches (p523)
great waves at some of Hanalei Bay's serviceable breaks.

2. Hanalei Bay (p523)
Kaua'i's most famous beach has something for almost everyone.

3. Na Pali Coast (p536)
This must-see coast is trekking heaven for hikers and kayakers alike.

Hanalei Surf Company OUTDOOR EQUIPMENT
(www.hanaleisurf.com; 5-5161 Kuhio Hwy, Hanalei Center; ⌚8am-9pm) Surf, surf, surf is the MO here. Surfer-girl earrings, bikinis, rashies and guys' boardshorts, slippers and all the surf gear you might need: wax, shades and even the board itself.

aFeinPhoto Gallery GALLERY
(☎634-7890; www.afeinbergphotography.com; 4489 Aku Rd; ⌚noon-7pm) Wunderkind photographer Aaron Feinberg creates award-winning fine-art landscapes of Kaua'i and beyond.

Sand People GIFTS
(☎826-1008; www.sandpeople.com; 5-5161 Kuhio Hwy; ⌚9:30am-8pm Mon-Sat, from 10am Sun) The Kaua'i link in the state-wide chain, this cute and quirky gift gallery features funky collectibles like a variety of model VW Buses, Beetles and Wagoneers, and antique glass buoys, along with an unremarkable collection of beach wear and jewellery.

Information

Hanalei has no bank, but there is an ATM in the Ching Young Village's Big Save supermarket.

Post Office (☎800-275-8777; 5-5226 Kuhio Hwy) On the *makai* (seaward) side of the road, just west of the Big Save supermarket.

Getting There & Around

There's one road in and one road out. Everything in Hanalei is walkable. Parking can be a headache and absent-minded pedestrians even more so. Live like a local and hop on a bike.

Pedal'n Paddle (☎826-9069; www.pedalnpaddle.com; 5-5105 Kuhio Hwy, Ching Young Village; ⌚9am-6pm) For cruisers ($12/50 per day/week) and hybrid road bikes ($20/80).

Around Hanalei

Lumaha'i Beach

Countless Kaua'i lifers consider this their absolute favorite beach on an island blessed with dozens of choices. It's so damn cinematic that movie tours sometimes still claim that Lumaha'i Beach is where Burt Lancaster and Deborah Kerr kissed in *that* scene in *From Here to Eternity,* but it's not (the scene was shot at Halona Cove on O'ahu). And though it's tempting, while high on pure bliss nature buzz, to let your guard down, know that Lumaha'i enjoys an infamous status as one of the more dangerous swim spots, and many have drowned here.

Instead, stay dry and take the safe-but-magical stroll (which still requires being water savvy). There are two ways onto Lumaha'i Beach. The first and more scenic is a three-minute walk that begins at the parking area 0.75 miles past mile marker 4 on the Kuhio Hwy. The trail slopes to the left at the end of the retaining wall. On the beach, the lava-rock ledges are popular for sunbathing and photo ops, but beware: bystanders have been washed away by high surf and rogue waves.

The other way to access Lumaha'i is along the road at sea level at the western end of the beach, just before crossing the Lumaha'i River Bridge. The beach at this end is lined with ironwood trees.

Wainiha

Wainiha Valley remains as it did in the old days: a holdout for Native Hawaiians,

MANO A MANO

No doubt being attacked by a *mano* (shark) could be deadly: precautions, such as not swimming in murky, post-rain waters, should be taken to avoid them. Statistically speaking, you're more likely to die from a bee sting (or a cow) than a shark attack, and you should be more concerned about contracting leptospirosis or staphylococcus in those infamous muddy river waters than becoming a midday snack.

Rather than letting any primordial phobia of large, deep-water predators get you down, try considering the creature from an another perspective while in Hawaii: the *mano* as sacred. For many local families, the *mano* is their *'aumakua* (guardian spirit). *'Aumakua* are family ancestors whose *'uhane* (spirit form) lives on in the form of an animal, watching over members of their living *'ohana.* Revered for their ocean skill, *mano* were also considered the *'aumakua* of navigators. Even today, *mano 'aumakua* have been said to guide lost fishermen home, or toward areas of plentiful fish, to make for a bountiful sojourn.

though some vacation rentals have encroached into the area.

Sleeping & Eating

Coco Cabana Cottage COTTAGE $$

(826-5141; www.vrbo.com/153703; 4766 Ananalu Rd; per night $135, 3-night minimum, $125 cleaning fee;) A hot tub, chirping birds, airy ambience and the nearby, swimmable Wainiha River make for a lovely secluded stay. This cute little cottage is perfect for a couple wanting privacy and coziness, as is the two-person outdoor jungle shower.

The Guesthouse at River Estate VACATION RENTAL $$$

(826-5118, 800-390-8444; www.riverestate.com; house per night/week $275/1800;) Airy, huge and open – it's pricey, but one look and you'll see why. It's located mid-jungle and features a master bedroom with a king bed, a second room with queen bed, a decked-out kitchen, a wraparound lanai, air-con and anything else you could possibly need.

The Riverhouse at River Estate VACATION RENTAL $$$

(800-390-8444, 826-5118; www.riverestate.com; house per night/week $295/1975;) Resting on stilts 30ft above the Wainiha River, blessed with Brazilian hardwood floors and marble countertops, and a screened-in lanai which allows for mosquito-free BBQs or soaks in the (mini) hot tub, this place satisfies honeymooners and families alike.

Red Hot Mama's MEXICAN $

(5-6607 Kuhio Hwy; mains $8-11; 11am-5pm Sun-Fri, closed Sat) 'Mama' slings generous Tex-Mex burritos and tacos made with heaps of TLC at this roadside flavor factory. It's unclear whether the establishment's name describes levels of spice in their palatable pork, chicken, beef, fresh fish (the thinker's choice) or tofu products, or in their fearless hardworking leader. Consider it a must-stop after a Na Pali hike; you earned it.

Wainiha General Store SELF-CATERING $

(5-6600 Kuhio Hwy; 10am-dusk) If you've left Hanalei and need a few items, don't panic. The locally christened 'Last Chance General Store' offers beach necessities such as sunscreen, snorkel gear and basic picnic snack items, as well as a kiss of fresh produce. If you're hiking the Na Pali Coast, buy an extra bottle of water.

Shopping

7 Artists GALLERY

(5-6607 Kuhio Hwy, Wainiha; 10am-4pm) A gallery of local painters, a photographer and a jeweller. Our favorite is Michi, a formerly LA-based graffiti artist who paints beach and underwater scenes with a retro pop art sensibility.

Ha'ena

Remote, resplendent and idyllic, this is where the road ends amid lava pinnacles, lush forest and truly spectacular beaches. It's also the site of controversy, as many of the luxury homes on the point were built on top of ancient Hawaiian burial grounds (*'iwi kupuna*). In 2007 this topic was brought to the attention of the media, following more mobilization of the Hawaiian community, which has continued a program of peaceful civil disobedience. No Kaua'i adventure is complete without a drive to the end of road and at least a short hike along the roadless Na Pali Coast.

Beaches

Makua (Tunnels) Beach BEACH

(P) This is one of the North Shore's almost-too-beautiful beaches (named for the underwater caverns in and among the nearshore reef) and among the best snorkel spots on the island. It's also the north shore's most popular dive site. Although more suitable for the summer months, as the reef is adjacent to the beach, winter snorkelling is a possibility.

Use caution and check with the lifeguards if uncertain. Beware of a regular current flowing west toward the open sea. If you can score a parking spot at one the two unmarked lots (short dirt roads), you're lucky. The next best option is parking at Ha'ena State Park and walking down. As always, arrive early for the best snorkelling and parking options.

Ha'ena Beach Park BEACH

Not always ideal for swimming, as the winter's regularly pounding shorebreak creates a strong undertow, this beach is good for taking in some sun. During the summer months, however, the sea is almost always smooth and safe. Between October and May, ask the lifeguard about conditions before going in. To the left is **Cannons**, a particularly good summer wall dive.

Ha'ena

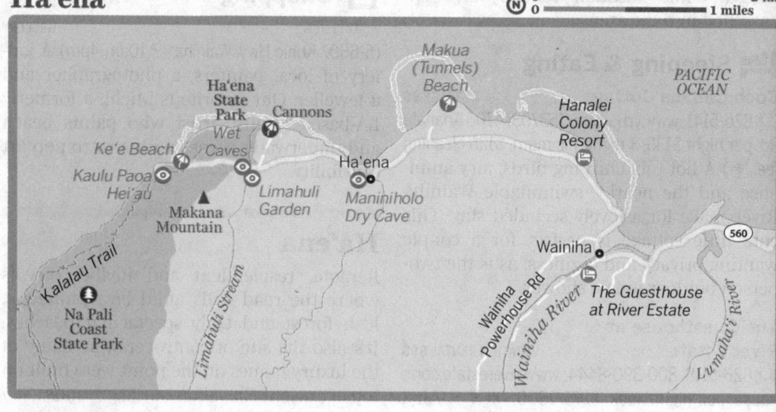

Sights & Activities

Limahuli Garden GARDENS
(☎826-1053; www.ntbg.org; 5-8291 Kuhio Hwy; self-guided/guided tour $15/30; ⏰9:30am-4pm Tue-Sat, guided tours 10am Tue-Fri) About as beautiful as it gets for living education, this 17-acre garden offers a pleasant overview of native botany and the *ahupua'a* (land division) system of management of ancient Hawai'i. Self-guided tours take about 1½ hours and allow you to take in the scenery meditatively.

Guided tours are held twice weekly (Wednesday and Thursday) in the low season and last 2½ hours. Occasional service projects allow a glimpse into the entire 985-acre preserve for native ecosystem restoration.

Maniniholo Dry Cave CAVE
Directly across from Ha'ena Beach Park, Maniniholo Dry Cave is deep, broad and high enough to explore. A constant seep of water from the cave walls keeps the dark interior dank. Drippy and creepy, the cave is named after the head fisherman of the *menehune* who, according to legend, built ponds and other structures overnight.

Hanalei Day Spa SPA
(☎826-6621; www.hanaleidayspa.com; Hanalei Colony Resort; massages from $105; ⏰11am-7pm Mon-Sat) If you need to revitalize, this spa offers some of the island's more competitively priced massage and body treatments. It's also the self-branded Ayurveda Center of Hawaii, so expect authentic Ayurvedic treatments here, along with deep-tissue, Thai massage and the Hawaiian classic, Lomi Lomi.

Sleeping

Ha'ena Beach Park is a popular and beautiful **camping** spot and base for exploring the North Shore, including the Na Pali Coast. Permits are required to camp; they can only be procured in Lihu'e.

There's an abundance of vacation rentals to be found, however. As always, **Vacation Rentals By Owner** (www.vrbo.com) is a good resource, as is **Kauai Vacation Rentals** (☎245-8841; www.kauaivacationrentals.com).

Hale Ho'omaha B&B **$$**
(☎800-851-0291, 826-7083; www.aloha.net/~hoomaha; 7083 Alamihi Rd; r $190; @ 📶) You'll be greeted by a parrot and two bejeweled Balinese sentries at the gate. Follow the staircase into the canopy, where you'll find a unique, four-room B&B. Shared amenities include an ozonated hot tub, high-end kitchen, enormous flat-screen HDTV, a guest-use computer and even an elevator.

Tropical Bamboo Hideaway VACATION RENTAL **$$$**
(☎800-325-5701, 826-0002; www.parrishkauai.com; 5-7107 Kuhio Hwy; per night $345-395; 📶) One of the more unique rentals in the area, this one-story, mostly bamboo, ranch-style home is stilted about 25ft high in the trees offering sea views from the lanai. There are two bedrooms, two bathrooms, wi-fi, a fat flat screen with premium channels, an open kitchen and bamboo beamed ceilings. It's quite something.

Hale Oli VACATION RENTAL **$$$**
(☎826-6585; www.oceanfrontrealty.com; 7097 Alimihi Rd; 2 br per night/week $275/1650) Perched

on stilts with nothing but greenery between the front lanai and Ha'ena's jutting mountains, and a Hawaiiana-meets-zen decor inside. The bathroom is compulsively clean and the back lanai has a spacious hot tub offering starry and foamy nights and a sliver of an ocean view.

Hanalei Colony Resort CONDO HOTEL **$$$**
(☎826-6235, 800-628-3004; www.hcr.com; 5-7130 Kuhio Hwy; 2br from $275;) It would be difficult to find a better location for a resort – this is the only one west of Princeville. Even if studios and larger condo units are scattered in several exceedingly charmless stucco out buildings, they are arced along an exquisite beach and bay, and the interiors are bright and updated. Walk-in rates drop to a reasonable $236.

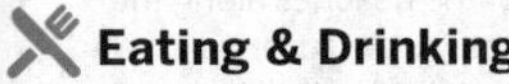

Eating & Drinking

Mediterranean Gourmet MEDITERRANEAN **$$**
(☎826-9875; www.kauaimedgourmet.com; 7132 Kuhio Hwy, Hanalei Colony Resort; lunch $12-17, dinner $20-35, luau per person $70; ⊙11am-3pm, 4:30-8:30pm; P) A taste of the Mediterranean literally on the Pacific (if the windows weren't there you'd get ocean mist on your face), this fish out of water offers dated elegance and an eclectic range of dishes from rosemary rack of lamb and stuffed grape leaves to pistachio-crusted ahi.

Be sure to leave room for dessert. Think baklava or cheesecake and a cup of muddy Turkish coffee. There's live music most nights and a luau on Tuesdays.

Na Pali Art Gallery & Coffee House CAFE
(☎826-1844; www.napaligallery.com; 5-7132 Kuhio Hwy, Hanalei Colony Resort; ⊙7am-5pm Mon-Sat & 7am-3pm Sun;) Order a latte or Kona coffee and peruse an assortment of local artists' paintings, jewelry (coveted Ni'ihau sunrise shell necklaces) and larimar (priced from $20 to $2000).

Ha'ena State Park

Wind-beaten Ha'ena State Park is sculpted into the narrow lava-rich coastline and burns with the allure, mystique and beauty usually associated with some divine tale. Pele (the goddess of lightning and fire) is said to have chosen the area as a home because of the water percolating through its wet and dry caves. The 230-acre park remains home to the 1280ft cliff commonly known in the tourism industry as 'Bali Hai,' its name in the film *South Pacific*. Its real name is Makana, which means 'gift.' Rather apt, for sure.

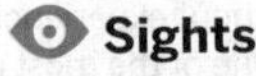

Sights

Ke'e Beach BEACH
Perhaps the most memorable North Shore sunsets happen at this spiritual place, where the first Hawaiians came to practice hula. It offers a refreshing dip after hiking the Kalalau Trail into the **Na Pali Coast State Park** in summer months. Be aware that Ke'e Beach has appeared calm to unsuspecting swimmers when it is, in fact, otherwise. Vicious currents have sucked some through a keyhole in its reef and out into the open sea. Summer brings car break-ins in the parking lot, so leave cars (especially those that are obviously rentals) free from visible valuables. There are showers and restrooms.

Wet Caves CAVE
Two wet caves are within the boundaries of Ha'ena State Park. The first, **Waikapala'e Wet Cave** (aka the Blue Room), is just a short walk from the road opposite the visitor-parking overflow area. Formed by constant wave-pounding many years ago, this massive cavern is as enchanting as it is spooky.

Though the Blue Room has been rather dry of late, when there is water, some slip in to experience the sunlight's blue reflection in the deeper chamber of the cave. Please note this water may have leptospirosis, the rocks are slippery and there is nothing to hold onto once in the water. The second cave, **Waikanaloa Wet Cave**, is on the south side of the main road.

WHEN IN DOUBT, DON'T GO OUT

The waters in Hawaii are as powerful as anywhere on the planet and can catch many a toe-dipper off guard in the blink of an eye. Strong undertows have the capability of sweeping even the most experienced mer-men off their feet and out to sea in a matter of seconds. Swimming with others and where lifeguards are present is always the safest way to go. Made evident by the knife-etched tally before the descent, Hanakapi'ai Beach (p537) has ended many a vacation – and life – too soon (over 30 in the last 40 years). Heed the warning.

THE NA PALI KAYAK TREK

The Na Pali Coast has reasonable claim to offering the most spectacular scenery of all of Kaua'i. Any trip to Kaua'i without experiencing it would be incomplete; and if you're able, kayaking it arguably offers one of the most unforgettable adventures on the planet.

Kayaking the Na Pali Coast is strenuous and dangerous, and therefore not for everyone. Going with a guide helps manage the dangers; going without means you're more than just familiar with sea (not river) kayaking. It also means you know better than to go alone. Always check several days of weather forecasting and ocean conditions before launching (☎245-3564). Hanakapi'ai Beach is about a mile in. About six more miles along and you can set up camp at Kalalau. If you start very early, you can aim for setting up camp at Miloli'i (with a permit), which is at the 11-mile point, two miles past Nu'alolo Kai. From there you have the often (seasonally) surfless, hot, flat stretch of Polihale, for what feels like much longer than 3 miles.

Always start on the North Shore, end on the Westside (due to currents) and never go in winter (potentially deadly swells).

Most outfitters offer a long day-trip that spans the entire Na Pali Coast from north to west shore. It's long, grueling and glorious. You can also rent kayaks for self-guided multi-day treks, but you'll have to reserve a campsite at one of the beaches along the way – in Kalalau or Miloli'i – up to a year in advance through the **Department of Land & Natural Resources** office in Lihu'e. If you require a guide, multi-day treks can get rather expensive (up to $800 for two people). Try the following operators:

Na Pali Kayak (☎826-6900, 866-977-6900; www.napalikayak.com; Kuhio Hwy; tours from $200) The Na Pali Coast trip is the only tour these folks lead and their guides have over a decade of experience paddling these waters.

Kayak Kaua'i (☎826-9844, 800-437-3507; www.kayakkauai.com; Kuhio Hwy; Na Pali day trips $216; ⏲8am-5pm, to 8pm summer) The original Na Pali kayaking outfitter. Their Na Pali Coast Odyssey – which spans the entire stretch from Ke'e to Polihale – is offered from May to September.

Kaulu Paoa Hei'au TEMPLE

The roaring surf worked as a teacher to those who first practiced the spiritual art of hula, chanting and testing their vocal horsepower against nature's decibel levels. Ke'e beach is home to one of the most cherished heiau, and it's also where the goddess Pele fell in love with Lohiau.

Leis and other offerings for Pele can be found on the ground and should be left as is. Enter the heiau through its entryway. Do not cross over its walls, as it is disrespectful and said to bring bad luck.

Na Pali Coast State Park

Roadless, pristine and hauntingly beautiful, this 22-mile-long stretch of stark cliffs, white sand beaches, turquoise coves and gushing waterfalls links the north and west shores and is arguably Kaua'i's most magnificent natural jewel. While the fit tackle the exposed, undulating, slippery trail from Ha'ena (11 miles to the Kalalau Valley), you can also experience this coastline by chopper, kayak, Zodiac or catamaran from either end. In the summer, some locals even swim from Ke'e Beach to Hanakapi'ai Beach and hike out! Kalalau, Honopu, 'Awa'awapuhi, Nu'alolo and Miloli'i are the five major valleys on the Na Pali Coast. Each seemingly more stunning than the last.

History

Archaeologists maintain that the extreme, remote Nualolo Valley housed a sophisticated civilization dating back more than a thousand years, after ancient weapons and hunting tools were excavated throughout the area. Irrigation ditches and agricultural terraces suggest the Kalalau Valley was home to the most advanced clan within the island chain. By the turn of the century, the majority of the inhabitants of the valley had relocated to more centrally located spots on the island.

Activities

For rewarding views of the Na Pali Coast, hiking along the 11-mile Kalalau coastal trail into Hanakapi'ai, Hanakoa and Kalalau Valleys from Ke'e beach in Ha'ena is an adventure that's sure not to disappoint. The Na Pali Coast can also be viewed from above on the westside of the island, in **Koke'e State Park**. And those views too are absolutely magnificent.

Kalalau Trail HIKING

How else could you brave the steep sea cliffs than by foot for 22 miles? Winding along the Na Pali (the cliffs) offers glimpses of some of the most pristine, extreme views from which to behold its deep, riveting pleats. This trail is without a doubt the best way to connect directly with the elements, though keep in mind that the trek – if you opt to complete the full 22-mile round-trip into the valley – is a steep, rough hike.

The three hiking options are Ke'e Beach to Hanakapi'ai Beach, Hanakapi'ai Beach to Hanakapi'ai Falls and Hanakapi'ai Beach to Kalalau Valley. There are hunters who can do the entire trail in and out in one day, but most people will either want to opt for the Hanakapi'ai Beach or Hanakapi'ai Falls hike or bring camping gear to make it to Kalalau Beach.

The state parks office in Lihu'e can provide a Kalalau Trail brochure with a map. Another good source sponsored by the county is **Kauai Explorer** (www.kauaiexplorer.com). Keep in mind that even if you're not planning to camp, a permit is officially required to continue on the Kalalau Trail beyond Hanakapi'ai. Free day-use hiking permits are available from the **Department of Land & Natural Resources** (www.camping.ehawaii.gov; camping per night $20, 5 night maximum) in Lihu'e, which also issues the required camping permits for the Hanakapi'ai (one-night maximum) and Kalalau (five-nights maximum) Valleys. You'll need ample advance time – possibly as much as six to 12 months – to get night permits.

Kalalau Trail

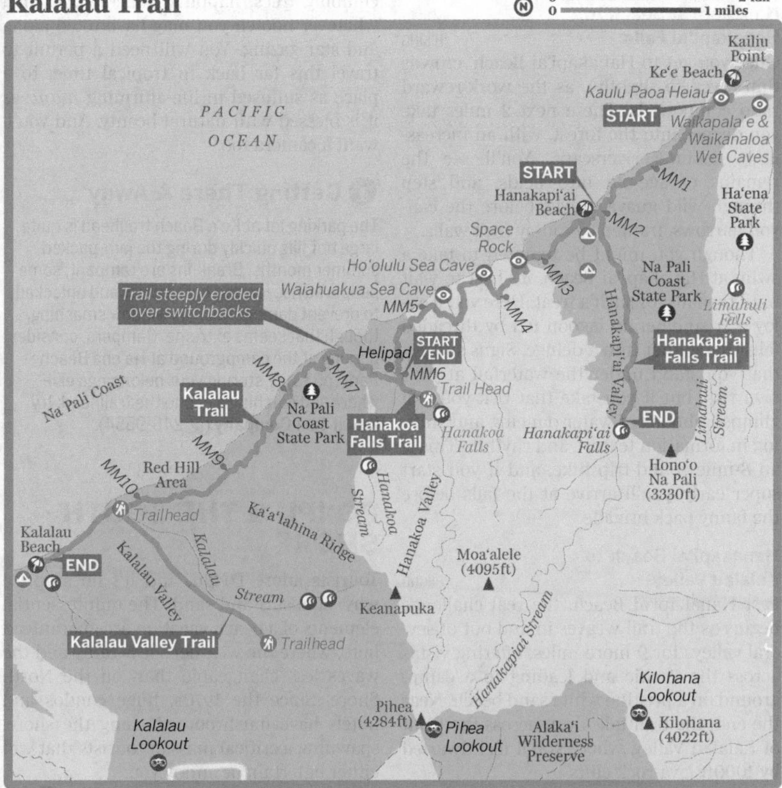

BE PREPARED

The Kalalau Trail (see p537) is seriously Rugged (yes, with a capital R) and therefore it's not for everyone. Being prepared is a tough call too, as you won't want to pack too much, but you will need to stay hydrated, prepped for rain and you *must* take your trash out with you. You may see hikers with machetes, walkie-talkies, climbing rope and reef shoes; but even the trekkers with the most bad-ass gear should know not to expect a rescue by emergency responders – these precipices are to be taken seriously. Anyone with a police scanner can tell you 'plenty story' about the braggart from the mainland who was warned by friends/family/an onlooker but said something along the lines of these famous last words: 'Naw, I'm from Colorado, this is nothing.' Finally, mosquitoes here are bloodthirsty and the sun can really ravage, so always wear insect repellent and sunblock.

Ke'e Beach to Hanakapi'ai Beach HIKING

Young buck surfers do love to paddle out at Hanakapi'ai, often hiking in barefoot with boards under their arm (the bastards!). It shouldn't take you more than two hours to complete this 4-mile (round-trip) trek, however. Locals suggest that you should never turn your back on the ocean here, especially near the river mouth.

Hanakapi'ai Beach to Hanakapi'ai Falls HIKING

Once you get to Hanakapi'ai Beach, crowds thin (ever so slightly), as the work-reward ratio compounds. These next 2 miles take you deeper into the forest, with an increasingly sublime riverscape. You'll see the remains of age-old taro fields, and step through wild guava groves before the canyon narrows, framed by mossy rock walls.

Though you might be tempted to take a swim at Hanakapi'ai Beach, it's best to wait until the falls for such a treat. Here you'll enjoy a crisp emerald lagoon fed by threaded falls that gather into a deluge. Signs suggest that you stand under the waterfall at your own risk, but if you take that risk you will glimpse ribbons of water dancing and shifting in formation texture and rhythm. This is an 8-mile round-trip hike, and if you start super early, you'll arrive at the falls before the fanny pack brigade.

Hanakapi'ai Beach to Kalalau Valley HIKING

Past Hanakapi'ai Beach, the real challenge begins as the trail weaves in and out of several valleys for 9 more miles, offering vistas across the Pacific and leading to a campground on a pristine white sand beach. Near the end, the trail takes you across the front of Kalalau Valley, where you'll feel dwarfed by 1000ft lava-rock cliffs.

The vibe at Kalalau camp is unforgettable. There is something of a semi-permanent hippie community that lives here – their camp decorated with flags, hammocks and Christmas lights – and most of the women and men who hang out here will sunbathe and swim naked. Feel free to join the freedom brigade, it may just feel good. Diversions include building fires, doodling, climbing trees, napping, snacking, sipping whatever hootch you may have toted along and star gazing. You will need a permit to travel this far back in tropical time, to a place as suffused in life-affirming *mana* as it is blessed with natural beauty. And you'll want a camera too.

Getting There & Away

The parking lot at Ke'e Beach trailhead is quite large but fills quickly during the jam-packed summer months. Break-ins are rampant; some people advise leaving cars empty and unlocked to prevent damage such as window smashing, though that seems extreme. Campers, consider parking at the campground at Ha'ena Beach Park (p533) or storing your belongings elsewhere and catching a cab to the trailhead; try **Kauai Taxi Company** (☎246-9554).

PO'IPU & THE SOUTH SHORE

Tourists adore Po'ipu, and it's no surprise why: sun, surf and sand. The quintessential elements of a beach vacation are guaranteed here, where the weather's less rainy and the waves less changeable than on the North Shore. Since the 1970s, huge condos and hotels have mushroomed along the shore, spawning a critical mass of tourists that will either entertain or annoy you.

The South Shore also boasts two world-renowned botanical gardens, as well as the undeveloped Maha'ulepu Coast, where lithified sand-dune cliffs and pounding surf make for an unforgettable walk. What's missing is a town center – or any town at all. Thus, you're bound to stop in Koloa, a former plantation town that's now the South Shore's lively little commercial center.

Koloa

POP 2144

On the South Shore, all roads lead to Koloa, which was a thriving plantation town until it withered after WWII, when sugar gave way to tourism. Today the quaint historic buildings are labeled with plaques and filled with galleries, affordable shops and restaurants – a welcome complement to the budget-breaking selection in Po'ipu. The adjacent residential towns of Lawa'i (population 2133) and Omao (population 1313) are low-key, neighborly and blooming with foliage.

When William Northey Hooper, an enterprising 24-year-old Bostonian, arrived on Kaua'i in 1835, he took advantage of two historical circumstances: the Polynesians' introduction of sugarcane to the islands and Chinese immigrants' knowledge of refining sugar. With financial backing from Honolulu businesspeople, he leased land in Koloa from the king and paid island *ali'i* (royalty) a stipend to release commoners from their traditional work obligations. He then hired the Hawaiians as wage laborers and Koloa became Hawaii's first plantation town.

Sights

As you cross the bridge between the two main historic buildings, be sure to pay your respects to the **Monkeypod Tree**, wrapped in lights. This gorgeous hulk was planted by Howard Yamamoto on this spot in 1925. Thank him, won't you?

★Lawai International Center TEMPLE

(☎639-4300; www.lawaicenter.org; 3381 Wawae Rd; admission by donation; ⏲2nd & last Sun of the month, tours depart at 10am, noon & 2pm) FREE

Magical. Enchanting. Stirring. Such words are often used to describe this quiet spiritual site. Originally the site of a Hawaiian heiau, in 1904 Japanese immigrants placed 88 miniature Shingon Buddhist shrines (about 2ft tall) along a steep hillside path to symbolize 88 pilgrimage shrines in Shikoku, Japan. For years, island pilgrims would journey here from as far as Hanalei and Kekaha.

But the site was abandoned by the 1960s, and half of the shrines lay scattered in shards. In the late 1980s, a hearty crew of volunteers, led by Lynn Muramoto, formed a nonprofit group, acquired the 32-acre property and embarked on a backbreaking project to repair or rebuild the shrines. Now, all 88 are beautifully restored, and there is a wonderful wooden temple, the Hall of Compassion, being constructed on the property as of this writing. You are welcome to take

LOCAL KNOWLEDGE

DRIVING WITH ALOHA

Lauded as the most scenic and breathtaking on the island, the drive to the 'end of the road' is impossibly beautiful. However, accidents have occurred from visitors pulling over for photo-ops – please avoid being 'that person.' (You'll likely see at least one other visitor pulling over.) If you're heading to the road's end (Ke'e Beach), take it slowly and enjoy the crossing of each of the seven one-lane bridges, the first of which is in Hanalei.

When crossing these bridges, do as the locals do:

- When the bridge is empty and you reach it first, you can go.
- If there's a steady stream of cars already crossing as you approach, then simply follow them.
- If traffic is 'heavy' and at least five cars have crossed ahead of you, yield to oncoming traffic. Your generosity will earn a *shaka* salute (see below).
- When you see cars approaching from the opposite direction, yield to the entire queue of approaching cars for at least five cars.
- Give the *shaka* sign ('hang loose' hand gesture, with index, middle and ring fingers downturned) as thanks to any opposite-direction drivers who have yielded.

a self-guided pilgrimage on the trail past all 88 Buddhist shrines as the center is a nondenominational sanctuary for all cultures. Among the luminaries who have found this property to be a source of comfort and healing is the famed baseball player and manager, Dusty Baker. Visits are allowed only on Sundays, twice-monthly.

Koloa History Center MUSEUM
(www.oldkoloa.com; Koloa Rd) FREE Hidden behind the first set of shops on Koloa Rd as you come from Po'ipu, this tiny, open-air museum has old barber chairs and kerosene dispensers, plows and saws, yolks and sewing machines, and a few legends tacked to the walls too. It's worth a quick peek.

Koloa Jodo Mission TEMPLE
(www.jodo.org; 2480 Waikomo Rd) East of town is the Koloa Jodo Mission, which follows Pure Land Buddhism, a devotional form popular in Japan since the 12th century. The Buddhist temple on the left is the original, which dates back to 1910, while the larger temple on the right is currently used for services.

St Raphael's Catholic Church CHURCH
(742-1955; 3011 Hapa Rd; mass 7am Mon-Fri, 5pm Sat, 9:30am Sun) Kaua'i's oldest Catholic church is the burial site of some of Hawaii's first Portuguese immigrants. The original church, built in 1854, was made of lava rock and coral mortar with walls 3ft thick – a type of construction visible in the ruins of the adjacent rectory.

When the church was enlarged in 1936 it was plastered over, creating a more typical whitewashed appearance. It is always open for visitors. Weekday mass is held in the old church. On weekends, services are held in the nearby new church.

Sugar Hill Monument MONUMENT
(www.oldkoloa.com; 5371 Koloa Rd) The story of old Koloa's plantation town history is told on eight plaques and the iron rendering of mill workers that make up this sugar cube of a monument.

Activities

Landlocked Koloa is home to two excellent ocean-sports outfits.

★Ocean Quest Fathom Five Divers DIVING
(742-6991; www.fathomfive.com; 3450 Po'ipu Rd; shore dives 1-/2-tanks $75/90, boat dives $125-350) They offer the whole range, from Ni'ihau boat dives ($350) and night dives to certification courses. Newbies can expect reassuring hand-holding during their introductory shore dives. Groups max out at six and they avoid mixing skill levels. Call well in advance.

Koloa Zipline ZIPLINING
(742-2894; www.koloazipline.com; 3477-A Weliweli Rd; per person $115-150; tours depart 8:30am, 9:30am, 1:30pm & 2:30pm) Take the plunge, and fold your bod into a cannon or a bullet. Zip upside down and enjoy superlative views from Kaua'i's newest, best and longest (in feet) zipline tour on the is-

HURRICANE CHICKENS (& ROOSTERS)

Before you get too annoyed at the thousands of wild chickens on Kaua'i, consider their back-story. The original chickens to populate Hawaii were jungle fowl *(moa),* introduced by the first Polynesians. These vividly colored birds later cross-bred with domestic chickens brought by Westerners. During plantation days, Kaua'i's wild-chicken population was kept in check by field fires (a regular event before harvest, to allow more efficient reaping). After the sugar industry began to go bust, the chicken population boomed.

When Hurricane 'Iwa and Hurricane 'Iniki struck in 1982 and 1992 respectively, they obliterated the cages of Kaua'i's fighting cocks, as well as those of the local chicken ranchers, adding thousands more chickens to the wild. With no mongoose or snake population to prey on fowl, wild chickens proliferated.

You'll see them perched in trees, running across fields, roaming parking lots and otherwise strutting their stuff across the island. Most locals have adopted an attitude of acceptance toward the chickens, but warn of their *lolo* (crazy) schedules: instead of crowing only at dawn, they cock-a-doodle-doo at random times and seem confused by a full moon or any late-night light. Before you book accommodations, ask whether there are chickens living within earshot. Or just wear earplugs.

land. The 8th line is the longest of them all. Check-in at Kaua'i ATV.

Snorkel Bob's SNORKELING

(742-2206; www.snorkelbob.com; 3236 Po'ipu Rd; rental mask, snorkel & fins per day/week $9/35; 8am-5pm) The king of snorkel gear rents and sells enough styles and sizes to assure a good fit. If, after renting, you want to buy an item, your rental payment deflects part of the cost.

Kaua'i ATV ATV

(742-2734, 877-707-7088; www.kauaiatv.com; 5330 Koloa Rd; tours $125-175; tours depart 7:30am, 9:30am, noon & 1:30pm) This outfit commendably offers two- and four-seater bio-diesel vehicles for a reasonable upgrade of $10 per person. Therefore, we recommend these ATV tours only if you opt for the green machines over the gas-powered ones. No matter the fuel formula, when riding in upcountry pastureland you're guaranteed to get dirty, whether merely dusty or soaked in mud. Use their loaner clothing.

Festivals & Events

Koloa Plantation Days Celebration LOCAL FESTIVAL

(652-3217; www.koloaplantationdays.com;) In July, the South Shore's biggest annual celebration spans nine days of family fun with the gamut of attractions (many free), including a parade, block party, rodeo, craft fair, canoe race, golf tournament, a ukulele contest and guided walks.

Sleeping

The following are in the Koloa, Omao and Lawa'i residential neighborhoods.

Boulay Inn INN $

(742-1120; www.boulayinn.com; 4175 Omao Rd; 1br $85;) Your money goes far in this airy one-bedroom guest apartment attached to a reasonably well-updated family home in quiet residential Omao. The 500-sq-ft space is comfy rather than fancy and sits atop a garage. Features include wraparound lanai, full kitchen, private phone line, high ceilings and free use of the washer-dryer. A cleaning fee ($50) is charged.

Yvonne's B&B B&B $

(742-2418; yvonne.e.johnson@gmail.com; 3857 Omao Rd; s/d $79/89, incl breakfast $89/109;) Stylishly decorated with a mixture of Hawaiian artifacts and retro furnishings, this B&B is perfect for a couple wanting a gregarious and obliging host or a single traveler craving a place to call home. Homemade breads and jams are regularly provided and the outdoor shower might have you reconsidering ever showering indoors again (although there is an indoor shower, too).

★ **Marjorie's Kaua'i Inn** INN $$

(332-8838, 800-717-8838; www.marjorieskauai-inn.com; Hailima St, Lawa'i; r incl breakfast $140-195;) There are magnificent vistas from this classy inn perched 400ft above the Lawa'i Valley, along with three rooms that show off stylish furnishings and include a large private lanai, along with a kitchenette. You're nowhere near the beach, but the elegant 50ft lap pool and poolside BBQ grill compensate nicely, as do breakfasts of waffles and quiche.

Cozy Kauai Cottage VACATION RENTAL $$

(742-1778, 877-742-1778; www.kauaivacation-properties.com/cottage.htm; 3794-A Omao Rd; s/d $90/115, cleaning fee $40;) A pastoral retreat with modern amenities, this simple, compact cottage (best for a single or couple) is efficiently arranged to include a full kitchen, separate bedroom and comfy living area. The hardwood floor, granite counters and dimmer lights add style, while lots of windows let in cool breezes. It's set well off the road, among the avocado trees.

Eating & Drinking

★ **Koloa Fish Market** SEAFOOD $

(742-6199; 5482 Koloa Rd; lunch $4-8 ; 10am-6pm Mon-Fri, to 5pm Sat) Line up with locals at this hole-in-the-wall serving outstanding *poke* (the Korean iteration has the most spice), Japanese-style bento, sushi rolls and Hawaiian plate lunches. Don't miss the thick-sliced, perfectly seared ahi and rich slabs of homemade *haupia* (coconut pudding). Cash only.

Koloa Deli DELI $

(742-9998; www.facebook.com/koloa.deli; 5470 Koloa Road; sandwiches $6-10; 7:30am-4pm Mon-Sat;) A new storefront deli across from the post office trafficking mostly in Boar's Head cold cuts and imported cheeses. They do a Godfather sub with salami, capocollo, mortadella and prosciutto, and a tangy spicy veggie sub too. Good for lunch on the run.

Koloa Mill Ice Cream & Coffee ICE CREAM $

(742-6544; www.koloamill.com; 6544 Koloa Rd; single-scoop ice cream $3.55; 7am-9pm)

Homemade cotton candy, Kaua'i coffee and nothing but the best Maui-born Roselani Ice Cream are always served with a smile. For the indecisive, start with the Pauwela Sunrise and go from there.

Kauai Food Truck FAST FOOD $
(5371 Koloa Rd; mains $7-8; 7am-3pm) Across the street from the main shopping strip, this venerable food truck churns out fish tacos, burgers and garlic shrimp at lunch and a pleasantly greasy breakfast sandwich and local coffee in the morning. It's parked behind the Sugar Hill Monument on the Old Mill site.

Pizzetta ITALIAN $$
(742-8881; www.pizzettarestaurant.com; 5408 Koloa Rd; calzones $12.95, pizza $17-25; 11am-10pm) If this family trattoria had *any* competition, we'd be more critical, but affordable eateries are scarce around here. Grab a decent gourmet pizza, such as the El Greco (sun-dried tomatoes, artichoke hearts and feta), that won't ravage your wallet. And finish your business with some delectable Papalani gelato. Expect a mainly touristy clientele.

Tomkat's TAVERN
(742-8887; 5402 Koloa Rd; 3pm-2am; live music 10pm-close) An old-fashioned bar and grill with a rather quaint garden courtyard. They do late-night drink specials and live music from 10pm until closing. They have a decent kitchen too.

Self-Catering

Sueoka Market SELF-CATERING $
(742-1611; 5392 Koloa Rd; 6:30am-8:30pm) An indie grocer that holds its own with the basics. It has a fine little produce and seafood selection, plus packaged Japanese takeout snacks.

Big Save SUPERMARKET $
(cnr Waikomo Rd & Koloa Rd; 6am-11pm) Has one of its best branches here. Don't miss the value-priced ahi *poke*.

Shopping

★ **Art House** GALLERY
(742-1400; www.arthousehawaii.com; 3440 Po'ipu Rd; 11am-6pm Mon-Sat, to 5pm Sun) Easily the best browse in town, this bright, happy art gallery features paintings, mixed media and groovy handicrafts from local artists – including the talented owner, Julie Berg. There's a small collection of sweet silver jewelry and funky handbags here too.

Island Soap & Candle Works SOUVENIRS
(888-528-7627; www.kauaisoap.com; 5428 Koloa Rd; 9am-9pm) For a delicious treat with zero calories, breathe deeply inside this flowery, fruity sensation of a shop. After all, the Morning Mint soap does look and smell like ice cream when it's being made, and papaya oatmeal smells delicious too. Established in 1984 to recreate the art of soap- and candlemaking, the company still makes everything by hand.

Christian Riso Fine Arts ART GALLERY
(742-2555; 5400 Koloa Rd; 9am-9pm Tue-Sun) Browsers are welcome at this informal gallery of paintings and drawings by island artists, fine jewelry (including Ni'ihau shell necklaces) and fun collectibles like hand-painted walking sticks and some rather fabulous antique masks. The shop specializes in custom framing using Hawaiian hardwoods such as koa and kamani.

Pohaku T's CLOTHING
(742-7500; www.pohaku.com; 3430 Po'ipu Rd; 10am-8pm Mon-Sat, to 6pm Sun) This well-stocked shop specializes in Kaua'i-made clothing, crafts and island-themed tees and tanks. Signature shirt designs feature classic island themes (petroglyphs, *honu* and navigational maps) on stonewashed or overdyed colors. Cotton aloha shirts are locally hand-sewn yet affordable.

Information

First Hawaiian Bank (742-1642; 3506 Waikomo Rd) At the east end of town.

Post Office (800-275-8777; 5485 Koloa Rd) Serves both Koloa and Po'ipu.

Getting There & Away

From the west, Koloa Rd (Hwy 530), which runs between Lawa'i and Koloa, is the best way in and out. From Lihu'e, take the scenic Maluhia Rd (Hwy 520) through the enchanting **Tree Tunnel**.

Po'ipu

POP 979

Po'ipu (which ironically translates as 'completely overcast' – don't worry, it isn't) is world renowned for its easy-access beaches and is somewhat drier and sunnier than the North Shore. But it's not just the climate that differs. While the north has a wilder feel –

A COAST LIKE NO OTHER

The windswept Maha'ulepu Coast resembles no other on Kaua'i: sand-dune cliffs, pounding surf and three pristine beaches still free from mass tourism. Known as Kaua'i's last undeveloped accessible coast, it lies just east of Shipwreck Beach.

The best way to explore the coast is hiking the **Maha'ulepu Heritage Trail**, a pleasant hike that runs for almost 4 miles from Shipwreck Beach to Ha'ula Beach (you can turn back at any point for a shorter, but still stunning, walk). To reach the trailhead, park in the Grand Hyatt lot at the end of Ainako St. From the beach, head east through the ironwood trees. Along the coast, you will pass spectacular cliffs, tide pools in rocky coves and even the ruins of a heiau.

The Maha'ulepu Coast comprises a string of beaches from west to east: **Maha'ulepu Beach (Gillin's Beach)**, **Kawailoa Bay** and **Ha'ula Beach**. Waters are choppy and better suited to experienced swimmers than once-a-year tourists, but hiking is enticing year-round. Near Maha'ulepu Beach you'll see the sole house on the entire coast, the **Gillin Beach House** (☎742-7561; www.gillinbeachhouse.com; per week from $3090), originally built in 1946 by Elbert Gillin, a civil engineer with the Koloa Sugar Plantation.

You can also access the **Makauwahi Cave Trail** (www.cavereserve.org; ⊙9am-2pm Sun) from here, which will take you inside the largest limestone cave in Hawaii. Visitors may only enter with a trained volunteer guide, who staff the cave on Sundays. Little known fact: they shot scenes for *Pirates of the Caribbean* in this sinkhole.

If you must drive, go past the Grand Hyatt, proceed for 1.5 miles on the unpaved road and turn right where it dead-ends at a gate (open 7:30am to 6pm, to 7pm summer). Continue past the gatehouse until you reach the beach parking area. Access hours are strictly enforced.

Two excellent resources are the Maha'ulepu Heritage Trail **website** (www.hikemahaulepu.org) and *Kaua'i's Geologic History: A Simplified Guide* by Chuck Blay and Robert Siemers. Also see **Malama Maha'ulepu** (www.malama-mahaulepu.org), a nonprofit group working to preserve the area, which is owned by Steve Case, the co-founder of America Online.

not to mention a certain hippie chic, cooler-than-thou quality – Po'ipu is just a simple, pleasant resort town, with condos galore, two aging yet still grand resorts, as well as some hidden, gorgeously wild beaches that rival the island's best scenery. It's ideal for families – especially those with young children, as several of the beaches are sheltered and the sea safe for *keiki*. And know that the quality of Po'ipu sunsets is reflected in the dizzy smiles of awe-drunk tourists, weaving and leaning against one another on the sand. Indeed, nature magic kisses this place goodnight with a flourish.

Alas, Po'ipu has no town center, though most commerce is centered around two shopping complexes, so a rental car – or at least a bicycle is advisable.

Beaches

Po'ipu Beach Park BEACH

(👪🐾) A go-to spot where there's something for everyone and the water is always clear and clean (according to Surfrider Foundation water testers, that is). Patrolled by resident *honu* (sea turtles) in the shallows, it's sheltered by a rock reef that attracts fish of all shapes and sizes.

The beach spills into two separate bays connected by that common reef outside and bisected by a sandbar. It's heart shaped in that way. There are also three nearby surf breaks and a gorgeous grassy lawn that connects to Brennecke's Beach just east. Add in the lifeguard, toilet and shower facilities, and those miracle sunsets and you have one safe, lively, family-friendly beach. It's located at the end of Ho'owili Rd. Parking is right across the street from the beach.

Brennecke's Beach BEACH

With a sandbar bottom and a notch of sand and sea wedged between two lava rock outcrops, this little beach attracts a cadre of bodyboarders, bobbing in the water, waiting for the next set at any time of day or year. No surfboards are allowed near shore, so bodyboarders rule.

If you want to join in, note that it's a shore break. Surf is highest in summer, but the

Po'ipu

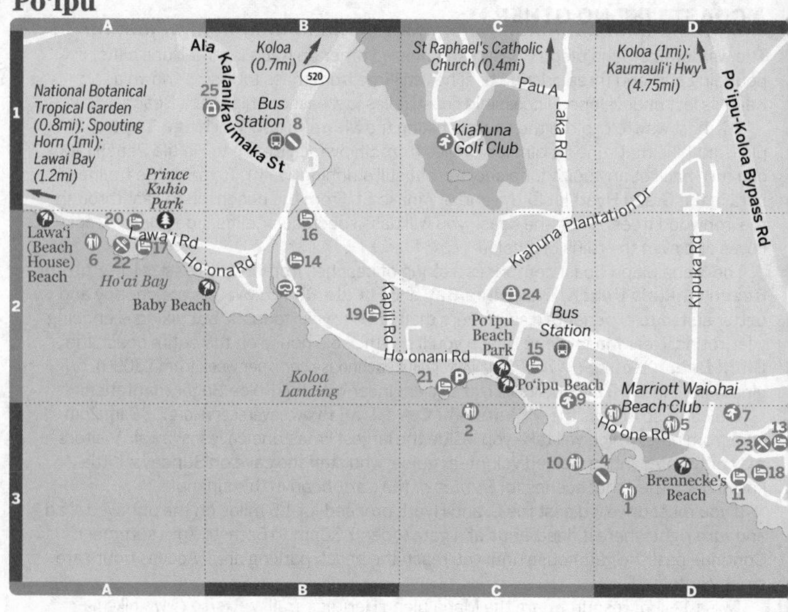

winter action can be respectable, too. Past the break, Brennecke's also happens to have the best snorkelling on the South Shore, with tumbling rock reefs on either edge of the bay, resident sea turtles and vast schools of fish. Further outside are some coral structures, teeming with life as well. Yet unless the water is super calm, it takes ocean skills and experience to enjoy these sites. Always check with the Po'ipu lifeguards before venturing out. Brennecke's flanks the eastern edge of Po'ipu Beach Park.

Po'ipu Beach BEACH

Despite its nicknames of Sheraton Beach and Kiahuna Beach, this long swath of sand is not private. It merely fronts the hotel and condo, both of which scored big-time with their location along Po'ipu Beach, which lies west of Po'ipu Beach Park.

The waters here are often too rough for kids, although an offshore reef tames the waves enough for strong swimmers and snorkelers. To get to the beach, drive to the end of Ho'onani Rd.

Shipwreck Beach BEACH

Unless you're an expert surfer, bodyboarder or bodysurfer, keep your feet dry at Shipwreck. Instead, come for an invigorating walk along the half-mile crescent of light gold sand. You'll most likely have company, as the Grand Hyatt Kaua'i Resort & Spa (p550) overlooks much of the beach along Keoneloa Bay.

Row after row of waves crashes close to the shore, giving this beach a rugged, untamed vibe. Toward the left of the bay looms **Makawehi Point**, a gigantic lithified sand dune, which you can ascend in 10 minutes.

In the movie *Six Days Seven Nights*, stunt doubles for Harrison Ford and Anne Heche leap off Makawehi Point. In real life, a few daredevils similarly dive off the rocky, 30ft cliff, as shown in thrilling YouTube clips, but no one mentions the severe casualties and deaths. In a word: don't. To get here, head toward the Grand Hyatt, turn *makai* (seaward) on Ainako St and park in the small lot at the end.

Baby Beach BEACH

(👪) Introduce tots to the ocean at this baby beach (there's another in Kapa'a), where the water is barely thigh-high. The sandy shore runs behind a row of beach homes on Ho'ona Rd (west of Koloa Landing), so access is easy but parking is tricky (don't block driveways). Look for the beach-access sign that marks a path to the beach.

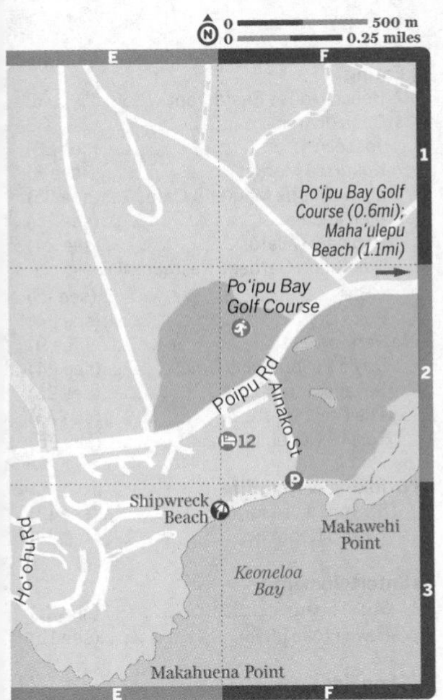

Lawa'i (Beach House) Beach — BEACH

Thanks to the nearby break PK's, this tiny beach gets some major action with snorkelers and surfers. Located almost adjacent to Lawa'i Rd (beside the iconic restaurant), it's not especially scenic or sandy. But during calm surf, the waters are rich snorkeling turf. There are restrooms, a shower and a smidge of public parking across the street.

Sights

Note that you can't see any beaches from Po'ipu Rd (all you see are condos and parking lots). To reach the beaches, you must turn *makai* (seaward) on side streets, such as Ho'owili Rd (Po'ipu Beach Park) and Kapili Rd (Sheraton Beach).

National Tropical Botanical Garden — GARDENS

(NTBG; ☎742-2623; www.ntbg.org; 4425 Lawa'i Rd; guided tour adult/child $45/20, self-guided tour $15/7.50; ⏰8:30am-5pm) If you're interested in plants and their preservation, a visit to these gardens is an education. The gardens are not just stunningly beautiful, they are also sanctuaries for native plants and living laboratories for staff scientists and international experts.

Of the two Po'ipu gardens, the 80-acre **Allerton Garden** is the showy star, but it requires a pricey guided tour. Tour guides are generally knowledgeable and enthusiastic, leisurely guiding groups (up to 20) through meticulously landscaped grounds. Highlights include otherworldly Moreton Bay fig trees (seen in Jurassic Park), golden bamboo groves, a pristine lagoon and valley walls blanketed with purple bougainvillea during summer. The artificial statuary and water elements somehow blend into the landscape.

The adjacent **McBryde Garden** is less manicured and fancy than Allerton Garden, showcasing palms, flowering and spice trees, orchids and rare native species, plus a pretty stream and waterfall. For budget travelers, the self-guided tour allows you to wander in the vast grounds without watching the clock.

Moir Gardens — GARDENS

(☎742-6411; 2253 Po'ipu Rd, Kiahuna Plantation; ⏰sunrise-sunset) FREE If cacti are your fancy, this modest garden on the grounds of the Kiahuna Plantation condo is worth a look-see. It's a low-key, approachable collection of mature cacti and succulents, interspersed with winding paths, a lily pond and colorful shocks of remarkable orchids.

The gardens, established in the 1930s, were originally the estate of Hector Moir, manager of Koloa Sugar Plantation, and Alexandra 'Sandie' Knudsen Moir. The Moirs were avid gardeners who switched from flowering plants to drought-tolerant ones that could naturally thrive in dry Po'ipu. A sideshow rather than a showstopper, it's worth a stroll if you're staying nearby or dining at the restaurant.

Spouting Horn Beach Park — OUTDOORS

A concrete pad and grassy picnic area set just above two blowholes in the lava rock reef where the surf juts through like a geyser, exhaling and spewing with beautiful violence. The bigger, circular hole furthest from the lookout is less dramatic than the closer one, which funnels the power more furiously.

There's a scrubby trail down to the outcrop but take care and don't get too close. You can get sucked into the sea with big surf. Also, the waves can be unpredictable, so you might need to wait for some action. Eruptions are typically under 30ft and last only seconds, but they can reach twice that height during big surf.

Po'ipu

Sights

- Galerie 103 .... (see 25)
- Moir Gardens .... (see 15)

Activities, Courses & Tours

- Anara Spa .... (see 12)
- 1 Cowshead D3
- 2 First Break C3
- Kauai Down Under Dive Team ..... (see 21)
- 3 Koloa Landing B2
- 4 Nukumoi Point D3
- 5 Nukumoi Surf Shop D3
- Outfitters Kaua'i .... (see 8)
- 6 PK's A2
- 7 Poipu Kai Tennis Club D3
- 8 Seasport Divers B1
- 9 Spa at Koa Kea Hotel & Resort C2
- 10 Waiohai C3

Sleeping

- 11 Aikane Po'ipu Beach Houses D3
- 12 Grand Hyatt Kaua'i Resort & Spa F2
- 13 Hideaway Cove Villas D3
- 14 Kauai Beach Inn B2
- 15 Kiahuna Plantation C2
- Koa Kea Hotel & Resort .... (see 9)
- 16 Koloa Landing B2
- 17 Kuhio Shores A2
- 18 Nihi Kai Villas D3
- 19 Po'ipu Kapili B2
- 20 Prince Kuhio Resort A2
- 21 Sheraton Kaua'i Resort C2

Eating

- 22 Beach House Restaurant A2
- 23 Casa di Amici D3
- Josselin's .... (see 25)
- Kukui'ula Market .... (see 8)
- Living Foods Market & Café .... (see 25)
- Merriman's .... (see 25)
- Papalani Gelato .... (see 24)
- Plantation Gardens Restaurant & Bar .... (see 15)
- Puka Dog .... (see 24)
- Red Salt .... (see 9)
- Roy's Po'ipu Bar & Grill .... (see 24)
- Savage Shrimp .... (see 25)
- The Dolphin .... (see 25)
- Tortilla Republic .... (see 25)

Drinking & Nightlife

- Stevenson's Library .... (see 12)
- Tortilla Republic .... (see 25)

Entertainment

- 'Auli'i Luau .... (see 21)
- Havaiki Nui Luau .... (see 12)

Shopping

- A Feinberg Gallery .... (see 25)
- Cariloha .... (see 24)
- Hawaiian Salt .... (see 25)
- Malie Organics .... (see 25)
- 24 Po'ipu Shopping Village C2
- 25 Shops at Kukui'ula B1

To get here, turn right off Po'ipu Rd onto Lawa'i Rd and continue for 1.75 miles.

Prince Kuhio Park PARK

The simple green space honoring Kaua'i's prince Jonah Kuhio Kalaniana'ole, born around here in 1871, still thrums with *mana*. Yes, the lawn is often brown and dry, which keeps visitors away, but this park contains the ruins of an ancient Hawaiian heiau and fishpond.

This is why you can often hear the echoing cries of Hawaiian dancers ring through the night as they rehearse in the moonlight (listen and enjoy, don't snoop). The park's namesake, Prince Kuhio, is revered to this day. He was the Territory of Hawaii's first delegate to the US Congress and he spearheaded the Hawaiian Homes Commission Act, which set aside 200,000 acres of land for indigenous Hawaiians, many of whom are still waiting for it.

Galerie 103 GALLERY

(☎ 742-0103; www.galerie103.com; 2829 Ala Kalanikaumaka, Shops at Kukui'ula, Suite 102/103; ⏰ noon-8pm Tue-Sat) For local art that goes beyond the easy-sell tropical motifs, visit this classy gallery that blurs the line between commercial enterprise and art museum. Owner and art photographer **Bruna Stude** (www.brunastude.com) has assembled an impressive collection of both emerging and established names, including some major artists who show regularly at the Met and Guggenheim in NYC.

Exhibits rotate every eight weeks and don't forget to visit its annex, A+. It's modeled after museum shops and offers more affordable drawings, ceramics, fiber art and other collectibles.

Activities

Diving

The Po'ipu coast offers the majority of the island's best dive sites, including **Sheraton Caverns**, a series of partially collapsed lava tubes 10ft or more in height, with shafts of glowing sunlight illuminating their dim, atmospheric interior; **General Store**, with sharks, octopuses, eels and the remains of an 1892 shipwreck; and **Nukumoi Point**, a shallow site as well as habitat for green sea turtles.

Dive boats and catamaran cruises usually depart from Kukui'ula Harbor, 0.5 miles east of Spouting Horn. In addition to the dive outfits listed here, consider nearby Ocean Quest Fathom Five Divers (p540).

Kauai Down Under Dive Team DIVING
(☎742-9534; www.kauaidownunderscuba.com; 2440 Ho'onani Rd, Sheraton Kaua'i Resort; 2-tank boat dives incl equipment rental $159; ⊙8am-6pm) With one instructor per four guests, personal attention is guaranteed. They offer introductory noncertified one-tank dives ($109), two-tank scooter dives ($169) and night dives ($99) for the truly adventurous, as well as a multitude of classes including the recommended pre-arrival online academic portion of the certification for those wanting to maximize playtime while on the island.

Seasport Divers DIVING
(☎742-9303, 800-685-5889; www.seasportdivers.com; 2827 Po'ipu Rd, Po'ipu Plaza; 2-tank dive $130, gear rental $30; ⊙check-in 7:30am & 12:45pm) This outfit leads a range of dives from shore or boat, including a three-tank dive to Ni'ihau ($315), offered only in summer. All dives are guided by instructor-level divemasters; any group with noncertified divers includes an additional instructor. Groups are limited to 18 but the count is typically eight to 12.

Koloa Landing SNORKELING
Koloa Landing, at the mouth of Waikomo Stream, was once Kaua'i's largest port. Nineteenth-century farmers used it to ship Kaua'i-grown sugar, oranges and sweet potatoes, and it was the third-busiest whaling port among the Hawaiian Islands, surpassed only by Honolulu and Lahaina, Maui.

The landing waned after the road system was built; it was abandoned in the 1920s. Today only a small boat ramp remains. Underwater, it's another story: Koloa Landing is popular for snorkeling and the best shore-diving spot on the South Shore. Its protected waters reach depths of about 30ft and it's generally calm all year. See underwater tunnels, a variety of coral and fish, sea turtles and monk seals. The best sights are located toward the west.

Surfing

Although the north and west shores get all the publicity, waves break on the South Shore in the summer time, and Po'ipu has three notable surf breaks.

PK's – short for its nameasake, Prince Kuhio – is soft breaking and generally good for beginners, unless a big swell rolls in. **Centers** is a shallower, hollow wave for more experienced surfers only. **Acid Drop** only breaks when the swell is big because it's deeper out, but when it's on it lives up to its name. Beware the bad trip.

Experienced surfers and bodyboarders can also attempt the breaks near the Sheraton (p550), but the waters are famous for sneaky sets (rogue waves that appear from nowhere) and the rocky coast makes it difficult to get offshore and back. **Cowshead**, the rocky outcropping at the west end of the beach, is an extremely challenging break unless you know how to approach the channel. Expert surfers can attempt offshore spots such as **First Break** in front of the Sheraton, but beginners should always remain inshore. **Waiohai**, at the east end of the beach in front of the **Marriott Waiohai Beach Club** time-share, is good for surfers of all levels and breaks left and right, but use caution, as the reef gets very shallow very quickly here.

Po'ipu is a popular spot for surf lessons. We recommend the following outfits, which all meet at the beach.

★Kaua'i Surf School SURFING
(☎651-6032; www.kauaisurfschool.com; 2hr lesson group/private $75/175; 👪) With 90 minutes of teaching and 30 minutes of free practice, you get your money's worth. A good outfit for children, with a special one-hour private lesson for kids aged four to 12. Also offers multiday surf clinics and surf escort services.

Garden Island Surf School SURFING
(☎652-4841; www.gardenislandsurfschool.com; Po'ipu Beach; 2hr lesson group/couple/private $75/120/150; ⊙lessons 8am, 10am, noon & 2pm) The lesson includes one hour with an instructor and one hour of free surfing. Four students per group; minimum age is eight for groups and five for privates. Meet on the beach between the Sheraton and Kiahuna condos.

Surf Lessons by Margo Oberg SURFING
(☎332-6100; www.surfonkauai.com; 2hr lesson group/semiprivate/private $68/90/125) Owned

and operated by a seven-time world champ and one of the longest-running surf schools on Kaua'i, this operation has a fine rep but classes can reach six.

Kelley's Surf School SURFING, SUP
(☎652-9979; www.kauaisurfandsup.com; surfing 2hr lesson/private/3hr tour $75/120/150, stand-up paddle boarding 2hr lesson/basic tour/elite tour $85/120/150;) Offers a kids' surf camp and family discounts, and has 30 years of experience to bring to the table.

Nukumoi Surf Shop SURFING
(☎742-8019; www.nukumoi.com; 2100 Ho'one Rd; surfboard rental per day from $25, SUP per hour/day from $20/60, bodyboards & snorkel set per day $6; ⏲7:45am-6:30pm Mon-Sat, 10:45am-6pm Sun) Po'ipu's most popular surf shop is conveniently located right across from Po'ipu Beach Park.

Golf & Tennis

Po'ipu Bay Golf Course GOLF
(☎742-8711, 800-858-6300; www.poipubaygolf.com; 2250 Ainako St; nonguest/guest $240/170, club rental $55) The South Shore's long-standing jewel, this Robert Trent Jones Jr–designed, 18-hole, par-72 course adjacent to the Grand Hyatt Kaua'i Resort & Spa covers 210 seaside acres and was the home of the PGA's Grand Slam of Golf from 1994 to 2006. Greens fees are reduced at noon (to $150) and further reduced at 2:30pm (to $95). The fee includes a cart.

Kiahuna Golf Club GOLF
(☎742-9595; www.kiahunagolf.com; 2545 Kiahuna Plantation Dr; greens fee incl cart before/after 3pm $103/72, club rental $52) This economical course is a relatively forgiving par-70, Robert Trent Jones Jr–designed 18 holes. Established in 1983, it's a compact, inland course using smaller targets and awkward stances to pose challenges.

Poipu Kai Tennis Club TENNIS
(☎742-8706; 1775 Po'ipu Rd; per person $20, racket rental $5; ⏲8am-noon, 2-6pm; clinics 8am Mon, Wed & Fri) Rent one of eight hard courts with an ocean view at this fine racquet club run by the greatest tennis pro in the history of the universe, the lovely Ms Hattie. They have tennis clinics, round robin tourneys and take reservations, but you can also just show up.

Other Activities

Outfitters Kaua'i ADVENTURE TOUR
(☎742-9667, 888-742-9887; www.outfitterskauai.com; 2827-A Po'ipu Rd, Po'ipu Plaza; bike rental per day $25-45; ⏲reservations taken 8am-9pm) Offers an array of sea-kayaking, cycling, zipline, waterfall and whale-watching tours. One of their coolest options is a stand up paddle tour (half-day per person $122) down a jungle stream through the Hule'ia National Wildlife Refuge. They rent bikes too.

CJM Country Stables HORSEBACK RIDING
(☎742-6096; www.cjmstables.com; Po'ipu Rd; 2hr rides $103-130; ⏲rides 9:30am & 2pm Mon-Sat, 1pm Wed & Fri) If you want a break from hoofin' it yourself, hop on a horse. The slow, nose-to-tail, follow-the-leader group rides may bore experienced riders – who should arrange private rides – but the terrain (the luscious Maha'ulelpu area) is wild and sublime, rain or shine.

Anara Spa SPA
(☎742-1234; www.anaraspa.com; 1571 Po'ipu Rd, Grand Hyatt Kaua'i Resort & Spa; massage per hr $160-235) Following its extreme makeover in 2007, the spa emerged as a 20,000-sq-ft tropical fantasyland, with gardens and waterfalls to soothe the eyes while the face and body indulges in a splurge-worthy menu of delicious services. Access to the lap pool and fitness center is free with a 50-minute spa treatment.

Spa at Koa Kea Hotel & Resort SPA
(☎828-8888; www.koakea.com; 2251 Po'ipu Rd; massage 50/80min from $120/175; ⏲8am-7pm) Offers five treatment rooms (including one for couples), a range of massage styles, and body scrubs and treatments utilize indigenous products such as *Awapuhi* root, red Kaua'i clay and local coffee. Reserve at least a day in advance.

Tours

Unless you're as water-phobic as a cat, we recommend a snorkeling tour to maximize your cruise experience. But if you're seeking a sunset tour, **Capt Andy's Sailing Adventures** (☎800-535-0830; www.napali.com; Waialo Rd, Port Allen Marina Center; adult/child $79/59) departs from Kukui'ula Harbor between 4pm and 5pm for a scenic two-hour cruise.

Festivals & Events

Prince Kuhio Celebration of the Arts CULTURAL
(☎240-6369; www.princekuhio.wetpaint.com; ⏲mid-late Mar) A 10-day-long celebration in March, held in honor of Prince Jonah Kuhio Kalaniana'ole, who was born in 1872 on the

site of Prince Kuhio Park. Events include canoe races, the sharing and explanation of Hawaiian proverbs from local elders, dance performance, concerts and even some amateur boxing matches.

Garden Isle Artisan Fair MUSIC, CRAFTS
(☎245-9021) When on Kaua'i, buy Kaua'i-made. At this triannual fair in mid-March, mid-August and mid-October, you'll find handcrafted items, Hawaiian music and local *grinds*. It's held in Po'ipu, Wailua and Kilauea. Call for details.

Sleeping

The majority of accommodations in Po'ipu are condos, available for all budget levels. Rates can vary depending on the owner or agency renting each unit; we list typical or average rates. Vacation-rental homes can offer more privacy and drive-up access. As you walk down the quiet residential stretch of Lawa'i Rd from Prince Kuhio Park to Spouting Horn Park, you'll see a number of particularly stunning villas dotting the rocky shore. The Parrish Collection (p549) manages a number of the homes here. So do Kauai Island Vacations (p549) and Garden Island Rentals (p549). The two major hotels in the area are the high-end Grand Hyatt Resort & Spa (p550) and business-class Sheraton Kaua'i (p550).

Check out the **Po'ipu Beach Resort Association** (www.poipubeach.org) for additional listings; note that condo links often go merely to agencies, however. If you decide on a specific condo, always check **Vacation Rentals by Owner** (www.vrbo.com) for additional rentals; owners might offer better deals than agencies.

That said, you don't incur extra fees if you book with agencies and they can steer you to appropriate properties, especially if you're seeking a vacation-rental home.

Agencies

Parrish Collection Kaua'i ACCOMMODATION SERVICES $$$
(☎742-1412, 800-325-5701; www.parrishkauai.com; Suite 1, 3176 Po'ipu Rd, Koloa) Well-established agency for condos and vacation homes. Friendly, accommodating staff also represent many of the top villas on Lawa'i Rd.

Kauai Island Vacations ACCOMMODATION SERVICES
(☎826-1111; www.kauaiislandvacations.com; homes from $525 per night) They represent a number of the best homes on the South Shore. Not cheap, but very high quality, tasteful and often soulful homes.

Po'ipu Connection Realty ACCOMMODATION SERVICES
(☎800-742-2260; www.poipuconnection.com) Rents units in the Prince Kuhio and Kuhio Shores condo developments, among others. Expect good prices and personalized service.

Po'ipu Beach Vacation Rentals ACCOMMODATION SERVICES
(☎742-2850; www.pbvacationrentals.com; condos/homes from per night $85/110) Good prices; limited selection includes condos and vacation homes.

Aikane Po'ipu Beach Houses ACCOMMODATION SERVICES
(☎742-1778, 877-742-1778; www.kauaivacationproperties.com/poipu.htm) Choose from a choice crop of dreamy beach houses near Brennecke's Beach.

Garden Island Rentals ACCOMMODATION SERVICES
(☎800-247-5599; www.kauaiproperties.com) They represent some of the fine homes on Lawa'i Rd in the Prince Kuhio area.

Properties

Prince Kuhio Resort CONDO $$
(☎888-747-2988; www.prince-kuhio.com; 5061 Lawa'i Rd; studio/1br from $75/115; ❄☒) This 90-unit condo is a budget property, so don't expect spiffy furnishings and floors. But it's great value for the location across the road from Lawa'i (Beach House) Beach. All units have full kitchens and breezy windows, while pleasantly landscaped grounds surround a decent-size pool. Units vary markedly in quality and include some rather odd, railcar floor-plans.

★ **Kuhio Shores** CONDO $$
(www.kuhioshores.net; 5050 Lawa'i Rd; condos from $180) Set on a grassy outcrop that juts into the sea opposite Prince Kuhio Park, this is a sleek, modern, three-story development of privately owned one- and two-bedroom condos that spill out onto patios or lanai with the most stunning vistas in Po'ipu. Inquiries can be made via their website only. Reserve well ahead.

Kauai Beach Inn B&B $$
(☎212-1942; www.kauaibeachinn.com; 2720 Ho'onani Rd; r $250; 📶) This two-year-old B&B in a cute, all-redwood 1930s plantation house

has just four rooms outfitted with flat-screen TVs and Jacuzzi tubs. Three have private lanai. Guests are served a massive gourmet breakfast each morning during which you can contemplate that resolute mango tree shading the property. Steep discounts for stays over four nights.

Hideaway Cove Villas CONDO $$
(☎635-8785, 866-849-2426; www.hideawaycove.com; 2307 Nalo Rd; studios $195-220, 1br $230-285, 2br $285-435;) A super cute garden property of all wood flats and condos with wood floors, beamed ceilings, high-dollar furnishings and wide verandas near Po'ipu Beach Park. It's professionally managed, and given that the units can sleep up to six comfortably, a good value. Cleaning fees range from $100 to $270.

Po'ipu Kapili CONDO $$
(☎742-6449, 800-443-7714; www.poipukapili.com; 2221 Kapili Rd; 1/2br from $225/350; P) An all-around winner, this 60-unit condo features gorgeously landscaped grounds and spacious units (1120 sq ft to 1820 sq ft) that are consistent in quality, with lots of hardwood, plush bedding, an extra bathroom, quality electronics and wired internet access. The closest sandy beach, fronting the Sheraton, is within walking distance.

Nihi Kai Villas CONDO $$
(☎742-1412, 742-2000; www.parrishkauai.com; 1870 Ho'one Rd; 1br from $145-210, 2br from $159-244; @) For moderate spenders who want walkable beach access, here's the ticket. Of the 70 units, half are managed by the on-site Parrish agency. They're comfortable, with full kitchens, two or more private lanai and washer-dryer. Not all units have wi-fi, but they all may access the property's tennis and paddle ball courts.

Kiahuna Plantation CONDO $$
(☎742-6411, 800-542-4862; www.outrigger.com; 2253 Po'ipu Rd; garden $169-249, seaview $199-269;) This aging beauty is still a hot property because it's among the rare accommodations flanking a swimmable beach. Of course, only a few units actually sit on the beach. Units are comfy, with fully equipped kitchen, living room and large lanai, but furnishings can be worn.

It's managed by four different management companies, which can be confusing. On-site agencies include Outrigger and Castle Resorts, but Kiahuna Beachside manages the best beachfront properties.

Sheraton Kaua'i Resort RESORT $$
(☎866-716-8109, 1-800-325-3535; www.sheraton-kauai.com; 2440 Ho'onani Rd; r from $209; P) The 394-room Sheraton offers a prime stretch of swimmable, sunset-perfect beach. Originally built in the 1960s and completely redone after the 1992 hurricane, rooms (and elevators) are dated but spacious with canopy beds blessed with plush linens, and though we don't love cottage cheese ceilings, the oceanfront rooms have amazing, reach-out-and-touch-the-sea views.

Grand Hyatt Kaua'i Resort & Spa RESORT $$$
(☎800-554-9288, 742-1234; www.grandhyattkauai.com; 1571 Po'ipu Rd; r from $309; P) Po'ipu's glamour gal is 602-rooms strong and loves to show off, with a soaring lobby, tropical gardens, huge spa, world-renowned golf course, oceanfront restaurants and meandering 'river pools.' Rooms are simple yet elegant with tropical wood crown mouldings, flat-screen TVs, marble entryway and bath, and rain shower heads. Adjacent Shipwreck Beach (p544) is a natural wonder.

Koa Kea Hotel & Resort RESORT $$$
(☎828-8888; www.koakea.com; 2251 Po'ipu Rd; r $349-1850;) With 121 rooms and a beachfront location, this high-end boutique hotel is gorgeously appointed. The Hawaiiana themed rooms are decorated with koa wood, leather lounge furniture, marble baths, soaker tubs and rain shower, and each boasts an unobstructed view from its private lanai. Still, if you were a nitpicker, you might say the ceilings are a touch low.

Koloa Landing CONDO $$$
(☎240-6600; www.koloalandingresort.com; 2641 Po'ipu Rd; 1br $279-309; P) The area's newest development, with their two final buildings still going up, this Grand Wyndham Resort offers private condos and vacation rentals, all of which are brand new and up-to-the-minute modern. The scope of the property is huge with villas scheduled for construction all the way to the seafront road.

Eating

Papalani Gelato ICE CREAM $
(www.papalanigelato.com; 2360 Kiahuna Plantation Dr, Po'ipu Shopping Village; single scoop $4; ⏲11am-9:30pm) Their mouthwatering flavors are all made on site. You can't go wrong with classic vanilla bean or pistachio gelato, but for local color, try the creamy sorbetto, made

with fresh, island-grown starfruit, lychee, mango, guava or avocado.

Savage Shrimp SEAFOOD $

(☎742-9600; www.savageshrimp.com; 2829 Ala Kalanikaumaka St, Shops at Kukui'ula; mains $10-12.50; ⏲11am-9pm) The garlicky crackle wafting from the kitchen makes it clear that their specialty is scampi. We're talking seven flavors of scampi, including Brazilian style made with coconut milk and orange juice, and a delectable Aloha style varietal sautéed with coconut milk, lemongrass and chili sauce. They do tacos and po'boys too.

Puka Dog FAST FOOD $

(www.pukadog.com; 2360 Kiahuna Plantation Dr; Polish sausage $6.75, veggie dog $7; ⏲10am-8pm;) Start with a Polish sausage or veggie dog and top it with a garlic-lemon chili sauce, one of several relishes sweetened with mango, pineapple, papaya, coconut, banana or star fruit, and a lilikoi mustard made in-house. The lemonade is deliciously famous too. Get yours with a minimalist quarter-scoop of sugar for best balance.

★Josselin's HAWAII REGIONAL CUISINE $$

(☎742-7117; www.josselins.com; 2829 Ala Kalanikaumaka St, Shops at Kukui'ula; dishes $8-36; ⏲5-10pm) Chef Jean-Marie Josselin is that rare artist in chef's clothing. A revered, award-winning contemporary of Wolfgang Puck, his boom and bust career is the stuff of pulp fiction and his food is culinary high art, yet somehow still understated and approachable. The salad dressings are tangy and bright, the Thai bisque is coconut creamy and his 36-hour braised pork belly is the finest dish on the island.

It's marinated in hoisin, agave, miso, orange zest and buttermilk, bagged and roasted for 36 hours, then plated with green apple kimchee and truffle oil potato foam. Don't be individualistic with this menu. Order and share liberally. We'll let you decipher the can't-miss sangria cart on your own.

Tortilla Republic MEXICAN $$

(☎742-8884; www.tortillarepublic.com; 2829 Ala Kalanikaumaka St, Shops at Kukui'ula; mains $12-32; ⏲margarita bar 7:30am-11pm, grill 5:30am-9pm Mon-Thu, to 10pm Fri, to 2am Sat) Bringing high-end yet traditional Mexican cooking to Po'ipu, the upstairs grill is a fine-dining scene featuring ancho chili-rubbed and grilled fresh catch, a fabulous pork chop al pastor, succulent carnitas and a shortrib chili verde. Best paired with one of their 75 tequila labels. The downstairs Margarita Bar serves live music on Tuesdays and Thursdays, and offers a decent brunch.

The Dolphin SEAFOOD $$

(☎742-1414; www.thedolphinkauai.com; 2829 Ala Kalanikaumaka St, Shops at Kukui'ula; mains $14-32; ⏲market 10am-7pm, restaurant 11:30am-3pm, 3:30am-9pm) Brand new at research time, this mall version of the Hanalei original comes complete with sushi bar, a terrific fish market, classic regional seafood mains and a lunch menu populated with shrimp tacos, teriyaki fish burgers and a really good seafood chowder.

Local secret: Gary Joseph Mitsui Jr, the Dolphin's longtime buyer of fish and manager of kitchens, owns the sushi bar on Thursday nights, turning out his famed Gary Yaki Special. Just order it. Then finish with the spicy *unagi nigiri*, a perfect balance of sweet and spicy.

Plantation Gardens Restaurant & Bar HAWAII REGIONAL $$

(☎742-2121; www.pgrestaurant.com; 2253 Po'ipu Rd, Kiahuna Plantation; appetizers $8-13, mains $22-30; ⏲5:30am-9pm) Set in a historic plantation house, this restaurant is lovely without trying too hard. The menu is mercifully concise and features locally grown ingredients, kiawe (a relative of the mesquite tree) grilling for a rich, smoky flavor and lots of fresh seafood. Lit by tiki torches at night, the setting is ideal for large gatherings.

Casa di Amici ITALIAN $$

(☎742-1555; www.casadiamici.com; 2301 Nalo Rd; dinner mains $24-30; ⏲from 6pm) Often overlooked due to an obscure location and chipped weatherbeaten front porch, this restaurant is an unpretentious gem. The chef focuses on using the highest quality ingredients, from locally grown greens to black truffles from Italy to homemade sausage. The menu's traditional Italian pastas and meats are joined by multicultural standouts such as the grilled miso-ginger ahi and paella risotto. Service can be spotty.

Red Salt FUSION $$$

(☎742-4288; www.koakea.com; 2251 Po'ipu Rd; mains $24-36; ⏲6:30am-11am, 6-10pm) They specialize in Hawaiian fusion dishes like pan-seared opah with king crab fries and a sake-spiked coconut broth, and a seared ahi plated with edamame cilantro risotto. Excellent sushi and sashimi are served in the elegant lounge on Friday and Saturday, and there's always that root beer float for dessert. Valet parking is free and they do breakfast too.

Beach House Restaurant SEAFOOD $$$
(☎742-1424; www.the-beach-house.com; 5022 Lawa'i Rd; mains lunch $11-19, dinner $26-40; ⏲11am-10pm) An iconic spot for a sunset splurge. Lunch is simple (think stir-fries and grilled fish sandwiches), but dinner is no joke. Start with ahi *poke*, and a Kaua'i beet salad sprinkled in guava salt and truffle oil, then *grind* a wasabi-crusted, miso-marinated or macadamia-butter-sautéed fresh catch. It's an institution for a reason.

Roy's Po'ipu Bar & Grill HAWAII REGIONAL $$$
(☎742-5000; www.roysrestaurant.com; 2360 Kiahuna Plantation Dr, Po'ipu Shopping Village; mains $26-43; ⏲5:30-9:30pm) Still wildly popular, though a link in a high-end national chain, Roy's continues to please the foodies. Signature dishes include melt-in-your-mouth *misoyaki* (miso-marinated) butterfish and pesto-steamed *ono* (white-fleshed wahoo) sizzled in cilantro-ginger-peanut oil, as well as a plethora of similarly original fusion dishes. The setting, however, is shopping mall chic.

Merriman's SEAFOOD $$$
(☎742-8385; www.merrimanshawaii.com; 2829 Ala Kalanikaumaka St, Shops at Kukui'ula; bar mains $10-15, mains $24-60; ⏲bar 11:30am-10pm, dining room 5:30-10pm) Join the casual crowd downstairs for pizza and gourmet burgers in their charming, and, at times, rollicking bar that spills onto the plaza. Or you can climb to the upscale seafood house where the raw bar comes stocked with *poke* and sashimi, and the ahi, mahi and *ono* are served either wok-charred, herb-grilled or macadamia-crusted.

Self-Catering

Living Foods Market & Café MARKET, CAFE $
(☎742-2323; www.livingfoodskauai.com; 2829 Ala Kalanikaumaka St, Shops at Kukui'ula; mains $10-18; ⏲7am-8pm, cafe to 4pm) Aptly tagged 'high dollar market' by locals, it's nevertheless a damn appetizing depot for gourmet groceries including imported cheeses, organic meats, fine wines, local produce and organic health and beauty staples. The cafe offers paninis, tasty pizzas (try the breakfast pizza), brioche French toast as well as a terrific coffee bar.

Kukui'ula Market MARKET $
(2827 Po'ipu Rd, Po'ipu Plaza; ⏲8am-8:30pm Mon-Fri, to 6:30pm Sat & Sun) This indie supermarket resembles a bodega from the outside, but stocks a good selection of basics and decent cuts of beef and ahi, though the produce section could use some love.

Drinking & Entertainment

Tortilla Republic CLUB
(☎742-8884; www.tortillarepublic.com; 2829 Ala Kalanikaumaka St, Shops at Kukui'ula; ⏲10pm-2am Sat) While they have live music in the downstairs bar on Tuesday and Thursday nights, Saturday runs deep into the night upstairs, where the tequila flows and DJs spin at 'Club Night.' It's a party quickly becoming legendary on the South Shore. Or is infamous a more accurate term? We'll let you decide. No flip-flops, shorts or T-shirts tolerated.

Stevenson's Library BAR
(www.grandhyattkauai.com; 1571 Po'ipu Rd, Grand Hyatt Kaua'i Resort & Spa; ⏲6-10:30pm) A rather austere koa-wood bar with chessboards on the tabletops and a drum kit on the bandstand that hints hopefully at jazz (Tuesday, Thursday and Saturday 8pm to 10pm). Drinks are mixed and muddled with tropical fruit. Sip yours while contemplating first editions sealed in glass bookcases next to antique china and ceramics from yesteryear.

Luau

Between the two choices here, the Sheraton's show gives you more for your money. Also consider driving to Lihu'e for Kilohana Plantation's new and different Luau Kalamaku (p489).

★'Auli'i Luau LUAU
(☎742-8205; www.sheraton-kauai.com; 2440 Ho'onani Rd, Sheraton Kaua'i Resort; adult/teen/child $100/68/47; ⏲check-in 6pm Fri) We rate the Sheraton's luau A (excellent) for oceanfront setting and B (good) for the food and show, which is the standard Polynesian revue. For a commercial luau, the audience size is relatively small at 200 to 300. Beware: the humorous emcee demands lots of audience participation.

Havaiki Nui Luau LUAU
(☎742-1234; www.grandhyattkauailuau.com; 1571 Po'ipu Rd, Grand Hyatt Kaua'i Resort & Spa; adult/teen/child $99/88/62; ⏲check-in 5:15pm Sun & Thu) The Havaiki Nui Luau is a well-oiled

production befitting the Grand Hyatt setting, but the price is steep, especially if rain forces the show indoors.

Shopping

The **Shops at Kukui'ula** (www.kukuiula.com; 2829 Ala Kalanikaumaka St) brought stodgy (at times) Po'ipu a much needed blast of chic high-end shopping, dining, and drinking (we're looking at you, tequila bar) when it opened less than three years ago. And it remains the only possible way to infect devout North Shore types with South Shore envy. The **Po'ipu Shopping Village** was the original Po'ipu meeting place, and while it's looking a bit tired, there's a fine restaurant and magnificent gelateria here, as well as a handful of fun shops to explore.

A Feinberg Gallery GALLERY
(☎639-3579; www.afeinphoto.com; 2829 Ala Kalanikaumaka St, Shops at Kukui'ula) Wunderkind photographer, Feinberg uses an array of filters to capture the magic of Hawaii's natural landscape, from rainbow eucalyptus trunks to thrashing waves and cascading falls. Colors generally pop and some are printed on aluminum which lends an otherworldly feel.

Hawaiian Salt CLOTHING
(☎742-6030; 2829 Ala Kalanikaumaka St, Shops at Kukui'ula; ⊙10am-9pm) The hipster choice for souvenir rags, this singular, designer-owned shop offers a superb array of T-shirts which come with original designs on three varieties of fabric, including a vintage cotton with a softer feel. They also carry flip-flops, Toms shoes and local art.

Malie Organics BEAUTY
(☎866-767-5727, 332-6220; www.malie.com; 2829 Ala Kalanikaumaka St, Shops at Kukui'ula; ⊙9am-4pm Mon-Fri) Launched in Kalaheo and now a sought-after global brand, the company crafts succulent body butters and exquisite flower essences from local organic ingredients.

Cariloha CLOTHING
(☎742-5220; www.cariloha.com; 2360 Kiahuna Plantation Dr, Po'ipu Shopping Village; ⊙9:30am-9:30pm Mon-Sat, 10am-7pm) A fabulous new eco-fashion chain with sportswear and stylish T-shirts made from super soft bamboo fabrics. They launched in the Caribbean; this is just one of three shops in the US and the only one in Hawaii.

Information

Bank of Hawaii (☎742-6800; 2360 Kiahuna Plantation Dr, Po'ipu Shopping Village; ⊙8:30am-4pm Mon-Thu, to 6pm Fri) Does not cash traveler's checks.

Po'ipu Beach Resort Association (www.poipubeach.org) For general information on Po'ipu and the whole South Shore.

Getting There & Around

To get here from Lihu'e, the quickest way is to exit on Maluhia Rd. Po'ipu, a sprawled-out town, demands a car to go anywhere besides the beach. Navigating is easy, with just two main roads: Po'ipu Rd along eastern Po'ipu and Lawa'i Rd along western Po'ipu.

The Kaua'i Bus (p480) runs through Koloa and into Po'ipu. It's an option to get here from other towns but has limited in-town value.

Kalaheo

POP 4595

From the highway, Kalaheo is a one-light cluster of eateries and little else. But along the backroads, this neighborly town – a cultural melting pot of Chinese, Japanese, Portuguese, Russian and Filipino families drawn here by the sugar economy – offers peaceful accommodations away from the tourist crowd. If you plan to hike at Waimea Canyon and Koke'e State Parks but also wish to visit Po'ipu beaches (a short drive away), Kalaheo's central location is ideal.

The town's post office and a handful of restaurants are clustered around the intersection of the Kau-muali'i Hwy and Papalina Rd.

Sights

Kukuiolono Park PARK
(854 Pu'u Rd; ⊙6:30am-6:30pm) Unless you stay in Kalaheo, you would probably miss this little park, which offers a nine-hole golf course, modest Japanese garden, sweeping views and grassy grounds for strolling or jogging. To get here, turn left onto Papalina Rd from Kaumuali'i Hwy (heading west).

In 1860 King Kamehameha III leased the land to Duncan McBryde, whose son, Walter, the pineapple baron, eventually purchased the 178-acre estate. He built the public golf course in 1929 and deeded the entire site for use as a public park upon his death. Walter McBryde is buried near the eighth hole.

THE CREATIVE COLLECTIVE

Bass-heavy house and hip-hop thump off the graffiti bombed walls in this spare dance space tucked behind the Union 76 station in Kalaheo. A tight mob of four- to seven-year-olds, most decked out in **Kuga** (www.kuga808.com) wear, circle up and freestyle, one at time. Their parents bob their heads, stomp their feet and giggle as the kids go all wild child, egged on by their teacher, leader and local arts visionary, Lila Metzger. A Kaua'i-born former pro surfer and model, Metzger, 32, left the island for Los Angeles at 17, where she fell in love with hip-hop and dance. But it wasn't until she returned to the island, four years later, that she found a crew – whom she describes as 'real B-Boys' – and together they started holding regular jams at Lydgate Park.

Soon she was tapped as a 'Red Bull Rider' (a sponsored break-dancer) and became a leader in Hawaii's emerging hip-hop scene. Yet Kaua'i's B-Boy apex was short lived as most of Metzger's crew were lured to professional dance gigs in Vegas and NYC. That's when Metzger founded Kuga, a nonprofit arts collective that's become a haven for south and Westside kids who don't necessarily identify with the island-dominant surf culture.

She teaches dance fundamentals to the young *keiki* (four to seven) and breakdancing to some of the older kids (eight to 12), the best of whom become Kuga Foot Soliders (10 per year). The Foot Soldiers perform at various events around the island, including the Kuga-sponsored Love Life Creative Festival (p486). In addition to the festival and Metzger's dance classes, Kuga has brought in two local artists who teach visual art (p554) classes to students.

But discovering great dancers and emerging artists isn't the whole point of Kuga. What Metzger wants is for island kids like her to feel good about themselves and where they come from. 'We get a lot of misfit kids,' says Metzger, 'and instead of feeling ripped off because they grew up on an island, Kuga is a place where they can express themselves in a nonjudgmental environment, find their voice, take risks and overcome their own obstacles.'

Hanapepe Valley Lookout VIEWPOINT
The scenic lookout that pops up shortly after mile marker 14 offers a view deep into Hanapepe Valley. The red-clay walls of the cliffs are topped by Kaua'i's last swath of green cane, like frosting on a cake. This sight is but a teaser of the dramatic vistas that await at Waimea Canyon.

While the sugar business has faded, Hanapepe Valley remains an agriculture stronghold with grazing cattle and local farmers growing taro, but look across the highway toward the ocean and you'll see the region's cash crop: coffee.

Activities

Kuga Visual Arts COURSE
(☎ 639-6889; www.kugava.com; Kaumuali'i Hwy; Ladies Art Night $10) This is where two young local artists teach visual art classes to students ages two to 17. Sessions last for five weeks and classes are held three times weekly. Each session has a theme: paints, mixed media or textiles.

Kuga Visual Arts also hold once monthly Ladies Art Nights at a nearby annex, on the last Saturday of the month. Local ladies love it, but visitors are most welcome. Call ahead to reserve your space.

Kukuiolono Golf Course GOLF
(☎ 332-9151; 854 Pu'u Rd , Kukuiolono Park; greens fee adult/child $9/3, club & cart rental $9 each; 6:30am-6:30pm, last tee time 4:30pm) Golf is practically free at Kukuiolono Golf Course, an unassuming nine-hole, par-36 course with spectacular ocean and valley views – and zero attitude. Grab a bucket of balls for $2 and hit the driving range – first-come, first-serve.

Kalaheo Yoga HEALTH & FITNESS
(☎ 652-3216; www.kalaheoyoga.com; 4427 Papalina Rd; per class $18, 3-class pass $48) A gorgeous and bright yoga space one block from the highway, which offers two to five classes daily including Pilates mat, qi gong and vinyasa flow classes.

Sleeping

Hale Ikena Nui B&B $
(☎ 800-550-0778, 332-9005; www.kauaivacationhome.com; 3957 Uluali'i St; d $75/95;) Locat-

ed at the end of a cul de sac, this spacious apartment (1000 sq ft) includes a living area with sofa-bed, full kitchen and washer-dryer. Singles can rent the B&B room, which includes a private bathroom and use of the main house.

Kalaheo Inn INN $

(☎332-6023; www.kalaheoinn.com; 4444 Papalina Rd; r $78-149) This cute, 15-room roadside inn has slightly different layouts in all the rooms. While atmosphere is lacking, on the whole they are reasonably clean, though walls are thin. Hint: room #7 is a split-level unit with nobody above or below you. They offer free snorkel gear to guests; some rooms have a kitchenette.

★Kauai Garden Cottages COTTAGE $$

(☎332-0877; www.kauaigardencottages.com; 5350 Pu'ulima Rd; ste $135; wi-fi) Perched high in the Kalaheo upcountry, this meticulously designed pair of suites gleam with rich Indonesian hardwood floors under soaring cathedral ceilings with cheerful stained-glass accents. The all-wood rooms are their own little pods, separate yet sheltered under one roof and adjoined by a vast lanai, cantilevered over a stunning green valley. Rent both rooms for only $200 nightly.

The owner, Thayne Taylor, is a boat captain, scuba instructor, musician and tech head who is the type of renaissance man worthy of a visit on his own.

Hale O Nanakai B&B $$

(☎652-8071; www.nanakai.com; 3726 Nanakai Pl; r $50-200; wi-fi) A baby blue family house turned four-room B&B with wall-to-wall carpeting, beamed ceilings, a comfy if slightly dated common living room, and spectacular seaviews. Rooms range in size, yet all but the cheapest digs have similar amenities including HDTV and queen or full-sized beds. The tiny Maile Room has but a single bed for the wandering ascetic.

Eating

Lanakila Kitchen HAWAII REGIONAL $

(☎332-5500; www.lanakilakitchen.org; 2-3687 Kaumali'i Hwy; meals $8-10; ⏲10am-5:30pm Mon-Thu, to 6pm Fri) A locals' haunt, this tiny bright cafe with a cause serves a steam table of curries, meat and fish dishes, which you can pick and mix for plate lunches. Think teriyaki *ono*, pork and peas, chicken curry and more. They also do soups, pies and ahi wraps. Proceeds go to an employment program for locals with disabilities.

★Kalaheo Café CAFE, SANDWICHES $$

(☎332-5858; www.kalaheo.com; 2-2560 Kaumuali'i Hwy; mains $5-13; ⏲6:30am-2:30pm, 5-8:30pm Tue-Sat) Rightfully beloved by locals, this fun roadside cafe serves egg and pancake breakfasts and a range of sandwiches at lunch, including pesto chicken breast and hot pastrami. Salads combine specialty ingredients like bulgur, beets and fresh local greens; dinner plates include miso-glazed fresh island catch, a chicken breast and couscous risotto, and a Thai veggie curry.

Kalaheo Steaks & Ribs STEAKHOUSE $$

(☎332-4444; www.kalaheosteakandribs.com; 4444 Papalina Rd; mains $16-32; ⏲5-9:30pm) Built and brushed to resemble an Old West saloon, this steakhouse has generated some buzz among locals. The prime rib is especially popular, but they do all the cuts of steak, St Louis–style ribs and steamed clams and *poke* for seafood lovers. It's set one block from the highway on the *makai* (seaward) side.

Pomodoro ITALIAN $$

(☎332-5945; www.pomodorokauai.com; Kaumuali'i Hwy, Rainbow Plaza; mains $16-27; ⏲5:30-9:30pm Mon-Sat) Unless you know it's there, you'd never expect such a romantic restaurant in an unmemorable business mall. But locals always cite Pomodoro for traditional dishes such as veal parmigiana and linguini with white or red clam sauce. With candlelit tables and white tablecloths, the setting is intimate yet neighborhood casual.

WAIMEA CANYON & THE WESTSIDE

Kaua'i doesn't get more local than the Westside, where revered traditions and local-style family pride reign supreme. Here, you're more likely to hear fluent Hawaiian, spot real-life *paniolo* (cowboys) and see old-school fishermen sewing their nets than anywhere else on the island. Deep, riveting red canyons and a seemingly infinite expanse of ocean offers the widest range of atmosphere and ambience found on Kaua'i. The least touristy and the most tried and true, the Westside isn't for everyone; it's good like that.

'Ele'ele & Numila

POP 2390

You might pass by the small town of Numila and its bigger, albeit still small, neighbor, 'Ele'ele, without a second thought. However, it's a pleasant, rural area, and offers a few convenient stops at the 'Ele'ele shopping center, including a **post office** (8am-4pm Mon-Fri, 9-11am Sat). The most noticeable of the bunch of small shops and restaurants is **Grinds Café** (335-6027; www.grindscafe.net; 4469 Waialo Rd, 'Ele'ele Shopping Center; mains $8.50-21.50; 6am-9pm), a diner for diner lovers, where skillets and platters are piled high and thick with rice, potatoes, tasty cuts of meat and fish, and fresh-made patty sausage and eggs. The pastries look good, the breads are all made in-house and they have espresso too.

Though it lacks the cachet imparted on the reputable Kona coffee, **Kaua'i Coffee Company** (335-0813, 800-545-8605; www.kauaicoffee.com; Halewili Rd; 9am-5pm; guided tours 10am, 1pm, and 3pm) produces a sturdy cup of joe. Take the self-guided tour of the gorgeous, rolling seaside plantation where berries are cooled by tradewinds. There's a bare bones **museum**, a cafe serving only the basics and a vast self-serve tasting patio where you can sample 20 plus varieties of coffee while watching a video describe cultivation and roasting techniques. The self-guided tour leads through a small slice of the property as do the guided tours, which are free, and take about 15 minutes. The entire plantation is powered by renewable energy.

Port Allen

Port Allen is essentially a Marina mini mall, packed with charter companies and wedged into a largely industrial port area. Aside from a damn fine brewery (p558), and the unique Glass Beach (p556), the principal reason for your arrival is to cruise the Na Pali Coast.

The majority of the island's Na Pali tours leave from Port Allen and, depending on the season, there is a variety of ways to experience this spectacular coastline – from snorkeling in the summer to whale-watching in the winter.

You'll either go by Zodiac (raft) or catamaran. The former offers little respite from the waves and sun; the latter offers shaded benches, a toilet and, of course, an unending supply of drinks and *pupu*.

Sights & Activities

Glass Beach BEACH

Trash as art – many a visitor has pored through the colorful well-worn remnants of glass along the shoreline of the aptly named Glass Beach, east of Port Allen. Glass 'pebbles,' along with abandoned metals (some with newfound patina, some not so much), have washed up from an old dumpsite nearby, showing that decades of weather, too, can make art.

The beach twinkles most romantically on sunny afternoons or under the full moon. To get to the little cove, take Aka'ula St, the last left before entering the Port Allen commercial harbor, go past the fuel-storage tanks and then curve to the right down a rutted dirt road that leads 100yd to the beach.

★ **Captain Andy's Sailing Adventures** BOAT TOUR

(335-6833, 800-535-0830; www.napali.com; Waialo Rd, Port Allen Marina Center; Na Pali Tours from adult/child $109/79) This outfit offers a high-end sailing experience aboard the Southern Star – their 65ft flagship catamaran – and a more rugged, adrenalin-addled Zodiac tour into the sea caves and secluded beaches of the Na Pali Coast. All travel at least as far as Kalalau, weather depending.

Holoholo Charters BOAT TOUR

(335-0815, 800-848-6130; www.holoholocharters.com; Waialo Rd, Port Allen Marina Center; Na Pali trips from adult/child $100/84; 6am-8pm) Among the best for delivering on its promises of sea-cave jaunts, *honu* sightings and augmented cultural lore. The 3½-hour sunset cruise offers the best deal. You'll save by booking online.

Catamaran Kahanu BOAT TOUR

(645-6176, 888-213-7711; www.catamarankahanu.com; Waialo Rd, Port Allen Marina Center; 5hr Na Pali cruise $135, 2hr whale-watching tour $89) Another favorite that includes demonstrations of Hawaiian basket-weaving and explanations of how 'fishing lines' are crafted from *ti* leaves (a native plant) and coconut fiber on the way out to sea. They offer discounts of up to $25 if you book online.

Blue Dolphin Charters BOAT TOUR

(335-5553, 877-511-1311; www.kauaiboats.com; Waialo Rd, Port Allen Marina Center; trips from $69) Offers a seven-hour snorkeling tour

Westside

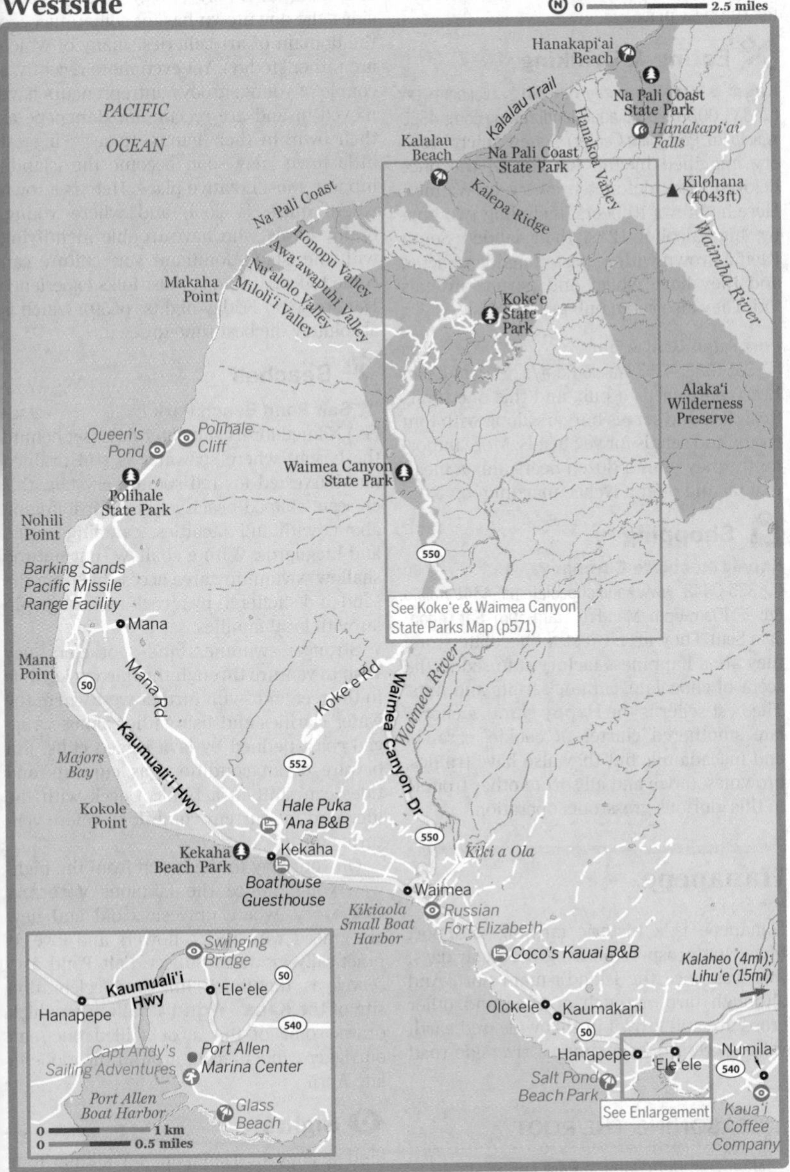

or five-hour Na Pali trip. For an additional $35, they'll take you on a one-tank dive. Their five-hour dinner cruise shoves off in the afternoon and they do a two-hour Po'ipu sunset and whale-watching cruise too. Book online for significant savings.

Kaua'i Sea Tours BOAT TOUR
(☎826-7254, 800-733-7997; www.kauaiseatours.com; Aka'ula St, Port Allen; adult/child catamaran from $144/104, raft from $140/100) Lets you opt for the Na Pali tour by catamaran or the

rougher, three-hour tour by raft. Book online for the best price.

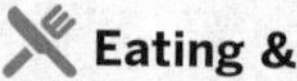

Eating & Drinking

Kauai Island Brewery & Grill MICROBREWERY
(335-0006; www.kauaiislandbrewing.com; 4350 Waialo Rd, Port Allen Center) A new microbrewery imagined by the founder of the once beloved, now defunct brewery in Waimea. Here he brews 10 beers, including two hoppy, high-alcohol IPAs, their lauded South Pacific Brown with a roasted malt character, and they have wheat and porter varietals too. They also serve pub grub.

Port Allen Grill & Bar PUB
(335-3188; 4353 Waialo Rd #7a; 11am-10pm) Every port needs a pub, and this one broils fresh fish and serves burgers along with tofu wraps and salads for veg heads. More importantly, they pour a dozen beers, mix a mean mai tai and offer a lychee martini too.

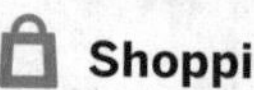

Shopping

Kauai Chocolate Company FOOD
(335-0448; www.kauaichocolate.us; 4341 Waialo Rd; 10am-6pm Mon-Fri, 11am-5pm Sat, noon-3pm Sun) They aren't just a chocolate store, they are a happiness factory suffused in the scent of chocolate, caramel, fruits and nuts. The best seller is the **Happy Honu**, a chocolate smothered cluster of cookie, caramel and macadamia, but they also have truffles, brownies, fudge and all sort of other trouble in this glorious grassroots operation.

Hanapepe

POP 2704

Hanapepe is a historic farming and port town that prospered during the sugar days; this was once the island's main port. And although taro, a touch of cane and other crops are still grown in this wide, red earth valley accessed by a sinuous riverside road and hemmed in by craggy cliffs on both sides, the downtown has for sometime been the domain of art galleries (many of which are rather stodgy). Yet even more recently, a couple of young, groovy entrepreneurs have moved in and are reclaiming Hanepepe as their own. In their hands, Kaua'i's 'biggest little town' may soon become the island's hippest, most creative place. Here is a town where quirk is cool, and where young, brainy locals who have trouble identifying with the island-dominant surf culture can come to feel at home. Most folks experience Hanapepe on Friday nights (p559), which is absolutely the best time to see it.

> **SEASONING THE ROOT**
>
> Near Salt Pond Beach Park (p558) families continue the tradition of salt panning in basins, just as their ancestors did hundreds of years ago. The spiritual task of collecting large, reddish crystals of Hawaiian salt means the local seasoning continues to be a source of Hawaiian pride.

Beaches

★**Salt Pond Beach Park** BEACH
() Named for its saltwater flats (set behind the beach) where seawater is still drained and harvested for red sodium crystals, this crescent-shaped beach is great for lounging about, with full facilities, camping access and lifeguards. With a shallow (but not too shallow) swimming area accessible from the sand and sheltered by a rock reef, it's popular with local families.

Stronger swimmers and snorkelers may wish to venture through the narrow keyhole in the reef and swim further west where the water clarifies and fish gather along a rugged coast defined by lava jagged cliffs. But beware ocean conditions as currents and tides can shift in a blink. Check with the lifeguard for current conditions before venturing out.

On your way to the beach from the highway, you'll notice the fabulous **Veterans Cemetery**, where gravesites old and new are graced with rocks, flowers and love. It practically glows at sunset. Salt Pond also serves as the finish line and celebration site of the **Kaua'i World Challenge**, which draws some of the most skilled one-man outrigger canoers from around the globe in late April.

Sights

Find a copy of Hanapepe's Walking Tour Map ($2), which describes the town's historic buildings.

Swinging Bridge LANDMARK
Built in 1911 and rebuilt after the 1992 hurricane, this narrow wood and cable suspension bridge spans the Hanapepe River just before it snakes inland between stark red-

earth cliffs, and it does swing and moan a bit in the wind. You'll find it tucked behind the Aloha Spice Company. No diving!

Arius Hopman Gallery GALLERY
(☎634-7858; www.hopmanart.com; 3840C Hanapepe Rd; ⏲10:30am-2pm Mon-Thu, 10:30am-2pm & 6-9pm Fri) An eye for recognizing, composing and presenting nature's beauty means Hopman's photography certainly beats any postcard shot taken on the island.

Art of Marbling/ Robert Bader Wood Sculpture GALLERY
(☎335-3553; 3890 Hanapepe Rd; ⏲10am-5pm Sat-Thu, to 9pm Fri) Becky J Wold's original silk scarves and sarongs hang from bamboo poles alongside her husband's wooden bowls and sculpture, making this gallery one of the most unique in town.

Dawn Traina Gallery GALLERY
(☎335-3993; 3840B Hanapepe Rd; ⏲6-9pm Fri or by appointment) Housed in one of the more understated galleries, her detailed research of Hawaiian culture shines through in drawings, paintings and other art.

Island Art Gallery GALLERY
(☎335-0591; 3876 Hanapepe Rd; ⏲10:30am-5pm Mon-Sat, 6-9pm Fri) This is a somewhat more adventurous, modern gallery than the rest. They feature artists who use techniques such as reverse acrylic painting or glass mosaic, along with the standard reproduction techniques, and they also have a few baubles and bracelets.

Activities

★Hanapepe Friday Night Art Walk ART FESTIVAL
(⏲6-9pm Fri) On any given Friday, old Hanapepe town offers an extended peek into its art world. Galleries keep later hours, offering a chance to stroll, peruse and dine on everything from Thai curries to grilled chicken to al pastor tacos, and the absolute best pies in Kaua'i (p488), if not the state.

The pace picks up around 5pm, when the main drag is transformed by its mix of musicians, art installations and visitors. Though art aficionados may snub some of the collections as less than cutting edge, there are some exceptional young entrepreneurs here delivering goods – if not art – that would do well in the most bustling of big city hipster hoods (we're looking at you, Machinemachine). The trick is to not judge and to take your time. You might just find a gem or three.

Birds in Paradise GLIDING
(☎822-5309; www.birdsinparadise.com; 3666 Kuiloko Rd, Port Allen Airport; 30/60/90min lesson $175/250/360) For a real adrenaline rush, take an ultralight-plane (something like a prop-powered glider) lesson. Thirty-minute flights allow you to see the Westside from above, hour-long flights take you into Waimea Canyon and along the Na Pali Coast, and 90-minute flights will get you around the entire island. Flights leave daily, weather permitting. Take the road for Salt Pond Beach Park to reach the airport.

Inter-island Helicopters HELICOPTER TOUR
(☎800-656-5009, 335-5009; www.interislandhelicopters.com; 3441 Kuiloko Rd; regular/waterfall flights $249/$310) Their doors-off flights provide insane Westside views, especially if the rain has been falling and the waterfalls are in full force. Its flight record, however, is less than perfect. They leave from the Port Allen airport in Hanapepe.

Sleeping

Though there aren't any hotels or rentals to speak of, Salt Pond Beach Park (p558) offers convenient camping.

Eating & Drinking

Hanapepe is a largely Native Hawaiian and longtime local community, which means it's a good place to sample local *grinds* on the cheap. Come with a thin wallet and an empty stomach and you'll do just fine.

★Little Fish Coffee CAFE $
(☎335-5000; www.facebook.com/LittleFishCoffee; 3900 Hanapepe Rd; eats $5-10, drinks $3-8; ⏲6:30am-5pm Mon-Fri, from 8am Sat; 📶) The colorful chalkboard menu at this crazy cute coffee shop – our favorite on the entire island, actually – lures you with espresso drinks and creative smoothies, homemade soups and bagel sandwiches. Sit inside among the retro art and music, or in the back garden splashed with both sun and shade. The kitchen closes at 2pm., but drinks flow till 5pm.

Hanapepe Naturals HEALTHY $
(☎335-5100; Awana Rd; meals $4.50-6.50; massage $70-105; ⏲9:30am-6pm; 🌱) A fabulous little health food shop serving vegetarian bowls of soup and stir-fries, kale salads,

tofu wraps and an entire menu of juices and smoothies. Their main business is bulk spices, teas and dehydrated foods, which they sell in health-food shops islandwide. The owner-operator is a gifted massage therapist and Ayurvedic practitioner. Ask about treatments.

Lappert's ICE CREAM $
(☎335-6121; www.lappertshawaii.com; 1-3555 Kaumuali'i Hwy; ⏲10am-6pm) The famed Hawaiian ice-cream chain started its operation right here along the highway at this quaint little roadside shop and factory. They are way too big for Hanapepe-based production now, but that humble shop still scoops the goodness and remains the business's headquarters, as it has since 1983.

Bobbie's HAWAII REGIONAL $
(☎334-5152; 3620 Hanapepe Rd; mains from $6.95; ⏲10am-3pm Mon-Wed, 10am-2:30pm & 5-8pm Thu-Sat) A small storefront greasy spoon lunch counter offering burgers, pulled pork sandwiches, fried shrimp and teriyaki chicken plates, as well as BBQ chicken on Friday nights. It's not good-for-you food, but it does taste pretty damn good.

Da Imu Hut Café CAFE $
(☎335-0200; 1-3529 Kaumuali'i Hwy; meals $7-11; ⏲10am-1:30pm & 5-8pm Mon-Fri) Set in a rather warehouse-sized Quonset hut on the highway, Da Imu is famous for its Monday-night Hawaiian buffets, but they serve up fried and teriyaki chicken dinners and Hawaiian-style BBQ pork combo plates every night. This is the perfect place to pick up lunch ($6.95) for a drive up to the canyon or a beach picnic.

Wong's Chinese Deli BAKERY, DELI $
(1-3543 Kaumuali'i Hwy; mains $7.50-9; ⏲9:30am-9pm Tue-Sun) This small Chinese counter cafe with a rather sprawling attached dining room allows you to pick and mix one to three dishes from their steam table. They do beef broccoli, lo mein, sweet-and-sour pork or chicken, and have crispy duck hanging under heat lamps too.

GIVE IT AWAY TO KEEP IT

While relishing all the tropical delight Kaua'i has to offer, an hour or two spent giving back may end up being your fondest memory. Here are a few welcomed volunteering opportunities:

Koke'e Resource Conservation Program (☎335-0045; www.krcp.org) Hands-on work restoring forested areas impacted by invasive species.

Kaua'i Forest Bird Recovery Project (☎335-5078; www.kauaiforestbirds.org; 3651 Hanapepe Rd) Restore native habitat of Kaua'i's endangered bird species.

National Botanical Tropical Gardens (☎332-7324; www.nbtg.org) Assist with general gardening and propagation.

Surfrider Foundation (www.surfriderkauai.ning.com) Beach clean-ups happen regularly across the island.

Shopping

You'll find the artists and entrepreneurs who put Hanapepe on the tourist radar in many of the old main-street galleries and workshops.

★Machinemachine CLOTHING
(www.machinemachineapparel.com; 3800 Hanapepe Rd; ⏲noon-5pm Tue-Thu & Sat, 6-9pm Fri) Shannon Hiramoto, a fifth-generation Kaua'i-born designer/imaginator, scours flea markets and thrift stores for age-old aloha wear and other knickknacks which she upcycles into comfy, funky, elegant dresses, skirts and excellent trucker hats. She has a devoted cult following, sells online and in 16 stores statewide, and does most of the sewing out of her Hanapepe workshop.

Set in an old mechanic's garage, the workshop alone is worthy of a trip to Hanapepe. Along with her special clothing line, you'll browse hacked up old signage, creative shell and chain jewelry, and framed paintings and drawings from young local talents. She has an increasingly popular **vintage collection** on the mezzanine, and even her yarn-wrapped hangers are cool. This effortlessly hip habitat, filled with quirky island soul, would do well in the most urban of environments, and on Kaua'i it is simply one of a kind. Hours do vary (those listed are merely approximations), but the workshop is always open on Friday nights.

Talk Story BOOKS
(☎335-6469; www.talkstorybookstore.com; 3785 Hanapepe Rd; ⏲10am-5pm Mon-Thu & Sat, to 9:30pm Fri) The island's one and only dedicated bookstore is an exceptionally quaint and funky indie paradise, the kind that will give you Amazonian regret and may even fill e-

reader enthusiasts with musty page-turning nostalgia.

New books by local authors are stocked up front, but it's mostly used fare here, with more than 40,000 books organized by both genre and, curiously, author gender. Why? Well, nobody actually knows, but take heart that only their fiction collection suffers such a strangely segregated fate. Oh, and say hello to Celeste if she rubs up and greets you.

Kauai Fine Arts GALLERY
(☎335-3778; www.brunias.com; 3751 Hanapepe Rd; ⏲9:30am-4:30pm Mon-Thu & Sat, to 9pm Fri) If you're sending something home or want to get your hands on a unique map – including navigational charts – this is a great little spot to peruse. Think fossilized shark teeth, antique and newer tiki carvings, quilts and prints of old Pan Am ads or long-gone old world maps.

Aloha Spice Company SPICES
(☎335-5960; www.alohaspice.com; 3865 Hanapepe Rd; ⏲10am-4:30pm Mon-Thu, to 9pm Fri, to 4pm Sat) You can smell the savory, smoky goodness as soon as the bells on the swinging front door announce your presence. In addition to local spices – all of which are packaged and shipped straight from the store – they also do creams and oils, wood products, nuts and chocolate, teapots and natural sodas. It's a delicious browse.

Banana Patch Studio ART GALLERY
(www.bananapatchstudio.com; 3865 Hanapepe Rd; ⏲10am-4:30pm Sat-Thu, to 9pm Fri) Sells Koi pond watercolors, vibrant island art and souvenir ceramic tiles.

Puahina Moku o Kaua'i CLOTHING
(☎335-9771; 4545 Kona Rd; ⏲11am-4pm Mon-Wed, 11am-4pm & 6-8:30pm Fri) With an eye for recognizing the need for traditional Hawaiian motifs fused with contemporary clothes (mostly for women), you'll find wearable keepsakes here. Look for originally designed shirts, skirts and tops adorning native *laua'e* and *ulu* (both symbolizing 'growth in excellence').

Amy-Lauren's Gallery GALLERY
(☎335-2827; www.amylaurensgallery.com; 3890 Hanapepe Rd; ⏲11am-5pm Mon-Fri, to 9pm Fri) Here's a chance to buy originals instead of giclée, though the latter are usually more affordable. This ambitious gallery, owned by a rather savvy young entrepreneur, doesn't necessarily deliver high art (they'd rather sell stuff), but in addition to tropical impressionist wannabes, they show poppier, livelier landscapes and portraiture than you'll find elsewhere in Hanapepe.

LOCAL KNOWLEDGE

STARRY STARRY NIGHT

With minimal city light interference, the west side of Kaua'i is an ideal locale to take in the night sky. The **Kaua'i Education Association for Science & Astronomy** (KEASA; ☎332-7827; www.keasa.org) holds free, monthly Starwatches on Saturdays closest to the new moon (the dark one). KEASA educators share both their gear and insights. Arrive at the Kaumakani Softball Field (between Hanapepe and Waimea) at sunset and prepare to have your mind blown. Space: it goes on forever.

Jacqueline on Kaua'i CLOTHING
(☎335-5797; 3837 Hanapepe Rd; custom shirts $60-200; ⏲9am-6pm Mon-Thu, Sat & Sun, to 9pm Fri) Friendly and eclectic, Jacqueline specializes in custom-made aloha shirts and can even make some cool dress shirts from vintage rice sacks. You choose the fabric, she does the rest. Expect a 24-hour turnaround.

Information

American Savings Bank (☎335-3118; 4548 Kona Rd)

Bank of Hawaii (☎335-5021; 3764 Hanapepe Rd) On the western end of Hanapepe Rd.

Getting There & Around

Veer *mauka* (inland) onto Hanapepe Rd at the 'Kaua'i's Biggest Little Town' sign.

Waimea

POP 9212

One of several Waimeas in Hawaii, this is not the legendary surfing mecca nor is it the upscale cowboy town. But in many ways, Kaua'i's Waimea is so much richer. Part humble Native Hawaiian hamlet, part big-dollar agriculture stronghold, it's also the original landing spot of Captain Cook and the access point to the sensational Waimea Canyon and Koke'e state parks.

Waimea means 'reddish-brown water,' which refers to the river that picks up salt from the canyon and colors the ocean red. It

Waimea

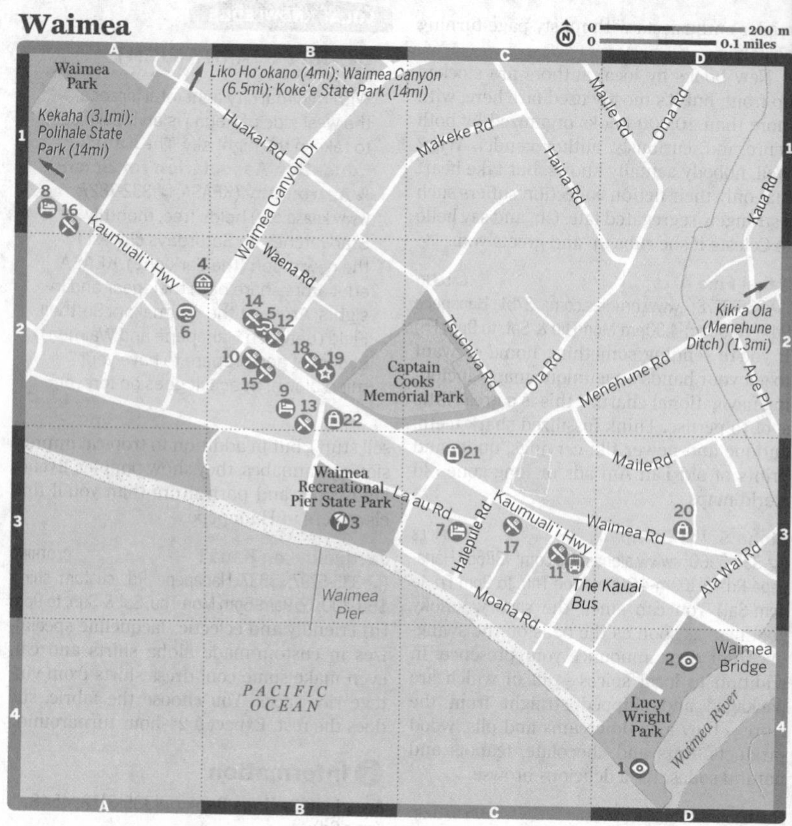

Waimea

Sights

1 Captain Cook Landing Site D4
2 Lucy Wright Park D4
3 Waimea Recreational Pier State Park B3
4 West Kaua'i Technology & Visitors Center A2

Activities, Courses & Tours

5 Na Pali Explorer B2
6 Na Pali Riders A2

Sleeping

7 Inn Waimea C3
8 Waimea Plantation Cottages A1
9 West Inn B2

Eating

10 Coconut Corner B2
11 Ishihara Market C3
12 Island Taco B2
13 Jo-Jo's Anuenue Shave Ice & Treats B2
14 Kaua'i Granola B2
15 Shrimp Station B2
16 The Grove Cafe A1
17 Wrangler's Steakhouse C3
18 Yumi's B2

Drinking & Nightlife

Da Java Hut .... (see 12)

Entertainment

19 Waimea Theater B2

Shopping

20 Aunty Lilikoi Passion Fruit Products D3
21 Fah Inn Fine Junque C3
22 Red Dirt Shirts B2

was at the Waimea River mouth where Captain Cook landed in 1778.

As is common in Hawaii, sugar played a role in the town's development and the skeleton of the old mill can still be seen amid the tech centers that house both the defense contractors working at the nearby Pacific Missile Range Facility and the island's recent and most controversial presence: multinational chemical companies developing genetically modified seeds for worldwide corn, soy and sunflower cultivation.

As the weather varies throughout the island, so do social climates. Waimea today – an echo of its multi-generational plantation history – remains a predominantly local Hawaii town, and one well worth experiencing, even as the lion's hare of tourists zip on through toward the state parks.

Sights

West Kaua'i Technology & Visitors Center — MUSEUM

(☎338-1332; www.wkbpa.org; 9565 Kaumuali'i Hwy; ⊙9:30am-5pm Mon-Fri) **FREE** A good historical orientation point to the Westside, this two-phase complex doubles as a visitor center and offers a free, three-hour historic Waimea walking tour at 9:30am Mondays. Registration is required. At 9:30am on Fridays they offer a lei-making class.

Lucy Wright Park — HISTORIC SITE

In the midst of a major dredging at research time, this park was the original **landing site** of Captain Cook on the Hawaiian Islands. Still, the people chose to name it in honor of Lucy Wright, a revered schoolteacher. Strong thinking, if you ask us. Descend at sunset and watch youth outrigger teams hammer through practice on the Waimea River.

Kiki a Ola (Menehune Ditch) — RUIN

Not much remains to be seen of this unique and still-functional aqueduct, and yet its archaeological significance begs repeating. It is the only example of pre-contact cut and dressed stonework in Hawaii, said to be the work of the *menehune* (the little people), who completed it within one night for the *ali'i* (royalty).

Russian Fort Elizabeth — HISTORIC SITE

Russia befriended Kaua'i's King Kaumuali'i in the early 1800s; the relationship stood to help Kaumuali'i overcome King Kamehameha, and the Russians to use Hawaii as an oceangoing stop during their reign as prominent fur traders.

This fort was begun in September 1816, but within a year was stopped – some say due to King Kamehameha's orders, and some to general suspicion of the Russians. Hawaiian troops used the fort until 1864. It was dismantled in 1865. Stroll the dusty trail that leads within the remains of the old foundation amid an otherwise rugged coastal moonscape.

Waimea Recreational Pier State Park — BEACH

(www.hawaiistateparks.org; La'au Rd) This wide black beach, flecked with microscopic green crystals called olivine, stretches between two rather stunning rock outcrops and is bisected by the namesake pier. It's especially lovely at sunset when the sun drops dead center and the sky explodes with color.

Activities

There are three snorkel outfits offering Na Pali Coast snorkel tours from Kikiaola Small Boat Harbor.

★Na Pali Riders — SNORKELING

(☎742-6331; www.napaliriders.com; 9600 Kaumuali'i Hwy; adult/child $129/99) Tours are hosted by Captain Chris Turner, who is passionate about what he does and likes to think of his tour as being in the style of *National Geographic*. Turner offers an intimate setting, healthy snacks and a CD of photographs and footage taken on the trip, along with the feeling that you're going out with some of your favorite ragamuffin friends.

Liko Ho'okano — SNORKELING

(☎338-0333, 888-732-5456; www.liko-kauai.com; 9875 Waimea Rd; 5hr cruise adult/child $140/95) Run by a Kaua'i-born-and-raised Native Hawaiian, whose ancestors hailed from the 'forbidden island' of Ni'ihau, this outfit sails its 49ft power catamaran to the Na Pali Coast. The maximum group size is 34 and tours go as far as Ke'e Beach.

Na Pali Explorer — SNORKELING

(☎338-9999, 877-335-9909; www.napali-explorer.com; Kaumuali'i Hwy; 4½hr tour adult/child $119/99; sportfishing per person $130) Offers snorkeling excursions from rigid-hull inflatable rafts, which have a hard bottom, inflatable sides and are smoother than the all-inflatable Zodiacs. Expect between 16 to 35 passengers. The 48ft raft includes a restroom and canopy for shade, and runs out of Waimea from October to April. They also offer sportfishing trips on their 41ft Concorde Sportfisher.

Pakalas SURFING

Between mile markers 21 and 22, you'll notice cars parked on the side of the highway in an area known as Makaweli. This is the access point to the fiercely defended local surf spot dubbed Pakalas, or Infinities, said to offer the 'longest lefts' anywhere on the island. It's also popular among tiger sharks, and seeing as it's one of the few locals' breaks remaining, leave it be and try the Kekaha or Polihale beach parks instead.

Festivals & Events

Waimea Town Celebration CULTURAL

(338-1332; www.wkbpa.org) An annual week-long festival in mid-February that includes rodeo, a canoe race, food, crafts, musical performances, a three-on-three basketball tourney and lei and hula competitions.

Waimea Lighted Christmas Parade PARADE

(338-9957; www.wkbpa.org/christmas.html; Kaumuali'i Hwy & Ala Wai Rd) Watch lighted floats cruise through Waimea town. The parade starts at dusk, usually held the last Saturday before Christmas.

Sleeping

★Waimea Plantation Cottages COTTAGE $$

(338-1625, 866-774-2924; www.waimea-plantation.com; 9400 Kaumuali'i Hwy; 1br/2br cottage from $199/255;) This is one of our favorite properties on the island. It features 57 rebuilt plantation cottages from the 1930s and 1940s, once used to house sugarcane labor. These are tin roof, clapboard, pastel brushed sweethearts with wide porches blessed with sea views and rattan seating. They're scattered over a wide lawn, studded with golden bamboo, swaying palm groves and a cathedral banyan tree.

Coco's Kaua'i B&B B&B $$

(639-1109, 338-0722; www.cocoskauai.com; btwn MM 21 & 22; cottages $120, incl breakfast $140; @) An appealing, off-the-grid retreat owned by one of the Robinson family descendants. You're still close to Waimea town, on the quiet side of a sugar plantation that's part of a greater 40,000 acres of agricultural land. The lone cottage features a king bed, kitchenette, private hot tub, BBQ and cowboys riding by on horses. There's a minimum two-night stay.

West Inn INN $$

(338-1107; www.thewestinn.com; 9690 Kaumuali'i Hwy; r $149; P) This brand-new inn set right across from Waimea Theater offers good value, spacious rooms with queen beds, high ceilings, granite counter tops, flat screens, microwave, mini fridge and wi-fi. The decor won't win any awards, but that's nit-picking. Laid-back management will gladly point out local surf breaks.

Inn Waimea INN $$

(338-0031; www.innwaimea.com; 4469 Halepule Rd; cottages $150-170, r $110-120; @) Situated in the heart of town, these suites and cottages were recently redone and feature clawfoot tubs and other antique furnishings. The two upstairs suites have their own lounge areas and the very reasonably priced two-bedroom cottages have a more modern decor. They also have a few vacation rentals in town, which they book for long-term stays.

Eating

★Island Taco MEXICAN $

(338-9895; www.islandfishtaco.com; 9643 Kaumuali'i Hwy; 1/2 tacos $8/15, burritos $11-15; 11am-5pm) At this roadside fusion taqueria tortillas are stuffed with wasabi-coated or Cajun-dusted seared ahi, fresh cabbage and rice. Or, if it's your pleasure, have the same trick done with tofu or teriyaki chicken instead. Service and vibe are perfectly sunny.

Ishihara Market DELI $

(9894 Kaumuali'i Hwy; plate lunch $8.75; 6am-8:30pm Mon-Fri, 7am-8:30pm Sat & Sun) It's an ad-hoc lesson in local cuisine perusing this historic market (c 1934) with an in-house deli, which is arguably the island's most local eatery. Trusty lunches are the sushi bento, spicy lobster salad and the archetypal spicy ahi *poke*. Daily specials and marinated ready-to-go meats are available for those wanting to barbecue.

Shrimp Station SEAFOOD $

(338-1242; www.shrimpstation.com; 9652 Kaumuali'i Hwy; meals $11-12; 11am-5:30pm;) Get your peel-and-eat shrimp seasoned in white wine, Thai lemongrass, sweet chile or Cajun sauce, or opt for a paper platter of beer- or coconut-battered shrimp instead. It also stocks kid-friendly ice cream and desserts such as push-up rainbow pops and

Häagen-Dazs bars. A walk-up window and picnic table seating help keep this a simple, inviting operation.

Kaua'i Granola BAKERY $
(☎338-0121; www.kauaigranola.com; 9633 Kaumuali'i Hwy; snacks $4-8; ⏰10am-5pm Mon-Sat) Lovely shop and cottage factory churning out an assortment of sugary roasted nut mixes and sinful cookies like the chocolate-dipped macadamia nut variety. Cheryl Salazar, the owner-operator, works the mixing bowl and the register with charm to spare. Around Christmas time, don't miss out on her aloha-shirt-clad and hula-skirted gingerbread men and women – they make adorable, edible gifts.

Jo-Jo's Anuenue Shave Ice & Treats SHAVE ICE $
(4491 Pokole Rd; ⏰9am-5pm; 👪) This rastified shack delivers icy flavor; all syrups are homemade without additives and won't knock you out with sweetness. The superstar item is the dragon-fruit *halo halo*. Best to find a nice seat (possibly Waimea landing just down the street) and savor the flavor. (Hint: it's the one not on the highway.)

Yumi's DINER $
(☎338-1731; 9691 Kaumuali'i Hwy; mains $6-11; ⏰7:30am-2:30pm Tue-Thu, 7am-1pm, 6-8pm Fri, 8am-1pm Sat) Waimea's classic diner, in business since 1978, serves greasy spoon fare and some excellent breakfasts. Try the French toast made with thick slices of Portuguese sweetbread.

Coconut Corner NOODLES $
(☎338-0444; 9640 Kaumuali'i Hwy; smoothies $7, mains $8-15; ⏰9:30am-6pm) A grab-bag snack stand where you can buy (overpriced) fresh fruit, enjoy tasty smoothies, shaved ice and a Thai-inspired noodle and wrap menu.

The Grove Cafe CAFE $$
(☎338-1625; www.waimea-plantation.com; 9400 Kaumuali'i Hwy, Waimea Plantation Cottages; mains $9-16; ⏰11am-4pm) More of a tavern with a dining room attached, it's not quite as elegant a place to eat as it appears from the roadside, but they do pub grub (nachos, wings and burgers) as well as local nibbles like *poke* and seared or broiled fish dishes. Food is decent if not fabulous.

Wrangler's Steakhouse STEAKHOUSE $$
(☎338-1218; www.innwaimea.com/wranglers.html; 9852 Kaumuali'i Hwy; dinner mains $18-27; ⏰11am-8:30pm Mon-Thu, 4-9pm Fri & Sat, 4-8:30pm Sun) Grab a plantation lunch (which starts from $9) in a *kaukau* tin full of shrimp tempura, teriyaki and BBQ meat, along with rice and kimchee. Included in that price is soup and salad. Steaks are good; the fresh fish less so. Save room for the peach cobbler, which may beckon you back.

Drinking & Entertainment

Da Java Hut CAFE
(9643 Kaumuali'i Hwy; ⏰6am-4pm) Hidden away behind Island Taco, this little drive-through joint serves Waimea's only espresso drinks. They do smoothies too. Cash only.

Waimea Theater CINEMA
(☎338-0282; www.waimeatheater.com; 9691 Kaumuali'i Hwy; adult/student/child $8/7/6; ⏰7:30pm Wed-Sun) Perfect for a rainy day or early evening reprieve from the sun and sea. Kaua'i is a bit behind with the new releases, but this is one of two functioning theaters on the island, so it's much appreciated. It's also historic, which makes it our favorite.

Shopping

★ **Fah Inn Fine Junque** VINTAGE
(☎338-9855; 9821 Kamaumali'i Hwy; ⏰11am-3pm Mon-Thu) The best vintage collectible shop on the island, where Dorris, the Tennessee-born matriarch and love beacon, tells old-timey stories with charm and an accent that perfectly mingles with the sweet Hawaiian melodies in the air. Rummage old ceramic bowls, glass buoys, maps, records, art and aloha wear in this tumbledown plantation shack near the school.

Aunty Lilikoi Passion Fruit Products GIFTS
(☎338-1296; www.auntylilikoi.com; 9875 Waimea Rd; ⏰10am-6pm) In 2008 Aunty Lilikoi did it again, taking the gold medal in the Napa Valley International Mustard Competition for her *liliko'i*-wasabi mustard, making it clear that if it's a product with *liliko'i* (passion fruit), Aunty's got it down.

Find something for almost any occasion: syrup (great for banana pancakes), some tremendous spice rubs, massage oil (the choice for honeymooners) and the tasty chap stick (ideal for après surf), all made with at least a kiss of, you guessed it, *liliko'i*.

Red Dirt Shirts CLOTHING
(www.dirtshirt.com; 4490 Pokole Rd; ⏰11am-6pm) With punny sayings like 'Older Than Dirt' and 'How's My Attitude?' these born-of-necessity shirts can be very useful if you

plan on hiking, as most of the dirt on the island wants to destroy your clothing. And you must have a beloved, cringe-worthy uncle who would sport a shirt that says 'Life's Short Play Dirty.'

Information

Aloha-N-Paradise (☎338-1522; www.alohanparadise.com; 9905 Waimea Rd; per 30min $4; ⏲7am-noon Mon-Fri, 8am-noon Sat; 📶) Next to the post office; offers internet access, wi-fi, lattes and $1000 paintings.

First Hawaiian Bank (☎338-1611; 4525 Panako Rd) On Waimea's central square.

West Kauai Medical Center (☎338-9431; www.kvmh.hhsc.org; 4643 Waimea Canyon Dr) Emergency services 24 hours.

West Kaua'i Technology & Visitors Center (☎338-1332; www.wkbpa.org/visitorcenter.html; 9565 Kaumuali'i Hwy; ⏲9:30am-4pm Mon, Tue & Thu, to 12:30pm Fri) Free internet access.

Getting There & Around

Heading west from Hanapepe leads you right into town. No taxi services run out of Waimea, but if you're in a jam **Pono Taxi and Kauai Tours** (☎634-4744; www.ponotaxi.com; per mile $3 plus per min 40¢) will service the entire island.

The Kaua'i Bus (www.kauai.gov; adult/senior & student $2/1; ⏲5:30am-8:30pm) Kekaha-Lihu'e line runs hourly from about 5:30am to 8:30pm. From Lihu'e you can transfer for buses that run to the South and North Shores.

Kekaha

POP 3537

Home to many military families, there's no town center here, but Kekaha Beach Park offers one of the most beautiful sunsets on the island. If you're looking for a town with a scenic beach near the base of Waimea Canyon, this is nice. It is, however, well removed from the action and too remote for some.

Kekaha is an old working-class sugar town turned military town, with a decommissioned old sugar mill at its heart and some stunning beach houses dotting the highway on the way to **Kekaha Beach Park**, now officially known as **Westside's MacArthur Park**. Set just west of town, this long fringe of powdery white sand was once ideal for running, walking or beachcombing. These days it depends upon the tides. In the last year alone, the southern edge of the beach has completely eroded, and they've had to move the lifeguard tower three times.

POLIHALE: DEPARTURE POINT

A massive expanse of beach – the end of one of the longest (15 miles) and widest (300 ft) in the state – Polihale is as mystical as it is enchanting. Loosely translated as 'home of the underworld,' Hawaiian belief holds Polihale as the place where souls depart for *Po* (the Hawaiian afterworld). The cliffs at the end of the beach are home to ancient Hawaiian ruins constructed over the ocean as the jumping-off place for spirits.

Of course, the sea (read: waves) is the big draw. Before jumping in, find a lifeguard and make sure it's OK, as the sea lacks the reef protection other beaches provide. When the surf is high, currents are extremely dangerous. Under the right conditions, however, it can be excellent for surfing and bodyboarding. The breaks here are known as **Davidson's** (at the east end of town) and **Intersections** at the northwest side of town. Davidson's is a good, crumbling beginner wave, susceptible to on-shore winds. Always remember to respect the locals who value the loneliness of this far out break, which pumps when either the North or South swells hit and wrap west. Locals call it *wrapping* and brag that Kekaha and nearby Polihale get as much as 350 days of surfing. North Shore heads beg to differ, of course, even as they make the drive all the way out here for a summer wave.

Kaumuali'i Hwy borders the coastline while Kekaha Rd, the town's main drag, lies parallel and a few blocks inland. All you'll find in town are a post office and a couple of stores. At its eastern end, Kekaha Rd and Kaumuali'i Hwy meet near the Kikiaola Small Boat Harbor, a state harbor with a launch ramp.

Sleeping

For more lodging listings, see **Vacation Rentals By Owner** (www.vrbo.com), which has a wide selection of choice beach houses along the west coast.

Boathouse Guesthouse INN $
(☎332-9744; www.seakauai.com; 4518A Nene St; r $85) Within walking distance of Kekaha Beach, this studio feels spacious and has its own covered lanai, kitchenette, king bed

and flat-screen TV. New Hawaiiana furnishings give it a welcome burst of life. Ideal for one person or a couple, with a washer-dryer on-site.

★ **Hale Puka 'Ana B&B** B&B $$
(652-6852; www.kekahakauaisunset.com; 8240A Elepaio Rd; ste $169-229;) The only oceanside B&B on the island is set in a gorgeous seafoam green house and offers three rooms with fine furnishings of cherrywood and bamboo, and two with private lanai and ocean views. Watch whales breach (November to March) while munching a superior breakfast. One hiccup: traffic noise. Book well ahead.

Canary House VACATION RENTAL $$
(406-624-6188; www.vrbo.com; 4518 Nene Rd; per night/week $190/1225) One of several stunning Kekaha rentals listed on vrbo.com, this lovely, bright, all-wood restored plantation manager's cottage has a sweet grassy yard, car port, wide front porch, crown mouldings and wood floors throughout.

Barking Sands

Between Kekaha Beach Park and Polihale State Park, the beach stretches for approximately 15 miles. However, since the terrorist attacks of September 11, 2001, consistent public access has been restricted. This is because it is home to the US Navy base Barking Sands Pacific Missile Range Facility. The missile-range facility at Barking Sands provides the above-ground link to a sophisticated sonar network that tracks more than 1000 sq miles of the Pacific. Established during WWII, it's been developed into the world's largest (possibly excluding blue whales) underwater listening device. Oh, and there are tasty waves here, even if they are only open to a select few. Bring your military ID. Casual tourists need not apply.

The navy is Kaua'i's largest employer and it controversially occupies and prohibits access to indigenous Hawaiian territory. Any move by the military to occupy more land generates fervent protest.

Barking Sands earned its nickname because on days both sunny and windy (with the planets lined up just right) the moving sands make sounds akin to those of barking dogs. (Please send us a recording if you hear them.)

Polihale State Park

Here is a 15-mile stretch of raw nectar. A beach thick, loamy and white that curls into dunes that climb into bluffs, with a turquoise bay that thrashes the looming majesty of the Na Pali cliffs. Yes, the northwesternmost end of the Na Pali Coast is unforgettable. Most folks come to surf **Echoes**, a tremendous big-wave break at the northernmost end. But if the currents aren't too rough, you'll be able to swim in **Queen's Pond** – a relatively shallow swirl of sea that lines up perpendicular to the road, which peters out on the bluffs above (we'll get to that road in a sec). Queen's Pond is sheltered by a reef, but surf and current rage outside, so don't meander too far from shore.

Here's the catch, this beach is only accessible by a rugged, rutted 4.8-mile-long dirt road that accesses the park from Mana village off Kaumuali'i Hwy. This road takes a beating from harsh conditions, which has made this state park something of a headache for the Department of Land & Natural Resources in the past. For the last couple of years an ambitious and altruistic local crew has taken it upon themselves to annually repair it.

Note that there aren't any car-rental vendors who offer insurance for visitors to drive here. In fact, some make you sign a special document swearing that you drive here at your (and your rented axle's) own risk. Truthfully, the road is not the island's most treacherous, and even low-riding rentals can almost always make the trip out and back unscathed. It's a no-brainer for high-clearance vehicles.

Whether you decide to drive here for a day trip or more, it's worth remembering that camping is, at times, allowed with a permit. However, the entryway, toilet and shower access is inconsistent – and finding a ride back should your rental transport fail is a risky proposition.

Waimea Canyon State Park

Of all Kaua'i's unique wonders, none can touch Waimea Canyon for utter grandeur. While one expects to find tropical beaches and gardens here, few expect a gargantuan chasm of ancient lava rock, 10 miles long and 2500ft deep, which Mark Twain first called the Grand Canyon of the Pacific. Flowing through the canyon is the Waimea River, Kaua'i's longest, which is fed by three eastern tributaries that bring reddish-brown waters from the mountaintop bog, Alaka'i Swamp.

Waimea Canyon was formed when Kaua'i's original shield volcano, Wai'ale'ale, slumped along an ancient fault line, creating a sharp east-facing line of cliffs. Then another shield volcano, Lihu'e, developed the island's east side, producing new lava flows that pounded against those cliffs. Thus the western canyon walls are taller, thinner and more eroded – the contrast is most theatrically apparent while hiking along the canyon floor. The black and red horizontal striations along the canyon walls represent successive volcanic eruptions; the red color indicates where water seeped through the rocks, creating mineral rust from the iron ore inside.

Drives on a clear day are phenomenal. But don't be disappointed by rain, as that's what makes the waterfalls gush. Sunny days following rain are ideal for prime views, though slick mud makes it a challenge.

The southern boundary of Waimea Canyon State Park is about 6 miles up the road from Waimea. You can reach the park by two roads: Waimea Canyon Dr (Hwy 550), which starts in Waimea just beyond mile marker 23, and Koke'e Rd (Hwy 552), which starts in Kekaha off Mana Rd. They merge between mile markers 6 and 7.

State officials generally prefer visitors to use Waimea Canyon Dr, which is 19 miles long and passes the canyon lookouts with terrific views into Kalalau Valley on the Na Pali Coast. Koke'e Rd is shorter by 3 miles and also offers scenic views, but not of the canyon.

Dangers & Annoyances

Rain creates hazardous conditions in the canyon. The red-dirt trails quickly become slick and river fords rise to impassable levels. Try hiking poles or a sturdy walking stick to ease the steep descent into the canyon.

Note the time of sunset and plan to return well before dark. The daylight will fade inside the canyon long before sunset.

While packing light is recommended, take enough water for your entire trip, especially the uphill return journey. Do not drink fresh water along the trails without treating it. Cell phones do not work here. If possible, hike with a companion or at least tell someone your expected return time.

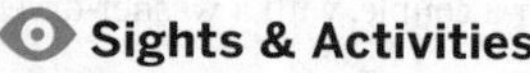

Sights & Activities

Waimea Canyon Drive OUTDOORS

In addition to jaw-dropping canyon vistas and ocean views, you can also see several fine specimens of native trees, including koa and ohia, as well as invasive species such as kiawe. The valuable hardwood koa proliferates at the **hunter's check station**. Look for the trees with narrow, crescent-shaped leaves.

Scenic Lookouts

Waimea Canyon Lookout, the most scenic of the lookout points, is located at 0.3 miles north of mile marker 10 and at an elevation of 3400ft. Keep your eyes peeled for the canyon running in an easterly direction off Waimea, which is Koai'e Canyon, an area accessible to backcountry hikers.

The 800ft waterscape known as **Waipo'o Falls** can be seen from a couple of small unmarked lookouts before mile marker 12 and then from a lookout opposite the picnic area shortly before mile marker 13. The picnic area includes BBQ pits, restrooms, drinking water, a pay phone and Camp Hale Koa, a Seventh Day Adventist camp. **Pu'u Hinahina Lookout**, at 3640ft, offers two lookouts near the parking lot at a marked turnoff between mile markers 13 and 14.

Hiking

Several rugged trails lead deep into Waimea Canyon: keep in mind they're shared with pig and deer hunters and that it's busiest during weekends and holidays.

The **Kukui trail** and its extension, the **Koai'e Canyon trail**, are two of the steepest on Kaua'i; they connect at Wiliwili Camp, 2000ft into the canyon. If the entire trek sounds too strenuous, hike just 1 mile down the Kukui Trail, where you'll reach a bench with an astounding view.

Iliau Nature Loop HIKING

(www.hawaiistateparks.org; Waimea Canyon Dr, Waimea Canyon State Park) This easy, mostly flat 0.3 mile loop was named for the *iliau*, a plant endemic to Kaua'i's Westside, which grows along the route and produces stalks up to 10ft high. Canyon walls, waterfalls and bursting *iliau* are all reasons to give it a try.

The marked trailhead for the 10-minute Iliau Nature Loop comes up shortly before mile marker 9. Be sure to pass the bench to the left and walk about three minutes for a top-notch vista into Waimea Canyon.

Kukui Trail HIKING

(www.hawaiistateparks.org; Waimea Canyon Dr, Waimea Canyon State Park) This narrow switchback trail drops 2000ft to the canyon floor and doesn't offer much in the way of sweeping views, though there is a river at the bottom. And don't let the fact that it's only 2.5 miles (five miles round-trip) fool you. The climb out is for seriously fit and agile hikers only.

Keep your eyes peeled for a small sign directing hikers to turn left. Hike the steep slope down, with the hill at your back. When you hear the sound of water, you're closing in on the picnic shelter and Wiliwili Camp area, where overnight camping is allowed but mostly patronized by boar hunters. To get here, find the Iliau Nature Loop trailhead just before mile marker 9. It officially starts just beyond at a hunter checking station on the right.

Waimea Canyon Trail HIKING

(www.hawaiistateparks.org; Waimea Canyon Dr, Waimea Canyon State Park) The 11.5-mile (one way) Waimea Canyon Trail starts at the bottom of Waimea Canyon at the end of Kukui Trail and leads out to Waimea town, fording the river along the way. An entry permit is required at the self-service box at the Kukui Trail register. You might see locals carrying inner tubes so they can float home the easy way.

Koai'e Canyon Trail HIKING

About 0.5 miles from the Kukui Trail in Waimea Canyon State Park is the Koai'e Canyon Trail, a moderate, 11-mile round-trip hike that takes you down the south side of the canyon to some reportedly hazardous swimming holes – including **Lonomea**, the last of the bunch, fed by a cascading waterfall.

Staying the night is an absolute must; this trail offers three camps. After the first, **Kaluaha'ulu Camp**, stay on the eastern bank of the river – do not cross it. Later you'll come upon the overgrown Na Ala Hele trailhead for the Koai'e Canyon Trail. Watch for greenery and soil that conceals drop-offs alongside the path. Next up is **Hipalau Camp**. After this camp the trail seems to disappear and can be tricky to find. Keep heading north, do not veer toward the river, but continue ascending at approximately the same point midway between the canyon walls and the river. Growing steeper, the trail then enters **Koai'e Canyon**, recognizable by the red-rock walls rising to the left. The last camp is the aforementioned **Lonomea**. Find the best views at the emergency helipad, a grassy area perfect for picnicking. When ready to leave, retrace your steps.

Cycling

Coast downhill for 13 miles, from the rim of Waimea Canyon (elevation 3500ft) to sea level with Outfitters Kaua'i (p548), which will supply necessary cruisers, helmets and snacks. Remember, you'll be a target for the setting sun during the afternoon ride. Tours cost $104 for adults and $84 for children.

Mountain bikers can also find miles of bumpy, 4WD hunting-area roads off Waimea Canyon Dr. Even when the yellow gates are closed on non-hunting days, cyclists are still allowed access – except for Papa'alai Rd, which is managed by the Department of Hawaiian Home Lands and open for hunting, but not recreational use.

Sleeping

All four camps on the canyon trails are part of the forest reserve system. They have open-air picnic shelters and pit toilets, but no other facilities; all freshwater must be treated before drinking.

Koke'e State Park

The expansive Koke'e State Park is a playground to those who revere the environment. Home to inspirational views, it offers an abundance of animal and plant life – everything from native timber to patches of non-native but still gorgeous California redwoods grow here. You'll also enjoy a welcome reprieve from the sun as you notice how the park's microclimates shift the ambient air temperature rather unexpectedly.

In ancient times, only Hawaiian birdcatchers resided up in this part of the island. The trail that once ran down the cliffs from Koke'e (ko-*keh*-eh) to Kalalau Valley on the Na Pali Coast is extraordinarily steep and has taken the life of at least one Western trekker. Though one of the park's locally revered charms is its choppy, almost impossible 4WD roads – which, unfortunately for tourists, happen to access the majority of the best trailheads – the state has reportedly been plotting (despite misgivings by many Kaua'i residents) to pave much of Koke'e. Advocates against this decision have argued it would rob the area of its reclusively rugged character.

Another potential moneymaker (of equally controversial status) is the state's plan to further modernize Koke'e by adding a helicopter landing pad, which would, in turn, increase air-tourism revenues.

This park's boundary starts beyond the **Pu'u Hinahina Lookout**. After mile marker 15, you'll pass a brief stretch of park cabins, a restaurant, a museum and campground.

Dangers & Annoyances

All of the suggestions for Waimea Canyon State Park also apply to Koke'e State Park. In addition, the higher elevation produces a cooler and wetter climate, so take appropriate attire.

Sights & Activities

Koke'e Museum MUSEUM

(335-9975; www.kokee.org; entry by donation $1; 9am-4:30pm) Here, you'll find detailed topographical maps, exhibits on local flora and fauna, local historical photographs and a tribute to the late photographer and educator David Boynton (and contributor to Lonely Planet), who died in 2007 when he was hiking along a cliff trail to one of his most cherished spots on the Na Pali coastline.

In addition to a handy trail map ($2), you can obtain a brochure for the short nature trail out back. It offers interpretive information corresponding to the trail's numbered plants and trees, including many native species.

Kalalau Lookout VIEWPOINT

Look for mile marker 18, where the ethereal 4000ft Kalalau Lookout stands up to the ocean, sun and winds with severe beauty. Hope for a clear day for ideal views, but know that even a rainy day can make for some settling clouds that could later disappear – followed by powerful waterfalls, and, of course, rainbows.

Though it might be hard to imagine, as the terrain is so extreme, as late as the 1920s Kalalau Valley was home to many residents – who farmed rice there, no less. The only way into the valley nowadays is along the coastal Kalalau Trail from Ha'ena on the North Shore or by kayak. The paved road continues another mile to **Pu'u o Kila Lookout**, where it dead-ends at a parking lot.

Hiking

Generally speaking, Koke'e is unspoiled. Its sheer size might make it a bit challenging to nail down where you want to start, and the 4WD-only roads which access the majority of trails present still another complication. Know that if you want to avoid hunters (and their dogs), it's best to opt for trails like Alaka'i Swamp or the Cliff Trail to Waipo'o Falls; though those might have some other hikers on it, they're still relatively remote. In total, Koke'e boasts 45 miles of trails that range from delving deep into the rainforest or merely skimming the perimeter, with views that can cause a vertiginous reaction in even the most avid mountain goat.

Trekking around Koke'e offers a rare view at an abundance of endemic species of wildlife and plants, including the largest population of Kaua'i's native fern, the fragrant *laua'e,* alluded to in many of the island's chants and traditions. Also here you might see some of Kaua'i's rare and endangered native forest birds.

The starting point for several scenic hikes, Halemanu Rd, is just north of mile marker 14 on Waimea Canyon Dr. Whether or not the road is passable in a non-4WD vehicle depends on recent rainfall. Note that many rental-car agreements are null and void when off-roading. One solid option to avoid having to deal with bad roads and lack of signage yourself is to hire a guide. Local guide and photographer **Jeffrey Courson** (639-9709; www.consciousjourneyskauai.com; half-/full-day $200/320; up to 4 people) has been hiking in Koke'e for over 30 years, knows the trails, roads, flora and fauna like the back of his hand, comes ready to drive in a 4WD vehicle and is quite simply a terrific resource and the kind of guide that will become a friend. He's highly recommended.

During summer weekends, trained volunteers lead **Wonder Walks**, guided hikes on various trails at Waimea Canyon and Koke'e State Parks. Contact the museum for schedules and reservations.

Honopu, Awa'awapuhi & Nu'alolo Cliffs Trails HIKING

These trails offer the best of the best. The **Awa'awapuhi Trail** (3.25 miles) and the more challenging **Nu'alolo Trail** (3.75 miles) are continuously maintained, while the **Honopu Trail** (2.5 miles) requires a guide. Yet all afford unforgettable vistas along 2000ft cliffs over the Na Pali Coast.

If you're undecided as to which trail to take, the Awa'awapuhi Trail is the least technical – though there are some steep steps where you might find yourself hugging a

Koke'e & Waimea Canyon State Parks

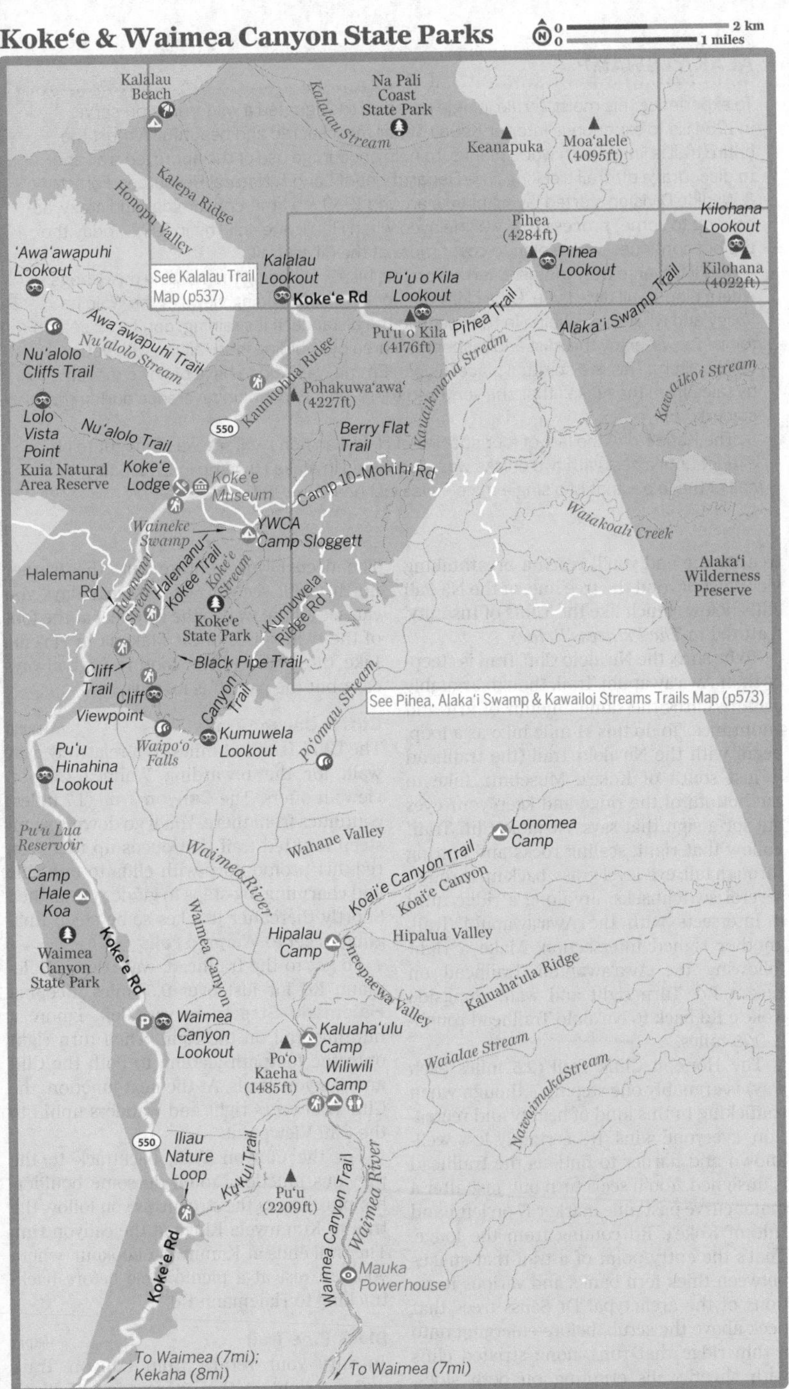

ALAKA'I SWAMP

To experience this moist, fertile, jungle paradise (designated a wilderness preserve in 1964) is to experience interior Kaua'i at her most sacred and beautiful. Almost the entire trail is linked with wood planks, to help encourage use of the approved trail and to discourage off-trail trekking. The Department of Land & Natural Resources' Forestry & Wildlife Division started laying planks around 1989 – a time-consuming (and crazy, according to some) process that was delayed when Hurricane 'Iniki hit in 1992. Today the project continues, with a plan to cover more of the Pihea Trail.

You'll traverse truly fantastic terrain on this hike – including memorably misty bogs where plants will dwarf you. On a clear day, look for outstanding views of the Wainiha Valley and whales breaching in the ocean in the distance. If it's raining, don't fret: search for rainbows, enjoy the mist and respect the area by avoiding loud talking with your fellow hikers. This is a spiritual place: Queen Emma was said to have been so moved by tales from the Alaka'i that she ventured there, only to chant in reverence during the sojourn.

The Kaua'i *'o'o*, the last of four species of Hawaiian honeyeaters, was thought to be extinct until a nest with two chicks was discovered in Alaka'i Swamp in 1971. Sadly, the call of the *'o'o* – that of a single male – was last heard in 1987.

tree. At the end you'll reach a breathtaking view, just beyond the tree line, of the Na Pali cliffs below (much like the 'Cliffs of Insanity' featured in *The Princess Bride*).

To be sure, the Nu'alolo Cliff Trail is steeper than Awa'awapuhi Trail, though arguably each requires the same amount of grit and endurance. To do this 11-mile hike as a loop, begin with the Nu'alolo Trail (the trailhead is just south of Koke'e Museum), hike to the bottom of the ridge and keep your eyes out for a sign that says 'Nu'alolo Cliff Trail.' Follow that right, scaling rocks and cutting through tall, eye-level grass, back up through several switchbacks, up along a ridge until it intersects with the Awa'awapuhi Trail, another signed intersection. Make a right following the Awa'awapuhi Trailhead on Koke'e Rd. Turn right and walk alongside Koke'e Rd back to Nu'alolo Trailhead roughly 0.75 miles.

The Honopu Cliffs Trail (2.5 miles each way) is arguably one step up – though when trafficking in this kind of beauty and recreation, everyone wins. It's certainly less well-known and harder to find, as the trailhead is unsigned. You'll see a turn out, just after a major curve past mile marker 17 on left hand side of Koke'e Rd coming from the lodge. That's the entry point of a trail that snakes between thick fern banks and various iterations of the archetypal Dr Seuss trees that peek above the scrub, before emerging onto a thin ridge that runs along striated cliffs with sheer walls erupting on both sides. The deeper you venture out, the further north you'll see. In fact, on clear days you can see all the way to the Ke'e reef at the foot of the twin spires of Mt Makana in Ha'ena. Like those above, the footing isn't always easy, but the pay off is massive.

Cliff & Canyon Trails HIKING

The **Cliff Trail** (0.1 miles) is a relatively easy walk for the rewarding Waimea Canyon views it offers. The **Canyon Trail** (1.7 miles) continues from there. You'll go down a semi-steep forested trail that opens up to a vast, red-dirt promontory with cliffs to one side and charming log-steps to guide you further. Shortly thereafter it takes some steep finagling to get to **Waipo'o Falls**.

To get to the trailhead, walk down Halemanu Rd for just over 0.5 miles. Keeping **Halemanu Stream** to your left, ignore a hunting trail on the right. Then turn right onto the footpath leading to both the Cliff and Canyon Trails. At the next junction, the Cliff Trail veers right and wanders uphill to the Cliff Viewpoint.

For the Canyon Trail, backtrack to the previous junction. You'll do some boulder-hopping across the stream, as you follow the trail to Kumuwela Ridge at the canyon rim. The trail ends at Kumuwela Lookout, where you can rest at a picnic table before backtracking to Halemanu Rd.

Black Pipe Trail HIKING

To vary your return from Canyon Trail, make a right at the intersection of Black

Pipe Trail and Canyon Trail at the top of the switchback where you leave the canyon rim. The 0.4 mile trail ends at Halemanu Rd, where you walk back to the Canyon trailhead.

Halemanu–Koke'e Trail HIKING

(www.hawaiistateparks.org; Halemanu Rd, Koke'e State Park) Another trail off Halemanu Rd, which starts further down the road than the Cliff and Canyon Trails, is Halemanu–Koke'e Trail (1.25 miles). An easy recreational nature trail, it passes through a native forest of koa and ohia trees, which provide a habitat for native birds.

One of the common plants found on this trail is banana poka, a member of the passionfruit family and an invasive pest. It has pretty pink flowers, but it drapes the forest with its vines and chokes out less aggressive native plants. The trail ends near YWCA Camp Sloggett, about 0.5 miles from Koke'e Lodge.

Pihea Trail to Alaka'i Swamp Trail HIKING

(www.hawaiistateparks.org; Koke'e Rd, Koke'e State Park) This 7.5-mile round-trip trek begins at Pu'u o Kila Lookout. A mere mile in and you'll see the **Pihea Lookout**. Past that and after a short scramble downhill the boardwalk begins. After another 1.5 miles you will come to a crossing with the Alaka'i Swamp Trail. A left at this crossing will put you on that trail to the **Kilohana Lookout**.

Continuing straight on the Pihea Trail will take you to the Kawaikoi campground along the Kawaikoi Stream. Most hikers start on the Pihea Trail because the trailhead is accessible by the paved road to Pu'u o Kila Lookout. For another trailhead, begin at the Alaka'i Swamp Trail starting point, but that requires 4WD. The trails are well maintained, with mile markers and signs. Note: the stretch between Alaka'i Crossing and Kilohana Lookout includes hundreds of steps, which can be hell on your knees.

Pihea, Alaka'i Swamp & Kawailoi Streams Trails

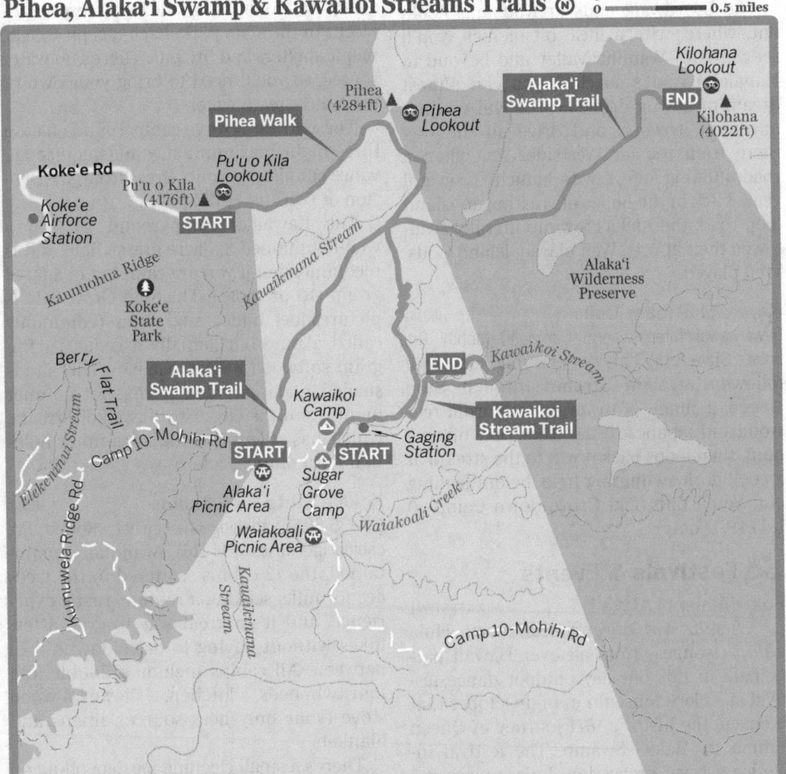

Alaka'i Swamp Trail HIKING
(www.hawaiistateparks.org) The Alaka'i Swamp trailhead (7 miles round-trip) begins on a ridge above Sugi Grove on Camp 10–Mohihi Rd. While this trailhead covers less steep terrain than the beginning of the Pihea trailhead, you will need a 4WD to get there, as well as the ability to follow a map along an unmarked dirt road.

Park in the clearing at the trailhead; the trail begins as a wide grassy path for roughly 0.5 miles to where the boardwalk begins and continues through small bogs and intermittent forests until you reach the Alaka'i Crossing, where the Pihea and Alaka'i Swamp trails intersect. Continuing straight through the crossing, the boardwalk becomes a series of steep steps to the Kawaikoi Stream and a steep series of switchbacks up the other side. You'll need to traverse a shallower second valley before the boardwalk becomes relatively flat, continuing through the almost otherworldly terrain of knee-high trees and tiny endemic carnivorous plants.

The boardwalk ends at Kilohana Lookout, where, with a little bit of luck, you'll see views of Wainiha Valley and beyond to Hanalei Bay. It's so close you can almost dream of having drinks at the Nui without having to traverse and drive all the way there from the far Westside. Yet, when a road-building effort was launched several years back in the hopes of creating an island loop road, the Alaka'i Swamp literally swallowed their efforts. Well played, Island Gods. Well played.

Kawaikoi Stream Trail HIKING
(www.hawaiistateparks.org; Camp 10–Mohihi Rd, Koke'e State Park) This easy 1.8-mile loop trail follows **Kawaikoi Stream** through **Sugi Grove**, a clutch of towering California redwood and Japanese cedar trees, rises up on a bluff, then loops back down to the stream at a cool, dark swimming hole, before leading out. You'll find Sugi Grove down Camp 10 Rd (4WD only).

Festivals & Events

Eo e Emalani I Alaka'i HULA FESTIVAL
(☎335-9975; www.kokee.org/details.html) Hula *halau* (troupes) from all over Hawaii participate in this one-day outdoor dance festival at Koke'e Museum in mid-October that reenacts the historic 1871 journey of Queen Emma to Alaka'i Swamp. The festival includes a royal procession, hula, music and crafts.

Sleeping & Eating

Even though it's Hawaii, don't be fooled into thinking you'll be warm all the time. Koke'e campgrounds are at an elevation of almost 4000ft and nights are cold. Take a sleeping bag, waterproof jacket, change of warm clothing, extra socks and hiking shoes (instead of sneakers).

Koke'e State Park Campground CAMPGROUND
(Koke'e Rd, Koke'e State Park) FREE The most accessible camping area is north of the meadow, just a few minutes' walk from Koke'e Lodge. The campsites sit in a grassy area beside the woods (perfect for laying out a blanket and taking a nap), along with picnic tables, drinking water, restrooms and showers.

Kawaikoi & Sugi Grove CAMPGROUND
(Camp 10–Mohihi Rd) FREE Further off the main track, these campgrounds are about 4 miles east of Koke'e Lodge, off the 4WD-only Camp 10–Mohihi Rd in the forest reserve adjacent to the state park. Each has pit toilets, picnic shelters and fire pits. There's no water source, so you'll need to bring your own or treat the stream water.

These forest-reserve campgrounds have a three-night maximum stay and require advance camping permits (free) from the Division of Forestry & Wildlife.

The Kawaikoi campground sits on a well-maintained 3.5-acre grassy field and is recommended if you are camping in a large group (10 or more). The Sugi Grove site is picturesque, under sugi trees (commonly called a pine but actually a cedar), a fragrant softwood native to Japan. This site is shaded, making it ideal during hot summer months, and is closer to Kawaikoi Stream, which has a few inviting swimming holes that local families adore.

Koke'e State Park Cabins CABIN $
(☎335-6061; thelodge@kokee.net; Koke'e Rd; cabins incl taxes $94-116) Minimally maintained, the 12 cabins scattered in the trees are for folks seeking a remote, rustic experience, and it's a great way to grab a few hikes without having to drive downhill in between. All cabins include a double and four twin beds, a kitchen, a shower, a wood stove (your only heat source), linens and blankets.

There's a small cleaning fee depending on length of stay. If you arrive after 4pm, when the lodge office closes, staff will leave your keys in an envelope with a map on the porch.

YWCA Camp Sloggett CAMPGROUND, CABIN **$**
(☎245-5959; www.campingkauai.com; campsites & dm per person $15, cabin Mon-Thu $125, Fri-Sun $150) Choose either a cabin or bunkhouse, or camp on the grass. The cabin has a king bed, full kitchen, a bathroom and a wood-burning fireplace, while the bunker has a kitchenette, two bathrooms and a fire pit. You provide the sleeping bags and towels. To tent camp, no reservations are needed.

To get here hang a right from Koke'e Rd, just past the lodge, at the YWCA sign and follow that dirt road for approximately a half mile.

Koke'e Lodge DINER **$**
(☎335-6061; Koke'e Rd; snacks $3-7; ⏰9am-2:30pm) This restaurant's one and only strong point is that it exists. But that goes a long way up in Koke'e, where you're a 30-minute drive away from all other options. Expect cereal, diner food and a gift shop with souvenirs and a small assortment of sundries for sale. But no dinner.

ℹ Information

Remember, the nearest place for provisions and gas is Waimea, 15 miles away. Should you need it, a **NASA Station**, a mile south down the road from the museum and lodge, has the closest cellular phone signal.

Koke'e Museum (☎335-9975; www.kokee.org; Koke'e Rd) Sells inexpensive trail maps ($2) and provides basic information on trail conditions; you can also call them for real-time mountain weather reports.

PAPAHĀNAUMOKUĀKEA MARINE NATIONAL MONUMENT

In a ground-breaking move, the Northwestern Hawaiian Islands (NWHI) became the USA's first Marine National Monument in 2006. Encompassing almost 140,000 sq miles, it's the largest protected marine area in the world and the USA's first Unesco World Heritage site designated for both natural and cultural reasons.

The NWHI begin more than 100 miles northwest of Kaua'i and stretch for 1200 miles. They're grouped into 10 island clusters, which contain atolls (low sandy islands formed on top of coral reefs) and some single-rock islands. From east to west, the clusters are Nihoa Island, Mokumanamana (Necker Island), French Frigate Shoals, Gardner Pinnacles, Maro Reef, Laysan Island, Lisianski Island, Pearl and Hermes Atoll, Midway Atoll and Kure Atoll.

The total land area of the NWHI is less than 5 sq miles. Human history on the islands extends back to when the first Polynesian voyagers arrived in the Hawaiian archipelago (Papahānaumokuākea is the Hawaiian name for 'earth mother'). In modern times, the most famous place has been Midway Atoll; it's currently the only island open to visitors.

Preserving an Ecological Balance

The NWHI contain the USA's largest and healthiest coral-reef system, home to 7000 marine species. Half of the fish species and a quarter of all species found here are endemic to Hawaii, with new ones discovered on every scientific voyage. This is a rare 'top predator-dominated ecosystem,' in which sharks, groupers, jacks and others make up over 54% of the biomass (which is three times greater than in the main Hawaiian Islands). The NWHI also support more than 14 million tropical seabirds, and they are the primary breeding ground for endangered green sea turtles and Hawaiian monk seals.

However, the islands are not pristine. Ocean currents bring over 50 tons of debris to the islands annually, and cleanups have removed over 700 tons of entangled fishing nets, plastic bottles and trash so far.

Today, the monument is jointly managed by the National Oceanic & Atmospheric Administration (NOAA), the US Fish & Wildlife Service (USFWS) and the state. The monument's 15-year management plan has raised concerns among some Native Hawaiians and environmental groups such as the Sierra Club. The plan exempts from its regulations the US military (which conducts missile tests and navy training exercises in the area) and allows for increasing visits to Midway and trips for scientific research – all of which could damage areas the monument is charged with preserving.

Nihoa & Mokumanamana

Nihoa and Mokumanamana, the two tiny islands closest to Kaua'i, were home to Native Hawaiians from around AD 1000 to 1700. More than 135 archaeological sites have been identified, including temple platforms, house sites, agricultural terraces, burial caves and carved stone images. As many as 175 people may have once lived on Nihoa and paddled over to Mokumanamana for religious ceremonies.

That anyone could live at all on these rocks is remarkable. Nihoa is only 1 sq km in size, and Mokumanamana is one-sixth that size. Nihoa juts from the sea steeply, like a broken tooth; it's the tallest among the NMHI, with 900ft sea cliffs. Two endangered endemic land birds live on Nihoa. The Nihoa finch, which, like the Laysan finch, is a raider of other birds' eggs, has a population of a few thousand. The Nihoa millerbird, related to the Old World warbler family, numbers fewer than 700.

French Frigate Shoals

Surrounded by over 230,000 acres of coral reef, the French Frigate Shoals contains the monument's greatest variety of coral. It's also where most of Hawaii's green sea turtles and Hawaiian monk seals breed. The 67-acre reef forms a classic comma-shaped atoll on top of an eroded volcano, in the center of which 120ft-high La Pérouse Pinnacle rises like a ship. Small, sandy Tern Island is dominated by an airfield, which was built as a refueling stop during WWII. Today, Tern Island has a USFWS field station housing scientific researchers and volunteers.

Laysan Island

Not quite 1.5 sq miles, Laysan is the second-biggest of the NWHI. The grassy island has the most bird species in the monument, and to see the huge flocks of Laysan albatross, shearwaters and curlews – plus the endemic Laysan duck chasing brine flies around a super-salty inland lake – you'd never know how close this island came to becoming a barren wasteland.

In the late 19th century, humans began frequenting Laysan to mine guano (bird droppings) to use as fertilizer. Poachers also killed hundreds of thousands of albatross for their feathers (to adorn hats) and took eggs for albumen, a substance used in photo processing. Albatross lay just one egg a year, so poaching could destroy an entire year's hatch.

Traders also built structures and brought pack mules and, oddly enough, rabbits for food. The rabbits ran loose and multiplied, and within 20 years their nibbling extirpated 22 of the island's 26 endemic plant species. Without plants, at least three endemic land birds – the Laysan rail, Laysan honeycreeper and Laysan millerbird – became extinct. Laysan finches and the last dozen Laysan ducks seemed doomed to follow.

In 1909, public outcry led President Theodore Roosevelt to create the Hawaiian Islands Bird Reservation, and the NWHI have been under some kind of protection ever since. By 1923 every last rabbit was removed from Laysan, and ecological rehabilitation began. With weed-abatement assistance, endemic plant life recovered, and so did the birds. The Laysan finch is again common, and the Laysan duck numbers about 600 (another small population has been established on Midway).

Nearly the same sequence of events unfolded on nearby Lisianski Island and, together, these islands are a stunning success story.

Midway Atoll

Midway Atoll was an important naval air station during WWII. It's best known as the site of a pivotal battle in June 1942, when US forces surprised an attacking Japanese fleet and defeated it. This victory is credited with turning the tide in the war's Pacific theater. Midway later became a staging point for Cold War air patrols and an underwater listening post to spy on Soviet submarines.

By 1996 the military transferred jurisdiction to the USFWS. Before leaving, it conducted an extensive clean-up program to remove debris, environmental contaminants, rats and non-native plants. Midway was then developed for tourism: barracks became hotel rooms, the mess hall a cafeteria and a beachfront restaurant and bar were added. A gym, movie theater, bowling alley and library were part of the original military facility. On Sand and Eastern Islands, various military structures have been designated National Historical Landmarks.

The ecological highlight at Midway is the more than two million seabirds that nest here, including the world's largest colony of Laysan albatross, which are so thick between November and July that they virtually blanket the ground. Midway's coral reefs are unusually rich and are frequented by Hawaiian monk seals and green sea turtles.

Visiting, Volunteering & Learning More

All tourist facilities on Midway Islands are managed by the **US Fish & Wildlife Service** (USFWS; www.fws.gov/midway), which issues permits only to organized groups. Check the website for a current list of tour operators and book your trip as far in advance as possible. You can also apply for long-term volunteer opportunities at **Tern Island Field Station** (www.fws.gov/hawaiianislands/getinvolved.html).

If you can't make the trip to the NWHI in person, you can virtually visit **Papahānaumokuākea Marine National Monument** (www.papahanaumokuakea.gov) and Midway Atoll's **Sand Island** (www.fws.gov/midway/tour.html) online, or drop by Hilo's Mokupapapa Discovery Center (p270) on the Big Island. Another excellent website is run by the **Northwestern Hawaiian Islands Multi-Agency Education Project** (www.hawaiianatolls.org). Or read Pamela Frierson's first-hand reports in *The Last Atoll: Exploring Hawai'i's Endangered Ecosystems*.

Kayakers paddling along the Na Pali Coast, Kaua'i (p536)

Understand Hawaii

Hawaii Today

The state motto, *Ua Mau ke Ea o ka 'Aina i Ka Pono* ('The life of the land is perpetuated in righteousness'), is not just an idealistic catchphrase. Hawaii's modern sovereignty movement, sustainability initiatives and antidevelopment activism are all rooted in *aloha 'aina* (literally, love and respect for the land), a traditional Hawaiian value deeply felt by almost everyone who lives here. This belief has nurtured widespread cooperation and commitment to overcoming the 21st-century challenges facing these ancient islands today.

Best in Print

Shark Dialogues (1995) Kiana Davenport's multigenerational family saga, stretching from ancient times into the plantation era.
Wild Meat & the Bully Burgers (1996) Lois-Ann Yamanaka's short-story novel about growing up local and speaking Hawaiian pidgin.
Hotel Honolulu (2001) Paul Theroux' satirical tale about a washed-up writer managing a Waikiki hotel.
'Olelo Noe'au (1997) *Kupuna* (elder) Mary Kawena Pukui's bilingual collection of Hawaiian proverbs and sayings, illustrated by Dietrich Varez.

Best on Film

The Descendants (2011) Contemporary island life, with all of its heartaches and blessings.
From Here to Eternity (1953) Classic WWII-era drama leading up to the Pearl Harbor attack.
Blue Crush (2002) Cheesy, but a local favorite for its surf cinematography.
50 First Dates (2004) Silly rom-com shot at gorgeous Windward O'ahu beaches.
Blue Hawaii (1961) Romp poolside with a ukulele-playing Elvis during Hawaii's tiki-tacky tourism boom.

Staying Hawaiian

Evolving from ancient Polynesian traditions, Hawaiian culture was attacked and suppressed in the two centuries after first Western contact with Captain Cook in 1778. But beginning with the 1970s Hawaiian Renaissance, a rebirth of Native Hawaiian cultural and artistic traditions, as well as the Hawaiian language, has taken hold. For more than three decades now there have been Hawaiian-language immersion programs in public schools, and Hawaiian culture–focused charter schools are popping up all over the place.

Today Hawaiian culture is about much more than just melodic place names and luau shows. Traditional arts like *lauhala* (pandanus leaf) weaving, *kapa* (pounded-bark cloth) making, and gourd and wood carving are all experiencing a revival. Healing arts like *lomilomi* ('loving touch') massage and *la'au lapa'au* (plant medicine) are being shared with students both within and beyond the Native Hawaiian community. Ancient heiau (temples) and fishponds are being restored, native forests replanted and endangered birds bred and released into the wild.

Being Hawaiian remains an important part of the identity of the islands, reflected in ways both large and small – in spontaneous hula at a concert, an *oli* (chant) sung before important occasions such as political inaugurations or development ground-breakings, the *lomilomi* treatment you receive at a spa, or listening to the word of the day in *'olelo Hawai'i* (the Hawaiian language) on local radio stations.

Although few island residents can agree on what shape the fragmented Native Hawaiian sovereignty movement should take, or even if it should exist at all, its grassroots political activism has achieved tangible results. Decades of protests and a federal lawsuit filed by sovereignty activists finally pressured the US military into returning the island of Kaho'olawe, which it had used for bombing practice since WWII, to the state in 1994. Sovereignty activists also helped spur the US federal government's official 1993 apology for its role in the unjust overthrow of the Kingdom of Hawai'i a century before.

Seeking Sustainability

Before the 19th-century arrival of foreign whalers, traders and Christian missionaries, the population of the Hawaiian Islands was somewhere between 200,000 and a million people – almost what it is today. It's mind-boggling to think about how all of those ancient people were sustainably supported using natural resource management practices and without metal or technology. As Hawaii's population swells – which it did by almost 200,000 between 2000 and 2012 – new housing developments sprawl, stressing the state's water resources, transportation systems, public schools and landfills.

Hawaii is less stable today than it was before first Western contact. That's because the islands have become wholly dependent on the outside world, meaning the US mainland and also foreign countries. Fully 80% of Hawaii's consumer goods, including up to a staggering 90% of its food, are imported. And despite being in a place blessed with a wealth of natural energy sources, 95% of Hawaii's power still comes from carbon-based fuels. In fact, the state spends more than $5 billion a year on oil and coal, all of it imported. Public transportation is limited or nonexistent on all islands except O'ahu, resulting in an average of one registered motor vehicle for each man, woman and child living here.

The future is far from decided, however. Hawaii is striving to become a pioneer in clean energy. In 2008 the Hawaii Clean Energy Initiative (HCEI) set the statewide goal of having a 70% self-sufficient energy economy by 2030. Public government and private industry are pursuing every renewable and clean energy option available – for example, wind farms and wave power on Maui, geothermal and biomass on the Big Island, algae-based biofuels and ocean thermal energy conversion (OTEC) on O'ahu and Kaua'i, and solar power and electric cars on Lana'i. In addition the state is modernizing its electricity grid and embarking on its most ambitious – and politically controversial – project yet: building a $5 billion light-rail system for Honolulu.

Diversifying the Economy

Hawaii is dependent on the outside world not only for its food and fuel, but for nearly its entire economy. After losing sugar and pineapple plantations to cheap imports from the developing world, Hawaii's eggs were pretty much left in one economic basket: tourism. When the global recession tanked the national economy in 2008, Hawaii's tourism went with

POPULATION: **1.4 MILLION**

GROSS STATE PRODUCT: **$68.9 BILLION**

MEDIAN ANNUAL HOUSEHOLD INCOME: **$67,116**

UNEMPLOYMENT: **5.2%**

if Hawaii were 100 people

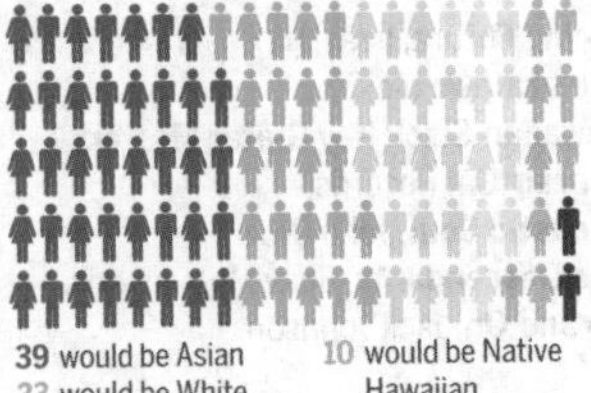

39 would be Asian
23 would be White
17 would be Mixed Race
10 would be Native Hawaiian
9 would be Latino
2 would be Black

belief systems

(% of population)

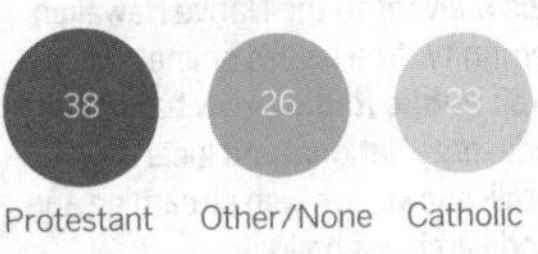

9 Buddhist
3 Mormon
1 Jewish

population per sq mile

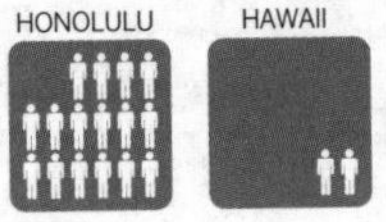

≈ 100 people

Best on TV

Hawaii Five-0 Detective Steve McGarrett redux, sans the suit and tie, in a contemporary crime drama shot entirely on O'ahu.

Magnum, PI Dated as it is, locals still watch it (if only to pick out the locations).

Rap's Hawai'i Rap Reiplinger was a local comedy icon in the '70s – his skit 'Room Service' is timeless.

Frank De Lima Pidgin-speaking comic whose parody songs and commercials still crack locals up – just search YouTube.

Best Music Albums

Facing Future, Israel (Iz) Kamakawiwo'ole

Hawaiian Slack Key Guitar Masters, Dancing Cat Records

Acoustic Soul, John Cruz

The Descendants, Sony Masterworks

On and On, Jack Johnson

Best Media

Honolulu Star-Advertiser (www.staradvertiser.com) Daily statewide newspaper covering breaking news, politics, sports, travel and more.

Ka Wai Ola (www.oha.org/kwo) Office of Hawaiian Affairs' newspaper on topics relevant to the Native Hawaiian community; free issues online.

Hawaii Public Radio (www.hawaiipublicradio.org) National and local news and talk shows; live web streaming and episode archives online.

OC16 (www.oc16.tv) Oceanic Cable channel 16 – 24-hour, all-local programming.

it. By year's end state revenue shortfalls soared to nearly $2 billion and then-governor Linda Lingle imposed extremely harsh budget cuts, including furloughs for state employees and shortened schedules for public schools.

Since 2011, Hawaii's economy has rebounded. In terms of statistical measures such as unemployment and outstanding debt, Hawaii is now in better shape than some US mainland states that have long been economic powerhouses. Current governor Neil Abercrombie intends to continue the state's push toward energy independence and food security (aka 'food sovereignty') by supporting small farmers and encouraging consumers to 'buy local' to mitigate Hawaii's dependency on imports and also tourism.

Nevertheless, tourism will likely be Hawaii's bread and butter for the foreseeable future, even though it comes at a price. Almost eight million visitors land on the islands each year – more than five times the resident population – overcrowding roads and beaches and driving up the price of real estate, not to mention fueling community resistance to new resort and housing developments. Some locals feel inundated by Hawaii's 'unofficial' residents, including part-time retirees and military personnel. Feelings are often mixed toward both tourism and the continued US military presence.

Many of those who live here acknowledge that Hawaii's current economic model is both unstable and unsustainable. Today the islands stand at a crossroads – Hawaii can either suffer the side effects of its dependence on tourism, imported goods and fossil fuels, or boldly move toward securing a more homegrown future.

History

Hawaii's discovery and colonization is one of humanity's great epic tales, starting with ancient Polynesians who found their way to these tiny islands – the world's most isolated – in the midst of Earth's largest ocean. Almost a millennium passed before Western explorers, whalers, missionaries and entrepreneurs arrived on ships. In the tumultuous 19th century, a melting pot of global immigrants came to work on Hawaii's plantations before the kingdom founded by Kamehameha the Great was overthrown, making way for US annexation.

Polynesian Voyagers

To ancient Polynesians, the Pacific Ocean was a passageway, not a barrier, and the islands it contained were connected, not isolated. Between AD 300 and 600, they made their longest journey yet and discovered the Hawaiian Islands. This would mark the northern reach of their migrations, which were so astounding that Captain Cook – the first Western explorer to take their full measure – could not conceive of how they did it, settling 'every quarter of the Pacific Ocean' and becoming 'by far the most extensive nation upon earth.'

Although the discovery of Hawaii may have been accidental, subsequent journeys were not. Polynesians were highly skilled seafarers, navigating over thousands of miles of open ocean without maps, and with only the sun, stars, wind and waves to guide them. In double-hulled wooden canoes, they imported to the islands their religious beliefs, social structures and over two dozen food plants and domestic animals. What they didn't possess is equally remarkable: no metals, no wheels, no alphabet or written language, and no clay to make pottery.

Almost nothing is known about the first wave of Polynesians (likely from the Marquesas Islands) who settled Hawai'i, except that the archaeological record shows they were here. A second wave of Polynesians from the Tahitian Islands began arriving around AD 1000, and they conquered the first peoples and obliterated nearly all traces of their history and culture. Later Hawaiian legends of the *menehune* – an ancient race of little

The paintings of acclaimed artist, historian and Polynesian Voyaging Society co-founder Herb Kawainui Kane give a glimpse into Hawaii's mythic and historical past, including in his illustrated book *Voyagers* (2005). Several dozen of his artworks are on display at King Kamehameha's Kona Beach Hotel on the Big Island.

TIMELINE

40–30 million BC

The first Hawaiian island, Kure, rises from the sea, appearing where the Big Island is today. Borne by wind, wing and wave, plants, insects and birds colonize the new land.

AD 300–600

The first wave of Polynesians, most likely from the Marquesas Islands, voyage by canoe to the Hawaiian Islands – a half-century before Vikings leave Scandinavia to plunder Europe.

1000–1300

Sailing from Tahiti, a second wave of Polynesians arrives. Their tools are made of stone, shells and bone, and they bring taro, sweet potato, sugarcane, coconut, chickens, pigs and dogs.

people who mysteriously built temples and great stoneworks overnight – may refer to these original inhabitants.

Ancient Hawai'i

When for unknown reasons trans-Pacific voyages from Polynesia stopped around AD 1300, ancient Hawaiian culture kept evolving in isolation retaining a family resemblance to cultures found throughout Polynesia. Hawaiian society was highly stratified, ruled by a chiefly class called *ali'i* whose power derived from their ancestry: they were believed to be descended from the gods. In ancient Hawai'i, clan loyalty trumped individuality, elaborate traditions of gifting and feasting conferred prestige, and a pantheon of shape-shifting gods animated the natural world.

Several ranks of *ali'i* ruled each island, and life was marked by frequent warfare as they jockeyed for power. The largest geopolitical division was the *mokupuni* (island), presided over by a member of the *ali'i*

HAWAII'S WAYFARING TRADITIONS REBORN

In 1976, a double-hulled wooden canoe and her crew set off from O'ahu's Windward Coast, aiming to recreate the journey of Hawaii's first human settlers and do what no one had done in over 600 years – sail 2400 miles to Tahiti without benefit of radar, compass, satellites or sextant. Launched by the Polynesian Voyaging Society, this modern reproduction of an ancient Hawaiian long-distance seafaring canoe was named *Hokule'a* ('Star of Gladness').

The canoe's Micronesian navigator, Mau Piailug, still knew the art of traditional Polynesian wayfaring at a time when such knowledge had been lost to Hawaiian culture. He knew how to use horizon or zenith stars – those that always rose over known islands – as a guide, then evaluate currents, winds, landmarks and time in a complex system of dead reckoning to stay on course. In the mind's eye, the trick is to hold the canoe still in relation to the stars while the island sails toward you.

Academic skeptics had long questioned whether Hawaii's early settlers really were capable of journeying back and forth across such vast, empty ocean. After 33 days at sea, the original crew of the *Hokule'a* proved those so-called experts wrong by reaching its destination, where it was greeted by 20,000 Tahitians. This historic achievement helped spark a revival of interest in Hawaii's Polynesian cultural heritage.

Since its 1976 voyage, the *Hokule'a* has served as a floating living-history classroom. The canoe has also made 10 more trans-oceanic voyages, sailing throughout Polynesia and to the US mainland, Canada, Micronesia and Japan. Its planned three-year voyage to circumnavigate the globe, expected to begin in mid-2013, will visit over 26 countries and travel more than 45,000 nautical miles, ending back in Hawaii in 2016. Learn more at http://hokulea.org.

1778–9

Captain Cook, the first foreigner known to reach the islands, visits Hawai'i twice. After being warmly welcomed, Cook loses his temper over a stolen boat and is killed by Hawaiians.

ROB REICHENFELD / GETTY IMAGES ©

➡ Statue of Captain Cook

1810

Kamehameha the Great negotiates peacefully to take control of Kaua'i, uniting all the islands in one kingdom for the first time. He establishes his royal court at Lahaina on Maui.

1819

Kamehameha I dies 'in the faith of his fathers.' A few months later, his son, the new king Liholiho, breaks the kapu (taboo) on eating with women, dramatically violating the Hawaiian religion.

nui (kingly class). Each island was further divided into *moku,* wedge-shaped areas of land running from the ridge of the mountains to the sea. Smaller, similarly wedge-shaped *ahupua'a* comprised each *moku*; they were mostly self-sustaining and had local chiefs.

Ranking just below *ali'i,* the kahuna (experts or masters) included priests, healers and skilled craftspeople – canoe makers, navigators etc. Also beneath the chiefs were the *konohiki,* who supervised natural resource management on land and sea within an *ahupua'a* and collected taxes from the *maka'ainana* (commoners), who did most of the physical labor. Occupying the lowest tier was a small class of outcasts or untouchables called *kaua,* who were a source of *pua'a waewae loloa* – 'long-legged pigs,' a euphemism for human sacrificial victims.

A culture of mutuality and reciprocity infused what was essentially a feudal agricultural society. Chiefs were custodians of their people, and humans custodians of nature, all of which was sacred – the living expression of mana (spiritual essence). Everyone played a part through work and ritual to maintain the health of the community and its comity with the gods. Ancient Hawaiians also developed rich traditions in art, music, dance, sport and competition.

Wanna know more? The community website www.hawaiihistory.org offers an interactive timeline of Hawaii's history and essays delving into every aspect of ancient Hawaiian culture, with evocative images and lots of links.

Captain Cook & First Western Contact

Starting in 1778, everything changed. It was the archetypal clash of civilizations: the British Empire, the most technologically advanced culture on the planet, sent an explorer on a mission. The Hawai'i he stumbled upon was, to his eyes, a place inhabited by heathens stuck in prehistoric times; their worship of pagan gods and human sacrifice seemed anathema to the Christian world view. But Hawai'i's geographic position and wealth of natural resources ensured these islands would quickly become a target of the West's civilizing impulse.

Captain James Cook had spent a decade traversing the Pacific over the course of three voyages. He sought the fabled 'Northwest Passage' linking the Pacific and Atlantic, but his were also voyages of discovery. He sailed with a complement of scientists and artists to document what they found. On the third voyage in 1778, and quite by accident, Cook sailed into the main Hawaiian Island chain. Ending nearly half a millennium of isolation, his arrival irrevocably altered the course of Hawaiian history.

Cook dropped anchor off O'ahu and, as he had elsewhere in the Pacific, bartered with the indigenous people for fresh water and food. While Cook was already familiar with Polynesians, Hawaiians knew nothing of Europeans, nor of the metal, guns and diseases their ships carried. Hawaiians thought of the natural world inseparable from the spiritual realm, while Cook embodied Enlightenment philosophy, in which God ruled in heaven and only humans walked the earth.

Restored Temples

- *Pu'uhonua o Honaunau National Historical Park (p214), Hawai'i the Big Island*
- *Pi'ilanihale Heiau (p402), Maui*
- *Ahu'ena Heiau (p179), Hawai'i the Big Island*
- *Kane'aki Heiau (p169), O'ahu*

1820

The first Christian missionaries arrive in Hawai'i. King Liholiho eventually allows missionary leader Hiram Bingham to establish the mission's headquarters in Honolulu.

1826

Missionaries formulate a 12-letter alphabet (plus glottal stop) for the Hawaiian language and set up the first printing press; it's said that Queen Ka'ahumanu learned to read in five days.

1828

Missionary Sam Ruggles plants the first coffee tree in the Kona district of the Big Island as a garden ornamental. Coffee doesn't succeed as a commercial crop until the 1840s.

1830

To control destructive herds of feral cattle (first introduced by British sea captain George Vancouver), Hawaiians recruit Spanish-Mexican cowboys, dubbed *paniolo,* who bring their guitars along with them.

When Cook returned to the islands almost a year later, he sailed around before eventually anchoring at Kealakekua Bay on the Big Island. Cook's ships were greeted by a thousand canoes, and Hawaiian chiefs and priests honored him with rituals and deference. Cook had landed at an auspicious time during the makahiki, a time of festival and celebration in honor of the god Lono, and some have theorized that the Hawaiians mistook Cook for the god. The Hawaiians were so unrelentingly gracious, in fact, that Cook and his men felt safe to move about unarmed.

Cook set sail some weeks later, but storms forced him to turn back. The mood in Kealakekua had changed, however. The makahiki had ended: no canoes met him and suspicion replaced welcome. A small series of minor conflicts provoked Cook into leading an armed party ashore to capture local chief Kalaniopu'u. When the Englishmen disembarked they were surrounded by angry Hawaiians. In an uncharacteristic fit of pique, Cook shot and killed a Hawaiian man. The Hawaiians immediately mobbed Cook, killing him on February 14, 1779.

CAPTAIN COOK

In *Blue Latitudes: Boldly Going Where Captain Cook Has Gone Before*, Tony Horwitz examines the controversial legacy of Captain Cook's South Seas voyages, weaving amusing real-life adventure tales together with bittersweet oral history.

Reign of Kamehameha the Great

In the years following Cook's death, a steady number of exploring and trading ships sought out the Kingdom of Hawai'i as a resupply spot. With the discovery of a deepwater anchorage in Honolulu Harbor in 1794, Hawai'i became the new darling of trans-Pacific commerce, first in the fur trade involving China, New England and the Pacific Northwest. The main commodity in the islands – salt – happened to be useful for curing hides. For Hawaiian chiefs, the main items of interest were firearms, which the Europeans willingly traded.

Bolstered with muskets and cannons, Kamehameha, a chief from the Big Island, began a campaign in 1790 to conquer all of the Hawaiian Islands. Other chiefs had tried and failed, but Kamehameha had Western guns; not only that, he was prophesied to succeed and possessed an unyielding determination and exceptional personal charisma. Within five years he united – bloodily – the main islands apart from Kaua'i (which eventually joined peacefully). The dramatic final skirmish in his campaign, the Battle of Nu'uanu, took place on O'ahu in 1795.

Kamehameha was a singular figure who reigned over the most peaceful era in Hawaiian history. A shrewd politician, he configured multi-island governance to mute competition among *ali'i*. A savvy businessman, he created a profitable monopoly on the sandalwood trade in 1810 while protecting the trees from overharvesting. He personally worked taro patches as an example to his people, and his most famous decree – Kanawai Mamalahoe, or 'Law of the Splintered Paddle' – established a kapu to protect travelers from harm.

1831

Lahainaluna Seminary, the first secondary school west of the Rocky Mountains, opens in Lahaina; its press later prints Hawai'i's first newspaper and first paper currency.

1843

The Kingdom of Hawai'i's only foreign invasion occurs when British naval officer George Paulet seizes O'ahu for five months; his illegal actions are disavowed by the British government.

1845

Kamehameha III, the first Hawaiian king to convert to Christianity, moves the capital of his kingdom from Lahaina on Maui to Honolulu. Mail service from San Francisco begins.

1846

At the height of the Pacific whaling era, a record 736 whaling ships stop over in the islands. Four of Hawai'i's 'Big Five' sugar plantation companies get their start supplying whalers.

Most importantly, Kamehameha I absorbed growing foreign influences while fastidiously honoring Hawai'i's indigenous customs. He did the latter even despite widespread doubts among his people about the justice of Hawaii's kapu system and traditional Hawaiian ideas about a divine social hierarchy. When Kamehameha died in 1819, he left the question of how to resolve these troubling issues to his son and heir, 22-year-old Liholiho. Within the year, Liholiho had broken with the indigenous religion in one sweeping, stunning act of repudiation.

Breaking Kapu & Destroying the Temples

One purpose of the kapu system Kamehameha I upheld was to preserve mana, or spiritual power. Mana could be strong or weak, won or lost; it expressed itself in one's talents and the success of a harvest or battle.The kapu system kept *ali'i* from mingling with commoners and men from eating with women. It also kept women from eating pork or entering *luakini heiau* (sacrificial temples). Chiefs could declare temporary kapu to help preserve their mana.

However, foreigners arriving in Hawai'i weren't accountable to the kapu system, and lesser *ali'i* saw they could possess power without following its dictates. Women saw that breaking kapu – for example, by dining with sailors – didn't incur the gods' wrath. Kamehameha the Great's most powerful wife, Ka'ahumanu, chafed under the kapu, as it kept women from becoming leaders equal to men. Eventually even Hawai'i's highest-ranking kahuna (priest), Hewahewa, couldn't defend the system.

Soon after Kamehameha's death, Hewahewa conspired with Kamehameha's favorite wife Ka'ahumanu, who ruled as *kahuna nui* (co-regent) with her stepson Liholiho, and Keopulani, who possessed more mana than any of Kamehameha's other royal wives. The trio arranged a feast where Liholiho would eat with women, thereby breaking the kapu. This act – effectively ending Hawai'i's religion – was nearly beyond the young king. He delayed for months, and drank himself into a stupor the day before.

Then to the shock of the gathered *ali'i* at the feast, Liholiho helped himself to food at the women's table. Hewahewa, signaling his approval, noted that the gods could not survive without kapu. 'Then let them perish with it!' Liholiho is said to have cried. For months afterward, Ka'ahumanu and others set fire to the temples and destroyed the *ki'i* (deity images). Many Hawaiians were relieved to be free from kapu, but some continued to venerate the old gods and secretly preserved *ki'i*.

Of Hawai'i's eight ruling monarchs, only King Kamehameha I begat children who eventually inherited the throne. His dynasty ended less than a century after it began with the death of Kamehameha V in 1872.

In *Legends and Myths of Hawaii*, King David Kalakaua (1836–91) captures the shimmering nature of ancient Hawaiian storytelling by seamlessly mixing history (of Kamehameha, Captain Cook, the burning of the temples) with living mythology.

Missionaries & Whalers Come Ashore

After Cook's expedition sailed back to Britain, news of his 'discovery' of Hawai'i soon spread throughout Europe and the Americas, opening the floodgates to seafaring explorers and traders. By the 1820s, whaling ships

1848

King Kamehameha III institutes the Great Mahele, a land redistribution act. Two years later, further legislation allows commoners and foreigners to own land in Hawai'i for the first time.

1852

The first indentured sugar-plantation laborers arrive from China; most are single men who, upon completing their contracts, often chose to stay in Hawai'i, starting businesses and families.

1868

The first Japanese contract laborers arrive to work the sugar plantations. The eruption of Mauna Loa volcano on the Big Island causes a magnitude-8 earthquake, Hawai'i's largest ever.

1873

A Belgian Catholic priest, Father Damien, arrives at Moloka'i's leprosy colony. He stays for 16 years, dying of leprosy (now called Hansen's disease) in 1889. He is sainted in 2009.

began pulling into Hawai'i's harbors for fresh water and food, supplies, liquor and women. To meet their needs, ever more shops, taverns and brothels sprang up around busy ports including at Honolulu on O'ahu, Lahaina on Maui and Koloa on Kaua'i. By the 1840s, the islands had become the unofficial whaling capital of the Pacific.

To the ire of 'dirty-devil' whalers, Hawai'i's first Christian missionary ship sailed into Honolulu's harbor on April 14, 1820, carrying staunch Calvinists who were set on saving the Hawaiians from their 'heathen ways.' Their timing could not have been more opportune, as Hawai'i's traditional religion had been abolished the year before, leaving Hawaiians with a spiritual vacuum. Both missionaries and the whalers hailed from New England, but soon were at odds: missionaries were intent on saving souls, while to many sailors there was 'no God west of the Horn.' Sailors repeatedly clashed, sometimes violently, with the missionaries, because they enjoyed all the pleasures that the Calvinists censured.

TRAVEL TIME

In the 19th century, New England missionaries needed six months to sail from Boston around Cape Horn to Hawai'i. Early 20th-century Matson steamships embarking from San Francisco took just five days to reach Honolulu.

The missionaries arrived expecting the worst of Hawai'i's indigenous 'pagans,' and in their eyes, that's what they found: public nudity, 'lewd' hula dancing, polygamy, gambling, drunkenness and fornication with sailors. To them, kahuna were witch doctors and Hawaiians hopelessly lazy. Because the missionaries' god was clearly powerful, Christianity attracted converts, notably Queen Ka'ahumanu. But many of these conversions were not deeply felt; Hawaiians often quickly abandoned the church's teachings, reverting to their traditional lifestyles.

The missionaries found one thing, however, that attracted avid, widespread interest: literacy. The missionaries established an alphabet for the Hawaiian language, and with this tool, Hawaiians learned to read with astonishing speed. In their oral culture, Hawaiians were used to prodigious feats of memory, and *ali'i* understood that literacy was a key to accessing Western culture and power. By the mid-1850s, Hawai'i had a higher literacy rate than the USA and supported dozens of Hawaiian-language newspapers.

The Great Mahele: Losing the Land

Amid often conflicting foreign influences, some Hawaiian leaders decided that the only way to survive in a world of more powerful nations was to adopt Western ways and styles of government. Hawai'i's absolute monarchy had previously denied citizens a voice in their government. Traditionally, no Hawaiian ever owned land, but the *ali'i* managed it in stewardship for all. None of this sat well with resident US expats, many of whose grandparents had fought a revolution for the right to vote and to own private property.

Born and raised in Hawai'i after Western contact, King Kamehameha III (Kauikeaouli) struggled to retain traditional Hawaiian society while

1879

King Kalakaua lays the cornerstone for 'Iolani Palace, a lavish, four-story building with an ornate throne room, running water and electric lights. It costs $350,000 and is completed in 1882.

1882

Macadamia trees are imported from Australia to the Big Island by William Purvis, who plants them as an ornamental. The nuts aren't grown commercially in Hawaii till the 1920s.

1884

The first pineapple plants are introduced to Hawai'i by Captain John Kidwell, but the industry doesn't take off until James Dole incorporates his O'ahu pineapple plantation in 1901.

➡ Pineapple harvesters

leveloping a political system better suited to foreign, frequently Ameri-
:an tastes. In 1840 Kauikeaouli promulgated Hawai'i's first constitution, vhich established a constitutional monarchy with limited citizen repre-
sentation. Given an inch, foreigners pressed for a mile, so Kauikeaouli 'ollowed up with a series of revolutionary land reform acts beginning vith the Great Mahele ('Great Division') of 1848.

It was hoped the Great Mahele would create a nation of small free-
ıolder farmers, but instead it was a disaster – for Hawaiians, at least. Confusion reigned over boundaries and surveys. Unused to the concept of private land and sometimes unable to pay the necessary tax, many Hawaiians simply failed to follow through on the paperwork to claim itles to the land they had lived on for generations. Many of those who lid – perhaps feeling that a taro farmer's life wasn't quite the attraction t once was – immediately cashed out, selling their land to eager and acquisitive foreigners.

Many missionaries ended up with sizable tracts of land, and more than a few left the church to devote themselves to their new estates.

DEFYING THE VOLCANO GODDESS

One of Christianity's early champions in the Hawaiian Islands was a chief on the Kona side of the Big Island. Her name was Kap'iolani (not to be confused with Queen Kap'iolani). People living near active Kilauea volcano, many of whom had experienced its deadly 1790 eruption, were less enthusiastic about worshiping the Christian god. They feared that if they failed to propitiate Pele, goddess of volcanoes and fire, the consequences might be dire.

When missionaries toured Kilauea in 1823, Hawaiians were astonished to see them flagrantly violate kapu by exploring the crater and eating *'ohelo* berries (a food reserved for Pele) with impunity. This primed the ground for chief Kapi'olani to challenge Pele directly and to prove that the Christian god was more powerful.

In 1824, the story goes, she walked about 60 miles from her home to the brink of the steaming crater and, dismissing pleas from her people and defying curses from the priests of Pele, descended into the vent at Halema'uma'u. Surrounded by roiling lava, Kapi'olani ate consecrated *'ohelo* berries, read passages from the Bible and threw stones into the volcano without retribution, demonstrating Pele's impotence before the missionaries' god.

The epic scene has become legendary, and it has been the subject of artwork such as Herb Kane's painting *Kapi'olani Defying Pele*. While the story is likely to have been embellished over the years, you can still appreciate how profound Kapi'olani's confidence in the new religion must have been to test the power of a goddess who was all too real for ancient Hawaiians.

1893
On January 17 the Hawaiian monarchy is overthrown by a group of US businessmen supported by military troops. Queen Lili'uokalani acquiesces under protest; not a shot is fired.

1895
Robert Wilcox leads a failed counter-revolution to restore Hawaii's monarchy. The deposed queen, charged with being a co-conspirator, is placed under house arrest at 'Iolani Palace.

1898
On July 7 President McKinley signs the resolution annexing Hawaii as a US territory; this is formalized by the 1900 Hawaiian Organic Act establishing a territorial government.

1900
A fire set to control an outbreak of bubonic plague in Honolulu's Chinatown blazes out of control. Meanwhile, the territory's Hawaiian population drops to its lowest point.

Within 30 to 40 years, despite supposed limits, foreigners owned fully three-quarters of the kingdom, and Hawaiians – who had already relinquished so much of their traditional culture so quickly during the 19th century – lost their sacred connection to the land. As historian Gavan Daws wrote in *Shoal of Time: A History of the Hawaiian Islands*, 'So the great division became the great dispossession.'

King Sugar & the Plantation Era

Ko (sugarcane) arrived in Hawai'i with the early Polynesian settlers. In 1835 Bostonian William Hooper saw a business opportunity to establish Hawaii's first sugar plantation. Hooper persuaded Honolulu investors to put up the money for his venture and then worked out a deal with Kamehameha III to lease agricultural land on Kaua'i. The next order of business was finding an abundant supply of low-cost labor, which was necessary to make sugar plantations profitable.

The natural first choice for plantation workers was Hawaiians, but even when willing, they were not enough. Due to introduced diseases like typhoid, influenza, smallpox and syphilis, the Hawaiian population had steadily and precipitously declined. An estimated 800,000 indigenous people lived on the islands before Western contact, but by 1800, the Hawaiian population had dropped by two-thirds, to around 250,000. By 1860, they numbered fewer than 70,000.

Wealthy plantation owners began to look overseas for a labor supply of immigrants accustomed to working long days in hot weather, and for whom the low wages would seem like an opportunity. In the 1850s, wealthy sugar-plantation owners began recruiting laborers from China, then Japan and Portugal. After annexing Hawaii in 1898, US restrictions on Chinese and Japanese immigration made O'ahu's plantation owners turn to Puerto Rico, Korea and the Philippines for laborers. All of these different immigrant groups, along with the shared pidgin language they developed and the uniquely mixed community created by plantation life, transformed Hawaii into the multicultural, multiethnic society it is today.

During California's Gold Rush and later the US Civil War, sugar exports to the mainland soared, making plantation owners wealthier and more powerful. Five sugar-related holding companies, known as the Big Five, came to dominate all aspects of the industry: Castle & Cooke, Alexander & Baldwin, C Brewer & Co, American Factors, and Theo H Davies & Co. All were run by haole white businessmen, many the sons and grandsons of missionaries, who eventually reached the same conclusion as their forebears: Hawaiians could not be trusted to govern themselves. So, behind closed doors, the Big Five developed plans to relieve Hawaiians of the job.

MOLOKA'I

For more than a century beginning in 1866, Moloka'i's Kalaupapa Peninsula was a brutal, deadly place of involuntary exile for those afflicted with leprosy (now called Hansen's disease). In *The Colony*, John Tayman tells the survivors' stories with dignity, compassion and unflinching honesty.

1909

In Hawaii's first major labor strike, 5000 Japanese plantation workers protest low pay and harsh treatment compared with other ethnic workers. The strike fails, winning no concessions.

1912

Duke Kahanamoku wins gold and silver medals in freestyle swimming at the Stockholm Olympics; he goes on to become an ambassador of surfing around the world.

1916

The US National Park Service is created by Congress; Hawai'i National Park is established, initially encompassing Haleakalā on Maui, and Kilauea and Mauna Loa on the Big Island.

1921

The Hawaiian Homes Commission Act is passed. It sets aside 200,000 acres for homesteading by Hawaiians with 50% or more native blood, granting 99-year leases costing $1 a year.

Downfall of the Merrie Monarch

King Kalakaua, who reigned from 1874 to 1891, fought to restore Hawaiian culture and indigenous pride. He resurrected hula and its attendant arts from near extinction. Along with his fondness for drinking, gambling and partying, it earned him the nickname 'the Merrie Monarch' – much to the dismay of Christian missionaries. Foreign businessmen considered these pastimes to be follies, but worse, Kalakaua was a mercurial decision-maker given to summarily replacing his entire cabinet on a whim.

Kalakaua spent money lavishly, piling up massive debts. Wanting Hawai'i's monarchy to equal any in the world, he commissioned 'Iolani Palace, holding an extravagant coronation there in 1883. He also saw Hawai'i playing a role on the global stage, and in 1881 embarked on a trip to meet foreign heads of state and develop stronger ties with Japan especially. When he returned to Hawai'i in November of that year, he became the first king to have traveled around the world.

Even so the days of the Hawaiian monarchy were numbered. The 1875 Treaty of Reciprocity, which had made Hawai'i-grown sugar profitable, had expired. Kalakaua refused to renew, as the treaty now contained a provision giving the US a permanent naval base at Pearl Harbor – a provision that Native Hawaiians regarded as a threat to the sovereignty of the kingdom. A secret anti-monarchy group called the Hawaiian League, led by a committee of mostly American lawyers and businessmen, 'presented' Kalakaua with a new constitution in 1887.

This new constitution stripped the monarchy of most of its powers, reducing Kalakaua to a figurehead, and it changed the voting laws to exclude Asians and allow only those who met income and property requirements to vote – effectively disenfranchising all but wealthy, mostly white business owners. Kalakaua signed under threat of violence, earning the 1887 constitution the moniker 'the Bayonet Constitution.' The US got its base at Pearl Harbor, and foreign businessmen consolidated their power.

Hawaii's Last Queen & Annexation

When Kalakaua died while visiting San Francisco, California in 1891, his sister and heir, Lili'uokalani, ascended the throne. The queen fought against foreign intervention and control, and she secretly drafted a new constitution to restore Hawaiian voting rights and the monarchy's powers. However, in 1893, before Lili'uokalani could present this, a hastily formed 'Committee of Safety' put in motion the Hawaiian League's long-brewing plans to overthrow the Hawaiian government.

First, the Committee of Safety requested support from US Minister John Stevens, who allowed American marines and sailors to come ashore in Honolulu Harbor 'only to protect American citizens in case of resistance.'

Farm-born and raised, Gerald Kinro brings personal insight and scholarship to *A Cup of Aloha*, an oral-history portrait of Kona's coffee industry. *Hawai'i's Pineapple Century* by Jan K Ten Bruggencate is another highly readable account of plantation life in Hawaii.

Part political statement, part historical treatise, *To Steal a Kingdom: Probing Hawaiian History* by Michael Dougherty takes a hard look at the legacy of Western colonialism and the lasting impacts of missionary culture.

1925

The first US military seaplane lands safely in Hawaii. Commercial flights don't start for more than a decade: Pan Am offers the first passenger flights to the islands in 1936.

1927

The $4-million, Moorish-style Royal Hawaiian hotel, dubbed the 'Pink Palace,' opens in Waikiki, and the arrival of the SS *Malolo* ('Flying Fish') luxury liner inaugurates a new era of steamship tourism.

1941

On December 7 Pearl Harbor is attacked by Japanese forces, catapulting the US into WWII. The sinking of the battleship USS *Arizona* kills all 1177 crew members aboard.

1946

On April 1 the most destructive tsunami in Hawaii history (generated by an earthquake in Alaska) kills 159 people across the islands and causes $26 million in property damage.

The Committee's own militia then surrounded 'Iolani Palace and ordered Queen Lili'uokalani to step down. With no standing army and wanting to avoid bloodshed, she acquiesced under protest.

Immediately after the coup, the Committee of Safety formed a provisional government and requested annexation by the US. Much to its surprise, US President Grover Cleveland refused: he condemned the coup as illegal, conducted under false pretext and against the will of the Hawaiian people, and he requested Lili'uokalani be reinstated. Miffed but unbowed, the Committee instead established their own government, the short-lived Republic of Hawaii.

For the next five years, Queen Lili'uokalani pressed her case (for a time while under house arrest at 'Iolani Palace) to no avail. In 1898, spurred by new US president, William McKinley, Congress annexed the Republic of Hawaii as a US territory. In part, the US justified this act of imperialism because the ongoing Spanish-American War had highlighted the strategic importance of the islands as a Pacific military base. Indeed, some feared that if America didn't take Hawaii, another Pacific Rim power – say, Japan – just might.

SHOAL OF TIME

Shoal of Time: A History of the Hawaiian Islands by Gavan Daws is an in-depth look at Hawaiian history, from Captain Cook's precipitous arrival in 1778 through the end of the Hawaiian monarchy and post-WWII statehood.

Matson Ships & Waikiki Beachboys

In 1901 WC Weedon, the owner of Waikiki Beach's first resort hotel, the Moana, went on a promotional tour of San Francisco with a stereopticon and daguerreotypes of palm-fringed beaches and smiling 'natives'. Just two years later, 2000 visitors a year were making the nearly five-day journey to Honolulu by sea. Travelers departed San Francisco aboard Matson Navigation Company's white-painted steamships, inaugurating the so-called 'White Ship Era' that continued until the mid-1930s, when flying made travel by ship passé. By the beginning of WWII, more than 30,000 visitors were landing in Hawaii each year.

The Hawaii of popular imagination – lei-draped visitors mangling the hula at a beach luau, tanned beachboys plying the surf in front of Diamond Head, the sounds of *hapa haole* (Hawaiian music with predominantly English lyrics) – was relentlessly commodified. More hotels sprouted along the strand at Waikiki, which had until the late 19th century been a wetland where the *ali'i* retreated for relaxation. The 1927 opening of the 'Pink Palace' (the Royal Hawaiian hotel) transformed Waikiki into a jet-setting tropical destination for the rich and famous, including celebrities of the day – Groucho Marx, Bing Crosby, Bette Davis, Clark Gable and even Shirley Temple.

This was also the era of Duke Kahanamoku, Olympic gold-medal swimmer, master waterman, movie star and unofficial 'ambassador of aloha.' He introduced the world beyond Hawaii's shores to the ancient sport of *he'e nalu* ('wave sliding'), called surfing. Duke was named af-

1949

Dockworkers stage a 177-day strike that halts all shipping to and from Hawaii; this is accompanied by plantation worker strikes that win concessions from the Big Five companies.

1959

Hawaii becomes the 50th US State. Hawaii's Daniel Inouye is the first Japanese American elected to the US Congress, which he serves in continuously until his death in 2012.

1961

Elvis Presley stars in the musical *Blue Hawaii*. Along with *Girls! Girls! Girls!* and *Paradise, Hawaiian Style*, Elvis' on-screen romps set the mood for Hawaii's post-statehood tourism boom.

1962

John Burns is elected governor as Democrats take control of all three branches of state government (including Hawaii's House and Senate), a grip on power they hold until 2002.

ter his father, who had been christened by Hawaiian princess Bernice Pauahi Bishop in honor of a Scottish lord. Duke Jr grew up swimming and surfing on Waikiki Beach, where he and his 'beachboys' taught tourists to surf, including heiress Doris Duke, who became the first woman to surf competitively.

Pearl Harbor & the 'Japanese Problem'

In the years leading up to WWII, the US government became obsessed with the Hawaiian territory's 'Japanese problem.' What, they wondered, were the true loyalties of 40% of Hawaii's population, the *issei* (first-generation Japanese immigrants), who had been born in Japan? During a war, would they fight for Japan or defend the US? Neither fully Japanese nor American, their children, island-born *nisei* (second-generation Japanese immigrants), also had their identity questioned.

On December 7, 1941, a surprise Japanese force of ships, submarines and aircraft bombed and attacked military installations across O'ahu. The main target was Pearl Harbor, the USA's most important Pacific naval base. This devastating attack, in which dozens of ships were damaged or lost and more than 3000 military and civilians were killed or injured, instantly propelled the US into WWII. In Hawaii the US Army took control of the islands, martial law was declared and civil rights were suspended.

A coalition of forces in Hawaii resisted immense federal government pressure, including from President Roosevelt, to carry out a mass internment of Japanese on the islands, similar to what was being done on the US West Coast. Around 1250 people were unjustly detained in internment camps on O'ahu, but the majority of Hawaii's 160,000 Japanese citizens were spared incarceration – although they did suffer racial discrimination and deep suspicions about their loyalties.

In 1943, the federal government was persuaded to reverse itself and approve the formation of an all-Japanese combat unit, the 100th Infantry Battalion. Thousands of *nisei* volunteers were sent, along with the all-Japanese 442nd Regimental Combat Team, to fight in Europe, where they became two of the most decorated units in US military history. By the war's end, Roosevelt proclaimed these soldiers were proof that 'Americanism is a matter of the mind and heart,' not 'race or ancestry.' The 1950s would test this noble sentiment. Still, Hawaii's multiethnic society emerged from WWII severely strained but not broken.

The popular radio program *Hawaii Calls* introduced the world to Hawaiian music. It broadcast from the banyan tree courtyard of Waikiki's Moana hotel between 1935 and 1975, and at its peak aired on 750 stations around the world. CD compilations are available through www.mele.com.

In *Strangers from a Different Shore*, Ronald Takaki tells the story of the USA's Asian immigrant communities, from Hawaii's plantation laborers to the effects of WWII on racial discrimination and modern attitudes toward multiculturalism.

A Long, Bumpy Road to Statehood

The end of WWII brought Hawaii closer to the center stage of American culture and politics. Three decades had already passed since Prince Jonah Kuhio Kalaniana'ole, Hawaii's first delegate to the US Congress,

1968

Hawaii Five-O begins its 12-year run, becoming one of American TV's longest-running crime dramas. The iconic theme song is kept when the prime-time TV series is relaunched in 2010.

1971

The Merrie Monarch hula festival, begun in 1964, holds its first competitive hula competition; part of a Hawaiian cultural renaissance, it becomes a proving ground for serious hula practitioners.

EMILY RIDDELL / GETTY IMAGES ©

➡ Merrie Monarch festival

1976

Native Hawaiian sovereignty activists illegally occupy the island of Kaho'olawe. The *Hokule'a* – a reproduction of an ancient Polynesian voyaging canoe – successfully sails to Tahiti and back.

introduced a Hawaii statehood bill in 1919, but it received a cool reception in Washington DC. Even after WWII, Hawaii was often viewed as too much of a racial melting pot for many US politicians to support statehood.

After WWII and during the Cold War, Southern Democrats in particular raised the specter that Hawaiian statehood would leave the US open not just to the 'Yellow Peril' (embodied, as they saw it, by imperialist Japan) but to Chinese and Russian communist infiltration through Hawaii's labor unions. Further, they feared that Hawaii would elect Asian politicians who would seek to end racial segregation, then still legal in the US. Conversely, proponents of statehood for Hawaii increasingly saw it as a necessary civil rights step to prove that the US actually practiced 'equality for all.'

In the late 1950s, Alaska narrowly beat out Hawaii to be admitted as the 49th state. With more than 90% of island residents voting for statehood, Hawaii finally became the USA's 50th state on August 21, 1959. A few years later, surveying Hawaii's relative ethnic harmony, President John Kennedy pronounced, 'Hawaii is what the world is striving to be.' In the 1960s, Hawaii's two Asian American senators – WWII veteran and *nisei* Daniel Inouye and Honolulu-born Hiram Fong – helped secure the passage of America's landmark civil rights legislation.

Statehood had an immediate economic impact and Hawaii's timing was remarkably fortuitous. The decline of sugar and pineapple plantations in the 1960s – due in part to the labor concessions won by Hawaii's unions – left the state scrambling economically. But the advent of the jet airplane meant tourists could become Hawaii's next staple crop. Tourism exploded, which led to a decades-long cycle of building booms. By 1970, over one million tourists each year were generating $1 billion annually for the state, surpassing both agriculture and federal military spending.

BITE-SIZE HISTORY

For a history of Hawaii you can finish on the flight over, *A Concise History of the Hawaiian Islands* by Phil Barnes captures a surprising amount of nuance in fewer than 90 pages.

Hawaiian Renaissance & Sovereignty Movement

By the 1970s, Hawaii's rapid growth meant new residents (mostly mainland 'transplants') and tourists were crowding island beaches and roads. Runaway construction was rapidly transforming resorts like Waikiki almost beyond recognition, and the relentless peddling of 'aloha' got some island-born and raised *kama'aina* wondering: what did it mean to be Hawaiian? Some Native Hawaiians turned to *kapuna* (elders) and the past to recover their heritage, and by doing so became more politically assertive.

In 1976, a group of activists illegally occupied Kaho'olawe, aka 'Target Island,' which the US government had taken during WWII and used for

1978
The 1978 Constitutional Convention establishes the Office of Hawaiian Affairs (OHA), which holds the Hawaiian Home Lands in trust to be used for the benefit of Native Hawaiians.

1983
Kilauea volcano begins its current eruption cycle, now the longest in recorded history; eruptions have destroyed the entire village of Kalapana, various residential subdivisions and a coastal road.

1992
On September 11 Hurricane 'Iniki slams into Kaua'i, demolishing almost 1500 buildings and damaging 5000, causing $1.8 billion in damage. Miraculously, only four people are killed.

1993
On the 100-year anniversary of the Hawaiian monarchy being overthrown, President Clinton signs the 'Apology Bill,' which acknowledges the US government's role in the kingdom's illegal takeover.

bombing practice ever since. During another protest occupation attempt in 1977, two activist members of the Protect Kaho'olawe 'Ohana (PKO) – George Helm and Kimo Mitchell – disappeared at sea, instantly becoming martyrs. Saving Kaho'olawe became a rallying cry, and it radicalized a nascent Native Hawaiian rights movement that continues today.

When the state held its landmark Constitutional Convention in 1978, it passed a number of important amendments of special importance to Native Hawaiians. For example, it made Hawaiian the official state language (along with English) and mandated that Hawaiian culture be taught in public schools. At the grassroots level, the islands were experiencing a revival of Hawaiian culture, with a surge in residents – of all ethnicities – joining hula *halau* (schools), learning to play Hawaiian music and rediscovering traditional crafts like feather lei-making.

Today asking the US federal government to recognize Native Hawaiians as an indigenous people, which would give them similar legal status as Native American tribes, is widely supported in Hawaii. But there is great controversy over what shape Hawaiian sovereignty should take and who exactly qualifies as Native Hawaiian. Even so, the issue of Hawaiian sovereignty, as retired US senator Daniel Akaka said, 'is important for all people of Hawaii…to finally resolve the longstanding issues from a dark period in Hawaii's history, the overthrow of the Kingdom of Hawai'i.'

2000

US Senator Daniel Akaka first introduces the Native Hawaiian Government Reorganization Act (the 'Akaka Bill'), asking for federal recognition of Native Hawaiians as indigenous people.

2002

Partly as a voter response to Democratic Party corruption scandals, mainland-born Linda Lingle is elected Hawaii's first Republican governor in 40 years. She is re-elected in 2006.

2006

Papahānaumokuākea Marine National Monument, protecting the rich, yet fragile reef ecosystem of the remote Northwestern Hawaiian Islands, is established. It's designated a World Heritage Site in 2010.

2012

Born and raised on O'ahu, US President Barack Obama is re-elected. Just as in the 2008 presidential election, Obama wins over 70% of the vote in Hawaii, the most of any state.

Hawaii's People

Whatever your postcard idyll might be – a paradise of white sandy beaches, emerald cliffs and azure seas; of falsetto-voiced ukulele strummers, bare-shouldered hula dancers and sun-bronzed surfers – it exists somewhere on these islands. But beyond the frame-edges of that magical postcard is a startling, different version of Hawaii, a real place where a multicultural mixed plate of everyday people work and live.

Island Life Today

Mary Kawena Pukui's *Folktales of Hawai'i* (1995), illustrated by island artist Sig Zane, is a delightful bilingual collection of ancient teaching stories and amusing tall tales.

FOLKTALES

Hawaii is a Polynesian paradise. But one with shopping malls, landfills and industrial parks, cookie-cutter housing developments, sprawling military bases and ramshackle small towns. In many ways, it's much like the rest of the USA. A first-time visitor stepping off the plane may be surprised to find a thoroughly modern place where the interstate highways and McDonald's look pretty much the same as back on 'da mainland.'

Underneath the veneer of the tourist industry and consumer culture is a different world, defined by and proud of its separateness, its geographical isolation and its unique blend of Polynesian, Asian and Western traditions. While those cultures don't always merge seamlessly, there are very few places in the world where so many different ethnicities, with no one group commanding a substantial majority, get along.

Perhaps it's because they live on tiny islands in the middle of a vast ocean that Hawaii residents strive to treat one another with aloha, act polite and respectful, and 'make no waves' (ie be cool). As the Hawaiian saying goes, 'We're all in the same canoe.' No no matter their race or background, island residents share a common bond: an awareness of living in one of the planet's most strikingly beautiful places.

Local vs Mainland Attitudes

Hawaii often feels overlooked by the other 49 states (except maybe Alaska, with which it shares the distinction of being the mainland's oddball younger sibling), yet it's protective of its separateness. This has both its advantages and disadvantages. On the up side, there's a genuine appreciation for Hawaii's uniqueness. On the down side, it reinforces an insider-outsider mentality that in its darkest moments manifests as exclusivity or blatant discrimination.

Mainland transplants tend to stick out, even after they've lived in the islands for some time. For example, as a rule loud assertiveness is discouraged in Hawaii, where it's better to avoid confrontation and 'save face' by keeping quiet. In a stereotype that's often true, the most vocal and passionate speakers – at a community meeting, a political rally – may be mainland activists who just moved in. No matter how long they live here, however, these folks will never be considered 'local.'

Locals take justifiable umbrage at outsiders who presume to know what's good for Hawaii better than they do. To get anywhere in Hawaii, it's better to show aloha – and a bit of deference – toward people who were island-born and raised, popularly called *kama'aina*.

Island Identity

Within Hawaii, life on O'ahu contrasts starkly with that on the Neighbor Islands. Honolulu is a cosmopolitan, global city – technologically savvy and fashion-conscious. It has the sports stadiums, the state's premier university and actual nightlife, even if it's comparatively tame. Kaua'i, Maui, Hawai'i the Big Island, Lana'i and especially Moloka'i are considered 'country.' That said, in a landscape as compressed as Hawaii, 'country' is a relative term. Rural areas tend not to be too far from the urban or suburban, and there are no vast swaths of uninterrupted wilderness like on the mainland.

In general, Neighbor Island residents tend to dress more casually and speak more pidgin. Status isn't measured by a Lexus but by a lifted pickup truck. *'Ohana* (extended family and friends) is important everywhere, but on islands beyond O'ahu it's often central. When locals first meet, they don't ask 'What do you do?' but 'Where you wen' grad?' (Where did you graduate from high school?). Like ancient Hawaiians comparing genealogies, locals often define themselves not by their accomplishments but by the communities to which they belong: island, town, high school.

Regardless of where they're from within the state, when two locals happen to meet outside Hawaii, there's often an automatic bond based on mutual affection and nostalgic longing for their island home – wherever they go, they belong to Hawaii's all-embracing *'ohana*.

What does it mean to be Hawaiian today? Read sharp-eyed journalist Sally-Jo Bowman's *The Heart of Being Hawaiian* (2008), a moving collection of articles and interviews that explore this question with unsentimental tenderness.

Multiculturalism

During the 2012 US presidential election, island residents were thrilled that someone from Hawaii was re-elected president ('*Hana hou*!' read the front-page headline in the *Honolulu Star-Advertiser* newspaper). Barack Obama, who spent most of his boyhood in Honolulu, was embraced by locals because his calm demeanor and respect for diversity represent Hawaii values. It also didn't hurt that he can bodysurf, and, more importantly, that he displayed true devotion to his *'ohana*. When his grandmother, who lived in Honolulu, died one day before the 2008 election, Obama suspended his campaign to visit her before she passed. To locals, these are the things that count.

WHO'S WHO

- Hawaiian – a person of Native Hawaiian ancestry. It's a faux pas to call just any Hawaii resident 'Hawaiian' (as you would a Californian or Texan), thus semantically ignoring the islands' indigenous people.
- Local – a person who grew up in Hawaii. Locals who move away retain their local 'cred,' at least in part. But transplant residents never become local, even once they've lived in the islands for many years. To call a transplant 'almost local' is a compliment, despite its emphasis on an insider-outsider mentality.
- *Malihini* – 'newcomer,' someone who's just moved to Hawaii and intends to stay.
- Resident – a person who lives, but might not have been born and raised, in Hawaii.
- Haole – white person (except local Portuguese); further subdivided as 'mainland' or 'local' haole. Can be insulting or playful, depending on the context.
- *Hapa* – a person of mixed ancestry; *hapa* is Hawaiian for 'half.' A common racial designation is *hapa haole* (part white and part other, such as Hawaiian and/or Asian).
- *Kama'aina* – literally a 'child of the land.' A person who is native to a particular place, eg a Hilo native is a *kama'aina* of Hilo, not Kona. The term connotes a deep connection to a place. In a commercial context, *kama'aina* discounts apply to any resident of Hawaii (ie anyone with a Hawaii driver's license).

What didn't matter to Hawaii is what the rest of the country seemed fixated on: his race. That Obama is of mixed-race parentage was barely worth mentioning. *Of course* he's mixed race – who in Hawaii isn't? One legacy of the plantation era is Hawaii's unselfconscious mixing of ethnicities; cultural differences are freely acknowledged, even carefully maintained, but they don't normally divide people. For residents, the relaxed lifestyle and inclusive cultural values are probably the most defining, best-loved aspects of island life. Depending on your perspective, Honolulu is either America's most Asian city or Polynesia's most American city.

Among the older generation of locals, plantation-era stereotypes still inform social hierarchies and interactions. During plantation days, whites were the wealthy plantation owners, and for years after minorities would joke about the privileges that came with being a haole *luna* (Caucasian boss). But in a growing generational divide, Hawaii's youth often dismiss these distinctions even as they continue to speak pidgin. As intermarriage increases, racial distinctions become even more blurred. It's not uncommon nowadays to meet locals who can rattle off four or five different ethnicities in their ancestry – Hawaiian, Chinese, Portuguese, Filipino and Caucasian, for example.

Hawaii is as ethnically diverse as California, Texas or Florida – and more racially intermixed – but it's noticeably missing large African American and Latino populations that help define those states and most multiculturalism on the mainland. Politically, the majority of Hawaii residents are middle-of-the-road Democrats who vote along party, racial/ethnic, seniority and local/nonlocal lines. As more mainland transplants arrive, conservative Republican candidates – such as Hawaii's former governor Linda Lingle – have stood a better chance.

WORKING-CLASS HAWAII

In *Folks You Meet in Longs and Other Stories* (2005), local newspaper columnist and playwright Lee Cataluna captures the flavor and the voice of working-class Hawaii in side-splittingly funny, exquisitely real monologues.

Ethnic Tension

In Hawaii, tensions among ethnicities, while they exist, are more benign and rarely violent compared with racial strife on the mainland. Among locals, island stereotypes are the subject of affectionate humor, eg talkative Portuguese, stingy Chinese, goody-goody Japanese and know-it-all haoles. Hawaii's comedians often use such stereotypes to hilarious comic effect. When racial conflict occurs, it's usually incidental to some other beef – if a white surfer cuts off a Hawaiian on a wave, the Hawaiian might curse the 'f'n haole.' But rarely is anyone insulted or attacked merely *because* of their race.

Things shift when nonlocals enter the picture, since they aren't always sensitive to Hawaii's colonial history and may not appreciate island ways. For instance, while the legitimacy of Hawaiian pidgin as a language has many challengers, the loudest critics are often mainlanders who don't speak it. In general, tourists and transplants are welcomed in the islands but have to earn trust by being *pono* – respectful and proper.

Religious Diversity & Sexual Orientation

The values of tolerance and acceptance extend beyond race – they apply also to religion and sexual orientation. The overwhelming majority of locals are Christian, but there are also substantial Buddhist communities as well as small populations of Jews, Muslims and Hindus. Mutual respect and acceptance among islanders of different faiths is the rule, not the exception. Even for devout Christians, religion often isn't a matter of rigid orthodoxy; many Hawaiians combine indigenous beliefs and ancient practices with modern Christianity.

For many years Hawaii has been politically behind the curve in its treatment of gay, lesbian and transgendered people (in part because so many residents are Christian, and there's a powerful Mormon influence), but in practice there is little visible discrimination. In fact, in traditional Hawaiian culture, the *mahu* (a transgendered or cross-dressing male) has been regarded as a figure of power and mystery. Already a premier destination for weddings, Hawaii became the seventh US state to legally recognize civil unions for same-sex couples in 2012.

Island Style

'On the islands, we do it island style,' sings local musician John Cruz in his slack key guitar anthem to life in Hawaii. While he doesn't say explicitly what 'island style' means, he doesn't have to; every local understands. Island style is easygoing, low-key, casual; even guitar strings are more relaxed. Islanders take pride in being laid-back – that everything happens on 'Hawaii time' (a euphemism for taking things slow or being late), that aloha shirts are preferred over suits and that a *tutu* (grandmother) will hold up a line to chat with the checkout person at Longs Drugs (and no one waiting seems to mind). 'Slow down! This ain't da mainland!' reads one popular bumper sticker.

Even in urban Honolulu, the 55th largest US city with a population of over 335,000, there's something of a small-town vibe. Shave ice, surfing, 'talking story,' ukulele, hula, baby luau, pidgin, broken-down 'rubbah slippah' (flip-flops) and particularly *'ohana* – these are touchstones of everyday life, which is relatively simple and often family-oriented. School sporting events are packed with eager parents, plus the gamut of aunties and uncles (whether they're actual relatives or not). Working overtime is not common; weekends are for play and potlucks at the beach.

To learn more about *mahu* in Polynesian culture and their experience in modern Hawaii, read Andrew Metzner's collection of spoken narratives, *'O Au No Keia: Voices from Hawai'i's Mahu and Transgender Communities* (2001).

HAOLE!

If you're a visitor (particularly a white-skinned one), you might hear this said – possibly in reference to you. It's a controversial word, one that, depending upon the context, can be descriptive, warm or insulting. Originally it meant 'foreigner,' describing anything (person or object) exotic to the islands, but later it came to denote Caucasian people.

No one's sure why ancient Hawaiians used the word to describe Captain Cook and his crew or what they meant by it. A popular explanation is that the British explorer didn't *honi* (share breath) with the natives. In ancient Polynesia and still today, Hawaiians often greet one another by touching noses and breathing together. Breath (*hā* in Hawaiian) is considered an expression of life force, and exchanging it is a gesture of respect and welcome. Instead the British kept their distance, shaking hands; thus it's reasoned the Hawaiians called them 'haole,' meaning 'without breath' – something of an insult. Another explanation is that the British would speak after praying, saying 'amen,' rather than breathing three times after *pule* (prayers), as the Hawaiians would.

Others challenge these explanations on linguistic grounds. In the Hawaiian language, glottal stops and long vowels are critical to a word's meaning. The word for 'without breath' is 'hā'ole,' not 'haole.' Transcriptions of ancient chants indicate that 'haole' meant 'foreign' and that it was used before the English arrived.

Regardless of how it happened, today the word means 'white person,' particularly one of European descent (excluding local Portuguese). If you're called haole, don't automatically let your lily-white skin turn red with anger; in many cases, it's a completely neutral descriptive term, as in 'See that haole guy over there?' Sometimes it's playful, as in 'Howzit haole boy/girl!' Some local white people will describe themselves as haole, often with self-deprecating humor.

At other times, it's clearly a racial slur. If someone calls you a 'stupid haole,' you can be reasonably sure they meant to insult both your intelligence and your race.

Hovering somewhere between is the phrase to 'act haole.' This describes people of any color who are condescending, presumptuous or demanding – deriving from islanders' experiences with pushy visitors and transplants. If someone tells you to 'stop acting haole,' you'd better dial it down a notch.

Hawaii leads the nation in shared housing: 32% of young adults live with parents or relatives, compared with 19% nationally. So don't be surprised by how many pairs of rubbah slippah are left by the front door at the next island home you visit!

Health, Wealth & Homelessness

By most social indicators, life is good. In 2012 Hawaii was ranked the fourth-healthiest state in the nation, with a low uninsured population. Over 75% of residents graduate from high school in four years, and nearly 30% have a bachelor's degree or higher (both above the national average). Unemployment, which dropped to 5.2% in early 2013, was much lower than the national average. Violent crimes occur 40 percent less often than on the mainland. Despite the mass quantities of Spam consumed in the islands, Hawaii had the fourth-lowest obesity rate in the US in 2011. In 2010 Hawaii's median annual household income ($58,507) ranked eighth and its poverty rate (9.6%) was fifth lowest among US states.

That last statistic, however, glosses over glaring inequity in the distribution of wealth. While there are a large number of wealthy locals and mainland transplants with magnificent estates and vacation homes skewing the average, there's a much larger number of locals, particularly Pacific Islanders, struggling with poverty and all the social ills that come with it. The state is currently trying to control one of the highest rates of ice (crystal methamphetamine) abuse in the US, a problem that leads to a significant percentage of the robberies and violent crimes.

Homelessness remains another serious concern: on average, 6000 people are homeless statewide. Most telling about the cost of living in Hawaii, however, is this statistic: up to 42% of homeless people are employed, but still can't make ends meet. Sprawling tent communities regularly pop up at beach parks and other public areas. Every now and then police disperse them, but the problem is never solved – only moved.

Costs of Living & Commuting

What makes Hawaii *no ka 'oi*, or 'the best'? Maybe it's that Hawaii residents have the longest life expectancy in the US: 81 years, compared with the national average of 78.

Honolulu has the third-highest cost of living among US cities (behind New York City's Manhattan and Brooklyn boroughs). Utility bills average three times higher than those on the mainland and grocery bills are exorbitant because over 85% of all food is imported. Limited land area (especially in a place where 20% of the land is controlled by the US military) leads to sky-high real-estate prices and many locals are unable to buy a home. Though home prices fell in 2008 as they did in the rest of the US, they didn't slide nearly as far. The median price of a home on O'ahu in 2012 was $600,000. One study found that nearly 50% of renters and homeowners spent 30% or more of their income on housing. The most affordable housing isn't close to the majority of jobs (near resort areas), resulting in long commutes and nightmarish traffic jams. Honolulu is currently debating – hotly – whether to build a multibillion-dollar light-rail system to relieve the congestion, which is only likely to get worse as more middle-class housing developments grow in the city's suburbs.

Hawaiians, Locals & Tourism

Hawaiians are still struggling with the colonial legacy that has marginalized them in their own homeland. They constitute a disproportionate number of Hawaii's homeless (over one-third) and impoverished. Their children, on average, lag behind state averages in reading and math and are more likely to drop out of school. Hawaiian charter schools were created to address this problem and they have demonstrated some remarkable success using alternative, culturally relevant approaches. However, many Hawaiians feel that some form of sovereignty is necessary to correct these deeply entrenched inequities.

These stresses – along with having to deal with a constant flow of tourists purchasing temporary paradise in resorts that many locals could never afford – can sap the aloha of residents. For many locals and

Hawaiians in particular, tourism is a Faustian bargain at best; with it comes jobs and economic stability, but many question whether it's worth the cost. In recent years, there's a hard-to-quantify feeling that life here isn't as good as it once was, which is partly why the state is so focused on developing a sustainability plan.

And yet, whatever difficulties arise, finding someone who'd prefer to live somewhere else is hardest of all. No matter what comes, locals say, 'lucky you live Hawaii.'

Hawaii's Cuisine

The word 'cuisine' almost sounds too formal for Hawaii. It suggests a need for a regimented approach to food that doesn't quite work for these laid-back islands. Here culinary traditions are enthusiastically off-the-cuff, with foreign flavors and cooking styles incorporated and shared – usually in heaping, savory portions. This no-worries fusion of global flavors is reflected nowhere better than in the state's most iconic dish: the plate lunch, a tasty insouciance that flouts any formal rules.

The Island 'Diet'

Edible Hawaiian Islands (www.ediblehawaiianislands.com), a colorful quarterly magazine focused on Hawaii's locavore movement and foodie trends, is available free at local restaurants, gourmet food shops and natural-foods grocery stores.

To understand Hawaii's gastronomy, it's helpful to think about the state's multicultural background. Before human contact, the only indigenous island edibles were ferns and *ohelo* berries. In their wooden canoes, Polynesians brought *kalo* (taro), *'ulu* (breadfruit), *'uala* (sweet potato), *mai'a* (banana), *ko* (sugarcane) and *niu* (coconut), as well as chickens, pigs and dogs for meat, and they harvested an abundance of seafood.

Starting with Captain Cook in 1779, Western explorers dropped off cattle and goats, while later missionaries imported tropical fruits such as pineapple and guava that now connote Hawaii. When the sugar industry rose in the late 1800s – bringing waves of immigrants from China, Japan, Portugal, Puerto Rico, Korea and the Philippines – Hawaii's cuisine developed an identity all of its own. It took immigrant imports like rice, *shōyu* (soy sauce), ginger and chili pepper, but never abandoned Hawaiian staples such as *kalua* pork and *poi* (steamed, mashed taro).

What does all this mean for visitors? Always sample the unknown, take another bite and travel the world on a single plate. Hawaii isn't a place to diet – it's the *broke da mout* (delicious) reward.

Local Food

Manapua, the local version of Chinese *bao* (steamed or baked filled bun), probably derives from either of two Hawaiian phrases: *mea 'ono pua'a* ('good pork thing') or *mauna pua'a* ('mountain of pork').

Cheap, tasty and filling, local food is the stuff of cravings and comfort. The classic example is Hawaii's ubiquitous plate lunch. Chunky layers of tender *kalua* pork, a dollop of smooth, creamy macaroni salad and two hearty scoops of white rice. Of course, the pork can be swapped for just about any other protein, maybe Korean-style *kalbi* short ribs, *mochiko* (batter-fried) chicken or *furikake*-encrusted mahimahi. A plate lunch is often eaten with throwaway chopsticks on disposable (and more often now biodegradable) plates. A favorite breakfast combo is fried eggs with spicy Portuguese sausage or Spam and, always, two-scoop rice.

Sticky white rice is more than a side dish in Hawaii. It's a culinary building block, an integral partner in everyday meals. Without rice, Spam *musubi* (rice ball) would just be a slice of canned meat. The *loco moco* (rice, fried egg and hamburger patty topped with gravy or other condiments) would be nothing more than an egg-covered hamburger. And without two-scoop rice, the plate lunch would be just a ho-hum conversation between meat and macaroni salad. Just so you know, sticky white rice means exactly that. Not fluffy rice. Not wild rice. And definitely *not* instant.

Snacks & Sweets

Pupu is the local term used for all kinds of snacks, munchies, appetizers or 'grazing' foods. Much more than just cheese and crackers, *pupu* represent the ethnic diversity of the islands, for example, boiled peanuts flavored with Chinese star anise or salted Japanese edamame (boiled fresh soybeans in the pod). Not to be missed is *poke*, a savory dish of bite-sized, cubed raw fish seasoned with *shōyu*, sesame oil, green onion, chili-pepper flakes, sea salt, *ogo* (seaweed) and/or *'inamona*, a Hawaiian condiment made of roasted, ground *kukui* (candlenut). *Poke* comes in many flavor varieties – ahi (yellowfin or bigeye tuna) is particularly popular.

Nowadays island kids veer toward mainland candy and gum to satisfy sweet teeth, but the traditional local treat is mouth-watering Chinese crack seed. It's preserved fruit (typically plum, cherry, mango or lemon) that, like Coca-Cola or curry, is impossible to describe. It can be sweet, sour, salty or licorice-spicy. Sold prepackaged at supermarkets, convenience stores and pharmacies like Longs Drugs or dished out by the pound at specialty shops, crack seed is mouthwatering and addictive.

On a hot day, nothing beats shave ice. It's *not* just a snow cone: the ice is shaved as fine as powdery snow, packed into a paper cup and drenched with sweet flavored syrups in an eye-popping rainbow of hues. For decadence, add a scoop of ice cream, sweet red azuki beans or soft *mochi* (Japanese pounded-rice cakes) underneath, or maybe *haupia* coconut cream or a dusting of powdered *li hing mui* (salty dried plums) on top.

Best Shave Ice

- *Matsumoto's (p160), O'ahu*
- *Scandinavian Shave Ice (p190), Hawai'i*
- *Itsu's Fishing Supplies (p278), Hawai'i*
- *Ululani's Hawaiian Shave Ice (p329), Maui*
- *Jo-Jo's Anuenue Shave Ice & Treats (p565), Kaua'i*

Hawaiian Traditions

With its earthy flavors and Polynesian ingredients, Hawaiian cooking is like no other. *Kalua* pig is traditionally roasted whole underground in an *imu*, a pit of red-hot stones layered with banana and *ti* leaves. Cooked this way, the pork is smoky, salty and succulent. Nowadays *kalua* pork is typically oven-roasted and seasoned with salt and liquid smoke. At commercial luau, a pig placed in an *imu* is usually only for show (it couldn't feed 300-plus guests).

Poi – a purplish paste made of pounded taro root, often steamed and fermented – was sacred to ancient Hawaiians. Taro is highly nutritious, low in calories, easily digestible and versatile to prepare. Tasting bland to mildly tart or even sour, *poi* is usually not eaten by itself, but as a starchy counterpoint to strongly flavored dishes such as *lomilomi* salmon (minced, salted salmon with diced tomato and green onion).

SPAM-TASTIC!

Hawaii may be the only place in the USA where you can eat Hormel's iconic canned meat with pride. Here in the nation's Spam capital, locals consume almost seven million cans per year.

Of course, Spam looks and tastes different in Hawaii. It is always eaten cooked (typically fried to a light crispiness in sugar-sweetened *shōyu*), not straight from the can, and often served as a tasty breakfast dish with eggs and rice.

A pork-based meat product, Spam was first canned in 1937 and introduced to Hawaii during WWII, when the islands were under martial law. During that period fresh meat imports were replaced by this standard GI ration. By the time the war ended, Hawaiians had developed an affinity for the fatty canned stuff.

One common preparation is Spam *musubi:* a block of rice with a slice of cooked Spam on top (or in the middle), wrapped with nori (Japanese dried seaweed). Created in the 1960s, it has become a classic, and thousands of *musubi* are sold daily at island grocers, lunch counters and convenience stores like 7-11.

Check out Honolulu's Waikiki Spam Jam (p113) festival in April. For Spam trivia, recipes, games and more, go to www.spam.com.

A common main dish is *laulau,* a bundle of pork or chicken and salted butterfish wrapped in taro or *ti* leaves and steamed until it has a soft spinach-like texture. Other traditional Hawaiian fare includes baked *'ulu* (breadfruit), with a mouthfeel similar to a potato; *'opihi,* tiny mollusks called limpet that are picked off reefs at low tide; *pipi kaula* (beef jerky); and *haupia,* a coconut-cream custard thickened with arrowroot or cornstarch.

Hawaii Regional Cuisine

Hawaii was once considered a culinary backwater. That is, until the early 1990s, when a handful of island chefs – including Alan Wong, Roy Yamaguchi, Sam Choy, Bev Gannon and Peter Merriman, all of whom still have their own popular local restaurants – created a new cuisine, borrowing liberally from Hawaii's multi-ethnic heritage. These chefs partnered with island farmers, ranchers and fishers to highlight fresh, local ingredients, and transformed childhood favorites into gourmet Pacific Rim masterpieces. Suddenly macadamia nut-crusted mahimahi, miso-glazed butterfish and *liliko'i* (passion fruit) anything were all the rage.

Star HRC Chefs

Roy's Waikiki (p119), O'ahu

Alan Wong's (p93), O'ahu

Merriman's (p248), Hawai'i

Hali'imaile General Store (p387), Maui

Josselin's Tapas Bar & Grill (p551), Kaua'i

This culinary movement was dubbed 'Hawaii Regional Cuisine' and its 12 pioneering chefs became celebrities. Back then HRC was rather exclusive, found only at destination and resort dining rooms; its hallmarks were Eurasian fusion preparations and elaborate plating. By the 2000s the focus began shifting toward island-grown, organic, seasonal and handpicked ingredients. Upscale restaurants are still the mainstay for star chefs, but now you'll find neighborhood bistros and even plate-lunch food trucks serving dishes inspired by HRC.

Hawaii's Locavore Movement

A whopping 85% to 90% of Hawaii's food is imported. Now, a growing number of small-scale farmers are trying to shift the agriculture industry away from corporate-scale, industrialized monocropping (eg sugar, pineapple) enabled by chemical fertilizers, pesticides and herbicides. Instead, family farms are growing diverse crops for high-end restaurants and also for sale locally, including at busy farmers markets.

Recent scientific and state governmental reports suggest, unsurprisingly, that an increase in production and consumption of locally grown food will benefit Hawaii in four areas: food security (popularly called 'food sovereignty'), the regional economy, the vitality of the land and water, and community pride. Furthering these goals is a grassroots political campaign to label and even exclude GMOs (genetically modified organisms) from the islands' food supply chain.

Learn more about local agriculture, farm tours and farmers markets at www.hiagtourism.org. It's not an exhaustive encyclopedia, but it's a good starting point.

But building a solid consumer market isn't easy. Locals tend to buy whatever is cheapest and often balk at paying for fruit they see falling off neighborhood trees. Supermarket chains typically prefer to stock blemish-free Sunkist oranges and California grapes. An exception is the Big Island's KTA Superstore, a mini-chain that carries 200 products – including milk, beef, produce and coffee – from dozens of local vendors under its Mountain Apple Brand.

Bottom line: the only way that small-scale farmers can thrive is to sell their products. Like the bumper stickers say, "Buy local. It matters!"

Island Drinks

Fruit trees thrive in Hawaii, so you'd expect to find fresh juices everywhere. Alas, most supermarket cartons contain imported purees or sugary 'juice drinks' like POG (passion fruit, orange and guava). Look for real, freshly squeezed or blended juices at health food stores, farmers markets, specialty juice bars and roadside fruit stands. Don't assume that the fruit is local, however.

Also bear in mind that the ancients never tasted that succulent mango or tangy pineapple. Hawaii's original intoxicants were plant-based Polynesian elixirs: *'awa*, a mild, mouth-numbing sedative made from the roots of the kava plant, and *noni* (Indian mulberry), which some consider a cure-all. Both of these drinks are pungent in smell and taste, so they're often mixed with other juices.

Coffee: Kona & Beyond

Hawaii was the first US state to grow coffee. World-famous Kona coffee wins raves for its mellow flavor that has no bitter aftertaste. The upland slopes of Mauna Loa and Hualalai in the Big Island's Kona district offer the ideal climate (sunny mornings and afternoon clouds with light seasonal showers) for coffee cultivation. While 100% Kona coffee has the most cachet, recent crops from Ka'u (the Big Island's southernmost district) have won accolades and impressed many aficionados, as have small-farm and estate-grown coffee from Maui, Kaua'i and Moloka'i.

Craft Beer, Island-Style

Once a novelty, a handful of microbreweries are now firmly established on Hawaii's biggest main islands. Brewmasters claim that the mineral content and purity of Hawaii's water makes for excellent-tasting beer. Another hallmark of local craft beers is the addition of a hint of tropical flavor, such as Kona coffee, honey or *liliko'i*.

Island microbreweries have lively brewpubs and tasting rooms, where you can try these popular pours: Longboard Island Lager and Pipeline Porter by Kona Brewing Company, on the Big Island (p191) and O'ahu (p131); Coconut Porter, Big Swell IPA and Wild Hog Stout by Maui Brewing Company (p341); Aloha Lager and Kiawe Honey Porter by Honolulu's Aloha Beer Company (p96); Belgian-style Golden Sabbath strong ale and Paniolo Pale Ale by the Big Island Brewhaus (p247); and Mehana Mauna Kea Pale Ale and Belgian-style Southern Cross winter ale, both made by Big Island-based Hawai'i Nui Brewing (p271).

HAWAII'S HOME-GROWN BOUNTY

Today outstanding island farms are lauded like designer brands on local restaurant menus. There are way too many notables to name, but here are a few:

➡ **Hawai'i the Big Island** – Hamakua Coast mushrooms and vanilla; tomatoes and salad greens from Hamakua Springs Country Farms; *kampachi* (yellowtail) from Kona Blue Water Farms; Kona Cold Lobsters; Big Island Abalone from the Kona coast; Kona coffee and chocolate; Mauna Kea Tea; Ka'u oranges and coffee; yellow-flesh Kapho Solo papayas from Puna.

➡ **Kaua'i** – goat cheese from the North Shore's Kaua'i Kunana Dairy; grass-fed beef from Medeiros Farm and Kauai Coffee Company coffee from Kalaheo; Kilauea honey and Kolo Kai Organic Farm's fresh ginger; Hanalei-grown taro; red-flesh Sunrise papayas.

➡ **O'ahu** – salad greens from 'Nalo Farms in Waimanalo; grass-fed beef from North Shore Cattle Co; tomatoes from North Shore Farms; Wailalua coffee, vanilla and chocolate; Manoa honey; sweet corn from Kahuku; 'Ewa-grown melons; orange-flesh Kamiya papayas.

➡ **Maui** – grass-fed beef from Maui Cattle Co; Ali'i Kula Lavender Farm, Surfing Goat Dairy cheese, 'Ulupalakua Ranch elk meat and Kula Country Farms' strawberries and onions, all from the Upcountry; Maui Brand natural cane sugar; Ka'anapali Estate's MauiGrown Coffee.

➡ **Moloka'i** – organic fruit and vegetables from Kumu Farms; coffee from Coffees of Hawaii; Pacifica Hawai'i sea salt; Moloka'i Meli honey; macadamia nuts from Purdy's.

CHEERS FOR HAWAII'S GREEN BEER

Maui Brewing Company and Kona Brewing Company beers aren't literally going green, but the folks who brew them are implementing some eco-conscious practices.

At Maui Brewing Company, vegetable oil used in the brewpub is converted to biodiesel fuel, which powers the cars of owners Garrett and Melanie Marrero as well as the delivery truck. Spent grain is given to local ranchers for composting, and the brewery's retail beers are sold in recyclable cans. Cans over glass? Yep, cans aren't breakable, so they're less of a threat on the beach. They also stop light damage and oxidation from affecting the beer's taste.

Kona Brewing Company hopped on the green bandwagon back in 2010 by installing a solar-energy generating system at its Big Island brewery and brewpub, as well as by producing the state's first certified green beer, Oceanic Organic Saison. The brewery also donates spent grain to local cattle ranches – that is, whatever it doesn't reuse as an ingredient in the brewpub's pizza dough and bread!

Wine & Cocktails

Hawaii isn't known for its wineries and vineyards, but wine enthusiasts need not despair. Upscale restaurants cater to connoisseurs looking to complement their meals with the right varietal from California to Europe, while wine bars are catching on in Honolulu and resort areas. Maui's Tedeschi Vineyards (p395) is known for its unique pineapple wines and Kaua'i's Nani Moon (p502) meadery for its honey wines, while the Big Island's Volcano Winery (p304) makes equally unusual guava-grape and macadamia nut-honey concoctions – they're not to everyone's taste, however.

Every beachfront and hotel bar mixes zany tropical cocktails topped with a fruit garnish and a little toothpick umbrella. Hawaii's legendary mai tai is a mix of dark and light rum, orange curaçao, orgeat and simple syrup with orange, lemon, lime and/or pineapple juices – learn how to mix a simple version yourself at Kaua'i's Koloa Rum Company (p489) tasting room.

Celebrating with Food

On O'ahu's North Shore, **Waialua Soda Works** (www.waialuasodaworks.com) bottles old-fashioned soda pop that's naturally flavored by tropical *liliko'i*, mango and pineapple, as well as Hawaii-grown vanilla and sugarcane.

Whether it's a 200-guest wedding or an intimate birthday party, a massive spread is almost mandatory in Hawaii. Most gatherings are informal, held at parks and beaches or in backyards, featuring a potluck buffet of homemade dishes. On major US holidays, mainstream mainland foods appear (eg Thanksgiving turkey) alongside local favorites such as rice (instead of mashed potatoes), sweet-potato tempura (instead of yams) and hibachi-grilled teriyaki beef (instead of roast beef).

Luau

In ancient Hawaii, a luau commemorated auspicious occasions, such as births, war victories or successful harvests. Modern luau celebrations, typically for weddings or a baby's first birthday, are often large banquet-hall gatherings of the *'ohana* (extended family and friends). The menu might be daring – including Hawaiian delicacies such as raw *'a'ama* (black crab) and *'opihi* (limpet) – but the entertainment low-key.

Hawaii's commercial luau started in the 1970s. Today, only these shows offer the elaborate Hawaiian feast and Polynesian dancing and fire eaters that folks expect. Bear in mind, the all-you-can-eat buffet of luau standards is toned down for the Western palate, with *kalua* pig, steamed mahimahi and teriyaki chicken. Most commercial luau are overpriced and overly touristy, but one stands out: Maui's Old Lahaina Luau (p330).

Food Festivals & Events

Festivals often showcase island-grown crops, such as the Kona Coffee Cultural Festival on the Big Island, Hana's East Maui Taro Festival, the Maui Onion Festival in Ka'anapali, O'ahu's Wahiawa Pineapple Festival, the Big Island Chocolate Festival in Kailua-Kona and the Kapa'a Coconut Festival on Kaua'i. Beer drinkers should mark their calendars for the Big Island's Kona Brewers Festival. And only in Hawaii will you find the Waikiki Spam Jam, held on O'ahu.

Gourmet culinary events are all the rage across the islands. On O'ahu, Restaurant Week Hawaii brings dining-out deals and special menus, while the Hawai'i Food & Wine Festival lets star chefs and island farmers shine in Honolulu and Ko Olina. Honolulu's Hawaii Fishing & Seafood Festival is a briny family-friendly feast. Maui hosts the Kapalua Wine & Food Festival for gourmands. Kaua'i's Spring Gourmet Gala in Lihu'e and Taste of Hawaii in Wailua bring top chefs to the island, while the Garden Island Range & Food Festival at Kilohana Plantation showcases cattle ranchers and farmers. The Big Island's A Taste of the Hawaiian Range agricultural festival happens at the Hilton Waikoloa Village resort.

Island Cookbooks

Roy's Feasts From Hawaii by Roy Yamaguchi

Hali'imaile General Store Cookbook by Beverly Gannon

Aloha Cuisine by Sam Choy

What Hawaii Likes to Eat by Muriel Muria and Betty Shimabukuro

Where To Eat & Drink

The dining scene in Honolulu, with its variety and quantity, is a lot different than the Neighbor Islands. On Kaua'i, you can count the number of established Japanese restaurants on one hand, while O'ahu's selection will number in the hundreds, from impeccable sushi bars to noodle shops to trendy *izakaya* (Japanese pubs serving tapas-style food). That said, the Big Island and especially Maui are closer to O'ahu as trendsetters, whether at casual farm-to-table cafés or star chef's dining rooms.

Across the islands, you'll find similar types of restaurants. For sit-down meals, there's a big divide between highbrow restaurants that could rival mainland counterparts and diner-type, family restaurants that serve local fare, loved for its familiar flavors and generous portions. When you're ready to splash out on a meal, pick a rave-reviewed foodie hotspot rather than a random oceanfront resort restaurant (where you're probably paying mainly for the view, not the food).

If calories are no concern, go for true local *grinds* (food) at '70s-style drive-ins, serving plate lunches, *loco moco* and the like. Ideal for picnics are *okazu-ya* (island-style Japanese take-out delicatessens); these are also the best places to find good, authentic Hawaiian food. Commercial luau buffets include all the notable Hawaiian dishes, but the quality can be mediocre and tastes often watered down for tourists.

ONLY IN HAWAII: MUST-TRY TASTES

➡ **Leonard's** (p117) *malasadas* – Sugar-coasted Portuguese doughnuts (no hole), often filled with flavored custard (O'ahu).

➡ **KCC Farmers Market** (p130) Artisanal food producers of everything from Hawaiian sea salt to guava jam (O'ahu).

➡ **Kanaka Kava** (p189) Thirst-quenching kava made from certified-organic *'awa* (Hawai'i).

➡ **Hanalei Taro & Juice Co** (p527) Taro-based smoothies, *mochi* cakes and veggie burgers (Kaua'i).

➡ **Aunty Lilikoi** (p565) Sweet syrups, spicy mustards and (inedible) massage oil, all made with *liliko'i* (passion fruit; Kaua'i).

EATING HAWAII'S FISH

Locals eat twice as much seafood as the per-capita US national average. Ahi is the local favorite, especially for eating raw in *poke* or lightly seared, but mahimahi and *ono* are also popular for cooking. Browse the **Hawaii Seafood** (www.hawaii-seafood.org) website to find out more about wild local fish, including seasonality, fishing methods, sustainability, nutrition notes and cooking tips.

Got a smartphone? Download the free Seafood Watch app from the Monterey Bay Aquarium, which provides at-a-glance information about ocean-friendly seafood, including sustainability specifics for various Hawaii fish. You can download free printable pocket guides from the website (www.montereybayaquarium.org/cr/seafoodwatch.aspx).

Fish species most commonly eaten in Hawaii include the following:

ahi – yellowfin or bigeye tuna; red flesh, excellent raw or rare

aku – skipjack tuna; red flesh, strong flavor; *katsuo* in Japanese

'ama'ama – mullet; delicate white flesh

awa – milkfish; tender white flesh

kajiki – Pacific blue marlin; firm white to pinkish flesh; *a'u* in Hawaiian

mahimahi – dolphinfish or dorado; firm pink flesh

moi – threadfish; flaky white flesh, rich flavor; reserved for royalty in ancient times

monchong – pomfret; mild flavor, firm pinkish-white flesh

nairagi – striped marlin; firm flesh, colored pink to deep red-orange; *a'u* in Hawaiian

'o'io – bonefish

onaga – red snapper; soft and moist; *'ula'ula* in Hawaiian

ono – wahoo; white-fleshed and flaky

opah – moonfish; firm and rich flesh, colored pink, orange, white or dark red

'opakapaka – pink snapper; delicate flavor, firm flesh, premium quality

'opelu – mackerel scad; pan-sized, delicious fried

papio – jack fish; also called *ulua*

shutome – swordfish; succulent and meaty, white to pinkish flesh

tako – octopus; chewy texture; *he'e* in Hawaiian

tombo – albacore tuna; light flesh, mild flavor, silky texture

Outside of Honolulu and Waikiki, especially on Neighbor Islands, restaurants typically close early (say, by 9pm or 10pm). For late-night dining, seek out bars and the rare 24-hour coffee shop or local diner.

Although it's now an island staple, salmon is not native to local waters. It's an imported fish, first introduced to Hawaii by whaling ships in the 19th century.

Self-Catering & Saving Money

In Hawaii, most groceries are imported. The everyday price of food averages 30% more than on the US mainland, so you may not save much money by cooking your own meals. You'll find fantastic prices on fresh seafood at local fish markets.

If you're not cooking for yourself, favorite budget eating picks include island bakeries, diners, sandwich shops, food trucks and plate-lunch take-out joints. At top-end dining rooms, like those found inside oceanfront resorts and golf-course clubhouses, stop by the bar during *pau hana* (happy hour), when *pupu* (appetizers) and drinks are often discounted.

Habits & Customs

When entertaining at home, locals typically serve meals potluck-style with a spread of flavorful dishes that may seem ridiculously clashing to the uninitiated palate. Locals may be laid-back, but they're punctual when it comes to meals. If you're invited to a local home, show up on time, bring dessert (ideally, from a local bakery) and remove your shoes at the door. Locals are generous with leftovers and might insist that you take a plate (along with homegrown fruits) with you.

Meals are early and start on the dot in Hawaii: typically 6am breakfast, noon lunch and 6pm dinner. Restaurants are jammed around mealtimes, but they clear out an hour or two later, as locals don't linger. Locals also tend to consider quantity as important as quality, and portion sizes reflect this attitude; feel free to split a meal or ask to take home leftovers.

Compared with the mainland, restaurant dress codes are relaxed ('island casual'), with no jackets or ties normally required. Tourists can get away with an aloha shirt and neat khaki shorts at most resorts, although locals usually don casual slacks when dining out.

Smoking is not allowed inside any restaurants in Hawaii. For tips on eating out with kids, see p55.

Best Plate Lunches

Ted's Bakery (p157), O'ahu

Super J's (p210), Hawai'i

Da Kitchen (p355), Maui

Blue Ginger Café (p432), Lana'i

Manae Goods & Grindz (p455), Moloka'i

Koloa Fish Market (p541), Kaua'i

Vegetarians & Vegans

Top-end restaurants almost always include meatless selections, such as grilled vegetables, garden pastas and creative uses of tofu. Hawaii's multitude of Asian eateries ensures plenty of vegetable and tofu dishes, plus gluten- or lactose-free options, even in rural towns. Healthy versions of traditional local fare are often available, including meal-sized salads and grilled-vegetable or tofu sandwiches and wraps.

Finding an exclusively vegetarian restaurant isn't as easy. Vegans, especially, must seek out the few eateries that use no animal products. When ordering, ask whether a dish is indeed meatless; soups and sauces often contain meat, chicken or fish broth. The most economical way to ensure no animal ingredients is to forage at farmers markets, as well as natural-foods grocery stores and health-food shops, which also stock food for special diets (eg gluten-free).

Food Glossary

Hawaii cuisine is multi-ethnic and so is the lingo.

adobo	Filipino chicken or pork cooked in vinegar, *shōyu*, garlic and spices
'awa	kava, a Polynesian plant used to make a mildly intoxicating drink
bentō	Japanese-style box lunch
broke da mout	delicious; literally 'broke the mouth'
char siu	Chinese barbecued pork
chirashizushi	assorted sashimi served over rice
crack seed	Chinese-style preserved fruit; a salty, sweet and/or sour snack
donburi	Japanese-style large bowl of rice topped with a protein (eg pork *katsu*)
furikake	catch-all Japanese seasoning or condiment, usually dry and sprinkled atop rice; in Hawaii, sometimes mixed into *poke*
grind	to eat
grinds	food (usually local); see *'ono kine grinds*
guava	fruit with green or yellow rind, moist pink flesh and lots of edible seeds
haupia	coconut-cream custard, often thickened with arrowroot or cornstarch
hulihuli chicken	rotisserie-cooked chicken with island-style barbecue sauce
imu	underground earthen oven used to cook *kalua* pig and other luau food
'inamona	roasted, ground *kukui* (candlenut), used as a condiment (eg mixed into *poke*)
izakaya	a Japanese pub serving tapas-style dishes

kalbi	Korean-style grilled dishes, typically marinated short ribs
kalo	Hawaiian word for taro, often pounded into *poi*
kalua	Hawaiian method of cooking pork and other luau food in an *imu*
kare-kare	Filipino oxtail stew
katsu	Japanese deep-fried cutlets, usually pork or chicken
kaukau	food
laulau	bundle of pork or chicken and salted butterfish, wrapped in taro and *ti* leaves and steamed
li hing mui	sweet-salty preserved plum a type of crack seed; also refers to the flavor powder
liliko'i	passion fruit
loco moco	hearty dish of rice, fried egg and hamburger patty topped with gravy or other condiments
lomilomi salmon	minced, salted salmon with diced tomato and green onion
luau	Hawaiian feast
mai tai	tiki-bar drink typically containing rum and tropical fruit juices
malasada	sugar-coated Portuguese fried doughnut (no hole), often filled with flavored custard
manapua	Chinese *bao* (baked or steamed buns) with *char siu* or other fillings
manjū	Japanese steamed or baked cake, often filled with sweet bean paste
miso	red, yellow or white Japanese fermented soybean paste
mochi	Japanese pounded-rice cake, sticky and sweet
musubi	Japanese *onigiri* (rice ball or triangle) wrapped in *nori*
noni	type of mulberry with smelly yellow fruit, used medicinally
nori	Japanese seaweed, usually dried
ogo	crunchy seaweed, sometimes added to *poke*; *limu* in Hawaiian
okazu-ya	Japanese take-out delicatessen, often specializing in home-style Hawaiian and local dishes
'ono	delicious
'ono kine grinds	good food
pau hana	happy hour (literally 'stop work')
phõ	Vietnamese soup, typically beef broth, noodles and fresh herbs
pipi kaula	Hawaiian beef jerky
poha	gooseberry
poi	staple Hawaiian starch made of steamed, mashed taro (*kalo*)
poke	cubed, marinated raw fish
ponzu	Japanese citrus sauce
pupu	snacks or appetizers
saimin	local-style noodle soup
shave ice	cup of finely shaved ice doused with sweet syrups
shōyu	soy sauce
star fruit	translucent green-yellow fruit with five ribs like the points of a star, and sweet, juicy pulp
taro	plant with edible corm used to make *poi* and with edible leaves eaten in *laulau*; *kalo* in Hawaiian
teishoku	Japanese set meal
teppanyaki	Japanese style of cooking with an iron grill
ume	Japanese pickled plum
uni	sea urchin

Hawaii's Arts & Crafts

Contemporary Hawaii is a garden of different cultural traditions, and the state capital of Honolulu is a fertile crossroads between East and West. Underneath it all beats a Hawaiian heart, pounding with an ongoing revival of Hawaii's indigenous language, artisan crafts, music and the hula. *E komo mai* (welcome) to these unique Polynesian islands, where storytelling and slack key guitar are among the sounds of everyday life.

Hula

Ancient Stories

In ancient Hawaii, hula sometimes was a solemn ritual, in which *mele* (songs, chants) were an offering to the gods or celebrated the accomplishments of *ali'i* (chiefs). At other times hula was lighthearted entertainment, in which chief and *kama'aina* (commoner) danced together, including at annual festivals such as the months-long makahiki held during harvest season. Most importantly, hula embodied the community – telling stories of and celebrating itself.

Dancers trained rigorously in *halau* (schools) under a *kumu* (teacher), so their hand gestures, facial expressions and synchronized movements were exact. In a culture without written language, chants were equally important, giving meaning to the movements and preserving Hawaii's oral history, anything from creation stories about gods and goddesses to the royal genealogies. Songs often contained *kaona* (hidden meanings), which could be spiritual, but also amorous or sexual.

Modern Revival

One can only imagine how hard Hawaii's earliest Christian missionaries blushed at the hula, which they disapproved of as licentious. Missionary efforts to suppress hula were aided by Christian convert Queen Ka'ahumanu, who banned public hula dancing in 1830.

The tradition might have been lost forever were it not for King Kalakaua. He revived hula dancing in the 1880s, saying famously, 'Hula is the language of the heart, and therefore the heartbeat of the Hawaiian people.' After the 'Merrie Monarch' died, the monarchy was soon overthrown, and hula faded again, until a 1960s and '70s Hawaiian cultural renaissance brought it back for good.

Today, hula *halau* run by revered *kumu* hula are thriving, as hula competitions blossom and some islanders adopt hula as a life practice.

Celebrating Hula

In hula competitions today, dancers vie in *kahiko* (ancient) and *'auana* (modern) categories.

Kahiko performances are raw and elemental, accompanied only by chanting and thunderous gourd drums; costumes are traditional, with *ti*-leaf leis, tapa skirts, primary colors and sometimes lots of skin.

Western contemporary influences – English-language lyrics, stringed instruments and smiling faces – may appear in *'auana* dances. Some hula troupes even flirt with postmodern dance styles.

HULA LESSONS

Can't resist the rhythms of the hula? Look for low-cost (or even free) introductory dance lessons at resort hotels, shopping malls and local community centers and colleges. No grass skirt required!

Hawaii's own Olympics of hula is the Big Island's Merrie Monarch Festival (p275), but authentic hula competitions and celebrations happen year-round on all the main islands. At touristy commercial luau, vigorously shaking hips and Vegas showgirl–style headdresses might be entertaining, but they're more related to Tahitian dance than to hula.

Island Music

The sounds of traditional Hawaiian music often feature falsetto singing and three instruments: steel guitar, slack key guitar and ukulele. If you tune your rental-car radio to today's island stations, you'll hear everything from US mainland hip-hop beats, country-and-western tunes and Asian pop hits to reggae-inspired 'Jawaiian' grooves. A few contemporary Hawaii-born singer-songwriters, most famously Jack Johnson, have achieved international stardom.

Browse classic and contemporary Hawaiian recordings online – including by Na Hoku Hanohano award-winning musicians – from Mountain Apple Company (www.mountainapplecompany.com) and Mele (www.mele.com).

Cowboy Heritage

Spanish and Mexican cowboys first introduced the guitar to Hawaiians in the 1830s. Fifty years later, O'ahu-born high-school student Joseph Kekuku started experimenting with playing a guitar flat on his lap while sliding a pocket knife or comb across the strings. He invented the Hawaiian steel guitar *(kika kila),* which lifts the strings off the fretboard using a movable steel slide, creating a signature smooth sound.

In the early 20th century, Kekuku and others introduced the islands' steel guitar sounds to the world. The steel guitar later inspired the creation of resonator guitars such as the Dobro, now integral to bluegrass, blues and other genres, and country-and-western music's lap and pedal steel guitar. Today Hawaii's most influential steel guitarists include Henry Kaleialoha Allen, Alan Akaka, Bobby Ingano and Gregory Sardinha.

The Jumping Flea

Heard all across the islands is the ukulele, derived from the *braguinha,* a Portuguese stringed instrument introduced to Hawaii in 1879. Ukulele means 'jumping flea' in Hawaiian, referring to the way players' deft fingers swiftly 'jump' around the strings. The ukulele is enjoying a revival as a young generation of virtuosos emerges, including teenaged Nick Acosta, who plays with just one hand, and genre-bending rockers led by Jake Shimabukuro, whose album *Peace Love Ukulele* (2011) topped Billboard's world music chart when it debuted.

Both the ukulele and the steel guitar contributed to the lighthearted *hapa haole* (Hawaiian music with predominantly English lyrics) popularized in Hawaii after the 1930s, of which 'My Little Grass Shack' and 'Lovely Hula Hands' are classic examples. For better or for worse, *hapa haole* songs became instantly recognizable as 'Hawaiian' thanks to Hollywood movies and the classic *Hawaii Calls* radio show, which broadcast worldwide from the banyan-tree courtyard of Waikiki's Moana hotel until 1975.

To find out more about slack key guitar, visit George Winston's Dancing Cat music label website (www.dancingcat.com) to listen to sound clips, browse bios of celebrated island guitarists and download a free e-book.

Slackin' Sounds

Since the mid-20th century, the Hawaiian steel guitar has usually been played with slack key *(ki ho'alu)* tunings, in which the thumb plays the bass and rhythm chords, while the fingers play the melody and improvisations, in a picked style. Traditionally, slack key tunings were closely guarded secrets among *'ohana* (extended family and friends).

The legendary guitarist Gabby Pahinui launched the modern slack key guitar era with his first recording of 'Hi'ilawe' in 1946. In the 1970s, Gabby and his legendary band the Sons of Hawai'i embraced the traditional Hawaiian sound. Along with other influential slack key guitarists such as

Sonny Chillingworth, they spurred a renaissance in Hawaiian music that continues to this day. The list of contemporary slack key masters is long and ever growing, including Keola Beamer, Ledward Ka'apana, Martin and Cyril Pahinui and Ozzie Kotani.

Traditional Hawaiian Crafts

In the 1970s, the Hawaiian renaissance sparked interest in artisan crafts. The most beloved traditional craft is lei-making, stringing garlands of flowers, leaves, berries, nuts or shells (for more about lei traditions, see p619). More lasting souvenirs include wood carvings, woven baskets and hats, and Hawaiian quilts. All of these crafts have become so popular with tourists that cheap imitation imports from across the Pacific have flooded into Hawaii, so shop carefully and buy local.

Kapa Hawaii (www.kapahawaii.net) celebrates the art of *kapa* with photo essays, news about workshops and events, and how-to tips for making, displaying and caring for this handmade fabric.

Woodworking

Ancient Hawaiians were expert woodworkers, carving canoes out of logs and hand-turning lustrous bowls from a variety of beautifully grained tropical hardwoods, such as koa, kou and milo. *Ipu* (gourds) were also dried and used as containers and as drums for hula. Contemporary woodworkers now take native woods to craft traditional bowls, exquisite furniture, jewelry and free-form sculptures. Hawaiian bowls are not decorated or ornate, but are shaped to bring out the natural beauty of the wood. The thinner and lighter the bowl, the finer the artistry and greater the value – and the price.

MODERN MELE

Ideally, this guidebook would come bundled with a CD and a ukulele. Instead here's a list of essential Hawaiian music albums, past and present:

- Israel Kamakawiwo'ole, *Facing Future* – 'Braddah Iz' touched Hawaii's soul with songs like 'Hawai'i '78,' while his version of 'Somewhere Over the Rainbow' has become world-famous. When Braddah Iz died in 1997, his body lay in state at the Capitol in Honolulu, an honor never before bestowed on a musician.
- *The Descendants* – Keola Beamer, Gabby Pahinui, Sonny Chillingworth and other slack key and steel guitar masters are showcased in this Hollywood movie soundtrack.
- Genoa Keawe, *Party Hulas* – Ukulele player 'Aunty Genoa' and her *ha'i* (voiced register-break singing technique) epitomized old-school Hawaiian hula music, and this sets the standard.
- Brothers Cazimero, *Some Call It Aloha...Don't Tell* – Kicking off the Hawaiian renaissance with Peter Moon's band Sunday Manoa, the dynamic duo of Robert and Roland blend melodic vocals with 12-string guitar and bass rhythms.
- Gabby Pahinui, *Gabby* – No self-respecting slack key music collection is complete without this seminal 1970s album.
- Dennis and David Kamakahi, *'Ohana* – Father Dennis and son David harmonize their musical gifts on Hawaiian slack key guitar and ukulele, respectively.
- Ledward Ka'apana, *Black Sand* – From a multi-talented master of the ukulele and both slack key and steel guitars, soothing instrumentals evoke the islands' natural beauty.
- Keali'i Reichel, *Ke'alaokamaile* – Charismatic vocalist and *kumu* hula, Reichel combines ancient chanting and soulful ballads in both Hawaiian and English.
- HAPA, *In the Name of Love* – Founded by a New Jersey slack key guitarist and a Hawaiian vocalist, HAPA's contemporary pop-flavored fusion has universal appeal.
- John Cruz, *One of These Days* – Cruz is an O'ahu-born singer-songwriter who crafts modern, blues-tinged riffs, most famously the hit song 'Island Style.'

Hawaii's Arts & Crafts

The beauty of the Hawaiian Islands will reawaken your senses with the flowing gestures of hula dancers, the melodious sounds of slack key guitars and ukuleles and the delicate artistry of a flower lei that set the soul in harmony with the natural world.

2

LINDA CHING / GETTY IMAGES ©

4

LONELY PLANET / GETTY IMAGES ©

1. Lei-Making (p619)
This most beloved of traditional Hawaiian crafts has experienced a resurgence since the 1970s.

2. Fabric Arts (p616)
Hawaii is famous for its vibrant fabrics that have evolved from the traditional art of making *kapa*.

3. Ukulele (p612)
This instrument, the name of which translates as 'jumping flea', is enjoying a revival in Hawaii.

4. Lauhala Hats (p616)
The leaves of the *hala* (pandanus) tree have been woven into many forms for centuries.

3

SUPERSTOCK / GETTY IMAGES ©

Fabric Arts

The making of *kapa* (pounded-bark cloth) for clothing and artworks, and *lauhala* weaving are two other ancient Hawaiian crafts.

Traditionally *lauhala* served as floor mats, canoe sails, protective capes and more. Weaving the *lau* (leaves) of the *hala* (pandanus) tree is the easier part, while preparing the leaves, which have razor-sharp spines, is messy work. Today the most common *lauhala* items are hats, placemats and baskets. Most are mass-produced, however. You can find handmade beauties at specialty stores like the Big Island's Kimura Lauhala Shop (p199) near Kailua-Kona.

Making *kapa* (called *tapa* elsewhere in Polynesia) is no less laborious. First, seashells are used to scrape away the rough outer bark of the *wauke* (paper mulberry) tree. Strips of softer inner bark are cut (traditionally with shark's teeth) and pounded with mallets until thin and pliable, further softened by soaking them in water to let them ferment between beatings. Softened bark strips are then layered atop one another and pounded together in a process called felting. Large sheets of finished *kapa* are colorfully dyed with plant materials and stamped or painted by hand with geometric patterns before being scented with flowers or oils.

In ancient times, *kapa* was worn as everyday clothing by both sexes, and used as blankets for everything from swaddling newborns to burying the dead. Today authentic handmade Hawaiian *kapa* cloth is rarely seen outside of museums, fine-art galleries and private collections.

Hawaiian Folktales, Proverbs & Poetry

Folktales of Hawai'i, illustrated by Sig Zane

'Olelo No'eau, illustrated by Dietrich Varez

Obake Files by Glen Grant

Island Writings

From Outsiders to Inside Views

Until the late 1970s, Hawaii literature was dominated by nonlocal Western writers observing Hawaii's exotic-seeming world from the outside. Best-selling titles include James Michener's historical saga, *Hawaii*, and Paul Theroux's caustically humorous *Hotel Honolulu*.

Since then, contemporary locally born writers have created an authentic literature of Hawaii that evokes island life from the inside. Leading this has been **Bamboo Ridge Press** (www.bambooridge.com), which for

QUILTING A HAWAIIAN STORY

With vibrant colors and graphic patterns, the appeal of Hawaiian appliqué quilting is easy to see. But look more closely and you'll discover the story behind the beauty.

Protestant missionaries introduced quilting to Hawaii in the early 19th century, but the craft has evolved since then. Traditional quilts typically have a solid color fabric, which is folded into fourths or eighths, cut into a repeating pattern derived from nature (remember making snowflakes in school?), and then appliquéd onto neutral foundation cloth.

If the quilt's center, or *piko* (navel), is open, it's said to be a gateway between the spiritual and physical worlds; a solid core embodies the strength of family. Fruits and plants have symbolic meaning, too: *'ulu* (breadfruit) represents prosperity and is traditionally the first quilt made, a pineapple signifies hospitality, taro equates to strength, a mango embodies wishes granted...

Don't look for human figures on a traditional quilt, though; they might come alive at night. Each original design is thought to contain the very spirit of the crafter. To prevent their souls from wandering, early Hawaiian quilts were buried with their makers.

The *'ohana* of one of the most highly regarded traditional Hawaiian quilters, the late Althea Poakalani Serrao, runs an encyclopedic website (www.poakalani.net) about Hawaiian quilting, including classes, shops, patterns, history and more.

Lisa Dunford

over 35 years has published contemporary local fiction and poetry in an annual journal and launched the careers of many Hawaii writers.

The **University of Hawai'i Press** (www.uhpress.hawaii.edu) and **Bishop Museum Press** (www.bishopmuseum.org/press) have also made space for local writers to have their voices heard, especially with insightful nonfiction writings about Hawaiian culture, history, nature and art.

Pidgin Beyond Plantations

In 1975, *All I Asking for Is My Body,* by Milton Murayama, vividly captured sugar plantation life for Japanese *nisei* (second-generation immigrants) around WWII. Murayama's use of pidgin opened the door to an explosion of vernacular literature. Lois-Ann Yamanaka has won widespread acclaim for her poetry (*Saturday Night at the Pahala Theatre,* 1993) and stories (*Wild Meat and the Bully Burgers,* 1996), in which pidgin embodies her characters like a second skin.

Indeed, redeeming pidgin – long dismissed by academics and disparaged by the upper class – has been a cultural and political cause for some. The hilarious stories (*Da Word,* 2001) and essays (*Living Pidgin,* 2002) of Lee Tonouchi, a prolific writer and playwright whose nickname is 'Da Pidgin Guerrilla,' argue that pidgin is not only essential to understanding local culture, but also a legitimate language. Another great introduction to pidgin is *Growing Up Local* (1998), an anthology of poetry and prose published by Bamboo Ridge Press.

New Voices

Other influential Hawaii writers who found their voices toward the end of the 20th century include Nora Okja Keller, whose first novel, *Comfort Woman,* won the 1998 American Book Award, and Kiana (born Diana) Davenport, whose *Shark Dialogues* (1994), *Song of the Exile* (2000) and *House of Many Gods* (2007) are sweeping multigenerational family tales entwined with Hawaii's own history.

Other contemporary Hawaii writers, especially women, abound. Some, like Mia King (*Sweet Life,* 2008), eschew purely ethnic or Hawaii-centered narratives, while others – like Kaui Hart Hemmings (*House of Thieves,* 2005) and Marie Hara (*An Offering of Rice,* 2007) – explode the 'paradise myth' as they explore conflcted issues of race and class. Hemmings' novel *The Descendants* (2007) has a dissolute Southern Gothic air, as the troubled *'ohana* of haole plantation owners and a Hawaiian princess almost lose their inheritance and their way.

PIDGIN

More than a pidgin dictionary, *Pidgin to Da Max,* by Douglas Simonson (aka Peppo), Pat Sasaki and Ken Sakata, is a side-splitting primer on local life that's knocked around forever because it (and its sequels) are so funny.

Hawaii on Screen

Nothing has cemented the fantasy of Edenic Hawaii in the popular imagination as firmly as Hollywood. Today, the 'dream factory' continues to peddle variations on a South Seas genre that first swept movie theaters in the 1930s. Whether the mood is silly or serious, whether Hawaii is used as a setting or a stand-in for someplace else, the story's familiar tropes hardly change, updating the original tropical castaways soap opera and providing a romantic gloss to the real history of colonization.

Hollywood first arrived in 1913, less than a decade after Thomas Edison journeyed to Hawaii to make movies that you can still watch today at Lahaina's Wo Hing Museum (p320) on Maui. By 1939, dozens of Hollywood movies had been shot here, including musical comedies like *Waikiki Wedding* (1937), in which Bing Crosby crooned the Oscar-winning song 'Sweet Leilani.' Later favorites include the WWII–themed *From Here to Eternity* (1953) and *South Pacific* (1958), and Elvis Presley's goofy postwar *Blue Hawaii* (1961).

Today, Hawaii actively encourages and supports the lucrative film industry by maintaining state-of-the-art production facilities and providing tax incentives. Hundreds of feature films have been shot in the state including box-office hits like *Raiders of the Lost Ark* (1981), *Jurassic Park* (1993), *Pearl Harbor* (2001), *50 First Dates* (2004) and *Pirates of the Caribbean: On Stranger Tides* (2011). Kaua'i is the most prolific island 'set' and has appeared in over 70 films. Today, avid fans can tour movie sites all over Kaua'i and also at Kualoa Ranch (p147) on O'ahu.

Hawaii has been home to many modern painters, notably Herb Kawainui Kane, and scores of visiting artists also have drawn inspiration from the islands' rich cultural heritage and landscapes. *Encounters with Paradise: Views of Hawaii and Its People, 1778-1941* by David Forbes is a vivid art-history tour.

Hawaii has hosted dozens of TV series since 1968, when the original *Hawaii Five-O*, an edgy cop drama unsentimentally depicting Honolulu's gritty side, debuted. In 2010 *Hawaii Five-O* was rebooted as a prime-time drama, filmed entirely on O'ahu. The island also served as the location for the hit series *Lost*, which, like *Gilligan's Island* (the pilot of which was filmed on Kaua'i), is about a group of island castaways trying to get home. To find *Lost* filming locations, visit www.lostvirtualtour.com.

For a complete Hawaii filmography and a list of hundreds of TV episodes filmed here, including what's currently being shot around the islands, check the Hawaii Film Office website (www.hawaiifilmoffice.com).

Lei

Greetings. Love. Honor. Respect. Peace. Celebration. Spirituality. Good luck. Farewell. A Hawaiian lei – a handcrafted garland of fresh tropical flowers – can signify all of these meanings, and many more. Lei-making may be Hawaii's most sensuous and transitory art form. Fragrant and ephemeral, lei embody the beauty of nature and the embrace of 'ohana (extended family and friends) and the community, freely given and freely shared.

The Art of the Lei

In choosing their materials, lei makers tell a story – since flowers and plants may embody Hawaiian places and myths – and express emotions. Traditional lei makers may use feathers, nuts, shells, seeds, seaweed, vines, leaves and fruit, in addition to more familiar fragrant flowers. The most commons methods of making lei are by knotting, braiding, winding, stringing or sewing the raw natural materials together.

Above Master lei maker at work

Worn daily, lei were integral to ancient Hawaiian society. In the islands' Polynesian past, lei were part of sacred hula dances and given as special gifts to loved ones, healing medicine to the sick and offerings to the gods, all practices that continue today. So powerful a symbol were they that on ancient Hawaii's battlefields, a lei could bring peace to warring armies.

Today, locals wear lei for special events, such as weddings, birthdays, anniversaries and graduations. It's no longer common to make one's own lei, unless you belong to a hula *halau* (school). For ceremonial hula, performers are often required to make their own lei, even gathering raw materials by hand.

On O'ahu, it's said that when passengers throw their lei into the sea as their departing ship passes Diamond Head, if the flowers of their lei then float back toward the beach, they're guaranteed to return to Hawaii someday.

Modern Celebrations

For visitors to Hawaii, the tradition of giving and receiving lei dates back to 19th-century steamships that brought the first tourists to the islands. Later, disembarking cruise ship passengers were greeted by vendors who would toss garlands around the necks of *malihini* (newcomers).

In 1927, the poet Don Blanding and Honolulu journalist Grace Tower Warren called for making May 1 a holiday to honor lei. Every year, Lei Day is still celebrated across the islands with Hawaiian music, hula dancing, parades, and lei-making workshops and contests.

The tradition of giving a kiss with a lei began during WWII, allegedly when a hula dancer at a USO club was dared by her friends to give a military serviceman a peck on the cheek when offering him a flower lei.

Lei: Dos & Don'ts

- Do not wear a lei hanging directly down around your neck. Instead, drape a closed (circular) lei over your shoulders, making sure equal lengths are hanging over front and back.
- When presenting a lei, bow your head slightly and raise the lei above your heart. Do not drape it with your own hands over the head of the recipient, as this isn't respectful; let them do it themselves.

ISLAND LEI TRADITIONS

Lei are a universal language in Hawaii, but some special lei evoke a particular island.

O'ahu The yellow-orange *'ilima* is the island's official flower, and a symbol of Laka, the Hawaiian goddess of hula dancing. Once favored by royalty, an *'ilima* lei may be made of up to a thousand small blossoms strung together.

Hawai'i the Big Island Lei made from lehua, flowers of the ohia plant, are most often colored red or pink. According to legend, the first Hawaiian lei was made of lehua and given by Hi'iaka, goddess of healing, to her sister Pele, goddess of fire and volcanoes.

Maui The *lokelani* (pink damask rose, or 'rose of heaven') is a soft, velvety and aromatic flower. It was imported by 19th-century Christian missionaries for their gardens in Lahaina. Today it's Maui's official flower, the only exotic species of flora so recognized in Hawaii.

Lana'i A yellowish-orange vine, *kaunaoa* is traditionally gathered from the island's windward shores, then twisted into a lei. One traditional Hawaiian chant sings of this plant growing on Lana'i like a feathered cape lying on a strong chief's shoulders.

Moloka'i *Kukui* (candelnut) lei are either made from the laboriously polished, dark-brown nuts of Hawaii's state tree (in which case, they're usually worn by men) or the tree's white blossoms, which are Moloka'i's official flower.

Kaua'i On the 'Garden Island,' leathery, anise-scented *mokihana* berries are often woven with strands of glossy, green maile vines. *Mokihana* trees grow on the rain-soaked western slopes of Mt Wai'ale'ale.

Lei on display in an O'ahu shop

➡ Don't give a closed lei to a pregnant woman, as it may bring bad luck; choose an open (untied) lei or *haku* (head) lei instead.

➡ Resist the temptation to wear a lei intended for someone else. That's bad luck.

➡ Never refuse a lei, and do not take one off in the presence of the giver.

➡ When you stop wearing your lei, don't throw it away. Untie the string, remove the bow and return the lei's natural elements to the earth (eg scatter flowers in the ocean, bury seeds or nuts).

Does an airport lei greeting to surprise your *ipo* (sweetheart) sound like fun? Several companies offer this service, including Greeters of Hawaii, which has been in the business of giving aloha since 1957.

Shopping for Lei

A typical Hawaiian lei costs anywhere from $10 for a single strand of orchids or plumeria to thousands of dollars for a 100% genuine Ni'ihau shell lei necklace. Beware that some *kukui* (candelnut) and *puka* shell lei are just cheap (even plastic) imports.

When shopping for a lei, ask the florist or shopkeeper for advice about what the most appropriate lei for the occasion is (eg for a bride, pick a string of pearl-like *pikake* jasmine flowers), and indicate if you're giving the lei to a man or a woman.

Land & Sea

It has been said that if Darwin had arrived first in Hawaii, a remote archipelago with spectacularly varied wildlife, he would have developed his theory of evolution in a period of weeks instead of years. On the other hand, few places have felt humanity's heavy footprint as deeply as Hawaii, which today holds the ignominious title of being the 'endangered species capital of the world' and faces serious environmental challenges.

Earth's Most Remote Paradise

Many people think of the Hawaiian Islands as tiny rafts of white sand and tiki bars sailing westward inch-by-inch to Japan. In fact, these islands are the palm-fringed tops of the planet's largest mountain range, something whales may appreciate more than humans do.

For 80 million years, a 'hot spot' beneath the earth's mantle has operated like a volcanic conveyor belt here, manufacturing a 1500-mile string of shield volcanoes that bubble out of the sea in the most geographically isolated spot on the planet, almost 2000 miles from the closest continent. This profound isolation has created a living textbook of evolution, with incredible biodiversity unmatched by anywhere else in the US.

Kilauea's ongoing eruption, which began in 1983, is the most voluminous outpouring of lava onto the volcano's east rift zone in 500 years. It has added 500 acres of new land to the Big Island – so far.

KILAUEA

Volcanoes & Hot Spots

The Hawaiian archipelago embraces over 50 volcanoes (and 137 islands and atolls), part of the larger, mostly submerged Hawaiian-Emperor Seamount chain that extends 3600 miles across the ocean. Hawaii's volcanoes are created by a rising column of molten rock – a 'hot spot' – under the Pacific Plate. As the plate moves northwest a few inches each year, magma pierces upward through the crust, creating volcanoes.

Each new volcano slowly creeps northwest past the hot spot that created it. As each volcanic island moves off the hot spot, it stops erupting and instead of adding more new land, it starts eroding. Wind, rain and waves add geologic character to the newly emerged islands, cutting deep valleys, creating sandy beaches and turning a mound of lava into a tropical paradise.

At the far northwestern end of the chain, the Hawaiian Islands have receded back below the ocean surface to become seamounts. Moving eastward from Kure Atoll, the islands get progressively taller and younger until you reach the Big Island of Hawai'i, the still-growing, 500,000-year-old baby of the Hawaiian group.

Straddling the hot spot today, the Big Island's Kilauea is the world's most active volcano. All Hawaiian volcanoes are shield volcanoes that erupt with effusive lava to create gently sloped, dome-shaped mountains, but they can also have a more explosive side, as Kilauea dramatically reminded onlookers and scientists in 2008.

Under the sea about 20 miles southeast of the Big Island, a new undersea volcano is erupting – Lo'ihi Seamount. Although you can't see it today, stick around: in 10,000 years or so, it will emerge from the water to become the newest island in the Hawaiian chain.

HAWAII BY THE NUMBERS

- Hawaii comprises 6423 sq miles of total land area, less than 0.2% of the total US landmass.
- Within the state, there are eight main islands, but only seven are populated.
- Beyond Kaua'i, the minuscule Northwestern Hawaiian Islands stretch for 1200 miles.
- On the Big Island, Ka Lae (South Point) is the USA's southernmost point, 18°55'N of the equator.

Wildlife

In the Beginning

Born of barren lava flows, the Hawaiian Islands were originally populated only by plants and animals that could traverse the Pacific – for example, seeds clinging to a bird's feather or fern spores that drifted thousands of miles through the air. Most species that landed here didn't survive. Scientists estimate that successful species were established maybe once every 70,000 years – and these included no amphibians, no browsing animals, no mosquitoes and only two mammals: a bat and a seal.

However, the flora and fauna that did succeed thrived on an unusually rich, diverse land, containing nearly every ecological or life zone. Without predators or much competition, new species dropped their defensive protections: thorns, poisons and strong odors disappeared. This evolutionary process accounts for why over 90% of native Hawaiian species are endemic, or unique to the islands, and why they fare so poorly against modern invaders and artificial environmental changes.

Hawaii is the northernmost point of the triangle of Pacific islands known as Polynesia ('many islands'); the other points are New Zealand and Rapa Nui (Easter Island).

Humans Invade

When Polynesians arrived, they introduced new animals and plants, including pigs, chickens, rats, coconuts, bananas, taro and about two dozen other plants, not to mention people. These 'Polynesian introductions' caused the first wave of species extinctions, including an estimated 50-plus birds that had disappeared by the time Captain Cook dropped off goats and melon, pumpkin and onion seeds in 1778. Later European, Asian and American immigrants imported more exotic (or 'alien') species, such as cattle that foraged at will, invasive ground covers and ornamental plants.

Today, Hawaii is the extinction capital of the USA, accounting for 75% of the nation's documented extinctions. Over two-thirds of Hawaii's known birds and half of its endemic plant species are already extinct. Yet recently the islands have become a unique laboratory in the global scientific effort to discover sustainable methods of conservation – preserving a diversity of wildlife, and by extension our own skins.

The endangered *'ope'ape'a* (Hawaiian hoary bat), one of Hawaii's two endemic mammals, has reddish-brown or grey, white-tinged fur, making it appear 'hoary' (grayed by age). With a foot-wide wingspan, these tree-dwellers exist predominantly around forests on the leeward sides of the Big Island and Kaua'i.

Animals

In modern times, nearly every animal introduced to the islands – whether rabbits, goats, sheep, pigs or horses – has led to environmental devastation. Some, like Maui's axis deer and the Big Island's cattle, were 'gifts' to Hawaiian kings that spun off out-of-control feral populations. The ubiquitous mongoose was originally introduced to control sugarcane rats, but has become a worse plague than the rats. Feral animals are the most destructive force in Hawaii today, and getting rid of them is central to re-establishing native landscapes and saving endangered species.

Land & Sea

In Hawaii what's going on underwater – where rainbow-colored tropical fish and sea turtles swim, migratory whales sing and monk seals dive – is just as thrilling as what awaits on land: fiery lava flowing into the Pacific and skyscraping mountain summits giving star-studded glimpses of the Milky Way.

MINT IMAGES - FRANS LANTING / GETTY IMAGES ©

DEBORAH RUST / GETTY IMAGES ©

1. Green Sea Turtle (p627)
The *honu*, sacred to Hawaiians, can be seen throughout the islands.

2. Lava
The Hawaiian islands were born from volcanic eruptions – and new ones continue to be formed.

3. Protea
Hawaii is home to many exotic flowers and trees, from hibiscus to banyans.

4. Gecko
Hawaii provides an ecosystem for animals both beautiful and strange.

RON DAHLQUIST / GETTY IMAGES ©

Feathered Friends

Many of Hawaii's birds are spectacular examples of adaptive radiation. For instance, all 56 species of endemic Hawaiian honeycreepers most likely evolved from a single finch ancestor. Today, over half of those bright-colored honeycreepers – along with two-thirds of all native birds – are extinct, the victims of more aggressive, non-native birds, predatory feral animals (like mongooses and pigs) and infectious avian diseases against which they have no natural immunity.

The endangered nene, Hawaii's state bird, is a long-lost cousin of the Canada goose. Nene usually nest in sparse vegetation on rugged lava flows, to which their feet adapted by losing most of their webbing. While eight other species of Hawaiian geese (now extinct) became flightless, nene remain strong flyers. There were once as many as 25,000 nene on all of the Hawaiian Islands, but by the 1950s there were only 30 left. Captive breeding and release programs have raised their numbers to over 2000 on the Big Island, Maui, Kaua'i and Moloka'i today.

The only hawk native to Hawaii, the *'io* was a symbol of royalty and often an *'aumakua* (protective deity). They are known to breed only on the Big Island; their numbers have held steady at over 3000 for the last decade. In 2008 the *'io* was proposed for delisting from the endangered species list, but a decision is still pending.

Hawaii for the Bird(er)s

- James Campbell National Wildlife Refuge (p*152*)
- Kealia Pond National Wildlife Refuge (p*361*)
- Haleakalā National Park (p*410*)
- Koke'e State Park (p*569*)
- Papahānaumokuākea Marine National Monument (p576)

Marine Superstars

Up to 10,000 migrating North Pacific humpback whales come to Hawaiian waters for calving each winter, and whale watching is a major attraction. The world's fifth-largest whale, the endangered humpback can reach lengths of 45ft and weigh up to 50 tons. Other whales (such as rarely seen blue and fin whales) also migrate through. By federal law, no one may approach a whale in Hawaiian waters closer than 100yd.

Hawaii is also home to a number of dolphins, most famously the spinner dolphin, named for its leaps from the water. These acrobats are nocturnal feeders that come into sheltered bays during the day to rest. Because they are extremely sensitive to human disturbance, federal guidelines recommend that swimmers do not approach any wild dolphins closer than 50yd.

HAWAII'S ANGRY BIRDS VS FERAL PIGS

How delicately interdependent are Hawaiian ecosystems? Consider how pigs are driving Hawaiian birds to extinction. Not directly, of course, but the chain of cause and effect is undeniable.

Feral pigs, most likely the descendants of domestic pigs brought by early Europeans, have caused widespread devastation to the islands' native wet forests. At Hawaii's national parks, pigs are considered public enemy number-one, with federally sponsored eradication and fencing programs. Outside of federal lands, eradication efforts are few, and one estimate is that there may be as many as one feral pig for every 33 state residents.

Pigs trample and kill native fauna, destroy the forest understory and spread far and wide the seeds of invasive plants. Pigs love native tree-fern stems, knocking them over and eating the plants' tender insides, while the bowl-like cavities left behind catch rainwater and create ideal breeding pools for mosquitoes.

Common mosquitoes – presumed to have arrived in Hawaii in water casks aboard whaling ships in 1826 – pick up avian malaria and avian pox (also introduced from the European continent) and spread it to native birds, particularly honeycreepers, who have lost their natural immunity to these diseases.

It's a simple equation: no feral pigs, far fewer mosquitoes, far less avian malaria and far more honeycreepers. What's not so simple is how to make that a reality statewide.

SACRED HONU

Hawaiians traditionally revere the green sea turtle, called *honu*. Often considered a personal *'aumakua* (protective deity), its image appears in petroglyphs (and today in tattoos). For ancient Hawaiians, sea turtles were a delicious and prized source of food, but their capture and consumption were typically governed by strict religious and traditional codes.

As with Hawaii's other two native species of sea turtles – the hawksbill and the leatherback – *honu* are endangered and protected by federal law. Adults can grow over 3ft long and weigh more than 200lb. Young turtles are omnivorous, but adults (unique among sea turtles) become strict vegetarians. This turns their fat green – hence their name.

Green sea turtles can be seen throughout the Hawaiian Islands, often while feeding in shallow lagoons, bays and estuaries. Their main nesting site is French Frigate Shoals in remote Papahānaumokuākea Marine National Monument. Up to 700 female turtles (90% of the total population) come to lay their eggs there each year.

If you spot a sea turtle hauled out on a beach in Hawaii, federal guidelines advise keeping back at least 20ft to avoid disturbing the animals or interfering with their natural activities. Always leave turtles a clear path from the beach back into the water and never touch, feed, chase or otherwise attempt to interact with them.

One of the Pacific's most endangered marine creatures is the Hawaiian monk seal, named for both the monastic cowl-like fold of skin at its neck and its solitary habits. Having migrated to the islands over 10 million years ago, the Hawaiian monk seal has evolved into a unique species that has been called a 'living fossil.' The Hawaiian name for the animal is *'ilio holo kai*, meaning 'the dog that runs in the sea.' Adults are over 7ft and 500lb of tough, some with the scars to prove they can withstand shark attacks. Once nearly driven to extinction, their population today numbers just over 1000.

Although monk seals once bred primarily in the remote Northwestern Hawaiian Islands, recently they have begun hauling out on beaches on the main islands. According to the National Oceanic and Atmospheric Administration (NOAA), people are now the biggest threat to the survival of Hawaiian monk seals. Humans who disturb seals that have hauled out on beaches to rest, molt or breed drive down an already endangered population. Federal guidelines advise staying back at least 50yd and avoiding all human-seal interactions. Areas of the beach around a hauled-out seal are often roped off to prevent close approach.

The Last Atoll: Exploring Hawai'i's Endangered Ecosystems, by Pamela Frierson, fascinatingly narrates explorations of the most remote points of the Hawaiian archipelago – it's the next best thing to sailing to Papahānaumokuākea Marine National Monument yourself.

Marine Wildlife 911

- Report Hawaiian monk seal sightings to NOAA's Fisheries Service by calling ☎(808) 220-7802.
- If you notice an entangled or injured seal or dolphin, or a whale or a dolphin swimming in very shallow ocean water, stay back and call the NOAA hotline at ☎(888) 256-9840.
- If you spot an obviously sick or injured, stranded or dead sea turtle, keep your distance and call ☎(808) 983-5730, or ☎(808) 288-5685 outside of normal business hours.

Tropical Fish

Hawaii's coral reefs constitute 84% of all US reefs, and they are home to over 500 fish species, of which over 20% are endemic. Protected coral reefs teem with vast numbers of tropical fish: bright yellow tangs, striped butterflyfish and Moorish Idols, silver needlefish, and gape-mouthed moray eels. Neon-colored wrasse, which have more species than any other Hawaiian reef fish, change sex (and color) as they mature.

The contrast between the variety and numbers of fish in the main islands and Papahānaumokuākea Marine National Monument is stunning. For instance, the weight of fish per acre in the Northwestern Hawaiian Islands is 2000lb, but it's 600lb in the main islands; meanwhile, predators like sharks and jacks are 15 times as numerous in the monument's shallow reefs.

Plants

Mile for mile, Hawaii has the highest concentration of ecological zones on earth. Whether you're in tropical rainforests or dry forests, high-altitude alpine deserts or coastal dunes, wetland marshes or grassy plains, extravagantly diverse flora occupies every island niche.

Of course, what you'll see today is not what the first Polynesians or ancient Hawaiians saw. Most 'Hawaiian' agricultural products were originally exotic imports – including papayas, pineapples, mangoes, bananas, macadamia nuts and coffee. Over half of Hawaii's native forest is now gone, mainly due to logging, conversion to agriculture and invasive plants. Of Hawaii's nearly 1300 endemic plant species, more than 100 are already extinct and over 300 remain endangered.

Ancient Hawaiians didn't have metals and never developed pottery, so plants fulfilled most of their needs. Ethnobotanist Beatrice Krauss delves into this fascinating history in *Plants in Hawaiian Culture* and *Plants in Hawaiian Medicine.*

Exotic Beauties

The classic hibiscus is native to Hawaii, but many varieties have also been introduced, so that now hundreds of varieties grow on the islands. However, it's perhaps fitting that Hawaii's state flower, the *pua aloalo* (yellow hibiscus), was added to the endangered species list in 1994. The *koki'o ke'oke'o,* a native white shrub or small tree that grows up to 30ft high, is the only known hibiscus in the world with a fragrance.

Strangely enough, while Hawaii's climate is ideal for growing orchids, there are only three native species. In the 19th century, Asian immigrants began importing orchids and today they're a thriving industry. Hawaii also blooms with scores of introduced ornamental and exotic tropical flowers, including blood-red anthurium with heart-shaped leaves, brilliant orange-and-blue bird-of-paradise and myriad heliconia.

Notable exotic trees include ironwood, a non-native conifer with drooping needles, which acts as a natural windbreak and prevents erosion from beaches; majestic banyan trees, which have a canopy of hanging aerial roots with trunks large enough to swallow small children; and towering monkeypods, a common shade tree that has dark glossy green leaves, powder-puff pink flowers and longish seed pods.

Going Native

Perhaps the most bewitching of native Hawaiian trees is the koa, growing over 50ft high and nowadays found only at higher elevations. This rich hardwood has been used to make canoes, surfboards and even ukuleles. Endemic *wiliwili* is a lightweight wood also popular for making surfboards and canoes. Hawaii was once rich in fragrant *'iliahi* (sandalwood) forests, but these were almost entirely sold off to foreign traders in the 19th century.

The widespread and versatile ohia is one of the first plants to colonize lava flows. Its distinctive tufted flowers (lehua), consisting of petalless groups of red, orange, yellow, pink and white stamens, are considered sacred to Pele, goddess of fire and volcanoes. Native forests of ohia and *hapu'u* (tree ferns) are vital, endangered habitats. Brought by early Polynesian settlers, the *kukui* (candlenut tree) has light silver-tinged foliage that stands out brightly in the forest; the oily nuts from Hawaii's state tree can be burned like candles and are used for making lei and lotions.

Flowering native coastal plants include *pohuehue* (beach morning-glory), with its glossy green leaves and pink flowers, found just above the wrack line; beach *naupaka*, a shrub with oval green leaves and small pinkish-white, five-petaled flowers that look as if they've been torn in half (by a broken-hearted lover, according to Hawaiian legend); and the low-growing *'ilima*, its delicate yellow-orange blossoms strung into lei.

Hawaii's Parks & Preserves

Hawaii has two national parks: Haleakalā National Park on Maui and Hawai'i Volcanoes National Park on the Big Island (www.nps.gov/state/HI/). Both have volcanoes as centerpieces, contain an astonishing range of environments and provide some of the best hiking in the islands. A Unesco World Heritage Site since 1987, the latter welcomes 1.35 million visitors a year, making it Hawaii's most popular attraction.

In addition, the islands have five national historical parks, sites and memorials, most helping to preserve Hawaiian culture. Three are on the Big Island, most popularly Pu'uhonua o Honaunau (Place of Refuge) National Historical Park. On Moloka'i, Kalaupapa National Historical Park is a unique living-history interpretive site. O'ahu claims the USS *Arizona* Memorial at Pearl Harbor, part of the larger World War II Valor in the Pacific National Monument. Hawaii also has nine national wildlife refuges (www.fws.gov/pacific/refuges) on the main islands; their primary focus is preserving endangered plants and waterbirds.

Incredibly, Hawaii has over 50 state parks, monuments and recreational areas (www.hawaiistateparks.org). These diverse natural and historic areas include stunners such as Waimea Canyon on Kaua'i and Diamond Head on O'ahu. Each island also has county-managed beach parks and natural areas, as well as privately run botanical gardens, zoos and aquariums.

Hawaii Books for Nature Lovers

A World Between Waves, edited by Frank Stewart

Hawaii: The Islands of Life by the Nature Conservancy with Gavan Daws

Environmental Report Card

Wild Hawaii

Among the most dire environmental problems facing Hawaii are feral exotic animals and the continual introduction and uncontrolled proliferation of invasive, habitat-modifying plants. Even in Hawaii's protected natural areas, including national parks and state reserves, continual funding cuts hamper eradication and rehabilitation efforts.

Hawaii wildlife conservation reports can be depressing reading, but success stories prove that with enough effort and the right conditions, nature can rehabilitate itself. The nonprofit **Nature Conservancy** (www.nature.org/hawaii) is deeply involved in Hawaii; read its ecological assessment and biodiversity conservation plan (www.hawaiiecoregionplan.info) online.

Land Development

Since the 1960s, mass tourism has posed challenges to Hawaii's natural environment with the rampant development of land-hungry resorts and water-thirsty golf courses. Sprawling subdivisions also strain Hawaii's limited watershed and nearly full landfills. Meanwhile, ongoing construction often uncovers and disturbs archaeological sites such as heiau (temples), petroglyphs and burial grounds. Protecting these important Hawaiian cultural sites and repatriating *'iwi kupuna* (human remains) can delay road building and construction for years.

Mainland tech billionaire Larry Ellison, who bought 98% of the island of Lana'i in 2012, has announced plans to turn the island into a 'laboratory for sustainability' – but so far without holding community meetings to ask if residents are willing to drive electric cars, work on organic farms and drink water from desalination plants. Lana'i's previous owner David Murdock, retains rights to develop a controversial wind farm on the former pineapple plantation island. Wind-farm opposition group **Friends of Lana'i** (http://friendsoflanai.org) argues that environmentally and culturally sensitive areas would be destroyed, and that there are better renewable energy alternatives for such a small island.

Future development of the sacred volcanic summits of Mauna Kea and Haleakalā are another hot-button topic. Many environmental and Native

HAWAII'S TOP 15 NATURAL AREAS

PROTECTED AREA	FEATURES	ACTIVITIES	BEST TIME TO VISIT
O'ahu			
Hanauma Bay Nature Preserve	enormous coral reef in volcanic ring	snorkeling, swimming	year-round
Malaekahana State Recreation Area	sandy beach, offshore bird sanctuary	swimming, snorkeling, camping, birding	May-Oct
Hawai'i, the Big Island			
Hawai'i Volcanoes National Park	lava tubes, volcanic craters, fern forests, petroglyphs	hiking, camping	year-round
Kealakekua Bay State Historical Park	calm waters, coral reefs, sea caves	snorkeling, diving	year-round
Mauna Kea	Hawaii's highest peak, ancient Hawaiian sites	hiking, stargazing	year-round
Maui			
Haleakalā National Park (Kipahulu area)	bamboo forest, waterfalls, cascading pools	hiking, swimming	year-round
Haleakalā National Park (summit area)	cloud forest, eroded volcanic summit, nene	hiking, camping, birding	year-round
Wai'anapanapa State Park	black-sand beach, caves	hiking, sunrise-watching	year-round
Lana'i			
Hulopo'e Beach	pristine bay, white-sand beach, spinner dolphins	swimming, snorkeling	year-round
Moloka'i			
Kalaupapa National Historical Park	remote peninsula, steep sea cliffs, historic Hansen's Disease colony	hiking, mule riding, guided tours	year-round
Kamakou Preserve	rainforest, striking valley vistas, montane bog	hiking, bird-watching	May-Oct
Kaua'i			
Koke'e State Park	clifftop vistas, waterfalls, swamp, rainforest	scenic lookouts, hiking, birding	May-Sep
Na Pali Coast State Park	waterfalls, beaches, Hawaii's most famous trek	hiking, backpacking, camping, swimming, snorkeling	Apr-Sep
Waimea Canyon State Park	unbeatable views of the 'Grand Canyon of the Pacific'	scenic lookouts, hiking, cycling, mountain biking	Apr-Sep
Papahānaumokuākea Marine National Monument			
Midway Atoll	Laysan albatross colony, rich coral reefs, marine wildlife, WWII history	birding, snorkeling, guided tours	Nov-Jul

Hawaiian groups adamantly oppose building any new astronomical or solar observatories on either peak. In 2010, Mauna Kea's final environmental impact statement (EIS) paved the way for building a new Thirty Meter Telescope (www.tmt.org) near its summit. In 2012, the state's Board of Land and Natural Resources granted a permit to construct the world's largest optical solar telescope atop Haleakalā.

Farm & Military Cleanup

Vast tracts of Hawaii's native forest were long ago cleared to make way for the monocrop industries of sugarcane and pineapple. In the past, corporate agribusiness in Hawaii has been found guilty of violating Environmental Protection Agency (EPA) guidelines regarding soil and groundwater contamination on the islands. In 2010 – almost 15 years after being added to the EPA's Superfund national priority list – O'ahu's Del Monte Corp plantation was finally cleaned up. Some other former agricultural land has been successfully placed under conservation easement protections for future generations. Statewide issues yet to be resolved include water pollution caused by agricultural runoff and debates over whether GMOs (genetically modified organisms) should be outlawed.

Long-standing friction over the US military presence also continues, especially on O'ahu. Unfortunately, the military has not always fully complied with environmental regulations, while some training maneuvers have negatively impacted Native Hawaiian cultural sites and local communities. For example, in 2002 it was discovered that the army dumped tons of conventional weapons off the Wai'anae Coast in western O'ahu; it took almost a decade for 'Ordnance Reef,' littered with military munitions, to be cleaned up. In 2008, conflicts with environmental and Native Hawaiian groups over the military's plans to conduct maneuvers with Stryker combat vehicles on O'ahu and the Big Island had to be settled by lawsuit.

By the Sea

In contrast to the land, Hawaii's coral reefs are comparatively healthy. Overfishing is a major concern, however. Three-quarters of Hawaii's reef fish have been depleted during the last century. Not surprisingly, the species most in danger are those fish popular for aquariums or eating. Some islands have banned laying gill nets and encouraged sustainable fishing practices.

Hawaii's shorelines are still in danger. The threat of rising seas due to global warming and persistent beach erosion are raising alarm bells. Scientific studies have found that 25% of beaches on O'ahu and Maui have been lost in the last 50 years. Meanwhile, if sea levels rise one to three feet by the end of this century as predicted, half of Waikiki's hotels will find themselves standing in the ocean.

Curious about Hawaii's environmental health? Get the lowdown from Environment Hawai'i (www.environment-hawaii.org), a watchdog group that publishes a monthly newsletter on a wide range of topics, from wildlife conservation to development. Browse top stories and recent issues online.

A multicultural grassroots environmental alliance, Kahea (www.kahea.org) tackles a wide range of ecological, developmental and cultural issues. Check for action alerts online.

Green Hawaii

Hawaii is a Polynesian paradise with astoundingly varied natural environments – from *mauka* (toward the mountains) to *makai* (toward the sea). It's also a high-profile test case of whether humans can achieve a sustainable relationship with nature. With growing ecotourism and a renaissance of Hawaiian traditions, *aloha 'aina* (respect and love for the land) runs strong. Conservation efforts, both state-funded and grassroots, are gaining strength, and environmentally responsible businesses are sprouting up statewide.

The Islands Go Green

Hawaii breathes green. From volcano summits and cloud forests to the ocean depths where whales sing, the natural beauty of this place swallows you up. Green is also a way of thinking and living on these islands, where residents spend many of their waking hours outdoors. Nearly everyone who lives here feels a close connection to the land and the sea.

Environmental concerns are entangled in just about every major issue facing Hawaii. Development is a notoriously contentious issue, due to the mixed impact that tourism, the military and agribusiness have had on Hawaii's natural environment and indigenous culture. Pressures, especially from tourism and a rising local population, on Hawaii's watershed, energy resources and landfills can be intense. While Hawaii's economy would not survive without these industries, some residents are asking what kind of jobs they really bring, and at what cost?

How to achieve a more diversified, 'greener' economy and sustainable future growth is the question on almost everyone's minds. Hawaii residents have repeatedly shown their support, although not unanimously, for 'green' initiatives at the ballot box, including renewable energy initiatives. Meanwhile, islanders of all backgrounds have become environmental activists – from Native Hawaiians restoring ancient fishponds to volunteers fighting to keep invasive plants at bay.

ORGANIC FARMS

A new crop of small organic farms are growing in Hawaii. The Hawai'i Agritourism Association (www.hiagtourism.org) showcases farms that you can visit and has an online map of farmers markets statewide.

Traveling Sustainably

More than 7 million tourists land of these shores every year – outnumbering residents five to one. But with these simple, sustainable travel practices, you can help these islands stay a paradise for years to come.

Eat & Drink Locally

Keep in mind that everything not grown or raised in Hawaii has to be shipped long-distance to the islands by boat or plane, which increases greenhouse emissions, not to mention prices. It's no wonder that weekly farmers markets and the locavore movement have encouraged residents to start buying more food grown and raised on the islands.

When shopping at grocery stores and choosing restaurants in Hawaii, look for places that feature locally grown produce and sustainably caught seafood. Takeout food containers and disposable silverware and chopsticks are a nightmare for Hawaii's limited landfills. Try to patronize places that use biodegradable takeout-ware, even if it costs you a bit extra.

Bottled water may be convenient, but tap water is perfectly fine to drink, so bring along a refillable container.

Sleeping Green

Many hotels in Hawaii have not yet embraced sustainable business practices. Even such simple eco-initiatives as switching to bulk soap dispensers and offering recycling bins are rare. Ask about a hotel's 'green' policies before booking your stay.

Once you've checked in, you can help by turning off all lights, electronics and air-conditioning units whenever you leave your hotel room. Hang-dry and reuse your towels, and display the card provided to request that linens not be changed daily. Bring your own toiletries in refillable containers instead of using plastic mini bottles of shampoo, conditioner etc.

Consider camping while you're in Hawaii or staying at an ecofriendly, locally owned B&B or guesthouse. Renting a condo, studio apartment, cottage or vacation home with a kitchen can also reduce your environmental impact, including by saving the water expended on daily housekeeping and the energy spent on round-the-clock services at hotels.

Recycle, Reduce & Reuse

Recycling bins are not common at hotels or on the street outside of major tourist areas like Waikiki on O'ahu, but you'll find them at many beaches, public parks and some museums and tourist attractions on the main islands. Momentum is growing to ban plastic shopping bags statewide; each of Hawaii's counties has already implemented its own plastic-bag ban. Help cut down on landfill waste by reusing your own cloth bags; sold at supermarkets, convenience stores and tourists shops, they also make colorful aloha-print souvenirs of your trip.

Carbon Offsetting

Avoid driving if you can walk, cycle or take public transportation. Public buses run limited, commuter-focused routes on Maui, Kaua'i, the Big Island and Moloka'i. On O'ahu, bus routes are more comprehensive, frequently running to many of the same places visitors want to go.

If you need to rent your own wheels during your trip, try to choose the most fuel-efficient vehicle. Book in advance for hybrid, electric or bio-fueled cars, now offered by some major international car-rental agencies as well as local independent businesses that maintain small fleets of Toyota Priuses, biodiesel VW Beetles, electric and Smart cars etc.

Looking for a carbon-offsetting program for your airline flights? ClimateCare (www.climatecare.org) funds pro-environment projects in the developing world.

GREEN BUSINESSES

The Hawaii Ecotourism Association (www.hawaiiecotourism.org) runs an ecotour certification program and puts together a directory of member 'green' businesses, including hotels. Self-selecting members don't have to meet any general sustainability criteria, however, so do your own research too.

Tread Lightly

So many travelers come to enjoy Hawaii's gorgeous scenery and myriad wildlife that only strict protections keep certain mega-popular places – like O'ahu's Hanauma Bay – from being loved to death. But many equally

SUSTAINABLE ICON

It seems like everyone's going 'green' these days, but how can you know which Hawaii businesses are actually ecofriendly and which are simply jumping on the sustainable bandwagon? Lonely Planet's sustainable icon (🍃) indicates listings that our authors are highlighting because they have proven to contribute to a greener future for Hawaii. Some are involved in environmental education and wildlife conservation, while others preserve Native Hawaiian cultural traditions or support the local food economy.

scenic and fragile areas have fewer regulations, or little oversight, and the question becomes: just because you can do something, should you?

Every step we take has an impact, but we can minimize the effect by being aware of our surroundings. So what are the best ways to experience Hawaii's natural beauty without harming it in the process? For some outdoor activities, there isn't a single definitive answer, but here are some universal guidelines and best practices to consider:

- **Coral-reef etiquette** When snorkeling or diving, never touch the coral reef. It's that simple. Coral polyps are living organisms, so oil from fingers and broken pieces create wounds and openings for infection and disease. Watch your fins; avoid stirring up clouds of sand, which can settle on and damage reef organisms. Don't feed fish.
- **Dive etiquette** Practice proper buoyancy control to avoid hitting the reef. Don't use reef anchors or ground boats over coral. Limit your time in caves, as air bubbles can collect on roofs and leave organisms high and dry.
- **Encountering sea turtles and marine mammals** Federal and state laws protect all wild marine mammals and turtles from 'harassment.' Legally, this usually means approaching them closer than 50yd (100yd for whales, or 20ft for turtles) or doing anything that disrupts their behavior. The most important actions to avoid are pursuing or touching wild dolphins, and disturbing seals or turtles resting on beaches.
- **Hiking** Scrub the soles of your shoes and wipe down your backpack and any outdoor gear *before* landing in Hawaii to avoid inadvertently importing invasive species via stray seeds. Prevent erosion by staying on marked hiking and mountain-biking trails. Respect 'No Trespassing – Kapu' and 'Private Property' signs, unless a trustworthy local resident says it's actually OK.
- **Helicopter rides** Some places in Hawaii you can't reach except by air. However, as air tours increase, aircraft noise disturbs visitors and island residents on the ground, and it stresses local bird populations. If you do fly, pick the most fuel-efficient helicopter possible, and consider carbon offsetting.

CLOSE ENCOUNTERS: DOLPHIN SWIMS

Signing up for a 'dolphin encounter' in Hawaii deserves careful consideration. Although many programs claim to be educational and ecofriendly, the effects of human-dolphin interaction can be far more complex. Some widely reported concerns:

- In the wild, acrobatic spinner dolphins are nocturnal feeders that come into sheltered bays during the day to rest; they are sensitive to human disturbance, and federal guidelines recommend that swimmers don't approach within 50yd. Some tour boats allow swimmers to approach the dolphins much closer than this.
- According to marine biologists, encountering humans can tire dolphins out, leaving them without enough critical energy to feed or defend themselves later. Repeated encounters with humans have driven some dolphins out of their natural habitats to seek less-safe resting places, where they may be predated upon.
- In captivity, dolphins are trained to perform for humans using a variety of techniques, ranging from positive behavioral training to food deprivation. They may also be exposed to human-borne illnesses and bacteria, and sustain damage to their dorsal fins by swimmers.
- The US National Marine Fisheries Service has reported that 'dolphin encounter' programs tend to make captive animals act more aggressively, especially if the human participants are nervous. Injuries to human participants, such as broken arms and ribs, have occurred.
- The Oscar-winning documentary *The Cove*, featuring an ex–dolphin trainer turned activist, looks at the 'dolphinarium' biz and the global industry of dolphin captivity. Learn more at www.thecovemovie.com.

➡ **4WDs & ATVs** Always stay on the road, track or pre-established trail. Off-roading, even on private land, can cause scars on the land that take decades to heal. Better yet, consider mountain biking or hiking as alternative low-impact transportation.

For more easy ideas about how to make your trip more sustainable and ecofriendly, pick up *50 Simple Things You Can Do to Save Hawai'i* by environmental studies professor Gail Grabowsky.

ECOFRIENDLY TRAVEL

Volunteering on Vacation

Volunteering provides an experience you'll never get by just passing through a place, and lets you give something back during your trip. There's always something to get involved in – even if it's for just an afternoon.

To find volunteer opportunities, check alternative local newspapers such as *Honolulu Weekly* (www.honoluluweekly.com/calendar) and talk to nonprofit organizations around the islands, including the following:

➡ GrowFood (www.growfood.org) Work exchanges on organic and sustainable farms.

➡ Habitat for Humanity (www.habitat.org) Building affordable housing in low-income communities.

➡ Haleakalā National Park (p418) Wilderness conservation day and overnight trips.

➡ Hawaii Food Bank (www.hawaiifoodbank.org) Feeding the hungry on O'ahu and Kaua'i.

➡ Hawaii Nature Center (www.hawaiinaturecenter.org) Trail maintenance and environmental restoration on O'ahu and Maui.

➡ Hawaii State Parks Partners (www.hawaiistateparks.org/partners) Natural and cultural resource preservation on the main islands.

➡ Hawai'i Volcanoes National Park (p309) Monthly reforestation projects and more.

➡ Hawai'i Wildlife Fund (http://wildhawaii.org) Species conservation and beach and marine-debris clean-up on Maui and the Big Island.

➡ Hawaiian Islands Humpback Whale National Marine Sanctuary (p48) Annual migratory whale counts and year-round volunteer opportunities.

➡ Kaho'olawe Island Reserve Commission (KIRC; http://kahoolawe.hawaii.gov) Restoring the island's natural environment and Native Hawaiian cultural sites.

➡ Koke'e Resource Conservation Program (www.krcp.org) Eradicating invasive exotic plants in Kaua'i's native forests.

➡ Malama Hawaii (www.malamahawaii.org) Educational events, environmental clean-up days and restoration projects statewide.

➡ Pacific Whale Foundation (www.volunteersonvacation.org) Online calendar of short- and long-term volunteer projects from *mauka* to *makai* on Maui.

➡ Preserve Hawai'i (http://preservehawaii.org/volunteer/) Online network of volunteer opportunities, from farming to wildlife protection, on the main islands.

➡ Sierra Club (http://sierraclub.org/) Educational volunteer service trips are all-inclusive working vacations for members.

➡ Surfrider Foundation (p48) Island chapters sponsor family-friendly coastal clean-up and habitat restoration days.

Wind farm above the hills of Ma'alaea (p361), Maui

Survival Guide

Directory A–Z

Accommodations

Reservations

A reservation guarantees your room, but most reservations require a deposit after which, if you change your mind after a certain date, your money may not be refunded. Ask about cancellation policies and other fine-print restrictions before making a deposit.

Peak vs Off-Peak Times

- During high season – mid-December through March or April, and June through August – lodgings are more expensive and in demand.
- Major holidays and special events command premium prices, and lodgings can book up a year ahead.
- In low or shoulder seasons, expect discounts and easier booking. Polite bargaining may be possible.
- Unless otherwise noted, all lodgings are open year-round.

Amenities

- Accommodations offering online computer terminals for guests are designated with the internet icon (@). An hourly fee may apply (eg at hotel business centers).
- The wi-fi icon (wi-fi) indicates that wireless internet access is offered. Look for free wi-fi hot spots in common areas (eg hotel lobby, poolside).
- In-room internet access at hotels is often wired (not wireless); a daily fee may apply.
- The swimming icon (swimming) appears where an indoor or outdoor pool is available.
- Air-conditioning (air-con) is a standard amenity at most hotels and resorts. At some hotels, condos, hostels, B&Bs and vacation rentals, only fans may be provided.

B&Bs & Vacation Rentals

B&B accommodations in Hawaii vary from spare bedrooms in residential homes to pull-out-all-the-stops romantic hideaways. Often family-run operations, B&Bs can provide more personal experiences than hotels but offer fewer services.

Despite their name, only some B&Bs offer breakfast or stock supplies – usually coffee, juice, fruit and bread or pastries – in guests' accommodations. Without a state-approved restaurant kitchen, B&Bs can be fined if caught making hot meals for guests.

B&Bs discourage unannounced drop-ins, so they sometimes do not appear on maps in this book. Same-day reservations are hard to get. Always try to book B&Bs in advance, because they tend to fill up weeks or months ahead of time. Many B&Bs have minimum-stay requirements of a few nights, though some will waive this if you pay a surcharge.

Typically, a vacation rental means renting an entire duplex, condo or house (with no on-site manager and no breakfast provided), but many B&Bs also rent stand-alone cottages and often all these kinds of properties are handled by the same rental agencies. Ask about cleaning fees, common for stays of less than five nights.

Sometimes B&Bs and vacation rentals will refuse credit cards, instead requiring payment by cash, traveler's checks or a personal check drawn on a US bank account.

For B&B and vacation rental listings statewide, try the following:

Affordable Paradise (☎261-1693; www.affordable-paradise.com)

BOOK YOUR STAY ONLINE

For more accommodations reviews by Lonely Planet authors, check out http://hotels.lonelyplanet.com. You'll find independent reviews, as well as recommendations on the best places to stay. Best of all, you can book online.

SLEEPING PRICE RANGES

The following price ranges refer to a double room with private bathroom in high season. Unless otherwise stated, breakfast and taxes of almost 14% are not included.

$	under $100
$$	$100 to $250
$$$	over $250

Air B&B (www.airbnb.com)

HomeAway (www.homeaway.com)

Pacific Islands Reservations (☎800-429-5711, 262-8133; www.pacificislandsreservations.com)

Purple Roofs (http://purpleroofs.com) Directory of gay-owned and gay-friendly B&Bs, vacation rentals, guesthouses and hotels.

Vacation Rentals by Owner (VRBO; www.vrbo.com)

Camping & Cabins

Hawaii has almost no full-service private campgrounds. The best public camping facilities are in national parks, next best are state parks and typically the least well cared-for are county parks. Campgrounds are less busy during the week than on weekends.

NATIONAL PARKS

Hawaii's two national parks – Maui's Haleakalā National Park and the Big Island's Hawai'i Volcanoes National Park – have free drive-up campgrounds that are first-come, first-served; most are grassy dispersed areas without many amenities. Permits required for backcountry campsites are usually available same-day for walk-up visitors. Advance reservations are strongly recommended for all cabin rentals.

STATE PARKS

➡ The five largest Hawaiian Islands offer camping at state parks (usually $18 to $30 per site per night, or $12 to $20 for Hawaii residents).

➡ State park campgrounds usually have picnic tables, BBQ grills, drinking water, toilets and outdoor cold-water showers.

➡ Some state parks also rent basic housekeeping cabins ($50 to $90 per night, or $30 to $60 for Hawaii residents).

➡ Obtain camping and cabin permits in person from any **Division of State Parks** (www.hawaiistateparks.org) office or book ahead online up to one year in advance. Permits are *not* available in person at campgrounds.

➡ On O'ahu, the **Division of State Parks (DSP) Headquarters** (☎587-0300; www.hawaiistateparks.org; Room 310, 1151 Punchbowl St, Honolulu; ⌚8am-3:15pm Mon-Fri) handles camping reservations for all islands.

COUNTY PARKS

Some county parks are wonderful, with white-sand beaches and good facilities, while others are run-down and dangerous. Keep in mind that just because you *can* camp somewhere doesn't necessarily mean you'll *want* to. Check out the campground in person or ask around before committing.

Condominiums

Usually more spacious than hotel rooms, condos are individually owned apartments typically furnished with everything a visitor needs, including a kitchen(ette). They're often less expensive than all but the cheapest hotel rooms, especially if you're traveling with family or friends.

➡ Most condo units have a multiday minimum stay, especially in high season.

➡ The weekly rental rate is often six times the daily rate, and the monthly rate three times the weekly.

➡ Ask about cleaning fees, a surcharge that depends on the length of stay.

➡ To save money, try booking condos directly first, then go through rental agencies.

➡ Search online for condo-rental classified ads at **HomeAway** (www.homeaway.com), **Vacation Rentals by Owner** (VRBO; www.vrbo.com), **Air B&B** (www.airbnb.com) and **Craigslist** (www.craigslist.org).

Hostels

Hawaii has only two hostels associated with **Hostelling International USA** (www.hiusa.org), both of which are in Honolulu. All of the main islands have a small selection of private hostels, usually in larger towns and cities. A few are friendly and well kept, but the majority are aimed at backpackers or seasonal surfers and can be well-worn crash pads. Most are spartan, offer a common kitchen, internet access and have bulletin boards and lockers.

SAFE CAMPING

For safety reasons, a few county and state parks are not recommended in this book because they either are very isolated or are late-night carousing spots. Theft and violence aimed at campers is uncommon, but you should still choose your campgrounds carefully. Check our reviews, then ask locals and park staff for advice.

PRACTICALITIES

- **Electricity** 110/120V, 50/60Hz
- **Newspapers** *Honolulu Star-Advertiser* (www.staradvertiser.com) is Hawaii's major daily
- **Radio** Hawaii has about 50 radio stations; National Public Radio (NPR) at lower end of the FM dial
- **Time** Hawaii-Aleutian Standard Time (HAST) is GMT-10. Hawaii doesn't observe Daylight Saving Time (DST). 'Island time' means taking things at a slower pace or occasionally being late.
- **TV & DVDs** All major US TV networks and cable channels, plus 24-hour tourist information; DVDs coded region 1 (US and Canada only)
- **Weights & Measures** Imperial

Dorm beds average $20 to $35 nightly, semiprivate or private rooms $50 to $80.

Hotels

It's common for hotels, particularly chains, to discount their published rack rates, typically by offering advance-purchase internet booking discounts. Otherwise rooms may be discounted by the season, week or day, depending on demand. Ask about special promotions and vacation packages when booking.

Be aware that descriptors such as 'oceanfront' and 'oceanview' are liberally used, even where a periscope may be required to spot the surf. An ocean view can easily cost 50% to 100% more than a parking-lot view (which is sometimes euphemistically called a 'garden view' or 'mountain view').

Resorts

Hawaii's resorts are tropical pleasure palaces designed to anticipate your every need and provide 'the best' of everything (to keep you on the property every minute of the day). Expect myriad dining options, bars with live entertainment, multiple swimming pools, children's activity programs, and modern fitness and business centers. Mandatory daily resort fees may be charged; inquire when booking.

Courses

Some resort hotels and shopping centers offer free or low-cost Hawaiian arts and cultural classes, and workshops in hula dancing, lei making and the like. Schedules are sporadic, so keep your eyes and ears open and ask your hotel concierge about what's on.

To learn how to surf, kayak, stand-up paddle or scuba dive, browse the Activities reviews in the island destination chapters of this book.

Road Scholar (☎800-454-5768; www.roadscholar.org) Formerly Elderhostel, Road Scholar offers learning vacations for those aged 50 or older. Some educational programs focus on Hawaii's history and culture, while others explore the natural environment. Typically lasting one to two weeks, programs cost from $1500 per person, including accommodations, meals, classes and activities, but not airfare to/from Hawaii.

Customs Regulations

Currently, each international visitor is allowed to bring into the USA duty-free:

- 1L of liquor (if you're over 21 years old)
- 200 cigarettes (1 carton) or 100 (non-Cuban) cigars (if you're over 18)

Amounts higher than $10,000 in cash, traveler's checks, money orders and other cash equivalents must be declared. For more complete, up-to-date information, check with **US Customs and Border Protection** (www.cbp.gov).

Most fresh fruits and plants are restricted from entry into Hawaii (to prevent the spread of invasive species), and customs officials are militant in enforcing this. Because Hawaii is a rabies-free state, the pet quarantine laws are draconian. For details, contact the **Hawaii Department of Agriculture** (http://hawaii.gov/hdoa).

Before leaving Hawaii, make sure that any fresh food or produce in your checked or carry-on baggage has been commercially

EATING PRICE RANGES

The following price ranges refer to an average main course dinner in a restaurant (lunch is cheaper, usually half-price) or a set meal at a casual take-out joint. Unless otherwise stated, taxes and tip are not included in the price.

$	under $12
$$	$12 to $30
$$$	over $30

packaged and approved for travel (else you'll be forced to surrender those pineapples at the airport). The same holds for flowers: make sure that any orchids, anthuriums or proteas are inspected and approved for travel. Call the **USDA Inspection Office** (☎861-8494) to find out which plants are allowed to be transported out of Hawaii to foreign countries.

Discount Cards

Free visitor magazines packed with discount coupons are widely available at airports, hotels and tourist hot spots. However, better deals on activities and tours may be available by booking online directly with the company.

Children, students, seniors, and active and retired military personnel usually receive discounts at museums and other sights; all but children need to present valid ID proving their status.

American Association of Retired Persons (AARP; www.aarp.org) Advocacy group for Americans aged 50 years and older offering member discounts (usually 10%) on hotels, car rentals and more; an annual membership costs $16.

American Automobile Association (AAA; ☎593-2221, from Neighbor Islands 800-736-2886, on US mainland 800-874-7532; www.aaa.com; 1130 N Nimitz Hwy, Honolulu; ⏲Honolulu office: 9am-5pm Mon-Fri, 9am-2pm Sat) Members of AAA and its foreign affiliates (eg CAA) qualify for small discounts (usually 10%) on car rentals, hotels and attractions; annual AAA membership from $57.

Student Advantage Card (www.studentadvantage.com) For international and US students, this card ($22.50 per year) gives discounts of 10% to 20% on some rental cars, shopping and hotels.

Electricity

Food

For more about Hawaii's cuisine, see p602.

Gay & Lesbian Travelers

The state of Hawaii has strong minority protections and a constitutional guarantee of privacy that extends to sexual behavior between consenting adults. Same-sex couples have the right to civil unions, granting equality with heterosexual couples.

Locals tend to be private about their personal lives, so you will not see much public hand-holding or open displays of same-sex affection. Everyday LGBTQ life is low-key – it's more about picnics and potlucks, not nightclubs. Even in Waikiki, the laid-back 'scene' is muted by US mainland standards.

That said, Hawaii remains a popular destination for LGBTQ travelers, who are served by a small network of B&Bs, guesthouses and hotels. Monthly magazine *Odyssey* (www.odysseyhawaii.com), free at gay-friendly businesses throughout Hawaii, covers the islandwide scene, as does *eXpression!* magazine (www.expression808.com).

For more information on LGBTQ Hawaii, including recommended places to stay, gay beaches, events and more, check these community resources:

Gay Hawaii (www.gayhawaii.com)

Out in Hawaii (www.outinhawaii.com)

Out Traveler (www.out-traveler.com) Gay-oriented Hawaii travel articles free online.

Pacific Ocean Holidays (☎923-2400; www.gayhawaii-vacations.com) Personalized Hawaii vacation packages for gay and lesbian travelers.

Purple Roofs (http://purpleroofs.com) Directory of gay-owned and gay-friendly B&Bs, vacation rentals, guesthouses and hotels.

Health

➡ For emergency medical assistance anywhere in Hawaii, call ☎911 or go directly to the emergency room (ER) of the nearest hospital. For nonemergencies, consider an urgent-care center or medical clinic.

➡ Some insurance policies require you to get preauthorization for medical treatment from a call center before seeking help. Keep all medical receipts and documentation for claims reimbursement later.

Environmental Hazards

MARINE ANIMALS

Marine spikes, such as those found on sea urchins, scorpionfish and lionfish, can cause severe localized pain. If this occurs, immediately immerse the affected area in hot water (as hot as can be tolerated). Keep topping up with hot water until the pain subsides and medical care can be reached. Do the same for cone shell stings.

Stings from jellyfish and Portuguese man-of-war (aka bluebottles) also occur in Hawaii's tropical waters (for more information, visit www.808jellyfish.com). Even touching a bluebottle hours after it's washed up onshore can result in burning stings. Jellyfish are often seen eight to 10 days after a full moon, when they float into Hawaii's shallow near-shore waters, often on the islands' leeward shores. If you are stung, douse the affected area in vinegar, or carefully peel off the tentacles with a gloved hand, then rinse the area well in sea water (not freshwater or urine), followed by rapid transfer to a hospital; antivenoms are available.

VOG

➡ Vog, a visible haze or smog caused by volcanic emissions on the Big Island, is usually dispersed by trade winds.

➡ Short-term exposure is not generally hazardous, however high sulfur-dioxide levels can create breathing problems for sensitive groups (eg anyone with asthma). Avoid vigorous physical exertion outdoors on voggy days.

➡ For more information on vog, see p303.

Infectious Diseases

DENGUE FEVER

➡ In Hawaii the last dengue fever outbreak was in 2002; for updates, consult the **Hawaii State Department of Health** (www.state.hi.us/doh).

➡ Dengue is transmitted by aedes mosquitoes, which bite preferentially during the daytime and breed primarily in artificial water containers.

➡ Dengue usually causes flu-like symptoms, including fever, muscle aches, joint pains, severe headaches, nausea and vomiting, often followed by a rash.

➡ If you suspect you've been infected, do not take aspirin or NSAIDs (eg ibuprofen), which can cause hemorrhaging. See a doctor for diagnosis and monitoring; severe cases may require hospitalization.

GIARDIASIS

➡ Symptoms of this parasitic infection of the small intestine include nausea, bloating, cramps and diarrhea and may last for weeks.

➡ To protect yourself, don't drink from waterfalls, ponds, streams and rivers, which may be contaminated by animal or human feces.

➡ Giardiasis is diagnosed by a stool test and treated with antibiotics.

LEPTOSPIROSIS

➡ Leptospirosis is acquired by exposure to water contaminated by the urine of infected animals, especially rodents.

➡ Outbreaks often occur after flooding, when overflow contaminates water sources downstream from livestock or wild animal habitats.

➡ Initial symptoms, which resemble a mild flu, usually subside uneventfully in a few days, but a minority of cases involve potentially fatal complications.

➡ Diagnosis is through blood and/or urine tests and treatment is with antibiotics.

➡ Minimize your risk by staying out of bodies of freshwater (eg pools, streams, waterfalls); avoid these entirely if you have open cuts or sores.

➡ On hiking trails, take warning signs about leptospirosis seriously. If you're camping, water purification and good hygiene are essential.

STAPHYLOCOCCUS

➡ Hawaii leads the nation in staphylococcus infections, having over twice the rate of infection as the US mainland. Some types of antibiotic-resistant staph infections can be fatal.

➡ Staph infections are caused by bacteria that enter the body through an open wound.

➡ To prevent infection, practice good hygiene (eg wash your hands frequently, shower or bathe daily, wear clean clothing). Apply antibiotic ointment (eg Neosporin) to any open cuts or sores and keep them out of recreational water; if they're on your feet, don't go barefoot, even on sand.

➡ If a wound becomes painful, looks red, inflamed or swollen, leaks pus or causes a rash or blisters, seek medical help immediately.

Insurance

Getting travel insurance to cover theft, loss and medical problems is highly recommended. Some insurance policies do not cover 'risky' activities such as scuba diving, trekking and motorcycling, so read the fine print

INTERNATIONAL VISITORS

Entering Hawaii

- Double-check current visa and passport requirements *before* coming to the USA.
- For current information about the USA's entry requirements for travelers and eligibility to enter, access the visa section of the **US Department of State website** (http://travel.state.gov) and also the travel section of the **US Customs & Border Protection website** (www.cbp.gov).
- Upon arrival in the USA, most foreign citizens (excluding for now, many Canadians) must register with the **Department of Homeland Security** (DHS; www.dhs.gov) US-VISIT program, which entails having electronic (inkless) fingerprints and a digital photo taken; the process usually takes less than a minute.

Passports

- A **machine-readable passport (MRP)** is required for all foreign citizens to enter the USA.
- Your passport must be valid for six months beyond your expected dates of stay in the USA.
- If your passport was issued or renewed after October 26, 2006, you need to have an 'e-passport' containing a digital photo and an integrated chip that stores biometric data.

Visas

- Currently, under the US **Visa Waiver Program (VWP)**, visas are not required for citizens of 37 countries for stays up to 90 days (no extensions).
- Under the VWP program you must have a return ticket (or onward ticket to any foreign destination) that's nonrefundable in the USA.
- All VWP travelers must register online at least 72 hours before arrival with the **Electronic System for Travel Authorization** (ESTA; https://esta.cbp.dhs.gov), which currently costs $14. Once approved, registration is valid for two years (or until your passport expires).
- Foreign visitors who don't qualify for the VWP must apply for a tourist visa. The process is not free, involves a personal interview and can take several weeks so apply early.
- The website www.usembassy.gov has links for all US embassies abroad. You're better off applying for a visa in your home country rather than while on the road.

Embassies & Consulates

Hawaii has no foreign embassies. O'ahu has a few consulates in Honolulu, including the following:

Australia (☎529-8100; Penthouse, 1000 Bishop St)
Japan (☎543-3111; 1742 Nu'uanu Ave)
Korea (☎595-6109; 2756 Pali Hwy)
Netherlands (☎531-6897; Suite 702, 745 Fort St Mall)
New Zealand (☎595-2200; 3929 Old Pali Rd)

Post

- The **US Postal Service** (USPS; ☎800-275-8777; www.usps.com) is inexpensive and reliable. Mail delivery to/from Hawaii usually takes slightly longer than on the US mainland.
- To send urgent or important letters and packages, **Federal Express** (FedEx; ☎800-463-3339; www.fedex.com) and **United Parcel Service** (UPS; ☎800-742-5877; www.ups.com) offer door-to-door delivery.

Make sure your policy at least covers hospital stays and an emergency flight home.

Paying for your airline ticket or rental car with a credit card may provide limited travel accident insurance. For more car-rental insurance options, see p652. If you already have private US health insurance or a homeowners or renters policy, find out what those policies cover and only get supplemental insurance. If you have prepaid a large portion of your vacation, trip cancellation insurance may be a worthwhile expense.

Worldwide travel insurance is available at www.lonelyplanet.com/travel-insurance. You can buy, extend and claim online any time – even if you're already on the road.

Internet Access

➡ In this book, the internet icon (@) indicates that an internet terminal is available, while the wi-fi icon (wi-fi) indicates a wi-fi hot spot; either may be free or fee-based.

➡ Most hotels and resorts, many coffee shops and a few bars, restaurants and other businesses offer public wi-fi hot spots (sometimes free only for paying customers). In-room internet access at Hawaii's hotels is often wired, not wireless.

➡ Cities and larger towns usually have cybercafes or business centers offering pay-as-you-go internet terminals (typically $6 to $12 per hour) and sometimes wi-fi (free or fee-based).

➡ Hawaii's **public libraries** (www.librarieshawaii.org) provide free internet access via computer terminals if you get a temporary nonresident library card ($10). A few library branches also offer free wi-fi (no card required).

Language

Hawaii has two official languages: English and Hawaiian. There's also an unofficial vernacular, pidgin, which has a laid-back, lilting accent and a colorful vocabulary that permeates the official tongues. To learn language basics, including some Hawaiian and pidgin terms, visit www.lonelyplanet.com/hawaiian-language for our free Hawaiian Language & Glossary download.

Legal Matters

If you are arrested, you have the right to an attorney; if you can't afford one, a public defender will be provided free. The **Hawaii State Bar Association** (☎537-9140; www.hawaiilawyerreferral.com) makes attorney referrals. International visitors may want to call their consulate for advice; police will provide the telephone number upon request.

Alcohol & Drugs

➡ Bars, clubs and liquor stores may require photo ID to prove you're of legal age (21 years) to buy alcohol.

➡ Drinking alcohol anywhere other than at a private residence or licensed premises (eg bar, restaurant) is illegal, which puts parks and beaches off-limits.

➡ The possession of marijuana and nonprescription narcotics is illegal. Foreigners convicted of a drug offense face immediate deportation.

Driving

➡ If you are stopped by the police while driving, be courteous. Don't get out of the car unless asked.

➡ Anyone driving with a blood alcohol level of 0.08% or higher is guilty of driving 'under the influence' (DUI), which carries severe penalties.

➡ Police can give roadside sobriety checks to assess if you've been drinking or using drugs. Refusing to be tested is legally considered the same as if you had taken and failed the test.

➡ It's illegal to carry open containers of alcohol inside a vehicle, even if they're empty. Store them inside the trunk.

Smoking

➡ Smoking is generally prohibited inside all public buildings, including airports, shopping malls, bars and nightclubs.

➡ On O'ahu, smoking has now been banned at some public beaches and parks, including Ala Moana Beach, Waikiki (Kahanamoku, Kuhio and Kapi'olani Beaches), Kapi'olani Park and Sandy Beach.

➡ There is no smoking allowed at restaurants, even on outdoor patios or at sidewalk tables.

➡ At hotels, you must specifically request a smoking room. Note that some properties are entirely nonsmoking by law, with high penalty fees for noncompliance.

Other Laws

➡ Public nudity (as at beaches) and hitchhiking are illegal in Hawaii but sometimes ignored by police. Hitching is never entirely safe, and we don't recommend it. Travellers who hitch should understand that they are taking a small but potentially serious risk.

➡ Due to security concerns about terrorism, never leave your bags unattended, especially at airports or bus stations.

Maps

Franko's Maps (www.frankosmaps.com) publishes a series of colorful, laminated and waterproof ocean sports and island sightseeing maps, including *Obama's O'ahu Guide* and *Pearl Harbor: Then and Now Historical Guide*. These maps are sold at many bookstores and outdoor outfitters.

Map geeks and backcountry hikers can buy topographical maps from bigger bookstores and national park visitor centers. Alternatively, download printable **US Geological Survey** (USGS; www.usgs.gov) maps for free online or order print copies for a fee. Pay attention to island topo map dates, as some were drawn decades ago.

Money

Hawaii has a 4.17% state sales tax tacked onto virtually everything, including meals, groceries and car rentals (which also entail additional state and local tax surcharges). Accommodations taxes total 13.96%.

ATMs

➡ ATMs are available 24/7 at most banks, shopping malls, airports and grocery and convenience stores.

➡ Expect a minimum surcharge of $2.25 per transaction, in addition to any fees charged by your home bank.

➡ Most ATMs are connected to international networks (Plus and Cirrus are the most common) and offer decent exchange rates.

Credit Cards

➡ Credit cards are widely accepted and even required for car rentals, hotel reservations etc. Some B&Bs and vacation rentals will refuse them.

➡ Visa, MasterCard and American Express are most commonly accepted, followed by Discover and JTB.

Moneychangers

➡ Exchange foreign currency at Honolulu International Airport or the main branches of bigger banks, such as the **Bank of Hawaii** (www.boh.com) or **First Hawaiian Bank** (www.fhb.com).

➡ Outside of cities and larger towns, exchanging money may be impossible, so make sure you carry enough cash and/or a credit card.

Tipping

Tipping is *not* optional; only withhold tips in cases of outrageously bad service.

Airport and hotel porters $2 to $3 per bag, minimum per cart $5 or $10

Bartenders 15% to 20% per round, minimum $1 per drink

Concierges Nothing for simple information, up to $20 for securing last-minute restaurant reservations etc

Housekeeping staff $3 to $5 per night, left under the card provided; more if you're messy

Parking valets At least $2 when your keys are returned

Restaurant servers and room service 15% to 20%, unless a gratuity is already charged

Taxi drivers 15% of metered fare, rounded up to the next dollar

Traveler's Checks

Traveler's checks are becoming obsolete. That said, traveler's checks in US dollars are still accepted like cash at many tourist-oriented businesses in Hawaii, such as hotels and restaurants. Cheaper places like grocery stores and fast-food chains usually refuse them.

Opening Hours

Standard opening hours year-round are as follows:

Banks 8:30am–4pm Mon–Fri; some open to 6pm Fri and 9am–noon or 1pm Sat

Bars noon–midnight daily; some open to 2am Thu–Sat

Businesses & government offices 8:30am–4:30pm Mon–Fri; some post offices open 9am–noon Sat

Restaurants breakfast 6–10am, lunch 11:30am–2pm, dinner 5–9:30pm

Shops 9am–5pm Mon–Sat, some also open noon–5pm Sun; shopping malls keep extended hours

Public Holidays

On the following national holidays, banks, schools and government offices (including post offices) close, and museums, transportation and other services operate on a Sunday schedule. Holidays falling on a weekend are usually observed the following Monday.

New Year's Day January 1

Martin Luther King Jr Day Third Monday in January

Presidents' Day Third Monday in February

Prince Kuhio Day March 26

Easter March or April

Memorial Day Last Monday in May

King Kamehameha Day June 11

Independence Day July 4

Statehood Day Third Friday in August

Labor Day First Monday in September

Columbus Day Second Monday in October

Veterans Day November 11

Thanksgiving Fourth Thursday in November

Christmas Day December 25

Safe Travel

Hawaii is generally a safe place to visit. Because tourism is so important, state officials have established the **Visitor Aloha Society of Hawaii** (VASH; ☎926-8274; www.visitoralohasocietyofhawaii.org), which provides non-monetary emergency aid to visitors who become the victims of accidents or crimes while vacationing. To qualify for VASH assistance, you must have a round-trip ticket back to the US mainland or abroad and be staying in Hawaii for less than 60 days.

Scams

The main scams directed toward visitors in Hawaii involve fake activity-operator booths and timeshare booths. Salespeople at the latter will offer you all sorts of deals, from free luaus to sunset cruises, if you'll just come to hear their 'no obligation' pitch. *Caveat emptor.*

Theft & Violence

The islands are notorious for thefts from parked cars, especially rentals (which are obviously tagged with bar-code stickers). Thieves can pop a trunk or pull out a door-lock assembly within seconds. They strike not only at remote trailheads when you've gone for a hike, but also at crowded beach and hotel parking lots where you'd expect safety in numbers.

As much as possible, do not leave anything valuable in your parked car, ever. If you must, pack all valuables out of sight *before* arriving at your destination, where thieves may be hanging out and waiting to see what you put in the trunk. Some locals leave their car doors unlocked with the windows rolled down to discourage break-ins and avoid costly damages (eg broken windows).

Stay attuned to the vibe on any beaches at night, even where police patrol (eg Waikiki), and in places like campgrounds (see p639) and roadside county parks, where drunks, drug users and gang members sometimes hang out. In rural areas of the islands, there may be pockets of resentment against tourists, so be respectful as you explore off the beaten path.

Flash Floods & Waterfalls

No matter how dry a streambed looks or how sunny the sky above is, a sudden rainstorm miles away can cause a flash flood in minutes, sending down a huge surge of debris-filled water that sweeps away everything in its path. Always check the weather report before setting out on a hike; this is crucial if you're planning on hiking through any narrow canyons or swimming in waterfalls or natural pools. Swimming underneath waterfalls is always risky due to the danger of falling rocks.

Tell-tale signs of an impending flash flood include sudden changes in water clarity (eg the stream turns muddy), rising water levels and/or floating debris, and a rush of wind, the sound of thunder or a low, rumbling roar. If you notice any of these signs, immediately get to higher ground (even a few feet could save your life). Don't run downstream or down-canyon – you can't beat a flash flood!

Tsunami

On average, tsunami (incorrectly called tidal waves – the Japanese term *tsunami* means 'harbor wave') occur only about once a decade in Hawaii, but they have killed more people statewide than all other natural disasters combined. Hawaii's tsunami warning system is tested on the first working day of each month at 11:45am for less than one minute, using the yellow speakers mounted on telephone poles around the islands. If you hear tsunami warning sirens at any other

KNOW BEFORE YOU GO: HAZARDS & TRESPASSING

Flash floods, rock falls, tsunami, earthquakes, volcanic eruptions, shark attacks, jellyfish stings and, yes, even possibly getting brained by a falling coconut — the potential dangers of traveling in Hawaii might seem alarming at first. But like the old saying goes, statistically you're more likely to get hurt crossing the street at home.

Of course, that's not to say that you shouldn't be careful. It's best to educate yourself first about potential risks to your health and safety. This advice becomes even more important when you're engaged in outdoor activities in a new and unfamiliar natural environment, whether that's an island snorkeling spot, a jungle waterfall, a high-altitude mountain or an active (and thus unpredictable) volcanic eruption zone.

Wherever you choose to explore on the islands, remember to mind your manners and watch your step. Hawaii has strict laws about trespassing on both private land and government land not intended for public use. Trespassing is always illegal, no matter how many other people you see doing it. As a visitor to the islands, it's important to respect all 'Kapu' or 'No Trespassing' signs. Always seek explicit permission from the land owner or local officials before venturing onto private or government-owned land that is closed to the public, regardless of whether it is fenced or signposted as such. Doing so not only respects the *kuleana* (rights) of residents and the sacredness of the land, but also helps assure your own safety.

time, head for higher ground immediately; telephone books have maps of evacuation zones. Turn on the radio or TV for news bulletins. For more information, visit the **Hawaii State Civil Defense** (www.scd.hawaii.gov) and **Pacific Disaster Center** (www.pdc.org) online.

Telephone

Cell Phones

Check with your service provider about using your phone in Hawaii. Among US providers, Verizon has the most extensive network; AT&T, Cingular and Sprint get decent reception. Cellular coverage is best on O'ahu, more spotty on Neighbor Islands and nonexistent in many rural areas, on hiking trails and at remote beaches.

International travelers need a multiband GSM phone in order to make calls in the USA. With an unlocked multiband phone, popping in a US prepaid rechargeable SIM card is usually cheaper than using your own network. SIM cards are available at any telecommunications or electronics store. If your phone doesn't work in the USA, these stores also sell inexpensive prepaid phones, including some airtime.

Dialing Codes

- All Hawaii phone numbers consist of a three-digit area code (808) followed by a seven-digit local number.
- To call long-distance from one Hawaiian Island to another, dial 1 + 808 + local number.
- Always dial 1 before toll-free numbers (800, 888 etc). Some toll-free numbers only work within Hawaii or from the US mainland (and possibly Canada).
- To call Canada from Hawaii, dial 1 + area code + local number (note international rates apply).
- To make all other international calls from Hawaii, dial 011 + country code + area code + local number.
- To call Hawaii from abroad, the international country code for the USA is 1.

Useful Numbers

- Emergency (police, fire, ambulance) 911
- Local directory assistance 411
- Long-distance directory assistance 1-(area code)-555-1212
- Toll-free directory assistance 1-800-555-1212
- Operator 0

Payphones & Phonecards

- Payphones are a dying breed, usually found at shopping centers, hotels and public places (eg beaches).
- Some payphones are coin-operated (local calls usually cost 50¢), while others only accept credit cards or phonecards.
- Private prepaid phone cards are available from convenience stores, newsstands, supermarkets and pharmacies.

Tourist Information

The most convenient place to pick up information is at the airport. In the arrivals areas there are staffed tourist-information desks and while you're waiting for your bags to appear on the carousel, you can peruse racks of free tourist brochures and magazines, such as **101 Things to Do** (www.101thingstodo.com) and **This Week** (www.thisweek.com), which contain discount coupons for activities, tours, restaurants etc.

For pretrip planning, browse the information-packed website of the Hawaii Visitors & Convention Bureau (www.gohawaii.com).

Travelers with Disabilities

- Bigger, newer hotels and resorts in Hawaii have elevators, TDD-capable phones and wheelchair-accessible rooms (reserve these well in advance).
- Telephone companies provide relay operators (TTY/TDD dial 711) for the hearing impaired.
- Many banks provide ATM instructions in Braille.
- Traffic intersections in cities and some towns have dropped curbs and audible crossing signals.
- Guide and service dogs are not subject to the same quarantine requirements as other pets; contact the Department of Agriculture's **Animal Quarantine Station** (808-483-7151; http://hawaii.gov/hdoa/ai/aqs/info) before arrival.

Transportation

- Where available on the islands, public transportation is wheelchair-accessible. Buses will usually 'kneel' if you're unable to use the steps – just let the driver know you need the lift or ramp.
- Some major car-rental agencies offer hand-controlled vehicles and vans with wheelchair lifts; reserve these well in advance.
- If you have a disability parking placard from home, bring it with you and hang it from your rental vehicle's rearview mirror when using designated disabled-parking spaces.

Wheelchair Getaways (800-638-1912; www.wheelchairgetaways.com) Rents wheelchair-accessible vans on Maui, Kaua'i and Hawai'i the Big Island.

Wheelers Van Rentals (800-456-1371; www.wheelersvanrentals.com) Wheelchair-accessible van rentals on O'ahu, Maui and Kaua'i.

HELPFUL RESOURCES

Access Aloha Travel (☎800-480-1143, 545-1143; www.accessalohatravel.com) Local travel agency that can help book wheelchair-accessible accommodations, rental vans, sightseeing tours and cruises.

Disability & Communication Access Board (☎586-8121; www.hawaii.gov/health/dcab/travel; Room 101, 919 Ala Moana Blvd, Honolulu) Online 'Traveler Tips' brochures provide information about airports, accessible transportation, beach wheelchairs, sightseeing, and medical and other support services on the main islands.

Volunteering

For volunteering opportunities, see p635 and browse the destination chapters.

Work

US citizens can pursue work in Hawaii as they would in any other state – the problem is finding a job. International visitors in the USA on tourist visas are strictly prohibited from taking employment. To work legally, foreigners must secure sponsorship from an employer or international work-exchange program and apply for a visa before leaving home.

Finding career professional employment is difficult because Hawaii has a tight labor market. The biggest exceptions are for teachers and medical professionals. Otherwise, joining the waitstaff of tourist restaurants and bars is the most likely employment opportunity. If you have foreign-language, scuba diving, fishing or guiding skills, investigate employment with resorts. Most housekeeping or groundskeeping jobs at hotels go to locals.

In addition to notice boards at hostels, coffee shops and natural-foods stores, check the classified ads in the **Honolulu Star-Advertiser** (www.staradvertiser.com) daily newspaper and online at **Craigslist** (www.craigslist.org). Continue surfing at **HireNet Hawaii** (www.hirenethawaii.com), run by Hawaii's **Department of Labor & Industrial Relations** (DLIR; ☎586-8700; http://hawaii.gov/labor; 830 Punchbowl St, Honolulu).

Transportation

GETTING THERE & AWAY

Roughly 99% of visitors to Hawaii arrive by air, and the majority of flights – both international and domestic – arrive at Honolulu International Airport on O'ahu. Nonstop and direct flights to the Neighbor Islands are increasingly available (but can be costly). Flights and tours can be booked online at www.lonelyplanet.com/bookings.

Air

All checked and carry-on bags leaving Hawaii for the US mainland and some foreign countries must be inspected by a US Department of Agriculture (USDA) X-ray machine. For more about Hawaii's strict import and export regulations, see Customs Regulations (p640).

Airports

The majority of incoming flights from overseas and the US mainland arrive at **Honolulu International Airport** (HNL; ☎836-6411; http://hawaii.gov/hnl; 300 Rodgers Blvd, Honolulu) (HNL) on O'ahu. Flights to Lana'i and Moloka'i usually originate from Honolulu or Maui.

The main Neighbor Island airports include the following:

Hawai'i the Big Island East Hawai'i **Hilo International Airport** (ITO; http://hawaii.gov/ito), West Hawai'i **Kona International Airport at Keahole** (KOA; http://hawaii.gov/koa)

Maui Kahului airport (OGG; www.hawaii.gov/ogg)

Lana'i Lana'i airport (LNY; http://hawaii.gov/lny)

Moloka'i Moloka'i airport (MKK; http://hawaii.gov/mkk)

Kaua'i Lihu'e airport (LIH; http://hawaii.gov/lih)

Tickets

Hawaii is a competitive market for US domestic and international airfares, which vary tremendously by season, day of the week and demand. Competition is highest among airlines flying to Honolulu from major US mainland cities, especially between Hawaiian Airlines and Alaska Airlines, while Allegiant Air serves smaller US regional airports.

The 'lowest fare' fluctuates constantly. In general, return fares from the US mainland to Hawaii cost from $350 (in low season from the West Coast) to $800 or more (in high season from the East Coast).

Vacation Packages

Offered by major airlines and online travel booking sites, vacation packages that include airfare, accommodations and possibly car rental, tours and activities may cost less than booking everything separately yourself. **Pleasant**

CLIMATE CHANGE & TRAVEL

Every form of transport that relies on carbon-based fuel generates CO_2, the main cause of human-induced climate change. Modern travel is dependent on airplanes, which might use less fuel per person than most cars but travel much greater distances. The altitude at which aircraft emit gases (including CO_2) and particles also contributes to their climate change impact. Many websites offer 'carbon calculators' that allow people to estimate the carbon emissions generated by their journey and, for those who wish to do so, to offset the impact of the greenhouse gases emitted with contributions to portfolios of climate-friendly initiatives throughout the world. Lonely Planet offsets the carbon footprint of all staff and author travel.

Holidays (☎800-742-9244; www.pleasantholidays.com) and **Apple Vacations** (☎800-517-2000; www.applevacations.com) offer competitive vacation packages from the US mainland.

Sea

Most cruises to Hawaii include stopovers in Honolulu and on Maui, Kaua'i and the Big Island. Cruises typically last two weeks, with fares starting around $100 per person per day, based on double occupancy; airfare to/from the departure point costs extra.

Popular cruise lines include the following:

Holland America (☎877-932-4259; www.holland-america.com) Departures from San Diego and Vancouver, British Columbia.

Princess (☎800-774-6237; www.princess.com) Departures mostly from Los Angeles but also San Francisco.

Royal Caribbean (☎866-562-7625; www.royalcaribbean.com) Typically departs from Vancouver, British Columbia; some cruises start in Honolulu and finish in Vancouver.

GETTING AROUND

Most interisland travel is by plane, but limited ferry services connect Maui with Moloka'i and Lana'i. Renting a car is usually necessary if you want to really explore; on Lana'i and Hawai'i the Big Island, a 4WD vehicle may come in handy for off-the-beaten-track adventures. Public transportation exists only on the bigger islands. That said, you'll probably find it time-consuming and difficult to get around on public buses, except on O'ahu.

Air

Hawaii's major airports handling most interisland air traffic are Honolulu (O'ahu), Kahului (Maui), Kailua-Kona and Hilo (Hawai'i the Big Island) and Lihu'e (Kaua'i).

Airlines in Hawaii

Two major interisland carriers – reliable Hawaiian Airlines and upstart go! (operated by Mesa Airlines) – offer frequent scheduled flights in jet planes between Honolulu and the main Neighbor Islands (Maui, Kaua'i and Hawai'i the Big Island). Flying between two Neighbor Islands may require changing planes in Honolulu.

Two smaller, commuter-oriented airlines – Island Air and Mokulele Airlines – provide scheduled service in both prop and jet planes to the main islands, as well as to Moloka'i and Lana'i. In mid-2013 Hawaiian Airlines plans to begin offering turboprop service to Moloka'i and Lana'i with its new subsidiary brand 'Ohana by Hawaiian.

Island Air and a few other tiny airlines – like Pacific Wings – are the only ones that fly to secondary airports, such as Hana on Maui and Waimea-Kohala on the Big Island. Many of these smaller airlines also offer charters. Flights in small turboprop planes fly so low they almost double as sightseeing excursions – fun!

Expect further schedule changes and possible shake-ups in the interisland flight biz. Currently the main interisland air carriers include the following:

Hawaiian Airlines (☎800-367-5320; www.hawaiianairlines.com) Flies nearly 200 daily routes between Honolulu, Kaua'i, Maui and the Big Island, with limited flights to Moloka'i and Lana'i.

go! (☎888-435-9462; www.iflygo.com) Flies frequently from its Honolulu hub to Kaua'i, Maui and both sides of the Big Island.

Island Air (☎800-388-1105; www.islandair.com) Flies turboprop jet planes from hubs in Honolulu (to all Neighbor Islands except the Big Island) and Maui (to all main islands but Lana'i).

Mokulele Airlines (☎866-260-7070; www.mokuleleairlines.com) Scheduled service in single-engine Cessnas to all of the main islands except Kaua'i.

Pacific Wings (☎888-575-4546; www.pacificwings.com) Flies single-engine Cessnas between all of the main islands except Kaua'i.

Tickets & Reservations

Interisland airfares vary wildly: expect to pay from $65 to $165 or more one way. Flights to islands with less frequent service, or which are furthest from each other, are more expensive. Round-trip fares are usually double the one-way fares without any additional discounts. The earlier you book your interisland ticket, the more likely you are to find a cheaper fare. Generally speaking, you're better off buying tickets directly on airline websites, which often post deals online.

While it's often possible to walk up and get on a flight among the four biggest islands (particularly to/from Honolulu), advance reservations are recommended, especially at peak times and also to secure the cheapest fares. Airline regulations concerning surfboards, bicycles and other oversized baggage vary and can be restrictive, not to mention expensive – ask before booking a flight.

Bicycle

Cycling around the islands is a great, nonpolluting way to travel. As a primary mode of transportation, cycling can be a challenge, however. All islands have narrow roads, dangerous traffic and changeable weather. Long-distance cycling is best done with a tour group, but if you're adventurous and in good shape, it can be done on your own. Smaller islands such as Kaua'i and Moloka'i are better suited to cycle touring than say, the Big Island.

Rental

➡ Usually only tourist resort areas and specialty bicycle shops rent beach cruisers, hybrid models and high-end road or mountain bikes.

➡ Rental rates average $20 to $40 per day (easily double that for high-tech road or mountain bikes); multiday and weekly discounts may be available.

➡ Some B&Bs, guesthouses and hostels rent or loan bicycles to guests.

Road Rules

➡ Generally, bicycles are required to follow the same laws and rules of the road as cars. Bicycles are prohibited on freeways and sidewalks.

➡ State law requires all cyclists under the age of 16 to wear helmets.

➡ For more bicycling information, as well as maps of current and proposed bike lanes, check with the **Hawaii Department of Transportation** (HDOT; http://hidot.hawaii.gov/highways/) online.

Transporting Bicycles

➡ Bringing your own bike to Hawaii costs $100 (or more) on flights from the US mainland, while interisland flights charge $35 (or more) to transport your bike.

➡ You can usually check your bicycle at the airline counter, the same as any baggage. It needs to be in a box or hard-sided case with the handlebars fixed sideways and the pedals removed.

➡ Some local buses are equipped with front-loading two-bicycle racks; let the driver know *before* loading your bicycle on or off the rack. If the bicycle rack is already full, ask about bringing your bicycle on board – otherwise, you'll have to wait until the next bus comes along (which can be problematic on the Big Island, Kaua'i and Maui).

Boat

Interisland ferry service is surprisingly limited in Hawaii. At the time of writing, only Moloka'i (p446) and Lana'i (p427) had regular, passenger-only public ferry service to/from Lahaina, Maui.

Norwegian Cruise Line (NCL; ☎866-234-7350; www.ncl.com) Norwegian Cruise Line is currently the only company offering cruises that both start and end in Hawaii. Seven-day interisland cruises make roundtrips from Honolulu and visit the four main islands (from $1200 per person, based on double occupancy).

Bus

O'ahu's islandwide public transportation system, called **TheBus** (☎848-5555; www.thebus.org), makes O'ahu the easiest island to get around without a car. Schedules are frequent, service is reliable and fares are inexpensive. That said, TheBus doesn't go everywhere – for example, to most hiking trailheads.

Public bus systems on the larger Neighbor Islands are more geared toward resident commuters; service is infrequent and limited to main towns, sometimes bypassing tourist destinations entirely.

➡ After O'ahu, the next best system is **Maui Bus** (☎871-4838; www.mauicounty.gov/bus) but it doesn't run to Hana or Haleakalā National Park.

➡ The Big Island's **Hele-On Bus** (☎961-8744; www.heleonbus.org) will get you around to many island towns, but schedules are too limited for sightseeing. It doesn't stop at Hawai'i Volcanoes National Park.

➡ **Kaua'i Bus** (☎246-8110; www.kauai.gov) can take visitors between the main island towns and as far north as Hanalei, but not to the Na Pali Coast, Waimea Canyon or Koke'e State Parks.

➡ On Moloka'i, the **MEO Bus** (www.meoinc.charityfinders.org; ⏲Mon-Fri) FREE trundles east and west of Kaunakakai every couple of hours, but it's definitely worth calling in advance to confirm schedules and seats.

Car

Most visitors to Hawaii rent their own vehicles, particularly on Neighbor Islands. If you're just visiting Honolulu and Waikiki, a car may be more of a hindrance than a help. Free parking is usually plentiful outside of cities and major towns. Some hotels and resorts, especially in Waikiki, may charge for overnight parking (up to $30 or more).

Automobile Associations

AAA has reciprocal agreements with automobile associations in other countries (eg CAAA). Bring your membership card from home.

American Automobile Association (AAA; ☎593-2221, from Neighbor Islands 800-736-2886; www.hawaii.aaa.com; 1130 N Nimitz Hwy, Honolulu; ⏲9am-5pm Mon-Fri, 9am-2pm Sat) On O'ahu, AAA's only Hawaii office provides members with free maps and travel information. AAA members also enjoy discounts on select car rentals, hotels and sightseeing attractions. For emergency roadside service and towing, members should call ☎800-222-4357.

Driver's Licenses

➡ US citizens with a driver's license from another state can legally drive in Hawaii if they are at least 18 years old.

- International visitors can legally drive in Hawaii with a valid driver's license issued by their home country (minimum age 18).
- Car-rental companies will generally accept foreign driver's licenses written in English. Otherwise, be prepared to present an International Driving Permit (IDP), obtainable in your home country, along with your foreign driver's license.

Fuel

- Gasoline (petrol) is readily available everywhere on the islands except along more remote roads (eg Saddle Rd on the Big Island, the Hana Hwy on Maui).
- Gas prices in Hawaii currently average $4.40 per US gallon. As a rule of thumb, expect to pay 60¢ more per gallon than on the US mainland.

Insurance

- Required by law, liability insurance covers any people or property that you might hit. For damage to the rental vehicle, a collision damage waiver (CDW) costs an extra $15 to $20 a day.
- If you decline CDW, you will be held liable for any damages up to the full value of the car.
- Even with CDW, you may be required to pay the first $100 to $500 for repairs; some agencies will also charge you for the rental cost of the car during the time it takes to be repaired.
- If you have collision coverage on your vehicle at home, it might cover damages to car rentals; ask your insurance agent before your trip.
- Some credit cards offer reimbursement coverage for collision damages if you rent the car with that credit card; check beforehand.
- Most credit-card coverage isn't valid for rentals over 15 days or for 'exotic' models (eg convertibles, 4WD Jeeps).

Rental

AGENCIES

- Most rental companies require that you be at least 25 years old, possess a valid driver's license and have a major credit card, not a debit or check card.
- A few major companies will rent to drivers between the ages of 21 and 24, typically for an underage surcharge of around $25 per day; call ahead to check.
- Without a credit card, many agencies simply won't rent you a vehicle, while others require prepayment by cash, traveler's checks or debit card with an additional refundable deposit of $500 per week, proof of return airfare and more.
- When picking up your vehicle, most agencies will request the name and phone number of the place where you're staying. Some agencies are reluctant to rent to visitors who list a campground as their address; a few specifically add 'No Camping Permitted' to rental contracts.

Most islands also have one or two independent car-rental agencies, and these are worth checking out – on Maui and Kaua'i, they're the only way to rent a biofuel or electric car, and on the Big Island, it's the only way to rent a 4WD that's allowed to drive to Mauna Kea's summit. Independent agencies are also more likely to rent to drivers under 25 and offer deals, especially on 4WD vehicles. See the Getting Around sections at the beginning of the island destination chapters for details.

Major car-rental agencies in Hawaii (some of which may offer 'green' hybrid models and eco-friendly Smart cars) that have branches on the four biggest islands include the following:

Advantage (☎800-777-5500; www.advantage.com) On O'ahu and Maui only.

Alamo (☎877-222-9075; www.alamo.com) Also on Moloka'i.

Avis (☎800-331-1212; www.avis.com)

Budget (☎800-527-0700; www.budget.com)

Dollar (☎800-800-4000; www.dollar.com) Also on Lana'i.

Enterprise (☎800-261-7331; www.enterprise.com)

Hertz (☎800-654-3131; www.hertz.com)

National (☎877-222-9058; www.nationalcar.com)

Thrifty (☎800-847-4389; www.thrifty.com)

RATES

- The daily rate for renting a small car usually ranges from $35 to $75, while typical weekly rates are $150 to $300.
- When getting quotes, always ask for the full rate including all taxes, fees and surcharges, which can easily add $10 or more per day.
- Rental rates usually include unlimited mileage, though if you drop off the car at a different location than where you picked it up, expect a hefty surcharge.
- If you belong to an automobile club or airline frequent-flyer or hotel rewards program, you may be eligible for discounts when booking car rentals.
- Check online travel booking sites, such as **Hawaii Discount Car Rental** (http://discounthawaiicarrental.com) and **Hotwire** (www.hotwire.com), as well as travel bidding sites like **Priceline** (www.priceline.com) for more car-rental deals.

RESERVATIONS

Always reserve rental cars in advance. With most car-rental companies there's little or no cancellation penalty if you change your mind before arrival. Walking up to the airport counter without a reservation will subject you to higher rates, and during busy periods it's not uncommon for all cars to be rented out, even in Honolulu. Joining the rental-car agency's rewards program in advance can help you shortcut long lines. Reserve child safety seats ($10 per day, or $50 per rental) when booking your car.

HAWAII'S HIGHWAY ADDRESSES

Street addresses on some island highways may seem to be random, but there's a logic at work. For hyphenated numbers, such as 4-734 Kuhio Hwy, the first part of the number identifies the local tax zone and section, while the second part identifies the actual street address. Thus, it's entirely possible for 4-736 to be followed by 5-002; you've just entered a new zone, that's all.

Road Conditions & Hazards

➡ The main hazards are drunk drivers and narrow, winding and/or steep roads that wash out after heavy rains. In rural areas, watch for livestock and wildlife.

➡ On narrow, unpaved or potholed roads, locals may hog both lanes and driver over the middle stripe until an oncoming car approaches.

➡ Don't drive your standard car on 4WD roads, which is usually prohibited by rental companies and will void insurance coverage. Ask your rental-car company about additional road restrictions on driving its vehicles.

➡ If you get into trouble with your car, towing is prohibitively expensive in Hawaii – avoid it at all costs.

Road Rules

Slow, courteous driving is the rule in Hawaii. Locals don't honk (unless they're about to crash), don't follow close (ie tailgate) and let other drivers pass. Do the same, and you may get an appreciative *shaka* (Hawaiian hand greeting sign) from other drivers.

➡ Drive on the right-hand side of the road.

➡ Speed limits are posted and enforced. If you're stopped for speeding, expect a ticket, as police rarely just give warnings.

➡ Turning right on red is allowed (unless a sign prohibits it), but island drivers often wait for the green light.

➡ At four-way stop signs, cars proceed in order of arrival. If two cars arrive simultaneously, the one on the right has the right of way. When in doubt, politely wave the other driver ahead.

➡ For one-lane-bridge crossings, one direction of traffic usually has the right of way while the other must obey the posted yield sign.

➡ Downhill traffic must yield to uphill traffic where there is no sign.

➡ Diamond-marked carpool lanes are reserved for high-occupancy vehicles during morning and afternoon rush hours.

➡ When emergency vehicles (ie police, fire or ambulance) approach from either direction, carefully pull over to the side of the road.

Safety Laws

➡ Talking or texting on a cell phone or mobile device while driving is illegal.

➡ Driving under the influence (DUI) of alcohol or drugs is a serious criminal offense (see p644).

➡ The use of seat belts is required for the driver, front-seat passengers and all children under age 18.

➡ Child safety seats are mandatory for children aged three and younger; children aged four to seven who are under 4ft 9in tall or weigh less than 80lbs must ride in a booster seat or be secured by a lap-only belt in the back seat.

Moped & Motorcycle

Moped and motorcycle rentals are not common in Hawaii, but are available in some tourist resort areas. Surprisingly, they can be more expensive to rent than cars. Rental mopeds cost from $35/175 per day/week, while motorcycles start around $100/400 per day/week, depending on the make and model; a sizeable credit-card deposit is usually required.

Road Rules

➡ You can legally drive a moped in Hawaii with a valid driver's license issued by your home state or country. Motorcyclists need to have a specially endorsed motorcycle license.

➡ The minimum age for renting a moped is 16; for a motorcycle it's 21.

➡ State law requires mopeds to be ridden by one person only and prohibits their use on sidewalks and freeways.

➡ Mopeds must always be driven in single file and may not be driven at speeds above 30mph.

Safety Tips

➡ Helmets are not legally required for anyone 18 years or older, but rental agencies often provide them free – use 'em.

➡ Riding on the rainy windward sides of the islands may require foul-weather gear.

Taxi

- The main islands have taxis with metered fares based on mileage, although a few drivers may offer flat rates.
- Taxi rates vary, as they're set by each county, but average $3 at flagfall, then $3 or more per additional mile (luggage and airport surcharges may apply).
- Taxis are readily available at most airports, hotels and resorts, but otherwise you'll probably need to phone one.

Tours

Several local companies offer half- and full-day sightseeing bus tours of each island. Specialized adventure tours, such as whale-watching cruises and snorkeling trips, are available on all the main islands. Helicopter tours are most popular on the Big Island, Kaua'i and Maui; for flightseeing charters, contact smaller island airlines directly (see p650). Most of these tours can be booked after arrival in Hawaii, but if your schedule is tight or you're visiting during peak travel times, reserve ahead.

Roberts Hawaii (☎800-831-5541, 539-9400; www.robertshawaii.com) If you want to visit another island while you're in Hawaii but only have a day to spare, consider an island-hopping tour.

Glossary

For food terms, see p609

'a'a – type of lava that is rough and jagged
ae'o – Hawaiian black-necked stilt
'ahinahina – silversword plant with pointed silver leaves
ahu – stone cairns used to mark a trail; an altar or shrine
ahupua'a – traditional land division, usually in a wedge shape that extends from the mountains to the sea (smaller than a *moku*)
'aina – land
'akala – Hawaiian raspberry or thimbleberry
'akohekohe – Maui parrotbill
'alae ke'oke'o – Hawaiian coot
'alae 'ula – Hawaiian moorhen
'alauahio – Maui creeper
ali'i – chief, royalty
ali'i nui – high chiefs, kingly class
aloha – the traditional greeting meaning love, welcome, good-bye
aloha 'aina – love of the land
'amakihi – small, yellow-green honeycreeper; one of the more common native birds
anchialine pool – contains a mixture of seawater and freshwater
'apapane – bright red native Hawaiian honeycreeper
a'u – swordfish, marlin
'aumakua – protective deity or guardian spirit, deified ancestor
'awa – see *kava*
'awa'awa – bitter
azuki bean – often served as a sweetened paste, eg as a topping for shave ice

braguinha – a Portuguese stringed instrument introduced to Hawaii in the late 19th century from which the ukulele is derived

e komo mai – welcome
'elepaio – Hawaiian flycatcher; a brownish native bird with a white rump

hā – breath
ha'i – voiced register-break technique used by women singers
haku – head
hala – pandanus tree; the leaves *(lau)* are used in weaving mats and baskets
hale – house
Haloa – the stillborn son of Papa and Wakea, Hawaiian earth mother and sky father deities
haole – Caucasian; literally, 'without breath'
hapa – portion or fragment; person of mixed blood
hapa haole – Hawaiian music with predominantly English lyrics
hapu'u – tree fern
hau – indigenous lowland hibiscus tree whose wood is often used for making canoe outriggers (stabilizing arms that jut out from the hull)
he'e nalu – wave sliding, or surfing
heiau – ancient stone temple; a place of worship in Hawaii
holua – sled or sled course
honi – to share breath
honu – turtle
ho'okipa – hospitality
ho'okupu – offering
ho'olaule'a – celebration, party
ho'onanea – to pass the time in ease, peace and pleasure
hukilau – fishing with a *seine,* involving a group of people who pull in the net
hula – Hawaiian dance form, either traditional or modern
hula 'auana – modern hula, developed after the introduction of Western music
hula halau – hula school or troupe
hula kahiko – traditional and sacred hula

'i'iwi – scarlet Hawaiian honeycreeper with a curved, salmon-colored beak
'iliahi – Hawaiian sandalwood
'ilima – native plant, a ground cover with delicate yellow-orange flowers; O'ahu's official flower
'ilio holo kai – 'the dog that runs in the sea'; Hawaiian monk seal

'io – Hawaiian hawk
ipo – sweetheart
ipu – spherical, narrow-necked gourd used as a hula implement
issei – first-generation immigrants to Hawaii who were born in Japan

kahili – a feathered standard, used as a symbol of royalty
kahuna – knowledgeable person in any field; commonly a priest, healer or sorcerer
kahuna lapa'au – healer
kahuna nui – high priest(ess) or royal co-regent
kalo lo'i – taro fields
kama'aina – person born and raised, or a longtime resident, in Hawaii; literally, 'child of the land'
kane/Kane – man; if capitalized, the name of one of four main Hawaiian gods
kapa – see *tapa*
kapu – taboo, part of strict ancient Hawaiian social and religious system
kapuna – elders
kaua – ancient Hawaiian lower class, outcasts
kaunaoa – a yellowish- orange vine used in Lana'i lei
kava – a mildly narcotic drink (*'awa* in Hawaiian) made from the roots of *Piper methysticum*, a pepper shrub
keiki – child
ki – see *ti*
ki ho'alu – slack key
kiawe – a relative of the mesquite tree introduced to Hawaii in the 1820s, now very common; its branches are covered with sharp thorns
kika kila – Hawaiian steel guitar
ki'i – see *tiki*
kilau – a stiff, weedy fern
kipuka – an area of land spared when lava flows around it; an oasis
ko – sugarcane
koa – native hardwood tree often used in making Native Hawaiian crafts and canoes
koki'o ke'oke'o – native Hawaiian white hibiscus tree
kokua – help, cooperation
koloa maoli – Hawaiian duck
kona – leeward side; a leeward wind
konane – a strategy game similar to checkers
konohiki – caretakers of ahupua'a
ko'olau – windward side
Ku – Polynesian god of many manifestations, including god of war, farming and fishing (husband of Hina)
kukui – candlenut, the official state tree; its oily nuts were once burned in lamps
kuleana – rights
kumu hula – hula teacher
Kumulipo – Native Hawaiian creation story or chant
kupuna – grandparent, elder
ku'ula/Ku'ula – a stone idol placed at fishing sites, believed to attract fish; if capitalized, the god of fishers

la'au lapa'au – plant medicine
lanai – veranda; balcony
lau – leaf
lauhala – leaves of the *hala* plant, used in weaving
lei – garland, usually of flowers, but also of leaves, vines, shells or nuts
leptospirosis – a disease acquired by exposure to water contaminated by the urine of infected animals, especially livestock
limu – seaweed
lokelani – pink damask rose, or 'rose of heaven'; Maui's official flower
loko i'a – fishpond
loko wai – freshwater pond
lolo – stupid, feeble-minded, crazy
lomi – to rub or soften
lomilomi – traditional Hawaiian massage; known as 'loving touch'
Lono – Polynesian god of harvest, agriculture, fertility and peace
loulu – native fan palms
luakini – a type of *heiau* dedicated to the war god Ku and used for human sacrifices
luau – traditional Hawaiian feast
luna – supervisor or plantation boss

mahalo – thank you
mahele – to divide; usually refers to the Great Mahele land reform act of 1848
mahu – a transgendered or cross-dressing male
mai ho'oka'awale – leprosy (Hansen's disease); literally, 'the separating sickness'
mai'a – banana
maile – native plant with twining habit and fragrant leaves; often used for lei
maka'ainana – commoners; literally, 'people who tend the land'
makaha – a sluice gate, used to regulate the level of water in a fishpond
makahiki – traditional annual wet-season winter festival dedicated to the agricultural god Lono
makai – toward the sea; seaward
make – to die
malihini – newcomer, visitor
mamo – a yellow-feathered bird, now extinct
mana – spiritual power
mauka – toward the mountains; inland
mele – song, chant
menehune – 'little people' who, according to legend, built many of Hawaii's fishponds, heiau and other stonework
milo – a native shade tree with beautiful hardwood
moa – jungle fowl
mokihana – a tree with leathery berries that faintly smell of licorice, used in lei
moku – wedge-shaped areas of land running from

the ridge of the mountains to the sea

mokupuni – low, flat island or atoll

mo'i – king

mo'o – water spirit, water lizard or dragon

muumuu – a long, loose-fitting dress introduced by the missionaries

na keiki – children

na'u – fragrant Hawaiian gardenia

naupaka – a native shrub with delicate white flowers

Neighbor Islands – the term used to refer to the main Hawaiian Islands except for O'ahu

nene – a native goose; Hawaii's state bird

nisei – second-generation Japanese immigrants

niu – coconut palm

no ka 'oi – the best

'ohana – family, extended family; close-knit group

'ohi'a lehua – native Hawaiian tree with tufted, feathery, pom-pom-like flowers

'olelo Hawai'i – the Hawaiian language

oli – chant

olona – a native shrub

'ope'ape'a – Hawaiian hoary bat

'opihi – an edible limpet

pahoehoe – type of lava that is quick and smooth-flowing

pakalolo – marijuana; literally, 'crazy smoke'

palaka – Hawaiian-style plaid shirt made from sturdy cotton

pali – cliff

paniolo – cowboy

Papa – earth mother

pau – finished, no more

pa'u – traditional horse riding, in which lei-bedecked women in flowing dresses ride for show (eg in a parade)

pau hana – 'stop work'; happy hour

Pele – goddess of fire and volcanoes; her home is in Kilauea Caldera

pidgin – distinct local language and dialect, originating from Hawaii's multiethnic plantation immigrants

pikake – jasmine flowers

piko – navel, umbilical cord

pili – a bunchgrass, commonly used for thatching traditional hale and heiau

pohaku – rock

pohuehue – beach morning glory (a flowering plant)

pono – righteous, respectful and proper

pua aloalo – yellow hibiscus

pua'a waewae loloa – 'long-legged pigs,' an ancient Hawaiian euphemism for human sacrificial victims

pueo – Hawaiian owl

puka – any kind of hole or opening; puka shells are small, white and strung into necklaces

pukiawe – native plant with red and white berries and evergreen leaves

pule – prayer, blessing, incantation or spell

pulu – the silken clusters encasing the stems of tree ferns

pupu – snack or appetizer; also a type of shell

pu'u – hill, cinder cone

pu'uhonua – place of refuge

raku – a style of Japanese pottery characterized by a rough, handmade appearance

rubbah slippah – flip-flops

sansei – third-generation Japanese immigrants

shaka – hand gesture used in Hawaii as a greeting or sign of local pride

shōji – translucent paper-covered wooden sliding doors

stink-eye – dirty look

taiko – Japanese drumming

talk story – to strike up a conversation, make small talk

tapa – cloth made by pounding the bark of paper mulberry, used for Native Hawaiian clothing (*kapa* in Hawaiian)

ti – common native plant; its long shiny leaves are used for wrapping food and making hula skirts (*ki* in Hawaiian)

tiki – wood- or stone-carved statue, usually depicting a deity (*ki'i* in Hawaiian)

tutu – grandmother or grandfather; also term of respect for any member of that generation

'ua'u – dark-rumped petrel

ukulele – a stringed musical instrument derived from the *braguinha,* which was introduced to Hawaii in the 1800s by Portuguese immigrants

'uli'uli – gourd rattle containing seeds and decorated with feathers, used as a hula implement

'ulu – breadfruit

'ulu maika – ancient Hawaiian stone bowling game

wahi pana – sacred or legendary place

Wakea – sky father

warabi – bracken fern

wauke – paper mulberry, used to make *tapa*

wiliwili – the lightest of the native woods

zendo – communal Zen meditation hall

Behind the Scenes

SEND US YOUR FEEDBACK

We love to hear from travelers – your comments keep us on our toes and help make our books better. Our well-traveled team reads every word on what you loved or loathed about this book. Although we cannot reply individually to postal submissions, we always guarantee that your feedback goes straight to the appropriate authors, in time for the next edition. Each person who sends us information is thanked in the next edition – the most useful submissions are rewarded with a selection of digital PDF chapters.

Visit **lonelyplanet.com/contact** to submit your updates and suggestions or to ask for help. Our award-winning website also features inspirational travel stories, news and discussions.

Note: We may edit, reproduce and incorporate your comments in Lonely Planet products such as guidebooks, websites and digital products, so let us know if you don't want your comments reproduced or your name acknowledged. For a copy of our privacy policy visit lonelyplanet.com/privacy.

OUR READERS

Many thanks to the travelers who used the last edition and wrote to us with helpful hints, useful advice and interesting anecdotes: Vanessa Dellow, Jennifer Dunkle, Barbara Easteal, Cinzia Glo, Molly Gras-Usry, Angela Kaminski, Sun Woong Kim, Trevor King, Martin L'Heureux, Heather Monell, Kent Murnaghan, Tori Rice, Ann Stout, Johannes Voit, Rochelle Walker, Joe Wichmann and Timothy Wilcox.

AUTHOR THANKS

Sara Benson

Thanks to all of the locals who shared savvy tips, especially Jan and Donn Pickett. Without Emily Wolman, Cat Craddock, Sasha Baskett, Alison Lyall, Mark Griffiths, David Carroll and my coauthors Adam Karlin, Adam Skolnick, Amy Balfour, Paul Stiles and Ryan Ver Berkmoes, this book wouldn't have seen such smooth sailing. Big thanks to Jonathan Hayes for company and Michael Connolly Jr for helping out.

Amy C Balfour

Mahalo to Emily Wolman for entrusting me with this fantastic assignment and Cat Craddock-Carrillo, who took the helm with finesse. Thanks also to style maestro Sasha Baskett, hiking expert and CA extraordinaire Sara Benson and my intrepid coauthors. Kudos to my Maui experts: Beckee Morrison, Sheryl Shinkawa Hasegawa, Daniel Sullivan, Melissa Chimera at Haleakalā National Park, and numerous guides and locals along the way.

Adam Karlin

Mahalo nui loa: Emily Wolman, for letting me tag along on this trip; Catherine Craddock-Carrillo for taking over when the call came; Sara Benson, for masterfully running the ship as coordinating author; my fellow coauthors, particularly Paul Stiles, my compadre on the Big Island; Charlie Ryan and Alayna Kilkuskie for some great hookups; Chris and Erica Ikeda for all of their aloha; Josh Lambus for invaluable advice; Mikio, Heather and Sam for being standup Big Island roadtrip buddies; Wayne and Ohnmar Karlin for selling me on Hawai'i in the first place; Rachel Houge, for the absolute time of my life – here's to many, many more adventures; and finally, all the Puna hippies who prayed against and prevented the 2012 Mayan Calendar Apocalypse. I spent Dec 21 driving over the world's biggest volcano, so if the end times were coming, I have a feeling my rented Ford Fusion and I would have been the first to go.

Adam Skolnick

Thanks to Gayle Newhouse, Sean Newhouse, Taj Jure and Marc-Andre Gagnon, Jeffrey

Courson and Hezar, Christian at Tahiti Nui, Evan Valiere, Brittany Valverde, Susan Dierker, Island Girl Activities, the Killermann Family, Camille Page and the Little Fish family, Lila Metzger, Jordan and Julie from Tortilla Republic and Art House, Pieter Ruig, Burton Breznick, Rebecca Bihr, and the two Shannons. Dye, you made me laugh and enjoy in the midst of madness. Hiramoto, you lit the way through the maelstrom. Thanks also to Emily, Cat, Sam and Paul Stiles for your guidance and assistance. It's a joy and privilege to work with and know you all!

Paul Stiles

Kudos to the team that put me on the Big Island and helped every step of the way: Emily, Catherine, Sarah, Adam. And many thanks to the huge cast of local characters who pitched in, especially Maris, Barbara and Gary, Chris, Jacqueline, Balbi, Jeff, Ira, and Eileen. *Mahalo.*

Ryan Ver Berkmoes

Teri Waros on Moloka'i was again infectious with her enthusiasm. My guides and others who talked story as we hiked up the Halawa Valley made it a memorable day. On Lana'i kudos to the many who shared their hopes and fears for an island on the cusp of change. And thanks to Alexis Averbuck who put my chicken in her golden pot.

ACKNOWLEDGMENTS

Climate map data adapted from Peel MC, Finlayson BL & McMahon TA (2007) 'Updated World Map of the Köppen-Geiger Climate Classification', *Hydrology and Earth System Sciences*, 11, 163344.
Cover photograph: Waikiki Beach, O'ahu (Danita Delimont Stock/AWL-images)

BEHIND THE SCENES

THIS BOOK

This 11th edition of Lonely Planet's *Hawaii* guidebook was researched and written by Sara Benson (coordinating author), Amy C Balfour, Adam Karlin, Adam Skolnick, Paul Stiles and Ryan Ver Berkmoes, with contributions by Lisa Dunford. The previous edition was written by Sara Benson, Amy C Balfour, Glenda Bendure, E Clark Carroll, Ned Friary, Conner Gorry, Ryan Ver Berkmoes, and Luci Yamamoto, with contributions by Michael Shapiro.

This guidebook was commissioned in Lonely Planet's Oakland office, and produced by the following:

Commissioning Editor Catherine Craddock-Carrillo
Coordinating Editor Elizabeth Jones
Senior Cartographers Mark Griffiths, Alison Lyall
Coordinating Layout Designer Carlos Solarte
Managing Editor Sasha Baskett
Managing Layout Designer Chris Girdler
Assisting Editors Michelle Bennett, Kate Daly, Carly Hall, Trent Holden, Kate Morgan, Christopher Pitts, Erin Richards,Helen Yeates
Assisting Cartographers Fatima Basic, Jeff Cameron, Robert Townsend
Assisting Layout Designer Wendy Wright
Cover Research Naomi Parker
Internal Image Research Kylie McLaughlin
Thanks to Anita Banh, Elin Berglund, Bruce Evans, Ryan Evans, Larissa Frost, Jane Hart, Genesys India, Jouve India, Laura Jane, Anne Mason, Kerrianne Southway, Raphael Richards, Angela Tinson, Branislava Vladisavljevic Gerard Walker, Emily K Wolman.

Index

Map Pages **000**
Photo Pages **000**

C

D

E

Map Pages **000**
Photo Pages **000**

I

Map Pages **000**
Photo Pages **000**

N

Map Pages **000**
Photo Pages **000**

O

P

Map Pages **000**
Photo Pages **000**

T

INDEX T-W

Y

Z

Map Legend

Sights

- Beach
- Bird Sanctuary
- Buddhist
- Castle/Palace
- Christian
- Confucian
- Hindu
- Islamic
- Jain
- Jewish
- Monument
- Museum/Gallery/Historic Building
- Ruin
- Sento Hot Baths/Onsen
- Shinto
- Sikh
- Taoist
- Winery/Vineyard
- Zoo/Wildlife Sanctuary
- Other Sight

Activities, Courses & Tours

- Bodysurfing
- Diving/Snorkelling
- Canoeing/Kayaking
- Course/Tour
- Skiing
- Snorkelling
- Surfing
- Swimming/Pool
- Walking
- Windsurfing
- Other Activity

Sleeping

- Sleeping
- Camping

Eating

- Eating

…king & Nightlife

- … Nightlife

Information

- Bank
- Embassy/Consulate
- Hospital/Medical
- Internet
- Police
- Post Office
- Telephone
- Toilet
- Tourist Information
- Other Information

Geographic

- Beach
- Hut/Shelter
- Lighthouse
- Lookout
- Mountain/Volcano
- Oasis
- Park
- Pass
- Picnic Area
- Waterfall

Population

- Capital (National)
- Capital (State/Province)
- City/Large Town
- Town/Village

Transport

- Airport
- Border crossing
- Bus
- Cable car/Funicular
- Cycling
- Ferry
- Metro station
- Monorail
- Parking
- Petrol station
- Subway station
- Taxi
- Train station/Railway
- Tram
- Underground station
- Other Transport

Note: Not all symbols displayed above appear on the maps in this book

Routes

- Tollway
- Freeway
- Primary
- Secondary
- Tertiary
- Lane
- Unsealed road
- Road under construction
- Plaza/Mall
- Steps
- Tunnel
- Pedestrian overpass
- Walking Tour
- Walking Tour detour
- Path/Walking Trail

Boundaries

- International
- State/Province
- Disputed
- Regional/Suburb
- Marine Park
- Cliff
- Wall

Hydrography

- River, Creek
- Intermittent River
- Canal
- Water
- Dry/Salt/Intermittent Lake
- Reef

Areas

- Airport/Runway
- Beach/Desert
- Cemetery (Christian)
- Cemetery (Other)
- Glacier
- Mudflat
- Park/Forest
- Sight (Building)
- Sportsground
- Swamp/Mangrove

Adam Skolnick

Kaua'i Adam writes about travel, culture, health and politics for Lonely Planet, *Outside*, *Men's Health* and *Travel & Leisure*. He has coauthored 19 Lonely Planet guidebooks to destinations in Europe, the US, Central America and Asia, and has never found an island or place he enjoys more than Kaua'i. You can read more of his work at www.adamskolnick.com or find him on Twitter (@adamskolnick).

Paul Stiles

Hawai'i the Big Island (North Kohala, Waimea, Mauna Kea & Saddle Rd, Hamakua Coast, Hilo, Hawai'i Volcanoes National Park & Ka'u) When he was 21, Paul bought an old motorcycle in London and drove it to Tunisia. That did it for him. Since then he has explored 60 countries. With a passion for exotic islands, he's covered Madagascar, Kaua'i and Borneo for Lonely Planet, and lived for four years in Tenerife, the tallest volcano in the Atlantic Ocean: great training for Hawaii. For this book he sampled everything in Hilo Farmers Market and discovered 'it's all good!'

Read more about Paul at:
lonelyplanet.com/members/paulwstiles

Ryan Ver Berkmoes

Lana'i, Moloka'i Ryan Ver Berkmoes first visited Moloka'i in 1987 and remembers being intoxicated by lush, rural scenery on the drive east (or maybe it was the fumes from the heaps of mangos fermenting along the side of the road). He's been back often, usually renting a beachside house where between novels he looks without envy at the busy lights of Maui across the channel. For this edition of *Hawaii*, Ryan also noted the many changes Larry Ellison is bringing to Lana'i, including the new grocery store dress code.

OUR STORY

A beat-up old car, a few dollars in the pocket and a sense of adventure. In 1972 that's all Tony and Maureen Wheeler needed for the trip of a lifetime – across Europe and Asia overland to Australia. It took several months, and at the end – broke but inspired – they sat at their kitchen table writing and stapling together their first travel guide, *Across Asia on the Cheap*. Within a week they'd sold 1500 copies. Lonely Planet was born.

Today, Lonely Planet has offices in Melbourne, London and Oakland, with more than 600 staff and writers. We share Tony's belief that 'a great guidebook should do three things: inform, educate and amuse'.

OUR WRITERS

Sara Benson

Coordinating Author, O'ahu, Papahānaumokuākea Marine National Monument After graduating from college in Chicago, Sara jumped on a plane to California with just one suitcase and $100 in her pocket. She then hopped across the Pacific to Japan, with stints living on Maui, Hawai'i the Big Island and O'ahu and tramping all around Kaua'i, Moloka'i and Lana'i. Sara is an avid hiker, backpacker and outdoor enthusiast who has worked as a seasonal ranger for the National Park Service and as a volunteer at Hawai'i Volcanoes National Park. Already the author of more than 50 travel and nonfiction books, Sara also cowrote Lonely Planet's *Discover Honolulu, Waikiki & O'ahu* guide. Follow her latest adventures online at www.indietraveler.blogspot.com, www.indietraveler.net, @indie_traveler on Twitter and indietraveler on Instagram.

Read more about Sara at:
lonelyplanet.com/members/Sara_Benson

Amy C Balfour

Maui Amy first visited Hawaii as a toddler. For this book, she snorkeled Molokini Crater, clutched the wheel on the Kahekili Hwy, ate a juicy burger beside a wild boar and watched the sunrise at Haleakalā. Amy has authored or coauthored more than a dozen books for Lonely Planet, including *California*, *Caribbean Islands* and *Southwest USA*. She has also written for *Backpacker*, *Every Day with Rachael Ray*, *Redbook*, *Southern Living* and *Women's Health*.

Read more about Amy at:
lonelyplanet.com/members/amycbalfour

Adam Karlin

Hawai'i the Big Island (Kailua-Kona & Around, South Kona Coast, North Kona Coast, South Kohala & Puna) Hawai'i was about as good as assignments get for Adam Karlin. He always gets asked this, so the answer is: yes, sometimes authors bring their significant others along on trips. He and his fiancée got an early honeymoon snorkeling with mantas, watching lava pour into the ocean, bathing in tide pools and endlessly exploring. He also celebrated his birthday on a Puna clifftop watching the waves, a full moon, and lava coming down the mountain. Adam sheepishly admits that sometimes writing for Lonely Planet is pretty damn awesome. He should know; he's written some 30 guidebooks for the company.

...ons Pty Ltd

...ated 2013